ANTHOLOGY OF LIVING THEATER

ANTHOLOGY OF LIVING THEATER

SECOND EDITION

Edwin Wilson

Alvin Goldfarb

McGraw Hill

Boston   Burr Ridge, IL   Dubuque, IA   Madison, WI
New York   San Francisco   St. Louis
Bangkok   Bogotá   Caracas   Lisbon   London   Madrid   Mexico City
Milan   New Delhi   Seoul   Singapore   Sydney   Taipei   Toronto

McGraw-Hill Higher Education &

A Division of The **McGraw-Hill** Companies

ANTHOLOGY OF LIVING THEATER

This book is printed on acid-free paper.

6 7 8 9 0 DOC/DOC 0 9 8 7 6 5 4

ISBN 0-07-231729-9

Publisher: *Phillip A. Butcher*
Associate editor: *Allison McNamara*
Marketing manager: *David S. Patterson*
Project manager: *Rebecca Nordbrock*
Production supervisor: *Melonie Salvati*
Freelance design coordinator: *Matthew Baldwin*
Cover design: *Andrew Curtis*
Photo research coordinator: *Sharon Miller*
Photo researcher: *Inge King*
Compositor: *Shepherd Incorporated*
Typeface: *10/12 Galliard*
Printer: *R. R. Donnelley & Sons Company*

Library of Congress Cataloging-in-Publication Data

Anthology of living theater / [edited by] Edwin Wilson, Alvin Goldfarb.--2nd ed.
    p. cm.
   Includes index.
   ISBN 0-07-231729-9 (alk. paper)
   1. Drama--Collections. I. Wilson, Edwin. II. Goldfarb, Alvin.
PN6112.A58   2001
808.82--dc21   00-055891

http://www.mhhe.com

CONTENTS

PREFACE

Anthology of Living Theater is intended as a companion volume to our three other books—*The Theater Experience, Theater: The Lively Art,* and *Living Theater.* Its use, however, need not be confined to those texts; it will prove valuable for any theater course in history, theory, criticism, play analysis, or directing, as well as any introduction to theater.

The 17 plays included offer the widest possible range in time periods, geographic areas, theatrical styles, and subject matter. The texts included in our anthology can be used as representative works for each of the historical periods discussed in *Living Theater.* Moreover, each play selected is not only representative of a period and a genre but exceptional for other reasons and can, therefore, also be used to highlight key issues in introduction to theater and the topics discussed in *Theater: The Lively Art* as well as *The Theater Experience.*

Antigone is a prime example of a classic Greek tragedy, but it also resonates with modern themes: a young woman's challenge to male authority and questions of pragmatism versus idealism. *The Menaechmus Brothers* is a typical Roman farce, but it is more than that, having served as the model for numerous subsequent plays, including Shakespeare's *Comedy of Errors* and the Rodgers and Hart musical *The Boys from Syracuse. Abraham and Isaac* is by common consent among the most poignant and best-constructed of the medieval religious plays. *Sotoba Komachi* is an excellent example of nō drama from Japan. William Shakespeare's *Hamlet* stands apart in popularity and complexity not only from Shakespeare's other works but from practically any other Renaissance play. Molière's *Tartuffe* occupies almost as lofty a place among comedies of the period, particularly—for English-speaking audiences—in Richard Wilbur's translation.

Unheralded until quite recently were the women playwrights of the late seventeenth and early eighteenth centuries. Though Aphra Behn has received more attention, we feel that Susanna Centlivre deserves a place of at least equal importance. Moreover, we are confident that those reading *The Busy Body* for the first time will delight in their discovery of a witty, inventive comedy.

From the works of the important early figures in modern realism—Henrik Ibsen, August Strindberg, and Anton Chekhov—it is not easy to select representative works. We have chosen Ibsen's *A Doll's House* and Chekhov's *The Cherry Orchard* for their insights into the human condition, especially as they foreshadow ideas and attitudes that are with us still. Equally important to twentieth-century theater have been the many departures from realism; among the early examples, Strindberg's *A Dream Play* pointed the way to expressionism, surrealism, and stream of consciousness.

One of the major figures of twentieth-century theater was Bertolt Brecht, who developed theories of epic theater and created many noteworthy plays. *The Good Woman of Setzuan* not only exemplifies his theories—including his ideas on Marxism—but is among the most accessible and fascinating of his works because of its relevance to the lives of people today.

Of the three best-known American playwrights just before and just after World War II—Eugene O'Neill, Tennessee Williams, and Arthur Miller—the most poetic is Williams. Both his lyricism and his acute dramatic sense are evident in the haunting, evocative *The Glass Menagerie*.

The most striking movement in the period immediately after World War II was theater of the absurd, and the undisputed leader of this movement was Samuel Beckett. *Krapp's Last Tape* provides an excellent introduction to the work and techniques of this seminal figure.

Among dramas of the past quarter-century, we have selected four texts representing significant aspects of the diversity that many consider the hallmark of contemporary theater; these plays illustrate today's multiculturalism, gender diversity, and performance art. Charles Ludlam's *The Mystery of Irma Vep* is an outrageously humorous takeoff on Victorian melodrama and other long-standing dramatic traditions and also addresses gay and gender issues. In addition, Ludlam's work forces the audience to reevaluate the categories of popular and high art as well as the conventions of theatrical performance. August Wilson's *Joe Turner's Come and Gone*, which takes place in Pittsburgh in 1911, is a poetic treatment of a cross section of African Americans who have migrated from the South and are facing a series of crises. Caryl Churchill's *Blue Heart* represents the intriguing mixture of styles that is common in postmodernist drama. Churchill is also one of the leading feminist playwrights of the past 30 years and is one of England's most political voices. Finally, *Freak* by John Leguizamo is a solo performance piece based on the author-performer's life. *Freak* focuses on living in New York City's multicultural society from the perspective of a Latino struggling to gain respect from his family. We have chosen to excerpt *Freak* in order to give readers the flavor of Leguizamo's comic performance art, recognizing that such works exist best on the stage.

For each play, we have provided an introduction consisting of three sections: information about the play, about the playwright, and about the period in which the play was written. These introductions provide context for the plays and offer important background material to make the plays more meaningful and accessible. We should also note that some of the texts have notes. The format for these notes is not uniform because we have tried, where possible, to use the notes from the original editors and/or translators so that the readers are given a consistent version of each text.

It is expected that instructors will select from the 17 plays in *Anthology of Living Theater* those works that best suit their individual courses. Some may choose to emphasize the sweep of history; others may focus on the more modern works, beginning with Ibsen and Strindberg. We hope, however, that as many plays as possible will be included, because we feel that each will prove rewarding in itself and an important experience in discovering theater.

ACKNOWLEDGMENTS

As always, many colleagues and others have helped make this book possible and to them we are deeply grateful. To all the readers of our other textbooks, *The Theater Experience, Theater: The Lively Art,* and *Living Theater,* who frequently suggested that we develop an anthology, we express our sincere appreciation. And to all those who have responded to surveys over the past year, we are immensely grateful for your feedback.

At Illinois State University, we would like to thank Georgia Bennett, who always eases the administrative burden on Provost Goldfarb and makes it possible for him to continue his scholarly career. Michelle Sullivan wrote excellent, early drafts of the biographies of a number of the playwrights and also provided invaluable assistance with research. Aaron Krall helped with research on John Leguizamo.

At McGraw-Hill we express our deepest thanks to our sponsoring editor, Cynthia Ward, and our current sponsoring editor, Allison McNamara. This anthology is a project that was discussed a number of times in the past but never undertaken until Cynthia and Allison exerted their leadership and patient supervision; Allison has done a remarkable job in guiding us through the details of this revision. We also want to express our thanks to our project manager, Rebecca Nordbrock, and our enormously talented photo researcher, Inge King.

Finally, we must thank our wives, Catherine Wilson and Elaine Goldfarb, for their patience, encouragement, and support. Dedicating books to them cannot fully acknowledge their importance to our lives and careers.

Edwin Wilson
Alvin Goldfarb

ANTHOLOGY OF LIVING THEATER

SOTOBA KOMACHI
Joe Turner's Co
TARTUFFE The Mystery of Ir
Hamlet
The Glass Menagerie The Busy
AK
ood Woman of Setzuan The Cherry Orc
A Do
HEART A DREAM PLAY
Abra Krapp's Last Tape
e Tu roth
SOTO
Mys
TA

INTRODUCTION:
HOW TO READ A PLAY

—ᴍ—

The Busy Body
Cherry Orchard FREAK The Glass
The Good Woman of Set
A Doll's House
A DRI
p's Last Tape BLUE HEART
e Menaechmus Brothers Abraham an
SOTOBA KOMACHI
Joe Turner's Come
gone
Hamlet TARTUFFE The Mystery of Ir
AK The Glass Menagerie The Busy
ood Woman of Setzuan The Cherry Orc
A Do
and Isaac A DREAM PLAY
The Menaechmus
Joe Turner's Come and Gone

Reading a play is an act of the imagination. In this, it is like reading a novel or a short story. When a novelist writes about a young American woman in a foreign country sitting with a friend at an outdoor café drinking expresso, or a secret agent on a dangerous mission trailing someone through an airport, or a group of hikers on a mountain pass suddenly caught in a deadly snowstorm, the reader visualizes these scenes in her or his mind's eye.

When a person reads a play on a printed page, the same thing happens. But something else happens as well: The reader must imagine the scene being played out *on the stage of a theater*. Unlike a novel or a short story, a printed play is not a completed work of art; rather, it is a blueprint for a production. The finished product is something quite different—a presentation on a stage before an audience. Some contemporary critics even suggest that a written script is only a *text*—that is, a basis—for performance and that the people staging the script can take whatever liberties they believe are necessary to create their own vision of the play.

Reading a play can be a double pleasure: It can have all the excitement afforded by reading a biography, a spy story, or a comic encounter, with the added reward of imagining that you are in a theater, watching a production unfold. Everyone understands how to read a book; but when you read a play, this second aspect—imagining it as a stage presentation—requires additional thought and information.

In some cases, before you read a play, it will be helpful to have background information. Reading a Greek play, for example, will be a more meaningful experience if you understand how the plays were produced and how the chorus, which is unique to Greek theater, is used. A medieval religious play or an Asian play will be easier to understand if you are aware of the style of the play and the way it was originally presented. This anthology includes some of this background information before each play. More can be learned, however, by consulting a theater textbook or speaking with an instructor who can provide crucial facts.

WHERE AND WHEN THE PLAY TAKES PLACE: THE SETTING AND CIRCUMSTANCES

When we begin to read a play, the first thing we must do is familiarize ourselves with the circumstances surrounding it. Looking at the title page and the description of the location, we discover when and where it takes place. Perhaps it takes place in ancient Greece, in Russia in the late nineteenth century, or in Pittsburgh, Pennsylvania, in 1911. We must also know whether this is fiction or fact: whether the play is based on a myth, an invented story, or a true event. It is possible, of course, that the play is based on an actual life or an actual happening but has been embellished or altered. For example, the author may want us to see a historical event as reflecting contemporary issues.

After learning when and where the play occurs, we next need to determine where the stage action occurs. Does the text tell us that it all happens in one room—a living room, a kitchen, a dining room—or that it ranges over a number of locations? We should try to create in our minds our own "stage set" as we begin to read. How do the spaces look? How large are they? What color are they? What kinds of furniture and other accessories are present?

It can be helpful to make your own *ground plan*. This is a blueprint of what the stage set would look like as seen from above: the placement of the walls, the doors, the furniture. In this way you can visualize where characters enter and leave the set and where they are located during specific scenes.

If the play covers a number of locations—as is the case, for instance, with a play by Shakespeare—how is this handled onstage? Is a relatively bare stage transformed simply by the addition of a few properties (called *props* in the theater), such as a throne, a dining room table, or a few trees? Perhaps there are different levels onstage on which the action unfolds. It is helpful, then, to have some mental picture of the setting.

Equally helpful is to have some idea of the kind of theater space in which the play is mounted. Theaters can be of different configurations and sizes. They can also be indoors or outdoors—Greek amphitheaters and many Shakespearean festivals are outdoors, for example. If the play is indoors, the stage and the auditorium can be arranged in one of several different ways.

A *proscenium,* or *picture-frame,* theater resembles a movie theater. All the seats face toward the stage, which is enclosed with a frame, the proscenium (a term originating in Renaissance Europe). This type of stage was prominent throughout Europe and the United States through the eighteenth and nineteenth centuries and the first half of the twentieth century. It works very well for plays that take place in interiors (the rooms of a house, for instance) because the picture-frame opening can serve as a "fourth wall" of a room whose other three walls will be created onstage. The proscenium stage is also ideal for spectacle. Behind the proscenium opening, elaborate stage effects can be created—ballrooms, street scenes, palaces—and these can be changed almost as if by magic because the stage machinery is hidden behind the picture frame that encloses the stage opening.

Another major arrangement is the *thrust stage*. In this case, the stage area "thrusts" out into the audience, which surrounds it on three sides. At the back of the thrust stage is a wall or some type of scenery. This is the kind of stage for which Shakespeare and his Spanish contemporary Lope de Vega wrote their plays. This type of stage is particularly good for episodic plays in which the action moves rapidly from place to place. In contemporary theater, the dramas of the German playwright Bertolt Brecht also work well on a thrust stage. Whereas all the Broadway theaters have proscenium stages, many of the regional professional theaters in the United States have thrust stages.

A third kind of stage is the *arena,* or *circle,* arrangement, in which the audience—in either a circle or a square—surrounds a playing area at the center. This type of stage affords a great deal of flexibility and intimacy to a production.

A fourth possibility is the use of *found spaces*. These are spaces not originally intended for theater, such as gymnasiums, garages, lofts, and cafeterias, which are transformed for theatrical purposes. Some texts call for the use of *site-specific* staging, that is, staging a play at actual locales appropriate for the setting of the script. For example, a text set in a factory building, in a stockyard, or on a street corner would be presented in those actual spaces.

As you begin to read a play, try to decide on which of these stages, or in which of these spaces, you would imagine the action unfolding. Also, try to conjecture whether the theater is small, seating perhaps 200 people; or larger, seating 1,000 spectators or even two or three times that many.

WHO THE PARTICIPANTS ARE: THE CHARACTERS

The next step in the adventure of reading a play is to familiarize yourself with the cast. At the beginning of a printed play, there is usually a list of the characters. Look at this carefully to see who the participants are. What are their ages and sexes? What are their occupations? What are their relationships to one another? You will really get to know the characters by seeing them in action once the play unfolds, but before you begin, it is helpful to know who they are and how they relate to one another.

Later, after you are well into the play, consider what strikes you most about various characters: how humorous they are, how evil, how noble, how human, how vulnerable. When you visualize characters, it sometimes helps to imagine flesh-and-blood performers you have seen playing individual roles on television, in films, or in the theater.

As you consider the characters, think about their functions in the play. Who is the main character—sometimes referred to as the *protagonist?* With whom is she or he in conflict? This character, the chief person opposing the protagonist, is sometimes referred to as the *antagonist.* Who are the minor characters who interact with the protagonist? These secondary characters are often called *foils.*

A number of contemporary critics suggest that we also consider how marginalized groups—people who are politically, economically, or socially disenfranchised—are represented by authors. For example, how are women presented? Are they dramatized as stereotypes? Are they less powerful than their male counterparts? Are they conceived in a way that reflects how men view women? (Contemporary criticism sometimes describes this as creating female characters through the "male gaze.") Are they presented as objects—that is, are they objectified? Similarly, how are minority groups—African Americans, Asian Americans, Native Americans, Hispanics, gays, lesbians—represented?

WHAT KIND OF PLAY IT IS: CATEGORIES AND GENRES

Sometimes we are told on the title page what kind of play we are reading: a tragedy, a comedy, a farce, a history. Having this information can often help us understand the basis on which we are supposed to experience it. If it is a serious play, we should expect to take a sober, thoughtful look at the events that take place. If it is a comedy, we know that we are meant to laugh and not to take the characters or the incidents very seriously. If it is a farce, we understand that there will be wild antics and that both the characters and the plot will be exaggerated.

The category to which a play is assigned is often referred to as its *genre* (pronounced "JAHN-ruh"), from a French word meaning "type." In the past, more emphasis was placed on the question of category or genre than is the case today.

Traditionally, a *tragedy* is defined as a play that involves serious action of universal significance and has important moral and philosophical implications. The hero or heroine is usually a person of royal or noble blood—or some other exceptional character—who suffers a tragic fate. The play usually ends unhappily.

As for *comedy,* a wide range of plays fall under this heading; but usually a comedy is a play that is light in tone, is designed to amuse and provoke laughter, is concerned with issues tending not to be serious, and has a happy ending. The most sophisticated kinds of comedy—intellectual comedy and comedies of manners—stress wit, satire, wordplay, and ideas. At the other end of the spectrum of comedy is *farce,* which is broad, often slapstick, and emphasizes plot twists and exaggerated characters.

Tragicomedy, a form that has come very much to the forefront in modern drama, is a mixture of tragedy and comedy. It is not tragedy with comic relief, such as *Hamlet* or *Macbeth,* but a true mixture of serious and comic elements. It is like a sweet-and-sour sauce.

Two other types that should be mentioned are *domestic drama,* which deals with everyday people in ordinary circumstances facing crises in their lives; and *melodrama,* which emphasizes effects—fear, suspense, moral judgment—and pits good characters against evil ones to achieve its ends.

The subject of domestic drama leads to two other categories: *realism* and *departures from realism.* The distinction between these two does not imply that one is truer or more genuine than another; rather, it is an aesthetic distinction. In realistic drama, all the elements in a play—language, characters, plot developments—conform to our observations of the way people speak and behave in daily life. Departures from realism, by contrast, uses devices that do not conform to our experience of everyday life: poetry rather than prose; otherworldly characters, such as ghosts or angels; and fantasy of all kinds.

In any discussion of genres and categories, it is important to remember that these are convenient guides; they are not ironclad divisions. They help us understand what the playwright, director, and performers are trying to do, but we should never try to categorize plays at the expense of experiencing them. Most plays do not fall neatly into a genre or category, and many plays mix genres. In this regard, there are questions you should ask as you are reading a play: Does the play clearly fit into any of the categories? Is it possible that the author has mixed genres, styles, realistic and nonrealistic elements, or high art and popular art?

A number of contemporary critics question traditional categorization altogether and suggest that a mixture of styles and disregard for distinctions is a key characteristic of present-day postmodernist art. There are also critics who argue that an appropriate way to categorize texts is by political point of view. For example, is the author a feminist, a Marxist, a gay activist? There are even subdivisions within these groups. When we approach a play in this way, a key question to ask is how the author's politics affect the way she or he structures the drama or represents the characters.

Possibly the best advice about categorization is to remain open-minded. Do not try to pigeonhole texts simplistically. Think about all the possible approaches to categorization, and see each drama as a unique work of art.

HOW THE PLAY UNFOLDS: ACTION AND THEME
The Play Begins

The first scene of a play should be a key to what is to follow. It should introduce you to the tone of the play—whether serious or comic—and to the characters and the main action. If the chief characters do not appear in the opening scene, they will probably be talked about in preparation for their appearance later. The chief conflicts of the play—what actions the characters are planning against each other, what tasks they have been commanded to undertake (by a god or a ghost, perhaps), what is at stake (a kingdom, turf in a neighborhood, control and power in a marriage)—will frequently be spelled out in the opening moments.

As you move into the play, all the things we have spoken of should be kept in mind: the kind of theater in which the play is presented; the stage set; the time and place of the action; the tendencies of the characters and their interplay with each other. Observe, as you progress, what information is revealed. Which characters seem to be the "good guys," the ones with whom you identify and who you hope will come out on top? Which are the "bad guys," the villains, the unjust ones, the selfish ones? In a struggle between two or more people, which character appears to have the upper hand? How does the power shift during the course of the play?

At the same time, note what is happening in the play, that is, what action is unfolding. Who seems to be the chief agent of the action? Who is the primary opponent of that agent? Are there surprises, or does there seem to be an inevitability about what takes place? Do you believe what is happening? Are the actions, the motivations, the emotions, and the words of the characters credible? If not, why not?

During the course of reading the play, you should at all times be aware of who is onstage. Take note of who enters and who exits and when this occurs. It may be important that, say, two people are alone onstage, or that they are being observed and overheard by another person or several people.

The Play Progresses

When you have begun to read the play, notice the language. Is the play written as conversation? If so, is the dialogue fresh, convincing, or even surprising? Or are the words predictable, ordinary, and trite? Is the language formal? If so, what makes it seem formal? Is it poetry? If so, what kind of poetry is it—stiff or flowing and musical? Perhaps you might read one or two sections out loud to get a better sense of the language. Whether conversational or poetic, does the language seem to lift the play up, or does it flatten the play out?

Earlier, we mentioned the importance of the first scene. As the play progresses, observe how the subsequent scenes follow each other. Does there seem to be a logical connection? If the play skips about—as Shakespeare's plays tend to do—can we still follow the action? Suppose that we leave one set of characters, go to another set, and then return to the first group. If you need to, you might make a scheme of this, to see how the scenes create a pattern of alternation and to trace each story as it unfolds. If there are two or more threads—a plot and a subplot, for instance, or several sets of characters—how are they related?

As you come to the end of the first act, and of each act after that, do you notice the play building to some sort of climax? Is a question posed in one act that must be answered in the next? Is there a threat or an impending conflict?

The Theme

Pause somewhere along the way—perhaps at the end of an act, or simply when the thought strikes you—to consider the *theme* of the play. What does the playwright appear to be concerned about, in terms of ideas, moral questions, values, and philosophical considerations? These matters usually come to the forefront not in direct speeches—though that may occur—but in the way different characters stand for ideas and represent different sides of a moral equation or dilemma. Perhaps the play is dealing with honor and duty to one's ancestors or to the gods. Perhaps it pits evil against good. Perhaps it takes up the subject of injustice. If it is a comedy, it may simply be dealing with human pretensions and pomposity. Once you think you have identified the theme or themes of the play, observe how the playwright develops this aspect as the action unfolds and the speeches of the characters address the subject.

Also remember that some contemporary critics believe that the playwright does not provide the meaning of a play. They argue that the response of the reader or viewer is more significant in bringing meaning to a text, and that no two readers or viewers—because of their differing backgrounds and orientations—will create the exact same reading of a script. Other critics note that a performance adds meaning to a script and that each artist who stages a work brings a unique reading of the text to his or her audience.

The Conclusion

As the play approaches its conclusion, note several things. First, does the play continue to hold your interest? Has the action become more and more exciting the closer you come to the end? Are you eager to follow it through to the end? Do you want to know how it comes out? Have the characters remained interesting? Are they complex? Have they fooled you or surprised you? Have they acted as you expected them to act? Has the theme become clear, and has it been explored in a provocative and interesting way?

Once you have finished reading the play, think back on what you have experienced. Can you describe how you felt as you were reading and how you feel now that you are finished? Has the play entertained you? Has the play made you think? Has it given you a new perspective? Have you learned anything?

Finally, what in the play has had the most impact on you: the emotion, the excitement and suspense of the story, your identification with the characters, the language, the ideas? Probably it is some combination of these. Also, perhaps there are certain aspects of the play that bothered you or that you did not understand. If so, you might reread those sections and discuss them with your friends and your instructor.

Ideally, in the end, you should have had not only a reading experience, but an imagined theater experience.

SOTOBA KOMACHI
Joe Turner's Co
gone
Hamlet
TARTUFFE
The Mystery of Ir
The Glass Menagerie
The Busy
AK
ood Woman of Setzuan
The Cherry Or
A Do
A DREAM PLAY
HEART
Krapp's Last Tape
Abra
roth
e Tu
SOTO
Mys

AN ANTHOLOGY OF PLAYS

TA

The Busy Body

Cherry Orchard

FREAK

The Glass

The Good Woman of Setz

A Doll's House

A DRI

p's Last Tape

BLUE HEART

e Menaechmus Brothers

Abraham an

SOTOBA KOMACHI

igone

Joe Turner's Come

Hamlet

TARTUFFE

The Mystery of Irr

AK

The Glass Menagerie

The Busy

ood Woman of Setzuan

The Cherry Orc

and Isaac

A DREAM PLAY

A Dol

The Menaechmus I

Joe Turner's Come and Gone

Introduction to *Antigone* by Sophocles

Translated from Greek and Edited by
Peter D. Arnott

Antigone   Left to right: Marshall Griffin (Attendant), Tara Fitzgerald as Antigone, Scott Frazer (Attendant), Old Vic Theatre, London. *(© Donald Cooper/PHOTOSTAGE)*

The Play   Written in 441 B.C., *Antigone* is based on a familiar Greek myth. Antigone is the daughter of King Oedipus. Before the start of the play's action, Antigone's two brothers, Eteocles and Polyneices, fight a war to see who will become king of Thebes; during this war, they kill one another. Antigone's uncle, Creon, then becomes king of Thebes and, blaming Polyneices for the conflict, issues an edict saying that he is not to be given an honorable burial.

As the play begins, Antigone tells her sister Ismene that she will defy her uncle. While Ismene cautions Antigone that such an action could result in her being put to death, Antigone argues that she will not be subservient to the king.

As the play progresses, Antigone attempts to bury Polyneices, but she is caught and brought before the king. In their confrontation, Antigone defies Creon and is sentenced to death. By the play's end, not only is Antigone dead; so, too, are Creon's wife and son, who have killed themselves. In the final scene, Creon is standing alone, bereft of all those he held dear.

Besides these characters, the play—like all classical Greek tragedies—also has a chorus. In *Antigone* the chorus represents the elders of Thebes. The chorus serves many functions: providing background information, raising philosophical questions, commenting on the action, and interacting with the principal figures.

Antigone has many of the traditional characteristics of classical Greek tragedy. Greek tragedy deals with reversals in fortune and the downfall of a royal figure. A much debated concept, put forth by the philosopher Aristotle, is that the downfall of the tragic protagonist is due to a tragic flaw, which is most often defined as either a character flaw or an error in judgment. The structure of classical tragedies is usually climactic; that is, the drama takes place within a short time, is set in one locale, and contains no secondary plot. In addition, these tragedies follow similar patterns in the unfolding of their scenes. First comes the *prologos,* the opening scene, which sets the action and provides background information. Next comes the *parados,* in which the chorus enters. Throughout the play itself, *episodes*—scenes in which characters confront each other—alternate with *choral odes.* The *exodos* is the final scene, in which all characters exit from the stage.

While *Antigone* fits the classical structure, critics point out that there are many possible interpretations of this play, some of which have modern implications. The play can be read as a battle between idealistic youth and conservative traditionalism. Some contemporary theater artists stage the play as a woman trapped in an oppressive society asserting independence against male dominance. Still others suggest that both Antigone and Creon are culpable, that their tragic flaw is their excessive pride—which the Greeks referred to as *hubris*—and that they are both responsible for the horrific outcome. These varied interpretations reflect the strength of *Antigone.*

The Playwright   Sophocles (ca. 496 B.C.–406 B.C.) was born at Colonus, near Athens, the son of a wealthy Athenian. He was devoted to his city-state, Athens, and refused many invitations to live at the courts of foreign kings. Sophocles was at various times a general, a civic leader, an ambassador, and a priest.

As a playwright, Sophocles was noted for his superb plot construction. The Greek philosopher Aristotle used Sophocles's *King Oedipus* as the model for his analysis of tragedy. Exploration of character and focus on the individual are also characteristics of Sophocles's plays. In addition, his poetry is widely admired for its lucidity and beauty. It is estimated that he wrote over 100 plays. He won first prize 18 times in the ancient Greek play contests, never finishing lower than second.

Sophocles is credited with introducing scene painting (though there is great debate about what the innovation actually was), increasing the chorus from 12 to 15 members, and adding a third actor to Greek tragedy.

Only seven complete tragedies by Sophocles survive: *Ajax* (ca. 450 to 440 B.C.), *Antigone* (ca. 441 B.C.), *King Oedipus* (ca. 430 B.C.), *Electra* (ca. 418 to 410 B.C.), *Trachiniae* (ca. 413 B.C.), *Philoctetes* (409 B.C.), and *Oedipus at Colonus* (ca. 406 B.C.).

The Period   The fifth century B.C. in Greece, referred to as the classical era and as the golden age of Greece, was a time of remarkable accomplishments. Athens, the center of Greek society, was the birthplace of democracy. During the fifth century B.C., Greek philosophers, historians, scientists, physicians, and mathematicians explored and tried to explain the world around them. Superb examples of architecture and art survive from this era. The achievements in theater were no less noteworthy.

Greek drama during this time was presented as part of religious festivals and staged in amphitheaters. Seating for approximately 15,000 spectators was set up on the side of a hill. At the base of the hillside was a circular playing space called the *orchestra,* and behind this was a scene house (*skene*), which served as the major piece of scenery (the standard scenic setting for Greek tragedy was a palace), as well as a place for actors to change clothes and for props to be stored. There were also devices for special effects, such as a wagon that could be wheeled out from the scene house and a crane on the roof of the skene, which could be used for flying.

All the characters in Greek drama, male and female, were portrayed by men. The performers, particularly the chorus, had to be accomplished at singing, dancing, and vocal projection. The actors were paid, and after 449 B.C. an acting contest was introduced. The number of actors taking speaking roles in a classical Greek tragedy was limited to three, but because the performers wore masks, each actor could play several roles in the same play.

The major element in Greek costuming was the mask, worn by all performers and probably constructed of wood and linen. Masks indicated the emotional state of the characters and made it possible for males to play females.

ANTIGONE

Sophocles

CHARACTERS

ANTIGONE, ISMENE } daughters of Oedipus
CREON, King of Thebes
EURYDICE, his wife
HAEMON, his son

TEIRESIAS, the blind prophet
GUARD, set to watch the corpse of Polyneices
FIRST MESSENGER
SECOND MESSENGER, from the house
CHORUS of THEBAN ELDERS

[In front of the palace at Thebes. Enter Antigone and Ismene.]

ANTIGONE. Ismene, my dear, my mother's child, my sister,
What part of Oedipus' sad legacy
Has Zeus not laid in full on us who live?
There is nothing bitter, nothing of disaster,
No shame, no humiliation I have not seen
In the number of your sufferings and mine.
And now what is this order which they say
Our leader has announced throughout the city?
Do you know? Have you heard? Or do I have to tell you
That what has happened to our enemies   10
Is threatening to fall upon our friends?
ISMENE. I have heard no word of friends, Antigone,
To bring me comfort or to bring me pain

10. **That what . . . friends:** The bodies of the warriors of Argos, who had aided Polyneices in his attempt on Thebes, had been left unburied; this punishment is now to be extended to Polyneices himself, although a Theban born.

Since the time we two were robbed of our two brothers,
Dead in one day, and by each other's hand.
And now the Argive army overnight
Has disappeared, I am no nearer knowing
Whether my luck has changed for good or bad.
ANTIGONE. I know, too well. That is why I wanted to bring you
Outside the courtyard, to talk to you alone.   20
ISMENE. What is it? Trouble, you do not need to tell me.
ANTIGONE. What else, when Creon singles out one brother
For a hero's grave, and lets the other rot?
They are saying he has laid Eteocles in the ground
With every rite and custom that is fitting
To give him honor with the dead below.
But Polyneices' body, that was killed
So pitifully, they say he has commanded
Should not be mourned or given burial
But lie unburied and unwept, a feast   30

For passing birds to gorge on at their pleasure.
And so, the rumor runs, has our good Creon
Decreed for you and me—for me, I say!
And is on his way here now, to spell it out
To those who have not heard. He does not take
This matter lightly. Anyone who disobeys
In any way will die by public stoning.
So there you have it. Now we shall soon find out
If you are a true-born daughter of your line,
Or if you will disgrace your noble blood!   40

ISMENE. But, my poor sister, if things are as you say,
  What ways and means have I to set them
    straight?
ANTIGONE. Ask yourself, will you work with me,
  help me do it?
ISMENE. What adventure is this? What do you have
  in mind?
ANTIGONE. Will you help this hand of mine to lift
  the dead?
ISMENE. You mean to bury him? Against the law?
ANTIGONE. Bury my brother? Yes—and bury yours,
  If you will not. No-one shall call me faithless.
ISMENE. You would not dare, when Creon has
    forbidden it!
ANTIGONE. He has no right to keep me from my
    own.   50
ISMENE. Oh sister, think of how our father died,
  Hated, despised, and driven by the sins
  He had himself laid bare, to turn his hand
  Against himself, and strike out both his eyes.
  And then his mother, wife—which shall I call her?
  Knotted a noose, and took away her life.
  Then the final blow, two brothers in one day,
  Unhappy pair, each shedding kinsman's blood,
  Lay hands on each other, and made one in
    death.
  Now we two are alone. Think how much
    worse   60
  Our deaths will be, if in despite of law
  We brave the king's commandment and his
    power.
  Let us not forget two things—that we were born
  Women, and so not meant to fight with men;
  And then, that we must do what our masters
    tell us—
  Obey in this, and other things far worse.
  I, then, will ask the kingdom of the dead
  To pardon me; since I am no free agent,
  I will yield to the powers that be. There is no
    sense
  In meddling in things outside our sphere.   70

ANTIGONE. I shall not persuade you. You would not
  be welcome
  To help me now, even if you wanted to.
  Be what you want to be; but I intend
  To bury him. It is a noble way to die.
  I shall lie with him for love, as he loved me,
  A criminal, but guiltless; for the dead
  Have longer claims upon me than the living.
  There is my lasting home. If you think fit
  To dishonor the gods' commandments, then
    you may.
ISMENE. I mean them no dishonor; but when it
  means   80
  Defying the state—I am not strong enough.
ANTIGONE. Let that be your excuse. Now I shall go
  To heap the earth on my beloved brother.
ISMENE. Antigone, no! I am so afraid for you!
ANTIGONE. You need not fear for me. Look after
  yourself.
ISMENE. At least tell no-one what you mean to do.
  Keep it a secret, I shall do the same.
ANTIGONE. Oh no, denounce me! You will be in far
  worse trouble
  For keeping silence, if you do not tell the
    world.
ISMENE. You have a hot heart where you should be
  shivering.   90
ANTIGONE. I know I am giving pleasure where I
  should.
ISMENE. Yes, if you can. But you ask too much of
  yourself.
ANTIGONE. When I have no more strength, then I
  shall stop.
ISMENE. No point in starting, when the cause is
  hopeless.
ANTIGONE. Go on like this and you will make me
  hate you,
  And the dead will hate you too; you give him
  cause.
  Leave me alone with my stupidity
  To face this dread unknown; whatever it is,
  Anything is better than to die a coward!
ISMENE. Then if your mind is made up, go. You are
  a fool,   100
  And yet your own will love you for it.

[Exit Antigone; Ismene retires within the palace. Enter chorus of Theban elders.]

CHORUS. Light of the morning sun, brightest that
  ever yet

Dawned upon the seven gates of Thebes;
Eye of the golden day, at last we see you
Rising over Dirke's streams,
Turning to rout the white-shielded warrior
That came from Argos in his array,
Winging his feet, and sending him flying home.

Polyneices' contentious quarrel
Was the cause of his coming here,   110
Winging over our country
Like an eagle clamoring,
Sheathed in snow-white feathers
With mail-clad men and waving plumes.

Over the housetops hovering, howling before
Our seven gates for blood to slake his spears;
But before he could suck his fill of Theban
Blood, before the Fire-god's flame
Leapt from the logs to embrace our ramparts,
He left, so loud the roaring of the war-cry   120
Behind him, as he fought the Theban dragon.

Zeus hates nothing more than a boastful
    tongue.
When he saw them coming, a mighty stream
Arrogant in their clanging gold
He brandished his thunderbolt and felled the
    man
Who had scaled our ramparts, and stood at his
    goal
With the cry of victory on his lips.

And over he tumbled, torch in hand,
He who a moment before
Had come at us like a man possessed,   130
Running berserk, with the hot breath of hatred.
Earth rang with his fall, and his threats went
    wide.
Then the God of War, our good yoke-fellow,
Lashed out, and assigned
To each of the rest their several deaths.

Seven captains stood before seven gates,
Matched against seven, and left their armor
In homage to Zeus, the arbiter of battles,
All but the ill-starred pair, who, born

Of one father and mother, leveled their spears   140
At each other; both won, and both fell dead.

But now the glorious name of Victory
Enters our chariot-proud
City, to laugh with us in our joy,
Let us put all memory of past war behind us
And visit the temples of the gods with song
And with nightlong dances; Bacchus, whose
    steps
Set the meadows dancing,
Come down to lead the procession!

[Enter Creon.]

But here comes our country's ruler,   150
Creon, Menoeceus' son, our new lord
By the gods' new dispensations.
What counsel can he be pondering
To summon the elders by general decree
To meet in special conference together?
CREON. Gentlemen, the state has been in troubled
    waters,
But now the gods have set us back on course.
My summons came to you, of all the people,
To meet here privately, because I knew
Your constant reverence for Laius' throne,   160
And then, when Oedipus became our king,
After his death, I saw their children
Secure in your unswerving loyalty.
And now this double blow has taken both
His sons in one day, each struck down by the
    other,
Each with his brother's blood upon his hands,
The throne and all its powers come to me
As next of kin in order of succession.
But you can never know what a man is made of,
His character or powers of intellect,   170
Until you have seen him tried in rule and office.
A man who holds the reins of government
And does not follow the wisest policies
But lets something scare him from saying what
    he thinks,
I hold despicable, and always have done.
Nor have I time for anyone who puts
His popularity before his country.
As Zeus the omnipotent will be my witness,
If I saw our welfare threatened; if I saw
One danger-signal, I would speak my mind,   180
And never count an enemy of my country
To be a friend of mine. This I believe:

---

105. Dirke: River on the west of Thebes.   **125. the man . . . ramparts:** A famous incident in the Theban story. Capaneus, one of the seven heroes who marched against the city, dared to defy Zeus and for his presumption was struck down at the moment of his triumph.

The state keeps us afloat. While she holds an
   even keel,
Then, and then only, can we make real friends.
By this creed I shall make Thebes prosperous;
And in accordance with it, I have published
My edict on the sons of Oedipus,
That Eteocles, who died a hero's death
While fighting to defend his fatherland
Should be entombed with every solemn rite   190
With which the glorious dead are sent to rest.
But his brother Polyneices, who returned
From exile, with intent to devastate
The country of his fathers, and to burn
The temples of his fathers' gods, to taste
His brother's blood, and make the rest of his
   slaves,
Concerning him, it is proclaimed as follows:
That nobody shall mourn or bury him,
But let his body lie for dogs and birds
To make their meal, so men may look and
   shudder.   200
Such is my policy; foul play shall never
Triumph over honest merit, if I can help it,
But the man who loves his city shall receive
Honor from me, in his life and in his death.
CHORUS. Such is your pleasure, Creon, son of
   Menoeceus,
Concerning our city's friend and enemy,
And you have the power to order as you wish,
Not only the dead, but the living too.
CREON. Then see to it my orders are obeyed.
CHORUS. Lay this responsibility on someone
   younger!   210
CREON. No, not to guard the corpse; that has been
   seen to.
CHORUS. Then what else are you asking me to do?
CREON. Not to side with anyone who disobeys me.
CHORUS. No man is fool enough to ask for death.
CREON. That is what you would get. But hope of
   gain
Has often led men on to their destruction.

[Enter Guard.]

GUARD. My lord, I won't say that I'm out of breath
From hurrying, or that I've run here all the
   way,
For several times my thoughts pulled me up
   short
And made me turn round to go back again.   220
There was a voice inside me kept on saying

"Why go, you fool? You're certain to be
   punished."
"Idiot, why hang about? If Creon hears
The news from someone else, you'll smart for it."
Arguing like this I went at snail's pace,
And so a short road turned into a long one.
But in the end, go forward won the day.
There's nothing to say, but all the same I'll
   say it.
I'm certain of one thing, at any rate,
That I can only get what's coming to me.   230
CREON. What is it that has put such fear in you?
GUARD. First let me say a word on my own account.
I didn't do it, nor did I see who did,
And it isn't right that I should take the blame
   for it.
CREON. A well-placed shot. You have covered
   yourself
Well against attack. I see you mean to surprise
   me.
GUARD. A man thinks twice before he tells bad
   news.
CREON. Then tell me, will you, and be on your way.
GUARD. Well, here it is: the corpse—someone has
   buried it.
And gone away; he sprinkled dry dust over   240
The flesh, and did whatever else was fitting.
CREON. What are you saying? What man has dared
   to do this?
GUARD. I don't know. There was no mark of a pick-
   axe,
No spade had been at work; the ground was
   hard,
Dry and unbroken; we could find no tracks
Of wheels; he left no trace, whoever did it.
And when the man who took the morning
   watch
Showed us, nobody knew what to make of it.
The corpse was out of sight—not in a tomb
But sprinkled with dust, as though someone
   had thrown it   250
To avoid bad luck. There was no sign of wild
   beasts
Or dogs around; the corpse was in one piece.
Then we all started cursing each other at once,
One sentry blaming the next; it would have
   come
To blows in the end, there was no-one there to
   stop us.
First one had done it, then the next man, then
   the next,

But we couldn't pin it down, all pleaded
  ignorance.
We were ready to take red-hot irons in our
  hands,
To walk through fire, to swear an oath to
  heaven
That we were innocent, had no idea   260
Of who had planned it all, or done the work.
In the end, when there was no more point in
  searching,
One man said something which made every one
  of us
Shiver, and hang our heads; we didn't see
How we could argue with him, or if we listened
How we could save our necks. He said we
  couldn't
Keep the thing dark, but we must come and tell
  you.
So we did; and I was the unlucky one.
The lot picked me to receive the prize.
So here I am—about as pleased to be here   270
As I know you are to see me. Nobody
Has any love for the one who brings bad news.
CHORUS. My lord, since he began, I have been
  wondering
  Could this perhaps have been the work of
  heaven?
CREON. Be quiet, before you make me lose my
  temper.
  Do you want to look like fools in your old age?
  What you suggest is intolerable,
  That the gods would give this corpse a second
  thought.
  Why should they try to hide his nakedness?
  In reward for services rendered? When he
  came   280
  To turn their marble halls and treasuries,
  To burn their land, make havoc of its laws?
  Or can you see the gods rewarding sinners?
  Never. No, there were people in this town
  Who took it hard from the first, and grumbled
  at me,
  Furtively tossing their heads, not submitting
  To the yoke as in duty bound, like contented
  men.
  It was these people—of that I am convinced—
  Who bribed the guards and urged them on to
  do it.
  Of all the institutions of mankind   290
  The greatest curse is money. It destroys
  Our cities, it takes men away from home,

Corrupts men's honest minds, and teaches
  them
To enter on disreputable courses.
It shows them how to lead immoral lives
And flout the gods in everything they do.
But every one of the bribers will be caught
Sooner or later, they may be sure of that.
But by the reverence I owe to Zeus,
I tell you this upon my solemn oath,   300
That if you do not find the author of
This burial, and produce him before my eyes,
Death alone will be too good for you; you will be
Left hanging, till you tell about this outrage.
Then, when you next go stealing, you will know
What you may take, and learn for once and all
Not to love money without asking where
It comes from. You will find ill-gotten gains
Have ruined many more than they have saved.
GUARD. May I speak? Or shall I just turn round and
  go?   310
CREON. Do you still need telling that your voice
  annoys me?
GUARD. Where does it hurt? In your ears or in your
  heart?
CREON. Is there any call for you to define my pain?
GUARD. The criminal troubles your mind, and I
  your ears.
CREON. Oh, you were born with a loose tongue, I
  can see.
GUARD. Maybe I was, but this I didn't do.
CREON. You did, and worse. You sold your life for
  money.
GUARD. How dreadful to judge by appearances,
  then be wrong.
CREON. Moralize as you please; but if you do not
  show me
  The men who did this thing, you will bear
  witness   320
  That dishonest winnings bring you into trouble.

[Exit Creon to the palace.]

GUARD. Well, I only hope he's caught; but whether
  he is
  Or not—it's in the hands of fortune now—
  You won't see me coming this way again.
  I never thought I'd get away with this.
  It's more than I hoped—the gods be praised for
  it.

[Exit.]

CHORUS. The world is full of wonderful things
    But none more so than man,
    This prodigy who sails before the storm-winds,
    Cutting a path across the sea's gray face   330
    Beneath the towering menace of the waves.
    And Earth, the oldest, the primeval god,
    Immortal, inexhaustible Earth,
    She too has felt the weight of his hand
    As year after year the mules are harnessed
    And plows go back and forwards in the fields.

    Merry birds and forest beasts,
    Fish that swim in the deep waters,
    Are gathered into the woven nets
    Of man the crafty hunter.   340
    He conquers with his arts
    The beasts that roam in the wild hill-country.
    He tames the horses with their shaggy manes
    Throwing a harness around their necks,
    And the tireless mountain bull.

    Speech he has made his own, and thought
    That travels swift as the wind,
    And how to live in harmony with others
    In cities, and how to shelter himself
    From the piercing frost, cold rain, when the
      open   350
    Fields can offer but a poor night's lodging.
    He is ever-resourceful; nothing that comes
    Will find him unready, save Death alone.
    Then he will call for help and call in vain,
    Though, often, where cure was despaired of, he
      has found one.

    The wit of man surpasses belief,
    It works for good and evil too;
    When he honors his country's laws, and the
      right
    He is pledged to uphold, then city
    Hold up your head; but the man   360
    Who yields to temptation and brings evil home
    Is a man without a city; he has
    No place in the circle of my hearth,
    Nor any part in my counsels.

[Enter Guard, leading Antigone prisoner.]

    But what is this? The gods alone know.
    Is it Antigone? She and no other.
    Oh unhappy daughter of
    Your wretched father Oedipus,

    What is it? Have they arrested you?
    Have you broken the royal commandment?   370
    Has your foolishness brought you to this?
GUARD. Here she is! This is the girl who did it!
    We caught her burying him. But where is
      Creon?
CHORUS. Here, coming from the palace, just in
      time.

[Enter from the palace Creon with attendants.]

CREON. Coming in time for what? What is it now?
GUARD. My lord, a man should never swear to
      anything.
    Second thoughts belie the first. I could have
      sworn
    I wouldn't have come back here again in a
      hurry
    After the tongue-lashing you gave me last time.
    But there's no pleasure like the one that
      comes   380
    As a surprise, the last thing you expected.
    So here I am, breaking my solemn oath,
    Bringing this girl, who was caught performing
    The final rites. We didn't draw lots this time.
    This piece of luck belongs to me, and no-one
      else.
    So now, my lord, she's yours, for you to
      examine
    And question as you wish. I've done my duty;
    It's someone else's problem from now on.
CREON. This girl? Where did you take her? What
      was she doing?
GUARD. Burying the man. That's all there is to
      know.   390
CREON. Are you serious? Do you know what you
      are saying?
GUARD. I saw her burying the corpse, the thing
    You had forbidden. What could be clearer than
      that?
CREON. You saw her? Captured her redhanded?
      How?
GUARD. It happened this way. When we returned to
      our posts
    With your dreadful threats still ringing in our ears
    We swept off every bit of dust that covered
    The corpse, and left the rotting carcass bare,
    Then sat down on the brow of a hill to
      windward
    Where the stench couldn't reach us. We kept
      ourselves lively   400

By threatening each other with what would
  happen
If anyone were careless in his duty.
And so time passed, until the sun's bright disk
Stood midway in the heavens, and the heat
Began to burn us. Suddenly a whirlwind
Raised a dust storm, a black blot on the sky,
Which filled the plain, played havoc with the
  leaves
Of every tree in sight, and choked the air.
We shut our eyes and bore it; heaven sends
These things to try us. When it had gone at
  last   410
There was the girl; she gave a shrill sharp cry
Like a bird in distress when it sees its bed
Stripped of its young ones and the nest
  deserted.
So she cried, when she saw the corpse left bare.
Raising her voice in grief, and calling down
Curses on the men who had done this thing.
Then at once she brought handfuls of dry dust,
Lifted a handsome vase, and poured from it
The three drink-offerings to crown the dead.
When we see it, out we run and close around
  her   420
In a moment. She was not at all put out.
We taxed her with what she had done, both then
And earlier; she admitted everything,
Which made me glad, but miserable too.
Nothing makes you happier than to get yourself
Out of trouble; but it's quite another thing
To get friends into it. But there's nothing
I wouldn't do, to keep myself from harm.
CREON. You there; yes, you, who dare not look me
  in the face;
  Do you admit this accusation or deny it?   430
ANTIGONE. Oh, I admit. I make no denial.
CREON. *[to the Guard]* Take yourself off, wherever
  you want to go,
  A free man. You are cleared of a serious charge.
  [to Antigone] Now tell me, you, and keep your
  answers brief
  Did you know there was an order forbidding
  this?
ANTIGONE. Yes. How could I help it? Everybody
  knew.
CREON. And yet you dared to go against the law?
ANTIGONE. Why not? It was not Zeus who gave the
  order,
  And Justice living with the dead below
  Has never given men a law like this.   440

Nor did I think that your pronouncements were
So powerful that mere man could override
The unwritten and unfailing laws of heaven.
These live, not for today and yesterday
But for all time; they came, no man knows
  whence.
There is no man's resolve I fear enough
To answer to the gods for breaking these.
I knew that I must die—how could I help it?
Even without your edict; but if I die
Before my time is up, I count it gain   450
For when a person lives as I do, in the midst
Of evils, what can death be but gain?
And so for me to happen on this fate
Is grief not worth a thought, but if I had left
My mother's son to lie a homeless corpse,
Then had I grieved. I do not grieve for this.
If what I do seems foolish in your sight
It may be that a fool condemns my folly.
CHORUS. This is her father's willful spirit in her,
  Not knowing how to bend before the storm.   460
CREON. Come, you must learn that over-stubborn
  spirits
  Are those most often humbled. Iron that has
  Been hardened in the fire and cannot bend
  You will find the first to snap and fly in pieces.
  I have known high-mettled horses brought to
  order
  By a touch on the bridle. Pride is not for those
  Who live their lives at their neighbour's beck
  and call.
This girl is already schooled in insolence
When she disobeyed the official proclamation
And now she adds insult to injury   470
By boasting of it, glorying in her crime.
I swear, she is the man and I the woman
If she keeps her victory and goes unpunished.
No! Even though she be my sister's child,
If she were bound to me by ties more close
Than anyone who shares our household prayers
She and that sister of hers will not escape
The ultimate fate; for I accuse her too
Of equal guilt in plotting this burial.
So go and call her. I saw her indoors just now 480
Delirious, not knowing what she was saying.

[Exeunt attendants to the palace.]

A guilty mind betrays itself beforehand
When men go plotting mischief in the dark.
But no less do I hate the criminal

Who is caught, and tries to glorify his crime.

ANTIGONE. What more would you take from me
than my life?

CREON. Not a thing. When I have that, I have all I
want.

ANTIGONE. Then what are you waiting for? Your
arguments
Fall on deaf ears; I pray they always will.
My loyalties are meaningless to you.   490
Yet, in the world's eyes, what could I have done
To earn me greater glory, than to give
My brother burial? Everybody here
Would cheer me, if they were not dumb with
fear.
But royalty, among so many blessings,
Has power to say and do whatever it likes.

CREON. These Thebans take a different view from
yours.

ANTIGONE. Not they. They only curb their tongues
for your sake.

CREON. Then why be different? Are you not
ashamed?

ANTIGONE. Ashamed? Of paying homage to a
brother?   500

CREON. Was not the man he killed your brother
too?

ANTIGONE. My brother, by one mother, by one
father.

CREON. Then why pay honors hateful in his eyes?

ANTIGONE. The dead man will not say he finds
them hateful.

CREON. When you honor him no higher than a
traitor?

ANTIGONE. It was his brother died, and not his slave.

CREON. Destroying Thebes; while he died to
protect it.

ANTIGONE. It makes no difference. Death asks these
rites.

CREON. But a hero asks more honor than a traitor.

ANTIGONE. Who knows? The dead may find no
harm in this.   510

CREON. Even death cannot change hatred into love.

ANTIGONE. But I was born for love, and not for
hate!

CREON. Then if you have to love, go down and love
The dead; while I live, no woman shall rule me!

[Enter attendants from the palace with Ismene.]

CHORUS. Look, the gates open and Ismene comes
Weeping for love and sisterhood.

Her brows are clouded, shadowing
Her face flushed red, and teardrops
Fall on her lovely cheek.

CREON. And you, a viper lurking in my house,   520
Were sucking my life's blood, while I,
unknowing,
Raised a twin scourge to drive me from my
throne.
Come, answer me. Will you confess your share
In this burial, or deny all knowledge of it?

ISMENE. I did it—if my sister will allow me.
Half the blame is mine. I take it on myself.

ANTIGONE. No! Justice will not let you! You
refused,
And I denied you any part in it.

ISMENE. But now you are in trouble. I am not
Ashamed to ride the storm out at your side.   530

ANTIGONE. Who did it, Hades and the dead can
witness.
I love not those who only talk of love.

ISMENE. No, sister, do not reject me. Let
Me die with you and sanctify the dead.

ANTIGONE. You shall not share my death. You had
no hand in this.
Do not say you had. My death will be enough.

ISMENE. What joy have I in life when you are gone?

ANTIGONE. Ask Creon. All your care has been for
him.

ISMENE. Why do you want to hurt me? It does no
good.

ANTIGONE. You are right. If I mock you it is for my
pain.   540

ISMENE. Then tell me how I can help you, even
now.

ANTIGONE. Save yourself. I do not grudge you your
escape.

ISMENE. Then is poor Ismene not to share your
fate?

ANTIGONE. It was you who chose to live, and I to
die.

ISMENE. At least I tried to move you from your
choice.

ANTIGONE. One side approved your wisdom, the
other mine.

ISMENE. And yet the offence is the same for both of
us.

ANTIGONE. Be of good heart. You live; but I have
been
Dead for a long time now, to serve the dead.

CREON. Here are two fools, one lately come to
folly,   550

The other since the day that she was born.

ISMENE. Indeed, my lord, such sense as nature
gives us

  Is not for ever. It goes in time of trouble.

CREON. Like yours, when you chose bad friends
and evil ways.

ISMENE. How can I bear to live without my sister?

CREON. Sister? You have no sister. She is dead.

ISMENE. But will you kill your son's appointed
bride?

CREON. I will. My son has other fields to plow.

ISMENE. He will never love another as he loved her.

CREON. No son of mine will wed an evil woman. 560

ISMENE. Haemon, my dearest! How your father
wrongs you!

CREON. Let us have no further talk of marriage.

CHORUS. You will do it, then? You will rob your
son of his bride?

CREON. Not I, but Death; yes, Death will break the
match.

CHORUS. The decision stands, then, that the girl
must die?

CREON. For you, and me. Let us have no more
delay.

  Servants, take them inside. From this time on
  They must be women, not let out alone.
  Even the boldest of us turns and runs
  The moment he can see death closing in.   570

[Exeunt attendants with Antigone and Ismene.]

CHORUS. Blessed are those whose days have not
tasted evil,

  For once the gods have set a house tottering
  The curse will never fade, but continues
  From generation unto generation,
  Like a storm rolling over the dark waters
  Driven by the howling Thracian gales,
  Stirring black mud from the bottom of the sea;
  And the wind-torn headlands answer back
  In a sullen roar, as the storm breaks over them.

  I look on the house of Labdacus   580
  And see how, from time immemorial,
  The sorrows of the living have been heaped
upon
  The sorrows of those that died before them.
  One generation does not set another

561. Haemon . . . wrongs you: It is uncertain whether this line is
spoken by Antigone or Ismene.

  Free, but some god strikes them down
  And they have no means of deliverance.
  Over the last root of the house of Oedipus
  Shone a ray of hope; but now this too has been
  Laid low by a handful of bloody dust
  Demanded by the gods of the underworld,   590
  By unthinking words, and the heart's delirium.

  Zeus, what man's transgression can restrain
your power,
  When neither Sleep, that encompasses all things,
  Nor the months' unwearied and god-ordered
march
  Can arrest it? You do not grow old with the
years
  But rule in shining splendor as Olympus' king.
  As it was in the past, this law will hold
  Tomorrow and until the end of time:
  That mortal life has a limited capacity.
  When it aims too high, then the curse will fall. 600

  For Hope, whose territory is unbounded,
  Brings comfort to many, but to many others
  Insane desires and false encouragement.
  A man may go blindly on his way
  Then walk into the fire and burn himself,
  And so disillusion comes.
  In his wisdom, someone coined the famous
saying
  That when a god leads a man's mind on
  To destruction, sooner or later he comes
  To believe that evil is good, good evil,   610
  And then his days of happiness are numbered.

[Enter Haemon.]

  But here is Haemon, your youngest son.
  Does he come to grieve for the doom that has
fallen
  Upon Antigone, his promised bride,
  To complain of the marriage that is taken from
him?

CREON. We shall not need second sight to tell us
that.
  My son, have you heard that sentence has been
passed
  On your betrothed? Are you here to storm at
me?
  Or have I your good will, whatever I do?

HAEMON. Father, I am in your hands. You in your
wisdom

Lay down for me the paths I am to follow.   620
There is no marriage in the world
That I would put before my good advisor.
CREON. Yes, keep this always in your heart, my son:
  Accept your father's word as law in all things.
  For that is why men pray to have
  Dutiful children growing up at home,
  To repay their father's enemies in kind
  And honor those he loves no less than he does.
  But a man is sowing troubles for himself
  And enemies' delight—what else?—when he 630
  Sires sons who bring no profit to their father.
  So, my son, do not be led by passing fancy
  To lose your head for a woman's sake. You
    know,
  The warmth goes out of such embraces, when
  An evil woman shares your home and bed.
  False friends are deadlier than a festered wound.
  So turn from her with loathing; let her find
  A husband for herself among the dead.
  For now that I have caught her, the only one
  Of all the city to disobey me openly,   640
  My people shall not see me break my word.
  I shall kill her. Let her plead the sacred ties
  Of kinship! If I bring up my own family
  To flout me, there will be no holding others.
  A man who sees his family obey him
  Will have authority in public matters.
  But if anyone offends, or violates the laws,
  No word of praise shall he ever have from me.
  Whoever the state appoints must be obeyed,
  In little things or great things, right or wrong. 650
  I should have confidence that such a man
  Would be as good a ruler as a subject
  And in a hail of spears would stand his ground
  Where he was put, a comrade you could trust.
  But disobedience is the worst of evils;
  It is this that ruins cities, it is this
  That makes homes desolate, turns brothers in
    arms
  To headlong rout. But those who are preserved
  Owe their lives, the greater part of them, to
    discipline.
  And so we must stand up for law and order, 660
  Not let ourselves be worsted by a woman.
  If yield we must, then let us yield to a man.
  Let no-one call us woman's underlings.
CHORUS. Unless the years have robbed me of my wits
  You seem to have sound sense in what you say.
HAEMON. Father, the gods endow mankind with
  reason,

The highest quality that we possess,
It is not for me to criticize your words.
I could not do it, and would hate to try.
And yet, two heads are sometimes better than
  one;   670
At least, it is my place to watch, on your behalf,
All that men do and say and criticize.
Fear of your frown prevents the common man
From saying anything that would displease you,
But I can hear these murmurs in the dark,
The feeling in the city for this girl.
"No woman" they say "has ever deserved death
  less,
Or died so shamefully in a noble cause.
When her brother fell in the slaughter, she
  would not
Leave him unburied, to provide a meal   680
For carrion dogs or passing birds of prey.
Is she not, then, deserving golden honors?"
This is what men are whispering to each other.
Father, there is nothing dearer to my heart
Than your continuing prosperity.
What finer ornament could children have
Than a father's proud success—or he, than
  theirs?
So wear an open mind; do not suppose
That you are right, and everyone else is wrong.
A man who thinks he has monopoly   690
Of wisdom, no rival in speech or intellect,
Will turn out hollow when you look inside him.
However wise he is, it is no disgrace
To learn, and give way gracefully.
You see how trees that bend to winter floods
Preserve themselves, save every twig unbroken,
But those that stand rigid perish root and
  branch,
And also how the man who keeps his sails
Stretched taut, and never slackens them,
  overturns
And finishes his voyage upside down.   700
Let your anger rest; allow us to persuade you.
If a young man may be permitted his opinion
I should say it would be best for everyone
To be born omniscient; but otherwise—
And things have a habit of falling out
  differently—
It is also good to learn from good advice.
CHORUS. My lord, if he speaks to the point you
  ought to listen,
  And Haemon, you to him. There is sense on
  both sides.

CREON. And is a man my age to be taught
  What I should think by one so young as this? 710
HAEMON. Nothing that is not right; young though
    I may be,
  You should judge by my behavior, not my age.
CREON. What sort of behavior is it to honor rebels?
HAEMON. I would never suggest that the guilty
    should be honored.
CREON. And is she not infected with this disease?
HAEMON. The people of Thebes unanimously deny
    it.
CREON. Will the city tell me how I am to rule?
HAEMON. Listen to that! Who is being childish
    now?
CREON. Is the state to listen to any voice but mine?
HAEMON. There is no state, when one man is its
    master.   720
CREON. Is not the state supposed to be the ruler's?
HAEMON. You would do well as the monarch of a
    desert.
CREON. It seems the woman has a champion here.
HAEMON. Then you are the woman! It is you I care
    about!
CREON. Insolent cub! Will you argue with your
    father?
HAEMON. I will, when I see you falling into error.
CREON. Am I wrong to respect my own
    prerogatives?
HAEMON. It is no respect, when you offend the
    gods.
CREON. How contemptible, to give way to a
    woman!
HAEMON. At least I do not give way to
    temptation.   730
CREON. But every word you say is a plea for her.
HAEMON. And for you, and for me, and for the
    gods below.
CREON. You will never marry her this side of the
    grave.
HAEMON. Then she will die—and take somebody
    with her.
CREON. So! Do you dare to go so far? Are you
    threatening me?
HAEMON. Is it threatening, to protest a wrong
    decision?
CREON. You shall pay for this. A fine one to teach
    wisdom!
HAEMON. If you were not my father, I should call
    you a fool.
CREON. You woman's slave; do not try to wheedle
    me!

HAEMON. Would you stop everyone from speaking
    but yourself?   740
CREON. Indeed! I tell you, by the gods above us,
  You shall pay for using such language to your
    father.

[To the attendants.]

  Bring this abomination out, and let her die
  Here, in his presence, at her bridegroom's side.
HAEMON. No, she will never perish at my side,
  So do not think it. From this moment on
  Your eyes will never see my face again.
  So rave away, to those who have more patience!

[Exit.]

CHORUS. My lord, he has gone away in angry haste.
  Young tempers are fierce when anything
    provokes them.   750
CREON. Let him do or dream all men can do and
    more.
  He shall never save those girls from punishment.
CHORUS. Do you mean to put the two of them to
    death?
CREON. You are right to ask. Not her whose hands
    are clean.
CHORUS. And how do you intend to kill the other?
CREON. I shall take her where nobody ever comes
  And shut her in a rocky vault alive,
  With the minimum of food that is permitted
  To stop pollution falling on the city.
  There she may pray to Death, the only god   760
  She worships, and perhaps he may forgive her.
  If not, she will learn—but when it is too late—
  That honoring the dead is wasted effort.

[Exit.]

CHORUS. Love, whom we fight but never conquer,
  Love, the ravager of proud possessions
  Who keep eternal vigilance
  In the softness of a young girl's cheek,
  You go wherever the wide seas go
  And among the cottages of country-dwellers.
  None of the immortal gods can escape you,   770
  Nor man, whose life is as a single day,
  And, to whoever takes you in, comes madness.

  The minds of honest men you lead
  Out of the paths of virtue to destruction.

Father is at odds with son
And it is you who set this quarrel in their hearts.
One glance from the eyes of a ready bride
Bright with desire, and a man is enslaved.
On the throne of the eternal laws
Love has a place, for there the goddess Aphrodite   780
Decides men's fates, and there is no
   withstanding her.

[Enter attendants with Antigone bound.]

It is my turn now; at a sight like this
The voice of the laws cannot hold me back
Or stop the tears from pouring down my cheeks.
Here comes Antigone, on her way
To the bridal-chamber where all must go to
   rest.
ANTIGONE. See me, citizens of my fatherland, as I
     go out   790
   On my last journey; as I look my last on the
     sunlight,
   Never to see it again; Death, who puts all to
     sleep,
   Takes me as I am,
   With life still in me, to the shores of the
     midnight lake,
   A bride with no choir to accompany her way,
   With no serenade at the bedroom door;
   I am to marry with the King of Darkness!
CHORUS. And so you go with honor and praise
   Below to the caverns of the dead;
   No sickness has wasted you away,
   You do not pay the wages of the sword,
   But will go to death a law unto yourself
   As no human being has done before you.   800
ANTIGONE. I have heard of one, a stranger among
     us from Phrygia,
   Tantalus' daughter, and her sad end on Mount
     Sipylus,
   Growing slowly into stone as a tree is wrapped
     with ivy.
   And the story goes

That her body pines in unceasing snow and rain
   And tears from her streaming eyes pour upon
     her breast.
   Her fate is mine; like her I go to rest.
CHORUS. But she was a goddess, born of gods,
   And we are mortals, mortal born.
   When a woman has to die, it is   810
   A great distinction, for her to share
   The lot of those who are one removed from
     gods,
   Both here, and in the manner of her death.
ANTIGONE. Oh, you make fun of me! Gods of my
     fathers!
   Must you laugh in my face? Can you not wait
     till I am gone?
   Oh, my city; Thebans, proud in your
     possessions;
   Chariot-thundering plain, you at least will bear
     witness
   How no friends mourn for my passing, by what
     laws
   I go to my rock-barred prison, my novel tomb.
   Luckless Antigone, an alien in both worlds,   820
   Among the living and among the dead!
CHORUS. You have driven yourself to the furthest
     limit of daring
   And run, my child, against the high throne
   Where justice sits; and great has been your fall.
   Perhaps you are paying the price of your
     father's sin.
ANTIGONE. You have touched the memory bitterest
     in my mind,
   The dirge for my father that is never finished,
   For the fate of us all, the famous house of
     Labdacus.
   Oh, the curse born
   In a mother's bed; doomed mother, sleeping
     with her son,   830
   My father. Poor Antigone, what parents
     brought you
   Into this world! Now I go to join them,
     accursed, unwed.
   Oh, my brother, how ill-fated was your
     marriage.
   Your dead hand has reached out to destroy the
     living.

---

780. Aphrodite: Goddess of love, or, more accurately, of sexual desire. **792. A bride . . . bedroom door:** According to Greek custom bride and groom were accompanied home by singing friends, who also sang outside the wedding chamber in the evening.
802. Tantalus' daughter: Niobe, daughter of the king of Phrygia in Asia Minor, turned into stone as punishment for boasting [of] herself [as] superior to the gods.

833. Oh, my brother: Not Oedipus, but Polyneices, whose marriage with the daughter of the king of Argos had cemented the alliance against Thebes.

CHORUS. Pious actions are a sort of piety.
  But a man who has authority in his keeping
  Can permit no offence against authority.
  Your own willful temper has destroyed you.
ANTIGONE. Friendless, unwept, without a wedding
    song,
  They call for me, and I must tread my road.   840
  Eye of heaven, light of the holy sun,
  I may look on you no longer.
  There is no friend to lament my fate,
  No-one to shed a tear for me.

[Enter Creon.]

CREON. Let me tell you, if songs and dirges before
    dying
  Did any good, we should never hear the end of
    them.
  Take her, and be quick about it. Lock her up
  In her cavern tomb, as I have ordered you,
  And leave her alone—to die, if she prefers,
  Or live in her tomb, for that will be her home. 850
  Whatever becomes of her our hands are clean.
  But in this world she has a place no longer.
ANTIGONE. Tomb, bridal-chamber, my eternal
    home
  Hewn from the rock, where I must go to meet
  My own, those many who have died, and been
  Made welcome by Persephone in the shadow-
    world.
  I am the last, my death the worst of all
  Before my allotted span of years has run.
  But as I go I have this hope in heart,
  That my coming may be welcome to my
    father,   860
  My mother; welcome, dearest brother, to you.
  For when you died, with my own hands I
    washed
  And robed your bodies, and poured offerings
  Over your graves. Now this is my reward,
  Polyneices, for rendering such services to you.
  Yet wisdom would approve my honoring you.
  If I were a mother; if my husband's corpse
  Were left to rot, I never should have dared
  Defy the state to do what I have done.
  What principle can justify such words?   870
  Why, if my husband died I could take another;

Someone else could give me a child if I lost the
    first;
  But Death has hidden my mother and father
    from me.
  No brother can be born to me again.
  Such was the principle by which I chose
  To honor you; and for this Creon judges me
    guilty
  Of outrage and transgression, brother mine!
  And now he seizes me to lead me off,
  Robbed of my bride-bed and my marriage song.
  I shall never marry, never be a mother.   880
  And so, in misery, without a friend,
  I go still living to the pit of death.
  Which one of heaven's commandments have I
    broken?
  Why should I look to the gods any longer
  After this? To whom am I to turn for help
  When doing right has branded me a sinner?
  If the gods approve what is happening to me,
  After the punishment I shall know my fault,
  But if my judges are wrong, I wish them no
    worse
  Than that they have unjustly done to me.   890
CHORUS. Still the same tempestuous spirit
  Carrying her along.
CREON. Then those who are charged with taking
    her
  Shall have cause to repent their slowness.
ANTIGONE. Oh, that word has brought me
  Very near my death.
CREON. I can offer you no hope.
  Your punishment stands unchanged.
ANTIGONE. City of my father in the land of
    Thebes,   900
  The time has come, they take me away.
  Look, princes of Thebes; this is the last
  Daughter of the house of your kings.
  See what I suffer, and at whose hands,
  For doing no less than heaven bids us do.

---

856. **Persephone:** Queen of the dead.   867. **If I were a mother . . . born to me again:** This passage is possibly spurious, and omitted by some editors.

905. **Danae:** The chorus adduce from mythology parallels to Antigone's plight. **Danae** was imprisoned by her father in a brazen tower to avert a prophecy that she would bear a son who would grow up to kill him. But **Zeus**, king of the gods, appeared to her in a shower of golden rain and fathered her son Perseus, who grew up to fulfill the prophecy. **Lycurgus**, son of **Dryas**, persecuted the worshippers of Dionysus, and as punishment for his insolence was driven mad by the god and died. **Cleopatra** married **Phineus**, King of Salmydessos in Thrace, and bore him two sons. Phineus later imprisoned her and took a new wife, who blinded the boys.

[Exeunt attendants, leading off Antigone.]

[Enter Teiresias, led by a boy.]

CHORUS. So Danae in her beauty endured the change
    From the bright sky to the brazen cell,
    And there she was hidden, lost to the living
      world.
    Yet she was of proud birth too, my daughter,
    And the seed of Zeus was trusted to her keeping
    That fell in golden rain.   910
    But the power of fate is terrible.
    Wealth cannot keep you from its reach, nor war,
    Nor city walls, nor the dark sea-beaten ships.
    And the king of the Edonians, the fiery-tempered
    Son of Dryas, was held in bondage
    For his savage taunts, at Dionysus' will,
    Clapped in a rocky cell; and so the full
    Flowering of his madness passed from him
      gradually
    And he came to recognize
    The god he had insulted in his frenzy.   920
    He had sought to stop the women when the
      god was in them
    And the Bacchic torches, and enraged the
      piping Muses.

    And by the Dark Rocks at the meeting of two
      waters
    Lie the shores of Bosporos and Thracian
      Salmydessos.
    Here was a sight for the eyes
    Of the city's neighbour, Ares—
    The two sons of Phineus, blinded
    By stepmother's fury, their sightless eyes
    Appealing for vengeance, calling down a curse
    On her bloody hands and the shuttle turned
      dagger.   930

    Pining in grief they bewailed their cruel fate.
    How sad their mother's marriage; but her line
    Went back to the ancient family
    Of Erechtheus—she was a child
    Of the North Wind, nursed in distant caves,
    Who played with her father's storms, a child of
      the gods
    Running swift as a steed upon the high hills.
    Yet on her too the gray Fates laid their hand,
      my daughter.

923. Dark Rocks: At the entrance of what is now the Black
Sea. **924. Bosporos:** Narrow strip of water separating Greece from
Asia Minor. **926. Ares:** God of war. **934. Erechtheus:** Legendary
king of Athens.

TEIRESIAS. Princes of Thebes, we have come here
    side by side,
    One pair of eyes for both of us. That is how   940
    Blind men must walk, supported by a guide.
CREON. What news have you for us, old Teiresias?
TEIRESIAS. I will tell you. Listen when the prophet
    speaks.
CREON. I have never yet disregarded your advice.
TEIRESIAS. And so have kept Thebes safely on her
    course.
CREON. I know my debt to you, and acknowledge
    it.
TEIRESIAS. Then listen. Once more you stand on the
    verge of doom.
CREON. What do you mean? I shudder at your
    words.
TEIRESIAS. You will know, when you hear the
    warnings of my art.
    As I took my place upon my ancient seat   950
    Of augury, where all the birds come flocking,
    I heard a noise I had never heard before,
    Their cries distorted in a scream of fury,
    And I knew that they were clawing, killing each
      other;
    The whirring of wings told a tale too clear.
    I was frightened, and went at once to light the
      altar
    And offer sacrifice; but from my offerings
    No flame sprang up. Fat melted on the thighs
    And oozed in slow drops down to quench the
      embers
    And smoked and spluttered; and the gall was
      scattered   960
    Into the air. The streaming thighs were raw,
    Bare of the fat which once enfolded them.
    And so my rites had failed. I asked a sign
    And none was given, as I learnt from this boy
      here.
    He is my guide, as I am guide to others.
    Your counsels brought this sickness on our
      state.
    The altars of our city and our homes
    Are all defiled by dogs and birds of prey
    Who feed on Oedipus' unhappy son.
    And so the gods no longer accept our prayers, 970
    Our sacrifices, our burnt offerings.
    The birds no longer warn us with their cries;
    They have drunk the fat blood of a slaughtered
      man.

Think on these things, my son. To err is human,
But when we err, then happy is the man
Who is not stubborn, and has sense enough
To remedy the fault he has committed.
Give the dead his due, and do not stab a man
When he is down. What good to kill him twice?
I have your interests at heart, and speak   980
To help you. No advisor is more welcome
Than when you profit from his good advice.

CREON. You circle me like archers, all of you,
    And I am made your target! Even the prophets
    Conspire against me. They have long been
      using me
    As merchandise, a thing to buy and sell!
    If profit is what you seek, go look abroad!
    There is silver in Sardis, gold in India.
    But you will not bury this man in his grave,
    No, not if the eagles of great Zeus himself   990
    Should lay his flesh before their master's throne.
    Not even that defilement frightens me
    Enough to bury him, for well I know
    No human being can defile the gods.
    The wisest of us, old Teiresias,
    Sink to the depths, when they hide their evil
      thoughts
    In fair-phrased speeches for the sake of money.

TEIRESIAS. If men only knew, would only realize—

CREON. Knew what? Another pronouncement! Let
    us hear!

TEIRESIAS. Good counsel is worth more than
    worldly riches.   1000

CREON. Just as stupidity is the greatest harm.

TEIRESIAS. Yet that is the sickness that has tainted
    you.

CREON. I do not want to call a prophet names.

TEIRESIAS. But you do, when you say my prophecies
    are false.

CREON. Men of your tribe were always money-
    seekers.

TEIRESIAS. And men of yours have always been
    dictators.

CREON. Have you forgotten you are speaking to
    your king?

TEIRESIAS. No. It was because of me that you saved
    Thebes.

CREON. You are a wise prophet but in love with
    evil.

TEIRESIAS. You will move me to tell the unutterable
    secret.   1010

CREON. Tell it—as long as there is no profit in it!

TEIRESIAS. I do not think so—as far as you are
    concerned.

CREON. You will make no money out of my
    decision.

TEIRESIAS. Then listen well. Before the sun's swift
    wheels
    Have numbered many more days of your life,
    You will surrender corpse for corpses, one
    Begotten from the seed of your own loins,
    Because you have sent this world to join the
      next
    And cruelly lodged the living in the grave,
    But keep Death's property on earth,
      unburied,   1020
    Robbed of its honor, an unhallowed corpse.
    This is not for you to say, nor for the gods
    In heaven, but in doing this you wrong them.
    And so the Avengers, Furies sent by Death
    And by the gods, lie in waiting to destroy you
    And snare you in the evils you have worked.
    So watch, and you will see if I am bribed
    To say these things. Before much time is out
    The cries of men and womenfolk will fill your
      house.
    And hatred rises against you in every city   1030
    Whose mangled sons were left for burial
    To dogs, or beasts, or birds of prey, who bore
    Their stinking breath to every soldier's home.
    Archer you call me; then these are the arrows
    I send into your heart, since you provoke me,
    Sure arrows; you will not escape their sting.
    Boy, take me to my home again, and leave him
    To vent his fury on some younger man,
    And learn to moderate his tongue, and bear
    A better spirit in his breast than now.   1040

[Exit.]

CHORUS. He has gone, my lord; his prophecies
    were fearful.
    As long as I remember, since my hair
    Has turned from black to white, this man has
     never
    Made one false prophecy about our city.

CREON. I know it as well as you. My mind is
    troubled.
    To yield is fatal; but to resist and bring
    A curse on my proud spirit—that too is hard.

---

988. Sardis: City of Asia Minor containing the royal treasury.

1024. Furies: Supernatural pursuers of the wrongdoer.

CHORUS. Son of Menoeceus, you must listen to
    good advice.
CREON. What's to be done? Tell me and I will do it.
CHORUS. Go free the girl from her prison in the
    rocks   1050
    And give the corpse an honorable tomb.
CREON. Is this your advice? You think that I should
    yield?
CHORUS. Yes, lord, as quickly as you can. The gods
    Move fast to cut short man's stupidity.
CREON. It is hard; but I resign my dear resolve.
    We cannot fight against necessity.
CHORUS. Go do it now; do not leave it to another.
CREON. I will go as I am. Servants, be off with you,
    Each and every one; take axes in your hands
    And go to the hill you can see over there.   1060
    Now that my judgment has been reversed
    I shall be there to free her, as I imprisoned her.
    Perhaps after all the gods' ways are the best
    And we should keep them till our lives are done.

[Exit.]

CHORUS. You who are known by many names,
    Who blessed the union of Cadmus' daughter,
    Begotten by Zeus the Thunderer, guarding
    The land of Italy famed in story,
    King of Eleusis, in the land-locked plain
    Of Deo where the wanderer finds welcome, 1070
    Bacchus whose home is Thebes, mother-city of
      Bacchanals,
    By Ismenus' tranquil waters where the fierce
      dragon's teeth were sown.

    The fitful gleam of the torchlight finds you
    Amid the smoke on the slopes of the forked
      mountains
    Where tread your worshippers, the nymphs
    Of Corycia, by Castalia's stream.
    From Nysa's ivy-mantled slopes,
    From the green shore carpeted with vines
    You come, and they are no human lips that cry
    Your name, as you make your progress through
      the ways of Thebes.   1080

    For it is she you honor above all other cities,
    And your mother too, who died by a bolt from
      heaven.
    And now the whole city labors under
    This grievous malady, come with healing feet
    Down from the slopes of Parnassus or the
      sounding sea.

    Conductor of the stars, whose breath is made of
      fire,
    Lord of the voices that cry aloud in the night,
    Son born of Zeus, appear to us, oh lord,
    With the Thyiads your servants who in nightly
      abandon
    Dance before you, Iacchus, the bringer of all
      blessings.   1090

[Enter Messenger.]

MESSENGER. You will live by Amphion's and
    Cadmus' walls,
    No man's estate is ever so assured
    That I would set it down as good or bad.
    Fortune can raise us, fortune cast us down,
    Depending on our luck, from day to day,
    But for how long? No man can see the future.
    For Creon was once blessed, as I count blessings;
    He saved the land of Cadmus from its enemies,
    Became its sole and undisputed king
    And ruled, proud father of a princely line.   1100
    Now everything is gone. A man who forfeits
    All of life's pleasures I can count no longer
    Among the living, but as dead in life.
    So stack your house with treasures as you will
    And live in royal pomp; when joy is absent
    I would not give the shadow of a breath
    For all the rest, compared with joy alone.
CHORUS. What is this new royal grief you come to
    tell us?
MESSENGER. Death; and the living must answer to
    the dead.
CHORUS. Who killed? And who has been killed? Tell
    us.   1110
MESSENGER. Haemon, and by a hand he knew too
    well.
CHORUS. By his father's hand? Or was it by his own?
MESSENGER. His own, in anger for his father's
    murder.

1066. Cadmus' daughter: Semele. **1069. Eleusis:** Home of the mystery-cult devoted to Demeter, goddess of the crops, and her daughter Persephone. The worship of Dionysus had infiltrated into this rite. **1070. Deo:** Demeter. **1076. Corycia:** Cave on Mt. Parnassus. **Castalia:** Fountain on Mount Parnassus sacred to the Muses. **1077. Nysa:** Legendary scene of the nursing of Dionysus.

1091. Amphion: Legendary musician whose lyre-playing charmed the stones to build a wall around Thebes.

CHORUS. Oh prophet, how much truth was in your
    words.
MESSENGER. That is how things are. For the rest you
    must decide.

[Enter Eurydice.]

CHORUS. And here is Eurydice, the unhappy wife
    Of Creon; she is coming from the palace.
EURYDICE. People of Thebes, I heard what you
    were saying
  As I was going from my house to offer
  Devotions at the goddess Pallas' shrine.   1120
  I stood there with my hand about to draw
  The bolt, and my ears were greeted by this tale
  Of family disaster. Terrified,
  I fell back swooning in my servants' arms.
  But tell again what you were telling then.
  The first grief is over. I shall listen now.
MESSENGER. Dear lady, I shall tell you what I saw
  Omitting nothing, exactly as it happened.
  Why should I give false comfort? You would
    soon
  Know I was lying. Truth is always best.   1130
  I attended on your husband to direct his way
  Across the plain, where Polyneices' corpse,
  Mangled by dogs, still lay unburied.
  We prayed the goddess of the roads, and Pluto,
  To have mercy on us and restrain their wrath,
  Performed the ritual washing of the corpse,
  Cut branches and cremated what was left of him
  And raised a hillock of his native soil
  Above him; then made for the cavern, where
    the girl
  Waited for Death to share her rocky bed.   1140
  Far off, one of us heard a piercing cry
  Coming from that unholy bridal chamber
  And came to report it to our master Creon.
  As he approached, a cry of anguish came
  To greet him, half-heard words; he groaned
    aloud
  And in his grief said "Creon, you are doomed;
  Can my fear be true? Is the path I tread today
  To be the bitterest path I ever trod?
  The voice that greets me is my son's; men, run
    ahead,
  Make for the tomb; there is an opening   1150
  Where someone has wrenched the stones away.
    Squeeze inside

1134. Pluto: God of the underworld.

  To the cell-mouth, see if it is Haemon's voice
  I hear, or if the gods are mocking me."
  And so, at our despairing master's bidding,
  We made the search, and in the farthest corner
  Of the tomb we saw her, hanged by the neck
  In a noose of twisted linen, soft as silk,
  While Haemon stood with his arms clasped
    round her waist
  Weeping for his bride now with the dead,
  For his father's actions and his foredoomed
    marriage.   1160
  When he saw him his father gave a fearful cry
  And went to him and called to him through his
    tears
  "Oh Haemon, what is this that you have done?
  What has possessed you? Have you gone insane?
  Come out, my son, I beg you, I implore you."
  But the boy glared back at him wild-eyed,
  Spat in his face, and without a word of answer
  Drew his cross-hilted sword and thrust at him
  But missed, as he jumped aside. Then in wild
    remorse
  The poor wretch threw his weight upon the
    point   1170
  And drove it half into his side. As long as sense
  Was left him, he clasped the girl in a limp
    embrace
  And as his breath came hard, a jet of blood
  Spurted from his lips, and ran down her pallid
    cheek.
  The bodies lie in each others arms. He has
  Claimed his bride—in the next world, not in
    this—
  And he has given proof to all mankind
  That of all human ills, bad counsel is the worst.

[Exit Eurydice to the palace.]

CHORUS. What would you make of this? Eurydice
  Has vanished without a word, good or bad. 1180
MESSENGER. It alarms me too. Yet I nourish the
    hope
  That now she knows her loss she does not think
    it proper
  To mourn in public, but has gone inside
  To set her maids to mourn for her
    bereavement.
  She has learnt discretion and will not be foolish.
CHORUS. I am not so sure. To me this unnatural
    silence
  Is as ominous as the wildest excess of grief.

MESSENGER. Well, I shall go in and see, in case
　　She is keeping some dark purpose hidden from
　　　　us
　　In her grief-torn heart. You are right to be
　　　　concerned.　　　　　　　　　　　　　1190
　　It is just as dangerous to be too quiet.

[Exit.]

CHORUS. But here is Creon coming himself
　　Bringing testimony all too plain,
　　The work of his and no other's madness,
　　If I may speak out, and his own wrongdoing.

[Enter Creon with servants bearing the body of Haemon.]

CREON. Oh deadly end of stubborn sins
　　Born in the blindness of understanding!
　　See here, a son dead, a father who killed him.
　　Oh the fatal workings of my mind;
　　My son, to die so young,　　　　　　　　1200
　　So soon to be taken from me
　　By my folly, not by yours.
CHORUS. Perhaps you see now too late what was
　　best.
CREON. Yes, I have learned my bitter lesson.
　　Some god must have chosen that moment
　　To crush me under his heavy hand
　　And hurl me into cruelty's ways,
　　Riding roughshod over all I held dear.
　　Oh, mankind, you were born to suffer!

[Enter Second Messenger from the palace.]

MESSENGER. Master, you do not come empty-
　　handed; but there is　　　　　　　　　　1210
　　More in store for you. You bear one load of
　　　　grief
　　But soon you will see another, in your home.
CREON. My grief is here; is any worse to come?
MESSENGER. Your wife is dead—true mother to her
　　son
　　To the last, poor lady—by a wound still fresh.
CREON. Oh Death, ever-open door,
　　Do you have no mercy on me?
　　You who bring this tale of death and sorrow
　　What is this you are saying to me?
　　What news is this, my boy?　　　　　　1220
　　My wife is dead? One more
　　To add to the pile of corpses?
MESSENGER. See for yourself. It is no longer hidden.

[The body of Eurydice is brought out.]

CREON. Oh, here is another, a second blow.
　　What has fate in store for me after this?
　　I have but this moment lifted
　　My child in my arms, and again
　　I see a corpse brought out to greet me.
　　Oh wretched mother; oh my child.
MESSENGER. There she lies at the altar, knife-point
　　in her heart.　　　　　　　　　　　　　1230
　　She mourned the noble fate of Megareus,
　　The first to die, then his; then closed her eyes
　　For ever, and with her dying breath called down
　　A curse on you for murdering her sons.
CREON. I am shaken with fear. Will nobody take
　　His two-edged sword and run me through?
　　For, oh, I am sick at heart.
　　Sorrow has made me his own.
MESSENGER. Yes, she whose body you see lying here
　　Laid the deaths of both sons at your door.　1240
CREON. And what was the violent manner of her
　　leaving?
MESSENGER. Her own hand drove the knife into her
　　heart
　　When she had heard them singing her son's
　　dirge.
CREON. Nobody else can bear the guilt,
　　No-one can take the blame from me.
　　I killed you, I, your unhappy father,
　　This is the truth.
　　Servants, take me away from this place.
　　Let me stay not a moment longer.
　　Creon has ceased to exist.　　　　　　　1250
CHORUS. Good advice, if there can be any good in
　　evil.
　　In present trouble the shortest way is best.
CREON. Let it come. What better fate could I ask
　　Than the fate which ushers in my life's last day?
　　Let it come, the best of all;
　　Let me never see tomorrow's dawn.
CHORUS. All in its proper time. We have things to
　　see to
　　Here and now. The future is in other hands.
CREON. But everything I want was in that prayer.
CHORUS. Save your prayers. Whatever is going to
　　happen　　　　　　　　　　　　　　　　1260
　　Is already fated. Nobody can change it.

1231. **Megareus:** A minor incident in the siege of Thebes, which Sophocles could expect his audience to know. Megareus, son of Creon, sacrificed himself in an attempt to appease the gods' wrath against the city.

CREON. Come, take this hot-headed fool away,
   A fool who killed you, my son, in my
      blindness,
   And you too, who are lying here; poor fool.
   I do not know
   Which way I am to take, where to lean;
   My hands can do nothing right;
   I am crushed beneath my fate.

[Exit.]

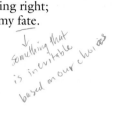

something that is inevitable based on our choices

CHORUS. To be happy it is first of all necessary
   To be wise, and always remember   1270
   To give the gods their due.
   The measure of a proud man's boasting
   Shall be the measure of his punishment
   And teach him late in life
   The nature of true wisdom.

[The chorus exits.]

Introduction to
The Menaechmus Brothers
by Plautus

Translated from Latin by E. F. Watling

The Comedies of Plautus (Venice, 1517). *(Bettmann/CORBIS)*

The Play   *The Menaechmus Brothers* was probably first staged in 146 B.C. Its author, the Roman playwright Plautus, uses mistaken identity to create a comedy that emphasizes wordplay, physicality, and sexual humor. The play opens with a prologue, delivered by an actor who addresses the audience directly. He asks us to pay careful attention to the story line and tells us that the Menaechmus twin brothers were separated while infants and explains how one twin—from Syracuse—is now in Epidamnus searching for his lost sibling. He also reminds us that we are in the theater and that the setting requires the audience to use its imagination.

When the action of the play begins, we first meet Menaechmus of Epidamnus and a parasitic friend, "Sponge." In their conversation, these two establish a number of the plot's complicated threads. For example, under his outer clothes Menaechmus is wearing one of his wife's prettiest dresses, which he is going to give to his mistress, Erotium. Later, when Erotium sends the dress out to be altered, and when Menaechmus's wife looks for the dress and cannot find it, all kinds of comic complications develop. A bit later, Menaechmus's twin from Syracuse, with his servant, comes on the scene and is mistaken for his brother by both the wife and the mistress, at which point Menaechmus of Syracuse becomes hopelessly confused—but at the same time takes advantage of the situation.

The Menaechmus Brothers is a typical example of Roman comedy. Roman comedy—often referred to as New Comedy—frequently dealt with domestic situations, particularly the trials and tribulations of romance and marriage. The characters are recognizable, recurring stock types, including servants and masters—and the parasites, who live off others and are motivated by sensual desires.

The impact of this form throughout theater history is clear. For example, Shakespeare's *Comedy of Errors* is an adaptation of *The Menaechmus Brothers,* as is the Rodgers and Hart musical *The Boys from Syracuse.* For that matter, Roman New Comedy is the direct ancestor of such twentieth-century forms as Hollywood's 1930s screwball comedies and television's situation comedies.

The Playwright Plautus (ca. 254–184 B.C.) was born in Umbria and at an early age went to Rome, where he became an actor. When he began writing his own plays, Plautus used his familiarity with song, dance, and native Italian farce and combined it with characters and plots of New Comedy, which was derived from Hellenistic Greece. His comedies, like Greek New Comedy, did not have a chorus and did not deal with contemporary political or social issues. Instead, they focused on domestic plotlines. Plautus's plays may have resembled modern musical comedies; it is believed that a good portion of the dialogue was sung.

Plautus was probably the most popular of all Roman writers. According to Cicero, Plautus was "choice, urbane, talented, and witty." Because of Plautus's reputation as the master of comedy, over 100 plays were attributed to him, but no more than 45 are now considered authentic. Twenty of his plays and fragments of one more have survived. Besides *The Menaechmus Brothers,* his well-known plays include *The Rope, Casina, The Pot of Gold, The Captives, The Haunted House,* and *The Girl from Persia.* The dates of individual plays by Plautus are unknown, but they are all presumed to have been written between 205 and 184 B.C.

The Period Rome was founded, according to legend, around 750 B.C. For over 200 years, it was ruled by kings; but around 500 B.C. the kings were overthrown and a republic—which would last until 27 B.C.—was established. After a number of governmental upheavals and considerable expansion, Rome became an empire, with one supreme ruler. This imperial form of government continued for several centuries, during which most of the Western world was unified under Roman rule.

Throughout their long history, the Romans were always practical. Their laws dealing with property, marriage, and inheritance continue to influence Western civilization. The Romans were also great engineers and architects, building aqueducts and roadways. Religion was important to the Romans, who worshiped gods that were counterparts of the Greek deities, as well as a large number of other divinities. After warring with the Greeks in the third century B.C., the Romans introduced theater into their religious festivals and later their civic festivals.

Roman theater production differed slightly from that of Greece. Festivals were under the jurisdiction of a local government official who hired acting troupes. The head of a troupe—who was usually the lead actor—made financial arrangements, bought plays from authors, hired musicians, and obtained costumes. Acting companies had at least six members, all males. Actors were admired for their physicalizations and their vocal abilities. Actors in comedies and tragedies, as in Greece, wore masks.

Permanent theaters were not constructed in Rome until 55 B.C.; thus the plays of Plautus were presented in temporary spaces, though these were probably similar in configuration to the permanent ones built later. A Roman theater had the same three units as a Greek theater: a semicircular, sloped seating area; an orchestra, also semicircular; and a stage house. The Roman structures, however, differed from Greek theaters in that they were freestanding, not built into hillsides, with the tiered audience section connected to the very ornate stage house to form a single unit. There was a large, raised stage in front of the stage house.

Scholars point out that there were many entertainments in Rome which may have been more popular than theater, including gladiator battles, chariot races, staged sea battles, and combats between animals and humans. Large arenas were built for many of these entertainments.

THE MENAECHMUS BROTHERS

Plautus

CHARACTERS

MENAECHMUS, a young married man living in Epidamnus
SOSICLES, his twin brother, also generally known by the name Menaechmus
PENICULUS, nicknamed The Sponge, a cadging friend of Menaechmus's
EROTIUM, Menaechmus's mistress

MESSENIO, slave of Sosicles
CYLINDRUS, cook in the house of Erotium
A MAID, in the house of Erotium
THE WIFE of Menaechmus
THE FATHER of Menaechmus's wife
A DOCTOR
Slaves and baggage-porters

SCENE: Epidamnus, outside the houses of Menaechmus and Erotium.
A Prologue is spoken by an unnamed character.

PROLOGUE

First, friends, a hearty welcome to you all—
And to myself. My business is to call
Plautus before your . . . ears, not eyes, today;
So please attend to what he has to say.
And please attend to me, while I unfold,
Briefly, the tale that here is to be told.

You know our comic writers have a way
Of claiming that what happens in the play
Takes place in Athens, that it may appear
To have a truly Grecian atmosphere.
For this play's setting—you must take my word

It happened in . . . the place where it occurred.
The story breathes a Grecian air, you'll see,
Though not of Attica, but Sicily.
So much for preface to my argument.
Now for the argument—which I present
In generous measure, bags and bushels packed
And running over, a whole barn in fact,
Because I have so much to *give away*
In setting out the story of the play.

In Syracuse a merchant, it appears,
Begat twin sons, who from their earliest years
Were so alike that neither nurse nor mother
Could ever tell one baby from the other,

So little was the difference between them,
As I was told by somebody who'd seen them—
I never saw them, I would have you know.
Now, when the boys were seven years old or so,
Their father planned a business trip abroad,
Loaded a ship and, with one child aboard,
Sailed to Tarentum, leaving the twin brother
At home, in Syracusa, with his mother.
Tarentum was *en fête* when they got there;
Hundreds of folk had come to see the fair.
And wandering in the crowd, the little lad
One day got separated from his dad.
An Epidamnian trader found the child
And took him off to Epidamnus. Wild
With desperate grief at losing his dear son,
The father, ere a few more days were done,
Fell sick and died upon Tarentine land.
When in due course the tidings came to hand
At Syracuse, and the grandfather knew
His son was dead, his grandson missing too,
He changed the name of the surviving brother
(Because, in fact, he much preferred the other)
And *Sosicles,* the one at home, became
Menaechmus—which had been his brother's
    name.
That was the name of the grandfather too
(I do know that, from hearing much ado
About a debt he owed). I hope that's clear . . .
But don't forget . . . the twins, when they
    appear,
Will both be called Menaechmus. Now again
I move to Epidamnus *[He takes a few steps.]* to
    explain
The rest of this affair . . . *[He breaks off, and
    continues prosaically.]*

Anybody got any commissions for me in
Epidamnus? Now's the time to say so, if you
have. Don't be afraid. Give me your orders—
and of course the necessary funds for the
business. No money, no business. And what
happens to your money if you give it me is no
business of yours either! . . . *[Indicating the scene
on the stage.]* All this is Epidamnus—as long as
this play lasts, anyway. In another play it will be
another place, I expect. Same with the houses—
they may be occupied by a young man one day,
an old man the next; rich man, poor man,
beggarman, king, client, or clairvoyant . . . But
to get back to where I was—while still
remaining where I am! . . .

This Epidamnian trader, he who stole
The boy, was childless; money was his whole
Life and existence, but he had no son
To leave it to when his day's work was done.
So he adopts the boy, and when of age
Gives him a wife, dowry, and heritage.
He died. While on a country walk, they say,
Outside the city, on a stormy day,
Trying to cross a torrent, in he fell;
And thus the thief was carried off to hell,
Who carried off the boy! The adopted heir
Inherited a large estate, and there *[showing the
    house]*
Menaechmus lives today. Now watch; for here
You'll see the twin from Syracuse appear
In Epidamnus, with one slave behind him,
To search for his twin brother—and to find him.[1]

*[Peniculus enters from the town, about to pay a visit to the
house of Menaechmus.]*

PENICULUS. My name is Peniculus—or Sponge, as
    the young fellows call me—Sponge, because
    whenever I eat I wipe the table clean! . . .
      You know, it's ridiculous for people to
    throw prisoners into chains and put fetters on
    runaway slaves—at least I think so; because if
    a man is in trouble, and you give him more
    trouble, he'll be all the more anxious to
    escape and commit more crimes. They always
    get themselves out of their chains by some
    means or other; if they're in fetters, they file
    away the ring or smash the bolt off with a
    stone; it's child's play. If you really want to
    keep a man from running away, the best way
    to do it is with food and drink; keep his nose
    down to a full table; give him anything he asks
    for, every day; I guarantee he'll never run
    away then, not even if he's on a capital charge;
    you'll have no difficulty in keeping him, as
    long as you keep him in that sort of
    confinement. Food—it's a marvellously
    effective kind of strait-jacket; the more you
    stretch it the closer it clings . . .
      Take me, now; I'm just on my way to my
    friend Menaechmus. I've been his bond-slave
    for some time now, and I'm still offering

---

1. The prologue establishes the premise of the play and also jokes about Greek society and the conventions of theater.

myself voluntarily to imprisonment. I tell you, that man doesn't just give you a meal; he builds you up, makes you a new man; there isn't a doctor to touch him. That's the sort of host he is; has a tremendous appetite himself, gives banquets fit for Harvest Festival,[2] piles the tables so high with culinary contraptions, you have to stand on your couch to reach anything off the top.

But alas, as far as I am concerned, there has been an intermission for many days past. All this time I have been housebound and homebound in the company of my own dear ones—and everything I buy or eat comes *very* dear, I can assure you! Moreover, I'm now running out of my dearly bought supplies. So I'm paying a call on my dear patron . . . Ah, the door's opening . . . and it's Menaechmus himself coming out . . . *[He retires to a corner.]*

[Menaechmus, a young man, appears at the door of his house, finishing off an altercation with his wife, who is just inside.]

MENAECHMUS. . . . And if you weren't such a mean, stupid, obstinate, and impossible female, you wouldn't want to do anything that you see your husband dislikes . . . If you go on like this any longer, I'll divorce you and pack you off to your father . . . Every time I choose to go out of doors you try to stop me and call me back, pester me with questions, what am I going to fetch, what have I brought back, what did I do when I was out. I might as well have married an immigration officer, the way I have to declare every blessed thing I've done or am doing . . . I've spoiled you, that's what it is. But I give you due warning: in consideration of my providing you with servants, food, clothes, jewellery, household linen, and finery, everything you could possibly need, you will kindly behave yourself or there'll be trouble— and you will cease spying on your husband's movements . . . *[Turning away from the door.]* Come to that, if you want something to spy on, you can have it . . . I'm going to take my girl out tonight and get an invitation to supper somewhere.

PENICULUS. He may think it's his wife he's telling off, but I'm the one he's getting at. If he's not going to be home for supper, that's one in the eye for me, not his wife.

MENAECHMUS. Good; that's done it! My language has frightened her from the door. Now then, all you *loving* husbands . . . aren't you going to load me with gifts and congratulations for my heroic fight? . . . *[He now reveals that he is wearing one of his wife's gowns under his cloak.]* Look, I've just stolen this gown of my wife's and I'm taking it to my girl! That's the way to treat 'em . . . that's a slap in the face for the sharp-eyed wardress! A beautiful, neat, ingenious masterly trick, my friends! That's going to cost the wretched woman something—or cost me, for that matter, since I've got to say goodbye to it . . . Ah well, let's say I've filched some booty from the enemy for the benefit of my friends.

PENICULUS. What about me, boy? Do I get a share of the booty?

MENAECHMUS. *[Hearing but not seeing him.]* Damn it! Someone else spying on me?

PENICULUS. No, someone protecting you; don't be alarmed.

MENAECHMUS. Who's there?

PENICULUS. Me.

MENAECHMUS. Oh, it's you, my old friend On-the-Spot, my dear Mr. Come-in-Time. How are you?

PENICULUS. Very well, thanks, how are you? *[They shake hands.]*

MENAECHMUS. What are you doing now?

PENICULUS. Holding my guardian angel by the hand.

MENAECHMUS. You couldn't have found me at a more favourable moment.

PENICULUS. I know. I'm like that. I can tell a favourable moment to the nearest second.

MENAECHMUS. Would you like to see a sight to gladden your eyes?

PENICULUS. It depends who cooked it. Show me the leavings and I'll tell you if there was anything wrong with the cooking.

MENAECHMUS. Did you ever see a mural painting . . . the eagle abducting Ganymede, or Venus seducing Adonis?

PENICULUS. Often. But why should such paintings interest me particularly?

MENAECHMUS. *[Posing in a graceful attitude in the female gown.]* Behold . . . do I look like anything like them?

2. Reference to a spring festival at which spectacular public banquets were held.

PENICULUS. What on earth are you dressed up like that for?

MENAECHMUS. Say I'm a smart fellow.

PENICULUS. *[Ignoring the inexplicable eccentricity.]* Where are we going to eat?

MENAECHMUS. First say what I told you to say.

PENICULUS. *[Obediently.]* You're a smart fellow.

MENAECHMUS. Is that all you can say?

PENICULUS. And a most amusing fellow.

MENAECHMUS. Anything else?

PENICULUS. Good Lord, no, nothing else—until I know what it's in aid of. You've got some quarrel with your wife, I suspect, so I shall have to be careful where I tread.

MENAECHMUS. Don't worry; we're going to bury our troubles and burn up the day in some place the wife doesn't know about.

PENICULUS. Come on, then; now you're talking sense. Say the word and I'll light the pyre; the day's already dead down to the waist. What are we waiting for?

MENAECHMUS. Only for you to stop talking.

PENICULUS. Knock my eye out if I utter another word except at your orders.

MENAECHMUS. Come away from this door.

PENICULUS. *[Moving a little, but keeping an anxious eye on the house door.]* All right.

MENAECHMUS. *[Also cautiously watching the door.]* Farther this way.

PENICULUS. If you like.

MENAECHMUS. Come on, there's nothing to be afraid of. You can turn your back on the lioness's den.

PENICULUS. What about you? You'd do well as a chariot-racer.

MENAECHMUS. Why a chariot-racer?

PENICULUS. The way you keep looking over your shoulder to see if the enemy is gaining on you . . .

MENAECHMUS. Look, tell me something—

PENICULUS. Me? I'll tell you anything you like, or deny it if you prefer.

MENAECHMUS. Are you good at smelling? Can you identify a thing by its scent?

PENICULUS. Why? Do you want to propose me for the College of Augurs?[3]

MENAECHMUS. Smell this dress . . . What does it smell of? *[Offering him the skirt of the gown.]* You don't want to?

PENICULUS. I'd rather smell the upper part of a woman's garment; elsewhere the nose detects a somewhat unwashed odour.

MENAECHMUS. Smell this part, then . . . Oh, you *are* a fussy man.

PENICULUS. I should hope so.

MENAECHMUS. Well, what does it smell of?

PENICULUS. It smells of . . . *[knowing Menaechmus's intentions]* stolen goods, secret amours, and a free lunch. I hope there'll be—

MENAECHMUS. Right you are! Lunch is the word. This gown is going to my girl Erotium, and I'll have lunch laid on at her place, for her, for me, and for you.

PENICULUS. Good enough.

MENAECHMUS. There we will carouse until tomorrow's dawn.

PENICULUS. Grand! It's a pleasure to listen to you. Shall I knock at the door? *[That is, of the neighbouring house where Erotium lives.]*

MENAECHMUS. Please do . . . No, wait.

PENICULUS. *[Disappointed.]* Oh, now you've pushed the loving cup a mile off.

MENAECHMUS. Knock gently.

PENICULUS. Why? The doors aren't made of Samian pottery, are they? *[He thumps the door.]*

[The door immediately opens and Erotium is seen to be about to come out.]

MENAECHMUS. Wait, wait, for goodness sake! Here she comes herself . . . Oh, see how the sun is dimmed beside the radiance of that lovely person!

EROTIUM. Menaechmus, my sweetheart! Welcome!

PENICULUS. No welcome for me?

EROTIUM. You don't count.

PENICULUS. Like on the battlefield—camp-followers don't count.

MENAECHMUS. That's right; and today I have planned an engagement for myself at your house.

EROTIUM. You shall have it.

MENAECHMUS. He and I are going to have a drinking battle; and whichever proves himself the superior fighter on the bottle-field, becomes your conscript. You shall be umpire and choose which you will have for your—night. Oh my darling, when I look at you, how I hate my wife!

EROTIUM. Meanwhile you apparently feel compelled to wear her clothes. What is this?

3. Governmentally supported prophets of Rome.

MENAECHMUS. Spoils from my wife for your adornment, my rose.

EROTIUM. That puts you head and shoulders above any other of my suitors, darling.

PENICULUS. Just like her sort, to talk pretty when she sees something to get her hands on . . . If you loved him, my dear, you ought to have bitten his nose off by now.

MENAECHMUS. *[Removing his cloak to get rid of the gown.]* Hold this, Peniculus. I must hand over my promised gift.

PENICULUS. Give it here. But wait a bit; won't you give us a dance in that thing?

MENAECHMUS. Me dance? Are you out of your mind?

PENICULUS. One of us is, I'm not sure which. All right, if you won't dance, take it off.

MENAECHMUS. I risked my life getting hold of this today . . . I doubt if Hercules[4] ran such a risk when abstracting Hippolyta's girdle[5] . . . Here you are, a present for the only girl in the world who likes to do what I like.

EROTIUM. *[Taking the gown.]* You set an example to all true lovers.

PENICULUS. All who are hell-bent to ruin themselves.

MENAECHMUS. I bought it for my wife a year ago; four hundred drachmas[6] it cost me.

PENICULUS. Four hundred down the drain, as I figure it.

MENAECHMUS. Now then, do you know what I want you to do for me?

EROTIUM. I know. I'll see to it.

MENAECHMUS. Good. Tell your people to prepare lunch for the three of us—and send to the market for something toothsome . . say, pork kidneys, or smoked ham, or pig's head . . . something of that kind, a nicely done dish to give me a vulture's appetite. And the sooner the better.[7]

EROTIUM. You shall have it, my love.

MENAECHMUS. We'll get off to town. We shan't be long; and then we can do some drinking while the things are cooking.

EROTIUM. Come back as soon as you like. We'll be ready for you.

MENAECHMUS. Don't waste any time, then. Come along, Sponge . . . *[He hurries off.]*

PENICULUS. I'm with you . . . and watching you. I wouldn't lose sight of you today for all the treasures of heaven. *[He follows.]*

EROTIUM. *[At her door.]* Tell Cylindrus I want him out here at once, please.

[Cylindrus, her cook, appears.]

Take a basket, and some money. Here . . . here's three pounds for you.

CYLINDRUS. Three pounds . . . that's right, ma'am.

EROTIUM. Get us something to eat; enough for three, please; not too little, and not too much.

CYLINDRUS. Three. What kind of three?

EROTIUM. I and Menaechmus and his table-companion.

CYLINDRUS. That's more like ten. These table-companions can easily do the work of eight men each.

EROTIUM. I've told you how many guests there are; go and do your business.

CYLINDRUS. Very good, ma'am. Consider the meal cooked, call the guests in.

EROTIUM. Don't be long.

CYLINDRUS. I'll be back in two shakes.

[He hurries off to market. Erotium goes indoors.]

[The twin Menaechmus, who exactly resembles his brother and was originally called Sosicles (as we shall call him), has now arrived by sea and comes from the harbour with this slave Messenio and other slaves carrying baggage.]

SOSICLES. Messenio, I don't believe sea-farers can ever enjoy a greater pleasure than their first sight of land from the ocean.

MESSENIO. For my part, I'd say the pleasure would be greater if it were your own homeland you were sighting. Can you tell me, sir, what we're doing now in Epidamnus? Are we going to circulate round all the islands, like the sea itself?

SOSICLES. I have come to look for my twin brother.

MESSENIO. And how long do you propose to go on looking for him? We've been at it now for six years. The Danube, Spain, Massilia, Illyria, all over the Atlantic, the Greek colonies, and the entire coast of Italy—we've visited the lot. You would have found a needle by this time, long

---

4. Mythical Greek hero known for his strength.   5. Amazon queen whose girdle Hercules had to battle for as one of his assigned tasks.   6. Ancient Greek silver coin.   7. Many of these foods were prohibited by law.

ago, if it were there to find. We're looking for a dead man among the living; if he were alive, we should have found him long before this.

SOSICLES. Very well, then, I am looking for someone who can give me certain news, someone who can say he knows for certain that my brother is dead. If it be so, I shall search no longer; but short of that, I shall never give up the quest as long as I live. No one but I knows how much I love him.

MESSENIO. Might as well look for a knotted bullrush . . . Why don't we go home, master? We're not writing a book of our travels, are we?

SOSICLES. Kindly do what you're told, eat what you're given, and mind your manners. I don't want any more of your impudence; and I'm not arranging my plans to suit you.

MESSENIO. *[Aside.]* There you are, you see. That's to remind me I'm a slave. He puts it in a nutshell. All the same, I can't hold my tongue . . . Sir, Menaechmus, I've just been looking at our purse, and I must say there's a bit of a drought in the reservoir. As far as I can see, if you don't make tracks for home, you'll be down to nothing, and then . . . looking for your brother . . . will be rather a bother. Do you know what sort of people live here? In Epidamnus you'll find all the worst drunkards and debauchees; the place is full of sharks and swindlers; and as for the harlots, I'm told they're the most seductive in the world. That's why it's called Epidamnus—anyone that lands up here is doomed to damnation.

SOSICLES. I'll be careful. Give me that purse.

MESSENIO. What do you want with the purse?

SOSICLES. I don't trust you after what you just said.

MESSENIO. Me? What are you afraid of?

SOSICLES. Lest you see me damned in Epidamnus. You're rather too fond of the women, Messenio; and I'm rather quick-tempered, and not always responsible for my actions. If I take charge of the money, it'll save us from both dangers—you from putting a foot wrong, and me from having to be angry with you.

MESSENIO. Take it, and welcome. Mind you don't lose it.

[Cylindrus returns from market with his provisions.]

CYLINDRUS. I've done some good shopping . . . got just what I wanted. I shall have a nice meal to offer the party . . . Hullo, there *is* Menaechmus! Oh dear, I shall catch it . . . guests waiting outside the door before I can get back with the provisions. I'd better go and speak to him . . . Good morning, sir.

SOSICLES. Who in the world may you be?

CYLINDRUS. Who am I? Don't you know me, then?

SOSICLES. I swear I don't.

CYLINDRUS. *[Passing this off with a grin.]* Are your fellow-guests with you?

SOSICLES. What fellow-guests?

CYLINDRUS. Your table-companion.

SOSICLES. My table-companion?

CYLINDRUS. *[Aside.]* The man is surely off his head.

MESSENIO. Didn't I tell you the place was swarming with swindlers?

SOSICLES. Who is this table-companion of mine you're expecting, young fellow?

CYLINDRUS. Your . . . Sponge.

MESSENIO. Sponge? I've got that here in the kitbag.

CYLINDRUS. I'm afraid you're a bit early for lunch. I've only just got back from market.

SOSICLES. *[Kindly, thinking he has to do with a lunatic.]* I say, young man, can you tell me how much a pig costs here—a perfect one, suitable for sacrifice?

CYLINDRUS. About . . . two drachmas.

SOSICLES. Here's two drachmas for you . . . go and make the offerings and get yourself absolved, at my expense. It's clear you must be a lunatic, whoever you are, to come pestering a perfect stranger.

CYLINDRUS. Well! I'm Cylindrus. Surely you know me by name?

SOSICLES. You may be Cylindrus or Coriendrus or what you please, but go to hell. I don't know you and I don't want to know you.

CYLINDRUS. Well, I know you; your name is Menaechmus.

SOSICLES. Now you're talking like a sane man, I will say. That is my name. But where have you met me?

CYLINDRUS. Where have I met you? Aren't you the lover of my mistress Erotium?

SOSICLES. I certainly am not, and I haven't the slightest idea who you are.

CYLINDRUS. Not know who I am, after all the times I've served you with drink at your parties at our place?

MESSENIO. God help me! Why haven't I got something to break this fellow's head with?

SOSICLES. How can you have served me with drink, when I've never seen or set foot in Epidamnus till this day?

CYLINDRUS. You haven't?

SOSICLES. I swear I haven't.

CYLINDRUS. Aren't you the occupant of that house there?

SOSICLES. May the gods damn the occupants of that house there!

CYLINDRUS. *[Aside.]* It's he that's off his head, cursing himself like that . . . Excuse me, Menaechmus—

SOSICLES. What now?

CYLINDRUS. If you want my advice, I think you should take that two drachmas you offered me just now . . . it's you that must be out of your mind, sir, calling down curses on your own head . . . the best thing would be to buy a pig for yourself . . .

MESSENIO. By all the gods, this fellow's unbearable. I'm sick and tired of him.

CYLINDRUS. *[Chatting on cheerfully to the audience.]* It's just his way; he often pulls my leg like this. He can be ever so amusing—when his wife's not there . . . I say, Menaechmus . . . Menaechmus!

SOSICLES. Well?

CYLINDRUS. Do you think I've got enough food here for the three of you—or should I get some more—for you and the lady and your table-companion?

SOSICLES. What lady, what table-companion are you talking about?

MESSENIO. What devil has got into you, man, to pester my master like this?

CYLINDRUS. I'm not concerned with you. I don't know you. I'm talking to this gentleman. I know him.

MESSENIO. I know you're a raving lunatic, and that's a fact.

CYLINDRUS. Anyway, I must go and get these things cooked. It won't take long, so don't go far away. With your leave, sir—

SOSICLES. You have my leave to go and be hanged.

CYLINDRUS. And you'd better go and . . . lie down, while I apply the powers of Vulcan to these articles. I'll go in, then, and let Erotium know you're standing out here . . . then she can ask you in . . . so you needn't hang about outside the door . . . *[He goes into the house.]*

SOSICLES. Has he gone at last? He has. Upon my word, Messenio, I begin to perceive that you spoke only too truly.

MESSENIO. You'll have to be careful, sir. I shouldn't wonder if this is some harlot's house, from what that mad fellow said.

SOSICLES. But how extraordinary that he should know my name!

MESSENIO. Bless you, no, nothing extraordinary in that. It's a way these women have; they send their slave boys or girls down to the port, and if there's a foreign ship in, they find out where she's from, and the master's name and everything; then they freeze on to him, and never let him out of their sight; and once they've got him hooked they send him home squeezed dry. And if I'm not mistaken, there's a pirate ship in *that* port at this moment *[pointing to Erotium's house]* and we'd do well to give her a wide berth.

SOSICLES. *[Sceptical.]* I'm sure that's very good advice.

MESSENIO. I'll believe it's good advice when I see you taking good heed of it.

SOSICLES. Say no more now, I hear the door opening. Let's see who comes out. *[He hides in some corner.]*

MESSENIO. I'll get rid of this meantime *[the bag he is carrying]*. Hey, galley-slaves, look after this stuff. *[He joins Sosicles.]*

[Erotium appears at the door, speaking to someone within.]

EROTIUM. No, don't shut the door; leave it as it is. See that everything is ready in there; make sure we have all that we need. Spread the couches and burn some perfumes; a gentleman likes to have things nice and comfortable. The more comfortable they are, the worse for his pocket, and the better for us! . . . The cook said my friend was waiting out here; where has he got to, I wonder? . . . *[Spying Sosicles.]* Ah, there he is—my most valuable and helpful friend! And of course he gets the consideration he deserves here; he's quite at home in this house . . . I'll go nearer and speak first . . . Darling! Why in the world are you standing out in the street, when the door's wide open for you! You know this house is more of a home to you than your own. We've got everything ready as you ordered, just as you like it; you won't be kept waiting. Lunch is prepared as you wished; we can sit down to it as soon as you like.

SOSICLES. Who is the woman talking to?

EROTIUM. She is talking to you, of course.

SOSICLES. *[Coming further into view.]* And what have you, or did you ever have, to do with me?

EROTIUM. Is it not you, above all other men, whom by the will of Venus I must most honour and worship, as you well deserve, since it is to you alone and to your generous hand I owe all my good fortune?

SOSICLES. The woman is either insane or intoxicated, Messenio. I've never seen her before, and she greets me as her dearest friend.

MESSENIO. What did I tell you? That's the way things are here. This is only a shower of leaves; you'll have trees falling on your head if we stay here three days. She's just like all the harlots here, experts at wheedling the money out of you. Let me have a word with her . . . Hey, woman, listen to me.

EROTIUM. I beg your pardon?

MESSENIO. Where have you seen this gentleman before?

EROTIUM. In the same place where he has often seen me, here, in Epidamnus.

MESSENIO. Here in Epidamnus? A man who has never set foot in the place till this day?

EROTIUM. Huh! Very funny! . . . Won't you come in, Menaechmus darling? You'll be much more comfortable inside.

SOSICLES. Blest if she doesn't call me by my right name too! I'm hanged if I know what this means.

MESSENIO. It means she's got wind of that purse you're carrying.

SOSICLES. Yes, that's very thoughtful of you, by Jove.[8] Here, you take it. I'll soon find out whether it's me or my purse she's in love with.

EROTIUM. Come along, let's go in to lunch.

SOSICLES. It's very kind of you; but . . . please excuse me.

EROTIUM. Then why did you ask me to cook a lunch for you, not an hour ago?

SOSICLES. I? Asked you to cook lunch for me?

EROTIUM. Of course you did; for you and your table-companion.

SOSICLES. Damn it, what table-companion? . . . The woman is undoubtedly mad.

EROTIUM. Your friend The Sponge.

SOSICLES. Sponge? The one I clean my shoes with?

EROTIUM. Oh you know, the man who was with you just now—when you brought me the robe you'd stolen from your wife.

SOSICLES. What *is* all this? I gave you a robe—stolen from my wife? Are you in your right mind? . . . This woman must be dreaming on her feet, like a horse.

EROTIUM. Why do you have to mock at everything I say, and deny everything you've done?

SOSICLES. Just kindly tell me what it is that I am supposed to have done and am denying.

EROTIUM. You denied that you had given me, this very morning, a robe belonging to your wife.

SOSICLES. And I still deny it. What's more, I haven't got a wife and never had one, and I have never before in the whole of my life put a foot inside the gate of this town. I have had lunch on board my ship, then I came ashore and here I've met you.

EROTIUM. *[Now thinking he must be mad.]* Oh, just think of it! Oh dear, this is terrible . . . What do you mean by a ship?

SOSICLES. *[Explaining whimsically.]* Well, it's a sort of a wooden affair . . . gets a lot of knocking about, nailing and banging with a hammer . . . full of bolts and pegs, like a furrier's drying-frame.

EROTIUM. Oh for heaven's sake, stop joking and come in with me.

SOSICLES. My good woman, it's someone else you're looking for, not me.

EROTIUM. As if I didn't know you perfectly well! You're Menaechmus, son of Moschus; born, by all accounts, in Sicily, the country which was ruled first by Agathocles, then by Phintias, then by Liparo, and after his death by Hiero who is the present king.[9]

SOSICLES. All that is perfectly correct, madam.

MESSENIO. Jupiter! Do you think she comes from these parts? She seems to know all about you.

SOSICLES. Upon my word, I don't think I can go on refusing her invitation.

MESSENIO. Mind what you're about. You're done for if you cross that doorstep.

---

8. Another name for Jupiter, the chief Roman god.

9. These may or may not be actual rulers; scholars are uncertain.

SOSICLES. Shut up. This is going to be all right. I'll agree to everything she says, in return for a little hospitality . . . *[He returns to Erotium, confidentially.]* Look, my dear, I had a good reason for contradicting you just now. I was afraid this man of mine might tell my wife about the dress and about our lunch party. I'm ready to come in as soon as you like.

EROTIUM. Are you going to wait for your friend?

SOSICLES. I am not; he can go to blazes; and if he does come I don't want him admitted.

EROTIUM. That'll suit me all right! But there's something else I'd like you to do for me, darling.

SOSICLES. Anything you say, beloved.

EROTIUM. That robe you've given me—could you take it to a dressmaker to have it refashioned with some improvements which I would like added?

SOSICLES. Of course I will. That's a good idea; it'll make it look different and my wife won't know it if she sees you wearing it in the street.

EROTIUM. You can take it away when you go.

SOSICLES. I'll do that.

EROTIUM. Let's go in, then.

SOSICLES. I'll be with you directly. I just want to have a word with my man first.

[Erotium goes in.]

Messenio! Come here.

MESSENIO. What are you up to? You ought to think what you're doing.

SOSICLES. Why ought I?

MESSENIO. Because—

SOSICLES. All right, I know; you needn't tell me.

MESSENIO. More fool you, then.

SOSICLES. I've captured a prize; so far so good. Get along and find a billet for those men, as soon as you can. Then come back and meet me here before sunset.

MESSENIO. You don't know what you're letting yourself in for, master—those women . . .

SOSICLES. That's quite enough, now. It's my funeral, not yours, if I make a fool of myself. This woman is the fool, an ignorant fool; from what I've seen so far, there's booty waiting for us here.

[He goes into the house.]

MESSENIO. No, you're not going in there? . . . Oh, damn and blast it, he's properly done for now. That pirate ship has got our little boat in tow for destruction. I'm the fool, though, to expect to be able to control my master; he bought me to obey orders, not give them . . . *[He turns to the slaves.]* Come on, you lot; let's be off, so that I can get back here at the time he said.

[He takes them off with the baggage.]

[An hour or two later, Peniculus returns from the town.]

PENICULUS. Well, that was the most stupid and fatal thing I have ever done in all the thirty odd years of my life—to go and get myself mixed up in that public meeting, fool that I was. While I was standing there gaping, Menaechmus must have slipped off and gone back to his mistress—not wanting to take me with him, of course. Gods confound the man who first invented public meetings, that device for wasting the time of people who have no time to waste. There ought to be a corps of idle men enrolled for that sort of business, every one of them to answer his name when called or pay a fine on the spot. After all, there are plenty of men who don't need more than one meal a day and have nothing else to do— never get invited out to eat, or invite their friends in; they could very well spend their time on meetings and committees. If things were managed that way, I wouldn't have lost that lunch today; I'm pretty sure he meant to give it me, sure as I'm alive. I think I'll go in, anyway; there's always the attractive prospect of left-overs . . . *[The door opens and Sosicles is about to come out, carrying the gown, and wearing a garland at a rakish angle on his head.]* But what's this? Menaechmus is coming out, with a garland on his head. They've cleared away, then, and I'm just in time to escort him home. I'll see what he's up to first, then I'll go and speak to him.

[Sosicles is speaking back to Erotium within.]

SOSICLES. Now you go and have a nice sleep, there's a good girl. I'll see that you get this back in plenty of time today, all nicely cleaned and altered. In fact it'll look so different you won't know it's the same one.

PENICULUS. Well, I'll be blowed, and he's off to the dressmaker's with that gown! Eaten all the lunch and drunk all the wine, and his table-friend left outside all this time! I'll jolly well get even with him for this treatment or I'm not the man I think I am. Just you wait, young man.

SOSICLES. *[Coming out.]* Oh gods above, did ever a man expect less of your bounty and receive more in one day than I have? Lunch, drinks, a woman, and . . . this for a prize, which its rightful owner is not going to see again.

PENICULUS. I can't quite catch what he's saying from here. Is it about the trick he's played me, now that he's got his belly full?

SOSICLES. The girl says I stole this from my wife and gave it to her! I could see there was some mistake, but I immediately agreed with her, as if we were on familiar terms; anything she said, I fell in with it. In short . . . I never had a better time at less expense.

PENICULUS. I'm going to talk to him. I'm dying to have a scrap with him.

SOSICLES. Now who's this coming my way?

PENICULUS. And what have you got to say for yourself, you base, vain, fickle and flighty, false and faithless, crooked and inconstant man? What have I done to deserve such infamous treatment at your hands? I know how you gave me the slip down in town not an hour ago, how you put away a luncheon without me there to assist at the obsequies. How dare you? Had not I as much right to be at the graveside as you?

SOSICLES. I don't know what business you have to be pitching into me, young fellow, when you don't know me and I've never seen you before. Unless you want me to give you the punishment your impudence deserves.

PENICULUS. As if you hadn't punished me enough already, by Jupiter!

SOSICLES. Perhaps you will be good enough to tell me your name at any rate?

PENICULUS. Is that your idea of a joke, pretending not to know my name?

SOSICLES. I swear I've never seen or met you till this minute, to the best of my knowledge. All I can say is, whoever you are, I shall be obliged if you will cease to annoy me.

PENICULUS. Come on, Menaechmus; wake up.

SOSICLES. I am quite awake, thank you.

PENICULUS. Do you mean to say you don't know me?

SOSICLES. If I did, I wouldn't deny it.

PENICULUS. You don't know me—your table-companion?

SOSICLES. It's quite clear to me, your brain is out of order.

PENICULUS. Tell me, didn't you steal that gown from your wife today and give it to Erotium?

SOSICLES. Damn it, I haven't got a wife and I never stole a gown and never gave one to Erotium.

PENICULUS. Have you gone mad? Oh dear, this is the end. Didn't I see you come out of your house this morning wearing that gown?

SOSICLES. God blast you, do you think we're all pansies like you? You mean to say you saw me wearing a woman's gown?

PENICULUS. I do, so help me.

SOSICLES. Oh go to . . . where you belong. Or go and get yourself certified, lunatic.

PENICULUS. That settles it. I'm going to tell your wife everything that's happened, and no one shall stop me. You'll find this high-handed treatment will recoil on your own head. I'll make you pay for eating up that lunch, you see if I don't. *[He goes into Menaechmus's house.]*

SOSICLES. What *does* all this mean? It seems that everyone I set eyes on is determined to make a fool of me . . . I hear someone coming.

[A Maid comes out of Erotium's house.]

MAID. Oh, Menaechmus, my mistress asks if you will be so very kind as to take this bracelet to the jeweller's at the same time and get him to add an ounce of gold to it and have it remodelled.

SOSICLES. With pleasure; tell her I'll do that and anything else she wants me to do—anything she wants.

MAID. You know this bracelet, of course?

SOSICLES. I don't know anything about it, except that it's a gold one.

MAID. It's the one you stole, so you said, some time ago from your wife's chest when she wasn't looking.

SOSICLES. I certainly never did.

MAID. Goodness, don't you recognize it? You had better give it back to me, in that case.

SOSICLES. No, wait a minute. Yes, of course I remember now. Yes, it is the one I gave her. This is it all right. And where are the armlets I gave her at the same time?

MAID. You never gave her any armlets.

SOSICLES. Didn't I? No, you're quite right. This was all I gave her.

MAID. Shall I say you'll look after it?

SOSICLES. Yes, you can say I'll look after it. I'll get the gown and the bracelet back to her at the same time.

MAID. If you'd like to do something for me, love, you could get me some gold earrings made—say about two pounds worth of gold—pendants, you know—then I'd be glad to see you next time you visit us, wouldn't I?

SOSICLES. I'll do that with pleasure—if you can give me the gold. I'll pay for the making.

MAID. Oh—I thought you could provide the gold. I can pay you back later.

SOSICLES. No, you provide the gold, and I'll pay you back—with interest.

MAID. But I haven't any gold.

SOSICLES. Then give it me when you have some.

MAID. I'd better be going, then—

SOSICLES. Say I'll take care of these things . . . [The Maid goes in.] . . . and get them sold as soon as possible for what they'll fetch! Has she gone? Oh yes, the door's shut . . . How all the gods love, aid, and exalt me! But I mustn't stop here. I must get away while I can from this den of vice. Get moving, Menaechmus! About turn, quick march. I'd better get rid of this garland too . . . I'll throw it away . . . over on this side . . . so that if anyone is after me they'll think I've gone that way. Now I'll go and find that man of mine, if I can, and tell him how good the gods have been to me.

[He goes away to the town.]

[Peniculus and the wife of Menaechmus come out of the neighbouring house.]

WIFE. How much longer am I expected to put up with this kind of marriage, I'd like to know, with my husband quietly robbing me of all I possess to make presents for his mistress?

PENICULUS. Don't say any more now. You're about to catch him red-handed, I promise you. Come this way. I've just seen him, drunk and with a garland on his head, taking your stolen gown to the dressmaker's . . . Oh look, here is the very garland he was wearing . . . now do you believe me? He must have gone this way, then, so you can follow his tracks if you want to. [Looking in the opposite direction to that taken by Sosicles.] Here he is too, by Jove, on his way back . . . that's fine! He hasn't got the gown, though.

WIFE. How shall I deal with him?

PENICULUS. Just as usual; give it him hot. That's what I would do. Come over here and stalk him from cover.

[They retire into an alley. Menaechmus comes along the street.]

MENAECHMUS. What fools we are to cling to this idiotic and supremely boring custom! Yet we do, and the more important we are, the more we cling to it. To have a large following of clients is everybody's ambition. Whether the clients are honest men or worthless, is immaterial; nobody bothers about that; a client's wealth is what matters, not his reputation for honesty. A decent poor man is of no account at all, but a rich rogue is considered a most desirable client. Yet look at the trouble a lawless and unscrupulous client can cause his patron. He will deny his debts, and be for ever going into court; he is avaricious, fraudulent, having made his fortune by usury and perjury; his whole mind is bent on such things. When his day of trial comes, it's a day of trial for the patron too (for we have to plead for the malefactors), whether the case is before a jury or judge or magistrate. That is the way I have been worried to death by a client today, and prevented from getting on with anything I wanted to do. The man button-holed me and wouldn't let me go. I had to put up a defence in court of all his countless crimes; I offered all kinds of involved and complicated terms of settlement; and just when I had more or less succeeded in getting the parties to agree to a decision by wager, what must the fellow do but demand a guarantor? Oh dear! . . . and a more manifest villain I have never seen exposed; there were three unshakeable witnesses for every one of his misdeeds. Gods curse the wretched man, for spoiling my day! Curse me too, for ever going near the forum[10] this morning. A perfectly good day wasted— lunch ordered, and my mistress no doubt anxiously awaiting me. I've hurried away from town as soon as I possibly could; and now, I suppose, she will be angry with me—unless the gift of the gown has placated her; the one I stole from my wife, you remember, and gave to Erotium.

PENICULUS. *[To the Wife.]* What do you think of that?

WIFE. I am cruelly married to a cruel husband.

PENICULUS. You heard what he said all right?

WIFE. I heard all right.

MENAECHMUS. My best plan will be to go in and join the party and have a good time.

PENICULUS. *[Coming forward.]* Just a minute. You're going to have a bad time first.

WIFE. Yes, indeed you are. You're going to pay heavy interest on that property you've borrowed.

PENICULUS. There's a nice surprise for you.

WIFE. Did you think you could get away with a mean trick like that?

MENAECHMUS. I don't know what you're talking about, my dear.

WIFE. You don't?

MENAECHMUS. Shall we ask *him* to explain? *[Taking her hand.]*

WIFE. Take your dirty hands off me, please.

PENICULUS. That's the way to talk to him.

MENAECHMUS. What have you got against me?

WIFE. As if you didn't know.

PENICULUS. He knows all right, but he pretends he doesn't, the scoundrel.

MENAECHMUS. What *are* you talking about?

WIFE. A robe—

MENAECHMUS. A robe?

WIFE. Yes, a robe, a wrap, which somebody—

MENAECHMUS. A wrap?

PENICULUS. What are you trembling at?

MENAECHMUS. I'm not trembling at anything.

PENICULUS. Well, you look as if you'd taken the rap! And who ate up the lunch behind my back? *[To Wife.]* Let him have it.

MENAECHMUS. I wish you'd shut up. *[Trying to make signals to Peniculus.]*

PENICULUS. I certainly won't shut up. *[To Wife.]* He's trying to tip me the wink to keep quiet, you see.

MENAECHMUS. Damn it. I'm not tipping you any winks or nods.

PENICULUS. There's boldness for you—to deny what's plainly visible.

MENAECHMUS. Woman, I swear by Jupiter and all the gods—if that will satisfy you—that *I did not wink or nod at that man!*

PENICULUS. All right, you didn't nod at "that man"; she'll take your word for it. Now let's get back—

MENAECHMUS. Back where?

PENICULUS. Back to the dressmaker's, I suggest, and get that gown back.

MENAECHMUS. What gown?

PENICULUS. *[After looking at the Wife, who is too upset to reply.]* It's no use my saying any more, if she's not going to play.

WIFE. *[Sobbing.]* I'm . . . so . . . unhappy . . .

MENAECHMUS. What are you unhappy about, my dear? Tell me, please. Has one of the servants been troublesome? Have the men or women been answering you back? If so, please tell me, and I'll have them punished.

WIFE. Stupid man!

MENAECHMUS. She *is* upset about something. I don't like to see her—

WIFE. St . . . stupid man!

MENAECHMUS. There's someone in the house you're angry with, I'm sure.

WIFE. *Stupid man!*

MENAECHMUS. It surely can't be me . . . can it?

WIFE. Oh? Sense at last, then?

MENAECHMUS. But I've done nothing wrong.

WIFE. Stupid man again!

MENAECHMUS. *[Trying to fondle her.]* My dear, do tell me what is troubling you.

PENICULUS. Trying to play the sweet hubby with you now!

MENAECHMUS. *[To Peniculus.]* Can't you mind your own business? I'm not talking to you, am I?

WIFE. Take your hands off me, please.

PENICULUS. Serve you right. Let's see you again eating up the lunch in my absence, and playing

---

10. Marketplace or public place of ancient Roman city, forming the center of judicial and public business.

the drunken fool with me in front of the house with a garland on your head.

MENAECHMUS. Heavens above! I tell you I haven't had any lunch, nor put a foot inside that house this day!

PENICULUS. You haven't?

MENAECHMUS. By the head of Hercules, I haven't.

PENICULUS. He's the most brazen liar I've ever known . . . Haven't I just seen you out here in the street with a wreath of roses on your head—when you told me my brain was out of order, pretended you didn't know me, and said you were a stranger here?

MENAECHMUS. But, good heavens, I parted from you some time ago, and have only just now come home.

PENICULUS. Go on, you can't fool me. And you didn't reckon on my being able to pay you out, did you? Well, I have. I've told your wife all about it.

MENAECHMUS. What have you told her?

PENICULUS. Oh, I forget. You'd better ask her yourself.

MENAECHMUS. What is it all about, my dear? What has he told you? What has been happening? Can't you speak? Can't you tell me what it is?

WIFE. Still asking me that? As if you didn't know.

MENAECHMUS. I wouldn't ask, would I, if I knew?

PENICULUS. What a double-faced scoundrel the man is! . . . You'll never get away with it, my lad. She knows all about it. I gave her all the details myself.

MENAECHMUS. *What* details?

WIFE. Very well, since you have no shame and no wish to confess voluntarily, just listen to this. I'll tell you why I am angry, and what this man has told me. A gown has been stolen and taken out of the house.

MENAECHMUS. A gown? I've been robbed of a gown?

PENICULUS. The rascal's still trying to twist you, you see . . . No, *you've* not been robbed, *she* has. If you've been robbed, we shall never see it again, that's certain.

MENAECHMUS. You keep out of this . . . Explain to me, my dear.

WIFE. A gown, I repeat, is missing from the house.

MENAECHMUS. Who can have taken it?

WIFE. The man who removed it can best answer that, I should think.

MENAECHMUS. And who would he be?

WIFE. His name is Menaechmus.

MENAECHMUS. Really? What a rotten thing to do. Who is this Menaechmus?

WIFE. *You* are this Menaechmus.

MENAECHMUS. Am I?

WIFE. You are.

MENAECHMUS. And who is my accuser?

WIFE. I am.

PENICULUS. So am I. And I add that you gave it to your mistress Erotium.

MENAECHMUS. I gave it to her?

WIFE. Yes, *you* did, *you* did.

PENICULUS. If you like, we'll bring on an owl to keep repeating "yoo, yoo"; we're tired of it.

MENAECHMUS. No, no, my dear, I never gave it away. By Jupiter and all the gods I swear—

PENICULUS. You'd much better swear that we are telling the truth.

MENAECHMUS. I didn't give it outright; I only lent it.

WIFE. Did you indeed? And have you ever known me lend your cloaks or tunics outside the house? It's a woman's place to lend out women's clothes, and a man's the men's. Perhaps you will kindly bring the gown back.

MENAECHMUS. I will certainly see that it comes back.

WIFE. It will certainly be in your interest to do so. You're not coming into this house again until you bring the gown with you. I'm going home.

PENICULUS. And what do I get for what I've done for you in this business?

WIFE. I'll do as much for you, when something is stolen from your house.

[She goes into her house.]

PENICULUS. That'll be never; there's nothing in my house that I'm likely to lose. May the gods blast you both, wife and husband! I'll get along to town; it's obvious I'm no longer a friend of this family.

[He goes off.]

MENAECHMUS. She thinks she's got her own back, does she—shutting me out of the house? As if I didn't know of another place, and a better one, where I shall be welcome. All right, my lady, if

you don't want me, I shall have to grin and
bear it. Erotium will want me; she won't shut
me out; she'll shut me in, both of us together.
I'll go now, and beg her to let me have the
gown back—tell her I'll buy her a better one.
[He knocks at her door.] Hey there! Is there a
doorkeeper here? Open please, and let someone
ask Erotium to come out here.

EROTIUM. *[Within.]* Who is asking for me?

MENAECHMUS. Someone who loves you more than
his own life.

[Erotium comes out.]

EROTIUM. Menaechmus, my dear! Don't wait
outside, come in.

MENAECHMUS. No, stay. Let me tell you what I've
come for.

EROTIUM. I know quite well what you've come
for—so that you and I may enjoy ourselves.

MENAECHMUS. The fact is . . . darling, will you
please let me have that gown back, the one I
gave you this morning. My wife has found out
all about the whole affair. I'll buy you another
one worth twice as much, any kind you like.

EROTIUM. But I have just given it you, not half an
hour ago, to take to the dressmaker; and the
bracelet you were to take to the jeweller to be
remade.

MENAECHMUS. You gave me the gown and a
bracelet? You're mistaken; you never did any
such thing. After giving it you this morning, I
went off to town, and now I have just come
back; this is the first time I've seen you since
then.

EROTIUM. Oh? I can see through that little game all
right. I put the things into your charge and
now you've thought up a nice way to do me
out of them.

MENAECHMUS. Good heavens, no! I'm not trying to
do you out of anything, by asking for it back. I
told you, my wife has found out—

EROTIUM. And I never asked for it in the first
place, did I? It was your idea to bring it to me;
you said it was a present for me; now you want
it back. It's all the same to me; you can keep
it, take it back, wear it yourself, let your wife
wear it, or lock it up in a cupboard for all I
care. If that's all you think of me, after all I've
done for you, you're not coming into this
house any more, I give you my word—not

without ready money in your hand. You can't
muck about with me like that, young man.
You can go and find someone else to make a
fool of. *[She goes in.]*

MENAECHMUS. Oh, no, please, you can't be as angry
as all that. Please, wait, listen, come back!
You're not going? Oh do come back, just for
my sake! . . . She's gone. The door's locked.
Now I'm properly locked out. No one will
believe a word I say, either at home or at my
mistress's. I don't know what I'm going to do
now . . . I shall have to go and find a friend
somewhere to advise me.

[He goes off to the town.]

*[Later, Sosicles returns from town, with the gown under his
arm.]*

SOSICLES. I was a fool to let Messenio have the
purse and money this morning. He'll have
gone to ground in some grog-shop by now, I
expect . . .

[The Wife looks out of her house.]

WIFE. I wonder if there's any sign of my husband
coming home . . . Oh yes, there he is. I'm
saved! He's bringing the gown back.

SOSICLES. I wish I knew where the man had got
to.

WIFE. I'll go and give him a suitable welcome . . .
Well, you sinner, aren't you ashamed to appear
in my sight with that thing on you?

SOSICLES. I beg your pardon? Is anything the
matter, madam?

WIFE. Heartless creature! Are you still daring to
bandy words with me?

SOSICLES. Why shouldn't I address you, pray? Have
I committed any crime?

WIFE. Still asking me that? Oh, you're utterly
shameless.

SOSICLES. Have you ever heard, madam, why the
Greeks used to call Hecuba[11] a bitch?

WIFE. I certainly haven't.

SOSICLES. It was because Hecuba used to do exactly
what you are doing, pour every kind of abuse

11. Queen of Troy, who survived the war as a slave and eventually
was turned into a fiery-eyed dog. She appears in *The Trojan Women*
by Euripides.

on anyone she came across. So she came to be called The Bitch—and rightly too.

WIFE. Oh! I won't put up with this infamous conduct any longer. I'd rather live and die without a husband than endure such outrageous behaviour.

SOSICLES. And what business is it of mine, whether you can endure your married life or intend to part from your husband? Is it perhaps the custom here to babble your affairs to any stranger that comes along?

WIFE. Babble! I tell you I won't stand it any longer. I'll get a divorce sooner than suffer such treatment for the rest of my life.

SOSICLES. Well, bless me, I've no objection. Get a divorce, and remain divorced, for the rest of your life, or as long as Jupiter is king.

WIFE. An hour ago you denied having stolen that gown, and here you are with it before my eyes. Aren't you ashamed of that?

SOSICLES. Oh my goodness, woman, what wicked impudence! Do you really claim that this gown was stolen from you, when it was given to me by another lady for me to take to the repairer's?

WIFE. Oh! I shall . . . I shall send for my father and tell him all about your wicked doings. *[She goes to the door.]* Decio! Go and find my father, and bring him back with you. Tell him it's urgent . . . I'll soon expose all your evil practices!

SOSICLES. I think you must be mad. What are these evil practices of mine?

WIFE. Stealing my clothes, and stealing my jewels, your wife's property, out of the house, and carrying them off to your mistress! Isn't that something to "babble" about?

SOSICLES. My good woman, if you know of any medicine that would help me to swallow your venomous insults more easily, I should be glad if you would tell me of it. I haven't the faintest idea who you think I am; and I know no more of you than I do of Hercules's grandfather-in-law.[12]

WIFE. Mock me if you like; you won't mock him so lightly—my father, who will be here in a minute. *[Looking down the street.]* There he is, do you see? Perhaps you know him?

SOSICLES. Oh yes, I know him as well as Calchas! I met him that day when I first met you.[13]

WIFE. Not know me indeed! Not know my father!

SOSICLES. Bring me your grandfather if you like; I shan't know him either.

WIFE. Huh! Just like you too. Just what I would expect from your conduct.

[The Wife's Father comes slowly along the street. As he is assumed to be still some way off, he has time for a good grumble before reaching the others.]

FATHER. I'm coming, I'm coming, as fast as an old man can, and as fast the need may be . . . but it isn't easy . . . don't I know it? I'm not as nippy as I used to be . . . the years tell on me . . . more weight to carry and less strength. Yes, age is a bad business, a dead loss. It brings you nothing but troubles, and plenty of them. I could tell you what they are, but it would take far too long. . . . What chiefly worries me at this moment is, what on earth does my daughter want, suddenly sending for me like this? She hasn't given me the least idea what she wants me for. Why should she demand my presence so urgently? . . . I think I've a pretty good idea what it's all about, though. She's had some quarrel with her husband, I expect. They're like that—these women who expect their husbands to be at their beck and call; with a good dowry behind them, they're terrors. Not that the husbands are always blameless, if it comes to that. Still, there are limits to what a wife should have to put up with; and you can be sure a woman doesn't send for her father without good reason— some misconduct on the husband's part or a serious quarrel. Well, we shall soon know . . . Ah yes, there she is outside the house . . . and her husband, in no good temper by the looks of him. Just as I thought, I'll get a word with her first. *[He beckons to her.]*

WIFE. I'll go to him . . . Oh, father, I'm glad to see you.

FATHER. I'm glad to see you. I hope you're well. All well here, eh? Nothing wrong, I hope, to bring me over here? You look a bit downcast, though; why is that? And why is he standing

---

12. Joke using mythology to suggest that he has no idea who the wife is.

13. Calchus was Agamemnon's prophet during the Trojan war.

over there looking so grumpy? I believe you've been having a bit of a tiff over something or other. Have you? Come on, out with it, tell me whose fault it was, and don't make a long tale of it.

WIFE. It is not I that have done anything wrong, you can make your mind easy on that, father. But I cannot live here any longer; I simply cannot stand it; you must take me away.

FATHER. What's the trouble, then?

WIFE. I am being treated like dirt.

FATHER. By whom?

WIFE. By my husband, the husband you found for me.

FATHER. So that's it—a bit of a squabble. How many times have I told you that I won't have you, either of you, running to me with your complaints?

WIFE. How can I avoid it, father?

FATHER. Do you want me to tell you?

WIFE. If you please.

FATHER. I've told you dozens of times; it's your business to try to please your husband, not keep spying on everything he does, always wanting to know where he's going and what he's up to.

WIFE. What he's up to is making love to the harlot next door.

FATHER. I don't blame him; and I warrant he'll go on loving her all the more, the more you keep on at him like this.

WIFE. Drinking there too.

FATHER. And do you think you have a right to stop him drinking, there or anywhere else he chooses? I never heard such impudence, girl. I suppose you think you can also stop him accepting invitations to supper, or inviting friends to his own house? Do you expect a husband to be your slave? You might as well expect him to do the housework for you, or sit with the women and spin.

WIFE. I see I've brought you here to plead for my husband, not for me. My advocate has gone over to the other side.

FATHER. My dear girl, if he commits any criminal offence, I shall have a lot more to say to him than I have said to you. He keeps you in clothes, jewellery, and all the servants and provisions you could possibly need; your best plan is to accept the situation sensibly.

WIFE. Even if he robs me, steals my clothes and jewels out of my cupboards, empties my wardrobe behind my back to make presents to his strumpets?

FATHER. Ah well, he has no right to do that—if that is what he is doing. But if he isn't, you have no right to accuse an innocent man.

WIFE. I tell you, father, at this very moment he has a gown and a bracelet of mine, which he had given to that woman, and which he is only now bringing back because I found out about it.

FATHER. Oh dear . . . I'd better learn the truth about this, from his own lips. I'll have a word with him . . . Now then, Menaechmus, what's this that you two are quarreling about? I want to know. Why are you moping over here, and she in a temper over there?

SOSICLES. Whoever you are, old gentleman, and whatever your name may be, I swear by Jupiter and all the gods above—

FATHER. Good heavens, what's coming?

SOSICLES. —that I have never done the slightest wrong to that woman who keeps accusing me of having stolen and abstracted a garment from her house—

WIFE. A wicked lie!

SOSICLES. —and if I have ever put a foot inside that house, may I be the damnedest of all damned creatures on earth!

FATHER. Why, you imbecile, have you taken leave of your senses, to utter such a curse upon yourself, and say you have never set foot inside the house you live in?

SOSICLES. Are you now saying that I live in that house too?

FATHER. Well, do you deny it?

SOSICLES. I most certainly deny it.

FATHER. Then you are telling a flat lie—unless you've moved out of the house since yesterday . . . Daughter, come over here . . . have you and your husband moved out of this house?

WIFE. Where in the world should we move to, and why, for goodness sake?

FATHER. I'm hanged if I know.

WIFE. He's pulling your leg, of course. Can't you see that?

FATHER. Come now, Menaechmus, that's enough of your joking; let's come to the point.

SOSICLES. What point? What has my business got to do with you? I don't know who you are or

---

where you come from or how I am supposed to be concerned with you or with this woman who has done nothing but insult me ever since I met her.

WIFE. *[In alarm.]* Look at him father! His eyes are turning green; all his face is turning green; and that glitter in his eyes—look!

SOSICLES. *[Aside.]* If they are going to declare me insane, the best thing I can do is to pretend to be insane; perhaps that will frighten them off. *[He acts accordingly.]*

WIFE. Now he's gaping and flinging himself about. Oh father, what ever shall I do?

FATHER. Come away, my dear, come away as far as possible from him.

SOSICLES. *[Raving.]* Euhoe! Euhoe! Bacchus[14] ahoy! Wilt thou have me go hunt in the woods away? I hear thee, I hear thee, but here I must stay. I am watched by a witch, a wild female bitch, on my left, and behind her a smelly old goat, a lying old dotard whose lies have brought many an innocent creature to ruin . . .

FATHER. Ay, ruin on you!

SOSICLES. Now the word of Apollo[15] commands me, commands me to burn out her eyes with firebrands blazing . . .

WIFE. Ah!! Father, father, he is threatening to burn out my eyes!

SOSICLES. Woe is me, when madmen themselves call me mad.

FATHER. Here, girl!

WIFE. Yes?

FATHER. What are we going to do? Shall I get some servants here? Yes, that's it; I'll get some men here to carry him home and tie him up before he can do any worse harm.

SOSICLES. Now what am I going to do? They'll have me carried off to their house if I don't think of something quickly . . . *[Making to attack the Wife.]* I hear thee, Apollo, bid me strike this woman's face and spare not, if she will not speedily avoid my sight and begone to whatever hell she chooses. Thy will be done, Apollo!

FATHER. Go inside, girl, go inside at once before he murders you!

WIFE. I'm going. Watch him, father. Don't let him get away. Oh! What terrible things for a poor wife to hear! . . .

[She escapes into the house.]

SOSICLES. That's got rid of her nicely. Now for this wicked whiskered tottering Tithonus,[16] so-called son of Cygnus[17] . . . At thy command, Apollo, I shall pound his body to bits, smash every bone and limb with his own walking-stick . . .

FATHER. You dare touch me, or come a step nearer, and you'll be sorry for it.

SOSICLES. I obey, Apollo. With a two-edged axe I will mash this old man's flesh and bones to mincemeat . . .

FATHER. My goodness, I must look out for myself, or I'm afraid he really will do me as much harm as he threatens.

SOSICLES. More commands, Apollo? Ay, now thou biddest me harness my fierce wild horses and mount my chariot to ride down this aged toothless stinking lion . . . So be it . . . now I am in my chariot, now I hold the reins, here is the goad in my hands . . . Gallop apace, my steeds! Let me hear the ring of your hoofs! Swift be the flight of your feet on your tireless courses!

FATHER. You keep your horses away from me!

SOSICLES. Apollo, Apollo! Still thou art bidding me charge on the foeman who stands in my path and destroy him . . . *[The old man stands his ground and grapples with the madman.]* . . . Ah! Who is this who seizes me by the hair and drags me from my car? Who is this who defies and obstructs thy orders, thy royal commands, O Apollo! . . .

[He gives up the battle and falls to the ground.]

FATHER. Well I never! He must have had a terribly sudden and serious stroke. He was perfectly well a few minutes ago, and now raving mad. I've never seen a man taken so suddenly. Good gods, what ever shall I do? I'd better go and find a doctor as quick as I can . . .

[He hurries off.]

SOSICLES. Have they gone at last? I got rid of those two pests who have turned a sane man into a

---

14. God of wine and revelry.   15. God of sunlight and prophesy.   16. Lover of the Roman goddess of dawn.   17. Swan constellation.

raving lunatic? . . . My best plan now is to get back to my ship while the going's good. You won't tell him, friends, will you? Don't tell the old man, if he comes back, which way I've gone. Goodbye. *[He goes.]*

[Later. The Father returns, wearily.]

FATHER. All this time I've been waiting for the doctor to get back from his rounds. My bottom's numb with sitting, and my eyes sore with watching out for him. At last the tiresome fellow finished with his patients and came home. Tells me he had to set a broken leg for Aesculapius and mend an arm for Apollo—whatever he meant by that . . . Oh, now I come to think of it, I wonder if I've summoned a stonemason instead of a doctor? Anyway, here he comes now . . . Hurry up, man; can't you move faster than an insect?

[The Doctor arrives.]

DOCTOR. Now, sir, what did you say was the nature of the illness? Is it a case of possession or hallucination? Are there any symptoms of lethargy or hydropsical condition?

FATHER. I've brought you here to tell me that, and to cure him.

DOCTOR. There'll be no difficulty about that; we'll cure him all right, I can promise you.

FATHER. I want him to have the most careful attention.

DOCTOR. I'll care for him most carefully. I shall be sighing over him every minute of the day.

FATHER. Look, here he comes. Let's watch his behaviour.

[They stand aside. Menaechmus comes from the town.]

MENAECHMUS. Upon my word, I don't know when I spent a more fatal and frustrating day. All my carefully concealed schemes have been exposed by that satellite of mine. Like a Ulysses,[18] he has plotted against his lord, and made me look a cowering guilty fool. I'll get even with the fellow, if I live; I'll put an end

to his life—if you can call it his life—my life, I should say, since it's my food and money he's been living on! Anyway, I'll stop his breath. As for that woman, she has behaved just as you would expect from her kind. I ask her to let me have the gown returned to my wife, and she says it was a gift to her. Oh dear, what a life!

FATHER. Do you hear what he's saying?

DOCTOR. He's saying what an unhappy creature he is.

FATHER. Go and speak to him, do.

DOCTOR. Good afternoon, Menaechmus. Oh dear me, you shouldn't have your arm uncovered like that. Don't you know that is the worst possible thing for your complaint?

MENAECHMUS. Why don't you go and hang yourself?

FATHER. Do you notice anything?

DOCTOR. I should think I do! It'll take bushels of hellebore[19] to get the better of this malady . . . Tell me, Menaechmus—

MENAECHMUS. Tell you what?

DOCTOR. Just one question—do you drink white wine or red?

MENAECHMUS. Oh go to blazes!

DOCTOR. *[To Father.]* Yes, indeed, the fit is coming on him again.

MENAECHMUS. Why don't you ask me whether I eat pink, purple, or yellow bread? Whether I eat birds with scales or fish with feathers?

FATHER. Ts, Ts! Listen to his raving. Can't you give him a dose of something immediately to save him from going completely mad?

DOCTOR. All in good time. I'll ask him some more questions.

FATHER. You'll kill us all with your rigmarole.

DOCTOR. Tell me, young man, do you ever feel your eyes scaling over?

MENAECHMUS. Imbecile, do you take me for a lobster?

DOCTOR. And another thing: have you noticed any rumbling in the bowels?

MENAECHMUS. They don't rumble when I'm full; they rumble when I'm empty.

DOCTOR. Well, I don't see anything unreasonable in that answer. Do you sleep all night? Do you fall asleep easily when you get into bed?

---

18. Roman name for the Greek leader of the Trojan War, who wandered for ten years after the war before returning home.

19. Type of herb.

MENAECHMUS. I sleep soundly enough—if I've paid all my bills. Oh, Jupiter and all the gods blast you and your silly questions!

DOCTOR. Madness coming on again. Be careful when he talks like that.

FATHER. He's talking as sanely as Nestor,[20] compared with what he was a little time ago; then he was calling his wife a crazy bitch.

MENAECHMUS. I was?

FATHER. You certainly were—in your madness, of course.

MENAECHMUS. I was mad?

FATHER. You were; you threatened to run me down with a chariot and four. I saw you. I can bring eye-witness evidence against you.

MENAECHMUS. Oh, can you? And I can prove you stole the sacred crown off Jupiter's head and were put in prison for it; I have evidence that when you were let out you were flogged at the stake; and I know how you murdered your father and sold your mother. Take that slander back in your teeth to convince you I'm a sane man.

FATHER. For heaven's sake, doctor, whatever you're going to do, do it quickly. You can surely see he's out of his mind.

DOCTOR. Yes . . . well . . . this is what I would advise you to do. Have him brought over to my house.

FATHER. Do you think that will be best?

DOCTOR. I certainly do. There I shall be able to supervise his treatment.

FATHER. Just as you please.

DOCTOR. *[To Menaechmus.]* I'll put you on to hellebore for three weeks.

MENAECHMUS. I'll put you on to a rack and have you pricked with goads for a month.

DOCTOR. Go and find some men to carry him to my house.

FATHER. How many men will it take, do you think?

DOCTOR. Judging by his present condition of insanity, not less than four.

FATHER. I'll have them here directly. You keep an eye on him, doctor, meanwhile.

DOCTOR. Oh, I must go home and see to the necessary preparations. You tell your men to bring him along.

FATHER. Very well. We'll get him to your house immediately.

DOCTOR. I'll go, then.

FATHER. Goodbye.

[They go their ways.]

MENAECHMUS. Exit doctor. Exit father-in-law. Now I am alone. Jupiter! Whatever can have possessed those two to pronounce me insane? Me—who have never had a day's illness in my life! I'm not insane at all, nor am I looking for a fight or a quarrel with anybody. I'm just as sane as every other sane man I see; I know my friends when I see them, I talk to them normally. Then why are they trying to make out that I am insane—unless it's they who are insane? Now what do I do? I'd like to go home, but wife says no. Next door there's no welcome for me either. What a damnable business! I shall just have to wait here; they'll let me in at nightfall, I should hope. *[He sits down at his own doorstep.]*

[Messenio comes from the town.]

MESSENIO. It's the mark of a good slave, I always say—one who can be trusted to watch and provide for his master's welfare, plan and organize his affairs—that he attends to his master's business just as well in his master's absence as in his presence, or better. Every right-thinking slave ought to value his own back more than his own throat, look after his shins rather than his belly. He'll remember, if he has any sense, how their masters reward worthless, idle, and dishonest slaves: floggings, chains, the treadmill, sweating, starving, freezing stiff—that's what you get for laziness. I'd rather take the trouble to keep out of that sort of trouble. That's why I've decided to be a good slave, not a bad one. I can bear a lash of the tongue more easily than a lash of the whip; and I'd much rather eat corn than grind it. So I do as my master tells me, carry out his orders in an efficient and orderly manner; and I find it pays me. Others can do as they think best; I'm going to do my duty. That's my resolution—to play safe, do no wrong, and always be where I'm wanted. The way to be a useful slave is to

---

20. Elder statesman of the Greeks at Troy.

be afraid of trouble even when you've done no wrong; the ones who are not afraid of anything, even when they *have* deserved trouble—they've got something to be afraid of! I shan't have much to fear. It won't be long before my master rewards me for my services. Anyway, that's my idea of service—making sure my own back doesn't suffer. So now I've done everything he told me, seen the baggage and the slaves settled at an inn, and come back here to meet him. I'll knock at the door and let him know I'm here, so that I can rescue him safely out of this den of thieves. Although I'm very much afraid the struggle may be over and I have come too late.

[As he goes up to Erotium's door, the Father comes back with four strong slaves.]

FATHER. Now you men, you have your orders and I repeat them again, and by heaven and earth I charge you to observe them diligently. I want that man picked up and carried at once to the doctor's house; see to it, unless you care nothing for the comfort of your own legs and sides. And don't, any of you, take the slightest notice of anything *he* may threaten to do to you. Well? Jump to it. What are you waiting for? He ought to be on your backs and away by now. I'll go along to the doctor's; I shall be ready to meet you there when you arrive.

[He goes. The slaves grapple with Menaechmus.]

MENAECHMUS. Help! Murder! What's happening? Why am I being set on like this? What do you want? Have you lost something? Why are you attacking me? Where are you dragging me? Where are you carrying me? Help, help, people of Epidamnus! Citizens, help! Let me go, can't you!

MESSENIO. Almighty gods! What do I see? My master man-handled and carried off by a gang of ruffians!

MENAECHMUS. Won't anyone come to my aid?

MESSENIO. I will, master. I'll fight 'em. Oh, men of Epidamnus, look at this horrible wicked outrage—my master being kidnapped in the street, in broad daylight, a freeborn visitor abducted in your peaceful city! Drop him, you villains!

MENAECHMUS. [Taking Messenio for a stranger.] Oh thank you, my man, whoever you are; help me, for goodness sake; don't let them do this outrageous thing to me.

MESSENIO. I'll help you, I'll defend you, I'll put up a fight for you. I'll not see you die—sooner die myself. Go on, sir, knock his eye out—that one that's got you by the arm. I'll plant a crop of fisticuffs among these other faces . . . You try to carry this man off and it will be the worse for you. Drop him!

MENAECHMUS. I've got my fingers in this one's eye.

MESSENIO. Leave him with an empty socket in his head. You villains! You robbers! You thugs!

SLAVES. Murder! Help!

MESSENIO. Let him go!

MENAECHMUS. How dare you attack me! [To Messenio.] Tear the skin off them!

[The slaves are by this time routed, and decamp.]

MESSENIO. Get out of it, the lot of you; off with you to hell. [Clouting the last of them.] And here's one for you . . . a prize for being the last . . . I gave their faces a good doing over, didn't I? Gave 'em all I wanted to. By jingo, sir, it was a lucky thing I got here just in time to help you.

MENAECHMUS. May the gods bless you, my good fellow—[aside] whoever you may be. But for you, I doubt if I should have lived to see this day's end.

MESSENIO. I'm sure you can't refuse to give me my freedom after this, master.

MENAECHMUS. I? Give you your freedom?

MESSENIO. Surely, after I've saved your life, master.

MENAECHMUS. What *do* you mean? You're under some misapprehension, my good man.

MESSENIO. I am? Why?

MENAECHMUS. I'll take my oath, by Jupiter above, you're not one of my servants.

MESSENIO. Don't talk—

MENAECHMUS. I mean it. No slave of mine ever did so much for me as you have done.

[Messenio is puzzled for a moment; then, taking Menaechmus at his word:]

MESSENIO. You mean. . . ? I'm no longer a slave of yours? I can go free, then?

MENAECHMUS. You have my permission to go free and to go wherever you please.

MESSENIO. Is that an order sir?

MENAECHMUS. It's certainly an order, so far as I have any power to give you orders.

MESSENIO. Hail, one time master, now my patron! [Shaking hands with himself, as if being congratulated by his master's friends.] "Congratulations, Messenio, on your freedom" . . . "Thank you, sir, it's very kind of you" . . . But I say, master . . . please, to please me, just go on giving me orders the same as when I was your slave. I still want to go on living with you. I'll go home with you when you go.

MENAECHMUS. Indeed you won't!

MESSENIO. I'll pop round to the inn and collect the baggage and your purse and bring them back here. The purse with our travelling money is safely sealed up in the trunk; I'll have it back here in a jiffy.

MENAECHMUS. [Amused.] Do, by all means.

MESSENIO. You'll find the money's all there just as you gave it to me. Wait here for me.

[He dashes off.]

MENAECHMUS. This is a day of wonders and no mistake! First I'm told I'm not myself, then I'm shut out in the street, and now comes this fellow saying he's my slave, so I set him free and he says he's going to bring me a purse full of money! If he does, I shall certainly tell him to clear off and be as free as he likes and go wherever he likes. I don't want him coming to claim the money back again when he comes to his senses. And that doctor and my father-in-law said I was out of my senses. It makes no sense to me. It's like a bad dream . . . However, I'll go and call on my mistress again, even if she is in a bad temper with me, and see if I can get her to let me have my wife's gown back. [He knocks at Erotium's door, and is admitted.]

[Messenio had not gone far when he met his real master again, and back they come.]

SOSICLES. Have you the impudence to tell me you have met me anywhere else today since we parted here and I told you to come back to find me here?

MESSENIO. What, and haven't I just rescued you from four men who were trying to carry you off, here in front of this house? And you were howling for help to heaven and earth, and up I came and by force of my own fists got you away safe in spite of the lot of them. And for having saved your life you gave me my freedom. And then I said I was going to fetch the money and our baggage, and meanwhile you, it seems, took a short cut to intercept me and try to pretend none of this ever happened.

SOSICLES. Are you telling me I have given you your freedom?

MESSENIO. Of course you have.

SOSICLES. Oh dear, no. You can rest assured I would rather become a slave myself than ever let you out of my hands.

[Menaechmus comes out of Erotium's house, with a parting shot at someone within.]

MENAECHMUS. I have *not* taken a gown and a bracelet from here today; swear if you like by your own bright eyes that I have, it won't alter the fact—bitches!

MESSENIO. Gods preserve us! What do I see?

SOSICLES. What do you see?

MESSENIO. Your living image.

SOSICLES. What do you mean?

MESSENIO. Your double. As like as two peas.

SOSICLES. There is certainly a remarkable resemblance—so far as I can tell what I look like.

MENAECHMUS. [Seeing Messenio.] Oh there you are again, my preserver, whoever you are.

MESSENIO. If you please, young sir, be good enough to tell me your name . . . for heaven's sake . . . if you have no objection.

MENAECHMUS. Well, bless me, I can't grudge you that much after what you've done for me. My name is Menaechmus.

SOSICLES. But that is my name!

MENAECHMUS. I am a Sicilian—from Syracuse.

SOSICLES. That is my home town.

MENAECHMUS. No, really?

SOSICLES. It's the truth.

MESSENIO. [Now thoroughly confused, aside.] Of course, I know him [Menaechmus] now; he's my master; I'm his slave, but I thought I was the other man's. [To Menaechmus.] The fact is, sir, I thought this man was you . . . and I'm afraid I've caused him a bit of trouble. *[To Sosicles.]* I hope you'll pardon me, sir, if I unwittingly said anything stupid to you.

SOSICLES. You seem to me to be talking utter nonsense. Don't you remember coming ashore here with me today?

MESSENIO. Did I? Yes, you're quite right. You must be my master, then. *[To Menaechmus.]* You'll have to find another slave, sir. *[To Sosicles.]* Pleased to meet you, sir. *[To Menaechmus.]* Good day to you, sir. This is Menaechmus, of course.

MENAECHMUS. But *I* am Menaechmus.

SOSICLES. What *are* you talking about? You Menaechmus?

MENAECHMUS. Certainly I am. Menaechmus, son of Moschus.

SOSICLES. Son of my father?

MENAECHMUS. No, sir, son of my own father. I don't want to claim yours or deprive you of him.

MESSENIO. Gods above! *[He goes aside.]* Oh gods, make what I think I expect come true—more than could ever be hoped for! If I'm not mistaken, these are the twin brothers. They both claim the same father and home. I'll speak to my master alone . . . Menaechmus!

MENAECHMUS *and* SOSICLES. Yes?

MESSENIO. No, not both of you. The one that came here with me by sea.

MENAECHMUS. Not me.

SOSICLES. No, me.

MESSENIO. You then. Come here, sir, please.

SOSICLES. Here I am. What do you want?

MESSENIO. That man, sir, is either an impostor—or your twin brother. I've never seen two men more alike; you and him—he and you—water is not more like water nor milk like milk than you two are. What's more, he says he's from the same country and has the same father as you. We must go and ask him some more questions.

SOSICLES. By the gods, Messenio, that's a wonderful idea. Thank you. Go on, and stand by me, do. If you find that he is my brother, you are a free man.

MESSENIO. That's what I hope.

SOSICLES. And I.

MESSENIO. *[To Menaechmus.]* Excuse me, sir; I think you said your name was Menaechmus?

MENAECHMUS. I did.

MESSENIO. Well, this gentleman's name is Menaechmus too. And you said you were born in Syracuse, I believe; so was he. And your father was Moschus, you said? So was his. Now, this is where you can both do something for me, and for yourselves too.

MENAECHMUS. You have earned the right to ask, and be granted, any favour you desire. I am a free man, but I am willing to serve you as your bought slave.

MESSENIO. I have every hope, sir, of finding that you two are twin brothers, owning one father, one mother, and one birthday.

MENAECHMUS. That sounds like a miracle. I hope you can make your promise good.

MESSENIO. I am sure I can; if you will both be good enough to answer my questions.

MENAECHMUS. Ask away. I'll tell you anything I know.

MESSENIO. Your name is Menaechmus?

MENAECHMUS. It is.

MESSENIO. And yours the same?

SOSICLES. It is.

MESSENIO. And your father, you say, was Moschus?

MENAECHMUS. That is correct.

SOSICLES. So was mine.

MESSENIO. You are a Syracusan?

MENAECHMUS. Yes.

MESSENIO. And you?

SOSICLES. You know I am.

MESSENIO. Good. So far all the indications agree. Now for some further points. Can you tell me what is the earliest thing you remember about your life at home?

MENAECHMUS. I remember my father taking me to Tarentum on a business trip, and how I lost my father one day in the crowd and so got kidnapped.

SOSICLES. Jupiter Almighty, preserve me!

MESSENIO. No exclamations, please. Wait for your turn to speak . . . How old were you when you left home with your father?

MENAECHMUS. Seven years old. I was just beginning to lose my first teeth. That was the last time I saw my father.

MESSENIO. Next question: how many sons did your father have at that time?

MENAECHMUS. To the best of my recollection, two.

MESSENIO. You and another one—which was the elder?

MENAECHMUS. Neither.

MESSENIO. Neither? How could that be?

MENAECHMUS. We were twins—both of us.

SOSICLES. Gods be praised, I am saved!

MESSENIO. If you keep interrupting, I shall stop talking.

SOSICLES. No, please, I'll keep quiet.

MESSENIO. Tell me now, were you and your twin brother both given the same name?

MENAECHMUS. Oh no; I was called Menaechmus, as I still am; my brother was called Sosicles.

SOSICLES. That settles it! I cannot refrain any longer from embracing him. Brother, my twin brother, greeting! I am Sosicles.

MENAECHMUS. Then how have you since got the name of Menaechmus?

SOSICLES. After the news reached us that you were lost and our father dead, our grandfather changed my name and had me called Menaechmus after you.

MENAECHMUS. That sounds possible. Tell me one thing more.

SOSICLES. What?

MENAECHMUS. What was our mother's name?

SOSICLES. Teuximarcha.

MENAECHMUS. It's true! Bless you, my brother! Given up for lost, and found again after all these years!

SOSICLES. Bless you, brother. At last my sad and weary search is ended and I rejoice to have found you.

MESSENIO. Now I see why that woman called you by your brother's name, and invited you to lunch. She must have thought you were he.

MENAECHMUS. Gad, yes, that's quite right. I did ask to be given lunch here today. I was eluding my wife, having just borrowed one of her gowns to give to my mistress.

SOSICLES. Is this the gown you are referring to?

MENAECHMUS. That's the one. How did you get hold of it?

SOSICLES. Your mistress insisted on my going in to lunch with her, and said I had given her the gown. I had an excellent lunch, enjoyed myself with wine and woman, and came away with the gown and a gold bracelet.

MENAECHMUS. I am delighted to have put a bit of good luck in your way. The woman obviously thought it was me she was entertaining.

MESSENIO. Well, sir, does the offer of freedom which you made to me still stand?

MENAECHMUS. Of course, a very fair and just request. Brother, will you grant it, for my sake?

SOSICLES. Messenio, you are a free man.

MENAECHMUS. Messenio, I congratulate you on your freedom.

MESSENIO. Thank you sirs . . . *[Aside.]* But it'll need more than congratulations to keep me a free man for life.

SOSICLES. Well, brother, after this satisfactory solution to our troubles, shall we return home together?

MENAECHMUS. I shall be happy to do so, brother. But first I shall hold an auction and sell all I have here. Let me welcome you to my house meanwhile.

SOSICLES. I shall be delighted.

MESSENIO. *[Seizing a good chance.]* May I ask you one other thing, gentlemen?

MENAECHMUS. What is that?

MESSENIO. Let me be your auctioneer.

MENAECHMUS. You shall.

MESSENIO. Shall I announce the sale immediately?

MENAECHMUS. Let us say a week today.

MESSENIO. *[Proclaiming.]* Sale by auction—this day week in the forenoon—the property of Menaechmus—sale will include—slaves, household effects, house, land, etcetera—and a wife, should there be any purchaser. All to be sold at an agreed price, cash down. *[Confidentially.]* And I doubt if the whole lot will fetch more than—fifty thousand. So farewell, friends; let's hear your loud applause.

Introduction to *Abraham and Isaac*
Anonymous

Adapted from medieval English by the Editors

Sacrifice of Abraham   Engraving by Henry Moses. *(Bettmann/CORBIS)*

The Play   *Abraham and Isaac* is a medieval English mystery play. Mystery plays (or cycle plays) usually dramatized a series of biblical events that could stretch from the stories of the Old Testament—including Adam and Eve in the garden of Eden, Noah and the flood, and Abraham and Isaac—to the stories of Christ in the New Testament. Sometimes these cycles would close with an imaginative representation of the last judgment. We have examples of these plays from a number of English towns, such as York, Coventry, and Townley. However, the best-known version of *Abraham and Isaac,* the Brome version, does not come from a known cycle. It is a single play that takes its name from a manuscript found in Brome Manor in Suffolk, England.

   Abraham and Isaac presents the biblical tale of the sacrifice of Isaac. Abraham is told by an angel of God to sacrifice his child, Isaac, as an offering to God. When Abraham takes Isaac to a mountaintop to sacrifice him, an angel intervenes, telling Abraham that God does not wish the death of his child; instead, Abraham slaughters a ram. The Brome play closes with a doctor recapitulating the religious implications of the tale.

Abraham and Isaac illustrates most of the standard techniques of medieval mystery plays. One such technique is *anachronism:* taking things out of their actual time periods. For example, Abraham and Isaac frequently refer to Christ, even though chronologically, their story comes first. In addition, Abraham and Isaac are not presented as the founding patriarchs of the Jewish people; instead, they are represented as medieval Christian serfs.

In fact, many of the issues pertinent to Judaism found in the original tale are changed. Abraham, in the medieval version, has many children, as would a medieval Christian serf. In the biblical tale, the death of Isaac, who is Abraham's only son and who was born when Abraham was very old, would have resulted in the end of the newly established Jewish people. The goal of the Brome dramatist is to present a play that makes Abraham and Isaac contemporaneous with the medieval world but also draws parallels between the sacrifice of Isaac and the death of Jesus. Hence, the playwright removes the Jewish implications of the Old Testament tale.

Although mystery plays use serious biblical tales, they frequently also incorporate popular comic and melodramatic techniques. In *Abraham and Isaac,* Isaac's fear is to some extent represented comically, and the delays in his sacrifice are highly melodramatic.

Medieval cycle plays introduced the episodic form into Western drama. Episodic structure is characterized—as the term suggests—by numerous episodes and is expansive in terms of place, time, and number of characters. In *Abraham and Isaac,* for example, there are several shifts in settings.

The Playwright   The authors of the English cycle plays are anonymous. (However, we do know the authors of some of the mystery plays written on the continent of Europe.) The English playwrights were probably not professional authors but members of the trade guilds that produced the plays during this era. Often, the plays were rewritten by later authors.

The Period   Society in the early Middle Ages was highly agrarian. The nobility controlled local areas, where most people worked as serfs. Gradually, several hundred years after the fall of the Roman Empire, towns began to emerge, and with them, trade and crafts. Learning also slowly revived. The strongest force during this period was the Roman Catholic Church, which dominated not only religion but education and frequently, politics as well.

The church was also central in reviving theater early in the Middle Ages. Out of musical additions to the services grew liturgical dramas, which dramatized biblical tales and were staged by clergy in Latin in the churches.

Later in the Middle Ages, sometime in the twelfth and thirteenth centuries, vernacular drama developed—drama that was written not in Latin, but in the everyday language of the people. Vernacular dramas still dealt with biblical and religious tales; in fact, the mystery plays were vernacular dramas. However, they were more elaborate and were staged as a cycle of plays, usually in the springtime. They were presented in town squares. In England and Spain, movable wagons were used, although scholars debate their appearance and mode of operation. In other parts of Europe, a platform stage was set up; behind it were the scenic units for each of the plays.

The actors were amateurs who belonged to craft guilds or laypeople who belonged to religious organizations. These groups were also responsible for producing the individual plays. Frequently, they provided their own costumes, which were for the most part contemporary dress, not historically accurate clothing. A professional pageant master was hired to oversee the organization of this elaborate theatrical event. Special effects—such as water to re-create Noah's flood—were also popular, so a professional specialist was sometimes hired to oversee these.

ABRAHAM AND ISAAC

Anonymous

CHARACTERS

ABRAHAM
ISAAC, his son

GOD and his ANGELS
DOCTOR, as epilogue

[On the upper stage, God and his Angels; on the lower stage, Abraham and Isaac.]

SCENE 1

[Near Abraham's dwelling. Enter Abraham and Isaac.]

ABRAHAM. *[Kneeling.]* Father of heaven omnipotent,
  With all my heart to thee I call:
  Thou hast given me both land and revenue,
  And my livelihood thou hast me sent;
  I thank thee highly, evermore, for all.

  First of the earth thou madest Adam,
  And Eve also to be his wife;
  All other creatures of them two came.
  And now thou hast granted to me, Abraham,
  Here in this land to lead my life.

  In my age thou hast granted me this,
  That this young child with me shall live:
  I love nothing so much, indeed,
  Except thine own self, dear Father of bliss,
  As Isaac here, my own sweet son.

I have other children more,
  The which I love not half so well;
  This fair sweet child he cheers me so
  In every place where that I go,
  That no trouble here may I feel.

  And therefore, Father of heaven, I thee pray
  For his health and also for his grace;
  Now, Lord, keep him both night and day,
  That never trouble nor any fear
  Come to my child in no place.

[Abraham rises and speaks to Isaac.]

  Now come on, Isaac, my own sweet child;
  Go we home and take our rest.
ISAAC. Abraham, my own father so mild,
  To follow you I am full glad,
  Both early and late.
ABRAHAM. Come on, sweet child. I love thee best
  Of all the children that ever I begat.

[Abraham and Isaac cross to another place.]

SCENE 2

[Heaven.]

GOD. My angel, fast hasten thee thy way,
  And unto earth below anon thou go;
  Abraham's heart now will I test,
  Whether that he be steadfast or no.

Editor's note: This version of Abraham and Isaac is based on the Brome manuscript and is essentially the same as the original. Each line has been retained and its meaning preserved. In a few instances, however, archaic expressions have been replaced by modern words or terms. For example, the word "iwis," which appears regularly in the original, has been replaced by its modern equivalent, "indeed."

Say I commanded him for to take
Isaac, his young son, that he loves so well.
And with his blood, sacrifice he make,
If any of my friendship he will have.

Show him the way unto the hill
Where that his sacrifice shall be;
I shall challenge now his good will,
Whether he loves better his child or me.
All men shall take example by him
My commandments how they shall keep.

SCENE 3

[Abraham's dwelling. Abraham kneels.]

ABRAHAM. Now, Father of heaven, that formed all
    things,
  My prayers I make to thee again,
  For this day my burnt-offering
  Here must I give to thee, most certain.
  Ah, Lord God, almighty King,
  What manner of beast will make thee most glad?

If I had thereof true knowing,
  It should be done with all my might,
  Full soon anon;
  To do what pleases thee on a hill,
  Verily it is my will,
  Dear Father, God in Trinity.

[The Angel appears.]

ANGEL. Abraham, Abraham, wilt thou rest?
  Our Lord commandeth thee for to take
  Isaac, thy young son, that thou lovest best,
  And with his blood sacrifice that thou make.
  Into the Land of Vision thou go,
  And offer thy child unto thy Lord;
  I shall thee lead and show also.
  Unto God's behest, Abraham, accord,
  And follow me upon this green.
ABRAHAM. Welcome to me be my Lord's emissary,
  And his command I will not withstand;
  Yet Isaac, my young son in this land,
  A full dear child to me has been.

I had rather, if God had been pleased,
  For to have given up all the goods that I have,
  Than Isaac my son should have been slain,
  So God in heaven my soul might save!

I loved never thing so much in earth,
And now I must the child go kill.
Ah, Lord God, my conscience is strongly stirred!
And yet, my dear Lord, I am sore afraid
To begrudge anything against your will.

I love my child as my life,
But yet I love my God much more;
For though my heart would make any strife,
Yet will I not spare child nor wife,
But do after my Lord's command.

Though I love my son never so well,
Yet smite off his head soon I shall.
Ah, Father of heaven, to thee I kneel;
A hard death my son shall feel,
For to honour thee, Lord, withal.

ANGEL. Abraham, Abraham, this is well said!
  And all these commandments look that thou
    keep,
  But in thy heart be nothing dismayed.
ABRAHAM. Nay, nay, forsooth, I am well satisfied,
  To please my God with the best that I have.

For though my heart be heavy with regret,
  To see the blood of my own dear son,
  Yet for all this I will not stop,
  But Isaac, my son, I will go get,
  And come as fast as ever we can.

[The Angel departs. Abraham crosses to the other side of the stage where Isaac is kneeling in prayer.]

Now, Isaac, my own son dear,
  Where art thou, child? Speak to me.
ISAAC. My father, sweet father, I am here,
  And make my prayers to the Trinity.
ABRAHAM. Rise up, my child, and fast come
    hither,
  My gentle son that art so wise—
  For we two, child, must go together,
  And unto my Lord make sacrifice.
ISAAC. I am full ready, my father, lo!
  Even at your hands I stand right here,
  And whatsoever ye bid me do,
  It shall be done with glad cheer,
  Full well and fine.
ABRAHAM. Ah, Isaac, my own son so dear,
  God's blessing I give thee, and mine.

Hold this kindling upon thy back,
And here myself fire shall bring.

ISAAC. Father, all of this here will I pack;
I am full glad to do your bidding.
ABRAHAM. *[Aside.]*
Ah, Lord of heaven, my hands I wring!
This child's words sorely wound my heart.

Now, Isaac, son, go we our way
Unto yon mount, with all our main.

ISAAC. Go we, my dear father. As fast as I may,
To follow you I am full glad,
Although I be young and weak.
ABRAHAM. *[Aside.]*
Ah, Lord, my heart breaketh in twain!
This child's words, they be so tender.

SCENE 4

[The hill.]

ABRAHAM. Ah, Isaac, son, anon lay it down;
No longer upon thy back it hold,
For I must preparations make
To honour my Lord God as I should.
ISAAC. Lo, my dear father, where it is.

[Isaac lays down the firewood.]

To cheer you always I draw me near;
But, father, I marvel much at this,
Why that ye look so sad.

And also father, evermore dread I:
Where is your live beast that ye should kill?
Both fire and wood we have ready,
But beast have we none on this hill.
A beast, I know well, must be dead
Your sacrifice for to make.

ABRAHAM. Dread thee not, my child, I thee advise;
Our Lord will send me unto this place,
Some kind of beast for to take,
Through his sweet messenger.
ISAAC. Yea, father, but my heart beginneth to
quake
To see that sharp sword in your hand.
Why bear ye your sword drawn so?
Of your countenance I have much wonder.

ABRAHAM. *[Aside.]*
Ah, Father of heaven, I'm filled with woe!
This child here breaks my heart asunder.
ISAAC. Tell me, my dear father ere that you cease,
Bear ye your sword drawn for me?
ABRAHAM. Ah, Isaac, sweet son, peace! peace!
For, indeed, thou break'st my heart in three.
ISAAC. Now truly, somewhat, father, ye think,
That ye mourn thus more and more.
ABRAHAM. *[Aside.]*
Ah, Lord of heaven, let thy grace descend,
For my heart was never half so sore.
ISAAC. I pray you, father, please let me know,
Whether shall I suffer any harm or no.
ABRAHAM. Indeed, sweet son, I may not tell thee
yet;
My heart is now so full of woe.
ISAAC. Dear father, I pray you, hide it not from me,
But some of your thought that ye tell me.
ABRAHAM. Ah, Isaac, Isaac, I must kill thee!
ISAAC. Kill me father? Alas, what have I done?
If I have trespassed against you in any way,
With a rod ye may make me full mild;
But with your sharp sword kill me nought,
For indeed, father, I am but a child.
ABRAHAM. I am full sorry thy blood for to spill,
But truly, my child, I may not choose.
ISAAC. Now I would my mother were here on this
hill!
She would kneel for me on both her knees
To save my life.
And since that my mother is not here,
I pray you, father, look not so sad,
And kill me not with your knife.
ABRAHAM. Forsooth, son, but unless I thee kill,
I should grieve God right sore, I dread.
It is his commandment and also his will
That I should do this same deed.
He commanded me, son, for certain,
To make my sacrifice with thy blood.
ISAAC. And is it God's will that I should be slain?
ABRAHAM. Yea, truly, Isaac, my son so good;
And therefore my hands I wring.
ISAAC. Now, father, against my Lord's will
I will never complain, loud nor still;
He might have sent me a better destiny
If it had been his pleasure.
ABRAHAM. Forsooth, son, but if I did not this
deed,
Grievously displeased our Lord will be.
ISAAC. Nay, nay, father, God forbid
That ever ye should displease him for me.

Ye have other children, one or two,
The which by nature ye should love well.
I pray you, father, make ye no woe;
For, be I once dead and from you go,
I shall be soon out of your mind.

Therefore do our Lord's bidding,
And when I am dead, then pray for me.
But, good father, tell ye my mother nothing;
Say that I am in another country dwelling.
ABRAHAM. Ah, Isaac, Isaac, blessed may thou be!
My heart beginneth strongly to rebel,
To see the blood of thy blessed body.
ISAAC. Father, since it may be no other wise,
Let it pass over as well as I.
But, father, ere I go unto my death,
I pray you bless me with your hand.

[Isaac kneels.]

ABRAHAM. Now, Isaac, with all my breath
My blessing I give thee upon this land,
And God's also thereto, indeed.
Isaac, Isaac, son, up thou stand,
Thy fair sweet mouth that I may kiss.
ISAAC. Now farewell, my own father so fine,
And greet well my mother in earth;
But I pray you, father, to hide my eyes,
That I see not the stroke of your sharp sword,
That my flesh shall defile.
ABRAHAM. Son thy words make me to weep full sore;
Now, my dear son Isaac, speak no more.
ISAAC. Ah, my own dear father, wherefore?
We shall speak together here but a while.

And since that I must needs be dead,
Yet my dear father, to you I pray,
Smite but few strokes at my head,
And make an end as soon as ye may,
And tarry not too long.

ABRAHAM. Thy meek words, child, make me afraid;
So "Welaway!" may be my song,

Except all only God's will.
Ah, Isaac, my own sweet child,
Yet kiss me again upon this hill!
In all this world is none so mild.

ISAAC. Now truly, father, all this tarrying
It doth my heart nought but harm;

I pray you, father, make an ending.
ABRAHAM. Come up, sweet son, unto my arm.
I must bind thy hands two,
Although thou be never so mild.

[Abraham begins to bind Isaac.]

ISAAC. Ah, mercy, father! Why should ye do so?
ABRAHAM. That thou shouldst not hinder me, my
child.
ISAAC. Nay, indeed, father, I will not stop you.
Do with me as you will;
Stay with the purpose that ye have set you,
For God's love keep to it still.

I am full sorry this day to die,
But yet I wish not my God to grieve;
Boldly do with me as you wish,
My fair sweet father, I give you leave.

But, father, I pray you evermore,
Tell ye my mother not at all
If she knew it, she would weep full sore,
For indeed, my father, she loveth me full well;
God's blessing may she have!

Now farewell, my mother so sweet!
We two be like no more to meet.

ABRAHAM. Ah, Isaac, son, thou mak'st me to
weep,
And with thy words thou upsetest me.
ISAAC. Indeed, father, I am sorry to grieve you.
I cry you mercy of that I have done,
And for all my sins that ever angered you;
Now, dear father, forgive me that I have
done.
God of heavens be with me!
ABRAHAM. Ah, dear child, leave off thy moans!
In all thy life thou grieved me never once;
Now blessed be thou, body and bones,
That ever thou were bred and born!
Thou hast been to me child full good.
But indeed, child, though I mourn never so
deeply,
Yet must I needs here at the last
In this place shed all thy blood.

Therefore, my dear son, here shall thou lie;

[Abraham lifts Isaac onto the altar.]

Unto my work I must proceed.
Indeed I had as lief myself to die,
If God were pleased with the deed
That I my own body should offer.

ISAAC. Ah, mercy, father, mourn ye no more!
Your weeping maketh my heart sore,
As my own death that I shall suffer.
Your kerchief, father, place ye about my eyes.

ABRAHAM. So I shall, my sweetest child in earth.

ISAAC. Now yet, good father, have this in mind,
And smite me not often with your sharp sword,
But hastily that it be quickly done.

[Here Abraham lays a cloth on Isaac's face, thus saying:]

ABRAHAM. Now farewell, my child, so full of grace.

ISAAC. Ah, father, father, turn downward my face,
For of your sharp sword I am ever afraid.

ABRAHAM. To do this deed I am full sorry,
But, Lord, thy command I will not withstand.

ISAAC. Ah, Father of heaven, to thee I cry:
Lord, receive me into thy hand!

ABRAHAM. Lo, now is the time come, certain,
That my sword in his neck shall bite.
Ah, Lord, my heart riseth against it;
I may not find it in my heart to smite;
My heart will not allow me to do it,
Yet fain I would work my Lord's will;
But this young innocent lieth so still,
I may not find it in my heart him to kill.
Oh, Father of heaven, what shall I do?

ISAAC. Ah, mercy, father, why tarry ye so,
And let me lie thus long on this heath?
Now would I to God the stroke were done!
Father, I pray you heartily, shorten my woe,
And let me not look longer to my death.

ABRAHAM. Now, heart, why wouldest not thou
break in three?
Yet shall thou not make me to my God
ungracious.
I will no longer for your sake delay,
For that my God aggrieved would be;
Now receive the stroke, my own dear child.

[Here Abraham makes as if to strike, and the Angel takes the sword in his hand suddenly.]

ANGEL. I am an angel, thou mayst gladly see,
That from heaven to thee is sent.
Our Lord thanks thee a hundred times
For the keeping of his commandment.

He knoweth thy will and also thy heart,
That thou worship him above all things;
And some of thy heaviness for to depart,
A fair ram yonder I did bring.

He standeth tied, lo, among the briars.
Now, Abraham, amend thy mood,
For Isaac, thy young son that here is,
This day thou shall not shed his blood.

Go, make thy sacrifice with yon ram.
Now farewell, blessed Abraham,
For unto heaven I go now home;
The way is full straight.
Take up thy son so free.

[The Angel exits.]

ABRAHAM. Ah, Lord, I thank thee of thy great grace!
Now am I eased in every way.
Arise up, Isaac, my dear son, arise;
Arise up, sweet child, and come to me.

ISAAC. Ah, mercy father! Why smite ye nought?
Ah, smite on, father, once with your knife.

ABRAHAM. Peace, my sweet sir, and take no
thought,
For our Lord of heaven hath granted thy life
By his angel now,
That thou shalt not die this day, son, truly.

ISAAC. Ah, father, full glad then were I—
Indeed, father, I say, indeed!—
If this tale were true.

ABRAHAM. A hundred times, my son fair of hue,
For joy thy mouth now will I kiss.

ISAAC. Ah, my dear father, Abraham,
Will not God be wrath that we do thus?

ABRAHAM. No, no, certainly, my sweet son,
For yon same ram he hath us sent
Hither down to us.

Yon beast shall die in thy stead,
In the worship of our Lord alone.
Go, fetch him hither, my child, indeed.

ISAAC. Father, I will go seize him by the head,
And bring yon beast with me anon.

[Isaac unties the ram.]

Ah, sheep, sheep, blessed might thou be,
That ever thou were sent down hither!

Thou shalt this day die for me
In the worship of the holy Trinity.
Now come fast and go we together
To my father in haste,
Though thou be never so gentle and good,
Yet had I rather thou shed'st thy blood,
Indeed, sheep, than I.

[Isaac leads the ram to Abraham.]

Lo, father, I have quickly brought here
This gentle sheep, and him to you I give;
But, Lord God, I thank thee with all my heart,
For I am glad that I shall live,
And kiss once my dear mother.

ABRAHAM. Now be right merry, my sweet child,
For this quick beast that is so mild
Here I shall offer before all other.
ISAAC. And I will fast begin to blow;
This fire shall burn a full good speed.
But, father, if I stoop down low,
Ye will not kill me with your sword, I trow?
ABRAHAM. No, hardly, sweet son. Have no dread;
My mourning is past.
ISAAC. Yea, but I would that sword were in a fire
For indeed, father, it makes me full ill afraid.

[Here Abraham makes his offering, kneeling and saying thus:]

ABRAHAM. Now, Lord God of heaven in Trinity,
Almighty God omnipotent,
My offering I make in the worship of thee,
And with this quick beast I thee present.
Lord, receive thou my intent,
As thou art God and ground of our grace.

[God speaks to Abraham.]

GOD. Abraham, Abraham, well may thou speed,
And Isaac, thy young son thee by!
Truly, Abraham, for this deed
I shall multiply both your seed
As thick as stars be in the sky,
Both more and less;
And as thick as gravel in the sea.,
So thick multiplied your seed shall be;
This grant I you for your goodness.

Of you shall come fruit in great abundance,
And ever be in bliss without end.

For ye fear me as God alone,
And keep my commandments every one,
My blessing I give, wheresoever ye go.

ABRAHAM. Lo, Isaac, my son, how think ye
By this work that we have wrought?
Full glad and blithe we may be,
Against the will of God that we grudged nought
Upon this fair heath.
ISAAC. Ah, father, I thank our Lord in every way,
That my wit served me so well
For to fear God more than my death.
ABRAHAM. Why, beloved son, were thou afraid?
Tell me heartily, child, what you think.
ISAAC. Yea, by my faith, father, now be it said,
I was never so afraid before
As I have been at yon hill.
But, by my faith, father, I swear
I will nevermore come there
But it be against my will.
ABRAHAM. Yea, come on with me, my own sweet son,
And homeward fast now let us go.
ISAAC. By my faith, father, I thereto agree!
I had never such good will to go home,
And to speak with my dear mother.
ABRAHAM. Ah, Lord of heaven, I thank thee,
For now may I lead home with me
Isaac, my young son so free,
The gentlest child above all others—
This may I well avow.
Now go we forth, my blessed son.
ISAAC. I grant, father, and let us go;
For, by my troth, were I at home,
I would never for me out yonder go.
I pray God give us grace evermore,
And all those that we be beholden to.

[Abraham and Isaac exit. Enter Doctor.]

DOCTOR. *[Speaking as an epilogue.]*
Lo, sovereigns and sirs, now have we showed
This solemn story to great and small.
It is a good lesson for learned and unlearned,
And the wisest of us all,
Without any omission.
For this story showeth you here
How we should keep, to our power,
God's commandments without complaining.

Think ye, sirs, if God sent an angel,
And commanded you your child to slay,

By your troth, is there any of you
That either would grudge or strive against it?
How think ye now, sirs, of that?
I think there be three or four or more.

And these women that weep so sorrowfully
When that their children die and from them go,
As nature takes its kind.
It is but folly, I may well avow,
To grudge against God or to grieve you,
For ye shall never see him harmed, well I know,
By land nor water. Have this in mind,

And grudge not against our Lord God,
In happiness or woe, whichever he you send,
Though ye be never so hard bestead;
For when he will, he may it amend,
His commandments truly if ye keep with good
   heart,
As this story hath now showed you before,
And faithfully serve him while ye be sound,
That ye may please God both even and morn.
Now Jesus, that weareth the crown of thorn,
Bring us all to heaven's bliss.

Introduction to *Sotoba Komachi* by Kan'ami Kiyotsugu

Translated by Arthur Waley

The Play *Sotoba Komachi,* written by Kan'ami (1333–1384), is based on a well-known Japanese legend and is an excellent example of traditional nō drama. In this legend, Komachi, a beautiful but cruel woman, is pursued by a man named Shii no Shosho. She tells him that he must call on her for 100 nights in a row, and for 99 nights he comes, in all kinds of weather. But on the hundredth night, with a terrible snowstorm raging, he dies at her doorstep.

As the play begins, seemingly in gloomy autumn, we see two priests enter, discussing the virtues of following Buddha. They then come upon an old woman, Komachi, approaching her hundredth year, and engage in a religious debate with her. She sits on a fallen religious monument, and the priests argue that this act is sacrilegious. She argues that there can be no sacrilege because all things in life and nature are holy, including even a wrecked life such as hers.

Although she appears to win this argument, Komachi is then quickly struck by madness. She imagines that she is once more in the storm that raged on the hundredth night of her lover's visits, and that he is once again lying dead at her feet.

At this point, the character of Komachi mimes the release of her emotions in a wild, mad dance, theatrically fusing words, music, and movement. The priest narrates the past occurrence while the performer playing Komachi physicalizes it, using highly symbolic gestures and movements. For a brief time during this dance, she relives the glorious days of her youth, becoming young again.

Komachi's agony as she gives release to her emotions is an expiation of her sins. At the conclusion of the play, there is an indication that she will receive a form of salvation. This theme is embraced in an overall theme: that ultimately—in the cosmic vision of life—evil and good, self-gratification and purity become one.

Nō drama developed in the fourteenth century, became the dominant form of serious Japanese theater, and would remain dominant until well past 1600, when it was supplanted in the popular taste by bunraku (puppet theater) and kabuki.

Nō is a remarkable synthesis of various theatrical forms into a single, total experience. The plays are philosophically sophisticated and are constructed around a series of organizational principles based on musical, psychological, and mimetic—or imitative—movements, which change gradually from a slow to a fast tempo.

The stories are from literary or historical sources. Nō characters are generally based on figures already familiar to the audience. A nō play reveals some working out of passions felt by a character, who often appears as a ghost or spirit.

The major roles in nō are the *shite,* or main character; the *waki,* or explainer; and the *tsure,* an accompanying role. There are various smaller roles as well, sometimes including a *kyogen,* or comic character.

A typical nō play, like *Sotoba Komachi,* is divided into two parts. In the first part, for example, a Buddhist priest on a pilgrimage might visit a famous site related to the life of the main character. The priest may find there a character who will say something about the legend of the protagonist. In the second part of the play, the chief character will appear, revealing to the priest that the person in the first part was actually herself or himself in disguise, and will then describe some profound experience in her or his life. Usually, this recitation will end with a dance or in some other powerful way. Generally, the second half of a nō play provides a unique combination of poetry, movement, and music.

The Playwright   Kan'ami was a talented nō actor and manager, who oversaw a touring troupe of actors in the middle to late fourteenth century. He was known for the nō dramas he wrote and for his improvements in staging methods.

One presentation of Kan'ami's troupe was seen by the shogun Ashikaga Yoshimitsu (1358–1408), a man of wealth, prestige, and enormous enthusiasm for the arts. Fascinated by what he saw, he lent support to Kan'ami's troupe, and also arranged to have Kan'ami's talented son, Zeami Motokiyo (1363–1443), who was then an 11-year-old actor, educated at court.

Zeami became the director of his father's troupe when Kan'ami died in 1384. He continued to improve nō, borrowing elements from earlier forms of dance drama. Zeami's 200 plays, 124 of which remain in the nō repertory, incorporated his innovations.

The Period   By the fifth century after Christ, the southern portions of Japan had been consolidated and a series of capitals had been established in the vicinity of present-day Kyoto. By that time, the Japanese had established a religion known as Shinto, which was closely bound to nature and spirit worship. With the growing influence on the Japanese aristocracy of the Tang dynasty in China (618–906), Buddhism became a prevailing influence, first in court circles and then in the country as a whole. Both Shinto and Buddhism had a strong influence on the development of theater in Japan, and particularly the nō drama.

The nō stage has remained roughly the same since the time of Zeami and his successors. The stage has a bridge 20 to 40 feet long, called the *hashigakari,* which leads from the actors' dressing rooms offstage to the stage proper. The main playing space is about 18 square feet, is roofed, and has a ceremonial pine tree painted on the rear wall. At the back of the playing space is a narrow section for four or five musicians. Nō theaters were originally outdoors, but a modern nō theater is placed inside a larger shell as though it were a giant stage set.

Nō actors move in a highly stylized way that has important elements of both dance and pantomime. During the performance of a nō text, actors alternate sections of chanting with a heightened speech that might be compared to recitative in Western opera.

Costumes made for nō are usually of great elegance, and the masks worn by the chief character are among the most beautiful, subtle, and effective ever created for any theater.

SOTOBA KOMACHI

Kan'ami Kiyotsugu

CHARACTERS

A PRIEST OF THE KOYASAN
ONO NO KOMACHI

SECOND PRIEST
CHORUS

PRIEST. We who on shallow hills have built our home
 In the heart's deep recess seek solitude.

[Turning to the audience.]

 I am a priest of the Koyasan. I am minded to go up to the Capital to visit the shrines and sanctuaries there.
 The Buddha of the Past is gone.
 And he that shall be Buddha has not yet come into the world.
SECOND PRIEST. In a dream-lull our lives are passed; all, all
 That round us lies
 Is visionary, void.
 Yet got we by rare fortune at our birth
 Man's shape, that is hard to get;
 And dearest gift was given us, harder to win,
 The doctrine of Buddha, seed of our Salvation.
 And me this only thought possessed,
 How I might bring that seed to blossom, till at least
 I drew this sombre cassock across my back.
 And knowing now the lives before my birth,
 No love I owe
 To those that to this life engendered me,
 Nor seek a care (have I not disavowed
 Such hollow bonds?) from child by me begot.
 A thousand leagues
 Is little road
 To the pilgrim's feet.
 The fields his bed,
 The hills his home
 Till the travel's close.

PRIEST. We have come so fast that we have reached the pine-woods of Abeno, in the country of Tsu. Let us rest in this place.

[They sit down by the Waki's pillar.]

KOMACHI. Like a root-cut reed,
 Should the tide entice,
 I would come, I think; but now
 No wave asks; no stream stirs.
 Long ago I was full of pride;
 Crowned with nodding tresses, halcyon locks,
 I walked like a young willow delicately wafted
 By the winds of Spring.
 I spoke with the voice of a nightingale that has sipped the dew.
 I was lovelier than the petals of the wild-rose open-stretched
 In the hour before its fall.
 But now I am grown loathsome even to sluts,
 Poor girls of the people, and they and all men
 Turn scornful from me.
 Unhappy months and days pile up their score;
 I am old; old by a hundred years.
 In the City I fear men's eyes,
 And at dusk, lest they should cry "Is it she?"
 Westward with the moon I creep
 From the cloud-high City of the Hundred Towers.
 No guard will question, none challenge
 Pilgrim so wretched: yet must I be walking
 Hid ever in shadow of the trees.
 Past the Lovers' Tomb,
 And the Hill of Autumn
 To the River of Katsura, the boats, the moonlight.

[She shrinks back and covers her face, frightened at being known.]

Who are those rowing in the boats?
Oh, I am weary. I will sit on this tree-stump
and rest awhile.
PRIEST. Come! The sun is sinking; we must hasten
on our way. Look, look at that beggar there! It
is a holy Stupa that she is sitting on! I must tell
her to come off it.
Now, then, what is that you are sitting on? Is it
not a holy Stupa, the worshipful Body of
Buddha?
Come off it and rest in some other place.
KOMACHI. Buddha's worshipful body, you say? But
I could see no writing on it, nor any figure
carved.
I thought it was only a tree-stump.
PRIEST. Even the little black tress on the hillside
When it has put its blossoms on
Cannot be hid;
And think you that this tree
Cut fivefold in the fashion of Buddha's holy form
Shall not make manifest its power?
KOMACHI. I too am a poor withered bough.
But there are flowers at my heart,
Good enough, maybe, for an offering.
But why is this called Buddha's body?
PRIEST. Hear then! This Stupa is the Body of the
Diamond Lord. It is the symbol of his
incarnation.
KOMACHI. And in what elements did he choose to
manifest his body?
PRIEST. Earth, water, wind, fire and space.
KOMACHI. Of these five man also is compounded.
Where then is the difference?
PRIEST. The forms are the same, but not the virtue.
KOMACHI. And what is the virtue of the Stupa?
PRIEST. "He that has looked once upon the Stupa,
shall escape forever from the Three Paths of
Evil."
KOMACHI. "One thought can sow salvation in the
heart." Is that of less price?
SECOND PRIEST. If your heart has seen salvation,
how comes it that you linger in the World?
KOMACHI. It is my body that lingers, for my heart
left it long ago.
PRIEST. You have no heart at all, or you would have
known the Body of Buddha.
KOMACHI. It was because I knew it that I came to
see it!

SECOND PRIEST. And knowing what you know, you
sprawled upon it without a word of prayer?
KOMACHI. It was on the ground already. What harm
could it get by my resting on it?
PRIEST. It was an act of discord.
KOMACHI. Sometimes from discord salvation
springs.
SECOND PRIEST. From the malice of Daiba. . . .[1]
KOMACHI. As from the Mercy of Kwannon.[2]
PRIEST. As from the wisdom of Handoku. . . .[3]
KOMACHI. From the folly of Monju.[4]
SECOND PRIEST. That which is called Evil
KOMACHI. Is Good.
PRIEST. That which is called Illusion
KOMACHI. Is Salvation.
SECOND PRIEST. For Salvation
KOMACHI. Cannot be planted like a tree.
PRIEST. And the Heart's Mirror
KOMACHI. Hangs in the void.
CHORUS. [*Speaking for Komachi.*]
"Nothing is real.
Between Buddha and Man
Is no distinction, but a seeming of difference
planned
For the welfare of the humble, the ill-
instructed,
Whom he has vowed to save.
Sin itself may be the ladder to salvation."
So she spoke, eagerly; and the priests,
"A saint, a saint is this decrepit, outcast soul."
And bending their heads to the ground,
Three times did homage before her.
KOMACHI. I now emboldened
Recite a riddle, a jesting song.
"Were I in Heaven
The Stupa were an ill seat;
But here in the world without,
What harm is done?"
CHORUS. The Priests would have rebuked her;
But they have found their match.
PRIEST. Who are you? Pray tell us the name you
had, and we will pray for you when you are
dead.
KOMACHI. Shame covers me when I speak my
name; but if you will pray for me, I will try to
tell you. This is my name; write it down in
your prayer list: I am the ruins of Komachi,

1. A wicked disciple who in the end attained to Illumination. 2.
The Goddess of Mercy. 3. A disciple so witless that he could not
recite a single verse of Scripture. 4. God of Wisdom.

daughter of Ono no Yoshizane, Governor of
the land of Dewa.

PRIESTS. Oh piteous, piteous! Is this
Komachi that once
Was a bright flower,
Komachi the beautiful, whose dark brows
Linked like young moons;
Her face white-farded ever;
Whose many, many damask robes
Filled cedar-scented halls?

KOMACHI. I made verses in our speech
And in the speech of the foreign Court.

CHORUS. The cup she held at the feast
Like gentle moonlight dropped its glint on her
sleeve.
Oh how fell she from splendor,
How came the white of winter
To crown her head?
Where are gone the lovely locks, double-
twined,
The coils of jet?
Lank wisps, scant curls wither now
On wilted flesh;
And twin-arches, moth-brows tinge no more
With the hue of far hills. "Oh cover, cover
From the creeping light of dawn
Silted seaweed locks that of a hundred years
Lack now but one.
Oh hide me from my shame."

[Komachi hides her face.]

CHORUS. *[Speaking for the Priest.]* What is it you carry
in the wallet string at your neck?

KOMACHI. Death may come to-day—or hunger
tomorrow.
A few beans and a cake of millet:
That is what I carry in my bag.

CHORUS. And in the wallet on your back?

KOMACHI. A garment stained with dust and sweat.

CHORUS. And in the basket on your arm?

KOMACHI. Sagittaries white and black.

CHORUS. Tattered cloak.[5]

KOMACHI. Broken hat. . . .

CHORUS. She cannot hide her face from our eyes:
And how her limbs

KOMACHI. From rain and dew, hoar-frost and snow?

CHORUS. *[Speaking for Komachi while she mimes the
action they describe.]* Not rags enough to wipe the
tears from my eyes!
Now, wandering along the roads
I beg an alms of those that pass.
And when they will not give,
An evil rage, a very madness possesses me.
My voice changes.
Oh terrible!

KOMACHI. *[Thrusting her hat under the Priests' noses and
shrieking at them menacingly.]* Grr! You priests,
give me something: give me something . . .
Ah!

PRIEST. What do you want?

KOMACHI. Let me go to Komachi.

*[The spirit of her lover Shosho has now entirely possessed
her.]*[6]

PRIEST. But you told us you were Komachi.
What folly is that you are talking?

KOMACHI. No. No. . . . Komachi was very beautiful.
Many letters came to her, many messages,
Thick as raindrops out of a black summer sky.
But she sent no answer, not even an empty
word.
And now in punishment she has grown old:
She has lived a hundred years—
I love her, oh I love her!

PRIEST. You love Komachi? Say then, whose spirit
has possessed you?

KOMACHI. There were many who set their hearts on
her,
But among them all
It was Shosho who loved her best
Shii no Shosho of the Deep Grass.

CHORUS. *[Speaking for Komachi, i.e., for the spirit of
Shosho.]*
The wheel goes back; I live again through the
cycle of my woes.
Again I travel to the shaft-bench.
The sun . . . what hour does he show?
Dusk. . . . Alone in the moonlight
I must go my way.
Though the watchmen of the barriers
Stand across my path,
They shall not stop me!

---

5. The words which follow suggest the plight of her lover Shosho
when he traveled to her house "a hundred nights all but one," to cut
his notch on the bench.

6. Translator's note: This "possession scene" lasts very much longer
on the stage than the brief words would suggest.

[Attendants robe Komachi in the Court hat and traveling-cloak of Shosho.]

    Look, I go!

KOMACHI. Lifting the white skirts of my trailing dress.

CHORUS. [*Speaking for Komachi, while she, dressed as her lover Shosho, mimes the night-journey.*]

    Pulling down over my ears the tall, nodding hat,
    Tying over my head the long sleeves of my hunting cloak,
    Hidden from the eyes of men,
    In moonlight, in darkness,
    On rainy nights I traveled; on windy nights,
    Under a shower of leaves; when the snow was deep,

KOMACHI. And when water dripped at the roof-eaves,—tok, tok . . .

CHORUS. Swiftly, swiftly coming and going, coming and going . . .
    One night, two nights, three nights,
    Ten nights (and this was harvest night) . . .
    I never saw her, yet I traveled;
    Faithful as the cock who marks each day the dawn,
    I carved my marks on the bench.
    I was to come a hundred times;
    There lacked but one . . .

KOMACHI. [*Feeling the death-agony of Shosho.*] My eyes dazzle. Oh the pain, the pain!

CHORUS. Oh the pain! and desperate,
    Before the last night had come,
    He died,—Shii no Shosho the Captain.

[Speaking for Komachi, who is now no longer possessed by Shosho's spirit.]

    Was it his spirit that possessed me,
    Was it his anger that broke my wits?
    If this be so, let me pray for the life hereafter,
    Where alone is comfort;
    Piling high the sands
    Till I be burnished as gold.[7]
    See, I offer my flower to Buddha,[8]
    I hold it in both hands.
    Oh may He lead me into the Path of Truth,
    Into the Path of Truth.

7. The color of the saints in heaven.   8. Her "heart-flower," i.e., poetic talent.

Introduction to *Hamlet*
by William Shakespeare

Edited and with notes by Tucker Brooke
and Jack Randall Crawford

Hamlet   Campbell Scott as Hamlet, Huntington Theatre. *(© T. Charles Erickson)*

The Play   Shakespeare's *Hamlet,* written about 1601, is often cited as the quintessential tragedy; unfortunately, this sometimes suggests to readers that it is esoteric and difficult to understand. But Shakespeare was a playwright of the people, who strove to write popular plays that would attract audiences of all classes. Like all Shakespeare's great works, *Hamlet* has many popular elements, including supernatural appearances, comic characters, swordplay, and intrigue, which make the play immensely accessible to audiences.

   Hamlet is a revenge tragedy, and the opening scenes quickly establish the dramatic premise. As the play begins, two sentinels standing watch on the parapet of the castle appear onstage, soon to be joined by Hamlet's friend Horatio. The three men discuss a ghost that has been appearing every night. The ghost, that of Hamlet's father, then appears, frightening the sentinels and Horatio.

The following scene shifts to the interior of the castle: King Claudius enters. He is the brother of Hamlet's father, the dead king, and he has married Hamlet's mother, Queen Gertrude. Also, in this scene we are introduced to Hamlet.

The action of the play, as in all suspenseful dramas, is full of twists and turns. In the next scene, Hamlet himself sees the ghost of his father, who says that Hamlet must avenge his father's murder at the hands of Claudius. Hamlet later has a group of strolling players present a drama, which proves that Claudius did murder Hamlet's father. In one of the play's most famous scenes, Hamlet confronts his mother in her bedroom, berates her for marrying his uncle, and thrusts his sword through a curtain, thinking that Claudius is hiding behind it. But the person concealed turns out to be Polonius, the father of Ophelia, the woman who loves Hamlet. Hamlet is then sent away by Claudius, who plots to have him killed at sea. Ophelia goes mad and kills herself. Hamlet returns, having escaped during an encounter with pirates at sea. The play closes with almost everyone killed: Hamlet and Laertes—Polonius's son—in a duel; Gertrude by poisoning; Claudius by stabbing.

Hamlet has the characteristics of all Shakespeare's great tragedies. The verse is full of metaphors, and the music of the language is extraordinary. The soliloquies—in which Hamlet speaks his inner thoughts aloud—are among the most famous speeches in the history of dramatic literature. Shakespeare was also a master of episodic plot construction, and this too is clearly illustrated in *Hamlet*.

In addition, Shakespeare's tragedies present noble characters caught in circumstances that are understandable and recognizable to all audiences. Hamlet suffers in the realms of politics, love, and family. His complex characterization has led to innumerable interpretations, some quite modern in point of view. In the twentieth century, classical and popular actors—such as Sarah Bernhardt, Laurence Olivier, Kenneth Branagh, and Mel Gibson—have created unique readings of this text.

The Playwright   William Shakespeare (1564–1616) appeared on the theater scene around 1590. Shakespeare was a native of Stratford-upon-Avon; his father was a prosperous glove-maker and town alderman, and his mother was the daughter of a prominent landowner and farmer. Shakespeare was educated in Stratford; he then married Anne Hathaway, who was several years older than he and who bore him three children.

At some point after the third child was born, Shakespeare left his family and went to London, where he worked first as an actor and shortly after that, as a playwright.

Shakespeare was an expert in many aspects of theater. He was an actor and a member of a dramatic company, the Lord Chamberlain's Men (which was London's leading troupe and after 1603 was known as the King's Men). He understood the technical and business elements of theater. As a writer, he excelled in several genres, including tragedy, comedy, and history. His tragedies include *Romeo and Juliet* (1595), *Julius Caesar* (1599), *Hamlet* (1601), *Othello* (1604), *Macbeth* (1605–1606), and *King Lear* (1605–1606). His comedies include *The Comedy of Errors* (1592), *A Midsummer Night's Dream* (1595), *As You Like It* (1599), and *Twelfth Night* (1601). Among his well-known histories are *Richard III* (1592–1593), *Henry IV, Parts 1 and 2* (1597–1598), and *Henry V* (1599). He is also noted for a number of plays that are referred to as problem dramas because they defy categorization by genre.

The Globe Theater, where Shakespeare's plays were produced, burned in 1613; shortly after that, Shakespeare retired to Stratford and became one of its leading citizens. He died three years later.

The Period   *Hamlet* was written during the English Renaissance. This is often called the Elizabethan period because its major political figure was Elizabeth I, who reigned during the 45 years from 1558 to 1603. Under her rule, England was united after long periods of religious and political strife. Throughout the English Renaissance, explorations abroad were undertaken, wealth accumulated, and literature flourished. The English were intrigued by language—Queen Elizabeth herself was an amateur linguist—and at the heart of the English Renaissance in literature and arts was theater.

The plays of Shakespeare and his contemporaries were presented in outdoor public theaters—of which the most famous was the Globe—or indoor spaces, referred to as private theaters. The stage in a public theater was a raised platform, probably surrounded on three sides by the audience. On this platform stage, locales could be changed quickly through the introduction of props and through descriptions spoken by the characters.

Behind the platform stage was a stage house, known as the tiring house. The configuration of this building is much debated; but it served as a place for changing costumes and storing props, and it also functioned as the basic scenic background. Doors provided entrances and exits, and there was probably some sort of upper playing area for balcony scenes. There was also an upper level for musicians, as well as a roof that extended out from the stage house and protected the stage.

The exact shape of the public theaters varied; their audience capacity was about 3,000. Spectators were accommodated in a standing area on the ground floor as well as in galleries and boxes. (The indoor private theaters were much smaller and had seats on the house floor.)

Acting companies—such as the Lord Chamberlain's Men, in which Shakespeare was an actor—had approximately 25 members and were made up exclusively of males; all the female roles were played by boys. In these companies, some individuals received shares of the profits; some were hired for a contracted period of time and at a contracted wage; and some young performers were apprenticed with accomplished actors. An acting company rarely produced the same play two days in a row, and each company had to be able to revive plays in its repertoire on very short notice. Actors were costumed primarily in contemporary clothing; the Elizabethans were not concerned with historical accuracy.

HAMLET

William Shakespeare

CHARACTERS

CLAUDIUS, the new king of Denmark
HAMLET, son to the late king and nephew to the present king

FORTINBRAS, prince of Norway
POLONIUS, a lord and high official (probably Lord Chamberlain)

LAERTES, his son
HORATIO, the friend of Hamlet
VOLTIMAND, courtier
CORNELIUS, courtier
ROSENCRANTZ, courtier
GUILDENSTERN, courtier
OSRIC, courtier
MARCELLUS, a Danish officer
FRANCISCO, soldier on sentry duty
BERNARDO, soldier on sentry duty

REYNALDO, servant to Polonius
A Norwegian captain
Players on tour
Two clowns, gravediggers
English ambassador, a priest, a gentleman, soldiers,
    sailor, messenger, and various attendants
GERTRUDE, queen of Denmark and mother of
    Hamlet
OPHELIA, daughter of Polonius
GHOST of Hamlet's father

SCENE: the royal castle of Elsinore (Helsingør), Denmark, and its environs

Act I

SCENE 1

Elsinore. Platform of the Castle

[Enter Bernardo and Francisco, two Sentinels.]

BERNARDO. Who's there?
FRANCISCO. Nay, answer me; stand, and unfold
    yourself.
BERNARDO. Long live the king!
FRANCISCO. Bernardo?   4
BERNARDO. He.
FRANCISCO. You come most carefully upon your hour.
BERNARDO. 'Tis now struck twelve; get thee to bed,
    Francisco.
FRANCISCO. For this relief much thanks; 'tis bitter
    cold,   8
    And I am sick at heart.
BERNARDO. Have you had quiet guard?
FRANCISCO.   Not a mouse
    stirring.
BERNARDO. Well, good night.
    If you do meet Horatio and Marcellus,   12
    The rivals of my watch, bid them make haste.

[Enter Horatio and Marcellus.]

FRANCISCO. I think I hear them. Stand, ho! Who is
    there?

HORATIO. Friends to this ground.
MARCELLUS.   And liegemen to
    the Dane.
FRANCISCO. Give you good night.
MARCELLUS.   O, farewell, honest
    soldier.   16
    Who hath reliev'd you?
FRANCISCO.   Bernardo hath my place.
    Give you good night. *[Exit Francisco.]*
MARCELLUS.   Holla! Bernardo!
BERNARDO.   Say,—
    What, is Horatio there?
HORATIO.   A piece of him.
BERNARDO. Welcome, Horatio; welcome, good
    Marcellus.   20
MARCELLUS. What, has this thing appear'd again
    tonight?
BERNARDO. I have seen nothing.
MARCELLUS. Horatio says 'tis but our fantasy,
    And will not let belief take hold of him   24
    Touching this dreaded sight twice seen of us.
    Therefore I have entreated him along
    With us to watch the minutes of this night,
    That if again this apparition come,   28
    He may approve our eyes and speak to it.
HORATIO. Tush, tush! 'twill not appear.
BERNARDO.   Sit down
    awhile,
    And let us once again assail your ears,

I.1. **Note. Platform:** level space on castle ramparts. **13. rivals:** partners.

17. Give you: God give you. **23. fantasy:** imagination. **29. approve:** confirm. **31. assail your ears:** i.e., try to tell you.

That are so fortified against our story,   32
What we have two nights seen.
HORATIO.   Well, sit we
    down,
And let us hear Bernardo speak of this.
BERNARDO. Last night of all,
    When yond same star that's westward from the
        pole   36
    Had made his course t' illume that part of
        heaven
    Where now it burns, Marcellus and myself,
    The bell then beating one,—

[Enter Ghost.]

MARCELLUS. Peace! break thee off; look, where it
    comes again!   40
BERNARDO. In the same figure, like the king that's
    dead.
MARCELLUS. Thou art a scholar; speak to it, Horatio.
BERNARDO. Looks 'a not like the king? mark it,
    Horatio.
HORATIO. Most like: it harrows me with fear and
    wonder.   44
BERNARDO. It would be spoke to.
MARCELLUS.   Question it,
    Horatio.
HORATIO. What art thou that usurp'st this time of
    night,
    Together with that fair and warlike form
    In which the majesty of buried Denmark   48
    Did sometimes march? by heaven I charge thee,
        speak!
MARCELLUS. It is offended.
BERNARDO.   See! it stalks away.
HORATIO. Stay! speak, speak! I charge thee, speak!

[Exit Ghost.]

MARCELLUS. 'Tis gone, and will not answer.   52
BERNARDO. How now, Horatio! you tremble and
    look pale.
    Is not this something more than fantasy?
    What think you on 't?
HORATIO. Before my God, I might not this
    believe   56
    Without the sensible and true avouch
    Of mine own eyes.

MARCELLUS.   Is it not like the king?
HORATIO. As thou art to thyself:
    Such was the very armor he had on   60
    When he the ambitious Norway combated;
    So frown'd he once, when, in an angry parle,
    He smote the sledded pole-axe on the ice.
    'Tis strange.   64
MARCELLUS. Thus twice before, and jump at this
    dead hour,
    With martial stalk hath he gone by our watch.
HORATIO. In what particular thought to work I
    know not;
    But in the gross and scope of my opinion,   68
    This bodes some strange eruption to our state.
MARCELLUS. Good now, sit down, and tell me, he
    that knows,
    Why this same strict and most observant
        watch
    So nightly toils the subject of the land;   72
    And why such daily cast of brazen cannon,
    And foreign mart for implements of war;
    Why such impress of shipwrights, whose sore
        task
    Does not divide the Sunday from the week;   76
    What might be toward, that this sweaty haste
    Doth make the night joint-laborer with the day:
    Who is't that can inform me?
HORATIO.   That can I;
    At least, the whisper goes so. Our last king,   80
    Whose image even but now appear'd to us,
    Was, as you know, by Fortinbras of Norway,
    Thereto prick'd on by a most emulate pride,
    Dar'd to the combat; in which our valiant
        Hamlet   84
    (For so this side of our known world esteem'd
        him,)
    Did slay this Fortinbras; who by a seal'd
        compact,
    Well ratified by law and heraldry,
    Did forfeit with his life all those his lands   88
    Which he stood seiz'd of, to the conqueror;
    Against the which a moiety competent   *equal*
    Was gaged by our king, which had return'd

---

43. **'a:** dialect form of 'he' (sometimes 'it'). **mark:** observe
closely. **49. sometimes:** formerly. **57. sensible:** involving the use
of one of the senses. **avouch:** assurance.

62. **parle:** verbal encounter. **63. sledded:** weighted (as a sledge-
hammer). **pole-axe:** battle-ax. **65. jump:** just. **67. thought:** train
of thinking. **68. gross and scope:** general drift. **72. toils:** causes
to toil. **subject:** people, subjects. **73. cast:** founding. **74. mart:**
traffic. **75. impress:** enforced service. **77. toward:** in
preparation. **83. prick'd on:** incited. **emulate:** ambitious. **85.
this side . . . world:** i.e., all Europe. **89. seiz'd of:** possessed
of. **90. moiety competent:** equal amount. **91. gaged:** staked.

To the inheritance of Fortinbras,   92
Had he been vanquisher; as, by the same
   cov'nant,
And carriage of the article design'd,
His fell to Hamlet. Now, sir, young Fortinbras,
Of unimproved mettle hot and full,   96
Hath in the skirts of Norway here and there
Shark'd up a list of lawless resolutes,
For food and diet, to some enterprise
That hath a stomach in 't; which is no other,
As it doth well appear unto our state,   101
But to recover of us by strong hand
And terms compulsatory, those foresaid lands
So by his father lost. And this, I take it,   104
Is the main motive of our preparations,
The source of this our watch and the chief head
Of this post-haste and romage in the land.
BERNARDO. I think it be no other but e'en so;   108
   Well may it sort that this portentous figure
   Comes armed through our watch, so like the
     king
   That was and is the question of these wars.
HORATIO. A mote it is to trouble the mind's eye. 112
   In the most high and palmy state of Rome,
   A little ere the mightiest Julius fell,
   The graves stood tenantless and the sheeted dead
   Did squeak and gibber in the Roman streets. 116
   [Astounding portents fill'd the element,]
   As stars with trains of fire and dews of blood,
   Disasters in the sun; and the moist star
   Upon whose influence Neptune's empire stands
   Was sick almost to doomsday with eclipse;   120
   And even the like precurse of fear'd events,
   As harbingers preceding still the fates
   And prologue to the omen coming on,
   Have heaven and earth together demonstrated
   Unto our climatures and countrymen.   125

[Enter Ghost again.]

But, soft, behold! lo, where it comes again!
I'll cross it, though it blast me. Stay, illusion!

If thou hast any sound, or use of voice,   128
Speak to me!   *[It spreads his arms.]*
If there be any good thing to be done,
That may to thee do ease and grace to me,
Speak to me!   132
If thou art privy to thy country's fate,
Which happily foreknowing may avoid,
O speak!
Or if thou hast uphoarded in thy life   136
Extorted treasure in the womb of earth,
For which, they say, you spirits oft walk in
   death,

[The cock crows.]

   Speak of it: stay, and speak! Stop it,
     Marcellus.   139
MARCELLUS. Shall I strike at it with my partisan?
HORATIO. Do, if it will not stand.
BERNARDO.   'Tis here!
HORATIO.   'Tis here!

[Exit Ghost.]

MARCELLUS. 'Tis gone!
   We do it wrong, being so majestical,
   To offer it the show of violence;   144
   For it is, as the air, invulnerable,
   And our vain blows malicious mockery.
BERNARDO. It was about to speak when the cock
   crew.
HORATIO. And then it started like a guilty thing
   Upon a fearful summons. I have heard,   149
   The cock, that is the trumpet to the morn,
   Doth with his lofty and shrill-sounding throat
   Awake the god of day; and at his warning,   152
   Whether in sea or fire, in earth or air,
   Th' extravagant and erring spirit hies
   To his confine; and of the truth herein
   This present object made probation.   156
MARCELLUS. It faded on the crowing of the cock.
   Some say that ever 'gainst that season comes
   Wherein our Saviour's birth is celebrated,
   This bird of dawning singeth all night
     long   160

---

94. **carriage:** import. **design'd:** drawn up.   96. **unimproved mettle:** untested courage. **hot and full:** exceedingly ardent.   97. **skirts:** outskirts.   98. **Shark'd up:** picked up at haphazard. **resolutes:** desperadoes.   103. **compulsatory:** involving compulsion.   106. **head:** origin.   107. **romage:** commotion, bustle.   109. **sort:** fit.   112. **mote:** minute particle of dust.   113. **palmy state:** flourishing sovereignty.   118. **As:** such as.   119. **Disasters:** unfavorable omens. **moist star:** moon.   121. **precurse:** heralding.   122. **still:** constantly.   123. **prologue:** introduction. **omen:** catastrophe.   127: **cross:** meet, face.

129. **s.d. his:** its (the ghost's).   131. **[do] grace:** do honor to.   134. **happily:** haply.   154. **extravagant:** vagrant. **erring:** wandering. **hies:** hastens.   155. **confine:** place of confinement.   156. **probation:** proof.   158. **'gainst that:** by the time that.

And then, they say, no spirit dare stir abroad;
The nights are wholesome; then no planets strike,
No fairy takes, nor witch hath power to charm,
So hallow'd and so gracious is that time.   164
HORATIO. So have I heard and do in part believe it.
But, look, the morn in russet mantle clad,
Walks o'er the dew of yon high eastward hill.
Break we our watch up; and by my advice   168
Let us impart what we have seen to-night
Unto young Hamlet, for, upon my life,
This spirit, dumb to us, will speak to him.
Do you consent we shall acquaint him with it,
As needful in our loves, fitting our duty?   173
MARCELLUS. Let's do 't, I pray; and I this morning
     know
Where we shall find him most conveniently.

[Exeunt.]

SCENE II

The King's Council Chamber

[Flourish. Enter Claudius King of Denmark, Gertrude the Queen, members of the Council, Polonius and his son Laertes, Voltimand and Cornelius, Hamlet, cum aliis.]

Claudius

KING. Though yet of Hamlet our dear brother's death
The memory be green, and that it us befitted
To bear our hearts in grief and our whole
     kingdom
To be contracted in one brow of woe,   4
Yet so far hath discretion fought with nature
That we wish wisest sorrow think on him,
Together with remembrance of ourselves.
Therefore our sometime sister, now our
     queen,   8
Th' imperial jointress of this warlike state,
Have we, as 'twere with a defeated joy,
With an auspicious and a dropping eye,
With mirth in funeral and with dirge in
     marriage,   12

In equal scale weighing delight and dole,
Taken to wife. Nor have we herein barr'd
Your better wisdoms, which have freely gone
With this affair along. For all, our thanks.   16
Now follows that you know young Fortinbras,
Holding a weak supposal of our worth,
Or thinking by our late dear brother's death
Our state to be disjoint and out of frame,   20
Colleagued with this dream of his advantage.
He hath not fail'd to pester us with message,
Importing the surrender of those lands
Lost by his father with all bands of law   24
To our most valiant brother. So much for him.
Now for ourself and for this time of meeting.
Thus much the business is: we have here writ
To Norway, uncle of young Fortinbras,   28
Who, impotent and bed-rid, scarcely hears
Of this his nephew's purpose, to suppress
His further gait herein in that the levies,
The lists and full proportions are all made   32
Out of his subject; and we here dispatch
You, good Cornelius, and you, Voltimand,
For bearers of this greeting to old Norway,
Giving to you no further personal power   36
To business with the king more than the scope
Of these delated articles allow.
Farewell and let your haste commend your
     duty.
CORNELIUS. ⎱In that and all things will we show our
VOLTIMAND. ⎰duty.   40
KING. We doubt it nothing: heartily farewell.

[Exeunt Voltimand and Cornelius.]

And now, Laertes, what's the news with you?
You told us of some suit; what is 't, Laertes?
You cannot speak of reason to the Dane,   44
And lose your voice. What wouldst thou beg,
     Laertes,
That shall not be my offer, not thy asking?
The head is not more native to the heart,
The hand more instrumental to the mouth,   48

---

163. **takes:** bewitches. 164. **gracious:** instinct with goodness. 166. **russet:** gray or reddish-brown (betokening dull weather).
I. ii. **Note:** Flourish: a trumpet call. 4. **one brow of woe:** unanimity of sorrow. 9. **jointress:** joint possessor. 10. **defeated:** dispirited. 11. **an auspicious:** one happy. **a dropping:** one tearful.

13. **dole:** grief. 17. **Now . . . know:** I must next inform you. 18. **weak supposal:** low opinion. 20. **disjoint:** at loose ends. **frame:** order. 21. **Colleagued . . . advantage:** conspired with himself to profit by this imaginary opportunity. 23. **Importing:** bearing as its purport. 24. **bands:** assurances. 31. **gait:** proceeding. **in that:** because. 32. **proportions:** supplies, forces. 33. **his subject:** liegemen of Norway. 38. **delated:** expressly stated. 45. **lose your voice:** speak to no purpose. 47. **native:** closely and congenitally connected. 48. **instrumental:** serviceable.

Than is the throne of Denmark to thy father.
What wouldst thou have, Laertes?

LAERTES.   Dread my lord,
Your leave and favor to return to France;
From whence though willingly I came to
      Denmark,   52
To show my duty in your coronation,
Yet now, I must confess, that duty done,
My thoughts and wishes bend again toward
      France
And bow them to your gracious leave and
      pardon.   56

KING. Have you your father's leave? What says
      Polonius?

POLONIUS. He hath, my lord, wrung from me my
      slow leave
By laborsome petition, and at last
Upon his will I seal'd my hard consent.   60
I do beseech you, give him leave to go.

KING. Take thy fair hour, Laertes; time be thine,
And thy best graces spend it at thy will.
But now, my cousin Hamlet, and my son—   64

HAMLET. *[Aside.]* A little more than kin, and less
      than kind.

KING. How is it that the clouds hang on you?

HAMLET. Now so, my lord; I am too much i' th'
      sun.

QUEEN. Good Hamlet, cast thy nighted color
      off,   68
And let thine eye look like a friend on
      Denmark.
Do not for ever with thy vailed lids
Seek for thy noble father in the dust.
Thou know'st 'tis common; all that lives must
      die,   72
Passing through nature to eternity.

HAMLET. Ay, madam, it is common.

QUEEN.   If it be,
Why seems it so particular with thee?

HAMLET. Seems, madam! Nay, it is; I know not
      'seems.'   76
'Tis not alone my inky cloak, good mother,
Nor customary suits of solemn black,
Nor windy suspiration of forc'd breath,

No, nor the fruitful river in the eye,   80
Nor the dejected havior of the visage,
Together with all forms, moods, shapes of grief
That can denote me truly. These indeed seem,
For they are actions that a man might play: 84
But I have that within which passes show;
These but the trappings and the suits of woe.

KING. 'Tis sweet and cómmendable in your nature,
      Hamlet,
To give these mourning duties to your
      father.   88
But, you must know, your father lost a father;
That father lost, lost his, and the survivor bound
In filial obligation for some term
To do obsequious sorrow; but to perséver   92
In obstinate condolement is a course
Of impious stubbornness; 'tis unmanly grief.
It shows a will most incorrect to heaven,
A heart unfortified, a mind impatient,   96
An understanding simple and unschool'd:
For what we know must be and is as common
As any the most vulgar thing to sense,
Why should we in our peevish opposition   100
Take it to heart? Fie! 'tis a fault to heaven,
A fault against the dead, a fault to nature,
To reason most absurd, whose common theme
Is death of fathers, and who still hath cried,   104
From the first corse till he that died to-day,
'This must be so.' We pray you, throw to earth
This unprevailing woe, and think of us
As of a father; for let the world take note,   108
You are the most immediate to our throne,
And with no less nobility of love
Than that which dearest father bears his son
Do I impórtune you. For your intent   112
In going back to school in Wittenberg,
It is most retrograde to our desire;
And we beseech you, bend you to remain
Here in the cheer and comfort of our eye,   116
Our chiefest courtier, cousin, and our son.

QUEEN. Let not thy mother lose her prayers,
      Hamlet.
I pray thee, stay with us; go not to Wittenberg.

---

50. **Dread my lord:** my revered lord. 51. **leave and favor:** kind permission. 56. **leave and pardon:** indulgence [to depart]. 60. **hard:** given with difficulty. 63. **graces:** virtues. 64. **cousin:** nephew. 70. **vailed:** down-cast. 72. **common:** the common lot. 75. **particular:** personal. 79. **windy suspiration:** tempestuous sighing. **forc'd:** against one's will.

80. **fruitful:** copious. 81. **havior:** behavior. 83. **denote:** portray. 90. **bound:** was bound. 92. **obsequious:** dutiful. 93. **condolement:** sorrowing. 95. **incorrect to:** unchastened toward. 99. **vulgar . . . sense:** common experience. 105. **corse:** corpse. 106. **throw to earth:** drop (like a burden on one's back). 107. **unprevailing:** unavailing. 109. **most immediate:** next in succession. 114. **retrograde:** contrary. 115. **bend:** incline.

HAMLET. I shall in all my best obey you,
   madam.   120
KING. Why, 'tis a loving and a fair reply!
   Be as ourself in Denmark.—Madam, come.
   This gentle and unforc'd accord of Hamlet
   Sits smiling to my heart; in grace whereof,   124
   No jocund health that Denmark drinks to-day,
   But the great cannon to the clouds shall tell,
   And the king's rouse the heavens shall bruit
      again,
   Re-speaking earthly thunder. Come away.   128

[Flourish. Exeunt all but Hamlet.]

HAMLET. O that this too too solid flesh would melt,
   Thaw and resolve itself into a dew!
   Or that the Everlasting had not fix'd
   His canon 'gainst self-slaughter! O God!
      God!   132
   How weary, stale, flat, and unprofitable
   Seem to me all the uses of this world.
   Fie on 't! fie! 'tis an unweeded garden,
   That grows to seed; things rank and gross in
      nature   136
   Possess it merely. That it should come to this!
   But two months dead! nay, not so much, not
      two.
   So excellent a king, that was to this
   Hyperion to a satyr; so loving to my
      mother   140
   That he might not beteem the winds of heaven
   Visit her face too roughly. Heaven and earth!
   Must I remember? why, she would hand on
      him,
   As if increase of appetite had grown   144
   By what it fed on; and yet, within a month,—
   Let me not think on 't! Frailty, thy name is
      woman.
   A little month; or ere those shoes were old
   With which she follow'd my poor father's body,
   Like Niobe, all tears; why she,—   149
   O God! a beast, that wants discourse of reason,
   Would have mourn'd longer,—married with my
      uncle,
   My father's brother, but no more like my father
   Than I to Hercules. Within a month,   153

Ere yet the salt of most unrighteous tears
Had left the flushing in her galled eyes,
She married. O most wicked speed, to post
With such dexterity to incestuous sheets.   157
It is not, nor it cannot come to, good.—
But break, my heart, for I must hold my
   tongue.

[Enter Horatio, Marcellus and Bernardo.]

HORATIO. Hail to your lordship!
HAMLET.   I am glad to see
   you well.
   Horatio! or I do forget myself.
HORATIO. The same, my lord, and your poor
   servant ever.
HAMLET. Sir, my good friend; I'll change that name
   with you.
   And what make you from Wittenberg, Horatio?
   Marcellus?   165
MARCELLUS. My good lord.—
HAMLET. I am very glad to see you. *[To Bernardo.]*
   Good even, sir.
   But what, in faith, make you from
      Wittenberg?
HORATIO. A truant disposition, good my lord.   169
HAMLET. I would not hear your enemy say so,
   Nor shall you do my ear that violence,
   To make it truster of your own report   172
   Against yourself; I know you are no truant.
   But what is your affair in Elsinore?
   We'll teach you to drink deep ere you depart.
HORATIO. My lord, I came to see your father's
   funeral.   176
HAMLET. I prithee, do not mock me, fellow-
   student.
   I think it was to see my mother's wedding.
HORATIO. Indeed, my lord, it follow'd hard upon.
HAMLET. Thrift, thrift, Horatio! the funeral bak'd
   meats   180
   Did coldly furnish forth the marriage tables.
   Would I had met my dearest foe in heaven
   Or ever I had seen that day, Horatio?
   My father, methinks I see my father.   184
HORATIO. Where, my lord?

---

127. rouse: revelry, 'carousing.' **bruit:** echo. **130. resolve:** dissolve. **132. canon:** divine law. **134. uses:** usages. **137. merely:** entirely. **141. beteem:** allow. **150. discourse of reason:** reasoning power.

155. left the flushing: ceased to produce redness. **galled:** sore with weeping. **156. post:** hasten. **157. dexterity:** facility. **163. change that name:** share the name of friend. **169. disposition:** temperament. **180. bak'd meats:** meat pies. **181. coldly:** when cold. **182. dearest:** direst. **183. Or:** before.

HAMLET.   In my mind's eye,
    Horatio.
HORATIO. I saw him once; 'a was a goodly king.
HAMLET. 'A was a man! take him for all in all,
    I shall not look upon his like again.   188
HORATIO. My lord, I think I saw him yesternight.
HAMLET. Saw? Who?
HORATIO. My lord, the king your father.
HAMLET.   The king,
    my father?
HORATIO. Season your admiration for a while   192
    With an attent ear, till I may deliver,
    Upon the witness of these gentlemen,
    This marvel to you.
HAMLET.   For God's love, let me hear.
HORATIO. Two nights together had these
    gentlemen,   196
    Marcellus and Bernardo, on their watch,
    In the dead waste and middle of the night,
    Been thus encounter'd: a figure like your father,
    Armed at point exactly, cap-a-pe,   200
    Appears before them, and with solemn march
    Goes slow and stately by them. Thrice he walk'd
    By their oppress'd and fear-surprised eyes,
    Within his truncheon's length; whilst they,
        distill'd   204
    Almost to jelly with the act of fear,
    Stand dumb and speak not to him. This to me
    In dreadful secrecy impart they did,
    And I with them the third night kept the watch;
    Where, as they had deliver'd, both in time,   209
    Form of the thing, each word made true and
        good,
    The apparition comes. I knew your father;
    These hands are not more like.
HAMLET.   But where was
    this?
MARCELLUS. My lord, upon the platform where we
    watch.   213
HAMLET. Did you not speak to it?
HORATIO.   My lord, I did;
    But answer made it none; yet once methought
    It lifted up it head and did address   216
    Itself to motion, like as it would speak;
    But even then the morning cock crew loud,
    And at the sound it shrunk in haste away
    And vanish'd from our sight.

HAMLET.   'Tis very
    strange.   220
HORATIO. As I do live, my honor'd lord, 'tis true;
    And we did think it writ down in our duty
    To let you know of it.
HAMLET. Indeed, indeed, sirs, but this troubles
    me.   224
    Hold you the watch to-night?
ALL.   We do, my lord.
HAMLET. Arm'd, say you?
ALL.   Arm'd, my lord.
HAMLET.   From top
    to toe?
ALL. My lord, from head to foot.
HAMLET. Then saw you not his face.   228
HORATIO. O yes, my lord; he wore his beaver up.
HAMLET. What! look'd he frowningly?
HORATIO. A countenance more in sorrow than in
    anger.
HAMLET. Pale or red?   232
HORATIO. Nay, very pale.
HAMLET.   And fix'd his eyes upon
    you?
HORATIO. Most constantly.
HAMLET.   I would I had been
    there.
HORATIO. It would have much amaz'd you.
HAMLET.   Very like.   236
    Stay'd it long?
HORATIO. While one with moderate haste
    Might tell a hundreth.
BOTH.   Longer, longer.
HORATIO. Not when I saw 't.
HAMLET.   His beard was grizzled,
    no?
HORATIO. It was, as I have seen it in his life,   240
    A sable silver'd.
HAMLET.   I will watch to-night;
    Perchance 'twill walk again.
HORATIO.   I warr'nt it will.
HAMLET. If it assume my noble father's person,
    I'll speak to it, though hell itself should
        gape   244
    And bid me hold my peace. I pray you all,
    If you have hitherto conceal'd this sight,
    Let it be tenable in your silence still;
    And whatsomever else shall hap to-night,   248

---

192. **Season:** temper, qualify. **admiration:** wonder.   **193. attent:** attentive.   **200. at point:** in full readiness. **cap-a-pe:** from head to foot.   **204. truncheon:** officer's staff. **distill'd:** melted.   **205. act:** operation.   **216. it:** its.

229. beaver: face-guard of a helmet.   **238. tell:** count. **hundreth:** hundred (a Norse form).   **239. grizzled:** grey.   **241. sable:** heraldic term for black.   **247. Let . . .tenable:** see that you keep it.   **248. whatsomever:** whatever

Give it an understanding, but no tongue.
I will require your loves. So, fare you well.
Upon the platform, 'twixt eleven and twelve,
I'll visit you.
ALL.   Our duty to your honor.   252
HAMLET. Your loves, as mine to you. Farewell.

[Exeunt all but Hamlet.]

My father's spirit in arms! all is not well;
I doubt some foul play. Would the night were
    come!
Till then sit still, my soul: foul deeds will rise,   256
Though all the earth o'erwhelm them, to men's
    eyes.

[Exit.]

SCENE III

Polonius' Apartment in the Castle

[Enter Laertes and Ophelia, his sister.]

LAERTES. My necessaries are embark'd; farewell:
    And, sister, as the winds give benefit
    And convoy is assistant, do not sleep,
    But let me hear from you.
OPHELIA.   Do you doubt that?   4
LAERTES. For Hamlet, and the trifling of his favor,
    Hold it a fashion and a toy in blood,
    A violet in the youth of primy nature,
    Forward, not permanent, sweet, not lasting,   8
    The perfume and suppliance of a minute;
    No more.
OPHELIA.   No more but so?
LAERTES.   Think it no more:
    For nature crescent does not grow alone
    In thews and bulk, but as this temple waxes,   12
    The inward service of the mind and soul
    Grows wide withal. Perhaps he loves you now,
    And now no soil nor cautel doth besmirch
    The virtue of his will; but you must fear.   16

His greatness weigh'd, his will is not his own,
For he himself is subject to his birth.
He may not, as unvalu'd persons do,
Carve for himself, for on his choice depends   20
The safety and health of this whole state;
And therefore must his choice be circumscrib'd
Unto the voice and yielding of that body
Whereof he is the head. Then if he says he loves
    you,   24
It fits your wisdom so far to believe it
As he in his particular act and place
May give his saying deed; which is no further
Than the main voice of Denmark goes withal.   28
Then weigh what loss your honor may sustain,
If with too credent ear you list his songs,
Or lose your heart, or your chaste treasure open
To his unmaster'd importunity.   32
Fear it, Ophelia, fear it, my dear sister;
And keep you in the rear of your affection,
Out of the shot and danger of desire.
The chariest maid is prodigal enough   36
If she unmask her beauty to the moon;
Virtue itself 'scapes not calumnious strokes;
The canker galls the infants of the spring
Too oft before their buttons be disclos'd,   40
And in the morn and liquid dew of youth
Contagious blastments are most imminent.
Be wary then; best safety lies in fear:
Youth to itself rebels, though none else near.   44
OPHELIA. I shall the effect of this good lesson keep,
    As watchman to my heart. But, good my brother,
    Do not, as some ungracious pastors do,
    Show me the steep and thorny way to heaven,
    Whiles, like a puff'd and reckless libertine,   49
    Himself the primrose path of dalliance treads,
    And recks not his own rede.
LAERTES.   O fear me not.

[Enter Polonius.]

I stay too long, but here my father comes.   52
A double blessing is a double grace;
Occasion smiles upon a second leave.

19. **unvalu'd:** untitled. 23. **voice and yielding:** approval and compliance. 26. **place:** position as a prince. 27. **deed:** effect. 30. **credent:** trustful. **list:** listen to. 32. **unmaster'd:** unrestrained. 36. **chariest:** most scrupulous. 39. **canker:** caterpillar. **galls:** injures. **infants:** young plants. 40. **buttons:** buds. **disclos'd:** opened. 41. **liquid dew:** while the dew is still fresh. 42. **blastments:** blights. 47. **ungracious:** graceless. 49. **puff'd:** bloated from excess. 50. **primrose path:** path of pleasure. 51. **recks:** heeds. **rede:** counsel. **fear me not:** don't worry about me. 54. **Occasion:** opportunity. **smiles upon:** favors me with.

2. **give benefit:** are favorable. 3. **convoy:** means of conveyance. 6. **fashion:** mere form. **toy in blood:** passing amorous fancy. 7. **primy:** spring-like. 8. **Forward:** precocious. 9. **suppliance:** diversion. 11. **crescent:** growing. 12. **thews:** bodily strength. **temple:** body. 14. **withal:** also. 15. **soil:** blemish. **cautel:** trickery. 16. **virtue of his will:** his virtuous intentions.

POLONIUS. Yet here, Laertes? aboard, aboard, for
    shame!
    The wind sits in the shoulder of your sail,   56
    And you are stay'd for. There, my blessing with
      thee!
    And these few precepts in thy memory
    Look thou cháracter. Give thy thoughts no
      tongue,
    Nor any unproportion'd thought his act.   60
    Be thou familiar, but by no means vulgar;
    Those friends thou hast, and their adoption
      tried,
    Grapple them unto thy soul with hoops of steel;
    But do not dull thy palm with entertainment 64
    Of each new-hatch'd, unfledg'd comráde.
      Beware
    Of entrance to a quarrel, but, being in,
    Bear 't that th' opposed may beware of thee.
    Give every man thy ear, but few thy voice;   68
    Take each man's censure, but reserve thy
      judgment.
    Costly thy habit as thy purse can buy,
    But not express'd in fancy; rich, not gaudy;
    For the apparel oft proclaims the man,   72
    And they in France of the best rank and station
    Are of a most select and generous clef in that.
    Neither a borrower, nor a lender be;
    For loan oft loses both itself and friend,   76
    And borrowing dulleth edge of husbandry.
    This above all: to thine own self be true,
    And it must follow, as the night the day,
    Thou canst not then be false to any man.   80
    Farewell; my blessing season this in thee!
LAERTES. Most humbly do I take my leave, my
    lord.
POLONIUS. The time invites you; go, your servants
    tend.
LAERTES. Farewell, Ophelia; and remember well
    What I have said to you.
OPHELIA.   'Tis in my memory
    lock'd,
    And you yourself shall keep the key of it.   86
LAERTES. Farewell.

[Exit Laertes.]

POLONIUS. What is 't, Ophelia, he hath said to you?
OPHELIA. So please you, something touching the
    Lord Hamlet.
POLONIUS. Marry, well bethought:
    'Tis told me, he hath very oft of late
    Given private time to you; and you yourself 92
    Have of your audience been most free and
      bounteous.
    If it be so,—as so 'tis put on me,
    And that in way of caution,—I must tell you,
    You do not understand yourself so clearly 96
    As it behoves my daughter and your honor.
    What is between you? give me up the truth.
OPHELIA. He hath, my lord, of late made many
    tenders
    Of his affection to me.
POLONIUS. Affection! pooh! you speak like a green
    girl,
    Unsifted in such perilous circumstance.
    Do you believe his tenders, as you call them?
OPHELIA. I do not know, my lord, what I should
    think.   104
POLONIUS. Marry, I'll teach you: think yourself a
    baby,
    That you have ta'en these tenders for true pay,
    Which are not sterling. Tender yourself more
      dearly;
    Or (not to crack the wind of the poor phrase,
    Running it thus) you'll tender me a fool.   109
OPHELIA. My lord, he hath impórtun'd me with love
    In honorable fashion.
POLONIUS. Ay, fashion you call it. Go to, go to. 112
OPHELIA. And hath given countenance to his
    speech, my lord,
    With almost all the holy vows of heaven.
POLONIUS. Ay, springes to catch woodcocks. I do
    know,
    When the blood burns, how prodigal the
      soul   116
    Lends the tongue vows: these blazes, daughter,
    Giving more light than heat, extinct in both,
    Even in their promise, as it is a-making,
    You must not take for fire. From this time 120
    Be somewhat scanter of your maiden presence;
    Set your entreatments at a higher rate

---

59. character: inscribe. **60. unproportion'd:** inordinate. **61. familiar:** friendly. **64. dull thy palm:** make yourself less sensitive to true friendship. **65. unfledg'd:** immature. **69. censure:** opinion. **71. express'd in fancy:** singular in design. **74. generous:** aristocratic. **clef:** musical key, tone. **77. husbandry:** thrift. **81. season this:** make my admonition palatable. **83. tend:** are in waiting.

92. private time: time in private visits. **94. put on:** impressed on. **99. tenders:** offers. **101. green:** inexperienced. **102. Unsifted:** untried. **circumstance:** state of affairs. **107. sterling:** legal currency. **115. springes:** snares. **122. entreatments:** interviews.

Than a command to parley. For Lord Hamlet,
Believe so much in him: that he is young, 124
And with a larger tether may he walk
Than may be given you. In few, Ophelia,
Do not believe his vows, for they are brokers,
Not of that dye which their investments show,
But mere implorators of unholy suits, 129
Breathing like sanctified and pious bawds,
The better to beguile. This is for all:
I would not, in plain terms, from this time
    forth,
Have you so slander any moment leisure, 133
As to give words or talk with the Lord Hamlet.
Look to 't, I charge you; come your ways.
OPHELIA. I shall obey, my lord.

[Exeunt.]

SCENE IV

The Platform of the Castle

[Enter Hamlet, Horatio, and Marcellus.]

HAMLET. The air bites shrewdly; it is very cold.
HORATIO. It is a nipping and an eager air.
HAMLET. What hour now?
HORATIO.   I think it lacks of twelve.
MARCELLUS. No, it is struck. 4
HORATIO. Indeed? I heard it not: it then draws near
    the season
    Wherein the spirit held his wont to walk.

[A flourish of trumpets, and two pieces (of ordnance) go off.]

What does this mean, my lord?
HAMLET. The king doth wake to-night and takes his
    rouse, 8
    Keeps wassail, and the swaggering up-spring
    reels;
    And, as he drains his draughts of Rhenish down,
    The kettle-drum and trumpet thus bray out
    The triumph of his pledge.

HORATIO.   Is it a custom? 12
HAMLET. Ay, marry, is 't:
    But to my mind, though I am native here
    And to the manner born, it is a custom
    More honor'd in the breach than the
        observance. 16
    This heavy-headed revel east and west
    Makes us traduc'd and tax'd of other nations;
    They clepe us drunkards, and with swinish
        phrase
    Soil our addition; and indeed it takes 20
    From our achievements, though perform'd at
        height,
    The pith and marrow of our attribute.
    So, oft it chances in particular men,
    That for some vicious mole of nature in them, 24
    As, in their birth, (wherein they are not guilty,
    Since nature cannot choose his origin),
    By the o'ergrowth of some complexion,
    Oft breaking down the pales and forts of
        reason, 28
    Or by some habit that too much o'er-leavens
    The form of plausive manners; that these men,
    Carrying, I say, the stamp of one defect,
    Being nature's livery, or fortune's star,— 32
    His virtues else, be they are pure as grace,
    As infinite as man may undergo,
    Shall in the general censure take corruption
    From that particular fault. The dram of eale 36
    Doth all the noble substance oft adulter
    To his own scandal.

[Enter Ghost.]

HORATIO.   Look, my lord, it comes!
HAMLET. Angels and ministers of grace defend us!
    Be thou a spirit of health or goblin damn'd, 40
    Bring with thee airs from heaven or blasts from
        hell,
    Be thy intents wicked or charitable,
    Thou com'st in such a questionable shape

---

126. **In few:** briefly.   127. **brokers:** go-betweens, procurers.   **128.
investments:** vestments, clothes.   129. **implorators:** solici-
tors.   133. **slander:** bring reproach upon.
2. **eager:** sharp.   8. **wake:** hold a revel by night.   9. **Keeps wassail:**
holds a drinking-bout.   **up-spring:** wild dance of German origin.   10. **Rhenish:** Rhine wine.   12. **pledge:** toast.

18. **traduc'd and tax'd:** defamed and censured.   19. **clepe:** call.
swinish phrase: name of 'pigs.'   20. **Soil our addition:** blemish our
good name.   21. **at height:** to the maximum.   22. **attribute:** reputation.   24. **mole:** blemish.   27. **complexion:** natural tendency,
'humor.'   28. **pales:** defensive enclosures.   29. **o'er-leavens:** makes
too light.   30. **plausive:** pleasing.   32. **nature's livery:** a natural attribute.   **fortune's star:** the position in which one is placed by
fortune.   34. **undergo:** bear the weight of.   36. **dram:** minute
quantity.   **eale:** e'il, evil.   38. **scandal:** shame.   39. **ministers of
grace:** messengers of God.   40. **spirit of health:** good spirit.   **goblin:**
evil spirit.   43. **questionable:** inviting question.

That I will speak to thee. I'll call thee Hamlet, 44
King, father, royal Dane! O answer me:
Let me not burst in ignorance, but tell
Why thy canóniz'd bones, hearsed in death,
Have burst their cerements; why the
sepulchre, 48
Wherein we saw thee quietly inurn'd,
Hath op'd his ponderous and marble jaws,
To cast thee up again? What may this mean,
That thou, dead corse, again in cómplete
steel 52
Revisits thus the glimpses of the moon,
Making night hideous; and we fools of nature
So horridly to-shake our disposition
With thoughts beyond the reaches of our
souls? 56
Say, why is this? wherefore? what should we do?

[Ghost beckons Hamlet.]

HORATIO. It beckons you to go away with it,
As if it some impartment did desire
To you alone.
MARCELLUS. Look, with what courteous
action 60
It waves you to a more removed ground:
But do not go with it.
HORATIO. No, by no means.
HAMLET. It will not speak. Then, I will follow it.
HORATIO. Do not, my lord.
HAMLET. Why, what should be the fear? 64
I do not set my life at a pin's fee;
And for my soul, what can it do to that,
Being a thing immortal as itself?
It waves me forth again; I'll follow it. 68
HORATIO. What if it tempt you toward the flood,
my lord,
Or to the dreadful summit of the cliff
That beetles o'er his base into the sea,
And there assume some other horrible form, 72
Which might deprive your sovereignty of reason
And draw you into madness? think of it;
The very place puts toys of desperation,

Without more motive, into every brain 76
That looks so many fadoms to the sea
And hears it roar beneath.
HAMLET. It waves me still. Go on! I'll follow thee.
MARCELLUS. You shall not go, my lord.
HAMLET. Hold off your hands! 80
HORATIO. Be rul'd; you shall not go.
HAMLET. My fate cries
out,
And makes each petty arture in this body
As hardy as the Némean lion's nerve.
Still am I call'd. Unhand me, gentlemen! 84
By heaven, I'll make a ghost of him that lets me.
I say, away!—Go on! I'll follow thee.

[Exeunt Ghost and Hamlet.]

HORATIO. He waxes desperate with imagination.
MARCELLUS. Let's follow; 'tis not fit thus to obey
him.
HORATIO. Have after. To what issue will this come?
MARCELLUS. Something is rotten in the state of
Denmark.
HORATIO. Heaven will direct it.
MARCELLUS. Nay, let's follow him.

[Exeunt.]

SCENE V

A More Remote Part of the Platform

[Enter Ghost and Hamlet.]

HAMLET. Whither wilt thou lead me? speak; I'll go
no further.
GHOST. Mark me.
HAMLET. I will.
GHOST. My hour is almost come,
When I to sulphurous and tormenting flames
Must render up myself.
HAMLET. Alas, poor ghost. 4
GHOST. Pity me not, but lend thy serious hearing
To what I shall unfold.
HAMLET. Speak; I am bound to
hear.

---

47. canóniz'd: buried according to the Church's rule. **hearsed:** coffined. **48. cerements:** waxen grave-clothes. **49. inurn'd:** interred. **53. glimpses of the moon:** the earth by night. **54. fools of nature:** stupid in nature's presence. **55. to-shake our disposition:** shatter our composure. **56. reaches:** capacities. **59. impartment:** communication. **65. at . . . fee:** at even a trifling value. **69. flood:** sea. **71. beetles:** overhangs threateningly. **73. deprive . . . reason:** dethrone reason from its sovereignty. **75. toys of desperation:** whims involving thoughts of self-destruction.

77. fadoms: fathoms. **82. arture:** artery. **83. nerve:** sinew, tendon. **85. lets:** hinders. **89. issue:** outcome.

GHOST. So art thou to revenge, when thou shalt hear.

HAMLET. What? 8

GHOST. I am thy father's spirit,

Doom'd for a certain term to walk the night,

And for the day confin'd to fast in fires,

Till the foul crimes done in my days of nature

Are burnt and purg'd away. But that I am forbid

To tell the secrets of my prison-house,

I could a tale unfold whose lightest word

Would harrow up thy soul, freeze thy young
blood, 16

Make thy two eyes, like stars, start from their
spheres,

Thy knotted and combined locks to part,

And each particular hair to stand an end,

Like quills upon the fretful porpentine. 20

But this eternal blazon must not be

To ears of flesh and blood. List, list, oh list!

If thou didst ever thy dear father love—

HAMLET. O God! 24

GHOST. Revenge his foul and most unnatural
murther.

HAMLET. Murther!

GHOST. Murther most foul, as in the best it is;

But this most foul, strange, and unnatural. 28

HAMLET. Haste me to know't, that I, with wings as
swift

As meditation or the thoughts of love,

May sweep to my revenge.

GHOST.   I find thee apt;

And duller shouldst thou be than the fat
weed 32

That roots itself in ease on Lethe wharf,

Wouldst thou not stir in this. Now, Hamlet, hear:

'Tis given out that, sleeping in my orchard,

A serpent stung me. So the whole ear of
Denmark 36

Is by a forged process of my death

Rankly abus'd; but know, thou noble youth,

The serpent that did sting thy father's life

Now wears his crown.

HAMLET.   O my prophetic soul! 40

My uncle?

GHOST. Ay, that incestuous, that adulterate beast,

With witchcraft of his wit, with traitorous gifts,—

O wicked wit and gifts, that have the power 44

So to seduce!—won to his shameful lust

The will of my most seeming-virtuous queen.

O Hamlet, what a falling-off was there!

From me, whose love was of that dignity 48

That it went hand in hand even with the vow

I made to her in marriage; and to decline

Upon a wretch whose natural gifts were poor

To those of mine! 52

But virtue, as it never will be mov'd,

Though lewdness court it in a shape of heaven,

So lust, though to a radiant angel link'd,

Will sate itself in a celestial bed, 56

And prey on garbage.

But soft! methinks I scent the morning air;

Brief let me be. Sleeping within my orchard,

My custom always of the afternoon, 60

Upon my secure hour thy uncle stole,

With juice of cursed hebona in a vial,

And in the porches of my ears did pour

The leperous distilment; whose effect 64

Holds such an enmity with blood of man

That swift as quicksilver it courses through

The natural gates and alleys of the body,

And with a sudden vigor it doth posset 68

And curd, like eager droppings into milk,

The thin and wholesome blood. So did it
mine;

And a most instant tetter bark'd about,

Most lazar-like, with vile and loathsome crust,

All my smooth body. 73

Thus was I, sleeping, by a brother's hand,

Of life, of crown, of queen, at once dispatch'd;

Cut off even in the blossom of my sin, 76

Unhousel'd, disappointed, unanel'd,

No reckoning made, but sent to my account

With all my imperfections on my head.

HAMLET. O horrible! O horrible! most horrible! 80

GHOST. If thou hast nature in thee, bear it not;

Let not the royal bed of Denmark be

A couch for luxury and damned incest.

But, howsomever thou pursu'st this act, 84

---

17. **spheres:** orbits. 18. **knotted:** neatly arranged. **combined:** smoothly combed. 19. **an:** on. 20. **porpentine:** porcupine. 21. **eternal blazon:** revelation of eternity. 25. **unnatural:** i.e., for one brother to kill another. 31. **apt:** ready to learn. 33. **wharf:** bank. 35. **orchard:** garden. 37. **process:** narrative. 38. **abus'd:** deceived. 42. **adulterate:** adulterous.

62. **hebona:** yew, notorious for its poisonous properties, but henbane and ebony are also involved. 64. **leperous:** causing leprosy. 67. **gates and alleys:** streets and lanes. 68. **posset:** curdle. 69. **eager:** sour. 71. **instant:** instantaneous. **tetter:** skin eruption. **bark'd about:** covered (as with bark). 72. **lazar-like:** leprous-like. 75. **dispatch'd:** bereft. 77. **Unhousel'd:** without having received the Holy Communion. **disappointed:** unprepared. **unanel'd:** without having received extreme unction. 78. **reckoning:** confession and absolution. 83. **luxury:** lasciviousness.

Taint not thy mind, nor let thy soul contrive
Against thy mother aught. Leave her to heaven,
And to those thorns that in her bosom lodge,
To prick and sting her. Fare thee well at once! 88
The glow-worm shows the matin to be near,
And 'gins to pale is uneffectual fire;
Adieu, adieu, adieu! Remember me. *[Exit.]*
HAMLET. O all you host of heaven! O earth! What
    else?   92
And shall I couple hell? O fie! Hold, hold, my
    heart!
And you, my sinews, grow not instant old,
But bear me stiffly up. Remember thee?
Ay, thou poor ghost, while memory holds a
    seat   96
In this distracted globe. Remember thee?
Yea, from the table of my memory
I'll wipe away all trivial fond records,
All saws of books, all forms, all pressures
    past,   100
That youth and observation copied there;
And thy commandment all alone shall live
Within the book and volume of my brain,
Unmix'd with baser matter: yes, by heaven!   104
O most pernicious woman!
O villain, villain, smiling, damned villain!
My tables! Meet it is I set it down,
That one may smile, and smile, and be a
    villain;   108
At least I'm sure it may be so in Denmark.

[Writing.]

So; uncle, there you are. Now to my word.
It is 'Adieu, adieu! remember me.'
I have sworn 't.   112
HORATIO AND MARCELLUS WITHIN. My lord! my lord!

[Enter Horatio and Marcellus.]

MARCELLUS.   Lord Hamlet!
HORATIO. Heaven secure him!
HAMLET.   So be it!
HORATIO. Illo, ho, ho, my lord!
HAMLET. Hillo, ho, ho, boy! come, bird, come.

MARCELLUS. How is 't, my noble lord?
HORATIO.   What news, my lord?   117
HAMLET. O wonderful!
HORATIO.   Good my lord, tell it.
HAMLET. No; you will reveal it.
HORATIO. Not I, my lord, by heaven!
MARCELLUS.   Nor I, my lord.   120
HAMLET. How say you, then? would heart of man
    once think it?
    But you'll be secret?
BOTH.   Ay, by heaven, my lord.
HAMLET. There's ne'er a villain dwelling in all
    Denmark,
    But he's an arrant knave.   124
HORATIO. There needs no ghost, my lord, come
    from the grave,
    To tell us this.
HAMLET.   Why, right; you are in the right;
    And so, without more circumstance at all,
    I hold it fit that we shake hands and part;   128
    You, as your business and desire shall point
    you,—
    For every man hath business and desire,
    Such as it is,—and, for my own poor part,
    I will go pray.   132
HORATIO. These are but wild and whirling words,
    my lord.
HAMLET. I am sorry they offend you, heartily;
    Yes, faith, heartily.
HORATIO.   There's no offence, my lord.
HAMLET. Yes, by Saint Patrick, but there is,
    Horatio,   136
    And much offence, too. Touching this vision
    here,
    It is an honest ghost, that let me tell you.
    For your desire to know what is between us,
    O'ermaster 't as you may. And now, good
    friends.   140
    As you are friends, scholars, and soldiers,
    Give me one poor request.
HORATIO. What is 't, my lord? we will.
HAMLET. Never make known what you have seen
    tonight.   144
BOTH. My lord, we will not.
HAMLET.   Nay, but swear 't.
HORATIO.   In faith,
    My lord, not I.

---

89. matin: morning. **90. uneffectual:** heatless. **97. distracted
globe:** confused head. **98. table:** writing-tablet. **99. fond:** foolish. **100. saws:** maxims. **pressures:** impressions—as of a
seal. **110. word:** watch-word. **115. Illo, ho, ho:** falconer's hunting call. **116. come, bird, come:** call which falconers use to their
hawk in the air.

---

124. arrant: thoroughgoing. **127. circumstance:** formality. **133.
whirling:** eddying, incoherent. **140. O'ermaster 't:** conquer it.

MARCELLUS.   Nor I, my lord, in faith.

HAMLET. Upon my sword.

MARCELLUS.   We have sworn, my lord, already.

HAMLET. Indeed, upon my sword, indeed.   148

GHOST. Swear.   *[Ghost cries under the stage.]*

HAMLET. Ha, ha, boy! sayst thou so? art thou there, true-penny?

  Come on,—you hear this fellow in the cellarage,—

  Consent to swear.

HORATIO.   Propose the oath, my lord.   152

HAMLET. Never to speak of this that you have seen.

  Swear by my sword.

GHOST. Swear.

HAMLET. *Hic et ubique?* then we'll shift our ground.   156

  Come hither, gentlemen, and lay your hands

  Again upon my sword. Swear by my sword

  Never to speak of this that you have heard.

GHOST. Swear by his sword.   160

HAMLET. Well said, old mole! canst work i' th' earth so fast?

  A worthy pioner! once more remove, good friends.

HORATIO. O day and night, but this is wondrous strange!

HAMLET. And therefore as stranger give it welcome.   164

  There are more things in heaven and earth, Horatio,

  Than are dreamt of in your philosophy.

But come;

Here, as before, never, so help you mercy,   168

How strange or odd soe'er I bear myself,—

As I perchance hereafter shall think meet

To put an antic disposition on,—

That you, at such times seeing me, never shall,   172

With arms encumber'd thus, or this head-shake,

Or by pronouncing of some doubtful phrase,

As, 'Well, well, we know,' or, 'We could an if we would;'

Or, 'If we list to speak,' or, 'There be, an if they might;'   176

Or such ambiguous giving out, to note

That you know aught of me. This do swear,

So grace and mercy at your most need help you.

GHOST. Swear.   *[They swear.]*

HAMLET. Rest, rest, perturbed spirit! So, gentlemen,   181

With all my love I do commend me to you:

And what so poor a man as Hamlet is

May do t' express his love and friending to you,   184

God willing, shall not lack. Let us go in together;

And still your fingers on your lips, I pray.

The time is out of joint. O cursed spite,

That ever I was born to set it right!   188

Nay, come, let's go together.

[Exeunt.]

Act II

SCENE I

Polonius' Apartment in the Castle

[Enter old Polonius with his man Reynaldo.]

POLONIUS. Give him this money and these notes, Reynaldo.

REYNALDO. I will, my lord.

POLONIUS. You shall do marvel's wisely, good Reynaldo,

Before you visit him, to make inquire   4

Of his behavior.

REYNALDO.   My lord, I did intend it.

POLONIUS. Marry, well said, very well said. Look you, sir,

Inquire me first what Danskers are in Paris;

150. true-penny: honest fellow.   **156.** *Hic et ubique:* here and everywhere.   **162. pioner:** digger, miner.
1. notes: instructions.

170. meet: proper.   **171. antic:** fantastic.   **173. encumber'd:** folded.   **174. doubtful:** ambiguous.   **176. an if:** an intensive form of 'if.'   **177. to note:** to give a sign.   **187. spite:** vexatious circumstance.
3. marvel's: marvelously.   **4. inquire:** investigation.   **7. Danskers:** Danes.

And how, and who, what means, and where
    they keep,   8
What company, at what expense; and finding
By this encompassment and drift of question
That they do know my son, come you more
    nearer
Than your particular demands will touch it. 12
Take you, as 'twere, some distant knowledge of
    him;
As thus, 'I know his father, and his friends,
And in part him.' Do you mark this, Reynaldo?
REYNALDO. Ay, very well, my lord.   16
POLONIUS. 'And in part him; but,' you may say,
    'not well:
But if 't be he I mean, he's very wild,
Addicted so and so'; and there put on him
What forgeries you please: marry, none so rank
As may dishonor him; take heed of that; 21
But, sir such wanton, wild, and usual slips
As are companions noted and most known
To youth and liberty.
REYNALDO.   As gaming, my lord? 24
POLONIUS. Ay, or drinking, fencing, swearing,
    Quarrelling, drabbing,—you may go so far.
REYNALDO. My lord, that would dishonor him.
POLONIUS. Faith, no, as you may season it in the
    charge.   28
You must not put another scandal on him,
That he is open to incontinency.
That's not my meaning; but breathe his faults
    so quaintly
That they may seem the taints of liberty, 32
The flash and outbreak of a fiery mind,
A savageness in unreclaimed blood,
Of general assault.
REYNALDO.   But, my good lord,—
POLONIUS. Wherefore should you do this?
REYNALDO.   Ay, my lord, 36
I would know that.
POLONIUS.   Marry, sir, here's my drift;
And I believe it is a fetch of warrant.
You laying these slight sullies on my son,

As 'twere a thing a little soil'd i' th'
    working,   40
Mark you,
Your party in converse, him you would sound,
Having ever seen in the prenominate crimes
The youth you breathe of guilty, be assur'd, 44
He closes with you in this consequence:
'Good sir,' or so, or 'friend,' or 'gentleman,'
According to the phrase or the addition
Of man and country—
REYNALDO.   Very good, my lord. 48
POLONIUS. And then, sir, does 'a this,—'a does,—
    what was
I about to say? By the mass I was about to say
    something. Where did I leave?
REYNALDO. At 'closes in the consequence,' 52
    At 'friend or so,' and 'gentleman.'
POLONIUS. At 'closes in the consequence'? Ay,
    marry;
He closes thus: 'I know the gentleman;
I saw him yesterday, or th' other day, 56
Or then, or then, with such or such; and, as you
    say,
There was 'a gaming, there o'ertook in 's rouse,
There falling out at tennis'; or perchance,
'I saw him enter such a house of sale,' 60
Videlicet, a brothel, or so forth.
See you now;
Your bait of falsehood takes this carp of truth;
And thus do we of wisdom and of reach, 64
With windlasses and with assays of bias,
By indirections find directions out.
So by my former lecture and advice
Shall you my son. You have me, have you
    not?   68
REYNALDO. My lord, I have.
POLONIUS.   God we wi' ye; fare ye
    well.
REYNALDO. Good my lord!
POLONIUS. Observe his inclination in yourself.
REYNALDO. I shall, my lord. 72
POLONIUS. And let him ply his music.
REYNALDO.   Well, my lord.

---

8. keep: live. **10. encompassment:** 'talking round' a subject. **question:** conversation. **12. particular demands:** concrete questions. **13. Take:** assume. **19. put on:** impute to. **20. forgeries:** invented tales. **rank:** excessive. **22. wanton:** unrestrained. **26. drabbing:** wenching. **28. season:** flavor. **charge:** accusation. **30. incontinency:** habitual loose behavior. **31. breathe . . . quaintly:** hint . . . cleverly. **32. taints of liberty:** blemishes due to high spirits. **34. savageness:** wildness. **unreclaimed:** untamed. **35. Of general assault:** to which all are liable. **38. fetch of warrant:** justifiable trick. **39. sullies:** blemishes.

43. prenominate: aforesaid. **45. closes . . . consequence:** confides in you as follows. **51. leave:** leave off. **58. o'ertook in 's rouse:** unable to hold his liquor. **61. *Videlicet:*** namely. **64. reach:** resourcefulness. **65. windlasses:** round-about ways. **assays of bias:** indirect approaches. **66. indirections:** devious courses. **directions:** the straight facts. **67. lecture:** instruction. **71. in yourself:** for yourself. **73. ply:** keep up.

POLONIUS. Farewell!   *[Exit Reynaldo.]*

[Enter Ophelia.]

              How now, Ophelia! what's
  the matter.
OPHELIA. O my lord, my lord! I have been so
  affrighted.
POLONIUS. With what, i' th' name of God?   76
OPHELIA. My lord, as I was sewing in my closet,
  Lord Hamlet, with his doublet all unbrac'd,
  No hat upon his head; his stockings foul'd,
  Ungarter'd, and down-gyved to his ankle;—   80
  Pale as his shirt, his knees knocking each other,
  And with a look so piteous in purport
  As if he had been loosed out of hell
  To speak of horrors, he comes before me.   84
POLONIUS. Mad for thy love?
OPHELIA.   My lord, I do not know;
  But truly I do fear it.
POLONIUS.   What said he?
OPHELIA. He took me by the wrist and held me hard,
  Then goes he to the length of all his arm,   88
  And, with his other hand thus o'er his brow,
  He falls to such perusal of my face
  As 'a would draw it. Long stay'd he so.
  At last, a little shaking of mine arm,   92
  And thrice his head thus waving up and down,
  He rais'd a sigh so piteous and profound
  As it did seem to shatter all his bulk
  And end his being. That done, he lets me go, 96
  And with his head over his shoulder turn'd,
  He seem'd to find his way without his eyes,
  For out o'doors he went without their help,
  And to the last bended their light on me.   100
POLONIUS. Come, go with me. I will go seek the
  king.
  This is the very ecstasy of love,
  Whose violent property fordoes itself
  And leads the will to desperate undertakings 104
  As oft as any passion under heaven
  That does afflict our natures. I am sorry.
  What! have you given him any hard words of late?
OPHELIA. No, my good lord; but, as you did
  command,   108
  I did repel his letters and denied
  His access to me.

POLONIUS.   That hath made him mad.
  I am sorry that with better heed and judgment
  I had not coted him. I fear'd he did but
    trifle,   112
  And meant to wrack thee, but beshrew my
    jealousy!
  By heaven, it is proper to our age
  To cast beyond ourselves in our opinions
  As it is common for the younger sort   116
  To lack discretion. Come, go we to the king.
  This must be known, which, being kept close,
    might move
  More grief to hide than hate to utter love.
  Come.   *[Exeunt.]*

SCENE II

The Lobby in the Castle

*[Flourish. Enter King and Queen, Rosencrantz and Guilden-
stern, cum aliis.]*

KING. Welcome, dear Rosencrantz and Guildenstern.
  Moreover that we much did long to see you,
  The need we have to use you did provoke
  Our hasty sending. Something have you heard 4
  Of Hamlet's transformation. So I call it,
  Sith nor th' exterior nor the inward man
  Resembles that it was. What it should be,
  More than his father's death, that thus hath put
    him   8
  So much from th' understanding of himself,
  I cannot dream of. I entreat you both,
  That being of so young days brought up with
    him,
  And since so neighbor'd to his youth and
    havior,   12
  That you vouchsafe your rest here in our court
  Some little time; so by your companies
  To draw him on to pleasures and to gather,
  So much as from occasion you may glean,   16
  Whether aught to us unknown afflicts him thus,
  That, open'd, lies within our remedy.

---

77. closet: sitting room. **78. doublet:** close-fitting coat. **unbrac'd:**
unfastened. **80. down-gyved:** hanging down like gyves or fetters.
90. perusal: scrutiny. **95. bulk:** frame. **102. ecstasy:**
madness. **103. property:** nature. **fordoes:** destroys.

112. coted: observed (obsolete form of 'quote'). **113. wrack:**
ruin. **beshrew:** curse. **jealousy:** suspicion, mistrust. **114. our age:**
us old folk. **115. cast . . . ourselves:** be over subtle.
11. of so young days: from such early youth. **12. neighbor'd
. . . havior:** near in age and occupation. **13. vouchsafe your rest:**
please to reside. **17. not in Folio. 18. open'd:** revealed.

QUEEN. Good gentlemen, he hath much talk'd of
you;
And sure I am two men there are not living　20
To whom he more adheres. If it will please you
To show us so much gentry and good will
As to expend your time with us awhile,
For the supply and profit of our hope,　24
Your visitation shall receive such thanks
As fits a king's remembrance.
ROSENCRANTZ. 　　　　　　Both your majesties
Might, by the sovereign power you have of us,
Put your dread pleasures more into command
Than to entreaty.
GUILDENSTERN. 　　　But we both obey,　29
And here give up ourselves in the full bent,
To lay our service freely at your feet
To be commanded.　32
KING. Thanks, Rosencrantz and gentle
Guildenstern.
QUEEN. Thanks, Guildenstern and gentle
Rosencrantz;
And I beseech you instantly to visit
My too much changed son. Go, some of you,　36
And bring these gentlemen where Hamlet is.
GUILDENSTERN. Heavens make our presence and
our practices
Pleasant and helpful to him!
QUEEN. 　　　　　　　　Ay, amen!

[Exeunt Rosencrantz and Guildenstern (attended).]

[Enter Polonius.]

POLONIUS. Th' ambassadors from Norway, my
good lord,　40
Are joyfully return'd.
KING. Thou still hast been the father of good news.
POLONIUS. Have I, my lord? Assure you, my good
liege,
I hold my duty as I hold my soul,　44
Both to my God and to my gracious king;
And I do think—or else this brain of mine
Hunts not the trail of policy so sure
As it hath us'd to do—that I have found　48
The very cause of Hamlet's lunacy.
KING. O speak of that! that do I long to hear.

POLONIUS. Give first admittance to th' ambassadors;
My news shall be the fruit to that great feast.　52
KING. Thyself do grace to them, and bring them in.

[Exit Polonius.]

He tells me, my dear Gertrude, he hath found
The head and source of all your son's
distemper.
QUEEN. I doubt it is no other but the main:　56
His father's death and our o'erhasty marriage.
KING. Well, we shall sift him.

[Enter Polonius, Voltimand, and Cornelius.]

　　　　　　　　　　Welcome, my good
friends!
Say, Voltimand, what from our brother
Norway?
VOLTIMAND. Most fair return of greetings and
desires.
Upon our first, he sent out to suppress
His nephew's levies, which to him appear'd
To be a preparation 'gainst the Polack;
But, better look'd into, he truly found　64
It was against your highness: whereat griev'd
That so his sickness, age, and impotence
Was falsely borne in hand, sends out arrests
On Fortinbras; which he in brief obeys,　68
Receives rebuke from Norway, and, in fine,
Makes vow before his uncle never more
To give th' assay of arms against your majesty.
Whereon old Norway, overcome with joy,　72
Gives him three thousand crowns in annual fee,
And his commission to employ those soldiers,
So levied as before, against the Polack;
With an entreaty, herein further shown,　76

[Giving a paper.]

That it might please you to give quiet pass
Through your dominions for this enterprise,
On such regards of safety and allowance
As therein are set down.
KING. 　　　　　　　It likes us well;　80
And at our more consider'd time we'll read,
Answer, and think upon this business.

---

22. **gentry:** courtesy.　24. **supply and profit:** aid and successful outcome.　26. **as . . . remembrance:** as is suitable to a king's gratitude.　30. **in the full bent:** to the utmost degree (an archery term).　47. **policy:** conduct of public affairs.

52. **fruit:** dessert.　56. **main:** chief point.　60. **desires:** good wishes.　67. **borne in hand:** deluded.　69. **in fine:** in conclusion.　71. **assay:** trial.　80. **likes:** pleases.　81. **consider'd:** fit for considering.

Meantime we thank you for your well-took
  labor.
Go to your rest; at night we'll feast together.
Most welcome home.

[Exeunt ambassadors.]

POLONIUS.   This business is well ended. 85
  My liege, and madam, to expostulate
  What majesty should be, what duty is,
  Why day is night, night night, and time is time,
  Were nothing but to waste night, day, and
    time.
  Therefore, since brevity is the soul of wit,
  And tediousness the limbs and outward
    flourishes,
  I will be brief. Your noble son is mad. 92
  Mad call I it; for to define true madness,
  What is 't but to be nothing else but mad?
  But let that go.
QUEEN.   More matter, with less art.
POLONIUS. Madam, I swear I use no art at all. 96
  That he is mad, 'tis true; 'tis true 'tis pity;
  And pity 'tis 'tis true: a foolish figure,
  But farewell it, for I will use no art.
  Mad let us grant him, then; and now remains
  That we find out the cause of this effect, 101
  Or rather say, the cause of this defect,
  For this effect defective comes by cause.
  Thus it remains, and the remainder thus.
  Perpend. 105
  I have a daughter (have while she is mine)
  Who, in her duty and obedience, mark,
  Hath given me this. Now, gather and surmise.

[Reads the letter.]

  "To the celestial, and my soul's idol, the most
    beautified Ophelia.—" 109
  That's an ill phrase, a vile phrase; 'beautified' is a
  vile phrase; but you shall hear. Thus:
  "In her excellent white bosom, these, &c.—" 112
QUEEN. Came this from Hamlet to her?
POLONIUS. Good madam, stay awhile; I will be
    faithful.
  "Doubt thou the stars are fire;
  Doubt that the sun doth move; 116

Doubt truth to be a liar;
But never doubt I love.
Oh dear Ophelia! I am ill at these numbers: I
  have not art to reckon my groans; but that I
  love thee best, O most best, believe it.
  Adieu.
Thine evermore, most dear lady, whilst this
  machine is to him,

                                  Hamlet."

This in obedience hath my daughter shown me,
And more above,—hath his solicitings,
As they fell out by time, by means, and place,
All given to mine ear.
KING.   But how hath she 128
  Receiv'd his love?
POLONIUS.   What do you think of me?
KING. As a man faithful and honorable.
POLONIUS. I would fain prove so. But what might
    you think,
  When I had seen this hot love on the
    wing,— 132
  As I perceiv'd it, (I must tell you that)
  Before my daughter told me,—what might you,
  Or my dear majesty, your queen here, think,
  If I had play'd the desk or table-book, 136
  Or given my heart a winking, mute and dumb,
  Or look'd upon this love with idle sight?
  What might you think? No, I went round to
    work,
  And my young mistress thus I did bespeak: 140
  'Lord Hamlet is a prince, out of thy star;
  This must not be:' and then I prescripts gave her,
  That she should lock herself from his resort,
  Admit no messengers, receive no tokens. 144
  Which done, she took the fruits of my advice;
  And he, repelled,—a short tale to make,—
  Fell into a sadness, thence into a fast,
  Thence to a watch, thence into a weakness, 148
  Thence to a lightness, and by this declension
  Into the madness wherein now he raves,
  And all we mourn for.

---

119. ill at: unskilled at making. **numbers:** verses. **120. reckon:**
number metrically, scan. **123. machine:** bodily frame. **126. more
above:** more too. **127. fell out:** occurred. **means:** opportunities of
access. **137. winking:** a short nap, i.e., allowed my heart to connive. **139. round:** straightforwardly. **140. bespeak:** address. **141. out of thy star:** above the position allotted thee by fortune. **142. prescripts:** positive orders. **148. watch:** state of
sleeplessness. **149. lightness:** lightheadedness. **declension:** downward course.

---

86. expostulate: set forth one's views. **90. wit:** judgment, understanding. **91. flourishes:** embellishments. **98. figure:** figure of
rhetoric. **105. Perpend:** consider. **109. beautified:** beautiful, or,
accomplished.

KING. Do you think 'tis this?

QUEEN. It may be, very like. 152

POLONIUS. Hath there been such a time,—I'd fain know that,—
That I have positively said, 'Tis so,'
When it prov'd otherwise?

KING. Not that I know.

POLONIUS. Take this from this, if this be otherwise. 156

[Pointing to his head and shoulder.]

If circumstances lead me, I will find
Where truth is hid, though it were hid indeed
Within the center.

KING. How may we try it further?

POLONIUS. You know sometimes he walks four hours together 160
Here in the lobby.

QUEEN. So he does indeed.

POLONIUS. At such a time I'll loose my daughter to him.
Be you and I behind an arras then.
Mark the encounter; if he love her not, 164
And be not from his reason fallen thereon,
Let me be no assistant for a state,
But keep a farm and carters.

KING. We will try it.

[Enter Hamlet reading a book.]

QUEEN. But look, where sadly the poor wretch comes reading. 168

POLONIUS. Away! I do beseech you, both away.
I'll board him presently. O, give me leave.

[Exeunt King and Queen.]

How does my good Lord Hamlet?

HAMLET. Well, God-a-mercy. 172

POLONIUS. Do you know me, my lord?

HAMLET. Excellent well. You are a fishmonger.

POLONIUS. Not I, my lord.

HAMLET. Then I would you were so honest a man. 176

POLONIUS. Honest, my lord?

HAMLET. Ay, sir; to be honest, as this world goes, is to be one man picked out of ten thousand.

POLONIUS. That's very true, my lord. 180

HAMLET. For if the sun breed maggots in a dead dog, being a god kissing carrion,—Have you a daughter?

POLONIUS. I have, my lord.

HAMLET. Let her not walk i' the sun. Conception is a blessing, but as your daughter may conceive, friend, look to 't. 186

POLONIUS. *[Aside.]* How say you by that? Still harping on my daughter. Yet he knew me not at first; 'a said I was a fishmonger. 'A is far gone; and truly in my youth I suffered much extremity for love, very near this. I'll speak to him again. What do you read, my lord? 192

HAMLET. Words, words, words.

POLONIUS. What is the matter, my lord?

HAMLET. Between who?

POLONIUS. I mean the matter that you read, my lord. 196

HAMLET. Slanders, sir; for the satirical rogue says here that old men have grey beards, that their faces are wrinkled, their eyes purging thick amber and plumtree gum, and that they have a plentiful lack of wit, together with most weak hams. All which, sir, though I most powerfully and potently believe, yet I hold it not honesty to have it thus set down; for yourself, sir, shall grow old as I am, if, like a crab, you could go backward. 205

POLONIUS. *[Aside.]* Though this be madness, yet there is method in 't. Will you walk out of the air, my lord?

HAMLET. Into my grave? 208

POLONIUS. Indeed, that's out of the air. *[Aside.]* How pregnant sometimes his replies are! a happiness that often madness hits on, which reason and sanity could not so prosperously be delivered of. I will leave him and suddenly contrive the means of meeting between him and my daughter. My honorable lord, I will most humbly take my leave of you. 215

HAMLET. You cannot take from me anything that I will more willingly part withal,—except my life, except my life, except my life.

POLONIUS. Fare you well, my lord. *[Going.]*

HAMLET. These tedious old fools!

---

159. **center:** middle point of the earth. 163. **arras:** hanging tapestry. 170. **board:** accost. **presently:** immediately.

194. **matter:** substance. 199. **purging:** discharging. 203. **honesty:** decency. 210. **pregnant:** full of meaning. **happiness:** appropriateness. 212. **prosperously:** successfully. 217. **withal:** with.

[Enter Guildenstern and Rosencrantz.]

POLONIUS. You go to seek the Lord Hamlet? There
    he is.

ROSENCRANTZ. *[To Polonius.]* God save you, sir!   222

[Exit Polonius.]

GUILDENSTERN. My honored lord!

ROSENCRANTZ. My most dear lord!

HAMLET. My excellent good friends! How dost
    thou, Guildenstern? Ah, Rosencrantz! Good
    lads, how do you both?   227

ROSENCRANTZ. As the indifferent children of the
    earth.

GUILDENSTERN. Happy in that we are not over
    happy; on Fortune's cap we are not the very
    button.

HAMLET. Nor the soles of her shoe?   231

ROSENCRANTZ. Neither, my lord.

HAMLET. Then you live about her waist, or in the
    middle of her favors?

GUILDENSTERN. Faith, her privates we.   235

HAMLET. In the secret parts of Fortune? O, most
    true; she is a strumpet. What news?

ROSENCRANTZ. None, my lord, but that the world's
    grown honest.   239

HAMLET. Then is doomsday near; but your news is
    not true. Let me question more in particular.
    What have you, my good friends, deserved at
    the hands of Fortune, that she sends you to
    prison hither?

GUILDENSTERN. Prison, my lord!   244

HAMLET. Denmark's a prison.

ROSENCRANTZ. Then is the world one.

HAMLET. A goodly one; in which there are many
    confines, wards, and dungeons, Denmark being
    one o' the worst.   249

ROSENCRANTZ. We think not so, my lord.

HAMLET. Why, then, 'tis none to you; for there is
    nothing either good or bad but thinking makes
    it so. To me it is a prison.   253

ROSENCRANTZ. Why, then your ambition makes it
    one; 'tis too narrow for your mind.

HAMLET. O God, I could be bounded in a nutshell,
    and count myself a king of infinite space, were it
    not that I have bad dreams.   258

GUILDENSTERN. Which dreams, indeed, are
    ambition, for the very substance of the

ambitious is merely the shadow of a
    dream.   261

HAMLET. A dream itself is but a shadow.

ROSENCRANTZ. Truly, and I hold ambition of so airy
    and light a quality that it is but a shadow's   264
    shadow.

HAMLET. Then are our beggars bodies, and our
    monarchs and outstretched heroes the beggars'
    shadows. Shall we to the court? for, by my fay, I
    cannot reason.

BOTH. We'll wait upon you.   268

HAMLET. No such matter. I will not sort you with
    the rest of my servants, for, to speak to you like
    an honest man, I am most dreadfully attended.
    But, in the beaten way of friendship, what make
    you at Elsinore?

ROSENCRANTZ. To visit you, my lord; no other
    occasion.   274

HAMLET. Beggar that I am, I am even poor in
    thanks, but I thank you: and sure, dear friends,
    my thanks are too dear a halfpenny. Were you
    not sent for? Is it your own inclining? Is it a free
    visitation? Come, come, deal justly with me:
    come, come; nay, speak.

GUILDENSTERN. What should we say my lord?   280

HAMLET. Why anything, but to the purpose. You
    were sent for; and there is a kind of confession in
    your looks which your modesties have not craft
    enough to color. I know the good kind and
    queen have sent for you.   285

ROSENCRANTZ. To what end, my lord?

HAMLET. That you must teach me. But let me
    conjure you, by the rights of our fellowship, by
    the consonancy of our youth, by the obligation
    of our ever-preserved love, and by what more
    dear a better proposer could charge you withal,
    be even and direct with me, whether you were
    sent for or no.   292

ROSENCRANTZ. *[Aside to Guildenstern.]* What say you?

HAMLET. Nay, then, I have an eye of you. If you
    love me, hold not off.

GUILDENSTERN. My lord, we were sent for.   296

HAMLET. I will tell you why; so shall my
    anticipation prevent your discovery, and your

---

264. quality: nature. **266. outstretched:** strutting. **267. fay:** faith. **reason:** argue. **268. wait upon:** attend. **269. sort:** class. **272. beaten:** well-worn, reliable. **278. free:** voluntary. **284. color:** disguise. **287. conjure:** adjure. **289. consonancy:** harmony. **290. better proposer:** more skillful exhorter. **292. even:** straightforward. **294. have an eye of you:** have an eye upon you. **298. prevent:** precede. **discovery:** disclosure.

---

228. indifferent: ordinary, average.

secrecy to the king and queen moult no feather. I have of late,—but wherefore I know not,—lost all my mirth, forgone all custom of exercises; and indeed it goes so heavily with my disposition that this goodly frame, the earth, seems to me a sterile promontory; this most excellent canopy, the air, look you, this brave o'erhanging firmament, this majestical roof fretted with golden fire, why, it appeareth nothing to me but a foul and pestilent congregation of vapors. What a piece of work is a man! How noble in reason! how infinite in faculties! in form and moving how express and admirable! in action 310
how like an angel! in apprehension how like a god! the beauty of the world, the paragon of animals. And yet to me what is this quintessence of dust? Man delights not me; no, nor woman neither, though by your smiling you seem to say so.

ROSENCRANTZ. My lord, there was no such stuff in my thoughts. 316

HAMLET. Why did ye laugh, then, when I said 'man delights not me'?

ROSENCRANTZ. To think, my lord, if you delight not in man, what lenten entertainment the players shall receive from you. We coted them on the way; and hither are they coming, to offer you service. 322

HAMLET. He that plays the king shall be welcome, his majesty shall have tribute of me; the adventurous knight shall use his foil and target; the lover shall not sigh gratis; the humorous man shall end his part in peace; the clown shall make those laugh whose lungs are tickle o' the sere; and the lady shall say her mind freely, or the blank verse shall halt for 't. What players are they? 330

ROSENCRANTZ. Even those you were wont to take delight in, the tragedians of the city.

HAMLET. How chances it they travel? Their residence, both in reputation and profit, was better both ways.

ROSENCRANTZ. I think their inhibition comes by the means of the late innovation. 336

HAMLET. Do they hold the same estimation they did when I was in the city? Are they so followed?

ROSENCRANTZ. No, indeed are they not. 339

HAMLET. How comes it? Do they grow rusty?

ROSENCRANTZ. Nay, their endeavor keeps in the wonted pace: but there is, sir, an aery of children, little eyases, that cry out on the top of question, and are most tyrannically clapped for 't. These are now the fashion, and so berattle the common stages (so they call them) that many wearing rapiers are afraid of goose-quills, and dare scarce come thither. 347

HAMLET. What, are they children? who maintains 'em? how are they escoted? Will they pursue the quality no longer than they can sing? Will they not say afterwards, if they should grow themselves to common players (as it is most like, if their means are no better) their writers do them wrong to make them exclaim against their own succession? 354

ROSENCRANTZ. Faith, there has been much to-do on both sides, and the nation holds it no sin to tarre them to controversy. There was for a while no money bid for argument, unless the poet and the player went to cuffs in the question. 359

HAMLET. Is 't possible?

GUILDENSTERN. O, there has been much throwing about of brains.

HAMLET. Do the boys carry it away?

ROSENCRANTZ. Ay, that they do, my lord—Hercules and his load too. 365

HAMLET. It is not very strange; for my uncle is king of Denmark, and those that would make mouths at him while my father lived give twenty, forty, fifty, a hundred ducats apiece for his picture in little. 'Sblood, there is something

---

305. brave: splendid. 306. fretted: adorned. 309. faculties: powers. express: well-modeled. 311. apprehension: understanding. 316. stuff: matter. 320. lenten: meagre. 321. coted: passed. 325. foil and target: sword and shield. 326. humorous man: actor of whimsical characters. 328. tickle o' the sere: yield easily to any impulse. 330. halt: limp. 333. residence: remaining at headquarters.

335. inhibition: hindrance. 337. estimation: reputation. 342. aery: nest. 343. eyases: young hawks. cry . . . question: deal pungently with the latest gossip. 344. tyrannically: outrageously. 345. berattle: decry. 346. many wearing rapiers: many men of quality. afraid of goose-quills: afraid of being satirized. 349. escoted: maintained. 350. quality: profession. 352. common players: professional players. 354. succession: future, inheritance. 357. tarre: incite. 358. argument: subject-matter, plot. 359. cuffs: blows. 363. carry it away: carry the day. 367. mouths: grimaces. 370. in little: in a miniature. 'Sblood: God's blood.

in this more than natural, if philosophy could find it out. *[A flourish.]*

GUILDENSTERN. There are the players. 372

HAMLET. Gentlemen, you are welcome to Elsinore. Your hands! come then; th' appurtenance of welcome is fashion and ceremony. Let me comply with you in this garb, lest my extent to the players (which, I tell you, must show fairly outwards) should more appear like entertainment than yours. You are welcome; but my uncle-father and aunt-mother are deceived.

GUILDENSTERN. In what, my dear lord? 380

HAMLET. I am but mad north-north-west. When the wind is southerly, I know a hawk from a handsaw.

[Enter Polonius.]

POLONIUS. Well be with you, gentlemen! 383

HAMLET. Hark you, Guildenstern, and you too! at each ear a hearer. That great baby you see there is not yet out of his swaddling-clouts.

ROSENCRANTZ. Happily he is the second time come to them, for they say an old man is twice a child. 388

HAMLET. I will prophesy he comes to tell me of the players; mark it.—You say right, sir; o' Monday morning. 'Twas then indeed.

POLONIUS. My lord, I have news to tell you.

HAMLET. My lord, I have news to tell you. When Roscius was an actor in Rome,— 394

POLONIUS. The actors are come hither, my lord.

HAMLET. Buzz, buzz!

POLONIUS. Upon my honor,—

HAMLET.

Then came each actor on his ass,—

POLONIUS. The best actors in the world, either for tragedy, comedy, history, pastoral, pastoral-comical, historical-pastoral, (tragical-historical, tragical-comical-historical-pastoral), scene individable, or poem unlimited: Seneca cannot be too heavy, nor Plautus too light.

For the law of writ and the liberty, these are the only men. 405

HAMLET. O Jephthah, judge of Israel, what a treasure hadst thou!

POLONIUS. What a treasure had he, my lord?

HAMLET. Why,

One fair daughter and no more,
The which he loved passing well.

POLONIUS. *[Aside.]* Still on my daughter. 412

HAMLET. Am I not i' in right, old Jephthah?

POLONIUS. If you call me Jephthah, my lord, I have a daughter that I love passing well.

HAMLET. Nay, that follows not. 416

POLONIUS. What follows, then, my lord?

HAMLET. Why,

As by lot, God wot.

And then, you know, 420

It came to pass, as most like it was.—

The first row of the pious chanson will show you more, for look where my abridgment comes. 423

[Enter four or five Players.]

You are welcome, masters; welcome, all. I am glad to see thee well. Welcome, good friends. O, my old friend? Why thy face is valanced since I saw thee last: com'st thou to beard me in Denmark? What, my young lady and mistress! By 'r lady, your ladyship is nearer to heaven than when I saw you last by the altitude of a chopine. Pray God, your voice, like a piece of uncurrent gold, be not cracked within the ring. Masters, you are all welcome. We'll e'en to 't like French falconers, fly at anything we see: we'll have a speech straight. Come, give us a taste of your quality; come, a passionate speech. 435

PLAYER. What speech, my good lord?

374. appurtenance: proper accompaniment. **375. comply:** observe the formalities of courtesy. **376. garb:** manner. **extent:** showing of kindness. **378. entertainment:** hospitality. **386. swaddling-clouts:** bandages in which newborn children were wrapped. **396. Buzz, buzz:** an exclamation of contempt.

406. Jephthah: hero of an old ballad quoted below. **421. 'as most like it was':** as was most probable. **422. row:** stanza, or column of print. **chanson:** song. **423. abridgment:** something to cut short my talk. **426. valanced:** 'curtained,' with a beard. **430. chopine:** a Venetian raised shoe worn by women. **431. uncurrent:** not passable as lawful coinage. **434. straight:** immediately.

HAMLET. I heard thee speak me a speech once,
but it was never acted; or, if it was, not above
once; for the play, I remember, pleased not
the million; 'twas caviary to the general: but it
was (as I received it, and others, whose
judgments in such matters cried in the top of
mine) an excellent play, well digested in the
scenes, set down with as much modesty as
cunning. I remember one said there were no
sallets in the lines to make the matter savory,
nor no matter in the phrase that might indict
the author of affection; but called it an honest
method, as wholesome as sweet, and by very
much more handsome than fine. One speech
in 't I chiefly loved; 'twas Æneas' tale to
Dido; and thereabout of it especially, where
he speaks of Priam's daughter. If it live in
your memory, begin at this line: let me see, let
me see:—   452

"The rugged Pyrrhus, like th' Hyrcanian
beast,—"

'Tis not so. It begins with Pyrrhus:—

"The rugged Pyrrhus, he, whose sable arms,
Black as his purpose, did the night resemble
When he lay couched in the ominous horse,
Hath now this dread and black complexion
    smear'd
With heraldry more dismal. Head to foot
Now is he total gules, horridly trick'd   460
With blood of fathers, mothers, daughters,
    sons,
Bak'd and impasted with the parching streets,
That lend a tyrannous and a damned light
To their lords' murther. Roasted in wrath and
    fire,
And thus o'er-sized with coagulate gore,
With eyes like carbuncles, the hellish Pyrrhus
Old grandsire Priam seeks."

So proceed you.   468

POLONIUS. 'Fore God, my lord, well spoken! with
good accent and good discretion.
PLAYER.   "Anon, he finds him
Striking too short at Greeks; his antique sword,
Rebellious to his arm, lies where it falls,   472
Repugnant to command. Unequal match'd,
Pyrrhus at Priam drives, in rage strikes wide;
But with the whiff and wind of his fell sword
Th' unnerved father falls. Then senseless
    Ilium,   476
Seeming to feel this blow, with flaming top
Stoops to his base, and with a hideous crash
Takes prisoner Pyrrhus' ear: for lo, his sword,
Which was declining on the milky head   480
Of reverend Priam, seem'd i' th' air to stick.
So as a painted tyrant Pyrrhus stood,
And like a neutral to his will and matter,
Did nothing.   484
But as we often see against some storm
A silence in the heavens, the rack stand still,
The bold winds speechless and the orb below
As hush as death, anon the dreadful thunder 488
Doth rend the region; so, after Pyrrhus' pause,
A roused vengeance sets him new a-work;
And never did the Cyclops' hammers fall
On Mars's armor, forg'd for proof eterne,   492
With less remorse than Pyrrhus' bleeding sword
Now falls on Priam.
Out, out, thou strumpet Fortune! All you gods,
In general synod take away her power,   496
Break all the spokes and fellies from her wheel,
And bowl the round nave down the hill of
    heaven
As low as to the fiends!"
POLONIUS. This is too long.   500
HAMLET. It shall to the barber's, with your beard.
Prithee, say on: he's for a jig or a tale of
bawdry, or he sleeps. Say on; come to Hecuba.
PLAYER. But who, O who, had seen the mobled
queen—
HAMLET. 'The mobled queen'?   505

---

442. **cried in the top of:** spoke with a louder voice of authority than. 443. **digested:** arranged. 444. **modesty:** moderation. **cunning:** skill in technique. 447. **indict:** convict. **affection:** affectation. 449. **fine:** elaborately fashioned. 460. **total gules:** red all over. **trick'd:** spotted. 462. **impasted:** made into a crust. 465. **o'er-sized:** covered with something like size, a kind of glue. 466. **carbuncles:** glittering red stones, rubies.

473. **Repugnant to:** resisting. 475. **fell:** cruel. 476. **senseless:** incapable of feeling. 482. **painted tyrant:** picture of an oppressor. 483. **a neutral:** one indifferent. **matter:** task. 485. **against:** just before. 486. **rack:** mass of cloud. 488. **anon:** presently. 489. **region:** the air. 491. **Cyclops':** Vulcan's workmen's. 492. **proof eterne:** eternal impenetrability. 496. **synod:** assembly. 497. **fellies:** the pieces of wood of which the circumference is made. 498. **nave:** hub. 502. **jig:** lively dance, often accompanied by coarse comic verses or dialogue. 504. **mobled:** muffled.

POLONIUS. That's good; 'mobled queen' is good.

PLAYER. Run barefoot up and down, threat'ning the
flames   507
With bisson rheum,—a clout upon that head
Where late the diadem stood, and for a robe,
About her lank and all o'er-teemed loins,
A blanket, in the alarm of fear caught up,—   511
Who this had seen, with tongue in venom
steep'd,
'Gainst Fortune's state would treason have
pronounc'd.
But if the gods themselves did see her then,
When she saw Pyrrhus make malicious sport
In mincing with his sword her husband's
limbs,
The instant burst of clamor that she made
(Unless things mortal move them not at all)
Would have made milch the burning eyes of
heaven   519
And passion in the gods.

POLONIUS. Look! wh'er he has not turned his
color and has tears in 's eyes. Prithee, no
more.   522
HAMLET. 'Tis well. I'll have thee speak out the rest
of this soon. Good my lord, will you see the
players well bestowed? Do you hear, let them
be well used, for they are the abstract and brief
chronicles of the time. After your death you
were better have a bad epitaph than their ill
report while you live.
POLONIUS. My lord, I will use them according to
their desert.   530
HAMLET. God's bodkin, man, much better! Use
every man after his desert, and who shall 'scape
whipping? Use them after your own honor and
dignity: the less they deserve,
the more merits is in your bounty. Take them
in.   535
POLONIUS. Come, sirs.
HAMLET. Follow him, friends: we'll hear a play
tomorrow. *[Exit Polonius (with all the Players but the
First).]* Dost thou hear me, old friend; can you
play the Murther of Gonzago?   540
PLAYER. Ay, my lord.

HAMLET. We'll ha 't to-morrow nigh
for a need, study a speech of som
sixteen lines, which I would set d
in 't, could you not?
PLAYER. Ay, my lord.
HAMLET. Very well. Follow that lord, and look you
mock him not. *[Exit Player. To Rosencrantz and
Guildenstern.]* My good friends, I'll leave you till
night. You are welcome to Elsinore.   550
ROSENCRANTZ. Good my lord!
HAMLET. Ay, so! Goodbye to you!

[Exeunt Rosencrantz and Guildenstern. Manet Hamlet.]

Now I am alone.
O what a rogue and peasant slave am I!
Is it not monstrous that this player here,   554
But in a fiction, in a dream of passion,
Could force his soul so to his own conceit
That from her working all the visage wann'd,
Tears in his eyes, distraction in 's aspect,   558
A broken voice, and his whole function suiting
With forms to his conceit? and all for nothing!
For Hecuba?
What's Hecuba to him or he to Hecuba,   562
That he should weep for her? What would he do
Had he the motive and the cue for passion
That I have? He would drown the stage with
tears,
And cleave the general ear with horrid
speech,   566
Make mad the guilty and appal the free,   *guiltless*
Confound the ignorant, and amaze indeed
The very faculties of eyes and ears.
Yet I,   *dull spirited*   *mope about* 570
A dull and muddy-mettled rascal, peak,
Like John-a-dreams, unpregnant of my cause,
And can say nothing; no, not for a king,
Upon whose property and most dear life   574
A damn'd defeat was made. Am I a coward?
Who calls me villain? breaks my pate across?
Plucks off my beard and blows it in my face?   577

---

543. **for a need:** in case of necessity.   552. **s.d. Manet:** remains on
the stage.   553. **peasant:** base.   556. **conceit:** imagination.   557.
wann'd: grew pale.   559. **function:** action of the body. **suiting:** fitting.   560. **forms:** bodily expression.   566. **horrid:** horrible.   567. **free:** free from offence, guiltless.   571. **muddy-mettled:**
dull-spirited. **peak:** mope about.   572. **John-a-dreams:** dreamy fellow. **unpregnant of:** not quickened by.   575. **defeat:**
destruction.

---

508. **bisson rheum:** blinding tears. **clout:** piece of cloth.   510.
o'er-teemed: exhausted by excessive child-bearing.   519. **milch:**
milky, moist.   521. **turned . . . color:** grown pale.   525. **bestowed:** lodged.   526. **abstract:** summary.

Tweaks me by the nose? gives me the lie i' th'
   throat,
As deep as to the lungs? Who does me this, ha?
'Swounds, I should take it, for it cannot be
But I am pigeon-liver'd, and lack gall
To make oppression bitter, or ere this   582
I should ha' fatted all the region kites
With this slave's offal. Bloody, bawdy villain!
Remorseless, treacherous, lecherous, kindless
   villain!   585
(O! vengeance!)
Why, what an ass am I! This is most brave
That I, the son of a dear murthered,
Prompted to my revenge by heaven and hell,
Must like a whore unpack my heart with words,
And fall a-cursing like a very drab,   591
A scullion! Fie upon it, foh!
About, my brains!—Hum,—. I have heard,
That guilty creatures sitting at a play   594

Have by the very cunning of the scene
Been struck so to the soul that presently
They have proclaim'd their malefactions;
For murther, though it have no tongue, will
   speak
With most miraculous organ. I'll have these
   players
Play something like the murther of my father
Before mine uncle. I'll observe his looks,
I'll tent him to the quick. If 'a do blench,   602
I know my course. The spirit that I have seen
May be a de'il, and the de'il hath power
T' assume a pleasing shape;—yea, and perhaps
Out of my weakness and my melancholy   606
(As he is very potent with such spirits)
Abuses me to damn me. I'll have grounds
More relative than this. The play's the thing 609
Wherein I'll catch the conscience of the king.
   [Exit.]

Act III

SCENE I

A Room in the Castle

*[Enter King, Queen, Polonius, Ophelia, Rosencrantz,
Guildenstern, and Lords.]*

KING. And can you by no drift of conference
   Get from him why he puts on this confusion,
   Grating so harshly all his days of quiet
   With turbulent and dangerous lunacy?   4
ROSENCRANTZ. He does confess he feels himself
   distracted,
   But from what cause 'a will by no means speak.
GUILDENSTERN. Nor do we find him forward to be
   sounded,
   But with a crafty madness keeps aloof,   8

When we would bring him on to some confession
   Of his true state.
QUEEN.   Did he receive you well?
ROSENCRANTZ. Most like a gentleman.
GUILDENSTERN. But with much forcing of his
   disposition.   12
ROSENCRANTZ. Niggard of question, but of our
   demands
   Most free in his reply.
QUEEN.   Did you assay him
   To any pastime?
ROSENCRANTZ. Madam, it so fell out that certain
   players   16
   We o'er-raught on the way; of these we told him,
   And there did seem in him a kind of joy
   To hear of it. They are about the court,
   And, as I think, they have already order   20
   This night to play before him.
POLONIUS.   'Tis most true;
   And he beseech'd me to entreat your majesties
   To hear and see the matter.

580. **'Swounds:** God's wounds.   **581. But:** but that. **pigeon-liver'd:**
meek.   **582. make oppression bitter:** make me feel the bitterness of
oppression.   **583. region kites:** vultures of the air.   **585. kindless:**
unnatural.   **592. scullion:** the lowest household servant.   **593.
About, my brains:** let me think less wildly.
1. drift of conference: turn of the conversation.   **2. confusion:** distraction.   **3. Grating:** harassing.   **7. forward:** ready, disposed.

602. tent: probe. **blench:** start aside.   **604. de'il:** devil.   **609. relative:** relevant, to the purpose.
12. forcing of his disposition: constraint.   **13. Niggard of question:** sparing of conversation.   **14. assay:** tempt.   **17. o'er-raught:**
overtook.

KING. With all my heart; and it doth much content me   24
    To hear him so inclin'd.
    Good gentlemen, give him a further edge,
    And drive his purpose into these delights.
ROSENCRANTZ. We shall, my lord.

[Exeunt Rosencrantz and Guildenstern.]

KING.   Sweet Gertrude, leave us too;
    For we have closely sent for Hamlet hither,   29
    That he, as 'twere by accident, may here
    Affront Ophelia.
    Her father and myself (lawful espials)   32
    Will so bestow ourselves that, seeing unseen.
    We may of their encounter frankly judge,
    And gather by him, as he is behav'd,
    If 't be th' affliction of his love or no   36
    That thus he suffers for.
QUEEN.   I shall obey you.
    And for your part, Ophelia, I do wish
    That your good beauties be the happy cause
    Of Hamlet's wildness; so shall I hope your virtues   40
    Will bring him to his wonted way again,
    To both your honors.
OPHELIA.   Madam, I wish it may.

[Exit Queen.]

POLONIUS. Ophelia, walk you here. Gracious, so please you,
    We will bestow ourselves. *[To Ophelia.]* Read on this book,   44
    That show of such an exercise may color
    Your loneliness. We are oft to blame in this;
    'Tis too much prov'd that with devotion's visage
    And pious action we do sugar o'er   48
    The devil himself.
KING. *[Aside.]*   O 'tis too true!
    How smart a lash that speech doth give my conscience!
    The harlot's cheek, beautied with plastering art,
    Is not more ugly to the thing that helps it   52

Than is my deed to my most painted word.
    O heavy burthen!
POLONIUS. I hear him coming; let's withdraw, my lord.

[Exeunt King and Polonius.]

[Enter Hamlet.]

HAMLET. To be, or not to be, that is the question: 56
    Whether 'tis nobler in the mind to suffer
    The slings and arrows of outrageous fortune,
    Or to take arms against a sea of troubles
    And by opposing end them. To die: to sleep.   60
    No more; and by a sleep to say we end
    The heart-ache and the thousand natural shocks,
    That flesh is heir to: 'tis a consummation
    Devoutly to be wish'd. To die: to sleep.   64
    To sleep? perchance to dream. Ay, there's the rub;
    For in that sleep of death what dreams may come,
    When we have shuffled off this mortal coil,
    Must give us pause. There's the respect   68
    That makes calamity of so long life;
    For who would bear the whips and scorns of time,
    Th' oppressor's wrong, the proud man's contumely,
    The pangs of dispriz'd love, the law's delay,   72
    The insolence of office, and the spurns
    That patient merit of th' unworthy takes,
    When he himself might his quietus make
    With a bare bodkin? Who would fardels bear, 76
    To grunt and sweat under a weary life,
    But that the dread of something after death,
    The undiscover'd country form whose bourn
    No traveller returns, puzzles the will,   80
    And makes us rather bear those ills we have
    Than fly to others that we know not of?
    Thus conscience does make cowards of us all,
    And thus the native hue of resolution   84
    Is sicklied o'er with the pale cast of thought,
    And enterprises of great pitch and moment

---

26. edge: incitement. **29. closely:** privately. **31. Affront:** meet. **32. espials:** spies. **34. frankly:** freely. **40 wildness:** madness. **43. Gracious . . . you:** if it please your Grace. **45. exercise:** religious devotion. **47. too much prov'd:** found by too frequent experience. **52. to:** in comparison with. **the thing:** the beautifying cosmetic.

65. rub: obstacle. **67. shuffled off:** sloughed off. **mortal coil:** turmoil of mortal life. **68. give us pause:** cause us to hesitate. **respect:** consideration. **72. dispriz'd:** held in contempt. **73. office:** people holding official position. **spurns:** insults. **75. quietus:** release from life. **76. fardels:** burdens. **79. bourn:** boundary. **80. puzzles:** frustrates. **83. conscience:** the ability to think. **84. native hue:** healthy complexion. **85. cast:** tinge. **86. pitch and moment:** elevation and importance.

With this regard their currents turn awry,
And lose the name of action.—Soft you
  now!   88
The fair Ophelia! Nymph, in thy orisons
Be all my sins remember'd.
OPHELIA.   Good my lord,
How does your honor for this many a day?
HAMLET. I humbly thank you; well, well, well.   92
OPHELIA. My lord, I have remembrances of yours,
That I have long to re-deliver;
I pray you now, receive them.
HAMLET.   No, not I.
I never gave you aught.   96
OPHELIA. My honor'd lord, you know right well
  you did;
And, with them, words of so sweet breath
  compos'd
As made the things more rich. Their perfume
  lost,
Take these again, for to the noble mind   100
Rich gifts wax poor when givers prove unkind.
There, my lord.
HAMLET. Ha, ha! are you honest?
OPHELIA. My lord!   104
HAMLET. Are you fair?
OPHELIA. What means your lordship?
HAMLET. That if you be honest and fair, your
  honesty should admit no discourse to your
  beauty.   108
OPHELIA. Could beauty, my lord, have better
  commerce than with honesty?
HAMLET. Ay, truly; for the power of beauty will
  sooner transform honesty from what it is to a
  bawd than the force of honesty can translate
  beauty into his likeness. This was sometimes a
  paradox, but now the time gives it proof. I did
  love you once.   115
OPHELIA. Indeed, my lord, you made me believe
  so.
HAMLET. You should not have believed me, for
  virtue cannot so inoculate our old stock but we
  shall relish of it. I loved you not.
OPHELIA. I was the more deceived.   120
HAMLET. Get thee to a nunnery. Why wouldst
  thou be a breeder of sinners? I am myself

indifferent honest, but yet I could accuse me
of such things that it were better my mother
had not borne me. I am very proud,
revengeful, ambitious, with more offences at
my beck than I have thoughts to put them in,
imagination to give them shape, or time to act
them in. What should such fellows as I do
crawling between earth and heaven? We are
arrant knaves all; believe none of us. Go thy
ways to a nunnery.—Where's your father?   131
OPHELIA. At home, my lord.
HAMLET. Let the doors be shut upon him, that he
  may play the fool nowhere but in 's own house.
  Farewell.
OPHELIA. O help him, you sweet heavens!   136
HAMLET. If thou dost marry, I'll give thee this
  plague for thy dowry: be thou as chaste as ice,
  as pure as snow, thou shalt not escape calumny.
  Get thee to a nunnery. Go; farewell. Or if thou
  wilt needs marry, marry a fool; for wise men
  know well enough what monsters you make of
  them. To a nunnery, go, and quickly too.
  Farewell.   143
OPHELIA. O heavenly powers, restore him!
HAMLET. I have heard of your paintings too, well
  enough. God hath given you one face, and
  you make yourselves another. You jig, you
  amble, and you lisp. You nickname God's
  creatures, and make your wantonness your
  ignorance. Go to, I'll no more on 't; it hath
  made me mad. I say, we will have no mo
  marriage. Those that are married already, all
  but one, shall live; the rest shall keep as they
  are. To a nunnery, go.

[Exit Hamlet.]

OPHELIA. O what a noble mind is here o'er-
  thrown!   154
The courtier's soldier's, scholar's, eye, tongue,
  sword;
Th' expectancy and rose of the fair state,
The glass of fashion and the mould of form,
Th' observ'd of all observers, quite, quite
  down!

---

87. regard: consideration. **currents:** courses. **89. orisons:** prayers. **91. for this many a day:** all this long time. **103. honest:** sincere. **107. honest:** here in a special sense of 'chaste'. **110. commerce:** intercourse. **115. paradox:** absurdity. **time:** present age. **118. inoculate:** engraft. **119. relish:** taste.

122. indifferent: tolerably. **126. beck:** command. **145. your paintings:** i.e., that women paint their faces. **148. nickname:** travesty. **149–150. make your wantonness your ignorance:** affect ignorance as a mask for wantonness. **150. on 't:** of it. **151. mo:** more. **156. expectancy and rose:** hope and pride. **157. glass:** mirror. **mould:** model.

And I, of ladies most deject and wretched,   159
That suck'd the honey of his music vows,
Now see that noble and most sovereign reason,
Like sweet bells jangled, out of tune and harsh;
That unmatch'd form and feature of blown
    youth   163
Blasted with ecstasy. O woe is me,
T' have seen what I have seen, see what I see!

[Enter King and Polonius.]

KING. Love! his affections do not that way tend;
    Nor what he spake, though it lack'd form a
      little,   167
    Was not like madness. There's something in his
      soul
    O'er which his melancholy sits on brood,
    And I do doubt, the hatch and the disclose
    Will be some danger; which for to prevent,   171
    I have in quick determination
    Thus set it down: he shall with speed to England
    For the demand of our neglected tribute.
    Haply the seas and countries different   175
    With variable objects shall expel
    This something-settled matter in his heart,
    Whereon his brain's still-beating puts him thus
    From fashion of himself. What think you on 't?
POLONIUS. It shall do well: but yet do I believe   180
    The origin and commencement of his grief
    Sprung from neglected love. How now,
      Ophelia!
    You need not tell what Lord Hamlet said;
    We heard it all. My lord, do as you please;   184
    But if you hold it fit, after the play
    Let his queen mother all alone entreat him
    To show his grief. Let her be round with
      him.   187
    And I'll be plac'd (so please you) in the ear
    Of all their conference. If she find him not,
    To England send him, or confine him where
    Your wisdom best shall think.
KING.   It shall be so.
    Madness in great ones must not unwatch'd go.

[Exeunt.]

---

161. **sovereign:** supreme.   163. **feature:** proportion of the whole body. **blown:** full-blown.   164. **Blasted:** withered.   170. **disclose:** opening of the shell, coming to life.   176. **variable objects:** variety of interests.   177. **something-settled:** somewhat settled.   178. **still-beating:** constant hammering.   179. **fashion of himself:** his ordinary manner.   189. **find:** see through, interpret.

SCENE II

A Hall in the Castle

[Enter Hamlet and three of the Players.]

HAMLET. Speak the speech, I pray you, as I
    pronounced it to you, trippingly on the tongue;
    but if you mouth it, as many of our players do, I
    had as lief the town-crier spoke my lines. Nor do
    not saw the air too much with your hand, thus;
    but use all gently, for in the very torrent,
    tempest, and (as I may say) whirlwind of your
    passion, you must acquire and beget a
    temperance that may give it smoothness. O it
    offends me to the soul to hear a robustious
    periwig-pated fellow tear a passion to tatters, to
    very rags, to split the ears of the groundlings,
    who for the most part are capable of nothing
    but inexplicable dumb-shows and noise. I would
    have such a fellow whipped for o'er-doing
    Termagant. It out-herods Herod: pray you,
    avoid it.   15
PLAYER. I warrant your honor.
HAMLET. Be not too tame neither, but let your
    own discretion be your tutor. Suit the action to
    the word, the word to the action, with this
    special observance, that you o'erstep not the
    modesty of nature; for anything so overdone is
    from the purpose of playing, whose end, both
    at the first and now, was and is to hold, as
    'twere, the mirror up to nature, to show virtue
    her own feature, scorn her own image, and the
    very age and body of the time his form and
    pressure. Now this overdone, or come tardy
    off, though it makes the unskilful laugh, cannot
    but make the judicious grieve, the censure of
    the which one must in your allowance
    o'erweigh a whole theater of others. O there be
    players that I have seen play and heard others
    praise, and that highly (not to speak it

---

2. **trippingly:** rapidly, but with neat articulation.   3. **mouth:** speak loudly with false emphasis and indistinctness.   8. **acquire and beget:** achieve yourself and inspire in your hearers. **temperance:** moderation.   10. **robustious:** boisterous. **periwig-pated:** wearing a wig.   13. **capable of:** able to enjoy.   21. **from:** alien to.   25–26. **very age . . . pressure:** even the contemporary and actual quality of the present time.   26. **pressure:** impressed character, stamp.   27. **come tardy off:** inadequately done.   29. **the which one:** one of whom.   30. **allowance:** estimation.

profanely) that, neither having the accent of
Christians nor the gait of Christian, pagan, nor
man, have so strutted and bellowed that I have
thought some of nature's journeymen had
made men and not made them well, they
imitated humanity so abominably.

PLAYER. I hope we have reformed that indifferently
with us, sir.　　　　　　　　　　　　　　　38

HAMLET. O reform it altogether. And let those that
play your clowns speak no more than is set
down for them; for there be of them that will
themselves laugh, to set on some quantity of
barren spectators to laugh too, though in the
mean time some necessary question of the play
be then to be considered. That's villainous, and
shows a most pitiful ambition in the fool that
uses it. Go, make you ready.

[Exeunt Players.]

[Enter Polonius, Guildenstern, and Rosencrantz.]

How now, my lord? will the king hear this piece
of work?

POLONIUS. And the queen too, and that
presently.　　　　　　　　　　　　　　　48

HAMLET. Bid the players make haste. *[Exit Polonius.]*
Will you two help to hasten them?

ROSENCRANTZ. Ay, my lord.　　　　　　　51

[Exeunt they two.]

HAMLET. What, ho! Horatio!

[Enter Horatio.]

HORATIO. Here, sweet lord, at your service.

HAMLET. Horatio, thou art e'en as just a man
As e'er my conversation cop'd withal.　　　55

HORATIO. O, my dear lord,—

HAMLET.　　　　　　　　Nay, do not think I
flatter;

For what advancement may I hope from thee,
That no revénue hast but thy good spirits
To feed and clothe thee? Why should the poor
be flatter'd?　　　　　　　　　　　　　59

No, let the candied tongue lick ábsurd pomp,
And crook the pregnant hinges of the knee
Where thrift may follow fawning. Dost thou
hear?
Since my dear soul was mistress of her choice
And could of men distinguish, her election　64
Hath seal'd thee for herself; for thou hast been
As one, in suffering all, that suffers nothing,
A man that fortune's buffets and rewards　67
Hast ta'en with equal thanks; and bless'd are
those
Whose blood and judgment are so well
co-mingled
That they are not a pipe for fortune's finger
To sound what stop she please. Give me that
man　　　　　　　　　　　　　　　71
That is not passion's slave, and I will wear him
In my heart's core, ay, in my heart of heart,
As I do thee. Something too much of this.
There is a play to-night before the king.　75
One scene of it comes near the circumstance
Which I have told thee of my father's death.
I prithee, when thou seest that act afoot,
Even with the very comment of thy soul　79
Observe my uncle. If his occulted guilt
Do not itself unkennel in one speech,
It is a damned ghost that we have seen,
And my imaginations are as foul　　　　83
As Vulcan's stithy. Give him heedful note,
For I mine eyes will rivet to his face,
And after we will both our judgments join
In censure of his seeming.

HORATIO.　　　　　　　　Well, my lord.　87
If 'a steal aught the whilst this play is playing,
And 'scape detecting, I will pay the theft.

HAMLET. They are coming to the play. I must be
idle.
Get you a place.　　　　　　　　　　91

*[Enter King, Queen, Polonius, Ophelia, Rosencrantz,
Guildenstern, and other Lords attendant, with his Guard
carrying torches. Danish March. Sound a Flourish.]*

---

35. **journeymen:** laborers not yet master of their trade.　**41. there
be of them:** there are some.　**42. barren:** barren of wit.　**54. just:**
fair-minded, righteous.　**55. cop'd withal:** came in contact with.

60. **candied:** flattering. **lick:** pay court to (like a dog). **absurd:** silly.
61. **pregnant hinges.** easily bent joints.　**62. thrift:** profit.　**64.
election:** choice.　**65. seal'd:** registered unchangeably.　**69. blood:**
passions.　**71. stop:** a hole in wind instruments for controlling the
sound.　**79. very comment:** most intense observation.　**80. occulted:** hidden.　**81. itself unkennel:** come to light (like a fox
driven from its hole).　**84. stithy:** blacksmith's shop, forge.　**87.
censure:** careful criticism. **seeming:** appearance.　**90. be idle:** act
mad.

KING. How fares our cousin Hamlet?

HAMLET. Excellent, i' faith; of the chameleon's
dish. I eat the air, promise-crammed. You
cannot feed capons so.   95

KING. I have nothing with this answer, Hamlet.
These words are not mine.

HAMLET. No, nor mine now. *[To Polonius.]* My
lord, you played once i' th' university, you
say?   99

POLONIUS. That did I, my lord, and was accounted
a good actor.

HAMLET. What did you enact?   102

POLONIUS. I did enact Julius Caesar. I was killed i'
the Capitol. Brutus killed me.

HAMLET. It was a brute part of him to kill so capital
a calf there. Be the players ready?   106

ROSENCRANTZ. Ay, my lord; they stay upon your
patience.

QUEEN. Come hither, my dear Hamlet, sit by me.

HAMLET. No, good mother, here's metal more
attractive.   110

POLONIUS. *[To the King.]* O ho! do you mark that?

HAMLET. Lady, shall I lie in your lap?

OPHELIA. No, my lord.

HAMLET. I mean, my head upon your lap?

OPHELIA. Ay, my lord.   115

HAMLET. Do you think I meant country matters?

OPHELIA. I think nothing, my lord.

HAMLET. That's a fair thought to lie between
maids' legs.

OPHELIA. What is, my lord?   120

HAMLET. Nothing.

OPHELIA. You are merry, my lord.

HAMLET. Who, I?

OPHELIA. Ay, my lord.   124

HAMLET. O God, your only jig-maker. What should
a man do but be merry? for look you how
cheerfully my mother looks, and my father died
within's two hours.   128

OPHELIA. Nay, 'tis twice two months, my lord.

HAMLET. So long? Nay, then, let the de'il wear
black, for I'll have a suit of sables. O heavens!
die two months ago, and not forgotten yet?
Then there's hope a great man's memory may
outlive his life half a year; but, by 'r lady, 'a
must build churches then, or else shall 'a

suffer not thinking on with the hobby-horse,
whose epitaph is, 'For O! for, O! the hobby-
horse is forgot.'   137

[Hautboys play. The dumb-show enters.]

*[Enter a King and a Queen very lovingly, the Queen em-
bracing him. She kneels and makes show of protestation
unto him. He takes her up and declines his head upon her
neck; lays him down upon a bank of flowers. She, seeing
him asleep, leaves him. Anon comes in a fellow, takes off
his crown, kisses it, and pours poison in the King's ears, and
exits. The Queen returns, finds the King dead, and makes
passionate action. The Poisoner, with some two or three
Mutes, comes in again, seeming to lament with her. The
dead body is carried away. The Poisoner woos the Queen
with gifts; she seems loath and unwilling awhile, but in the
end accepts his love.   Exeunt.]*

OPHELIA. What means this, my lord?

HAMLET. Marry, this is miching Malicho; it means
mischief.   140

OPHELIA. Belike this show imports the argument of
the play.

[Enter Prologue.]

HAMLET. We shall know by this fellow. The players
cannot keep counsel; they'll tell all.   144

OPHELIA. Will 'a tell us what this show meant?

HAMLET. Ay, or any show that you will show him.
Be not you ashamed to show, he'll not
shame to tell you what it means.   148

OPHELIA. You are naught, you are naught. I'll mark
the play.

PROLOGUE. For us and for our tragedy.   151
Here stooping to your clemency,
We beg your hearing patiently.

HAMLET. Is this a prologue, or the posy of a ring?

OPHELIA. 'Tis brief, my lord.

HAMLET. As woman's love.

[Enter (Player) King and Queen.]

P. KING. Full thirty times hath Phoebus' cart gone
round   157

135. suffer not thinking on: be forgotten. **136. hobby-horse:** one
of the participants in the morris dance. **Directions. Hautboys:**
wooden double-reed instruments of high pitch. **Mutes:** actors without
speaking parts (but here all are mutes). **139. miching Malicho:**
skulking mischief. **141. imports the argument:** amounts to a synop-
sis. **144. counsel:** secret. **149. naught:** wanton. **152. stooping:**
bowing. **154. posy:** motto. **157. cart:** chariot.

96. have nothing with: can make nothing of. **105. brute part:**
stupid act. **107. stay upon:** wait for. **patience:** leisure. **116.
country matters:** uncouth conduct. **125. your only jig-maker:** I
am the best jig-maker there is; cf. n. on II. ii. 502. **128. within's:**
within this. **131. suit of sables:** suit of rich furs.

Neptune's salt wash and Tellus' orbed ground,
And thirty dozen moons with borrow'd sheen
About the world have times twelve thirties
   been,
Since love our hearts and Hymen did our hands
Unite commutual in most sacred bands.   162
P. QUEEN. So many journeys may the sun and moon
Make us again count o'er ere love be done!
But, woe is me! you are so sick of late,   165
So far from cheer and from your former state,
That I distrust you. Yet though I distrust,
Discomfort you, my lord, it nothing must;
For women fear too much, even as they love,
And women's fear and love hold quantity,
In neither aught, or in extremity.   171
Now what my love is, proof hath made you
   know;
And as my love is siz'd, my fear is so.
Where love is great, the littlest doubts are fear;
Where little fears grow great, great love grows
   there.   175
P. KING. Faith, I must leave thee, love, and shortly
   too.
My operant powers their functions leave to do,
And thou shalt live in this fair world behind,
Honor'd, belov'd; and haply one as kind   179
For husband shalt thou—
P. QUEEN.   O confound the rest!
Such love must needs be treason in my breast.
In second husband let me be accurst;
None wed the second but who kill'd the first.
HAMLET. *[Aside.]* That's wormwood, wormwood.
P. QUEEN. The instances that second marriage move
Are base respects of thrift, but none of love;
A second time I kill my husband dead,   187
When second husband kisses me in bed.
P. KING. I do believe you think what now you
   speak,
But what we do determine oft we break.
Purpose is but the slave of memory,   191
Of violent birth, but poor validity;
Which now, like fruit unripe, sticks on the tree,
But fall unshaken when they mellow be.
Most necessary 'tis that we forget   195

To pay ourselves what to ourselves is debt;
What to ourselves in passion we propose,
The passion ending, doth the purpose lose.
The violence of either grief or joy   199
Their own enactures with themselves destroy;
Where joy most revels grief doth most
   lament,
Grief joys, joy grieves, on slender accident.
This world is not for aye, nor 'tis not strange
That even our loves should with our fortunes
   change,   204
For 'tis a question left us yet to prove
Whether love lead fortune or else fortune love.
The great man down, you mark his favorite
   flies;   207
The poor advanc'd makes friends of enemies.
And hitherto doth love on fortune tend,
For who not needs shall never lack a friend;
And who in want a hollow friend doth try   211
Directly seasons him his enemy.
But, orderly to end where I begun,
Our wills and fates do so contrary run
That our devices still are overthrown,   215
Our thoughts are ours, their ends none of our
   own.
So think thou wilt no second husband wed,
But die thy thoughts when thy first lord is
   dead.
P. QUEEN. Nor earth to me give food, nor heaven
   light!   219
Sport and repose lock from me day and night!
To desperation turn my trust and hope!
An anchor's cheer in prison be my scope!
Each opposite that blanks the face of joy   223
Meet what I would have well, and it destroy!
Both here and hence pursue me lasting strife,
If, once a widow, ever I be wife!
HAMLET. If she should break it now!   227
P. KING. 'Tis deeply sworn. Sweet, leave me here
   awhile;
My spirits grow dull, and fain I would beguile
The tedious day with sleep.   *[Sleeps.]*
P. QUEEN.   Sleep rock thy brain;
And never come mischance between us twain!
                                [Exit.]
HAMLET. Madam, how like you this play?   233

---

158. **wash:** sea.   159. **borrow'd sheen:** reflected light.   162. **commutual:** an intensive form of 'mutual'.   167. **I distrust you:** I have misgivings on your account.   170. **quantity:** proportion.   171. **In . . extremity:** nothing of either, or else an excess.   177. **operant:** vital.   185. **instances:** motives, inducements. **move:** suggest.   192. **validity:** strength.

200. **enactures:** fulfillments.   211. **hollow:** insincere.   216. **ends:** results.   219. **Nor . . .nor:** neither . . .nor.   220. **Sport:** pleasure.   222. **anchor's:** anchorite's.   223. **opposite:** contrary thing. **blanks:** blanches, makes pale.

QUEEN. The lady doth protest too much, me-thinks.

HAMLET. O, but she'll keep her word.   235

KING. Have you heard the argument? Is there no
offence in 't?

HAMLET. No, no, they do but jest,—poison in jest.
No offence i' th' world.

KING. What do you call the play?

HAMLET. The Mouse-trap. Marry, how? Tropically.
This play is the image of a murther done in
Vienna. Gonzago is the duke's name; his wife,
Baptista. You shall see anon. 'Tis a knavish
piece of work: but what of that? Your majesty
and we that have free souls, it touches us not.
Let the galled jade wince, our withers are
unwrung.   247

[Enter Player as Lucianus.]

This is one Lucianus, nephew to the King.

OPHELIA. You are as good as a chorus, my lord.

HAMLET. I could interpret between you and your
love, if I could see the puppets dallying.   251

OPHELIA. You are keen, my lord, you are keen.

HAMLET. It would cost you a groaning to take off
mine edge.   254

OPHELIA. Still better, and worse.

HAMLET. So you must take your husbands. Begin,
murtherer; leave thy damnable faces, and begin.
Come; the croaking raven doth bellow for
revenge.

LUCIANUS. Thoughts black, hands apt, drugs fit,
and time agreeing;
Confederate season, else no creature seeing.
Thou mixture rank, of midnight weeds
collected,
With Hecate's ban thrice blasted, thrice
infected,
Thy natural magic and dire property,   263
On wholesome life usurps immediately.

[Pours the poison in his ears.]

HAMLET. 'A poisons him i' the garden for his estate.
His name's Gonzago. The story is extant,
and written in very choice Italian. You shall
see anon how the murtherer gets the love of
Gonzago's wife.   268

OPHELIA. The king rises.

HAMLET. What, frighted with false fire?

QUEEN. How fares my lord?

POLONIUS. Give o'er the play.   272

KING. Give me some light! Away!

POLONIUS. Lights, lights, lights!

[Exeunt all but Hamlet and Horatio.]

HAMLET.

Why, let the stricken deer go weep,
The hart ungalled play,   276
For some must watch while some must sleep:
Thus runs the world away.

Would not this, sir, and a forest of feathers (if
the rest of my fortunes turn Turk with me)
with two Provincial roses on my razed
shoes, get me a fellowship in a cry of
players?

HORATIO. Half a share.

HAMLET. A whole one, I.   284

For thou dost know, O Damon dear,
This realm dismantled was
Of Jove himself; and now reigns here
A very, very—pajock.   288

HORATIO. You might have rimed.

HAMLET. O good Horatio, I'll take the ghost's
word for a thousand pound. Didst perceive?

HORATIO. Very well, my lord.   292

HAMLET. Upon the talk of the poisoning?

HORATIO. I did very well note him.

HAMLET. Ah, ha! Come, some music! come, the
recorders!   296

For if the king like not the comedy,
Why then, belike he likes it not, perdy.

Come, some music!

[Enter Rosencrantz and Guildenstern.]

---

241. **Tropically:** figuratively. 242. **image:** representation. 247. **galled jade:** horse sore from chafing. **withers:** shoulders. 247. **unwrung:** not galled. 260. **Confederate season:** time conspiring to assist.

272. **Give o'er:** stop. 279. **forest of feathers:** an allusion to the plumes worn by actors. 280. **turn Turk:** play the renegade. 281. **Provincial roses:** rosettes imitating the damask rose. **razed:** slashed, i.e., with cuts or openings. 282. **fellowship:** partnership. **cry:** company. 288. **pajock:** scarecrow. 296. **recorders:** wind instruments of the flute type. 298. **perdy:** a corruption of *par dieu.*

GUILDENSTERN. Good my lord, vouchsafe me a
     word with you.   300

HAMLET. Sir, a whole history.

GUILDENSTERN. The king, sir,—

HAMLET. Ay, sir, what of him?   303

GUILDENSTERN. Is in his retirement marvellous
     distempered.

HAMLET. With drink, sir?

GUILDENSTERN. No, my lord, with choler.   306

HAMLET. Your wisdom should show itself more
     richer to signify this to the doctor; for, for me
     to put him to his purgation would perhaps
     plunge him into more choler.   310

GUILDENSTERN. Good my lord, put your discourse
     into some frame, and start not so wildly from
     my affair.

HAMLET. I am tame, sir; pronounce.

GUILDENSTERN. The queen, your mother, in most
     great affliction of spirit, hath sent me to you.

HAMLET. You are welcome.   316

GUILDENSTERN. Nay, good my lord, this courtesy
     is not of the right breed. If it shall please you
     to make me a wholesome answer, I will do
     your mother's commandment; if not, your
     pardon and my return shall be the end of my
     business.   321

HAMLET. Sir, I cannot.

ROSENCRANTZ. What, my lord?

HAMLET. Make you a wholesome answer. My wit's
     diseased; but, sir such answer as I can make,
     you shall command; or, rather, as you say, my
     mother. Therefore no more, but to the matter.
     My mother, you say,—   328

ROSENCRANTZ. Then, thus she says: your behavior
     hath struck her into amazement and
     admiration.

HAMLET. O wonderful son, that can so 'stonish a
     mother! But is there no sequel at the heels of
     this mother's admiration? Impart.   333

ROSENCRANTZ. She desires to speak with you in her
     closet ere you go to bed.

HAMLET. We shall obey, were she ten times our
     mother. Have you any further trade with us?

ROSENCRANTZ. My lord, you once did love me.

HAMLET. And do still, by these pickers and stealers.

ROSENCRANTZ. Good my lord, what is your cause of
     distemper? You do surely bar the door upon
     your own liberty, if you deny your griefs to your
     friend.   342

HAMLET. Sir, I lack advancement.

ROSENCRANTZ. How can that be when you have the
     voice of the king himself for your succession in
     Denmark?

[Enter the Players, with recorders.]

HAMLET. Ay, sir, but 'While the grass grows,'—
     the proverb is something musty.—O, the
     recorders! Let me see one. To withdraw with
     you,—Why do you go about to recover the
     wind of me, as if you would drive me into a
     toil?   350

GUILDENSTERN. O! my lord, if my duty be too bold,
     my love is too unmannerly.

HAMLET. I do not well understand that. Will you
     play upon this pipe?

GUILDENSTERN. My lord, I cannot.   355

HAMLET. I pray you.

GUILDENSTERN. Believe me, I cannot.

HAMLET. I do beseech you.

GUILDENSTERN. I know no touch of it, my lord.

HAMLET. It is as easy as lying. Govern these
     ventages with your fingers and thumb, give it
     breath with your mouth, and it will discourse
     most eloquent music. Look you, these are the
     stops.

GUILDENSTERN. But these cannot I command to
     any utterance of harmony. I have not the
     skill.   365

HAMLET. Why, look you now, how unworthy a
     thing you make of me. You would play upon
     me; you would seem to know my stops; you
     would pluck out the heart of my mystery; you
     would sound me from my lowest note to the
     top of my compass. And there is much music,
     excellent voice, in this little organ, yet cannot
     you make it speak. 'Sblood, do you think I am
     easier to be played on than a pipe? Call me what
     instrument you will, though you can fret me,
     yet you cannot play upon me.   375

---

304. distempered: disordered   **306. choler:** anger.   **309. purga-**
tion: purging.   **312. frame:** sensible form.   **313. pronounce:**
speak.   **318. of the right breed:** pure-bred, genuine.   **319.**
wholesome: sincere.   **339. pickers and stealers:** hands.

342. liberty: freedom of action.   **344. voice:** vote.   **348. with-**
draw with: speak privately with.   **349. recover the wind of:** get
advantage of.   **350. toil:** snare.   **359. know no touch:** have no
skill at all.   **360. ventages:** holes, stops.   **370. compass:** range of
voice.

[Enter Polonius.]

God bless you, sir!

POLONIUS. My lord, the queen would speak with
    you, and presently.

HAMLET. Do you see yonder cloud, that's almost in
    shape of a camel?   380

POLONIUS. By the mass, and 'tis like a camel, indeed.

HAMLET. Methinks it is like a weasel.

POLONIUS. It is backed like a weasel.   383

HAMLET. Or like a whale?

POLONIUS. Very like a whale.

HAMLET. Then I will come to my mother by and by.
    [Aside.] They fool me to the top of my bent.
    [Aloud.] I will come by and by.   388

POLONIUS. I will say so.   *[Exit.]*

HAMLET. By and by is easily said. Leave me, friends.

[Exeunt all but Hamlet.]

'Tis now the very witching time of night,   391
When churchyards yawn and hell itself breathes
    out
Contagion to this world. Now could I drink
    hot blood,
And do such bitter business as the day   394
Would quake to look on. Soft! now to my
    mother!
O heart, lose not thy nature; let not ever
The soul of Nero enter this firm bosom.
Let me be cruel, not unnatural;   398
I will speak daggers to her, but use none.
My tongue and soul in this be hypocrites:
How in my words somever she be shent,
To give them seals never, my soul, consent!   402

[Exit.]

SCENE III

A Room in the Castle

[Enter King, Rosencrantz, and Guildenstern.]

KING. I like him not, nor stands it safe with us
    To let his madness range. Therefore prepare you.
    I your commission will forthwith dispatch,
    And he to England shall along with you.   4
    The terms of our estate may not endure
    Hazard so near us as doth hourly grow
    Out of his braves.

GUILDENSTERN. We will ourselves provide.
    Most holy and religious fear it is   8
    To keep those many many bodies safe
    That live and feed upon your majesty.

ROSENCRANTZ. The single and peculiar life is bound
    With all the strength and armor of the mind   12
    To keep itself from noyance; but much more
    That spirit upon whose weal depends and rests
    The lives of many. The cesse of majesty
    Dies not alone, but like a gulf doth draw   16
    What's near it with it. It is a massy wheel,
    Fix'd on the summit of the highest mount,
    To whose huge spokes ten thousand lesser things
    Are mortis'd and adjoin'd; which, when it
        falls,   20
    Each small annexment, petty consequence,
    Attends the boisterous ruin. Never alone
    Did the king sigh, but with a general groan.   23

KING. Arm you, I pray you, to this speedy voyage;
    For we will fetters put about this fear,
    Which now goes too free-footed.

ROSENCRANTZ.   We will haste us.

[Exeunt Gentlemen.]

[Enter Polonius.]

POLONIUS. My lord, he's going to his mother's closet.
    Behind the arras I'll convey myself   28
    To hear the process. I'll warr'nt she'll tax him
        home;
    And, as you said, and wisely was it said,
    'Tis meet that some more audience than a
        mother,
    Since nature makes them partial, should o'erhear
    The speech, of vantage. Fare you well, my
        liege.   33

---

386. by and by: at once. **387. top . . . bent:** limit of my endurance. **391. witching:** when spells are cast. **401. How . . . somever:** c.f. I. v. 84. **shent:** rebuked. **402. give them seals:** confirm them by making words into deeds.

1. like him not: distrust him. **2. range:** rove, roam. **3. forthwith dispatch:** prepare at once. **5. terms:** condition. **7. braves:** defiances. **8. fear:** caution. **11. single and peculiar:** individual and private. **13. noyance:** harm. **14. weal:** welfare. **15. cesse:** decease. **16. gulf:** whirlpool. **21. annexment:** appendage. **22. Attends:** accompanies. **24. Arm:** prepare. **29. process:** interview. **tax . . . home:** censure effectually. **33. of vantage:** in addition.

I'll call upon you ere you go to bed
And tell you what I know.
KING.   Thanks, dear my lord.

[Exit Polonius.]

O my offence is rank, it smells to heaven!   36
It hath the primal eldest curse upon 't;
A brother's murther. Pray can I not.
Though inclination be as sharp as will,
My stronger guilt defeats my strong intent,   40
And, like a man to double business bound,
I stand in pause where I shall first begin,
And both neglect. What if this cursed hand
Were thicker than itself with brother's blood,   44
Is there not rain enough in the sweet heavens
To wash it white as snow? Whereto serves
   mercy
But to confront the visage of offence?
And what's in prayer but this twofold force,   48
To be forestalled, ere we come to fall,
Or pardon'd, being down? Then I'll look up;
My fault is past. But, O, what form of prayer
Can serve my turn? 'Forgive me my foul
   murther?'   52
That cannot be, since I am still possess'd
Of those effects for which I did the murther,
My crown, mine own ambition, and my queen.
May one be pardon'd and retain th' offence?   56
In the corrupted currents of this world
Offence's gilded hand may shove by justice,
And oft 'tis seen the wicked prize itself
Buys out the law; but 'tis not so above.   60
There is no shuffling, there the action lies
In his true nature, and we ourselves compell'd
Even to the teeth and forehead of our faults
To give in evidence. What then? what rests?   64
Try what repentance can. What can it not?
Yet what can it, when one cannot repent?
O wretched state! O bosom black as death!
O limed soul, that struggling to be free   68
Art more engage'd! Help, angels! make assay!

Bow, stubborn knees; and heart with strings of
   steel
Be soft as sinews of the new-born babe.
All may be well.   *[He kneels.]*

[Enter Hamlet.]

HAMLET. Now might I do it pat, now 'a is
   praying!   73
And now I'll do 't. And so 'a goes to heaven;
And so am I reveng'd? That would be
   scann'd.
A villain kills my father, and for that,   76
I, his sole son, do this same villain send
To heaven.
Why, this is hire and salary, not revenge.
'A took my father grossly, full of bread,   80
With all his crimes broad blown, as flush as
   May;
And how his audit stands who knows save
   heaven?
But in our circumstance and course of
   thought
'Tis heavy with him. And am I then
   reveng'd,   84
To take him in the purging of his soul,
When he is fit and season'd for his passage?
No.
Up, sword, and know thou a more horrid
   hent;   88
When he is drunk asleep, or in his rage,
Or in th' incestuous pleasure of his bed,
At game a-swearing, or about some act
That has no relish of salvation in 't.   92
Then trip him, that his heels may kick at
   heaven,
And that his soul may be as damn'd and black
As hell, whereto it goes. My mother stays.—
This physic but prolongs thy sickly days.   *[Exit.]*
KING. *[Rising.]* My words fly up, my thoughts remain
   below.   97
Words without thoughts never to heaven go.
   [Exit.]

---

37. primal: primeval. **44. thicker than itself:** made more than double its normal thickness. **47. confront:** oppose directly. **49. forestalled:** prevented in anticipation. **54. effects:** i.e., things acquired by an action. **55. ambition:** i.e., the realization of ambition (so also *offence* in 56). **58. gilded hand:** hand using bribes of gold. **59. wicked prize:** reward of wickedness. **60. Buys out:** corrupts. **61. shuffling:** trickery. **lies:** used in its legal sense. **63. teeth and forehead:** very face. **64. rests:** remains. **68. limed:** caught with bird-lime. **69. engag'd:** entangled.

73. pat: to a nicety. **75. would:** requires to. **scann'd:** examined, considered. **79. hire and salary:** i.e., a reward. **80. full of bread:** without opportunity to fast. **81. broad blown:** in full bloom. **flush:** lusty. **82. audit:** account. **83. in . . . thought:** according to our vague ideas. **86. passage:** i.e., to the other world. **88. know . . . hent:** let me grasp you at a more horrid moment. **92. relish:** flavor. **96. physic:** medicine, i.e., the postponement.

SCENE IV

The Queen's Closet

[Enter Queen and Polonius.]

POLONIUS. 'A will come straight. Look you lay
   home to him. Tell him his pranks have been too
   broad to bear with,
   And that your Grace hath screen'd and stood
     between
   Much heat and him. I'll silence me e'en here.   4
   Pray you, be round with him.
HAMLET. *[Within.]* Mother, mother, mother!
QUEEN.   I'll warrant you;
   Fear me not. Withdraw, I hear him coming.

[Polonius hides behind the arras.]

[Enter Hamlet.]

HAMLET. Now, mother, what's the matter?   8
QUEEN. Hamlet, thou hast thy father much
   offended.
HAMLET. Mother, you have my father much
   offended.
QUEEN. Come, come, you answer with an idle
   tongue.
HAMLET. Go, go, you question with a wicked
   tongue.   12
QUEEN. Why, how now, Hamlet!
HAMLET.   What's the matter
   now?
QUEEN. Have you forgot me?
HAMLET.   No, by the rood, not
   so.
   You are the queen, your husband's brother's
     wife;
   And,—would it were not so!—you are my
     mother.   16
QUEEN. Nay then, I'll set those to you that can speak.
HAMLET. Come, come, and sit you down; you shall
   not budge.
   You go not till I set you up a glass
   Where you may see the inmost part of you.   20
QUEEN. What wilt thou do? thou wilt not murther
   me?

   Help, help, ho!
POLONIUS. What, ho! help! help! help!
HAMLET. How now! a rat? Dead, for a ducat, dead!

[Kills Polonius through the arras.]

POLONIUS. O, I am slain!
QUEEN.   O me, what hast thou
   done?
HAMLET. Nay, I know not. Is it the king?
QUEEN. O, what a rash and bloody deed is this!
HAMLET. A bloody deed! almost as bad, good
   mother,   29
   As kill a king, and marry with his brother.
QUEEN. As kill a king?
HAMLET.   Ay, lady, 'twas my word.

[Lifts up the arras and discovers Polonius.]

   Thou wretched, rash, intruding fool, farewell!
   I took thee for thy better. Take thy fortune;   33
   Thou find'st to be too busy is some danger.
   [To the Queen.] Leave wringing of your hands.
     Peace! sit you down,
   And let me wring your heart; for so I shall
   If it be made of penetrable stuff,   37
   If damned custom have not braz'd it so
   That it be proof and bulwark against sense.
QUEEN. What have I done that thou dar'st wag thy
   tongue
   In noise so rude against me?
HAMLET.   Such an act   41
   That blurs the grace and blush of modesty,
   Calls virtue hypocrite, takes off the rose
   From the fair forehead of an innocent love
   And sets a blister there, makes marriage vows
   As false as dicers' oaths. O, such a deed   46
   As from the body of contraction plucks
   The very soul, and sweet religion makes
   A rhapsody of words! Heaven's face does glow,
   Yea, this solidity and compound mass,   50
   With tristful visage as against the doom,
   Is thought-sick at the act.
QUEEN.   Ay me! what act,
   That roars so loud and thunders in the index?

---

24. for: i.e., I wager. **38. braz'd:** made it brazen. **39. proof
and bulwark:** an impenetrable defence. **sense:** feeling. **47. contraction:** marriage contract. **49. rhapsody:** meaningless
string. **50. this solidity and compound mass:** the solid and
composite earth. **51. tristful:** sad. **doom:** doomsday. **53. index:**
table of contents, prelude.

---

1. lay home: talk plainly. **2. broad:** free, unrestrained. **4. heat:**
anger. **silence me:** withdraw into silence. **14. rood:** cross.

HAMLET. Look here, upon this picture, and on
      this,   54
   The counterfeit presentment of two brothers.
   See what a grace was seated on this brow:
   Hyperion's curls, the front of Jove himself.   57
   An eye like Mars, to threaten and command,
   A station like the herald Mercury
   New-lighted on a heaven-kissing hill,
   A combination and a form indeed,   61
   Where every god did seem to set his seal,
   To give the world assurance of a man.
   This was your husband. Look you, now, what
      follows.
   Here is your husband, like a mildew'd ear   65
   Blasting his wholesome brother. Have you eyes?
   Could you on this fair mountain leave to feed,
   And batten on this moor? Ha! have you eyes?
   You cannot call it love, for at your age   69
   The heyday in the blood is tame, it's humble,
   And waits upon the judgment; and what
      judgment
   Would step from this to this? Sense sure you
      have,
   Else could you not have motion; but sure that
      sense
   Is apoplex'd, for madness would not err,
   Nor sense to ecstasy was ne'er so thrall'd
   But it reserv'd some quantity of choice   76
   To serve in such a difference. What devil was't
   That thus hath cozen'd you at hoodman-blind?
   Eyes without feeling, feeling without sight,
   Ears without hands or eyes, smelling sans all,
   Or but a sickly part of one true sense   81
   Could not so mope.
   O shame! where is thy blush? Rebellious hell,
   If thou canst mutine in a matron's bones,
   To flaming youth let virtue be as wax   85
   And melt in her own fire: proclaim no shame
   When the compulsive ardor gives the charge,
   Since frost itself as actively doth burn,
   And reason panders will.
QUEEN.   O Hamlet, speak no
      more!

Thou turn'st mine eyes into my very soul;   90
   And there I see such black and grained spots
   As will not leave their tint.
HAMLET.   Nay, but to live   92
   In the rank sweat of an enseamed bed,
   Stew'd in corruption, honeying and making
      love
   Over the nasty sty,
QUEEN.   O speak to me no more!
   These words like daggers enter in my ears.   96
   No more, sweet Hamlet!
HAMLET.   A murtherer and a
      villain;
   A slave that is not twentieth part the tithe
   Of your precedent lord; a vice of kings;
   A cutpurse of the empire and the rule,
   That from the shelf the precious diadem
      stole,   101
   And put it in his pocket!
QUEEN.   No more!

[Enter Ghost.]

HAMLET. A king of shreds and patches,—
   Save me, and hover o'er me with your wings,
   You heavenly guards! What would your
      gracious figure?
QUEEN. Alas! he's mad!   106
HAMLET. Do you not come your tardy son to chide,
   That, laps'd in time and passion, lets go by
   Th' important acting of your dread command?
   O, say.
GHOST.   Do not forget. This visitation   110
   Is but to whet thy almost blunted purpose.
   But, look, amazement on thy mother sits.
   O, step between her and her fighting soul.
   Conceit in weakest bodies strongest works.
   Speak to her, Hamlet.
HAMLET.   How is it with you, lady?
QUEEN. Alas, how is 't with you,
   That you bend your eye on vacancy   117
   And with th' incorporal air do hold discourse?
   Forth at your eyes your spirits wildly peep;
   And, as the sleeping soldiers in th' alarm,

---

55. **counterfeit presentment**: portrayed likeness. 57. **front**: forehead. 59. **station**: poise. 65. **ear**: ear of wheat. 68. **batten**:
grow fat. **moor**: a barren upland. 70. **heyday**: youthful high
spirits. 72. **Sense**: control of the physical senses. 74. **apoplex'd**:
atrophied. 75. **thrall'd**: enslaved. 76. **quantity of choice**: power
to choose. 78. **cozen'd**: cheated. **hoodman-blind**: blind man's
bluff. 80. **sans**: without. 82. **mope**: act aimlessly. 84. **mutine**:
rise in mutiny. 87. **charge**: command. 89. **panders**: ministers to
the gratifications of.

91. **grained**: ingrained. 92. **leave their tinct**: lose their
color. 93. **enseamed**: greasy. 94. **honeying**: talking
sweetly. 98. **tithe**: tenth part (i.e., not one two-hundreth). 99.
precedent: former. **vice**: buffoon. 100. **cutpurse**: pickpocket.
108. **laps'd in time and passion**: frittering away time and
energy. 109. **important**: urgent. 114. **Conceit**: imagination. 118. **incorporal**: incorporeal.

Your bedded hair, like life in excrements,   121
Start up and stand an end. O gentle son,
Upon the heat and flame of thy distemper
Sprinkle cool patience. Whereon do you look?
HAMLET. On him, on him! Look you, how pale he
    glares!
His form and cause conjoin'd, preaching to
    stones,   126
Would make them capable.—Do not look upon
    me;
Lest with this piteous action you convert
My stern effects. Then what I have to do
Will want true color,—tears perchance for
    blood.   130
QUEEN. To whom do you speak this?
HAMLET.   Do you see nothing there?
QUEEN. Nothing at all; yet all that is I see.
HAMLET. Nor did you nothing hear?
QUEEN.   No, nothing but ourselves.
HAMLET. Why, look you there! look, how it steals
    away!
My father, in his habit as he liv'd!   135
Look, where he goes, even now, out at the
    portal.

[Exit Ghost.]

QUEEN. This is the very coinage of your brain: 137
This bodiless creation ecstasy
Is very cunning in.
HAMLET.   Ecstasy!
My pulse, as yours, doth temperately keep time,
And makes as healthful music. It is not
    madness   141
That I have utter'd. Bring me to the test,
And I the matter will re-word, which madness
Would gambol from. Mother, for love of grace,
Lay not that flattering unction to your soul,   145
That not your trespass but my madness speaks.
It will but skin and film the ulcerous place,
Whiles rank corruption, mining all within,   148
Infects unseen. Confess yourself to heaven;
Repent what's past; avoid what is to come;

And do not spread the compost on the weeds
To make them ranker. Forgive me this my
    virtue,   152
For in the fatness of these pursy times
Virtue itself of vice must pardon beg,
Yea, curb and woo for leave to do him good.
QUEEN. O Hamlet, thou hast cleft my heart in
    twain.
HAMLET. O throw away the worser part of it,   157
And live the purer with the other half.
Good night; but go not to my uncle's bed;
Assume a virtue, if you have it not.
That monster, custom, who all sense doth eat
Of habits evil, is angel yet in this,
That to the use of actions fair and good
He likewise gives a frock or livery   164
That aptly is put on. Refrain to-night,
And that shall lend a kind of easiness
To the next abstinence: the next more easy;
For use almost can change the stamp of nature,
And either tame the devil or throw him out
With wondrous potency. Once more, good
    night,
And when you are desirous to be bless'd,
I'll blessing beg of you. For this same lord,   172
I do repent; but heaven hath pleas'd it so,
To punish me with this, and this with me,
That I must be their scourge and minister.
I will bestow him, and will answer well   176
The death I gave him. So, again, good night.
I must be cruel only to be kind:
Thus bad begins and worse remains behind.
One word more, good lady.
QUEEN.   What shall I do?   180
HAMLET. Not this, by no means, that I bid you do:
Let the bloat king tempt you again to bed,
Pinch wanton on your cheek, call you his
    mouse;
And let him, for a pair of reechy kisses,   184
Or paddling in your neck with his damn'd
    fingers,
Make you to ravel all this matter out,
That I essentially am not in madness,
But mad in craft, 'Twere good you let him
    know;   188

121. **bedded:** smooth, flatly brushed. **hair:** hairs. **life in excrements:** dead tissue come alive. **122. an end:** on end. **126. conjoin'd:** united. **127. capable:** capable of feeling. **128. convert:** translate. **129. My stern effects:** the sternness of my deeds. **130. want true color:** not be what it should. **135. habit . . . liv'd:** familiar costume. **143. re-word:** repeat word for word. **144. gambol from:** skip away from. **grace:** God. **145. unction:** salve. **148. mining:** undermining.

153. **fatness:** grossness. **pursy:** corpulent. **155. curb and woo:** bow and beg. **him:** i.e., vice. **163. use:** habitual practice. **171. be bless'd:** become blessed. **176. answer:** account for. **182. bloat:** bloated. **183. wanton:** wantonly. **184. reechy:** greasy. **185. paddling:** playing fondly. **187. essentially:** in my essential nature.

For who that's but a queen, fair, sober, wise,
Would from a paddock, from a bat, a gib,
Such dear concernings hide? who would do so?
No, in despite of sense and secrecy,   192
Unpeg the basket on the house's top,
Let the birds fly, and, like the famous ape,
To try conclusions in the basket creep,
And break your own neck down.   196
QUEEN. Be thou assur'd, if words be made of
     breath,
And breath of life, I have no life to breathe
What thou hast said to me.
HAMLET. I must to England; you know that?
QUEEN.   Alack!
     I had forgot. 'Tis so concluded on.   201
HAMLET. There's letters seal'd, and my two school-
     fellows,
Whom I will trust as I will adders fang'd,

They bear the mandate; they must sweep my
     way
And marshall me to knavery. Let it work,   205
For 'tis the sport to have the enginer
Hoist with his own petar; and t' shall go hard
But I will delve one yard below their mines,   208
And blow them at the moon. O 'tis most
     sweet,
When in one line two crafts directly meet!
This man shall set me packing.
I'll lug the guts into the neighbor room.—   212
Mother, good night indeed.—This counsellor
Is now most still, most secret, and most grave,
Who was in life a foolish prating knave.
Come, sir, to draw toward an end with you.   216
Good night, mother.

[Exit Hamlet tugging in Polonius.]

Act IV

SCENE I

A Room in the Castle

[Enter King and Queen, with Rosencrantz and Guildenstern.]

KING. There's matter in these sighs, these profound
     heaves,
You must translate. 'Tis fit we understand them.
Where is your son?
QUEEN. Bestow this place on us a little while.   4

[Exeunt Rosencrantz and Guildenstern.]

Ah, mine own lord, what have I seen to-night!
KING. What, Gertrude? How does Hamlet?
QUEEN. Mad as the sea and wind, when both
     contend
Which is the mightier. In his lawless fit,   8
Behind the arras hearing something stir,
Whips out his rapier, cries, 'A rat! a rat!'

And in this brainish apprehension kills
The unseen good old man.
KING.   O heavy deed!   12
It had been so with us had we been there.
His liberty is full of threats to all;
To you yourself, to us, to every one.
Alas, how shall this bloody deed be answer'd?   16
It will be laid to us, whose providence
Should have kept short, restrain'd, and out of
     haunt,
This mad young man. But so much was our love,
We would not understand what was most fit,   20
But like the owner of a foul disease,
To keep it from divulging, let it feed
Even on the pith of life. Where is he gone?
QUEEN. To draw apart the body he hath kill'd,   24
O'er whom his very madness, like some ore
Among a mineral of metals base,
Shows itself pure. 'A weeps for what is done.

---

190. **paddock:** toad. **gib:** tom-cat.   191. **dear concernings:** affairs dearly concerning one.   195. **conclusions:** experiments.   196. **down:** in the fall.
1. **heaves:** prolonged sighs.

204. **mandate:** command. **sweep my way:** clear my path.   205. **marshal:** conduct.   206. **enginer:** maker of military engines, sapper.   207. **Hoist:** blown up. **petar:** small bomb.   207–208. **'t shall . . . will:** it shall not be for lack of trying if I do not.   11. **brainish apprehension:** insane illusion.   12. **heavy:** grievous.   17. **providence:** foresight.   18. **short:** tethered. **out of haunt:** out of company.   22. **divulging:** becoming known.   26. **mineral:** mine.

KING. O Gertrude, come away!
  The sun no sooner shall the mountains touch
  But we will ship him hence; and this vile deed
  We must with all our majesty and skill
  Both countenance and excuse. Ho,
    Guildenstern!   32

[Enter Rosencrantz and Guildenstern.]

  Friends both, go join you with some further
    aid.
  Hamlet in madness hath Polonius slain,
  And from his mother's closet hath he dragg'd
    him.
  Go seek him out; speak fair, and bring the body
  Into the chapel. I pray you haste in this.   37

[Exeunt Gentlemen.]

  Come, Gertrude, we'll call up our wisest friends;
  And let them know both what we mean to do
  and what's untimely done. [So, haply, slander,]
  Whose whisper o'er the world's diameter,   41
  As level as the cannon to his blank
  Transports his poison'd shot, may miss our name,
  And hit the woundless air. O, come away!   44
  My soul is full of discord and dismay.

[Exeunt.]

SCENE II

Another Room in the Castle

[Enter Hamlet.]

HAMLET. Safely stowed.
GENTLEMEN WITHIN. Hamlet! Lord Hamlet!
HAMLET. What noise? who calls on Hamlet?
  O, here they come.   4

[Enter Rosencrantz and Guildenstern.]

ROSENCRANTZ. What have you done, my lord, with
  the dead body?
HAMLET. Compounded it with dust, whereto 'tis kin.

ROSENCRANTZ. Tell us where 'tis, that we may take
  it thence
  And bear it to the chapel.   8
HAMLET. Do not believe it.
ROSENCRANTZ. Believe what?
HAMLET. That I can keep your counsel and not
  mine own. Besides, to be demanded of a
  sponge, what replication should be made by the
  son of a king?
ROSENCRANTZ. Take you me for a sponge, my
  lord?   14
HAMLET. Ay, sir, that soaks up the king's
  countenance, his rewards, his authorities. But
  such officers do the king best service in the end.
  He keeps them, like an ape an apple, in the
  corner of his jaw; first mouthed, to be last
  swallowed. When he needs what you have
  gleaned, it is but squeezing you, and, sponge,
  you shall be dry again.   21
ROSENCRANTZ. I understand you not, my lord.
HAMLET. I am glad of it. A knavish speech sleeps in
  a foolish ear.
ROSENCRANTZ. My lord, you must tell us where the
  body is, and go with us to the king.   26
HAMLET. The body is with the king, but the king is
  not with the body. The king is a thing—
GUILDENSTERN. A thing, my lord!
HAMLET. Of nothing. Bring me to him. (Hide fox,
  and all after.)

[Exeunt.]

SCENE III

Another Room in the Castle

[Enter King and two or three.]

KING. I have sent to seek him and to find the body.
  How dangerous is it that this man goes loose!
  Yet must not we put the strong law on him:
  He's lov'd of the distracted multitude,   4
  Who like not in their judgment but their eyes;
  And where 'tis so, th' offender's scourge is
    weigh'd,

36. fair: courteously.   **41. diameter:** extent from side to side.   **42. level:** straight. **blank:** white spot in the centre of a target.

12. to be demanded of: on being questioned by.   **13. replication:** reply.   **16. countenance:** favor. **authorities:** offices of authority.   **30. Hide fox, and all after:** signal cry in a children's game.   **6. scourge:** punishment.

But never the offence. To bear all smooth and
even,
This sudden sending him away must seem   8
Deliberate pause. Diseases desperate grown
By desperate appliance are reliev'd
Or not at all.

[Enter Rosencrantz.]

                          How now! what hath befall'n?
ROSENCRANTZ. Where the dead body is bestow'd,
my lord,   12
We cannot get from him.
KING.   But where is he?
ROSENCRANTZ. Without, my lord, guarded, to know
your pleasure.
KING. Bring him before us.
ROSENCRANTZ. Ho, Guildenstern! bring in my
lord.   16

[Enter Hamlet and Guildenstern.]

KING. Now, Hamlet, where's Polonius?
HAMLET. At supper.
KING. At supper! Where?   19
HAMLET. Not where he eats, but where 'a is eaten. A
certain convocation of politic worms are e'en at
him. Your worm is your only emperor for diet:
we fat all creatures else to fat us, and we fat
ourselves for maggots. Your fat king and your
lean beggar is but variable service,—two dishes,
but to one table. That's the end.
KING. Alas, alas!   27
HAMLET. A man may fish with the worm that hath
eat of a king, and eat of the fish that hath fed of
that worm.
KING. What dost thou mean by this?   31
HAMLET. Nothing, but to show you how a king may
go a progress through the guts of a beggar.
KING. Where is Polonius?   34
HAMLET. In heaven. Send thither to see. If your
messenger find him not there, seek him i' th'
other place yourself. But, indeed, if you find
him not within this month, you shall nose him
as you go up the stairs into the lobby.   39
KING. *[To some Attendants.]* Go seek him there.
HAMLET. 'A will stay till you come.

[Exeunt Attendants.]

KING. Hamlet, this deed, for thine especial safety,—
Which we do tender, as we dearly grieve   43
For that which thou hast done,—must send
thee hence
With fiery quickness. Therefore prepare
thyself.
The bark is ready and the wind at help,
Th' associates tend, and everything is bent   47
For England.
HAMLET.   For England?
KING.   Ay, Hamlet.
HAMLET.   Good.
KING. So is it, if thou knew'st our purposes.
HAMLET. I see a cherub that sees them. But, come;
for England! Farewell, dear mother.
KING. Thy loving father, Hamlet.
HAMLET. My mother. Father and mother is man
and wife, man and wife is one flesh, and so, my
mother.
Come, for England!   *[Exit.]*
KING. Follow him at foot; tempt him with speed
aboard.
Delay it not, I'll have him hence to-night.   57
Away! for everything is seal'd and done
That else leans on th' affair. Pray you, make
haste.   59

[Exeunt Rosencrantz and Guildenstern.]

And, England, if my love thou hold'st at
aught,—
As my great power thereof may give thee sense,
Since yet thy cicatrice looks raw and red
After the Danish sword, and thy free awe   63
Pays homage to us,—thou mayst not coldly set
Our sovereign process, which imports at full,
By letters cóngruing to that effect,
The present death of Hamlet. Do it, England;
For like the hectic in my blood he rages,   68
And thou must cure me. Till I know 'tis done,
Howe'er my haps, my joys were ne'er begun.

[Exit.]

---

7. **bear:** execute. **smooth and even:** pleasantly and equably. **9. Deliberate pause:** judicially considered. **10. appliance:** remedy. **21. convocation:** assembly. **politic:** crafty. **25. variable service:** variety of courses. **33. progress:** state journey.

47. **bent:** prepared. **56. at foot:** close behind. **59. leans on:** depends upon. **61. thereof may give thee sense:** may make you think of it. **62. cicatrice:** scar. **63. free awe:** awe still felt but no longer enforced by arms. **64. set:** esteem. **65. process:** formal command. **66. cóngruing:** agreeing. **68. hectic:** wasting fever. **70. haps:** fortunes.

SCENE IV

Open Country Near the Castle

[Enter Fortinbras with his army over the stage.]

FORTINBRAS. Go, captain, from me greet the Danish
    king.
  Tell him that by his licence Fortinbras
  Craves the conveyance of a promis'd march
  Over his kingdom. You know the rendezvous. 4
  If that his majesty would aught with us,
  We shall express our duty in his eye,
  And let him know so.
CAPTAIN.   I will do't, my lord.
FORTINBRAS. Go softly on.

[Exit with army, leaving Captain.]

[Enter Hamlet, Rosencrantz, & c.]

HAMLET. Good sir, whose powers are these?
CAPTAIN. They are of Norway, sir.
HAMLET. How purpos'd, sir, I pray you?
CAPTAIN. Against some part of Poland.   12
HAMLET. Who commands them sir?
CAPTAIN. The nephew of old Norway, Fortinbras.
HAMLET. Goes it against the main of Poland, sir,
  Or for some frontier?   16
CAPTAIN. Truly to speak, and with no addition,
  We to go gain a little patch of ground
  That hath in it no profit but the name.
  To pay five ducats, five, I would not farm it; 20
  Nor will it yield to Norway or the Pole
  A ranker rate, should it be sold in fee.
HAMLET. Why, then the Polack never will defend it.
CAPTAIN. Yes, it is already garrison'd.   24
HAMLET. Two thousand souls and twenty thousand
    ducats
  Will not debate the question of this straw.
  This is th' imposthume of much wealth and peace,
  That inward breaks, and shows no cause
    without   28
  Why the man dies, I humbly thank you, sir.
CAPTAIN. God we wi' you, sir.   *[Exit.]*

ROSENCRANTZ.   Will 't please you go,
  my lord?
HAMLET. I'll be with you straight. Go a little before.

[Exeunt all except Hamlet.]

  How all occasions do inform against me   32
  And spur my dull revenge! What is a man,
  If his chief good and market of his time
  Be but to sleep and feed? A beast, no more.
  Sure he that made us with such large
    discourse,   36
  Looking before and after, gave us not
  That capability and godlike reason
  To fust in us unus'd. Now whether it be
  Bestial oblivion, or some craven scruple   40
  Of thinking too precisely on th' event
  (A thought, which quarter'd, hath but one part
    wisdom,
  And ever three parts coward) I do not know
  Why yet I live to say 'This thing's to do,'   44
  Sith I have cause and will and strength and means
  To do 't. Examples gross as earth exhort me:
  Witness this army of such mass and charge,
  Led by a delicate and tender prince,   48
  Whose spirit with divine ambition puff'd
  Makes mouths at the invisible event,
  Exposing what is mortal and unsure
  To all that fortune, death and danger dare,   52
  Even for an egg-shell. Rightly to be great
  Is not to stir without great argument,
  But greatly to find quarrel in a straw
  When honor's at the stake. How stand I then,
  That have a father kill'd, a mother stain'd,   57
  Excitements of my reason and my blood,
  And let all sleep, while, to my shame, I see
  The imminent death of twenty thousand men,
  That for a fantasy and trick of fame   61
  Go to their graves like beds, fight for a plot
  Whereon the numbers cannot try the cause,
  Which is not tomb enough and continent   64
  To hide the slain? O, from this time forth,
  My thoughts be bloody, or be nothing worth!

[Exit.]

---

3. the conveyance of: escort during the course of. **6. in his eye:** in his presence. **8. softly:** slowly. **9. power:** troops. **15. main:** chief part. **17. no addition:** without adding fine words. **22. ranker:** richer. **sold in fee:** sold absolutely. **26. debate:** bring to a settlement. **straw:** trifling matter. **27. imposthume:** abscess.

34. market of: way to dispose of. **36. large discourse:** latitude of comprehension. **39. fust:** become mouldy. **40. Bestial oblivion:** animal-like forgetfulness. **41. event:** outcome. **44. to do:** i.e., still undone. **46. gross:** weighty. **47. charge:** expense. **54. argument:** cause. **58. Excitements:** incentives. **61. trick:** trifle. **64. continent:** (a sufficient) receptacle.

SCENE V

A Room in the Castle

[Enter Queen, Horatio, and a Gentleman.]

QUEEN. I will not speak with her.
GENTLEMAN. She is importunate, indeed distract:
　　Her mood will needs be pitied.
QUEEN. 　　　　　　　　　　　What would she
　　　　have?
GENTLEMAN. She speaks much of her father; says she
　　　　hears　　　　　　　　　　　　　　　　　4
　　There's tricks i' th' world; and hems, and beats
　　　　her heart;
　　Spurns enviously at straws, speaks things in
　　　　doubt
　　That carry but half sense. Her speech is
　　　　nothing,
　　Yet the unshaped use of it doth move　　　　8
　　The hearers to collection. They aim at it,
　　And botch the words up fit to their own
　　　　thoughts;
　　Which, as her winks and nods and gestures yield
　　　　them,
　　Indeed would make one think there might be
　　　　thought,
　　Though nothing sure, yet much unhappily.　　13
HORATIO. 'Twere good she were spoken with, for
　　　　she may strew
　　Dangerous conjectures in ill-breeding minds.
QUEEN. Let her come in.　　　　　*[Exit Gentleman.]*
　　To my sick soul, as sin's true nature is,　　　17
　　Each toy seems prologue to some great
　　　　amiss.
　　So full of artless jealousy is guilt,
　　It spills itself in fearing to be spilt.　　　20

[Enter Ophelia distracted.]

OPHELIA. Where is the beauteous majesty of
　　　　Denmark?
QUEEN. How now, Ophelia!

OPHELIA. *[She sings.]*

　　　　How should I your true love know
　　　　From another one?　　　　　　　　　24
　　　　By his cockle hat and staff,
　　　　And his sandal shoon.

QUEEN. Alas! sweet lady, what imports this song?
OPHELIA. Say you? nay, pray you, mark. *[Song.]*　28

　　　　　　He is dead and gone, lady,
　　　　　　He is dead and gone;
　　　　　　At his head a grass-green turf;
　　　　　　At his heels a stone.　　　　　32

O, ho!
QUEEN. Nay, but Ophelia,—
OPHELIA. Pray you, mark.

　　　White his shroud as the mountain snow,—　36

[Enter King.]

QUEEN. Alas! look here, my lord.
OPHELIA.

　　　　Larded all with sweet flowers;
　　　　Which bewept to the ground did—not—go
　　　　With true-love showers.　　　　　40

KING. How do you, pretty lady?
OPHELIA. Well, God 'ild you! They say the owl was
　　　a baker's daughter. Lord! we know what we are,
　　　but know not what we may be. God be at your
　　　table!　　　　　　　　　　　　　　　45
KING. Conceit upon her father.
OPHELIA. Pray, let's have no words of this; but
　　　when they ask you what it means, say you
　　　this:

　　　　To-morrow is Saint Valentine's Day,　　49
　　　　All in the morning betime,
　　　　And I a maid at your window,
　　　　To be your Valentine.　　　　　52
　　　　Then up he rose, and donn'd his clo'es,
　　　　And dupp'd the chamber door;
　　　　Let in the maid, that out a maid
　　　　Never departed more.　　　　　56

---

2. **importunate:** persistent. **5. tricks:** deceptions. **6. Spurns:**
kicks. **enviously:** spitefully. **in doubt:** ambiguous. **8. unshaped:**
artless. **9. collection:** inference. **aim:** guess. **11. Which:** the
words. **yield them:** interpret her words. **13. nothing:** not at all.
much: very. **15. ill-breeding:** plotting ill. **18. great amiss:**
calamity. **19. artless jealousy:** foolish anxiety. **20. spills:** ruins.

25. cockle hat: pilgrim's hat. **26. shoon:** shoes. **38. Larded:** gar-
nished. **42. God 'ild:** God reward. **54. dupp'd:** opened.

KING. Pretty Ophelia!

OPHELIA. Indeed, la, without an oath, I'll make an
end on 't:

> By Gis and by Saint Charity,
> Alack, and fie for shame! 60
> Young men will do 't, if they come to 't:
> By Cock they are to blame.
> Quoth she, before you tumbled me,
> You promis'd me to wed. 64

He answers:

> So would I ha' done, by yonder sun,
> An thou hadst not come to my bed.

KING. How long hath she been thus? 67

OPHELIA. I hope all will be well. We must be
patient; but I cannot choose but weep to think
they would lay him i' th' cold ground. My
brother shall know of it: and so I thank you for
your good counsel. Come, my coach!
Goodnight, ladies; good night, sweet ladies;
good night, good night. *[Exit.]*

KING. Follow her close. Give her good watch, I
pray you. *[Exit Horatio.]*
O, this is the poison of deep grief; it springs 76
All from her father's death. O Gertrude,
Gertrude!
When sorrows come, they come not single
spies,
But in battalions. First, her father slain;
Next, your son gone, and he most violent
author 80
Of his own just remove; the people muddied,
Thick and unwholesome in their thoughts and
whispers
For good Polonius' death,—and we have done
but greenly,
In hugger-mugger to inter him; poor Ophelia
Divided from herself and her fair judgment, 85
Without the which we are pictures, or mere
beasts.
Last, and as much containing as all these,
Her brother is in secret come from France, 88
Feeds on his wonder, keeps himself in clouds,

And wants no buzzers to infect his ear
With pestilent speeches of his father's death;
Wherein necessity, of matter beggar'd, 92
Will nothing stick our person to arraign
In ear and ear. O my dear Gertrude, this,
Like to a murdering-piece, in many places
Gives me superfluous death. *[A noise within.]*

QUEEN. Alack! what noise is this?

KING. Attend!

[Enter a Messenger.]

Where are my Switzers? Let them guard the
door. 97
What is the matter?

MESSENGER. Save yourself, my lord!
The ocean, overpeering of his list,
Eats not the flats with more impetuous haste
Than young Laertes, in a riotous head, 101
O'erbears your officers. The rabble call him lord,
And as the world were now but to begin,
Antiquity forgot, custom not known, 104
The ratifiers and props of every word,
They cry, 'Choose we! Laertes shall be king!'
Caps, hands, and tongues applaud it to the
clouds,
'Laertes shall be king, Laertes king!' 108

[A noise within.]

QUEEN. How cheerfully on the false trail they cry!
O, this is counter, you false Danish dogs!

KING. The doors are broke.

[Enter Laertes with others.]

LAERTES. Where is the king? Sirs, stand you all
without.

ALL. No, let's come in. 113

LAERTES. I pray you, give me leave.

ALL. We will! we will!

LAERTES. I thank you: keep the door. *[Mob retires.]*
O thou vile king!
Give me my father.

---

59. **by Gis:** by Jesus. 62. **Cock:** perversion of 'God' in oaths. 81. **remove:** removal. **muddied:** stirred up. 83. **greenly:** foolishly. 84. **In hugger-mugger:** secretly. 89. **wonder:** doubt. **in clouds:** in gloom, or, invisible.

90. **buzzers:** tale-bearers. 92. **Wherein:** i.e., in which pestilent speeches. **necessity:** poverty (of argument). 93. **nothing stick:** not at all hesitate. 94. **In ear and ear:** in many ears. 95. **murdering-piece:** small 'anti-personnel' cannon. 97. **Switzers:** Swiss guards. 99. **overpeering:** rising above. **list:** boundary. 101. **head:** hostile advance. 110. **counter:** following the trail in a direction opposite to that which the game has taken.

QUEEN.   Calmly, good Laertes.   117
LAERTES. That drop of blood that's calm proclaims
    me bastard,
    Cries cuckold to my father, brands the harlot
    Even here, between the chaste unsmirched
      brows
    Of my true mother.
KING.   What is the cause, Laertes?
    That thy rebellion looks so giantlike!   122
    Let him go, Gertrude; do not fear our person.
    There's such divinity doth hedge a king
    That treason can but peep to what it would,
    Acts little of his will. Tell me, Laertes,   126
    Why thou art thus incens'd. Let him go,
      Gertrude.
    Speak, man.
LAERTES. Where is my father?
KING.   Dead.
QUEEN.   But not by him.
KING. Let him demand his fill.   129
LAERTES. How came he dead? I'll not be juggled
    with.
    To hell, allegiance! vows, to the blackest devil!
    Conscience and grace, to the profoundest pit!
    I dare damnation. To this point I stand,   133
    That both the worlds I give to negligence.
    Let come what comes! only I'll be reveng'd
    Most thoroughly for my father.
KING.   Who shall stay
    you?
LAERTES. My will, not all the world: 137
    And for my means, I'll husband them so well,
    They shall go far with little.
KING.   Good Laertes,
    If you desire to know the certainty
    Of your dear father, is 't writ in your
      revenge,   141
    That, swoopstake, you will draw both friend
      and foe,
    Winner and loser?
LAERTES. None but his enemies.
KING.   Will you know them
    then?
LAERTES. To his good friends thus wide I'll ope my
    arms;   145

And like the kind life-rendering pelican,
Repast them with my blood.
KING.   Why, now you
    speak
    Like a good child and a true gentleman.
    That I am guiltless of your father's death,   149
    And am most sensibly in grief for it,
    It shall as level to your judgment peer
    As day does to your eye.
[A noise within. Voices.] Let her come in.
LAERTES. How now! what noise is that?

[Enter Ophelia.]

    O heat, dry up my brains! tears seven times salt,
    Burn out the sense and virtue of mine eye!
    By heaven, thy madness shall be paid with
      weight,
    Till our scale turn the beam. O rose of May!
    Dear maid, kind sister, sweet Ophelia!   158
    O heavens! is 't possible a young maid's wits
    Should be as mortal as an old man's life?
    (Nature is fine in love, and where 'tis fine   161
    It sends some precious instance of itself
    After the thing it loves.)
OPHELIA. *[Sings.]*

      They bore him barefac'd on the bier;
      Hey non nonny, nonny, hey nonny;   165
      And in his grave rain'd many a tear—

    Fare you well, my dove!
LAERTES. Hadst thou my wits, and didst persuade
    revenge,
    It could not move thus.   169
OPHELIA.

      You must sing, a-down a-down,
      And you call him a-down-a.

    O how the wheel becomes it! It is the false
    steward that stole his master's daughter.   173
LAERTES. This nothing's more than matter.
OPHELIA. There's rosemary, that's for
    remembrance; pray you, love, remember: and
    there is pansies, that's for thoughts.   177

---

119. cuckold: husband with an unfaithful wife. **125. peep:** look from tiptoe (as over a hedge). **132. grace:** God's grace. **134. both the worlds:** this world and the next. **137. My will:** as regards my will. **140. certainty:** the real truth. **142. swoopstake:** indiscriminately.

147. Repast: feed. **150. sensibly:** feelingly. **151. peer:** show itself. **155. sense and virtue:** feeling and power. **156. paid with weight:** heavily paid for. **157. of May:** early-blooming, delicate.

LAERTES. A document in madness, thoughts and
    remembrance fitted.
OPHELIA. There's fennel for you, and columbines;
    there's rue for you, and here's some for me; we
    may call it herb of grace o' Sundays. O, you
    must wear your rue with a difference. There's a
    daisy; I would give you some violets, but they
    withered all when my father died. They say he
    made a good end.   185

        For bonny sweet Robin is all my joy.

LAERTES. Thought and affliction, passion, hell itself,
    She turns to favor and to prettiness.   188
OPHELIA.

      And will 'a not come again?   *[Song.]*
      And will 'a not come again?
      No, no, he is dead;
      Go to thy deathbed,   192
      He never will come again.
      His beard was as white as snow
      All flaxen was his poll,
      He is gone, he is gone,   196
      And we castaway moan:
      God ha' mercy on his soul!

    And of all Christian souls, I pray God. God be
      wi' you!   *[Exit Ophelia.]*
LAERTES. Do you see this, O God?   201
KING. Laertes, I must cómmune with your grief,
    Or you deny me right. Go but apart,
    Make choice of whom your wisest friends you
      will,   204
    And they shall hear and judge 'twixt you and
      me.
    If by direct or by collateral hand
    They find us touch'd, we will our kingdom
      give,
    Our crown, our life, and all that we call
      ours   208
    To you in satisfaction; but if not,
    Be you content to lend your patience to us,

    And we shall jointly labor with your soul
    To give it due content.
LAERTES.   Let this be so.   212
    His means of death, his óbscure burial,
    No trophy, sword, nor hatchment o'er his
      bones,
    No noble rite nor formal ostentation,
    Cry,—to be heard as 'twere from heaven to
      earth,—
    That I must call 't in question.
KING.   So you shall;   217
    And where th' offence is let the great axe fall.
    I pray you go with me.

[Exeunt.]

SCENE VI

Another Room in the Castle

[Enter Horatio with an Attendant.]

HORATIO. What are they that would speak with
    me?
ATTENDANT. Seafaring men, sir. They say they have
    letters for you.
HORATIO. Let them come in. *[Exit Attendant.]*
    I do not know from what part of the world   4
    I should be greeted, if not from Lord Hamlet.

[Enter Sailor.]

SAILOR. God bless you, sir.
HORATIO. Let him bless thee too.
SAILOR. 'A shall, sir, an 't please him. There's a
    letter for you, sir. It came from th' ambassador
    that was bound for England,—if your name be
    Horatio, as I am let to know it is.   11
HORATIO. *[Reads the letter.]* "Horatio, when thou
    shalt have overlooked this, give these fellows
    some means to the king: they have letters for
    him. Ere we were two days old at sea, a pirate of
    very warlike appointment gave us chase.

---

178. **document:** lesson.   179. **fennel:** emblem of flattery.
columbines: emblems of thanklessness.   180. **rue:** emblem of repentance.   182. **daisy:** emblem of dissemblers.   183. **violets:** emblems of faithfulness.   187. **passion:** suffering.   188. **favor:**
charm.   195. **poll:** head ('pow' in dialect).   197. **castaway:** be-
reaved ones.   202. **commune:** consult.   203. **right:** equitable
treatment.   204. **whom your:** whichever.   206. **collateral:** indirect.   207. **touch'd:** implicated.

213. **means:** manner.   214. **trophy:** memorial emblem. **hatch-
ment:** tablet displaying armorial bearings.   215. **ostentation:** ceremony.   216. **Cry:** cry out, proclaim. **to be heard:** so loud as to be
heard.   217. **call't in question:** demand an explanation.
13. **overlooked:** perused.   16. **appointment:** equipment.

Finding ourselves too slow of sail, we put on a
compelled valor, and in the grapple I boarded
them. On the instant they got clear of our ship,
so I alone became their prisoner. They have
dealt with me like thieves of mercy, but they
knew what they did; I am to do a good turn for
them. Let the king have the letters I have sent,
and repair thou to me with as much speed as
thou wouldst fly death. I have words to speak in
thine ear will make thee dumb; yet are they too
much light for the bore of the matter. These
good fellows will bring thee where I am.
Rosencrantz and Guildenstern hold their course
for England. Of them I have much to tell thee.
Farewell!

> He that thou knowest thine,
>> Hamlet."

Come, I will give you way for these your
   letters,   32
And do 't the speedier that you may direct me
To him from whom you brought them.

[Exeunt.]

SCENE VII

A Room in the Castle

[Enter King and Laertes.]

KING. Now must your conscience my acquittance
   seal,
And you must put me in your heart for friend,
Sith you have heard, and with a knowing ear,
That he which hath your noble father slain   4
Pursu'd my life.
LAERTES. It well appears; but tell me
Why you proceeded not against these feats,
So crimeful and so capital in nature,
As by your safety, greatness, wisdom, all
   things,   8
You mainly were stirr'd up.
KING.   O, for two special
   reasons,

Which may to you perhaps seem much
   unsinew'd,
But yet to me they're strong. The queen his
   mother
Lives almost by his looks, and for myself,—   12
My virtue or my plague, be it either which,—
She's so conjunctive to my life and soul
That, as the star moves not but in his sphere,
I could not but by her. The other motive   16
Why to a public count I might not go
Is the great love the general gender bear him,
Who, dipping all his faults in their affection,
Work like the spring that turneth wood to
   stone,—   20
Convert his gyves to graces; so that my arrows,
Too slightly timber'd for so loud a wind,
Would have reverted to my bow again,
And not where I had aim'd them.   24
LAERTES. And so have I a noble father lost,
A sister driven into desperate terms,
Whose worth, if praises may go back again,
Stood challenger-on-mount of all the age   28
For her perfections. But my revenge will come.
KING. Break not your sleeps for that. You must not
   think
That we are made of stuff so flat and dull
That we can let our beard be shook with danger
And think it pastime. You shortly shall hear
   more.   33
I lov'd your father, and we love ourself,
And that, I hope, will teach you to imagine,—

[Enter a Messenger with letters.]

How now, what news?
MESSENGER.   Letters, my lord, from
   Hamlet.
These to your majesty; this to the queen.   37
KING. From Hamlet? who brought them?
MESSENGER. Sailors, my lord, they say; I saw them
   not.
They were given me by Claudio, he receiv'd
   them   40
Of him that brought them.

---

23. **repair:** come. 25. **bore:** literally, calibre, hence importance. 32. **way:** passage.
3. **knowing:** convinced. 5. **Pursu'd:** sought. 7. **capital:** punishable by death. 8. **your safety:** regard for your safety. **greatness:** position. **wisdom:** intelligence in general. 9. **mainly:** strongly.

10. **unsinew'd:** weak. 13. **be . . . which:** whichever it be. 14. **conjunctive:** closely united. 16. **could not but by her:** could not move except beside her (could not live without her). 17. **count:** legal indictment. 18. **general gender:** common people. 21. **gyves:** leg-irons, marks of shame. 22. **Too slightly timber'd:** too light. 23. **reverted:** returned. 28. **challenger-on-mount:** mounted challenger, ready in the lists.

KING.   Laertes, you shall
   hear them.—
   Leave us.   *[Exit Messenger.]*
   "High and mighty, you shall know I am set
   naked on your kingdom. To-morrow shall I
   beg leave to see your kingly eyes; when I
   shall (first asking your pardon thereunto)
   recount the occasion of my sudden and more
   strange return."
   What should this mean? Are all the rest come
   back?   48
   Or is it some abuse, and no such thing?
LAERTES. Know you the hand?
KING.   'Tis Hamlet's character. 'Naked'!
   And in a postscript here, he says, 'alone.'   51
   Can you advise me?
LAERTES. I'm lost in it, my lord. But let him come!
   It warms the very sickness in my heart
   That I shall live and tell him to his teeth,   55
   'Thus didest thou.'
KING.   If it be so, Laertes,—
   As how should it be so? how otherwise?—
   Will you be rul'd by me?
LAERTES.   Ay, my lord;
   So you will not o'er-rule me to a peace.   59
KING. To thine own peace. If he be now return'd,
   As checking at his voyage, and that he means
   No more to undertake it, I will work him
   To an exploit now ripe in my device,   63
   Under the which he shall not choose but fall;
   And for his death no wind of blame shall
     breathe,
   But even his mother shall uncharge the practice
   And call it accident.
LAERTES.   My lord, I will be rul'd;   67
   The rather, if you could devise it so
   That I might be the organ.
KING.   It falls right.
   You have been talk'd of since your travel much,
   And that in Hamlet's hearing, for a quality   71
   Wherein, they say, you shine. Your sum of parts
   Did not together pluck such envy from him
   As did that one, and that, in my regard,
   Of the unworthiest siege.
LAERTES.   What part is that, my lord? 75

KING. A very riband in the cap of youth,
   Yet needful too, for youth no less becomes
   The light and careless livery that it wears
   Than settled age his sables and his weeds   79
   Importing health and graveness. Two months
     since
   Here was a gentleman of Normandy.
   I've seen myself, and serv'd against, the French,
   And they can well on horseback; but this
     gallant
   Had witchcraft in 't. He grew unto his seat,
   And to such wondrous doing brought his
     horse,
   As had he been incorps'd and demi-natur'd
   With the brave beast. So far he topp'd my
     thought,   87
   That I, in forgery of shapes and tricks,
   Come short of what he did.
LAERTES.   A Norman was 't?
KING. A Norman.
LAERTES. Upon my life, Lamound.
KING.   The very same.   91
LAERTES. I know him well. He is the brooch indeed
   And gem of all the nation.
KING. He made confession of you,
   And gave you such a masterly report   95
   For art and exercise in your defence,
   And for your rapier most especially,
   That he cried out, 'twould be a sight indeed
   If one could match you. The scrimers of their
     nation,
   He swore, had neither motion, guard, nor
     eye,   100
   If you oppos'd them. Sir, this report of his
   Did Hamlet so envenom with his envy
   That he could nothing do but wish and beg   103
   Your sudden coming o'er, to play with you.
   Now, out of this,—
LAERTES.   What out of this, my lord?
KING. Laertes, was your father dear to you?
   Or are you like the painting of a sorrow,   107
   A face without a heart?
LAERTES.   Why ask you this?
KING. Not that I think you did not love your
   father,

---

43. naked: without resources. **49. abuse:** imposture. **50. character:** handwriting. **61. checking:** stopping short. **66. uncharge:** acquit of guilt. **practice:** stratagem. **69. organ:** instrument. **falls:** happens. **75. siege:** rank. **part:** attribute.

76. riband: ribbon. **78. livery:** garb. **79. weeds:** garments. **80. health:** prosperity. **83. can well:** are skilled. **87. topp'd:** surpassed. **94. confession:** report. **96. art and exercise:** theory and practice. **defence:** science of defence. **99. scrimers:** fencers. **104. play:** fence.

But that I know love is begun by time,
And that I see, in passages of proof,   111
Time qualifies the spark and fire of it.
There lives within the very flame of love
A kind of wick or snuff that will abate it,
And nothing is at a like goodness still,   115
For goodness, growing to a plurisy,
Dies in his own too-much. There we would do,
We should do when we would, for this 'would'
    changes,
And hath abatements and delays as many   119
As there are tongues, are hands, are accidents;
And then this 'should' is like a spendthrift's
    sigh,
That hurts by easing. But, to the quick o' th'
    ulcer:
Hamlet comes back. What would you
    undertake
To show yourself in deed your father's son   124
More than in words?
LAERTES.   To cut his throat i' th'
    church.
KING. No place, indeed, should murther
    sanctuarize;
Revenge should have no bounds. But, good
    Laertes,   127
Will you do this: keep close within your
    chamber?
Hamlet return'd shall know you are come
    home.
We'll put on those shall praise your excellence,
And set a double varnish on the fame   131
The Frenchman gave you,—bring you, in fine,
    together,
And wager on your heads. He, being remiss,
Most generous, and free from all contriving,
Will not peruse the foils; so that with ease,   135
Or with a little shuffling, you may choose
A sword unbated, and in a pass of practice
Requite him for your father.
LAERTES.   I will do 't;
And for that purpose I'll anoint my sword.   139
I bought an unction of a mountebank
So mortal that, but dip a knife in it,
Where it draws blood no cataplasm so rare,
Collected from all simples that have virtue   143

Under the moon, can save the thing from death
That is but scratch'd withal. I'll touch my point
With this contagion, that if I gall him slightly,
It may be death.
KING.   Let's further think of this,   147
Weigh what convenience both of time and
    means
May fit us to our shape. If this should fail,
And that our drift look through our bad
    performance,
'Twere better not assay'd. Therefore this
    project   151
Should have a back or second, that might hold,
If this should blast in proof. Soft! let me see.
We'll make a solemn wager on your cunnings.
I ha t':   155
When in your motion you are hot and dry,—
As make your bouts more violent to that end,—
And that he calls for drink, I'll have prepar'd
    him
A chalice for the nonce, whereon but sipping,
If he by chance escape your venom'd stuck,   160
Our purpose may hold there. But stay! what
    noise?

[Enter Queen.]

    How, sweet queen?
QUEEN. One woe doth tread upon another's
    heel,   163
So fast they follow. Your sister's drown'd,
    Laertes.
LAERTES. Drown'd! O, where?
QUEEN. There is a willow grows aslant a brook,
That shows his hoar leaves in the glassy stream.
There with fantastic garlands did she come   168
Of crowflowers, nettles, daisies, and long
    purples,
That liberal shepherds give a grosser name,
But our cold maids do dead men's fingers call
    them.   171
There, on the pendent boughs her coronet
    weeds
Clambering to hang, an envious sliver broke,
When down her weedy trophies and herself

116. plurisy: fulness. 119. abatements: diminutions. 130. put on: instigate. those: certain persons who. 133. remiss: easygoing. 135. peruse: inspect. 137. unbated: not blunted. pass of practice: treacherous thrust. 139. anoint: smear. 142. cataplasm: poultice. 143. simples: medicinal herbs.

149. our shape: part we purpose to act. 153. blast in proof: burst when tested (as of a cannon). 154. cunnings: skill. 156. motion: bodily exertion. 159. for the nonce: for the purpose. 160. stuck; thrust. 167. hoar: greyish-white. 169. crowflowers: buttercups. long purples: early purple. 170. liberal: free-spoken. 172. coronet: garlanded.

Fell in the weeping brook. Her clothes spread
    wide,   175
And mermaid-like awhile they bore her up;
Which time she chanted snatches of old tunes,
As one incapable of her own distress,
Or like a creature native and indu'd   179
Unto that element; but long it could not be
Till that her garments, heavy with their drink,
Pull'd the poor wretch from her melodious lay
To muddy death.
LAERTES.   Alas, then, she is drown'd? 183
QUEEN. Drown'd, drown'd.

LAERTES. Too much of water hast thou, poor
    Ophelia,
And therefore I forbid my tears; but yet
It is our trick, nature her custom holds,   187
Let shame say what it will. When these are gone,
The woman will be out. Adieu, my lord!
I have a speech of fire, that fain would blaze,
But that this folly douts it.   *[Exit.]*
KING.   Let's follow, Gertrude.
How much I had to do to calm his rage!   192
Now fear I this will give it start again.
Therefore let's follow.   *[Exeunt.]*

Act V

SCENE I

A Churchyard near Elsinore

[Enter two Clowns.]

[FIRST] CLOWN. Is she to be buried in Christian
    burial when she wilfully seeks her own
    salvation?
OTHER. I tell thee she is. Therefore make her grave
    straight. The crowner hath sat on her and finds
    it Christian burial.   5
CLOWN. How can that be, unless she drowned
    herself in her own defence?
OTHER. Why, 'tis found so.
CLOWN. It must be *se offendendo;* it cannot be else.
    For here lies the point: if I drown myself
    wittingly, it argues an act, and an act hath three
    branches; it is to act, to do, to perform. Argal,
    she drowned herself wittingly.
OTHER. Nay, but hear you, goodman delver,— 14
CLOWN. Give me leave. Here lies the water; good.
    Here stands the man; good. If the man go to
    this water and drown himself, it is, will he, nill
    he, he goes; mark you that! But if the water
    come to him and drown him, he drowns not

himself. Argal, he that is not guilty of his own
    death shortens not his own life.   21
OTHER. But is this law?
CLOWN. Ay, marry, is 't; crowner's quest law. 23
OTHER. Will you ha' the truth on 't? If this had not
    been a gentlewoman, she should have been
    buried out o' Christian burial.   26
CLOWN. Why, there thou sayest; and the more pity
    that great folk should have countenance in this
    world to drown or hang themselves more than
    their even Christen. Come, my spade! There is
    no ancient gentlemen but gardeners, ditchers,
    and gravemakers. They hold up Adam's
    profession.   32
OTHER. Was he a gentleman?
CLOWN. 'A was the first that ever bore arms.
OTHER. Why, he had none.   35
CLOWN. What! art a heathen? How dost thou
    understand the Scripture? The Scripture says,
    Adam digged; could he dig without arms? I'll
    put another question to thee. If you answerest
    me not to the purpose, confess thyself—
OTHER. Go to.   41
CLOWN. What is he that builds stronger than
    either the mason, the shipwright, or the
    carpenter.
OTHER. The gallows-maker; for that frame outlives
    a thousand tenants.   45

---

178. incapable: having no understanding.   **179. indu'd:** endowed
with qualities fitting her.
4. straight: at once. **crowner:** coroner. **sat on:** passed on.   **11.
branches:** divisions.   **12. Argal:** corruption of *ergo,* therefore.   **14.
goodman delver:** Mr. Sexton.

187. trick: hereditary trait.   **191. douts:** extinguishes.
23. quest: inquest.   **30. even Christen:** fellow Christian.   **41. Go
to:** out with it!

CLOWN. I like thy wit well. In good faith the gallows does well, but how does it well? It does well to those that do ill. Now thou dost ill to say the gallows is built stronger than the church. Argal, the gallows may do well to thee. To 't again; come!

OTHER. Who builds stronger than a mason, a shipwright, or a carpenter?   52

CLOWN. Ay, tell me that, and unyoke.

OTHER. Marry, now I can tell.

CLOWN. To 't.

OTHER. Mass, I cannot tell.   56

[Enter Hamlet and Horatio afar off.]

CLOWN. Cudgel thy brains no more about it, for your dull ass will not mend his pace with beating; and when you are asked this question next, say, 'a gravemaker.' The houses he makes lasts till doomsday. Go, get thee to Yaughan and fetch me a stoup of liquor.

[Exit other Clown.]

[Clown digs and sings.]

In youth, when I did love, did love,
    Methought it was very sweet.
To contract—oh—the time, for—ah—my behove,
O methought there—ah—was nothing—ah—
    meet.

HAMLET. Has this fellow no feeling of his business,
    that he sings at grave-making?   68

HORATIO. Custom hath made it in him a property of easiness.

HAMLET. 'Tis e'en so; the hand of little employment hath the daintier sense.   72

CLOWN.

But age, with his stealing steps,   *[Song.]*
Hath claw'd me in his clutch,
And hath shipp'd me intil the land,
As if I had never been such.   76

[Throws up a skull.]

HAMLET. That skull had a tongue in it and could sing once. How the knave jowls it to the ground, as if 't were Cain's jaw-bone, that did the first murther! This might be the pate of a politician which this ass now o'erreaches, one that would circumvent God, might it not?   82

HORATIO. It might, my lord.

HAMLET. Or of a courtier, which could say, 'Good morrow, sweet lord! How dost thou, good lord?' This might be my Lord Such-a-one, that praised my Lord Such-a-one's horse when 'a went to beg it, might it not?   88

HORATIO. Ay, my lord.

HAMLET. Why, e'en so, and now my Lady Worm's: chapless, and knocked about the mazzard with a sexton's spade. Here's fine revolution, an we had the trick to see 't. Did these bones cost no more the breeding but to play at loggats with 'em? Mine ache to think on 't.   95

CLOWN. *[Song.]*

A pick-axe and a spade, a spade,
For and a shrouding sheet;
O, a pit of clay for to be made
For such a guest is meet.

[Throws up another skull.]

HAMLET. There's another! Why may not that be the skull of a lawyer? Where be his quiddities now, his quillets, his cases, his tenures, and his tricks? Why does he suffer this rude knave now to knock him about the sconce with a dirty shovel, and will not tell him of his action of battery? Hum! This fellow might be in 's time a great buyer of land, with his statutes, his recognizances, his fines, his double vouchers, his recoveries. (Is this the fine of his fines, and the recovery of his recoveries,) to have his fine pate full of fine dirt? Will his vouchers vouch him no more of his purchases, and double ones too, than the length and breadth of a pair of indentures? The very conveyances of his lands will scarcely lie in this box, and must th' inheritor himself have no more, ha?

78. **jowls:** dashes. 79. **Cain's jaw-bone, that:** the jaw-bone of Cain, who. 87. **went:** went about, attempted. 91. **chapless:** lacking the lower jaw. **mazzard:** head. 101. **quiddities:** subtleties. 102. **quillets:** minute distinctions. 104. **sconce:** head. 108. **fine:** end. 112. **indentures:** mutual agreements.

62. **stoup:** two quart measure. 65. **contract:** shorten (with pleasure). **behove:** benefit. 66. **meet:** good enough. 72. **sense:** sensibility. 75. **intil:** into.

HORATIO. Not a jot more, my lord.   115

HAMLET. Is not parchment made of sheep skins?

HORATIO. Ay, my lord, and of calves' skins too.   117

HAMLET. They are sheep and calves which seek out assurance in that. I will speak to this fellow. Whose grave 's this, sirrah?

CLOWN. Mine, sir,

> O, a pit of clay for to be made   122
> For such a guest is meet.

HAMLET. I think it be thine indeed, for thou liest in 't.

CLOWN. You lie out 't, sir, and therefore 't is not yours. For my part, I do not lie in 't, yet it is mine.   128

HAMLET. Thou does lie in 't, to be in 't and say it is thine. 'Tis for the dead, not for the quick. Therefore thou liest.

CLOWN. 'Tis a quick lie, sir. 'Twill away again from me to you.

HAMLET. What man dost thou dig it for?   134

CLOWN. For no man, sir.

HAMLET. What woman, then?

CLOWN. For none, either.

HAMLET. Who is to be buried in 't?   138

CLOWN. One that was a woman, sir; but, rest her soul, she's dead.

HAMLET. How absolute the knave is! we must speak by the card, or equivocation will undo us. By the Lord, Horatio, this three years I have took note of it; the age is grown so picked that the toe of the peasant comes so near the heel of the courtier he galls his kibe.—How long hast thou been grave-maker?   146

CLOWN. Of all the days i' th' year, I came to 't that day that our last King Hamlet overcame Fortinbras.

HAMLET. How long is that since?   149

CLOWN. Cannot you tell that? Every fool can tell that. It was that very day that young Hamlet was born,— he that is mad and sent into England.   152

HAMLET. Ay, marry! Why was he sent into England?

CLOWN. Why, because 'a was mad. 'A shall recover his wits there; or if 'a do not, 'tis no great matter there.   156

HAMLET. Why?

CLOWN. 'Twill not be seen in him there. There the men are as mad as he.   159

HAMLET. How came he mad?

CLOWN. Very strangely, they say.

HAMLET. How, strangely?   162

CLOWN. Faith, e'én with losing his wits.

HAMLET. Upon what ground?

CLOWN. Why, here in Denmark. I have been sexton here, man and boy, thirty years.   166

HAMLET. How long will a man lie i' th' earth ere he rot?

CLOWN. Faith, if 'a be not rotten before 'a die (as we have many pocky corses now-a-days, that will scarce hold the laying in) 'a will last you some eight year or nine year. A tanner will last you nine year.

HAMLET. Why he more than another?   173

CLOWN. Why, sir, his hide is so tanned with his trade that 'a will keep out water a great while, and your water is a sore decayer of your whoreson dead body. Here's a skill now hath lien you i' th' earth three-and-twenty years.   178

HAMLET. Whose was it?

CLOWN. A whoreson mad fellow's it was. Whose do you think it was?

HAMLET. Nay, I know not.   182

CLOWN. A pestilence on him for a mad rogue! 'a poured a flagon of Rhenish on my head once. This same skull, sir, was Sir Yorick's skull, the king's jester.

HAMLET. This!

CLOWN. E'en that.   188

HAMLET. Let me see. *[Takes the skull.]* Alas, poor Yorick! I knew him, Horatio; a fellow of infinite jest, of most excellent fancy. He hath borne me on his back a thousand times; and now, how abhorred in my imagination it is! My gorge rises at it. Here hung those lips that I have kissed I know not how oft. Where be your gibes now? your gambols? your songs? your flashes of merriment, that were wont to set the table on a roar? Not one now, to mock your own grinning; quite chapfallen. Now get you to my lady's chamber, and tell her, let her paint an inch thick, to this favor she must come. Make her laugh at that. Prithee, Horatio, tell me one thing.

---

119. assurance: security.   141. absolute: precise.   142. by the card: with precision.   144. picked: fastidious.   146. kibe: chilblain.

176. sore: grievous. whoreson: plagued.   177. lien: lain.
200. favor: appearance.

HORATIO. What's that, my lord?   202

HAMLET. Dost thou think Alexander looked o' this fashion i' th' earth?

HORATIO. E'en so.

HAMLET. And smelt so? pah!   206

[Puts down the skull.]

HORATIO. E'en so, my lord.

HAMLET. To what base uses we may return, Horatio! Why may not imagination trace the noble dust of Alexander till 'a find it stopping a bunghole?   210

HORATIO. 'Twere to consider too curiously, to consider so.

HAMLET. No, faith, not a jot; but to follow him thither with modesty enough, and likelihood to lead it; as thus: Alexander died, Alexander was buried, Alexander returneth to dust; the dust is earth. Of earth we make loam, and why of that loam, whereto he was converted, might they not stop a beer-barrel?

Imperious Caesar, dead and turn'd to clay,
Might stop a hole to keep the wind away.   220
O that that earth, which kept the world in awe,
Should patch a wall t' expel the winter's flaw!

But soft! but soft awhile! Here comes the king.

[Enter King, Queen, Laertes, a Priest, and a coffin, with Lords attendant.]

The queen, the courtiers! Who is this they
    follow?   224
And with such maimed rites? This doth betoken
The corse they follow did with desperate hand
Fordo it own life. 'Twas of some estate.
Couch we awhile, and mark.   228

[Retires with Horatio.]

LAERTES. Where ceremony else?

HAMLET.   That is Laertes,
   A very noble youth. Mark.

LAERTES. What ceremony else?

PRIEST. Her obsequies have been as far enlarg'd   232
   As we have warranty. Her death was doubtful,

And but that great command o'ersways the
    order,
She should in ground unsanctified been
    lodg'd
Till the last trumpet; for charitable prayers,   236
Shards, flints, and pebbles should be thrown on
    her.
Yet here she is allow'd her virgin crants,
Her maiden strewments, and the bringing home
Of bell and burial.   240

LAERTES. Must there no more be done?

PRIEST.   No more be
    done.
We should profane the service of the dead
To sing a requiem and such rest to her
As to peace-parted souls.

LAERTES.   Lay her i' th' earth, 244
And from her fair and unpolluted flesh
May violets spring! I tell thee, churlish priest,
A ministering angel shall my sister be
When thou liest howling.

HAMLET.   What! the fair Ophelia? 248

QUEEN. *[Scattering flowers.]* Sweets to the sweet!
    farewell!
I hop'd thou shouldst have been my Hamlet's
    wife.
I thought thy bride-bed to have deck'd, sweet
    maid,
And not have strew'd thy grave.

LAERTES.   O treble woe 252
Fall ten times treble on that cursed head
Whose wicked deed thy most ingenious sense
Depriv'd thee of. Hold off the earth awhile,
Till I have caught her once more in mine arms.

[Leaps in the grave.]

Now pile your dust upon the quick and dead,
Till of this flat a mountain you have made   258
T' o'er-top old Pelion or the skyish head
Of blue Olympus.

HAMLET. *[Advancing.]* What is he whose grief
Bears such emphasis? whose phrase of
    sorrow   261
Conjures the wandering stars, and makes them
    stand

---

211. **curiously:** minutely.   214. **modesty:** moderation. **likelihood:** probability.   222. **flaw:** squall of wind.   227. **Fordo it:** undo its. **estate:** rank.   228. **Couch:** remain concealed.   232. **enlarg'd:** extended.   233. **warranty:** warrant. **doubtful:** suspicious.

235. **been:** have been.   237. **Shards:** fragments of pottery.   238. **crants:** garland.   239. **strewments:** flowers strewn on a grave.   244. **peace-parted:** piously deceased.   254. **ingenious:** delicately sensitive.   262. **wandering stars:** planets.

Like wonder-wounded bearers? This is I,
Hamlet the Dane. *[Hamlet leaps in after Laertes.]*
LAERTES.   The devil take thy soul!   264

[Grapples with him.]

HAMLET. Thou pray'st not well.
   I prithee take thy fingers from my throat;
   For though I am not splenetive and rash,
   Yet have I in me something dangerous,   268
   Which let thy wisdom fear. Hold off thy hand!
KING. Pluck them asunder.
QUEEN.   Hamlet! Hamlet!
ALL. Gentlemen!
HORATIO.   Good my lord, be quiet.

[The Attendants part them, and they come out of the grave.]

HAMLET. Why, I will fight with him upon this
     theme
   Until my eyelids will no longer wag.
QUEEN. O my son, what theme?
HAMLET. I lov'd Ophelia. Forty thousand brothers
   Could not with all their quantity of love   276
   Make up my sum. What wilt thou do for her?
KING. O, he is mad, Laertes.
QUEEN. For love of God, forbear him.
HAMLET. 'Swounds, show me what thou't do.
   Woo't weep? woo't fight? woo't fast? woo't tear
     thyself.   281
   Woo't drink up eisel? eat a crocodile?
   I'll do 't. Dost thou come here to whine?
   To outface me with leaping in her grave?   284
   Be buried quick with her, and so will I.
   And if thou prate of mountains, let them throw
   Millions of acres on us, till our ground,
   Singeing his pate against the burning zone,   288
   Make Ossa like a wart! Nay, an thou'lt mouth,
   I'll rant as well as thou.
QUEEN.   This is mere madness,
   And thus a while the fit will work on him.
   Anon, as patient as the female dove,   292
   When that her golden couplets are disclos'd,
   His silence will sit drooping.
HAMLET.   Hear you, sir.
   What is the reason that you use me thus?

I lov'd you ever,—but it is no matter.   296
Let Hercules himself do what he may,
The cat will mew and dog will have his day. *[Exit.]*
KING. I pray thee, good Horatio, wait upon him.

[Exit Horatio.]

[To Laertes.] Strengthen your patience in our last
   night's speech.   300
We'll put the matter to the present push.—
Good Gertrude, set some watch over your son.
This grave shall have a living monument.
An hour of quiet shortly shall we see;   304
Till then, in patience our proceeding be.

[Exeunt.]

SCENE II

The Hall in the Castle

[Enter Hamlet and Horatio.]

HAMLET. So much for this, sir; now shall you see
   the other.
   You do remember all the circumstance?
HORATIO. Remember it, my lord!
HAMLET. Sir, in my heart there was a kind of
   fighting   4
   That would not let me sleep. Methought I lay
   Worse than the mutines in the bilboes.
     Rashly,—
   And prais'd be rashness for it (let us know,
   Our indiscretion sometimes serves us well   8
   When our deep plots do pall; and that should
     learn us
   There's a divinity that shapes our ends,
   Rough-hew them how we will)—
HORATIO.   That is most
   certain.
HAMLET. Up from my cabin,   12
   My sea gown scarf'd about me, in the dark
   Grop'd I to find out them, had my desire,
   Finger'd their packet, and in fine withdrew
   To mine own room again; making so bold   16

---

267. **splenetive:** quick-tempered.   **279. forbear him:** leave him alone.   **281. Woo't:** wilt thou.   **282. eisel:** vinegar (associated with gall).   **288. burning zone:** 'coelum igneum,' heavenly region of fire.

300. **in:** in the thought of.   **301. present push:** immediate trial.   **303. living:** lasting.
6. **mutines:** mutineers. **bilboes:** shackles.   **9. pall:** fail.   **15. Finger'd:** pilfered.

(My fears forgetting manners) to unseal
Their grand commission, where I found, Horatio,
(Ah, royal knavery!) an exact command,—
Larded with many several sorts of reasons   20
Importing Denmark's health and England's too,
With, ho! such bugs and goblins in my life,—
That, on the supervise, no leisure bated,
No, not to stay the grinding of the axe,   24
My head should be struck off.

HORATIO.   Is 't possible?

HAMLET. Here's the commission: read it at more leisure.
But wilt thou hear now how I did proceed?

HORATIO. I beseech you.   28

HAMLET. Being thus be-netted round with villainies,
Ere I could make a prologue to my brains
They had begun the play. I sat me down,
Devis'd a new commission, wrote it fair.—   32
I once did hold it, as our statists do,
A baseness to write fair and labor'd much
How to forget that learning, but, sir, now
It did me yeoman's service. Wilt thou know   36
Th' effect of what I wrote?

HORATIO.   Ay, good my lord.

HAMLET. An earnest conjuration from the king,
As England was his faithful tributary,
As love between them like the palm might flourish,   40
As peace should still her wheaten garland wear
And stand a comma 'tween their amities,
And many such-like 'As'es of great charge,
That, on the view and knowing of these contents,   44
Without debatement further, more or less,
He should those bearers put to sudden death,
Not shriving-time allow'd.

HORATIO.   How was this seal'd?

HAMLET. Why, even in that was heaven ordinant.   48
I had my father's signet in my purse,
Which was the model of that Danish seal.—
Folded the writ up in the form of th' other,
Subscrib'd it, gave 't th' impression, plac'd it safely,   52

The changeling never known. Now, the next day
Was our sea-fight, and what to this was sequent
Thou know'st already.

HORATIO. So Guilderstern and Rosencrantz go to 't.   56

HAMLET. Why, man, they did make love to this employment;
They are not near my conscience. Their defeat
Does by their own insinuation grow.
'Tis dangerous when the baser nature comes   60
Between the pass and fell-incensed points
Of mighty opposites.

HORATIO.   Why, what a king is this!

HAMLET. Does it not, think thee, stand me now upon?
He that hath kill'd my king and whor'd my mother,   64
Popp'd in between th' election and my hopes,
Thrown out his angle for my proper life,
And with such cozenage—is 't not perfect conscience
To quit him with this arm? and is 't not to be damn'd
To let this canker of our nature come   69
In further evil?

HORATIO. It must be shortly known to him from England
What is the issue of the business there.   72

HAMLET. It will be short. The interim is mine,
And a man's life's no more than to say 'One.'
But I am very sorry, good Horatio,
That to Laertes I forgot myself,   76
For by the image of my cause I see
The portraiture of his. I'll court his favors:
But sure the bravery of his grief did put me
Into a towering passion.

HORATIO.   Peace! who comes here? 80

[Enter young Osric.]

OSRIC. Your lordship is right welcome back to Denmark.

HAMLET. I humbly thank you, sir. *[Aside to Horatio.]*
Dost know this water-fly?   84

HORATIO. *[Aside to Hamlet.]* No, my good lord.

---

23. supervise: perusal. **bated:** deducted. **29. be-netted:** ensnared. **33. statists:** statesmen. **36. yeoman's service:** good and faithful service. **41. wheaten garland:** emblem of peace. **42. comma:** bond of connection. **47. shriving-time:** time for absolution. **48. ordinant:** controlling. **50. model:** exact likeness. **52. Subscrib'd:** signed. **impression:** i.e., of the seal.

53. changeling: substitute. **59. insinuation:** intrusion. **61. fell-incensed:** cruelly angered. **62. opposites:** opponents. **63. stand . . . upon:** vitally concern. **66. angle:** fishing-hook. **proper:** own. **67. cozenage:** cheating. **79. bravery:** ostentatious display.

HAMLET. *[Aside to Horatio.]* Thy state is the more gracious, for 'tis a vice to know him. He hath much land, and fertile. Let a beast be lord of beasts, and his crib shall stand at the king's mess. 'Tis a chough, but, as I say, spacious in the possession of dirt. 90

OSRIC. Sweet lord, if your lordship were at leisure, I should impart a thing to you from his majesty.

HAMLET. I will receive it, sir, with all diligence of spirit. Put your bonnet to his right use; 'tis for the head. 95

OSRIC. I thank your lordship. It is very hot.

HAMLET. No, believe me, 'tis very cold; the wind is northerly. 98

OSRIC. It is indifferent cold, my lord, indeed.

HAMLET. But yet methinks it is very sultry and hot for my complexion. 101

OSRIC. Exceedingly, my lord. It is very sultry, as 'twere,—I cannot tell how. But, my lord, his majesty bade me signify to you that 'a has laid a great wager on your head. Sir, this is the matter,— 105

HAMLET. I beseech you, remember—

[Hamlet moves him to put on his hat.]

OSRIC. Nay, good my lord, for my ease, in good faith. Sir, here is newly come to court Laertes,— believe me, an absolute gentleman, full of most excellent differences, of very soft society and great showing. Indeed, to speak feeling of him, he is the card or calendar of gentry, for you shall find in him the continent of what part a gentleman would see. 113

HAMLET. Sir, his definement suffers no perdition in you; though, I know, to divide him inventorially would dozy th' arithmetic of memory, and yet but yaw neither, in respect of his quick sail. But, in the verity of extolment, I take him to be a soul of great article, and his infusion of such dearth and rareness as, to make true diction of him, his semblable is his mirror, and who else would trace him his umbrage, nothing more. 122

OSRIC. Your lordship speaks most infallibly of him.

HAMLET. The concernancy, sir? Why do we wrap the gentleman in our more rawer breath?

OSRIC. Sir?

HORATIO. Is 't not possible to understand in another tongue? You will to 't, sir, really. 128

HAMLET. What imports the nomination of this gentleman?

OSRIC. Of Laertes? 131

HORATIO. His purse is empty already. All 's golden words are spent.

HAMLET. Of him, sir.

OSRIC. I know you are not ignorant— 135

HAMLET. I would you did, sir; yet in faith, if you did, it would not much approve me. Well sir.

OSRIC. You are not ignorant of what excellence Laertes is—

HAMLET. I dare not confess that, lest I should compare with him in excellence; but to know a man well were to know himself. 142

OSRIC. I mean, sir, for his weapon; but in the imputation laid on him by them, in his meed he's unfellowed.

HAMLET. What's his weapon?

OSRIC. Rapier and dagger. 147

HAMLET. That's two of his weapons, but,—well.

OSRIC. The king, sir, hath wagered with him six Barbary horses, against the which he has impawned, as I take it, six French rapiers and poniards, with their assigns; as girdle, hanger, and so. Three of the carriages, in faith, are very dear to fancy, very responsive to the hilts, most delicate carriages and of very liberal conceit. 155

HAMLET. What call you the carriages?

HORATIO. I knew you must be edified by the margent, ere you had done.

OSRIC. The carriages, sir, are the hangers. 159

HAMLET. The phrase would be more germane to the matter, if we could carry a cannon by our sides. I would it might be hangers till then. But, on; six Barbary horses against six French

---

89. chough: small chattering bird. **109. absolute:** perfect. **110. differences:** distinguishing features. **soft:** gentle. **112. card:** map. **114. definement:** description. **perdition:** loss. **115. divide inventorially:** catalogue. **116. dozy:** make giddy. **117. yaw:** stagger. **neither:** too. **119. great article:** large scope. **infusion:** character imparted by nature. **121. semblable:** like. **122. trace:** follow. **umbrage:** shadow.

124. concernancy: relevance. **125. more rawer:** too unskilled. **128. You will to 't:** You will acquire the art. **129. nomination:** naming. **137. approve me:** commend me. **141. compare with:** vie with. **144. imputation:** reputation. **meed:** merit, worth. **145. unfellowed:** without an equal. **151. impawned:** staked. **152. assigns:** appurtenances. **hanger:** strap from which a sword is suspended. **153. carriages:** hangers. **154. dear to fancy:** unusual in design. **delicate:** finely wrought. **155. liberal conceit:** tasteful design.

swords, their assigns, and three liberal-conceited carriages; that's the French bet against the Danish. Why is this all impawned, as you call it?

OSRIC. The king, sir, hath laid that in a dozen passes between yourself and him, he shall not exceed you three hits. He hath laid on twelve for nine, and it would come to immediate trial, if your lordship would vouchsafe the answer. 171

HAMLET. How if I answer no?

OSRIC. I mean, my lord, the opposition of your person in trial.

HAMLET. Sir, I will walk here in the hall. If it please his majesty, it is the breathing time of day with me. Let the foils be brought, the gentleman willing, and the king hold his purpose, I will win for him an I can; if not, I will gain nothing but my shame and the odd hits. 180

OSRIC. Shall I deliver you so?

HAMLET. To this effect, sir, after what flourish your nature will. 183

HAMLET. I commend my duty to your lordship.

HAMLET. Yours, yours. *[Exit Osric.]* He does well to commend it himself; there are no tongues else for 's turn. 187

HORATIO. This lapwing runs away with the shell on his head.

HAMLET. 'A did comply, sir, with his dug before 'a sucked it. Thus has he—and many more of the same bevy, that I know the drossy age dotes on—only got the tune of the time and outward habit of encounter, a kind of yesty collection which carries them through and through the most fond and winnowed opinions, and do but blow them to their trial, the bubbles are out. 197

[Enter a Lord.]

LORD. My lord, his majesty commended him to you by young Osric, who brings back to him that you attend him in the hall. He sends to know if your pleasure hold to play with Laertes, or that you will take longer time. 202

HAMLET. I am constant to my purposes; they follow the king's pleasure. If his fitness speaks, mine is ready, now or whensoever, provided I be so able as now.

LORD. The king and queen and all are coming down. 208

HAMLET. In happy time.

LORD. The queen desires you to use some gentle entertainment to Laertes before you fall to play.

HAMLET. She well instructs me. *[Exit Lord.]*

HORATIO. You will lose this wager, my lord.

HAMLET. I do not think so. Since he went into France, I have been in continual practice. I shall win at the odds, but thou wouldst not think how ill all 's here about my heart. But it is no matter. 217

HORATIO. Nay, good my lord,—

HAMLET. It is but foolery, but it is such a kind of gain giving as would perhaps trouble a woman. 220

HORATIO. If your mind dislike anything, obey it. I will forestall their repair hither and say you are not fit. 222

HAMLET. Not a whit, we defy augury; there is special providence in the fall of a sparrow. If it be now, 'tis not to come; if it be not to come, it will be now; if it be not now, yet it will come: the readiness is all. Since no man has aught of what he leaves, what is 't to leave betimes? Let be.

[Enter King, Queen, Laertes and Lords, with other Attendants with foils and gauntlets. A table and flagons of wine on it.]

KING. Come, Hamlet, come, and take this hand from me.

[The King puts the hand of Laertes into that of Hamlet.]

HAMLET. Give me your pardon, sir. I've done you wrong;
But pardon 't, as you are a gentleman.
This presence knows, and you must needs have heard,
How I am punish'd with a sore distraction.
What I have done, 234

---

176. **breathing time:** exercise period. 188. **lapwing:** plover, a vivacious little bird. 188–189. **with . . . head:** almost before he is hatched. 190. **comply:** use fine language. 192. **drossy:** frivolous. 193. **tune:** mood. 193–194. **outward . . . encounter:** superficial mannerisms. 194. **yesty:** frothy.

209. **In happy time:** at an appropriate time. 220. **gaingiving:** foreboding. 232. **presence:** royal assembly.

That might your nature, honor, and exception
Roughly awake, I here proclaim was madness.
Was 't Hamlet wrong'd Laertes? Never
     Hamlet.
If Hamlet from himself be ta'en away,   238
And when he's not himself does wrong Laertes,
Then Hamlet does it not; Hamlet denies it.
Who does it then? His madness. If't be so,
Hamlet is of the faction that is wrong'd;   242
His madness is poor Hamlet's enemy.
Sir, in this audience,
Let my disclaiming from a purpos'd evil
Free me so far in your most generous thoughts,
That I have shot my arrow o'er the house,   247
And hurt my brother. *asking for forgiveness*

Hamlet talks
like there is
2 Hamlets

LAERTES.   I am satisfied in nature,
Whose motive in this case should stir me most
To my revenge; but in my terms of honor   250
I stand aloof, and will no reconcilement
Till by some elder masters of known honor
I have a voice and precedent of peace,
To keep my name ungor'd. But till that time,
I do receive your offer'd love like love,   255
And will not wrong it.
HAMLET.   I embrace it freely,
And will this brothers' wager frankly play.
Give us the foils. Come on.
LAERTES.   Come, one for me.
HAMLET. I'll be your foil, Laertes. In mine
     ignorance
Your skill shall, like a star i' th' darkest night,
Stick fiery off indeed.
LAERTES.   You mock me, sir.
HAMLET. No, by this hand.   262
KING. Give them the foils, young Osric. Cousin
     Hamlet,
You know the wager?
HAMLET.   Very well, my lord;
Your Grace has laid the odds o' th' weaker side.
KING. I do not fear it. I have seen you both;
But since he is better'd, we have therefore odds.
LAERTES. This is too heavy; let me see another.
HAMLET. This likes me well. These foils have all a
     length?
OSRIC. Ay, my good lord.   270

[Prepare to play.]

KING. Set me the stoups of wine upon that table.
If Hamlet give the first or second hit,
Or quit in answer of the third exchange,
Let all the battlements their ordnance fire.   274
The king shall drink to Hamlet's better breath;
And in the cup an union shall he throw,
Richer than that which four successive kings
In Denmark's crown have worn. Give me the
     cups;   278
And let the kettle to the trumpet speak,
The trumpet to the cannoneer without,
The cannons to the heavens, the heaven to
     earth:
'Now the king drinks to Hamlet!'
         Come, begin *[Trumpets the while.]*
And you, the judges, bear a wary eye.
HAMLET. Come on sir.
LAERTES.   Come, my lord.   *[They play.]*
HAMLET.   One.
LAERTES.   No.
HAMLET.   Judgment.
OSRIC. A hit, a very palpable hit.

[Drum, trumpets and shot. Flourish. A piece goes off.]

LAERTES.   Well; again.
KING. Stay; give me drink. Hamlet, this pearl is
     thine.
Here's to thy health. Give him the cup.   287

[Trumpets sound; and shot goes off.]

HAMLET. I'll play this bout first; set it by awhile.
Come.— *[They play.]* Another hit! What say you?
LAERTES. A touch, a touch, I do confess't.   290
KING. Our son shall win.
QUEEN.   He's fat and scant of breath.
Here, Hamlet, take my napkin, rub thy brows.
The queen carouses to thy fortune, Hamlet.

[Takes Hamlet's cup.]

HAMLET. Good madam!
KING.   Gertrude, do not drink! 294
QUEEN. I will, my lord; I pray you, pardon me.
KING. *[Aside.]* It is the poison'd cup! it is too late.
HAMLET. I dare not drink yet, madam, By and by.
QUEEN. Come, let me wipe thy face.   298

---

235. exception: disapproval.   **253. voice:** opinion.   **254. ungor'd:**
uninjured.   **261. stick . . . off:** stand out in relief.

276. union: pearl.   **279. kettle:** kettledrum.   **291. fat:** out of
training.   **292. napkin:** handkerchief.

says he forgives him

LAERTES. My lord, I'll hit him now.

KING.   I do not think 't.

LAERTES. *[Aside.]* And yet it is almost against my
    conscience.

HAMLET. Come, for the third! Laertes, you but
    dally;

    I pray you, pass with your best violence.   302

    I am afeard you make a wanton of me.

LAERTES. Say you so? come on.   *[Play.]*

OSRIC. Nothing, neither way.

LAERTES. Have at you now.

[In scuffling they change rapiers.]

KING.   Part them! they are incens'd.

HAMLET. Nay, come again!   *[The Queen falls.]*

OSRIC.   Look to the queen there. Ho!

HORATIO. They bleed on both sides. How is it, my
    lord?

OSRIC. How is 't Laertes?

LAERTES. Why, as a woodcock to mine own springe,
    Osric.   310

    I am justly kill'd with mine own treachery.

HAMLET. How does the queen?

KING.   She sounds to see them bleed.

QUEEN. No, no, the drink, the drink! O my dear
    Hamlet!   313

    The drink, the drink! I am poison'd.   *[Dies.]*

HAMLET. O villainy! Ho! let the door be lock'd.
    Treachery! seek it out.   *[Laertes falls.]*

LAERTES. It is here, Hamlet. Hamlet, thou art slain;
    No medicine in the world can do thee good. 318
    In thee there is not half an hour's life.
    The treacherous instrument is in thy hand,
    Unbated and envenom'd. The foul practice
    Hath turn'd itself on me. Lo, here I lie,   322
    Never to rise again. Thy mother's poison'd.
    I can no more. The king, the king's to blame.

HAMLET. The point envenom'd too?
    Then, venom, to thy work!   *[Hurts the King.]*

ALL.   Treason! treason!   326

KING. O yet defend me, friends; I am but hurt.

HAMLET. Here, thou incestuous, murd'rous,
    damned Dane,
    Drink off this potion! Is thy union here!   329
    Follow my mother.   *[King dies.]*

LAERTES.   He is justly serv'd;
    It is a poison temper'd by himself.

Exchange forgiveness with me, noble Hamlet:
Mine and my father's death come not upon
    thee,
Nor thine on me!   *[Dies.]*

HAMLET. Heaven make thee free of it! I follow
    thee.   335
    I am dead, Horatio. Wretched queen, adieu!
    You that look pale and tremble at this chance,
    That are but mutes or audience to this act,   338
    Had I but time (as this fell sergeant, death,
    Is strict in his arrest) O, I could tell you—
    But let it be. Horatio, I am dead;   341
    Thou liv'st. Report me and my cause aright
    To the unsatisfied.

HORATIO.   Never believe it!
    I am more an antique Roman than a Dane.
    Here's yet some liquor left.

HAMLET.   As th' art a man, 345
    Give me the cup! let go! by heaven, I'll have 't!
    O good Horatio, what a wounded name
    (Things standing thus unknown) shall live
    behind me.
    If thou didst ever hold me in thy heart,   349
    Absent thee from felicity awhile,
    And in this harsh world draw they breath in pain,
    To tell my story.

[A march afar off and shout within.]

    What warlike noise is this?

[Enter Osric.]

OSRIC. Young Fortinbras, with conquest come from
    Poland,   353
    To the ambassadors of England gives
    This warlike volley.

HAMLET.   O, I die, Horatio;
    The potent poison quite o'er-crows my spirit.
    I cannot live to hear the news from England, 357
    But I do prophesy th' election lights
    On Fortinbras. He has my dying voice.
    So tell him, with th' occurrents, more or less,
    Which have solicited—The rest is silence. *[Dies.]*

HORATIO. Now cracks a noble heart. Good night,
    sweet prince,   362
    And flights of angels sing thee to thy rest!
    Why does the drum come hither?

---

302. pass: thrust. **303. wanton:** pampered child. **312. sounds:** swoons. **331. temper'd:** compounded.

339. sergeant: sheriff's officer. **356. o'er-crows:** triumphs over. **360. occurrents:** incidents. **361. solicited:** moved. **363. flights:** troops.

[Enter Fortinbras, and English Ambassador, with drum, colors, and Attendants.]

FORTINBRAS. Where is this sight?

HORATIO.   What is it you would see?   365
If aught of woe or wonder, cease your search.

FORTINBRAS. This quarry cries on havoc. O proud
     death,
What feast is toward in thine eternal cell,
That thou so many princes at a shot   369
So bloodily hast struck?

AMBASSADOR.   The sight is dismal,
And our affairs from England come too late.
The ears are senseless that should give us hearing,
To tell him his commandment is fulfill'd,   373
That Rosencrantz and Guildenstern are dead.
Where should we have our thanks?

HORATIO.   Not from his mouth,
Had it th' ability of life to thank you.   376
He never gave commandment for their death.
But since, so jump upon this bloody question,
You from the Polack wars, and you from
     England,
Are here arriv'd, give order that these bodies
High on a stage be placed to the view,   381
And let me speak to th' yet unknowing world
How these things came about. So shall you hear
Of carnal, bloody, and unnatural acts,
Of accidental judgments, casual slaughters,   385

Of deaths put on by cunning and forc'd cause,
And, in this upshot, purposes mistook
Fall'n on th' inventors' heads. All this can I
Truly deliver.

FORTINBRAS.   Let us haste to hear it,   389
And call the noblest to the audience.
For me, with sorrow I embrace my fortune.
I have some rights of memory in this kingdom,
Which now to claim my vantage doth invite
     me.   393

HORATIO. Of that I shall have also cause to speak,
And from his mouth whose voice will draw on
     more.
But let this same be presently perform'd,
Even while men's minds are wild, lest more
     mischance
On plots and errors happen.

FORTINBRAS.   Let four captains   398
Bear Hamlet like a soldier to the stage;
For he was likely, had he been put on,
To have prov'd most royal. And for his passage
The soldiers' music and the rites of war   402
Speak loudly for him!
Take up the bodies. Such a sight as this
Becomes the field, but here shows much amiss.
Go bid the soldiers shoot.   406

[Exeunt marching, after the which a peal of ordnance are shot off.]

367. **quarry:** heap of slain. **cries on havoc:** proclaims merciless. 381. **stage:** platform. 385. **casual:** unpremeditated.

386. **forc'd:** unreal. 392. **rights of memory:** ancient claims. 395. **draw on more:** be seconded by others. 400. **been put on:** been put to the proof, tried.

Introduction to *Tartuffe* by Molière

Translated by Richard Wilbur

Tartuffe   Michele Farr as Elmire, Richard Kinter as Orgon, Utah Shakespearean Festival. *(© John Running)*

The Play   Molière's *Tartuffe* was a highly controversial play. Molière read it to Louis XIV in 1665, and the king liked it; but before it could be presented publicly, it provoked an uproar. Although the play was presented once, in the summer of 1667, Louis XIV was out of the country at the time, and in his absence the religious authorities had it closed down. Finally, in 1669, it was given royal approval for performance.

The reason for the controversy was its subject matter: religious hypocrisy. The comedy focuses on Orgon, a man who has been duped by the religious hypocrite Tartuffe. Orgon is so thoroughly fooled that he pays no attention to his family, or to his saucy maid Dorine, when they tell him how dishonest and disreputable Tartuffe is. In fact, Orgon expects his daughter Mariane to marry the hypocrite, despite her protests. When Orgon's wife, Elmire, tells him that Tartuffe has tried to seduce her, he refuses to believe her. And when Orgon's son, Damis, confirms his stepmother's accusations, Orgon disowns him. Only when Orgon learns for himself the truth about Tartuffe does he realize his error. This occurs in the scene in which Orgon, hiding under a table, hears Tartuffe again trying to seduce Elmire.

Orgon's discovery, however, is seemingly too late. He has already handed his house and fortune over to the hypocrite. In addition, Orgon has given Tartuffe papers he has hidden for a friend who is disloyal to the king; and Tartuffe hands these incriminating letters over to authorities. At the end of the play, however, an officer for the king announces that Louis XIV has seen through the hypocrite, has ordered Tartuffe's arrest, and has pardoned Orgon.

While much of the historic debate revolved around the representation of Tartuffe and his religious hypocrisy—a representation which threatened religious figures of the time—Molière's real focus is on Orgon. Molière examines a character who allows himself to be duped into becoming an arrogant and domineering father and husband. Molière's interest seems to be in human beings who cannot see through charlatans and whose obsession with these frauds is comic but also potentially destructive.

Molière's work was highly influenced by the popular Italian *commedia dell'arte.* He uses many of the same stock characters: foolish comic lovers (Mariane and Valère, the young man she truly wishes to marry), a bossy servant (Dorine), and a foolish father and husband (Orgon). He creates exaggerated character types, such as Orgon and Tartuffe, and makes fun of their eccentricities. As the playwright himself said in defense of *Tartuffe,* "If it be the aim of comedy to correct man's vices, then I do not see for what there should be a privileged class"—that is, religious hypocrites and fanatics.

Molière was a master of slapstick, as in the scene when Orgon hides under a table to eavesdrop on his wife and Tartuffe. Molière's use of rhyming couplets in many of his plays, including *Tartuffe,* also creates a comic sensibility about the characters' exaggerated patterns of speech.

Molière frequently used a *deus ex machina*—an arbitrary or coincidental solution—to resolve his comically contrived plots, such as the arrival of the king's officer who reveals Louis XIV's wise insights. However, while the king's intervention here may seem arbitrary in terms of plot, this *deus ex machina* clearly reflects Molière's belief that a wise monarch could not be fooled by religious hypocrisy or fanaticism.

Finally, readers should note that Molière adhered to many of the French neoclassical practices, such as structuring plays so that they adhered to the unities of time, place, and action.

The Playwright Molière (1622–1673) was born Jean-Baptiste Poquelin, the son of an upholsterer in the service of the king. Molière studied to become a lawyer but left school in 1643, changed his name, and founded the Théâtre Illustre with the Béjart family of actors. The theater went bankrupt in 1645, and Molière was imprisoned for debt. Forced out of Paris by poor economic conditions, the troupe played in the provinces until 1658.

During this 12-year period, Molière became an accomplished comic actor as well as a playwright. As a leader in the company, along with his mistress Madeleine Béjart (whose daughter he later married), Molière was able to develop a disciplined ensemble. In 1658, an influential patron secured a royal audience for the company. Louis XIV was impressed by Molière's work, and the group was allowed to share a theater in Paris with an Italian *commedia* troupe. The king made Molière's troupe the "King's Men" in 1665, and the dramatist wrote many court pageants and plays. Indeed, Molière wrote about one-third of the troupe's presentations.

By 1672, however, Louis XIV became more interested in opera and dance, and Molière had to work harder for financial stability. Exhausted and suffering from a lung ailment, Molière collapsed during a performance of *The Imaginary Invalid* (1673) and died a few hours later. Because he was an actor, and France at that time had laws preventing actors from receiving Christian burial, his funeral was held at night.

Molière remains one of the most popular dramatists of all time. In such plays as *The School for Wives* (1662), *The Misanthrope* (1666), *The Doctor in Spite of Himself* (1666), *The Miser* (1668), and *The Would-Be Gentleman* (1670) he combined farcical humor with a gift for witty dialogue and a keen sense of human indiscretions.

The Period   Renaissance theater did not reach its zenith in France until the seventeenth century, later than in Italy and England. This was partly due to continuous religious unrest. With religious and political stability established in the 1600s, French society was able to flourish under Louis XIV, who ruled from 1643 to 1715. Among the significant accomplishments of France during this period was its exploration of the New World.

The French were the first Europeans to construct a permanent theater building. This was the Hôtel de Bourgogne, built in 1548 for the presentation of religious plays. When religious drama was outlawed in the same year that the building was completed, the space was rented to touring professional companies. The Bourgogne, a long narrow building with a platform stage, was the sole permanent indoor theater in Paris for nearly a century, until the Théâtre du Marais, a converted tennis court, opened in 1634.

Italian influence on French theater architecture became evident in 1641, when Cardinal Richelieu, a leading religious and political figure, erected the Palais Cardinal, renamed the Palais Royal after his death. This is the theater that Molière's troupe eventually used. The Palais Cardinal was the first proscenium-arch theater in France and also had Italian-style machinery to shift painted-perspective scenery.

Another major theater building of the French neoclassical period was the Comédie Française, which housed the national theater. Louis XIV had founded the French national theater in 1680 by merging the leading theater companies in Paris, but the company did not move into its own building until 1689. Sight lines in this theater were much improved over those of the earlier spaces.

Acting companies in French neoclassical theaters, such as Molière's, were organized under a sharing plan and had women members. Rehearsals were supervised by the playwright or a leading performer or both, but troupes spent little time on rehearsals. Once a play was introduced, the troupe was expected to be able to revive it at a moment's notice, and the bill at theaters was changed daily. This was similar to the conditions under which English Renaissance companies worked.

TARTUFFE

Molière

CHARACTERS

MADAME PERNELLE, Orgon's mother

ORGON, Elmire's husband

ELMIRE, Orgon's wife

DAMIS, Orgon's son, Elmire's stepson

MARIANE, Orgon's daughter, Elmire's
    stepdaughter, in love with Valère

VALÈRE, in love with Mariane

CLÉANTE, Orgon's brother-in-law

TARTUFFE, a hypocrite

DORINE, Mariane's lady's-maid

MONSIEUR LOYAL, a bailiff

A POLICE OFFICER

FLIPOTE, Madame Pernelle's maid

SCENE: Throughout, Orgon's house in Paris.

Act 1

SCENE I

[*Madame Pernelle and Flipote, her maid; Elmire, Mariane, Dorine, Damis, Cléante*]

MADAME PERNELLE. Come, come, Flipote; it's time I
    left this place.

ELMIRE. I can't keep up, you walk at such a pace.

MADAME PERNELLE. Don't trouble, child; no need to
    show me out.

    It's not your manners I'm concerned about.

ELMIRE. We merely pay you the respect we owe.   5

    But Mother, why this hurry? Must you go?

MADAME PERNELLE. I must. This house appalls me.
    No one in it

    Will pay attention for a single minute.

    Children, I take my leave much vexed in spirit.

    I offer good advice, but you won't hear it.   10

    You all break in and chatter on and on.

    It's like a madhouse with the keeper gone.

DORINE. If . . .

MADAME PERNELLE.
           Girl, you talk too much, and I'm
    afraid

    You're far too saucy for a lady's-maid.

    You push in everywhere and have your say.   15

DAMIS. But . . .

MADAME PERNELLE.
           You, boy, grow more foolish
    every day.

    To think my grandson should be such a dunce!

    I've said a hundred times, if I've said it once,

    That if you keep the course on which you've
    started,

    You'll leave your worthy father broken-
    hearted.   20

MARIANE. I think . . .

MADAME PERNELLE. And you, his sister, seem so pure,

    So shy, so innocent, and so demure.

    But you know what they say about still waters.

    I pity parents with secretive daughters.

ELMIRE. Now, Mother . . .

MADAME PERNELLE.   And as for you, child, let
    me add   25

    That your behavior is extremely bad,

    And a poor example for these children, too.

    Their dear, dead mother did far better than
    you.

    You're much too free with money, and I'm
    distressed

    To see you so elaborately dressed.   30

    When it's one's husband that one aims to
    please,

    One has no need of costly fripperies.

CLÉANTE. Oh, Madam, really . . .

MADAME PERNELLE. You are her brother, Sir,
And I respect and love you; yet if I were
My son, this lady's good and pious spouse, 35
I wouldn't make you welcome in my house.
You're full of worldly counsels which, I fear,
Aren't suitable for decent folk to hear.
I've spoken bluntly, Sir; but it behooves us
Not to mince words when righteous fervor
moves us. 40

DAMIS. Your man Tartuffe is full of holy speeches . . .

MADAME PERNELLE. And practices precisely what he preaches.
He's a fine man, and should be listened to.
I will not hear him mocked by fools like you.

DAMIS. Good God! Do you expect me to submit 45
To the tyranny of that carping hypocrite?
Must we forgo all joys and satisfactions
Because that bigot censures all our actions?

DORINE. To hear him talk—and he talks all the time—
There's nothing one can do that's not a crime. 50
He rails at everything, your dear Tartuffe.

MADAME PERNELLE. Whatever he reproves deserves reproof.
He's out to save your souls, and all of you
Must love him, as my son would have you do.

DAMIS. Ah no, Grandmother, I could never take 55
To such a rascal, even for my father's sake.
That's how I feel, and I shall not dissemble.
His every action makes me seethe and tremble
With helpless anger, and I have no doubt
That he and I will shortly have it out. 60

DORINE. Surely it is a shame and a disgrace
To see this man usurp the master's place—
To see this beggar who, when first he came,
Had not a shoe or shoestring to his name
So far forget himself that he behaves 65
As if the house were his, and we his slaves.

MADAME PERNELLE. Well, mark my words, your souls would fare far better
If you obeyed his precepts to the letter.

DORINE. You see him as a saint. I'm far less awed;
In fact, I see right through him. He's a fraud. 70

MADAME PERNELLE. Nonsense!

DORINE. His man Laurent's the same, or worse;
I'd not trust either with a penny purse.

MADAME PERNELLE. I can't say what his servant's morals may be;
His own great goodness I can guarantee.
You all regard him with distaste and fear 75
Because he tells you what you're loath to hear,
Condemns your sins, points out your moral flaws,
And humbly strives to further Heaven's cause.

DORINE. If sin is all that bothers him, why is it
He's so upset when folk drop in to visit? 80
Is Heaven so outraged by a social call
That he must prophesy against us all?
I'll tell you what I think: if you ask me,
He's jealous of my mistress' company.

MADAME PERNELLE. Rubbish! *[To Elmire.]* He's not alone, child, in complaining 85
Of all of your promiscuous entertaining.
Why, the whole neighborhood's upset, I know,
By all these carriages that come and go,
With crowds of guests parading in and out
And noisy servants loitering about. 90
In all of this, I'm sure there's nothing vicious;
But why give people cause to be suspicious?

CLÉANTE. They need no cause; they'll talk in any case.
Madam, this world would be a joyless place
If, fearing what malicious tongues might say, 95
We locked our doors and turned our friends away.
And even if one did so dreary a thing,
D'you think those tongues would cease their chattering?
One can't fight slander; it's a losing battle;
Let us instead ignore their tittle-tattle. 100
Let's strive to live by conscience' clear decrees,
And let the gossips gossip as they please.

DORINE. If there is talk against us, I know the source:
It's Daphne and her little husband, of course.
Those who have greatest cause for guilt and shame 105
Are quickest to besmirch a neighbor's name.
When there's a chance for libel, they never miss it;
When something can be made to seem illicit
They're off at once to spread the joyous news,
Adding to fact what fantasies they choose. 110
By talking up their neighbor's indiscretions
They seek to camouflage their own transgressions,

Hoping that others' innocent affairs
Will lend a hue of innocence to theirs,
Or that their own black guilt will come
　　to seem　　　　　　　　　　　　　115
Part of a general shady color-scheme.
MADAME PERNELLE. All that is quite irrelevant. I
　　doubt
That anyone's more virtuous and devout
Than dear Orante; and I'm informed that she
Condemns your mode of life most
　　vehemently.　　　　　　　　　　120
DORINE. Oh, yes, she's strict, devout, and has no
　　taint
Of worldliness; in short, she seems a saint.
But it was time which taught her that disguise;
She's thus because she can't be otherwise.
So long as her attractions could enthrall,　　125
She flounced and flirted and enjoyed it all,
But now that they're no longer what they were
She quits a world which fast is quitting her,
And wears a veil of virtue to conceal
Her bankrupt beauty and her lost appeal.　　130
That's what becomes of old coquettes today:
Distressed when all their lovers fall away,
They see no recourse but to play the prude,
And so confer a style on solitude.
Thereafter, they're severe with everyone,　　135
Condemning all our actions, pardoning none,
And claiming to be pure, austere, and zealous
When, if the truth were known, they're merely
　　jealous,
And cannot bear to see another know
The pleasures time has forced them to forgo. 140
MADAME PERNELLE. *[Initially to Elmire.]*
That sort of talk is what you like to hear;
Therefore you'd have us all keep still, my dear,
While Madam rattles on the livelong day.
Nevertheless, I mean to have my say.
I tell you that you're blest to have Tartuffe　145
Dwelling, as my son's guest, beneath this roof;
That Heaven has sent him to forestall its wrath
By leading you, once more, to the true path;
That all he reprehends is reprehensible,
And that you'd better heed him, and be
　　sensible.　　　　　　　　　　150
These visits, balls, and parties in which you revel
Are nothing but inventions of the Devil.
One never hears a word that's edifying:
Nothing but chaff and foolishness and lying,
As well as vicious gossip in which one's
　　neighbor　　　　　　　　　　155

Is cut to bits with epee, foil, and saber.
People of sense are driven half-insane
At such affairs, where noise and folly reign
And reputations perish thick and fast.
As a wise preacher said on Sunday last,　　160
Parties are Towers of Babylon, because
The guests all babble on with never a pause;

And then he told a story which, I think . . .

[To Cléante.]

I heard that laugh, Sir, and I saw that wink!
Go find your silly friends and laugh some
　　more!　　　　　　　　　　165
Enough; I'm going; don't show me to the
　　door.
I leave this household much dismayed and vexed;
I cannot say when I shall see you next.

[Slapping Flipote.]

Wake up, don't stand there gaping into space!
I'll slap some sense into that stupid face.　　170
Move, move, you slut.

SCENE II

[Cléante, Dorine.]

CLÉANTE.　　　　　　　I think I'll stay behind;
I want no further pieces of her mind.
How that old lady . . .
DORINE.　　　　　　Oh, what wouldn't she say
If she could hear you speak of her that way!
She'd thank you for the *lady,* but I'm sure　5
She'd find the *old* a little premature.
CLÉANTE. My, what a scene she made, and what a
　　din!
And how this man Tartuffe has taken her in!
DORINE. Yes, but her son is even worse deceived;
His folly must be seen to be believed.　　10
In the late troubles, he played an able part
And served his king with wise and loyal heart,
But he's quite lost his senses since he fell
Beneath Tartuffe's infatuating spell.
He calls him brother, and loves him as his life,　15
Preferring him to mother, child, or wife.
In him and him alone will he confide;
He's made him his confessor and his guide;

talk about Orgon

He pets and pampers him with love more
    tender
Than any pretty maiden could engender,   20
Gives him the place of honor when they dine,
Delights to see him gorging like a swine,
Stuffs him with dainties till his guts distend,
And when he belches, cries "God bless you,
    friend!"
In short, he's mad; he worships him; he
    dotes;   25
His deeds he marvels at, his words he quotes,
Thinking each act a miracle, each word
Oracular as those that Moses heard.
Tartuffe, much pleased to find so easy a
    victim,
Has in a hundred ways beguiled and tricked
    him,   30
Milked him of money, and with his permission
Established here a sort of Inquisition.
Even Laurent, his lackey, dares to give
Us arrogant advice on how to live;
He sermonizes us in thundering tones   35
And confiscates our ribbons and colognes.
Last week he tore a kerchief into pieces
Because he found it pressed in a *Life of Jesus:*
He said it was a sin to juxtapose
Unholy vanities and holy prose.   40

SCENE III

[Elmire, Mariane, Damis, Cléante, Dorine.]

ELMIRE. *[To Cléante.]* You did well not to follow; she
    stood in the door
And said *verbatim* all she'd said before.
I saw my husband coming. I think I'd best
Go upstairs now, and take a little rest.
CLÉANTE. I'll wait and greet him here; then I must
    go.   5
I've really only time to say hello.
DAMIS. Sound him about my sister's wedding,
    please.
I think Tartuffe's against it, and that he's
Been urging Father to withdraw his blessing.
As you well know, I'd find that most
    distressing.   10
Unless my sister and Valère can marry,
My hopes to wed *his* sister will miscarry,
And I'm determined . . .
DORINE.   He's coming.

SCENE IV

[Orgon, Cléante, Dorine.]

ORGON.   Ah, Brother, good-day.
CLÉANTE. Well, welcome back. I'm sorry I can't
    stay.
    How was the country? Blooming, I trust, and
    green?
ORGON. Excuse me, Brother; just one moment.

[To Dorine.]

                  Dorine . . .

[To Cléante.]

    To put my mind at rest, I always learn   5
    The household news the moment I return.

[To Dorine.]

    Has all been well, these two days I've been
    gone?
    How are the family? What's been going on?
DORINE. Your wife, two days ago, had a bad fever,
    And a fierce headache which refused to leave
    her.   10
ORGON. Ah. And Tartuffe?
DORINE.   Tartuffe? Why, he's
    round and red,
    Bursting with health, and excellently fed.
ORGON. Poor fellow!
DORINE.   That night, the mistress was
    unable
    To take a single bite at the dinner-table.
    Her headache-pains, she said, were simply
    hellish.   15
ORGON. Ah. And Tartuffe?
DORINE.   He ate his meal with
    relish,
    And zealously devoured in her presence
    A leg of mutton and a brace of pheasants.
ORGON. Poor fellow!
DORINE.   Well, the pains continued
    strong,
    And so she tossed and tossed the whole night
    long,   20
    Now icy-cold, now burning like a flame.
    We sat beside her bed till morning came.
ORGON. Ah. And Tartuffe?

DORINE. Why, having eaten, he rose
    And sought his room, already in a doze,
    Got into his warm bed, and snored away   25
    In perfect peace until the break of day.
ORGON. Poor fellow!
DORINE.   After much ado, we talked her
    Into dispatching someone for the doctor.
    He bled her, and the fever quickly fell.
ORGON. Ah. And Tartuffe?
DORINE.   He bore it very well.   30
    To keep his cheerfulness at any cost,
    And make up for the blood *Madame* had lost,
    He drank, at lunch, four beakers full of port.
ORGON. Poor fellow!
DORINE.   Both are doing well, in short.
    I'll go and tell *Madame* that you've
         expressed   35
    Keen sympathy and anxious interest.

SCENE V

[Orgon, Cléante.]

CLÉANTE. That girl was laughing in your face, and
         though
    I've no wish to offend you, even so
    I'm bound to say that she had some excuse.
    How can you possibly be such a goose?
    Are you so dazed by this man's hocus-pocus   5
    That all the world, save him, is out of focus?
    You've given him clothing, shelter, food, and care;
    Why must you also . . .
ORGON.   Brother, stop right there.
    You do not know the man of whom you speak.
CLÉANTE. I grant you that. But my judgment's not
         so weak   10
    That I can't tell, by his effect on others . . .
ORGON. Ah, when you meet him, you two will be
         like brothers!
    There's been no loftier soul since time began.
    He is a man who . . . a man who . . . an
         excellent man.
    To keep his precepts is to be reborn,   15
    And view this dunghill of a world with scorn.
    Yes, thanks to him I'm a changed man indeed.
    Under his tutelage my soul's been freed
    From earthly loves, and every human tie:
    My mother, children, brother, and wife could
         die,   20
    And I'd not feel a single moment's pain.

CLÉANTE. That's a fine sentiment, Brother; most
         humane.
ORGON. Oh, had you seen Tartuffe as I first knew
         him,
    Your heart, like mine, would have surrendered
         to him.
    He used to come into our church each day   25
    And humbly kneel nearby, and start to pray.
    He'd draw the eyes of everybody there
    By the deep fervor of his heartfelt prayer;
    He'd sigh and weep, and sometimes with a
         sound
    Of rapture he would bend and kiss the
         ground;   30
    And when I rose to go, he'd run before
    To offer me holy-water at the door.
    His serving-man, no less devout than he,
    Informed me of his master's poverty;
    I gave him gifts, but in his humbleness   35
    He'd beg me every time to give him less.
    "Oh, that's too much," he'd cry, "too much by
         twice!
    I don't deserve it. The half, Sir, would suffice."
    And when I wouldn't take it back, he'd share
    Half of it with the poor, right then and
         there.   40
    At length, Heaven prompted me to take
         him in
    To dwell with us, and free our souls from sin.
    He guides our lives, and to protect my honor
    Stays by my wife, and keeps an eye upon her;
    He tells me whom she sees, and all she does,   45
    And seems more jealous than I ever was!
    And how austere he is! Why, he can detect
    A mortal sin where you would least suspect;
    In smallest trifles, he's extremely strict.
    Last week, his conscience was severely
         pricked   50
    Because, while praying, he had caught a flea
    And killed it, so he felt, too wrathfully.
CLÉANTE. Good God, man! Have you lost your
         common sense—
    Or is this all some joke at my expense?
    How can you stand there and in all
         sobriety . . .   55
ORGON. Brother, your language savors of impiety.
    Too much free-thinking's made your faith
         unsteady,
    And as I've warned you many times already,
    'Twill get you into trouble before you're
         through.

CLÉANTE. So I've been told before by dupes like
 you: 60
 Being blind, you'd have all others blind as well;
 The clear-eyed man you call an infidel,
 And he who sees through humbug and pretense
 Is charged, by you, with want of reverence.
 Spare me your warnings, Brother; I have no
  fear 65
 Of speaking out, for you and Heaven to hear,
 Against affected zeal and pious knavery.
 There's true and false in piety, as in bravery,
 And just as those whose courage shines the most
 In battle, are the least inclined to boast, 70
 So those whose hearts are truly pure and lowly
 Don't make a flashy show of being holy.
 There's a vast difference, so it seems to me,
 Between true piety and hypocrisy:
 How do you fail to see it, may I ask? 75
 Is not a face quite different from a mask?
 Cannot sincerity and cunning art,
 Reality and semblance, be told apart?
 Are scarecrows just like men, and do you hold
 That a false coin is just as good as gold? 80
 Ah, Brother, man's a strangely fashioned creature
 Who seldom is content to follow Nature,
 But recklessly pursues his inclination
 Beyond the narrow bounds of moderation,
 And often, by transgressing Reason's laws, 85
 Perverts a lofty aim or noble cause.
 A passing observation, but it applies.
ORGON. I see, dear Brother, that you're profoundly
 wise;
 You harbor all the insight of the age.
 You are our one clear mind, our only sage, 90
 The era's oracle, its Cato too,
 And all mankind are fools compared to you.
CLÉANTE. Brother, I don't pretend to be a sage,
 Nor have I all the wisdom of the age.
 There's just one insight I would dare to
  claim: 95
 I know that true and false are not the same;
 And just as there is nothing I more revere
 Than a soul whose faith is steadfast and sincere,
 Nothing that I more cherish and admire
 Than honest zeal and true religious fire, 100
 So there is nothing that I find more base
 Than specious piety's dishonest face—
 Than these bold mountebanks, these histrios
 Whose impious mummeries and hollow shows
 Exploit our love of Heaven, and make a jest 105
 Of all that men think holiest and best;

 These calculating souls who offer prayers
 Not to their Maker, but as public wares,
 And seek to buy respect and reputation
 With lifted eyes and sighs of exaltation; 110
 These charlatans, I say, whose pilgrim souls
 Proceed, by way of Heaven, toward earthly
  goals,
 Who weep and pray and swindle and extort,
 Who preach the monkish life, but haunt the
  court,
 Who make their zeal the partner of their
  vice— 115
 Such men are vengeful, sly, and cold as ice,
 And when there is an enemy to defame
 They cloak their spite in fair religion's name,
 Their private spleen and malice being made
 To seem a high and virtuous crusade, 120
 Until, to mankind's reverent applause,
 They crucify their foe in Heaven's cause.
 Such knaves are all too common; yet, for the
  wise,
 True piety isn't hard to recognize,
 And, happily, these present times provide
  us 125
 With bright examples to instruct and guide us.
 Consider Ariston and Périandre;
 Look at Oronte, Alcidamas, Clitandre;
 Their virtue is acknowledged; who could
  doubt it?
 But you won't hear them beat the drum about
  it. 130
 They're never ostentatious, never vain,
 And their religion's moderate and humane;
 It's not their way to criticize and chide:
 They think censoriousness a mark of pride,
 And therefore, letting others preach and
  rave, 135
 They show, by deeds, how Christians should
  behave.
 They think no evil of their fellow man,
 But judge of him as kindly as they can.
 They don't intrigue and wangle and conspire;
 To lead a good life is their one desire; 140
 The sinner wakes no rancorous hate in them;
 It is the sin alone which they condemn;
 Nor do they try to show a fiercer zeal
 For Heaven's cause than Heaven itself could
  feel.
 These men I honor, these men I advocate 145
 As models for us all to emulate.
 Your man is not their sort at all, I fear:

And, while your praise of him is quite sincere,
I think that you've been dreadfully deluded.
ORGON. Now then, dear Brother, is your speech
    concluded?   150
CLÉANTE. Why, yes.
ORGON.   Your servant, Sir. *[He turns to go.]*
CLÉANTE.   No, Brother; wait.
There's one more matter. You agreed of late
That young Valère might have your daughter's
    hand.
ORGON. I did.
CLÉANTE.   And set the date, I understand.
ORGON. Quite so.
CLÉANTE.   You've now postponed it; is that
    true?   155
ORGON. No doubt.
CLÉANTE.   The match no longer pleases
    you?
ORGON. Who knows?
CLÉANTE.   D'you mean to go back on
    your word?
ORGON. I won't say that.
CLÉANTE.   Has anything occurred

Which might entitle you to break your pledge?
ORGON. Perhaps.
CLÉANTE.   Why must you hem, and haw, and
    hedge?   160
The boy asked me to sound you in this affair . . .
ORGON. It's been a pleasure.
CLÉANTE.   But what shall I tell
    Valère?
ORGON. Whatever you like.
CLÉANTE.   But what have you
    decided?
What are your plans?
ORGON.   I plan, Sir, to be guided
    By Heaven's will.
CLÉANTE.   Come, Brother, don't talk
    rot.   165
You've given Valère your word; will you keep it,
    or not?
ORGON. Good day.
CLÉANTE.   This looks like poor Valère's
    undoing;
I'll go and warn him that there's trouble
    brewing.

Act II

SCENE I

[Orgon, Mariane.]

ORGON. Mariane.
MARIANE.   Yes, Father?
ORGON.   A word with you;
    come here,
MARIANE. What are you looking for?
ORGON. *[Peering into a small closet.]* Eavesdroppers,
    dear.
I'm making sure we shan't be overheard.
Someone in there could catch our every word.
Ah, good, we're safe. Now, Mariane, my
    child,   5
You're a sweet girl who's tractable and mild,
Whom I hold dear, and think most highly of.
MARIANE. I'm deeply grateful, Father, for your love.
ORGON. That's well said, Daughter; and you can
    repay me
If, in all things, you'll cheerfully obey me.   10
MARIANE. To please you, Sir, is what delights me best.

ORGON. Good, good. Now, what d'you think of
    Tartuffe, our guest?
MARIANE. I, Sir?
ORGON.   Yes. Weigh your answer; think it
    through.
MARIANE. Oh, dear. I'll say whatever you wish me to.
ORGON. That's wisely said, my Daughter. Say of
    him, then,   15
That he's the very worthiest of men,
And that you're fond of him, and would rejoice
In being his wife, if that should be my choice.
Well?
MARIANE. What?
ORGON.   What's that?
MARIANE.   I . . .
ORGON.   Well?
MARIANE.   Forgive me, pray.
ORGON. Did you not hear me?
MARIANE.   Of *whom*, Sir,
    must I say   20
That I am fond of him, and would rejoice
In being his wife, if that should be your choice?

ORGON. Why, of Tartuffe.

MARIANE.   But, Father, that's false,
    you know.
    Why would you have me say what isn't so?

ORGON. Because I am resolved it shall be true.   25
    That it's my wish should be enough for you.

MARIANE. You can't mean, Father . . .

ORGON.   Yes, Tartuffe
    shall be
    Allied by marriage to this family,
    And he's to be your husband, is that clear?
    It's a father's privilege . . .   30

SCENE II

[Dorine, Orgon, Mariane.]

ORGON. *[To Dorine.]*   What are you doing
    in here?
    Is curiosity so fierce a passion
    With you, that you must eavesdrop in this
        fashion?

DORINE. There's lately been a rumor going about—
    Based on some hunch or chance remark, no
        doubt—   5
    That you mean Mariane to wed Tartuffe.
    I've laughed it off, of course, as just a spoof.

ORGON. You find it so incredible?

DORINE.   Yes, I do.
    I won't accept that story, even from you.

ORGON. Well, you'll believe it when the thing is
    done.   10

DORINE. Yes, yes, of course. Go on and have your
    fun.

ORGON. I've never been more serious in my life.

DORINE. Ha!

ORGON.   Daughter, I mean it; you're to be his
    wife.

DORINE. No, don't believe your father; it's all a
    hoax.

ORGON. See here, young woman . . .

DORINE.   Come, Sir, no
    more jokes;   15
    You can't fool us.

ORGON.   How dare you talk that way?

DORINE. All right, then; we believe you, sad to
    say.
    But how a man like you, who looks so wise
    And wears a moustache of such splendid size,
    Can be so foolish as to . . .

ORGON.   Silence, please!   20
    My girl, you take too many liberties.
    I'm master here, as you must not forget.

DORINE. Do let's discuss this calmly; don't be
    upset.
    You can't be serious, Sir, about this plan.
    What should that bigot want with Mariane?   25
    Praying and fasting ought to keep him busy.
    And then, in terms of wealth and rank, what is
    he?
    Why should a man of property like you
    Pick out a beggar son-in-law?

ORGON.   That will do.
    Speak of his poverty with reverence.   30
    His is a pure and saintly indigence
    Which far transcends all worldly pride and pelf.
    He lost his fortune, as he says himself,
    Because he cared for Heaven alone, and so
    Was careless of his interests here below.   35
    I mean to get him out of his present straits
    And help him to recover his estates—
    Which, in his part of the world, have no small
    fame.
    Poor though he is, he's a gentleman just the
    same.

DORINE. Yes, so he tells us; and, Sir, it seems to
    me   40
    Such pride goes very ill with piety.
    A man whose spirit spurns this dungy earth
    Ought not to brag of lands and noble birth;
    Such worldly arrogance will hardly square
    With meek devotion and the life of prayer.   45
    . . . But this approach, I see, has drawn a blank;
    Let's speak, then, of his person, not his rank.
    Doesn't it seem to you a trifle grim
    To give a girl like her to a man like him?
    When two are so ill-suited, can't you see   50
    What the sad consequence is bound to be?
    A young girl's virtue is imperiled, Sir,
    When such a marriage is imposed on her;
    For if one's bridegroom isn't to one's taste,
    It's hardly an inducement to be chaste,   55
    And many a man with horns upon his brow
    Has made his wife the thing that she is now.
    It's hard to be a faithful wife, in short,
    To certain husbands of a certain sort,
    And he who gives his daughter to a man she
    hates   60
    Must answer for her sins at Heaven's gates.
    Think, Sir, before you play so risky a role.

ORGON. This servant-girl presumes to save my soul!

DORINE. You would do well to ponder what I've
　　said.

ORGON. Daughter, we'll disregard this
　　dunderhead.　　　　　　　　　　　　　　65
　　Just trust your father's judgment. Oh, I'm
　　　aware
　　That I once promised you to young Valère;
　　But now I hear he gambles, which greatly
　　　shocks me;
　　What's more, I've doubts about his
　　　orthodoxy.
　　His visits to church, I note, are very few.　70

DORINE. Would you have him go at the same hours
　　as you,
　　And kneel nearby, to be sure of being seen?

ORGON. I can dispense with such remarks, Dorine.

[To Mariane.]

　　Tartuffe, however, is sure of Heaven's blessing,
　　And that's the only treasure worth possessing.　75
　　This match will bring you joys beyond all
　　　measure;
　　Your cup will overflow with every pleasure;
　　You two will interchange your faithful loves
　　Like two sweet cherubs, or two turtle-doves.
　　No harsh word shall be heard, no frown be
　　　seen,　　　　　　　　　　　　　　　　80
　　And he shall make you happy as a queen.

DORINE. And she'll make him a cuckold, just wait
　　and see.

ORGON. What language!

DORINE.　　　　　　　Oh, he's a man of destiny;
　　He's *made* for horns, and what the stars
　　　demand
　　Your daughter's virtue surely can't withstand.　85

ORGON. Don't interrupt me further. Why can't you
　　learn
　　That certain things are none of your concern?

DORINE. It's for your own sake that I interfere.

*[She repeatedly interrupts Orgon just as he is turning to
speak to his daughter.]*

ORGON. Most kind of you. Now, hold your tongue,
　　d'you hear?

DORINE. If I didn't love you . . .

ORGON.　　　　　　　　　　Spare me your
　　affection.　　　　　　　　　　　　　　90

DORINE. I'll love you, Sir, in spite of your
　　objection.

ORGON. Blast!

DORINE.　　　　I can't bear, Sir, for your honor's
　　sake,
　　To let you make this ludicrous mistake.

ORGON. You mean to go on talking?

DORINE.　　　　　　　　　　　If I didn't
　　protest
　　This sinful marriage, my conscience couldn't
　　rest.　　　　　　　　　　　　　　　　95

ORGON. If you don't hold your tongue, you little
　　shrew . . .

DORINE. What, lost your temper? A pious man like
　　you?

ORGON. Yes! Yes! You talk and talk. I'm maddened
　　by it.
　　Once and for all, I tell you to be quiet.

DORINE. Well, I'll be quiet. But I'll be thinking
　　hard.　　　　　　　　　　　　　　　100

ORGON. Think all you like, but you had better
　　guard
　　That saucy tongue of yours, or I'll . . .

[Turning back to Mariane.]

　　　　　　　　　　　　　　　　Now,
　　child,
　　I've weighed this matter fully.

DORINE. *[Aside.]*　　　　　　It drives me wild
　　That I can't speak.

[Orgon turns his head, and she is silent.]

ORGON.　　　　　　Tartuffe is no young dandy,
　　But, still, his person . . .

DORINE. *[Aside.]*　　　　　Is as sweet as candy.　105

ORGON. Is such that, even if you shouldn't care
　　For his other merits . . .

[He turns and stands facing Dorine, arms crossed.]

DORINE. *[Aside.]*　　　　　　They'll make a lovely
　　pair.
　　If I were she, no man would marry me
　　Against my inclination, and go scot-free.
　　He'd learn, before the wedding-day was
　　　over,　　　　　　　　　　　　　　　110
　　How readily a wife can find a lover.

ORGON. *[To Dorine.]* It seems you treat my orders as
　　a joke.

DORINE. Why, what's the matter? 'Twas not to you
　　I spoke.

ORGON. What *were* you doing?

DORINE.   Talking to myself,
    that's all.

ORGON. Ah! *[Aside.]* One more bit of impudence
    and gall,   115
    And I shall give her a good slap in the face.

*[He puts himself in position to slap her; Dorine, whenever
he glances at her, stands immobile and silent.]*

    Daughter, you shall accept, and with good
       grace,
    The husband I've selected . . . Your wedding
       day . . .

[To Dorine.]

    Why don't you talk to yourself?

DORINE.   I've nothing to
    say.

ORGON. Come, just one word.

DORINE.   No thank you, Sir. I
    pass.   120

ORGON. Come, speak; I'm waiting.

DORINE.   I'd not be such
    an ass.

ORGON. *[Turning to Mariane.]* In short, dear Daughter,
    I mean to be obeyed,
    And you must bow to the sound choice I've
       made.

DORINE. *[Moving away.]* I'd not wed such a monster,
    even in jest.

[Orgon attempts to slap her, but misses.]

ORGON. Daughter, that maid of yours is a thorough
    pest;   125
    She makes me sinfully annoyed and nettled.
    I can't speak further; my nerves are too
       unsettled.
    She's so upset me by her insolent talk,
    I'll calm myself by going for a walk.

SCENE III

[Dorine, Mariane.]

DORINE. *[Returning.]* Well, have you lost your
    tongue, girl? Must I play
    Your part, and say the lines you ought to say?

    Faced with a fate so hideous and absurd,
    Can you not utter one dissenting word?

MARIANE. What good would it do? A father's power
    is great.   5

DORINE. Resist him now, or it will be too late.

MARIANE. But . . .

DORINE.   Tell him one cannot love at a
    father's whim;
    That you shall marry for yourself, not him;
    That since it's you who are to be the bride,
    It's you, not he, who must be satisfied;   10
    And that if his Tartuffe is so sublime,
    He's free to marry him at any time.

MARIANE. I've bowed so long to Father's strict
    control,
    I couldn't oppose him now, to save my soul.

DORINE. Come, come, Mariane. Do listen to
    reason, won't you?   15
    Valère has asked your hand. Do you love him,
    or don't you?

MARIANE. Oh, how unjust of you! What can you
    mean
    By asking such a question, dear Dorine?
    You know the depth of my affection for him;
    I've told you a hundred times how I adore
    him.   20

DORINE. I don't believe in everything I hear;
    Who knows if your professions were sincere?

MARIANE. They were, Dorine, and you do me
    wrong to doubt it;
    Heaven knows that I've been all too frank
    about it.

DORINE. You love him, then?

MARIANE.   Oh, more than I can
    express.   25

DORINE. And he, I take it, cares for you no less?

MARIANE. I think so.

DORINE.   And you both, with equal fire,
    Burn to be married?

MARIANE.   That is our one desire.

DORINE. What of Tartuffe, then? What of your
    father's plan?

MARIANE. I'll kill myself, if I'm forced to wed that
    man.   30

DORINE. I hadn't thought of that recourse. How
    splendid!
    Just die, and all your troubles will be ended!
    A fine solution. Oh, it maddens me
    To hear you talk in that self-pitying key.

MARIANE. Dorine, how harsh you are! It's most
    unfair.   35

You have no sympathy for my despair.
DORINE. I've none at all for people who talk drivel
  And, faced with difficulties, whine and snivel.
MARIANE. No doubt I'm timid, but it would be
      wrong . . .
DORINE. True love requires a heart that's firm and
      strong.   40
MARIANE. I'm strong in my affection for Valère,
  But coping with my father is his affair.
DORINE. But if your father's brain has grown so
      cracked
  Over his dear Tartuffe that he can retract
  His blessing, though your wedding day was
      named,   45
  It's surely not Valère who's to be blamed.
MARIANE. If I defied my father, as you suggest,
  Would it not seem unmaidenly, at best?
  Shall I defend my love at the expense
  Of brazenness and disobedience?   50
  Shall I parade my heart's desires, and flaunt . . .
DORINE. No, I ask nothing of you. Clearly you
      want
  To be Madame Tartuffe, and I feel bound
  Not to oppose a wish so very sound.
  What right have I to criticize the match?   55
  Indeed, my dear, the man's a brilliant catch.
  Monsieur Tartuffe! Now, there's a man of
      weight!
  Yes, yes, Monsieur Tartuffe, I'm bound to state,
  Is quite a person; that's not to be denied;
  'Twill be no little thing to be his bride.   60
  The world already rings with his renown;
  He's a great noble—in his native town;
  His ears are red, he has a pink complexion,
  And all in all, he'll suit you to perfection.
MARIANE. Dear God!
DORINE.   Oh, how triumphant you will
      feel   65
  At having caught a husband so ideal!
MARIANE. Oh, do stop teasing, and use your
      cleverness
  To get me out of this appalling mess.
  Advise me, and I'll do whatever you say.
DORINE. Ah no, a dutiful daughter must obey   70
  Her father, even if he weds her to an ape.
  You've a bright future; why struggle to escape?
  Tartuffe will take you back where his family
      lives,
  To a small town aswarm with relatives—
  Uncles and cousins whom you'll be charmed to
      meet.   75

You'll be received at once by the elite,
  Calling upon the bailiff's wife, no less—
  Even, perhaps, upon the mayoress,
  Who'll sit you down in the *best* kitchen chair.
  Then, once a year, you'll dance at the village
      fair   80
  To the drone of bagpipes—two of them, in
      fact—
  And see a puppet-show, or an animal act.
  Your husband . . .
MARIANE.   Oh, you turn my blood to ice!
  Stop torturing me, and give me your advice.
DORINE. *[Threatening to go.]* Your servant, Madam.
MARIANE.   Dorine, I beg of you . . .   85
DORINE. No, you deserve it; this marriage must go
      through.
MARIANE. Dorine!
DORINE.   No.
MARIANE.   Not Tartuffe! You know I
      think him . . .
DORINE. Tartuffe's your cup of tea, and you shall
      drink him.
MARIANE. I've always told you everything, and
      relied . . .
DORINE. No. You deserve to be tartuffified.   90
MARIANE. Well, since you mock me and refuse to
      care,
  I'll henceforth seek my solace in despair:
  Despair shall be my counsellor and friend,
  And help me bring my sorrows to an end.

[She starts to leave.]

DORINE. There, now, come back; my anger has
      subsided.   95
  You do deserve some pity, I've decided.
MARIANE. Dorine, if Father makes me undergo
  This dreadful martyrdom, I'll die. I know.
DORINE. Don't fret; it won't be difficult to discover
  Some plan of action . . . But here's Valère,
      your lover.   100

SCENE IV

[Valère, Mariane, Dorine.]

VALÈRE. Madam, I've just received some wondrous
      news
  Regarding which I'd like to hear your views.
MARIANE. What news?

VALÈRE. You're marrying Tartuffe.
MARIANE. I find
That Father does have such a match in mind.
VALÈRE. Your father, Madam . . .
MARIANE. . . . has just this
minute said 5
That it's Tartuffe he wishes me to wed.
VALÈRE. Can he be serious?
MARIANE. Oh, indeed he can;
He's clearly set his heart upon the plan.
VALÈRE. And what position do you propose to take,
Madam?
MARIANE. Why—I don't know.
VALÈRE. For heaven's sake— 10
You don't know?
MARIANE. No.
VALÈRE. Well, well!
MARIANE. Advise
me, do.
VALÈRE. Marry the man. That's my advice to you.
MARIANE. That's your advice?
VALÈRE. Yes.
MARIANE. Truly?
VALÈRE. Oh,
absolutely.
You couldn't choose more wisely, more
astutely.
MARIANE. Thanks for this counsel; I'll follow it, of
course. 15
VALÈRE. Do, do; I'm sure 'twill cost you no
remorse.
MARIANE. To give it didn't cause your heart to
break.
VALÈRE. I gave it, Madam, only for your sake.
MARIANE. And it's for your sake that I take it, Sir.
DORINE. *[Withdrawing to the rear of the stage.]*
Let's see which fool will prove the stubborner. 20
VALÈRE. So! I am nothing to you, and it was flat
Deception when you . . .
MARIANE. Please, enough of that.
You've told me plainly that I should agree
To wed the man my father's chosen for me,
And since you've deigned to counsel me so
wisely, 25
I promise, Sir, to do as you advise me.
VALÈRE. Ah, no, 'twas not by me that you were
swayed.
No, your decision was already made;
Though now, to save appearances, you protest
That you're betraying me at my behest. 30
MARIANE. Just as you say.

VALÈRE. Quite so. And I now see
That you were never truly in love with me.
MARIANE. Alas, you're free to think so if you
choose.
VALÈRE. I choose to think so, and here's a bit of
news:
you've spurned my hand, but I know where to
turn 35
For kinder treatment, as you shall quickly learn.
MARIANE. I'm sure you do. Your noble qualities
Inspire affection . . .
VALÈRE. Forget my qualities, please.
They don't inspire you overmuch, I find.
But there's another lady I have in mind 40
Whose sweet and generous nature will no scorn
To compensate me for the loss I've borne.
MARIANE. I'm no great loss, and I'm sure that you'll
transfer
Your heart quite painlessly from me to her.
VALÈRE. I'll do my best to take it in my stride. 45
The pain I feel at being cast aside
Time and forgetfulness may put an end to.
Or if I can't forget, I shall pretend to.
No self-respecting person is expected
To go on loving once he's been rejected. 50
MARIANE. Now, that's a fine, high-minded sentiment.
VALÈRE. One to which any sane man would assent.
Would you prefer it if I pined away
In hopeless passion till my dying day?
Am I to yield you to a rival's arms 55
And not console myself with other charms?
MARIANE. Go then; console yourself; don't hesitate.
I wish you to; indeed, I cannot wait.
VALÈRE. You wish me to?
MARIANE. Yes.
VALÈRE. That's the final straw.
Madam, farewell. Your wish shall be my law. 60

[He starts to leave, and then returns: this repeatedly.]

MARIANE. Splendid.
VALÈRE. *[Coming back again.]*
This breach, remember,
is of your making;
It's you who've driven me to the step I'm
taking.
MARIANE. Of course.
VALÈRE. *[Coming back again.]*
Remember, too, that I
am merely
Following your example.

MARIANE.   I see that clearly.
VALÈRE. Enough. I'll go and do your bidding,
    then.   65
MARIANE. Good.
VALÈRE. *[Coming back again.]*
          You shall never see my face again.
MARIANE. Excellent.
VALÈRE. *[Walking to the door, then turning about.]*
                Yes?
MARIANE.   What?
VALÈRE.   What's that? What
    did you say?
MARIANE. Nothing. You're dreaming.
VALÈRE.   Ah. Well, I'm
    on my way.
    Farewell, *Madame.*

[He moves slowly away.]

MARIANE.   Farewell.
DORINE. *[To Mariane.]*   If you ask me,
    Both of you are as mad as mad can be.   70
    Do stop this nonsense, now. I've only let you
    Squabble so long to see where it would get you.
    Whoa there, Monsieur Valère!

[She goes and seizes Valère by the arm; he makes a great show of resistance.]

VALÈRE.   What's this, Dorine?
DORINE. Come here.
VALÈRE.   No, no, my heart's too full of
    spleen.
    Don't hold me back; her wish must be
    obeyed.   75
DORINE. Stop!
VALÈRE.   It's too late now; my decision's made.
DORINE. Oh, pooh!
MARIANE. *[Aside.]* He hates the sight of me, that's
    plain.
    I'll go, and so deliver him from pain.
DORINE. *[Leaving Valère, running after Mariane.]*
    And now *you* run away! Come back.
MARIANE. No, no.
    Nothing you say will keep me here. Let go!   80
VALÈRE. *[Aside.]* She cannot bear my presence, I
    perceive.
    To spare her further torment, I shall leave.
DORINE. *[Leaving Mariane, running after Valère.]*
    Again! You'll not escape, Sir; don't you try it.
    Come here, you two. Stop fussing, and be quiet.

[She takes Valère by the hand, then Mariane, and draws them together.]

VALÈRE. *[To Dorine.]* What do you want of me?
MARIANE. *[To Dorine.]* What is the point of this?   85
DORINE. We're going to have a little armistice.

[To Valère.]

    Now, weren't you silly to get so overheated?
VALÈRE. Didn't you see how badly I was treated?
DORINE. *[To Mariane.]* Aren't you a simpleton, to
    have lost your head?
MARIANE. Didn't you hear the hateful things he
    said?   90
DORINE. *[To Valère.]* You're both great fools. Her
    sole desire, Valère,
    Is to be yours in marriage. To that I'll swear.

[To Mariane.]

    He loves you only, and he wants no wife
    But you, Mariane. On that I'll stake my life.
MARIANE. *[To Valère.]* Then why you advised me so, I
    cannot see.   95
VALÈRE. *[To Mariane.]* On such a question, why ask
    advice of *me?*
DORINE. Oh, you're impossible. Give me your
    hands, you two.

[To Valère.]

    Yours first.
VALÈRE. *[Giving Dorine his hand.]*
              But why?
DORINE. *[To Mariane.]* And now a hand from you.
MARIANE. *[Also giving Dorine her hand.]*
    What are you doing?
DORINE.   There: a perfect fit.
    You suit each other better than you'll admit.   100

[Valère and Mariane hold hands for some time without looking at each other.]

VALÈRE. *[Turning toward Mariane.]*
    Ah, come, don't be so haughty. Give a man
    A look of kindness, won't you, Mariane?

[Mariane turns toward Valère and smiles.]

DORINE. I tell you, lovers are completely mad!

VALÈRE. *[To Mariane.]* Now come, confess that you
    were very bad
    To hurt my feelings as you did just now.   105
    I have a just complaint, you must allow.
MARIANE. *You* must allow that you were most
    unpleasant . . .
DORINE. Let's table that discussion for the
    present;
    Your father has a plan which must be stopped.
MARIANE. Advise us, then; what means must we
    adopt?   110
DORINE. We'll use all manner of means, and all at
    once.

[To Mariane.]

    Your father's addled; he's acting like a dunce.
    Therefore you'd better humor the old fossil.
    Pretend to yield to him, be sweet and docile,
    And then postpone, as often as necessary,   115
    The day on which you have agreed to marry.
    You'll thus gain time, and time will turn the
    trick.
    Sometimes, for instance, you'll be taken sick,
    And that will seem good reason for delay;
    Or some bad omen will make you change the
    day—   120
    You'll dream of muddy water, or you'll pass
    A dead man's hearse, or break a looking-glass.
    If all else fails, no man can marry you
    Unless you take his ring and say "I do."
    But now, let's separate. If they should find   125
    Us talking here, our plot might be divined.

[To Valère.]

    Go to your friends, and tell them what's
    occurred,
    And have them urge her father to keep his
    word.
    Meanwhile, we'll stir her brother into action,
    And get Elmire, as well, to join our faction.   130
    Good-bye.
VALÈRE. *[To Mariane.]*
                Though each of us will do his best,
    It's your true heart on which my hopes shall
    rest.
MARIANE. *[To Valère.]* Regardless of what Father may
    decide,
    None but Valère shall claim me as his bride.
VALÈRE. Oh, how those words content me! Come
    what will . . .   135
DORINE. Oh, lovers, lovers! Their tongues are never
    still.
    Be off, now.
VALÈRE. *[Turning to go, then turning back.]*
    One last word . . .
DORINE.   No time to chat:
    You leave by this door; and *you* leave by that.

[Dorine pushes them, by the shoulders, toward opposing doors.]

Act III

SCENE I

[Damis, Dorine.]

DAMIS. May lightning strike me even as I speak,
    May all men call me cowardly and weak,
    If any fear or scruple holds me back
    From settling things, at once, with that great
    quack!
DORINE. Now, don't give way to violent
    emotion.   5
    Your father's merely talked about this notion,
    And words and deeds are far from being one.
    Much that is talked about is never done.
DAMIS. No, I must stop that scoundrel's
    machinations;
    I'll go and tell him off; I'm out of patience.   10
DORINE. Do calm down and be practical. I had
    rather
    My mistress dealt with him—and with your
    father.
    She has some influence with Tartuffe, I've
    noted.
    He hangs upon her words, seems most devoted,
    And may, indeed, be smitten by her charm.   15
    Pray Heaven it's true! 'Twould do our cause no
    harm.
    She sent for him, just now, to sound him out

On this affair you're so incensed about;
She'll find out where he stands, and tell him
    too,
What dreadful strife and trouble will ensue   20
If he lends countenance to your father's plan.
I couldn't get in to see him, but his man
Says that he's almost finished with his prayers.
Go, now. I'll catch him when he comes
    downstairs.

DAMIS. I want to hear this conference, and I
    will.   25

DORINE. No, they must be alone.

DAMIS.   Oh, I'll keep still.

DORINE. Not you. I know your temper. You'd start
    a brawl,
And shout and stamp your foot and spoil it all.
Go on.

DAMIS.   I won't; I have a perfect right . . .

DORINE. Lord, you're a nuisance! He's coming; get
    out of sight.   30

[Damis conceals himself in a closet at the rear of the stage.]

SCENE II

[Tartuffe, Dorine.]

TARTUFFE. *[Observing Dorine, and calling to his
    manservant offstage.]*
Hang up my hair-shirt, put my scourge in place,
And pray, Laurent, for Heaven's perpetual
    grace.
I'm going to the prison now, to share
My last few coins with the poor wretches there.

DORINE. *[Aside.]* Dear God, what affection! What a
    fake!   5

TARTUFFE. You wished to see me?

DORINE.   Yes . . .

TARTUFFE. *[Taking a handkerchief from his pocket.]*
                        For mercy's sake,
Please take this handkerchief, before you speak.

DORINE. What?

TARTUFFE.   Cover that bosom, girl. The flesh is
    weak,
And unclean thoughts are difficult to control.
Such sights as that can undermine the soul.   10

DORINE. Your soul, it seems, has very poor
    defenses,
And flesh makes quite an impact on your senses.
It's strange that you're so easily excited;

My own desires are not so soon ignited,
And if I saw you naked as a beast,   15
Not all your hide would tempt me in the least.

TARTUFFE. Girl, speak more modestly; unless you do,
I shall be forced to take my leave of you.

DORINE. Oh, no, it's I who must be on my way;
I've just one little message to convey.   20
Madame is coming down, and begs you, Sir,
To wait and have a word or two with her.

TARTUFFE. Gladly.

DORINE. *[Aside.]*   *That* had a softening effect!
I think my guess about him was correct.

TARTUFFE. Will she be long?

DORINE.   No: that's her step I
    hear.   25
Ah, here she is, and I shall disappear.

SCENE III

[Elmire, Tartuffe.]

TARTUFFE. May Heaven, whose infinite goodness
    we adore,
Preserve your body and soul forevermore,
And bless your days, and answer thus the plea
Of one who is its humblest votary.

ELMIRE. I thank you for that pious wish, but
    please,   5
Do take a chair and let's be more at ease.

[They sit down.]

TARTUFFE. I trust that you are once more well and
    strong?

ELMIRE. Oh, yes: the fever didn't last for long.

TARTUFFE. My prayers are too unworthy, I am sure,
To have gained from Heaven this most gracious
    cure;   10
But lately, Madam, my every supplication
Has had for object your recuperation.

ELMIRE. You shouldn't have troubled so. I don't
    deserve it.

TARTUFFE. Your health is priceless, Madam, and to
    preserve it
I'd gladly give my own, in all sincerity.   15

ELMIRE. Sir, you outdo us all in Christian charity.
You've been most kind. I count myself your
    debtor.

TARTUFFE. 'Twas nothing, Madam. I long to serve
    you better.

ELMIRE. There's a private matter I'm anxious to
    discuss.
    I'm glad there's no one here to hinder us.   20
TARTUFFE. I too am glad; it floods my heart with bliss
    To find myself alone with you like this.
    For just this chance I've prayed with all my
      power—
    But prayed in vain, until this happy hour.
ELMIRE. This won't take long, Sir, and I hope you'll
    be   25
    Entirely frank and unconstrained with me.
TARTUFFE. Indeed, there's nothing I had rather do
    Than bare my inmost heart and soul to you.
    First, let me say that what remarks I've made
    About the constant visits you are paid   30
    Were prompted not by any mean emotion,
    But rather by a pure and deep devotion,
    A fervent zeal . . .
ELMIRE.   No need for explanation.
    Your sole concern, I'm sure, was my salvation.
TARTUFFE. *[Taking Elmire's hand and pressing her*
    fingertips.]
    Quite so; and such great fervor do I feel . . .   35
ELMIRE. Ooh! Please! You're pinching!
TARTUFFE.   'Twas from excess of zeal.
    I never meant to cause you pain, I swear.
    I'd rather . . .

[He places his hand on Elmire's knee.]

ELMIRE.   What can your hand be doing there?
TARTUFFE. Feeling your gown: what soft, fine-
    woven stuff!
ELMIRE. Please, I'm extremely ticklish. That's
    enough.   40

[She draws her chair away; Tartuffe pulls his after her.]

TARTUFFE. *[Fondling the lace collar of her gown.]*
    My, my, what lovely lacework on your dress!
    The workmanship's miraculous, no less.
    I've not seen anything to equal it.
ELMIRE. Yes, quite. But let's talk business for a bit.
    They say my husband means to break his
      word   45
    And give his daughter to you, Sir. Had you
    heard?
TARTUFFE. He did once mention it. But I confess
    I dream of quite a different happiness.
    It's elsewhere, Madam, that my eyes discern
    The promise of that bliss for which I yearn.   50

ELMIRE. I see: you care for nothing here below.
TARTUFFE. Ah, well—my heart's not made of stone,
    you know.
ELMIRE. All your desires mount heavenward, I'm
    sure,
    In scorn of all that's earthly and impure.
TARTUFFE. A love of heavenly beauty does not
    preclude   55
    A proper love for earthly pulchritude;
    Our senses are quite rightly captivated
    By perfect works our Maker has created.
    Some glory clings to all that Heaven has made;
    In you, all Heaven's marvels are displayed.   60
    On that fair face, such beauties have been
      lavished,
    The eyes are dazzled and the heart is ravished;
    How could I look on you, O flawless creature,
    And not adore the Author of all Nature,
    Feeling a love both passionate and pure
    For you, his triumph of self-portraiture?   65
    At first, I trembled lest that love should be
    A subtle snare that Hell had laid for me;
    I vowed to flee the sight of you, eschewing
    A rapture that might prove my soul's undoing;
    But soon, fair being, I became aware   70
    That my deep passion could be made to square
    With rectitude, and with my bounden duty.
    I thereupon surrendered to your beauty.
    It is, I know, presumptuous on my part
    To bring you this poor offering of my heart,   75
    And it is not my merit, Heaven knows,
    But your compassion on which my hopes
      repose.
    You are my peace, my solace, my salvation;
    On you depends my bliss—or desolation;
    I bide your judgment and, as you think best,   80
    I shall be either miserable or blest.
ELMIRE. Your declaration is most gallant, Sir,
    But don't you think it's out of character?
    You'd have done better to restrain your
      passion
    And think before you spoke in such a
      fashion.   85
    It ill becomes a pious man like you . . .
TARTUFFE. I may be pious, but I'm human too:
    With your celestial charms before his eyes,
    A man has not the power to be wise.
    I know such words sound strangely, coming
      from me,   90
    But I'm no angel, nor was meant to be,
    And if you blame my passion, you must needs

Reproach as well the charms on which it feeds.
Your loveliness I had no sooner seen
Than you became my soul's unrivalled
    queen;   95
Before your seraph glance, divinely sweet,
My heart's defenses crumbled in defeat,
And nothing fasting, prayer, or tears might do
Could stay my spirit from adoring you.
My eyes, my sighs have told you in the past   100
What now my lips make bold to say at last,
And if, in your great goodness, you will deign
To look upon your slave, and ease his pain,—
If, in compassion for my soul's distress,
You'll stoop to comfort my unworthiness,   105
I'll raise to you, in thanks for that sweet manna,
An endless hymn, an infinite hosanna.
With me, of course, there need be no anxiety,
No fear of scandal or of notoriety.
These young court gallants, whom all the ladies
    fancy,   110
Are vain in speech, in action rash and chancy;
When they succeed in love, the world soon
    knows it;
No favor's granted them but they disclose it
And by the looseness of their tongues profane
The very altar where their hearts have lain.   115
Men of my sort, however, love discreetly,
And one may trust our reticence completely.
My keen concern for my good name insures
The absolute security of yours;
In short, I offer you, my dear Elmire,   120
Love without scandal, pleasure without fear.

ELMIRE. I've heard your well-turned speeches to the
    end,
And what you urge I clearly apprehend.
Aren't you afraid that I may take a notion
To tell my husband of your warm devotion,   125
And that, supposing he were duly told,
His feelings toward you might grow rather
    cold?

TARTUFFE. I know, dear lady, that your exceeding
    charity
Will lead your heart to pardon my temerity;
That you'll excuse my violent affection   130
As human weakness, human imperfection;
And that—O fairest!—you will bear in mind
That I'm but flesh and blood, and am not
    blind.

ELMIRE. Some women might do otherwise,
    perhaps,
But I shall be discreet about your lapse;   135

I'll tell my husband nothing of what's occurred
If, in return, you'll give your solemn word
To advocate as forcefully as you can
The marriage of Valère and Mariane,
Renouncing all desire to dispossess   140
Another of his rightful happiness,
And . . .

SCENE IV

[Damis, Elmire, Tartuffe.]

DAMIS. *[Emerging from the closet where he has been*
    hiding.]
No! We'll not hush up this vile affair;
I heard it all inside that closet there,
Where Heaven, in order to confound the pride
Of this great rascal, prompted me to hide.
Ah, now I have my long-awaited chance   5
To punish his deceit and arrogance,
And give my father clear and shocking proof
Of the black character of his dear Tartuffe.

ELMIRE. Ah no, Damis! I'll be content if he
Will study to deserve my leniency.   10
I've promised silence—don't make me break my
    word;
To make a scandal would be too absurd.
Good wives laugh off such trifles, and forget
    them;
Why should they tell their husbands, and upset
    them?

DAMIS. You have your reasons for taking such a
    course,   15
And I have reasons, too, of equal force.
To spare him now would be insanely wrong.
I've swallowed my just wrath for far too long
And watched this insolent bigot bringing strife
And bitterness into our family life.   20
Too long he's meddled in my father's affairs,
Thwarting my marriage-hopes, and poor
    Valère's.
It's high time that my father was undeceived,
And now I've proof that can't be
    disbelieved—
Proof that was furnished me by Heaven
    above.   25
It's too good not to take advantage of.
This is my chance, and I deserve to lose it
If, for one moment, I hesitate to use it.

ELMIRE. Damis . . .

DAMIS.   No, I must do what I think right.
Madam, my heart is bursting with delight,   30
And, say whatever you will, I'll not consent
To lose the sweet revenge on which I'm bent.
I'll settle matters without more ado;
And here, most opportunely, is my cue.

SCENE V

[Orgon, Damis, Tartuffe, Elmire.]

DAMIS. Father, I'm glad you've joined us. Let us
        advise you
Of some fresh news which doubtless will
        surprise you.
You've just now been repaid with interest
For all your loving-kindness to our guest.
He's proved his warm and grateful feelings
        toward you;   5
It's with a pair of horns he would reward you.
Yes, I surprised him with your wife, and heard
His whole adulterous offer, every word.
She, with her all too gentle disposition,
Would not have told you of his proposition;   10
But I shall not make terms with brazen lechery,
And feel that not to tell you would be
        treachery.
ELMIRE. And I hold that one's husband peace of
        mind
Should not be spoilt by tattle of this kind.
One's honor doesn't require it: to be
        proficient   15
In keeping men at bay is quite sufficient.
These are my sentiments, and I wish, Damis,
That you had heeded me and held your peace.

SCENE VI

[Orgon, Damis, Tartuffe.]

ORGON. Can it be true, this dreadful thing I hear?
TARTUFFE. Yes, Brother, I'm a wicked man, I fear:
A wretched sinner, all depraved and twisted,
The greatest villain that has ever existed.
My life's one heap of crimes, which grows each
        minute;   5
There's naught but foulness and corruption in it;
And I perceive that Heaven, outraged by me,
Has chosen this occasion to mortify me.

Charge me with any deed you wish to name;
I'll not defend myself, but take the blame.   10
Believe what you are told, and drive Tartuffe
Like some base criminal from beneath your roof;
Yes, drive me hence, and with a parting curse:
I shan't protest, for I deserve far worse.
ORGON. *[To Damis.]* Ah, you deceitful boy, how dare
        you try   15
To stain his purity with so foul a lie?
DAMIS. What! Are you taken in by such a bluff?
Did you not hear . . . ?
ORGON.   Enough, you rogue, enough!
TARTUFFE. Ah, Brother, let him speak: you're being
        unjust.
Believe his story; the boy deserves your trust. 20
Why, after all, should you have faith in me?
How can you know what I might do, or be?
Is it on my good actions that you base
Your favor? Do you trust my pious face?
Ah, no, don't be deceived by hollow shows;   25
I'm far, alas, from being what men suppose;
Though the world takes me for a man of worth,
I'm truly the most worthless man on earth.

[To Damis.]

Yes, my dear son, speak out now: call me the
        chief
Of sinners, a wretch, a murderer, a thief;   30
Load me with all the names men most abhor;
I'll not complain; I've earned them all, and more;
I'll kneel here while you pour them on my head
As a just punishment for the life I've led.
ORGON. *[To Tartuffe.]* This is too much, dear Brother.

[To Damis.]

Have you no heart?   35
DAMIS. Are you so hoodwinked by this rascal's
        art . . . ?
ORGON. Be still, you monster.

[To Tartuffe.]

                                Brother, I pray you, rise.

[To Damis.]

Villain!
DAMIS.   But . . .
ORGON.   Silence!

DAMIS.   Can't you realize . . . ?

ORGON. Just one word more, and I'll tear you limb
     from limb.

TARTUFFE. In God's name, Brother, don't be harsh
     with him.   40
    I'd rather far be tortured at the stake
    Than see him bear one scratch for my poor sake.

ORGON. [To Damis.] Ingrate!

TARTUFFE.   If I must beg you, on
     bended knee,
    To pardon him . . .

ORGON. [Falling to his knees, addressing Tartuffe.]

                        Such goodness cannot be!

[To Damis.]

    Now, *there's* true charity!

DAMIS.   What, you . . . ?

ORGON.   Villain,
     be still!   45
    I know your motives; I know you wish him ill:
    Yes, all of you—wife, children, servants, all—
    Conspire against him and desire his fall,
    Employing every shameful trick you can
    To alienate me from this saintly man.   50
    Ah, but the more you seek to drive him away,
    The more I'll do to keep him. Without delay,
    I'll spite this household and confound its pride
    By giving him my daughter as his bride.

DAMIS. You're going to force her to accept his
     hand?   55

ORGON. Yes, and this very night, d'you understand?
    I shall defy you all, and make it clear
    That I'm the one who gives the orders here.
    Come, wretch, kneel down and clasp his blessed
     feet,
    And ask his pardon for your black deceit.   60

DAMIS. I ask that swindler's pardon? Why, I'd
     rather . . .

ORGON. So! You insult him, and defy your father!
    A stick! A stick! *[To Tartuffe.]* No, no—release
     me, do.

[To Damis.]

    Out of my house this minute! Be off with you,
    And never dare set foot in it again.   65

DAMIS. Well, I shall go, but . . .

ORGON.   Well, go quickly,
     then.

    I disinherit you; an empty purse
    Is all you'll get from me—except my curse!

SCENE VII

[Orgon, Tartuffe.]

ORGON. How he blasphemed your goodness! What
     a son!

TARTUFFE. Forgive him, Lord, as I've already done.

[To Orgon.]

    You can't know how it hurts when someone
     tries
    To blacken me in my dear Brother's eyes.

ORGON. Ahh!

TARTUFFE.   The mere thought of such
     ingratitude   5
    Plunges my soul into so dark a mood . . .
    Such horror grips my heart . . . I gasp for
     breath,
    And cannot speak, and feel myself near death.

ORGON. [He runs, in tears, to the door through which he
     has just driven his son.]
    You blackguard! Why did I spare you? Why did
     I not
    Break you in little pieces on the spot?   10
    Compose yourself, and don't be hurt, dear
     friend.

TARTUFFE. These scenes, these dreadful quarrels,
     have got to end.
    I've much upset your household, and I perceive
    That the best thing will be for me to leave.

ORGON. What are you saying!

TARTUFFE.   They're all against me
     here;   15
    They'd have you think me false and insincere.

ORGON. Ah, what of that? Have I ceased believing
     in you?

TARTUFFE. Their adverse talk will certainly
     continue,
    And charges which you now repudiate
    You may find credible at a later date.   20

ORGON. No, Brother, never.

TARTUFFE.   Brother, a wife can sway
    Her husband's mind in many a subtle way.

ORGON. No, no.

TARTUFFE.   To leave at once is the solution;
    Thus only can I end their persecution.

ORGON. No, no, I'll not allow it; you shall
    remain.   25
TARTUFFE. Ah, well; 'twill mean much martyrdom
    and pain,
    But if you wish it . . .
ORGON.   Ah!
TARTUFFE.   Enough; so be it.
    But one thing must be settled, as I see it.
    For your dear honor, and for our friendship's
    sake,
    There's one precaution I feel bound to take. 30
    I shall avoid your wife, and keep away . . .
ORGON. No, you shall not, whatever they may say.
    It pleases me to vex them, and for spite

I'd have them see you with her day and night.
What's more, I'm going to drive them to
    despair   35
By making you my only son and heir;
This very day, I'll give to you alone
Clear deed and title to everything I own.
A dear, good friend, and son-in-law-to-be
Is more than wife, or child, or kin to me.   40
Will you accept my offer, dearest son?
TARTUFFE. In all things, let the will of Heaven be
    done.
ORGON. Poor fellow! Come, we'll go draw up the
    deed.
    Then let them burst with disappointed greed!

Act IV

SCENE I

[Cléante, Tartuffe.]

CLÉANTE. Yes, all the town's discussing it, and truly,
    Their comments do not flatter you unduly.
    I'm glad we've met, Sir, and I'll give my view
    Of this sad matter in a word or two.
    As for who's guilty, that I shan't discuss;   5
    Let's say it was Damis who caused the fuss;
    Assuming, then, that you have been ill-used
    By young Damis, and groundlessly accused,
    Ought not a Christian to forgive, and ought
    He not to stifle every vengeful thought?   10
    Should you stand by and watch a father make
    His only son an exile for your sake?
    Again I tell you frankly, be advised:
    The whole town, high and low, is scandalized;
    This quarrel must be mended, and my
    advice is   15
    Not to push matters to a further crisis.
    No, sacrifice your wrath to God above,
    And help Damis regain his father's love.
TARTUFFE. Alas, for my part I should take great joy
    In doing so. I've nothing against the boy.   20
    I pardon all, I harbor no resentment;
    To serve him would afford me much
    contentment.
    But Heaven's interest will not have it so:
    If he comes back, then I shall have to go.

    After his conduct—so extreme, so vicious—   25
    Our further intercourse would look suspicious.
    God knows what people would think! Why,
    they'd describe
    My goodness to him as a sort of bribe;
    They'd say that out of guilt I made pretense
    Of loving-kindness and benevolence—   30
    That, fearing my accuser's tongue, I strove
    To buy his silence with a show of love.
CLÉANTE. Your reasoning is badly warped and
    stretched,
    And these excuses, Sir, are most far-fetched.
    Why put yourself in charge of Heaven's cause? 35
    Does Heaven need our help to enforce its laws?
    Leave vengeance to the Lord, Sir; while we live,
    Our duty's not to punish, but forgive;
    And what the Lord commands, we should obey
    Without regard to what the world may say.   40
    What! Shall the fear of being misunderstood
    Prevent our doing what is right and good?
    No, no: let's simply do what Heaven ordains,
    And let no other thoughts perplex our brains.
TARTUFFE. Again, Sir, let me say that I've forgiven   45
    Damis, and thus obeyed the laws of Heaven;
    But I am not commanded by the Bible
    To live with one who smears my name with
    libel.
CLÉANTE. Were you commanded, Sir, to indulge
    the whim
    Of poor Orgon, and to encourage him   50

In suddenly transferring to your name
A large estate to which you have to claim?
TARTUFFE. 'Twould never occur to those who know
    me best
To think I acted from self-interest.
The treasures of this world I quite despise;   55
Their specious glitter does not charm my eyes;
And if I have resigned myself to taking
The gift which my dear Brother insists on
    making,
I do so only, as he well understands,
Lest so much wealth fall into wicked hands,   60
Lest those to whom it might descend in time
Turn it to purposes of sin and crime,
And no, as I shall do, make use of it
For Heaven's glory and mankind's benefit.
CLÉANTE. Forget these trumped-up fears. Your
    argument   65
Is one the rightful heir might well resent;
It *is* a moral burden to inherit
Such wealth, but give Damis a chance to bear it.
And would it not be worse to be accused
Of swindling, than to see that wealth
    misused?   70
I'm shocked that you allowed Orgon to broach
This matter, and that you feel no self-reproach:
Does true religion teach that lawful heirs
May freely be deprived of what is theirs?
And if the Lord has told you in your heart   75
That you and young Damis must dwell apart,
Would it not be the decent thing to beat
A generous and honorable retreat,
Rather than let the son of the house be sent,
For your convenience, into banishment?   80
Sir, if you wish to prove the honesty
Of your intentions . . .
TARTUFFE.   Sir, it is half-past three.
I've certain pious duties to attend to,
And hope my prompt departure won't offend
    you.
CLÉANTE. *[Alone.]* Damn.

SCENE II

[Elmire, Mariane, Cléante, Dorine.]

DORINE. Stay, Sir, and help Mariane, for Heaven's
    sake!
She's suffering so, I fear her heart will break.
Her father's plan to marry her off tonight

Has put the poor child in a desperate plight.
I hear him coming. Let's stand together,
    now,   5
And see if we can't change his mind, somehow,
About this match we all deplore and fear.

SCENE III

[Orgon, Elmire, Mariane, Cléante, Dorine.]

ORGON. Hah! Glad to find you all assembled here.

[To Mariane.]

This contract, child, contains your happiness,
And what it says I think your heart can guess.
MARIANE. *[Falling to her knees.]*
Sir, by that Heaven which sees me here
    distressed,
And by whatever else can move your breast,   5
Do not employ a father's power, I pray you,
To crush my heart and force it to obey you,
Nor by your harsh commands oppress me so
That I'll begrudge the duty which I owe—
And do not so embitter and enslave me   10
That I shall hate the very life you gave me.
If my sweet hopes must perish, if you refuse
To give me to the one I've dared to choose,
Spare me at least—I beg you, I implore—
The pain of wedding one whom I abhor;   15
And do not, by a heartless use of force,
Drive me to contemplate some desperate course.
ORGON. *[Feeling himself touched by her.]*
Be firm, my soul. No human weakness, now.
MARIANE. I don't resent your love for him. Allow
Your heart free reign, Sir; give him your
    property,   20
And if that's not enough, take mine from me;
He's welcome to my money; take it, do,
But don't, I pray, include my person too.
Spare me, I beg you; and let me end the tale
Of my sad days behind a convent veil.   25
ORGON. A convent! Hah! When crossed in their
    amours,
All lovesick girls have the same thought as yours.
Get up! The more you loathe the man, and
    dread him,
The more ennobling it will be to wed him.   30
Marry Tartuffe, and mortify your flesh!
Enough; don't start that whimpering afresh.

DORINE. But why . . . ?

ORGON.   Be still, there. Speak when
you're spoken to.

Not one more bit of impudence out of you.

CLÉANTE. If I may offer a word of counsel here . . .

ORGON. Brother, in counselling you have no
peer;   35

All your advice is forceful, sound, and clever;

I don't propose to follow it, however.

ELMIRE. *[To Orgon.]* I am amazed, and don't know
what to say;

Your blindness simply takes my breath away.

You are indeed bewitched, to take no warning   40

From our account of what occurred this
morning.

ORGON. Madam, I know a few plain facts, and one

Is that you're partial to my rascal son;

Hence, when he sought to make Tartuffe the
victim

Of a base lie, you dared not contradict him.   45

Ah, but you underplayed your part, my pet;

You should have looked more angry, more
upset.

ELMIRE. When men make overtures, must we reply

With righteous anger and a battle-cry?

Must we turn back their amorous advances   50

With sharp reproaches and with fiery glances?

Myself, I find such offers merely amusing,

And make no scenes and fusses in refusing;

My taste is for good-natured rectitude,

And I dislike the savage sort of prude   55

Who guards her virtue with her teeth and claws,

And tears men's eyes out for the slightest cause:

The Lord preserve me from such honor as that,

Which bites and scratches like an alley-cat!

I've found that a polite and cool rebuff   60

Discourages a lover quite enough.

ORGON. I know the facts, and I shall not be shaken.

ELMIRE. I marvel at your power to be mistaken.

Would it, I wonder, carry weight with you

If I could *show* you that our tale was true?   65

ORGON. Show me?

ELMIRE.   Yes.

ORGON.   Rot.

ELMIRE.   Come, what if I found a
way

To make you see the facts as plain as day?

ORGON. Nonsense.

ELMIRE.   Do answer me; don't be absurd.

I'm not now asking you to trust our word.

Suppose that from some hiding-place in here   70

You learned the whole sad truth by eye and
ear—

What would you say of your good friend, after
that?

ORGON. Why, I'd say . . . nothing, by Jehoshaphat!

It can't be true.

ELMIRE.   You've been too long deceived,

And I'm quite tired of being disbelieved.   75

Come now: let's put my statements to the test,

And you shall see the truth made manifest.

ORGON. I'll take that challenge. Now do your
uttermost.

We'll see how you make good your empty
boast.

ELMIRE. *[To Dorine.]* Send him to me.

DORINE.   He's crafty; it
may be hard   80

To catch the cunning scoundrel off his guard.

ELMIRE. No, amorous men are gullible. Their
conceit

So blinds them that they're never hard to cheat.

Have him come down.

[To Cléante and Mariane.]

          Please leave us, for a bit.

SCENE IV

[Elmire, Orgon.]

ELMIRE. Pull up this table, and get under it.

ORGON. What?

ELMIRE. It's essential that you be well-hidden.

ORGON. Why there?

ELMIRE. Oh, Heavens! Just do as you are bidden.

I have my plans; we'll soon see how they fare.

Under the table, now; and once you're there,   5

Take care that you are neither seen nor heard.

ORGON. Well, I'll indulge you, since I gave my
word

To see you through this infantile charade.

ELMIRE. Once it is over, you'll be glad we played.

[To her husband, who is now under the table.]

I'm going to act quite strangely, now, and you   10

Must not be shocked at anything I do.

Whatever I may say, you must excuse

As part of that deceit I'm forced to use.

I shall employ sweet speeches in the task
Of making that imposter drop his mask;   15
I'll give encouragement to his bold desires,
And furnish fuel to his amorous fires.
Since it's for your sake, and for his destruction,
That I shall seem to yield to his seduction,
I'll gladly stop whenever you decide   20
That all your doubts are fully satisfied.
I'll count on you, as soon as you have seen
What sort of man he is, to intervene,
And not expose me to his odious lust
One moment longer than you feel you must.   25
Remember: you're to save me from my plight
Whenever . . . He's coming! Hush! Keep out of
    sight!

SCENE V

[Tartuffe, Elmire, Orgon.]

TARTUFFE. You wish to have a word with me, I'm
    told.
ELMIRE. Yes. I've a little secret to unfold.
    Before I speak, however, it would be wise
    To close that door, and look about for spies.

[Tartuffe goes to the door, closes it, and returns.]

    The very last thing that must happen now   5
    Is a repetition of this morning's row.
    I've never been so badly caught off guard.
    Oh, how I feared for you! You saw how hard
    I tried to make that troublesome Damis
    Control his dreadful temper, and hold his
        peace.   10
    In my confusion, I didn't have the sense
    Simply to contradict his evidence;
    But as it happened, that was for the best,
    And all has worked out in our interest.
    This storm has only bettered your position;   15
    My husband doesn't have the least suspicion,
    And now, in mockery of those who do,
    He bids me be continually with you.
    And that is why, quite fearless of reproof,
    I now can be alone with my Tartuffe,   20
    And why my heart—perhaps too quick to yield—
    Feels free to let its passion be revealed.
TARTUFFE. Madam, your words confuse me. Not
    long ago,
    You spoke in quite a different style, you know.

ELMIRE. Ah, Sir, if that refusal made you smart,   25
    It's little that you know of woman's heart,
    Or what that heart is trying to convey
    When it resists in such a feeble way!
    Always, at first, our modesty prevents
    The frank avowal of tender sentiments;   30
    However high the passion which inflames us,
    Still, to confess its power somehow shames us.
    Thus we reluct, at first, yet in a tone
    Which tells you that our heart is overthrown,
    That what our lips deny, our pulse confesses,   35
    And that, in time, all noes will turn to yesses.
    I fear my words are all too frank and free,
    And a poor proof of woman's modesty;
    But since I'm started, tell me, if you will—
    Would I have tried to make Damis be still,   40
    Would I have listened, calm and unoffended,
    Until your lengthy offer of love was ended,
    And been so very mild in my reaction,
    Had your sweet words not given me
        satisfaction?
    And when I tried to force you to undo   45
    The marriage-plans my husband has in view,
    What did my urgent pleading signify
    If not that I admired you, and that I
    Deplored the thought that someone else might
        own
    Part of a heart I wished for mine alone?   50
TARTUFFE. Madam, no happiness is so complete
    As when, from lips we love, come words so
        sweet;
    Their nectar floods my every sense, and drains
    In honeyed rivulets through all my veins.
    To please you is my joy, my only goal;   55
    Your love is the restorer of my soul;
    And yet I must beg leave, now, to confess
    Some lingering doubts as to my happiness.
    Might not this be a trick? Might not the catch
    Be that you wish me to break off the match   60
    With Mariane, and so have feigned to love me?
    I shan't quite trust your fond opinion of me
    Until the feelings you've expressed so sweetly
    Are demonstrated somewhat more concretely,
    And you have shown, by certain kind
        concessions,   65
    That I may put my faith in your professions.
ELMIRE. *[She coughs, to warn her husband.]*
    Why be in such a hurry? Must my heart
    Exhaust its bounty at the very start?
    To make that sweet admission cost me dear,
    But you'll not be content, it would appear,   70

Unless my store of favors is disbursed
To the last farthing, and at the very first.
TARTUFFE. The less we merit, the less we dare to
   hope,
   And with our doubts, mere words can never
      cope.
   We trust no promised bliss till we receive it;   75
   Not till a joy is ours can we believe it.
   I, who so little merit your esteem,
   Can't credit this fulfillment of my dream,
   And shan't believe it, Madam, until I savor
   Some palpable assurance of your favor.   80
ELMIRE. My, how tyrannical your love can be,
   And how it flusters and perplexes me!
   How furiously you take one's heart in hand,
   And make your every wish a fierce command!
   Come, must you hound and harry me to
      death?   85
   Will you not give me time to catch my breath?
   Can it be right to press me with such force,
   Give me no quarter, show me no remorse,
   And take advantage, by your stern insistence,
   Of the fond feelings which weaken my
      resistance?   90
TARTUFFE. Well, if you look with favor upon my love,
   Why, then, begrudge me some clear proof
      thereof?
ELMIRE. But how can I consent without offense
   To Heaven, toward which you feel such
      reverence?
TARTUFFE. If Heaven is all that holds you back,
      don't worry.   95
   I can remove that hindrance in a hurry.
   Nothing of that sort need obstruct our path.
ELMIRE. Must one not be afraid of Heaven's wrath?
TARTUFFE. Madam, forget such fears, and be my
      pupil,
   And I shall teach you how to conquer
      scruple.   100
   Some joys, it's true, are wrong in Heaven's eyes;
   Yet Heaven is not averse to compromise;
   There is a science, lately formulated,
   Whereby one's conscience may be liberated,
   And any wrongful act you care to mention   105
   May be redeemed by purity of intention.
   I'll teach you, Madam, the secrets of that science;
   Meanwhile, just place on me your full reliance.
   Assuage my keen desires, and feel no dread:
   The sin, if any, shall be on my head.   110

[Elmire coughs, this time more loudly.]

You've a bad cough.
ELMIRE.   Yes, yes. It's bad indeed.
TARTUFFE. *[Producing a little paper bag.]*
   A bit of licorice may be what you need.
ELMIRE. No, I've a stubborn cold, it seems. I'm
      sure it
   Will take much more than licorice to cure it.
TARTUFFE. How aggravating.
ELMIRE.   Oh, more than I can
      say.   115
TARTUFFE. If you're still troubled, think of things
      this way:
   No one shall know our joys, save us alone,
   And there's no evil till the act is known;
   It's scandal, Madam, which makes it an offense,
   And it's no sin to sin in confidence.   120
ELMIRE. *[Having coughed once more.]* Well, clearly I
      must do as you require,
   And yield to your importunate desire.
   It is apparent, now, that nothing less
   Will satisfy you, and so I acquiesce.
   To go so far is much against my will;   125
   I'm vexed that it should come to this; but still,
   Since you are so determined on it, since you
   Will not allow mere language to convince you,
   And since you ask for concrete evidence, I
   See nothing for it, now, but to comply.   130
   If this is sinful, if I'm wrong to do it,
   So much the worse for him who drove me to it.
   The fault can surely not be charged to me.
TARTUFFE. Madam, the fault is mine, if fault there be,
   And . . .
ELMIRE.   Open the door a little, and peek out;   135
   I wouldn't want my husband poking about.
TARTUFFE. Why worry about the man? Each day he
      grows
   More gullible; one can lead him by the nose.
   To find us here would fill him with delight,
   And if he saw the worst, he'd doubt his
      sight.   140
ELMIRE. Nevertheless, do step out for a minute
   Into the hall, and see that no one's in it.

SCENE VI

[Orgon, Elmire.]

ORGON. *[Coming out from under the table.]*
   That man's a perfect monster, I must admit!
   I'm simply stunned. I can't get over it.

ELMIRE. What, coming out so soon? How
    premature!
  Get back in hiding, and wait until you're sure.
  Stay till the end, and be convinced completely;   5
  We mustn't stop till things are proved
    concretely.
ORGON. Hell never harbored anything so vicious!
ELMIRE. Tut, don't be hasty. Try to be judicious.
  Wait, and be certain that there's no mistake.
  No jumping to conclusions, for Heaven's
    sake!   10

[She places Orgon behind her, as Tartuffe reenters.]

SCENE VII

[Tartuffe, Elmire, Orgon.]

TARTUFFE. *[Not seeing Orgon.]*
  Madam, all things have worked out to
    perfection;
  I've given the neighboring rooms a full
    inspection;
  No one's about; and now I may at last . . .
ORGON. *[Intercepting him.]* Hold on, my passionate
    fellow, not so fast!
  I should advise a little more restraint.   5
  Well, so you thought you'd fool me, my dear
    saint!
  How soon you wearied of the saintly life—
  Wedding my daughter, and coveting my wife!
  I've long suspected you, and had a feeling
  That soon I'd catch you at your double-
    dealing.   10
  Just now, you've given me evidence galore;
  It's quite enough; I have no wish for more.
ELMIRE. *[To Tartuffe.]* I'm sorry to have treated you
    so slyly,
  But circumstances forced me to be wily.

TARTUFFE. Brother, you can't think . . .
ORGON.   No more
  talk from you;   15
  Just leave this household, without more ado.
TARTUFFE. What I intended . . .
ORGON.   That seems fairly
  clear.
  Spare me your falsehoods and get out of here.
TARTUFFE. No, I'm the master, and you're the one
    to go!
  This house belongs to me, I'll have you
    know,   20
  And I shall show you that you can't hurt *me*
  By this contemptible conspiracy,
  That those who cross me know not what they
    do,
  And that I've means to expose and punish you,
  Avenge offended Heaven, and make you
    grieve   25
  That ever you dared order me to leave.

SCENE VIII

[Elmire, Orgon.]

ELMIRE. What was the point of all that angry
    chatter?
ORGON. Dear God, I'm worried. This is no
    laughing matter.
ELMIRE. How so?
ORGON.   I fear I understood his drift.
  I'm much disturbed about that deed of gift.
ELMIRE. You gave him . . . ?
ORGON.   Yes, it's all been drawn
    and signed.   5
  But one thing more is weighing on my mind.
ELMIRE. What's that?
ORGON. I'll tell you; but first let's see if there's
  A certain strong-box in his room upstairs.

Act V

SCENE I

[Orgon, Cléante.]

CLÉANTE. Where are you going so fast?

ORGON. God knows!
CLÉANTE. Then wait;
  Let's have a conference, and deliberate
  On how this situation's to be met.
ORGON. That strong-box has me utterly upset;

This is the worst of many, many shocks. 5
CLÉANTE. Is there some fearful mystery in that box?
ORGON. My poor friend Argas brought that box to
  me
 With his own hands, in utmost secrecy;
 'Twas on the very morning of his flight.
 It's full of papers which, if they came to light, 10
 Would ruin him—or such is my impression.
CLÉANTE. Then why did you let it out of your
  possession?
ORGON. Those papers vexed my conscience, and it
  seemed best
 To ask the counsel of my pious guest.
 The cunning scoundrel got me to agree 15
 To leave the strong-box in his custody,
 So that, in case of an investigation,
 I could employ a slight equivocation
 And swear I didn't have it, and thereby,
 At no expense to conscience, tell a lie. 20
CLÉANTE. It looks to me as if you're out on a limb.
 Trusting him with that box, and offering him
 That deed of gift, were actions of a kind
 Which scarcely indicate a prudent mind.
 With two such weapons, he has the upper
  hand, 25
 And since you're vulnerable, as matters stand,
 You erred once more in bringing him to bay,
 You should have acted in some subtler way.
ORGON. Just think of it: behind that fervent face,
 A heart so wicked, and a soul so base! 30
 I took him in, a hungry beggar, and then . . .
 Enough, by God! I'm through with pious men:
 Henceforth I'll hate the whole false
  brotherhood,
 And persecute them worse than Satan could.
CLÉANTE. Ah, there you go—extravagant as ever! 35
 Why can you not be rational? You never
 Manage to take the middle course, it seems,
 But jump, instead, between absurd extremes.
 You've recognized your recent grave mistake
 In falling victim to a pious fake; 40
 Now, to correct that error, must you embrace
 An even greater error in its place,
 And judge our worthy neighbors as a whole
 By what you've learned of one corrupted soul?
 Come, just because one rascal made you
  swallow 45
 A show of zeal which turned out to be hollow,
 Shall you conclude that all men are deceivers,
 And that, today, there are no true believers?
 Let atheists make that foolish inference;

Learn to distinguish virtue from pretense, 50
Be cautious in bestowing admiration,
And cultivate a sober moderation.
Don't humor fraud, but also don't asperse
True piety; the latter fault is worse,
And it is best to err, if err one must, 55
As you have done, upon the side of trust.

SCENE II

[Damis, Orgon, Cléante.]

DAMIS. Father, I hear that scoundrel's uttered
  threats
 Against you; that he pridefully forgets
 How, in his need, he was befriended by you,
 And means to use your gifts to crucify you.
ORGON. It's true, my boy. I'm too distressed for
  tears. 5
DAMIS. Leave it to me, Sir; let me trim his ears.
 Faced with such insolence, we must not waver.
 I shall rejoice in doing you the favor
 Of cutting short his life, and your distress.
CLÉANTE. What a display of young
  hotheadedness! 10
 Do learn to moderate your fits of rage.
 In this just kingdom, this enlightened age,
 One does not settle things by violence.

SCENE III

[Madame Pernelle, Mariane, Elmire, Dorine, Damis, Orgon, Cléante.]

MADAME PERNELLE. I hear strange tales of very
  strange events.
ORGON. Yes, strange events which these two eyes
  beheld.
 The man's ingratitude is unparalleled.
 I save a wretched pauper from starvation,
 House him, and treat him like a blood relation, 5
 Shower him every day with my largesse,
 Give him my daughter, and all that I possess;
 And meanwhile the unconscionable knave
 Tries to induce my wife to misbehave;
 And not content with such extreme rascality, 10
 Now threatens me with my own liberality,
 And aims, by taking base advantage of
 The gifts I gave him out of Christian love,

To drive me from my house, a ruined man,
And make me end a pauper, as he began.   15
DORINE. Poor fellow!
MADAME PERNELLE. No, my son, I'll never bring
   Myself to think him guilty of such a thing.
ORGON. How's that?
MADAME PERNELLE. The righteous always were
   maligned.
ORGON. Speak clearly, Mother. Say what's on your
   mind.
MADAME PERNELLE. I mean that I can smell a rat, my
   dear.   20
   You know how everybody hates him, here.
ORGON. That has no bearing on the case at all.
MADAME PERNELLE. I told you a hundred times,
   when you were small,
   That virtue in this world is hated ever;
   Malicious men may die, but malice never.   25
ORGON. No doubt that's true, but how does it apply?
MADAME PERNELLE. They've turned you against him
   by a clever lie.
ORGON. I've told you, I was there and saw it done.
MADAME PERNELLE. Ah, slanderers will stop at
   nothing, Son.
ORGON. Mother, I'll lose my temper . . . For the
   last time,   30
   I tell you I was witness to the crime.
MADAME PERNELLE. The tongues of spite are busy
   night and noon,
   And to their venom no man is immune.
ORGON. You're talking nonsense. Can't you realize
   I saw it; saw it; saw it with my eyes?   35
   Saw, do you understand me? Must I shout it
   Into your ears before you'll cease to doubt it?
MADAME PERNELLE. Appearances can deceive, my
   son. Dear me,
   We cannot always judge by what we see.
ORGON. Drat! Drat!
MADAME PERNELLE. One often interprets things
   awry;   40
   Good can seem evil to a suspicious eye.
ORGON. Was I to see his pawing at Elmire
   As an act of charity?
MADAME PERNELLE.   Till his guilt is clear,
   A man deserves the benefit of the doubt.
   You should have waited, to see how things
   turned out.   45
ORGON. Great God in Heaven, what more proof
   did I need?
   Was I to sit there, watching, until he'd . . .
   You drive me to the brink of impropriety.

MADAME PERNELLE. No, no, a man of such
   surpassing piety
   Could not do such a thing. You cannot shake
   me.   50
   I don't believe it, and you shall not make me.
ORGON. You vex me so that, if you weren't my
   mother,
   I'd say to you . . . some dreadful thing or other.
DORINE. It's your turn now, Sir, not to be listened to;
   You'd not trust us, and now she won't trust
   you.   55
CLÉANTE. My friends, we're wasting time which
   should be spent
   In facing up to our predicament.
   I fear that scoundrel's threats weren't made in
   sport.
DAMIS. Do you think he'd have the nerve to go to
   court?
ELMIRE. I'm sure he won't; they'd find it all too
   crude   60
   A case of swindling and ingratitude.
CLÉANTE. Don't be too sure. He won't be at a loss
   To give his claims a high and righteous gloss;
   And clever rogues with far less valid cause
   Have trapped their victims in a web of laws.   65
   I say again that to antagonize
   A man so strongly armed was most unwise.
ORGON. I know it; but the man's appalling cheek
   Outraged me so, I couldn't control my pique.
CLÉANTE. I wish to Heaven that we could
   devise   70
   Some truce between you, or some compromise.
ELMIRE. If I had known what cards he held, I'd not
   Have roused his anger by my little plot.
ORGON. [To Dorine, as M. Loyal enters.]
   What is that fellow looking for? Who is he?
   Go talk to him—and tell him that I'm busy.   75

SCENE IV

[Monsieur Loyal, Madame Pernelle, Orgon, Damis, Mariane, Dorine, Elmire, Cléante.]

MONSIEUR LOYAL. Good day, dear sister. Kindly let
   me see
   Your master.
DORINE.   He's involved with company,
   And cannot be disturbed just now, I fear.
MONSIEUR LOYAL. I hate to intrude; but what has
   brought me here

Will not disturb your master, in any event.   5
Indeed, my news will make him most content.
DORINE. Your name?
MONSIEUR LOYAL.   Just say that I bring greetings
        from
    Monsieur Tartuffe, on whose behalf I've come.
DORINE. [To Orgon.] Sir, he's a very gracious man,
        and bears
    A message from Tartuffe, which, he declares,   10
    Will make you most content.
CLÉANTE.   Upon my word,
    I think this man had best be seen, and heard.
ORGON. Perhaps he has some settlement to suggest.
    How shall I treat him? What manner would be
        best?
CLÉANTE. Control your anger, and if he should
        mention   15
    Some fair adjustment, give him your full
        attention.
MONSIEUR LOYAL. Good health to you, good Sir.
        May Heaven confound
    Your enemies, and may your joys abound.
ORGON. [Aside, to Cléante.] A gentle salutation: it
        confirms
    My guess that he is here to offer terms.   20
MONSIEUR LOYAL. I've always held your family most
        dear;
    I served your father, Sir, for many a year.
ORGON. Sir, I must ask your pardon; to my shame,
    I cannot now recall your face or name.
MONSIEUR LOYAL. Loyal's my name; I come from
        Normandy,   25
    And I'm a bailiff, in all modesty.
    For forty years, praise God, it's been my boast
    To serve with honor in that vital post,
    And I am here, Sir, if you will permit
    The liberty, to serve you with this writ . . . 30
ORGON. To—*what*?
MONSIEUR LOYAL. Now, please, Sir, let us have no
        friction:
    It's nothing but an order of eviction.
    You are to move your goods and family out
    And make way for new occupants, without
    Deferment or delay, and give the keys . . .   35
ORGON. I? Leave this house?
MONSIEUR LOYAL.   Why yes, Sir, if you
        please.
    This house, Sir, from the cellar to the roof,
    Belongs now to the good Monsieur Tartuffe,
    And he is lord and master of your estate
    By virtue of a deed of present date,   40

Drawn in due form, with clearest legal
        phrasing . . .
DAMIS. Your insolence is utterly amazing!
MONSIEUR LOYAL. Young man, my business here is
        not with you,
    But with your wise and temperate father, who,
    Like every worthy citizen, stands in awe   45
    of justice, and would never obstruct the law.
ORGON. But . . .
MONSIEUR LOYAL.
                    Not for a million, Sir, would you
        rebel
    Against authority; I know that well.
    You'll not make trouble, Sir, or interfere
    With the execution of my duties here.   50
DAMIS. Someone may execute a smart tattoo
    On that black jacket of yours, before you're
        through.
MONSIEUR LOYAL. Sir, bid your son be silent. I'd
        much regret
    Having to mention such a nasty threat
    Of violence, in writing my report.   55
DORINE. [Aside.] This man Loyal's a most disloyal
        sort!
MONSIEUR LOYAL. I love all men of upright character,
    And when I agreed to serve these papers, Sir,
    It was your feelings that I had in mind.
    I couldn't bear to see the case assigned   60
    To someone else, who might esteem you less
    And so subject you to unpleasantness.
ORGON. What's more unpleasant than telling a man
        to leave
    His house and home?
MONSIEUR LOYAL.   You'd like a short reprieve?
    If you desire it, Sir, I shall not press you,   65
    But wait until tomorrow to dispossess you.
    Splendid. I'll come and spend the night here,
        then,
    Most quietly, with half a score of men.
    For form's sake, you might bring me, just
        before
    You go to bed, the keys to the front door.   70
    My men, I promise, will be on their best
    Behavior, and will not disturb your rest.
    But bright and early, Sir, you must be quick
    And move out all your furniture, every stick:
    The men I've chosen are both young and
        strong,   75
    And with their help it shouldn't take you long.
    In short, I'll make things pleasant and
        convenient,

And since I'm being so extremely lenient,
Please show me, Sir, a like consideration,
And give me your entire cooperation.   80

ORGON. *[Aside.]* I may be all but bankrupt, but I
    vow
I'd give a hundred louis, here and now,
Just for the pleasure of landing one good clout
Right on the end of that complacent snout.

CLÉANTE. Careful; don't make things worse.

DAMIS.   My
    bootsole itches   85
To give that beggar a good kick in the
    breeches.

DORINE. Monsieur Loyal, I'd love to hear the
    whack
Of a stout stick across your fine broad back.

MONSIEUR LOYAL. Take care: a woman too may go
    to jail if
She uses threatening language to a bailiff.   90

CLÉANTE. Enough, enough, Sir. This must not go on.
Give me that paper, please, and then begone.

MONSIEUR LOYAL. Well, *au revoir.* God give you all
    good cheer!

ORGON. May God confound you, and him who
    sent you here!

SCENE V

*[Orgon, Cléante, Mariane, Elmire, Madame Pernelle,
Dorine, Damis.]*

ORGON. Now, Mother, was I right or not? This writ
Should change your notion of Tartuffe a bit.
Do you perceive his villainy at last?

MADAME PERNELLE. I'm thunderstruck. I'm utterly
    aghast.

DORINE. Oh, come, be fair. You mustn't take
    offense   5
At this new proof of his benevolence.
He's acting out of selfless love, I know.
Material things enslave the soul, and so
He kindly has arranged your liberation
From all that might endanger your salvation.   10

ORGON. Will you not ever hold your tongue, you
    dunce?

CLÉANTE. Come, you must take some action, and at
    once.

ELMIRE. Go tell the world of the low trick he's
    tried.

The deed of gift is surely nullified
By such behavior, and public rage will not   15
Permit the wretch to carry out this plot.

SCENE VI

*[Valère, Orgon, Cléante, Elmire, Mariane, Madame Per-
nelle, Damis, Dorine]*

VALÈRE. Sir, though I hate to bring you more bad
    news,
Such is the danger that I cannot choose.
A friend who is extremely close to me
And knows my interest in your family
Has, for my sake, presumed to violate   5
The secrecy that's due to things of state,
And sends me word that you are in a plight
From which your one salvation lies in flight.
That scoundrel who's imposed upon you so
Denounced you to the King an hour ago   10
And, as supporting evidence, displayed
The strong-box of a certain renegade
Whose secret papers, so he testified,
You had disloyally agreed to hide.
I don't know just what charges may be
    pressed,   15
But there's a warrant out for your arrest;
Tartuffe has been instructed, furthermore,
To guide the arresting officer to your door.

CLÉANTE. He's clearly done this to facilitate
His seizure of your house and your estate.   20

ORGON. That man, I must say, is a vicious beast!

VALÈRE. You can't afford to delay, Sir, in the least.
My carriage is outside, to take you hence;
This thousand louis should cover all expense.
Let's lose no time, or you shall be undone;   25
The sole defense, in this case, is to run.
I shall go with you all the way, and place you
In a safe refuge to which they'll never trace
    you.

ORGON. Alas, dear boy, I wish that I could show
    you
My gratitude for everything I owe you.   30
But now is not the time; I pray the Lord
That I may live to give you your reward.
Farewell, my dears; be careful . . .

CLÉANTE.   Brother, hurry.
We shall take care of things; you needn't
    worry.

SCENE VII

[The Officer, Tartuffe, Valère, Orgon, Elmire, Mariane, Madame Pernelle, Dorine, Cléante, Damis.]

TARTUFFE. Gently, Sir, gently; stay right where you
    are.
  No need for haste; your lodging isn't far.
  You're off to prison, by order of the Prince.
ORGON. This is the crowning blow, you wretch;
    and since
  It means my total ruin and defeat,   5
  Your villainy is now at last complete.
TARTUFFE. You needn't try to provoke me; it's no
    use.
  Those who serve Heaven must expect abuse.
CLÉANTE. You are indeed most patient, sweet, and
    blameless.
DORINE. How he exploits the name of Heaven! It's
    shameless.   10
TARTUFFE. Your taunts and mockeries are all for
    naught;
  To do my duty is my only thought.
MARIANE. Your love of duty is most meritorious,
  And what you've done is little short of glorious.
TARTUFFE. All deeds are glorious, Madam, which
    obey   15
  The sovereign prince who sent me here today.
ORGON. I rescued you when you were destitute;
  Have you forgotten that, you thankless brute?
TARTUFFE. No, no, I well remember everything;
  But my first duty is to serve my King.   20
  That obligation is so paramount
  That other claims, beside it, do not count;
  And for it I would sacrifice my wife,
  My family, my friend, or my own life.
ELMIRE. Hypocrite!
DORINE. All that we most revere, he uses   25
  To cloak his plots and camouflage his ruses.
CLÉANTE. If it is true that you are animated
  By pure and loyal zeal, as you have stated,
  Why was this zeal not roused until you'd
    sought
  To make Orgon a cuckold, and been caught? 30
  Why weren't you moved to give your evidence
  Until your outraged host had driven you hence?
  I shan't say that the gift of all his treasure
  Ought to have damped your zeal in any
    measure;

But if he is a traitor, as you declare,   35
  How could you condescend to be his heir?
TARTUFFE. [To the Officer.]
  Sir, spare me all this clamor; it's growing shrill.
  Please carry out your orders, if you will.
OFFICER. Yes, I've delayed too long, Sir. Thank you
    kindly.
  You're just the proper person to remind me.   40
  Come, you are off to join the other boarders
  In the King's prison, according to his orders.
TARTUFFE. Who? I, Sir?
OFFICER.   Yes.
TARTUFFE.   To prison? This can't be
    true!
OFFICER. I owe an explanation, but not to you.

[To Orgon.]

Sir, all is well; rest easy, and be grateful.   45
We serve a Prince to whom all sham is hateful,
A Prince who sees into our inmost hearts,
And can't be fooled by any trickster's arts.
His royal soul, though generous and human,
Views all things with discernment and
    acumen;   50
His sovereign reason is not lightly swayed,
And all his judgments are discreetly weighed.
He honors righteous men of every kind,
And yet his zeal for virtue is not blind,
Nor does his love of piety numb his wits   55
And make him tolerant of hypocrites.
'Twas hardly likely that this man could cozen
A King who's foiled such liars by the dozen.
With one keen glance, the King perceived the
    whole
Perverseness and corruption of his soul,   60
And thus high Heaven's justice was displayed:
Betraying you, the rogue stood self-betrayed.
The King soon recognized Tartuffe as one
Notorious by another name, who'd done
So many vicious crimes that one could fill   65
Ten volumes with them, and be writing still.
But to be brief: our sovereign was appalled
By this man's treachery toward you, which he
    called
The last, worst villainy of a vile career,
And bade me follow the imposter here   70
To see how gross his impudence could be,
And force him to restore your property.
Your private papers, by the King's command,

I hereby seize and give into your hand.
The King, by royal order, invalidates   75
The deed which gave this rascal your estates,
And pardons, furthermore, your grave offense
In harboring an exile's documents.
By these decrees, our Prince rewards you for
Your loyal deeds in the late civil war,   80
And shows how heartfelt is his satisfaction
In recompensing any worthy action,
How much he prizes merit, and how he makes
More of men's virtues than of their mistakes.

DORINE. Heaven be praised!

MADAME PERNELLE.   I breathe again, at
     last.   85

ELMIRE. We're safe.

MARIANE.   I can't believe the danger's past.

ORGON. *[To Tartuffe.]*
     Well, traitor, now you see . . .

CLÉANTE.   Ah, Brother, please,
Let's not descend to such indignities.
Leave the poor wretch to his unhappy fate,
And don't say anything to aggravate   90
His present woes; but rather hope that he
Will soon embrace an honest piety,
And mend his ways, and by a true repentance
Move our just King to moderate his sentence.
Meanwhile, go kneel before your sovereign's
     throne   95
And thank him for the mercies he has shown.

ORGON. Well said: let's go at once and, gladly
     kneeling,
Express the gratitude which all are feeling.
Then, when that first great duty has been done,
We'll turn with pleasure to a second one,   100
And give Valère, whose love has proven so true,
The wedded happiness which is his due.

Introduction to *The Busy Body* by Susanna Centlivre

The Busy Body   (Billy Rose Theatre Collection/New York Public Library for the Performing Arts, Astor, Lenox, and Tilden Foundations)

The Play   *The Busy Body*, first staged in 1709, is a comedy of intrigue and disguises, in which young lovers, kept apart by older men, are eventually united. Sir George Airy is a young suitor in love with Miranda, whose inheritance is larger than his and whose guardian, Sir Francis Gripe, is also in love with her. Miranda pretends to be in love with her guardian. Meanwhile, Sir Francis's son, Charles, is in love with Isabinda. However, Isabinda's merchant father, Sir Jealous Traffick, who foolishly mimics Spanish customs, has promised her to a Spaniard and tries to keep her from all other men. In the midst of all of this intrigue is Marplot, the "busybody" of the title, who, in his attempts to discover the lovers' secrets, frequently undoes their plotting.

Like much Restoration and eighteenth-century English comedy, *The Busy Body* is reminiscent of Molière's comedies of characters; each character's name reflects a stock comic type. Marplot is the most obvious: This character's curiosity frequently comes close to marring the young lovers' plots. The plotline—young love blocked by older men—is also similar to that of many other plays of the era. Centlivre's play is, in fact, considered a bridge between bawdy, sexually explicit Restoration comedy and the more traditional morality of eighteenth-century English sentimental comedy.

Still, even in the eighteenth century, critics suggested that Centlivre's dramaturgical approach was unique, compared with the work of her male contemporaries. Richard Steele (1672–1729), himself a playwright, noted that "the plot and incidents of the play are laid with that subtlety of spirit which [is] peculiar to females of wit, and is very seldom well performed by those of the other sex, in whom craft in love is an act of invention, and not, as with women, the effect of nature and instinct." Modern feminist criticism of Centlivre's work frequently focuses on her representation of the female young lovers, who transcend the traditional objectified characterization; instead, they are much more the subject of the comedy and have a significant role in the dramatic action. Miranda, for example, is not only wealthier than George but much more successful at intrigue. Critics have also noted the interesting representation of a male gossip, whose foolishness nearly undoes the lovers.

The Playwright   There were many significant female dramatists in England during the Restoration and the early eighteenth century, including Aphra Behn (1640–1689), Mary Pix (1666–1706), Delariviere Manley (ca.1672–1724), and Catharine Trotter (1679–1749). Susanna Centlivre (ca.1670–1723) was the most commercially successful of these English female playwrights. She produced numerous letters, poems, 16 full-length plays, and three short farces. Five of her plays became standard works in the eighteenth- and nineteenth-century repertoire: *The Gamester* (1705), *The Basset Table* (1705), *The Busy Body* (1709), *The Wonder: A Woman Keeps Her Secret* (1714), and *A Bold Stroke for a Wife* (1718).

The details of Centlivre's early life are unclear. Some biographers report that she was born to a Mr. Freeman of Holbeach, Lincolnshire, who died when she was three. At 14, Centlivre supposedly ran away from home with a group of strolling players to escape a wicked stepmother. Other biographers suggest that Centlivre ran away with Anthony Hammond, who dressed her up as a man and took her with him to Cambridge. Shortly thereafter, she married a nephew of Sir Stephen Fox. She was widowed within a year and then married an army officer. Eighteen months later she was widowed again, when her second husband was killed in a duel.

After 1700, Centlivre's life is more accurately documented. Early in the century, she was actively involved in politics, working with the Whig party. She also returned to the stage, acting and writing plays. In 1707, she married Joseph Centlivre, a cook for Queen Anne, who had seen her playing a breeches role—that is, a role in which she was costumed as a man.

Centlivre wrote during a time when many audience members viewed female writers negatively. Like Aphra Behn, she was believed to be writing out of economic necessity, and she encountered so much hostility that she left the theater for two years. She returned with a new play, *The Busy Body*, in 1709. This comedy premiered to a small audience, but by the third night (a performance for the benefit of the author), the theater was filled.

After the success of *The Busy Body*, Centlivre, who had written a number of her earlier plays anonymously, never again hid her sexual identity.

The Period   *The Busy Body* is a transitional play, coming just after the end of the English Restoration and soon after the start of the eighteenth century. The background of the Restoration was a bitter civil war lasting from 1642 to 1649, when Charles I of England was removed from the throne by the Puritans and beheaded. For the next 11 years, England was a Commonwealth, governed by Oliver Cromwell with a Parliament that had been purged of all his opponents. When Cromwell died in 1658, his son was unable to keep control of the government; and in 1660 Charles II, who had been living in exile in France, was invited by a newly elected Parliament to return and rule England. The monarchy was thus restored, and the subsequent period in English history—usually dated from 1660 through 1700—is therefore called the Restoration.

The eighteenth century was a time of transition. Increased manufacturing and international trade affected populations worldwide. The major eighteenth-century mercantile powers were England and France, and decisions made in these two nations directly affected people in such places as North America, India, and Africa. One effect on Africa, for example, was a marked increase in the slave trade. Because of the growth in trade, western Europe prospered more than ever before, and ingenious and daring investors of capital became extremely wealthy. Profits from colonial trade filtered down to the emerging middle class, which included merchants and others in commercial enterprises and which then became a social as well as a political force.

There were also many new developments in learning and philosophy—so many that the eighteenth century is called the Age of Enlightenment, or simply the Enlightenment. The search for knowledge was supported by the educated middle class, and though France was its center, the Enlightenment had international reverberations. Two major political and social upheavals, the American Revolution (1775–1783) and the French Revolution (1789–1799), were based on ideals of the Enlightenment.

At the beginning of the eighteenth century, the time when Centlivre was writing her plays, there had been significant changes in the English theater. During the period of the Commonwealth, many members of the English nobility had been exiles in France; when the English monarchy was restored, these people took back with them the theatrical practices they had seen there. The theater of the English Restoration, therefore, combined aspects of English and continental Renaissance theater. Restoration drama contained elements of both Elizabethan plays and the dramas of the French neoclassical era. The Restoration playhouse also had native and continental elements: Its modified proscenium arch came from French and Italian practices, but its elongated apron and proscenium doors and boxes came from the theaters of Shakespeare's time. During the eighteenth century, the English playhouse changed somewhat. The number of proscenium doors and boxes decreased from four to two and the apron became shallower. Scenery was painted in perspective.

Women were introduced as professional performers in the Restoration theater, and in general the eighteenth century is remembered as an era of great actors and actresses, including Thomas Betterton (ca.1635–1710), Elizabeth Barry (1658–1713), Ann Bracegirdle (ca.1663–1748), Anne Oldfield (1683–1730), James Quin (1693–1766), Charles Macklin (1699–1797), and David Garrick (1717–1779), who was so innovative as an actor-manager that he is often cited as the first modern director.

The English drama of the eighteenth century included middle-class tragedy, comedy of intrigue, sentimental comedy, and ballad opera, which combined traditional dialogue with songs set to popular music and is sometimes considered an antecedent of musical comedy. The focus on the emerging middle class in much of this drama clearly reflected the economic transformations taking place in England in the 1700s.

THE BUSY BODY

Susanna Centlivre

CHARACTERS

Women

MIRANDA, an heiress worth £30,000, really in love with Sir George Airy, but pretends to be so with her guardian, Sir Francis Gripe.

ISABINDA, daughter to Sir Jealous Traffic, in love with Charles, but designed for a Spanish merchant by her father, and kept from the sight of all men.

PATCH, Isabinda's woman.

SCENTWELL, Miranda's woman.

Men

MARPLOT, a sort of a silly fellow, cowardly, but very inquisitive to know everybody's business, generally spoils all he undertakes, but without design.

SIR GEORGE AIRY, a gentleman of £4,000 a year, in love with Miranda.

SIR FRANCIS GRIPE, guardian to Miranda and Marplot, father to Charles, in love with Miranda.

CHARLES, friend to Sir George, in love with Isabinda.

SIR JEALOUS TRAFFICK, a merchant that has lived some time in Spain, a great admirer of Spanish customs, father to Isabinda.

WHISPER, manservant to Charles.

Act I

SCENE I

[The park. Sir George Airy meeting Charles.]

CHARLES. Ha! Sir George Airy! A-birding thus early! What forbidden game roused you so soon? For no lawful occasion could invite a person of your figure abroad at such unfashionable hours.

SIR GEORGE. There are some men, Charles, whom Fortune has left free from inquietude, who are diligently studious to find out ways and means to make themselves uneasy.

CHARLES. Is it possible that anything in nature can ruffle the temper of a man whom the four seasons of the year compliment with as many thousand pounds; nay, and a father at rest with his ancestors?

SIR GEORGE. Why there 'tis now! A man that wants money thinks none can be unhappy that has it; but my affairs are in such a whimsical posture, that it will require a calculation of my nativity[1] to find if my gold will relieve me, or not.

CHARLES. Ha, ha, ha! Never consult the stars about that. Gold has a power beyond them; gold unlocks the midnight councils; gold outdoes the wind, becalms the ship, or fills her sails. Gold is omnipotent below: it makes whole armies fight or fly; it buys even souls, and bribes the wretches to betray their country. Then what can the business be, that gold won't serve thee in?

SIR GEORGE. Why, I'm in love.

CHARLES. In love!—Ha, ha, ha, ha! In love, ha, ha, ha, with what, prithee? A cherubim?

SIR GEORGE. No, with a woman.

CHARLES. A woman, good, ha, ha, ha! And gold not help thee?

SIR GEORGE. But suppose I'm in love with two—

CHARLES. Aye, if thou'rt in love with two hundred, gold will fetch 'em, I warrant thee, boy. But who are they! Who are they! Come.

SIR GEORGE. One is a lady whose face I never saw, but witty as an angel; the other beautiful as Venus—

CHARLES. And a fool—

SIR GEORGE. For aught I know, for I never spoke to her, but you can inform me. I am charmed for the wit of one, and die for the beauty of the other.

CHARLES. And pray which are [you] in quest of now?

SIR GEORGE. I prefer the sensual pleasure; I'm for her I've seen, who is thy father's ward, Miranda.

CHARLES. Nay then I pity you; for the jew, my father, will no more part with her and 30,000 pounds, than he would with a guinea to keep me from starving.

SIR GEORGE. Now you see gold can't do everything, Charles.

CHARLES. Yes: for 'tis her gold that bars my father's gate against you.

SIR GEORGE. Why, if he is that avaricious wretch, how cam'st thou by such a liberal education?

CHARLES. Not a souse out of his pocket I assure you: I had an uncle who defrayed that charge, but for some little wildnesses of youth, though he made me his heir, left Dad my guardian 'til I came to years of discretion, which I presume the old gentleman will never think I am; and now he has got the estate into his clutches, it does me no more good that if it lay in Prester-John's[2] dominions.

SIR GEORGE. What, can'st thou find no strategem to redeem it?

CHARLES. I have made many essays to no purpose: though want, the mistress of invention still tempts me on, yet still the old fox is too cunning for me—I am upon my last project, which if it fails, then for my last refuge, a brown musket.

SIR GEORGE. What is't? Can I assist thee?

CHARLES. Not yet; when you can, I have confidence enough in you to ask it.

SIR GEORGE. I am always ready. But what does he intend to do with Miranda? Is she to be sold in private? Or will he put her up by way of auction, at who bids most? If so, egad I'm for him: my gold, as you say, shall be subservient to my pleasure.

CHARLES. To deal ingenuously with you, Sir George, I know very little of her, or home: for since my uncle's death, and my return from travel, I have never been well with my father; he thinks my expenses too great, and I his allowance too little; he never sees me, but he quarrels; and to avoid that, I shun his house as much as possible. The report is, he intends to marry her himself.

SIR GEORGE. Can she consent to it?

CHARLES. Yes, faith, so they say; but I tell you I am wholly ignorant of the matter. Miranda and I are like two violent members of a contrary party: I can scarce allow her beauty, though all the world does; nor she me civility, for that contempt: I fancy she plays the mother-in-law already, and sets the old gentleman on to do mischief.

SIR GEORGE. Then I've your free consent to get her.

CHARLES. Aye, and my helping hand if occasion be.

SIR GEORGE. Pugh, yonder's a fool coming this way, let's avoid him.

---

1. **calculation of my nativity:** astrological diagram.

2. **Prestor-John:** the richest king on earth.

CHARLES. What, Marplot? No, no, he's my instrument; there's a thousand conveniences in him; he'll lend me his money, when he has any, run of my errands, and be proud on't; in short, he'll pimp for me, lie for me, drink for me, do any thing but fight for me, and that I trust to my own arm for.

SIR GEORGE. Nay, then he's to be endured; I never knew his qualifications before.

[Enter Marplot with a patch across his face.]

MARPLOT. Dear Charles, yours—*[Aside.]*—Ha! Sir George Airy, the man in the world I have an ambition to be known to.—Give me thy hand dear boy—

CHARLES. A good assurance! But hark ye, how came your beautiful countenance clouded in the wrong place?

MARPLOT. I must confess 'tis a little mal-à-propos, but no matter for that; a word with you, Charles: prithee introduce me to Sir George—he is a man of wit, and I'd give ten guineas to—

CHARLES. When you have 'em you mean.

MARPLOT. Aye, when I have 'em; pugh, pox you cut the thread of my discourse—I would give ten guineas, I say, to be ranked in his acquaintance: well, 'tis a vast addition to a man's fortune, according to the rout of the world, to be seen in the company of leading men; for then we are all thought to be politicians, or Whigs, or Jacks,[3] or high-flyers,[4] or low-flyers,[5] or Levellers[6]—and so forth; for you must know, we all herd in parties now.

CHARLES. Then a fool for diversion is out of fashion, I find.

MARPLOT. Yes, without it be a mimicking fool, and they are darlings everywhere; but prithee, introduce me.

CHARLES. Well, on condition you'll give us a true account how you came by that mourning nose, I will.

MARPLOT. I'll do it.

CHARLES. Sir George, here's a gentleman has a passionate desire to kiss your hand.

SIR GEORGE. Oh, I honour men of the sword, and I presume this gentleman is lately come from Spain or Portugal[7]—by his scars.

MARPLOT. No, really, Sir George, mine sprung from civil duty: happening last night into the Groom-Porter's[8]—I had a strong inclination to go ten guineas with a sort of a, sort of a—kind of a milk-sop[9] as I thought. A pox of the dice he flung out, and my pockets being empty, as Charles knows they often are, he proved a surly North-Briton,[10] and broke my face for my deficiency.

SIR GEORGE. Ha! Ha! And did not you draw?

MARPLOT. Draw, sir! Why I did but lay my hand upon my sword, to make a swift retreat, and he roared out, 'Now the de'il a ma sol, sir, gin ye touch yer steel, I'se whip mine through yer wem.'

SIR GEORGE. Ha, ha, ha!

CHARLES. Ha, ha, ha! Safe was the word, so you walked off, I suppose.

MARPLOT. Yes: for I avoid fighting, purely to be serviceable to my friends, you know—

SIR GEORGE. Your friends are much obliged to you, sir; I hope you'll rank me in that number.

MARPLOT. Sir George, a bow from the side-box, or to be seen in your chariot, binds me ever yours.

SIR GEORGE. Trifles; you may command 'em when you please.

CHARLES. Provided he may command you—

MARPLOT. Me! why I live for no other purpose—Sir George, I have the honour to be caressed by most of the reigning toasts of the town; I'll tell them you are the finest gentleman—

SIR GEORGE. No, no prithee let me alone to tell the ladies—my parts—can you convey a letter upon occasion or deliver a message with an air of business, ha?

MARPLOT. With the assurance of a page, and the gravity of a statesman.

SIR GEORGE. You know, Miranda!

MARPLOT. What, my sister ward? Why her guardian is mine, we are fellow sufferers. Ah! He is a covetous, cheating, fancified curmudgeon; that Sir Francis Gripe is a damned old—

CHARLES. I suppose, friend, you forget that he is my father—

3. Jacks: followers of James II.   **4. high-flyers:** high churchmen.   **5. low-flyers:** low churchmen.   **6. Levellers:** Agrarian reformers.   **7. Spain or Portugal:** the war of Spanish succession was taking place at this time.   **8. Groom-Porter:** a gambling club.   **9. milk-sop:** an effeminate man.   **10. North-Briton:** Scot.

MARPLOT. I ask your pardon, Charles; but it is for your sake I hate him. Well, I say, the world is mistaken in him, his outside piety makes him every man's executioner; and his inside cunning makes him every heir's jailor. Egad, Charles, I'm half-persuaded that thou'rt some ward too, and never of his getting; for thou art as honest a debauchee as ever cuckolded man of quality.

SIR GEORGE. A pleasant fellow.

CHARLES. The dog is diverting sometimes, or there would be no enduring his impertinence. He is pressing to be employed and willing to execute, but some ill-fate generally attends all he undertakes, and he oftener spoils an intrigue than helps it—

MARPLOT. If I miscarry, 'tis none of my fault, I follow my instructions.

CHARLES. Yes; witness the merchant's wife.

MARPLOT. Pish, pox, that was an accident.

SIR GEORGE. What was it, prithee?

CHARLES. Why you must know, I had lent a certain merchant my hunting horses, and was to have met his wife in his absence: sending him along with my groom to make the compliment, and to deliver a letter to the lady at the same time; what does he do, but gives the husband the letter and offers her the horses.

MARPLOT. I remember you was even with me, for you denied the letter to be yours, and swore I had a design upon her which my bones paid for.

CHARLES. Come, Sir George, let's walk round, if you are not engaged; for I have sent my man upon a little earnest business, and I have ordered him to bring me the answer into the Park.

MARPLOT. Business, and I do not know it! Egad, I'll watch him.

SIR GEORGE. I must beg your pardon, Charles, I am to meet your father.

CHARLES. My father!

SIR GEORGE. Aye, and about the oddest bargain perhaps you ever heard of; but I'll not impart till I know the success.

MARPLOT. [Aside.] What can his business be with Sir Francis? Now would I give all the world to know it? Why the devil should not one know every man's concern!

CHARLES. Prosperity to't whate'er it be. I have private affairs too; over a bottle we'll compare notes.

MARPLOT. [Aside.] Charles knows I love a glass as well as any man, I'll make one: shall it be tonight? And I long to know their secrets.

[Enter Whisper.]

WHISPER. [To Charles.] Sir, sir, Mrs Patch says Isabinda's Spanish father has quite spoiled the plot, and she can't meet you in the Park, but he infallibly will go out this afternoon, she says; but I must step again to know the hour.

MARPLOT. [Aside.] What did Whisper say now? I shall go stark mad, if I'm not let into the secret.

CHARLES. Cursed misfortune! Come along with me, my heart feels pleasure at her name. Sir George, yours; we'll meet at the old place the usual hour.

SIR GEORGE. Agreed. I think I see Sir Francis yonder.

[Exit.]

CHARLES. Marplot, you must excuse me, I am engaged.

[Exit.]

MARPLOT. Engaged! Egad I'll engage my life I'll know what your engagement is.

[Exit. Enter Miranda, coming from a chair.]

MIRANDA. Let the chair wait: my servant that dodged Sir George said he was in the Park.

[Enter Patch.]

MIRANDA. Ha! Miss Patch alone! Did not you tell me you had contrived a way to bring Isabinda to the Park?

PATCH. Oh, madam, your ladyship can't imagine what a wretched disappointment we have met with: just as I had fetched a suit of my clothes for a disguise, comes my old master into his closet, which is right against her chamber-door; this struck us into a terrible fright.—At length I put on a grave face, and asked him if he was at leisure for his chocolate, in hopes to draw him out of his hole; but he snapped my nose off, 'No I shall be busy here these two hours.' At which my poor mistress, seeing no way of escape, ordered me to wait on your ladyship with the sad relation.

MIRANDA. Unhappy Isabanda! Was ever anything so unaccountable as the humour of Sir Jealous Traffic?

PATCH. Oh, madam, it's his living so long in Spain; he vows he'll spend half his estate, but he'll be a Parliament-man, on purpose to bring in a Bill for women to wear veils, and the other odious Spanish customs—he swears it is the height of impudence to have a woman seen bare-faced, even at church, and scarce believes there's a true-begotten child in the City.

MIRANDA. Ha, ha, ha! How the old fool torments himself! Suppose he could introduce his rigid rules—does he think we could not match them in contrivance? No, no, let the tyrant man make what laws he will, if there's a woman under the government, I warrant she finds a way to break 'em. Is his mind set upon the Spaniard for his son-in-law still?

PATCH. Aye, and he expects him by the next fleet, which drives his daughter to melancholy and despair; but, madam, I find you retain the same gay, cheerful spirit you had, when I waited in your ladyship.—My lady is mighty good-humoured too; and I have found a way to make Sir Jealous believe I am wholly in his interest, when my real design is to serve her: he makes me her jailor, and I set her at liberty.

MIRANDA. I knew thy prolific brain would be of singular service to her, or I had not parted with thee to her father.

PATCH. But, madam, the report is, that you are going to marry your guardian.

MIRANDA. It is necessary such a report should be, Patch.

PATCH. But is it true madam?

MIRANDA. That's not absolutely necessary.

PATCH. I thought it was only the old strain, coaxing him still for your own, and railing at all the young fellows-about-town. In my mind, now, you are as ill-plagued with your guardian, madam, as my lady is with her father.

MIRANDA. No, I have liberty, wench; that she wants. What would she give now to be in this déshabillé[11] in the open air; nay more, in pursuit of the young fellow she likes; for that's my case, I assure you.

PATCH. As for that, madam, she's even with you; for though she can't come abroad, we have a way to bring him home in spite of old Argus.[12]

MIRANDA. Now, Patch, your opinion of my choice, for here he comes.—Ha! My guardian with him: what can be the meaning of this? I'm sure Sir Francis can't know me in this dress—let's observe them.

[They withdraw. Enter Sir Francis Gripe and Sir George Airy.]

SIR FRANCIS. Verily, Sir George, thou wilt repent throwing away thy money so; for I tell thee sincerely, Miranda, my charge, does not love a young fellow; they are all vicious, and seldom make good husbands; in sober sadness she cannot abide them.

MIRANDA. *[Peeping.]* In sober sadness you are mistaken—what can this mean?

SIR GEORGE. Look ye, Sir Francis, whether she can or cannot abide young fellows, is not the business: will you take the fifty guineas?

SIR FRANCIS. In good truth—I will not; for I knew thy father: he was a hearty wary man, and I cannot consent that his son should squander away what he saved to no purpose.

MIRANDA. *[Peeping.]* Now, in the name of wonder, what bargain can he be driving about me for fifty guineas?

PATCH. I wish it ben't for the first night's lodging, madam.

SIR GEORGE. Well, Sir Francis, since you are so conscientious for my father's sake, then permit me the favour gratis.

MIRANDA. *[Peeping.]* The favour! O'my life, I believe 'tis as you said, Patch.

SIR FRANCIS. No, verily, if thou dost not buy thy experience, thou wilt never be wise; therefore give me a hundred, and try Fortune.

SIR GEORGE. The scruples arose, I find from the scanty sum—let me see—a hundred guineas—*[Takes them out of purse and chinks them.]*—Ha! They have a very pretty sound, and a very pleasing look—but then, Miranda—but if she should be cruel—

MIRANDA. *[Peeping.]* As ten to one I shall—

SIR FRANCIS. Aye, do consider on't, he he, he, he.

---

11. **déshabillé:** state of undress.

12. **Argus:** god with many eyes.

SIR GEORGE. No, I'll do't.

PATCH. Do't! What, whether you will or no, madam!

SIR GEORGE. Come to the point, here's the gold, sum up the condition—

[Sir Francis pulling out a paper.]

MIRANDA. *[Peeping.]* Aye, for heaven's sake do, for my expectation is on the rack.

SIR FRANCIS. Well, at your peril be it.

SIR GEORGE. Aye, aye, go on.

SIR FRANCIS. Imprimis,[13] you are to be admitted into my house, in order to move your suit to Miranda, for the space of ten minutes, without let or molestation, provided I remain in the same room.

SIR GEORGE. But out of earshot.

SIR FRANCIS. Well, well; I don't desire to hear what you say; ha, ha, ha; in consideration I am to have that purse and a hundred guineas.

SIR GEORGE. Take it—

[Gives him the purse.]

MIRANDA. *[Peeping.]* So, 'tis well 'tis no worse; I'll fit you both—

SIR GEORGE. And this agreement is to be performed today.

SIR FRANCIS. Aye, aye, the sooner the better. Poor fool, how Miranda and I shall laugh at him.— Well, Sir George, ha, ha, ha! Take the last sound of your guineas—*[Chinks them.]* ha, ha, ha!

[Exit.]

MIRANDA. *[Peeping.]* Sure he does not know I am Miranda.

SIR GEORGE. A very extraordinary bargain I have made truly, if she should be really in love with this old cuff[14] now—pshaw, that's morally impossible—but then what hopes have I to succeed, I never spoke to her—

MIRANDA. *[Peeping.]* Say you so? Then I am safe.

SIR GEORGE. What though my tongue never spoke, my eyes said a thousand things, and my hopes flattered me her's answered 'em. If I'm lucky— if not, it is but a hundred guineas thrown away.

[Miranda and Patch come forward.]

MIRANDA. Upon what, Sir George?

SIR GEORGE. Ha! My incognita[15]—upon a woman, madam.

MIRANDA. They are the worst things you can deal in, and damage the soonest; your very breath destroys 'em, and I fear you'll never see your return, Sir George, ha, ha.

SIR GEORGE. Were they more brittle than china, and dropped to pieces with a touch, every atom of her I have ventured at, if she is but mistress of my wit, balances ten times the sum—prithee let me see thy face.

MIRANDA. By no means; that may spoil your opinion of my sense—

SIR GEORGE. Rather confirm it, madam.

PATCH. So rob the lady of your gallantry, sir.

SIR GEORGE. No, child, a dish of chocolate in the morning never spoils my dinner; the other lady I design a set-meal; so there's no danger.—

MIRANDA. Matrimony! Ha, ha, ha! What crimes have you committed against the god of love that he should revenge 'em so severely to stamp husband upon your forehead?

SIR GEORGE. For my folly, in having so often met you here, without pursuing the laws of nature, and exercising her command—but I resolve, ere we part now, to know who you are,—where you live, and what kind of flesh and blood your face is. Therefore unmask, and don't put me to the trouble of doing it for you.

MIRANDA. My face is the same flesh and blood with my hand, Sir George, which if you'll be so rude to provoke—

SIR GEORGE. You'll apply it to my cheek—the ladies' favours are always welcome; but I must have that cloud withdrawn. *[Taking hold of her.]* Remember you are in the Park, child, and what a terrible thing would it be to lose this pretty white hand?

MIRANDA. And how will it sound in the chocolate-house that Sir George Airy rudely pulled off a lady's mask, when he had given her his honour that he never would directly or indirectly endeavour to know her till she gave him leave?

PATCH. I wish we were safe out.

SIR GEORGE. But if that lady thinks fit to pursue and meet me at every turn, like some troubled spirit,

---

13. **Imprimis:** to begin with.   14. **cuff:** an old miser.

15. **incognita:** unknown woman.

shall I be blamed if I enquire into the reality? I would have nothing dissatisfied in a female shape.

MIRANDA. *[Pauses.]* What shall I do?

SIR GEORGE. Aye, prithee consider, for thou shalt find me very much at thy service.

PATCH. Suppose, sir, the lady should be in love with you.

SIR GEORGE. Oh! I'll return the obligation in a moment.

PATCH. And marry her?

SIR GEORGE. Ha, ha, ha! That's not the way to love her, child.

MIRANDA. If he discovers me, I shall die—which way shall I escape?—let me see. *[Pauses.]*

SIR GEORGE. Well, madam—

MIRANDA. I have it—Sir George, 'tis fit you should allow something; if you'll excuse my face, and turn your back (if you look upon me, I shall sink, even masked as I am) I will confess why I have engaged you so often, who I am, and where I live.

SIR GEORGE. Well, to show you I'm a man of honour, I accept the conditions. Let me but once know those, and the face won't be long a secret to me.

PATCH. What mean you, madam?

MIRANDA. To get off.

SIR GEORGE. 'Tis something indecent to turn one's back upon a lady; but you command, and I obey. *[Turns his back.]* Come, madam, begin—

MIRANDA. *[Draws back a little while and speaks.]* First then it was my unhappy lot to see you at Paris, at a ball upon a Birthday; your shape and air charmed my eyes; your wit and complaisance my soul; and from that fatal night I loved you. *[Drawing back.]*

And when you left the place, grief seized me so,
No rest my heart, no sleep my eyes could know,
Last I resolved a hazardous point to try,
And quit the place in search of liberty.

[Exit.]

SIR GEORGE. Excellent—I hope she's handsome—Well, now, madam, to the other two things: your name, and where you live?—I am a gentleman, and this confession will not be lost upon me.—Nay, prithee don't weep, but go on—for I find my heart melts in thy behalf.—Speak quickly, or I shall turn about.—Not yet—Poor lady, she expects I should comfort her! And to do her justice, she has said enough to encourage me.

[Turns about.]

Ha! Gone! The devil. Jilted! Why what a tale has she invented of Paris, balls and birthdays.—Egad, I'd give ten guineas to know who the gipsy is—a curve on my folly—I deserve to lose her: What woman can forgive a man that turns his back!

The bold and resolute in love and war,
To conquer take the right and swiftest way:
The boldest lover soonest gains the fair,
As courage makes the rudest force obey.
Take no denial, and the dames adore ye,
Closely pursue them, and they fall before you.

[Exit.]

Act II

SCENE I

[Sir Francis Gripe's house. Enter Sir Francis Gripe and Miranda.]

SIR FRANCIS. Ha, ha, ha, ha, ha!

MIRANDA. Ha, ha, ha, ha, ha, ha, ha! Oh I shall die with laughing—The most romantic adventure. Ha, ha! What does the odious young fop mean? A hundred pieces to talk an hour with me! Ha, ha!

SIR FRANCIS. And I am to be by too; there's the jest: adod, if it had been in private, I should not have cared to trust the young dog.

MIRANDA. Indeed and indeed, but you might, guardie.—Now methinks there's nobody handsomer than you: so neat, so clean, so good-humoured and so loving—

SIR FRANCIS. Pretty rogue, pretty rogue; and so thou shalt find me, if thou dost prefer thy guardie before these caperers of the age; thou shalt outshine the Queen's box on an Opera night; thou shalt be the envy of the Ring (for I will carry thee to Hyde Park) and thy equipage shall surpass the—what d'ye call 'em—Ambassadors.

MIRANDA. Nay I am sure the discreet part of my sex will envy me more for the inside furniture, when you are in it, than my outside equipage.

SIR FRANCIS. A cunning baggage, i'faith thou art, and a wise one too: and to show thee thou hast not chose amiss, I'll this moment disinherit my son, and settle my whole estate upon thee.

MIRANDA. *[Aside.]* There's an old rogue now.—No guardie, I would not have your name be so black in the world.—You know my father's will runs, that I am not to possess my estate without your consent, till I'm five-and-twenty; you shall only abate the odd seven years, and make me mistress of my estate today, and I'll make you master of my person tomorrow.

SIR FRANCIS. Humph! That may not be safe.—No chargie, I'll settle it upon thee for pin-money; and that will be every bit as well, thou know'st.

MIRANDA. *[Aside.]* Unconscionable old wretch, bribe me with my own money—which way shall I get it out of his hands!

SIR FRANCIS. Well, what are thou thinking on, my girl, ha? How to banter Sir George?

MIRANDA. *[Aside.]* I must not pretend to banter; he knows my tongue too well.—No guardie, I have thought of a way will confound him more than all I could say if I should talk to him seven years.

SIR FRANCIS. How's that! Oh! I'm transported, I'm ravished, I'm mad—

MIRANDA. *[Aside.]* It would make you mad if you knew all.—I'll not answer him a word, but be dumb to all he says—

SIR FRANCIS. Dumb! Good. Ha, ha, ha! Excellent, ha, ha, ha! I think I have you now, Sir George. Dumb! He'll go distracted!—Well, she's the wittiest rogue.—Ha, ha? Dumb! I can but laugh, ha, ha! To think how damned mad he'll be when he finds he has given his money away for a dumb-show. Ha, ha, ha!

MIRANDA. Nay guardie, if he did but know my thoughts of him, it would make him ten times madder: ha, ha, ha!

SIR FRANCIS. Aye, so it would, chargie, to hold him in such derision, to scorn to answer him, to be dumb! Ha, ha, ha!

[Enter Charles.]

SIR FRANCIS. How now sirrah! Who let you in?

CHARLES. My necessity, sir.

SIR FRANCIS. Sir, your necessities are very impertinent, and ought to have sent before they entered.

CHARLES. Sir, I knew 'twas a word would gain admittance nowhere.

SIR FRANCIS. Then sirrah, how durst you rudely thrust that upon your father, which nobody else would admit?

CHARLES. Sure the name of a son is a sufficient plea. I ask this lady's pardon if I have intruded.

SIR FRANCIS. Aye, aye, ask her pardon and her blessing too, if you expect anything from me.

MIRANDA. I believe yours, Sir Francis, is a pursue of guineas, would be more material. Your son may have business with you, I'll retire.

SIR FRANCIS. I guess his business, but I'll dispatch him; I expect the knight every minute: you'll be in readiness?

MIRANDA. Certainly! My expectation is more upon the wing than yours, old gentleman.

[Exit.]

SIR FRANCIS. Well, sir!

CHARLES. Nay, it is very ill, sir; my circumstances are, I'm sure.

SIR FRANCIS. And what's that to me, sir; your management should have made them better.

CHARLES. If you please to entrust me with the management of my estate, I shall endeavour it, sir.

SIR FRANCIS. What, to set upon a card, and buy a lady's favour at the price of a thousand pieces, to rig out an equipage for a wench, or by your carelessness enrich your steward to sign for sheriff, or put up for parliament-man?

CHARLES. I hope, I should not spend it this way. However, I ask only for what my uncle left me; yours you may dispose of as you please, sir.

SIR FRANCIS. That I shall, out of your reach, I assure you, sir. Adod these young fellows think old men get estates for nothing but them to squander away, in dicing, wenching, drinking, dressing, and so forth.

CHARLES. I think I was born a gentleman sir! I'm sure my uncle bred me like one.

SIR FRANCIS. From which you would infer, sir, that gaming, whoring, and the pox, are requisites to a gentleman.

CHARLES. *[Aside.]* Monstrous! When I would ask him only for a support, he falls into these unmannerly reproaches; I must, though against my will, employ invention, and by stratagem relieve myself.

SIR FRANCIS. Sirrah, what is it you mutter sirrah, ha? *[Holds up his cane.]* I say you shan't have a groat out of my hands till I please—and maybe I'll never please, and what's that to you?

CHARLES. Nay, to be robbed or to have one's throat cut, is not much—

SIR FRANCIS. What's that sirrah? Would ye rob me, or cut my throat, ye rogue?

CHARLES. Heaven forbid, sir,—I said no such thing.

SIR FRANCIS. Mercy on me! What a plague it is to have a son of one-and-twenty, who wants to elbow one out of one's life to edge himself into the estate!

[Enter Marplot.]

MARPLOT. Egad, he's here—I was afraid I had lost him: his secret could not be with his father, his wants are public there—guardian—your servant Charles, I know by that sorrowful countenance of thine, the old man's fist is as close as his strong-box—but I'll help thee—

SIR FRANCIS. So: here's another extravagant coxcomb, that will spend his fortune before he comes to't; but he shall pay swinging interest, and so let the fool go on—Well, what! Does necessity bring you too sir?

MARPLOT. You have hit it, guardian—I want a hundred pounds.

SIR FRANCIS. For what?

MARPLOT. Pugh, for a hundred things: I can't for my life tell you for what.

CHARLES. Sir, I suppose I have received all the answer I am like to have.

MARPLOT. Oh, the devil, if he gets out before me, I shall lose him again.

SIR FRANCIS. Aye, sir, and you may be marching as soon as you please.—I must see a change in your temper ere you find one in mine.

MARPLOT. Pray, sir, dispatch me. The money, sir, I'm in mighty haste.

SIR FRANCIS. Fool, take this and go to the cashier; I shan't be long plagued with thee.

[Gives him a note.]

MARPLOT. Devil take the cashier, I shall certainly have Charles gone out before I come back again.

[Exit.]

CHARLES. Well, sir, I take my leave—but remember, you expose an only son to all the miseries of wretched poverty, which too often lays the plan for scenes of mischief.

SIR FRANCIS. Stay, Charles, I have a sudden thought come into my head, may prove to thy advantage.

CHARLES. Ha, does he relent?

SIR FRANCIS. My lady Wrinkle, worth forty thousand pounds, sets up for a handsome young husband; she praised thee t'other day; though the matchmakers can get twenty guineas for a sight of her, I can introduce thee for nothing.

CHARLES. My lady Wrinkle, sir! Why she has but one eye.

SIR FRANCIS. Then she'll see but half your extravagance, sir.

CHARLES. Condemn me to such a piece of deformity! Toothless, dirty, wry-necked, hunch-backed hag.

SIR FRANCIS. Hunch-backed! So much the better, then she has a rest for her misfortunes; for thou wilt load her swingingly. Now I warrant you think, this is no offer of a father; forty thousand pounds is nothing with you.

CHARLES. Yes, sir, I think it too much; a young beautiful woman with half the money would be more agreeable. I thank you, sir; but you chose better for yourself, I find.

SIR FRANCIS. Out of my doors, you dog; you pretend to meddle with my marriage, sirrah!

CHARLES. Sir, I obey—

SIR FRANCIS. But me no buts—be gone, sir: dare to ask me for money again—refuse forty thousand pounds! Out of my doors, I say, without reply.

[Exit Charles. Enter servant.]

SERVANT. One Sir George Airy enquires for you, sir.

[Enter Marplot running.]

MARPLOT. Ha! Gone! Is Charles gone, guardian?

SIR FRANCIS. Yes, and I desire your wise worship to walk after him.

MARPLOT. Nay, egad, I shall run, I tell you but that. Ah! Pox of this cashier for detaining me so long; where the devil shall I find him now? I shall certainly lose this secret.

[Exit hastily.]

SIR FRANCIS. What, is the fellow distracted?—Desire Sir George to walk up—now for a trial of skill that will make me happy, and him a fool; Ha, ha, ha! In my mind he looks like an ass already.

[Enter Sir George.]

SIR FRANCIS. Well, Sir George, do ye hold in the same mind, or would you capitulate? Ha, ha, ha! look, here are the guineas. *[Chinks them.]* Ha, ha, ha!

SIR GEORGE. Not if they were twice the sum, Sir Francis: therefore be brief, call in the lady, and take your post—*[Aside.]* If she's a woman, and not seduced by witchcraft to this old rogue, I'll make his heart ache; for if she has but one grain of inclination about her, I'll vary a thousand shapes but find it.

[Enter Miranda.]

SIR FRANCIS. Agreed—Miranda, there's Sir George, try your fortune.

[Takes out his watch.]

SIR GEORGE.

So from the eastern chambers breaks the sun,
Dispels the clouds, and gilds the vales below.

[Salutes her.]

SIR FRANCIS. Hold sir, kissing was not in our agreement.

SIR GEORGE. Oh! That's by way of prologue:—prithee, old mammon,[16] to thy post.

SIR FRANCIS. Well, young Timon,[17] 'tis now four exactly; one hour, remember, is your utmost limit, not a minute more.

[Retires to the rear of the stage.]

SIR GEORGE. Madam, whether you'll excuse or blame my love, the author of this rash proceeding depends upon your pleasure, as also the life of your admirer! Your sparkling eyes speak a heart susceptible of love; your vivacity a soul too delicate to admit the embraces of decayed mortality.

MIRANDA. *[Aside.]* Oh! that I durst speak—

SIR GEORGE. Shake off this tyrant guardian's yoke, assume yourself, and dash his bold aspiring hopes; the deity of his desires, avarice; a heretic in love, and ought to be banished by the Queen of Beauty. See, madam, a faithful servant kneels and begs to be admitted in the number of your slaves.

[Miranda gives him her hand to raise him.]

SIR FRANCIS. I wish I could hear what he says now. *[Running up.]* Hold, hold, hold, no palming, that's contrary to articles—

SIR GEORGE. 'Sdeath, sir keep your distance, or I'll write another article in your guts.

[Lays his hand to his sword.]

SIR FRANCIS. *[Going back.]* A bloody minded fellow!—

SIR GEORGE. Not answer me! Perhaps she thinks my address too grave: I'll be more free—can you be so unconscionable, madam, to let me say all these fine things to you without one single compliment in return? View me well, am I not a proper handsome, fellow, ha? Can you prefer that old, dry withered sapless log of sixty-five, to the vigorous, gay, sprightly love of twenty-four? With snoring only he'll awake thee, but I with ravishing delight would make thy senses dance in consort with the joyful minutes.—Ha! Not yet? Sure she is dumb?—Thus wou'd I steal and touch thy beauteous hand, *[Takes hold of her hand.]* till by degrees, I reached thy snowy breasts, then ravish kisses thus.

---

16. mammon: a man who seeks riches.

17. Timon: misanthrope, from Shakespeare's play.

[Embraces her in ecstasy.]

MIRANDA. *[Struggles and flings from him. Aside.]* Oh heavens! I shall not be able to contain myself.

SIR FRANCIS. *[Running up with his watch in his hand.]* Sure she did not speak to him—there's three-quarters of an hour gone, Sir George—adod, I don't like those close conferences—

SIR GEORGE. More interruptions—you will have it, sir.

[Lays his hand to his sword.]

SIR FRANCIS. *[Aside, going back.]* No, no, you shant have her neither.

SIR GEORGE. Dumb still—sure this old dog has enjoined her silence. I'll try another way. I must conclude, madam, that in compliance to your guardian's humour, you refuse to answer me.— Consider the injustice of his injunction. This single hour cost me an hundred pounds—and would you answer me, I could purchase the twenty-four so. However madam, you must give me leave to make the best interpretation I can for my money, and take the indication of your silence for the secret liking of my person; therefore, madam, I will instruct you how to keep your word inviolate to Sir Francis, and yet answer me to every question; as for example when I ask anything to which you would reply in the affirmative, gently nod your head: thus; and when in the negative: thus; *[Shakes his head.]* and in the doubtful: a tender sigh, thus. *[Sighs.]*

MIRANDA. *[Aside.]* How every action charms me— but I'll fit him for signs, I warrant him.

SIR FRANCIS. *[Aside.]* Ha, ha, ha, ha! Poor Sir George, Ha, ha, ha, ha!

SIR GEORGE. Was it by his desire that you are dumb, madam, to all that I can say?

MIRANDA. *[Nods.]*

SIR GEORGE. Very well! she's tractable, I find—and is it possible that you can love him!

MIRANDA. *[Nods.]*

SIR GEORGE. Miraculous! Pardon the bluntness of my questions, for my time is short; may I not hope to supplant him in your esteem?

MIRANDA. *[Sighs.]*

SIR GEORGE. Good, she answers me as I could wish.—You'll not consent to marry him then?

MIRANDA. *[Sighs.]*

SIR GEORGE. How! Doubtful in that—undone again—humph! But that may proceed from his

power to keep her out of her estate 'till twenty-five; I'll try that—come madam, I cannot think you hesitate on this affair out of any motive but your fortune. Let him keep it 'till those few years are expired; make me happy with your person, let him enjoy your wealth—

MIRANDA. *[Holds up her hands.]*

SIR GEORGE. Why, what sign is that now? Nay, nay madam, except you observe my lesson, I can't understand your meaning—

SIR FRANCIS. What a vengeance are they talking by signs? 'Ad I may be fooled here; what do you mean, Sir George?

SIR GEORGE. To cut your throat, if you dare mutter another syllable.

SIR FRANCIS. Od! I wish he were fairly out of my house.

SIR GEORGE. Pray madam, will you answer me to the purpose?

MIRANDA. *[Shakes her head and points to Sir Francis.]*

SIR GEORGE. What! Does she mean she won't answer me to the purpose, or is she afraid yon' old cuff should understand her signs?—Aye, it must be that; I perceive, madam, you are too apprehensive of the promise you have made to follow my rules; therefore I'll suppose your mind, and answer for you.—First, for myself, madam, that I am in love with you is an infallible truth. Now for you. *[Turns to her side.]* Indeed, Sir, and may I believe it?—*[In his own person, on one knee.]*—as certainly, madam, as that 'tis daylight, or that I die if you persist in silence.—Bless me with the music of your voice, and raise my spirits to their proper heaven; thus low let me entreat; ere I'm obliged to quit this place, grant me some token of a favourable reception to keep my hopes alive.—*[Arises hastily, turns to her side.]*—Rise, sir, and since my guardian's presence will not allow me privilege of tongue, read that, and rest assured you are not indifferent to me.—*[Offers her a letter.]* Ha!

MIRANDA. *[Strikes it down.]*

SIR GEORGE. Ha! Right woman! But no matter, I'll go on.

SIR FRANCIS. Ha! What's that, a letter?—Ha, ha, ha! Thou art baulked.

MIRANDA. *[Aside.]* The best assurance I ever saw—

SIR GEORGE. Ha! A letter! Oh! Let me kiss it with the same raptures that I would do the dear hand that touched it .*[Opens it.]* Now for a quick fancy, and a long extempore—what's here? *[Reads.]* "Dear Sir

George, this virgin muse I consecrate to you, which when it has received the addition of your voice, 'twill charm me into a desire of liberty to love, which you, and only you can fix." My angel! Oh you transport me! *[Kisses the letter.]* And see the power of your command; the god of love has set the verse already; the flowing numbers dance into a tune; and I'm inspired with a voice to sing it.

MIRANDA. *[Aside.]* I'm sure thou art inspired with impudence enough.

SIR GEORGE. *[Sings.]*

> Great love inspire him;
> Say I admire him.
> Give me the lover
> That can discover
> Secret devotion
> From silent motion;
> Then don't betray me,
> But hence convey me.

[Taking hold of Miranda.]

> With all my heart,
> This moment let's retire.

SIR FRANCIS. *[Coming up hastily.]* The hour is expired, sir, and you must take your leave. There my girl, there's the hundred pounds, which thou hast won; go, I'll be with you presently, Ha, ha, ha!

[Exit Miranda.]

SIR GEORGE. Ads-heart, madam, you won't leave me just in the nick, will you?

SIR FRANCIS. Ha, ha, ha! She has nicked you, Sir George, I think, ha, ha, ha! Have ye any more hundred pounds to throw away upon such courtship? Ha, ha, ha!

SIR GEORGE. He, he, he, he, a curse on your fleering jests—yes, however ill I succeeded, I'll venture the same wager, she does not value thee a spoonful of snuff.—Nay more, though you enjoined her silence to me, you'll never make her speak to the purpose with yourself.

SIR FRANCIS. Ha, ha, ha! Did not I tell thee thou wouldst repent thy money? Did not I say, she hated young fellows? Ha, ha, ha!

SIR GEORGE. And I'm positive she's not in love with Age.

SIR FRANCIS. Ha, ha! no matter for that, ha, ha! She's not taken with your youth, nor your rhetoric to boot, ha, ha!

SIR GEORGE. Whate'er her reasons are for disliking of me, I am certain she can be taken with nothing about thee.

SIR FRANCIS. Ha, ha, ha! How he swells with envy— poor man, poor man.—Ha, ha! I must beg your pardon, Sir George; Miranda will be impatient to have her share of mirth: verily we shall laugh at thee most egregiously;[18] ha, ha, ha!

SIR GEORGE. With all my heart, faith,—I shall laugh in my turn too.—For if you dare marry her, old Beelzebub, you will be cuckolded most egregiously: remember that and tremble—

> She that to age her beauteous self resigns,
> Shows witty management for close designs.
> Then if thou'rt graced with fair Miranda's bed,
> Actæon's[19] horns she means shall crown thy head.

[Exit.]

SIR FRANCIS.

> Ha, ha, ha! he is mad.
> These fluttering fops imagine they can wind,
> Turn and decoy to love all womankind:
> But here's a proof of wisdom in my charge,
> Old men are constant, young men live at large;
> The frugal hand can bills at sight defray,
> When he that lavish is, has nought to pay.

[Exit.]

SCENE II

[Sir Jealous Traffick's house. Enter Sir Jealous and Isabinda with Patch following.]

SIR JEALOUS. What, in the balcony again, notwithstanding my positive commands to the contrary!—Why don't you write a bill on your forehead, to show passengers there's something to be let—

ISABINDA. What harm can there be in a little fresh air, sir?

---

18. egregiously: immoderately.   **19. Actæon's horns:** cuckold's horns.

SIR JEALOUS. Is your constitution so hot, mistress, that it wants cooling, ha? Apply the virtuous Spanish rules, banish your taste, and thoughts of flesh, feed upon roots, and quench your thirst with water.

ISABINDA. That and a close room would certainly make me die of the vapours.

SIR JEALOUS. No, mistress, 'tis your high-fed, lusty, rambling, rampant ladies—that are troubled with the vapours: 'tis your ratafia,[20] persico,[21] cinnamon, citron, and spirit of clary,[22] cause such swi-mm-ing in the brain, that carries many a guinea[23] full tide to the doctor. But you are not to be bred this way; no galloping abroad, no receiving visits at home; for in our loose country, the women are as dangerous as the men.

PATCH. So I told her, sir; and that it was not decent to be seen in a balcony—but she threatened to slap my chaps,[24] and told me, I was her servant, not her governess.

SIR JEALOUS. Did she so? But I'll make her to know that you are her Duenna.[25] Oh! That incomparable custom of Spain! Why there's no depending upon old women in my country— for they are as wanton at eighty, as a girl of eighteen; and a man may as safely trust to Asgill's[26] translation as to his great grandmother's not marrying again.

ISABINDA. Or to the Spanish ladies' veils and duennas, for the safeguard of their honour.

SIR JEALOUS. Dare to ridicule the cautious conduct of that wise nation, and I'll have you locked up this fortnight without a peep-hole.

ISABINDA. If we had but the ghostly helps in England, which they have in Spain, I might deceive you if you did.—Sir, 'tis not the restraint, but the innate principles, secures the reputation and honour of our sex.—Let me tell you, sir, confinement sharpens the invention, as want of sight strengthens the other senses, and is often more pernicious than the recreation innocent liberty allows.

SIR JEALOUS. Say you so, mistress; who the devil taught you the art of reasoning? I assure you, they must have a greater faith than I pretend to,

that can think any woman innocent who requires liberty. Therefore, Patch, to your charge I give her; lock her up 'till I come back from 'Change: I shall have some sauntering coxcomb, with nothing but a red coat and feather, think by leaping into her arms, to leap into my estate.—But I'll prevent them; she shall be only Babinetto's.

PATCH. Really, sir, I wish you would employ anybody else in this affair; I lead a life like a dog, with obeying your commands. Come, madam, will you please to be locked up?

ISABINDA. *[Aside.]* Aye, to enjoy more freedom than he is aware of.

[Exit, with Patch.]

SIR JEALOUS. I believe this wench is very true to my interest; I am happy I met with her, if I can but keep my daughter from being blown upon till Signior Babinetto arrives; who shall marry her as soon as he comes, and carry her to Spain as soon as he has married her; she has a pregnant wit, and I'd no more have her an English wife than the grand signior's mistress.

[Exit. Enter Whisper.]

WHISPER. So, I saw Sir Jealous go out; where shall I find Mrs Patch now?

[Reenter Patch.]

PATCH. Oh, Mr Whisper! My lady saw you out as the window, and ordered me to bid you fly, and let your master know she's now alone.

WHISPER. Hush, speak softly; I go, I go: but hark ye, Mrs Patch, shall not you and I have a little confabulation, when my master and your lady are engaged?

PATCH. Aye, aye, farewell.

[Exit, shutting the door. Reenter Sir Jealous Traffick, meeting Whisper.]

SIR JEALOUS. Sure whilst I was talking with Mr Tradewell, I heard my door clap. *[Seeing Whisper.]* Ha! a man lurking about my house; who do you want there, sir?

WHISPER. Want—want, a pox! Sir Jealous! What must I say now?

SIR JEALOUS. Aye, want: have you a letter or message for anybody there?—O' my conscience this is some he-bawd—

WHISPER. Letter or message, sir?

SIR JEALOUS. Aye, letter or message, sir.

WHISPER. No, not I, sir.

SIR JEALOUS. Sirrah, sirrah, I'll have you set in the stocks, if you don't tell me your business immediately.

WHISPER. Nay, sir, my business—is not great matter of business neither; and yet 'tis business of consequence too.

SIR JEALOUS. Sirrah, don't trifle with me.

WHISPER. Trifle, sir! Have you found him, sir?

SIR JEALOUS. Found what, you rascal?

WHISPER. Why Trifle is the very lap-dog my lady lost, sir; I fancied I saw him run into this house. I'm glad you have him.—Sir, my lady will be overjoyed that I have found him.

SIR JEALOUS. Who is your lady, friend?

WHISPER. My Lady Lovepuppy, sir.

SIR JEALOUS. My Lady Lovepuppy! Then prithee carry thyself to her, for I know no other whelp that belongs to her; and let me catch you no more a-puppy-hunting about my doors, lest I have you pressed into the service, sirrah.

WHISPER. By no means, sir—your humble servant; I must watch whether he goes, or no, before I can tell my master.

[Exit.]

SIR JEALOUS. This fellow has the officious leer of a pimp; and I half suspect a design, but I'll be upon them before they think on me, I warrant 'em.

[Exit.]

SCENE III

[Charles's lodgings. Enter Charles and Marplot.]

CHARLES. Honest Marplot, I thank thee for this supply: I expect my lawyer with a thousand pounds I have ordered him to take up, and then you shall be repaid.

MARPLOT. Foh, foh, no more of that: here comes Sir George Airy. Cursedly out of humour at his disappointment: see how he looks! Ha, ha, ha!

[Enter Sir George.]

SIR GEORGE. Ah, Charles, I am so humbled in my pretensions to plots upon women, that I believe I shall never have courage enough to attempt a chamber-maid—I'll tell thee.

CHARLES. Ha, ha! I'll spare you the relation, by telling you.—Impatient to know your business with my father, when I saw you enter I slipped back into the next room, where I overheard every syllable.

SIR GEORGE. That I said.—I'll be hanged if you heard her answer.—But prithee tell me, Charles, is she a fool?

CHARLES. I ne'er suspected her for one; but Marplot can inform you better, if you'll allow him a judge.

MARPLOT. A fool! I'll justify she has more wit than all the rest of her sex put together; why she'll rally me till I han't one word to say for myself.

CHARLES. A mighty proof of her wit truly—

MARPLOT. There must be some trick in't, Sir George; egad I'll find it out, if it cost me the sum you paid for't.

SIR GEORGE. Do, and command me—

MARPLOT. Enough, let me alone to trace a secret—

[Enter Whisper, and speaks aside to his master.]

MARPLOT. The devil! Whisper here again! That fellow never speaks out. Is this the same, or a new secret?—Sir George, won't you ask Charles what news Whisper brings?

SIR GEORGE. Not I, sir; I suppose it does not relate to me.

MARPLOT. Lord, lord, how little curiosity some people have! Now my chief pleasure lies in knowing everybody's business.

SIR GEORGE. I fancy, Charles, thou hast some engagement upon thy hands: I have a little business too. Marplot, if it fall in your way to bring me any intelligence from Miranda, you'll find me at the Thatched House at six—

MARPLOT. You do me much honour.

CHARLES. You guess right, Sir George, wish me success.

SIR GEORGE. Better than attended me. Adieu.

[Exit.]

CHARLES. Marplot, you must excuse me—

MARPLOT. Nay, nay, what need of any excuse amongst friends: I'll go with you.

CHARLES. Indeed you must not.

MARPLOT. No! Then I suppose 'tis a duel, and I will go to secure you.

CHARLES. Well, but it is no duel, consequently no danger: therefore prithee be answered.

MARPLOT. What, is't a mistress then?—Mum!—You know I can be silent upon occasion.

CHARLES. I wish you could be civil too: I tell you, you neither must nor shall go with me. Farewell.

[Exit.]

MARPLOT. Why then,—I must and will follow you.

[Exit.]

Act III

SCENE I

[Outside the house of Sir Jealous. Enter Charles.]

CHARLES. Well, here's the house which holds the lovely prize quiet and serene: here no noisy footmen throng to tell my world, that beauty dwells within; no ceremonious visit makes the lover wait; no rival to give my heart a pang: who would not scale the window at midnight without fear of the jealous father's pistol, rather than fill up the train of a coquette, where every minute he is jostled out of place? *[Knocks softly.]* Mrs Patch. Mrs Patch!

[Enter Patch.]

PATCH. Oh, are you come, sir? All's safe.

CHARLES. So, in, then.

[They exit. Enter Marplot.]

MARPLOT. There he goes: who the devil lives here? Except I can find out that, I am as far from knowing his business as ever; 'gad I'll watch, it may be a bawdy-house, and he may have his throat cut; if there should be any mischief, I can make oath he went in. Well Charles, in spite of your endeavour to keep me out of the secret, I may save your life for aught I know. At that corner I'll plant myself, there I shall see whoever goes in, or comes out. 'Gad, I love discoveries.

[Exit.]

SCENE II

[Inside the house of Sir Jealous. Enter Charles, Isabinda, and Patch.]

WHISPER. Patch, look out sharp; have a care of Dad.

PATCH. I warrant you.

ISABINDA. Well, sir, if I may judge your love by your courage, I ought to believe you sincere; for you venture into the lion's den, when you come to see me.

CHARLES. If you'd consent whilst the furious beast is abroad, I'd free you from the reach of his paws.

ISABINDA. That would be but to avoid one danger by running into another; like poor wretches who fly the burning ship, and meet their fate in the water. Come, come Charles, I fear if I consult my reason, confinement and plenty is better than liberty and starving. I know you'd make the frolic pleasing for a little time, by saying and doing a world of tender things; but when our small substance is exhausted, and a thousand requisites for life are wanting, love, who rarely dwells with poverty, would also fail us.

CHARLES. Faith, I fancy not; methinks my heart has laid up a stock will last for life; to back which, I have taken a thousand pounds upon my uncle's estate; that surely will support us till one of our fathers relent.

ISABINDA. There's no trusting to that, my friend; I doubt your father will carry his humour to the grave, and mine till he sees me settled in Spain.

CHARLES. And can ye then cruelly resolve to stay till that cursed Don arrives, and suffer that youth, beauty, fire, and wit to be sacrificed to the arms of a dull Spaniard, to be immured, and forbid the sight of anything that's human?

ISABINDA. No, when it comes to the extremity, and no stratagem can relieve us, thou shalt 'list for a soldier, and I'll carry thy knapsack after thee.

CHARLES. Bravely resolved; the world cannot be more savage than our parents, and Fortune generally assists the bold: therefore consent now. Why should we put it to a future hazard? Who knows when we shall have another opportunity?

ISABINDA. Oh, you have your ladder of ropes, I suppose, and the closet-window stands just where it did, and if you han't forgot to write in characters, Patch will find a way for our assignations. Thus much of the Spanish contrivance my father's severity has taught me, I thank him; though I hate the nation, I admire their management in these affairs.

[Enter Patch.]

PATCH. Oh, madam, I see my master coming up the street.

CHARLES. Oh, the devil, would I had my ladder now, I thought you had not expected him till night; why, why, why, why, what shall I do, madam?

ISABINDA. Oh! For Heaven's sake! don't go that way, you'll meet him full in the teeth. Oh, unlucky moment!—

CHARLES. 'Adheart, can you shut me into no cupboard, ram me into a chest, ha?

PATCH. Impossible, sir, he searches every hole in the house.

ISABINDA. Undone for ever! If he sees you, I shall never see you more.

PATCH. I have thought on it: run to your chamber, madam; and, sir, come you along with me, I'm certain you may easily get down from the balcony.

CHARLES. My life, adieu—lead on guide.

[Exit.]

ISABINDA. Heaven preserve him.

[Exit.]

SCENE III

[The street outside the house of Sir Jealous. Enter Sir Jealous, with Marplot behind him.]

SIR JEALOUS. I don't know what's the matter, but I have a strong suspicion all is not right within; that fellow's sauntering about my door, and his tale of a puppy had the face of a lie methought. By St Iägo, if I should find a man in the house, I'd make mince-meat of him—

MARPLOT. Ah, poor Charles—Ha! Egad he is old—I fancy I might bully him, and make Charles have an opinion of my courage.

SIR JEALOUS. *[Feeling for his key.]* My own key shall let me in, I'll give them no warning.

MARPLOT. *[Going up to Sir Jealous.]* What's that you say, sir?

SIR JEALOUS. *[Turning quick upon him.]* What's that to you, sir?

MARPLOT. Yes, 'tis to me, sir: for the gentleman you threaten is a very honest gentleman. Look to't; for if he comes not as safe out of your house as he went in, I have half a dozen Myrmidons[27] hard by shall beat it about your ears.

SIR JEALOUS. Went in! What is he in then? Ah! a combination to undo me—I'll Myrmidon you, ye dog you—thieves, thieves!

[Beats Marplot all the while he cries "thieves."]

MARPLOT. Murder, murder; I was not in your house, sir.

[Enter Servant.]

SERVANT. What's the matter, sir?

SIR JEALOUS. The matter, rascal! Have you let a man into my house! But I'll flea him alive; follow me, I'll not leave a mouse-hole unsearched; if I find him, by St Iägo I'll equip him for the Opera.[28]

MARPLOT. A deuce of his cane, there's no trusting to age.—What shall I do to relieve Charles? Egad, I'll raise the neighbourhood—murder, murder—

[Charles drops down upon him from the balcony.]

27. **Myrmidons:** hoodlums. 28. **equip him for the Opera:** castrate him.

MARPLOT. Charles, faith I'm glad to see thee safe out with all my heart.

CHARLES. A pox of your bawling: how the devil came you here?

MARPLOT. Here! 'Gad, I have done you a piece of service; I told the old thunderbolt that the gentleman that was gone in, was—

CHARLES. Was it you that told him, sir? *[Laying hold of him.]* 'Sdeath, I could crush thee into atoms.

[Exit Charles.]

MARPLOT. What, will ye choke me for my kindness?—Will my enquiring soul never leave searching into other people's affairs till it gets squeezed out of my body? I dare not follow him now, for my blood, he's in such a passion—I'll to Miranda; if I can discover aught that may oblige Sir George, it may be a means to reconcile me again to Charles.

[Exit. Enter Sir Jealous and Servants.]

SIR JEALOUS. Are you sure you have searched everywhere?

SERVANT. Yes, from the top of the house to the bottom.

SIR JEALOUS. Under the beds, and over the beds?

SERVANT. Yes, and in them too; but found nobody sir.

SIR JEALOUS. Why, what could this rogue mean?

[Enter Isabinda and Patch.]

PATCH. *[Aside to Isabinda.]* Take courage, madam, I saw him safe out.

ISABINDA. Bless me! what's the matter, sir?

SIR JEALOUS. You know best—pray where's the man that was here just now?

ISABINDA. What man, sir: I saw none!

PATCH. Nor I, by the trust you repose in me; do you think I would let a man come within these doors, when you are absent?

SIR JEALOUS. Ah, Patch, she may be too cunning for thy honesty: the very scout that he had set to give warning, discovered it to me—and threatened me with half a dozen Myrmidons.—But I think I mauled the villain. These afflictions you draw upon me, mistress!

ISABINDA. Pardon me, sir, 'tis your own ridiculous humour draws you into these vexations, and gives every fool pretence to banter you.

SIR JEALOUS. No, 'tis your idle conduct, your coquettish flirting into the balcony.—Oh with what joy shall I resign thee into the arms of Don Diego Babinetto!

ISABINDA. *[Aside.]* And with what industry shall I avoid him!

SIR JEALOUS. Certainly that rogue had a message from somebody or other; but being balked by my coming, popped that sham upon me. Come along ye sots, let's see if we can find the dog again. Patch, lock her up; d'ye hear?

PATCH. Yes, sir.—Aye, walk till your heels ache, you'll find nobody, I'll promise you.

ISABINDA. Who could that scout be which he talks of?

PATCH. Nay, I can't imagine, without it was Whisper.

ISABINDA. Well, dear Patch, let's employ all our thoughts how to escape this horrid Don Diego, my very heart sinks at his terrible name.

PATCH. Fear not, madam, Don Carlo shall be the man, or I'll lose the reputation of contrivine;[29] and then what's a chamber-maid good for?

ISABINDA.

> Say'st thou so, my girl? Then—
> Let Dad be jealous, multiply his cares.
> While love instructs me to avoid the snares;
> I'll, spite of all his Spanish caution, show
> How much for love a British maid can do.

[Exit.]

SCENE IV

[Sir Francis Gripe's house. Enter Sir Francis and Miranda, meeting.]

MIRANDA. Well guardie, how did I perform the dumb scene?

SIR FRANCIS. To admiration—thou dear little rogue, let me buss thee for it; nay, adod I will, chargie, so muzzle, and tuzzle, and hug thee, I will, i'faith, I will.

---

29. **contrivine:** schemer.

[Hugging and kissing her.]

MIRANDA. Nay guardie, don't be so lavish; who would ride post, when the journey lasts for life?

SIR FRANCIS. Ah wag, ah wag—I'll buss thee again, for that.

MIRANDA. *[Aside.]* Faugh! How he stinks of tobacco! What a delicate bedfellow I should have!

SIR FRANCIS. Oh I'm transported! When, when, my dear, wilt thou convince the world of thy happy day? When shall we marry, ha?

MIRANDA. There's nothing wanting but your consent, Sir Francis.

SIR FRANCIS. My consent! What does my charmer mean?

MIRANDA. Nay, 'tis only a whim, but I'll have everything according to form—therefore when you sign an authentic paper, drawn up by an able lawyer, that I have your leave to marry, the next day makes me yours, guardie.

SIR FRANCIS. Ha, ha, ha! A whim indeed! Why is it not demonstration I give my leave when I marry thee?

MIRANDA. Not for your reputation, guardie: the malicious world will be apt to say you tricked me into a marriage, and so take the merit from my choice. Now I will have the act my own, to let the idle fops see how much I prefer a man loaded with years and wisdom.

SIR FRANCIS. Humph! Prithee leave out years, chargie, I'm not so old, as thou shalt find: adod, I'm young, there's a caper for ye.

[Jumps.]

MIRANDA. Oh, never excuse it; why, I like you the better for being old.—But I shall suspect you don't love me, if you refuse me this formality.

SIR FRANCIS. Not love thee, chargie! Adod, I do love thee better than, than, than, better than—what shall I say? Egad, better than money; i'faith I do.

MIRANDA. *[Aside.]* That's false, I'm sure.—To prove it, do this then.

SIR FRANCIS. Well, I will do it, chargie, provided I bring a licence at the same time.

MIRANDA. Aye and a parson too, if you please. Ha, ha, ha! I can't help laughing to think how all the young coxcombs about town will be mortified when they hear of our marriage.

SIR FRANCIS. So they will, so they will; ha, ha, ha!

MIRANDA. Well, I fancy I shall be so happy with my guardie!

SIR FRANCIS. If wearing pearls and jewels, or eating gold, as the old saying is, can make thee happy, thou shalt be so, my sweetest, my lovely, my charming, my—verily, I know not what to call thee.

MIRANDA. You must know, guardie, that I am so eager to have this business concluded, that I have employed my woman's brother, who is a lawyer in the Temple, to settle matters just to your liking; you are to give your consent to my marriage, which is to yourself, you know; but mum, you must take no notice of that. So then I will, that is, with your leave, put my writings into his hands; then tomorrow we come slap upon them with a wedding that nobody thought on; by which you seize me and my estate, and I suppose, make a bonfire of your own act and deed.

SIR FRANCIS. Nay, but chargie, if—

MIRANDA. Nay, guardie, no ifs—have I refused three northern lords, two British Peers, and half-a-score knights, to have put in your ifs?—

SIR FRANCIS. So thou hast indeed, and I will trust to thy management. Od, I'm all of a fire.

MIRANDA. *[Aside.]* 'tis a wonder the dry stubble does not blaze.

[Enter Marplot.]

SIR FRANCIS. How now, who sent for you, sir? What, is the hundred pound gone already?

MARPLOT. No, sir, I don't want money now.

SIR FRANCIS. No: that's a miracle! But there's one thing you want, I'm sure.

MARPLOT. Aye, what's that guardian?

SIR FRANCIS. Manners: what, had I no servants without?

MARPLOT. None that could do my business, guardian, which is at present with this lady.

MIRANDA. With me, Mr Marplot! What is it, I beseech you?

SIR FRANCIS. Aye, sir, what is it? Anything that relates to her may be delivered to me.

MARPLOT. I deny that.

MIRANDA. That's more than I do, sir.

MARPLOT. Indeed, madam! Why then to proceed. Fame says, that you and my most conscionable guardian here designed, contrived, plotted and agreed, to chouse a very civil, honest, honourable gentleman out of an hundred pound.

MIRANDA. That I contrived it!

MARPLOT. Aye you—you said never a word against it, so far you are guilty.

SIR FRANCIS. Pray tell that civil, honest, honourable gentleman, that if he has any more such sums to fool away, they shall be received like the last. Ha, ha, ha, ha! "Choused,"[30] quotha! But hark ye, let him know at the same time, that if he dared to report I tricked him of it, I shall recommend a lawyer to him shall show him a trick for twice as much. D'ye hear? Tell him that.

MARPLOT. So, and this is the way you use a gentleman and my friend?

MIRANDA. Is the wretch thy friend?

MARPLOT. The wretch! Look ye, madam, don't call names. Egad, I won't take it.

MIRANDA. Why, you won't beat me, will you? Ha, ha!

MARPLOT. I don't know whether I will or no.

SIR FRANCIS. Sir, I shall make a servant show you out at the window, if you are saucy.

MARPLOT. I am your most humble servant, guardian; I design to go out the same way I came in. I would only ask this lady, if she does not think in her soul Sir George Airy is not a fine gentleman?

MIRANDA. He dresses well.

SIR FRANCIS. Which is chiefly owing to his tailor and valet-de-chambre.

MARPLOT. The judicious part of the world allows him wit, courage, gallantry, and management; though I think he forfeited that character when he flung away a hundred pound upon your dumb ladyship.

SIR FRANCIS. Does that gall him? Ha, ha, ha!

MIRANDA. So, Sir George remaining in deep discontent, has sent you his trusty squire to utter his complaint: ha, ha, ha!

MARPLOT. Yes, madam; and you like a cruel, hard-hearted jew value it no more—than I would your ladyship, were I Sir George, you, you, you—

MIRANDA. Oh, don't call names, I know you love to be employed and I'll oblige you, and you shall carry him a message from me.

MARPLOT. According as I like it: what is it?

MIRANDA. Nay, a kind one you may be surer—first tell him, I have chose this gentleman to have and to hold, and so forth.

[Clapping her hand into Sir Francis's.]

SIR FRANCIS. *[Aside.]* Oh, the dear rogue, how I dote on her!

MIRANDA. And advise his impertinence to trouble me no more, for I prefer Sir Francis for a husband before all the fops in the universe.

MARPLOT. Oh lord, oh lord! She's bewitched, that's certain: here's a husband for eighteen—here's a shape—here's bones rattling in a leathern bag. *[Turning Sir Francis about.]* Here's buckram[31] and canvas to scrub you to repentance.

SIR FRANCIS. Sirrah, my cane shall teach you repentance presently.

MARPLOT. No faith, I have felt its twin brother from just such a withered hand too lately.

MIRANDA. One thing more; advise him to keep from the garden gate on the left hand; for if he dare to saunter there about the hour of eight, as he used to do, he shall be saluted with a pistol or blunderbuss.

SIR FRANCIS. Oh monstrous! Why chargie, did he use to come to the garden gate?

MIRANDA. The gardener described just such another man that always watched his coming out, and fain would have bribed him for his entrance.— Tell him he shall find a warm reception if he comes this night.

MARPLOT. Pistols and blunderbusses! Egad, a warm reception indeed; I shall take care to inform him of your kindness, and advise him to keep farther off.

MIRANDA. *[Aside.]* I hope he will understand my meaning better than to follow your advice.

SIR FRANCIS. Thou hast signed, sealed, and ta'en possession of my heart forever, chargie, ha, ha, ha! And for you, Mr Saucebox, let me have no more of your messages, if ever you design to inherit your estate, gentleman.

MARPLOT. Why, there 'tis now. Sure I shall be out of your clutches one day—well guardian, I say no more, but if you be not as arrant a cuckold, as e'er drove bargain upon the Exchange, or paid attendance to a court, I am the son of a whetstone;[32] and so your humble servant.

[Exit.]

MIRANDA. Don't forget the message; ha, ha!

---

30. **choused:** cheated   31. **buckram:** stiff, heavy cloth.   32. **whetstone:** sharpener.

SIR FRANCIS. I am so provoked—'tis well he's gone.

MIRANDA. Oh mind him not, guardie, but let's sign articles, and then—

SIR FRANCIS. And then—adod, I believe I am metamorphosed: my pulse beats high, and my blood boils, methinks—

[Kissing and hugging her.]

MIRANDA. Oh fie guardie, be not so violent: consider the market lasts all the year—well, I'll in and see if the lawyer be come, you'll follow.

[Exit.]

SIR FRANCIS. Aye, to the world's end, my dear. Well, Frank, thou art a lucky fellow in thy old age, to have such a delicate morsel, and thirty thousand pound in love with thee; I shall be the envy of bachelors, the glory of married men, and the wonder of the town. Some guardians would be glad to compound for part of the estate, at dispatching an heiress. But I engross the whole. Oh!

Mihi praeteritos referat si Jupiter annos.[33]

[Exit.]

SCENE V

[A tavern. Sir George and Charles with wine before them, Whisper waiting on them.]

SIR GEORGE. Nay, prithee don't be grave Charles: misfortunes will happen, ha, ha, ha! 'Tis some comfort to have a companion in our sufferings.

CHARLES. I am only apprehensive for Isabinda; her father's humour is implacable; and how far his jealousy may transport her to her undoing, shocks my soul to think.

SIR GEORGE. But since you escaped undiscovered by him, his rage will quickly lash into a calm, never fear it.

CHARLES. But who knows what that unlucky dog Marplot told him; nor can I imagine what

brought him thither; that fellow is ever doing mischief; and yet, to give him his due he never designs it. This is some blundering adventure, wherein he thought to show his friendship, as he calls it; a curse on him.

SIR GEORGE. Then you must forgive him; what said he?

CHARLES. Said? Nay, I had more mind to cut his throat, than to hear his excuses.

SIR GEORGE. Where is he?

WHISPER. Sir, I saw him go into Sir Francis Gripe's just now.

CHARLES. Oh! Then he's upon your business, Sir George, a thousand to one but he makes some mistake there too.

SIR GEORGE. Impossible, without he huffs the lady, and makes love to Sir Francis.

[Enter Drawer.]

DRAWER. Mr Marplot's below, gentlemen, and desires to know if he may have leave to wait upon ye.

CHARLES. How civil the rogue is, when he has done a fault!

SIR GEORGE. Ho! Desire him to walk up. Prithee Charles, throw off this chagrin, and be good company.

CHARLES. Nay, hang him, I'm not angry with him. Whisper, fetch me pen, ink and paper.

WHISPER. Yes, sir.

[Exit. Enter Marplot.]

CHARLES. Do but mark his sheepish look, Sir George.

MARPLOT. Dear Charles, don't overwhelm a man—already under insupportable affliction. I'm sure I always intend to serve my friends; but if my malicious stars deny the happiness, is the fault mine?

SIR GEORGE. Never mind him, Mr Marplot; he is eat up with spleen, but what says Miranda?

MARPLOT. Says—nay, we are all undone there too.

CHARLES. I told you so, nothing prospers that he undertakes.

MARPLOT. Why, can I help her having chose your father for better for worse?

CHARLES. So: there's another of Fortune's strokes. I suppose I shall be edged out of my estate with twins every year, let who will get 'em.

SIR GEORGE. What, is the woman really possessed?

33. Would Jupiter restore the years that are fled (Virgil, *Aeneid:* viii, 560).

MARPLOT. Yes, with the spirit of contradiction, she railed at you most prodigiously.

SIR GEORGE. That's no ill sign.

[Enter Whisper, with pen, ink, and paper.]

MARPLOT. You'd say it was no good sign, if you knew all.

SIR GEORGE. Why, prithee?

MARPLOT. Hark 'e, Sir George, let me warn you, pursue your old haunt no more, it may be dangerous.

[Charles sits down to write.]

SIR GEORGE. My old haunt, what d'you mean!

MARPLOT. Why in short, then since you will have it, Miranda vows if you dare approach the garden gate at eight o'clock, as you used, you shall be saluted with a blunderbuss, sir. These were her words, nay she bid me tell you so too.

SIR GEORGE. Ha! The garden gate at eight, as I used to do! There must be a meaning in this. Is there such a gate, Charles?

CHARLES. Yes, yes: it opens into the Park; I suppose her ladyship has made many a scamper through it.

SIR GEORGE. It must be an assignation then. Ha, my heart springs with joy, 'tis a propitious omen. My dear Marplot, let me embrace thee, thou art my friend, my better angel—

MARPLOT. What do you mean, Sir George?

SIR GEORGE. No matter what I mean. Here, take a bumper[34] to the garden gate, ye dear rogue you.

MARPLOT. You have reason to be transported, Sir George; I have saved your life.

SIR GEORGE. My life! Thou hast saved my soul, man.—Charles, if thou dost not pledge this health, mayst thou never taste the joys of love.

CHARLES. Whisper, be sure you take care how you deliver this. *[Gives him the letter.]* Bring me the answer to my lodgings.

WHISPER. I warrant you, sir.

MARPLOT. Whither does that letter go?—Now I dare not ask for my blood.

CHARLES. Now I'm for you.

SIR GEORGE. To the garden gate at the hour of eight, Charles, along, huzza!

CHARLES. I begin to conceive you.

MARPLOT. That's more than I do, egad—to the garden gate, huzza! *[Drinks.]* But I hope you design to keep far enough off it, Sir George.

SIR GEORGE. Aye, aye, never fear that; she shall see I despise her frown; let her use her blunderbuss against the next fool, she shan't reach me with the smoke, I warrant her. Ha, ha, ha!

MARPLOT. Ah, Charles, if you could receive a disappointment thus *en cavalier,*[35] one should have some comfort in being beat for you.

CHARLES. The fool comprehends nothing.

SIR GEORGE. Nor would I have him; prithee take him along with thee.

CHARLES. Enough: Marplot, you shall go home with me.

MARPLOT. I'm glad I'm well with him, however. Sir George, yours. Egad, Charles's asking me to go home with him gives me a shrewd suspicion there's more in the garden gate than I comprehend. Faith, I'll give him the drop, and away to guardian's, and find it out.

SIR GEORGE.

I kiss both your hands.—And now for the garden gate.
It's beauty gives the assignation there,
And love too powerful grows, t'admit of fear.

[Exit.]

Act IV

SCENE I

[Outside the house of Sir Jealous Traffick. Enter Whisper. Patch is peeping out the door.]

WHISPER. Ha, Mrs Patch, this is a lucky minute, to find you so readily; my master dies with impatience.

PATCH. My lady imagined so, and by her orders I have been scouting this hour in search of you, to

---

34. **bumper:** jug of wine.

35. *en cavalier:* in a cavalier manner.

inform you that Sir Jealous has invited some friends to supper with him tonight, which gives an opportunity to your master to make use of his ladder of ropes. The closet window shall be open, and Isabinda ready to receive him; bid him come immediately.

WHISPER. Excellent! He'll not disappoint, I warrant him. But hold, I have a letter here, which I'm to carry an answer of, I can't think what language the direction is.

PATCH. Foh, 'tis no language, but a character which the lovers intend to avert discovery. Ha, I hear my old master coming downstairs, it is impossible you should have an answer; away, and bid him come himself for that.—Begone, we are ruined if you're seen, for he has doubled his care since the last accident.

WHISPER. I go, I go.

[Exit.]

PATCH. There, go thou into my pocket. *[Puts it to her side, and it falls down.]* Now I'll up the back stairs, lest I meet him. Well, a dextrous chamber-maid is the ladies' best utensil, I say.

[Exit. Enter Sir Jealous with a letter in his hand.]

SIR JEALOUS. So, this is some comfort; this tells me that Señor Don Diego Babinetto is safely arrived; he shall marry my daughter the minute he comes, ha, ha! What's here? *[Picks up the letter which Patch dropped.]* A letter! I don't know to make of the superscription, I'll see what's within side. *[Opens it.]* Humph, 'tis Hebrew, I think. What can this mean? There must be some trick in it; this was certainly designed for my daughter, but I don't know that she can speak any language but her mother-tongue. No matter for that, this may be one of love's hieroglyphics, and I fancy I saw Patch's tail sweep by. That wench may be a slut, and instead of guarding my honour, betray it. I'll find it out I'm resolved. Who's there?

[Enter Servant.]

SIR JEALOUS. What answer did you bring from the gentlemen I sent you to invite?

SERVANT. That they'll all wait of you, sir, as I told you before; but I suppose you forgot, sir.

SIR JEALOUS. Did I so, sir? But I shan't forget to break your head, if any of them come, sir.

SERVANT. Come, sir! Why did you not send me to desire their company, sir?

SIR JEALOUS. But I send you now to desire their absence; say I have something extraordinary fallen out, which calls me abroad contrary to expectation, and ask their pardon; and d'ye hear, send the butler to me.

SERVANT. Yes, sir.

[Exit. Enter Butler.]

SIR JEALOUS. If this paper has a meaning, I'll find it.—Lay the cloth in my daughter's chamber, and bid the cook send supper thither presently.

BUTLER. Yes, sir,—Heyday, what's the matter now?

[Exit.]

SIR JEALOUS. He wants the eye of Argus, that has a young handsome daughter in this town; but my comfort is, I shall not be troubled long with her. He that pretends to rule a girl once in her teens, had better be at sea in a storm, and would be in less danger;

For let him do or counsel all he can,
She thinks and dreams of nothing else but Man.

[Exit.]

SCENE II

[Isabinda's chamber. Isabinda and Patch.]

ISABINDA. Are you sure nobody saw you speak to Whisper?

PATCH. Yes, very sure, madam; but I heard Sir Jealous coming downstairs, so clapped his letter into my pocket.

[Feels for the letter.]

ISABINDA. A letter? Give it me quickly.

PATCH. Bless me! What's become on't—I'm sure I put it—

[Searching still.]

ISABINDA. Is it possible thou could'st be so careless?—Oh! I'm undone forever, if it be lost.

PATCH. I must have dropped it upon the stairs. But why are you so much alarmed? If the worst happens, nobody can read it, madam, nor find out who it was designed for.

ISABINDA. If it falls into my father's hands, the very figure of a letter will produce ill consequences. Run and look for it upon the stairs this moment.

PATCH. Nay, I'm sure it can be nowhere else—

[As she is going out of the door, she meets the Butler entering.]

PATCH. How now, what do you want?

BUTLER. My master ordered me to lay the cloth here for his supper.

ISABINDA. *[Aside.]* Ruined, past redemption—

PATCH. You mistake sure: what shall we do?

ISABINDA. I thought he expected company tonight—Oh! Poor Charles! Oh, unfortunate Isabinda!

BUTLER. I thought so too, madam, but I suppose he has altered his mind.

[Lays the cloth, and exit.]

ISABINDA. The letter is the cause; this heedless action has undone me. Fly and fasten the closet-window, which will give Charles notice to retire. Ha! My father! Oh confusion!

[Enter Sir Jealous.]

SIR JEALOUS. Hold, hold, Patch, whither are you going? I'll have nobody stir out of the room till after supper.

PATCH. Sir, I was going to reach your easy chair.— Oh, wretched accident!

SIR JEALOUS. I'll have nobody stir out of the room. I don't want my easy chair.

ISABINDA. *[Aside.]* What will be the event of this?

SIR JEALOUS. Hark ye, daughter: do you know this hand?

ISABINDA. As I suspected—hand do you call it, sir? 'Tis some school-boy's scrawl.

PATCH. Oh invention! Thou chamber-maid's best friend, assist me.

SIR JEALOUS. Are you sure you don't understand it?

[Patch feels in her bosom, and shakes her coats.]

ISABINDA. Do you understand it, sir?

SIR JEALOUS. I wish I did.

ISABINDA. *[Aside.]* Thank heaven you do not.—Then I know no more of it that you do, indeed, sir.

PATCH. Oh lord, oh lord, what have you done, sir? Why the paper is mine, I dropped it out of my bosom.

[Snatching it from him.]

SIR JEALOUS. Ha! Yours mistress?

ISABINDA. *[Aside.]* What does she mean by owning it?

PATCH. Yes, sir, it is.

SIR JEALOUS. What is it? Speak.

PATCH. Yes, sir, it is a charm for the toothache.—I have worn it these seven years; 'twas given me by an angel for aught I know, when I was raving with the pain; for nobody knew from whence he came, nor whither he went. He charged me never to open it, lest some dire vengeance befall me, and heaven knows what will be the event. Oh! Cruel misfortune, that I should drop it, and you should open it.—If you had not opened it—

ISABINDA. *[Aside.]* Excellent wench!

SIR JEALOUS. Pox of your charms and whims for me; if that be all, 'tis well enough; there, there, burn it, and I warrant you no vengeance will follow.

PATCH. *[Aside.]* So, all's right again thus far.

ISABINDA. *[Aside.]* I would not lose Patch for the world—I'll take courage a little.—Is this usage for your daughter, sir? Must my virtue and conduct be suspected for every trifle? You immure me like some dire offender here, and deny me all the recreations which my sex enjoy, and the custom of the country and modesty allow; yet not content with that, you make my confinement more intolerable by your mistrusts and jealousies; would I were dead, so I were free from this.

SIR JEALOUS. Tomorrow rids you of this tiresome load—Don Diego Babinetto will be here, and then my care ends, and his begins.

ISABINDA. Is he come then? *[Aside.]* Oh how shall I avoid this hated marriage.

[Enter Servants with supper.]

SIR JEALOUS. Come, will you sit down?

ISABINDA. I can't eat, sir.

PATCH. *[Aside.]* No, I dare swear he has given her supper enough. I wish I could get into the closet—

SIR JEALOUS. Well, if you can't eat, then give me a song whilst I do.

ISABINDA. I have such a cold I can scarce speak, sir, much less sing. *[Aside.]*—How shall I prevent Charles coming in?

SIR JEALOUS. I hope you have the use of your fingers, madam. Play a tune upon your spinnet, whilst your woman sings me a song.

PATCH. *[Aside.]* I'm as much out of tune as my lady, if he knew all.

ISABINDA. I shall make excellent music.

[Isabinda sits down to play.]

PATCH. Really, sir, I'm so frighted about your opening this charm, that I can't remember one song.

SIR JEALOUS. Pish, hang your charm: come, come, sing anything.

PATCH. *[Aside.]* Yes, I'm likely to sing truly.— Humph, humph; bless me I cannot raise my voice, my heart pants so.

SIR JEALOUS. Why, what does your heart pant so, that you can't play neither? Pray what key are you in, ha?

PATCH. *[Aside.]* Ah, would the key were turned of you once.

SIR JEALOUS. Why don't you sing, I say?

PATCH. When madam has put her spinnet in tune, sir? Humph, humph—

ISABINDA. *[Rising.]* I cannot play sir, whatever ails me.

SIR JEALOUS. Zounds sit down and play me a tune, or I'll break your spinnet about your ears.

ISABINDA. What will become of me?

[Sits down and plays.]

SIR JEALOUS. Come mistress.

PATCH. Yes, sir.

[Sings, but horribly out of tune.]

SIR JEALOUS. Hey, hey, why you are a-top of the house, and you are down in the cellar. What is the meaning of this? Is it on purpose to cross me, ha?

PATCH. Pray, madam, take it a little lower, I cannot reach that note—nor any note I fear.

ISABINDA. Well, begin—Oh! Patch, we shall be discovered.

PATCH. I sing with the apprehension, madam— humph, humph—*[Sings.]*

[Charles pulls open the closet door.]

CHARLES.

> Music and singing.
> 'Tis thus the bright celestial court above
> Beguiles the hours with music and with love.
> Death! her father there!

[The women shriek.]

CHARLES. Then I must fly—

[Exit into the closet. Sir Jealous rises up hastily, seeing Charles slip back in the closet.]

SIR JEALOUS. Hell and furies, a man in the closet!—

PATCH. Ah! A ghost, a ghost—he must not enter the closet—

[Isabinda throws herself down before the closet door, as in a swoon.]

SIR JEALOUS. The devil! I'll make a ghost of him I warrant you.

[Strives to get by.]

PATCH. Oh sir, have a care, you'll tread upon my lady.—Who waits there? Bring some water. Oh! This comes of your opening the charm. Oh, oh, oh, oh. *[Weeps aloud.]*

SIR JEALOUS. I'll charm you, housewife, here lies the charm that conjured this fellow in, I'm sure on't; come out you rascal, do so. Zounds, take her from the door, or I'll spurn her from it, and break your neck downstairs.

ISABINDA. Oh, oh, where am I—*[Aside to Patch.]* He's gone, I heard him leap down.

PATCH. Nay, then let him enter—here, here madam, smell to this; come, give me your hand: come nearer to the window, the air will do you good.

SIR JEALOUS. I would she were in her grave. Where are you sirrah? Villain, robber of my honour! I'll pull you out of your nest.

[Goes into the closet.]

PATCH. You'll be mistaken, old gentleman, the bird is flown.

ISABINDA. I'm glad I have 'scaped so well. I was almost dead in earnest with the fright.

[Reenter Sir Jealous out of the closet.]

SIR JEALOUS. Whoever the dog were, he has escaped out of the window, for the sash is up, But though he has got out of my reach, you are not. And first Mrs Pander, with your charms for the toothache, get out of my house, go, troop; yet hold, stay, I'll see you out of my doors myself, but I'll secure your charge ere I go.

ISABINDA. What do you mean, sir? Was she not a creature of your own providing?

SIR JEALOUS. She was of the devil's providing for aught I know.

PATCH. What have I done, sir, to merit your displeasure?

SIR JEALOUS. I don't know which of you have done it; but you shall both suffer for it, till I can discover whose guilt it is. Go, get in there, I'll move you from this side of the house. *[Pushes Isabinda in at the door, and locks it: puts the key into his pocket.]* I'll keep the key myself; I'll try what ghost will get into that room. And now forsooth I'll wait on you downstairs.

PATCH. Ah, my poor lady—downstairs, sir! But I won't go out, sir, till I have looked up my clothes.

SIR JEALOUS. If thou wer't as naked as thou wer't born, thou should'st not stay to put on a smock. Come along, I say! When your mistress is married, you shall have your rags, and everything that belongs to you; but till then—

[Exit, pulling her out.]

PATCH. Oh! Barbarous usage for nothing!

[Patch and Sir Jealous reenter at the lower end of the stage.]

SIR JEALOUS. There, go, and come no more within sight of my habitation these three days, I charge you.

[Slams the door after her.]

PATCH. Did ever anybody see such an old monster?

[Enter Charles.]

PATCH. Oh! Mr Charles, your affairs and mine are in an ill posture.

CHARLES. I am inured to the frowns of Fortune: but what has befallen thee?

PATCH. Sir Jealous, whose suspicious nature's always on the watch; nay, even while one eye sleeps, the other keeps sentinel; upon sight of you, flew into such a violent passion, that I could find no stratagem to appease him; but in spite of all arguments, locked his daughter into his own apartment, and turned me out-of-doors.

CHARLES. Ha! Oh, Isabinda!

PATCH. And swears she shall neither see sun or moon, till she is Don Diego Babinetto's wife, who arrived last night, and is expected with impatience.

CHARLES. He dies: yes, by all the wrongs of love he shall; here will I plant myself, and through my breast he shall make his passage, if he enters.

PATCH. A most heroic resolution. There might be ways found out more to your advantage. Policy is often preferred to open force.

CHARLES. I apprehend you not.

PATCH. What think you personating this Spaniard, imposing upon the father, and marrying your mistress by his own consent.

CHARLES. Say'st thou so, my angel! Oh could that be done, my life to come would be too short to recompense thee. But how can I do that, when I ne'er know what ship he came in, or from what part of Spain; who recommends him, or how attended?

PATCH. I can solve all this. He is from Madrid, his father's name Don Pedro Questo Portento Babinetto. Here's a letter of his to Sir Jealous, which he dropped one day. You understand Spanish, and the hand may be counterfeited. You conceive me, sir.

CHARLES. My better genius, thou hast revived my drooping soul: I'll about it instantly. Come to my lodgings, and we'll concert matters.

[Exeunt.]

SCENE II

[A garden gate, open. Scentwell waiting inside. Enter Sir George Airy.]

SIR GEORGE. So, this is the gate, and most invitingly open. If there should be a blunderbuss here now, what a dreadful ditty would my fall make for fools! And what a jest for the wits! How my name would be roared about street! Well, I'll venture all.

SCENTWELL. *[Entering.]* Hist, hist! Sir George Airy—

SIR GEORGE. A female voice! Thus far I'm safe, my dear.

SCENTWELL. No, I'm not your dear, but I'll conduct you to her; give me your hand: you must go through many a dark passage and dirty step before you arrive—

SIR GEORGE. I know I must before I arrive at Paradise; therefore be quick, my charming guide.

SCENTWELL. For aught you know; come, come, your hand and away.

SIR GEORGE. Here, here, child, you can't be half so swift as my desires.

[Exeunt.]

SCENE III

[Inside the house. Enter Miranda.]

MIRANDA. Well, let me reason a little with my mad self. Now don't I transgress all rules to venture upon a man without the advice of the grave and wise? But then a rigid knavish guardian, who would have married me! To whom? Even to his nauseous self, or nobody. Sir George is what I have tried in conversation, enquired into his character, am satisfied in both. Then his love! Who would have given a hundred pounds only to have seen a woman he had not infinitely loved? So I find my liking him has furnished me with arguments enough of his side; and now the only doubt remains, whether he will come or no.

[Enter Scentwell.]

SCENTWELL. That's resolved, madam, for here's the knight.

[Exit.]

SIR GEORGE. And do I once more behold that lovely object, whose idea fills my mind, and forms my pleasing dreams!

MIRANDA. What! Beginning again in heroics!—Sir George, don't you remember how little fruit your last prodigal oration produced? Not one bare single word in answer.

SIR GEORGE. Ha! the voice of my Incognita.—Why did you take ten thousand ways to captivate a heart your eyes alone had vanquished?

MIRANDA. Prithee no more of these flights, for our time's but short, and we must fall to business. Do you think we can agree on that same terrible bugbear, Matrimony, without heartily repenting on both sides!

SIR GEORGE. It has been my wish since first my longing eyes beheld ye.

MIRANDA. And your happy ears drank in the pleasing news, I had thirty thousand pounds.

SIR GEORGE. Unkind! Did I not offer you in those purchased minutes to run the risk of your fortune, so you would but secure that lovely person to my arms?

MIRANDA. Well, if you have such love and tenderness, (since our wooing has been short) pray reserve it for our future days, to let the world see we are lovers after wedlock; 'twill be a novelty—

SIR GEORGE. Haste then, and let us tie the knot, and prove the envied pair—

MIRANDA. Hold, not so fast, I have provided better than to venture on dangerous experiments headlong.—My guardian, trusting to my dissembled love, has given up my fortune to my own disposal; but with this proviso, that he tomorrow morning weds me. He is now gone to Doctor's Commons[36] for a licence.

SIR GEORGE. Ha, a licence!

MIRANDA. But I have planted emissaries that infallibly take him down to Epsom, under pretence that a brother usurer of his is to make him his executor; the thing on earth he covets.

SIR GEORGE. 'Tis his known character.

MIRANDA. Now my instruments confirm him this man is dying, and he sends me word he goes this minute; it must be tomorrow ere he can be undeceived. That times is ours.

SIR GEORGE. Let us improve it then, and settle on our coming years, endless, endless happiness.

MIRANDA. I dare not stir till I hear he's on the road—then I, and my writings, the most material point, are soon removed.

36. Doctor's Commons: law center in London.

SIR GEORGE. I have one favour to ask, if it lies in your power, you would be a friend to poor Charles, though the son of this tenacious man: he is as free from all his vices, as nature and a good education can make him; and what now I have vanity enough to hope will induce you, he is the man on earth I love.

MIRANDA. I never was his enemy, and only put it on as it helped my designs on his father. If his uncle's estate ought to be in his possession, which I shrewdly suspect, I may do him a singular piece of service.

SIR GEORGE. You are all goodness.

[Enter Scentwell.]

SCENTWELL. Oh, madam, my master and Mr Marplot are just coming into the house.

MIRANDA. Undone, undone, if he finds you here in this crisis, all my plots are unravelled.

SIR GEORGE. What shall I do? Can't I get back into the garden?

SCENTWELL. Oh, no! He comes up those stairs.

MIRANDA. Here, here, here! Can you condescend to stand behind this chimney-board,[37] Sir George?

SIR GEORGE. Anywhere, anywhere, dear madam, without ceremony.

SCENTWELL. Come, come, sir; lie close—

[They put him behind the chimney-board. Enter Sir Francis and Marplot, Sir Francis peeling an orange.]

SIR FRANCIS. I could not go, though 'tis upon life and death, without taking leave of dear Chargie. Besides, this fellow buzzed in my ears, that thou might'st be so desperate to shoot that wild rake which haunts the garden gate; and that would bring us into trouble, dear—

MIRANDA. *[Frowning at Marplot, aside.]* So Marplot brought you back then; I am obliged to him for that, I'm sure—

MARPLOT. By her looks she means she's not obliged to me, I have done some mischief now, but what I can't imagine.

SIR FRANCIS. Well, chargie, I have had three messengers to come to Epsom to my neighbour Squeezum's, who, for all his vast riches, is departing. *[Sigh.]*

MARPLOT. Aye, see what all your usurers must come to.

SIR FRANCIS. Peace ye young knave! Some forty years hence I may think on't—But, chargie, I'll be with thee tomorrow, before those pretty eyes are open; I will, I will, chargie, I'll rouse you, i'faith.—Here Mrs Scentwell, lift up your lady's chimney-board, that I may throw my peel in, and not litter her chamber.

MIRANDA. Oh my stars! What will become of us now?

SCENTWELL. Oh, pray sir, give it me; I love it above all things in nature, indeed I do.

SIR FRANCIS. No, no, hussy; you have the green-pip[38] already, I'll have no apothecary's bills.

[Goes towards the chimney-board.]

MIRANDA. Hold, hold, hold, dear guardie, I have a, a, a, a, a, monkey, shut up there; and if you open it before the man comes that is to tame it, 'tis so wild 'twill break all my china, or get away, and that would break my heart; *[In a flattering tone.]* for I'm fond on't to distraction, next thee, dear guardie.

SIR FRANCIS. Well, well, chargie, I won't open it; she shall have her monkey, poor rogue; here, throw this peel out of the window.

[Exit Scentwell.]

MARPLOT. A monkey! Dear madam, let me see it; I can tame a monkey as well as the best of them all. Oh how I love the little miniatures of man!

MIRANDA. Be quiet, mischief, and stand farther from the chimney.—You shall not see my monkey—why sure—

[Striving with him.]

MARPLOT. For heaven's sake, dear madam, let me but peep, to see if it be as pretty as my Lady Fiddle-Faddle's. Has it got a chain?

MIRANDA. Not yet, but I design it one shall last its lifetime. Nay, you shall not see it!—Look, guardie, how he teases me!

SIR FRANCIS. *[Getting between him and the chimney.]* Sirrah, sirrah, let my chargie's monkey alone, or

---

37. **chimney-board:** wooden board put across front of fireplace to control downdrafts in summer.

38. **green-pip:** anorexia in adolescent girls.

Bambo shall fly about your ears. What, is there no dealing with you?

MARPLOT. Pugh, pox of this monkey! Here's a rout: I wish he may rival you.

[Enter a servant.]

SERVANT. Sir, they put two more horses to the coach, as you ordered, and 'tis ready at the door.

SIR FRANCIS. Well, I am going to be executor, better for thee, jewel. Bye chargie, one buss!—I'm glad thou hast got a monkey to divert thee a little.

MIRANDA. Thank'e dear guardie.—Nay, I'll see you to the coach.

SIR FRANCIS. That's kind, adod.

MIRANDA. *[To Marplot.]* Come along, Impertinence.

MARPLOT. *[Stepping back.]* Egad, I will see the monkey now. *[Lifts up the board, and discovers Sir George.]* Oh lord, oh lord! Thieves, thieves, murder!

SIR GEORGE. Damn'e, you unlucky dog! 'Tis I; which way shall I get out! Show me instantly, or I'll cut your throat.

MARPLOT. Undone, undone! At that door there. But hold, hold, break that china, and I'll bring you off.

[He runs off at the corner, and throws down some china. Reenter Sir Francis, Miranda, and Scentwell.]

SIR FRANCIS. Mercy on me! What's the matter?

MIRANDA. Oh you toad! What have you done?

MARPLOT. No great harm, I beg of you to forgive me. Longing to see the monkey, I did but just raise up the board, and it flew over my shoulders, scratched all my face, broke yon china, and whisked out of the window.

SIR FRANCIS. Was ever such an unlucky rogue! Sirrah, I forbid you my house. Call the servants to get the monkey again. I would stay myself to look it, but that you know my earnest business.

SCENTWELL. Oh my lady will be the best to lure it back; all them creatures love my lady extremely.

MIRANDA. Go, go, dear guardie, I hope I shall recover it.

SIR FRANCIS. Bye, bye, dearie. Ah, mischief, how you look now! Bye, bye.

[Exit.]

MIRANDA. Scentwell, see him in the coach, and bring me word.

SCENTWELL. Yes, madam.

MIRANDA. So, sir, you have done your friend a signal piece of service, I suppose.

MARPLOT. Why look you, madam, if I have committed a fault, thank yourself; no man is more serviceable when I am let into a secret, nor none more unlucky at finding it out. Who could divine your meaning? When you talked of a blunderbuss, who thought of a rendezvous? And when you talked of a monkey, who the devil dreamt of Sir George?

MIRANDA. A sign you converse but little with our sex, when you can't reconcile contradictions.

[Enter Scentwell.]

SCENTWELL. He's gone, madam, as fast as the coach-and-six can carry him.

[Enter Sir George.]

SIR GEORGE. Then I may appear.

MARPLOT. Dear Sir George, make my peace! On my soul, I did not think of you.

SIR GEORGE. I dare swear thou didst not. Madam, I beg you to forgive him.

MIRANDA. Well, Sir George, if he can be secret.

MARPLOT. Ods heart, madam, I'm as secret as a priest when I'm trusted.

SIR GEORGE. Why 'tis with a priest our business is at present.

SCENTWELL. Madam, here's Mrs Isabinda's woman to wait on you.

MIRANDA. Bring her up.

[Enter Patch.]

MIRANDA. How do'e Mrs Patch? What news from your lady?

PATCH. That's for your private ear, madam. Sir George, there's a friend of yours has an urgent occasion for your assistance.

SIR GEORGE. His name.

PATCH. Charles.

MARPLOT. Ha! Then there's something a-foot that I know nothing of. I'll wait on you, Sir George.

SIR GEORGE. A third person may not be proper, perhaps; as soon as I have dispatched my own

affairs, I am at his service. I'll send my servant
to tell him I'll wait upon him in half-an-hour.

MIRANDA. How come you employed in this
message, Mrs Patch?

PATCH. Want of business, madam: I am discharged
by my master, but hope to serve my lady still.

MIRANDA. How! Discharged! You must tell me the
whole story within.

PATCH. With all my heart, madam.

MARPLOT. [Aside.] Pish! Pox, I wish I were fairly out
of the house. I find marriage is the end of this
secret: and now I am half mad to know what
Charles wants him for.

SIR GEORGE. Madam, I'm double pressed by love
and friendship: this exigence admits of no delay.
Shall we make Marplot of the party?

MIRANDA. If you'll run the hazard, Sir George; I
believe he means well.

MARPLOT. Nay, nay, for my part, I desire to be let
into nothing; I'll be gone, therefore pray don't
mistrust me.

[Going.]

SIR GEORGE. So, now he has a mind to be gone to
Charles. But not knowing what affairs he may
have upon his hands at present, I'm resolved he
shan't stir.—No, Mr Marplot, you must not
leave us, we want a third person.

[Takes hold of him.]

MARPLOT. I never had more mind to be gone in my
life.

MIRANDA. Come along then; if we fail in the
voyage, thank yourself for taking this ill-starred
gentleman on board.

SIR GEORGE.

That vessel ne'er can unsuccessful prove,
Whose freight is beauty, and whose pilot Love.

[Exeunt.]

Act V

SCENE I

[Enter Miranda, Patch, and Scentwell.]

MIRANDA. Well, Patch, I have done a strange bold
thing; my fate is determined, and expectation
is no more. Now to avoid the impertinence
and roguery of an old man, I have thrown
myself into the extravagance of a young one; if
he should despise, slight, or use me ill, there's
no remedy from a husband but the grave; and
that's a terrible sanctuary to one of my age and
constitution.

PATCH. Oh fear not, madam, you'll find your
account in Sir George Airy; it is impossible a
man of sense should use a woman ill, endow'd
with beauty, wit and fortune. It must be the
lady's fault, if she does not wear the
unfashionable name of wife easy, when nothing
but complaisance and good humour is requisite
on either side to make them happy.

MIRANDA. I long till I am out of this house, lest any
accident should bring my guardian back.
Scentwell, put my best jewels into the little

casket, slip them into thy pocket, and let us
march off to Sir Jealous's.

SCENTWELL. It shall be done, madam.

[Exit Scentwell.]

PATCH. Sir George will be impatient, madam: if
their plot succeeds, we shall be received; if not,
he will be able to protect us. Besides, I long to
know how my young lady fares.

MIRANDA. Farewell, old Mammon, and thy detested
walls: 'twill be no more "Sweet Sir Francis"; I
shall be compelled to the odious talk of
dissembling no longer to get my own, and coax
him with the wheedling names of "my
precious," "my dear," "dear guardie." Oh
Heavens!

[Enter Sir Francis behind. Miranda starts with fright.]

SIR FRANCIS. Ah, my sweet chargie, don't be
frighted. But thy poor guardie has been abused,
cheated, fooled, betrayed, but nobody knows
by whom.

MIRANDA. *[Aside.]* Undone! Past redemption.

SIR FRANCIS. What, won't you speak to me, chargie?

MIRANDA. I am so surprised with joy to see you, I know not what to say.

SIR FRANCIS. Poor dear girl! But do'e know that my son, or some such rogue, to rob or murder me, or both, contrived this journey? For upon the road I met my neighbour Squeezum well, and coming to town.

MIRANDA. Good lack! Good lack! What tricks are there in this world.

[Enter Scentwell, with a diamond necklace in her hand, not seeing Sir Francis.]

SCENTWELL. Madam, be pleased to tie this necklace on, for I can't get into the—*[Seeing Sir Francis.]*

MIRANDA. The wench is a fool, I think! Could you not have carried it to be mended, without putting it in the box?

SIR FRANCIS. What's the matter?

MIRANDA. Only dear'e, I bid her, I bid her—Your ill-usage has put everything out of my head. But won't you go, guardie, and find out these fellows, and have them punished? And, and—

SIR FRANCIS. Where should I look them, child! No, I'll sit me down contented with my safety, nor stir out of my own doors till I go with thee to a parson.

MIRANDA. *[Aside.]* If he goes into his closet, I am ruined. Oh! Bless me, in this fright, I had forgot Mrs Patch.

PATCH. Aye, madam, I stay for your speedy answer.

MIRANDA. *[Aside.]* I must get him out of the house. Now assist me Fortune.

SIR FRANCIS. Mrs Patch! I profess I did not see you. How dost thou do, Mrs Patch? Well, don't you repent leaving my chargie.

PATCH. Yes, everybody must love her—but I came now—*[Aside to Miranda.]*—Madam, what did I come for? My invention is at the last ebb.

SIR FRANCIS. Nay, never whisper, tell me.

MIRANDA. She came, dear guardie, to invite me to her lady's wedding, and you shall go with me, guardie, 'tis to be done this moment, to a Spanish merchant: old Sir Jealous keeps on his humour, the first minute he sees her, the next he marries her.

SIR FRANCIS. Ha, ha, ha! I'd go if I thought the sight of matrimony would tempt chargie to perform her promise. There was a smile, there was a consenting look with those pretty twinklers, worth a million. Ods-precious, I am happier than the Great Mogul, the Emperor of China, or all the potentates that are not in the wars. Speak, confirm it, make me leap out of my skin.

MIRANDA. When one has resolved, 'tis in vain to stand, shall I shall I; if ever I marry, positively this is my wedding-day.

SIR FRANCIS. Oh! Happy, happy man.—Verily I will beget a son the first night, shall disinherit that dog Charles. I have estate enough to purchase a barony, and be the immortalising the whole family of the Gripes.

MIRANDA. Come then, guardie, give me thy hand, let's to this house of Hymen.
My choice is fixed, let good or ill betide.

SIR FRANCIS. The joyful bridegroom I,

MIRANDA. And I the happy bride.

[Exeunt.]

SCENE II

[Enter Sir Jealous meeting a servant.]

SERVANT. Sir, here's a couple of gentlemen enquire for you; one of them calls himself Señor Diego Babinetto.

SIR JEALOUS. Ha! Señor Babinetto! Admit 'em instantly!—Joyful minute: I'll have my daughter married tonight.

[Enter Charles in a Spanish habit, with Sir George dressed like a merchant.]

SIR JEALOUS. Señor, beso las menas vuestra merced es muy bien venido en esta tierra.[39]

CHARLES. Señor, soy muy humilde, y muy obligado cryado de vuestra merced: mi padre embia a vuestra merced, los mas profondos de sus respetos; y a commissionada este mercadel Ingles, de concluyr un negocio, que me haze el mas dichoso hombre del muhndo, haziendo me su yerno.[40]

---

39. Sir, I kiss your worship's hands; you are most welcome to this country. **40.** Sir, I am most humbly obliged for your worship's greeting. My father sends your worship his deepest respects. To settle the business he has commissioned this English merchant whom I consider the most trustworthy man in the world to have come to my notice.

SIR JEALOUS. I am glad on't, for I find I have lost much of my Spanish. Sir, I am your most humble servant. Señor Don Diego Babinetto has informed me that you are commissioned by Señor Don Pedro, etc., his worthy father.

SIR GEORGE. To see an affair of marriage consummated between a daughter of yours and Señor Diego Babinetto his son here. True, sir, such a trust is reposed in me, as that letter will inform you. *[Aside.]* I hope 'twill pass upon him.

[Gives him a letter.]

SIR JEALOUS. Aye, 'tis his hand. *[Seems to read.]*

SIR GEORGE. *[Aside.]* Good—you have counterfeited to a nicety, Charles.

CHARLES. *[Aside.]* If the whole plot succeeds as well, I'm happy.

SIR JEALOUS. Sir, I find by this, that you are a man of honour and probity; I think sir, he calls you Meanwell.

SIR GEORGE. Meanwell is my name, sir.

SIR JEALOUS. A very good name, and very significant.

CHARLES. *[Aside.]* Yes faith, if he knew all.

SIR JEALOUS. For to mean well is to be honest, and to be honest is the virtue of a friend, and a friend is the delight and support of human society.

SIR GEORGE. You shall find that I'll discharge the part of a friend in what I have undertaken, Sir Jealous.

CHARLES. *[Aside.]* But little does he think to whom.

SIR GEORGE. Therefore, sir, I must entreat the presence of your daughter, and the assistance of your chaplain; for Señor Don Pedro strictly enjoined me to see the marriage rites performed as soon as we should arrive, to avoid the accidental overtures of Venus!

SIR JEALOUS. Overtures of Venus!

SIR GEORGE. Aye, sir, that is, those little hawking females that traverse the Park, and the play-house, to put off their damaged ware—they fasten upon foreigners like leeches, and watch their arrival as carefully as the Kentish men do a ship-wreck. I warrant you they have heard of him already.

SIR JEALOUS. Nay, I know this town swarms with them.

SIR GEORGE. Aye, and then you know the Spaniards are naturally amorous, but very constant, the first faces fixes 'em; and it may be very dangerous to let him ramble ere he is tied.

CHARLES. *[Aside.]* Well hinted.

SIR JEALOUS. Pat to my purpose.—Well, sir, there is but one thing more, and they shall be married instantly.

CHARLES. *[Aside.]* Pray heaven that one thing more don't spoil all.

SIR JEALOUS. Don Pedro writ one word in his last but one, that he designed the sum of five thousand crowns by way of jointure for my daughter; and that it should be paid into my hand upon the day of marriage—

CHARLES. *[Aside.]* Oh! The devil.

SIR JEALOUS. —in order to lodge it in some of our funds in case she should become a widow, and return for England.

SIR GEORGE. *[Aside.]* Pox on't, this is an unlucky turn. What shall I say?

SIR JEALOUS. And he does not mention one word of it in this letter.

CHARLES. *[Aside.]* I don't know how he should.

SIR GEORGE. Humph! True, Sir Jealous, he told me such a thing, but, but, but, but,—he, he, he, he,—he did not imagine you would insist upon the very day; for, for, for, for money you know is dangerous returning by sea, an, an, an, an,—

CHARLES. *[Aside.]* Zounds, say we have brought it in commodities.

SIR GEORGE. And so, sir, he has sent it in merchandise, tobacco, sugars, spices, lemons, and so forth, which shall be turned into money with all expedition. In the mean time, sir, if you please to accept of my bond for performance—

SIR JEALOUS. It is enough, sir. I am so pleased with the countenance of Señor Diego, and the harmony of your name, that I'll take your word, and will fetch my daughter this moment. Within there!

[Enter servant.]

SIR JEALOUS. Desire Mr Tackum, my neighbour's chaplain, to walk thither.

SERVANT. Yes, sir.

[Exit.]

SIR JEALOUS. Gentlemen, I'll return in an instant.

CHARLES. Wondrous well, let me embrace thee.

SIR GEORGE. Egad that five thousand crowns had like to have ruined the plot.

CHARLES. But that's over! And if Fortune throws no more rubs in our way—

SIR GEORGE. Thou'lt carry the prize.—But hist, here he comes.

[Enter Sir Jealous, dragging in Isabinda.]

SIR JEALOUS. Come along, you stubborn baggage you, come along.

ISABINDA.

Oh, hear me, sir! Hear me but speak one word:
Do not destroy my everlasting peace:
My soul abhors this Spaniard you have chose,
Nor can I wed him without being cursed.

SIR JEALOUS. How's that!

ISABINDA.

Let this posture move your tender nature. *[Kneels.]*
Forever will I hang upon these knees:
Nor loose my hands till you cut off the hold,
If you refuse to hear me, sir.

CHARLES. *[Aside.]* Oh that I could discover myself to her!

SIR GEORGE. *[Aside.]* Have a care what you do. You had better trust to his obstinacy.

SIR JEALOUS. Did you ever see such a perverse slut? Off, I say! Mr Meanwell, pray help me a little.

SIR GEORGE. Rise, madam, and do not disoblige your father, who has provided a husband worthy of you, one that will love you equal with his soul, and one that you will love when once you know him.

ISABINDA. Oh! Never, never! Could I suspect that falsehood in my heart, I would this moment tear it from my breast, and straight present him with the treacherous part.

CHARLES. *[Aside.]* Oh my charming faithful dear!

SIR JEALOUS. Falsehood! Why who the devil are you in love with? Don't provoke me, or by St Iägo I shall beat you, huswife.

CHARLES. Heaven forbid; for I shall infallibly discover myself if he should.

SIR GEORGE. Have patience, madam! And look at him: why will ye prepossess yourself against a man that is master of all the charms you would desire in a husband?

SIR JEALOUS. Aye, look at him, Isabinda. Señor pase vind adelante.[41]

CHARLES. My heart bleeds to see her grieve, whom I imagined would with joy receive me. Señora oblique me vuestra merced de su mano.[42]

SIR JEALOUS. *[Pulling up her head.]* Hold up your head, hold up your head, huswife, and look at him: is there a properer, handsomer, better-shaped fellow in England, ye jade you? Ha! See, see the obstinate baggage shuts her eyes; by St Iägo, I have a good mind to beat 'em out.

[Pushes her down.]

ISABINDA.

Do, then, sir, kill me, kill me instantly.
'Tis much the kinder action of the two;
For 'twill be worse than death to wed him.

SIR GEORGE. Sir Jealous, you are too passionate. Give me leave, I'll try by gentle words to work her to your purpose.

SIR JEALOUS. I pray do, Mr Meanwell, I pray do; she'll break my heart. *[Weeps.]* There is in that, jewels of the value of £3000 which were her mother's, and a paper wherein I have settled one half of my estate upon her now, and the whole when I die; but provided she marries this gentleman; else by St Iägo I'll turn her out-of-doors to beg or starve. Tell her this, Mr Meanwell, pray do.

[Walks off.]

SIR GEORGE. Ha! This is beyond expectation!— Trust me, sir, I'll lay the dangerous consequence of disobeying you at this juncture before her, I warrant you.

CHARLES. *[Aside.]* A sudden joy runs through my heart like a propitious omen.

SIR GEORGE. Come, madam, do not blindly cast your life away just in the moment you would wish to save it.

ISABINDA. Pray, cease your trouble, sir, I have no wish but sudden death to free me from this hated Spaniard. If you are his friend, inform him what I say: my heart is given to another

---

41. Come forward, sir. **42.** Madam, oblige me with the favour of your hand.

youth, whom I love with the same strength of passion that I hate this Diego; with whom, if I am forced to wed, my own hand shall cut the Gordian knot.[43]

SIR GEORGE. Suppose this Spaniard, which you strive to shun, should be the very man to whom you'd fly?

ISABINDA. Ha!

SIR GEORGE. Would you not blame your rash resolve, and curse your eyes that would not look on Charles?

ISABINDA. Oh Charles! Oh, you have inspired new life, and collected every wandering sense. Where is he? Oh! Let me fly into his arms.

[Rises.]

SIR GEORGE. Hold, hold, hold. 'Sdeath, madam, you'll ruin all; your father believes him to be Señor Babinetto: compose yourself a little pray, madam.

[He runs to Sir Jealous.]

CHARLES. [Aside.] Her eyes declare she knows me.

SIR GEORGE. She begins to hear reason, sir; the fear of being turned out of doors has done it.

[Runs back to Isabinda.]

ISABINDA. 'Tis he! Oh, my ravished soul!

SIR GEORGE. Take heed, madam, you don't betray yourself. Seem with reluctance to consent, or you are undone.

[Runs to Sir Jealous.]

SIR GEORGE. Speak gently to her, I'm sure she'll yield, I see it in her face.

SIR JEALOUS. Well, Isabinda, can you refuse to bless a father, whose only care is to make you happy, as Mr Meanwell has informed you? Come, wipe thy eyes, nay prithee do, or thou wilt break thy father's heart. See, thou bring'st the tears in mine, to think of thy undutiful carriage to me. [Weeps.]

ISABINDA. Oh! Do not weep, sir, your tears are like a poignard[44] to my soul; do with me what you please, I am all obedience.

SIR JEALOUS. Ha! Then thou art my child again.

SIR GEORGE. 'Tis done, and now, friend, the day's thy own.

CHARLES. The happiest of my life, if nothing intervene.

SIR JEALOUS. And wilt thou love him?

ISABINDA. I will endeavour it, sir.

[Enter servant.]

SERVANT. Sir, here's Mr Tackum.

SIR JEALOUS. Show him into the parlour—Señor tome vind sueipora; cette momento les juntta les manos.[45]

[Gives her to Charles.]

CHARLES. Oh transport!—Señor yo la reciba como se devo un tesero tan grande.[46] Oh! My joy, my life, my soul.

[They embrace.]

ISABINDA. My faithful everlasting comfort.

SIR JEALOUS.

Now, Mr Meanwell, let's to the parson.
Who, by his art, will join this pair for life,
Make me the happiest father, her the happiest wife.

[Exeunt.]

SCENE III

[The street before Sir Jealous's door. Enter Marplot, alone.]

MARPLOT. I have hunted all over the town for Charles, but can't find him; and by Whisper's scouting at the end of the street, I suspect he must be in the house again. I am informed too, that he has borrowed a Spanish habit out of the play-house: what can it mean?

[Enter a servant of Sir Jealous's to him, out of the house.]

MARPLOT. Hark'e, sir, do you belong to this house?

SERVANT. Yes, sir.

43. Gordian knot: intricate problem.   44. poignard: dagger.

45. Sir, take your wife; from this very moment your hands are joined.   46. Sir, I welcome her to me as befits a treasure so great.

MARPLOT. Pray can you tell me if there be a gentleman in it in Spanish habit?

SERVANT. There's a Spanish gentleman within, that is just a-going to marry my young lady, sir.

MARPLOT. Are you sure he is a Spanish gentleman?

SERVANT. I am sure he speaks no English, that I hear of.

MARPLOT. Then that can't be him I want; for 'tis an English gentleman, though I suppose he may be dressed like a Spaniard, that I enquire after.

SERVANT. *[Aside.]* Ha! Who knows but this may be an imposter? I'll inform my master; for if he should be imposed upon, he'll beat us all round.—Pray, come in, sir, and see if this be the person you enquire for.

SCENE IV

[Inside the house. Enter Marplot.]

MARPLOT. So, this was a good contrivance: If this be Charles, now will he wonder how I found him out.

[Enter servant and Sir Jealous.]

SIR JEALOUS. What is your earnest business, blockhead, that you must speak with me before the ceremony's past? Ha! Who's this?

SERVANT. Why this gentleman, sir, wants another gentleman in a Spanish habit, he says.

SIR JEALOUS. In Spanish habit! 'Tis some friend of Señor Don Diego's, I warrant. Sir, I suppose you would speak with Señor Babinetto—

MARPLOT. Heyday! What the devil does he say now!—Sir, I don't understand you.

SIR JEALOUS. Don't you understand Spanish, sir?

MARPLOT. Not I, indeed, sir.

SIR JEALOUS. I thought you had known Señor Babinetto.

MARPLOT. Not I, upon my word, sir.

SIR JEALOUS. What then, you'd speak with his friend, the English merchant Mr Meanwell?

MARPLOT. Neither, sir not I.

SIR JEALOUS. *[In an angry tone.]* Why, who are you then, sir? And what do you want?

MARPLOT. Nay, nothing at all, not I, sir. Pox on him! I wish I were out. He begins to exalt his voice, I shall be beaten again.

SIR JEALOUS. Nothing at all, sir! Why then, what business have you in my house? Ha!

SERVANT. You said you wanted a gentleman in Spanish habit.

MARPLOT. Why, aye, but his name is neither Babinetto, nor Meanwell.

SIR JEALOUS. What is his name, then, sirrah? Ha? Now I look at you again, I believe you are the rogue that threatened me with half a dozen Myrmidons—Speak, sir, who is it you look for? Or, or—

MARPLOT. A terrible old dog!—Why, sir, only an honest young fellow of my acquaintance—I thought that here might be a ball, and that he might have been here in a masquerade; 'tis Charles, Sir Francis Gripe's son, because I know he used to come hither sometimes.

SIR JEALOUS. Did he so?—Not that I know of, I'm sure. Pray heaven that this be no Don Diego— If I should be tricked now—ha? My heart misgives me plaguily.—Within there! Stop the marriage!—Run, sirrah, call all my servants! I'll be satisfied that this is Señor Pedro's son, ere he has my daughter.

MARPLOT. Ha! Sir George! What have I done now?

[Enter Sir George with a drawn sword between the scenes.]

SIR GEORGE. Ha! Marplot here—oh the unlucky dog!—What's the matter, Sir Jealous?

SIR JEALOUS. Nay, I don't know the matter, Mr Meanwell—

MARPLOT. *[Going up to Sir George.]* Upon my soul, Sir George—

SIR JEALOUS. Nay, then, I'm betrayed, ruined, undone: thieves, traitors, rogues! *[Offers to go in.]* Stop the marriage, I say—

SIR GEORGE. I say go on, Mr Tackum—Nay, no entering here, I guard this passage, old gentleman; the act and deed were both your own, and I'll see 'em signed or die for't.

[Enter servants.]

SIR JEALOUS. A pox on the act and deed!—Fall on, knock him down.

SIR GEORGE. Aye, come on scoundrels! I'll prick your jackets for you.

SIR JEALOUS. Zounds, sirrah, I'll be revenged on you.

[Beats Marplot.]

SIR GEORGE. Aye, there your vengeance is due: ha, ha!

MARPLOT. Why, what do you beat me for? I han't married your daughter.

SIR JEALOUS. Rascals! Why don't you knock him down?

SERVANT. We are afraid of his sword, sir; if you'll take that from him, we'll knock him down presently.

[Enter Charles and Isabinda.]

SIR JEALOUS. Seize her then.

CHARLES. Rascals, retire; she's my wife, touch her if you dare, I'll make dogs-meat of you.

SIR JEALOUS. Ah! Downright English:—Oh, oh, oh, oh!

[Enter Sir Francis, Miranda, Patch, Scentwell, and Whisper.]

SIR FRANCIS. Into the house of joy we enter without knocking. Ha! I think 'tis the house of sorrow, Sir Jealous.

SIR JEALOUS. Oh, Sir Francis! Are you come? What, was this your contrivance to abuse, trick, and chouse me out of my child!

SIR FRANCIS. My contrivance! What do you mean?

SIR JEALOUS. No, you don't know your son there in Spanish habit?

SIR FRANCIS. How! My son in Spanish habit! Sirrah, you'll come to be hanged; get out of my sight, ye dog! Get out of my sight.

SIR JEALOUS. Get out of your sight, sir! Get out with your bags? Let's see what you'll give him now to maintain my daughter on.

SIR FRANCIS. Give him? He shall never be the better for a penny of mine—and you might have looked after your daughter better, Sir Jealous. Tricked, quotha! Egad, I think you designed to trick me. But look ye, gentleman, I believe I shall trick you both. This lady is my wife, do you see; and my estate shall descend only to the heirs of her body.

SIR GEORGE. Lawfully begotten by me—I shall be extremely obliged to you, Sir Francis.

SIR FRANCIS. Ha, ha, ha, ha! Poor Sir George! You see your project was of no use. Does not your hundred pound stick in your stomach? Ha, ha, ha!

SIR GEORGE. No faith, Sir Francis, this lady has given me a cordial for that.

[Takes her by the hand.]

SIR FRANCIS. Hold, sir, you have nothing to say to this lady.

SIR GEORGE. Nor you nothing to do with my wife, sir.

SIR FRANCIS. Wife sir!

MIRANDA. Aye really, guardian, 'tis even so. I hope you'll forgive my first offence.

SIR FRANCIS. What, have you choused me out of my consent, and your writings then, mistress, ha?

MIRANDA. Out of nothing but my own, guardian.

SIR JEALOUS. Ha, ha, ha! 'Tis some comfort at least to see you are over-reached as well as myself. Will you settle your estate upon your son now?

SIR FRANCIS. He shall starve first.

MIRANDA. That I have taken care to prevent. There sir, is the writings of your uncle's estate, which has been your due these three years.

[Gives Charles papers.]

CHARLES. I shall study to deserve this favour.

SIR FRANCIS. What, have you robbed me too, mistress! Egad I'll make you restore 'em— huswife, I will so.

SIR JEALOUS. Take care I don't make you pay the arrears, sir. 'Tis well it's no worse, since 'tis no better. Come young man, seeing thou hast outwitted me, take her, and bless thee both.

CHARLES. I hope, sir, you'll bestow your blessing, too, 'tis all I'll ask. *[Kneels.]*

SIR FRANCIS. Confound you all!

[Exit.]

MARPLOT. Mercy upon us, how he looks!

SIR GEORGE. Ha, ha! Ne'er mind his curses, Charles; thou'lt thrive not one jot the worse for 'em. Since this gentleman is reconciled, we are all made happy.

SIR JEALOUS. I always loved precaution, and took care to avoid dangers. But when a thing was past, I ever had philosophy enough to be easy.

CHARLES. Which is the true sign of a great soul; I loved your daughter, and she me, and you shall have no reason to repent her choice.

ISABINDA. You'll not blame me, sir, for loving my own country best.

MARPLOT. So, here's everybody happy, I find, but poor Pilgarlick.[47] I wonder what satisfaction I shall have, for being cuffed, kicked, and beaten in your service.

SIR JEALOUS. I have been a little too familiar with you, as things are fallen out; but since there's no help for't, you must forgive me.

MARPLOT. Egad, I think so—but provided that you be not so familiar for the future.

SIR GEORGE. Thou hast been an unlucky rogue.

MARPLOT. But very honest.

CHARLES. That I'll vouch for; and freely forgive thee.

SIR GEORGE. And I'll do you one piece of service more, Marplot. I'll take care that Sir Francis makes you master of your estate.

MARPLOT. That will make me as happy as any of you.

PATCH. Your humble servant begs leave to remind you, madam.

ISABINDA. Sir, I hope you'll give me leave to take Patch into favour again.

47. **Pilgarlick:** food.

SIR JEALOUS. Nay, let your husband look to that, I have done with my care.

CHARLES. Her own liberty shall always oblige me. Here's nobody but honest Whisper and Mrs Scentwell to be provided for now. It shall be left to their choice to marry, or keep their services.

WHISPER. Nay then, I'll stick to my master.

SCENTWELL. Coxcomb! And I prefer my lady before a footman.

SIR JEALOUS. Hark, I hear the music, the fiddlers smell a wedding. What say you, young fellows, will you have a dance?

SIR GEORGE. With all my heart; call 'em in.

[A dance.]

SIR JEALOUS. Now let us in and refresh ourselves with a cheerful glass, in which we will bury all animosities; and:

By my example let all parents move,
And never strive to cross their children's love;
But still submit that care to Providence above.

Introduction to *A Doll's House* by Henrik Ibsen

Translated by Eva Le Gallienne

A Doll's House   Janet McTeer as Nora, Owen Teale as Torvald, Playhouse Theatre, London. (© *Donald Cooper/PHOTOSTAGE.*)

The Play   As a realistic playwright, Henrik Ibsen sought to convince his audiences that the stage action in his dramas represented everyday life. But he went further than that: He felt that drama should tackle subjects that had been taboo in the theater—economic injustice, the sexual double standard, and unhappy marriages, all of which are touched on in *A Doll's House.* (We should note that many contemporary critics and translators suggest that the title *A Doll House* is a more accurate translation and better reflects the thematic issues of the text. We continue to use *A Doll's House* since that is the title of the Eva Le Galliene translation found in this anthology.)

Ibsen and the realistic dramatists who followed him often insisted that the purpose of drama was to call attention to social problems in order to bring about change. *A Doll's House* employs many of the traditional elements of the nineteenth-century well-made play, including clearly developed exposition, central secrets, and the use of theatrical devices such as a letter. Ibsen, however, subverts the traditional form by refusing to make simple moral judgments or resolve their dramatic action neatly, which was the norm in the well-made play of the era. Unlike popular well-made melodramas, realistic plays frequently implied that morality and immorality were relative and not clearly distinct or easily defined. Not surprisingly, Ibsen and other realists met a great deal of opposition in producing their plays and were constantly plagued by censorship.

A Doll's House was one of Ibsen's most controversial dramas. The play focuses on Nora, a wife who has saved her husband Torvald's life through an act of forgery. However, she discovers her unequal status in the home when her forgery is revealed in a letter sent to Torvald by a fired employee, Krogstad. Even when Krogstad rescinds the letter because he is to marry Nora's friend Mrs. Linde, Nora realizes that she can no longer live with Torvald in a relationship in which she is treated like a child. The play closes with Nora leaving her home, slamming the door behind her. Since Ibsen does not let us know what will happen to Nora or Torvald, the enigmatic ending implies the inability to dramatize a neat resolution to such a complex circumstance.

A Doll's House remains a frequently produced drama in the modern theater because it focuses on issues that remain unresolved in the twenty-first century: the role of women in marriage as well as the unequal treatment of women inside and outside the home. Furthermore, the play also dramatizes how the middle-class values held by Torvald strangle Nora's independence. Her husband's concern over reputation, financial status, and appropriate social behavior, as well as his desire to control his wife physically and emotionally, imprison Nora within her home. Nora's sense of entrapment is heightened by her growing sense of self-determination. The "doll's house" becomes the metaphor for the constraints society places upon women. When Nora slams the door, her act signals the call for the kinds of revolutionary changes that will be demanded at the end of the nineteenth and throughout the twentieth century.

The Playwright   As a playwright, Henrik Ibsen (1828–1906) is known for his mastery of dramatic technique, his psychological insights into human nature, and his poetic symbolism.

For much of his life, Ibsen was an outcast from the society that he dramatized. When he was born in Skien, Norway, in 1828, his father was a prosperous businessman; but in 1834 the business failed, and the family was forced to move outside the town. At 15, Ibsen left home to work as a pharmacist's apprentice; later he tried to qualify for the university. In 1852, at age 24, he became a producer at the theater in Bergen, Norway, and was commissioned to write one play a year for the theater's anniversary. While he was a producer at Bergen, he took a study tour of German and Danish theaters.

He moved to Christiana in 1857 to become artistic director of the Norwegian Theater there. When it went bankrupt, he secured a small government grant and, in 1864, left Norway. For the next 27 years, he lived in Rome, Dresden, and Munich. He returned to Norway in 1891, continuing to work in his careful, methodical way (he allowed himself two years to write and polish a play).

Ibsen was incapacitated by a stroke in 1900. After another stroke the following year, he remained an invalid, nearly helpless, until his death in 1906.

Ibsen's earliest plays, based on Norwegian history and mythology, are romantic verse dramas examining the extremes of the Norwegian national character. They include *Lady of Ostraat* (1855), *The Vikings of Helgeland* (1858), *The Pretenders* (1863), *Brand* (1866), and *Peer Gynt* (1867). The plays of his middle period—the realistic, social dramas for which he is best known—explore the interaction of people with society, dealing with such problems as unhappy marriages, the sexual double standard, infidelity, and the position of women. Among these realistic plays are *The Pillars of Society* (1877), *A Doll's House* (1879), *Ghosts* (1881), *An Enemy of the People* (1882), and *Hedda Gabler* (1891).

While still working in a realistic Norwegian setting, Ibsen moved toward symbolism and mysticism in his last plays. The dramas in this group include *The Wild Duck* (1884), *Rosmersholm* (1886), *The Master Builder* (1892), *John Gabriel Borkman* (1896), *The Lady from the Sea* (1898), and *When We Dead Awaken* (1899). Regardless of their period or style, Ibsen's plays all have a common theme: the individual amidst conflicting social pressures.

The Period   Possibly the most significant social development of the late nineteenth century was the rise of the working class. Politicians, social scientists, and artists focused on the concerns of the lower classes. An indication of the increased political power of the working class was the trend, throughout Europe, to allow larger numbers of people to vote. The growing suffragist movement, which sought voting rights for women, was tied to this political transformation. Furthermore, workers gained economic and political power by unionizing.

Scientific advances continued to alter Western lifestyles radically. Advances in medicine increased life expectancy. The work of Freud, Einstein, and Nietzsche, following the writings of Darwin and Marx earlier in the century, challenged accepted beliefs in religion, science, and politics. In psychology, Sigmund Freud established psychoanalysis. In physics, the work of people like Einstein altered our understanding of the universe. Many philosophers point out that as a result of the growth of modern scientific knowledge, Western society became more atheistic, and God and religion became less important in daily life. Einstein's term "relativity" provides a key: Things that were thought to be fixed became relative.

There were radical technological changes as well. Inventions, including Alexander Graham Bell's telephone, Thomas Edison's electric light, Wilbur and Orville Wright's flying machine, and the early automobile, made daily life easier. Some of the inventions of this period, such as recording devices, film, and radio, resulted in new electronic art forms.

This era of intellectual, moral, and scientific upheaval was reflected in theater. Between 1875 and 1915 one can see the emergence of two artistic impulses in theater that have stood in sharp contrast throughout the twentieth century. One of these impulses was realism. Realistic artists attempted to create onstage the illusion of everyday life. A strong countermovement was departures from realism, in which theatrical artists created seemingly abstract, illogical stage pictures that were rooted in the subconscious or in the world of dreams.

The leaders in establishing realism were Ibsen, the Swedish playwright August Strindberg (1849–1912), and the Russian Anton Chekhov (1860–1904). These dramatists and their fellow realists sought to convince their audiences that the stage action represented everyday life. This is not as revolutionary a concept for modern audiences, but in the late nineteenth century many theatergoers and critics were scandalized by realism because it touched a raw nerve. In the attempt to portray daily life, realists argued, no subject matter should be excluded from the stage. Among the taboo subjects dramatized by the realists were economic injustice, the sexual double standard, unhappy marriages, venereal disease, and religious hypocrisy. Rather than use stock characters, realists created complicated personalities molded by heredity and environment. The language of these characters was colloquial and conversational.

A DOLL'S HOUSE

Henrik Ibsen

CHARACTERS

TORVALD HELMER, a lawyer
NORA, his wife
DOCTOR RANK
MRS. KRISTINE LINDE
NILS KROGSTAD, an attorney

HELMER'S THREE SMALL CHILDREN
ANNE-MARIE,* nurse at the Helmers
HELENE, maid at the Helmers
A PORTER

SCENE: The action takes place in the Helmer residence.

Act I

SCENE: A comfortable room furnished with taste, but not expensively. In the back wall a door on the right leads to the hall, another door on the left leads to Helmer's study. Between the two doors a piano. In the left wall, center a door; farther downstage a window. Near the window a round table with an armchair and a small sofa. In the right wall upstage a door, and farther downstage a porcelain stove round which are grouped a couple of armchairs and a rocking chair. Between the stove and the door stands a small table. Engravings on the walls. A whatnot with china objects and various bric-a-brac. A small bookcase with books in fancy bindings. The floor is carpeted; a fire burns in the stove. A winter day.

NORA. Be sure and hide the Christmas tree carefully, Helene, the children mustn't see it till this evening, when it's all decorated. *[To the porter, taking out her purse.]* How much?
PORTER. Fifty. Ma'am.
NORA. Here you are. No—keep the change.

[The Porter thanks her and goes. Nora closes the door. She laughs gaily to herself as she takes off her outdoor things. Takes a bag of macaroons out of her pocket and eats a couple, then she goes cautiously to the door of her husband's study and listens.]

Yes—he's home. *[She goes over to the table right, humming to herself again.]*
HELMER. *[From his study.]* Is that my little lark twittering out there?
NORA. *[Busily undoing the packages.]* Yes, it is.

*For stage purposes, often ANNA-MARIA.

HELMER. Is that my little squirrel bustling about?

NORA. Yes.

HELMER. When did my squirrel get home?

NORA. Just this minute. *[She puts the bag of macaroons back in her pocket and wipes her mouth.]* Oh, Torvald, do come in here! You must see what I have bought.

HELMER. Now, don't disturb me! *[A moment afterwards he opens the door and looks in—pen in hand.]* Did you say "bought"? That—all *that?* Has my little spendthrift been flinging money about again?

NORA. But, Torvald, surely this year we ought to let ourselves go a bit! After all, it's the first Christmas we haven't had to be careful.

HELMER. Yes, but that doesn't mean we can afford to *squander* money.

NORA. Oh, Torvald, we can squander a bit, can't we? Just a little tiny bit? You're going to get a big salary and you'll be making lots and lots of money.

HELMER. After the first of the year, yes. But remember there'll be three whole months before my salary falls due.

NORA. We can always borrow in the meantime.

HELMER. Nora! *[Goes to her and pulls her ear playfully.]* There goes my little featherbrain! Let's suppose I borrowed a thousand crowns today, you'd probably squander it all during Christmas week; and then let's suppose that on New Year's Eve a tile blew off the roof and knocked my brains out—

NORA. *[Puts her hand over his mouth.]* Don't say such frightful things!

HELMER. But let's suppose it happened—then what?

NORA. If anything as terrible as *that* happened, I shouldn't care whether I owed money or not.

HELMER. But what about the people I'd borrowed from?

NORA. Who cares about them? After all they're just strangers.

HELMER. Oh, Nora, Nora! What a little woman you are! But seriously, Nora, you know my feelings about such things. I'll have no borrowing—I'll have no debts! There can be no freedom—no, nor beauty either—in a home based upon loans and credit. We've held out bravely up to now, and we shall continue to do so for the short time that remains.

NORA. *[Goes toward the stove.]* Just as you like, Torvald.

HELMER. *[Following her.]* Come, come; the little lark mustn't droop her wings. Don't tell me my little squirrel is sulking! *[He opens his purse.]* Nora! Guess what I have here!

NORA. *[Turns quickly.]* Money!

HELMER. There you are! *[He hands her some notes.]* Don't you suppose I know that money is needed at Christmas time.

NORA. *[Counts the notes.]* Ten, twenty, thirty, forty. Oh thank you, thank you, Torvald—this'll last me a long time!

HELMER. Better see that it does!

NORA. Oh, it will—I know. But do come here. I want to show you everything I've bought, and all so cheap too! Here are some new clothes for Ivar, and a little sword—and this horse and trumpet are for Bob, and here's a doll for Emmy—and a doll's bed. They're not worth much, but she's sure to tear them to pieces in a minute anyway. This is some dress material and handerchiefs for the maids. Old Anne-Marie really should have had something better.

HELMER. And what's in that other parcel?

NORA. *[With a shriek.]* No, Torvald! You can't see that until this evening!

HELMER. I can't, eh? But what about you—you little squanderer? Have you thought of anything for yourself?

NORA. Oh, there's nothing I want, Torvald.

HELMER. Of course there is!—now tell me something sensible you'd really like to have.

NORA. But there's nothing—really! Except of course—

HELMER. Well?

NORA. *[She fingers the buttons on his coat; without looking at him.]* Well—If you really want to give me something—you might —you might—

HELMER. Well, well, out with it!

NORA. *[Rapidly.]* You might give me some money, Torvald—just anything you feel you could spare; and then one of these days I'll buy myself something with it.

HELMER. But Nora—

NORA. Oh, please do, dear Torvald—I beg you to! I'll wrap it up in beautiful gold paper and hang it on the Christmas tree. Wouldn't that be fun?

HELMER. What's the name of the bird that eats up money?

NORA. The Spendthrift bird—I know! But do let's do as I say, Torvald!—it will give me a chance to choose something I really need. Don't you think that's a sensible idea? Don't you?

HELMER. *[Smiling.]* Sensible enough—providing you really *do* buy something for yourself with it. But I expect you'll fritter it away on a lot of unnecessary household expenses, and before I know it you'll be coming to me for more.

NORA. But, Torvald—

HELMER. You can't deny it, Nora dear. *[Puts his arm round her waist.]* The Spendthrift is a sweet little bird—but it costs a man an awful lot of money to support one!

NORA. How can you say such nasty things—I save all I can!

HELMER. Yes, I dare say—but that doesn't amount to much!

NORA. *[Hums softly and smiles happily.]* You don't know, Torvald, what expenses we larks and squirrels have!

HELMER. You're a strange little creature; exactly like your father. You'll go to any lengths to get a sum of money—but as soon as you have it, it just slips through your fingers. You don't know yourself what's become of it. Well, I suppose one must just take you as you are. It's in your blood. Oh, yes! such things are hereditary, Nora.

NORA. I only wish I had inherited a lot of Father's qualities.

HELMER. And I wouldn't wish you any different than you are, my own sweet little lark. But Nora, it's just occurred to me—isn't there something a little—what shall I call it—a little guilty about you this morning?

NORA. About me?

HELMER. Yes. Look me straight in the eye.

NORA. *[Looking at him.]* Well?

HELMER. *[Wags a threatening finger at her.]* Has my little sweet-tooth been breaking rules today?

NORA. No! What makes you think that?

HELMER. Are you sure the sweet-tooth didn't drop in at the confectioner's?

NORA. No, I assure you, Torvald—

HELMER. She didn't nibble a little candy?

NORA. No, really not.

HELMER. Not even a macaroon or two?

NORA. No, Torvald, I assure you—really—

HELMER. There, there! Of course I'm only joking.

NORA. *[Going to the table right.]* It would never occur to me to go against your wishes.

HELMER. Of course I know that—and anyhow—you've given me your word—*[Goes to her.]* Well, my darling, I won't pry into your little Christmas secrets. They'll be unveiled tonight under the Christmas tree.

NORA. Did you remember to ask Dr. Rank?

HELMER. No, it really isn't necessary. He'll take it for granted he's to dine with us. However, I'll ask him, when he stops by this morning. I've ordered some specially good wine. I am so looking forward to this evening, Nora, dear!

NORA. So am I—And the children will have such fun!

HELMER. Ah! How nice it is to feel secure; to look forward to a good position with an ample income. It's a wonderful prospect—isn't it, Nora?

NORA. It's simply marvelous!

HELMER. Do you remember last Christmas? For three whole weeks—you locked yourself up every evening until past midnight—making paper flowers for the Christmas tree—and a lot of other wonderful things you wanted to surprise us with. I was never so bored in my life!

NORA. I wasn't a bit bored.

HELMER. *[Smiling.]* But it all came to rather a sad end, didn't it, Nora?

NORA. Oh, do you have to tease me about that again! How could I help the cat coming in and tearing it all to pieces.

HELMER. Of course you couldn't help it, you poor darling! You meant to give us a good time—that's the main thing. But it's nice to know those lean times are over.

NORA. It's wonderful!

HELMER. Now I don't have to sit here alone, boring myself to death; and you don't have to strain your dear little eyes, and prick your sweet little fingers—

NORA. *[Claps her hands.]* No, I don't—do I, Torvald! Oh! How lovely it all is. *[Takes his arm.]* I want to tell you how I thought we'd arrange things after Christmas. *[The doorbell rings.]* Oh there's the bell. *[Tidies up the room a bit.]* It must be a visitor—how tiresome!

HELMER. I don't care to see any visitors, Nora—remember that.

HELENE. *[In the doorway.]* There's a lady to see you, Ma'am.

NORA. Well, show her in.

HELENE. *[To Helmer.]* And the Doctor's here too, Sir.

HELMER. Did he go straight to my study?

HELENE. Yes, he did, Sir.

[Helmer goes into his study. Helene ushers in Mrs. Linde who is dressed in traveling clothes, and closes the door behind her.]

MRS. LINDE. *[In subdued and hesitant tone.]* How do you do, Nora?

NORA. *[Doubtfully.]* How do you do?

MRS. LINDE. You don't recognize me, do you?

NORA. No, I don't think—and yet—I seem to— *[With a sudden outburst.]* Kristine! Is it really you?

MRS. LINDE. Yes; it's really I!

NORA. Kristine! And to think of my not knowing you! But how could I when—*[More softly.]* You've changed so, Kristine!

MRS. LINDE. Yes I suppose I have. After all—it's nine or ten years—

NORA. Is it *that* long since we met? Yes, so it is. Oh, these last eight years have been such happy ones! Fancy your being in town! And imagine taking that long trip in midwinter! How brave you are!

MRS. LINDE. I arrived by the morning boat.

NORA. You've come for the Christmas holidays, I suppose—what fun! Oh, what a good time we'll have! Do take off your things. You're not cold, are you? *[Helping her.]* There; now we'll sit here by the stove. No, you take the arm-chair; I'll sit here in the rocker. *[Seizes her hands.]* Now you look more like yourself again. It was just at first—you're a bit paler, Kristine—and perhaps a little thinner.

MRS. LINDE. And much, much older, Nora.

NORA. Well, perhaps a *little* older—a tiny, tiny bit—not much, though. *[She suddenly checks herself; seriously.]* Oh, but, Kristine! What a thoughtless wretch I am, chattering away like that—Dear, darling Kristine, do forgive me!

MRS. LINDE. What for, Nora, dear?

NORA. *[Softly.]* You lost your husband, didn't you, Kristine! You're a widow.

MRS. LINDE. Yes; my husband died three years ago.

NORA. Yes, I remember; I saw it in the paper. Oh, I *did* mean to write to you, Kristine! But I kept on putting it off, and all sorts of things kept coming in the way.

MRS. LINDE. I understand, dear Nora.

NORA. No, it was beastly of me, Kristine! Oh, you poor darling! What you must have gone through!—And he died without leaving you anything, didn't he?

MRS. LINDE. Yes.

NORA. And you have no children?

MRS. LINDE. No.

NORA. Nothing then?

MRS. LINDE. Nothing—Not even grief, not even regret.

NORA. *[Looking at her incredulously.]* But how is that possible, Kristine?

MRS. LINDE. *[Smiling sadly and stroking her hair.]* It sometimes happens, Nora.

NORA. Imagine being so utterly alone! It must be dreadful for you, Kristine! I have three of the loveliest children! I can't show them to you just now, they're out with their nurse. But I want you to tell me all about yourself—

MRS. LINDE. No, no; I'd rather hear about you, Nora—

NORA. No, I want you to begin. I'm not going to be selfish today. I'm going to think only of you. Oh! but one thing I *must* tell you. You haven't heard about the wonderful thing that's just happened to us, have you?

MRS. LINDE. No. What is it?

NORA. My husband's been elected president of the Joint Stock Bank!

MRS. LINDE. Oh, Nora—How splendid!

NORA. Yes; isn't it? You see, a lawyer's position is so uncertain, especially if he refuses to handle any cases that are in the least bit—shady; Torvald is very particular about such things—and I agree with him, of course! You can imagine how glad we are. He's to start at the Bank right after the New Year; he'll make a big salary and all sorts of percentages. We'll be able to live quite differently from then on—we'll have everything we want. Oh, Kristine! I'm so happy and excited! Won't it be wonderful to have lots and lots of money, and nothing to worry about!

MRS. LINDE. It certainly would be wonderful to have enough for one's needs.

NORA. Oh, not just for one's *needs*, Kristine! But heaps and heaps of money!

MRS. LINDE. *[With a smile.]* Nora, Nora, I see you haven't grown up yet! I remember at school you were a frightful spendthrift.

NORA. *[Quietly; smiling.]* Yes; that's what Torvald always says. *[Holding up her forefinger.]* But I haven't had much chance to be a spendthrift. We have had to work hard—both of us.

MRS. LINDE. You too?

NORA. Oh yes! I did all sorts of little jobs: needlework, embroidery, crochet—that sort of thing. *[Casually.]* And other things as well. I suppose you know that Torvald left the Government service right after we were married. There wasn't much chance of promotion in his department, and of course he had to earn more money when he had me to support. But that first year he overworked himself terribly. He had to undertake all sorts of odd jobs, worked from morning till night. He couldn't stand it; his health gave way and he became deathly ill. The doctors said he absolutely *must* spend some time in the South.

MRS. LINDE. Yes, I heard you spent a whole year in Italy.

NORA. Yes, we did. It wasn't easy to arrange, I can tell you. It was just after Ivar's birth. But of course we had to go. It was a wonderful trip, and it saved Torvald's life. But it cost a fearful lot of money, Kristine.

MRS. LINDE. Yes, it must have.

NORA. Twelve hundred dollars! Four thousand eight hundred crowns! That's an awful lot of money, you know.

MRS. LINDE. You were lucky to have it.

NORA. Well, you see, we got it from Father.

MRS. LINDE. Oh, I see. Wasn't it just about that time that your father died?

NORA. Yes, it was, Kristine. Just think! I wasn't able to go to him—I couldn't be there to nurse him! I was expecting Ivar at the time and then I had my poor sick Torvald to look after. Dear, darling Papa! I never saw him again, Kristine. It's the hardest thing I have had to go through since my marriage.

MRS. LINDE. I know you were awfully fond of him. And after that you went to Italy?

NORA. Yes; then we had the money, you see; and the doctors said we must lose no time; so we started a month later.

MRS. LINDE. And your husband came back completely cured?

NORA. Strong as an ox!

MRS. LINDE. But—what about the doctor then?

NORA. How do you mean?

MRS. LINDE. Didn't the maid say something about a doctor, just as I arrived?

NORA. Oh, yes; Dr. Rank. He's our best friend—it's not a professional call; he stops in to see us every day. No, Torvald hasn't had a moment's illness since; and the children are strong and well, and so am I. *[Jumps up and claps her hands.]* Oh Kristine, Kristine! How lovely it is to be alive and happy! But how disgraceful of me! Here I am talking about nothing but myself! *[Seats herself upon a footstool close to Kristine and lays her arms on her lap.]* Please don't be cross with me—Is it really true, Kristine, that you didn't love your husband? Why did you marry him, then?

MRS. LINDE. Well, you see—Mother was still alive; she was bedridden; completely helpless; and I had my two younger brothers to take care of. I didn't think it would be right to refuse him.

NORA. No, I suppose not. I suppose he had money then?

MRS. LINDE. Yes, I believe he was quite well off. But his business was precarious, Nora. When he died it all went to pieces, and there was nothing left.

NORA. And then—?

MRS. LINDE. Then I had to struggle along as best I could. I had a small shop for a while, and then I started a little school. These last three years have been one long battle—but it is over now, Nora. My dear mother is at rest—She doesn't need me any more. And my brothers are old enough to work, and can look after themselves.

NORA. You must have such a free feeling!

MRS. LINDE. No—only one of complete emptiness. I haven't a soul to live for! *[Stands up restlessly.]* I suppose that's why I felt I had to get away. I should think here it would be easier to find something to do—something to occupy one's thoughts. I might be lucky enough to get a steady job here—some office work, perhaps—

NORA. But that's so terribly tiring, Kristine; and you look so tired already. What you need is a rest. Couldn't you go to some nice watering-place?

MRS. LINDE. *[Going to the window.]* I have no father to give me the money, Nora.

NORA. *[Rising.]* Oh, please don't be cross with me!

MRS. LINDE. *[Goes to her.]* My dear Nora, you mustn't be cross with me! In my sort of position it's hard not to become bitter. One has no one to work for, and yet one can't give up the struggle. One must go on living, and it makes one selfish. I'm ashamed to admit it—but, just now, when you told me the good news about your husband's new position—I was glad—not so much for your sake as for mine.

NORA. How do you mean? Oh of course—I see! You think Torvald might perhaps help you.

MRS. LINDE. That's what I thought, yes.

NORA. And so he shall, Kristine. Just you leave it to me. I'll get him in a really good mood—and then bring it up quite casually. Oh, it would be such fun to help you!

MRS. LINDE. How good of you, Nora dear, to bother on my account! It's especially good of you—after all, you've never had to go through any hardship.

NORA. I? Not go through any—?

MRS. LINDE. [Smiling.] Well—Good Heavens—a little needlework, and so forth—You're just a child, Nora.

NORA. [Tosses her head and paces the room.] You needn't be so patronizing!

MRS. LINDE. No?

NORA. You're just like all the rest. You all think I'm incapable of being serious—

MRS. LINDE. Oh, come now—

NORA. You seem to think I've had no troubles—that I've been through nothing in my life!

MRS. LINDE. But you've just told me all your troubles, Nora dear.

NORA. I've only told you trifles! [Softly.] I haven't mentioned the important thing.

MRS. LINDE. Important thing? What do you mean?

NORA. I know you look down on me, Kristine; but you really shouldn't. You take pride in having worked so hard and so long for your mother.

MRS. LINDE. I don't look down on anyone, Nora; I can't help feeling proud and happy too, to have been able to make Mother's last days a little easier—

NORA. And you're proud of what you did for your brothers, too.

MRS. LINDE. I think I have a right to be.

NORA. Yes, so do I. But I want you to know, Kristine—that I, too, have something to be proud of.

MRS. LINDE. I don't doubt that. But what are you referring to?

NORA. Hush! We must talk quietly. It would be dreadful if Torvald overheard us! He must never know about it! No one must know about it, except you.

MRS. LINDE. And what is it, Nora?

NORA. Come over here. [Draws her down beside her on sofa.] Yes, I have something to be proud and happy about too. I saved Torvald's life, you see.

MRS. LINDE. Saved his life? But how?

NORA. I told you about our trip to Italy. Torvald would never have recovered if it hadn't been for that.

MRS. LINDE. Yes, I know—and your father gave you the necessary money.

NORA. [Smiling.] That's what everyone thinks—Torvald too; but—

MRS. LINDE. Well—?

NORA. Papa never gave us a penny. I raised the money myself.

MRS. LINDE. All that money! You?

NORA. Twelve hundred dollars. Four thousand eight hundred crowns. What do you think of that?

MRS. LINDE. But, Nora, how on earth did you do it? Did you win it in the lottery?

NORA. [Contemptuously.] The lottery! Of course not! Any fool could have done that!

MRS. LINDE. Where did you get it then?

NORA. [Hums and smiles mysteriously.] H'm; tra-la-la-la.

MRS. LINDE. You certainly couldn't have borrowed it.

NORA. Why not?

MRS. LINDE. A wife can't borrow without her husband's consent.

NORA. [Tossing her head.] Oh I don't know! If a wife has a good head on her shoulders—and has a little sense of business—

MRS. LINDE. I don't in the least understand, Nora—

NORA. Well, you needn't. I never said I borrowed the money. I may have got it in some other way. [Throws herself back on the sofa.] Perhaps I got it from some admirer. After all when one is as attractive as I am—!

MRS. LINDE. What a mad little creature you are!

NORA. I'm sure you're dying of curiosity, Kristine—

MRS. LINDE. Nora, are you sure you haven't been a little rash?

NORA. [Sitting upright again.] Is it rash to save one's husband's life?

MRS. LINDE. But mightn't it be rash to do such a thing behind his back?

NORA. But I couldn't tell him—don't you understand that! He wasn't even supposed to know how ill he was. The doctors didn't tell him—they came to me privately, told me his life was in danger and that he could only be saved by living in the South for a while. At first I tried persuasion; I cried, I begged, I cajoled—I said how much I longed to take a trip abroad like other young wives; I reminded him of my condition and told him he ought to humor me—and finally, I came right out and suggested that we borrow the money. But then, Kristine, he was almost angry; he said I was being frivolous and that it was his duty as my husband not to indulge my whims and fancies—I think that's what he called them. Then I made up my mind he must be saved in spite of himself—and I thought of a way.

MRS. LINDE. But didn't he ever find out from your father that the money was not from him?

NORA. No; never. You see, Papa died just about that time. I was going to tell him all about it and beg him not to give me away. But he was so very ill—and then, it was no longer necessary—unfortunately.

MRS. LINDE. And you have never confided all this to your husband?

NORA. Good heavens, no! That's out of the question! He's much too strict in matters of that sort. And besides—Torvald could never bear to think of owing anything to me! It would hurt his self-respect—wound his pride. It would ruin everything between us. Our whole marriage would be wrecked by it!

MRS. LINDE. Don't you think you'll ever tell him?

NORA. [Thoughtfully; half-smiling.] Perhaps some day— a long time from now when I'm no longer so pretty and attractive. No! Don't laugh! Some day when Torvald is no longer as much in love with me as he is now; when it no longer amuses him to see me dance and dress-up and act for him—then it might be useful to have something in reserve. [Breaking off.] Oh, what nonsense! That time will never come! Well—what do you think of my great secret, Kristine? Haven't I something to be proud of too? It's caused me endless worry, though. It hasn't been easy to fulfill my obligations. You know, in business there are things called installments, and quarterly interest—and they're dreadfully hard to meet on time. I've had to save a little here and there, wherever I could. I couldn't save much out of the housekeeping, for of course Torvald had to live well. And I couldn't let the

children go about badly dressed; any money I got for them, I spent on them, the darlings!

MRS. LINDE. Poor Nora! I suppose it had to come out of your own allowance.

NORA. Yes, of course. But after all, the whole thing was my doing. Whenever Torvald gave me money to buy some new clothes, or other things I needed, I never spent more than half of it; I always picked out the simplest cheapest dresses. It's a blessing that almost anything looks well on me—so Torvald never knew the difference. But it's been hard sometimes, Kristine. It's so nice to have pretty clothes— isn't it?

MRS. LINDE. I suppose it is.

NORA. And I made money in other ways too. Last winter I was lucky enough to get a lot of copying to do. I shut myself up in my room every evening and wrote far into the night. Sometimes I was absolutely exhausted—but it was fun all the same—working like that and earning money. It made me feel almost like a man!

MRS. LINDE. How much have you managed to pay off?

NORA. Well, I really don't know exactly. It's hard to keep track of things like that. All I know is— I've paid every penny I could scrape together. There were times when I didn't know which way to turn! [Smiles.] Then I used to sit here and pretend that some rich old gentleman had fallen madly in love with me—

MRS. LINDE. What are you talking about? *What* old gentleman?

NORA. I'm just joking! And then he was to die and when they opened his will, there in large letters were to be the words: "I leave all my fortune to that charming Nora Helmer to be handed over to her immediately."

MRS. LINDE. But who *is* this old gentleman?

NORA. Good heavens, can't you understand? There never *was* any such old gentleman; I just used to make him up, when I was at the end of my rope and didn't know where to turn for money. But it doesn't matter now—the tiresome old fellow can stay where he is as far as I am concerned. I no longer need him nor his money; for now my troubles are over. [Springing up.] Oh, isn't it wonderful to think of, Kristine. No more troubles! No more worry! I'll be able to play and romp about with the children; I'll be able to make a charming lovely home for

Torvald—have everything just as he likes it. And soon spring will be here, with its great blue sky. Perhaps we might take a little trip—I might see the ocean again. Oh, it's so marvelous to be alive and to be happy!

[The hall doorbell rings.]

MRS. LINDE. [Rising.] There's the bell. Perhaps I had better go.

NORA. No no; do stay! It's probably just someone for Torvald.

HELENE. [In the doorway.] Excuse me, Ma'am; there's a gentleman asking for Mr. Helmer—but the doctor's in there—and I didn't know if I should disturb him—

NORA. Who is it?

KROGSTAD. [In the doorway.] It is I, Mrs. Helmer.

[Mrs. Linde starts and turns away to the window.]

NORA. [Goes a step toward him, anxiously; in a low voice.] You? What is it? Why do you want to see my husband?

KROGSTAD. It's to do with Bank business—more or less. I have a small position in the Joint Stock Bank, and I hear your husband is to be the new president.

NORA. Then it's just—?

KROGSTAD. Just routine business, Mrs. Helmer; nothing else.

NORA. Then, please be good enough to go into his study.

[Krogstad goes. She bows indifferently while she closes the door into the hall. Then she goes to the stove and tends the fire.]

MRS. LINDE. Who was that man, Nora?

NORA. A Mr. Krogstad—he's a lawyer.

MRS. LINDE. I was right then.

NORA. Do you know him?

MRS. LINDE. I used to know him—many years ago. He worked in a law office in our town.

NORA. Yes, so he did.

MRS. LINDE. How he has changed!

NORA. He was unhappily married, they say.

MRS. LINDE. Is he a widower now?

NORA. Yes—with lots of children. There! That's better! [She closes the door of the stove and moves the rocking chair a little to one side.]

MRS. LINDE. I'm told he's mixed up in a lot of rather questionable business.

NORA. He may be; I really don't know. But don't let's talk about business—it's so tiresome.

[Dr. Rank comes out of Helmer's room.]

RANK. [Still in the doorway.] No, no, I won't disturb you. I'll go in and see your wife for a moment. [Sees Mrs. Linde.] Oh, I beg your pardon. I seem to be in the way here, too.

NORA. Of course not! [Introduces them.] Dr. Rank—Mrs. Linde.

RANK. Well, well, I've often heard that name mentioned in this house; didn't I pass you on the stairs when I came in?

MRS. LINDE. Yes; I'm afraid I climb them very slowly. They wear me out!

RANK. A little on the delicate side—eh?

MRS. LINDE. No; just a bit overtired.

RANK. I see. So I suppose you've come to town for a good rest—on a round of dissipation!

MRS. LINDE. I have come to look for work.

RANK. Is that the best remedy for tiredness?

MRS. LINDE. One has to live, Doctor.

RANK. Yes, I'm told that's necessary.

NORA. Oh, come now, Dr. Rank! You're not above wanting to live yourself!

RANK. That's true enough. No matter how wretched I may be, I still want to hang on as long as possible. All my patients have that feeling too. Even the *morally* sick seem to share it. There's a wreck of a man in there with Helmer now—

MRS. LINDE. [Softly.] Ah!

NORA. Whom do you mean?

RANK. A fellow named Krogstad, he's a lawyer—you wouldn't know anything about him. He's thoroughly depraved—rotten to the core—Yet even he declared, as though it were a matter of paramount importance, that he must live.

NORA. Really? What did he want with Torvald?

RANK. I've no idea; I gathered it was some Bank business.

NORA. I didn't know that Krog—that this man Krogstad had anything to do with the Bank?

RANK. He seems to have some sort of position there. [To Mrs. Linde.] I don't know if this is true in your part of the country—but there are men who make it a practice of prying about in other people's business, searching for individuals of doubtful character—and having discovered their secret, place them in positions of trust, where they can keep an eye on them, and make use of them at will. Honest men—men of strong moral fiber—they leave out in the cold.

MRS. LINDE. Perhaps the weaklings need more help.

RANK. [Shrugs his shoulders.] That point-of-view is fast turning society into a clinic.

[Nora, deep in her own thoughts, breaks into half-stifled laughter and claps her hands.]

RANK. Why should that make you laugh? I wonder if you've any idea what "society" is?

NORA. Why should I care about your tiresome old "society"? I was laughing at something quite different—something frightfully amusing. Tell me, Dr. Rank—will all the employees at the Bank be dependent on Torvald now?

RANK. Is *that* what strikes you as so amusing?

NORA. [Smiles and hums.] Never you mind! Never you mind! [Walks about the room.] What fun to think that we—that Torvald—has such power over so many people. [Takes the bag from her pocket.] Dr. Rank, how about a macaroon?

RANK. Well, well—Macaroons, eh? I thought they were forbidden here.

NORA. These are some Kristine brought—

MRS. LINDE. What! I—

NORA. Now, you needn't be so frightened. How could you possibly know that Torvald had forbidden them? He's afraid they'll spoil my teeth. Oh, well—just for once! Don't you agree, Dr. Rank? There you are! [Puts a macaroon into his mouth.] You must have one too, Kristine. And I'll have just one—just a tiny one, or at most two. [Walks about again.] Oh dear, I am so happy! There's just one thing in all the world that would give me the greatest pleasure.

RANK. What's that?

NORA. It's something I long to say in front of Torvald.

RANK. What's to prevent you?

NORA. Oh, I don't dare; it isn't nice.

MRS. LINDE. Not nice?

RANK. It might be unwise, then; but you can certainly say it to us. What is it you so long to say in front of Torvald?

NORA. I'd so love to say "Damn!—damn!—damn it all!"

RANK. Have you gone crazy?

MRS. LINDE. Good gracious, Nora—

RANK. Go ahead and say it—here he comes!

NORA. [Hides the macaroons.] Hush—sh—sh.

[Helmer comes out of his room; he carries his hat and overcoat.]

NORA. [Going to him.] Well, Torvald, dear, did you get rid of him?

HELMER. He has just gone.

NORA. Let me introduce you—this is Kristine, who has just arrived in town—

HELMER. Kristine? I'm sorry—but I really don't—

NORA. Mrs. Linde, Torvald, dear—Kristine Linde.

HELMER. Oh yes! I suppose you're one of my wife's school friends?

MRS. LINDE. Yes; we knew each other as children.

NORA. Imagine, Torvald! She came all that long way just to talk to you.

HELMER. How do you mean?

MRS. LINDE. Well, it wasn't exactly—

NORA. Kristine is tremendously good at office-work, and her great dream is to get a position with a really clever man—so she can improve still more, you see—

HELMER. Very sensible, Mrs. Linde.

NORA. And when she heard that you had become president of the Bank—it was in the paper, you know—she started off at once; you *will* try and do something for Kristine, won't you. Torvald? For my sake?

HELMER. It's by no means impossible. You're a widow, I presume?

MRS. LINDE. Yes.

HELMER. And you've already had business experience?

MRS. LINDE. A good deal.

HELMER. Then, I think it's quite likely I may be able to find a place for you.

NORA. [Clapping her hands.] There, you see! You see!

HELMER. You have come at a good moment, Mrs. Linde.

MRS. LINDE. How can I ever thank you—?

HELMER. [Smiling.] Don't mention it. [Puts on his overcoat.] But just now, I'm afraid you must excuse me—

RANK. I'll go with you. [Fetches his fur coat from the hall and warms it at the stove.]

NORA. Don't be long, Torvald, dear.

HELMER. I shan't be more than an hour.

NORA. Are you going too, Kristine?

MRS. LINDE. *[Putting on her outdoor things.]* Yes; I must go and find a place to live.

HELMER. We can all go out together.

NORA. *[Helping her.]* How tiresome that we're so cramped for room, Kristine; otherwise—

MRS. LINDE. Oh, you mustn't think of that! Good bye, dear Nora, and thanks for everything.

NORA. Good bye for the present. Of course you'll come back this evening. And you too, Dr. Rank—eh? If you're well enough? But of course you'll be well enough! Wrap up warmly now! *[They go out talking, into the hall; children's voices are heard on the stairs.]* Here they come! Here they come! *[She runs to the outer door and opens it. The nurse, Anne-Marie, enters the hall with the children.]* Come in, come in—you darlings! Just look at them, Kristine. Aren't they sweet?

RANK. No chattering in this awful draught!

HELMER. Come along, Mrs. Linde; you have to be a mother to put up with this!

[Dr. Rank, Helmer, and Mrs. Linde go down the stairs; Anne-Marie enters the room with the children; Nora comes in too, shutting the door behind her.]

NORA. How fresh and bright you look! And what red cheeks! Like apples and roses. *[The children chatter to her during what follows.]* Did you have a good time? Splendid! You gave Emmy and Bob a ride on your sled? Both at once? You *are* a clever boy, Ivar! Let me hold her for a bit, Anne-Marie. My darling little doll-baby. *[Takes the smallest from the nurse and dances with her.]* All right, Bobbie! Mama will dance with you too. You threw snow-balls, did you? I should have been in on that! Never mind, Anne; I'll undress them myself—oh, do let me—it's such fun. Go on into the nursery, you look half-frozen. There's some hot coffee in there on the stove. *[The nurse goes into the room on the left. Nora takes off the children's things and throws them down anywhere, while the children all talk together.]* Not really! You were chased by a big dog? But he didn't bite you? No; dogs don't bite tiny little doll-babies! Don't touch the packages, Ivar. What's in them? Wouldn't you like to know! No. No! Careful! It might bite! Come on, let's play. What will we play? Hide-and-seek? Let's play hide-and-seek. Bob, you hide first! Do you want me to? All right! I'll hide first then.

[She and the children play, laughing and shouting, all over the room and in the adjacent room to the left. Finally Nora hides under the table; the children come rushing in, look for her, but cannot find her, hear her half-suppressed laughter, rush to the table, lift up the cover and see her. Loud shouts of delight. She creeps out, as though to frighten them. More shouts. Meanwhile there has been a knock at the door leading into the hall. No one has heard it. Now the door is half-opened and Krogstad appears. He waits a little—the game continues.]

KROGSTAD. I beg your pardon, Mrs. Helmer—

NORA. *[With a stifled scream, turns round and half jumps up.]* Oh! What do you want?

KROGSTAD. Excuse me; the outer door was ajar—someone must have forgotten to close it—

NORA. *[Standing up.]* My husband is not at home, Mr. Krogstad.

KROGSTAD. I know that.

NORA. Then, what do you want here?

KROGSTAD. I want a few words with you.

NORA. With—? *[To the children, softly.]* Go in to Anne-Marie. What? No—the strange man won't do Mama any harm; when he's gone we'll go on playing. *[She leads the children into the right hand room, and shuts the door behind them; uneasy, in suspense.]* You want to speak to me?

KROGSTAD. Yes, I do.

NORA. Today? But it's not the first of the month yet—

KROGSTAD. No, it is Christmas Eve. It's up to you whether your Christmas is a merry one.

NORA. What is it you want? Today I can't possibly—

KROGSTAD. That doesn't concern me for the moment. This is about something else. You have a few minutes, haven't you?

NORA. I suppose so; although—

KROGSTAD. Good. I was sitting in the restaurant opposite, and I saw your husband go down the street—

NORA. Well?

KROGSTAD. —with a lady.

NORA. What of it?

KROGSTAD. May I ask if that lady was a Mrs. Linde?

NORA. Yes.

KROGSTAD. She's just come to town, hasn't she?

NORA. Yes. Today.

KROGSTAD. Is she a good friend of yours?

NORA. Yes, she is. But I can't imagine—

KROGSTAD. I used to know her too.

NORA. Yes, I know you did.

KROGSTAD. Then you know all about it. I thought as much. Now, tell me: is Mrs. Linde to have a place in the Bank?

NORA. How dare you question me like this, Mr. Krogstad—you, one of my husband's employees! But since you ask—you might as well know. Yes, Mrs. Linde is to have a position at the Bank, and it is I who recommended her. Does that satisfy you, Mr. Krogstad?

KROGSTAD. I was right, then.

NORA. [Walks up and down.] After all, one has a little influence, now and then. Even if one is only a woman it doesn't always follow that—people in subordinate positions, Mr. Krogstad, ought really to be careful how they offend anyone who—h'm—

KROGSTAD. —has influence?

NORA. Precisely.

KROGSTAD. [Taking another tone.] Then perhaps you'll be so kind, Mrs. Helmer, as to use your influence on *my* behalf?

NORA. What? How do you mean?

KROGSTAD. Perhaps you'll be good enough to see that I *retain* my subordinate position?

NORA. But, I don't understand. Who wants to take it from you?

KROGSTAD. Oh, don't try and play the innocent! I can well understand that it would be unpleasant for your friend to associate with me; and I understand too, whom I have to thank for my dismissal.

NORA. But I assure you—

KROGSTAD. Never mind all that—there is still time. But I advise you to use your influence to prevent this.

NORA. But Mr. Krogstad, I *have* no influence—absolutely none!

KROGSTAD. Indeed! I thought you just told me yourself—

NORA. You misunderstood me—*really* you did! You must know my husband would never be influenced by me!

KROGSTAD. Your husband and I were at the University together—I know him well. I don't suppose he's any more inflexible than other married men.

NORA. Don't you dare talk disrespectfully about my husband, or I'll show you the door!

KROGSTAD. The little lady's plucky.

NORA. I'm no longer afraid of you. I'll soon be free of all this—after the first of the year.

KROGSTAD. [In a more controlled manner.] Listen to me, Mrs. Helmer. This is a matter of life and death to me. I warn you I shall fight with all my might to keep my position in the Bank.

NORA. So it seems.

KROGSTAD. It's not just the salary; that is the least important part of it—It's something else—Well, I might as well be frank with you. I suppose you know, like everyone else, that once—a long time ago—I got into quite a bit of trouble.

NORA. I have heard something about it, I believe.

KROGSTAD. The matter never came to court; but from that time on, all doors were closed to me. I then went into the business with which you are familiar. I had to do something; and I don't think I've been among the worst. But now I must get away from all that. My sons are growing up, you see; for their sake I'm determined to recapture my good name. This position in the Bank was to be the first step; and now your husband wants to kick me back into the mud again.

NORA. But I tell you, Mr. Krogstad, it's not in my power to help you.

KROGSTAD. Only because you don't really want to; but I can compel you to do it, if I choose.

NORA. You wouldn't tell my husband that I owe you money?

KROGSTAD. And suppose I were to?

NORA. But that would be an outrageous thing to do! [With tears in her voice.] My secret—that I've guarded with such pride—such joy! I couldn't bear to have him find it out in such an ugly, hateful way—to have him find it out from you! I couldn't bear it! It would be too horribly unpleasant!

KROGSTAD. Only unpleasant, Mrs. Helmer?

NORA. [Vehemently.] But just you do it! You'll be the one to suffer; for then my husband will *really* know the kind of man you are—there'll be no chance of keeping your job then!

KROGSTAD. Didn't you hear my question? I asked if it were only unpleasantness you feared?

NORA. If my husband got to know about it, he'd naturally pay you off at once, and then we'd have nothing more to do with you.

KROGSTAD. [Takes a step towards her.] Listen, Mrs. Helmer: Either you have a very bad memory, or you know nothing about business. I think I'd better make the position clear to you.

NORA. What do you mean?

KROGSTAD. When your husband fell ill, you came to me to borrow twelve hundred dollars.

NORA. I didn't know what else to do.

KROGSTAD. I promised to find you the money—

NORA. And you did find it.

KROGSTAD. I promised to find you the money, on certain conditions. At that time you were so taken up with your husband's illness and so anxious to procure the money for your journey, that you probably did not give much thought to details. Perhaps I'd better remind you of them. I promised to find you the amount in exchange for a note, which I drew up.

NORA. Yes, and I signed it.

KROGSTAD. Very good. But then I added a clause, stating that your father would stand sponsor for the debt. This clause your father was to have signed.

NORA. Was to—? He did sign it.

KROGSTAD. I left the date blank, so that your father himself should date his signature. You recall that?

NORA. Yes, I believe—

KROGSTAD. Then I gave you the paper, and you were to mail it to your father. Isn't that so?

NORA. Yes.

KROGSTAD. And you must have mailed it at once; for five or six days later you brought me back the document with your father's signature; and then I handed you the money.

NORA. Well? Haven't I made my payments punctually?

KROGSTAD. Fairly—yes. But to return to the point: That was a sad time for you, wasn't it, Mrs. Helmer?

NORA. It was indeed!

KROGSTAD. Your father was very ill, I believe?

NORA. Yes—he was dying.

KROGSTAD. And he did die soon after, didn't he?

NORA. Yes.

KROGSTAD. Now tell me, Mrs. Helmer: Do you happen to recollect the date of your father's death: the day of the month, I mean?

NORA. Father died on the 29th of September.

KROGSTAD. Quite correct. I have made inquiries. Now here is a strange thing, Mrs. Helmer— *[Produces a paper.]* something rather hard to explain.

NORA. What do you mean? What strange thing?

KROGSTAD. The strange thing about it is, that your father seems to have signed this paper three days after his death!

NORA. I don't understand—

KROGSTAD. Your father died on the 29th of September. But look at this: his signature is dated October 2nd! Isn't that rather strange, Mrs. Helmer? *[Nora is silent.]* Can you explain that to me? *[Nora continues silent.]* It is curious, too, that the words 'October 2nd' and the year are not in your father's handwriting, but in a handwriting I seem to know. This could easily be explained, however; your father might have forgotten to date his signature, and someone might have added the date at random, before the fact of your father's death was known. There is nothing wrong in that. It all depends on the signature itself. It is of course genuine, Mrs. Helmer? It was your father himself who wrote his name here?

NORA. *[After a short silence, throws her head back and looks defiantly at him.]* No, it wasn't. *I* wrote father's name.

KROGSTAD. I suppose you realize, Mrs. Helmer, what a dangerous confession that is?

NORA. Why should it be dangerous? You will get your money soon enough!

KROGSTAD. I'd like to ask you a question: Why didn't you send the paper to your father?

NORA. It was impossible. Father was too ill. If I had asked him for his signature, he'd have wanted to know what the money was for. In his condition I simply could not tell him that my husband's life was in danger. That's why it was impossible.

KROGSTAD. Then wouldn't it have been wiser to give up the journey?

NORA. How could I? That journey was to save my husband's life. I simply couldn't give it up.

KROGSTAD. And it never occurred to you that you weren't being honest with me?

NORA. I really couldn't concern myself with that. You meant nothing to me—In fact I couldn't help disliking you for making it all so difficult—with your cold, business-like clauses and conditions—when you knew my husband's life was at stake.

KROGSTAD. You evidently haven't the faintest idea, Mrs. Helmer, what you have been guilty of. Yet let me tell you that it was nothing more and nothing worse that made me an outcast from society.

NORA. You don't expect me to believe that you ever did a brave thing to save your wife's life?

KROGSTAD. The law takes no account of motives.

NORA. It must be a very bad law, then!

KROGSTAD. Bad or not, if I produce this document in court, you will be condemned according to the law.

NORA. I don't believe that for a minute. Do you mean to tell me that a daughter has no right to spare her dying father worry and anxiety? Or that a wife has no right to save her husband's life? I may not know much about it—but I'm sure there must be something or other in the law that permits such things. You as a lawyer should be aware of that. You don't seem to know very much about the law, Mr. Krogstad.

KROGSTAD. Possibly not. But business—the kind of business we are concerned with—I *do* know something about. Don't you agree? Very well, then; do as you please. But I warn you: if I am made to suffer a second time, you shall keep me company. *[Bows and goes out through the hall.]*

NORA. *[Stands a while thinking, then tosses her head.]* What nonsense! He's just trying to frighten me. I'm not such a fool as all that! *[Begins folding the children's clothes. Pauses.]* And yet—? No, it's impossible! After all—I only did it for love's sake.

CHILDREN. *[At the door, left.]* Mamma, the strange man has gone now.

NORA. Yes, yes, I know. But don't tell anyone about the strange man. Do you hear? Not even Papa!

CHILDREN. No, Mamma; now will you play with us again?

NORA. No, not just now.

CHILDREN. But Mamma! You promised!

NORA. But I can't just now. Run back to the nursery; I have so much to do. Run along now! Run along, my darlings! *[She pushes them gently into the inner room, and closes the door behind them. Sits on the sofa, embroiders a few stitches, but soon pauses.]* No! *[Throws down the work, rises, goes to the hall door and calls out.]* Helene, bring the tree in to me, will you? *[Goes to table, right, and opens the drawer; again pauses.]* No, it's utterly impossible!

HELENE. *[Carries in the Christmas tree.]* Where shall I put it, Ma'am?

NORA. Right there; in the middle of the room.

HELENE. Is there anything else you need?

NORA. No, thanks; I have everything.

[Helene having put down the tree, goes out.]

NORA. *[Busy dressing the tree.]* We'll put a candle here—and some flowers here—that dreadful man! But it's just nonsense! There's nothing to worry about. The tree will be lovely. I'll do everything to please you, Torvald; I'll sing for you, I'll dance for you—

[Enter Helmer by the hall door, with a bundle of documents.]

NORA. Oh! You're back already?

HELMER. Yes. Has somebody been here?

NORA. No. Nobody.

HELMER. That's odd. I just saw Krogstad leave the house.

NORA. Really? Well—as a matter of fact—Krogstad was here for a moment.

HELMER. Nora—I can tell by your manner—he came here to ask you to put in a good word for him, didn't he?

NORA. Yes, Torvald.

HELMER. And you weren't supposed to tell me he'd been here— You were to do it as if of your own accord—isn't that it?

NORA. Yes, Torvald; but—

HELMER. Nora, Nora! How could you consent to such a thing! To have dealings with a man like that—make him promises! And then to lie about it too!

NORA. Lie!

HELMER. Didn't you tell me that nobody had been here? *[Threatens with his finger.]* My little bird must never do that again! A song-bird must sing clear and true! No false notes! *[Puts arm around her.]* Isn't that the way it should be? Of course it is! *[Lets her go.]* And now we'll say no more about it. *[Sits down before the fire.]* It's so cozy and peaceful here! *[Glances through the documents.]*

NORA. *[Busy with the tree, after a short silence.]* Torvald!

HELMER. Yes.

NORA. I'm so looking forward to the Stenborgs' fancy dress party, day after tomorrow.

HELMER. And I can't wait to see what surprise you have in store for me.

NORA. Oh, it's so awful, Torvald!

HELMER. *What* is?

NORA. I can't think of anything amusing. Everything seems so silly, so pointless.

HELMER. Has my little Nora come to *that* conclusion?

NORA. *[Behind his chair, with her arms on the back.]* Are you very busy, Torvald?

HELMER. Well—

NORA. What are all those papers?

HELMER. Just Bank business.

NORA. Already!

HELMER. The board of directors has given me full authority to do some reorganizing—to make a few necessary changes in the staff. I'll have to work on it during Christmas week. I want it all settled by the New Year.

NORA. I see. So that was why that poor Krogstad—

HELMER. H'm.

NORA. *[Still leaning over the chair-back and slowly stroking his hair.]* If you weren't so very busy, I'd ask you to do me a great, great favor, Torvald.

HELMER. Well, let's hear it! Out with it!

NORA. You have such perfect taste, Torvald; and I do so want to look well at the fancy dress ball. Couldn't you take me in hand, and decide what I'm to be, and arrange my costume for me?

HELMER. Well, well! So we're not so self-sufficient after all! We need a helping hand, do we?

NORA. Oh, please, Torvald! I know I shall *never* manage without your help!

HELMER. I'll think about it; we'll hit on something.

NORA. Oh, how sweet of you! *[Goes to the tree again; pause.]* Those red flowers show up beautifully! Tell me, Torvald; did that Krogstad do something very wrong?

HELMER. He committed forgery. Have you any idea of what that means?

NORA. Perhaps he did it out of necessity?

HELMER. Or perhaps he was just fool-hardy, like so many others. I am not so harsh as to condemn a man irrevocably for one mistake.

NORA. No of course not!

HELMER. A man has a chance to rehabilitate himself, if he honestly admits his guilt and takes his punishment.

NORA. Punishment—

HELMER. But that wasn't Krogstad's way. He resorted to tricks and evasions; became thoroughly demoralized.

NORA. You really think it would—?

HELMER. When a man has that sort of thing on his conscience his life becomes a tissue of lies and deception. He's forced to wear a mask—even with those nearest to him—his own wife and children even. And the children—that's the worst part of it, Nora.

NORA. Why?

HELMER. Because the whole atmosphere of the home would be contaminated. The very air the children breathed would be filled with evil.

NORA. *[Closer behind him.]* Are you sure of that?

HELMER. As a lawyer, I know it from experience. Almost all cases of early delinquency can be traced to dishonest mothers.

NORA. Why—only mothers?

HELMER. It usually stems from the mother's side; but of course it can come from the father too. We lawyers know a lot about such things. And this Krogstad has been deliberately poisoning his own children for years, by surrounding them with lies and hypocrisy—that is why I call him demoralized. *[Holds out both hands to her.]* So my sweet little Nora must promise not to plead his cause. Shake hands on it. Well? What's the matter? Give me your hand. There! That's all settled. I assure you it would have been impossible for me to work with him. It literally gives me a feeling of physical discomfort to come in contact with such people. *[Nora draws her hand away, and moves to the other side of the Christmas tree.]*

NORA. It's so warm here. And I have such a lot to do.

HELMER. *[Rises and gathers up his papers.]* I must try and look through some of these papers before dinner. I'll give some thought to your costume too. Perhaps I may even find something to hang in gilt paper on the Christmas tree! *[Lays his hand on her head.]* My own precious little song-bird! *[He goes into his study and closes the door after him.]*

NORA. *[Softly, after a pause.]* It can't be—! It's impossible. Of course it's impossible!

ANNE-MARIE. *[At the door, left.]* The babies keep begging to come in and see Mamma.

NORA. No, no! Don't let them come to me! Keep them with you, Anne-Marie.

ANNE-MARIE. Very well, Ma'am. *[Shuts the door.]*

NORA. *[Pale with terror.]* Harm my children!— Corrupt my home! *[Short pause. She throws back her head.]* It's not true! I know it's not! It could never, never be true!

CURTAIN

Act II

SCENE: The same room. In the corner, beside the piano, stands the Christmas tree, stripped and with the candles burnt out. Nora's outdoor things lie on the sofa. Nora, alone, is walking about restlessly. At last she stops by the sofa, and picks up her cloak.

NORA. *[Puts the cloak down again.]* Did someone come in? *[Goes to the hall and listens.]* No; no one; of course no one will come today, Christmas Day; nor tomorrow either. But perhaps— *[Opens the door and looks out.]* No, there's nothing in the mail-box; it's quite empty. *[Comes forward.]* Oh nonsense! He only meant to frighten me. There won't be any trouble. It's all impossible! Why, I—I have three little children!

[Anne-Marie enters from the left, with a large cardboard box.]

ANNE-MARIE. Well—I found the box with the fancy dress clothes at last, Miss Nora.

NORA. Thanks; put it on the table.

ANNE-MARIE. *[Does so.]* I'm afraid they're rather shabby.

NORA. If I had my way I'd tear them into a thousand pieces!

ANNE-MARIE. Good gracious! They can be repaired—just have a little patience.

NORA. I'll go and get Mrs. Linde to help me.

ANNE-MARIE. I wouldn't go out again in this awful weather! You might catch cold, Miss Nora, and get sick.

NORA. Worse things might happen—How are the children?

ANNE-MARIE. The poor little things are playing with their Christmas presents; but—

NORA. Have they asked for me?

ANNE-MARIE. They're so used to having Mamma with them.

NORA. I know, but, you see, Anne-Marie, I won't be able to be with them as much as I used to.

ANN-MARIE. Well, little children soon get used to anything.

NORA. You really think so? Would they forget me if I went away for good?

ANNE-MARIE. Good gracious!—for good!

NORA. Tell me something, Anne-Marie—I've so often wondered about it—how could you bear to part with your child—give it up to strangers?

ANNE-MARIE. Well, you see, I had to—when I came to nurse my little Nora.

NORA. Yes—but how could you *bear* to do it?

ANNE-MARIE. I couldn't afford to say "no" to such a good position. A poor girl who's been in trouble must take what comes. Of course *he* never offered to help me—the wicked sinner!

NORA. Then I suppose your daughter has forgotten all about you.

ANNE-MARIE. No—indeed she hasn't! She even wrote to me— once when she was confirmed and again when she was married.

NORA. *[Embracing her.]* Dear old Anne-Marie—you were a good mother to me when I was little.

ANNE-MARIE. But then my poor little Nora *had* no mother of her own!

NORA. And if ever my little ones were left without—you'd look after them, wouldn't you?—Oh, that's just nonsense! *[Opens the box.]* Go back to them. Now I must—Just you wait and see how lovely I'll look tomorrow!

ANNE-MARIE. My Miss Nora will be the prettiest person there! *[She goes into the room on the left.]*

NORA. *[Takes the costume out of the box, but soon throws it down again.]* I wish I dared go out—I'm afraid someone might come. I'm afraid something might happen while I'm gone. That's just silly! No one will come, I must try not to think— This muff needs cleaning. What pretty gloves— they're lovely! I must put it out of my head! One, two, three, four, five, six—*[With a scream.]* Ah! They're here!

[Goes toward the door, then stands irresolute. Mrs. Linde enters from the hall, where she has taken off her things.]

NORA. Oh, it's you, Kristine! There's no one else out there, is there? I'm so glad you have come!

MRS. LINDE. I got a message you'd been asking for me.

NORA. Yes, I just happened to be passing by. There's something I want you to help me with. Sit down here on the sofa. Now, listen: There's to be a fancy dress ball at the Stenborgs' tomorrow evening—they live just overhead—

and Torvald wants me to go as a Neapolitan peasant girl, and dance the tarantella; I learned it while we were in Capri.

MRS. LINDE. So you're going to give a real performance, are you?

NORA. Torvald wants me to. Look, here's the costume; Torvald had it made for me down there. But it's all torn, Kristine, and I don't know whether—

MRS. LINDE. Oh, we'll soon fix that. It's only the trimming that has come loose here and there. Have you a needle and thread? Oh, yes. Here's everything I need.

NORA. It's awfully good of you!

MRS. LINDE. *[Sewing.]* So you're going to be all dressed up, Nora—what fun! You know—I think I'll run in for a moment—just to see you in your costume— I haven't really thanked you for last night. I had such a happy time!

NORA. *[Rises and walks across the room.]* Somehow it didn't seem as nice to me as usual. I wish you'd come to town a little earlier, Kristine. Yes— Torvald has a way of making things so gay and cozy.

MRS. LINDE. Well—so have you. That's your father coming out in you! But tell me—is Doctor Rank always so depressed?

NORA. No; last night it was worse than usual. He's terribly ill, you see—tuberculosis of the spine, or something. His father was a frightful man, who kept mistresses and all that sort of thing— that's why his son has been an invalid from birth—

MRS. LINDE. *[Lets her sewing fall into her lap.]* Why, Nora! what do you know about such things?

NORA. *[Moving about the room.]* After all—I've had three children; and those women who look after one at childbirth know almost as much as doctors; and they love to gossip.

MRS. LINDE. *[Goes on sewing; a short pause.]* Does Doctor Rank come here every day?

NORA. Every single day. He's Torvald's best friend, you know— always has been; and he's *my* friend too. He's almost like one of the family.

MRS. LINDE. Do you think he's quite sincere, Nora? I mean—isn't he inclined to flatter people?

NORA. Quite the contrary. What gave you that impression?

MRS. LINDE. When you introduced us yesterday he said he had often heard my name mentioned here; but I noticed afterwards that your husband hadn't the faintest notion who I was. How could Doctor Rank—?

NORA. He was quite right, Kristine. You see Torvald loves me so tremendously that he won't share me with anyone; he wants me all to himself, as he says. At first he used to get terribly jealous if I even mentioned any of my old friends back home; so naturally I gave up doing it. But I often talk to Doctor Rank about such things—he likes to hear about them.

MRS. LINDE. Listen to me, Nora! In many ways you are still a child. I'm somewhat older than you, and besides, I've had much more experience. I think you ought to put a stop to all this with Dr. Rank.

NORA. Put a stop to what?

MRS. LINDE. To the whole business. You said something yesterday about a rich admirer who was to give you money—

NORA. One who never existed, unfortunately. Go on.

MRS. LINDE. Has Doctor Rank money?

NORA. Why yes, he has.

MRS. LINDE. And he has no one dependent on him?

NORA. No, no one. But—

MRS. LINDE. And he comes here every single day?

NORA. Yes—I've just told you so.

MRS. LINDE. It's surprising that a sensitive man like that should be so importunate.

NORA. I don't understand you—

MRS. LINDE. Don't try to deceive me, Nora. Don't you suppose I can guess who lent you the twelve hundred dollars?

NORA. You must be out of your mind! How could you ever think such a thing? Why, he's a friend of ours; he comes to see us every day! The situation would have been impossible!

MRS. LINDE. So it wasn't he, then?

NORA. No, I assure you. Such a thing never even occurred to me. Anyway, he didn't have any money at that time; he came into it later.

MRS. LINDE. Perhaps that was just as well, Nora, dear.

NORA. No—it would never have entered my head to ask Dr. Rank—Still—I'm sure that if I did ask him—

MRS. LINDE. But you won't, of course.

NORA. No, of course not. Anyway—I don't see why it should be necessary. But I'm sure that if I talked to Doctor Rank—

MRS. LINDE. Behind your husband's back?

NORA. I want to get that thing cleared up; after all, that's behind his back too. I must get clear of it.

MRS. LINDE. That's just what I said yesterday; but—

NORA. *[Walking up and down.]* It's so much easier for a man to manage things like that—

MRS. LINDE. One's own husband, yes.

NORA. Nonsense. *[Stands still.]* Surely if you pay back everything you owe—the paper is returned to you?

MRS. LINDE. Naturally.

NORA. Then you can tear it into a thousand pieces, and burn it up—the nasty, filthy thing!

MRS. LINDE. *[Looks at her fixedly, lays down her work, and rises slowly.]* Nora, you are hiding something from me.

NORA. You can see it in my face, can't you?

MRS. LINDE. Something's happened to you since yesterday morning, Nora, what is it?

NORA. *[Going towards her.]* Kristine—! *[Listens.]* Hush! Here comes Torvald! Go into the nursery for a little while. Torvald hates anything to do with sewing. Get Anne-Marie to help you.

MRS. LINDE. *[Gathers the things together.]* Very well; but I shan't leave until you have told me all about it. *[She goes out to the left, as Helmer enters from the hall.]*

NORA. *[Runs to meet him.]* Oh, I've missed you so, Torvald, dear!

HELMER. Was that the dressmaker—?

NORA. No, it was Kristine. She's helping me fix my costume. It's going to look so nice.

HELMER. Wasn't that a good idea of mine?

NORA. Splendid! But don't you think it was good of me to let you have your way?

HELMER. Good of you! To let your own husband have his way! There, there, you crazy little thing; I'm only teasing. Now I won't disturb you. You'll have to try the dress on, I suppose.

NORA. Yes—and I expect you've work to do.

HELMER. I have. *[Shows her a bundle of papers.]* Look. I've just come from the Bank—*[Goes towards his room.]*

NORA. Torvald.

HELMER. *[Stopping.]* Yes?

NORA. If your little squirrel were to beg you—with all her heart—

HELMER. Well?

NORA. Would you do something for her?

HELMER. That depends on what it is.

NORA. Be a darling and say 'Yes', Torvald! Your squirrel would skip about and play all sorts of pretty tricks—

HELMER. Well—out with it!

NORA. Your little lark would twitter all day long—

HELMER. She does that anyway!

NORA. I'll pretend to be an elf and dance for you in the moonlight, Torvald.

HELMER. Nora—you're surely not getting back to what we talked about this morning?

NORA. *[Coming nearer.]* Oh, Torvald, dear, I do most humbly beg you—!

HELMER. You have the temerity to bring that up again?

NORA. You must give in to me about this, Torvald! You *must* let Krogstad keep his place!

HELMER. I'm giving his place to Mrs. Linde.

NORA. That's awfully sweet of you. But instead of Krogstad—couldn't you dismiss some other clerk?

HELMER. This is the most incredible obstinacy! Because you were thoughtless enough to promise to put in a good word for him, am I supposed to—?

NORA. That's not the reason, Torvald. It's for your own sake. Didn't you tell me yourself he writes for the most horrible newspapers? He can do you no end of harm. Oh! I'm so afraid of him—

HELMER. I think I understand; you have some unpleasant memories—that's why you're frightened.

NORA. What do you mean?

HELMER. Aren't you thinking of your father?

NORA. Oh, yes—of course! You remember how those awful people slandered poor father in the newspapers? If you hadn't been sent to investigate the matter, and been so kind and helpful—he might have been dismissed.

HELMER. My dear Nora, there is a distinct difference between your father and me. Your father's conduct was not entirely unimpeachable. But mine is; and I trust it will remain so.

NORA. You never know what evil-minded people can think up. We could be so happy now, Torvald, in our lovely, peaceful home—you and I and the children! Oh! I implore you, Torvald—!

HELMER. The more you plead his cause the less likely I am to keep him on. It's already known at the Bank that I intend to dismiss Krogstad. If I were to change my mind, people might say I'd done it at the insistence of my wife—

NORA. Well—what of that?

HELMER. Oh, nothing, of course! As long as the obstinate little woman gets her way! I'd simply be the laughing-stock of the whole staff; they'd think I was weak and easily influenced—I should soon be made to feel the consequences. Besides—there is one factor that makes it quite impossible for Krogstad to work at the Bank as long as I'm head there.

NORA. What could that be?

HELMER. His past record I might be able to overlook—

NORA. Yes, you might, mightn't you, Torvald—?

HELMER. And I'm told he's an excellent worker. But unfortunately we were friendly during our college days. It was one of those impetuous friendships that subsequently often prove embarrassing. He's tactless enough to call me by my first name—regardless of the circumstances—and feels quite justified in taking a familiar tone with me. At any moment he comes out with "Torvald" this, and "Torvald" that! It's acutely irritating. It would make my position at the Bank intolerable.

NORA. You're surely not serious about this, Torvald?

HELMER. Why not?

NORA. But—it's all so petty.

HELMER. Petty! So you think I'm petty!

NORA. Of course not, Torvald—just the opposite; that's why—

HELMER. Never mind; you call my motives petty; so I must be petty too! Petty! Very well!—We'll put an end to this now—once and for all. [Helmer goes to the door into the hall and calls Helene.]

NORA. What do you want?

HELMER. [Searching among his papers.] I want this thing settled. [Helene enters.] Take this letter, will you? Get a messenger and have him deliver it at once! It's urgent. Here's some money.

HELENE. Very good, Sir. [Goes with the letter.]

HELMER. [Putting his papers together.] There, little Miss Obstinacy.

NORA. [Breathless.] Torvald—what was in that letter?

HELMER. Krogstad's dismissal.

NORA. Call her back, Torvald! There's still time. Call her back! For my sake, for your own sake, for the sake of the children, don't send that letter! Torvald, do you hear? You don't realize what may come of this!

HELMER. It's too late.

NORA. Too late, yes.

HELMER. Nora, dear; I forgive your fears—though it's not exactly flattering to me to think I could ever be afraid of any spiteful nonsense Krogstad might choose to write about me! But I forgive you all the same—it shows how much you love me. [Takes her in his arms.] And that's the way it should be, Nora darling. No matter what happens, you'll see—I have strength and courage for us both. My shoulders are broad—I'll bear the burden.

NORA. [Terror-struck.] How do you mean?

HELMER. The whole burden, my darling. Don't you worry any more.

NORA. [With decision.] No! You mustn't—I won't let you!

HELMER. Then we'll share it, Nora, as man and wife. That is as it should be. [Petting her.] Are you happy now? There! Don't look at me like a frightened little dove! You're just imagining things, you know—Now don't you think you ought to play the tarantella through—and practice your tambourine? I'll go into my study and close both doors, then you won't disturb me. You can make all the noise you like! [Turns round in doorway.] And when Rank comes, just tell him where I am. [He nods to her, and goes with his papers to his room, closing the door.]

NORA. [Bewildered with terror, stands as though rooted to the ground, and whispers.] He'd do it too! He'd do it—in spite of anything! But he mustn't—never, never! Anything but that! There must be some way out! What shall I do? [The hall bell rings.] Dr. Rank—! Anything but that—anything, *any*thing but that!

[Nora draws her hands over her face, pulls herself together, goes to the door and opens it. Rank stands outside hanging up his fur coat. During the following scene, darkness begins to fall.]

NORA. How are you, Doctor Rank? I recognized your ring. You'd better not go in to Torvald just now; I think he's busy.

RANK. How about you? [Enters and closes the door.]

NORA. You know I always have an hour to spare for you.

RANK. Many thanks, I'll make use of that privilege as long as possible.

NORA. What do you mean—as long as possible?

RANK. Does that frighten you?

NORA. No—but it's such a queer expression. Has anything happened?

RANK. I've been expecting it for a long time; but I never thought it would come quite so soon.

NORA. What is it you have found out? Doctor Rank, please tell me!

RANK. [Sitting down by the stove.] I haven't much time left. There's nothing to do about it.

NORA. [With a sigh of relief.] Oh! Then—it's about you—?

RANK. Of course. What did you think? It's no use lying to one's self. I am the most miserable of all my patients, Mrs. Helmer. These past few days I've been taking stock of my position—and I find myself completely bankrupt. Within a month, I shall be rotting in the church-yard.

NORA. What a ghastly way to talk!

RANK. The whole business is pretty ghastly, you see. And the worst of it is, there are so many ghastly things to be gone through before it's over. I've just one last examination to make, then I shall know approximately when the final dissolution will begin. There's something I want to say to you: Helmer's sensitive nature is repelled by anything ugly. I couldn't bear to have him near me when—

NORA. But Doctor Rank—

RANK. No, I couldn't bear it! I won't have him there—I shall bar my door against him—As soon as I am absolutely certain of the worst, I'll send you my visiting-card marked with a black cross; that will mean the final horror has begun.

NORA. Doctor Rank—you're absolutely impossible today! And I did so want you to be in a good humor.

RANK. With death staring me in the face? And why should I have to expiate another's sins! What justice is there in that? Well—I suppose in almost every family there are some such debts that have to be paid.

NORA. [Stopping her ears.] Don't talk such nonsense! Come along! Cheer up!

RANK. One might as well laugh. It's really very funny when you come to think of it—that my poor innocent spine should be made to suffer for my father's exploits!

NORA. [At table, left.] He was much addicted to asparagus-tips and pate de foie gras, wasn't he?

RANK. Yes; and truffles.

NORA. Oh, of course—truffles, yes. And I suppose oysters too?

RANK. Oh, yes! Masses of oysters, certainly!

NORA. And all the wine and champagne that went with them! It does seem a shame that all these pleasant things should be so damaging to the spine, doesn't it?

RANK. Especially when it's a poor miserable spine that never had any of the fun!

NORA. Yes, that's the biggest shame of all!

RANK. [Gives her a searching look.] H'm—

NORA. [A moment later.] Why did you smile?

RANK. No; you were the one that laughed.

NORA. No; you were the one that smiled, Doctor Rank!

RANK. [Gets up.] You're more of a rogue than I thought you were.

NORA. I'm full of mischief today.

RANK. So it seems.

NORA. [With her hands on his shoulders.] Dear, dear Doctor Rank, don't go and die and leave Torvald and me.

RANK. Oh, you won't miss me long! Those who go away—are soon forgotten.

NORA. [Looks at him anxiously.] You really believe that?

RANK. People develop new interests, and soon—

NORA. What do you mean—new interests?

RANK. That'll happen to you and Helmer when I am gone. You seem to have made a good start already. What was that Mrs. Linde doing here last evening?

NORA. You're surely not jealous of poor old Kristine!

RANK. Yes, I am. She will be my successor in this house. When I'm gone she'll probably—

NORA. Sh—hh! She's in there.

RANK. She's here again today? You see!

NORA. She's just helping me with my costume. Good heavens, you *are* in a unreasonable mood! [Sits on sofa.] Now do try to be good, Doctor Rank. Tomorrow you'll see how beautifully I'll dance; and then you can pretend I'm doing it all to please you—and Torvald too, of course—that's understood.

RANK. [After a short silence.] You know—sitting here talking to you so informally—I simply can't imagine what would have become of me, if I had never had this house to come to.

NORA. [Smiling.] You really *do* feel at home with us, don't you?

RANK. [In a low voice—looking straight before him.] And to be obliged to leave it all—

NORA. Nonsense! You're not going to leave anything.

RANK. *[In the same tone.]* And not to be able to leave behind one even the smallest proof of gratitude; at most a fleeting regret—an empty place to be filled by the first person who comes along.

NORA. And supposing I were to ask you for—? No—

RANK. For what?

NORA. For a great proof of your friendship.

RANK. Yes?—Yes?

NORA. No, I mean—if I were to ask you to do me a really tremendous favor—

RANK. You'd really, for once, give me that great happiness?

NORA. Oh, but you don't know what it is.

RANK. Then tell me.

NORA. I don't think I can, Doctor Rank. It's much too much to ask—it's not just a favor—I need your help and advice as well—

RANK. So much the better. I've no conception of what you mean. But tell me about it. You trust me, don't you?

NORA. More than anyone. I know you are my best and truest friend—that's why I can tell you. Well then, Doctor Rank, there is something you must help me prevent. You know how deeply, how intensely Torvald loves me; he wouldn't hesitate for a moment to give up his life for my sake.

RANK. *[Bending towards her.]* Nora—do you think he is the only one who—?

NORA. *[With a slight start.]* Who—what?

RANK. Who would gladly give his life for you?

NORA. *[Sadly.]* I see.

RANK. I was determined that you should know this before I—went away. There'll never be a better chance to tell you. Well, Nora, now you know, and you must know too that you can trust me as you can no one else.

NORA. *[Standing up; simply and calmly.]* Let me get by—

RANK. *[Makes way for her, but remains sitting.]* Nora—

NORA. *[In the doorway.]* Bring in the lamp, Helene. *(Crosses to the stove.)* Oh, dear Doctor Rank, that was really horrid of you.

RANK. *[Rising.]* To love you just as deeply as—as someone else does; is that horrid?

NORA. No—but the fact of your telling me. There was no need to do that.

RANK. What do you mean? Did you know—?

[Helene enters with the lamp; sets it on the table and goes out again.]

RANK. Nora—Mrs. Helmer—tell me, did you know?

NORA. Oh, how do I know what I knew or didn't know. I really can't say—How could you be so clumsy, Doctor Rank? It was all so nice.

RANK. Well, at any rate, you know now that I stand ready to serve you body and soul. So—tell me.

NORA. *[Looking at him]* After this?

RANK. I beg you to tell me what it is.

NORA. I can't tell you anything now.

RANK. But you must! Don't punish me like that! Let me be of use to you; I'll do anything for you—anything within human power.

NORA. You can do nothing for me now. Anyway—I don't really need help. I was just imagining things, you see. Really! That's all it was! *[Sits in the rocking chair, looks at him and smiles.]* Well—you're a nice one, Doctor Rank! Aren't you a bit ashamed, now that the lamp's been lit?

RANK. No; really not. But I suppose I'd better go now—for good?

NORA. You'll do no such thing! You must come here just as you always have. Torvald could never get on without you!

RANK. But how about *you?*

NORA. You know I always love to have you here.

RANK. Yes—I suppose that's what misled me. I can't quite make you out. I've often felt you liked being with me almost as much as being with Helmer.

NORA. Well—you see—There are the people one loves best—and yet there are others one would almost rather *be* with.

RANK. Yes—there's something in that.

NORA. When I was still at home, it was of course Papa whom I loved best. And yet whenever I could, I used to slip down to the servants' quarters. I loved being with them. To begin with, they never lectured me a bit, and it was such fun to hear them talk.

RANK. I see; and now you have me instead!

NORA. *[Jumps up and hurries toward him.]* Oh, dear, darling Doctor Rank. I didn't mean it like that! It's just that now, Torvald comes first—the way Papa did. *You* understand—!

[Helene enters from the hall.]

HELENE. I beg your pardon, Ma'am—*[Whispers to Nora, and gives her a card.]*

NORA. *[Glancing at card.]* Ah! *[Puts it in her pocket.]*

RANK. Anything wrong?

NORA. No, nothing! It's just—it's my new costume—

RANK. Isn't that your costume—there?

NORA. Oh, that one, yes. But this is a different one. It's one I've ordered—Torvald mustn't know—

RANK. So *that's* the great secret!

NORA. Yes, of course it is! Go in and see him, will you? He's in his study. Be sure and keep him there as long as—

RANK. Don't worry; He shan't escape me. *[Goes into Helmer's room.]*

NORA. *[To Helene.]* He's waiting in the kitchen?

HELENE. Yes, he came up the back stairs—

NORA. Why didn't you tell him I was busy?

HELENE. I did, but he insisted.

NORA. He won't go away?

HELENE. Not until he has spoken to you, Ma'am.

NORA. Very well, then; show him in; but quietly, Helene—and don't say a word to anyone; it's about a surprise for my husband.

HELENE. I understand, Ma'am. *[She goes out.]*

NORA. It's coming! It's going to happen after all! No, no! It can't happen. It *can't*!

[She goes to Helmer's door and locks it. Helene opens the hall door for Krogstad, and shuts it after him. He wears a traveling-coat, boots, and a fur cap.]

NORA. *[Goes towards him.]* Talk quietly; my husband is at home.

KROGSTAD. What's that to me?

NORA. What is it you want?

KROGSTAD. I want to make sure of something.

NORA. Well—what is it? Quickly!

KROGSTAD. I suppose you know I've been dismissed.

NORA. I couldn't prevent it, Mr. Krogstad. I did everything in my power, but it was useless.

KROGSTAD. So that's all your husband cares about you! He must realize what I can put you through, and yet, in spite of that, he dares to—

NORA. You don't imagine my husband knows about it?

KROGSTAD. No—I didn't really suppose he did. I can't imagine my friend Torvald Helmer showing that much courage.

NORA. I insist that you show respect when speaking of my husband, Mr. Krogstad!

KROGSTAD. With all due respect, I assure you! But am I right in thinking—since you are so anxious to keep the matter secret—that you have a clearer idea today than you had yesterday, of what you really did?

NORA. Clearer than *you* could ever give me!

KROGSTAD. Of course! I who know so little about the law—!

NORA. What do you want of me?

KROGSTAD. I just wanted to see how you were getting on, Mrs. Helmer. I've been thinking about you all day. You see—even a mere money-lender, a cheap journalist—in short, someone like me—is not entirely without feeling.

NORA. Then prove it; think of my little children.

KROGSTAD. Did you or your husband think of mine? But that's not the point. I only wanted to tell you not to take this matter too seriously. I shan't take any action—for the present, at least.

NORA. You won't, will you? I was sure you wouldn't!

KROGSTAD. It can all be settled quite amicably. It needn't be made public. It needn't go beyond us three.

NORA. But, my husband must never know.

KROGSTAD. How can you prevent it? Can you pay off the balance?

NORA. No, not immediately.

KROGSTAD. Have you any way of raising the money within the next few days?

NORA. None—that I will make use of.

KROGSTAD. And if you had, it would have made no difference. Even if you were to offer me the entire sum in cash—I still wouldn't give you back your note.

NORA. What are you going to do with it?

KROGSTAD. I shall simply keep it—I shall guard it carefully. No one, outside the three of us, shall know a thing about it. So, if you have any thought of doing something desperate—

NORA. I shall.

KROGSTAD.—of running away from home, for instance—

NORA. I shall!

KROGSTAD.—or perhaps even something worse—

NORA. How could you guess that?

KROGSTAD.—then put all such thoughts out of your head.

NORA. How did you know that I had thought of *that*?

KROGSTAD. Most of us think of *that,* at first. I thought of it, too; but I didn't have the courage—

NORA. *[Tonelessly.]* I haven't either.

KROGSTAD. *[Relieved.]* No; you haven't the courage for it either, have you?

NORA. No! I haven't, I haven't!

KROGSTAD. Besides, it would be a very foolish thing to do. You'll just have to get through one domestic storm—and then it'll all be over, I have a letter for your husband, here in my pocket—

NORA. Telling him all about it?

KROGSTAD. Sparing you as much as possible.

NORA. *[Quickly.]* He must never read that letter. Tear it up, Mr. Krogstad! I will manage to get the money somehow—

KROGSTAD. Excuse me, Mrs. Helmer, but I thought I just told you—

NORA. Oh, I'm not talking about the money I owe you. Just tell me how much money you want from my husband—I will get it somehow!

KROGSTAD. I want no money from your husband.

NORA. What *do* you want then?

KROGSTAD. Just this: I want a new start; I want to make something of myself; and your husband shall help me do it. For the past eighteen months my conduct has been irreproachable. It's been a hard struggle—I've lived in abject poverty; still, I was content to work my way up gradually, step by step. But now I've been kicked out, and now I shall not be satisfied to be merely reinstated—taken back on sufferance. I'm determined to make something of myself, I tell you. I intend to continue working in the Bank—but I expect to be promoted. Your husband shall create a new position for me—

NORA. He'll never do it!

KROGSTAD. Oh, yes he will; I know him—he'll do it without a murmur; he wouldn't dare do otherwise. And then—you'll see! Within a year I'll be his right hand man. It'll be Nils Krogstad, not Torvald Helmer, who'll run the Joint Stock Bank.

NORA. That will never happen.

KROGSTAD. No? Would you, perhaps—?

NORA. Yes! I have the courage for it now.

KROGSTAD. You don't frighten me! A dainty, pampered little lady such as you—

NORA. You'll see, you'll see!

KROGSTAD. Yes, I dare say! How would you like to lie there under the ice—in that freezing, pitch-black water? And in the spring your body would be found floating on the surface—hideous, hairless, unrecognizable—

NORA. You can't frighten me!

KROGSTAD. You can't frighten me either. People don't do that sort of thing, Mrs. Helmer. And, anyway, what would be the use? I'd still have your husband in my power.

NORA. You mean—afterwards? Even if I were no longer—?

KROGSTAD. Remember—I'd still have your reputation in my hands! *[Nora stands speechless and looks at him.]* Well, I've given you fair warning. I wouldn't do anything foolish, if I were you. As soon as Helmer receives my letter, I shall expect to hear from him. And just remember this: I've been forced back into my former way of life—and your husband is responsible. I shall never forgive him for it. Good-bye, Mrs. Helmer.

[Goes out through the hall. Nora hurries to the door, opens it a little, and listens.]

NORA. He's gone. He didn't leave the letter. Of course he didn't—that would be impossible! *[Opens the door further and further.]* What's he doing? He's stopped outside the door. He's not going down the stairs. Has he changed his mind? Is he—? *[A letter falls into the box. Krogstad's footsteps are heard gradually receding down the stairs. Nora utters a suppressed shriek, and rushes forward towards the sofa table; pause.]* It's in the letterbox! *[Slips shrinkingly up to the hall door.]* It's there!—Torvald, Torvald—now we are lost!

[Mrs. Linde enters from the left with the costume.]

MRS. LINDE. There, I think it's all right now. If you'll just try it on—?

NORA. *[Hoarsely and softly.]* Come here, Kristine.

MRS. LINDE. *[Throws down the dress on the sofa.]* What's the matter with you? You look upset.

NORA. Come here. Do you see that letter? Do you see it—in the letter-box?

MRS. LINDE. Yes, yes, I see it.

NORA. It's from Krogstad—

MRS. LINDE. Nora—you don't mean Krogstad lent you the money!

NORA. Yes; and now Torvald will know everything.

MRS. LINDE. It'll be much the best thing for you both, Nora.

NORA. But you don't know everything. I committed forgery—

MRS. LINDE. Good heavens!

NORA. Now, listen to me, Kristine; I want you to be my witness—

MRS. LINDE. How do you mean "witness"? What am I to—?

NORA. If I should go out of my mind—that might easily happen—

MRS. LINDE. Nora!

NORA. Or if something should happen to me— something that would prevent my being here—!

MRS. LINDE. Nora, Nora, you're quite beside yourself!

NORA. In case anyone else should insist on taking all the blame upon himself—the whole blame— you understand—

MRS. LINDE. Yes, but what makes you think—?

NORA. Then you must bear witness to the fact that that isn't true. I'm in my right mind now; I know exactly what I'm saying; and I tell you nobody else knew anything about it; I did the whole thing on my own. Just remember that.

MRS. LINDE. Very well—I will. But I don't understand at all.

NORA. No—of course—you couldn't. It's the wonderful thing—It's about to happen, don't you see?

MRS. LINDE. What "wonderful thing"?

NORA. The wonderful—wonderful thing! But it must never be allowed to happen—never. It would be too terrible.

MRS. LINDE. I'll go and talk to Krogstad at once.

NORA. No, don't go to him! He might do you some harm.

MRS. LINDE. There was a time—he would have done anything in the world for me.

NORA. He?

MRS. LINDE. Where does he live?

NORA. How do I know—? Yes—*[Feels in her pocket.]* Here's his card. But the letter, the letter—

HELMER. *[From his study; knocking on the door.]* Nora!

NORA. *[Shrieks in terror.]* Oh! What is it? What do you want?

HELMER. Don't be frightened! We're not coming in; anyway, you've locked the door. Are you trying on?

NORA. Yes, yes, I'm trying on. I'm going to look so pretty, Torvald.

MRS. LINDE. *[Who has read the card.]* He lives just round the corner.

NORA. But it won't do any good. It's too late now. The letter is in the box.

MRS. LINDE. I suppose your husband has the key?

NORA. Of course.

MRS. LINDE. Krogstad must ask for his letter back, unread. He must make up some excuse—

NORA. But this is the time that Torvald usually—

MRS. LINDE. Prevent him. Keep him occupied. I'll come back as quickly as I can. *[She goes out hastily by the hall door.]*

NORA. *[Opens Helmer's door and peeps in.]* Torvald!

HELMER. *[In the study.]* Well? May one venture to come back into one's own living-room? Come along, Rank—now we shall see— *[In the doorway.]* Why—what's this?

NORA. What, Torvald dear?

HELMER. Rank led me to expect some wonderful disguise.

RANK. *[In the doorway.]* That's what I understood. I must have been mistaken.

NORA. Not till tomorrow evening! Then I shall appear in all my splendor!

HELMER. But you look quite tired, Nora, dear. I'm afraid you've been practicing too hard.

NORA. Oh, I haven't practiced at all yet.

HELMER. You ought to, though—

NORA. Yes—I really should, Torvald! But I can't seem to manage without your help. I'm afraid I've forgotten all about it.

HELMER. Well—we'll see what we can do. It'll soon come back to you.

NORA. You will help me, won't you, Torvald? Promise! I feel so nervous—all those people! You must concentrate on me this evening— forget all about business. *Please,* Torvald, dear—promise me you will!

HELMER. I promise. This evening I'll be your slave—you sweet, helpless little thing—! Just one moment, though—I want to see—*[Going to hall door.]*

NORA. What do you want out there?

HELMER. I just want to see if there are any letters.

NORA. Oh, don't, Torvald! Don't bother about that now!

HELMER. Why not?

NORA. *Please* don't, Torvald! There aren't any.

HELMER. Just let me take a look—*[Starts to go.]*

[Nora, at the piano, plays the first bars of the tarantella.]

HELMER. *[Stops in the doorway.]* Aha!

NORA. I shan't be able to dance tomorrow if I don't rehearse with you!

HELMER. *[Going to her.]* Are you really so nervous, Nora, dear?

NORA. Yes, I'm terrified! Let's rehearse right away. We've plenty of time before dinner. Sit down and play for me, Torvald, dear; direct me—guide me; you know how you do!

HELMER. With pleasure, my darling, if you wish me to. *[Sits at piano.]*

[Nora snatches the tambourine out of the box, and hurriedly drapes herself in a long parti-colored shawl; then, with a bound, stands in the middle of the floor and cries out.]

NORA. Now play for me! Now I'll dance!

[Helmer plays and Nora dances. Rank stands at the piano behind Helmer and looks on.]

HELMER. *[Playing.]* Too fast! Too fast!

NORA. I can't help it!

HELMER. Don't be so violent, Nora!

NORA. That's the way it *should* be!

HELMER. *[Stops.]* No, no; this won't do at all!

NORA. *[Laughs and swings her tambourine.]* You see? What did I tell you?

RANK. I'll play for her.

HELMER. *[Rising.]* Yes, do—then I'll be able to direct her.

[Rank sits down at the piano and plays; Nora dances more and more wildly. Helmer stands by the stove and addresses frequent corrections to her; she seems not to hear. Her hair breaks loose, and falls over her shoulders. She does not notice it, but goes on dancing. Mrs. Linde enters and stands spellbound in the doorway.]

MRS. LINDE. Ah—!

NORA. *[Dancing.]* We're having such fun, Kristine!

HELMER. Why, Nora, dear, you're dancing as if your life were at stake!

NORA. It is! It is!

HELMER. Rank, stop! This is absolute madness. Stop, I say!

[Rank stops playing, and Nora comes to a sudden standstill.]

HELMER. *[Going toward her.]* I never would have believed it. You've forgotten everything I ever taught you.

NORA. *[Throws the tambourine away.]* I told you I had!

HELMER. This needs an immense amount of work.

NORA. That's what I said; you see how important it is! You must work with me up to the very last minute. Will you promise me, Torvald?

HELMER. I most certainly will!

NORA. This evening and all day tomorrow you must think of nothing but me. You mustn't open a single letter—mustn't even *look* at the mail-box.

HELMER. Nora! I believe you're still worried about that wretched man—

NORA. Yes—yes, I am!

HELMER. Nora—Look at me—there's a letter from him in the box, isn't there?

NORA. Maybe—I don't know; I believe there is. But you're not to read anything of that sort now; nothing must come between us until the party's over.

RANK. *[Softly, to Helmer.]* Don't go against her.

HELMER. *[Putting his arm around her.]* Very well! The child shall have her way. But tomorrow night, when your dance is over—

NORA. Then you'll be free.

[Helene appears in the doorway, right.]

HELENE. Dinner is served, Ma'am.

NORA. We'll have champagne, Helene.

HELENE. Very good, Ma'am. *[Goes out.]*

HELMER. Quite a feast, I see!

NORA. Yes—a real feast! We'll stay up till dawn drinking champagne! *[Calling out.]* Oh, and we'll have macaroons, Helene—lots of them! Why not—for once?

HELMER. *[Seizing her hand.]* Come, come! Not so violent! Be my own little lark again.

NORA. I will, Torvald. But now—both of you go in—while Kristine helps me with my hair.

RANK. *[Softly, as they go.]* Is anything special the matter? I mean—anything—?

HELMER. No, no; nothing at all. It's just this childish fear I was telling you about. *[They go out to the right.]*

NORA. Well?

MRS. LINDE. He's gone out of town.

NORA. I saw it in your face.

MRS. LINDE. He'll be back tomorrow evening. I left a note for him.

NORA. You shouldn't have bothered. You couldn't prevent it anyway. After all, there's a kind of joy in waiting for the wonderful thing to happen.

MRS. LINDE. I don't understand. What *is* this thing you're waiting for?

NORA. I can't explain. Go in and join them. I'll be there in a moment.

[Mrs. Linde goes into the dining room. Nora stands for a moment as though pulling herself together; then looks at her watch.]

NORA. Five o'clock. Seven hours till midnight. Twenty-four hours till the next midnight and then the tarantella will be over. Twenty-four and seven? I've thirty-one hours left to live.

[Helmer appears at the door, right.]

HELMER. Well! What has become of the little lark?

NORA. *[Runs to him with open arms.]* Here she is!

CURTAIN

Act III

SCENE: The same room. The table, with the chairs around it, has been moved to stage-center. A lighted lamp on the table. The hall door is open. Dance music is heard from the floor above. Mrs. Linde sits by the table absent-mindedly turning the pages of a book. She tries to read, but seems unable to keep her mind on it. Now and then she listens intently and glances towards the hall door.

MRS. LINDE. *[Looks at her watch.]* Where can he be? The time is nearly up. I hope he hasn't—*[Listens again.]* Here he is now. *[She goes into the hall and cautiously opens the outer door; cautious footsteps are heard on the stairs; she whispers.]* Come in; there is no one here.

KROGSTAD. *[In the doorway.]* I found a note from you at home. What does it mean?

MRS. LINDE. I simply *must* speak to you.

KROGSTAD. Indeed? But why here? Why in this house?

MRS. LINDE. I couldn't see you at my place. My room has no separate entrance. Come in; we're quite alone. The servants are asleep, and the Helmers are upstairs at a party.

KROGSTAD. *[Coming into the room.]* Well, well! So the Helmers are dancing tonight, are they?

MRS. LINDE. Why shouldn't they?

KROGSTAD. Well—why not!

MRS. LINDE. Let's have a talk, Krogstad.

KROGSTAD. Have we two anything to talk about?

MRS. LINDE. Yes. A great deal.

KROGSTAD. I shouldn't have thought so.

MRS. LINDE. But then, you see—you have never really understood me.

KROGSTAD. There wasn't much to understand, was there? A woman is heartless enough to break off with a man, when a better match is offered; it's quite an ordinary occurrence.

MRS. LINDE. You really think me heartless? Did you think it was so easy for me?

KROGSTAD. Wasn't it?

MRS. LINDE. You really believed that, Krogstad?

KROGSTAD. If not, why should you have written to me as you did?

MRS. LINDE. What else could I do? Since I was forced to break with you, I felt it was only right to try and kill your love for me.

KROGSTAD. *[Clenching his hands together.]* So that was it! And you did this for money!

MRS. LINDE. Don't forget I had my mother and two little brothers to think of. We couldn't wait for you, Krogstad; things were so unsettled for you then.

KROGSTAD. That may be; but, even so, you had no right to throw me over—not even for their sake.

MRS. LINDE. Who knows? I've often wondered whether I did right or not.

KROGSTAD. *[More softly.]* When I had lost you, I felt the ground crumble beneath my feet. Look at me. I'm like a shipwrecked man clinging to a raft.

MRS. LINDE. Help may be nearer than you think.

KROGSTAD. Help was here! Then you came and stood in the way.

MRS. LINDE. I knew nothing about it, Krogstad. I didn't know until today that I was to replace *you* at the Bank.

KROGSTAD. Very well—I believe you. But now that you do know, will you withdraw?

MRS. LINDE. No; I'd do you no good by doing that.

KROGSTAD. "Good" or not—I'd withdraw all the same.

MRS. LINDE. I have learnt to be prudent, Krogstad—I've had to. The bitter necessities of life have taught me that.

KROGSTAD. And life has taught me not to believe in phrases.

MRS. LINDE. Then life has taught you a very wise lesson. But what about deeds? Surely you must still believe in them?

KROGSTAD. How do you mean?

MRS. LINDE. You just said you were like a shipwrecked man, clinging to a raft.

KROGSTAD. I have good reason to say so.

MRS. LINDE. Well—I'm like a shipwrecked *woman* clinging to a raft. I have no one to mourn for, no one to care for.

KROGSTAD. You made your choice.

MRS. LINDE. I *had* no choice, I tell you!

KROGSTAD. What then?

MRS. LINDE. Since we're both of us shipwrecked, couldn't we join forces, Krogstad?

KROGSTAD. You don't mean—?

MRS. LINDE. Two people on a raft have a better chance than one.

KROGSTAD. Kristine!

MRS. LINDE. Why do you suppose I came here to the city?

KROGSTAD. You mean—you thought of me?

MRS. LINDE. I can't live without work; all my life I've worked, as far back as I can remember; it's always been my one great joy. Now I'm quite alone in the world; my life is empty—aimless. There's not much joy in working for one's self. You could help me, Nils; you could give me something and someone to work for.

KROGSTAD. I can't believe all this. It's an hysterical impulse—a woman's exaggerated craving for self-sacrifice.

MRS. LINDE. When have you ever found me hysterical?

KROGSTAD. You'd really be willing to do this? Tell me honestly—do you quite realize what my past has been?

MRS. LINDE. Yes.

KROGSTAD. And you know what people think of me?

MRS. LINDE. Didn't you just say you'd have been a different person if you'd been with me?

KROGSTAD. I'm sure of it.

MRS. LINDE. Mightn't that still be true?

KROGSTAD. You really mean this, Kristine, don't you? I can see it in your face. Are you sure you have the courage—?

MRS. LINDE. I need someone to care for, and your children need a mother. We two need each other, Nils. I have faith in your fundamental goodness. I'm not afraid.

KROGSTAD. [Seizing her hands.] Thank you—thank you, Kristine. I'll make others believe in me too—I won't fail you! But—I'd almost forgotten—

MRS. LINDE. [Listening.] Hush! The tarantella! You must go!

KROGSTAD. Why? What is it?

MRS. LINDE. Listen! She's begun her dance; as soon as she's finished dancing, they'll be down.

KROGSTAD. Yes—I'd better go. There'd have been no need for all that—but, of course, you don't know what I've done about the Helmers.

MRS. LINDE. Yes, I do, Nils.

KROGSTAD. And yet you have the courage to—?

MRS. LINDE. I know you were desperate—I understand.

KROGSTAD. I'd give anything to undo it!

MRS. LINDE. You can. Your letter's still in the mail-box.

KROGSTAD. Are you sure?

MRS. LINDE. Quite, but—

KROGSTAD. [Giving her a searching look.] Could that be it? You're doing all this to save your friend? You might as well be honest with me! Is that it?

MRS. LINDE. I sold myself once for the sake of others, Nils; I'm not likely to do it again.

KROGSTAD. I'll ask for my letter back unopened.

MRS. LINDE. No, no.

KROGSTAD. Yes, of course. I'll wait till Helmer comes; I'll tell him to give me back the letter—I'll say it refers to my dismissal—and ask him not to read it—

MRS. LINDE. No, Nils; don't ask for it back.

KROGSTAD. But wasn't that actually your reason for getting me to come here?

MRS. LINDE. Yes, in my first moment of fear. But that was twenty-four hours ago, and since then I've seen incredible things happening here. Helmer must know the truth; this wretched business must no longer be kept secret; it's time those two came to a thorough understanding; there's been enough deceit and subterfuge.

KROGSTAD. Very well, if you like to risk it. But there's one thing I can do, and at once—

MRS. LINDE. *[Listening.]* You must go now. Make haste! The dance is over; we're not safe here another moment.

KROGSTAD. I'll wait for you downstairs.

MRS. LINDE. Yes, do; then you can see me home.

KROGSTAD. Kristine! I've never been so happy!

[Krogstad goes out by the outer door. The door between the room and the hall remains open.]

MRS. LINDE. *[Arranging the room and getting her outdoor things together.]* How different things will be! Someone to work for, to live for; a home to make happy! How wonderful it will be to try!—I wish they'd come—[Listens.] Here they are! I'll get my coat—[Takes bonnet and cloak. Helmer's and Nora's voices are heard outside, a key is turned in the lock, and Helmer drags Nora almost by force into the hall. She wears the Italian costume with a large black shawl over it. He is in evening dress and wears a black domino, open.]

NORA. *[Struggling with him in the doorway.]* No, no! I don't want to come home; I want to go upstairs again; I don't want to leave so early!

HELMER. Come—Nora dearest!

NORA. I beg you, Torvald! Please, *please*—just one hour more!

HELMER. Not one single minute more, Nora darling; don't you remember our agreement? Come along in, now; you'll catch cold. *[He leads her gently into the room in spite of her resistance.]*

MRS. LINDE. Good evening.

NORA. Kristine!

HELMER. Why, Mrs. Linde! What are you doing here so late?

MRS. LINDE. Do forgive me. I did so want to see Nora in her costume.

NORA. Have you been waiting for me all this time?

MRS. LINDE. Yes; I came too late to catch you before you went upstairs, and I didn't want to go away without seeing you.

HELMER. *[Taking Nora's shawl off.]* And you *shall* see her, Mrs. Linde! She's worth looking at I can tell you! Isn't she lovely?

MRS. LINDE. Oh, Nora! How perfectly—!

HELMER. Absolutely exquisite, isn't she? That's what everybody said. But she's obstinate as a mule, is my sweet little thing! I don't know what to do with her. Will you believe it, Mrs. Linde, I had to drag her away by force?

NORA. You'll see—you'll be sorry, Torvald, you didn't let me stay, if only for another half-hour.

HELMER. Do you hear that, Mrs. Linde? Now, listen to this: She danced her tarantella to wild applause, and she deserved it, too, I must say— though, perhaps, from an artistic point of view, her interpretation was a bit too realistic. But never mind—the point is, she made a great success, a phenomenal success. Now—should I have allowed her to stay on and spoil the whole effect? Certainly not! I took my sweet little Capri girl—my capricious little Capri girl, I might say—in my arms; a rapid whirl round the room, a low curtsey to all sides, and—as they say in novels—the lovely apparition vanished! An exit should always be effective, Mrs. Linde; but I can't get Nora to see that. Phew! It's warm here. *[Throws his domino on a chair and opens the door to his room.]* Why—there's no light on in here! Oh no, of course— Excuse me—[Goes in and lights candles.]

NORA. *[Whispers breathlessly.]* Well?

MRS. LINDE. *[Softly.]* I've spoken to him.

NORA. And—?

MRS. LINDE. Nora—you must tell your husband everything—

NORA. *[Tonelessly.]* I knew it!

MRS. LINDE. You have nothing to fear from Krogstad; but you must speak out.

NORA. I shan't.

MRS. LINDE. Then the letter will.

NORA. Thank you, Kristine. Now I know what I must do. Hush—!

HELMER. *[Coming back.]* Well, have you finished admiring her, Mrs. Linde?

MRS. LINDE. Yes, and now I must say good-night.

HELMER. Oh—must you be going already? Does this knitting belong to you?

MRS. LINDE. *[Takes it.]* Oh, thank you; I almost forgot it.

HELMER. So you knit, do you?

MRS. LINDE. Yes.

HELMER. Why don't you do embroidery instead?

MRS. LINDE. Why?

HELMER. Because it's so much prettier. Now watch! You hold the embroidery in the left hand—so— and then, in the right hand, you hold the needle, and guide it—so—in a long graceful curve—isn't that right?

MRS. LINDE. Yes, I suppose so—

HELMER. Whereas, knitting can never be anything but ugly. Now, watch! Arms close to your sides, needles going up and down—there's something

Chinese about it!—That really was splendid champagne they gave us.

MRS. LINDE. Well, good-night, Nora; don't be obstinate any more.

HELMER. Well said, Mrs. Linde!

MRS. LINDE. Good-night, Mr. Helmer.

HELMER. *[Accompanying her to the door.]* Good-night, good-night; I hope you get home safely. I'd be only too glad to—but you've such a short way to go. Good-night, good-night. *[She goes; Helmer shuts the door after her and comes forward again.]* Well—thank God we've got rid of her; she's a dreadful bore, that woman.

NORA. You must be tired, Torvald.

HELMER. I? Not in the least.

NORA. But, aren't you sleepy?

HELMER. Not a bit. On the contrary, I feel exceedingly lively. But what about you? You seem to be very tired and sleepy.

NORA. Yes, I am very tired. But I'll soon sleep now.

HELMER. You see! I was right not to let you stay there any longer.

NORA. Everything you do is always right, Torvald.

HELMER. *[Kissing her forehead.]* There's my sweet, sensible little lark! By the way, did you notice how gay Rank was this evening?

NORA. Was he? I didn't get a chance to speak to him.

HELMER. I didn't either, really; but it's a long time since I've seen him in such a jolly mood. *[Gazes at Nora for a while, then comes nearer her.]* It's so lovely to be home again—to be here alone with you. You glorious, fascinating creature!

NORA. Don't look at me like that, Torvald.

HELMER. Why shouldn't I look at my own dearest treasure?—at all this loveliness that is mine, wholly and utterly mine—mine alone!

NORA. *[Goes to the other side of the table.]* You mustn't talk to me like that tonight.

HELMER. *[Following.]* You're still under the spell of the tarantella—and it makes you even more desirable. Listen! The other guests are leaving now. *[More softly.]* Soon the whole house will be still, Nora.

NORA. I hope so.

HELMER. Yes, you do, don't you, my beloved. Do you know something—when I'm out with you among a lot of people—do you know why it is I hardly speak to you, why I keep away from you, and only occasionally steal a quick glance at

you; do you know why that is? It's because I pretend that we love each other in secret, that we're secretly engaged, and that no one suspects there is anything between us.

NORA. Yes, yes; I know your thoughts are always round me.

HELMER. Then, when it's time to leave, and I put your shawl round your smooth, soft, young shoulders—round that beautiful neck of yours—I pretend that you are my young bride, that we've just come from the wedding, and that I'm taking you home for the first time— that for the first time I shall be alone with you—quite alone with you, in all your tremulous beauty. All evening I have been filled with longing for you. As I watched you swaying and whirling in the tarantella—my pulses began to throb until I thought I should go mad; that's why I carried you off—made you leave so early—

NORA. Please go, Torvald! Please leave me. I don't want you like this.

HELMER. What do you mean? You're teasing me, aren't you, little Nora? Not want me—! Aren't I your husband—?

[A knock at the outer door.]

NORA. *[Starts.]* Listen—!

HELMER. *[Going toward the hall.]* Who is it?

RANK. *[Outside.]* It is I; may I come in a moment?

HELMER. *[In a low tone, annoyed.]* Why does he have to bother us now! *[Aloud.]* Just a second! *[Opens door.]* Well! How nice of you to look in.

RANK. I heard your voice, and I thought I'd like to stop in a minute. *[Looks round.]* These dear old rooms! You must be so cozy and happy here, you two!

HELMER. I was just saying how gay and happy you seemed to be, upstairs.

RANK. Why not? Why shouldn't I be? One should get all one can out of life; all one can, for as long as one can. That wine was excellent—

HELMER. Especially the champagne.

RANK. You noticed that, did you? It's incredible how much I managed to get down.

NORA. Torvald drank plenty of it too.

RANK. Oh?

NORA. It always puts him in such a jolly mood.

RANK. Well, why shouldn't one have a jolly evening after a well-spent day?

HELMER. Well-spent! I'm afraid mine wasn't much to boast of!

RANK. [Slapping him on the shoulder.] But mine was, you see?

NORA. Did you by any chance make a scientific investigation, Doctor Rank?

RANK. Precisely.

HELMER. Listen to little Nora, talking about scientific investigations!

NORA. Am I to congratulate you on the result?

RANK. By all means.

NORA. It was good then?

RANK. The best possible, both for the doctor and the patient—certainty.

NORA. [Quickly and searchingly.] Certainty?

RANK. Absolute certainty. Wasn't I right to spend a jolly evening after that?

NORA. You were quite right, Doctor Rank.

HELMER. I quite agree! Provided you don't have to pay for it, tomorrow.

RANK. You don't get anything for nothing in this life.

NORA. You like masquerade parties, don't you, Dr. Rank?

RANK. Very much—when there are plenty of amusing disguises—

NORA. What shall we two be at our next masquerade?

HELMER. Listen to her! Thinking of the next party already!

RANK. We two? I'll tell you. You must go as a precious talisman.

HELMER. How on earth would you dress that!

RANK. That's easy. She'd only have to be herself.

HELMER. Charmingly put. But what about you? Have you decided what you'd be?

RANK. Oh, definitely.

HELMER. Well?

RANK. At the next masquerade party I shall be invisible.

HELMER. That's a funny notion!

RANK. There's a large black cloak—you've heard of the invisible cloak, haven't you? You've only to put it around you and no one can see you any more.

HELMER. [With a suppressed smile.] Quite true!

RANK. But I almost forgot what I came for. Give me a cigar, will you, Helmer? One of the dark Havanas.

HELMER. Of course—with pleasure. [Hands cigar case.]

RANK. [Takes one and cuts the end off.] Thanks.

NORA. [Striking a wax match.] Let me give you a light.

RANK. I thank you. [She holds the match. He lights his cigar at it.] And now. I'll say good-bye!

HELMER. Good-bye, good-bye, my dear fellow.

NORA. Sleep well, Doctor Rank.

RANK. Thanks for the wish.

NORA. Wish me the same.

RANK. You? Very well, since you ask me—Sleep well. And thanks for the light. [He nods to them both and goes out.]

HELMER. [In an undertone.] He's had a lot to drink.

NORA. [Absently.] I dare say. [Helmer takes his bunch of keys from his pocket and goes into the hall.] Torvald! What do you want out there?

HELMER. I'd better empty the mail-box; it's so full there won't be room for the papers in the morning.

NORA. Are you going to work tonight?

HELMER. No—you know I'm not.—Why, what's this? Someone has been at the lock.

NORA. The lock—?

HELMER. Yes—that's funny! I shouldn't have thought that the maids would—Here's a broken hair-pin. Why—it's one of yours, Nora.

NORA. [Quickly.] It must have been the children—

HELMER. You'll have to stop them doing that— There! I got it open at last. [Takes contents out and calls out towards the kitchen.] Helene?—Oh, Helene; put out the lamp in the hall, will you? [He returns with letters in his hand, and shuts the door to the hall.] Just look how they've stacked up. [Looks through them.] Why, what's this?

NORA. [At the window.] The letter! Oh, Torvald! No!

HELMER. Two visiting cards—from Rank.

NORA. From Doctor Rank?

HELMER. [Looking at them.] Doctor Rank, physician. They were right on top. He must have stuck them in just now, as he left.

NORA. Is there anything on them?

HELMER. There's a black cross over his name. Look! What a gruesome thought. Just as if he were announcing his own death.

NORA. And so he is.

HELMER. What do you mean? What do you know about it? Did he tell you anything?

NORA. Yes. These cards mean that he has said good-bye to us for good. Now he'll lock himself up to die.

HELMER. Oh, my poor friend! I always knew he hadn't long to live, but I never dreamed it would be quite so soon—! And to hide away like a wounded animal—

NORA. When the time comes, it's best to go in silence. Don't you think so, Torvald?

HELMER. *[Walking up and down.]* He'd become such a part of us. I can't imagine his having gone for good. With his suffering and loneliness he was like a dark, cloudy background to our lives—it made the sunshine of our happiness seem even brighter—Well, I suppose it's for the best—for him at any rate. *[Stands still.]* And perhaps for us too, Nora. Now we are more than ever dependent on each other. *[Takes her in his arms.]* Oh, my beloved wife! I can't seem to hold you close enough. Do you know something, Nora. I often wish you were in some great danger—so I could risk body and soul—my whole life—everything, everything, for your sake.

NORA. *[Tears herself from him and says firmly.]* Now you must read your letters, Torvald.

HELMER. No, no; not tonight. I want to be with you, my beloved wife.

NORA. With the thought of your dying friend—?

HELMER. Of course—You are right. It's been a shock to both of us. A hideous shadow has come between us—thoughts of death and decay. We must try and throw them off. Until then—we'll stay apart.

NORA. *[Her arms round his neck.]* Torvald! Good-night! Good-night!

HELMER. *[Kissing her forehead.]* Good-night, my little song-bird; Sleep well! Now I'll go and read my letters. *[He goes with the letters in his hand into his room and shuts the door.]*

NORA. *[With wild eyes, gropes about her, seizes Helmer's domino, throws it round her, and whispers quickly, hoarsely, and brokenly.]* I'll never see him again. Never, never, never. *[Throws her shawl over her head.]* I'll never see the children again. I'll never see them either—Oh the thought of that black, icy water! That fathomless—! If it were only over! He has it now; he's reading it. Oh, not yet—please! Not yet! Torvald, goodbye—! Good-bye to you and the children!

[She is rushing out by the hall; at the same moment Helmer flings his door open, and stands there with an open letter in his hand.]

HELMER. Nora!

NORA. *[Shrieks.]* Ah—!

HELMER. What does this mean? Do you know what is in this letter?

NORA. Yes, yes, I know. Let me go! Let me out!

HELMER. *[Holds her back.]* Where are you going?

NORA. *[Tries to break away from him.]* Don't try to save me, Torvald!

HELMER. *[Falling back.]* So it's true! It's true what he writes? It's too horrible! It's impossible—it can't be true.

NORA. It *is* true. I've loved you more than all the world.

HELMER. Oh, come now! Let's have no silly nonsense!

NORA. *[A step nearer him.]* Torvald—!

HELMER. Do you realize what you've done?

NORA. Let me go—I won't have you suffer for it! I won't have you take the blame!

HELMER. Will you stop this play-acting! *[Locks the outer door.]* You'll stay here and give an account of yourself. Do you understand what you have done? Answer me! Do you understand it?

NORA. *[Looks at him fixedly, and says with a stiffening expression.]* I think I'm beginning to understand for the first time.

HELMER. *[Walking up and down.]* God! What an awakening! After eight years to discover that you who have been my pride and joy—are no better than a hypocrite, a liar—worse than that—a criminal! It's too horrible to think of! *[Nora says nothing, and continues to look fixedly at him.]* I might have known what to expect. I should have foreseen it. You've inherited all your father's lack of principle—be silent!—all of your father's lack of principle, I say!—no religion, no moral code, no sense of duty. This is my punishment for shielding him! I did it for your sake; and this is my reward!

NORA. I see.

HELMER. You've destroyed my happiness. You've ruined my whole future. It's ghastly to think of! I'm completely in the power of this scoundrel; he can force me to do whatever he likes, demand whatever he chooses; order me about at will; and I shan't dare open my mouth! My entire career is to be wrecked and all because of a lawless, unprincipled woman!

NORA. If I were no longer alive, then you'd be free.

HELMER. Oh yes! You're full of histrionics! Your father was just the same. Even if you "weren't alive," as you put it, what good would that do me? None whatever! He could publish the story all the same; I might even be suspected of collusion. People might say I was behind it all—that I had prompted you to do it. And to think I have you to thank for all this—you whom I've done nothing but pamper and spoil since the day of our marriage. Now do you realize what you've done to me?

NORA. *[With cold calmness.]* Yes.

HELMER. It's all so incredible, I can't grasp it. But we must try and come to some agreement. Take off that shawl. Take it off, I say! Of course, we must find some way to appease him—the matter must be hushed up at any cost. As far as we two are concerned, there must be no change in our way of life—in the eyes of the world, I mean. You'll naturally continue to live here. But you won't be allowed to bring up the children—I'd never dare trust them to you—God! to have to say this to the woman I've loved so tenderly—There can be no further thought of happiness between us. We must save what we can from the ruins—we can save appearances, at least—*[A ring; Helmer starts.]* What can that be? At this hour! You don't suppose he—! Could he—? Hide yourself, Nora; say you are ill.

[Nora stands motionless. Helmer goes to the door and opens it.]

HELENE. *[Half dressed, in the hall.]* It's a letter for Mrs. Helmer.

HELMER. Give it to me. *[Seizes the letter and shuts the door.]* It's from him. I shan't give it to you. I'll read it myself.

NORA. Very well.

HELMER. *[By the lamp.]* I don't dare open it; this may be the end—for both of us. Still—I must know. *[Hastily tears the letter open; reads a few lines, looks at an enclosure; with a cry of joy.]* Nora! *[Nora looks inquiringly at him.]* Nora!—I can't believe it—I must read it again. But it's true—it's really true! Nora, I am saved! I'm saved!

NORA. What about me?

HELMER. You too, of course; we are both of us saved, both of us. Look!—he's sent you back your note—he says he's sorry for what he did and apologizes for it—that due to a happy turn of events he—Oh, what does it matter what he says! We are saved, Nora! No one can harm you now. Oh, Nora, Nora—; but let's get rid of this hateful thing. I'll just see—*[Glances at the I.O.U.]*

No, no—I won't even look at it; I'll pretend it was all a horrible dream. *[Tears the I.O.U. and both letters in pieces. Throws them into the fire and watches them burn.]* There! Now it's all over—He said in his letter you've known about this since Christmas Eve—you must have had three dreadful days, Nora!

NORA. Yes. It's been very hard.

HELMER. How you must have suffered! And you saw no way out but—No! We'll forget the whole ghastly business. We'll just thank God and repeat again and again: It's over; all over! Don't you understand, Nora? You don't seem to grasp it: It's over. What's the matter with you? Why do you look so grim? My poor darling little Nora, I understand; but you mustn't worry—because I've forgiven you, Nora; I swear I have; I've forgiven everything. You did what you did because you loved me—I see that now.

NORA. Yes—that's true.

HELMER. You loved me as a wife should love her husband. You didn't realize what you were doing—you weren't able to judge how wrong it was. Don't think this makes you any less dear to me. Just you lean on me; let me guide you and advise you; I'm not a man for nothing! There's something very endearing about a woman's helplessness. And try and forget those harsh things I said just now. I was frantic; my whole world seemed to be tumbling about my ears. Believe me, I've forgiven you, Nora—I swear it—I've forgiven everything.

NORA. Thank you for your forgiveness, Torvald. *[Goes out, to the right.]*

HELMER. No! Don't go. *[Looking through the doorway.]* Why do you have to go in there?

NORA. *[Inside.]* I want to get out of these fancy-dress clothes.

HELMER. *[In the doorway.]* Yes, do, my darling. Try to calm down now, and get back to normal, my poor frightened little song-bird. Don't you worry—you'll be safe under my wings—they'll protect you. *[Walking up and down near the door.]* How lovely our home is, Nora! You'll be sheltered here; I'll cherish you as if you were a little dove I'd rescued from the claws of some dreadful hawk. You'll see—your poor fluttering little heart will soon grow calm again. Tomorrow all this will appear in quite a different light—things will be just as they were. I won't have to keep on saying I've forgiven you—you'll be able to sense it. You don't really think I could ever drive you away, do you? That I could even so much as reproach you for anything? You'd understand if you could see into my heart. When a man forgives his wife whole-heartedly—as I have you—it fills him with such tenderness, such peace. She seems to belong to him in a double sense; it's as though he'd brought her to life again; she's become more than his wife—she's become his child as well. That's how it will be with us, Nora—my own bewildered, helpless little darling. From now on you mustn't worry about anything; just open your heart to me; just let me be both will and conscience to you. *[Nora enters in everyday dress.]* What's all this? I thought you were going to bed. You've changed your dress?

NORA. Yes, Torvald; I've changed my dress.

HELMER. But what for? At this hour?

NORA. I shan't sleep tonight.

HELMER. But, Nora dear—

NORA. *[Looking at her watch.]* It's not so very late—Sit down, Torvald; we have a lot to talk about. *[She sits at one side of the table.]*

HELMER. Nora—what does this mean? Why that stern expression?

NORA. Sit down. It'll take some time. I have a lot to say to you. *[Helmer sits at the other side of the table.]*

HELMER. You frighten me, Nora. I don't understand you.

NORA. No, that's just it. You don't understand me; and I have never understood you either—until tonight. No, don't interrupt me. Just listen to what I have to say. This is to be a final settlement, Torvald.

HELMER. How do you mean?

NORA. *[After a short silence.]* Doesn't anything special strike you as we sit here like this?

HELMER. I don't think so—why?

NORA. It doesn't occur to you, does it, that though we've been married for eight years, this is the first time that we two—man and wife—have sat down for a serious talk?

HELMER. What do you mean by serious?

NORA. During eight whole years, no—more than that—ever since the first day we met—we have never exchanged so much as one serious word about serious things.

HELMER. Why should I perpetually burden you with all my cares and problems? How could you possibly help me to solve them?

NORA. I'm not talking about cares and problems. I'm simply saying we've never once sat down seriously and tried to get to the bottom of anything.

HELMER. But, Nora, darling—why should you be concerned with serious thoughts?

NORA. That's the whole point! You've never understood me—A great injustice has been done me, Torvald; first by Father, and then by you.

HELMER. What a thing to say! No two people on earth could ever have loved you more than we have!

NORA. *[Shaking her head.]* You never loved me. You just thought it was fun to be in love with me.

HELMER. This is fantastic!

NORA. Perhaps. But it's true all the same. While I was still at home I used to hear Father airing his opinions and they became my opinions; or if I didn't happen to agree, I kept it to myself—he would have been displeased otherwise. He used to call me his doll-baby, and played with me as I played with my dolls. Then I came to live in your house—

HELMER. What an expression to use about our marriage!

NORA. *[Undisturbed.]* I mean—from Father's hands I passed into yours. You arranged everything according to your tastes, and I acquired the same tastes, or I pretended to—I'm not sure which—a little of both, perhaps. Looking back on it all, it seems to me I've lived here like a beggar, from hand to mouth. I've lived by performing tricks for you, Torvald. But that's the way you wanted it. You and Father have done me a great wrong. You've prevented me from becoming a real person.

HELMER. Nora, how can you be so ungrateful and unreasonable! Haven't you been happy here?

NORA. No, never. I thought I was; but I wasn't really.

HELMER. Not—not happy!

NORA. No; only merry. You've always been so kind to me. But our home has never been anything but a play-room. I've been your doll-wife, just as at home I was Papa's doll-child. And the children in turn, have been my dolls. I thought it fun when you played games with me, just as they thought it fun when I played games with them. And that's been our marriage, Torvald.

HELMER. There may be a grain of truth in what you say, even though it is distorted and exaggerated.

From now on things will be different. Play-time is over now; tomorrow lessons begin!

NORA. Whose lessons? Mine, or the children's?

HELMER. Both, if you wish it, Nora, dear.

NORA. Torvald, I'm afraid you're not the man to teach me to be a real wife to you.

HELMER. How can you say that?

NORA. And I'm certainly not fit to teach the children.

HELMER. Nora!

NORA. Didn't you just say, a moment ago, you didn't dare trust them to me?

HELMER. That was in the excitement of the moment! You mustn't take it so seriously!

NORA. But you were quite right, Torvald. That job is beyond me; there's another job I must do first: I must try and educate myself. You could never help me to do that; I must do it quite alone. So, you see—that's why I'm going to leave you.

HELMER. *[Jumping up.]* What did you say—?

NORA. I shall never get to know myself—I shall never learn to face reality—unless I stand alone. So I can't stay with you any longer.

HELMER. Nora! Nora!

NORA. I am going at once. I'm sure Kristine will let me stay with her tonight—

HELMER. But, Nora—this is madness! I shan't allow you to do this. I shall forbid it!

NORA. You no longer have the power to forbid me anything. I'll only take a few things with me—those that belong to me. I shall never again accept anything from you.

HELMER. Have you lost your senses?

NORA. Tomorrow I'll go home—to what *was* my home, I mean. It might be easier for me there, to find something to do.

HELMER. You talk like an ignorant child, Nora—!

NORA. Yes. That's just why I must educate myself.

HELMER. To leave your home—to leave your husband, and your children! What do you suppose people would say to that?

NORA. It makes no difference. This is something I *must* do.

HELMER. It's inconceivable! Don't you realize you'd be betraying your most sacred duty?

NORA. What do you consider that to be?

HELMER. Your duty towards your husband and your children—I surely don't have to tell you that!

NORA. I've another duty just as sacred.

HELMER. Nonsense! What duty do you mean?

NORA. My duty towards myself.

HELMER. Remember—before all else you are a wife and mother.

NORA. I don't believe that anymore. I believe that before all else I am a human being, just as you are—or at least that I should try and become one. I know that most people would agree with you, Torvald—and that's what they say in books. But I can no longer be satisfied with what most people say—or what they write in books. I must think things out for myself—get clear about them.

HELMER. Surely your position in your home is clear enough? Have you no sense of religion? Isn't that an infallible guide to you?

NORA. But don't you see, Torvald—I don't really know what religion is.

HELMER. Nora! How *can* you!

NORA. All I know about it is what Pastor Hansen told me when I was confirmed. He taught me what he thought religion was—said it was *this* and *that*. As soon as I get away by myself, I shall have to look into that matter too, try and decide whether what he taught me was right—or whether it's right for *me*, at least.

HELMER. A nice way for a young woman to talk! It's unheard of! If religion means nothing to you, I'll appeal to your conscience; you must have some sense of ethics, I suppose? Answer me! Or have you none?

NORA. It's hard for me to answer you, Torvald. I don't think I know—all these things bewilder me. But I *do* know that I think quite differently from you about them. I've discovered that the law, for instance, is quite different from what I had imagined; but I find it hard to believe it can be right. It seems it's criminal for a woman to try and spare her old, sick, father, or save her husband's life! I can't agree with that.

HELMER. You talk like a child. You have no understanding of the society we live in.

NORA. No, I haven't. But I'm going to try and learn. I want to find out which of us is right—society or I.

HELMER. You are ill, Nora; you have a touch of fever; you're quite beside yourself.

NORA. I've never felt so sure—so clear-headed—as I do tonight.

HELMER. "Sure and clear-headed" enough to leave your husband and your children?

NORA. Yes.

HELMER. Then there is only one explanation possible.

NORA. What?

HELMER. You don't love me any more.

NORA. No; that is just it.

HELMER. Nora!—What are you saying!

NORA. It makes me so unhappy, Torvald; for you've always been so kind to me. But I can't help it. I don't love you any more.

HELMER. *[Mastering himself with difficulty.]* You feel "sure and clear-headed" about this too?

NORA. Yes, utterly sure. That's why I can't stay here any longer.

HELMER. And can you tell me how I lost your love?

NORA. Yes, I can tell you. It was tonight—when the wonderful thing didn't happen; I knew then you weren't the man I always thought you were.

HELMER. I don't understand.

NORA. For eight years I've been waiting patiently; I knew, of course, that such things don't happen every day. Then, when this trouble came to me—I thought to myself: Now! Now the wonderful thing will happen! All the time Krogstad's letter was out there in the box, it never occurred to me for a single moment that you'd think of submitting to his conditions. I was absolutely convinced that you'd defy him—that you'd tell him to publish the thing to all the world; and that then—

HELMER. You mean you thought I'd let my wife be publicly dishonored and disgraced?

NORA. No. What I thought you'd do, was to take the blame upon yourself.

HELMER. Nora—!

NORA. I know! You think I never would have accepted such a sacrifice. Of course I wouldn't! But my word would have meant nothing against yours. That was the wonderful thing I hoped for, Torvald, hoped for with such terror. And it was to prevent that, that I chose to kill myself.

HELMER. I'd gladly work for you day and night, Nora—go through suffering and want, if need be—but one doesn't sacrifice one's honor for love's sake.

NORA. Millions of women have done so.

HELMER. You think and talk like a silly child.

NORA. Perhaps. But you neither think nor talk like the man I want to share my life with. When you'd recovered from your fright—and you never thought of me, only of yourself—when you had nothing more to fear—you behaved as though none of this had happened. I was your little lark again, your little doll—whom you would have to guard more carefully than ever, because she was so weak and frail *[Stands up.]* At that moment it suddenly dawned on me that I had been living here for eight years with a stranger and that I'd borne him three children. I can't bear to think about it! I could tear myself to pieces!

HELMER. *[Sadly.]* I see, Nora—I understand; there's suddenly a great void between us—Is there no way to bridge it?

NORA. Feeling as I do now, Torvald—I could never be a wife to you.

HELMER. But, if I were to change? Don't you think I'm capable of that?

NORA. Perhaps—when you no longer have your doll to play with.

HELMER. It's inconceivable! I *can't* part with you, Nora. I can't endure the thought.

NORA. *[Going into room on the right.]* All the more reason it should happen. *[She comes back with outdoor things and a small traveling-bag, which she places on a chair.]*

HELMER. But not at once, Nora—not now! At least wait till tomorrow.

NORA. *[Putting on cloak.]* I can't spend the night in a strange man's house.

HELMER. Couldn't we go on living here together? As brother and sister, if you like—as friends.

NORA. *[Fastening her hat.]* You know very well that wouldn't last, Torvald. *[Puts on the shawl.]* Good-bye. I won't go in and see the children. I know they're in better hands than mine. Being what I am—how can I be of any use to them?

HELMER. But surely, some day, Nora—?

NORA. How can I tell? How do I know what sort of person I'll become?

HELMER. You are my wife, Nora, now and always!

NORA. Listen to me, Torvald—I've always heard that when a wife deliberately leaves her husband as I am leaving you, he is legally freed from all responsibility towards her. At any rate, I release you now from all responsibility. You mustn't feel yourself bound, any more than I shall. There must be complete freedom on both sides. Here is your ring. Now give me mine.

HELMER. That too?

NORA. That too.

HELMER. Here it is.

NORA. So—it's all over now. Here are the keys. The servants know how to run the house—better than I do. I'll ask Kristine to come by tomorrow, after I've left town; there are a few things I brought with me from home; she'll pack them up and send them on to me.

HELMER. You really mean it's over, Nora? *Really* over? You'll never think of me again?

NORA. I expect I shall often think of you; of you—and the children, and this house.

HELMER. May I write to you?

NORA. No—never. You mustn't! Please!

HELMER. At least, let me send you—

NORA. Nothing!

HELMER. But, you'll let me help you, Nora—

NORA. No, I say! I can't accept anything from strangers.

HELMER. Must I always be a stranger to you, Nora?

NORA. [Taking her traveling-bag.] Yes. Unless it were to happen—the most wonderful thing of all—

HELMER. What?

NORA. Unless we both could change so that—Oh, Torvald! I no longer *believe* in miracles, you see!

HELMER. Tell me! Let *me* believe! Unless we both could change so that—?

NORA.—So that our life together might truly be a marriage. Good-bye. [She goes out by the hall door.]

HELMER. [Sinks into a chair by the door with his face in his hands.] Nora! Nora! [He looks around the room and rises.] She is gone! How empty it all seems! [A hope springs up in him.] The most wonderful thing of all—?

[From below is heard the reverberation of a heavy door closing.]

CURTAIN

Introduction to *The Cherry Orchard* by Anton Chekhov

Translated by Constance Garnett

The Cherry Orchard   Standing, left to right: Alec McCowen (Gaev), Sean Murray(Trofimov); seated, left to right: Kate Duchene (Varya), Penelope Wilton (Mme. Ranyevskaya), Lucy Whybrow (Anya); on floor: David Troughton (Lopakhin). Royal Shakespeare Company, Swan Theatre. *(© Donald Cooper/ PHOTOSTAGE)*

The Play   The year 1904, when Anton Chekhov's *The Cherry Orchard* was first produced, was a time of change in Russia. Though many people did not yet realize it, the landowning aristocracy that owed allegiance to the czar, the ruler of Russia, was in its last days. In less than two decades there would be a revolution; land would be confiscated, and the czar and his family would be executed. Chekhov's play *The Cherry Orchard* proved to be prophetic in its chronicling of the changes that were to come in the lives of the aristocracy.

As *The Cherry Orchard* opens, Madame Andreyevna Lyubov (also known as Madame Ranevsky) has just returned to her country estate in Russia from five years in Paris. She is accompanied by her daughter Anya, age 17, and her brother Gaev, an ineffectual aristocrat. Lyubov's estate, with its famous cherry orchard, is heavily mortgaged, and the mortgage is about to be foreclosed. Greeting Lyubov is Lopahin, a merchant whose father was a serf on the estate. Lopahin is supposed to marry Varya, Lyubov's adopted daughter. Anya tells Varya that their mother cannot accept the change in their fortunes but is continuing to give money away that she does not have. In Act II, Lopahin tells Madam Lyubov that she can avert the forced sale of the estate if she will tear down the house and the cherry orchard and develop the land for summer villas, but Lyubov and Gaev cannot bear the thought of destroying the beautiful orchard. Lyubov even talks of hiring an orchestra for a dance, and she discourages Gaev's plan to work in a bank.

In Act III, a dance is being held in Lyubov's house; it is also the evening of the sale of the estate. After a time, Lopahin returns to announce that he has bought the estate, whereupon Lyubov sits down, crushed and weeping. In Act IV we return to the scene of Act I, which took place in the nursery. Now the nursery is stripped bare, in anticipation of the family's departure. Lopahin promises Lyubov that he will marry Varya, but when he is left alone with Varya, he once again fails to propose to the weeping girl. Finally everyone leaves but Lyubov and Gaev, who say a last tearful farewell to their home and their beloved orchard. We hear the sound of an ax cutting down the trees of the cherry orchard.

In *The Cherry Orchard* Chekhov achieves the remarkable dramatic effects for which he is famous. First, he has created an extraordinary cast of characters. Chekhov had unusual insight into human attitudes and behavior and was able to translate his perceptions into dramatic terms. Second, he "orchestrates" his characters, blending them into a rich tapestry of relationships and interconnections. Chekhov deliberately avoids melodramatic effects, direct statements, and political didacticism. Everything is done indirectly, subtly, and with nuances and shadings rather than obvious, overt strokes. Another characteristic evident in *The Cherry Orchard* is his blending of the tragic and comic. This results in a form of tragicomedy in which the two strains intermingle. Tragicomedy was to become a predominant form of theater in the twentieth century, but Chekhov was one of the first to incorporate the tragicomic sensibility so completely in his plays.

The Playwright When he first arrived in Saint Petersburg in 1885 to finish his medical studies, Anton Chekhov was astonished to discover that he was a famous writer. The short stories that he had been writing casually to support his family and pay for his education had been highly acclaimed. As a result, he resolved to improve his work habits and concentrate on literature as a career.

As a schoolboy in Taganrog, Russia, Chekhov had acted and written for the local theater. During his last years in school, his father, a grocer, had gone into bankruptcy, and the family fled to Moscow to escape the creditors. The son's literary sketches, written for magazines in Moscow and Saint Petersburg, helped support the family and allowed him to continue studying for a medical degree. Though Chekhov did finish medical school, he never entered active practice because of his literary career.

In 1887 Chekhov's first successful play, *Ivanov*, was produced in Moscow. An earlier drama, *Platonov*, written while he was a student, had been rejected by the Moscow theaters. His third play, *The Wood Demon*, written under the influence of Tolstoy's philosophy, was a failure in 1889. He also wrote several short farces—or "jokes," as he called them—in his late twenties. It was seven years before Chekhov's next play, *The Seagull*, was produced; during the intervening time, he perfected his dramatic techniques.

Although the initial production of *The Seagull* was not a success, the Moscow Art Theater, headed by Konstantin Stanislavski, produced it successfully in 1898. The

Moscow Art Theater also produced Chekhov's next three plays, *Uncle Vanya* (1899), *The Three Sisters* (1900), and *The Cherry Orchard* (1904). These productions were successful, but Chekhov criticized Stanislavski for neglecting the humor in his plays.

Chekhov contracted tuberculosis when he was 23, and in the last years of his life he was forced to leave his estate outside Moscow and move south to Yalta for the sake of his health. In 1901, he married Olga Knipper, an actress with the Moscow Art Theater. He was elected to the Russian Academy of Science, but resigned when his friend, the writer Maxim Gorki, was expelled. He died in 1904 at age 44 at Baden-weiler, Germany, where he had gone in an attempt to regain his health.

The Period   *The Cherry Orchard* was written 25 years after Ibsen's *A Doll's House.* Many of the historic developments cited in that drama's introduction as influences on Ibsen are also significant in examining the work of Anton Chekhov. (Readers should review that material.) In addition, Chekhov's plays, like Ibsen's, are realistic works.

We should also note that *The Cherry Orchard* clearly reflects the changes in Russian society at the beginning of the twentieth century. The play allows the audience to see the economic tensions in Russia and the significant transformations taking place in its class structure. The aristocracy is withering (represented by Ranevsky and her family), while a new bourgeois class (represented by Lopahin) is emerging. But there is also developing rhetoric about the need for a revolution led by the working class. Such discussions are found in speeches made by the student Trofimov. Chekhov's play seems to foreshadow the impending 1917 Bolshevik Revolution, which would transform Russian society.

THE CHERRY ORCHARD

Anton Chekhov

CHARACTERS

MADAME RANEVSKY (LYUBOV ANDREYEVNA), the owner of the Cherry Orchard
ANYA, her daughter, aged 17
VARYA, her adopted daughter, aged 24
GAEV (LEONID ANDREYEVITCH), brother of Madame Ranevsky
LOPAHIN (YERMOLAY ALEXEYEVITCH), a merchant
TROFIMOV (PYOTR SERGEYEVITCH), a student

SEMYONOV-PISHTCHIK, a landowner
CHARLOTTA IVANOVNA, a governess
EPIHODOV (SEMYON PANTALEYEVITCH), a clerk
DUNYASHA, a maid
FIRS, an old valet, aged 87
YASHA, a young valet
VAGRANT
STATION MASTER
POST OFFICE CLERK
VISITORS, SERVANTS

SCENE: The action takes place on the estate of Madame Ranevsky.

Act I

A room, which has always been called the nursery. One of the doors leads into Anya's room. Dawn, sun rises during the scene. May, the cherry trees in flower, but it is cold in the garden with the frost of early morning. Windows closed.

[Enter Dunyasha with a candle and Lopahin with a book in his hand.]

LOPAHIN. The train's in, thank God. What time is it?

DUNYASHA. Nearly two o'clock. *[Puts out the candle.]* It's daylight already.

LOPAHIN. The train's late! Two hours, at least. *[Yawns and stretches.]* I'm a pretty one; what a fool I've been. Came here on purpose to meet them at the station and dropped asleep. . . . Dozed off as I sat in the chair. It's annoying. . . . You might have waked me.

DUNYASHA. I thought you had gone *[listens]*. There, I do believe they're coming!

LOPAHIN. *[Listens.]* No, what with the luggage and one thing and another *[a pause]*. Lyubov Andreyevna has been abroad five years; I don't know what she is like now. . . . She's a splendid woman. A good-natured, kind-hearted woman. I remember when I was a lad of fifteen, my poor father—he used to keep a little shop here in the village in those days—gave me a punch in the face with his fist and made my nose bleed. We were in the yard here, I forget what we'd come about—he had had a drop. Lyubov Andreyevna—I can see her now—she was a slim young girl then—took me to wash my face, and then brought me into this very room, into the nursery. "Don't cry, little peasant," says she, "it will be well in time for your wedding day." . . . *[A pause.]* Little peasant. . . . My father was a peasant, it's true, but here am I in a white waistcoat and brown shoes, like a pig in a bun shop. Yes, I'm a rich man, but for all my money, come to think, a peasant I was, and a peasant I am. *[Turns over the pages of the book.]* I've been reading this book and I can't make head or tail of it. I fell asleep over it. *[A pause.]*

DUNYASHA. The dogs have been awake all night, they feel that the mistress is coming.

LOPAHIN. Why, what's the matter with you, Dunyasha?

DUNYASHA. My hands are all of a tremble. I feel as though I should faint.

LOPAHIN. You're a spoilt soft creature, Dunyasha. And dressed like a lady too, and your hair done up. That's not the thing. One must know one's place.

[Enter Epihodov with a nosegay; he wears a pea-jacket and highly polished creaking topboots; he drops the nosegay as he comes in.]

EPIHODOV. *[Picking up the nosegay.]* Here! the gardener's sent this, says you're to put it in the dining-room. *[Gives Dunyasha the nosegay.]*

LOPAHIN. And bring me some kvass.

DUNYASHA. I will. *[Goes out.]*

EPIHODOV. It's chilly this morning, three degrees of frost, though the cherries are all in flower. I can't say much for our climate. *[Sighs.]* I can't. Our climate is not often propitious to the occasion. Yermolay Alexeyevitch, permit me to call your attention to the fact that I purchased myself a pair of boots the day before yesterday, and they creak, I venture to assure you, so that there's no tolerating them. What ought I to grease them with?

LOPAHIN. Oh, shut up! Don't bother me.

EPIHODOV. Every day some misfortune befalls me. I don't complain, I'm used to it, and I wear a smiling face.

[Dunyasha comes in, hands Lopahin the kvass.]

EPIHODOV. I am going. *[Stumbles against a chair, which falls over.]* There! *[As though triumphant.]* There you see now, excuse the expression, an accident like that among others . . . It's positively remarkable. *[Goes out.]*

DUNYASHA. Do you know, Yermolay Alexeyevitch, I must confess, Epihodov has made me a proposal.

LOPAHIN. Ah!

DUNYASHA. I'm sure I don't know. . . . He's a harmless fellow, but sometimes when he begins talking, there's no making anything of it. It's all very fine and expressive, only there's no understanding it. I've a sort of liking for him too. He loves me to distraction. He's an unfortunate man; every day there's something. They tease him about it—two and twenty misfortunes they call him.

LOPAHIN. *[Listening.]* There! I do believe they're coming.

DUNYASHA. They are coming! What's the matter with me? . . . I'm cold all over.

LOPAHIN. They really are coming. Let's go and meet them. Will she know me? It's five years since I saw her.

DUNYASHA. *[In a flutter.]* I shall drop this very minute. . . . Ah, I shall drop.

[There is a sound of two carriages driving up to the house. Lopahin and Dunyasha go out quickly. The stage is left empty. A noise is heard in the adjoining rooms. Firs, who has driven to meet Madame Ranevsky, crosses the stage hurriedly leaning on a stick. He is wearing old-fashioned livery and a high hat. He says something to himself, but not a word can be distinguished. The noise behind the scenes goes on increasing. A voice: "Come, let's go in here." Enter Lyubov Andreyevna, Anya, and Charlotta Ivanovna with a pet dog on a chain, all in traveling dresses. Varya in an out-door coat with a kerchief over her head, Gaev, Semyonov-Pishtchik, Lopahin, Dunyasha with bag and parasol, servants with other articles. All walk across the room.]

ANYA. Let's come in here. Do you remember what room this is, mamma?

LYUBOV. *[Joyfully, through her tears.]* The nursery!

VARYA. How cold it is, my hands are numb. *[To Lyubov Andreyevna.]* Your rooms, the white room and the lavender one, are just the same as ever, mamma.

LYUBOV. My nursery, dear delightful room. . . . I used to sleep here when I was little. . . . *[Cries.]* And here I am, like a little child. . . . *[Kisses her brother and Varya, and then her brother again.]* Varya's just the same as ever, like a nun. And I knew Dunyasha. *[Kisses Dunyasha.]*

GAEV. The train was two hours late. What do you think of that? Is that the way to do things?

CHARLOTTA. *[To Pishtchik.]* My dog eats nuts, too.

PISHTCHIK. *[Wonderingly.]* Fancy that!

[They all go out except Anya and Dunyasha.]

DUNYASHA. We've been expecting you so long. *[Takes Anya's hat and coat.]*

ANYA. I haven't slept for four nights on the journey. I feel dreadfully cold.

DUNYASHA. You set out in Lent, there was snow and frost, and now? My darling! *[Laughs and kisses her.]* I *have* missed you, my precious, my joy. I must tell you . . . I can't put it off a minute. . . .

ANYA. *[Wearily.]* What now?

DUNYASHA. Epihodov, the clerk, made me a proposal just after Easter.

ANYA. It's always the same thing with you. . . . *[Straightening her hair.]* I've lost all my hairpins. . . . *[She is staggering from exhaustion.]*

DUNYASHA. I don't know what to think, really. He does love me, he does love me so!

ANYA. *[Looking toward her door, tenderly.]* My own room, my windows just as though I had never gone away. I'm home! To-morrow morning I shall get up and run into the garden. . . . Oh, if I could get to sleep! I haven't slept all the journey, I was so anxious and worried.

DUNYASHA. Pyotr Sergeyevitch came the day before yesterday.

ANYA. *[Joyfully.]* Petya!

DUNYASHA. He's asleep in the bath house, he has settled in there. I'm afraid of being in their way, says he. *[Glancing at her watch.]* I was to have waked him, but Varvara Mihalovna told me not to. Don't you wake him, says she.

[Enter Varya with a bunch of keys at her waist.]

VARYA. Dunyasha, coffee and make haste. . . . Mamma's asking for coffee.

DUNYASHA. This very minute. *[Goes out.]*

VARYA. Well, thank God, you've come. You're home again. *[Petting her.]* My little darling has come back! My precious beauty has come back again!

ANYA. I have had a time of it!

VARYA. I can fancy.

ANYA. We set off in Holy Week—it was so cold then, and all the way Charlotta would talk and show off her tricks. What did you want to burden me with Charlotta for?

VARYA. You couldn't have traveled all alone, darling. At seventeen!

ANYA. We got to Paris at last, it was cold there—snow. I speak French shockingly. Mamma lives on the fifth floor, I went up to her and there were a lot of French people, ladies, an old priest with a book. The place smelt of tobacco and so comfortless. I felt sorry, oh! so sorry for mamma all at once, I put my arms round her neck, and hugged her and wouldn't let her go. Mamma was as kind as she could be, and she cried. . . .

VARYA. *[Through her tears.]* Don't speak of it, don't speak of it!

ANYA. She had sold her villa at Mentone, she had nothing left, nothing. I hadn't a farthing left either, we only just had enough to get here. And mamma doesn't understand! When we had dinner at the stations, she always ordered the most expensive things and gave the waiters a whole rouble. Charlotta's just the same. Yasha too must have the same as we do; it's simply awful. You know Yasha is mamma's valet now, we brought him here with us.

VARYA. Yes, I've seen the young rascal.

ANYA. Well, tell me—have you paid the arrears on the mortgage?

VARYA. How could we get the money?

ANYA. Oh, dear! Oh, dear!

VARYA. In August the place will be sold.

ANYA. My goodness!

LOPAHIN. *[Peeps in at the door and moos like a cow.]* Moo! *[Disappears.]*

VARYA. *[Weeping.]* There, that's what I could do to him. *[Shakes her fist.]*

ANYA. *[Embracing Varya, softly.]* Varya, has he made you an offer? *[Varya shakes her head.]* Why, but he loves you. Why is it you don't come to an understanding? What are you waiting for?

VARYA. I believe that there never will be anything between us. He has a lot to do, he has no time for me . . . and takes no notice of me. Bless the man, it makes me miserable to see him. . . . Everyone's talking of our being married, everyone's congratulating me, and all the while there's really nothing in it; it's all like a dream. *[In another tone.]* You have a new brooch like a bee.

ANYA. *[Mournfully.]* Mamma bought it. *[Goes into her own room and in a lighthearted childish tone.]* And you know, in Paris I went up in a balloon!

VARYA. My darling's home again! My pretty is home again!

[Dunyasha returns with the coffeepot and is making the coffee.]

VARYA. *[Standing at the door.]* All day long, darling, as I go about looking after the house, I keep dreaming all the time. If only we could marry you to a rich man, then I should feel more at rest. Then I would go off by myself on a pilgrimage to Kiev, to Moscow . . . and so I would spend my life going from one holy place to another. . . . I would go on and on. . . . What bliss!

ANYA. The birds are singing in the garden. What time is it?

VARYA. It must be nearly three. It's time you were asleep, darling. *[Going into Anya's room.]* What bliss!

[Yasha enters with a rug and a traveling bag.]

YASHA. *[Crosses the stage, mincingly.]* May one come in here, pray?

DUNYASHA. I shouldn't have known you, Yasha. How you have changed abroad.

YASHA. H'm! . . . And who are you?

DUNYASHA. When you went away, I was that high. *[Shows distance from floor.]* Dunyasha, Fyodor's daughter. . . . You don't remember me!

YASHA. H'm! . . . You're a peach! *[Looks round and embraces her: she shrieks and drops a saucer. Yasha goes out hastily.]*

VARYA. *[In the doorway, in a tone of vexation.]* What now?

DUNYASHA. *[Through her tears.]* I have broken a saucer.

VARYA. Well, that brings good luck.

ANYA. *[Coming out of her room.]* We ought to prepare mamma: Petya is here.

VARYA. I told them not to wake him.

ANYA. *[Dreamily.]* It's six years since father died. Then only a month later little brother Grisha was drowned in the river, such a pretty boy he was, only seven. It was more than mamma could bear, so she went away, went away without looking back. *[Shuddering.]* . . . How well I understand her, if only she knew! *[A pause.]* And Petya Trofimov was Grisha's tutor, he may remind her.

[Enter Firs: he is wearing a pea-jacket and a white waist-coat.]

FIRS. *[Goes up to the coffeepot, anxiously.]* The mistress will be served here. *[Puts on white gloves.]* Is the coffee ready? *[Sternly to Dunyasha.]* Girl! Where's the cream?

DUNYASHA. Ah, mercy on us! *[Goes out quickly.]*

FIRS. *[Fussing round the coffeepot.]* Ech! you good-for-nothing! *[Muttering to himself.]* Come back from Paris. And the old master used to go to Paris too . . . horses all the way. *[Laughs.]*

VARYA. What is it, Firs?

FIRS. What is your pleasure? *[Gleefully.]* My lady has come home! I have lived to see her again! Now I can die! *[Weeps with joy.]*

[Enter Lyubov Andreyevna, Gaev and Semyonov-Pishtchik; the latter is in a short-waisted full coat of fine cloth, and full trousers. Gaev, as he comes in, makes a gesture with his arms and his whole body, as though he were playing billiards.]

LYUBOV. How does it go? Let me remember. Hit off the red!

GAEV. That's it—in off the white! Why, once, sister, we used to sleep together in this very room, and now I'm fifty-one, strange as it seems.

LOPAHIN. Yes, time flies.

GAEV. What do you say?

LOPAHIN. Time, I say, flies.

GAEV. What a smell of patchouli!

ANYA. I'm going to bed. Good-night, mamma. *[Kisses her mother.]*

LYUBOV. My precious darling. *[Kisses her hands.]* Are you glad to be home? I can't believe it.

ANYA. Good-night, uncle.

GAEV. *[Kissing her face and hands.]* God bless you! How like you are to your mother! *[To his sister.]* At her age you were just the same, Lyuba.

[Anya shakes hands with Lopahin and Pishtchik, then goes out, shutting the door after her.]

LYUBOV. She's quite worn out.

PISHTCHIK. Aye, it's a long journey, to be sure.

VARYA. *[To Lopahin and Pishtchik.]* Well, gentlemen? It's three o'clock and time to say good-bye.

LYUBOV. *[Laughs.]* You're just the same as ever, Varya *[Draws her to her and kisses her.]* I'll just drink my coffee and then we will all go and rest. *[Firs puts a cushion under her feet.]* Thanks, friend. I am so fond of coffee, I drink it day and night. Thanks, dear old man. *[Kisses Firs.]*

VARYA. I'll just see whether all the things have been brought in. *[Goes out.]*

LYUBOV. Can it really be me sitting here? *[Laughs.]* I want to dance about and clap my hands. *[Covers her face with her hands.]* And I could drop asleep in a moment! God knows I love my country, I love it tenderly; I couldn't look out of the window in the train, I kept crying so. *[Through her tears.]* But I must drink my coffee, though. Thank you. Firs, thanks, dear old man. I'm so glad to find you still alive.

FIRS. The day before yesterday.

GAEV. He's rather deaf.

LOPAHIN. I have to set off for Harkov directly, at five o'clock. . . . It is annoying! I wanted to have a look at you, and a little talk. . . . You are just as splendid as ever.

PISHTCHIK. *[Breathing heavily.]* Handsomer, indeed. . . . Dressed in parisian style . . . completely bowled me over.

LOPAHIN. Your brother, Leonid Andreyevitch here, is always saying that I'm a low-born knave, that I'm a money-grubber, but I don't care one straw for that. Let me talk. Only I do want you to believe in me as you used to. I do want your wonderful tender eyes to look at me as they used to in the old days. Merciful God! My father was a serf of your father and of your grandfather, but you—you—did so much for me once, that I've forgotten all that; I love you as though you were my kin . . . more than my kin.

LYUBOV. I can't sit still, I simply can't. . . . *[Jumps up and walks about in violent agitation.]* This happiness is too much for me. . . . You may laugh at me, I know I'm silly. . . . My own bookcase. *[Kisses the bookcase.]* My little table.

GAEV. Nurse died while you were away.

LYUBOV. *[Sits down and drinks coffee.]* Yes, the Kingdom of Heaven be hers! You wrote me of her death.

GAEV. And Anastasy is dead. Squinting Petruchka has left me and is in service now with the police captain in the town. *[Takes a box of caramels out of his pocket and sucks one.]*

PISHTCHIK. My daughter, Dashenka, wishes to be remembered to you.

LOPAHIN. I want to tell you something very pleasant and cheering. *[Glancing at his watch.]* I'm going directly . . . there's no time to say much . . . well, I can say it in a couple of words. I needn't tell you your cherry orchard is to be sold to pay your debts; the 22nd of August is the date fixed for the sale; but don't you worry, dearest lady, you may sleep in peace, there is a way of saving it. . . . This is what I propose. I beg your attention! Your estate is not twenty miles from the town, the railway runs close by it, and if the cherry orchard and the land along the river bank were cut up into building plots and then let on lease for summer villas, you would make an income of at least 25,000 roubles a year out of it.

GAEV. That's all rot, if you'll excuse me.

LYUBOV. I don't quite understand you, Yermolay Alexeyevitch.

LOPAHIN. You will get a rent of at least 25 roubles a year for a three-acre plot from summer visitors, and if you say the word now, I'll bet you what you like there won't be one square foot of ground vacant by the autumn, all the plots will be taken up. I congratulate you; in fact, you are saved. It's a perfect situation with that deep river. Only, of course, it must be cleared—all the old buildings, for example, must be removed, this house too, which is really good for nothing and the old cherry orchard must be cut down.

LYUBOV. Cut down! My dear fellow, forgive me, but you don't know what you are talking about. If there is one thing interesting—remarkable indeed—in the whole province, it's just our cherry orchard.

LOPAHIN. The only thing remarkable about the orchard is that it's a very large one. There's a crop of cherries every alternate year, and then there's nothing to be done with them, no one buys them.

GAEV. This orchard is mentioned in the "Encyclopædia."

LOPAHIN. *[Glancing at his watch.]* If we don't decide on something and don't take some steps, on the 22nd of August the cherry orchard and the whole estate too will be sold by auction. Make up your minds! There is no other way of saving it, I'll take my oath on that. No, No!

FIRS. In old days, forty or fifty years ago, they used to dry the cherries, soak them, pickle them, make jam too, and they used—

GAEV. Be quiet, Firs.

FIRS. And they used to send the preserved cherries to Moscow and to Harkov by the waggon-load. That brought the money in! And the preserved cherries in those days were soft and juicy, sweet and fragrant. . . . They knew the way to do them then. . . .

LYUBOV. And where is the recipe now?

FIRS. It's forgotten. Nobody remembers it.

PISHTCHIK. *[To Lyubov Andreyevna.]* What's it like in Paris? Did you eat frogs there?

LYUBOV. Oh, I ate crocodiles.

PISHTCHIK. Fancy that now!

LOPAHIN. There used to be only the gentlefolks and the peasants in the country, but now there are these summer visitors. All the towns, even the small ones, are surrounded nowadays by these summer villas. And one may say for sure, that in another twenty years there'll be many more of these people and that they'll be everywhere. At present the summer visitor only drinks tea in his verandah, but maybe he'll take to working his bit of land too, and then your cherry orchard would become happy, rich and prosperous. . . .

GAEV. *[Indignant.]* What rot!

[Enter Varya and Yasha.]

VARYA. There are two telegrams for you, mamma. *[Takes out keys and opens an old-fashioned bookcase with a loud crack.]* Here they are.

LYUBOV. From Paris. *[Tears the telegrams, without reading them.]* I have done with Paris.

GAEV. Do you know, Lyuba, how old that bookcase is? Last week I pulled out the bottom drawer and there I found the date branded on it. The bookcase was made just a hundred years ago. What do you say to that? We might have celebrated its jubilee. Though it's an inanimate object, still it is a *book* case.

PISHTCHIK. *[Amazed.]* A hundred years! Fancy that now.

GAEV. Yes. . . . It is a thing. . . . *[Feeling the bookcase.]* Dear, honoured, bookcase! Hail to thee who for more than a hundred years hast served the pure ideals of good and justice; thy silent call to fruitful labour has never flagged in those hundred years, maintaining [in tears] in the generations of man, courage and faith in a brighter future and fostering in us ideals of good and social consciousness. [A pause.]

LOPAHIN. Yes. . . .

LYUBOV. You are just the same as ever, Leonid.

GAEV. [A little embarrassed.] Hit off the right into the pocket!

LOPAHIN. [Looking at his watch.] Well, it's time I was off.

YASHA. [Handing Lyubov Andreyevna medicine.] Perhaps you will take your pills now.

PISHTCHIK. You shouldn't take medicines, my dear madam . . . they do no harm and no good. Give them here . . . honoured lady. [Takes the pillbox, pours the pills into the hollow of his hand, blows on them, puts them in his mouth and drinks off some kvass.] There!

LYUBOV. [In alarm.] Why, you must be out of your mind!

PISHTCHIK. I have taken all the pills.

LOPAHIN. What a glutton! [All laugh.]

FIRS. His honour stayed with us in Easter week, ate a gallon and a half of cucumbers. . . . [Mutters.]

LYUBOV. What is he saying?

VARYA. He has taken to muttering like that for the last three years. We are used to it.

YASHA. His declining years.

[Charlotta Ivanovna, a very thin, lanky figure in a white dress with a lorgnette in her belt, walks across the stage.]

LOPAHIN. I beg your pardon, Charlotta Ivanovna, I have not had time to greet you. [Tries to kiss her hand.]

CHARLOTTA. [Pulling away her hand.] If I let you kiss my hand, you'll be wanting to kiss my elbow, and then my shoulder.

LOPAHIN. I've no luck today! [All laugh.] Charlotta Ivanovna, show us some tricks!

LYUBOV. Charlotta, do show us some tricks!

CHARLOTTA. I don't want to. I'm sleepy. [Goes out.]

LOPAHIN. In three weeks' time we shall meet again. [Kisses Lyubov Andreyevna's hand.] Good-bye till then—I must go. [To Gaev.] Good-bye. [Kisses Pishtchik.] Good-bye. [Gives his hand to Varya, then to Firs and Yasha.] I don't want to go. [To Lyubov Andreyevna.] If you think over my plan for the villas and make up your mind, then let me know; I will lend you 50,000 roubles. Think of it seriously.

VARYA. [Angrily.] Well, do go, for goodness sake.

LOPAHIN. I'm going, I'm going. [Goes out.]

GAEV. Low-born knave! I beg pardon, though . . . Varya is going to marry him, he's Varya's fiancé.

VARYA. Don't talk nonsense, uncle.

LYUBOV. Well, Varya, I shall be delighted. He's a good man.

PISHTCHIK. He is, one must acknowledge, a most worthy man. And my Dashenka . . . says too that . . . she says . . . various things. [Snores, but at once wakes up.] But all the same, honoured lady, would you oblige me . . . with a loan of 240 roubles . . . to pay the interest on my mortgage tomorrow?

VARYA. [Dismayed.] No, no.

LYUBOV. I really haven't any money.

PISHTCHIK. It will turn up. [Laughs.] I never lose hope. I thought everything was over, I was a ruined man, and lo and behold—the railway passed through my land and . . . they paid me for it. And something else will turn up again, if not to-day, then tomorrow . . . Dashenka'll win two hundred thousand . . . she's got a lottery ticket.

LYUBOV. Well, we've finished our coffee, we can go to bed.

FIRS. [Brushes Gaev, reprovingly.] You have got on the wrong trousers again! What am I to do with you?

VARYA. [Softly.] Anya's asleep. [Softly opens the window.] Now the sun's risen, it's not a bit cold. Look, mamma, what exquisite trees! My goodness! And the air! The starlings are singing!

GAEV. [Opens another window.] The orchard is all white. You've not forgotten it, Lyuba? That long avenue that runs straight, straight as an arrow, how it shines on a moonlight night. You remember? You've not forgotten?

LYUBOV. [Looking out of the window into the garden.] Oh, my childhood, my innocence! It was in this nursery I used to sleep, from here I looked out into the orchard, happiness waked with me every morning and in those days the orchard was just the same, nothing has changed. [Laughs with delight.] All, all white! Oh, my orchard! After the dark gloomy autumn, and the cold winter; you are young again, and full of happiness, the heavenly angels have never left you. . . . If I could cast off the burden that weighs on my heart, if I could forget the past!

GAEV. H'm! and the orchard will be sold to pay our debts; it seems strange. . . .

LYUBOV. See, our mother walking . . . all in white, down the avenue! *[Laughs with delight.]* It is she!

GAEV. Where?

VARYA. Oh, don't, mamma!

LYUBOV. There is no one. It was my fancy. On the right there, by the path to the arbour, there is a white tree bending like a woman. . . .

[Enter Trofimov wearing a shabby student's uniform and spectacles.]

LYUBOV. What a ravishing orchard! White masses of blossom, blue sky. . . .

TROFIMOV. Lyubov Andreyevna! *[She looks round at him.]* I will just pay my respects to you and then leave you at once. *[Kisses her hand warmly.]* I was told to wait until morning, but I hadn't the patience to wait any longer. . . .

[Lyubov Andreyevna looks at him in perplexity.]

VARYA. *[Through her tears.]* This is Petya Trofimov.

TROFIMOV. Petya Trofimov, who was your Grisha's tutor. . . . Can I have changed so much?

[Lyubov Andreyevna embraces him and weeps quietly.]

GAEV. *[In confusion.]* There, there, Lyuba.

VARYA. *[Crying.]* I told you, Petya, to wait till tomorrow.

LYUBOV. My Grisha . . . my boy . . . Grisha . . . my son!

VARYA. We can't help it, mamma, it is God's will.

TROFIMOV. *[Softly through his tears.]* There . . . there.

LYUBOV. *[Weeping quietly.]* My boy was lost . . . drowned. Why? Oh, why, dear Petya? *[More quietly.]* Anya is asleep in there, and I'm talking loudly . . . making this noise. . . . But, Petya? Why have you grown so ugly? why do you look so old?

TROFIMOV. A peasant woman in the train called me a mangy-looking gentleman.

LYUBOV. You were quite a boy then, a pretty little student, and now your hair's thin—and spectacles. Are you really a student still? *[Goes towards the door.]*

TROFIMOV. I seem likely to be a perpetual student.

LYUBOV. *[Kisses her brother, then Varya.]* Well, go to bed. . . . You are older too, Leonid.

PISHTCHIK. *[Follows her.]* I suppose it's time we were asleep. . . . Ugh! my gout. I'm staying the night! Lyubov Andreyevna, my dear soul, if you could . . . to-morrow morning . . . 240 roubles.

GAEV. That's always his story.

PISHTCHIK. 240 roubles . . . to pay the interest on my mortgage.

LYUBOV. My dear man, I have no money.

PISHTCHIK. I'll pay it back, my dear . . . a trifling sum.

LYUBOV. Oh, well, Leonid will give it you. . . . You give him the money, Leonid.

GAEV. Me give it him! Let him wait till he gets it!

LYUBOV. It can't be helped, give it him. He needs it. He'll pay it back.

[Lyubov Andreyevna, Trofimov, Pishtchik, and Firs go out. Gaev, Varya, and Yasha remain.]

GAEV. Sister hasn't got out of the habit of flinging away her money. *[To Yasha.]* Get away, my good fellow, you smell of the henhouse.

YASHA. *[With a grin.]* And you, Leonid Andreyevitch, are just the same as ever.

GAEV. What's that? *[To Varya.]* What did he say?

VARYA. *[To Yasha.]* Your mother has come from the village; she has been sitting in the servants' room since yesterday, waiting to see you.

YASHA. Oh, bother her!

VARYA. For shame!

YASHA. What's the hurry? She might just as well have come to-morrow. *[Goes out.]*

VARYA. Mamma's just the same as ever, she hasn't changed a bit. If she had her own way, she'd give away everything.

GAEV. Yes. *[A pause.]* If a great many remedies are suggested for some disease, it means that the disease is incurable. I keep thinking and racking my brains; I have many schemes, a great many, and that really means none. If we could only come in for a legacy from somebody, or marry our Anya to a very rich man, or we might go to Yaroslavl and try our luck with your old aunt, the Countess. She's very, very rich, you know.

VARYA. *[Weeps.]* If God would help us.

GAEV. Don't blubber. Aunt's very rich, but she doesn't like us. First, sister married a lawyer instead of a nobleman. . . .

[Anya appears in the doorway.]

GAEV. And then her conduct, one can't call it virtuous. She is good, and kind, and nice, and I love her, but, however one allows for extenuating circumstances, there's no denying that she's an immoral woman. One feels it in her slightest gesture.

VARYA. *[In a whisper.]* Anya's in the doorway.

GAEV. What do you say? *[A pause.]* It's queer, there seems to be something wrong with my right eye. I don't see as well as I did. And on Thursday when I was in the district Court . . .
[Enter Anya.]

VARYA. Why aren't you asleep, Anya?

ANYA. I can't get to sleep.

GAEV. My pet. *[Kisses Anya's face and hands.]* My child *[Weeps.]* You are not my niece, you are my angel, you are everything to me. Believe me, believe . . .

ANYA. I believe you, uncle. Everyone loves you and respects you . . . but, uncle dear, you must be silent . . . simply be silent. What were you saying just now about my mother, about your own sister? What made you say that?

GAEV. Yes, yes . . . *[Puts his hand over his face.]* Really, that was awful! My God, save me! And to-day I made a speech to the bookcase . . . so stupid! And only when I had finished, I saw how stupid it was.

VARYA. It's true, uncle, you ought to keep quiet. Don't talk, that's all.

ANYA. If you could keep from talking, it would make things easier for you, too.

GAEV. I won't speak *[Kisses Anya's and Varya's hands.]* I'll be silent. Only this is about business. On Thursday I was in the district Court; well, there was a large party of us there and we began talking of one thing and another, and this and that, and do you know, I believe that it will be possible to raise a loan on an I.O.U. to pay the arrears on the mortgage.

VARYA. If the Lord would help us!

GAEV. I'm going on Tuesday; I'll talk of it again. *[To Varya.]* Don't blubber. *[To Anya.]* Your mamma will talk to Lopahin; of course, he won't refuse her. And as soon as you're rested you shall go to Yaroslavl to the Countess, your great-aunt. So we shall all set to work in three directions at once, and the business is done. We shall pay off arrears, I'm convinced of it *[Puts a caramel into his mouth.]* I swear on my honour, I swear by anything you like, the estate shan't be sold. *[Excitedly.]* By my own happiness, I swear it! Here's my hand on it, call me the basest, vilest of men, if I let it come to an auction! Upon my soul I swear it!

ANYA. *[Her equanimity has returned; she is quite happy.]* How good you are, uncle, and how clever! *[Embraces her uncle.]* I'm at peace now! Quite at peace! I'm happy!

[Enter Firs.]

FIRS. *[Reproachfully.]* Leonid Andreyevitch, have you no fear of God? When are you going to bed?

GAEV. Directly, directly. You can go, Firs. I'll . . . yes, I will undress myself. Come, children, bye-bye. We'll go into details to-morrow, but now go to bed. *[Kisses Anya and Varya.]* I'm a man of the eighties. They run down that period, but still I can say I have had to suffer not a little for my convictions in my life. It's not for nothing that the peasant loves me. One must know the peasant! One must know how . . .

ANYA. At it again, uncle!

VARYA. Uncle dear, you'd better be quiet.

FIRS. *[Angrily.]* Leonid Andreyevitch!

GAEV. I'm coming. I'm coming. Go to bed. Potted the shot—there's a shot for you! A beauty! *[Goes out, Firs hobbling after him.]*

ANYA. My mind's at rest now. I don't want to go to Yaroslavl, I don't like my great-aunt, but still my mind's at rest. Thanks to uncle. *[Sits down.]*

VARYA. We must go to bed. I'm going. Something unpleasant happened while you were away. In the old servants' quarters there are only the old servants, as you know—Efimyushka, Polya and Yevstigney—and Karp too. They began letting stray people in to spend the night—I said nothing. But all at once I heard they had been spreading a report that I gave them nothing but pease pudding to eat. Out of stinginess, you know. . . . And it was all Yevstigney's doing. . . . Very well, I said to myself. . . . If that's how it is, I thought, wait a bit. I sent for Yevstigney. . . . *[Yawns.]* He comes. . . . "How's this, Yevstigney," I said, "you could be such a fool as to? . . ." *[Looking at Anya.]* Anitchka! *[A pause.]* She's asleep. *[Puts her arm round Anya.]* Come to bed . . . come along! *[Leads her.]* My darling has fallen asleep! Come. . . . *[They go.]*

[Far away beyond the orchard a shepherd plays on a pipe. Trofimov crosses the stage and, seeing Varya and Anya, stands still.]

VARYA. Sh! asleep, asleep. Come, my own.
ANYA. *[Softly, half asleep.]* I'm so tired. Still those bells. Uncle . . . dear . . . mamma and uncle. . . .

VARYA. Come, my own, come along.

[They go into Anya's room.]

TROFIMOV. *[Tenderly.]* My sunshine! My spring!

CURTAIN

Act II

The open country. An old shrine, long abandoned and fallen out of the perpendicular; near it a well, large stones that have apparently once been tombstones, and an old garden seat. The road to Gaev's house is seen. On one side rise dark poplars; and there the cherry orchard begins. In the distance a row of telegraph poles and far, far away on the horizon there is faintly outlined a great town, only visible in very fine clear weather. It is near sunset. Charlotta, Yasha, and Dunyasha are sitting on the seat. Epihodov is standing near, playing something mournful on a guitar. All sit plunged in thought. Charlotta wears an old forage cap; she has taken a gun from her shoulder and is tightening the buckle on the strap.

CHARLOTTA. *[Musingly.]* I haven't a real passport of my own, and I don't know how old I am, and I always feel that I'm a young thing. When I was a little girl, my father and mother used to travel about to fairs and give performances—very good ones. And I used to dance *salto-mortale* and all sorts of things. And when papa and mamma died, a German lady took me and had me educated. And so I grew up and became a governess. But where I came from, and who I am, I don't know. . . . Who my parents were, very likely they weren't married . . . I don't know. *[Takes a cucumber out of her pocket and eats.]* I know nothing at all. *[A pause.]* One wants to talk and has no one to talk to . . . I have nobody.
EPIHODOV. *[Plays on the guitar and sings.]* "What care I for the noisy world! What care I for friends or foes!" How agreeable it is to play on the mandolin!

DUNYASHA. That's a guitar, not a mandolin. *[Looks in a hand-mirror and powders herself.]*
EPIHODOV. To a man mad with love, it's a mandolin. *[Sings.]* "Were her heart but aglow with love's mutual flame." *[Yasha joins in.]*
CHARLOTTA. How shockingly these people sing! Foo! Like jackals!
DUNYASHA. *[To Yasha.]* What happiness, though, to visit foreign lands.
YASHA. Ah, yes! I rather agree with you there. *[Yawns, then lights a cigar.]*
EPIHODOV. That's comprehensible. In foreign lands everything has long since reached full complexion.
YASHA. That's so, of course.
EPIHODOV. I'm a cultivated man, I read remarkable books of all sorts, but I can never make out the tendency I am myself precisely inclined for, whether to live or to shoot myself, speaking precisely, but nevertheless I always carry a revolver. Here it is. . . . *[Shows revolver.]*
CHARLOTTA. I've had enough, and now I'm going. *[Puts on the gun.]* Epihodov, you're a very clever fellow, and a very terrible one too, all the women must be wild about you. Br-r-r! *[Goes.]* These clever fellows are all so stupid; there's not a creature for me to speak to. . . . Always alone, alone, nobody belonging to me . . . and who I am, and why I'm on earth, I don't know. *[Walks away slowly.]*
EPIHODOV. Speaking precisely, not touching upon other subjects, I'm bound to admit about myself, that destiny behaves mercilessly to me, as a storm to a little boat. If, let us suppose, I am mistaken, then why did I wake up this morning, to quote an example, and look round, and there on my chest was a spider of fearful magnitude . . . like this. *[Shows with both hands.]* And then I take up a

jug of kvass, to quench my thirst, and in it there is something in the highest degree unseemly of the nature of a cockroach. *[A pause.]* Have you read Buckle? *[A pause.]* I am desirous of troubling you, Dunyasha, with a couple of words.

DUNYASHA. Well, speak.

EPIHODOV. I should be desirous to speak with you alone. *[Sighs.]*

DUNYASHA. *[Embarrassed.]* Well—only bring me my mantle first. It's by the cupboard. It's rather damp here.

EPIHODOV. Certainly. I will fetch it. Now I know what I must do with my revolver. *[Takes guitar and goes off playing on it.]*

YASHA. Two and twenty misfortunes! Between ourselves, he's a fool. *[Yawns.]*

DUNYASHA. God grant he doesn't shoot himself! *[A pause.]* I am so nervous, I'm always in a flutter. I was a little girl when I was taken into our lady's house, and now I have quite grown out of peasant ways, and my hands are white, as white as a lady's. I'm such a delicate, sensitive creature, I'm afraid of everything. I'm so frightened. And if you deceive me, Yasha, I don't know what will become of my nerves.

YASHA. *[Kisses her.]* You're a peach! Of course a girl must never forget herself; what I dislike more than anything is a girl being flighty in her behavior.

DUNYASHA. I'm passionately in love with you, Yasha; you are a man of culture—you can give your opinion about anything. *[A pause.]*

YASHA. *[Yawns.]* Yes, that's so. My opinion is this: if a girl loves anyone, that means that she has no principles. *[A pause.]* It's pleasant smoking a cigar in the open air. *[Listens.]* Someone's coming this way . . . it's the gentlefolk *[Dunyasha embraces him impulsively.]* Go home, as though you had been to the river to bathe; go by that path, or else they'll meet you and suppose I have made an appointment with you here. That I can't endure.

DUNYASHA. *[Coughing softly.]* The cigar has made my head ache. . . . *[Goes off.]*

[Yasha remains sitting near the shrine. Enter Lyubov Andreyevna, Gaev, and Lopahin.]

LOPAHIN. You must make up your mind once for all—there's no time to lose. It's quite a simple question, you know. Will you consent to letting the land for building or not? One word in answer: Yes or no? Only one word!

LYUBOV. Who is smoking such horrible cigars? *[Sits down.]*

GAEV. Now the railway line has been brought near, it's made things very convenient. *[Sits down.]* Here we have been over and lunched in town. Hit off the white! I should like to go home and have a game.

LYUBOV. You have plenty of time.

LOPAHIN. Only one word! *[Beseechingly.]* Give me an answer!

GAEV. *[Yawning.]* What do you say?

LYUBOV. *[Looks in her purse.]* I had quite a lot of money here yesterday, and there's scarcely any left today. My poor Varya feeds us all on milk soup for the sake of economy; the old folks in the kitchen get nothing but pease pudding, while I waste my money in a senseless way. *[Drops purse, scattering gold pieces.]* There, they have all fallen out! *[Annoyed.]*

YASHA. Allow me, I'll soon pick them up. *[Collects the coins.]*

LYUBOV. Pray do, Yasha. And what did I go off to the town to lunch for? Your restaurant's a wretched place with its music and the tablecloth smelling of soap. . . . Why drink so much, Leonid? And eat so much? And talk so much? Today you talked a great deal again in the restaurant, and all so inappropriately. About the era of the 'seventies, about the decadents. And to whom? Talking to waiters about decadents!

LOPAHIN. Yes.

GAEV. *[Waving his hand.]* I'm incorrigible; that's evident. *[Irritably to Yasha.]* Why is it you keep fidgeting about in front of us!

YASHA. *[Laughs.]* I can't help laughing when I hear your voice.

GAEV. *[To his sister.]* Either I or he . . .

LYUBOV. Get along! Go away, Yasha.

YASHA. *[Gives Lyubov Andreyevna her purse.]* Directly. *[Hardly able to suppress his laughter.]* This minute . . . *[Goes off.]*

LOPAHIN. Deriganov, the millionaire, means to buy your estate. They say he is coming to the sale himself.

LYUBOV. Where did you hear that?

LOPAHIN. That's what they say in town.

GAEV. Our aunt in Yaroslavl has promised to send help; but when, and how much she will send, we don't know.

LOPAHIN. How much will she send? A hundred thousand? Two hundred?

LYUBOV. Oh, well! . . . Ten or fifteen thousand, and we must be thankful to get that.

LOPAHIN. Forgive me, but such reckless people as you are—such queer, unbusiness-like people—I never met in my life. One tells you in plain Russian your estate is going to be sold, and you seem not to understand it.

LYUBOV. What are we to do? Tell us what to do.

LOPAHIN. I do tell you every day. Every day I say the same thing. You absolutely must let the cherry orchard and the land on building leases; and do it at once, as quick as may be—the auction's close upon us! Do understand! Once make up your mind to build villas, and you can raise as much money as you like, and then you are saved.

LYUBOV. Villas and summer visitors—forgive me saying so—it's so vulgar.

GAEV. There I perfectly agree with you.

LOPAHIN. I shall sob, or scream, or fall into a fit. I can't stand it! You drive me mad! *[To Gaev.]* You're an old woman!

GAEV. What do you say?

LOPAHIN. An old woman! *[Gets up to go.]*

LYUBOV. *[In dismay.]* No, don't go! Do stay, my dear friend! Perhaps we shall think of something.

LOPAHIN. What is there to think of?

LYUBOV. Don't go, I entreat you! With you here it's more cheerful, anyway. *[A pause.]* I keep expecting something, as though the house were going to fall about our ears.

GAEV. *[In profound dejection.]* Potted the white! It fails—a kiss.

LYUBOV. We have been great sinners. . . .

LOPAHIN. You have no sins to repent of.

GAEV. *[Puts a caramel into his mouth.]* They say I've eaten up my property in caramels. *[Laughs.]*

LYUBOV. Oh, my sins! I've always thrown my money away recklessly like a lunatic. I married a man who made nothing but debts. My husband died of champagne—he drank dreadfully. To my misery I loved another man, and immediately—it was my first punishment—the blow fell upon me, here, in the river . . . my boy was drowned and I went abroad—went away for ever, never to return, not to see that river again. . . . I shut my eyes, and fled, distracted, and *he* after me . . . pitilessly, brutally. I bought a villa at Mentone, for *he* fell

ill there, and for three years I had no rest day or night. His illness wore me out, my soul was dried up. And last year, when my villa was sold to pay my debts, I went to Paris and there he robbed me of everything and abandoned me for another woman; and I tried to poison myself. . . . So stupid, so shameful! . . . And suddenly I felt a yearning for Russia, for my country, for my little girls. . . . *[Dries her tears.]* Lord, Lord, be merciful! Forgive my sins! Do not chastise me more! *[Takes a telegram out of her pocket.]* I got this today from Paris. He implores forgiveness, entreats me to return. *[Tears up the telegram.]* I fancy there is music somewhere. *[Listens.]*

GAEV. That's our famous Jewish orchestra. You remember, four violins, a flute and a double bass.

LYUBOV. That still in existence? We ought to send for them one evening, and give a dance.

LOPAHIN. *[Listens.]* I can't hear. . . . *[Hums softly.]* "For money the Germans will turn a Russian into a Frenchman." *[Laughs.]* I did see such a piece at the theatre yesterday! It was funny!

LYUBOV. And most likely there was nothing funny in it. You shouldn't look at plays, you should look at yourselves a little oftener. How grey your lives are! How much nonsense you talk.

LOPAHIN. That's true. One may say honestly, we live a fool's life. *[Pause.]* My father was a peasant, an idiot; he knew nothing and taught me nothing, only beat me when he was drunk, and always with his stick. In reality I am just such another blockhead and idiot. I've learnt nothing properly. I write a wretched hand. I write so that I feel ashamed before folks, like a pig.

LYUBOV. You ought to get married, my dear fellow.

LOPAHIN. Yes . . . that's true.

LYUBOV. You should marry our Varya, she's a good girl.

LOPAHIN. Yes.

LYUBOV. She's a good-natured girl, she's busy all day long, and what's more, she loves you. And you have liked her for ever so long.

LOPAHIN. Well? I'm not against it. . . . She's a good girl. *[Pause.]*

GAEV. I've been offered a place in the bank: 6,000 roubles a year. Did you know?

LYUBOV. You would never do for that! You must stay as you are.

[Enter Firs with overcoat.]

FIRS. Put it on, sir, it's damp.

GAEV. [Putting it on.] You bother me, old fellow.

FIRS. You can't go on like this. You went away in the morning without leaving word. [Looks him over.]

LYUBOV. You look older, Firs!

FIRS. What is your pleasure?

LOPAHIN. You look older, she said.

FIRS. I've had a long life. They were arranging my wedding before your papa was born. . . . [Laughs.] I was the head footman before the emancipation came. I wouldn't consent to be set free then; I stayed on with the old master. . . . [A pause.] I remember what rejoicings they made and didn't know themselves what they were rejoicing over.

LOPAHIN. Those were fine old times. There was flogging anyway.

FIRS. [Not hearing.] To be sure! The peasants knew their place, and the masters knew theirs; but now they're all at sixes and sevens, there's no making it out.

GAEV. Hold your tongue, Firs. I must go to town tomorrow. I have been promised an introduction to a general, who might let us have a loan.

LOPAHIN. You won't bring that off. And you won't pay your arrears, you may rest assured of that.

LYUBOV. That's all his nonsense. There is no such general.

[Enter Trofimov, Anya, and Varya.]

GAEV. Here come our girls.

ANYA. There's mamma on the seat.

LYUBOV. [Tenderly.] Come here, come along. My darlings! [Embraces Anya and Varya.] If you only knew how I love you both. Sit beside me, there, like that. [All sit down.]

LOPAHIN. Our perpetual student is always with the young ladies.

TROFIMOV. That's not your business.

LOPAHIN. He'll soon be fifty, and he's still a student.

TROFIMOV. Drop your idiotic jokes.

LOPAHIN. Why are you so cross, you queer fish?

TROFIMOV. Oh, don't persist!

LOPAHIN. [Laughs.] Allow me to ask you what's your idea of me?

TROFIMOV. I'll tell you my idea of you, Yermolay Alexeyevitch: you are a rich man, you'll soon be a millionaire. Well, just as in the economy of nature a wild beast is of use, who devours everything that comes in his way, so you too have your use.

[All laugh.]

VARYA. Better tell us something about the planets, Petya.

LYUBOV. No, let us go on with the conversation we had yesterday.

TROFIMOV. What was it about?

GAEV. About pride.

TROFIMOV. We had a long conversation yesterday, but we came to no conclusion. In pride, in your sense of it, there is something mystical. Perhaps you are right from your point of view; but if one looks at it simply, without subtlety, what sort of pride can there be, what sense is there in it, if man in his physiological formation is very imperfect, if in the immense majority of cases he is coarse, dull-witted, profoundly unhappy? One must give up glorification of self. One should work, and nothing else.

GAEV. One must die in any case.

TROFIMOV. Who knows? And what does it mean—dying? Perhaps man has a hundred senses, and only the five we know are lost at death, while the other ninety-five remain alive.

LYUBOV. How clever you are, Petya!

LOPAHIN. [Ironically.] Fearfully clever!

TROFIMOV. Humanity progresses, perfecting its powers. Everything that is beyond its ken now will one day become familiar and comprehensible; only we must work, we must with all our powers aid the seeker after truth. Here among us in Russia the workers are few in number as yet. The vast majority of the intellectual people I know, seek nothing, do nothing, are not fit as yet for work of any kind. They call themselves intellectual, but they treat their servants as inferiors, behave to the peasants as though they were animals, learn little, read nothing seriously, do practically nothing, only talk about science and know very little about art. They are all serious people, they all have severe faces, they all talk of weighty matters and air their theories, and yet the vast majority of us—ninety-nine percent—live like

savages, at the least thing fly to blows and
abuse, eat piggishly, sleep in filth and stuffiness,
bugs everywhere, stench and damp and moral
impurity. And it's clear all our fine talk is only
to divert our attention and other people's.
Show me where to find the crèches there's so
much talk about, and the reading-rooms? They
only exist in novels: in real life there are none of
them. There is nothing but filth and vulgarity
and Asiatic apathy. I fear and dislike very serious
faces. I'm afraid of serious conversations. We
should do better to be silent.

LOPAHIN. You know, I get up at five o'clock in the
morning, and I work from morning to night;
and I've money, my own and other people's,
always passing through my hands, and I see
what people are made of all round me. One has
only to begin to do anything to see how few
honest, decent people there are. Sometimes
when I lie awake at night, I think: "Oh! Lord,
thou hast given us immense forests, boundless
plains, the widest horizons, and living here we
ourselves ought really to be giants."

LYUBOV. You ask for giants! They are no good except
in story-books; in real life they frighten us.

*[Epihodov advances in the background, playing on the
guitar.]*

LYUBOV. *[Dreamily.]* There goes, Epihodov.
ANYA. *[Dreamily.]* There goes Epihodov.
GAEV. The sun has set, my friends.
TROFIMOV. Yes.
GAEV. *[Not loudly, but, as it were, declaiming.]* O nature,
divine nature, thou art bright with eternal
lustre, beautiful and indifferent! Thou, whom
we call mother, thou dost unite within thee life
and death! Thou dost give life and dost destroy!
VARYA. *[In a tone of supplication.]* Uncle!
ANYA. Uncle, you are at it again!
TROFIMOV. You'd much better be hitting off the
red!
GAEV. I'll hold my tongue, I will.

*[All sit plunged in thought. Perfect stillness. The only thing
audible is the muttering of Firs. Suddenly there is a sound in
the distance, as it were from the sky—the sound of a breaking harp-string, mournfully dying away.]*

LYUBOV. What is that?

LOPAHIN. I don't know. Somewhere far away a
bucket fallen and broken in the pits. But
somewhere very far away.
GAEV. It might be a bird of some sort—such as a
heron.
TROFIMOV. Or an owl.
LYUBOV. *[Shudders.]* I don't know why, but it's
horrid. *[A pause.]*
FIRS. It was the same before the calamity—the owl
hooted and the samovar hissed all the time.
GAEV. Before what calamity?
FIRS. Before the emancipation. *[A pause.]*
LYUBOV. Come, my friends, let us be going;
evening is falling. *[To Anya.]* There are tears in
your eyes. What is it, darling? *[Embraces her.]*
ANYA. Nothing, mamma; it's nothing.
TROFIMOV. There is somebody coming.

*[The wayfarer appears in a shabby white forage cap and an
overcoat; he is slightly drunk.]*

WAYFARER. Allow me to inquire, can I get to the
station this way?
GAEV. Yes. Go along that road.
WAYFARER. I thank you most feelingly. *[Coughing.]*
The weather is superb. *[Declaims.]* My brother,
my suffering brother! . . . Come out to the
Volga! Whose groan do you hear? . . . *[To
Varya.]* Mademoiselle, vouchsafe a hungry
Russian thirty kopeks.

[Varya utters a shriek of alarm.]

LOPAHIN. *[Angrily.]* There's a right and a wrong way
of doing everything!
LYUBOV. *[Hurriedly.]* Here, take this. *[Looks in her
purse.]* I've no silver. No matter—here's gold for
you.
WAYFARER. I thank you most feelingly! *[Goes off.]*

[Laughter.]

VARYA. *[Frightened.]* I'm going home—I'm going
. . . Oh, mamma, the servants have nothing to
eat, and you gave him gold!
LYUBOV. There's no doing anything with me. I'm
so silly! When we get home, I'll give you all I
possess. Yermolay Alexeyevitch, you will lend
me some more . . .!
LOPAHIN. I will.

LYUBOV. Come, friends, it's time to be going. And Varya, we have made a match of it for you. I congratulate you.

VARYA. [Through her tears.] Mamma, that's not a joking matter.

LOPAHIN. "Ophelia, get thee to a nunnery!"

GAEV. My hands are trembling; it's a long while since I had a game of billiards.

LOPAHIN. "Ophelia! Nymph, in thy orisons be all my sins remember'd.'"

LYUBOV. Come, it will soon be supper-time.

VARYA. How he frightened me! My heart's simply throbbing.

LOPAHIN. Let me remind you, ladies and gentlemen: on the 22nd of August the cherry orchard will be sold. Think about that! Think about it!

[All go off, except Trofimov and Anya.]

ANYA. [Laughing.] I'm grateful to the wayfarer! He frightened Varya and we are left alone.

TROFIMOV. Varya's afraid we shall fall in love with each other, and for days together she won't leave us. With her narrow brain she can't grasp that we are above love. To eliminate the petty and transitory which hinders us from being free and happy—that is the aim and meaning of our life. Forward! We go forward irresistibly towards the bright star that shines yonder in the distance. Forward! Do not lag behind, friends.

ANYA. [Claps her hands.] How well you speak! [A pause.] It is divine here to-day.

TROFIMOV. Yes, it's glorious weather.

ANYA. Somehow, Petya, you've made me so that I don't love the cherry orchard as I used to. I used to love it so dearly. I used to think that there was no spot on earth like our garden.

TROFIMOV. All Russia is our garden. The earth is great and beautiful—there are many beautiful places in it. [A pause.] Think only, Anya, your grandfather, and great-grandfather, and all your ancestors were slave-owners—the owners of living souls—and from every cherry in the orchard, from every leaf, from every trunk there are human creatures looking at you. Cannot you hear their voices? Oh, it is awful! Your orchard is a fearful thing, and when in the evening or at night one walks about the orchard, the old bark on the trees glimmers dimly in the dusk, and the old cherry trees seem to be dreaming of centuries gone by and tortured by fearful visions. Yes! We are at least two hundred years behind, we have really gained nothing yet, we have no definite attitude to the past, we do nothing but theorise or complain of depression or drink vodka. It is clear that to begin to live in the present we must first expiate our past, we must break with it; and we can expiate it only by suffering, by extraordinary unceasing labour. Understand that, Anya.

ANYA. The house we live in has long ceased to be our own, and I shall leave it, I give you my word.

TROFIMOV. If you have the house keys, fling them into the well and go away. Be free as the wind.

ANYA. [In ecstasy.] How beautifully you said that!

TROFIMOV. Believe me, Anya, believe me! I am not thirty yet, I am young, I am still a student, but I have gone through so much already! As soon as winter comes I am hungry, sick, careworn, poor as a beggar, and what ups and downs of fortune have I not known! And my soul was always, every minute, day and night, full of inexplicable forebodings. I have a foreboding of happiness, Anya. I see glimpses of it already.

ANYA. [Pensively.] The moon is rising.

[Epihodov is heard playing still the same mournful song on the guitar. The moon rises. Somewhere near the poplars Varya is looking for Anya and calling "Anya! where are you?"]

TROFIMOV. Yes, the moon is rising. [A pause.] Here is happiness—here it comes! It is coming nearer and nearer; already I can hear its footsteps. And if we never see it—if we may never know it—what does it matter? Others will see it after us.

VARYA'S VOICE. Anya! Where are you?

TROFIMOV. That Varya again! [Angrily.] It's revolting!

ANYA. Well, let's go down to the river. It's lovely there.

TROFIMOV. Yes, let's go. [They go.]

VARYA'S VOICE. Anya! Anya!

CURTAIN

Act III

A drawing-room divided by an arch from a larger drawing-room. A chandelier burning. The Jewish orchestra, the same that was mentioned in Act II, is heard playing in the anteroom. It is evening. In the larger drawing-room they are dancing the grand chain. The voice of Semyonov-Pishtchik: "Promenade à une paire!" Then enter the drawing-room in couples first Pishtchik and Charlotta Ivanovna, then Trofimov and Lyubov Andreyevna, third Anya with the Post-Office Clerk, fourth Varya with the Station Master, and other guests. Varya is quietly weeping and wiping away her tears as she dances. In the last couple is Dunyasha. They move across the drawing-room. Pishtchik shouts: "Grand rond, balancez!" *and* "Les cavaliers à genou et remerciez vos dames."

[Firs in a swallowtail coat brings in seltzer water on a tray. Pishtchik and Trofimov enter the drawing-room.]

PISHTCHIK. I am a full-blooded man; I have already had two strokes. Dancing's hard work for me, but as they say, if you're in the pack, you must bark with the rest. I'm as strong, I may say, as a horse. My parent, who would have his joke—may the Kingdom of Heaven be his!—used to say about our origin that the ancient stock of the Semyonov-Pishtchiks was derived from the very horse that Caligula made a member of the senate. *[Sits down.]* But I've no money, that's where the mischief is. A hungry dog believes in nothing but meat. . . . *[Snores, but at once wakes up.]* That's like me . . . I can think of nothing but money.

TROFIMOV. There really is something horsy about your appearance.

PISHTCHIK. Well . . . a horse is a fine beast . . . a horse can be sold.

[There is a sound of billiards being played in an adjoining room. Varya appears in the arch leading to the larger drawing-room.]

TROFIMOV. *[Teasing.]* Madame Lopahin! Madame Lopahin!

VARYA. *[Angrily.]* Mangy-looking gentleman!

TROFIMOV. Yes, I am a mangy-looking gentleman, and I'm proud of it!

VARYA. *[Pondering bitterly.]* Here we have hired musicians and nothing to pay them! *[Goes out.]*

TROFIMOV. *[To Pishtchik.]* If the energy you have wasted during your lifetime in trying to find the money to pay your interest, had gone to something else, you might in the end have turned the world upside down.

PISHTCHIK. Nietzsche, the philosopher, a very great and celebrated man . . . of enormous intellect . . . says in his works that one can make forged banknotes.

TROFIMOV. Why, have you read Nietzsche?

PISHTCHIK. What next . . . Dashenka told me. . . . And now I am in such a position, I might just as well forge banknotes. The day after tomorrow I must pay 310 roubles—130 I have procured . . . *Feels in his pockets, in alarm.* The money's gone! I have lost my money! *[Through his tears.]* Where's the money? *[Gleefully.]* Why, here it is behind the lining. . . . It has made me hot all over.

[Enter Lyubov Andreyevna and Charlotta Ivanovna.]

LYUBOV. *[Hums the Lezginka.]* Why is Leonid so long? What can he be doing in town? *[To Dunyasha.]* Offer the musicians some tea.

TROFIMOV. The sale hasn't take place, most likely.

LYUBOV. It's the wrong time to have the orchestra, and the wrong time to give a dance. Well, never mind. *[Sits down and hums softly.]*

CHARLOTTA. *[Gives Pishtchik a pack of cards.]* Here's a pack of cards. Think of any card you like.

PISHTCHIK. I've thought of one.

CHARLOTTA. Shuffle the pack now. That's right. Give it here, my dear Mr. Pishtchik. Eins, zwei, drei—now look, it's in your breast pocket.

PISHTCHIK. *[Taking a card out of his breast pocket.]* The eight of spades! Perfectly right! *[Wonderingly.]* Fancy that now!

CHARLOTTA. *[Holding pack of cards in her hands, to Trofimov.]* Tell me quickly which is the top card.

TROFIMOV. Well, the queen of spades.

CHARLOTTA. It is! *[To Pishtchik.]* Well, which card is uppermost?

PISHTCHIK. The ace of hearts.

CHARLOTTA. It is! *[Claps her hands, pack of cards disappear.]* Ah! what lovely weather it is today!

[A mysterious feminine voice which seems coming out of the floor answers her. "Oh, yes, it's magnificent weather, madam."]

CHARLOTTA. You are my perfect ideal.

VOICE. And I greatly admire you too, madam.

STATION MASTER. *[Applauding.]* The lady ventriloquist—bravo!

PISHTCHIK. *[Wonderingly.]* Fancy that now! Most enchanting Charlotta Ivanovna. I'm simply in love with you.

CHARLOTTA. In love? *[Shrugging shoulders.]* What do you know of love, guter Mensch, aber schlechter Musikant?

TROFIMOV. *[Pats Pishtchik on the shoulder.]* You dear old horse. . . .

CHARLOTTA. Attention, please! Another trick! *[Takes a traveling rug from a chair.]* Here's a very good rug; I want to sell it. *[Shaking it out.]* Doesn't anyone want to buy it?

PISHTCHIK. *[Wonderingly.]* Fancy that!

CHARLOTTA. Eins, zwei, drei! *[Quickly picks up rug she has dropped; behind the rug stands Anya; she makes a curtsey, runs to her mother, embraces her and runs back into the larger drawing-room amidst general enthusiasm.]*

LYUBOV. *[Applauds.]* Bravo! Bravo!

CHARLOTTA. Now again! Eins, zwei, drei! *[Lifts up the rug; behind the rug stands Varya, bowing.]*

PISHTCHIK. *[Wonderingly.]* Fancy that now!

CHARLOTTA. That's the end. *[Throws the rug at Pishtchik, makes a curtsey, runs into the larger drawing-room.]*

PISHTCHIK. *[Hurries after her.]* Mischievous creature! Fancy! *[Goes out.]*

LYUBOV. And still Leonid doesn't come. I can't understand what he's doing in the town so long! Why, everything must be over by now. The estate is sold, or the sale has not taken place. Why keep us so long in suspense?

VARYA. *[Trying to console her.]* Uncle's bought it. I feel sure of that.

TROFIMOV. *[Ironically.]* Oh, yes!

VARYA. Great-aunt sent him an authorization to buy it in her name, and transfer the debt. She's doing it for Anya's sake, and I'm sure God will be merciful. Uncle will buy it.

LYUBOV. My aunt in Yaroslavl sent fifteen thousand to buy the estate in her name, she doesn't trust us—but that's not enough even to pay the arrears. *[Hides her face in her hands.]* My fate is being sealed today, my fate. . . .

TROFIMOV. *[Teasing Varya.]* Madame Lopahin.

VARYA. *[Angrily.]* Perpetual student! Twice already you've been sent down from the University.

LYUBOV. Why are you angry, Varya? He's teasing you about Lopahin. Well, what of that? Marry Lopahin if you like, he's a good man, and interesting; if you don't want to, don't! Nobody compels you, darling.

VARYA. I must tell you plainly, mamma, I look at the matter seriously; he's a good man, I like him.

LYUBOV. Well, marry him. I can't see what you're waiting for.

VARYA. Mamma. I can't make him an offer myself. For the last two years, everyone's been talking to me about him. Everyone talks; but he says nothing or else makes a joke. I see what it means. He's growing rich, he's absorbed in business, he has no thoughts for me. If I had money, were it ever so little, if I had only a hundred roubles, I'd throw everything up and go far away. I would go into a nunnery.

TROFIMOV. What bliss!

VARYA. *[To Trofimov.]* A student ought to have sense! *[In a soft tone with tears.]* How ugly you've grown, Petya! How old you look! *[To Lyubov Andreyevna, no longer crying.]* But I can't do without work, mamma; I must have something to do every minute.

[Enter Yasha.]

YASHA. *[Hardly restraining his laughter.]* Epihodov has broken a billiard cue! *[Goes out.]*

VARYA. What is Epihodov doing here? Who gave him leave to play billiards? I can't make these people out. *[Goes out.]*

LYUBOV. Don't tease her, Petya. You see she has grief enough without that.

TROFIMOV. She is so very officious, meddling in what's not her business. All the summer she's given Anya and me no peace. She's afraid of a love affair between us. What's it to do with her? Besides, I have given no grounds for it. Such triviality is not in my line. We are above love!

LYUBOV. And I suppose I am beneath love. *[Very uneasily.]* Why is it Leonid's not here? If only I could know whether the estate is sold or not! It seems such an incredible calamity that I really don't know what to think. I am distracted . . . I shall scream in a minute . . . I shall do something stupid. Save me, Petya, tell me something, talk to me!

TROFIMOV. What does it matter whether the estate is sold today or not? That's all done with long ago. There's no turning back, the path is overgrown. Don't worry yourself, dear Lyubov Andreyevna. You mustn't deceive yourself; for once in your life you must face the truth!

LYUBOV. What truth? You see where the truth lies, but I seem to have lost my sight, I see nothing. You settle every great problem so boldly, but tell me, my dear boy, isn't it because you're young—because you haven't yet understood one of your problems through suffering? You look forward boldly, and isn't it that you don't see and don't expect anything dreadful because life is still hidden from your young eyes? You're bolder, more honest, deeper than we are, but think, be just a little magnanimous, have pity on me. I was born here, you know, my father and mother lived here, my grandfather lived here, I love this house. I can't conceive of life without the cherry orchard, and if it really must be sold, then sell me with the orchard. [Embraces Trofimov, kisses him on the forehead.] My boy was drowned here. [Weeps.] Pity me, my dear kind fellow.

TROFIMOV. You know I feel for you with all my heart.

LYUBOV. But that should have been said differently, so differently. [Takes out her handkerchief, telegram falls on the floor.] My heart is so heavy today. It's so noisy here, my soul is quivering at every sound, I'm shuddering all over, but I can't go away; I'm afraid to be quiet and alone. Don't be hard on me, Petya . . . I love you as though you were one of ourselves. I would gladly let you marry Anya—I swear I would—only, my dear boy, you must take your degree, you do nothing—you're simply tossed by fate from place to place. That's so strange. It is, isn't it? And you must do something with your beard to make it grow somehow. [Laughs.] You look so funny!

TROFIMOV. [Picks up the telegram.] I've no wish to be a beauty.

LYUBOV. That's a telegram from Paris. I get one every day. One yesterday and one to-day. That savage creature is ill again, he's in trouble again. He bets forgiveness, beseeches me to go, and really I ought to go to Paris to see him. You look shocked, Petya. What am I to do, my dear

boy, what am I to do? He is ill, he is alone and unhappy, and who'll look after him, who'll keep him from doing the wrong thing, who'll give him his medicine at the right time? And why hide it or be silent? I love him, that's clear. I love him! I love him! He's a millstone about my neck, I'm going to the bottom with him, but I love that stone and can't live without it. [Presses Trofimov's hand.] Don't think ill of me, Petya, don't tell me anything, don't tell me . . .

TROFIMOV. [Through his tears.] For God's sake forgive my frankness: why, he robbed you!

LYUBOV. No! No! No! You mustn't speak like that. [Covers her ears.]

TROFIMOV. He is a wretch! You're the only person that doesn't know it! He's a worthless creature! A despicable wretch!

LYUBOV. [Getting angry, but speaking with restraint.] You're twenty-six or twenty-seven years old, but you're still a schoolboy.

TROFIMOV. Possibly.

LYUBOV. You should be a man at your age! You should understand what love means! And you ought to be in love yourself. You ought to fall in love! [Angrily.] Yes, yes, and it's not purity in you, you're simply a prude, a comic fool, a freak.

TROFIMOV. [In horror.] The things she's saying!

LYUBOV. I am above love! You're not above love, but simply as our Firs here says, "You are a good-for-nothing." At your age not to have a mistress!

TROFIMOV. [In horror.] This is awful! The things she is saying! [Goes rapidly into the larger drawing-room clutching his head.] This is awful! I can't stand it! I'm going. [Goes off, but at once returns.] All is over between us! [Goes off into the anteroom.]

LYUBOV. [Shouts after him.] Petya! Wait a minute! You funny creature! I was joking! Petya! [There is a sound of somebody running quickly downstairs and suddenly falling with a crash. Anya and Varya scream, but there is a sound of laughter at once.]

LYUBOV. What has happened?

[Anya runs in.]

ANYA. [Laughing.] Petya's fallen downstairs! [Runs out.]

LYUBOV. What a queer fellow that Petya is!

[The Station Master stands in the middle of the larger room and reads "The Magdalene," by Alexey Tolstoy. They listen *to him, but before he has recited many lines strains of a waltz are heard from the anteroom and the reading is broken off. All dance. Trofimov, Anya, Varya, and Lyubov Andreyevna come in from the anteroom.]*

LYUBOV. Come, Petya—come, pure heart! I beg your pardon. Let's have a dance! *[Dances with Petya.]*

[Anya and Varya dance. Firs comes in, puts his stick down near the side door. Yasha also comes into the drawing room and looks on at the dancing.]

YASHA. What is it, old man?

FIRS. I don't feel well. In old days we used to have generals, barons and admirals dancing at our balls, and now we send for the post-office clerk and the station master and even they're not overanxious to come. I am getting feeble. The old master, the grandfather, used to give sealing-wax for all complaints. I have been taking sealing-wax for twenty years or more. Perhaps that's what's kept me alive.

YASHA. You bore me, old man! *[Yawns.]* It's time you were done with.

FIRS. Ach, you're a good-for-nothing! *[Mutters.]*

[Trofimov and Lyubov Andreyevna dance in the larger room and then onto the stage].

LYUBOV. *Merci.* I'll sit down a little. *[Sits down.]* I'm tired.

[Enter Anya.]

ANYA. *[Excitedly.]* There's a man in the kitchen has been saying that the cherry orchard's been sold today.

LYUBOV. Sold to whom?

ANYA. He didn't say to whom. He's gone away.

[She dances with Trofimov, and they go off into the larger room.]

YASHA. There was an old man gossiping there, a stranger.

FIRS. Leonid Andreyevitch isn't here yet, he hasn't come back. He has his light overcoat on, *demisaison,* he'll catch cold for sure. Ach! Foolish young things!!

LYUBOV. I feel as though I should die. Go, Yasha, find out to whom it has been sold.

YASHA. But he went away long ago, the old chap. *[Laughs.]*

LYUBOV. *[With slight vexation.]* What are you laughing at? What are you pleased at?

YASHA. Epihodov is so funny. He's a silly fellow, two and twenty misfortunes.

LYUBOV. Firs, if the estate is sold, where will you go?

FIRS. Where you bid me, there I'll go.

LYUBOV. Why do you look like that? Are you ill? You ought to be in bed.

FIRS. *[Ironically.]* Me go to bed and who's to wait here? Who's to see to things without me? I'm the only one in all the house.

YASHA. *[To Lyubov Andreyevna.]* Lyubov Andreyevna, permit me to make a request of you; if you go back to Paris again, be so kind as to take me with you. It's positively impossible for me to stay here. *[Looking about him; in an undertone.]* There's no need to say it, you see for yourself—an uncivilised country, the people have no morals, and then the dullness! The food in the kitchen's abominable, and then Firs runs after one muttering all sorts of unsuitable words. Take me with you, please do!

[Enter Pishtchik.]

PISHTCHIK. Allow me to ask you for a waltz, my dear lady. *[Lyubov Andreyevna goes with him.]* Enchanting lady, I really must borrow of you just 180 roubles. *[Dances.]* Only 180 roubles. *[They pass into the larger room.]*

YASHA. *[Hums softly.]* "Knowest thou my soul's emotion."

[In the larger drawing-room, a figure in a gray top hat and check trousers is gesticulating and jumping about. Shouts of "Bravo, Charlotta Ivanovna."]

DUNYASHA. *[She has stopped to powder herself.]* My young lady tells me to dance. There are plenty of gentlemen, and too few ladies, but dancing makes me giddy and makes my heart beat. Firs, the post office clerk said something to me just now that quite took my breath away.

[Music becomes more subdued.]

FIRS. What did he say to you?

DUNYASHA. He said I was like a flower.

YASHA. *[Yawns.]* What ignorance! *[Goes out.]*

DUNYASHA. Like a flower. I am a girl of such delicate feelings, I am awfully fond of soft speeches.

FIRS. Your head's being turned.

[Enter Epihodov.]

EPIHODOV. You have no desire to see me, Dunyasha. I might be an insect. *[Sighs.]* Ah! life!

DUNYASHA. What is it you want?

EPIHODOV. Undoubtedly you may be right. *[Sighs.]* But of course, if one looks at it from that point of view, if I may so express myself, you have, excuse my plain speaking, reduced me to a complete state of mind. I know my destiny. Every day some misfortune befalls me and I have long ago grown accustomed to it, so that I look upon my fate with a smile. You gave me your word, and though I—

DUNYASHA. Let us have a talk later, I entreat you, but now leave me in peace, for I am lost in reverie. *[Plays with her fan.]*

EPIHODOV. I have a misfortune every day, and if I may venture to express myself, I merely smile at it, I even laugh.

[Varya enters from the larger drawing-room.]

VARYA. You still have not gone, Epihodov. What a disrespectful creature you are, really! *[To Dunyasha.]* Go along, Dunyasha! *[To Epihodov.]* First you play billiards and break the cue, then you go wandering about the drawing-room like a visitor!

EPIHODOV. You really cannot, if I may so express myself, call me to account like this.

VARYA. I'm not calling you to account, I'm speaking to you. You do nothing but wander from place to place and don't do your work. We keep you as a counting-house clerk, but what use you are I can't say.

EPIHODOV. *[Offended.]* Whether I work or whether I talk, whether I eat or whether I play billiards, is a matter to be judged by persons of understanding and my elders.

VARYA. You dare to tell me that! *[Firing up.]* You dare! You mean to say I've no understanding. Begone from here! This minute!

EPIHODOV. *[Intimidated.]* I beg you to express yourself with delicacy.

VARYA. *[Beside herself with anger.]* This moment! Get out! Away! *[He goes towards the door, she following him.]* Two and twenty misfortunes! Take yourself off! Don't let me set eyes on you! *[Epihodov has gone out, behind the door his voice, "I shall lodge a complaint against you."]* What! You're coming back? *[Snatches up the stick Firs has put down near the door.]* Come! Come! Come! I'll show you! What! You're coming? Then take that! *[She swings the stick, at the very moment that Lopahin comes in.]*

LOPAHIN. Very much obliged to you!

VARYA. *[Angrily and ironically.]* I beg your pardon!

LOPAHIN. Not at all! I humbly thank you for your kind reception!

VARYA. No need of thanks for it. *[Moves away, then looks round and asks softly.]* I haven't hurt you?

LOPAHIN. Oh, no! Not at all! There's an immense bump coming up, though!

VOICES FROM LARGER ROOM. Lopahin has come! Yermolay Alexeyevitch!

PISHTCHIK. What do I see and hear? *[Kisses Lopahin.]* There's a whiff of cognac about you, my dear soul, and we're making merry here too!

[Enter Lyubov Andreyevna.]

LYUBOV. Is it you, Yermolay Alexeyevitch? Why have you been so long? Where's Leonid?

LOPAHIN. Leonid Andreyevitch arrived with me. He is coming.

LYUBOV. *[In agitation.]* Well! Well! Was there a sale? Speak!

LOPAHIN. *[Embarrassed, afraid of betraying his joy.]* The sale was over at four o'clock. We missed our train—had to wait till half-past nine. *[Sighing heavily.]* Ugh! I feel a little giddy.

[Enter Gaev. In his right hand he has purchases; with his left hand he is wiping away his tears.]

LYUBOV. Well, Leonid? What news? *[Impatiently, with tears.]* Make haste, for God's sake!

GAEV. *[Makes her no answer, simply waves his hand. To Firs, weeping.]* Here, take them; there's anchovies, Kertch herrings. I have eaten nothing all day. What I have been through! *[Door into the billiard room is open. There is heard a knocking of balls and the voice of Yasha saying "Eighty-seven." Gaev's expression changes; he leaves off weeping.]* I am fearfully tired. Firs, come and help me change my things. *[Goes to his own room across the larger drawing-room.]*

PISHTCHIK. How about the sale? Tell us, do!

LYUBOV. Is the cherry orchard sold?

LOPAHIN. It is sold.

LYUBOV. Who has bought it?

LOPAHIN. I have bought it. *[A pause. Lyubov is crushed; she would fall down if she were not standing near a chair and table.]*

[Varya takes keys from her waistband, flings them on the floor in middle of drawing-room and goes out.]

LOPAHIN. I have bought it! Wait a bit, ladies and gentlemen, pray. My head's a bit muddled, I can't speak. *[Laughs.]* We came to the auction. Deriganov was there already. Leonid Andreyevitch only had 15,000 and Deriganov bid 30,000, besides the arrears, straight off. I saw how the land lay. I bid against him. I bid 40,000, he bid 45,000, I said 55, and so he went on, adding 5 thousands and I adding 10. Well . . . so it ended. I bid 90, and it was knocked down to me. Now the cherry orchard's mine! Mine! *[Chuckles.]* My God, the cherry orchard's mine! Tell me that I'm drunk, that I'm out of my mind, that it's all a dream. *[Stamps his feet.]* Don't laugh at me! If my father and my grandfather could rise from their graves and see all that has happened! How their Yermolay, ignorant, beaten Yermolay, who used to run about barefoot in winter, how that very Yermolay has bought the finest estate in the world! I have bought the estate where my father and grandfather were slaves, where they weren't even admitted into the kitchen. I am asleep, I am dreaming! It is all fancy, it is the work of your imagination plunged in the darkness of ignorance. *[Picks up keys, smiling fondly.]* She threw away the keys; she means to show she's not the housewife now. *[Jingles the keys.]* Well, no matter. *[The orchestra is heard tuning up.]* Hey, musicians! Play! I want to hear you. Come, all of you, and look how Yermolay Lopahin will take the axe to the cherry orchard, how the trees will fall to the ground! We will build houses on it and our grandsons and great-grandsons will see a new life springing up there. Music! Play up!

[Music begins to play. Lyubov Andreyevna has sunk into a chair and is weeping bitterly.]

LOPAHIN. *[Reproachfully.]* Why, why didn't you listen to me? My poor friend! Dear lady, there's no turning back now. *[With tears.]* Oh, if all this could be over, oh, if our miserable disjointed life could somehow soon be changed!

PISHTCHIK. *[Takes him by the arm, in an undertone.]* She's weeping, let us go and leave her alone. Come. *[Takes him by the arm and leads him into the larger drawing-room.]*

LOPAHIN. What's that? Musicians, play up! All must be as I wish it. *[With irony.]* Here comes the new master, the owner of the cherry orchard! *[Accidentally tips over a little table, almost upsetting the candelabra.]* I can pay for everything!

[Goes out with Pishtchik. No one remains on the stage or in the larger drawing-room except Lyubov, who sits huddled up, weeping bitterly. The music plays softly. Anya and Trofimov come in quickly. Anya goes up to her mother and falls on her knees before her. Trofimov stands at the entrance to the larger drawing-room.]

ANYA. Mamma! Mamma, you're crying, dear, kind, good mamma! My precious! I love you! I bless you! The cherry orchard is sold, it is gone, that's true, that's true! But don't weep, mamma! Life is still before you, you have still your good, pure heart! Let us go, let us go, darling, away from here! We will make a new garden, more splendid than this one; you will see it, you will understand. And joy, quiet, deep joy, will sink into your soul like the sun at evening! And you will smile, mamma! Come, darling, let us go!

CURTAIN

Act IV

SCENE: Same as in Act I. There are neither curtains on the windows nor pictures on the walls: only a little furniture remains piled up in a corner as if for sale. There is a sense of desolation; near the outer door and in the background of the scene are packed trunks, traveling bags, etc. On the left the door is open, and from here the voices of Varya and Anya are audible. Lopahin is standing waiting. Yasha is holding a tray with glasses full of champagne. In front of the stage Epihodov is tying up a box. In the background behind the scene a hum of talk from the peasants who have come to say good-bye. The voice of Gaev: "Thanks, brothers, thanks!"

YASHA. The peasants have come to say good-bye. In my opinion, Yermolay Alexeyevitch, the peasants are good-natured, but they don't know much about things.

[The hum of talk dies away. Enter across front of stage Lyubov Andreyevna and Gaev. She is not weeping but is pale; her face is quivering—she cannot speak.]

GAEV. You gave them your purse, Lyuba. That won't do—that won't do!
LYUBOV. I couldn't help it! I couldn't help it!

[Both go out.]

LOPAHIN. *[In the doorway, calls after them.]* You will take a glass at parting? Please do. I didn't think to bring any from the town, and at the station I could only get one bottle. Please take a glass. *[A pause.]* What? You don't care for any? *[Comes away from the door.]* If I'd known, I wouldn't have bought it. Well, and I'm not going to drink it. *[Yasha carefully sets the tray down on a chair.]* You have a glass, Yasha, anyway.
YASHA. Good luck to the travelers, and luck to those that stay behind! *[Drinks.]* This champagne isn't the real thing, I can assure you.
LOPAHIN. It cost eight roubles the bottle. *[A pause.]* It's devilish cold here.
YASHA. They haven't heated the stove to-day—it's all the same since we're going. *[Laughs.]*
LOPAHIN. What are you laughing for?
YASHA. For pleasure.
LOPAHIN. Though it's October, it's as still and sunny as though it were summer. It's just right for building! *[Looks at his watch; says in doorway.]* Take note, ladies and gentlemen, the train goes in forty-seven minutes; so you ought to start for the station in twenty minutes. You must hurry up!

[Trofimov comes in from out of doors wearing a greatcoat.]

TROFIMOV. I think it must be time to start, the horses are ready. The devil only knows what's become of my goloshes; they're lost. *[In the doorway.]* Anya! My goloshes aren't here. I can't find them.
LOPAHIN. And I'm getting off to Harkov. I am going in the same train with you. I'm spending all the winter at Harkov. I've been wasting all my time gossiping with you and fretting with no work to do. I can't get on without work. I don't know what to do with my hands, they flap about so queerly, as if they didn't belong to me.
TROFIMOV. Well, we're just going away, and you will take up your profitable labours again.
LOPAHIN. Do take a glass.
TROFIMOV. No, thanks.
LOPAHIN. Then you're going to Moscow now?
TROFIMOV. Yes. I shall see them as far as the town, and to-morrow I shall go on to Moscow.
LOPAHIN. Yes, I daresay, the professors aren't giving any lectures, they're waiting for your arrival.
TROFIMOV. That's not your business.
LOPAHIN. How many years have you been at the University?
TROFIMOV. Do think of something newer than that—that's stale and flat. *[Hunts for goloshes.]* You know we shall most likely never see each other again, so let me give you one piece of advice at parting: don't wave your arms about—get out of the habit. And another thing, building villas, reckoning up that the summer visitors will in time become independent farmers—reckoning like that, that's not the thing to do either. After all, I am fond of you: you have fine delicate fingers like an artist, you've a fine delicate soul.
LOPAHIN. *[Embraces him.]* Good-bye, my dear fellow. Thanks for everything. Let me give you money for the journey, if you need it.
TROFIMOV. What for? I don't need it.
LOPAHIN. Why, you haven't got a halfpenny.
TROFIMOV. Yes, I have, thank you. I got some money for a translation. Here it is in my pocket. *[Anxiously.]* But where can my goloshes be!
VARYA. *[From the next room.]* Take the nasty things! *[Flings a pair of goloshes on to the stage.]*
TROFIMOV. Why are you so cross, Varya? h'm! . . . But those aren't my goloshes.
LOPAHIN. I sowed three thousand acres with poppies in the spring, and now I have cleared

forty thousand profit. And when my poppies were in flower, wasn't it a picture! So here, as I say, I made forty thousand, and I'm offering you a loan because I can afford to. Why turn up your nose? I am a peasant—I speak bluntly.

TROFIMOV. Your father was a peasant, mine was a chemist—and that proves absolutely nothing whatever. *[Lopahin takes out his pocket-book.]* Stop that—stop that. If you were to offer me two hundred thousand I wouldn't take it. I am an independent man, and everything that all of you, rich and poor alike, prize so highly and hold so dear, hasn't the slightest power over me—it's like so much fluff fluttering in the air. I can get on without you. I can pass by you. I am strong and proud. Humanity is advancing toward the highest truth, the highest happiness, which is possible on earth, and I am in the front ranks.

LOPAHIN. Will you get there?

TROFIMOV. I shall get there. *[A pause.]* I shall get there, or I shall show others the way to get there.

[In the distance is heard the stroke of an ax on a tree.]

LOPAHIN. Good-bye, my dear fellow; it's time to be off. We turn up our noses at one another, but life is passing all the while. When I am working hard without resting, then my mind is more at ease, and it seems to me as though I too know what I exist for; but how many people there are in Russia, my dear boy, who exist, one doesn't know what for. Well, it doesn't matter. That's not what keeps things spinning. They tell me Leonid Andreyevitch has taken a situation. He is going to be a clerk at the bank—6,000 roubles a year. Only, of course, he won't stick to it—he's too lazy.

ANYA. *[In the doorway.]* Mamma begs you not to let them chop down the orchard until she's gone.

TROFIMOV. Yes, really, you might have the tact. *[Walks out across the front of the stage.]*

LOPAHIN. I'll see to it! I'll see to it! Stupid fellows! *[Goes out after him.]*

ANYA. Has Firs been taken to the hospital?

YASHA. I told them this morning. No doubt they have taken him.

ANYA. *[To Epihodov, who passes across the drawing-room.]* Semyon Pantaleyevitch, inquire, please, if Firs has been taken to the hospital.

YASHA. *[In a tone of offence.]* I told Yegor this morning—why ask a dozen times?

EPIHODOV. Firs is advanced in years. It's my conclusive opinion no treatment would do him good; it's time he was gathered to his fathers. And I can only envy him. *[Puts a trunk down on a cardboard hatbox and crushes it.]* There now, of course—I knew it would be so.

YASHA. *[Jeeringly.]* Two and twenty misfortunes!

VARYA. *[Through the door.]* Has Firs been taken to the hospital?

ANYA. Yes.

VARYA. Why wasn't the note for the doctor taken too?

ANYA. Oh, then, we must send it after them. *[Goes out.]*

VARYA. *[From the adjoining room.]* Where's Yasha? Tell him his mother's come to say good-bye to him.

YASHA. *[Waves his hand.]* They put me out of all patience! *[Dunyasha has all this time been busy about the luggage. Now, when Yasha is left alone, she goes up to him.]*

DUNYASHA. You might just give me one look, Yasha. You're going away. You're leaving me. *[Weeps and throws herself on his neck.]*

YASHA. What are you crying for? *[Drinks the champagne.]* In six days I shall be in Paris again. Tomorrow we shall get into the express train and roll away in a flash. I can scarcely believe it! *Vive la France!* It doesn't suit me here—it's not the life for me; there's no doing anything. I have seen enough of the ignorance here. I have had enough of it. *[Drinks champagne.]* What are you crying for? Behave yourself properly, and then you won't cry.

DUNYASHA. *[Powders her face, looking in a pocket-mirror.]* Do send me a letter from Paris. You know how I loved you, Yasha—how I loved you! I am a tender creature, Yasha.

YASHA. Here they are coming!

[Busies himself about the trunks, humming softly. Enter Lyubov Andreyevna, Gaev, Anya, and Charlotta Ivanovna.]

GAEV. We ought to be off. There's not much time now. *[Looking at Yasha.]* What a smell of herrings!

LYUBOV. In ten minutes we must get into the carriage. *[Casts a look about the room.]* Farewell, dear house, dear old home of our fathers! Winter will pass and spring will come, and then you will be no more; they will tear you down!

How much those walls have seen! *[Kisses her daughter passionately.]* My treasure, how bright you look! Your eyes are sparkling like diamonds! Are you glad! Very glad?

ANYA. Very glad! A new life is beginning, mamma.

GAEV. Yes, really, everything is all right now. Before the cherry orchard was sold, we were all worries and wretched, but afterward, when once the question was settled conclusively, irrevocably, we all felt calm and even cheerful. I am a bank clerk now—I am a financier—hit off the red. And you, Lyuba, after all, you are looking better; there's no question of that.

LYUBOV. Yes. My nerves are better, that's true. *[Her hat and coat are handed to her.]* I'm sleeping well. Carry out my things, Yasha. It's time. *[To Anya.]* My darling, we shall soon see each other again. I am going to Paris. I can live there on the money your Yaroslavl auntie sent us to buy the estate with—hurrah for auntie!—but that money won't last long.

ANYA. You'll come back soon, mamma, won't you? I'll be working up for my examination in the high school, and when I have passed that, I shall set to work and be a help to you. We will read all sorts of things together, mamma, won't we? *[Kisses her mother's hands.]* We will read in the autumn evenings. We'll read lots of books, and a new wonderful world will open out before us. *[Dreamily.]* Mamma, come soon.

LYUBOV. I shall come, my precious treasure. *[Embraces her.]*

[Enter Lopahin. Charlotta softly hums a song.]

GAEV. Charlotta's happy; she's singing!

CHARLOTTA. *[Picks up a bundle like a swaddled baby.]* Bye, bye, my baby. *[A baby is heard crying: "Ooah! ooah!"]* Hush, hush, my pretty boy! *[Ooah! ooah!]* Poor little thing! *[Throws the bundle back.]* You must please find me a situation. I can't go on like this.

LOPAHIN. We'll find you one, Charlotta Ivanovna. Don't you worry yourself.

GAEV. Everyone's leaving us. Varya's going away. We have become of no use all at once.

CHARLOTTA. There's nowhere for me to be in the town. I must go away. *[Hums.]* What care I . . .

[Enter Pishtchik.]

LOPAHIN. The freak of nature!

PISHTCHIK. *[Gasping.]* Oh! . . . let me get my breath. . . .I'm worn out . . . my most honoured . . . Give me some water.

GAEV. Want some money, I suppose? Your humble servant! I'll go out of the way of temptation *[Goes out.]*

PISHTCHIK. It's a long while since I have been to see you . . . dearest lady. *[To Lopahin.]* You are here . . . glad to see you . . . a man of immense intellect . . . take . . . here *[Gives Lopahin]* 400 roubles. That leaves me owing 840.

LOPAHIN. *[Shrugging his shoulders in amazement.]* It's like a dream. Where did you get it?

PISHTCHIK. Wait a bit . . . I'm hot . . . a most extraordinary occurrence! Some Englishmen came along and found in my land some sort of white clay. *[To Lyubov Andreyevna.]* And 400 for you . . . most lovely . . . wonderful. *[Gives money.]* The rest later. *[Sips water.]* A young man in the train was telling me just now that a great philosopher advises jumping off a housetop. "Jump!" says he; "the whole gist of the problem lies in that." *[Wonderingly.]* Fancy that, now! Water, please!

LOPAHIN. What Englishmen?

PISHTCHIK. I have made over to them the rights to dig the clay for twenty-four years . . . and now, excuse me . . . I can't stay . . . I must be trotting on. I'm going to Znoikovo . . . to Kardamanovo . . . I'm in debt all round. *[Sips.]* . . . To your very good health! . . . I'll come in on Thursday.

LYUBOV. We are just off to the town, and to-morrow I start for abroad.

PISHTCHIK. What! *[In agitation.]* Why to the town? Oh, I see the furniture . . . the boxes. No matter . . . *[Through his tears.]* . . . no matter . . . men of enormous intellect . . . these Englishmen.. . . Never mind . . . be happy. God will succour you . . . no matter . . . everything in this world must have an end. *[Kisses Lyubov Andreyevna's hand.]* If the rumour reaches you that my end has come, think of this . . . old horse, and say: "There once was such a man in the world . . . Semyonov-Pishtchik . . . the Kingdom of Heaven be his!" . . . Most extraordinary weather . . . yes. *[Goes out in violent agitation, but at once returns and says in the doorway.]* Dashenka wishes to be remembered to you. *[Goes out.]*

LYUBOV. Now we can start. I leave with two cares in my heart. The first is leaving Firs ill. *[Looking at her watch.]* We have still five minutes.

ANYA. Mamma, Firs has been taken to the hospital. Yasha sent him off this morning.

LYUBOV. My other anxiety is Varya. She is used to getting up early and working; and now, without work, she's like a fish out of water. She is thin and pale, and she's crying, poor dear! *[A pause.]* You are well aware, Yermolay Alexeyevitch, I dreamed of marrying her to you, and everything seemed to show that you would get married. *[Whispers to Anya and motions to Charlotta and both go out.]* She loves you—she suits you. And I don't know—I don't know why it is you seem, as it were, to avoid each other. I can't understand it!

LOPAHIN. I don't understand it myself, I confess. It's queer somehow, altogether. If there's still time, I'm ready now at once. Let's settle it straight off, and go ahead; but without you, I feel I shan't make her an offer.

LYUBOV. That's excellent. Why, a single moment's all that's necessary. I'll call her at once.

LOPAHIN. And there's champagne all ready too. *[Looking into the glasses.]* Empty! Someone's emptied them already. *[Yasha coughs.]* I call that greedy.

LYUBOV. *[Eagerly.]* Capital! We will go out. Yasha, *allez!* I'll call her in. *[At the door.]* Varya, leave all that; come here. Come along! *[Goes out with Yasha.]*

LOPAHIN. *[Looking at his watch.]* Yes.

[A pause. Behind the door, smothered laughter and whispering, and, at last, enter Varya.]

VARYA. *[Looking a long while over the things.]* It is strange, I can't find it anywhere.

LOPAHIN. What are you looking for?

VARYA. I packed it myself, and I can't remember. *[A pause.]*

LOPAHIN. Where are you going now, Varvara Mihailova?

VARYA. I? To the Ragulins. I have arranged to go to them to look after the house—as a housekeeper.

LOPAHIN. That's in Yashnovo? It'll be seventy miles away *[A pause.]* So this is the end of life in this house!

VARYA. *[Looking among the things.]* Where is it? Perhaps I put it in the trunk. Yes, life in this house is over—there will be no more of it.

LOPAHIN. And I'm just off to Harkov—by this next train. I've a lot of business there. I'm leaving Epihodov here, and I've taken him on.

VARYA. Really!

LOPAHIN. This time last year we had snow already, if you remember; but now it's so fine and sunny. Though it's cold, to be sure—three degrees of frost.

VARYA. I haven't looked. *[A pause.]* And besides, our thermometer's broken. *[A pause.]*

[Voice at the door from the yard: "Yermolay Alexeyevitch!"]

LOPAHIN. *[As though he had long been expecting this summons.]* This minute!

[Lopahin goes out quickly. Varya sitting on the floor and laying her head on a bag full of clothes, sobs quietly. The door opens. Lyubov Andreyevna comes in cautiously.]

LYUBOV. Well? *[A pause.]* We must be going.

VARYA. *[Has wiped her eyes and is no longer crying.]* Yes, mamma, it's time to start. I shall have time to get to the Ragulins today, if only you're not late for the train.

LYUBOV. *[In the doorway.]* Anya, put your things on.

[Enter Anya, then Gaev and Charlotta Ivanovna. Gaev has on a warm coat with a hood. Servants and cabmen come in. Epihodov bustles about the luggage.]

LYUBOV. Now we can start on our travels.

ANYA. *[Joyfully.]* On our travels!

GAEV. My friends—my dear, my precious friends! Leaving this house for ever, can I be silent? Can I refrain from giving utterance at leave-taking to those emotions which now flood all my being?

ANYA. *[Supplicatingly.]* Uncle!

VARYA. Uncle, you mustn't!

GAEV. *[Dejectedly.]* Hit into the pocket . . . I'll be quiet. . . .

[Enter Trofimov and afterward Lopahin.]

TROFIMOV. Well, ladies and gentlemen, we must start.

LOPAHIN. Epihodov, my coat!

LYUBOV. I'll stay just one minute. It seems as though I have never seen before what the walls, what the ceilings in this house were like, and now I look at them with greediness, with such tender love.

GAEV. I remember when I was six years old sitting in that window on Trinity Day watching my father going to church.

LYUBOV. Have all the things been taken?

LOPAHIN. I think all. *[Putting on overcoat, to Epihodov.]* You, Epihodov, mind you see everything is right.

EPIHODOV. *[In a husky voice.]* Don't you trouble, Yermolay Alexeyevitch.

LOPAHIN. Why, what's wrong with your voice?

EPIHODOV. I've just had a drink of water, and I choked over something.

YASHA. *[Contemptuously.]* The ignorance!

LYUBOV. We are going—and not a soul will be left here.

LOPAHIN. Not till the spring.

VARYA. *[Pulls a parasol out of a bundle, as though about to hit someone with it. Lopahin makes a gesture as though alarmed.]* What is it? I didn't mean anything.

TROFIMOV. Ladies and gentlemen, let us get into the carriage. It's time. The train will be in directly.

VARYA. Petya, here they are, your goloshes, by that box. *[With tears.]* And what dirty old things they are!

TROFIMOV. *[Putting on his goloshes.]* Let us go, friends!

GAEV. *[Greatly agitated, afraid of weeping.]* The train—the station! Double baulk, ah!

LYUBOV. Let us go!

LOPAHIN. Are we all here? *[Locks the side-door on left.]* The things are all here. We must lock up. Let us go!

ANYA. Good-bye, home! Good-bye to the old life!

TROFIMOV. Welcome to the new life!

[Trofimov goes out with Anya. Varya looks round the room and goes out slowly. Yasha and Charlotta Ivanovna, with her dog, go out.]

LOPAHIN. Till the spring, then! Come, friends, till we meet! *[Goes out.]*

[Lyubov Andreyevna and Gaev remain alone. As though they had been waiting for this, they throw themselves on each other's necks, and break into subdued smothered sobbing, afraid of being overheard.]

GAEV. *[In despair.]* Sister, my sister!

LYUBOV. Oh, my orchard!—my sweet, beautiful orchard! My life, my youth, my happiness, good-bye! good-bye!

VOICE OF ANYA. *[Calling gaily.]* Mamma!

VOICE OF TROFIMOV. *[Gaily, excitedly.]* Aa—oo!

LYUBOV. One last look at the walls, at the windows. My dear mother loved to walk about this room.

GAEV. Sister, sister!

VOICE OF ANYA. Mamma!

VOICE OF TROFIMOV. Aa—oo!

LYUBOV. We are coming. *[They go out.]*

[The stage is empty. There is the sound of the doors being locked up, then of the carriages driving away. There is silence. In the stillness there is the dull stroke of an ax in a tree, clanging with a mournful lonely sound. Footsteps are heard. Firs appears in the doorway on the right. He is dressed as always—in a pea-jacket and white waistcoat, with slippers on his feet. He is ill.]

FIRS. *[Goes up to the doors, and tries the handles.]* Locked! They have gone. . . . *[Sits down on sofa.]* They have forgotten me. . . . Never mind . . . I'll sit here a bit. . . I'll be bound Leonid Andreyevitch hasn't put his fur coat on and has gone off in his thin overcoat. *[Sighs anxiously.]* I didn't see after him. . . . These young people . . . *[Mutters something that can't be distinguished.]* Life has slipped by as though I hadn't lived. *[Lies down.]* I'll lie down a bit. . . . There's no strength in you, nothing left you—all gone! Ech! I'm good for nothing. *[Lies motionless.]*

[A sound is heard that seems to come from the sky, like a breaking harp-string, dying away mournfully. All is still again, and there is heard nothing but the strokes of the ax far away in the orchard.]

CURTAIN

Introduction to *A Dream Play* by August Strindberg

Translated by Walter Johnson

A Dream Play   Penny Downie as Indra's Daughter. (© *Donald Cooper/PHOTOSTAGE*)

The Play   In the discussion of *A Doll's House*, we pointed out that the two predominant approaches to drama, beginning in the late nineteenth century and continuing to the present, have been realism and departures from realism. From the outset of realism, there was a strong countermovement of nonrealism and antirealism. One reason is that realistic drama, for all its advantages, excludes a number of effective and long-standing theatrical devices, including music, dance, symbolism, poetry, fantasy, and the supernatural.

It is worth noting that two of the dramatists who inaugurated modern realism, Henrik Ibsen and August Strindberg, also wrote plays that departed decidedly from realism. The two best known of Strindberg's works in this form are *A Dream Play* (1902) and *The Ghost Sonata* (1907). As the title of *A Dream Play* indicates, the dramatic action evokes the world of a dream. We see a Christlike goddess, the Daughter of Indra, journeying through a variety of human situations and experiencing continual suffering. Behind the events in *A Dream Play*, Strindberg had carefully worked out a very elaborate structure, a scheme that followed the seasons—spring, summer, autumn, winter—and other logical developments, but these appear in a seemingly random arrangement of incidents.

The scenes are not always causally related but rather are a series of stages or, to emphasize the Christian imagery, "stations" in the Daughter of Indra's journey,

279

analogous to the stations of the cross. Places, time, and characters transform suddenly and unexpectedly. Characters such as the Officer, the Attorney, the Poet, He, She, and the Dean of Philosophy are representative more of types than of individuals; thus they are referred to by titles rather than by names.

Symbols abound: A castle grows out of a dunghill; a shawl contains all human suffering; two lands are referred to as Foulgut and Fairhaven; and the Attorney's face has become hideously lined by the torment of those who have engaged him. *A Dream Play* deals with many of the concerns found in Strindberg's realistic dramas—the destructiveness of marriage, materialism, and the class struggle—but he dramatizes these concerns, as he says in the play's preface, in "the disconnected but apparently logical form of a dream. Everything can happen; everything is possible and likely."

The Playwright   The Swedish playwright August Strindberg (1849–1912) had an unhappy, insecure childhood as the son of a steamship agent and a former waitress and servant. His youthful unhappiness was a prelude to a troubled adulthood, including frequent bouts with mental illness, but he was able to use these experiences as the basis of his writings.

After some intermittent study at the University of Uppsala in Sweden, Strindberg returned to Stockholm and worked as a teacher, librarian, and journalist while revising *Master Olaf,* his first play. In 1875, he met Siri von Essen, a soldier's wife, whom he married in 1877. Their stormy marriage, which lasted until 1891, provided many situations for his novels and plays, particularly the dramas *The Father* (1887) and *Miss Julie* (1888)—both naturalistic works examining the battle between the sexes. In his preface to *Miss Julie,* Strindberg described the realistic characterization and production methods that he wanted for the play.

In 1884 Strindberg was prosecuted for blasphemy when he published *Married,* a collection of his stories. This increased his paranoia and his dislike for Sweden, and as a result he spent much time abroad, particularly in Paris, until 1897. When his second marriage failed in 1894, he went through a period of severe stress and mental instability—often referred to as his "inferno crisis," after *Inferno,* an autobiographical book about this time in his life—before undergoing a conversion to religious mysticism. His plays written after 1897, such as *To Damascus* (1898) and *A Dream Play* (1902), are expressionistic in form, using symbolism and unrealistic shifts in their action, and are steeped in his new beliefs. The plays from this period were to be influential on the surrealist movement and, after that, on theater of the absurd.

Several of Strindberg's later plays cover events in Swedish history, a possible reflection of his return to Stockholm in 1899. Here Strindberg, who had once again embraced the radical ideas of his youth, wrote many social and political treatises for the press. In 1902 he married Harriet Bosse, a young actress, but that marriage also failed, in 1904.

Some of Strindberg's most experimental and influential plays were written for the Intimate Theater in Stockholm, which he and the director August Falck ran for a time. His chamber plays, like *The Ghost Sonata* (1907), reflected his interest in music, particularly Beethoven, and his preoccupation with removing facades to reveal grotesque elements beneath the surface. When he died in 1912, the Swedish Academy ignored him, as it had always done, but his compatriots mourned him as their greatest writer.

The Period   The historical period of *A Dream Play* is the same as that of *The Cherry Orchard.* In fact, *A Dream Play* was produced only two years earlier than Chekhov's play. These were the years immediately following the many revolutionary discoveries and pronouncements of the nineteenth century—from Darwin, Marx, and Freud—and just before the work of Albert Einstein. This was also a time of scientific break-throughs: the telephone, the electric light, and early automobiles and airplanes.

It was against a background of intellectual ferment and of pioneering work in psychological analysis, then, that Strindberg did his work. Sigmund Freud was maintaining, for example, that psychological motivations could be discovered and that seemingly illogical subconscious processes, such as dreams, could be analyzed and explained. People are ruled, Freud argued, as much by subconscious thoughts and desires as by conscious ones. Similar ideas found their way into Strindberg's dramas, particularly *A Dream Play* and *The Ghost Sonata.*

Theatrical production of this period followed two somewhat contradictory paths. On the one hand there were commercial productions: popular new plays and revivals of Shakespeare that found a large paying audience both in Great Britain and on the European continent. But the challenging new plays of writers like Ibsen and Strindberg often could not find commercial producers and were frequently subject to censorship by the authorities.

Thus a number of independent theaters were established throughout Europe to produce controversial realistic dramas. These theaters were exempted from government censorship because they were organized as subscription companies, with theatergoers being treated almost like members of a private club. Since they were not striving for commercial success, these theater companies presented their plays to small audiences interested in the new dramatic forms. Some of them also popularized realistic production techniques. The four major independent theaters were the Théâtre Libre in France, the Freie Bühne in Germany, the Independent Theatre in England, and the Moscow Art Theater in Russia.

Like the realists, the symbolists also needed independently organized theater companies to produce their plays. In France, two independent theater companies—Théâtre d'Art and the Théâtre de l'Oeuvre—were dedicated to antirealistic drama and production style.

A DREAM PLAY

August Strindberg

AN EXPLANATORY NOTE

In this dream play, as in his earlier dream plays *To Damascus,*[1] the author has tried to imitate the disconnected but apparently logical form of a dream. Everything can happen; everything is possible and likely. Time and space do not exist; on an insignificant basis of reality the imagination spins and weaves new patterns: a blending of memories, experiences, free inventions, absurdities, and improvisations.

The characters split, double, redouble, evaporate, condense, scatter, and converge. But one consciousness remains above all of them: the dreamer's; for

1. The trilogy To Damascus, written between 1898 and 1904, is extremely subjective and deals with Strindberg's conversion from agnosticism to Strindbergian Christianity. (Footnotes are taken from the translator's notes.)

him there are no secrets, no inconsequence, no scruples, no law. He does not judge, does not acquit, simply relates; and as the dream is usually painful, less frequently cheerful, a note of sadness and sympathy for every living creature runs through the swaying story. Sleep, the liberator, appears often as painful, but, when the torture is at its very peak, waking comes, reconciling suffering with reality, which however painful it may be still at this moment is a delight compared with the tormenting dream.

CHARACTERS

(Voice of) FATHER INDRA	POET
INDRA'S DAUGHTER	HE
GLAZIER	SHE *(doubles with Victoria's voice)*
OFFICER	PENSIONER
FATHER	UGLY EDITH
MOTHER	EDITH'S MOTHER
LINA	NAVAL OFFICER
DOORKEEPER	ALICE
BILLSTICKER	SCHOOLMASTER
PROMPTER	NILS
POLICEMAN	HUSBAND
LAWYER	WIFE
DEAN OF PHILOSOPHY	BLIND MAN
DEAN OF THEOLOGY	FIRST COALHEAVER
DEAN OF MEDICINE	SECOND COALHEAVER
DEAN OF LAW	GENTLEMAN
CHANCELLOR	LADY
KRISTIN	SINGERS AND DANCERS *(members of the opera company)*
QUARANTINE MASTER	CLERKS, GRADUATES, MAIDS, SCHOOLBOYS,
ELDERLY FOP	CHILDREN, CREW, RIGHTEOUS PEOPLE
COQUETTE	
FRIEND	

PROLOGUE

[Cloud formations resembling castles and citadels in ruins on crumbling slate hills form the backdrop. The constellations Leo, Virgo, and Libra can be seen, and among them is the planet Jupiter shining brightly. Indra's daughter is standing on the uppermost cloud.]

INDRA'S VOICE. *[From above.]* Where are you, Daughter? Where?
INDRA'S VOICE. You have gone astray, my child; take care, you're sinking. . . . How did you get here?
INDRA'S DAUGHTER.

I followed the flash of lightning from high Ether and took a cloud as my coach . . .

But the cloud sank, and I'm headed down . . .
Tell me, Father Indra,[2] what regions have I come to?
Why is it so close, so hard to breathe?

INDRA'S VOICE.

You have left the second world and gone into the third
from çukra; the morning star[3]
you have departed and are entering
the dusty atmosphere of Earth;
note the seventh house of the Sun called the Scales[4]
where the morning star stands in autumn
when Day and Night weigh the same . . .

2. Indra was one of the eight gods keeping watch over the world.
3. Venus is the morning star. 4. In the zodiac, Virgo and Scorpio represent a pair of scales.

INDRA'S DAUGHTER.

> You spoke of Earth . . . Is that this dark
> and heavy world lighted by the Moon?

INDRA'S VOICE.

> It is the densest and heaviest
> of the spheres wandering in space.

INDRA'S DAUGHTER.

> Doesn't the sun ever shine here?

INDRA'S VOICE.

> Of course, it does, but not always . . .

INDRA'S DAUGHTER.

> The cloud is parting, and I can see the earth

INDRA'S VOICE.

> What do you see, my child?

INDRA'S DAUGHTER.

> I see . . . it's beautiful . . . with green forests,
> blue waters, white mountains, and yellow fields . . .

INDRA'S VOICE.

> Yes, it's beautiful as everything Brahma[5] created . . .
> but it was still more beautiful in the dawn of time;
> then something happened, a breakdown in its orbit,
> perhaps something else, a rebellion
> accompanied by crimes that had to be suppressed . . .

INDRA'S DAUGHTER.

> I hear sounds from there . . .
> What creatures dwell down there?

INDRA'S VOICE.

> Descend and see . . . I will not
> slander the Creator's children,
> but what you hear is their language.

5. Brahma is the first figure in the Hindu trinity, creator of the world.

INDRA'S DAUGHTER.

> It sounds like . . . it does not have a happy ring.

INDRA'S VOICE.

> I imagine! For their mother tongue
> is complaint. Yes! The earthlings
> are a dissatisfied, ungrateful lot . . .

INDRA'S DAUGHTER.

> Don't say that; now I hear shouts of joy,
> and shots and booms; I see the lightning
> flash—Bells are ringing, fires lighted,
> and thousand times thousand voices
> sing out in praise and thanks to heaven . . . *[Pause.]*
> you judge them too severely, Father . . .

INDRA'S VOICE.

> Descend and see and hear . . .
> then come back and tell me
> if their complaints and laments are justified . . .

INDRA'S DAUGHTER.

> I will descend, but come with me, Father!

INDRA'S VOICE.

> No. I cannot breathe down there . . .

INDRA'S DAUGHTER.

> The cloud is sinking . . . it's getting stifling . . .
> I'm suffocating . . .
> It isn't air but smoke and water I'm breathing . . .
> so heavy, it pulls me down, down . . .
> and now I already feel its sway . . .
> the third world is not the best . . .

INDRA'S VOICE.

> No, not the best, but not the worst;
> It is Dust, it revolves as all the others do . . .
> that's why the earthlings at times get dizzy,
> on the verge between folly and madness.
> Have courage, my child! It is but a test.

INDRA'S DAUGHTER. *[On her knees as the cloud sinks.]*
I'm sinking!

I

[The backdrop represents a mass of gigantic white, pink, scarlet, sulphur yellow, and violet hollyhocks in bloom; over their tops can be seen the gilded roof of a castle[6] with a flower bud resembling a crown uppermost. Along the bottom of the castle walls, heaps of straw covering cleaned-out stable litter. The side wings which remain throughout the play are stylized wall paintings, at the same time rooms, architecture, and landscapes. The Glazier and Indra's daughter come onstage.]

DAUGHTER. The castle's still growing out of the earth . . . Do you see how much it has grown since last year?

GLAZIER. *[To himself.]* I've never seen that castle before . . . I've never heard that a castle grows . . . but *[To the Daughter with firm conviction.]*—yes, it has grown four feet, but that's because they've manured it . . . and if you'll look, you'll see a wing has shot out on the sunny side.

DAUGHTER. It really ought to bloom soon . . . it's past midsummer . . .

GLAZIER. Don't you see the flower up there?

DAUGHTER. Yes, I do! *[Claps her hands.]* Tell me, Father, why do flowers grow out of the dirt?

GLAZIER. *[Devoutly.]* They don't thrive in dirt; they hurry as fast as they can up into the light to bloom and die!

DAUGHTER. Do you know who lives in that castle?

GLAZIER. I did know, but I've forgotten.

DAUGHTER. I think there's a prisoner in there . . . and he's waiting for me to set him free.

GLAZIER. But at what price?

DAUGHTER. You don't bargain about your duty. Let's go into the castle! . . .

GLAZIER. Yes, let's!

•

[They go toward the back, which slowly opens to the sides. The setting is now a plain, bare room with a table and some chairs. An Officer in an extremely unusual contemporary uniform is sitting on one chair. He is rocking the chair and striking his sword against the table.]

DAUGHTER. *[Goes up to the Officer and takes the sword gently out of his hand.]* No, no! Don't do that!

OFFICER. *Agnes,* let me keep my sword!

DAUGHTER. No, you'll ruin the table! *[To the Glazier.]* Go down into the harness room and put in the pane. I'll see you later!

[Glazier goes.]

•

DAUGHTER. You're a prisoner in your rooms; I've come to set you free!

OFFICER. I've been waiting for that, but I wasn't sure you'd want to.

DAUGHTER. The castle is strong, it has seven walls, but—I'll manage! . . . Do you want to or don't you?

OFFICER. Frankly: I don't know . . . either way I'll be hurt! Every joy in life has to be paid for doubly in sorrow. It's difficult here, but if I'm to purchase freedom, I'll have to suffer threefold. Agnes,[7] I'd rather put up with it—if only I get to see you!

DAUGHTER. What do you see in me?

OFFICER. The beauty which is the harmony in the universe. There are lines in your figure the like of which I can find only in the course of the solar system, in the beautiful melody of strings, in the vibrations of light. You're a child of heaven . . .

DAUGHTER. So are you!

OFFICER. Why then should I tend horses? Look after stables and have litter hauled out?

DAUGHTER. So you'll long to get away from here.

OFFICER. I do long, but it's very hard to get out of this.

DAUGHTER. But it's your duty to seek freedom in light!

OFFICER. Duty? Life has never admitted having any duties toward me.

DAUGHTER. You feel unjustly treated by life, do you?

OFFICER. Yes! It has been unjust!

•

[Voices can now be heard behind the screen, which is immediately drawn aside. The Officer and the Daughter look in that direction, then stop, their gestures and expressions

---

6. The golden top of a calvary barracks, visible form Strindberg's window in Stockholm.

7. The reason for giving Andra's daughter the name Agnes is uncertain, but the name itself stands for purity.

frozen. *The Mother, who is ill, is sitting by a table. In front of her is burning a candle which she trims now and then with snuffers. Piles of newly sewn undershirts, which she marks with marking ink and quill pen. A brown wardrobe-cupboard to the left.]*

FATHER. *[Gently handing her a silk mantilla.]* Don't you want it?

MOTHER. A silk mantilla for me, dear! What's the use—I'm soon going to die!

FATHER. Do you believe what the doctor says?

MOTHER. Even what he says, but most of all I believe what my inner voice says.

FATHER. *[Sadly.]* So it is serious! . . . And you think of your children, first and last!

MOTHER. Why, they were my life, my justification . . . my joy, and my sorrow . . .

FATHER. Kristina, forgive me . . . for everything!

MOTHER. For what? Forgive me dear; we've tortured each other. Why? We don't know! We couldn't do anything else! . . . But here are the children's new undershirts . . . See to it they change twice a week, on Wednesday and Sunday, and that Lovisa washes them . . . all over . . . Are you going out?

FATHER. I have to be at a staff meeting. At eleven o'clock.

MOTHER. Ask Alfred to come in before you leave.

FATHER. *[Points at the Officer.]* Why, he's here, dear!

MOTHER. Imagine . . . I'm beginning to lose my eyesight, too . . .
Yes, it's getting dark . . . *[Trims the candle.]* Alfred! Come!

[Father, nodding good-bye, goes out right through the wall. The Officer goes up to the Mother.]

MOTHER. Who's the girl over there?

OFFICER. *[Whispering.]* It's Agnes!

MOTHER. Oh, it's Agnes? You know what they say? . . . That she's the god Indra's daughter, who has to come down to Earth to learn how human beings really have it . . . But don't say anything! . . .

OFFICER. She is a child of god!

MOTHER. *[Out loud.]* Alfred, I'm leaving you and your brothers and sisters soon. . . . Let me tell you one thing that will help you through life.

OFFICER. *[Sad.]* Tell me, Mother!

MOTHER. Just this: Never quarrel with God!

OFFICER. What do you mean, Mother?

MOTHER. Don't go about feeling mistreated by life.

OFFICER. But when I am mistreated?

MOTHER. You're thinking about the time you were unfairly punished for taking a coin that was later found.

OFFICER. Yes! And that wrong has given a warped twist to my life ever since . . .

MOTHER. Yes. But go over to that cupboard.

OFFICER. *[Ashamed.]* So you know! It's . . .

MOTHER. *Swiss Family Robinson*[8] . . . which . . .

OFFICER. Don't say any more . . .

MOTHER. Which your brother was punished for . . . and which had torn to pieces and hidden!

OFFICER. Imagine—that cupboard's still there after twenty years . . . Why, we've moved many times, and my mother died ten years ago!

MOTHER. Well, so what? You always have to question everything, and so you ruin the best in life for yourself . . . Look, there's Lina.

LINA. *[Enters.]* Ma'am, thank you very much, but I can't go to the christening . . .

MOTHER. Why not child?

LINA. I haven't anything to wear.

MOTHER. You may borrow my mantilla.

LINA. Goodness no, that won't do!

MOTHER. I don't understand. I'll never go to any party again . . .

●

OFFICER. What will Father say? It was a present from him . . .

MOTHER. How small-minded . . .

●

FATHER. *[Sticks his head in.]* Are you going to lend my present to the maid?

MOTHER. Don't say that . . . Remember, I was a servant, too . . . Why do you hurt an innocent person?

FATHER. Why do you hurt me, your husband . . .

MOTHER. This life! When you do something nice, there's always someone to whom it's ugly . . . If you do something good for someone, you hurt someone else. Ugh, this life!

[She trims the candle so that it goes out. The stage becomes dark, and the screen is replaced.]

●

DAUGHTER. Human beings are to be pitied!

8. For many years a favorite novel for children.

OFFICER. You've found that out!

DAUGHTER. Yes, life is hard, but love conquers all. Come and see!

[They go toward the back.]

•

[The backdrop is drawn up; a new one can now be seen, representing an old shabby fire wall. In the middle of the wall is a gate opening on a path which ends in a bright green plot in which is a gigantic blue monkshood (aconite). To the left by the gate sits the Doorkeeper with a shawl over her head. She is crocheting a bedspread with a star pattern. To the right is a bulletin board which the Billposter is cleaning; next to him is a dip net with a green handle. Still farther to the right is a door with an airhole in the shape of a four-leaf clover. To the left of the gate is a slim linden with a coal-black trunk and a few pale green leaves; next to it a cellar opening.]

DAUGHTER. *[Goes up to the Doorkeeper.]* Isn't the bedspread finished yet?

DOORKEEPER. No, my dear; twenty-six years aren't enough for a project like this!

DAUGHTER. And your fiancé never came back?

DOORKEEPER. No, but that wasn't his fault. He *had* to leave . . . poor fellow . . . thirty years ago!

DAUGHTER. *[To the Billposter.]* Wasn't she in the ballet? Up there in the opera?

BILLPOSTER. Yes, she was number one . . . but when *he* left, he sort of took her dancing along . . . so she didn't get any more roles . . .

DAUGHTER. All of you complain, at least with your eyes, and with your voices . . .

BILLPOSTER. I'm not complaining much . . . now when I've got a dip net and a green box!

DAUGHTER. That makes you happy?

BILLPOSTER. Yes, very happy, very . . . that was my childhood dream, and now it has come true. I'm past fifty, of course . . .

DAUGHTER. Fifty years for a dip net and a box . . .

BILLPOSTER. A *green* box, a *green* one . . .

DAUGHTER. *[To the Doorkeeper.]* Give me the shawl now so I may sit here observing human beings! But stand behind me to tell me what I need to know.

[The Daughter puts on the shawl and sits down by the gate.]

DOORKEEPER. Today's the last day of the opera season . . . they're finding out if they're engaged for next year . . .

DAUGHTER. What about those who aren't?

DOORKEEPER. Yes, Good Lord, that's something to see . . . Well, I draw the shawl over my head . . .

DAUGHTER. Poor human beings!

DOORKEEPER. Look, there comes one! . . . She's not among the chosen . . . Look, how she's crying . . .

•

[The Singer rushes in from the right out through the gate with her handkerchief over her eyes. Stops for a moment on the path outside the gate, leans her head against the wall, and then rushes out.]

DAUGHTER. Human beings are to be pitied! . . .

DOORKEEPER. But look at him: that's how a happy human being looks!

[The Officer enters through the gate; he is dressed in a frock coat and a top hat and is carrying a bouquet of roses. Radiantly happy.]

He's going to marry Miss Victoria![9] . . .

OFFICER. *[Downstage; looks up, sings.]* Victoria!

DOORKEEPER. She's coming right away!

OFFICER. Fine! The carriage is waiting, the table has been set, the champagne's on ice . . . May I? *[Embraces both the Daughter and the Doorkeeper. Sings.]* Victoria!

WOMAN'S VOICE. *[From above. Sings.]* I'm here!

OFFICER. *[Begins to walk back and forth.]* Fine! I'm waiting!

•

DAUGHTER. Do you know me?

OFFICER. No, I know only one woman . . . Victoria! I've been here for seven years waiting for her[10] . . . at noon when the sun hits the chimneys and in the evening when darkness begins to fall . . . Look at the pavement there—you can see traces of the faithful lover! Hurrah, she's mine! *[Sings.]* Victoria! *[He gets no answer.]* Well, she's getting dressed! *[To the Billposter.]* There's your dip net, I see! Everybody at the opera's wild about dip nets . . . or about fish, rather! The silent fish—

9. Victoria has the same meaning as Siri, the name of Strindberg's first wife. Victoria is the ideal woman. 10. Two of Strindberg's wives were actresses, and he may have waited for them in the corridor outside the theater.

because they can't sing . . . What does a thing like that cost?

BILLPOSTER. It's quite expensive!

OFFICER. *[Sings.]* Victoria! . . . *[Shakes the linden.]* Look, it's budding again. The eighth time! . . . *[Sings.]* Victoria! . . . now she's combing her hair . . . *[To the Daughter.]* Ma'am, let me go up to fetch my bride.

DOORKEEPER. No one's admitted onstage.

OFFICER. I've walked about here seven years! Seven times three hundred and sixty-five make two thousand five hundred fifty-five! *[Stops; pokes at the door with the four-leaf hole.]* . . . And I've looked at that door two thousand five hundred fifty-five times without knowing where it leads to! And that four-leaf hole that's to let in light . . . For whom is it to let in light? Is there someone on the other side? Does someone live there?

DOORKEEPER. I don't know. I've never seen it opened . . .

OFFICER. It looks like a pantry door I saw when I was four and went with the maid on Sunday afternoon visits. Visits with other maids, but I never got beyond the kitchens, and I sat between the water barrel and the salt container; I've seen so many kitchens in my day, and the pantries were always in the entrance with round holes and a four-leaf clover in the door . . . But surely the opera doesn't have any pantry since they don't have any kitchen. *[Sings.]* Victoria! . . . She'll surely not go out some other way, ma'am?

DOORKEEPER. No, there isn't any other way.

OFFICER. Fine, then I'll see her!

[Theater people rush out and are looked over by the Officer.]

•

OFFICER. She'll have to be here soon! . . Ma'am! That blue monkshood out there. I've seen it since I was a child . . . Is it the same one? . . . I remember it in a parsonage when I was seven . . . there are two doves, blue doves under that hood . . . but that time a bee went into the hood . . . I thought: now I've got you! so I grabbed the flower; but the bee stung me, and I cried . . . but the pastor's wife came and put mud on it . . . then we got wild strawberries and milk for dinner! . . . I think it's already getting dark. *[To the Billposter.]* Where are you going?

BILLPOSTER. I'm going home to eat dinner.

[Goes.]

OFFICER. *[Puts his hand to his eyes.]* Dinner? At this time of day? Please! . . May I just go in to telephone to "the growing castle"?

DAUGHTER. Why, what do you have in mind?

OFFICER. I'm going to tell the glazier to put in double panes—it'll soon be winter, and I'm so terribly cold!

[Goes in.]

•

DAUGHTER. *[To the Doorkeeper.]* Who is Miss Victoria?

DOORKEEPER. The woman he loves!

DAUGHTER. Right! He doesn't care what she is to us and others. She *is* only what she is for him! . . .

[It grows dark suddenly.]

DOORKEEPER. *[Lighting her lantern.]* It's growing dark quickly today.

DAUGHTER. To the gods a year is as a minute!

DOORKEEPER. And to human beings a minute can be long as a year!

OFFICER. *[Comes out again. He looks worn; the roses have withered.]* She hasn't come yet?

DOORKEEPER. No.

OFFICER. She'll *come!* . . . She'll surely come! *[Pacing.]* . . . That's right—I'd probably be wise if I canceled dinner anyway . . . since it's evening . . . Yes, yes, I'll do that!

[Goes in to telephone.]

•

DOORKEEPER. *[To the Daughter.]* May I have my shawl now?

DAUGHTER. No, dear, I'll relieve you; I'll do your job . . . I want to know human beings and life to find out if it's as hard as they say.

DOORKEEPER. But you mustn't fall asleep on this job, never fall asleep, neither night nor day . . .

DAUGHTER. Not sleep at night?

DOORKEEPER. Yes, you can, if you have the bell cord tied to your arm . . . for there are night watchmen on the stage, and they're replaced every third hour . . .

DAUGHTER. Why, that's torture . . .

DOORKEEPER. So it seems to you, but we others are glad to get a job like this, and if you knew how envied I am . . .

DAUGHTER. Envied? They envy someone who's tortured?

DOORKEEPER. Yes! . . . But you see what's harder than keeping awake at night and drudgery, drafts, and cold, and damp is to have, as I do, all the unhappy ones up there confide in me . . . They come to me. Why? Probably they see in the lines of my face the inscription carved by suffering which invites confiding . . . In that shawl, dear, is the agony of thirty years, my own and others! . . .

DAUGHTER. It is heavy, and it burns like nettles . . .

DOORKEEPER. Put it on since you want to . . . When it gets too heavy, call me, and I'll come and relieve you.

DAUGHTER. Farewell. What you can do, I surely can.

DOORKEEPER. We'll see! . . . But be kind to my young friends and don't weary of their complaints.

[Goes out by way of the path. It becomes pitch-black onstage. The scenery is changed so that the linden is stripped of leaves. The blue monkshood has withered; and when it turns light again, the green at the end of the path is autumn brown. The Officer comes out when it turns light. His hair and his beard are now gray. His clothes are shabby, his collar is dirty and limp. Only the stems of the bouquet of roses remain. He paces back and forth.]

OFFICER. To judge by all the signs, summer's past and fall's almost here. I can tell by looking at the linden and the monkshood . . . *[Walks about.]* But fall is *my* spring, for then the theater opens again! And then she has to come! Dear lady, may I sit on this chair for a while?

DAUGHTER. Yes, my friend—I'll stand.

OFFICER. *[Sits down.]* If I could only sleep a little, it would be better . . . *[He falls asleep for a moment, then rushes up to start walking about, stops in front of the door with the four-leaf hole, and pokes at it.]* This door that doesn't give me any peace . . . What's back of it? There has to be something! *[From up above can be heard soft music in dance measure.]* There! Now they've started rehearsing! *[The stage is lighted intermittently as if by a lighthouse beam.]* What's that? *[Speaks in time with the blinking light.]* Light and dark; light and dark?

DAUGHTER. *[Imitating him.]* Day and night; day and night! . . . A kindly providence wants to shorten your waiting. So the days flee, pursuing the nights.

[The light onstage becomes steady. The Billposter enters with his dip net and billposting equipment.]

OFFICER. It's the billposter and the dip net . . . Was the fishing good?

BILLPOSTER. Oh, yes! The summer was warm and a bit long . . . the dip net was good enough, but not *just* the way I'd wanted it . . .

OFFICER. *[Emphasizing.]* Not just the way I'd wanted it . . . That's marvelously put! Nothing is the way I'd wanted it . . . because the idea is greater than the act—superior to the object.

[Walks about striking the rose bouquet on the walls so that the last leaves and petals fall.]

BILLPOSTER. Hasn't she come down yet?

OFFICER. No, not yet, but she'll come soon . . . Do you know what's back of that door?

BILLPOSTER. No, I've never seen it open.

OFFICER. I'll telephone for a locksmith to open it!

[Goes in to telephone. The billposter puts up a poster and then is going out to the right.]

DAUGHTER. What was wrong with the dip net?

BILLPOSTER. Wrong? Well, there wasn't anything really wrong . . . but it wasn't just what I'd wanted, so I didn't enjoy it so much . . .

DAUGHTER. How had you wanted it?

BILLPOSTER. How? . . . I can't say . . .

DAUGHTER. Let me say it . . . You had wanted it as it wasn't. Green, yes, but not *that* green.

BILLPOSTER. You do understand! You know everything—that's why all of them come to you with their troubles . . . Would you listen to mine, too? . . .

DAUGHTER. Gladly . . . Come in here and tell me . . .

[Goes into the Doorkeeper's cage. The Billposter stands outside the window speaking.]

●

[It becomes pitch-dark again; then it turns light, and the linden gets green leaves again, and the monkshood blooms;

the sun illuminates the foliage along the path. The Officer comes out; he is old and white-haired; he is ragged, his shoes are worn out; he is carrying the remains of the bouquet. He walks back and forth slowly, like an old man. He reads the playbill. A Ballet Girl comes in from the right.]

OFFICER. Has Miss Victoria gone?

GIRL. No, she hasn't.

OFFICER. Then I'll wait. She'll come soon, I hope?

GIRL. [Seriously.] She's sure to.

OFFICER. Don't go—then you'll see what's back of this door—I've sent for the locksmith.

GIRL. It'll really be fun to see the door opened. That door and the growing castle. Do you know the growing castle?

OFFICER. Do I? Why, I was a prisoner in it.

GIRL. Well, were you the one? But why did they have so many horses there?

OFFICER. It was a stable castle, of course . . .

GIRL.[Hurt.] How stupid I am! not able to understand that!

[Goes.]

●

[A member of the chorus enters from the right.]

OFFICER. Has Miss Victoria gone?

CHORUS GIRL. No, she hasn't. She never goes.

OFFICER. That's because she loves me! . . . You mustn't go before the locksmith who's going to open the door comes.

CHORUS GIRL. Oh, is the door going to be opened? What fun! . . . I just want to ask the doorkeeper something.

[The Prompter enters from the right.]

OFFICER. Has Miss Victoria gone?

PROMPTER. No, not that I know.

OFFICER. There, you see! Didn't I say she's waiting for me! Don't go—the door's going to be opened.

PROMPTER. What door?

OFFICER. Is there more than one door?

PROMPTER. Oh, I know—the one with the four-leaf opening . . . Then I'll certainly stay! I'm just going to talk with the doorkeeper a little.

●

[The Ballet Girl, the Chorus Girl, and the Prompter station themselves next to the Billposter outside the Doorkeeper's

window. They all talk to the Daughter in turn. The Glazier enters through the gate.]

OFFICER. Are you the locksmith?

GLAZIER. No, he had calls to make, and a glazier will do just as well.

OFFICER. Yes, of course . . . of course, but do you have your diamond?

GLAZIER. Naturally! What's a glazier without a diamond?

OFFICER. Nothing! So let's go to work.

[Strikes his hands together. All of the rest gather with him in a circle about the door. Chorus members dressed as Meistersinger,[11] and supers as dancers in Aida join the group from the right.]

●

OFFICER. Locksmith—or glazier—do your duty!

[The glazier comes forward with his diamond.]

OFFICER. A moment like this seldom recurs in a lifetime, so, my friends, I beg you . . . to consider carefully . . .

POLICEMAN. [Comes up.] In the name of the law I forbid the opening of this door!

OFFICER. Oh lord, what a fuss when we want to do something new and great . . . But we'll take it to court . . . To the lawyer, then! We'll find out if the laws will hold up! To the lawyer!

●

[The scene changes into a Lawyer's office without lowering the curtain thus: the gate remains functioning as the gate to the office railing, which extends directly across the stage. The Doorkeeper's room remains as the Lawyer's writing nook but is open to the front of the stage; the linden stripped of leaves is a combination hat- and clotheshanger; the bulletin board is covered with official notices and judgments in legal cases; the door with the four-leaf hole is now part of a cupboard containing documents.

The Lawyer in tails and white tie is sitting to the left inside the gate at a desk covered with papers. His appearance testifies to extremely great suffering: his face is chalk-white and heavily lined, the shadows on it verge on violet; he is ugly, and his face reflects all the sorts of crimes and vices with which his profession has forced him to deal.

One of his two Clerks has only one arm, the other is one-eyed.

11. Male singers in Wagner's opera.

The people who have gathered to see "the opening of the door" remain, but now as if they were clients waiting to see the Lawyer. They look as if they had been standing there forever. The Daughter (wearing the shawl) and the Officer are on the level closest to the audience.]

LAWYER. *[Going up to the Daughter.]* May I have the shawl, my dear . . . I'll hang it up in here until I get the fire in the tile stove going; then I'll burn it with all its sorrows and miseries . . .

DAUGHTER. Not yet . . . I want it really full . . . first . . . and above all I want to gather in it your afflictions, all you have received in confidence about crimes, vices, thefts, backbiting, slander, libel . . .

LAWYER. Your shawl wouldn't do for all that, my friend! Look at these walls. Isn't it as if all sins have soiled the wallpaper? Look at these papers on which I record the accounts of wrongdoing . . . look at me . . . Never does a person who smiles come here—only evil looks, bared teeth, shaking fists . . . And all of them spray their evil, their envy, their suspicions over me . . . See! My hands are black, and can never be washed. Do you see how cracked and bleeding they are? . . . I can never wear clothes for more than a few days, for they smell of other people's crimes . . . Sometimes I fumigate with sulphur in here, but that doesn't help. I sleep in the next room, and dream only about crime . . . Just now I have a murder trial going in court . . . That's bearable, I suppose, but do you know what's worse than everything else? . . . Separating husband and wife! Then it's as if earth itself and heaven above cried out . . . cried treason against the source of life, the spring of what is good, against love . . . And, you see, when reams of paper have been filled with their accusations against each other, and a sympathetic person takes one of them aside in private, takes him by his ear, and smiling asks the simple question: What do you really have against your husband—or your wife?— he—or she—stands there without an answer and doesn't know! Once—well, it had to do with a green salad, I think, and another time with a word, usually with nothing. But the pangs, the suffering! I have to hear them . . . Look at me! Do you think I could win a woman's love when I look like a criminal? And do you think anyone wants to be my friend

when I have to collect the debts, the financial debts, of everyone in town? . . . It's hard to be a human being!

DAUGHTER. Human beings are to be pitied!

LAWYER. That's right. And what people live on is a puzzle to me. They get married on an income of two thousand when they need four thousand . . . They borrow, of course; all of them borrow! So they walk a sort of tightrope until they die . . . then the estate is never clear of debt. Who finally has to pay? I don't know.

DAUGHTHER. The One who feeds the birds!

LAWYER. Yes! But if the One who feeds the birds would descend to His earth to see how the poor children of man have it, He'd probably pity us . . .

DAUGHTER. Human beings are to be pitied!

LAWYER. Yes, that's the truth! *[To the Officer.]* What do you wish?

OFFICER. I only wanted to ask if Miss Victoria had gone.

LAWYER. No, she hasn't, you can be absolutely sure . . . Why are you poking at my cupboard?

OFFICER. I thought the door was so like . . .

LAWYER. Oh no, no, no!

[Church bells can be heard ringing.]

OFFICER. Is there a funeral?

LAWYER. No, it's commencement[12]—the candidates are receiving their doctor's degrees. I was just about to go up to get my doctor of laws' degree. Perhaps you'd like to graduate and get a laurel wreath?

OFFICER. Wel-l-l, why not? That would always be a little break from monotony . . .

LAWYER. Perhaps we should proceed to the solemn rites at once?—Just go and change your clothes.

[The Officer goes out; the stage becomes dark—the following changes take place: the railing remains and now serves as the balustrade for the sanctuary in a church; the billboard becomes a bulletin board listing psalms; the linden-clotheshanger becomes a candelabra; the lawyer's desk the Chancellor's lectern; the door with the four-leaf opening now leads into the sacristy. The singers from Die Meistersinger become Heralds carrying scepters, and the Dancers carry the laurel wreaths.[13]

12. A traditional Swedish university commencement is a highly formal ceremony.   13. The laurel wreath, used since Greek and Roman times as a symbol of achievement, has long been important in Swedish life.

The rest of the people make up the audience.

The backdrop is raised. The new one represents a single large organ with keyboard below and a mirror above.

Music is heard. To the sides the four faculties—philosophy (arts and sciences), theology, medicine, and law. The stage is empty for a moment. The Heralds enter from the right.

The Dancers follow with laurel wreaths in their outstretched hands.

Three Candidates enter, one after the other, from the left and are crowned by the Dancers and then go out to the right.

The Lawyer comes forward to be crowned.

The Dancers turn away, refusing to crown him, and go out.

The Lawyer, shaken, leans against a pillar. Everyone else leaves. The Lawyer is alone.

DAUGHTER. *[Enters with a white veil over her head and shoulders.]* Look, I've washed the shawl . . . But why are you standing here? Didn't you get the wreath?

LAWYER. No, I wasn't worthy.

DAUGHTER. Why? Because you've defended the poor, put in a good word for the criminal, lightened the burden for the guilty, got respite for the condemned . . . Poor human beings . . . They aren't angels; but they're to be pitied.

LAWYER. Don't say anything bad about human beings; why, I'm to plead their case . . .

DAUGHTER. *[Leaning on the organ.]* Why do they slap their friends in the face?

LAWYER. They don't know any better.

DAUGHTER. Let's teach them! Do you want to? With me!

LAWYER. They won't learn! . . . If only our complaint could reach the gods in heaven . . .

DAUGHTER. It will reach the throne! *[Places herself by the organ.]* Do you know what I see in this mirror? . . . The world right side to! . . . Yes, since it's reversed in itself!

LAWYER. How did it get reversed?

DAUGHTER. When the copy was made . . .

LAWYER. That's it! The copy . . . I always sensed it was an imperfect copy . . . and when I began

to remember the original, I became dissatisfied with everything . . . People called that dissatisfaction the devil's fragments of glass in my eye . . . and other things . . .

DAUGHTER. It's certainly mad! Look at the four faculties! The government that's to preserve the community pays all four of them: theology, the doctrine about God, which is always attacked and ridiculed by philosophy, which says it's wisdom itself! And medicine, which always questions the validity of philosophy and doesn't consider theology one of the sciences but calls it superstition . . . And they sit in the same council which is to teach the students respect—for the university. Why, it's an insane asylum! And pity the poor soul who gets sane first!

LAWYER. Those who learn that first are the theologians. As preliminary studies they get philosophy, which teaches them theology is nonsense; then they learn in theology that philosophy is nonsense. Madmen, aren't they?

DAUGHTER. And law, the servant of all, except the servants!

LAWYER. Justice, which when it wants to be just, becomes the death of the just! . . . The court of justice, which often is unjust!

DAUGHTER. What a mess you've made for yourselves, children of man! Child!—Come here; I'll give you a wreath . . . that will be more becoming for you! *[Places a crown of thorns[14] on his head.]* Now I'll play for you!

[She sits down at the piano and plays a Kyrie,[15] but instead of organ music human voices are heard.]

CHILDREN'S VOICES. Eternal Lord! *[The last note is extended.]*

WOMEN'S VOICES. Have mercy on us! *[The last note is extended.]*

MEN'S VOICES. *[Tenors.]* Save us, for the sake of Thy mercy! *[The last note is extended.]*

MEN'S VOICES. *[Basses.]* Spare Thy children, oh Lord, and be not angry with us!

•

ALL. Have mercy! Hear us! Pity us mortals!— Eternal God, why art Thou so far away? . . .

---

14. A symbol of Christ's suffering. 15. The petition "Lord, have mercy upon us" in the church service.

Out of the depths we cry: Mercy, oh God! Do not make Thy children's burden too heavy! Hear us! Hear us!

•

[The stage becomes dark. The Daughter gets up, approaches the Lawyer. Through a change in lighting the organ becomes Fingal's Cave.[16] The sea dashes in swells under the basalt pillars and produces a harmonious sound of waves and wind.]

LAWYER. Where are we?
DAUGHTER. What do you hear?
LAWYER. I hear drops falling . . .
DAUGHTER. They are the tears when human beings weep . . . What else do you hear?
LAWYER. Sighs . . . cries . . . moans . . .
DAUGHTER. Mortals' laments have come this far . . . not farther. But why this eternal grumbling? Hasn't life anything to be happy about?

LAWYER. Yes, the most delightful which is also the most bitter: love! Mate and home! The highest and the lowest!
DAUGHTER. Let me try it!
LAWYER. With me?
DAUGHTER. With you! You know the rocks, the stumbling blocks. Let's avoid them!
LAWYER. I'm poor!
DAUGHTER. What difference does that make if we love each other? And a little beauty doesn't cost anything.
LAWYER. I have dislikes which you probably don't have.
DAUGHTER. We'll have to compromise.
LAWYER. If we weary?
DAUGHTER. Then our child will come and give us a diversion that's always new!
LAWYER. You want to marry me—poverty-stricken and ugly, despised, rejected?
DAUGHTER. Yes! Let's join our destinies!
LAWYER. So be it!

II

[A very simple room next to the Lawyer's office. To the right a large double bed with a canopy; next to it a window. To the left a sheet-iron stove with cooking utensils on it. Kristin is pasting strips along the inner windows. At the back an open door to the office; poor people waiting to be heard can be seen out there.]

KRISTIN. I paste! I paste![17]
DAUGHTER. [Pale and worn, is sitting by the stove.] You're shutting out the air! I'm suffocating! . . .
KRISTIN. Now there's only one little crack left!
DAUGHTER. Air, air! I can't breathe!
KRISTIN. I paste, I paste!
LAWYER. That's right, Kristin! Heat is expensive!
DAUGHTER. It's as if you were gluing my mouth shut!
LAWYER. [Stands in the door with a document in his hand.] Is the baby asleep?
DAUGHTER. Yes, at last!
LAWYER. [Gently.] His crying frightens my clients away.

DAUGHTER. [Friendly.] What can we do about it?
LAWYER. Nothing.
DAUGHTER. We'll have to get a larger apartment.
LAWYER. We haven't any money.
DAUGHTER. May I open the window? This bad air is suffocating me!
LAWYER. Then the heat will go out, and we'll have to freeze.
DAUGHTER. That's terrible! . . . May we scrub out there then?
LAWYER. You're not strong enough to scrub, nor am I, and Kristin has to paste; she has to paste the whole house, every last crack—in the ceiling, the floors, the walls.
DAUGHTER. I was prepared for poverty, not for dirt!
LAWYER. Poverty is always relatively dirty.
DAUGHTER. This is worse than I imagined!
LAWYER. We're not the worst off. We still have food in our pot!
DAUGHTER. But what food!
LAWYER. Cabbage is inexpensive, nourishing, and good.
DAUGHTER. For the one who likes cabbage. I can't stand it!

16. A cave in the Hebrides west of Scotland with pillars and a roof of basalt.   17. For many years pasting strips of paper over windows was a common practice to keep out the cold in winter.

LAWYER. Why didn't you say so?

DAUGHTER. Because I loved you! I wanted to sacrifice my taste!

LAWYER. Then I'll have to sacrifice my taste for cabbage. The sacrifices have to be mutual.

DAUGHTER. What shall we eat then? Fish? But you hate fish.

LAWYER. And it's expensive.

DAUGHTER. This is harder than I thought.

LAWYER. *[Friendly.]* Yes, you see how hard it is . . . And our child, who was to be our bond and blessing . . . becomes our ruin!

DAUGHTER. Darling! I'm dying in this air, in this room with its view of the backyard, with endless hours of our child's crying—without sleep, with those people out there, and their complaining, squabbling, and accusations . . . I'll die in here!

LAWYER. Poor little flower, without light, without air . . .

DAUGHTER. And you say there are people who are worse off.

LAWYER. I'm one of those who are envied in this neighborhood.

DAUGHTER. Everything would be all right if I could only have a bit of beauty in our home.

LAWYER. I know you mean a flower, a heliotrope especially, but that costs one and a half—that's the price of six quarts of milk or two pecks of potatoes.

DAUGHTER. I'd gladly go without food if I could only get my flower!

LAWYER. There's a kind of beauty that doesn't cost anything, and the lack of which in his home is the biggest torture for a man with a sense of beauty.

DAUGHTER. What's that?

LAWYER. If I tell you, you'll get angry!

DAUGHTER. We've agreed not to get angry!

LAWYER. We've agreed . . . Everything will do, Agnes, except the short, hard accents . . . Do you know them? Not yet.

DAUGHTER. We'll never hear them!

LAWYER. Not so far as I'm concerned.

DAUGHTER. So tell me!

LAWYER. Well: when I come into a home, I first see how the curtains hang . . . *[Goes up to the window and straightens the curtain.]* . . . If it hangs like a rope or a rag . . . then I leave pretty soon . . . Then I look at the chairs . . . if they're in their places, I stay! *[Moves a chair into its proper place against the wall.]* Then I look at the candles in their holders . . . If they lean, the house is off base. *[Straightens a candle on the bureau.]* . . . It's this bit of beauty, my dear, that doesn't cost anything.

DAUGHTER. *[Inclines her head downward.]* Not the short accents, Axel.

LAWYER. They weren't short!

DAUGHTER. Yes, they were!

LAWYER. What the hell! . . .

DAUGHTER. What sort of language is that?

LAWYER. Forgive me, Agnes. But I have suffered from your slovenliness as you suffer from dirt. And I haven't dared to put things into their places myself, for you'd get as angry then as if I scolded you . . . Ugh! Shall we stop?

DAUGHTER. It's terribly hard to be married . . . it's harder than anything else. One has to be an angel, I think.

LAWYER. Yes, I think so.

DAUGHTER. I think I'm beginning to hate you!

LAWYER. Too bad for us if you do! . . . But let's prevent hate. I promise never to criticize your housekeeping . . . though it's torture to me.

DAUGHTER. And I'll eat cabbage, though it's agony for me.

LAWYER. So, a life together in agony. The one's pleasure, the other's pain!

DAUGHTER. Human beings are to be pitied!

LAWYER. You do understand that?

DAUGHTER. Yes, but in God's name let's avoid the rocks now that we know them so well!

LAWYER. Let's. Why, we're humane and enlightened people; we can forgive and overlook!

DAUGHTER. Why, we can smile at trifles!

LAWYER. We, only we, can! . . . Do you know I read in the *Morning News!* . . . by the way—where is the paper?

DAUGHTER. *[Embarrassed.]* What paper?

LAWYER. *[Harshly.]* Do I take more than one!

DAUGHTER. Smile and don't speak harshly now . . . I started the fire with your paper . . .

LAWYER. *[Violently.]* What the hell!

DAUGHTER. Smile! . . . I burned it because it made fun of what I consider sacred . . .

LAWYER. What isn't sacred for me. Huh . . . *[Hits his fist into his other hand, beside himself.]* I'll smile, I'll smile so my molars show . . . I'll be humane, and conceal my thoughts and say yes to everything, and evade and play the hypocrite!

So you burned my paper! So-o! *[Rearranges the curtain on the bed.]* There! Now I'll straighten up so you'll be angry . . . Agnes, this is simply impossible!

DAUGHTER. It certainly is!

LAWYER. And just the same we have to stick it out, not because of our vows but for the sake of our child.

DAUGHTER. That's true. For the child's . . . *[Sighs.]* We must stick it out!

LAWYER. And now I have to go out to my clients. Listen to them—they're buzzing with impatience to tear at each other, to get each other fined and imprisoned . . . lost souls . . .

DAUGHTER. Poor, poor human beings. And this pasting! *[She bows her head in silent despair.]*

KRISTIN. I paste, I paste!

[The lawyer stands at the door, fingering the doorknob nervously.]

DAUGHTER. How that lock squeaks; it's as if you were crushing my heart . . .

LAWYER. I crush, I crush . . .

DAUGHTER. Don't do it!

LAWYER. I crush . . .

DAUGHTER. No!

LAWYER. I . . .

OFFICER. *[Enters from the office, takes hold of the knob.]* Permit me!

LAWYER. *[Lets go the knob.]* Go ahead. Since you got your degree!

OFFICER. Everything in life is mine now! All careers are open to me, Parnassus[18] has been climbed, the laurel wreath has been worn, immortality, honor, everything mine!

LAWYER. How are you going to support yourself?

OFFICER. Support myself?

LAWYER. You'll need food, shelter, and clothing, I suspect.

OFFICER. There'll always be a way, just so one has someone who loves one.

LAWYER. I can imagine . . . Yes, imagine . . . Paste, Kristin! Paste! Until they can't breathe!

[Goes out backward, nodding.]

KRISTIN. I paste, I paste! Until they can't breathe!

OFFICER. Are you coming along now?

DAUGHTER. Right away. But where?

OFFICER. To Fairhaven![19] It's summer there, the sun is shining there, youth is there and children and flowers; singing and dancing, parties and rejoicing!

DAUGHTER. Then I want to go there!

OFFICER. Come!

●

LAWYER. *[Comes in again.]* I'm returning to my first hell . . . this was the second . . . and the greatest! The most delightful is the greatest hell . . . Look at that—she has dropped hairpins on the floor again! . . . *[Picks one up.]*

OFFICER. Imagine, he has discovered the hairpins, too!

LAWYER. Too? . . . Look at this one. It has two prongs but is one pin! There are two, but it's one! If I straighten it out, there's only one! If I bend it, there are two without ceasing to be one. That means: the two are one! But if I break it—here! Then they're two! Two! *[Breaks the hairpin and throws the pieces away.]*

OFFICER. You've seen all this . . . But before you can break them off, the prongs have to diverge. If they converge, it holds up.

LAWYER. And if they're parallel—they never meet—it's neither one nor two.

OFFICER. The hairpin is the most perfect of all created things! A straight line that equals two parallel ones.

LAWYER. A lock that closes when it's open!

OFFICER. Open, closes—a braid of hair that remains open when it's bound . . .

LAWYER. It's like this door. When I shut it, I open the way out for you, Agnes!

[Goes out, shutting the door.]

●

DAUGHTER. So?

[Change onstage: the bed with its canopy becomes a tent; the stove remains; the backdrop is raised; to the right in the foreground one sees burned-over mountains with red heather and stumps black and white after a forest fire; red

18. Mountain in Greece sacred to Apollo; represents intellectual achievements.

19. Fairhaven means Beautiful Bay and contrasts with Foulstrand, which means Shame Sound.

pigpens and outhouses. Below, an open gymnasium in which people are exercised on machines resembling instruments of torture. To the left in the foreground, part of the quarantine building's open shed with hearths, furnace walls, and plumbing pipes. The middle area is a sound. The back of the stage is a beautiful shore with trees in foliage, piers (decorated with flags) to which white boats are tied; some of them have their sails hoisted, some not. Small Italian villas, pavilions, kiosks, marble statues can be seen among the foliage.[20]]

[Quarantine Master, in blackface, is walking on the shore.]

OFFICER. *[Comes up to him and shakes his hand.]* Well, if it isn't Ordström![21] So you've landed here?

MASTER. Yes, I'm here.

OFFICER. Is this Fairhaven?

MASTER. No, that's over there. This is Foulstrand!

OFFICER. Then we've come to the wrong place!

MASTER. We?—Aren't you going to introduce me?

OFFICER. No, it's not proper. *[Softly.]* It's Indra's own daughter, you see.

MASTER. Indra's? I thought it was Waruna *[the supreme god]* himself! . . . Well, aren't you amazed my face is black?

OFFICER. My boy, I'm over fifty—at that age one doesn't get amazed any more—I assumed right away you were going to a masquerade this afternoon.

MASTER. Absolutely right! I hope you'll come along.

OFFICER. Most likely, for it . . . it doesn't look too attractive here . . . What sort of people live here?

MASTER. The sick live here; those who are healthy live over there.

OFFICER. I suppose there are only poor people here.

MASTER. No, old man, the rich are here. Look at the man on that rack! He has eaten too much goose liver with truffles and drunk too much burgundy that his feet have become malformed!

OFFICER. Malformed?

MASTER. Yes! . . . And the one lying on the guillotine over there; he has consumed so much Hennessy[22] that his backbone has to be ironed out!

OFFICER. That can't be good either!

MASTER. In general the ones who live on this side all have some form of misery to hide. Look at the one who's coming, for example!

[An older fop is wheeled in in a wheelchair, accompanied by a sixty-year-old coquette, dressed in the latest fashion and attended by Her Friend, who is forty.]

OFFICER. It's the major! Our schoolmate!

MASTER. Don Juan! You see, he's still in love with the old wreck by his side. He doesn't see she has aged, that she's ugly, faithless, cruel!

OFFICER. Well, that's love! I'd never have believed that flighty soul capable of loving so profoundly and seriously.

MASTER. You do have a nice attitude!

OFFICER. I've been in love—with Victoria—yes, I still haunt the corridor waiting for her . . .

MASTER. Are you the one in the corridor?

OFFICER. Yes, I am.

MASTER. Well, have you got the door opened yet?

OFFICER. No, we're still in court about it . . . The billposter is out with his dip net, of course, so hearing testimony has been delayed . . . in the meanwhile the glazier has put in panes in the castle which has grown a half story . . . It has been an unusually good year this year . . . warm and wet.

MASTER. But you still haven't had it as warm as I have!

OFFICER. How warm do you keep the ovens?

MASTER. When we disinfect people who may have cholera, we keep them at 144 degrees.

OFFICER. Is cholera raging again?

MASTER. Didn't you know?

OFFICER. Of course I knew, but I so often forget what I know!

MASTER. I often wish I could forget, myself mostly; that's why I like masquerades, dressing up, and amateur theatricals.

OFFICER. What have you been up to?

MASTER. If I tell, they say I'm bragging; if I keep still, I'm called a hypocrite!

OFFICER. Is that why you've blackened your face?

MASTER. Yes! A little blacker than I am!

OFFICER. Who's that coming?

MASTER. Oh, he's a poet. Who's going to have his mudbath!

[The Poet enters with his eyes directed toward the sky and a pail of mud in his hand.]

20. The quarantine and coalheaver scenes are echoes of Strindberg's trip in 1884 to Italy, which he found to be a far from perfect country.   **21.** A stream of words; the man is obviously talkative.   **22.** Hennessey cognac.

MASTER. Heavens, you'd think he'd need a bath in light and air!

MASTER. No, he's always way up there in the heights so he gets homesick for mud . . . wallowing in dirt makes his skin as hard as a pig's. He doesn't feel the gadflies' stings after that!

OFFICER. What a strange world of contradictions this is!

•

POET. *[Ecstatically.]* Of clay the god Ptah[23] created man on a potter's wheel, a lathe—*[Skeptically.]*—or what the hell have you!—*[Ecstatically.]* Of clay the sculptor creates his more or less immortal masterpieces—*[Skeptically.]*—which most often are pure junk! *[Ecstatically.]* Of clay are created these vessels so needed in the pantry, which have the name dishes in common, plates—*[Skeptically.]*—as far as that goes I don't care much what they're called! *[Ecstatically.]* This is the clay! When it's mixed with water and flows, it's called mud—*C'est mon affaire!* *[Calls.]* Lina!

•

[Lina enters with a pail.]

POET. Lina, let Miss Agnes see you! She knew you ten years ago when you were a young, happy, let's say pretty girl . . *[To the Daughter.]* See what she looks like now! Five children, drudgery, yelling, starving, beatings! See how her beauty has perished, how her joy has disappeared, while she has been doing her duty, which should have given her the inner satisfaction that reflects itself in the harmonious lines of a face and in the quiet glow of the eyes . . .

MASTER. *[Places his hand over the Poet's mouth.]* Keep still! Keep still!

POET. That's what they all say! And if one keeps still, they say: speak! Perverse human beings!

•

DAUGHTER. *[Goes up to Lina.]* Tell me your complaints!

LINA. No, I don't dare to—then I'd have it still worse!

DAUGHTER. Who is that cruel?

LINA. I don't dare to say—then I'll get a beating!

POET. That's how it can be! But I will tell you even if that black fellow wants to knock my teeth out! . . . I'll tell you that there is injustice sometimes . . . Agnes, daughter of God! . . . Do you hear music and dancing up there on the hillside? Fine! . . . It's Lina's sister, who has come home from the city where she went astray . . . you understand . . . Now they're butchering the fatted calf,[24] but Lina who stayed at home has to carry the pail to feed the pigs! . . .

DAUGHTER. There's rejoicing in her home because the one who has gone astray has given up her wickedness—not only because she has come home! Remember that!

POET. But then put on a dinner and ball every evening for this blameless woman who has never gone astray! Do that! . . . But people don't . . . instead when Lina has a little leisure, she has to go to church and get scolded because she isn't perfect. Is that justice?

DAUGHTER. Your questions are so hard to answer because . . . there are so many unknowns . . .

POET. The caliph Harun the Just[25] understood that, too! He sat quietly on his throne and never saw how they had it down below. The complaints finally reached his noble ear. Then one fine day he stepped down, disguised himself, and went about unrecognized among the crowds of people to see how it was with justice.

DAUGHTER. You surely don't think I'm Harun the Just?

OFFICER. Let's talk about something else . . . Company's coming!

[A white dragon-shaped boat with a light blue silk sail with a golden yard and golden mast with a rose-red pennant glides forward on the sound from the left. At the helm with their arms about each other sit He and She.]

OFFICER. Look at that—perfect happiness, total bliss, the ecstasy of young love!

[The stage becomes lighter.]

HE. *[Stands up in the boat and sings.]*

Hail thee, lovely bay,
where I spent my early years

---

23. Egyptian god considered creator of the world.

24. Refers to account of prodigal son in New Testament. 25. Celebrated in the *Arabian Nights* as a model of integrity.

where I dreamt my first dreams of love,
here you have me once again,
but not alone as then!
Groves and bays,
skies and sea,
hail her!
My true love, my bride!
My sun, my life!

[The flags on the docks at Fairhaven dip in greeting, white handkerchiefs from villas and shores wave, and a chord played by harps and violins sounds over the water.]

POET. See how they radiate light! Listen to the melody from across the water! Eros!

OFFICER. It is Victoria!

MASTER. What?

OFFICER. It's his Victoria; I have mine! And mine, no one else may see! . . . Raise the quarantine flag now; I'm going to pull in the net.

[Master waves a yellow flag.]

OFFICER. *[Pulls on a line so that the boat turns toward Foulstrand.]* Hold it there!

[He and She now notice the ghastly landscape and express their horror.]

MASTER. Yes, yes! It's hard. But everyone, every last one who comes from an infected area has to come here.

POET. Imagine, being able to talk like that, being able to do that when one sees two human beings who have met in love. Don't touch them! Don't touch love! That's the greatest crime! . . . Poor souls! Everything beautiful has to go down, down into the mud!

[He and She step ashore, sorrow-stricken and ashamed.]

HE. What have we done?

MASTER. You don't have to have done anything to be hit by the small discomforts of life.

SHE. That's how short happiness and joy are!

HE. How long do we have to stay here?

MASTER. Forty days and nights![26]

SHE. Then we'd rather drown ourselves!

HE. Live here, among the scorched hills and the pigpens?

26. Refers to an account of the flood in the Book of Genesis.

POET. Love conquers all, even sulphur fumes and carbolic acid!

•

QUARANTINE MASTER. *[Lights the stove; blue sulphur vapors rise.]* Now I'm lighting the sulphur. Please step in!

SHE. My blue dress will lose its color!

MASTER. Yes, it'll turn white! Your red roses will turn white, too!

HE. And your cheeks as well! In forty days!

SHE. *[To Officer.]:* That will please you!

OFFICER. No, it won't! . . . Your happiness did cause my suffering, but . . . that doesn't matter—I now have my degree and am tutoring over there . . . *[Sighs.]* . . . and this fall I'll have a place in a school . . . teaching boys the same lessons I had in all of my childhood, in all of my youth, and now I'm going to do the same lessons through all my years of maturity and finally through all of my old age . . . the same lessons: How much is two times two? How many times does two go into four? . . . Until I'm retired with a pension and have to go—without anything to do, waiting for my meals and the papers—until at last they bring me to the crematory and burn me up . . . Don't you have anyone who's ready to be pensioned out here? I suspect that's the worst next to two times two is four. Starting school again just when one has received his degree; asking the same questions until he dies . . . *[An older man walks by with his hands behind his back.]* There goes a pensioner waiting to die! Probably a captain who didn't become a major or a law clerk who didn't get to be a judge—many are called, but few are chosen . . . He's waiting and waiting for breakfast . . .

PENSIONER. No, for the paper! The morning paper!

OFFICER. And he's only fifty-four years old; he can live for twenty-five more years waiting for his meals and his paper . . . Isn't that terrible?

PENSIONER. What isn't terrible? Tell me that!

OFFICER. Yes, let him who can tell us that! . . . Now, I'm going to teach boys two times two is four: How many times does two go into four? *[He puts his hands to his head in despair.]* And Victoria, whom I love and for whom I wished the greatest happiness on earth . . . Now she has happiness, the greatest she knows, and I suffer . . . suffer . . . suffer!

SHE. Do you think I can be happy when I see you suffer? How can you think that? Maybe my being a prisoner here for forty days and nights will relieve your suffering a little. Does it?

OFFICER. Yes, and no. I can't be happy when you're suffering!

HE. And do you think my happiness can be built on your agony?

OFFICER. We are to be pitied—all of us!

[All raise their hands toward heaven and utter a cry of pain resembling a dissonant chord.]

DAUGHTER. Eternal God, hear them! Life is evil! Human beings are to be pitied!

[All cry out as before.]

•

[The stage becomes pitch-black for a moment, during which the actors leave or change places. When the lights come on again, the shore of Foulstrand²⁷ can be seen at the back in shadow. The sound lies in the middle area, and Fairhaven in the foreground, both fully lighted up. To the right, a corner of the clubhouse with its windows open; couples can be seen dancing inside. On an empty box outside stand three Maids, their arms about each other, looking in at the dance. On the porch is a bench on which Ugly Edith is sitting, bareheaded, depressed, with her heavy head of hair disheveled. In front of her an open piano.

To the left a yellow wooden house.

Two lightly clad Children are tossing a ball back and forth outside the clubhouse.

In the foreground a dock with white boats and flagpoles with flags waving. Out on the sound a warship rigged with cannon openings is anchored.

But the whole landscape is in its winter dress with snow on leafless trees and the ground.

The Daughter and the Officer enter.]

•

DAUGHTER. Here there's peace and happiness during vacation time. Work is over, there's a party every day; people are dressed in their holiday clothes; music and dancing even in the

forenoon. *[To the Maids.]* Why don't you go in and dance, children?

MAIDS. We?

OFFICER. Why, they're servants!

DAUGHTER. That's true! . . . But why is Edith sitting there instead of dancing?

[Edith hides her face in her hands.]

OFFICER. Don't ask her! She has been sitting there for three hours without being asked . . .

[He goes into the yellow house to the left.]

DAUGHTER. What a cruel pleasure!

MOTHER. *[Comes out, wearing a low-cut dress, goes up to Edith.]* Why don't you go in as I've told you?

EDITH. Because . . . I can't ask for a dance. I know I'm ugly . . . that's why no one wants to dance with me, but you could quit reminding me about that! *[Edith begins to play Johann Sebastian Bach's Toccata and Fugue No. 10 on the piano.]*

Christ Ky – ri – é!

[The waltz from the dance indoors can be heard softly at first, but then becomes louder as if competing with Bach's Toccata. Edith plays the waltz down, however, and brings it to silence. Dancers appear in the door and listen to her music; everyone on stage stands listening with rapt attention.]

•

A NAVAL OFFICER. *[Puts his arm about Alice, one of the dancers, and leads her down to the dock.]* Come quickly!

[Edith breaks off playing, stands up, and looks at the Naval Officer and Alice with despair. Remains standing as if turned to stone.]

[The wall of the yellow house is lifted away. One can see three schoolbenches with boys on them; among them sits

---

27. "Shane Sound"; contrasts with Fairhaven.

the Officer, looking uneasy and troubled. The Schoolmaster with glasses, chalk, and cane is standing in front of them.]

SCHOOLMASTER. [To the Officer.] Well, my boy, can you tell me how much two times two is?

[Officer remains seated, searching painfully in his memory without finding the answer.]

SCHOOLMASTER. You should stand up when a question is put to you.

OFFICER. [Tortured, gets up.] Two . . . times two . . . Let me see! . . . It's two twos!

MASTER. So! You haven't studied your lesson!

OFFICER. [Ashamed.] Yes, I have, but . . . I know the answer, but I can't say it . . .

MASTER. You're trying to get out of it! You know but *can't* say it. Maybe I can help you! [Pulls the Officer's hair.]

OFFICER. It's terrible, it is terrible!

MASTER. Yes, it's terrible a big boy hasn't the ambition . . .

OFFICER. [Humiliated.] A *big* boy! Yes, I am big, much bigger than these boys; I'm grown up; I've finished school—[As if awakening.] Why, I have my degree . . . Why am I sitting here? Didn't I get my degree?

SCHOOLMASTER. Yes, you did, but you're to sit here maturing, you see . . . you're to mature . . . Isn't that right?

OFFICER. [His hand to his forehead.] Yes, that's right . . . One should mature . . . Two times two . . . is two . . . and I'll prove it by analogy, the highest form of proof! Listen . . . One times one is one, so two times two is two. What applies to the one applies to the other!

SCHOOLMASTER. The proof is absolutely correct according to the laws of logic, but the answer is wrong!

OFFICER. What's in keeping with the laws of logic can't be wrong! Let's test it! One goes into one once, so two goes into two twice.

SCHOOLMASTER. Absolutely correct by analogy. But how much is one times three?

OFFICER. Three!

SCHOOLMASTER. So two times three is also three!

OFFICER. [Thoughtfully.] No, that can't be right . . . it can't . . . or . . . [Sits down, in despair.] No, I'm not mature yet.

SCHOOLMASTER. No, you're not mature by a long shot . . .

OFFICER. But how long will I have to sit here?

SCHOOLMASTER. How long? Do you think time and space exist? . . . Assume that time exists. Then you should be able to say what time is! What is time?

OFFICER. Time . . . [Considers.] I can't say me, but I know what it is: ergo, I can know how much two times two is without my being able to say it! Can you say what time is, sir?

SCHOOLMASTER. Of course I can!

ALL THE BOYS. Go—tell us!

SCHOOLMASTER. Time? . . . Let me see! [Stands motionless with his finger to his nose.] While we're speaking, time flies. So time is something that flies while I speak!

ONE BOY. [Gets up.] You're talking now, sir, and while you're talking, I fly, so I'm time! [Flees.]

SCHOOLMASTER. That's absolutely right according to the laws of logic!

OFFICER. But then the laws of logic are crazy, for Nils who fled can't be time!

SCHOOLMASTER. That, too, is absolutely right according to the laws of logic, though it is crazy.

OFFICER. Then logic is crazy!

SCHOOLMASTER. It really looks like it! But if logic is crazy, the whole world is crazy . . . Then to hell with sitting here teaching you nonsense! . . . If anyone offers to treat us to a drink, we'll go swimming!

OFFICER. That is *posterus prius,* or the world turned backside to, because usually one goes swimming first and then has a drink! You old fogey!

SCHOOLMASTER. Don't be arrogant, Doctor!

OFFICER. Use my military title, please! I'm an officer, and I don't understand why I'm sitting here among schoolboys being scolded . . .

SCHOOLMASTER. [Lifts his finger.] We should mature!

•

QUARANTINE MASTER. [Enters.] The quarantine's beginning!

OFFICER. There you are! Can you imagine that fellow has me sitting on the school bench though I have my degree?

QUARANTINE MASTER. Well, why don't you leave?

OFFICER. Why not? . . . Leave? That's not so easy!

SCHOOLMASTER. No, I imagine not. Try!

OFFICER. [To the Quarantine Master.] Save me! Save me from his eyes!

QUARANTINE MASTER. Come along! . . . Just come and help us dance . . . We have to dance before the epidemic breaks out. We have to!

OFFICER. Is the ship leaving then?

QUARANTINE MASTER. The ship is to leave first! . . . There'll be weeping then, of course!

OFFICE. Always weeping: when it comes, and when it leaves . . . Let's go!

[They go out. The Schoolmaster silently continues teaching.]

•

[The Maids, who have been standing at the dance-hall window, move sadly toward the dock; Edith, who has stood as if turned to stone by the piano, follows them slowly.]

DAUGHTER. *[To the Officer.]* Isn't there a single happy human being in this paradise?

OFFICER. Yes, there are two newlyweds over there. Listen to them!

•

[The newlyweds enter.]

HUSBAND. *[To the Wife.]* My happiness is so great I could wish to die . . .

WIFE. Why die?

HUSBAND. Because in the midst of happiness grows the seed of unhappiness; it consumes itself as the flame of fire . . . it can't burn forever but must go out; this presentiment of the end destroys bliss while at its very height.

WIFE. Let's die together, right now!

HUSBAND. Die? All right! For I fear happiness! It's deceitful!

[They go toward the water.]

•

DAUGHTER. *[To the Officer.]* Life is evil! Human beings are to be pitied!

OFFICER. Look at that fellow who's coming! He's the most envied of all the mortals in this place! *[The Blindman is led in.]* He owns these hundred Italian villas; he owns all these firths, bays, shores, forests, and fish in the water, the birds in the air, and the wildlife in the forest. These thousand people are his paying guests, and the sun rises on his sea and sets on his lands . . .

DAUGHTER. Well, does he complain, too?

OFFICER. Yes, and with good reason—he can't see!

QUARANTINE MASTER. He's blind! . . .

DAUGHTER. The one most envied of all!

OFFICER. Now he's to see the ship sail—his son is on board.

•

BLINDMAN. I don't see, but I hear! I hear how the anchor tears the bottom as when one pulls a fishhook out of a fish and its heart comes along through its throat! . . . My son, my only child, is going to foreign countries by way of the wide sea; I can follow him only with my thoughts . . . now I hear the anchor chain grating . . . and . . . there's something fluttering and crackling like washing on a clothesline . . . wet handkerchiefs probably . . . and I hear sobbing and sighing as when people are crying . . . if it's the washing of the waves against the ship or girls on the shore . . . the deserted and the ones who can't be comforted . . . I once asked a child why the sea was salt, and the child, whose father was on a long journey, answered at once: The sea is salt because the sailors weep so much. Why do the sailors weep so much, then? . . . Well, he answered, because they're always going away . . . and therefore they always dry their handkerchiefs up on the masts! . . . Why does a human being weep when he's sad? I then asked . . . Well, said the child, his glasses have to be washed occasionally so he can see more clearly! . . .

[The ship has hoisted its sails and is gliding away; the girls on shore wave their handkerchiefs and, alternately, dry their tears. Now the signal "yes" is hoisted on the topmast—a red ball on a white field. Alice waves jubilantly by way of answer.]

DAUGHTER. *[To the Officer.]* What does that flag mean?

OFFICER. It means "yes." It's the lieutenant's "yes" in red—the red blood of his heart—inscribed on the blue cloth of the sky!

DAUGHTER. What does "no" look like then?

OFFICER. It's blue as the tainted blood in blue veins . . . but do you see how Alice is rejoicing?

DAUGHTER. And how Edith is weeping! . . .

BLINDMAN. Meeting and parting! Parting and meeting! That is life! I met his mother. And she's gone! I still had my son. And now he has gone!

DAUGHTER. He'll surely come back.

BLINDMAN. Who is it talking to me? I've heard that voice before, in my dreams, in my youth, when summer vacation began, when I was just married, when my child was born. Every time life smiled, I heard that voice like the sighing of the south wind, like music on a harp above, as I imagine the chorus of angels greeting Christmas night . . .

[Lawyer enters, goes up to the Blindman, and whispers to him.]

BLINDMAN. Really!

LAWYER. Yes, that's how it is! *[Goes up to the Daughter.]* Now you've seen most things, but you haven't tried the worst.

DAUGHTER. What can that be?

LAWYER. Repetition . . . doing the same thing again and again! . . . Going back! Redoing one's lessons! . . . Come!

DAUGHTER. Where?

LAWYER. To your duties!

DAUGHTER. What are they?

LAWYER. They're everything you loathe! Everything you don't want to do but have to do! They're doing without, giving up, forsaking, and leaving . . . everything unpleasant, repulsive, painful . . .

DAUGHTER. Aren't there any pleasant duties?

LAWYER. They become pleasant when they're fulfilled . . .

DAUGHTER. When they don't exist any more . . . So duty is everything unpleasant! What's pleasant then?

LAWYER. What's pleasant is sin.

DAUGHTER. Sin?

LAWYER. Which is to be punished, yes! If I've had a pleasant day and evening, I have the pangs of hell and a bad conscience the next day!

DAUGHTER. How strange!

LAWYER. Yes, I wake up in the morning with a headache, and the repetition begins . . . in reverse. In such a way that everything that last night was beautiful, pleasant, clever, memory today presents as evil, vile, stupid. Pleasure sort of rots, and joy goes to pieces. What human beings call success always becomes the cause of the next defeat. The successes I've had in life became my ruination. You see, human beings have an instinctive horror of other people's success; they think fate is unjust to favor one person, so they try to restore the balance by rolling stones in one's way. Being talented is extremely dangerous, for you can easily starve to death! In the meanwhile, return to your duties or I'll sue you, and we'll go through all three courts—one, two, three!

DAUGHTER. Return? To the stove, with the pot filled with cabbage, the baby's clothes . . .

LAWYER. Yes, indeed! We have a big washing today; we're going to wash all the handkerchiefs, you see . . .

DAUGHTER. *[Sighs.]* Am I going to do it over again?

LAWYER. All of life is only repetitions . . . Look at the teacher in there . . . He got his doctor's degree yesterday, was crowned with the laurel wreath, they fired cannon shots in his honor, he climbed Parnassus, and was embraced by the king . . . and today he begins school over again, asks how much is two times two, and will be doing that until he dies . . . However, come back . . . to your home!

DAUGHTER. I'd rather die!

LAWYER. Die? You mayn't! First, it's so disgraceful your body'll be outraged, and afterward . . . you're damned! . . . It's a mortal sin!

DAUGHTER. It isn't easy to be a human being!

•

ALL. Right!

•

DAUGHTER. I'll not return to degradation and dirt with you! . . . I want to return to where I came from, but . . . first the door must be opened so I learn the secret . . . I want the door opened!

LAWYER. Then you must retrace your steps, go back the same way, and bear all the horrors of the process, the repetitions, the circumlocutions, the reiterations . . .

DAUGHTER. So be it, but I'll go alone into the wilderness to find myself again. We'll meet again! *[To the Poet.]* Come with me!

[Cries of agony from the back, in the distance.]

DAUGHTER. What was that?

LAWYER. The damned at Foulstrand!

DAUGHTER. Why do they complain more than usual today?

LAWYER. Because the sun is shining here, because there's music here, dancing here, youth here. Then they feel their agony so much more deeply.

DAUGHTER. We must set them free!

LAWYER. Try! A liberator did come once, but He was hanged on a cross!

DAUGHTER. By whom?

LAWYER. By all the right-thinking people!

DAUGHTER. Who are they?

LAWYER. Don't you know all the right-thinking? Then you're going to get to know them.

DAUGHTER. Were they the ones who refused to grant you your degree?

LAWYER. Yes.

DAUGHTER. Then I know them!

•

[A shore on the Mediterranean. To the left in the foreground can be seen a white wall, over which branches of fruit-bearing orange trees are hanging. At the back, villas and a casino with a terrace. To the right, a large pile of coal with two wheelbarrows. At the back to the right, a strip of the blue sea.

Two Coalheavers, naked to their waists, black on their faces, on their hands, and on the other exposed parts of their bodies, are sitting, hopeless, each on a wheelbarrow. The Daughter and the Lawyer come in at the back.]

DAUGHTER. This is paradise!

FIRST COALHEAVER. This is hell!

SECOND COALHEAVER. Over 115 degrees in the shade!

FIRST COALHEAVER. Shall we take a dip?

SECOND COALHEAVER. Then the police will come. Bathing's forbidden here.

FIRST COALHEAVER. Can't we take an orange from the tree?

SECOND COALHEAVER. No, then the police will come.

FIRST COALHEAVER. But I can't work in this heat; I'll give up the whole thing.

SECOND COALHEAVER. Then the police will come and take you! . . . [Pause.] And besides you'll have nothing to eat . . .

FIRST COALHEAVER. Nothing to eat? We who work the most get to eat the least; and the rich who don't do anything have the most! . . . Shouldn't one—without getting too close to the truth—say it's unjust? . . . What does that daughter of the gods over there say?

•

DAUGHTER. I haven't the answer! . . . But tell me: what have you done to be so black and to have so hard a lot?

FIRST COALHEAVER. What have we done? We were born to poor and rather worthless parents . . . Probably punished a couple of times!

DAUGHTER. Punished?

FIRST COALHEAVER. Yes! The unpunished sit up there in the casino eating seven courses with wine.

DAUGHTER. [To the Lawyer.] Can that be true?

LAWYER. For the most part, yes! . . .

DAUGHTER. You mean every human being at some time or other has deserved imprisonment?

LAWYER. Yes!

DAUGHTER. Even you?

LAWYER. Yes!

•

DAUGHTER. Is it true the poor can't bathe in the sea here?

LAWYER. Yes, not even with their clothes on. Only the ones who intend to drown themselves get out of paying. But they're likely to get beaten up at the police station!

DAUGHTER. Couldn't they go outside the city limits, out into the country, to bathe?

LAWYER. There isn't any free land—it's all fenced in.

DAUGHTER. Out in the open, I mean.

LAWYER. There isn't any open . . . it's all taken.

DAUGHTER. Even the sea, the great, wide sea . . .

LAWYER. Everything! You can't go on a boat at sea and land anywhere without its being recorded and paid for. Lovely, isn't it!

DAUGHTER. This isn't paradise!

LAWYER. No, I assure you it isn't!

DAUGHTER. Why don't human beings do something to improve their situation . . .

LAWYER. They do, of course, but all reformers end up either in prison or in the insane asylum . . .

DAUGHTER. Who puts them in prison?

LAWYER. All the right-thinking, all the decent . . .

DAUGHTER. Who puts them in the insane asylum?

LAWYER. Their own despair over seeing how hopeless their efforts are.

DAUGHTER. Hasn't anyone thought there are secret reasons for its being as it is?

LAWYER. Yes, those who are well off always think that!

DAUGHTER. That it's fine as it is? . . .

FIRST COALHEAVER. And all the same we're the foundations of society; if you don't get any coal, the fire in the kitchen stove goes out, the fire in the fireplace, the machine in the factory; the lights go out on the street, in the stores, in the homes; darkness and cold fall upon you . . . And that's why we sweat like hell to carry the black coal . . . What do you give in return?

LAWYER. *[To the Daughter.]* Help them . . . *[Pause.]* That it can't be absolutely equal for all, I understand, but how can it be so unequal?

•

[A Gentleman and a Lady walk across the stage.]

LADY. Are you coming to play a game?

GENTLEMAN. No, I have to take a little walk so I can eat dinner.

•

FIRST COALHEAVER. So he *can* eat dinner?

SECOND COALHEAVER. So he *can?* . .

[The Children enter; scream with horror when they see the black laborers.]

FIRST COALHEAVER. They scream when they see us! They scream . . .

SECOND COALHEAVER. Damn it! . . . I suppose we'll have to bring out the scaffolds soon and go to work on this rotten body . . .

FIRST COALHEAVER. Damn it! I say, too! Ugh!

•

LAWYER. *[To the Daughter.]* Of course it's crazy! People aren't so bad . . .

DAUGHTER. But? . . .

LAWYER. But the administration . . .

DAUGHTER. *[Covers her face and goes.]* This is not paradise!

COALHEAVERS. No, it's hell. That's what it is!

III

———

[Fingal's Cave. Long, green waves roll slowly into the cave; in the foreground a red sounding buoy rocks on the waves. The buoy sounds only at indicated places. The music of the winds. The music of the waves.]

POET. Where have you brought me?

DAUGHTER. Far from the noise and wailing of human beings, to the end of the sea, to this cave we call the Ear of Indra, since they say the Lord of Heaven listens here to the complaints of mortals!

POET. What? Here?

DAUGHTER. Do you see how this cave is shaped like a seashell? Yes, you do. Don't you know your ear is shaped like a shell? You know, but you haven't thought about it. *[She picks up a seashell from the shore.]* As a child, didn't you hold a shell to your ear and listen . . . You hear that in the little shell; imagine what can be heard in this big one! . . .

POET. *[Listening.]* I can't hear anything but the sighing of the wind . . .

DAUGHTER. Then I'll be its interpreter. Listen! The lamentation of the winds!

[Recites to soft music.]

Born under the clouds of heaven
We were chased by the bolts of Indra
down unto the dusty earth . . .
The litter on the fields soiled our feet;
the dust of the highways,
the smoke of the cities,
vile human breaths,
the smell of food and wine
we had to bear . . .
Out on the wide sea we fled
to give our lungs air,
to shake our wings,
and wash our feet.
Indra, Lord of Heaven,
hear us!
Hear when we sigh!
The earth is not clean,
life is not good,
human beings not evil,
nor are they good.
They live as they can,
one day at a time.

The sons of dust wander in dust,
born of dust
they return to dust.
They have feet to walk,
but not wings.
They become dusty.
Is the blame theirs
or yours?

we are like flames of fire,
we are wet flames.
Quenching, burning,
washing, bathing,
breeding, bearing.
We, we the waves
that rock the winds
to sleep!

POET. That's what I heard once . . .
DAUGHTER. Sh-h! The winds are still singing!

[Recites to soft music.]

We, the winds, children of the air,
carry the laments of mankind.
If you heard us
in the chimney on autumn evenings,
in the openings of the stove,
in the cracks by the windows,
when the rain wept on the roofs,
or on a winter evening
in a snowy fir forest
on the stormy sea
if you heard moans and sighs
in sails and rigging . . .
It was we, the winds,
children of the air,
who from human hearts
through which we've passed
have learned these melodies of torment . . .
in sickrooms, on battlefields,
most in children's rooms
where the newborn whimper,
wailing, screaming
over the pain of existence.
It is we, we the winds
who whine and moan!

POET. It seems to me I've . . .
DAUGHTER. Sh-h! The waves are singing.

[Recites to soft music.]

It is we, we, the waves,
that rock the winds
to rest!
Green cradles, we the waves.
We are wet and salt;

DAUGHTER. False and faithless waves: everything that isn't burned on earth is drowned—in the waves. Look at that! [Points to a rubbish heap.] See what the sea has stolen and crushed . . . Only the figureheads of sunken ships remain . . . and their names: *Justice, Friendship, The Golden Peace, Hope*—that's all that's left of *Hope* . . . deceitful *Hope!* . . . Beams, oarlocks, bailers! And look, the lifebuoy . . . it saves itself, but lets the man in distress perish!

POET. [Searching in the rubbish heap.] The nameboard of the ship *Justice* is here. That was the one that left Fairhaven with the blindman's son aboard. So it sank! And on board was Alice's fiancé, Edith's hopeless love.

DAUGHTER. The blindman? Fairhaven? I must have dreamed that! And Alice's fiancé, ugly Edith, Foulstrand, and the quarantine, sulphur and carbolic acid, the commencement in the church, the lawyer's office, the corridor and Victoria, the growing castle, and the officer . . . I've dreamed that . . .

POET. I put it into poetry once . . .

DAUGHTER. Then you know what poetry is . . .

POET. Then I know what dreaming is . . . What is poetry?

DAUGHTER. Not reality, but more than reality . . . not dreaming, but waking dreams . . .

POET. And the children of man think we poets only play . . . invent and make up!

DAUGHTER. And that is good, my friend; otherwise the world would be laid waste for lack of encouragement. Everyone would lie on his back looking at the sky; no one would put his hand to the plow and spade, plane or hoe.

POET. And this you say, Daughter of Indra, you who by half belong up there . . .

DAUGHTER. You may well reproach me; I've been too long down here bathing in mud as you do

. . . My thoughts cannot fly any more; there's
clay on my wings . . . soil on my feet . . . and
I myself—*[Lifts her arms.]*—I'm sinking, sinking
. . . Help me, Father, God of Heaven! *[Silence.]*
I don't hear His answer any more! Ether won't
carry the sound from His lips to the shell of my
ear . . . the silver thread has broken . . . *[Sighs.]*
I am earthbound!

POET. Do you intend to ascend . . . soon?

DAUGHTER. As soon as I have burned my body . . .
for the waters of the sea cannot cleanse me.
Why do you ask?

POET. Because . . . I have a prayer . . . a
petition . . .

DAUGHTER. What sort of petition . . .

POET. A petition from mankind to the ruler of the
world, put together by a dreamer!

DAUGHTER. To be delivered by . . .

POET. Indra's daughter . . .

DAUGHTER. Can you recite your poem?

POET. Yes, I can.

DAUGHTER. Say it then.

POET. Better you do it!

DAUGHTER. Where will I read it?

POET. In my thoughts, or here! *[Hands her a roll of
paper.]*

DAUGHTER. Fine! Then I'll recite it!

[Accepts the paper but reads by heart.]

"Why were you born with pain,
why do you torment your mother,
child of man, when you are giving
her the joy of becoming a mother,
the joy above all joys?
Why do you awaken to life,
why do you greet light,
with a cry of anger and of pain?
Why don't you smile at life,
child of man, when the gift of
life is happiness itself?
Why are we born like beasts,
we who are divine and human?
The spirit would want a garment
other than this of blood and filth!
Is the image of God to cut its teeth . . ."
Sh-h! . . . the creature blames not the Creator!
No one has yet solved the riddle of life! . . .
"And so begins the wandering
over thorns, thistles, stones;
if you walk on a beaten path

they say at once it's forbidden;
if you pick a flower, you
learn at once it's someone else's;
if your way is through a field
and you have to go directly,
you're tramping down another's crop;
others will tramp on yours
to make the difference less!
Every joy which you enjoy
brings sorrow to all others,
but your sorrow makes no one happy,
because sorrow is heaped on sorrow!
So goes the journey until your death,
which becomes another's bread." . . .
Is that how you intend to approach,
son of dust, the highest god? . . .

POET.

How shall the son of dust find
words bright, pure, light enough
to be able to rise from earth . . .
Child of God, will you convert
our lamentation into the speech
the Immortals grasp best?

DAUGHTER. *[Pointing at the buoy.]* What's that floating
there? . . . A buoy?

DAUGHTER. Yes.

POET. It looks like a lung with a voice box!

DAUGHTER. It's the watchman of the sea. When
danger threatens, it sings.

POET. It seems to me the sea is rising and the waves
are beginning to roll . . .

DAUGHTER. Most likely!

POET. *[Sighs.]* What do I see? A ship . . . outside
the reef.

DAUGHTER. What ship can it be?

POET. I think it's the ghost ship.[28]

DAUGHTER. What's that?

POET. *The Flying Dutchman.*

DAUGHTER. That one? Why is he punished so
severely, and why doesn't he ever land?

POET. Because he had seven faithless wives.

DAUGHTER. Should he be punished for that?

POET. Yes! All right-thinking people condemned
him . . .

DAUGHTER. Strange world! . . . How can he be
freed from his sentence?

POET. Freed? Better watch out for setting free . . .

---

28. Refers to legend about the Flying Dutchman, a sea captain condemned to sail the seas on a ghost ship because of his godlessness.

DAUGHTER. Why?

POET. Because . . . No, it isn't the *Dutchman*. It's an ordinary ship in distress . . . Why doesn't the buoy sing? . . . See, the sea's rising, the waves are high; soon we'll be shut up in the cave! . . . Now the ship's bell's ringing! We'll soon get another figure-head . . . Scream, buoy; do your duty, watchman . . . *[The buoy sings a four-part chord in fifths and sixths resembling foghorns.]* . . . The crew is waving to us . . . but we ourselves are perishing!

DAUGHTER. Don't you want to be set free!

POET. Yes, of course, I do, but not now . . . and not in water!

CREW. *[Sings in four-part.]* Christ Kyrie!

POET. Now they're calling, and the sea's calling. But no one hears!

CREW. Christ Kyrie!

DAUGHTER. Who's coming out there?

POET. Walking on the water? There's only one who walks on water. It isn't Peter,[29] the rock, for he sank like a stone . . .

[A white glow can be seen on the water.]

CREW. Christ Kyrie!

DAUGHTER. Is it He?

POET. It is He, the crucified one . . .

DAUGHTER. Why—tell me, why was He crucified?

POET. Because He wanted to set free . . .

DAUGHTER. Who—I've forgotten—who crucified Him?

POET. All the right-thinking.

DAUGHTER. What a strange world!

POET. The sea's rising! Darkness is upon us! . . . The storm's getting worse.

•

[Crew scream.]

POET. The members of the crew are screaming with terror when they see their redeemer . . . And . . . they're jumping overboard out of fear of their savior . . . *[The Crewmen scream again.]* Now they're screaming because they have to die! Scream when they're born, and scream when they die! *[The rising waves threaten to drown them in the cave.]*

DAUGHTER. If I were sure it is a ship . . .

POET. Honestly . . . I don't think it is. . . . It's a two-story house with trees outside . . . and a telephone tower . . . It's the modern tower of Babel[30] which sends lines up there . . . to inform those above . . .

DAUGHTER. Child, human thought doesn't need any metal wire to get there . . . The prayer of the devout makes its way through all the worlds . . . It's certainly no tower of Babel, for if you want to take heaven by storm you must do it by means of your prayers.

POET. No, it's not a house . . . not a telephone tower . . Do you see that?

DAUGHTER. What do you see?

POET. I see a snow-covered heath, a training field . . . the winter sun shines behind a church on the hill, and the tower casts its long shadow on the snow . . . a troop of soldiers is marching onto the field; they march on the tower, up the spire; now they're on the cross, but I sense that the first one who steps on the cock must die . . . now they're getting close . . . the corporal's in the van . . . *[Laughs.]* . . . a cloud is rolling across the heath, past the sun, of course . . . now it's all gone . . . the water in the cloud put out the fire in the sun! The sunlight created the dark image of the tower, but the cloud's dark image choked the tower's . . .

[While the above was being said, the stage had again become the theater corridor.]

---

29. In Matthew 24, Jesus walked on water but Peter failed to do so because of his lack of faith.

30. In Genesis 11, God punished the builders of the tower of Babel by making them speak many different languages.

DAUGHTER. *[To the Doorkeeper.]* Has the lord chancellor arrived yet?

DOORKEEPER. No.

DAUGHTER. Have the deans?

DOORKEEPER. No.

DAUGHTER. Summon them at once, then—the door's to be opened . . .

DOORKEEPER. Is that so urgent?

DAUGHTER. Yes, it is! For there's a suspicion that the solution to the puzzle of the world is kept in there . . . So summon the deans of the four faculties and the lord chancellor!

[The Doorkeeper blows a whistle.]

DAUGHTER. And don't forget the glazier and his diamond, or nothing will get done!

[Theater people enter from the left as early in the play.]

OFFICER. *[Comes in from the back dressed in frock coat and top hat and carrying a bouquet of roses. He is radiantly happy.]* Victoria!

DOORKEEPER. She'll soon be here!

OFFICER. Fine! The carriage is ready, the table's set, the champagne's on ice . . . May I embrace you, ma'am?

WOMAN'S VOICE. *[From above, sings.]* I'm here!

OFFICER. *[Walking about.]* Fine! I'm waiting.

•

POET. I seem to have lived through this before . . .

DAUGHTER. I, too.

POET. Perhaps I dreamt it?

DAUGHTER. Or composed it, perhaps?

POET. Or composed it.

DAUGHTER. Then you know what poetry is.

POET. Then I know what dreaming is.

DAUGHTER. It seems to me we've stood elsewhere saying these words before.

POET. Then you can soon determine what reality is!

DAUGHTER. Or dreaming!

POET. Or poetry!

•

[The Lord Chancellor and the Deans of theology, philosophy, medicine, and law, respectively, enter.][31]

31. Swedish universities still maintain the division into these four faculties.

CHANCELLOR. It's the question of the door, of course! What do you, dean of the theological faculty, think?

DEAN OF THEOLOGY. I don't think, I believe . . . credo . . .

DEAN OF PHILOSOPHY. I think . . .

DEAN OF MEDICINE. I know . . .

DEAN OF LAW. I doubt until I have evidence and witnesses.

CHANCELLOR. Now they're going to squabble again! . . . What do you, dean of theology, believe?

DEAN OF THEOLOGY. I believe this door must not be opened, because it conceals dangerous truths . . .

DEAN OF PHILOSOPHY. The truth is never dangerous.

DEAN OF MEDICINE. What is truth?

DEAN OF LAW. What can be proved by two witnesses!

DEAN OF THEOLOGY. Anything and everything can be proved with two false witnesses—by a perverter of the law.

DEAN OF PHILOSOPHY. Truth is wisdom, and knowledge is philosophy itself . . . Philosophy is the science of sciences, the knowledge of all knowledge, and all the other sciences are the servants of philosophy.

DEAN OF MEDICINE. The only science is natural science—philosophy isn't a science. It's merely empty speculations.

DEAN OF THEOLOGY. Bravo!

DEAN OF PHILOSOPHY. *[To Dean of Theology.]* You say bravo! What are you really? You're the eternal enemy of all knowledge, you're the opposite of science, you're ignorance and darkness . . .

DEAN OF MEDICINE. Bravo!

DEAN OF THEOLOGY. *[To Dean of Medicine.]* You say bravo, you who don't see farther than your nose in your magnifying glass, you who only believe in your deceptive senses, in your eye, for example, which can be farsighted, shortsighted, blind, dimsighted, cross-eyes, one-eyed, color blind, blind to red, blind to green . . .

DEAN OF MEDICINE. Fool!

DEAN OF THEOLOGY. Ass!

[They rush at each other.]

CHANCELLOR. Quiet! One raven shouldn't hack out the eyes of the other!

DEAN OF PHILOSOPHY. If I were to select between those two, theology and medicine, I'd select— neither!

DEAN OF LAW. And if I were to judge you three, I'd convict—all of you! . . . You can't agree on a single point, and never have been able to. But back to the matter at hand! What are your views on this door and its opening, lord chancellor!

CHANCELLOR. Views? I haven't any views. The government has simply appointed me to see you don't break each other's arms and legs in council . . while you're bringing up young people. Views? No, I watch out for views. I once had a few, but they were immediately disproved; views are immediately disproved—by one's opponent, of course! . . . Perhaps we may now open the door even at the risk that it conceals dangerous truths?

DEAN OF LAW. What is truth? Where is truth?

DEAN OF THEOLOGY. I am the truth and the life . . .

DEAN OF PHILOSOPHY. I am the knowledge of all knowledge . . .

DEAN OF MEDICINE. I am exact knowledge . . .

DEAN OF LAW. I doubt!

[They rush at each other.]

•

DAUGHTER. Teachers of youth, blush for shame!

DEAN OF LAW. Lord chancellor, representative of the government, head of our faculty, punish this woman for her offence. She had told you to blush for shame. That is an insult, and she has called you teachers of youth in a contemptuous, ironic sense, and that is libelous!

DAUGHTER. Poor young people!

DEAN OF LAW. She pities the young—that amounts to accusing us, lord chancellor. Punish her for her offence!

DAUGHTER. Yes, I accuse you, all of you for sowing doubt and dissension in the mind of the young.

DEAN OF LAW. Listen: she is making the young doubt our authority, and she accuses us of causing doubt. Isn't that a criminal act? I ask all right-thinking people.

ALL THE RIGHT-THINKING. Yes, it's criminal!

DEAN OF LAW. All right-thinking people have condemned you! Go in peace with your gain! Or—

DAUGHTER. My gain? Or? Or what?

DEAN OF LAW. Or you'll be stoned.

POET. Or crucified.

DAUGHTER. I am going. Come with me, and you'll get the answer to the riddle!

POET. Which riddle?

DAUGHTER. What does he mean by "my gain"?

POET. Probably nothing. It's what we call talk. He was just talking.

DAUGHTER. But he hurt me deeply by saying that!

POET. That's probably why he said it . . . People are like that.

•

ALL THE RIGHT-THINKING. Hurrah! The door has been opened!

•

CHANCELLOR. What was hidden back of the door?

GLAZIER. I can't see anything.

CHANCELLOR. He can't see anything! No, I can believe that! . . . Deans! What was concealed back of the door?

DEAN OF THEOLOGY. Nothing! That's the solution to the riddle of the world . . . In the beginning God created heaven and earth out of nothing.

DEAN OF PHILOSOPHY. Out of nothing comes nothing.

DEAN OF MEDICINE. Bosh! That's nothing.

DEAN OF LAW. I doubt. And here there's a fraud. I appeal to all right-thinking people!

DAUGHTER. *[To the Poet.]* Who are the right-thinking?

POET. Let him say who can. Usually all the right-thinking are just one person. Today it's I and mine, tomorrow it's you and yours. A person's labeled that, or, more accurately, a person labels himself that.

•

ALL THE RIGHT-THINKING. They've deceived us!

CHANCELLOR. Who has deceived you?

ALL THE RIGHT-THINKING. The daughter!

CHANCELLOR. *[To the Daughter.]* Will you please tell us what you intended by the opening of this door?

DAUGHTER. No, my friends! If I told you, you wouldn't believe it.

DEAN OF MEDICINE. Why, there's nothing there.

DAUGHTER. As you say! But you didn't understand that nothing!

DEAN OF MEDICINE. It's nonsense what she's saying.

ALL. Bosh!

DAUGHTER. *[To the Poet.]* They're to be pitied.

POET. Are you serious!

DAUGHTER. I'm always serious.

POET. Do you pity the right-thinking, too?

DAUGHTER. Them perhaps most of all.

POET. And the deans, too?

DAUGHTER. Even them, and not least! Four heads, four minds in one body! Who created that monster?

ALL. She doesn't answer!

CHANCELLOR. Strike her, then!

DAUGHTER. I have answered.

CHANCELLOR. Listen, she's answering.

ALL. Strike her! She's answering.

DAUGHTER. "Either she answers, or she doesn't answer: strike her!" . . . Come, seer. *[To the Poet.]* I'm going—far away from here!—to tell you the riddle—but out in the wilderness, where no one can hear us, no one can see us! Because . . .

•

LAWYER. *[Comes forward, takes the Daughter by her arm.]* Have you forgotten your duties?

DAUGHTER. Goodness no! But I have higher duties.

LAWYER. And your child?

DAUGHTER. My child! So?

LAWYER. Your child is calling for you.

DAUGHTER. My child! *[Sadly.]* I am earthbound! . . . And this torment in my heart, this anguish . . . What is it?

LAWYER. Don't you know?

DAUGHTER. No!

LAWYER. They're pangs of conscience.

DAUGHTER. Pangs of conscience?

LAWYER. Yes! And they appear after every neglected duty, after every pleasure, even the most innocent—if there are any innocent pleasures, which I rather doubt; and after every suffering one has caused his neighbor.

DAUGHTER. And there's no cure?

LAWYER. Yes, but only one! That's to do one's duty right away . . .

DAUGHTER. You look like a demon when you utter the word *duty!* But when one has—as I do— two duties to fulfill?

LAWYER. One fulfills first one, then the other!

DAUGHTER. The highest first . . . so you look after my child, then I'll do my duty . . .

LAWYER. Your child suffers from missing you . . . Can you understand that someone suffers because of you?

DAUGHTER. Now my soul is disturbed . . . it split into two, and I'm torn in two directions!

LAWYER. Those are life's little difficulties, you see!

DAUGHTER. Oh, how it tears!

•

POET. If you had any idea how I've spread sorrow and destruction through fulfilling my calling— note "calling"—which is the highest duty, you wouldn't want to take me by the hand!

DAUGHTER. What do you mean?

POET. My father had built his hopes on me—his only son, who would carry on his business . . . I ran away from the college of business administration . . . My father died of grief. My mother wanted me to become a minister . . . I couldn't become a minister . . . she disowned me . . . I had a friend who had stood by me in my most difficult times . . . My friend behaved like a tyrant against those I spoke for and sang for. I had to strike down my friend and benefactor to save my own soul. Since then I don't have inner peace any more; people call me an infamous scoundrel; it doesn't help that my conscience says: You did the right thing, for the next minute my conscience says: You did wrong! Life is like that!

DAUGHTER. Come with me into the wilderness!

POET. But your child!

DAUGHTER. *[Pointing at all those present.]* These are my children! Each one by himself is good, but all you have to do to turn them into demons is to bring them together . . . Farewell!

[Outside the castle; the same scenery as in the first tableau in the first act. But the ground at the base of the castle is now covered with flowers (blue monkshood, aconite). At the very peak on the tower of the castle roof is a chrysanthemum bud ready to burst. The castle windows are illuminated with candlelight.]

•

DAUGHTER. The moment isn't far off when with the help of fire I will ascend to Ether again . . . That is what you mortals call death, and what you approach with fear.

POET. Fear of the unknown.

DAUGHTER. Which you know.

POET. Who does?

DAUGHTER. Everyone! Why don't you believe your prophets?

POET. Prophets have never been believed. How does that happen? And "if God has spoken, why don't human beings believe?" His convincing power ought to be irresistible!

DAUGHTER. Have you always doubted?

POET. No. I've had certainty many times, but after a while, it has gone its way as a dream does when one awakens.

DAUGHTER. Is isn't easy to be a human being!

POET. You understand and admit that?

DAUGHTER. Yes!

POET. Wait! Wasn't it Indra who once sent His son down here to hear the complaints of mankind?

DAUGHTER. Yes, it was. How was He received?

POET. How did He carry out His mission? To answer with a question.

DAUGHTER. To answer with another . . . Wasn't the lot of man better after His stay on earth? Tell me truthfully!

POET. Better? . . . Yes, a little. Very little! . . . But instead of asking questions, won't you explain the riddle?

DAUGHTER. Yes. But to what point? You'll not believe me.

POET. I'll believe you, for I know who you are!

DAUGHTER. Well, then, I will tell you. In the morning of time before the sun shone, Brahma, the primordial divine force, let Maja,[32] mother of the world, seduce him in order to increase and multiply. This, the union of the divine and the earthly, was heaven's fall from grace. The world, life, and human beings are therefore only phantoms, appearances, visions . . .

POET. My vision!

DAUGHTER. A true vision! . . . But to free themselves from the earthly, Brahma's descendants seek self-denial and suffering . . . There you have suffering as the savior . . . But this longing for suffering is in conflict with the instinct to enjoy or love . . . Do you yet understand what love is with its greatest pleasure in the greatest suffering, the most pleasant in the most bitter? Do you understand what woman is? Woman, through whom sin and death entered into life?

POET. I understand . . . And the end? . . .

DAUGHTER. What you feel . . . The struggle between the pain of joy and the joy of suffering . . . the penitent's anguish and the voluptuary's pleasures . . .

POET. A struggle, then?

DAUGHTER. Struggle between opposites generates power, just as fire and water produce steam . . .

POET. But peace? And rest?

DAUGHTER. Sh-h! You may not ask any more, and I may not answer! . . . The altar is adorned for the sacrifice . . . the flowers keep watch . . . the candles are lighted . . . white sheets are at the windows . . . pine boughs[33] in the entrance . . .

POET. You say this as calmly as if suffering no longer existed for you!

DAUGHTER. No! . . . I have suffered all your sufferings, but a hundredfold, for my perceptions are finer . . .

POET. Tell me your sorrows!

DAUGHTER. Poet, could you tell me yours so there wouldn't be an extra word, could your words for once really express your thoughts?

POET. No, you're right! I seemed like someone deaf and dumb to myself, and when the crowd listened with admiration to my song, I thought it only words . . . that's why, you see, I always blushed with shame when they praised me.

DAUGHTER. So you want me to? Look me in the eye!

POET. I can't bear your look . . .

DAUGHTER. How could you bear my words if I were to speak my language? . . .

POET. Tell me, though, before you leave: what caused you most suffering here on earth?

DAUGHTER. Existing—being alive; feeling my sight weakened by an eye, my hearing dulled by an ear, and my thought, my airy light thought bound in the labyrinths of layers of fat. Why, you've seen a brain . . . what twisted, creeping ways . . .

POET. Yes, that's why the thinking of all right-thinking people is twisted.

DAUGHTER. Malicious, always malicious, but all of you are . . .

POET. How can one be anything else?

DAUGHTER. Now I shake the dust from my feet . . . the earth the clay . . .

[She takes off her shoes and puts them into the fire.]

DOORKEEPER. *[Enter, puts her shawl into the fire.]* Perhaps I may burn up my shawl, too? *[Exits.]*

32. Earth goddess in the Vedic religion.

33. Hanging white sheets in front of the windows and strewing evergreens on the front walk are Swedish funeral customs.

OFFICER. *[Enters.]* And I my roses—only the thorns remain! *[Exits.]*

BILLPOSTER. *[Enters.]* The posters may go, but never the dip net! *[Exits.]*

GLAZIER. *[Enters.]* The diamond that opened the door! Farewell! *[Exits.]*

LAWYER. *[Enters.]* The documents in the big case concerning the pope's beard or the decrease in water in the sources of the Ganges! *[Exits.]*

QUARANTINE MASTER. *[Enters.]* A little contribution—the black mask that made me a black man against my will! *[Exits.]*

VICTORIA. *[Enters.]* My beauty, my sorrow! *[Exits.]*

EDITH. *[Enters.]* My ugliness, my sorrow! *[Exits.]*

BLINDMAN. *[Enters; sticks his hand into the fire.]* I give my hand for my eye! *[Exits.]*

DON JUAN. *[Enters in his wheelchair, accompanied by His Mistress and Her Friend.]* Hurry up, hurry up, life is short! *[The three exit.]*

●

POET. I read that when life comes close to its end, everything and everyone rushes by in a single procession . . . Is this the end?

DAUGHTER. Yes, it's mine! Farewell!

POET. Give me a parting word!

DAUGHTER. No, I can't! Do you think your words could express our thoughts?

●

THEOLOGIAN. *[Enters, raging.]* I'm disavowed by God, I'm persecuted by people, I'm deserted by the government and ridiculed by my colleagues! How can I believe when no one else believes . . . how can I defend a god who doesn't defend his own? It's all nonsense!

[Throws a book on the fire and exits.]

POET. *[Grabs the book from the fire.]* Do you know what that was? . . . A book of martyrs, a calendar with a martyr for each day in the year.

DAUGHTER. Martyr?

POET. Yes, someone who has been tortured for his faith! Tell me why! Do you think everyone who's tortured suffers, and everyone who's

killed feels pain? Why, suffering is redemption, and death release.

KRISTIN. *[With strips of paper.]* I paste, I paste until there isn't anything more to paste . . .

POET. And if heaven itself were rent, you'd try to paste it together . . . Go!

KRISTIN. Aren't there any inner windows over there in the castle!

POET. No, not there.

KRISTIN. *[Going.]* Then I'll go!

●

DAUGHTER.

Our parting comes, and the end as well;
farewell, child of man, you the dreamer,
you the poet who best understands living;
on wings hovering above the earth,
you dive at times into the dust
not to stay in it but to touch it!

. . . .
. . . .

Now when I'm going . . . in the moment of parting
When one must part from a friend, a place,
how our longing for what one has loved rises
and regret over what one has broken . . .
Now I feel all the agony of being,
that's how it's to be a human being . . .
One misses even what one has not valued,
one regrets even what one has not broken . . .
One wants to leave, and one wants to stay . . .
So the halves of the heart are torn apart,
and feelings are torn as between horses
by contradiction, indecision, disharmony . . .

. . . .
. . . .

Farewell! Tell your fellows I remember them,
where I'm now going, and in your name
I shall bear their complaints to the throne.
Farewell!

[She goes into the castle. Music is heard. The backdrop is lighted by the burning castle and shows a wall of human faces, asking, sorrowing, despairing . . . When the castle burns, the flower bud on the roof bursts into a gigantic chrysanthemum. Curtain.]

Introduction to
The Good Woman of Setzuan
by Bertolt Brecht

Translated by Eric Bentley and Maja Apelman

The Good Woman of Setzuan Left to right: Steve Memran, Sanaa Lathan, Stephen De Rosa. Yale School of Drama. *(© T. Charles Erickson)*

The Play The German playwright Bertolt Brecht established many of the conventions of what he called "epic theater," a sweeping, panoramic theater intended to teach political and moral lessons. Brecht's basic goal was to point up the need for social change; in particular, he propagandized for socialism. Brecht believed that the members of the audience should be intellectually, not emotionally, involved in a stage production and should be highly aware of the fact that they were in a theater. For example, he wanted lighting instruments and other theatrical elements made visible to the audience. He also attacked realistic acting, instructing performers to present their roles as if telling a story so that the audience would not identify too closely with the characters. Nevertheless, the major characters in his plays are so full of life that it is difficult not to sympathize with them.

The *Good Woman of Setzuan* (1938–1940), whose original German title is *The Good Person of Setzuan,* offers an excellent example of Brecht's theatrical

313

approach. A play with many scenes and numerous characters, covering an extensive period of time, it has the sweep of epic theater. It also embodies other techniques of Brecht's: It is set in a somewhat mythical foreign country—in this case, a city in China—and the story is told in the form of a parable.

Three gods have come to earth looking for one good person; unless such a person can be found, the world cannot continue to exist. In the town of Setzuan they ask a water seller to find them a place to stay, but everyone turns them down except a prostitute, Shen Te. As a reward, they give her money to open a tobacco shop, but immediately her family and a horde of other parasites descend on her. To protect herself, she invents a tough cousin, Shui Ta. Pretending to be Shui Ta, she drives the spongers away.

Shen Te falls in love with an unemployed, ne'er-do-well aviator, Yang Sun, and becomes pregnant by him; but the selfish Yang Sun is interested only in her money and deserts her. As Shen Te, the young woman must disappear while pregnant, but as Shui Ta she develops a successful tobacco factory. Eventually Shui Ta is accused of having murdered Shen Te, and the gods hold court to decide his fate. He reveals that he is also Shen Te. The gods are relieved, because they believe they have found one good person: Shen Te. However, she screams for their help as they leave, since she recognizes that she can survive only as Shui Ta. Brecht's moral is that good people cannot exist in a world based on wealth; they must become hardened like Shui Ta. Only when the economic system is changed can goodness survive on its own.

The Playwright   Bertolt Brecht (1898–1956), who was educated in his native Bavaria, was bored by regular schooling but loved to write. When he graduated from college in 1917, he began to study medicine in Munich before being drafted as an orderly in 1918. Brecht's father offered to publish his first play, *Baal* (1918), but only if the Brecht family name was not mentioned, a condition the playwright refused. In 1922, Brecht's play *Drums in the Night* was awarded the Kleist Prize, one of Germany's highest literary honors.

Brecht settled in Berlin in 1924, where he worked for a time with the directors Max Reinhardt and Erwin Piscator, but mostly with smaller experimental groups. One of Brecht's friends was the composer Kurt Weill, with whom he wrote *The Threepenny Opera* (1928), a modern version of *The Beggar's Opera*. During the time he was in Berlin, Brecht became a Marxist. At this time he began to develop his theories of theater. Forced by the Nazis to flee Germany in 1933, he lived in Denmark, Sweden, and the United States, where he did some film writing in Hollywood.

During his years of exile, Brecht had time to refine his ideas on epic theater. He also wrote such noteworthy plays as *Mother Courage* (1938), *Galileo* (1938–1939), *The Good Woman of Setzuan* (1938–1940), *The Resistible Rise of Arturo Ui* (1941), and *The Caucasian Chalk Circle* (1944–1945). In 1947 Brecht was called before the House Committee on Un-American Activities because of leftist ideas, and he left the United States shortly after his appearance before the committee.

He then settled in East Berlin, where the government gave him his own theater, the Berliner Ensemble, which opened in 1949 with *Mother Courage.* For the next seven years he and his wife, the actress Helene Weigel, worked to develop epic theater; and when Brecht died in 1956, his wife took over the company, which had developed into one of the foremost acting troupes in the world.

Brecht remains a controversial figure. Many have judged him to be one of the most innovative dramatists and theoreticians of twentieth-century theater. Others criticize him for his habit of appropriating the work of others—particularly female collaborators—without acknowledging their contributions when his plays were produced and published. Also, though Brecht was an avowed Marxist, he managed his financial affairs with the self-interest of a full-fledged capitalist.

The Period   The period from 1915 to 1945—from the year after the beginning of World War I to the end of World War II—was obviously a time of unusual unrest for the Western world. On the one hand, the world was being brought closer together through the communications provided by radio, telephone, and motion pictures. On the other hand, some nations were guarding their independence and sovereignty as other nations attempted to take them over. Drastic political and economic changes led to instability, and the theater during these three decades mirrored that turbulence. Many of the theatrical movements we discuss were defined by their relationship to emerging political, social, or economic ideologies.

This era of unrest was ushered in by the First World War, which resulted in nearly 8.5 million deaths. The ultimate cost of the conflict, which American President Woodrow Wilson had called "the war to end all wars," was not, however, immediately apparent. When the war ended in 1918, most people believed President Wilson's idealistic pronouncements, and attempts were made to organize a workable League of Nations and a World Court. The isolationist policy of the United States—that is, its determination to stay out of foreign affairs—prevented it from joining the League of Nations, and that in turn prevented the organization from becoming a viable international force. Furthermore, fervent nationalism kept many of the member countries from giving the League of Nations any real power.

Unrest in Europe contributed to the Russian Revolution in 1917, which led to the establishment of the Soviet government. Before it took control, however, the new communist regime was forced to fight a costly civil war.

Throughout Europe and America, economic problems developed. In the 1920s rampant inflation and the depression that followed proved to be another cost of the earlier political turmoil. Many nations' economies were destroyed; monetary systems were devalued.

Many historians believe that this political and economic unrest in Europe set the stage for the rise of totalitarianism, a form of government under which the individual is totally subservient to the state. Between the world wars, there were fascist totalitarian dictatorships in Italy (Benito Mussolini) and Germany (Adolph Hitler), nationalist dictatorships in several other countries, and a communist totalitarian dictatorship in the Soviet Union.

Given the nationalistic fervor of the totalitarian dictators, the chaotic economic situation, and the widespread political instability, many historians believe that the Second World War was inevitable. The six-year war was more horrible than any of its predecessors, with over 35 million people losing their lives. The concentration camps became mechanized death factories, used to exterminate innocent victims of anti-Semitism and of the war. The atomic bomb proved that humanity was capable of developing weaponry that could annihilate the human race. World War II posed unanswerable questions: How could civilized, rational societies wreak such irrational destruction? Were individuals responsible for societal actions? How could the wartime genocide be explained?

Editors' note: This translation of *The Good Woman of Setzuan*, which was prepared by Eric Bentley with the assistance of his then wife, Maja Apelman, is of historical significance in that it was the first version of the play ever published in any language. For that reason, Bentley noted in a postscript to the translation that it was "made from German manuscripts which may not exactly correspond with future German editions of the play."

THE GOOD WOMAN OF SETZUAN

Bertolt Brecht

CHARACTERS

WONG, a water seller

THREE GODS

SHEN TE, a prostitute, later a shopkeeper

MRS. SHIN, former owner of Shen Te's shop

FAMILY OF EIGHT (husband, wife, brother, sister-in-law, grandfather, nephew, niece, boy)

UNEMPLOYED MAN

CARPENTER

MRS. MI TZU, Shen Te's landlady

YANG SUN, an unemployed pilot, later a factory manager

OLD WHORE

POLICEMAN

OLD MAN

OLD WOMAN, his wife

MR. SHU FU, a barber

MRS. YANG, mother of Yang Sun

GENTLEMEN, VOICES, CHILDREN (3), etc.

SHUI TA, Shen Te impersonating a male "cousin"

PROLOGUE

[A street. It is evening. Wong, the water seller, introduces himself to the audience.]

WONG. I sell water here in the city of Setzuan. It's a difficult business. When water is scarce, I have to go a long way to find any. And when it is plentiful, I am without income. But in our province there is nothing unusual about poverty. It is generally said that only the gods can still help us. From a cattle buyer who moves around a good deal, I learn to my unutterable joy that some of the highest gods are on their way to our province and may be expected here in Setzuan too. Heaven is said to be very disturbed by all the complaints that have been going up. For three days I have been waiting here at the entrance of the town, especially toward evening, so that I may be the first to greet them. Later, I'd hardly have the opportunity to do so. The gods will be surrounded by important people. They'll be in constant demand. If only I recognize them! After all they needn't come together. Perhaps they'll come separately so as not to be so conspicuous. It can't be those people over there, they are coming from work. *[He looks at passing workers.]* Their shoulders are crushed from all the carrying they do. That fellow there can't possibly be a god either, he has ink on his fingers. At best he's an office worker at a cement factory. Even those gentlemen there *[Two gentlemen pass.]* don't seem like gods to me. They look like people who're always beating somebody, which gods don't need to do. But look at those three! They're quite a different matter. They're well fed, show no sign of having any occupation, and have dust on their shoes, which means they come from far away. They must be gods. Dispose of me, illustrious ones!

[He throws himself down before them.]

THE FIRST GOD. *[Pleased.]* Have we been expected here?

WONG. *[Giving them a drink.]* For a long time. But I was the only one who *knew* you were coming.

THE FIRST GOD. Well, we need somewhere to stay the night. Do you know a place?

WONG. *A* place? Countless places! The whole town is at your service, illustrious ones! What sort of a place do you wish?

[The Gods look meaningfully at each other.]

THE FIRST GOD. Take the nearest house, my son! Try the very nearest house first.

WONG. I'm a little afraid of making enemies of other mighty men if I favor one of them in particular. Few people can help us, you see, but almost everyone can hurt us.

THE FIRST GOD. Well then, we order you: take the nearest house!

WONG. That is Mr. Fo over there! Wait just one moment!

[He runs to a house and knocks at the door. It is opened, but one can see that he is rejected. He returns, hesitantly.]

WONG. That's annoying. Mr. Fo is not at home just now, and his servants don't dare do anything without orders from him, he's so very strict. He will certainly have a fit when he learns who they turned away, won't he?

THE GODS. *[Smiling.]* He certainly will.

WONG. Well then, another moment! The house next door belongs to the widow Su. She'll be beside herself with joy.

[He runs to the house but apparently is rejected there too.]

WONG. I'll have to inquire over there. She says she has only one little tiny room and it isn't prepared. I can well understand she's ashamed because some corners of the house aren't so clean. That's what women are like, it's a disgrace. I'll go at once to Mr. Tscheng.

THE SECOND GOD. The little room will be enough. Tell her we're coming.

WONG. Even if it isn't clean? It may be swarming with spiders!

THE SECOND GOD. That doesn't matter. Where there are spiders, there aren't so many flies.

THE THIRD GOD. Never mind. *[Friendly, to Wong.]* Go to Mr. Tscheng or some other place, my son. Spiders, after all, rather disgust me.

[Wong knocks again somewhere and is admitted.]

VOICE FROM THE HOUSE. Spare us your gods! We have other troubles!

WONG. *[Back with the Gods.]* Mr. Tscheng is quite upset. He has the whole house full of relations and doesn't dare show his face, illustrious ones! Between ourselves I believe there are bad people among them whom he doesn't want you to see. He is too afraid of your judgment, that's the thing.

THE THIRD GOD. Are we so terrible, then?

WONG. Only with bad people, isn't that so? It's well known, isn't it, that the province Kwan has been afflicted with floods for decades?

THE SECOND GOD. Really? Why?

WONG. Well, because there's no religion there!

THE SECOND GOD. Nonsense. It's because they neglected the dam!

THE FIRST GOD. Sst! *[To Wong.]* Are you still hoping, my son?

WONG. How can you ask such a thing? I only need to go one house farther along. From there on, there'll be plenty to choose from. Everyone's just itching to put you up. Accidental circumstances, you understand. I go!

[He begins to leave and then, undecided, remains standing in the street.]

THE SECOND GOD. What did I say?

THE THIRD GOD. Of course it may really be "accidental circumstances."

THE SECOND GOD. In Schun, in Kwan, and in Setzuan—"accidental circumstances" every time? There aren't any religious people left, that's the naked truth, and you don't want to face it. Our mission has failed, why not admit it?

THE FIRST GOD. We might run across some good people at any moment. We mustn't expect things to be too cozy.

THE THIRD GOD. The resolution said: "The world can remain as it is if enough people are found living lives worthy of human beings. Good people, in other words. The water seller himself is such a person unless I'm very much mistaken. *[He goes up to Wong, who is still standing undecided.]*

THE SECOND GOD. He *is* very much mistaken. When this water man gave us a drink from his measuring cup, I noticed something. Here's the cup. *[He shows it to the First God.]*

THE FIRST GOD. It has two bottoms.

THE SECOND GOD. A swindler!

THE FIRST GOD. All right, count *him* out. But what does it matter if *one* person is rotten? We'll find enough yet who'll meet our conditions. We have to find *one!* For two thousand years, they've been shouting: "The world can't go on as it is, no one on earth can *be* good and *stay* good." And now at last we've got to name the people who can keep our commandments.

THE THIRD GOD. *[To Wong.]* Is it so difficult to find a place?

WONG. Not for you! What are you thinking of? It's all my fault a place wasn't found right away. I'm not going about it properly.

THE THIRD GOD. Surely, that's not so.

[He goes back.]

WONG. They're noticing already. *[He accosts a gentleman.]* Pardon me, worthy sir, for accosting you, but three of the highest gods, whose imminent arrival has been discussed for years by all Setzuan, have now actually appeared. They need a place to sleep. Do not pass by! See for yourself. One look will suffice. Don't wait, for heaven's sake. It's a chance in a lifetime! Be the first to ask the gods under your roof before they're snapped up by someone else. They will accept.

[The gentleman has passed by.]

WONG. *[Turning to another.]* My dear sir, you've heard what's going on. Do you, perhaps, have spare rooms? They don't have to be palatial. It's the good intention that counts.

THE MAN. How should I know what kind of gods you've got there? A fellow that lets people into his house likes to know what he's getting.

[He goes into a tobacco store. Wong runs back to the Three Gods.]

WONG. I've found a gentleman who'll certainly take you.

[He sees his cup on the ground, looks toward the Gods in confusion, takes it, and runs back again.]

THE FIRST GOD. That doesn't sound encouraging.

WONG. *[As the Man is coming out of the store again.]* Well, what about the rooms for the night?

THE MAN. How do you know I don't live at an inn?

THE FIRST GOD. He's getting nowhere. We can cross Setzuan off the list too.

WONG. They're three of the very greatest gods! Really. Their statues in the temples are very well done. If you go quickly and invite them, they might accept!

THE MAN. *[Laughing.]* You must be trying to find a place for a nice bunch of crooks. *[Exit.]*

WONG. *[Abusing him.]* You squinting scoundrel! Have you no religion? You'll all roast in boiling oil for your indifference! The gods spit on you! But you'll regret it! You'll have to pay. The whole pack of you, fourth cousins included. You've brought disgrace to all Setzuan. *[Pause.]* And now only Shen Te the prostitute is left. She can't say no.

[He calls "Shen Te!" Above, Shen Te looks out of the window.]

WONG. They're here. I can't find any place to put them. Can't you take them for the night?

SHEN TE. I don't think so, Wong. I'm expecting a gentleman. How is it you can't find any other place?

WONG. I can't tell you now. Setzuan is one big dung heap.

SHEN TE. When he comes I'd have to hide. Then ~~maybe he'd go away again. He's expecting to~~ take me out.

WONG. In the meantime, couldn't we come up?

SHEN TE. Well, you don't have to shout. Can we be open with them?

WONG. No! They mustn't find out about your profession. We'd better wait downstairs. You won't go out with the gentleman then?

SHEN TE. I'm not so well off. And if I don't pay my rent by tomorrow morning, I'll be thrown out.

WONG. This is no time for calculations.

SHEN TE. I'm not so sure. Stomachs rumble even on the emperor's birthday. But all right, I'll take them in. *[She can be seen putting out the light.]*

THE FIRST GOD. I think it's hopeless.

[They step up to Wong.]

WONG. *[Starting as he sees them standing behind him.]* A place has been found. *[He wipes the sweat off.]*

THE GODS. It has? Let's see it then.

WONG. There's no hurry. Take your time. The room still has to be fixed.

THE THIRD GOD. Well then, we'll sit down here and wait.

WONG. I'm afraid there's too much traffic right here. Perhaps we should go over there?

THE SECOND GOD. We like to look at people. That's what we're here for.

WONG. But . . . there's a draft.

THE SECOND GOD. Oh, we're pretty tough.

WONG. Perhaps you'd like me to show you Setzuan by night? We might take a little walk.

THE THIRD GOD. We've done quite a bit of walking today already. *[Smiling.]* But if you want to get us away from here, you need only say so.

[They go back.]

THE THIRD GOD. Is this all right with you?

[They sit down on a doorstep. Wong sits down on the ground at a little distance.]

WONG. *[Taking a deep breath.]* You're staying with a single girl. She's the best woman—the best human being—in Setzuan.

THE THIRD GOD. That's nice.

WONG. *[To the audience.]* When I picked up the cup a little while ago, they looked at me so strangely. Did they notice something? I don't dare look them in the eyes any more.

THE THIRD GOD. You're quite exhausted.

WONG. A little. From running.

THE FIRST GOD. Do people have a hard time of it here?

WONG. *Good* people do.

THE FIRST GOD. *[Seriously.]* And you?

WONG. I know what you mean. I'm not good. But I don't have an easy time either.

[In the meantime a gentleman has turned up in front of Shen Te's house. He has whistled several times. Each time Wong starts.]

THE THIRD GOD. *[Softly, to Wong.]* I think he's gone now.

WONG. *[Confused.]* Yes.

[He gets up and runs to the square, leaving his carrying pole behind. But in the meantime the waiting man has left, and Shen Te has stepped through the door and, softly calling "Wong!" has gone down the street. Wong, now softly calling "Shen Te!" gets no reply.]

WONG. She's left me in the lurch. She's gone off to get her rent together and now I've no place for the illustrious ones. They're tired and still waiting. I can't go back again and say nothing doing. My own little place, a sewer pipe, is out of the question. Moreover, the gods wouldn't want to stay with a fellow when they're seen through his dishonest dealings. I won't go back. Not for anything in the world. But my carrying pole is lying there. What'll I do? I don't dare to get it. Since I didn't succeed in doing anything for the gods, whom I revere, I'll leave Setzuan and hide from their sight.

[He rushes off. Shen Te returns. She is looking for Wong on the other side and sees the Gods.]

SHEN TE. Are you the illustrious ones? My name is Shen Te. It would please me very much if you'd be content with my simple room.

THE THIRD GOD. Where has the water seller gone to?

SHEN TE. I must have missed him.

THE FIRST GOD. He probably thought you weren't coming and didn't dare return to us.

THE THIRD GOD. *[Picking up the carrying pole.]* We'll leave this at your house. He'll be needing it.

[Led by Shen Te, they go into the house. It grows dark, then light again. It is dawn. Again led by Shen Te, who lights their way with a lamp, the Gods pass through the door. They are taking leave.]

THE FIRST GOD. My dear Shen Te, we must thank you for your hospitality. We shall not forget that it was you who took us in. Return the carrying pole to the water seller and tell him that we want to thank him too for showing us a good human being.

SHEN TE. I'm not good. I have to confess something: when Wong asked me to put you up I hesitated.

THE FIRST GOD. Hesitating doesn't matter if only you win out. You must know that you did more than give us a place to sleep. Many—even some of us gods—have been doubting whether good people still exist. To decide that question is the main object of our journey. Now that we've found a good human being, we shall joyously continue on our way. Goodbye!

SHEN TE. Stop, illustrious ones! I'm not at all sure that I'm good. I'd like to be good of course, but how am I to pay my rent? Well, I'll confess it to you: I sell myself in order to live, and even so I can't get along. There are many others who have to do the same. I'm ready to do anything; but who isn't? I'd be happy to honor my father and my mother and speak the truth. It would be nice not to covet my neighbor's house. It would be pleasant to attach myself to one man and be faithful to him. I too should like not to exploit anyone, not to rob the helpless. But how? How? Even when I break only a *few* of the commandments, I can hardly survive.

THE FIRST GOD. All these, Shen Te, are but the doubts of a good woman.

THE THIRD GOD. Farewell, Shen Te! And give my best regards to the water seller. He was a good friend to us.

THE SECOND GOD. I fear he's none the better for it.

THE THIRD GOD. Best of luck to you!

THE FIRST GOD. Above all, be good, Shen Te! Farewell!

[They turn to go. They are already waving.]

SHEN TE. *[Worried.]* But I'm not sure of myself, illustrious ones! How can I be good when everything is so expensive?

THE SECOND GOD. We can't do anything about that. We mustn't meddle with economics!

THE THIRD GOD. Stop! Just one moment! Might she not fare better if she were a little richer?

THE SECOND GOD. We can't give her anything. We couldn't account for it up above.

THE FIRST GOD. Why not?

[They put their heads together and talk excitedly.]

THE FIRST GOD. *[Embarrassed, to Shen Te.]* You say you can't pay your rent. We're not paupers and of course we'll pay for the room. Here! *[He gives her money.]* But don't tell anyone we paid. Such an action could be misinterpreted.

THE SECOND GOD. It certainly could.

THE FIRST GOD. But it's allowable. We *can* pay for the room without misgiving. There's nothing against it in the resolution. Well, goodbye!

[The Gods quickly go.]

1

[A small tobacco store. The store is not as yet completely furnished and has not opened.]

SHEN TE. *[To the audience.]* It's now three days since the gods went away. They said they wanted to pay me for the night's lodging. And when I looked to see what they'd given me, I saw that it was more than a thousand silver dollars. With the money I bought myself a tobacco store. Yesterday I moved in here and I hope now to be able to do a lot of good. There, for instance, is Mrs. Shin, the former owner of the store. Yesterday she came to ask for rice for her children. Today I see her again coming across the square with her pot.

[Enter Mrs. Shin. The two women bow to each other.]

SHEN TE. Good morning, Mrs. Shin.

MRS. SHIN. Good morning, Miss Shen Te. How do you like it in your new home?

SHEN TE. Very much. How did your children spend the night?

MRS. SHIN. Oh dear, in a strange house, if you can call that shack a house! The youngest is coughing already.

SHEN TE. That's bad.

MRS. SHIN. You don't know what's bad. You're well off. But you'll learn quite a lot in this dump. What a slum this neighborhood is!

SHEN TE. Didn't you tell me the workers from the cement factory come here at noon?

MRS. SHIN. Yes, but otherwise there isn't a soul that buys here, not even the neighbors.

SHEN TE. You didn't tell me that when you sold me the store.

MRS. SHIN. Don't start blaming me now! First you rob me and my children of our home and then you call it a dump! And a slum! That's the limit! *[She cries.]*

SHEN TE. *[Quickly.]* I'll get your rice right away.

MRS. SHIN. I also wanted to ask you to lend me some money.

SHEN TE. *[Pouring rice into Mrs. Shin's pot.]* I can't. You know I haven't sold anything.

MRS. SHIN. But I need it. What am I to live off? You took everything away from me and now you cut my throat! I'll leave my children on your doorstep, you cutthroat! *[She tears the pot out of Shen Te's hands.]*

SHEN TE. Don't be angry! You'll spill the rice!

[Enter an elderly couple and a shabbily dressed young man.]

THE WIFE. Ah, my dear Shen Te, we've heard you're so well off now. You've become a businesswoman! Imagine, we're without a roof over our heads. Our tobacco store has gone to pieces. We were wondering whether we couldn't spend the night with you. You know my nephew? He's come too. He never leaves us.

THE NEPHEW. *[Looking around.]* A nice store!

MRS. SHIN. What sort of people are *they*?

SHEN TE. They put me up when I first came in from the country. *[To the audience.]* When the little money I had was gone, they threw me out on the street. Perhaps they're afraid now that I'll say no.

> They are poor.
> They have no shelter.
> They have no friends.
> They need somebody.
> How could one say no?

[Friendly, to the newcomers.] Welcome! I'll gladly give you shelter. Though I only have one very small room behind the store.

THE HUSBAND. That'll be enough. Don't worry.

THE WIFE. *[While she brings tea to Shen Te.]* We better settle down here, so we won't be in your way. I suppose you've chosen a tobacco store in memory of your first home. We'll be able to give you some hints. That's another reason why we came.

MRS. SHIN. *[Sneering.]* I hope customers will come too!

THE WIFE. I guess that's meant for us.

THE HUSBAND. Psst! Here comes a customer.

[A ragged man comes in.]

THE RAGGED MAN. Excuse me. I am unemployed.

[Mrs. Shin laughs.]

SHEN TE. Can I help you?

THE UNEMPLOYED. I hear you're opening up tomorrow. Things sometimes get damaged when you're unpacking. Don't you have a spare cigarette?

THE WIFE. What nerve, begging for tobacco! He might at least ask for bread!

THE UNEMPLOYED. Bread is expensive. A few puffs at a cigarette and I'll be a new man. I'm all in.

SHEN TE. *[Giving him cigarettes.]* That's important, to be a new man. I'll open the store with you as my first customer. You'll bring me luck.

[The unemployed quickly lights a cigarette, inhales, and goes off, coughing.]

THE WIFE. My dear Shen Te, was that right?

MRS. SHIN. If you open up like this, in three days there'll be no store left.

THE HUSBAND. I bet he still had money in his pocket.

SHEN TE. But he said he hadn't.

THE NEPHEW. How do you know he wasn't lying?

SHEN TE. *[Angrily.]* How do I know he *was* lying?

THE WIFE. *[Shaking her head.]* She can't say no! You're too good, Shen Te. If you want to keep your store, you must learn to say no, now and then.

THE HUSBAND. Why don't you say it's not yours? Say it belongs to a relative who insists on an exact settlement of accounts. Can't you do that?

MRS. SHIN. That could be done if one wasn't always pretending to be a benefactress.

SHEN TE. *[Laughing.]* Scold, scold, scold! If you're not careful I'll give you notice and pour the rice back.

THE WIFE. *[Horrified.]* The rice is yours, too?

SHEN TE. *[To the audience.]*

> They are bad.
> They are nobody's friend.
> They begrudge everyone his rice.
> They need everything themselves.
> Who could scold them?

[Enter a little man.]

MRS. SHIN. *[Seeing him and hurriedly starting to go.]* I'll see you tomorrow. *[Exit.]*

THE LITTLE MAN. *[Calling after her.]* Stop, Mrs. Shin! It's you I'm looking for.

THE WIFE. Does she come regularly? Does she have any claim on you?

SHEN TE. She has no claim, but she's hungry: that's more than a claim.

THE LITTLE MAN. *She* knows why she's running. You're the new owner? Oh, you're filling up the shelves already. But they don't belong to you, see! Unless you pay for them. The rascals who were here before didn't pay for them. *[To the others.]* I'm the carpenter, you see.

SHEN TE. But I thought they belonged to the furnishings, which I paid for.

THE CARPENTER. Fraud! It's all a fraud! You're working together with that Shin woman of course. I demand my hundred silver dollars as sure as my name's Lin To.

SHEN TE. How am I to pay it? I have no more money!

THE CARPENTER. Then I'll have you arrested. You'll pay at once or I'll have you arrested.

THE HUSBAND. *[Prompting Shen Te.]* Cousin!

SHEN TE. Can't it wait till next month?

THE CARPENTER. *[Shouting.]* No!

SHEN TE. Don't be hard, Mr. Lin To. I can't settle all claims at once. *[To the audience.]*

A little indulgence and strength is redoubled.
Look, the cart horse stops and sniffs the grass:
Connive at this and the horse will pull better.
A little patience in June and the tree is heavy with
    peaches in August.
How should we live together without patience?
A short postponement, and the farthest goals are
    reached.

[To the Carpenter.] Be patient just for a little while, Mr. Lin To!

THE CARPENTER. And who's patient with me and my family? *[He moves a shelf from the wall as if he wanted to take it with him.]* Pay up, or I take the shelves away!

THE WIFE. My dear Shen Te, why don't you let your cousin settle this affair? *[To the Carpenter.]* Write down your claim and Miss Shen Te's cousin will pay.

THE CARPENTER. Cousin! I know these cousins!

THE NEPHEW. Don't laugh like that! I know him personally.

THE HUSBAND. What a man! Sharp as a knife!

THE CARPENTER. All right, he'll get my bill! *[He puts down a shelf, sits on it, and writes out his bill.]*

THE WIFE. *[To Shen Te.]* If you don't stop him, he'll tear the shirt off your body to get his measly shelves. Never recognize a claim, justified or not, or in two minutes you'll be swamped with claims, justified or not. Throw a piece of meat into a garbage can, and all the mangy dogs of the district will be at each other's throats in your back yard. What are our law courts for?

SHEN TE. If his work doesn't support him, the law courts won't. He's done some work and doesn't want to go empty-handed. And he's got a family. It's too bad. I can't pay him. What will the gods say?

THE HUSBAND. You did your share when you took *us* in. That's more than enough.

[Enter a limping man and a pregnant woman.]

THE LIMPING MAN. *[To the couple.]* Oh, here you are! You're nice relatives! Leaving us standing on the street corner.

THE WIFE. *[Embarrassed, to Shen Te.]* That's my brother Wung and my sister-in-law. *[To the two of them.]* Stop grumbling. Go and sit quietly in the corner and don't disturb our old friend, Miss Shen Te. You can stay here, she's got nothing against it. *[To Shen Te.]* I think we've got to take these two in. My sister-in-law is in her fifth month. Or don't you agree?

SHEN TE. Oh, yes. Welcome!

THE WIFE. *[To the two.]* Say thank you. The cups are back there. *[To Shen Te.]* They just wouldn't have known *where* to go. A good thing you got the store!

SHEN TE. *[Laughing, and bringing tea, she says to the audience.]* Yes, a good thing I did!

[Enter the Landlady, Mrs. Mi Tzu, a blank in her hand.]

THE LANDLADY. Miss Shen Te, I am the landlady, Mrs. Mi Tzu. I hope we'll get on well together. Here is the lease. *[While Shen Te is reading through the lease.]* The opening of a little store is a beautiful moment, isn't it, ladies and gentlemen? *[She looks around.]* There're still a few small gaps on the shelves, but it'll be all right. You'll be able to bring me some references, won't you?

SHEN TE. Is that necessary?

THE LANDLADY. I've no idea who you are.

THE HUSBAND. Perhaps we can vouch for Miss Shen Te? We've known her since she came to town and will go through fire for her at any time.

THE LANDLADY. And who are you?

THE HUSBAND. I am the tobacco dealer Ma Fu.

THE LANDLADY. Where's your store?

THE HUSBAND. At the moment I don't have a store. I've just sold it.

THE LANDLADY. I see. *[To Shen Te.]* And don't you know anyone else who could give me some information about you?

THE WIFE. *[Prompting.]* Cousin! Cousin!

THE LANDLADY. You've got to have somebody to speak for you if you're coming into my house. This a respectable house, my dear. Without some assurance I can't even sign the lease with you.

SHEN TE. *[Slowly, with downcast eyes.]* I have a cousin.

THE LANDLADY. Oh, you have a cousin. On the square? Then we can go over there right away. What does he do?

SHEN TE. He isn't living here. He's in another town.

THE WIFE. Didn't you say he was in Shung?

SHEN TE. Mr. . . . Shui Ta. In Shung.

THE HUSBAND. But I know him! A tall thin fellow?

THE NEPHEW. *[To the Carpenter.] You* were negotiating with Miss Shen Te's cousin too! About the shelves!

THE CARPENTER. *[Surly.]* I'm just writing out a bill for him. Here it is! *[He hands it over.]* Tomorrow morning I'll be back. *[Exit.]*

THE NEPHEW. *[Calling after him and glancing at the Landlady.]* Don't worry, the cousin will pay!

THE LANDLADY. *[Examining Shen Te closely.]* Well, I'll be very pleased to meet him too. Good morning! *[Exit.]*

THE WIFE. *[After a pause.]* Now the cat's out of the bag. You can be sure she'll know everything about you tomorrow morning.

THE SISTER-IN-LAW. *[Softly to the Nephew.]* This thing won't last long!

[Enter a boy leading an old man.]

THE BOY. *[Calling over his shoulder.]* Here they are.

THE WIFE. Good evening, Grandfather. *[To Shen Te.]* The good old man! He must have worried about us. And the boy, hasn't he grown? He eats like ten men. Well, who else did you bring, for heaven's sake?

THE HUSBAND. *[Looking outside.]* Only our niece.

THE SISTER-IN-LAW. *[Softly to the Nephew while a young girl comes in.]* The rats climb onto the sinking ship!

THE WIFE. *[To Shen Te.]* A young relative from the country. I hope we aren't too many for you. We weren't quite as many when you were living with us, were we? Yes, we got more and more. The less we had, the more there were of us. And the more there were of us, the less we had. But now we'll lock up, or there won't be a moment's peace. *[She locks the door and they all sit down.]* We mustn't disturb you in your business, that's the main thing. Or how can the fire be kept burning? We thought we might arrange matters something like this: during the day the young ones will go off and only grandfather, the sister-in-law, and maybe I myself will stay. The others will look in at the most once or twice during the day, all right? Light the lamp over there and make yourself at home.

THE NEPHEW. *[Humorously.]* If only the cousin doesn't pop up tonight all of a sudden. The strict Mr. Shui Ta!

[The Sister-in-law laughs.]

THE BROTHER. *[Reaching for a cigarette.]* One cigarette won't matter much.

THE HUSBAND. I'm sure it won't.

[They all help themselves to cigarettes. The Brother hands round a jug of wine.]

THE NEPHEW. The cousin will pay for it.

THE GRANDFATHER. *[Seriously to Shen Te.]* Good evening! *[Shen Te is confused by the belated greeting and bows. In one hand she holds the Carpenter's bill, in the other the lease.]*

THE WIFE. Couldn't you sing something to entertain our hostess a little?

THE NEPHEW. Grandfather will start!

[They sing.]

The Song of the Smoke

THE GRANDFATHER.

There was a time—before old age had bleached my hair—

I hoped I might survive by being clever.

But when does cleverness alone suffice

To fill a poor man's belly? Never, never!
That's why I said: let go!
Watch the grey smoke float
Ever into colder coldness: so
Sails your boat.

THE HUSBAND.

I saw the honest, conscientious man oppressed
So by the crooked path I tried to go.
But that path also leads us only downward
And what to do I don't pretend to know.
And so I say: let go!
Watch the grey smoke float
Ever into colder coldness: so
Sails your boat.

THE NIECE.

The old, I hear, have nothing left to hope for.
Since only time can heal, they're in a fix.
But for the young, I hear, the door is open.
It opens, so they tell me, upon nix.
So I too say: let go!
Watch the grey smoke float
Ever into colder coldness: so
Sails your boat.

THE NEPHEW. Where did you get the wine?
THE SISTER-IN-LAW. He pawned the bag of tobacco.
THE HUSBAND. What? That tobacco was the only thing left to us! We didn't even touch it to pay for our lodgings! You swine!
THE BROTHER. Do you call me a swine because my wife is cold? And you had a drink yourself? Give me the jug this minute!

[They fight. The shelves fall over.]

SHEN TE. *[Imploring them.]* Oh, spare the store! Don't destroy everything! It's a gift of the gods! Take what there is, but don't destroy it all!
THE WIFE. *[Skeptically.]* The store is smaller than I thought. Perhaps we shouldn't have mentioned it to Auntie and the others. If they come too, it'll be very crowded.
THE SISTER-IN-LAW. Our hostess is cooling off already.

[There are voices outside and a knocking on the door.]

SHOUTS FROM OUTSIDE. Open up! It's us!

THE WIFE. Is that you, Auntie? What are we going to do?
SHEN TE. O hope! My beautiful store! I bought it yesterday and today it's done for.

The little lifeboat
Is swiftly sent down
Too many people greedily
Reach for it as they drown.

SHOUTS FROM OUTSIDE. Open up!

1•A

[Below a bridge. The water seller crouches by the river.]

WONG. *[Looking around.]* Everything's quiet. It's four days now that I've been hiding out. They can't find me, because I'm keeping my eyes open. I fled along their road on purpose. On the second day, they passed the bridge, I heard their steps above me. Now they must be a long way off, and I'm safe.

[He lies back and falls asleep. Music. The slope becomes transparent and the Gods appear.]

WONG. *[Raising his arm to his face as if about to be struck.]* Don't say anything! I know it all! I found no one who wants to take you, not in a single house! Now you know! Now you can go on!
THE FIRST GOD. But you did find someone. When you were away, she came. She took us in for the night, she watched over our sleep, and when we left her in the morning she showed us the way with a lamp. You mentioned her to us as a good woman and she was good.
WONG. So it was Shen Te who took you in?
THE THIRD GOD. Of course.
WONG. And I had so little faith, I ran away! Only because I thought: "She can't come. Because she's not well off, she can't come."
THE GODS.

O weak one!
O well-disposed but weak man!
Where there is need, he thinks, there is no goodness!
Where there is danger, he thinks, there is no courage!
O weakness always to believe the worst!
O hasty judgment! Frivolous despair!

WONG. I'm very ashamed, illustrious ones!

THE FIRST GOD. And now, water seller, do us a favor and go back quickly to the city of Setzuan. Look up the good Shen Te there and gives us a report on her. She's well off now. She's supposed to have got some money for a little store so she can follow the inclinations of her heart. Show an interest in her goodness. No one can be good for long when goodness is not in demand. We will continue our journey. We will search and find other people who resemble our good woman from Setzuan: the talk about good people being no longer able to live on our earth will stop. *[They disappear.]*

2

[The tobacco store. People sleeping everywhere. The lamp is still burning. A knocking.]

THE WIFE. *[Getting up, sleepily.]* Shen Te! Someone's knocking! Where is she, anyway?

THE NEPHEW. I guess she's getting breakfast. The cousin will pay for it!

[The Wife laughs and shuffles to the door. Enter a young man, followed by the Carpenter.]

THE YOUNG MAN. I'm the cousin.

THE WIFE. *[Falling from the clouds.]* What?!

THE YOUNG MAN. My name is Shui Ta.

THE GUESTS. *[Shaking each other awake.]* Her cousin! But that was a joke, she doesn't *have* a cousin! Someone's here saying he's her cousin! I don't believe it, so early in the morning!

THE NEPHEW. If you're our hostess's cousin, go and get us some breakfast quickly!

SHUI TA. *[Putting out the light.]* The first customers will soon be here. Please get dressed so that I can open my store.

THE HUSBAND. *Your* store? I thought the store belonged to our friend Shen Te. *[Shui Ta shakes his head.]* What, it isn't her store at all?

THE SISTER-IN-LAW. Then she's cheated us! Where is she, anyway?

SHUI TA. She's been delayed. She wants me to tell you that, now *I'm* here, she can no longer do anything for you.

THE WIFE. *[Deeply affected.]* And we thought she was good!

THE NEPHEW. Don't believe him! Look for her!

THE HUSBAND. That's what we'll do. *[He organizes the search.]* You and you and you and you, look for her everywhere. Grandfather and us, we'll stay here to hold the fort. In the meantime the boy can get us something to eat. *[To the Boy.]* You see the bakery over there on the corner? Sneak over and stuff your shirt full.

THE SISTER-IN-LAW. Take a few of the little light cakes too!

THE HUSBAND. But be careful, don't let the baker catch you! And don't run into the policeman!

[The Boy nods and goes off. The others finish dressing.]

SHUI TA. This store has been your refuge. Won't you give it a bad reputation if you steal from the bakery?

THE NEPHEW. Don't pay any attention to him. We'll find her soon enough. She'll give him a piece of her mind.

[The Nephew, the Brother, the Sister-in-law, and the Niece go out.]

THE SISTER-IN-LAW. *[As she leaves.]* Leave us some of the breakfast!

SHUI TA. *[Calmly.]* You won't find her. My cousin regrets of course that she can't abide by the law of hospitality for an unlimited period. But unfortunately there are too many of you. This is a tobacco store and Miss Shen Te has to live off it.

THE HUSBAND. Our Shen Te just couldn't say a thing like that.

SHUI TA. Perhaps you're right. *[To the Carpenter.]* The unfortunate thing is that the need in this city is too great for a single person to manage. In that regard, nothing has changed, unfortunately, since someone eleven hundred years ago composed these lines:

> The governor, asked what was needed
> To help the freezing people of the town, made answer:
> "A blanket ten thousand feet long
> Which would simply cover all the suburbs."

[He starts to clean up the store.]

THE CARPENTER. I see you're trying to put your cousin's affairs in order. There's a little debt, recognized by witnesses, and it needs settling. For the shelves. One hundred silver dollars.

SHUI TA. [Taking the bill out of his pocket, not unfriendly.] Don't you think one hundred silver dollars a little much?

THE CARPENTER. No. And I can't make any deductions. I have a wife and children to support.

SHUI TA. [Severely.] How many children?

THE CARPENTER. Four.

SHUI TA. Then I offer you twenty silver dollars.

[The Husband laughs.]

THE CARPENTER. Are you crazy? The shelves are walnut!

SHUI TA. Then take them away.

THE CARPENTER. What d'you mean?

SHUI TA. They cost too much. I beg you, take the walnut shelves away.

THE WIFE. Well said! [She laughs too.]

THE CARPENTER. [Uncertainly.] I demand that someone call Miss Shen Te. She seems to be a better person than you.

SHUI TA. Certainly. She's ruined.

THE CARPENTER. [Resolutely taking some shelves and carrying them to the door.] You can pile up your tobacco goods on the floor! It suits me!

SHUI TA. [To the Husband.] Help him!

THE HUSBAND. [He also grabs a shelf and, grinning, carries it to the door.] Out with the shelves!

THE CARPENTER. You dog, do you want my family to starve?

SHUI TA. Once more I offer you twenty silver dollars. I don't want to pile up my tobacco goods on the floor.

THE CARPENTER. A hundred!

[Shui Ta looks indifferently out of the window. The Husband prepares to carry out more shelves.]

THE CARPENTER. At least don't smash them against the door post, idiot! [Desperately.] But they were made to measure! They fit this dump and nowhere else! The boards are spoiled, mister!

SHUI TA. Exactly. That's why I'm offering you only twenty silver dollars. Because the boards are spoiled.

[The Wife squeals with pleasure.]

THE CARPENTER. [Suddenly tired.] I can't keep it up. Take the shelves and pay what you want.

SHUI TA. Twenty silver dollars.

[He places two large coins on the table. The Carpenter takes them.]

THE HUSBAND. [Carrying back the shelves.] It's enough for a heap of spoiled boards!

THE CARPENTER. Enough, maybe, to get drunk on!

[Exit.]

THE HUSBAND. We got rid of *him*!

THE WIFE. [Weeping with merriment and drying her tears.] "They're walnut!" "Take them away!" "One hundred silver dollars! I have four children!" "Then I'll pay twenty!" "But they're spoiled." "Exactly! Twenty silver dollars!"—That's how one has to treat those scamps.

SHUI TA. Yes. [Earnestly.] Go away quickly!

THE HUSBAND. Us?

SHUI TA. Yes, you. You're thieves and parasites. If you go fast without wasting time talking back, you can still save yourselves.

THE HUSBAND. It's best just not to answer him at all. Let's not shout on an empty stomach. I'd like to know where the boy is.

SHUI TA. Yes, where's the boy? I told you before, I don't want him in my store with stolen cakes. [Suddenly shouting.] Once more: Go!

[They remain seated.]

SHUI TA. [Calmly again.] As you wish.

[He goes to the door and bows low. A Policeman appears in the doorway.]

SHUI TA. I presume I am addressing the officer in charge of this neighborhood?

THE POLICEMAN. Yes, Mr. . . .

SHUI TA. Shui Ta. [They smile at each other.] Nice weather today!

THE POLICEMAN. A little warm, maybe?

SHUI TA. A little warm, maybe.

THE HUSBAND. [Softly to the wife.] If he gabbles until the boy comes back, we're done for!

[He tries secretly to make some signs at Shui Ta.]

SHUI TA. *[Without paying attention to him.]* It makes a difference whether one thinks of the weather from a cool store or from the dusty street.

THE POLICEMAN. A big difference.

THE WIFE. *[To the Husband.]* Don't worry! The boy won't come when he sees the policeman standing in the doorway.

SHUI TA. Why don't you come in? It's really cooler in here. My cousin and I have opened a store. We attach the greatest importance, let me tell you, to being on good terms with the authorities.

THE POLICEMAN. *[Entering.]* You are very kind, Mr. Shui Ta. Yes, it's really cool in here.

THE HUSBAND. *[Softly.]* He's taking him in, specially so the boy won't see him.

SHUI TA. Visitors. Distant acquaintances of my cousin, I hear. They are on a journey. *[They bow.]* We were just about to take leave.

THE HUSBAND. *[Hoarsely.]* Well, we'll be going now.

SHUI TA. I shall tell my cousin that you want to thank her for the rooms but that you had no time to await her return.

[A noise from the streets and shouts of: "Stop thief!"]

THE POLICEMAN. What's that?

[The Boy is in the doorway. Various kinds of cakes are falling out of his shirt. The Wife waves him desperately back. He turns and starts to go.]

THE POLICEMAN. Stop, you! *[He takes hold of the Boy.]* Where did you get these cakes?

THE BOY. Over there.

THE POLICEMAN. Oh, theft, is it?

THE WIFE. We didn't know anything about it. The boy did it on his own. *[To the Boy.]* You good-for-nothing!

THE POLICEMAN. Mr. Shui Ta, can you clarify the situation?

[Shui Ta is silent.]

THE POLICEMAN. Aha. You're all coming to the station with me.

SHUI TA. I'm most distressed that such a thing could have happened in my establishment.

THE WIFE. He was watching when the boy went away!

SHUI TA. I can assure you, officer, I should hardly have asked you in if I'd wanted to conceal a theft.

THE POLICEMAN. That's right. And you will also understand Mr. Shui Ta, that it's my duty to take those people away. *[Shui Ta bows.]* Go on with you! *[He drives them out.]*

THE GRANDFATHER. *[Solemnly from the doorway.]* Good day!

[Exeunt all except Shui Ta, who continues to tidy up. Enter the Landlady.]

THE LANDLADY. So you're her cousin! What does it mean that the police are dragging people away from my house? What right has your Miss Shen Te to turn this store into a house of assignation? That's what happens if one takes in people who only yesterday lived in a two-bit hotel and went begging for bread to the corner bakery! You see, I know everything!

SHUI TA. Yes, I see. You've been told bad things about my cousin. She is accused of having gone hungry! It's a notorious fact that she lived in poverty. She's got the worst possible reputation: that of being poor.

THE LANDLADY. She was a common . . .

SHUI TA. Pauper. Let's not mince words.

THE LANDLADY. Oh, please, no sentimental rubbish. I'm speaking about her conduct, and her earnings. There must have been earnings, or this store wouldn't be here. Several elderly gentlemen must have taken care of that. How does one get a store at all? Sir, this is a respectable house! The people who pay rent here don't wish to live under the same roof with such a person. Yes, sir. *[Pause.]* I'm not a monster but I've got to be careful.

SHUI TA. *[Coldly.]* Mrs. Mi Tzu, I'm busy. Just tell me how much it'll cost us to live in this respectable house.

THE LANDLADY. You're a cool customer, I must say.

SHUI TA. *[Taking the lease from the counter.]* The rent is very high. I assume from the contract that it's payable by the month.

THE LANDLADY. *[Quickly.]* Not for people like your cousin!

SHUI TA. What do you mean?

THE LANDLADY. I mean that people like your cousin must pay the half-yearly rent of two hundred silver dollars in advance.

SHUI TA. Two hundred silver dollars! Sheer usury! How am I to get it? I can't count on a large turnover here. My only hope lies in the sack makers at the cement factory. I've been told they smoke a lot because their work is exhausting. But then, *they* don't earn much either.

THE LANDLADY. You should have thought of that earlier.

SHUI TA. Mrs. Tzu, have a heart! It's true, my cousin has made the unpardonable mistake of giving shelter to unfortunate persons. But she can improve. I'll see to it that she improves. And, tell me, how could you find a better tenant than one who knows the depths because she comes from them? She'll work her fingers to the bone to pay the rent on time. She'll do everything, sacrifice everything, sell everything, shun nothing, and all the time she'll be as humble as a little mouse and as quiet as a fly. She'll give way to you in anything before she'll go back where she came from. Such a tenant is worth her weight in gold.

THE LANDLADY. Two hundred silver dollars payable in advance or she'll go back on the streets where she came from!

[Enter the Policeman.]

THE POLICEMAN. Don't let me disturb you, Mr. Shui Ta!

THE LANDLADY. The police certainly display a great interest in this store.

THE POLICEMAN. Mrs. Mi Tzu, I hope you haven't got the wrong impression. Mr. Shui Ta has done us a service and I'm coming solely to thank him for it in the name of the police.

THE LANDLADY. Well, that's nothing to me. I hope, Mr. Shui Ta, that my proposal will be agreeable to your cousin. I like to be on good terms with my tenants. Good day, gentlemen.

[Exit.]

SHUI TA. Good day, Mrs. Mi Tzu.

THE POLICEMAN. Are you having difficulties with Mrs. Mi Tzu?

SHUI TA. She's demanding the rent in advance because my cousin doesn't seem to her respectable.

THE POLICEMAN. And you don't have the money? *[Shui Ta is silent.]* But surely a man like you, Mr. Shui Ta, can get credit?

SHUI TA. Perhaps. But how can a woman like Shen Te get credit?

THE POLICEMAN. Aren't you staying?

SHUI TA. No. I can't come back either. I can lend her a helping hand only on my trip through town. I can only ward off the worst. Soon she'll have to rely on herself again. I'm wondering what will happen then? I'm worried.

THE POLICEMAN. Mr. Shui Ta, I'm sorry you're in difficulties with the rent. I must admit that at first we looked at this store with mixed feelings. But your courageous behavior a little while ago showed us what you're made of. The authorities soon find out who they can trust.

SHUI TA. *[Bitterly.]* Officer, in order to save this little store, which my cousin regards as a gift of the gods, I'm ready to go to the very limit permitted by law. But hardness and cunning help only against inferiors. The lines are drawn cleverly. I feel like the man who dealt with the rats, only to find himself with rivers to cross. *[After a little pause.]* Do you smoke?

THE POLICEMAN. *[Putting two cigars into his pocket.]* Us fellows at the station would hate to lose you, Mr. Shui Ta. But you've got to understand Mrs. Mi Tzu. Shen Te—let's not beat about the bush—lived by selling herself to men. You can object: what else could she have done? How, for instance, was she to pay her rent? But the fact remains: it isn't respectable. Why not? First: one doesn't sell love—beware of the love that's for sale! Second: it's respectable to go with someone you love but not with someone who's paying for it! Third: the proverb says, not a handful of rice but for love! Well, you'll answer, what good is all this wisdom once the milk is spilt? What can she do? She's got to get hold of her half-year's rent or she'll be back on the streets. And how's she to get hold of the rent? Mr. Shui Ta, I have to tell you, I don't know. *[He's busy thinking.]* Mr. Shui Ta, I've got it! Find her a husband.

[Enter a little old woman.]

THE OLD WOMAN. A good cheap cigar for my husband. We'll have been married forty years tomorrow, you see, and we're having a little celebration.

SHUI TA. *[Politely.]* Forty years, and you still want to celebrate!

THE OLD WOMAN. As far as our means allow! We own the carpet store across from here. I hope we'll be good neighbors. We should be. Times are bad.

SHUI TA. *[Showing her various boxes.]* A very old saying, I fear.

THE POLICEMAN. Mr. Shui Ta, we need capital. Well, I propose a marriage.

SHUI TA. *[Apologetically to the Old Woman.]* I've let myself be persuaded to bother this gentleman with my personal worries.

THE POLICEMAN. We can't pay the half-year's rent. Very well. We marry a little money.

SHUI TA. That won't be easy.

THE POLICEMAN. Why not? She's a good match. She's got a small, growing store. *[To the Old Woman.]* What do *you* think about it?

THE OLD WOMAN. *[Undecidedly.]* Yes . . .

THE POLICEMAN. An ad in the paper!

THE OLD WOMAN. *[Reticently.]* If the young lady agrees . . .

THE POLICEMAN. What should she have against it? I'll make out the ad. One good turn deserves another. Don't think the authorities aren't concerned with the struggling small businessman! You lend us a helping hand and in return we make up a matrimonial ad for you! Ha! ha! ha!

[He eagerly takes out his notebook, wets the stump of a pencil, and writes away.]

SHUI TA. *[Slowly.]* It's not a bad idea.

THE POLICEMAN. "What . . . decent . . . man with small capital . . . widower . . . not excluded . . . wishes . . . marriage . . . into flourishing tobacco store?" And then we'll add: "am . . . pretty . . . pleasant appearance." How's that?

SHUI TA. If you don't think that's an exaggeration . . .

THE OLD WOMAN. *[Kindly.]* Not at all. I've seen her.

[The Policeman tears the page out of his notebook and hands it to Shui Ta.]

SHUI TA. With horror I see how much luck one needs to keep above water. How many ideas! How many friends! *[To the Policeman.]* Despite my determination, I was at the end of my tether as far as the store rent was concerned. But then you came and helped me with good advice. Truly, now I see a way out.

3

[Evening in the city park. A young man—Yang Sun—in ragged clothes follows with his eyes an airplane which seems to be describing a curve high over the city park. He takes a rope out of his pocket and looks carefully around. As he is going toward a large willow, two prostitutes come along. The one is already old, the other is the niece from the family that has imposed itself on Shen Te.]

THE YOUNG ONE. Good evening, young gentleman. Coming with me, dearie?

SUN. Perhaps, ladies. If you buy me something to eat.

THE OLD ONE. You're nuts, aren't you? *[To the Young One.]* Let's go on. We're only wasting our time with him. He's the unemployed pilot.

THE YOUNG ONE. But no one else will be left in the park, it'll rain in a minute.

THE OLD ONE. You never know.

[They go on. Sun, looking about, pulls out his rope and throws it round a willow branch. But again he is disturbed. The two prostitutes are coming quickly back. They don't see him.]

THE YOUNG ONE. It's going to pour.

[Shen Te comes walking along.]

THE OLD ONE. Look, here comes the monster! She brought disaster to you and your family!

THE YOUNG ONE. It wasn't her. It was her cousin. She took us in and later offered to pay for the cakes. I have nothing against her.

THE OLD ONE. But I have! *[Loudly.]* Ah, here's our dear rich sister! She's got a store but she still wants to snatch our boy friends away.

SHEN TE. Now don't bite my head off! I'm going to the tearoom by the pond.

THE YOUNG ONE. Is it true you're going to marry a widower with three children?

SHEN TE. Yes, I'm meeting him there.

SUN. *[Impatiently.]* Won't you get going, you whores! Can't a man be at peace even here?

THE OLD ONE. Shut your trap!

[Exeunt the two prostitutes.]

SUN. *[Calling after them.]* Vultures! *[To the audience.]* Even at this remote spot they don't tire of fishing for victims! Even in the bushes, even when it's raining, they desperately search for customers!

SHEN TE. *[Angrily.]* Why do you swear at them? *[She notices the rope.]* Oh!

SUN. What are you gaping at?

SHEN TE. What's the rope for?

SUN. Go on, sister, go on! I've no money, nothing, not even a penny. And if I had a penny, I wouldn't buy you. First I'd buy a cup of water.

[It starts raining.]

SHEN TE. What's the rope for? You mustn't do that!

SUN. What's that to you? Clear off!

SHEN TE. It's raining.

SUN. Don't you try to come under this tree.

SHEN TE. *[Who stays standing in the rain without moving.]* No.

SUN. Sister, leave it, it won't help you. You can't do business with me. You're too ugly for me anyway. Crooked legs.

SHEN TE. That isn't true.

SUN. Don't show them! If it's raining, for heaven's sake come under the tree!

[She goes slowly under the tree and sits down.]

SHEN TE. Why did you want to do it?

SUN. Do you want to know? Then I'll tell you: to get rid of you. *[Pause.]* Do you know what it is to be a flier?

SHEN TE. Yes, I've seen pilots in a tearoom.

SUN. No, you haven't. Perhaps you've seen a couple of conceited idiots with leather helmets, fellows with no ear for a motor, no sense for a machine. They only get into a plane because they know how to bribe the manager at the airport. Tell one of them: "Take your plane two thousand feet up, let it fall down through the clouds, and then catch it with one flick of the wrist," and he'll say: "That's not in the contract." If you fly, and you don't land your plane as if you were landing on your own rear end, you are not a flier but a fool. I am a flier. And I'm also the biggest fool for reading all those books on flying in the school at Peking

and missing out on one page of one book which says that there's no need for fliers any more. And so I'm a flier without a plane, a mail pilot without mail. *You* can't understand what that means.

SHEN TE. I think I can.

SUN. No, I'm telling you, you can't understand it. That means you can't understand it.

SHEN TE. *[Half laughing, half crying.]* When we were children we had a crane with a lame wing. He was friendly and didn't mind our jokes. He strutted along behind us, crying out to us not to run too fast. But in the fall and in the spring when large swarms of cranes were flying over the village, he became very restless. And I could understand why. *[She weeps.]*

SUN. Don't howl.

SHEN TE. No.

SUN. It hurts the complexion.

SHEN TE. I'm stopping.

[She dries her tears with her sleeve. Leaning against the tree, and without turning toward her, he reaches for her face.]

SUN. You don't even know how to wipe your face properly.

[He wipes it for her with a handkerchief. Pause.]

SUN. If you *had* to stay here so I wouldn't hang myself, you might at least open your mouth.

SHEN TE. I don't know anything.

SUN. Why exactly do you want to cut me down from the tree, sister?

SHEN TE. I'm frightened. I'm sure you only wanted to do it because the evening is so gloomy. *[To the audience.]*

    In our country
    There should be no gloomy evenings.
    High bridges over the river
    The hour between night and morning
    And the long winter: they too are dangerous.
    For with all the misery
    A little is enough
    And men throw away
    The unbearable life.

SUN. Talk about yourself.

SHEN TE. What about me? I have a little store.

SUN. [Mocking.] Oh, you don't walk the streets, you have a store!

SHEN TE. [Determinedly.] I have a store now, but, before, I was on the streets.

SUN. And the store was a gift of the gods, I suppose?

SHEN TE. Yes.

SUN. One nice evening they were standing there and saying: Here's some money?

SHEN TE. [Laughing softly.] One morning.

SUN. You're not exactly entertaining.

SHEN TE. [After a pause.] I can play the zither a little, and I can mimic people. [In a low voice she imitates a man of dignity.] "Well, think of that, I must have left my money at home!" But then I got the store. And the first thing I did was to give away my zither. Now, I said to myself, I can be as dumb as a fish and it won't make any difference.

> I'm rich now, I said.
> I walk alone, I sleep alone.
> For a whole year, I said,
> I'll have nothing to do with a man.

SUN. But now you're marrying one? The one in the tearoom by the pond?

[Shen Te is silent.]

SUN. What exactly do you know of love?

SHEN TE. Everything.

SUN. Nothing, sister. [Pause.] Or perhaps you liked it?

SHEN TE. No.

SUN. [Without turning toward her, he strokes her face with his hand.] Is that pleasant?

SHEN TE. Yes.

SUN. You're easily satisfied, I must say. What a town!

SHEN TE. Don't you have any friends?

SUN. Lots, but none who want to hear I'm still without a job. They make a face as if someone was complaining that there's still water in the ocean. Do *you* have a friend maybe?

SHEN TE. [Hesitantly.] A cousin.

SUN. Then beware of him.

SHEN TE. He's only been here once. Now he's gone away and he'll never be back. But why are you talking so despairingly? To speak without hope, they say, is to speak without goodness.

SUN. Just go on talking. A voice, after all, is a voice.

SHEN TE. [Eagerly.] Despite the great misery, there are still kind people. Once, when I was little, I fell down with a load of brushwood. An old man picked me up. He gave me a penny too. I've often thought of that. Especially those who don't have much to eat like to give some away. People probably like to show what they can do, and how could they show it better than by being kind? Being wicked is just being clumsy. When someone sings a song or builds a machine or plants some rice, that's really a sort of kindness. And you're kind, too.

SUN. It doesn't seem hard to be kind in your eyes.

SHEN TE. No. Just now I felt a raindrop.

SUN. Where?

SHEN TE. Between the eyes.

SUN. Nearer the right one or nearer the left?

SHEN TE. Nearer the left.

SUN. Good. [After a while, sleepily.] And you're through with men?

SHEN TE. [Smiling.] But my legs aren't crooked.

SUN. Perhaps not.

SHEN TE. Definitely not.

SUN. [Tired, leaning against the tree.] I haven't eaten anything for two days or drunk anything for one. So I couldn't love you, sister, even if I wanted to.

SHEN TE. It's lonely in the rain.

[Wong, the water seller, appears. He sings.]

The Song of the Water Seller in the Rain

> I'm selling water, water,
> And I stand here in the rain.
> For such a little water
> I've suffered too much pain.
> And I shout: "Buy water!"
> But nobody's buying
> Parched and dying
> And drinking and paying!
> Buy water, you dogs!
> O how I wish the rain would stop!
> Last night in bed I dreamt again
> That seven years passed without any rain.
> I doled out water by the drop.

> O how they shouted: "Water, water!"
> Each man who came to my place
> I looked him over to see whether
> I really liked his face.
> How their tongues hung out!

[Laughing.]

And now reclining on their backs
The little plants and such
Drink at the udder of the clouds
And never ask: How much?
And I shout: "Buy water!"
But nobody's buying
Parched and dying
And drinking and paying!
Buy water, you dogs!

[The rain has stopped. Shen Te sees Wong and runs toward him.]

SHEN TE. Oh, Wong, are you back again? I've got your carrying pole at home.

WONG. Thank you very much for keeping it! How are you, Shen Te?

SHEN TE. I'm well. I've met a clever and brave man. And I'd like to buy a cup of your water.

WONG. Put your head back and open your mouth and you'll have as much water as you want. The willow over there is still dripping.

SHEN TE.

But I want your water, Wong,
The water carried from far
The water that has made you tired
The water that will be hard to sell because it is raining.
And I need it for the gentleman over there.
He is a pilot.
A pilot is bolder than other men.
In the clouds' company!
Braving the great storms
He flies through the skies
And brings to friends in far-off lands
The friendly mail.

[She pays and runs over to Sun with the cup.]

SHEN TE. *[Calling back, laughing, to Wong.]* He's fallen asleep. Despair and rain and I have made him tired.

3•A

[Wong's sleeping quarters in a sewer pipe. The water seller is asleep. Music. The sewer pipe becomes transparent and the Gods appear to the dreaming Wong.]

WONG. *[Radiantly.]* I've seen her, illustrious ones! She's still the same!

THE FIRST GOD. We're glad to hear it.

WONG. She loves! She's shown me her friend. She's really well off.

THE FIRST GOD. That's good to hear. Let's hope it will give her strength in her striving toward the good.

WONG. Absolutely! She does as many good deeds as she can.

THE FIRST GOD. What sort of good deeds? Tell us about it, my dear Wong!

WONG. She has a kind word for everyone.

THE FIRST GOD. *[Eagerly.]* Yes, and . . .?

WONG. It seldom happens that anyone leaves her little store without tobacco just because he has no money.

THE FIRST GOD. That doesn't sound bad. Anything else?

WONG. She gave lodging to a family of eight!

THE FIRST GOD. *[Triumphantly to the Second.]* Eight! *[To Wong.]* And something else perhaps?

WONG. She bought a cup of water from me, even though it was raining.

THE FIRST GOD. Of course, all these smaller good deeds. That's understood.

WONG. But they run into money. A little store doesn't make so much.

THE FIRST GOD. Yes, surely. But a prudent gardener can produce miracles even on a tiny plot.

WONG. She really does that! Every morning she hands out rice, and believe me, it takes more than half her earnings!

THE FIRST GOD. *[A little disappointed.]* I'm not saying anything. And for a beginning, I'm not dissatisfied.

WONG. Just think, times aren't exactly good! Once, her store got into difficulties and she had to call a cousin to her aid.

As soon as there was a place that was shielded from the wind
The ruffled birds of the whole wintry sky
Came flying and fought for the place
And the hungry fox bit through the thin wall
And the one-legged wolf tipped the small dish over.

In short, she couldn't manage all the business herself any more. But they all agree that she's a good girl. Everywhere she's called the Angel of the Suburbs already. So much good comes from her store. Whatever the carpenter Lin To may say!

THE FIRST GOD. What does that mean? Does the carpenter Lin To speak badly of her?

WONG. Oh, he only says that the shelves in the store weren't paid for in full.

THE SECOND GOD. What are you saying now? A carpenter wasn't paid? In Shen Te's store? How could she allow that?

WONG. I guess she didn't have the money.

THE SECOND GOD. All the same one pays what one owes. The mere appearance of injustice has to be avoided. First the letter of the commandment must be fulfilled. Then the spirit.

WONG. But it was only her cousin, illustrious one, not she herself!

THE SECOND GOD. Then that cousin must never cross her threshold again!

WONG. [Downcast.] I understand, illustrious one! In defense of Shen Te, let me at least say that her cousin is considered a highly respectable businessman. Even the police value him.

THE FIRST GOD. Well, we don't want to damn this cousin without having heard him. I admit I don't understand anything about business. Perhaps one should make inquiries to find out what is customary. But anyway, business—is it so very necessary? They're always doing business nowadays! Did the Seven Good Kings do business? Did the Kung the Just sell fish? What does business have to do with an honest and dignified life?

THE SECOND GOD. [With a bad cold.] In any case such a thing must not happen again. [He turns to go. The two other Gods turn too.]

THE THIRD GOD. [The last to turn away, embarrassed.] You must forgive our harsh tone today. We're over-tired and haven't slept enough. Lodgings for the night! The wealthy give us the very best of recommendations to the poor, but the poor don't have enough room.

THE GODS. [Moving away, grumbling.] Weak, the best of them! Nothing decisive! Little, little! Everything from the heart, of course, but it doesn't amount to much! At least, she should see that . . .

[One no longer hears them.]

WONG. [Calling after them.] Oh, don't be angry, illustrious ones! Don't ask too much all at once!

4

[The square in front of Shen Te's tobacco store. A barber's shop, a carpet store, and Shen Te's tobacco store. It is morning. In front of Shen Te's store, two of the family of eight, the Grandfather and the Sister-in-law, are waiting. Waiting also are the Unemployed and Mrs. Shin.]

THE SISTER-IN-LAW. She didn't come home last night!

MRS. SHIN. Unbelievable behavior! At last this crazy cousin has gone away and madam deigns, now and then at least, to give us a little bit of rice out of all her abundance. But already she's staying out all night, loitering around, God knows where!

[Loud voices are heard from the barber's. Wong stumbles out, followed by the fat barber, Mr. Shu Fu, who is carrying a heavy curling iron.]

MR. SHU FU. I'll teach you to bother my customers with your smelly water! Take your cup and get going!

[Wong reaches for the cup held out by Mr. Shu Fu, who hits him on the hand with the curling iron. Wong cries out with pain.]

MR. SHU FU. There you have it! Let it be a lesson to you! [He goes puffing back into his store.]

THE UNEMPLOYED. [Picking up the cup and handing it to Wong.] You can report him to the police for hitting you like that.

WONG. My hand's smashed.

THE UNEMPLOYED. Is something broken?

WONG. I can't move it.

THE UNEMPLOYED. Sit down and pour a little water over it!

[Wong sits down.]

MRS. SHIN. You get the water cheap, anyway.

THE SISTER-IN-LAW. You can't even get a little linen rag here at eight in the morning. She's got to go out! Adventures! What a scandal!

MRS. SHIN. [Gloomily.] She's forgotten us!

[Shen Te comes down the street carrying a dish of rice.]

SHEN TE. [To the audience.] I've never seen the town in the early morning before. At this hour I used to lie in bed with a dirty blanket over my head, afraid of waking up. Today I walked among the newspaper boys, among the men who rinse the pavement with water, and among the ox carts that bring fresh vegetables from the country. I've walked a long way from Sun's neighborhood over here, but I've been getting merrier at every step. I've always been told that if you're in love you walk on clouds, but the best thing is walking on the earth, on the pavement. I tell you, in the morning rows of houses look like rubbish heaps with lights on them. The sky is pink and transparent because there's no dust yet. I tell you, you miss much if you don't love, if you don't see your Setzuan at the hour when it rises from sleep like a sober old craftsman pumping his lungs full of fresh air and reaching for his tools, as the poets say. *[To the waiting people.]* Good morning! Here's the rice! *[She distributes the rice, then notices Wong.]* Good morning, Wong. I'm quite light-headed today. On the way home I looked at myself in every shop window, and now I feel like buying a shawl. *[After hesitating a little.]* I'd so much like to be beautiful. *[She quickly goes into the carpet store.]*

MR. SHU FU. *[Who has stepped out again, to the audience.]* I'm quite surprised to note how beautiful Miss Shen Te looks today. She's the owner of the tobacco store across the street and I've never really noticed her before. I've been looking at her for three minutes and I think I'm already in love with her. An incredibly attractive person. *[To Wong.]* Clear off, you rascal! *[He goes back into his store. Shen Te, the Old Woman, and her husband the carpet dealer step out of the carpet store. Shen Te is wearing a shawl; the carpet dealer is holding out a mirror.]*

THE OLD WOMAN. It's very pretty and not expensive because it has a little hole at the bottom.

SHEN TE. *[Looking at the shawl on the Old Woman's arm.]* The green one's nice too.

THE OLD WOMAN. *[Smiling.]* But unfortunately not the least bit damaged.

SHEN TE. Yes, that's a shame. I can't spend too much, with my small store. I only take in a little and the expenses are great.

THE OLD WOMAN. It's good deeds that cost you so much. Be careful. In the beginning, every dish of rice counts, doesn't it?

SHEN TE. *[Trying on the shawl with the little hole in it.]* Well, that's how things are. But at the

moment I'm light-headed. I wonder if this color suits me?

THE OLD WOMAN. That's a question to put to a *man*.

SHEN TE. *[Turning to the Old Man.]* Does it suit me?

THE OLD MAN. Why don't you ask . . .

SHEN TE. *[Very politely.]* No, I'm asking you.

THE OLD MAN. *[Also politely.]* The shawl suits you. But wear it with the dull side turned out.

[Shen Te pays.]

THE OLD WOMAN. If you don't like it, you can always exchange it. *[She pulls her aside.]* Does he have any money?

SHEN TE. *[Laughing.]* Oh no!

THE OLD WOMAN. Then how will you be able to pay the rent?

SHEN TE. The rent? I'd completely forgotten it!

THE OLD WOMAN. I thought as much. And next Monday is the first of the month. I'd like to talk something over with you. You know my husband and I had a few doubts about the marriage ad after we got to know you. We decided to help you out if it comes to the worst. We've put aside a little money and can lend you two hundred silver dollars. If you wish you can pledge us your stock of tobacco. Of course we don't need a written agreement.

SHEN TE. Do you really want to lend money to a light-headed person like me?

THE OLD WOMAN. Well, to be honest, we might not lend it to your cousin—who's definitely not light-headed. But we don't worry about lending it to you.

THE OLD MAN. *[Stepping up to them.]* Settled?

SHEN TE. I wish the gods could have heard your wife just now, Mr. Ma. They're looking for good people who're happy. And you must be happy helping me, for it was love that got me into trouble.

[The old couple smile at each other.]

THE OLD MAN. Here's the money.

[He hands her an envelope. Shen Te takes it and bows. The old couple bow too. They go back into their store.]

SHEN TE. *[To Wong, holding up her envelope.]* This is the rent for half a year! Isn't it just like a miracle? And how do you like my new shawl, Wong?

WONG. Did you buy it for the fellow I saw in the city park?

[Shen Te nods.]

MRS. SHIN. Maybe you better take a look at his smashed hand? Never mind telling him your doubtful adventures!

SHEN TE. *[Taken aback.]* What's the matter with your hand?

MRS. SHIN. The barber smashed it with a curling iron in front of our eyes.

SHEN TE. *[Horrified at her negligence.]* And I didn't notice anything! You must go to the doctor this minute or your hand will get stiff and you'll never be able to work properly again. What a terrible misfortune! Quick, get up! Go, quickly!

THE UNEMPLOYED. It's not the doctor he should go to but the judge! He can demand compensation from the barber, he's rich.

WONG. You think there's a chance?

MRS. SHIN. If it's really smashed. But is it?

WONG. I think so. It's swollen up already. Maybe I could get a pension?

MRS. SHIN. Of course you've got to have a witness.

WONG. But you *all* saw it! You could *all* testify?

[He looks round. The Unemployed, the Grandfather, and the Sister-in-law sit by the wall of the house and eat. Nobody looks up.]

SHEN TE. *[To Mrs. Shin.]* But you saw it yourself!

MRS. SHIN. I don't want anything to do with the police.

SHEN TE. *[To the Sister-in-law.]* What about you?

THE SISTER-IN-LAW. Me? I wasn't looking!

MRS. SHIN. Of course you were! I saw you! But you're afraid because the barber's a big shot.

SHEN TE. *[To the Grandfather.]* I'm sure *you'll* testify!

THE SISTER-IN-LAW. His testimony won't be accepted. He's gaga.

SHEN TE. *[To the Unemployed.]* It might be a matter of pension for life.

THE UNEMPLOYED. I've been picked up twice for begging. *My* testimony would only do him harm.

SHEN TE. *[Not quite believing.]* So none of you want to say what happened? His hand was smashed in broad daylight, all of you were watching, and nobody wants to speak! *[Angrily.]*

Unhappy men!
Your brother is assaulted and you shut your eyes!
He is hit and cries aloud and you are silent?
The beast prowls, chooses his victim, and you say:
He's spared us because we do not show displeasure.
What sort of a city is this? What sort of people are you?
When injustice is done there should be revolt in the city.
And if there is no revolt, it were better that the city should perish in fire before night falls!

Wong, if no one present will be your witness, I will. I'll say *I* saw it.

MRS. SHIN. That'll be perjury.

WONG. I don't know if I can accept this. Though maybe I'll have to. *[Looking at his hand, worried.]* Do you think it's swollen enough? I think maybe the swelling's gone down now?

THE UNEMPLOYED. *[Reassuring him.]* No, the swelling definitely hasn't gone down.

WONG. Hasn't it? No, I guess it's *more* swollen, if anything. Maybe my wrist is broken after all! I'd better run to the judge this minute.

[Carefully holding his hand and looking at it all the time, he runs off. Mrs. Shin runs into the barber's shop.]

THE UNEMPLOYED. She wants to get on the right side of the barber.

THE SISTER-IN-LAW. We can't change the world.

SHEN TE. *[Discouraged.]* I didn't want to scold you. I'm only afraid. No, I *did* want to scold. Get out of my sight!

[The Unemployed, the Sister-in-law, and the Grandfather go off, eating and sulking.]

SHEN TE. *[To the audience.]*

They no longer answer.
Where one puts them they stay
And if one sends them away
They quickly go.
Nothing moves their hearts.
Only the smell of food can make them look up.

[An oldish woman comes running in.]

THE OLDISH WOMAN. *[Out of breath.]* Are you Miss Shen Te? My son. Has told me everything. I am. Sun's mother, Mrs. Yang. Just think, he has. A chance now. To get a job as flier. This morning. Just now a letter. Came from Peking. From the manager of the airmail service.

SHEN TE. He can fly again? Oh, Mrs. Yang!

MRS. YANG. But the job. Costs a lot of money. Five hundred silver dollars.

SHEN TE. That's a lot, but money mustn't stand in the way of a thing like that. After all, I've got the store!

MRS. YANG. If you could only do something!

SHEN TE. *[Embracing her.]* If only I could!

MRS. YANG. You would give a talented young man a chance?

SHEN TE. How can they prevent a man from being useful? *[After a pause.]* Only I won't get enough for the store, and these two hundred silver dollars cash are just borrowed. Take them with you at once. I'll pay them back by selling my tobacco stock. *[She gives her the old couple's money.]*

MRS. YANG. Oh, Miss Shen Te, that really is help at the right moment! And they were calling him the Dead Flier of Setzuan, they were all convinced he'd never do any more flying!

SHEN TE. But we need three hundred silver dollars more for the job. We've got to think, Mrs. Yang. *[Slowly.]* I know someone who might be able to help me. Someone who helped me out once before. I didn't really want to call him again, he's so hard and cunning. It would certainly have to be the last time. But a flier's got to fly, that's clear.

[Distant sound of engines.]

MRS. YANG. If the man you're talking about could get the money! Look, that's the morning mail plane, going to Peking!

SHEN TE. *[Decisively.]* Wave, Mrs. Yang! I'm sure the pilot can see us! *[She waves with her shawl.]* You wave too!

MRS. YANG. *[Waving.]* You know the pilot who's flying up there?

SHEN TE. No. I know the pilot who *shall* be up there. He gave up hope but he *shall* fly, Mrs. Yang. One at least shall raise himself above this misery and above us all! *[To the audience.]*

Yang Sun, my lover,
In the clouds' company!

Braving the great storms
Flying through the skies
And bringing to friends in distant lands
The friendly mail.

4•A

[Before the curtain. Shen Te appears with the suit and mask of Shui Ta in her hands. She sings.]

The Song of the Defenselessness of the Gods and Good Men

In our country
The useful man needs luck.
Only if he finds strong helpers
Can he prove himself useful.
Good men can't help themselves
And the gods are powerless.
Why don't the gods have mines and cannon
Battleships, bombers, and tanks?
Bring down the bad and save the good?
Shouldn't we all give thanks?

[She puts on Shui Ta's suit and takes a few steps in his manner.]

Good men
Cannot long remain good in our country.
Where plates are empty, the diners fight.
Alas, the commandments of the gods
Are no use against want.
Why don't the gods appear in our markets
And, smiling, distribute the plentiful food?
Let every man eat and drink at his pleasure
And be to his brother loving and good?

[She puts on the mask of Shui Ta and now sings with his voice.]

To procure a dinner
You must be hard as builders of empire.
Without trampling down twelve others
You cannot help one poor man.
Why then don't the gods speak up in their heaven
And say that they owe the good world to good men?
Why don't they stand by good men with their bombers
Fire their guns and suffer no suffering then?

5

[*The tobacco store. Shui Ta sits behind the counter reading the paper. He doesn't pay the least attention to Mrs. Shin, who is cleaning up and talking at the same time.*]

MRS. SHIN. A little store like this soon comes to ruin when certain rumors start spreading in the neighborhood. Believe me. It's high time that a decent man like you started looking into this dubious affair between Miss Shen Te and that Yang Sun from Yellow Street. Don't forget Mr. Shu Fu, the barber next door, a man with twelve houses and only one wife, and she's old, only yesterday confessed a certain interest in Miss Shen Te. A very flattering interest, I thought. He even inquired about her means. And that, if I may say so, proves real affection.

[*Since she gets no answer, she finally goes out with the bucket.*]

SUN'S VOICE. [*From outside.*] Is that Miss Shen Te's store?
MRS. SHIN'S VOICE. Yes, this is it. But today her cousin's here.

[*With the light steps of Shen Te, Shui Ta runs to a mirror. She is just about to start fixing her hair when she notices the mistake in the mirror. She turns away laughing softly. Enter Yang Sun. Behind him comes the inquisitive Mrs. Shin. She goes past him into the back room.*]

SUN. I'm Yang Sun. [*Shui Ta bows.*] Is Shen Te here?
SHUI TA. No, she's not.
SUN. I guess you know what our relationship is? [*He begins to inspect the store.*] A real live store! I always thought she was just talking big. [*He looks with satisfaction into the little boxes and china jars.*] Man, I'm going to fly again! [*He takes a cigar and Shui Ta gives him a light.*] D'you think we can squeeze another three hundred silver dollars out of the store?
SHUI TA. May I ask if you intend to sell it right away?
SUN. Well, do we have the three hundred in cash? [*Shui Ta shakes his head.*] It was decent of her to come right out with the two hundred. But with three hundred still missing, they won't be much use.

SHUI TA. Perhaps it was rather rash of her to promise you the money. It may cost her the store. Haste, they say, is the name of the wind that knocks down the scaffolding.
SUN. I need the money quickly or not at all. And the girl isn't one to keep you waiting either. For one thing or another, you get me?
SHUI TA. I get you.
SUN. Uh-huh.
SHUI TA. May I know what the five hundred silver dollars will be used for?
SUN. Sure. I see I'm to be sounded out. The manager at the Peking airport is a friend of mine from flying school. He can get me the job if I cough up five hundred silver dollars.
SHUI TA. Is not that sum unusually high?
SUN. No. He'll have to fire one of his present pilots. For negligence. And the fellow he has in mind isn't negligent, because he's got a large family. You understand. All this, by the way, in confidence. Shen Te needn't know it.
SHUI TA. Perhaps not. Just one thing—won't that manager sell *you* out next month?
SUN. Not me. There won't be any negligence in my work. I was unemployed long enough.
SHUI TA. [*Nodding.*] The hungry dog pulls the cart home faster. [*He scrutinizes him.*] The responsibility is very great. Mr. Yang Sun, you ask my cousin to give up her small possessions, to leave all her friends in this town, and to put her entire fate into your hands. I assume you intend to marry Shen Te?
SUN. I'd be prepared to.
SHUI TA. But isn't it a pity, then, to get rid of the store for a few silver dollars. We won't get much for it if we have to sell at once. The two hundred silver dollars you have in your hands would pay the rent for half a year. Wouldn't that tempt you to continue in the tobacco business?
SUN. Would it tempt *me*? Is Yang Sun, the flier, to be seen standing behind the counter: "Do you wish a strong cigar or a mild one, worthy sir?" That's no business for the Yang Sun's, not in this century!
SHUI TA. Allow me to ask, is flying very profitable?
SUN. [*Pulling a letter out of his pocket.*] Sir, I'd get two hundred and fifty silver dollars a month! Look at the letter yourself. Here's the stamp and the postmark. Peking.
SHUI TA. Two hundred and fifty silver dollars? That's a lot.

SUN. Do you think I fly for nothing?

SHUI TA. The job seems to be good. Mr. Yang Sun, my cousin has commissioned me to help you to this post which means so much to you. From her own point of view, I cannot see any good reason why she shouldn't follow the inclinations of her heart. She has every right to experience the joys of love. I'm prepared to turn everything here to money. Here comes the landlady, Mrs. Mi Tzu, whom I'll ask to advise me about the sale.

THE LANDLADY. *[Entering.]* Good day, Mr. Shui Ta. I suppose it's about the rent which is due the day after tomorrow?

SHUI TA. Mrs. Mi Tzu, circumstances have arisen which make it look doubtful whether my cousin will keep her store. She's planning to marry, and her future husband *[he introduces Yang Sun.]* Mr. Yang Sun, will take her to Peking where they are to start a new life. If I can get enough for my tobacco, I shall sell out.

THE LANDLADY. How much do you need?

SUN. Three hundred down.

SHUI TA. *[Quickly.]* No, five hundred!

THE LANDLADY. *[To Sun.]* Perhaps I'll be able to help you. How much did your tobacco cost?

SHUI TA. My cousin paid a thousand silver dollars for it and very little has been sold.

THE LANDLADY. A thousand silver dollars! She was gypped of course. I'll tell you something: I'll pay you three hundred silver dollars for the whole store if you move out the day after tomorrow.

SUN. We'll do that. It'll work, old man!

SHUI TA. It's too little.

SUN. It's enough!

SHUI TA. I've got to have at least five hundred.

SUN. What for?

SHUI TA. *[To the landlady.]* Allow me to talk something over with my cousin's fiancé. *[Aside to Sun.]* All the tobacco here has been pledged to two old people for the two hundred silver dollars which were given to you yesterday.

SUN. Is there a written agreement?

SHUI TA. No.

SUN. *[To the Landlady.]* We can manage with three hundred.

THE LANDLADY. But I've got to know whether the store is in debt.

SUN. You answer!

SHUI TA. The store is not in debt.

SUN. When can the three hundred be had?

THE LANDLADY. The day after tomorrow, and you can still think it over. You'll get more if you don't sell in such a rush. I'll pay three hundred, but only because I want to do my share in what seems to be a case of young love. *[Exit.]*

SUN. *[Calling after her.]* We'll make the deal! Little boxes, jars and sacks, everything for three hundred and the pain's over. *[To Shui Ta.]* Perhaps some other place we can get more by the day after tomorrow?

SHUI TA. Not in such a short time. We won't have one silver dollar apart from the three hundred of Mrs. Mi Tzu. You have the money for the trip and the first few weeks?

SUN. Sure.

SHUI TA. How much is that?

SUN. I'll dig it up, anyway, even if I have to steal it!

SHUI TA. Oh, I see, this money too has to be dug up?

SUN. Don't fall out of your shoes, old man, I'll get to Peking somehow.

SHUI TA. It can't be so cheap for two people.

SUN. *Two* people? I'm leaving the girl behind. At first, she'll only be a millstone round my neck.

SHUI TA. I see.

SUN. Why d'you look at me as if I was a leaking oil tank? You've got to manage the best you can.

SHUI TA. And how is my cousin to live?

SUN. Can't *you* do something for her?

SHUI TA. I'll try. *[Pause.]* I wish, Mr. Yang Sun, you'd hand over to me the two hundred silver dollars and would leave them here till you can show me two tickets to Peking.

SUN. My dear man, I wish you'd mind your own business.

SHUI TA. Miss Shen Te . . .

SUN. Just leave the girl to me.

SHUI TA. . . . might not want to sell her store when she learns that . . .

SUN. She'll want to. Even then.

SHUI TA. And you're not afraid of my interference?

SUN. My dear sir!

SHUI TA. You seem to forget she's a human being and has got some sense.

SUN. *[Amused.]* What certain people think about their female relatives and the effect of reasonable persuasion has always been a source of wonder to me. Have you ever heard of the power of love? The tickling of the flesh? You want to talk reason to her? She doesn't know what reason is! On the other hand, the poor creature's been abused all her life. I've only to put my hand on her shoulder and say "you're coming with me" and she hears bells and wouldn't know her own mother.

SHUI TA. *[With difficulty.]* Mr. Yang Sun!

SUN. Mr. What's-your-name!

SHUI TA. My cousin is devoted to you because . . .

SUN. Shall we say because I've got my hand on her bosom? Put that in your pipe and smoke it! *[He takes another cigar, then puts a few in his pocket, and finally takes the whole box under his arm.]* Don't you go to her with empty hands. We'll stick to the marriage. And she'll bring the three hundred or you'll bring them. Either she or you! *[Exit.]*

MRS. SHIN. *[Putting her head out of the back room.]* Not exactly pleasant. And all of Yellow Street knows he's got the girl completely under his thumb.

SHUI TA. *[Crying out.]* The store's gone! He isn't in love! I'm lost! *[He begins to run round like an imprisoned animal, repeating, "The store's gone!" until he stops suddenly and begins to talk to Mrs. Shin.]* Shin, you grew up in the gutter and so did I. Are we frivolous? No. Do we lack the necessary brutality? No. I'm ready to take you by the throat and shake you till you spit out the last crumb of cheese you've stolen from me. You know that. The times are terrible, this town is hell, but gradually we manage to crawl up the smooth walls. Then bad luck overtakes one or another of us: he is in love. That's enough, he's lost. One weakness and you're finished. How are you to free yourself of *all* weaknesses, and especially of the deadliest of weaknesses, love? Love is absolutely impossible! It's much too expensive! But then, tell me yourself, can one live and be *always* on the watch? What sort of a world is this?

> Caresses turn to strangulation.
> The sigh of love turns to a cry of fear.
> Why are the vultures circling over there?
> A girl is going to meet her lover.

MRS. SHIN. I think I had better go and get the barber right away. You've got to talk with the barber. He's a man of honor. The barber, he's the right one for your cousin.

[Receiving no answer, she runs off. Shui Ta runs around again until Mr. Shu Fu enters, followed by Mrs. Shin, who, however, on a sign from Mr. Shu Fu, is forced to withdraw.]

SHUI TA. *[Hurrying toward him.]* My dear sir, I know from hearsay that you have hinted at a certain interest in my cousin. Let me set aside all the laws of propriety and reserve: Miss Shen Te is at the moment in great danger.

MR. SHU FU. Oh!

SHUI TA. Only a few hours ago the possessor of her own store, my cousin is now little more than a beggar. Mr. Shu Fu, this store is ruined.

MR. SHU FU. Mr. Shui Ta, the charm of Miss Shen Te lies not in the goodness of her store but in the goodness of her heart. The name which this neighborhood has given to the young lady tells all. They call her the Angel of the Suburbs!

SHUI TA. My dear sir, this goodness has cost my cousin two hundred silver dollars on a single day. We have to put a stop to that.

MR. SHU FU. Allow me to express a different opinion: we've got to open the gates wide to this goodness. It's in the nature of the young lady to do good. Every morning I affectionately watch her feeding four people. What does that signify? Why can't she feed four hundred? I hear, for instance, that she's racking her brains about how to shelter some homeless people. My cabins behind the cattle run are empty. They're at her disposal. And so on and so forth . . . Mr. Shui Ta, might I hope that Miss Shen Te would lend an ear to certain ideas which have come to me in the last few days? Ideas like these?

SHUI TA. Mr. Shu Fu, she will listen to such high thoughts with admiration.

[Enter Wong with the Policeman. Mr. Shu Fu turns around and studies the shelves.]

WONG. Is Miss Shen Te here?

SHUI TA. No.

WONG. I am Wong, the water seller. I guess you're Mr. Shui Ta?

SHUI TA. Quite right. Good day, Wong.

WONG. I'm a friend of Shen Te's.

SHUI TA. You're one of her oldest friends, I know.

WONG. *[To the Policeman.]* You see? *[To Shui Ta.]* I'm coming because of my hand.

THE POLICEMAN. It's smashed all right. There's no doubt about it.

SHUI TA. *[Quickly.]* I see you need a sling. *[He gets a shawl from the back room and throws it to Wong.]*

WONG. But that's her new shawl.

SHUI TA. She no longer needs it.

WONG. But she bought it to please a certain person.

SHUI TA. As things have turned out, that is no longer necessary.

WONG. [Making himself a sling out of the shawl.] She's my only witness.

THE POLICEMAN. Your cousin's supposed to've seen how the barber Shu Fu hit the water seller with the curling iron. D'you know anything about it?

SHUI TA. I only know that my cousin wasn't present when the incident occurred.

WONG. That's a misunderstanding! Just wait till Shen Te's here and everything will be cleared up. Shen Te'll bear witness to everything. Where is she?

SHUI TA. [Seriously.] Mr. Wong, you call yourself my cousin's friend. My cousin has a lot of worries right now. She's been terribly exploited from all sides. In the future, she won't be able to afford the smallest weakness. I'm convinced you won't ask her to lose all she has by making her say anything but the truth in this matter.

WONG. [Confused.] But *she* advised me to go to the judge.

SHUI TA. Was the judge supposed to heal your hand? [Mr. Shu Fu turns round.] Mr. Wong, it's one of my principles never to meddle in the quarrels of my friends. [Shui Ta bows to Mr. Shu Fu, who returns the bow.]

WONG. [Taking off the sling and putting it back, sadly.] I understand.

THE POLICEMAN. And now I guess I can go again. You went to a decent man—the wrong fellow for your swindling. You better be a bit more careful next time, with your accusations. If Mr. Shu Fu didn't put mercy before justice, you could be jailed for libel. Off with you now.

[Exeunt.]

SHUI TA. I beg you to excuse this occurrence.

MR. SHU FU. It's excused. [Urgently.] And this affair with a "certain person" [he points to the shawl] is really over? Completely finished?

SHUI TA. Completely. She's seen through him. Of course, it'll take time till she's got over everything.

MR. SHU FU. We shall be careful. Delicate.

SHUI TA. There are some fresh wounds.

MR. SHU FU. She'll go to the country.

SHUI TA. For some weeks. However, before that she'll be glad to talk everything over with someone she can trust.

MR. SHU FU. At a small dinner in a small but good restaurant.

SHUI TA. In a discreet way. I'll hurry to inform my cousin. She'll be reasonable. She's very worried about the store, which she regards as a gift of the gods. Be patient for a few minutes. [Exit into the back room.]

MRS. SHIN. [Putting her head in.] May I congratulate you?

MR. SHU FU. Mrs. Shin, you may let Miss Shen Te's protégés know today that I am giving them shelter in the cabins behind the cattle run.

[She nods, grinning.]

MR. SHU FU. [Getting up, to the audience.] What do you think of me, ladies and gentlemen? Could anyone do more? Could anyone be less selfish? More farsighted? A small dinner! What vulgar and clumsy thoughts this would bring into the minds of most people. But nothing like that will happen. Nothing. She won't be touched. Not even casually. Not even accidentally while passing the salt! Nothing but ideas will be exchanged. Two souls will find each other over the flowers on the table, white chrysanthemums by the way. [He makes a note of that.] No, we won't exploit an unfortunate situation. We won't turn a disappointment to our advantage. Understanding and assistance will be offered. And almost without a sound. A single glance might perhaps acknowledge it. A glance which could also mean more.

MRS. SHIN. So everything went as you wished, Mr. Shu Fu?

MR. SHU FU. Oh, just as I wished! There'll presumably be a few changes in this district. A certain person has been shown the door and some of the plots against this shop will be spoiled. Certain people who still dare to harm the reputation of the chastest girl in this city will get into trouble with me in the future. What do you know about this Yang Sun?

MRS. SHIN. He's the dirtiest, laziest . . .

MR. SHU FU. He's nothing. He doesn't exist. He can't be found, Mrs. Shin.

[Enter Sun.]

SUN. What's going on here?

MRS. SHIN. Mr. Shu Fu, d'you want me to call Mr. Shui Ta? He won't want strangers loitering around in the store.

MR. SHU FU. Miss Shen Te is having an important talk with Mr. Shui Ta and mustn't be interrupted.

SUN. What, she's here? I didn't see her go in! What sort of a talk is that? I've got to be in on it!

MR. SHU FU. [Preventing him from going into the back room.] You'll have to be patient, my dear sir. I think I know who you are. Please take note that Miss Shen Te and I are about to announce our engagement.

SUN. What?

MRS. SHIN. That surprises you, doesn't it?

[Sun is fighting with the barber to get into the back room when Shen Te steps out of it.]

MR. SHU FU. Excuse me, dear Shen Te. Perhaps you could explain . . .

SUN. What's the matter, Shen Te? Are you crazy?

SHEN TE. [Breathlessly.] Sun, my cousin and Mr. Shu Fu have come to an agreement: I'm to listen to Mr. Shu Fu's ideas about how to help the people in the neighborhood. [Pause.] My cousin wants to part us.

SUN. And you agree?

SHEN TE. Yes.

[Pause.]

SUN. Did they tell you I'm a bad man?

[Shen Te is silent.]

SUN. Maybe I *am* a bad man, Shen Te. And that's why I need you. I'm low. Without money, without manners. But I fight back. They're driving you into misfortune, Shen Te. [He goes over to her and speaks in an undertone.] Just look at him! Do you have no eyes in your head? [With his hand on her shoulder.] Poor creature, *now* what did they want you to do? Make a reasonable match! Without me they'd just have sacrificed you. Admit that, but for me, you would have gone away with him!

SHEN TE. Yes.

SUN. A man you don't love.

SHEN TE. Yes.

SUN. Have you forgotten everything? How it was raining?

SHEN TE. No.

SUN. How you cut me from the tree? How you bought a cup of water? How you promised me the money so I could fly again?

SHEN TE. [Trembling.] What do you want?

SUN. I want you to come with me.

SHEN TE. Mr. Shu Fu, forgive me, I want to go away with Sun.

SUN. We're lovers, you know. [He leads her to the door.] Where is the key to the store? [He takes it from her pocket and hands it to Mrs. Shin.] Leave it outside the door when you're through. Come on, Shen Te.

MR. SHU FU. But this is rape! [Shouting to the back.] Mr. Shui Ta!

SUN. Tell him not to shout so much in here.

SHEN TE. Please don't call my cousin, Mr. Shu Fu. He doesn't agree with me, I know. But he's not right, I can feel it. [To the audience.]

> I want to go with the one I love
> I don't want to reckon what it will cost
> I don't want to consider if it is wise
> I want to go with the one I love.

SUN. That's it.

[Exeunt.]

5•A

[Before the curtain. Shen Te, in her wedding outfit and on the way to her wedding, turns to the audience.]

SHEN TE. I've had a terrible experience. As I was stepping out of the house, gay and full of expectation, the carpet dealer's old wife was standing on the street. She was trembling all over, and she told me that her husband had fallen sick from excitement and worry about the money they'd lent me. She thought it best that I return the money to her now in any case. Of course I promised it to her. She was very relieved, wished me the best of luck with tears in her eyes and asked me to forgive her because she couldn't altogether trust my cousin, nor, unfortunately, Sun. I had to sit down when she'd gone, I was so alarmed by my own behavior. With my emotions in an uproar, I threw myself again into the arms of Yang Sun. I couldn't resist his voice and his caresses. The bad things he said to Shui Ta didn't teach Shen Te anything. Sinking into his arms, I thought: the gods wanted me to be good to myself too.

To let no one perish, not even one's self,
To fill everyone with happiness, even one's self,
That is good.

How could I simply forget those two good old people? Like a small hurricane, Sun just swept away my store and all my friends in the direction of Peking. But he's not bad and he loves me. As long as I'm with him, he won't do anything bad. What men say between themselves doesn't count. He just wants to seem big and powerful and above all hard-boiled. When I tell him that the old people won't be able to pay their taxes, he'll understand everything. He's rather go and work in the cement factory than owe his flying to a crime. Of course flying's a great passion with Sun. Shall I be strong enough to bring out the good in him? Now, on the way to my wedding, I waver between fear and joy. *[She goes quickly off.]*

6

[A side room of a cheap restaurant in the suburbs. A waiter pours out wine for the wedding party. Near Shen Te are the Grandfather, the Sister-in-law, the Niece, Mrs. Shin, and the Unemployed. In the corner, alone, stands a Priest. Down stage, Sun is talking with his mother, Mrs. Yang. He is wearing a dinner jacket.]

SUN. Something unpleasant, Mamma. She just told me in all innocence that she can't sell the store for me. Somebody or other is bringing a claim because they lent her the two hundred silver dollars which she gave to you. And her cousin said that there wasn't any written agreement.

MRS. YANG. What did you say to her? Of course you can't marry her now.

SUN. There's no sense in talking with her about these things. She's got a thick head. I've sent for her cousin.

MRS. YANG. But he wants to marry her to the barber.

SUN. I've put an end to that marriage. The barber's been insulted. Her cousin will soon understand that if I don't hand over the two hundred, the creditors will seize the store and the store will be gone, but if I don't get the three hundred, my job will be gone too.

MRS. YANG. I'll look for him outside the restaurant. Go to your bride, now, Sun!

SHEN TE. *[Pouring wine, to the audience.]* I wasn't mistaken in him. I couldn't see a trace of disappointment in his face. He's perfectly cheerful though it must be a heavy blow for him to have to give up flying. I love him very much. *[She waves Sun over.]* Sun, you haven't drunk a toast with the bride!

SUN. What shall we drink to?

SHEN TE. Let's drink to the future.

[They drink.]

SUN. When the bridegroom's tuxedo will no longer be borrowed!

SHEN TE. But when the bride's dress will still get rained on now and then.

SUN. To everything we wish for!

SHEN TE. That it may quickly come true!

MRS. YANG. *[On the way out, to Mrs. Shin.]* I'm delighted with my son. I've always impressed it on him that he can get whoever he wants. Why, he's a trained mechanic and flier. And what does he tell me now? "I'm marrying for love, Mamma," he says, "money isn't everything." It's a love match! *[To the Sister-in-law.]* It has to happen once, hasn't it? But it's hard for a mother, it's hard. *[Calling back to the Priest.]* Don't cut it too short. If you take as much time for the ceremony as you took to haggle about the price, it'll be dignified all right. *[To Shen Te.]* We've got to postpone things a little still, my dear. One of our most beloved guests hasn't arrived yet. *[To all.]* Excuse me, please. *[Exit.]*

THE SISTER-IN-LAW. We'll gladly be patient as long as there's wine.

[They all sit down.]

THE UNEMPLOYED. We're not missing anything.

SUN. *[Loud and jokingly before the guests.]* And before the marriage I've still got to give you a little quiz. A not unnecessary thing when a wedding is held at such short notice. *[To the guests.]* I've no idea what sort of a wife I'm getting. That worries me. *[To Shen Te.]* For instance, can you make five cups of tea with three tea leaves?

SHEN TE. No.

SUN. I see I won't be getting any tea. Can you sleep on a sack of straw the size of the book the priest is reading?

SHEN TE. With someone else?

SUN. Alone.

SHEN TE. In that case, no.

SUN. I'm horrified at the wife I'm getting.

[They all laugh. Behind Shen Te, Mrs. Yang steps into the doorway. With a shrug of her shoulders, she tells Sun that there's no sign of the expected guest.]

MRS. YANG. *[To the Priest, who has shown her his watch.]* Don't be in such a hurry. It can be a matter of minutes. I can see they're drinking and smoking and no one's in a hurry. *[She sits down by the guests.]*

SHEN TE. Don't we have to talk about how we're going to arrange everything?

MRS. YANG. Oh, please, let's not talk shop. Shoptalk introduces a *common* note into the celebration, doesn't it?

[The entrance bell rings. They all look to the door but no-body enters.]

SHEN TE. Who's your mother waiting for, Sun?

SUN. That's a surprise for you. By the way, how's your cousin Shui Ta? I got on with him. A very sensible man! What a brain! Why don't you say anything?

SHEN TE. I don't know. I don't want to think of him.

SUN. Why not?

SHEN TE. Because you *shouldn't* get on well with him. If you love me, you can't love him.

SUN. Then may the three devils fetch him: the Fog-devil, the Engine-trouble-devil, and the Empty-gas-tank devil! Drink, you stubborn girl! *[He makes her drink.]*

THE SISTER-IN-LAW. *[To Mrs. Shin.]* Something's wrong here.

MRS. SHIN. What else did you expect?

THE PRIEST. *[Resolutely stepping up to Mrs. Yang, a watch in his hand.]* I've got to go, Mrs. Yang. I've got another wedding to attend to, and tomorrow morning a funeral.

MRS. YANG. D'you think I like all this postponing? We were hoping to manage with one pitcher of wine. But look how it's coming to an end! *[Loudly to Shen Te.]* My dear Shen Te, I can't understand where your cousin can be all this time!

SHEN TE. My cousin?

MRS. YANG. But, my dear, it's him we're waiting for! I'm just old fashioned enough to think that such a close relative of the bride should be present at the wedding.

SHEN TE. Oh Sun, is it because of the three hundred silver dollars?

SUN. *[Without looking at her.]* Can't you hear? She's old fashioned. Well, I'm considerate. We'll wait another fifteen minutes and if he hasn't come then because the three devils have got him, we'll start!

MRS. YANG. I guess you all know already that my son is getting a job, as a mail pilot. I'm very pleased about it. In these times, we have to make good money.

THE SISTER-IN-LAW. It's to be in Peking, isn't it?

MRS. YANG. Yes, in Peking.

SHEN TE. You've got to tell your mother, Sun, that Peking is out of the question.

SUN. Your cousin will tell her, if he agrees with you. Between us: I don't agree.

SHEN TE. *[Appalled.]* Sun!

SUN. How I hate this Setzuan. What a town! Do you know what they all look like when I half close my eyes? Horses! They fret and screw their necks up: what's thundering there above them? How's that? They're no longer needed? What, their time's up already? Let them bite themselves to death in their horse town! O to get out of here!

SHEN TE. But I've promised the money to the old couple.

SUN. Yes, you told me. And since you do stupid things like that, it's lucky your cousin's coming. Drink, and leave business to us! We'll fix it up.

SHEN TE. *[Horrified.]* But my cousin can't come.

SUN. What do you mean?

SHEN TE. He can't come!

SUN. And how do you figure our future? Tell me that.

SHEN TE. I thought you still had the two hundred silver dollars. We could return them tomorrow and keep the tobacco, which is worth a lot more. Then we'll sell it together in front of the cement factory since we can't pay the half year's rent.

SUN. Forget it! Forget it fast, sister! *I* am to stand on the street and sell tobacco to cement workers, I, Yang Sun, the flier! I'd rather run through all two hundred in one night! I'd rather throw it in the river! And your cousin knows me! I've arranged it with him. He's to bring the three hundred to the wedding.

SHEN TE. My cousin can't come.

SUN. And I thought he couldn't stay away.

SHEN TE. He can't be where I am.

SUN. How mysterious!

SHEN TE. Sun, you've got to know it: he's not your friend. I'm the one that loves you. My cousin Shui Ta doesn't love anybody. He's my friend, but he's not friend to my friends. He was thinking of the job at Peking when he agreed to your getting the old couple's money. But he won't bring you the three hundred silver dollars to the wedding.

SUN. And why not?

SHEN TE. [Looking into his eyes.] He says you only bought one ticket to Peking.

SUN. Yes, that was so yesterday, but just look what I can show him today! [He pulls two pieces of paper halfway out of his breast pocket.] The old woman needn't see. Here's two tickets to Peking. One for me and one for you. Do you still think your cousin's against the marriage?

SHEN TE. No. The job's good. And I don't have my store any more.

SUN. Because of you I sold our furniture.

SHEN TE. Don't go on! Don't show me the tickets! I'm too afraid I might simply go with you. But I can't give you the three hundred silver dollars, Sun. What's to become of the old couple?

SUN. And what's to become of me? [Pause.] Better drink some more! Or are you a cautious person? I don't want a cautious wife. If I drink, I'll fly again. And you, if you drink, you might possibly understand me.

SHEN TE. Don't think I don't understand you. You want to fly and I can't help you.

SUN. "Here's a plane, my darling, but it's only got one wing!"

SHEN TE. Sun, we can't get the job at Peking honestly. That's why I need the two hundred silver dollars which you got from me. Give them to me now, Sun!

SUN. "Give them to me now, Sun!" What exactly are you talking about? Are you my wife or aren't you? You're betraying me, you know that, don't you? Luckily for both of us, things don't depend on you. Everything's arranged.

MRS. YANG. [Icily.] Sun, are you sure the bride's cousin is coming? Since he's still not here it might almost seem that he has something against this marriage.

SUN. What are you thinking of Mamma? We're bosom friends! I'll open the door wide so he'll find us right away when he comes to be his friend Sun's best man. [He goes to the door and kicks it open. Then he returns, staggering somewhat since he has already drunk too much, and sits down again beside Shen Te.] We're waiting. Your cousin's got more sense than you. Love, he says wisely, goes with living! And, more important than that, he knows what it means to you: no more store and no marriage either!

[Everyone is waiting.]

MRS. YANG. Now!

[Steps can be heard and everyone looks toward the door. But the steps pass.]

MRS. SHIN. It's going to be a scandal. I can feel it. I can smell it. The bride is waiting for the wedding but the groom's waiting for her cousin.

SUN. The cousin's taking his time.

SHEN TE. [Softly.] Oh, Sun!

SUN. To sit here with the tickets in my pocket and next to me a fool who doesn't know arithmetic. I can foresee the day when you'll send the police to my house to get the two hundred silver dollars.

SHEN TE. [To the audience.] He is bad and he wants me to be bad too. Here I am, I love him, and he waits for the cousin. But around me are the frail: the old woman with her sick husband, the poor who in the morning wait for their rice at my door, and an unknown man from Peking who is worried about his job. And they all protect me by trusting me.

SUN. [Staring at the glass pitcher in which there is no wine left.] The glass pitcher of wine is our clock. We're poor people and when the guests have drunk the wine, the clock's run down forever.

[Mrs. Yang beckons him to be silent, for steps can again be heard.]

THE WAITER. *[Entering.]* Do you want another pitcher of wine, Mrs. Yang?

MRS. YANG. No, I think we've got enough. Wine only makes you warm, doesn't it?

MRS. SHIN. It's expensive too, I'd say.

MRS. YANG. Drinking always makes me perspire.

THE WAITER. Might I ask, then, for a settlement of the bill?

MRS. YANG. *[Not hearing him.]* Ladies and gentlemen, I ask you to be patient a little longer, the cousin *must* be on his way. *[To the waiter.]* Don't spoil the festivities!

THE WAITER. I can't let you leave without settling the bill.

MRS. YANG. But I'm known here!

THE WAITER. Exactly.

MRS. YANG. It's outrageous, the service today. What d'you say to that, Sun?

THE PRIEST. I take my leave. *[He goes off, ponderously.]*

MRS. YANG. *[Desperately.]* Just stay where you are! The priest's coming back in a few minutes.

SUN. Never mind, Mamma. Ladies and gentlemen, since the priest's gone away, we can't keep you.

THE SISTER-IN-LAW. Come on, grandfather!

THE GRANDFATHER. *[Earnestly emptying his glass.]* To the bride!

THE NIECE. *[To Shen Te.]* Don't hold it against him. He wants to be friendly. He likes you.

MRS. SHIN. What a disgrace!

[All the guests go off.]

SHEN TE. Shall I go too, Sun?

SUN. No, you'll wait. *[He drags her by her bridal ornaments, messing them up.]* Isn't it your wedding? I'm still waiting and the old woman's waiting too. *She* wants to see her falcon *[he points at himself]* in the clouds! However, I almost believe now that it'll be Saint Nevernever Day before she'll step to her door and see his plane thundering over her house. *[To the empty seats, as if the guests were still present.]* Ladies and gentlemen, what's the matter with the conversation? Don't you like it here? The wedding, after all, is only postponed a bit because of the important guest who's expected and because the bride doesn't yet know the meaning of love. For your entertainment, I, the bridegroom, will sing you a song. *[He sings.]*

The Song of Saint Nevernever Day

On a certain day, as is very well known,
Everyone will cry "Hooray,
The poor woman's son is on the golden throne!"
And the day's Saint Nevernever Day.
On Saint Nevernever Day
He'll sit on the golden throne.

And on that day goodness will pay
And badness will cost you your head
And merit and gain will smile and play
While exchanging salt and bread.
On Saint Nevernever Day
While exchanging salt and bread.

And the grass will look down at the sky
And the pebbles will roll up the stream
And men will be good without batting an eye
They will make of our earth a dream.
On Saint Nevernever Day
They will make of our earth a dream.

And on that day I shall be a flier
And you'll be one of the best
And you, idle man, will have work at last
You, woman, will get your rest.
On Saint Nevernever Day
You, woman, will get your rest.

And because we can hardly wait for that time
All this will begin, I know,
Not at night, at seven or eight or nine,
But at the first cock crow.
On Saint Nevernever Day
At the very first cock crow.

MRS. YANG. He won't come now.

[The three sit there, two of them looking toward the door.]

6•A

[Wong's sleeping quarters. Again the Gods appear to Wong in a dream. He has fallen asleep over a large book. Music.]

WONG. I'm glad you've come, illustrious ones!
Permit me a question which disturbs me deeply.
In the ruined hut of a priest who has moved

away to become a laborer in the cement factory, I found a book and in it a strange passage. I absolutely must read it to you. Here it is. [With his left hand he turns the pages of an imaginary book above the real book which is lying in his lap. He lifts up the imaginary book to read from while the real book remains where it is.] "In Sung there is a place called Thorngrove. Catalpas, cypresses, the mulberry trees grow there. Now trees which are one or two spans in circumference are cut down by those who want sticks to make dog kennels with. Those of three or four feet in circumference are cut down by rich families in search of boards for coffins. Those of seven or eight feet in circumference are cut down by people seeking beams for their luxury villas. Thus none of the trees lives its allotted span, for all perish before their time is up by saw and ax. Such are the tribulations of usefulness.

THE THIRD GOD. In that case the one men have least use for would be the best.

WONG. No, only the happiest. It's the worst but also the happiest.

THE FIRST GOD. The things people write!

THE SECOND GOD. Why does this parable affect you so deeply, water seller?

WONG. Because of Shen Te, illustrious one! She has come to grief in her love because she followed the commandment, love thy neighbor! Perhaps she is really *too* good for this world, illustrious ones!

THE FIRST GOD. Nonsense, weak and wretched man! Lice and doubts, it seems, have almost eaten you up.

WONG. Certainly, illustrious one, forgive me! I only thought you might be able to intervene.

THE FIRST GOD. That's quite impossible. Our friend here [He points to the Third God, who has a black eye.] intervened in a quarrel only yesterday. You can see the consequences.

WONG. But her cousin had to be called in again. He's an incredibly skillful man, as I found out for myself, but not even he could achieve anything. The store seems to be lost.

THE THIRD GOD. [A bit worried.] Perhaps we should help after all?

THE FIRST GOD. I'm of the opinion that she should help herself.

THE SECOND GOD. [Sternly.] The worse the situation of a good man, the better he shows himself. Suffering ennobles!

THE FIRST GOD. All our hopes rest on her.

THE THIRD GOD. Things aren't what they might be with our search. Now and then we find some good beginnings, gratifying intentions, many high principles, but all that hardly constitutes a good human being. And when we do find halfway good people, they don't live in a dignified, human way. [Confidentially.] Things are especially bad with our sleeping quarters. You can see where we spend the nights by the straw sticking to our clothes.

WONG. Just one thing, couldn't you at least . . .

THE GODS. No. We're onlookers. We firmly believe that our good woman will find her own way on this dark earth. The heavier the burden the greater will be her strength! Just wait, water seller, and, you'll see, everything will come to a good . . .

[The figures of the Gods have grown paler, their voices softer, all the time. Now they disappear and their voices are no longer heard.]

7

[The yard behind Shen Te's tobacco store. On a cart there are a few house furnishings. Shen Te and Mrs. Shin are taking down the washing from the line.]

MRS. SHIN. I can't understand why you don't fight for your store tooth and nail.

SHEN TE. What? I can't even pay the rent. The old couple's two hundred silver dollars have to be returned today but since I've given them to someone else, I'll have to sell my tobacco to Mrs. Mi Tzu.

MRS. SHIN. Everything's gone then. No husband, no tobacco, no place to stay! That's what happens when somebody wants to be better than other people. What are you going to live off now?

SHEN TE. I don't know. Perhaps I can earn a little by sorting tobacco.

MRS. SHIN. What are Mr. Shui Ta's pants doing here? He must have gone away from here naked!

SHEN TE. He's got another pair of trousers.

MRS. SHIN. I thought you said he'd gone for good? Why did he leave his pants behind?

SHEN TE. Perhaps he doesn't need them any more.

MRS. SHIN. Shall I pack them away?

SHEN TE. No.

[Mr. Shu Fu comes running in.]

MR. SHU FU. Don't say anything. I know all. You sacrificed your love and happiness so as not to ruin two old people who trusted you. It's not in vain that this neighborhood, this suspicious and malevolent neighborhood, calls you the Angel of the Suburbs. Your fiancé couldn't rise to your moral level, so you left him. And now you're closing your store, this little haven for so many! I can't let that pass. Morning after morning I watched from my doorstep the little crowd of wretched people in front of your store and you distributing rice with your own hands. Will that never happen again? Must the good woman of Setzuan perish? Or, if only you'd permit me to assist you with your good works! No, don't say anything! I don't want any assurances. No avowals that you wish to accept my help! But here. [He pulls out a checkbook and signs a check which he puts on her cart.] I'm making out a blank check to you. You can fill it out as you wish, for any sum. And now I go, quietly and modestly, making no claims, on tiptoe, full of veneration, selflessly. [Exit.]

MRS. SHIN. [Examining the check.] You're saved! The likes of you are lucky: you always find some idiot. But now fall to! Fill it out for a thousand silver dollars and I'll take it to the bank before he comes to his senses.

SHEN TE. Put the washing basket on the cart. I can pay the laundry bill without the check.

MRS. SHIN. What? You don't want to take the check? It's a crime! Is it just because you think you'd have to marry him? Sheer madness! People like him *want* to be led by the nose! It's the greatest bliss they know. Or do you still want to hold on to your flier when Yellow Street and the whole neighborhood know how badly he treated you?

SHEN TE. It all comes from poverty. [To the audience.]

I saw him puff up his cheeks in his sleep. They were bad cheeks.
But in the morning I held his coat against the light and saw the walls through it.
When I heard his cunning laugh, I grew afraid.
But when I saw his shoes full of holes, I loved him dearly.

MRS. SHIN. So you're defending him after everything that's happened. I've never seen anyone quite as crazy. [Angrily.] I shall breathe more easily when we're rid of you in this neighborhood.

SHEN TE. [Staggering while taking down the wash.] I'm a bit dizzy.

MRS. SHIN. [Taking the wash from her.] Do you often get dizzy when you stretch or bend? If only there isn't a little visitor on the way! [She laughs.] What a pretty mess! If that's what's happened, it's all up with the big check! It wasn't meant for an occasion of that sort. [She goes to the back with a basket. Shen Te looks after her without moving. Then she looks at her body, feels it, and a great joy comes over her face.]

SHEN TE. [Softly.] O joy! A human being is growing in my womb. Nothing can be seen yet. But he's there already. The world awaits him secretly. In the towns, people are saying: Someone's coming now who's got to be reckoned with. [In pantomime she introduces her little son to the audience.] A flier!

Welcome a new conqueror of unknown mountains and unreachable regions!
One who brings the mail from man to man over the unpassable deserts!

[She begins to walk up and down, leading her little son by the hand.]

Come, son, look at the world! Here, that's a tree. Bow to it, greet it. [She shows him how to bow.] That's it: now you know each other. Stop, here comes the water seller. A friend. Give him your hand. Don't be afraid. A glass of fresh water for my son, please. It's warm today. [She gives him the glass.] O dear, the policeman! We'll make a big circle around him. Perhaps we'll get a few cherries over there in the rich Mr. Feh Pung's garden. But we mustn't be seen there. Come, fatherless boy! You too want cherries! Easy, easy, son! [They walk carefully, looking around.] No, over here, the bushes will hide us. No, you can't go straight at them like that. [He seems to pull her away. She resists.] We've got to be reasonable. [Suddenly she gives in.] All right, if you really must go straight at them . . . [She lifts him up.] Can you reach the cherries? Push them in your mouth, that's a safe place for them. [She *takes a cherry from him and puts it in her mouth.]* Tastes pretty good. O heavens, the policeman! Now we've got to run! *[They flee.]* There's the street. Quiet now, we'll walk slowly so we won't be noticed. As if not the least thing had happened. *[She sings, walking along with the child.]*

> For no reason a plum
> Attacked a bum.
> But the man, very quick,
> Bit the plum in the neck.

[Wong, the water seller, has come in, leading a child by the hand. He watches Shen Te with wonder. Wong coughs.]

SHEN TE. Oh, Wong! Hello.

WONG. Shen Te, I've heard you're not so well off. You even had to sell your store to pay your debts. But here's a child without a roof over his head. He was running about in the stockyards. He seems to be one of Lin To's children. You remember the carpenter? He lost his shop a few weeks ago and has been drinking ever since. His children go hungry and hang around the streets. What can be done for them?

SHEN TE. *[Taking the child from him.]* Come, little man! *[To the audience.]*

> You there! Someone is asking for shelter.
> A bit of tomorrow is asking for a today!
> His friend, the conqueror, whom you know,
> Is his advocate.

[To Wong.] He can easily live in Mr. Shu Fu's cabins where I also may be going. I'm to have a baby too. But don't tell anyone or Yang Sun will hear it, and we'd only be in his way. Look for Mr. Lin To downtown, and tell him to come here.

WONG. Thanks a lot, Shen Te. I knew you'd find something. *[To the child.]* You see, someone who's *good* always knows a way out. I'll run quickly and get your father. *[He starts to go.]*

SHEN TE. Oh Wong, now it comes back to me: how's your hand? I *wanted* to take the oath for you but my cousin . . .

WONG. Don't worry about my hand. Look, I've already learned to get along without my right hand. I hardly need it any more. *[He shows her how he can handle his pole without using his right hand.]* Watch how I do it!

SHEN TE. But it mustn't grow stiff! There, take the cart, sell everything, and go to the doctor with the money. I'm ashamed to have let you down like this. And what will you think of my accepting the cabins from the barber?

WONG. The homeless can live there now. And so can you. That's more important than my hand. Now I'm going to get the carpenter. *[Exit.]*

SHEN TE. Promise me you'll go to the doctor!

[Mrs. Shin has returned and has been waving to her.]

MRS. SHIN. Are you crazy? Giving away the cart with your very last possessions! What's his hand to you? If the barber hears of it, he'll chase you out of the only shelter you can get. You haven't paid me for the laundry!

SHEN TE. Why are you so bad?

> You tread on your fellow man.
> Isn't it a strain?
> Your veins swell with your efforts to be greedy.
> Extended naturally, a hand gives and receives with equal ease.
> Grabbing greedily, it has to strain. Alas!
> What an enticement, to give! How pleasant, to be kind!
> A good word slips out like a sigh of contentment.

[Mrs. Shin goes angrily off.]

SHEN TE. *[To the child.]* Sit down and wait till your father comes.

[The child sits on the ground. Enter the Husband and Wife who came to live with Shen Te on the day her store opened. They are dragging large sacks.]

THE WIFE. Are you alone, Shen Te? *[Since Shen Te nods, she calls in her Nephew, who is also carrying a sack.]* Where's your cousin?

SHEN TE. He's gone away.

THE WIFE. And is he coming back?

SHEN TE. No. I'm giving up the store.

THE WIFE. We know that. That's why we came. We've got a few sacks of raw tobacco here which someone owed us and we'd like to ask you to move them to your new home together with your new belongings. We haven't got a place yet to take them to and we'd be so noticeable on the street. I don't see how you

can deny us this small favor after all the trouble
we got into in your store.

SHEN TE. I'll gladly do you the favor.

THE HUSBAND. And if someone should ask whose
sacks these are, you can say they're yours.

SHEN TE. Who should ask me?

THE WIFE. [*Looking at her sharply.*] The police, for
instance. They are prejudiced against us and
want to ruin us. Where should we put the sacks?

SHEN TE. I don't know, just now I'd rather not do
anything that might get me in jail.

THE WIFE. That's just like you. We're to lose the
few miserable sacks of tobacco too, the only
things we saved!

[*Shen Te maintains a stubborn silence.*]

THE HUSBAND. Just think, this tobacco could start
us in the manufacturing business. We could go
a long way!

SHEN TE. All right, I'll keep the sacks for you. For
the time being, we'll put them in the back
room.

[*She goes in with them. The child looks after her. Then,
shyly glancing about, he goes to the garbage can and fishes
around in it. He starts to eat out of it. Shen Te and the others come back.*]

THE WIFE. You understand, I guess, that we depend
on you completely.

SHEN TE. Yes. [*She sees the child and grows rigid.*]

THE HUSBAND. We'll look for you the day after
tomorrow in Mr. Shu Fu's cabins.

SHEN TE. Go now, quickly. I'm not well.

[*She pushes them off. Exeunt the three.*]

SHEN TE. He is hungry. He's fishing in the garbage
can. [*She picks up the child and, in the following
speech, expresses her horror at the fate of poor children.
She shows the audience the little gray mouth. She
asserts her determination under no circumstances to
treat her own child with such cruelty. During her speech
the musicians start playing "The Song of the
Defenselessness of the Gods and Good Men."*]

O son! O flier! Into what a world will you come?
They want to let you fish in the garbage can, even
you!
Only look at the little gray mouth!

[*She shows the child to the audience.*]

How do you treat your offspring?
Have you no mercy on the fruit of your womb?
No pity for yourselves, unhappy men?
I shall defend my own even if I have to be a tigress to
do it!
Having seen this, from now on, I divorce myself from
everybody!
I will not rest till I have saved my son, if only him!
What I have learned in my school, the gutter,
With fisticuffs and deceit,
Will now be of use to you, my son!
I will be good to you, and a tigress, a wild beast
To all others,
If I have to.
And I *shall* have to.

[*She goes off to change into the cousin's clothes.*]

SHEN TE. [*Going.*] Once more it has to be. The last
time, I hope.

[*She has taken with her Shui Ta's trousers. The returning
Mrs. Shin looks after her curiously. Enter the Sister-in-law
and the Grandfather. The music continues softly.*]

THE SISTER-IN-LAW. The store's closed. The
furniture's in the yard. That's the end.

MRS. SHIN. The results of frivolity, sensuality, and self-
love. And where's the journey to? Down, down,
down! Into Mr. Shu Fu's cabins. With you.

THE SISTER-IN-LAW. She'll have a nice surprise!
We've come to complain! Damp rat holes with
rotten floors! The barber only offered them to
us because his soap supplies got moldy there. "I
have shelter for you, what do you say to that?"
Shame! we say to that!

[*Enter the Unemployed.*]

THE UNEMPLOYED. Is it true, Shen Te's moving away?

THE SISTER-IN-LAW. Yes, she wanted to sneak off.
No one was supposed to find out.

MRS. SHIN. She's ashamed because she's ruined.

THE UNEMPLOYED. [*Excitedly.*] She's got to call her
cousin! Advise her to call her cousin! He's the
only one who can still do something.

THE SISTER-IN-LAW. That's true. He's stingy enough
but at least he'll save her store and then she'll
help us again.

THE UNEMPLOYED. I wasn't thinking of us, I was thinking of her. But, you're right, she should call him for our sake too.

[Enter Wong with the Carpenter. He leads two children by the hand.]

THE CARPENTER. I really can't thank you enough. [To the others.] We're getting a place to live.

MRS. SHIN. Where?

THE CARPENTER. Mr. Shu Fu's cabins! And it was little Feng who brought the change about! [He sees Feng.] Well, here you are! "Here is someone asking for shelter," Miss Shen Te is supposed to have said, and at once she got us a place to stay. [To the two children.] Thank your brother, you two! [The Carpenter and his children gaily bow to the child.] Our thanks, little friend!

[Shui Ta has entered.]

SHUI TA. May I ask what you all want here?

THE UNEMPLOYED. Mr. Shui Ta!

WONG. Good day, Mr. Shui Ta. I didn't know you'd come back. You know the carpenter, Mr. Lin To. Miss Shen Te has promised him a place in Mr. Shu Fu's cabins.

SHUI TA. Mr. Shu Fu's cabins are not available.

THE CARPENTER. So we can't live there?

SHUI TA. The space is reserved for something else.

THE SISTER-IN-LAW. Does that mean *we* have to get out too?

SHUI TA. I'm afraid so.

THE SISTER-IN-LAW. But where are we all to go?

SHUI TA. [Shrugging his shoulders.] As I understand Miss Shen Te, who has gone on a journey, it is not her intention to withdraw her aid completely. However, in the future, things will be ordered a bit more reasonably. No more food without services rendered in return. Instead, everyone will be given the opportunity to work himself up in an honest way. Miss Shen Te has decided to give you all work. Those of you who want to follow me now into Shu Fu's cabins will not be led into nothingness.

THE SISTER-IN-LAW. Does that mean we're all supposed to work for Shen Te now?

SHUI TA. Yes. You'll be making tobacco. In the room inside are three bales of goods. Get them!

THE SISTER-IN-LAW. Don't forget we owned a store once. We prefer to work for ourselves. We have our own tobacco.

SHUI TA. [To the Unemployed and the Carpenter.] Perhaps *you* will want to work for Shen Te since you don't have your own tobacco.

[The Carpenter and the Unemployed go in dejectedly. The Landlady enters.]

THE LANDLADY. Well, Mr. Shui Ta, how're things with the sale? Here I have three hundred silver dollars.

SHUI TA. Mrs. Mi Tzu, I've decided not to sell, but to sign the lease.

THE LANDLADY. What? All of a sudden you don't need the money for the flier?

SHUI TA. No.

THE LANDLADY. And do you have the rent?

SHUI TA. [Taking the barber's check from the cart and filling it out.] Here I have a check for ten thousand silver dollars, made out by Mr. Shu Fu, who's interested in my cousin. Mrs. Mi Tzu, look for yourself. The two hundred silver dollars for the next half year's rent will be in your hands before 6 P.M. And now, Mrs. Mi Tzu, allow me to continue my work. I'm very busy today and have to ask your pardon.

THE LANDLADY. Oh I see, Mr. Shu Fu steps into the flier's shoes! Ten thousand silver dollars! Nevertheless, Mr. Shui Ta, the young girls of today surprise me. They are fickle. And superficial too.

[She goes out. The Carpenter and the Unemployed drag in the sacks.]

THE CARPENTER. I don't know why I'm dragging your sacks.

SHUI TA. It's enough that I know. Your son here has a healthy appetite. He wants to eat, Mr. Lin To.

THE SISTER-IN-LAW. [Seeing the sacks.] Has my brother-in-law been here?

MRS. SHIN. Yes.

THE SISTER-IN-LAW. I thought so. I know these sacks. That's our tobacco!

SHUI TA. You better not say that so loud. This is my tobacco, as you can see from the fact that it was standing in my room. If you have any doubts, we can go to the police and remove them. Is that what you want?

THE SISTER-IN-LAW. [Angrily.] No.

SHUI TA. It seems you don't have tobacco of your own after all. Under these circumstances you will perhaps grasp the saving hand which Miss Shen Te is holding out to you? Be so kind now as to show me the way to Mr. Shu Fu's cabins.

[Taking the Carpenter's youngest child by the hand, Shui Ta goes off, followed by the Carpenter, his other children, the Sister-in-law, the Grandfather, and the Unemployed. The Sister-in-law, the Carpenter, and the Unemployed drag the sacks.]

WONG. He's a bad man. But Shen Te is good.

MRS. SHIN. I don't know. A pair of pants is missing from the clothes line and her cousin's wearing them. That must mean something. I'd like to know what.

[Enter the old couple.]

THE OLD WOMAN. Isn't Miss Shen Te here?

MRS. SHIN. [Absent-mindedly.] Gone away.

THE OLD WOMAN. That's strange. She was going to bring us something.

WONG. [Sadly looking at his hand.] She was going to help me too. My hand's getting all stiff. I'm sure she'll be back soon. The cousin has never stayed long.

MRS. SHIN. He hasn't, has he?

7•A

[Wong's sleeping quarters. Music. In his dream, the water seller tells the Gods his fears. The Gods are still on their long journey. They seem tired. Stopping for a moment, they look over their shoulders toward the water seller.]

WONG. Before your sudden appearance woke me, illustrious ones, I was dreaming. I saw my dear sister Shen Te in great distress in the rushes by the river at the place where those who commit suicide are found. She was staggering strangely and held her head low as if she were dragging something soft but heavy which was pulling her down in the mud. When I called to her, she told me she had to take the package of rules to the other shore without getting it wet since that would wipe away the writing. Actually I couldn't see that she was carrying anything. But

I remembered with fear that you, the gods, had spoken to her about the great virtues, in gratitude for her taking you in when you were hard put to it for sleeping quarters, O shame! I'm sure you'll understand my worries.

THE THIRD GOD. What do you suppose?

WONG. Somewhat fewer rules, illustrious ones! A little relaxation of the book of rules, benevolent ones, in view of the bad times.

THE THIRD GOD. As for instance, Wong, as for instance?

WONG. As for instance that only goodwill be required, instead of love, or . . .

THE THIRD GOD. But that would be even more difficult, unhappy one!

WONG. Or fairness instead of justice.

THE THIRD GOD. But that would mean more work!

WONG. Then just propriety instead of honor.

THE THIRD GOD. But, don't you see, that would mean *more* work, not less, you skeptic! [Tired, they wander on.]

8

[Shui Ta's tobacco factory. Shui Ta has established a small tobacco factory in Mr. Shu Fu's cabins. Behind bars, fearfully close together, are several families, especially women and children. Among them are the Sister-in-law, the Grandfather, the Carpenter, and his children. Enter Mrs. Yang followed by Yang Sun.]

MRS. YANG. [To the audience.] I have to tell you how the wisdom and strength of the universally respected Mr. Shui Ta has transformed my son Yang Sun from a depraved scamp into a useful person. As the whole neighborhood found out, Mr. Shui Ta opened a small but soon flourishing tobacco factory near the cattle runs. Three months ago I found it necessary to visit him there with my son. After a short time he received me.

[Shui Ta comes out of the factory and goes to Mrs. Yang.]

SHUI TA. How can I help you, Mrs. Yang?

MRS. YANG. Mr. Shui Ta, I'd like to put in a word for my son. This morning the police were out at our house and we were told that you have brought an action in the name of Miss Shen Te for breach of promise of marriage. You also claim that Sun dishonestly got his hands on two hundred silver dollars.

SHUI TA. Quite right, Mrs. Yang.

MRS. YANG. Mr. Shui Ta, for the sake of the gods, couldn't you be merciful once more? The money's gone. He ran through it in two days when nothing came of the flying job. I know he's a good-for-nothing. He'd already sold my furniture and wanted to go to Peking without his old Mamma. [She weeps.] Miss Shen Te thought very highly of him once.

SHUI TA. What do you have to say, Mr. Yang Sun?

SUN. [Darkly.] The money's gone.

SHUI TA. Mrs. Yang, because of my cousin's incomprehensible weakness for your depraved son, I'm prepared to give him another chance. She told me that she expected honest work to produce an improvement. He can have a job in my factory. We will deduct the two hundred silver dollars from his salary bit by bit.

SUN. Then it's the factory or the jail?

SHUI TA. Take your choice.

SUN. And I guess I can't talk with Shen Te?

SHUI TA. No.

SUN. Where's my place?

MRS. YANG. A thousand thanks, Mr. Shui Ta! You are infinitely kind. The gods will reward you. [To Sun.] You've departed from the right path. Now try your hand at honest work till you can face your mother again!

[Sun follows Shui Ta into the factory. Mrs. Yang returns to the footlights.]

MRS. YANG. The first weeks were hard for Sun. The work didn't agree with him. He had little opportunity to distinguish himself. But in the third week a small incident came to his aid.

[Sun and the former Carpenter Lin To are each dragging two bales of tobacco.]

THE CARPENTER. [He stops, groaning, and sits down on a bale.] I can hardly go on. I'm not young enough for this work.

SUN. [Sitting down too.] Why don't you just throw the sacks in their faces?

THE CARPENTER. And how're we to live? To get a bare living I've even got to use the children. If Miss Shen Te could see this! She was good.

SUN. She was all right. If conditions hadn't been so lousy, we could have made out quite nicely together. I'd like to know where she is. We better go on. *He* usually comes about this time.

[They get up. Sun sees Shui Ta approaching.]

SUN. Give me one of your sacks, you cripple! [Sun takes one of the bales from Lin To.]

THE CARPENTER. Thanks a lot! Now if *she* were here and saw how you help an old man you'd soon be in favor. Oh dear!

[Enter Shui Ta.]

MRS. YANG. And of course Mr. Shui Ta saw right away what it means to be a good worker not shrinking from any job. And he stepped in.

SHUI TA. Stop, you! What's going on? Are you only carrying one sack?

THE CARPENTER. I'm a bit tired today, Mr. Shui Ta, and Yang Sun was kind enough to . . .

SHUI TA. You're going back to take three bales, my friend. What Yang Sun can do, you can do. Yang Sun has the right attitude and you have not.

MRS. YANG. [While the former Carpenter gets two more bales.] Of course, not a word to Sun but Mr. Shui Ta was wise to the situation. And the following Saturday when the wages were being paid out . . .

[A table is brought in and Shui Ta arrives with a bag of money. Standing next to the foreman—the former Unemployed—he pays the wages. Sun steps up to the table.]

THE UNEMPLOYED. Yang Sun, six silver dollars.

SUN. Excuse me, it can't be more than five. Only five silver dollars. [He takes the list held by the foreman.] Please look, here are marked *six* working days. That's a mistake. I was absent one day because of some court business. [Hypocritically.] I don't want to get anything I don't deserve, however lousy the pay is!

THE UNEMPLOYED. Okay, five silver dollars! [To Shui Ta.] A rare case, Mr. Shui Ta!

SHUI TA. How can it say six days here if it was only five?

THE UNEMPLOYED. I must have made a mistake, Mr. Shui Ta. [To Sun, coldly.] It won't happen again.

SHUI TA. [Calling Sun aside.] I noticed the other day that you're a strong man and don't hold your strength back. You give it to the firm. Today I see you're even honest. Does it often happen that the foreman makes mistakes in favor of the employees?

SUN. He's got friends among the workers and they look on him as one of themselves.

SHUI TA. I see. Well, one good turn deserves another. Would you like some little recompense?

SUN. No. But perhaps I may point to the fact that I'm also intelligent. I've had an education, you know. The foreman means well enough by the workers but he's uneducated and can't understand what the firm needs. Give me a trial period of one week, Mr. Shui Ta, and I think I'll be able to prove to you that my intelligence can be worth more to the firm than my physical strength.

MRS. YANG. Those were daring words, but that evening I said to my son: You're a flier. Show that, even where you are now, you can rise! Fly, my falcon! And, really, education and intelligence can do great things! How can you belong to the better sort of people without them? My son worked true miracles in Mr. Shui Ta's factory!

[Sun stands with his legs apart behind the workers. Above their heads is a basket of raw tobacco which they are handing along.]

SUN. You there, I don't call that honest work! This basket has got to move faster! [To a child.] Sit on the floor where you don't take up so much room! And you, yes you over there, you can easily take on the pressing too! Lazy dogs, what're you getting paid for? Hurry up the basket! The devil! Put grandfather on one side and let him pick with the children! No more laziness now! To my beat, the whole thing!

[He claps the rhythm with his hands and the basket moves faster.]

MRS. YANG. And no enmity, no abuse from uneducated people—and there was plenty of it—could stop my son from doing his duty.

[One of the workers starts The Song of the Eighth Elephant.]

The Song of the Eighth Elephant

Seven elephants had Mr. Dschin
And then there was Number Eight.
Seven were wild, Number Eight was tame
Number Eight guarded the gate.
Run faster!
Mr. Dschin has a forest park
It must be cleared before nightfall
And now it will soon be dark!

Seven elephants were clearing the forest
Mr. Dschin rode Number Eight.
And when the seven toiled all day
Number Eight would quietly wait.
Dig faster!
Mr. Dschin has a forest park
It must be cleared before nightfall
And now it will soon be dark!

Seven elephants had had enough
Of felling trees each day till late.
Mr. Dschin was angry at the seven, but he
Gave a bushel of rice to Number Eight.
What does it mean?
Mr. Dschin has a forest park
It must be cleared before nightfall
And now it will soon be dark!

Seven elephants they hadn't a tusk
Number Eight had a tusk which he used.
And when Number Eight cut the other seven up
Mr. Dschin stood there and was amused.
Keep on digging!
Mr. Dschin has a forest park
It must be cleared before nightfall
And now it will soon be dark!

[Smoking a cigar, Shui Ta has come casually strolling forward. Yang Sun, laughing, has joined in the refrain of the third stanza and speeded up the tempo of the last by clapping his hands.]

MRS. YANG. We really can't thank Mr. Shui Ta enough. Almost without lifting a finger, with wisdom and strength alone, he's brought out all the good that lay hidden in Sun. He didn't make him fantastic promises like his cousin whom they praise so highly. He just forced him into honest work. Today, Sun is quite a different person. You'll have to admit that! A noble man is like a bell. If you ring it, it rings, and if you don't, it don't, as the saying goes.

9

[Shen Te's tobacco store. The store has become an office with club chairs and fine carpets. It is raining. Shui Ta, now fat, is sending away the Old Man and his wife. Mrs. Shin, amused, looks on. She is obviously in new clothes.]

SHUI TA. I'm sorry I can't tell you when she'll be back.
THE OLD WOMAN. We got a letter today with the two hundred silver dollars which we once lent her. It had no return address. But the letter must have come from Shen Te. We'd like to write to her. What's her address?
SHUI TA. I'm sorry I don't know either.
THE OLD MAN. Let's go.
THE OLD WOMAN. She's got to come back sometime.

[Shui Ta bows. The two old people go off, uncertain and worried.]

MRS. SHIN. They got their money too late. Now they've lost their store because they couldn't pay their taxes.
SHUI TA. Why didn't they come to me?
MRS. SHIN. People don't like to come to you. At first, I guess, they were waiting for Shen Te to come back, because they had nothing in writing. Then at the critical moment the old man got a fever and his wife stayed with him day and night.
SHUI TA. [He has to sit down; he is beginning to feel sick.] I'm dizzy again.
MRS. SHIN. [Attending to him.] You're in your seventh month! The excitement isn't good for you. You can be glad you've got me. No one can get along without help from others. Well, I'll be at your side when your hardest hour comes. [She laughs.]
SHUI TA. [Weakly.] Can I count on it, Mrs. Shin?
MRS. SHIN. I'll say. Of course it'll cost you a bit. Open your collar, you'll feel better.
SHUI TA. [Wretchedly.] It's all for the child's sake, Mrs. Shin.
MRS. SHIN. All for the child.
SHUI TA. I'm getting fat too fast. It must draw attention.

MRS. SHIN. They put it down to your wealth.
SHUI TA. And what'll happen to the little one?
MRS. SHIN. You ask that three times a day. It'll be taken care of. It'll have the best that money can buy.
SHUI TA. Yes. [Anxiously.] And it must never see Shui Ta.
MRS. SHIN. Never. Always Shen Te.
SHUI TA. But the rumors in the neighborhood! The things the water seller says! The store is watched!
MRS. SHIN. As long as the barber doesn't know anything, nothing's lost. Drink some of this water.

[Enter Sun in a smart suit and with a businessman's briefcase. He looks surprised at finding Shui Ta in Mrs. Shin's arms.]

SUN. I guess I'm intruding.
SHUI TA. [Getting up with difficulty and going to the door, staggering.] Until tomorrow, Mrs. Shin!

[Mrs. Shin, putting on her gloves, smiles and goes off.]

SUN. Gloves! Where from, what for, and how? Is she fleecing you maybe? [Since Shui Ta does not answer.] Are even you susceptible to the tender emotions? Funny. [He takes a sheet of paper out of his briefcase.] Anyway, you haven't been at your best, lately, not as you used to be. Moods. Indecisions. Are you ill? The business suffers. Here's another letter from the police. They want to close the factory. They say that at the very most they can only permit twice the lawful number of workers. You've got to do something now, Mr. Shui Ta.

[Shui Ta looks at him absent-mindedly for a moment. Then he goes into the back room and returns with a bag. He pulls out a new bowler hat and throws it on the desk.]

SHUI TA. The firm wishes its representatives to be decently dressed.
SUN. Did you buy that for me?
SHUI TA. [Indifferently.] Try it on and see if it fits.

[Sun is surprised but puts it on. Shui Ta looks him over and puts the bowler in place.]

SUN. Your servant! But don't evade me again! You've got to discuss the new project with the barber today.

SHUI TA. The barber's demanding impossible conditions.

SUN. Of what kind? If only you'd tell me.

SHUI TA. *[Evasively.]* The cabins are good enough.

SUN. Yes, good enough for the rabble working there. But not good enough for the tobacco. It gets damp. Before the meeting I'll have a talk with Mrs. Mi Tzu about *her* buildings. If we have them, we can fire this bunch of beggars, abortions, and walking scarecrows. They're not good enough. We'll have a cup of tea, I'll stroke Mrs. Mi Tzu's fat knees, and we'll get her buildings half price.

SHUI TA. *[Sharply.]* No. In the interest of the firm's reputation, I want your behavior always to be personally reserved and coolly businesslike.

SUN. Why are you so irritated? Are those unpleasant rumors bothering you?

SHUI TA. I don't pay any attention to rumors.

SUN. Then it must be the rain again. Rain always makes you irritable and melancholy. I'd like to know why.

WONG'S VOICE. *[From outside.]*

I'm selling water, water,
As I stand here in the rain.
For such a little water
I've suffered too much pain.
And now I shout: "Buy water!"
But no one's buying
Parched and dying
And drinking and paying . . .

SUN. Here's that damned water seller. He'll be starting his heckling again.

WONG'S VOICE. *[From outside.]* Aren't there any good people left in the city of Setzuan? Not even here on the square where the good Shen Te used to live? Where is she who even when it was raining bought a little water from me in the gladness of her heart many months ago? Where is she now? Has no one seen her? Has no one heard from her? She went into this house one evening and never came out again.

SUN. Shall I shut his trap for him? What's it to him where she is? By the way, I think you're only keeping it secret so that *I* won't find out.

WONG. *[Entering.]* Mr. Shui Ta, I'm asking you again when Shen Te will come back. It's six months now since she went away. *[Shui Ta is silent.]* In the meantime much has happened which she would never have put up with. *[Shui Ta is still silent.]* Mr. Shui Ta, there are rumors in the district that something must have happened to Shen Te. We, her friends, are very worried. Have the goodness to give us her address!

SHUI TA. Unfortunately, I'm not free at the moment, Mr. Wong. Come back next week.

WONG. *[Excitedly.]* In the mornings there used to be rice at her door. For the needy. It has been there again lately!

SHUI TA. And what do people conclude from this?

WONG. That Shen Te hasn't gone away at all, but . . .

SHUI TA. But what? *[Wong is silent.]* Then I'll give you my answer. And it is final. If you're Shen Te's friend, Mr. Wong, ask about her as little as possible. That's my advice.

WONG. Nice advice! Mr. Shui Ta, Shen Te told me before her disappearance that she was pregnant!

SUN. What?

SHUI TA. *[Quickly.]* It's a lie!

WONG. *[Very earnestly to Shui Ta.]* Mr. Shui Ta, you mustn't believe that Shen Te's friends will stop asking about her. A good person isn't so easily forgotten. There aren't many. *[Exit.]*

[Motionless, Shui Ta looks after him, then goes quickly into the back room.]

SUN. *[To the audience.]* Shen Te pregnant! I'm beside myself! I've been swindled! She must have told her cousin right away and that scoundrel sent her away immediately! "Pack your suitcase and disappear before the child's father gets wind of it." It's absolutely unnatural. It's inhuman. I have a son, a Yang appears on the scene, and what happens? The girl disappears and I'm left here to slave! *[He gets angry.]* I'm put off with a hat! *[He stamps on it.]* Criminal! Thief! Kidnapper! And the girl's virtually without a protector!

[Sobbing can be heard from the back room. He stands still.]

Did I hear sobbing? Who is it? It's stopped. What sobs are these? That cunning dog Shui Ta doesn't sob! Who sobs then? And what does it mean that the rice is said to be at the door in the mornings? Is the girl here after all? Is he just hiding her? Who else could be sobbing? That would be just the thing I want! If she's pregnant I've got to find her!

[*Shui Ta returns from the back room. He goes to the door and looks out into the rain.*]

SUN. Well, where is she?

SHUI TA. [*Putting up his hand and listening.*] Just a moment! It's nine o'clock. But one can't hear a thing today. The rain's too heavy.

SUN. [*Ironically.*] And what do you want to hear?

SHUI TA. The mail plane.

SUN. Stop fooling.

SHUI TA. I was once told that you wanted to fly? Have you lost that desire?

SUN. I'm not complaining about my present position, if that's what you mean. I don't care for night work, you know. Flying the mail is night work. The firm's become very dear to me, so to speak. It is after all the firm of my one-time future wife, even if she has gone away. And she has, hasn't she?

SHUI TA. Why do you ask?

SUN. Maybe because her affairs still don't leave me altogether unmoved.

SHUI TA. That might interest my cousin.

SUN. In any case, I'm still sufficiently concerned in her affairs not to close my eyes if, for instance, she were kept under lock and key.

SHUI TA. By whom?

SUN. By you!

[*Pause.*]

SHUI TA. What would you do?

SUN. I might, to begin with, start arguing about my position in the firm.

SHUI TA. Oh, I see. And if the firm, that is, if *I* should give you an adequate position, could I count on your giving up all further investigations concerning your one-time future wife?

SUN. Perhaps.

SHUI TA. And what sort of new position are you thinking of?

SUN. The top one. I'd be thinking of throwing you out, for example.

SHUI TA. And if, instead of me, the firm threw *you* out?

SUN. I'd probably come back. And not alone.

SHUI TA. But?

SUN. With the police.

SHUI TA. With the police. And suppose the police found no one here?

SUN. Then I suppose they'd search this back room. Mr. Shui Ta, my longing for the lady of my heart is insatiable. I feel I must do something in order to fold her in my arms again. [*Calmly.*] She's pregnant and needs someone around. I've got to talk it over with the water seller. [*He goes.*]

[*Shui Ta looks after him without moving. Then he quickly returns to the back room. He brings out various belongings of Shen Te's, underwear, dresses, toilet articles. He looks a long time at the shawl which Shen Te bought from the Old Man and his wife. He then makes all these things up into a bundle and, hearing a noise, hides it under the table. Enter the Landlady and Mr. Shu Fu. They greet Shui Ta and put away their umbrellas and rubbers.*]

THE LANDLADY. Fall's coming on, Mr. Shui Ta.

MR. SHU FU. A sad season!

THE LANDLADY. And where's your charming secretary? A terrible lady-killer! But I guess you don't know that side of him. All the same he knows how to combine charm with attention to business in a way which can only be to your advantage.

SHUI TA. [*Bowing.*] Won't you take a seat?

[*They sit down and start smoking.*]

SHUI TA. My friends, an unforeseen incident which might have certain consequences forces me to speed up the negotiations. Negotiations concerning the future of the project I've been working on. Mr. Shu Fu, my factory is in difficulties.

MR. SHU FU. It always is.

SHUI TA. But now the police are openly threatening to close it if I can't point to negotiations for a new project. Mr. Shu Fu, it's a question of my cousin's one piece of property. Now you've always displayed the liveliest interest in my cousin.

MR. SHU FU. Mr. Shui Ta, I have a deep aversion to talking about your constantly expanding projects. I speak about a small dinner with your cousin; you hint at financial difficulties. I put cabins for the homeless at your cousin's disposal; you establish a factory there. I hand her a check; you present it. Your cousin disappears; you ask for ten thousand silver dollars, remarking that my cabins are too small. Sir, where *is* your cousin?

SHUI TA. Mr. Shu Fu, don't worry. I can inform you today that she'll be back very soon.

MR. SHU FU. Soon? When? You've been saying "soon" for weeks.

SHUI TA. I'm not demanding new signatures from you. I've merely asked whether you'd show more interest in my project if my cousin returned.

MR. SHU FU. I've told you a thousand times that I'm ready to discuss everything with your cousin and nothing with you. However, it seems that you want to put obstacles in the way of such a discussion.

SHUI TA. Not any more.

MR. SHU FU. When will it take place then?

SHUI TA. *[Uncertainly.]* In three months.

MR. SHU FU. *[Annoyed.]* Then I'll sign in three months.

SHUI TA. But everything has to be prepared.

MR. SHU FU. You can prepare everything, Shui Ta, if you're convinced that your cousin will really come at this time.

SHUI TA. Mrs. Mi Tzu, are you, for your part, ready to confirm to the police that I may have your workrooms?

THE LANDLADY. Certainly, if you'll let me have your secretary. You've known for weeks that's my condition. *[To Mr. Shu Fu.]* The young man's so efficient in business and I need a manager.

SHUI TA. You've got to understand that I can't do without Mr. Yang Sun just now, with all the difficulties I'm having. And my health has been failing me lately. I was ready from the beginning to let you have him, but . . .

THE LANDLADY. Yes, but?

[Pause.]

SHUI TA. All right, he'll call on you tomorrow, in your office.

MR. SHU FU. I am very glad that you were able to reach this decision, Shui Ta. Should Miss Shen Te really come back, the young man's presence would be highly improper. As we know, he once exerted a most harmful influence over her.

SHUI TA. *[Bowing.]* Doubtless. Please excuse my long hesitation over the question of my cousin Shen Te and Mr. Yang Sun. It is not worthy of a businessman. But they were once very close to each other.

THE LANDLADY. You're excused.

SHUI TA. *[Looking toward the door.]* My friends, let us now reach a settlement. In this once small and shabby store where the poor people of the neighborhood bought the good Shen Te's tobacco, we, her friends, are resolving to establish twelve beautiful new stores which in the future will sell Shen Te's good tobacco. I'm told people are calling me the Tobacco King of Setzuan. Actually I carried on this business solely in my cousin's interests. It will belong to her, her children, and her grandchildren.

[The noise of a crowd can be heard from outside. Enter Sun, Wong, and the Policeman.]

THE POLICEMAN. Mr. Shui Ta, I'm very sorry the excited state of this neighborhood forces me to follow up a report originating in your own firm. According to this report you are depriving your cousin Miss Shen Te of her freedom.

SHUI TA. It's not true.

THE POLICEMAN. Mr. Yang Sun here testifies that from the room behind your office he heard sobbing which could only come from a female.

THE LANDLADY. That's ridiculous. I and Mr. Shu Fu, two respected citizens of this city whose evidence could hardly be doubted by the police, can testify that no one has been sobbing here. We are quietly smoking our cigars.

THE POLICEMAN. Unfortunately I have orders to inspect the room in question.

[Shui Ta opens the door. The Policeman bows and steps into the doorway. He looks into the room, then turns round and smiles.]

THE POLICEMAN. There's really nobody in there.

SUN. *[Who has been following him.]* But I heard sobbing! *[His eye lights on the table under which Shui Ta has pushed the bundle. He spots the bundle.]* That wasn't there before! *[Opening it, he shows Shen Te's dresses and other things.]*

WONG. Those are Shen Te's things! *[He runs to the door and calls out.]* Her clothes have been discovered here!

THE POLICEMAN. *[Taking the things.]* You declare that your cousin's gone away. A bundle of things of hers is found hidden under your table. Where can the girl be reached, Mr. Shui Ta?

SHUI TA. I don't know her address.

THE POLICEMAN. That is most regrettable.

SHOUTS FROM THE CROWD. Shen Te's things have been found! The Tobacco King has murdered the girl and put her out of the way!

THE POLICEMAN. Mr. Shui Ta, I shall have to ask you to follow me to the station.

SHUI TA. *[Bowing to the Landlady and Mr. Shu Fu.]* I have to apologize for this scandal, my friends. But there are still judges in Setzuan. I'm convinced that everything will shortly be cleared up. *[He goes out, the Policeman at his back.]*

WONG. A terrible crime has been committed!

SUN. *[Dismayed.]* But I heard sobbing!

9•A

[Wong's sleeping quarters. Music. For the last time the Gods appear to the water seller in his dream. They have changed considerably. There are unmistakable signs of a long journey, extreme exhaustion, and manifold unhappy experiences. One has had his hat struck off his head, one has lost a leg in a fox trap, and all three go barefoot.]

WONG. At last you've come! Terrible things have been happening in Shen Te's tobacco store, illustrious ones! Shen Te went away again many months ago! Her cousin seized everything! Today he's been arrested. He's supposed to have murdered her to get her store. But I don't believe it. I had a dream in which she came and told me that her cousin's holding her prisoner. Oh, illustrious ones, you must come back at once and find her.

THE FIRST GOD. This is terrible. Our whole search has come to grief. We didn't find many good people and those we found lived in a way quite unworthy of human beings. We'd already decided to confine ourselves to Shen Te.

THE SECOND GOD. If she's still good!

WONG. She certainly is, but she's disappeared!

THE FIRST GOD. Then all is lost.

THE SECOND GOD. Restrain yourself.

THE FIRST GOD. What good would that do? If she can't be found, we've got to retire. What sort of world did we find? Misery, vulgarity, and waste everywhere! Even the countryside has fallen away from us. The lovely trees are decapitated by telephone wires and on the other side of the mountains we see heavy smoke clouds and hear the thunder of cannon. And nowhere a good man who can pull through!

THE THIRD GOD. Alas, water seller, our commandments seem to be deadly. I fear that all our moral rules have to be done away with. People keep busy just saving their skins. Good intentions bring them to the brink of the abyss, and good deeds throw them into it. *[To the other two Gods.]* The world can't be lived in, you've got to admit!

THE SECOND GOD. *[Vehemently.]* No, it's people who are worthless!

THE THIRD GOD. The world is too cold!

THE SECOND GOD. People are too weak!

THE FIRST GOD. Dignity, my friends, dignity! Brothers, we mustn't despair. We did find one human being who was good and stayed good. She's only disappeared. Let's hurry and find her! One is enough! Didn't we say that everything can still turn out well if there's one human being who can stand this world? Just one?

[They quickly disappear.]

10

[A courtroom. Groups: Mr. Shu Fu and the Landlady. Sun and his mother. Wong, the Carpenter, the Grandfather, the Young Prostitute, the Old Man and Woman. Mrs. Shin, the Policeman. The Unemployed, the Sister-in-law.]

THE OLD MAN. He's too powerful.

WONG. He wants to open twelve new stores.

THE CARPENTER. How can the judge give a fair sentence if the accused's friends—the barber Shu Fu and the landlady Mi Tzu—are also *his* friends?

THE SISTER-IN-LAW. Mrs. Shin was seen last night carrying a fat goose into the judge's kitchen by order of Mr. Shui Ta. The fat was dripping through the basket.

THE OLD WOMAN. *[To Wong.]* Our poor Shen Te will never be found.

WONG. No, only the gods can discover the truth.

THE POLICEMAN. Order! The judges are coming!

[Enter the three Gods in judges' robes. As they walk by the footlights on their way to their seats, one can hear them whispering.]

THE THIRD GOD. We'll be found out. The certificates are very badly forged.

THE SECOND GOD. And people will wonder about the judge's sudden indigestion.

THE FIRST GOD. No, that's only natural. He ate half a goose.

MRS. SHIN. These are *new* judges!

WONG. And very good ones!

[The third and last God hears this, turns round, and smiles at Wong. The Gods sit down. The First God beats on the table with a hammer. The Policeman brings in Shui Ta who is whistled at but walks with lordly steps.]

THE POLICEMAN. Be prepared for a surprise. It isn't the just Fu Yi Tcheng. But the new judges look very mild too.

[Shui Ta sees the Gods and faints.]

THE YOUNG PROSTITUTE. What's the matter? The Tobacco King has fainted.

THE SISTER-IN-LAW. Yes, at the sight of the new judges!

WONG. He seems to know them! I don't understand that.

THE FIRST GOD. Are you the tobacco merchant Shui Ta?

SHUI TA. *[Weakly.]* Yes.

THE FIRST GOD. You have been accused of doing away with your own cousin Miss Shen Te, in order to take possession of her business. Do you plead guilty?

SHUI TA. No.

THE FIRST GOD. *[Turning the pages of documents.]* We'll first hear the policeman of this neighborhood on the reputation of the accused and on the reputation of his cousin.

THE POLICEMAN. *[Stepping forward.]* Miss Shen Te was a girl who liked to please everyone, who lived and let live, as the saying goes. Mr. Shui Ta, on the other hand, is a man of principle. The generosity of Miss Shen Te forced him at times to strict measures. However, unlike the girl, he was always on the side of the law, your honor. Once, people to whom his cousin trustfully gave shelter were unmasked by him as a band of thieves. Another time he saved Miss Shen Te at the last moment from plain perjury. I know Mr. Shui Ta to be a respectable and law-abiding citizen.

THE FIRST GOD. Are there others present who want to testify that the accused is incapable of his supposed crime?

[Mr. Shu Fu and the Landlady step forward.]

THE POLICEMAN. *[Whispering to the Gods.]* Mr. Shu Fu, a very influential gentleman.

MR. SHU FU. Mr. Shui Ta has the reputation of a highly respected businessman here in Setzuan. He is Vice-President of the Chamber of Commerce and is about to be made justice of the peace.

WONG. *[Interrupting.]* By you! You're doing business with him!

THE POLICEMAN. *[Whispering.]* A disagreeable character.

THE LANDLADY. As President of the Community Chest I'd like to call the attention of the court to this fact: Mr. Shui Ta is not only about to give to his numerous employees the best possible rooms, well-lighted and healthy, but is also making regular contributions to our home for the disabled.

THE POLICEMAN. *[Whispering.]* Mrs. Mi Tzu, a close friend of the judge Fu Yi Tcheng!

THE FIRST GOD. Yes, yes, but now we've got to hear whether anyone has *less* favorable evidence to bring forward.

[Wong, the Carpenter, the Old Man and Woman, the Unemployed, the Sister-in-law, and the Young Prostitute step forward.]

THE POLICEMAN. The scum of the neighborhood.

THE FIRST GOD. Well, what do you know of the general behavior of Shui Ta?

SHOUTS. *[Jumbled.]* He's ruined us!

__ He blackmailed me!

__ He led us off on the wrong track!

__ Exploited the helpless!

__ Lied!

__ Cheated!

__ Murdered!

THE FIRST GOD. Accused, what have you to say?

SHUI TA. I have simply enabled my cousin to exist, your honor. I only came when she was in danger of losing her little store. I had to come three times. I never wanted to stay. But the last time circumstances forced me to remain. I never had anything but trouble. My cousin was popular; I did the dirty work. That's why I'm hated.

THE SISTER-IN-LAW. You certainly are. Take our case, your honor! *[To Shui Ta.]* I won't mention the sacks.

SHUI TA. Why not? Why not?

THE SISTER-IN-LAW. *[To the Gods.]* Shen Te gave us shelter and *he* had us arrested.

SHUI TA. You stole cakes!

THE SISTER-IN-LAW. Now he pretends to be interested in the baker's cakes! He wanted the store for himself!

SHUI TA. The store wasn't a public refuge, selfish creatures!

THE SISTER-IN-LAW. But we had no place to stay!

SHUI TA. There were too many of you!

WONG. And they *[pointing to the Old Man and Woman]* were selfish too?

THE OLD MAN. We put our savings into Shen Te's store. Why did you make us lose *our* store?

SHUI TA. Because my cousin was helping a flier to fly. I was to get the money!

WONG. Maybe she wanted to help him to fly. What interested you was the well-paid job in Peking. The store wasn't good enough for you!

SHUI TA. The rent was too high!

MRS. SHIN. That's true enough.

SHUI TA. And my cousin knew nothing about business!

MRS. SHIN. That's true too! She was also in love with the flier.

SHUI TA. Shouldn't she be allowed to love?

WONG. Certainly! And why did you want to force her to marry a man she did not love, the barber over there?

SHUI TA. The man she loved was a scoundrel.

WONG. *[Pointing to Sun.]* Him?

SUN. *[Jumping up.]* And because he was a scoundrel you took him into your office!

SHUI TA. To improve you! To improve you!

THE SISTER-IN-LAW. To make him into a slave-driver!

WONG. And when he was improved, didn't you sell him to her? *[Pointing to the Landlady.]* She shouted it around every place!

SHUI TA. Because she wouldn't give me her ~~buildings unless she had him to stroke her~~ knees!

THE LANDLADY. That's a lie! Don't talk of my buildings ever again. I'll have nothing more to do with you. Murderer! *[She rustles off, insulted.]*

SUN. *[Insisting on getting his word in.]* Your honor, I must speak on his behalf!

THE SISTER-IN-LAW. Naturally. You're in his employ.

THE UNEMPLOYED. He's the worst slave-driver I've ever known. He's absolutely depraved.

SUN. Your honor, the accused may have made whatever you say of me, but he's not a murderer. A few minutes before he was arrested I heard Shen Te's voice in his back room!

THE FIRST GOD. *[Avidly.]* So she's alive? Tell us exactly what you heard?

SUN. *[Triumphantly.]* Sobbing, your honor, sobbing!

THE THIRD GOD. And you recognized her?

SUN. Absolutely. How could I fail to recognize her voice?

MR. SHU FU. Sure, *you* made her sob often enough!

SUN. And yet I made her happy. But then he *[pointing to Shui Ta]* wanted to sell her to you!

SHUI TA. *[To Sun.]* Because you didn't love her!

WONG. No. For the money!

SHUI TA. But what was the money needed for, your honor? *[To Sun.]* You wanted her to sacrifice all her friends, but the barber offered his cabins and his money to help the poor. Moreover, I *had* to get her engaged to him so that she could still be good.

WONG. Why didn't you let her be good when the big check was signed? Why did you send Shen Te's friends into the dirty sweatshops of your factory, Tobacco King?

SHUI TA. For the child's sake!

THE CARPENTER. And *my* children? What did you do with *my* children?

[Shui Ta is silent.]

WONG. Now you're silent! The gods gave the store to Shen Te as a little fountain of goodness. She always wanted to do good and you always came and spoiled it.

SHUI TA. *[Beside himself.]* Because otherwise the fountain would have dried up, fool!

MRS. SHIN. That's true, your honor!

WONG. What good is a fountain if you can't get at the water?

SHUI TA. Good deeds mean ruin!

WONG. *[Wildly.]* But bad deeds mean a good life, don't they? What did you do with the good Shen Te, bad man? How many good people are there, illustrious ones? *She* was good! When that man over there smashed my hand, she wanted to testify for me. And now I testify for her. She was good, I swear! *[He raises his hand in an oath.]*

THE THIRD GOD. What's the matter with your hand, water seller? It's all stiff.

WONG. *[Pointing to Shui Ta.]* It's his fault, his alone! She wanted to give me money for the doctor but then *he* came along! You were her deadly enemy!

SHUI TA. I was her only friend!

ALL. Where is she?

SHUI TA. Gone away!

WONG. Where to?

SHUI TA. I won't tell!

ALL. And why did she have to go away?

SHUI TA. *[Shouting.]* Because you would have torn her to shreds! *[Sudden quiet. He sinks onto a chair.]* I can't go on. I'll explain everything. If the hall is cleared and only the judges remain, I will make a confession.

ALL. He's confessing! He's found out!

THE FIRST GOD. *[Beating on the table with the hammer.]* Let the hall be cleared!

[The Policeman clears the hall.]

MRS. SHIN. *[Laughing as she goes.]* There'll be a surprise!

SHUI TA. Have they gone? All of them? I can no longer keep silence. I recognized you, illustrious ones!

THE SECOND GOD. What did you do with our good woman of Setzuan?

SHUI TA. Let me confess the terrible truth: I am she!

THE SECOND GOD. Shen Te!

SHEN TE.

Yes, it is I. Shui Ta and Shen Te. I am both.
Your former injunction to be good and yet to live
Tore me like lightning in halves.
I don't know how it happened.
To be good to others and to myself—
I couldn't do both at the same time.
To help others and to help myself was too hard.
Alas, your world is difficult! Too much misery, too much despair!
The hand that is extended to a beggar, the beggar at once tears off!
Whoever helps the lost is lost himself!
For who could long refuse to be bad when he who eats no meat must die?
All the things that were needed—where should I have taken them from?
From myself! But then I perished!
A load of good intentions weighed me down to the ground.
Yet when I was unjust I walked mightily about and ate good meat!

Something must be wrong with your world.
Why is malice well rewarded? Why do punishments await the good?
Oh, how I should have loved to pamper myself!
And there was also a secret knowledge in me.
My foster-mother washed me in water from the gutter:
That gave me a sharp eye.
Yet pity pained me so, I was an angry wolf at the sight of misery.
Then I felt how I was changing and kind words turned to ashes in my mouth.
And yet I wished to be an Angel to the Suburbs.
To give was a delight. A happy face, and I walked on clouds.
Condemn me: everything I did I did to help my neighbor,
To love my lover, and to save my little son from want.
For your great plans, O gods! I was too poor and small.

THE FIRST GOD. *[With all signs of horror.]* Don't go on, unhappy woman! What should we think, we who are so happy to have found you again!

SHEN TE. But I've got to tell you that I am the bad man whose crimes everyone was talking about!

THE FIRST GOD. The good woman whose good deeds everyone was talking about!

SHEN TE. The bad man too!

THE FIRST GOD. A misunderstanding! Several unfortunate occurrences! Some heartless neighbors! An excess of zeal!

THE SECOND GOD. But how is she to go on living?

THE FIRST GOD. She can do it. She's strong, well built. She can stand a lot.

THE SECOND GOD. But didn't you hear what she said?

THE FIRST GOD. *[Vehemently.]* It was confused, very confused! And incredible, highly incredible! Should we admit our commandments to be deadly? Should we renounce our commandments? *[Sullenly.]* Never! Should the world be changed? How? By whom? No! Everything is in order! *[He suddenly beats on the table with the hammer.]*

And now . . . *[He makes a sign and music is heard. Rosy light.]* let us return.
This little world has much engaged us.
Its joy and its sorrow have refreshed and pained us.

Up there, however, beyond the stars.
We shall gladly think of you, Shen Te, the good
 woman
Who bears witness to our spirit down below,
Who, in cold darkness, carries a little lamp!
Goodbye! Do it well!

*[He makes a sign and the ceiling opens. A pink cloud
comes down. On it the Three Gods rise, very slowly.]*

SHEN TE. Oh, don't, illustrious ones! Don't go
 away! Don't leave me! How can I face the good
 old couple who've lost their store and the water
 seller with his stiff hand? And how can I defend
 myself from the barber whom I do not love and
 from Sun whom I do love? And I am with child.
 Soon there'll be a little son who'll want to eat. I
 can't stay here!

*[She turns with a hunted look toward the door which will
let her tormentors in.]*

THE FIRST GOD. You can do it. Just be good and
 everything will turn out well!

*[Enter the witnesses. They look with surprise at the judges
floating on their pink cloud.]*

WONG. Show respect! The gods have appeared
 among us! Three of the highest gods have come
 to Setzuan to find a good human being. They
 had found one already, but . . .
THE FIRST GOD. No "but"! Here she is!
ALL. Shen Te!
THE FIRST GOD. She has not perished. She was only
 hidden. She will stay with you. A good human
 being!
SHEN TE. But I need my cousin!
THE FIRST GOD. Not too often!
SHEN TE. At least once a week!
THE FIRST GOD. Once a month. That's enough!
SHEN TE. Oh, don't go away, illustrious ones! I
 haven't told you everything! I need you
 desperately!

[The Gods sing.]

The Trio of the Vanishing Gods on the Cloud

We, alas, may never stay
More than a fleeting year
If you watch your treasure long
'Twill always disappear.
Down here the golden light of truth
With shadow is alloyed
That is why we take our leave
And go back to our void.

SHEN TE. Help! *[Her cries continue through the song.]*

Our anxious search is over now
Let us to heaven ascend
The good, good woman of Setzuan
Praising, praising to the end!

*[As Shen Te stretches out her arms to them in desperation,
they disappear above, smiling and waving.]*

EPILOGUE

*[One of the actors walk out in front of the curtain and
apologetically addresses the audience.]*

Ladies and gentlemen, don't be angry! Please!
We know the play is still in need of mending.
A golden legend floated on the breeze,
The breeze dropped, and we got a bitter ending.
Being dependent on your approbation
We wished, alas! our work might be commended.
We're disappointed too. With concentration
We see the curtain closed, the plot unended.
In your opinion, then, what's to be done?
Change human nature or—the world? Well: which?
Believe in bigger, better gods or—none?
How can we mortals be both good and rich?
The right way out of the calamity
You must find for yourselves. Ponder, my friends,
How man with man may live in amity
And good men—women also—reach good ends.
There must, there must, be *some* end that would
 fit.
Ladies and gentlemen, help us look for it!

Introduction to *The Glass Menagerie* by Tennessee Williams

The Glass Menagerie   Danny Swartz as the Gentleman Caller, Heather Robison as Laura. The Acting Company. *(© T. Charles Erickson)*

The Play   *The Glass Menagerie,* which opened originally in 1945, has been revived frequently since then. Set in the Depression era—the 1930s—the play deals with a Southern family, the Wingfields, transplanted to Saint Louis. The members of the family are the mother, Amanda, a former Southern belle who cannot accept the fact that the family now lives in near poverty; the son, Tom, who works at a shoe warehouse; and the daughter, Laura, a painfully shy girl with a slight limp, who entertains herself by playing with a collection of glass animals, from which the play takes its title. These character types will recur in later dramas by Williams.

In this play, Tom serves as a narrator, speaking directly to the audience, telling about the past events in the family's life, describing his own desire to escape the suffocating influence of his mother, and setting the stage for the scenes. The scenes themselves, which take place in the Wingfields' cramped apartment, alternate with Tom's narrative. The character of Tom resembles the author, Tennessee Williams; and the other characters and the events in the play parallel people and incidents in Williams's own life, though they have been transformed and dramatized.

In the story, the Wingfields are struggling through the Depression, having been abandoned by the father. Amanda is trying to persuade Tom to work toward success in business and to find a "gentleman caller" for Laura, someone who will court and marry her as gentlemen did when Amanda was a young woman in Mississippi. Tom, however, is a dreamer who writes poetry and plans to run away from the tedium of his job in the warehouse. Laura is highly introverted and fearful of leaving the apartment; she cherishes her collection of glass animals, particularly her unicorn. In one of the final scenes of the play, Tom does bring home a gentleman caller—a man he works with, who turns out to be a former classmate of Laura's and someone she has always admired, but who also turns out to be engaged to marry somebody else. Since the play is presented as a memory being narrated by Tom, we discover that after this incident Tom abandoned his family; he is now trying to rid himself of his guilty feelings.

The Glass Menagerie combines many of the dramatic forms prevalent in the first half of the twentieth century. On the surface, the play is a realistic family drama. However, in presenting the action through the eyes of Tom Wingfield, Williams uses expressionistic techniques. Expressionism is a form of drama in which the audience sees the action through the eyes of the protagonist, and here, the poetic quality and the selected reality of the play are clearly influenced by Tom's memories. In addition, Williams, who worked with the German director Erwin Piscator while Piscator was in exile in New York during World War II, was influenced by the epic techniques that Piscator and Brecht developed. The narrator and the titles that begin each scene are epic devices.

The Playwright Tennessee Williams was one of the foremost twentieth-century American playwrights. He had a series of critical and popular successes from the 1940s through the 1960s, including *The Glass Menagerie* (1945), *A Streetcar Named Desire* (1947), *Summer and Smoke* (1948), *The Rose Tattoo* (1950), *Cat on a Hot Tin Roof* (1954), *Sweet Bird of Youth* (1959), and *The Night of the Iguana* (1961). Both *A Streetcar Named Desire* and *Cat on a Hot Tin Roof* won the Pulitzer Prize.

A common theme running through these works is the plight of society's outcasts, outsiders trapped in a hostile environment. (Recent biographical studies suggest that Williams's own sense of being an outsider, due to his homosexuality, influenced his dramaturgy.) These characters are usually victims who are unable to comprehend their world, and Williams evokes compassion for them through the use of lyrical and poetic language as well as symbolism. His most popular plays are fairly realistic, but in his later dramas—such as *The Seven Descents of Myrtle* (1968)—he increasingly used nonrealistic techniques.

Williams had a long wait for his critical and commercial success. The son of a traveling shoe salesman, he was born in Columbus, Mississippi, and grew up in Saint Louis. He entered the University of Missouri in 1929, but financial difficulties forced him to leave school. After several years and many jobs, he received his B.A. from the University of Iowa in 1938.

In 1939, Williams received a citation from the Group Theater for his collection of one-act plays, *American Blues.* The Theater Guild production of his full-length drama *Battle of Angels* closed in Boston in 1940 after a brief run. He spent six months as a contract writer for Metro-Goldwyn-Mayer in 1943, and it was while he was in Hollywood that he wrote the first draft of *The Glass Menagerie.*

In his later years, Williams himself became somewhat of an outsider, at least to theater. His late full-length plays were failures, though some of his shorter plays, for example, *Small Craft Warnings* (1973), had extended runs off-Broadway. His work, including *The Glass Menagerie,* continues to be performed frequently and to influence other American playwrights. In addition, there have been many recent revivals of his dramas in England.

The Period   Like Brecht, Williams was influenced by the chaotic world that surrounded him. He, too, was affected by the events between World War I and World War II. *The Glass Menagerie* is set during the Depression, and there are hints, through Tom's narration, of the coming renewed world war. Williams's play focuses on the economic difficulties of the Wingfield household. In addition, the play begins to question many of the traditional values held by Americans. Like Arthur Miller's *Death of a Salesman* (1949), *The Glass Menagerie* questions the American dream.

Williams's play is clearly influenced by developments in American drama and theater between the wars. During the early decades of the century—after the initial objections—realistic plays began to be presented commercially. In the United States, however, for a long time these plays were produced by small, independent groups like those that developed in France, Germany, and England.

These small American theaters were part of what was called the little theater movement, which flourished between the world wars. The Provincetown Playhouse, the Neighborhood Playhouse, and the Washington Square Players, all founded in 1915 as alternatives to commercial theater, often presented experimental, nonrealistic work; they also offered a haven to controversial or unknown realistic drama. The Provincetown Playhouse, in particular, supported the early work of the playwright Eugene O'Neill (1888–1953), who experimented with realistic and nonrealistic techniques.

In terms of realism, the most important producing group between World War I and World War II was the Group Theater, a noncommercial company in New York's Broadway district. The Group Theater was dedicated to presenting socially relevant drama and to introducing Stanislavski's system to the United States. Its founding members were Lee Strasberg (1901–1982), Cheryl Crawford (1902–1986), and Harold Clurman (1901–1980); and its acting company included a number of performers who became well known in movies as well as on the stage. Its resident playwright was Clifford Odets (1906–1963), a leading realist in the 1930s; Odets's plays include *Awake and Sing* (1935) and *Golden Boy* (1937). The Group Theater disbanded in 1941, but its influence on realistic acting, directing, and playwriting continued for many years.

One additional experiment in American theater between the wars should be noted. During the Depression, President Franklin Delano Roosevelt established the Works Progress Administration (WPA), which organized governmentally subsidized agencies to put the unemployed back to work. The Federal Theater Project, headed by Hallie Flanagan Davis (1890–1969), a college professor, was one of these agencies. For four years the Federal Theater Project supported theatrical ventures throughout the United States and helped revitalize interest in theater outside New York City. The Federal Theater developed the "living newspaper," a form that dramatized current events, often using epic techniques. The Federal Theater also assisted aspiring African-American theaters and artists, supporting, for example, an all-black production of *Macbeth* directed by Orson Welles (1915–1985). The government, for political reasons, discontinued funding the project in 1939 (many members of Congress had claimed that the project was sympathetic to communism).

Being familiar with the Group Theater, the Theater Guild, and Piscator, Tennessee Williams was clearly influenced by the dynamic state of American theater between the world wars.

THE GLASS MENAGERIE

Tennessee Williams

CHARACTERS

AMANDA WINGFIELD, the mother
LAURA WINGFIELD, her daughter

TOM WINGFIELD, her son
JIM O'CONNOR, the gentleman caller

SCENE—An alley in St. Louis.

Part I—Preparation for a Gentleman Caller.
Part II—The Gentleman Calls.
Time—Now and the Past.

SCENE I

The Wingfield apartment is in the rear of the building, one of those vast hive-like conglomerations of cellular living-units that flower as warty growths in overcrowded urban centers of lower-middle-class population and are symptomatic of the impulse of this largest and fundamentally enslaved section of American society to avoid fluidity and differentiation and to exist and function as one interfused mass of automatism.

The apartment faces an alley and is entered by a fire-escape, a structure whose name is a touch of accidental poetic truth, for all of these huge buildings are always burning with the slow and implacable fires of human desperation. The fire-escape is included in the set—that is, the landing of it and steps descending from it.

The scene is memory and is therefore nonrealistic. Memory takes a lot of poetic license. It omits

some details; others are exaggerated, according to the emotional value of the articles it touches, for memory is seated predominantly in the heart. The interior is therefore rather dim and poetic.

At the rise of the curtain, the audience is faced with the dark, grim rear wall of the Wingfield tenement. This building, which runs parallel to the footlights, is flanked on both sides by dark, narrow alleys which run into murky canyons of tangled clotheslines, garbage cans, and the sinister latticework of neighboring fire-escapes. It is up and down these side alleys that exterior entrances and exits are made, during the play. At the end of Tom's opening commentary, the dark tenement wall slowly reveals (by means of a transparency) the interior of the ground-floor Wingfield apartment.

Downstage is the living room, which also serves as a sleeping room for Laura, the sofa unfolding to make her bed. Upstage, center, and divided by a wide arch or second proscenium with transparent faded portieres (or second curtain), is the dining room. In an old-fashioned what-not in the living room are seen scores of transparent glass animals. A blown-up photograph of the father hangs on the wall of the living room, facing the audience, to the left of the archway. It is the face of a very handsome young man in a doughboy's First World War cap. He is gallantly smiling, ineluctably smiling, as if to say, "I will be smiling forever."

The audience hears and sees the opening scene in the dining room through both the transparent fourth wall of the building and the transparent gauze portieres of the dining-room arch. It is during this revealing scene that the fourth wall slowly ascends, out of sight. This transparent exterior wall is not brought down again until the very end of the play, during Tom's final speech.

The narrator is an undisguised convention of the play. He takes whatever license with dramatic convention is convenient to his purposes.

[Tom enters dressed as a merchant sailor from alley, stage left, and strolls across the front of the stage to the fire-escape. There he stops and lights a cigarette. He addresses the audience.]

TOM. Yes, I have tricks in my pocket, I have things up my sleeve. But I am the opposite of a stage magician. He gives you illusion that has the appearance of truth. I give you truth in the pleasant disguise of illusion. To begin with, I turn back time. I reverse it to that quaint period, the thirties, when the huge middle class of America was matriculating in a school for the blind. Their eyes had failed them, or they had failed their eyes, and so they were having their fingers pressed forcibly down on the fiery Braille alphabet of a dissolving economy. In Spain there was revolution. Here there was only shouting and confusion. In Spain there was Guernica. Here there were disturbances of labor, sometimes pretty violent, in otherwise peaceful cities such as Chicago, Cleveland, Saint Louis. . . . This is the social background of the play.

[Music.]

The play is memory. Being a memory play, it is dimly lighted, it is sentimental, it is not realistic. In memory everything seems to happen to music. That explains the fiddle in the wings. I am the narrator of the play, and also a character in it. The other characters are my mother, Amanda; my sister, Laura; and a gentleman caller who appears in the final scenes. He is the

most realistic character in the play, being an emissary from a world of reality that we were somehow set apart from. But since I have a poet's weakness for symbols, I am using this character also as a symbol; he is the long delayed but always expected something that we live for. There is a fifth character in the play who doesn't appear except in this larger-than-life photograph over the mantel. This is our father who left us a long time ago. He was a telephone man who fell in love with long distances; he gave up his job with the telephone company and skipped the light fantastic out of town. . . . The last we heard of him was a picture post-card from Mazatlan, on the Pacific coast of Mexico, containing a message of two words—"Hello—Good-bye!" and no address. I think the rest of the play will explain itself. . . .

[Amanda's voice becomes audible through the portieres.]

[Legend on screen: "Où sont les neiges."]

[He divides the portieres and enters the upstage areas.]

[Amanda and Laura are seated at a drop-leaf table. Eating is indicated by gestures without food or utensils. Amanda faces the audience. Tom and Laura are seated in profile.]

[The interior has lit up softly and through the scrim we see Amanda and Laura seated at the table in the upstage area.]

AMANDA. *[Calling.]* Tom?
TOM. Yes, Mother.
AMANDA. We can't say grace until you come to the table!
TOM. Coming, Mother. *[He bows slightly and withdraws, reappearing a few moments later in his place at the table.]*
AMANDA. *[To her son.]* Honey, don't *push* with your *fingers*. If you have to push with something, the thing to push with is a crust of bread. And chew—chew! Animals have sections in their stomachs which enable them to digest food without mastication, but human beings are supposed to chew their food before they swallow it down. Eat food leisurely, son, and really enjoy it. A well-cooked meal has lots of delicate flavors that have to be held in the mouth for appreciation. So chew your food and give your salivary glands a chance to function!

[Tom deliberately lays his imaginary fork down and pushes his chair back from the table.]

TOM. I haven't enjoyed one bite of this dinner because of your constant directions on how to eat it. It's you that makes me rush through meals with your hawk-like attention to every bite I take. Sickening—spoils my appetite—all this discussion of animals' secretion—salivary glands—mastication!

AMANDA. *[Lightly.]* Temperament like a Metropolitan star! *[He rises and crosses downstage.]* You're not excused from the table.

TOM. I'm getting a cigarette.

AMANDA. You smoke too much.

[Laura rises.]

LAURA. I'll bring in the blancmange.

[He remains standing with his cigarette by the portieres during the following.]

AMANDA. *[Rising.]* No, sister, no, sister—you be the lady this time and I'll be the darky.

LAURA. I'm already up.

AMANDA. Resume your seat, little sister—I want you to stay fresh and pretty—for gentlemen callers!

LAURA. I'm not expecting any gentlemen callers.

AMANDA. *[Crossing out to kitchenette. Airily.]* Sometimes they come when they are least expected! Why, I remember one Sunday afternoon in Blue Mountain—*[Enters kitchenette.]*

TOM. I know what's coming!

LAURA. Yes. But let her tell it.

TOM. Again?

LAURA. She loves to tell it.

[Amanda returns with bowl of dessert.]

AMANDA. One Sunday afternoon in Blue Mountain—your mother received—*seventeen*!—gentlemen callers! Why, sometimes there weren't chairs enough to accommodate them all. We had to send the nigger over to bring in folding chairs from the parish house.

TOM. *[Remaining at portieres.]* How did you entertain those gentlemen callers?

AMANDA. I understood the art of conversation!

TOM. I bet you could talk.

AMANDA. Girls in those days *knew* how to talk, I can tell you.

TOM. Yes?

[Image: Amanda as a girl on a porch, greeting callers.]

AMANDA. They knew how to entertain their gentlemen callers. It wasn't enough for a girl to be possessed of a pretty face and a graceful figure—although I wasn't slighted in either respect. She also needed to have a nimble wit and a tongue to meet all occasions.

TOM. What did you talk about?

AMANDA. Things of importance going on in the world! Never anything coarse or common or vulgar. *[She addresses Tom as though he were seated in the vacant chair at the table though he remains by portieres. He plays this scene as though he held the book.]* My callers were gentlemen—all! Among my callers were some of the most prominent young planters of the Mississippi Delta—planters and sons of planters!

[Tom motions for music and a spot of light on Amanda.]

[Her eyes lift, her face glows, her voice becomes rich and elegiac.]

[Screen legend: "Où sont les neiges."]

There was young Champ Laughlin who later became vice-president of the Delta Planters Bank. Hadley Stevenson who was drowned in Moon Lake and left his widow one hundred and fifty thousand in Government bonds. There were the Cutrere brothers, Wesley and Bates. Bates was one of my bright particular beaux! He got in a quarrel with that wild Wainright boy. They shot it out on the floor of Moon Lake Casino. Bates was shot through the stomach. Died in the ambulance on his way to Memphis. His widow was also well-provided for, came into eight or ten thousand acres, that's all. She married him on the rebound—never loved her—carried my picture on him the night he died! And there was that boy that every girl in the Delta had set her cap for! That beautiful, brilliant young Fitzhugh boy from Greene County!

TOM. What did he leave his widow?

AMANDA. He never married! Gracious, you talk as though all of my old admirers had turned up their toes to the daisies!

TOM. Isn't this the first you've mentioned that still survives?

AMANDA. That Fitzhugh boy went North and made a fortune—came to be known as the Wolf of Wall Street! He had the Midas touch, whatever he touched turned to gold! And I could have been Mrs. Duncan J. Fitzhugh, mind you! But—I picked your *father*!

LAURA. *[Rising.]* Mother, let me clear the table.

AMANDA. No, dear, you go in front and study your typewriter chart. Or practice your shorthand a little. Stay fresh and pretty!—It's almost time for our gentlemen callers to start arriving. *[She flounces girlishly toward the kitchenette.]* How many do you suppose we're going to entertain this afternoon?

[Tom throws down the paper and jumps up with a groan.]

LAURA. *[Alone in the dining room.]* I don't believe we're going to receive any, Mother.

AMANDA. *[Reappearing, airily.]* What? No one—not one? You must be joking! *[Laura nervously echoes her laugh. She slips in a fugitive manner through the half-open portieres and draws them gently behind her. A shaft of very clear light is thrown on her face against the faded tapestry of the curtains. Music: "The Glass Menagerie" under faintly. Lightly.]* Not one gentlemen caller? It can't be true! There must be a flood, there must have been a tornado!

LAURA. It isn't a flood, it's not a tornado, Mother. I'm just not popular like you were in Blue Mountain. . . . *[Tom utters another groan. Laura glances at him with a faint, apologetic smile. Her voice catching a little.]* Mother's afraid I'm going to be an old maid.

[The scene dims out with "Glass Menagerie" Music.]

SCENE II

"Laura, Haven't You Ever Liked Some Boy?"

    On the dark stage the screen is lighted with the image of blue roses.

    Gradually Laura's figure becomes apparent and the screen goes out.

    The music subsides.

    Laura is seated in the delicate ivory chair at the small clawfoot table.

    She wears a dress of soft violet material for a kimono—her hair tied back from her forehead with a ribbon.

    She is washing and polishing her collection of glass.

    Amanda appears on the fire-escape steps. At the sound of her ascent, Laura catches her breath, thrusts the bowl of ornaments away and seats herself stiffly before the diagram of the typewriter keyboard as though it held her spellbound. Something has happened to Amanda. It is written in her face as she climbs to the landing: a look that is grim and hopeless and a little absurd.

    She has on one of those cheap or imitation velvety-looking cloth coats with imitation fur collar. Her hat is five or six years old, one of those dreadful cloche hats that were worn in the late twenties, and she is clasping an enormous black patent-leather pocketbook with nickel clasp and initials. This is her full-dress outfit, the one she usually wears to the D.A.R.

    Before entering she looks through the door.

    She purses her lips, opens her eyes wide, rolls them upward and shakes her head.

    Then she slowly lets herself in the door. Seeing her mother's expression Laura touches her lips with a nervous gesture.

LAURA. Hello, Mother, I was—*[She makes a nervous gesture toward the chart on the wall. Amanda leans against the shut door and stares at Laura with a martyred look.]*

AMANDA. Deception? Deception? *[She slowly removes her hat and gloves, continuing the swift suffering stare. She lets the hat and gloves fall on the floor—a bit of acting.]*

LAURA. *[Shakily.]* How was the D.A.R. meeting? *[Amanda slowly opens her purse and removes a dainty white handkerchief which she shakes out delicately and delicately touches to her lips and nostrils.]* Didn't you go to the D.A.R. meeting, Mother?

AMANDA. *[Faintly, almost inaudibly.]*—No.—No. *[Then more forcibly.]* I did not have the strength—to go to the D.A.R. In fact, I did not have the courage! I wanted to find a hole in the ground and hide myself in it forever! *[She crosses slowly to the wall and removes the diagram of the typewriter keyboard. She holds it in front of her for a second, staring at it sweetly and sorrowfully—then bites her lips and tears it in two pieces.]*

LAURA. *[Faintly.]* Why did you do that, Mother? *[Amanda repeats the same procedure with the chart of the Gregg Alphabet.]* Why are you—

AMANDA. Why? Why? How old are you, Laura?

LAURA. Mother, you know my age.

AMANDA. I thought that you were an adult; it seems that I was mistaken. *[She crosses slowly to the sofa and sinks down and stares at Laura.]*

LAURA. Please don't stare at me, Mother.

[Amanda closes her eyes and lowers her head. Count ten.]

AMANDA. What are we going to do, what is going to become of us, what is the future?

[Count ten.]

LAURA. Has something happened, Mother? *[Amanda draws a long breath and takes out the handkerchief again. Dabbing process.]* Mother, has—something happened?

AMANDA. I'll be all right in a minute. I'm just bewildered—*[Count five.]*—by life. . . .

LAURA. Mother, I wish that you would tell me what's happened!

AMANDA. As you know, I was supposed to be inducted into my office at the D.A.R. this afternoon. *[Image: a swarm of typewriters.]* But I stopped off at Rubicam's Business College to speak to your teachers about your having a cold and ask them what progress they thought you were making down there.

LAURA. Oh. . . .

AMANDA. I went to the typing instructor and introduced myself as your mother. She didn't know who you were. Wingfield, she said. We don't have any such student enrolled at the school! I assured her she did, that you had been going to classes since early in January. "I wonder," she said, "if you could be talking about that terribly shy little girl who dropped out of school after only a few days' attendance?" "No," I said, "Laura, my daughter, has been going to school every day for the past six weeks!" "Excuse me," she said. She took the attendance book out and there was your name, unmistakably printed, and all the dates you were absent until they decided that you had dropped out of school. I still said,

"No, there must have been some mistake! There must have been some mix-up in the records!" And she said, "No—I remember her perfectly now. Her hands shook so that she couldn't hit the right keys! The first time we gave a speed-test, she broke down completely— was sick at the stomach and almost had to be carried into the washroom! After that morning she never showed up any more. We phoned the house but never got any answer"—while I was working at Famous and Barr, I suppose, demonstrating those—Oh! I felt so weak I could barely keep on my feet! I had to sit down while they got me a glass of water! Fifty dollars' tuition, all of our plans—my hopes and ambitions for you—just gone up the spout, just gone up the spout like that. *[Laura draws a long breath and gets awkwardly to her feet. She crosses to the victrola and winds it up.]* What are you doing?

LAURA. Oh! *[She releases the handle and returns to her seat.]*

AMANDA. Laura, where have you been going when you've gone out pretending that you were going to business college?

LAURA. I've just been going out walking.

AMANDA. That's not true.

LAURA. It is. I just went walking.

AMANDA. Walking? Walking? In winter? Deliberately courting pneumonia in that light coat? Where did you walk to, Laura?

LAURA. All sorts of places—mostly in the park.

AMANDA. Even after you'd started catching that cold?

LAURA. It was the lesser of two evils, Mother. *[Image: Winter scene in park.]* I couldn't go back up. I—threw up—on the floor!

AMANDA. From half past seven till after five every day you mean to tell me you walked around in the park, because you wanted to make me think that you were still going to Rubicam's Business College?

LAURA. It wasn't as bad as it sounds. I went inside places to get warmed up.

AMANDA. Inside where?

LAURA. I went in the art museum and the bird-houses at the Zoo. I visited the penguins every day! Sometimes I did without lunch and went to the movies. Lately I've been spending most of my afternoons in the Jewel-box, that big glass house where they raise the tropical flowers.

AMANDA. You did all this to deceive me, just for the deception? *[Laura looks down.]* Why?

LAURA. Mother, when you're disappointed, you get that awful suffering look on your face, like the picture of Jesus' mother in the museum!

AMANDA. Hush!

LAURA. I couldn't face it.

[Pause. A whisper of strings.]

[Legend: "The crust of humility."]

AMANDA. *[Hopelessly fingering the huge pocketbook.]* So what are we going to do the rest of our lives? Stay home and watch the parades go by? Amuse ourselves with the glass menagerie, darling? Eternally play those worn-out phonograph records your father left as a painful reminder of him? We won't have a business career—we've given that up because it gave us nervous indigestion! *[Laughs wearily.]* What is there left but dependency all our lives? I know so well what becomes of unmarried women who aren't prepared to occupy a position. I've seen such pitiful cases in the South—barely tolerated spinsters living upon the grudging patronage of sister's husband or brother's wife!—stuck away in some little mousetrap of a room— encouraged by one in-law to visit another— little birdlike women without any nest—eating the crust of humility all their life! Is that the future that we've mapped out for ourselves? I swear it's the only alternative I can think of! It isn't a very pleasant alternative, is it? Of course—some girls *do marry.* *[Laura twists her hands nervously.]* Haven't you ever liked some boy?

LAURA. Yes. I liked one once. *[Rises.]* I came across his picture a while ago.

AMANDA. *[With some interest.]* He gave you his picture?

LAURA. No, it's in the year-book.

AMANDA. *[Disappointed.]* Oh—a high-school boy.

[Screen image: Jim as high-school hero bearing a silver cup.]

LAURA. Yes. His name was Jim. *[Laura lifts the heavy annual from the claw-foot table.]* Here he is in *The Pirates of Penzance.*

AMANDA. *[Absently.]* The what?

LAURA. The operetta the senior class put on. He had a wonderful voice and we sat across the aisle from each other Mondays, Wednesdays and Fridays in the Aud. Here he is with the silver cup for debating! See his grin?

AMANDA. *[Absently.]* He must have had a jolly disposition.

LAURA. He used to call me—Blue Roses.

[Image: Blue roses.]

AMANDA. Why did he call you such a name as that?

LAURA. When I had that attack of pleurosis—he asked me what was the matter when I came back. I said pleurosis—he thought that I said Blue Roses! So that's what he always called me after that. Whenever he saw me, he'd holler, "Hello, Blue Roses!" I didn't care for the girl that he went out with. Emily Meisenbach. Emily was the best-dressed girl at Soldan. She never struck me, though, as being sincere . . . It says in the Personal Section—they're engaged. That's—six years ago! They must be married by now.

AMANDA. Girls that aren't cut out for business careers usually wind up married to some nice man. *[Gets up with a spark of revival.]* Sister, that's what you'll do!

[Laura utters a startled, doubtful laugh. She reaches quickly for a piece of glass.]

LAURA. But, Mother—

AMANDA. Yes? *[Crossing to photograph.]*

LAURA. *[In a tone of frightened apology.]* I'm crippled!

[Image: Screen.]

AMANDA. Nonsense! Laura, I've told you never, never to use that word. Why, you're not crippled, you just have a little defect—hardly noticeable, even! When people have some slight disadvantage like that, they cultivate other things to make up for it—develop charm—and vivacity—and—*charm!* That's all you have to do! *[She turns again to the photograph.]* One thing your father had *plenty of*—was *charm!*

[Tom motions to the fiddle in the wings.]

[The scene fades out with music.]

SCENE III

[Legend on screen: "After the fiasco—"]

[Tom speaks from the fire-escape landing.]

TOM. After the fiasco at Rubicam's Business College, the idea of getting a gentleman caller for Laura began to play a more important part in Mother's calculations. It became an obsession. Like some archetype of the universal unconscious, the image of the gentleman caller haunted our small apartment. . . . *[Image: Young man at door with flowers.]* An evening at home rarely passed without some allusion to this image, this spectre, this hope. . . . Even when he wasn't mentioned, his presence hung in Mother's preoccupied look and in my sister's frightened, apologetic manner—hung like a sentence passed upon the Wingfields! Mother was a woman of action as well as words. She began to take logical steps in the planned direction. Late that winter and in the early spring—realizing that extra money would be needed to properly feather the nest and plume the bird—she conducted a vigorous campaign on the telephone, roping in subscribers to one of those magazines for matrons called *The Homemaker's Companion,* the type of journal that features the serialized sublimations of ladies of letters who think in terms of delicate cup-like breasts, slim, tapering waists, rich, creamy thighs, eyes like wood-smoke in autumn, fingers that soothe and caress like strains of music, bodies as powerful as Etruscan sculpture.

[Screen image: Glamour magazine cover.]

[Amanda enters with phone on long extension cord. She is spotted in the dim stage.]

AMANDA. Ida Scott? This is Amanda Wingfield! We *missed* you at the D. A. R. last Monday! I said to myself: She's probably suffering with that sinus condition! How is that sinus condition? Horrors! Heaven have mercy!—You're a Christian martyr, yes, that's what you are, a Christian martyr! Well, I just now happened to notice that your subscription to the *Companion's* about to expire! Yes, it expires with the next issue, honey!—just when that wonderful new serial by Bessie Mae Hopper is getting off to such an exciting start. Oh, honey, it's something that you can't miss! You remember how *Gone With the Wind* took everybody by storm? You simply couldn't go out if you hadn't read it. All everybody *talked* was Scarlett O'Hara. Well, this is a book that critics already compare to *Gone With the Wind.* It's the *Gone With the Wind* of the post-World War generation!—What?—Burning?—Oh, honey, don't let them burn, go take a look in the oven and I'll hold the wire! Heavens—I think she's hung up!

[Dim out.]

[Legend on screen: "You think I'm in love with Continental Shoemakers?"]

[Before the stage is lighted, the violent voices of Tom and Amanda are heard.]

[They are quarreling behind the portieres. In front of them stands Laura with clenched hands and panicky expression.]

[A clear pool of light on her figure throughout this scene.]

TOM. What in Christ's name am I—
AMANDA. *[Shrilly.]* Don't you use that—
TOM. Supposed to do!
AMANDA. Expression! Not in my—
TOM. Ohhh!
AMANDA. Presence! Have you gone out of your senses?
TOM. I have, that's true, *driven* out!
AMANDA. What is the matter with you, you—big—big—IDIOT!
TOM. Look—I've got *no thing,* no single thing—
AMANDA. Lower your voice!
TOM. In my life here that I can call my own! Everything is—
AMANDA. Stop that shouting!
TOM. Yesterday you confiscated my books! You had the nerve to—
AMANDA. I took that horrible novel back to the library—yes! That hideous book by that insane Mr. Lawrence. *[Tom laughs wildly.]* I cannot control the output of diseased minds or people who cater to them—*[Tom laughs still more wildly.]* BUT I WON'T ALLOW SUCH FILTH BROUGHT INTO MY HOUSE! No, no, no, no, no!

TOM. House, house! Who pays rent on it, who makes a slave of himself to—

AMANDA. *[Fairly screeching.]* Don't you DARE to—

TOM. No, no, *I* mustn't say things! *I've* got to just—

AMANDA. Let me tell you—

TOM. I don't want to hear any more! *[He tears the portieres open. The upstage area is lit with a turgid smoky red glow.]*

[Amanda's hair is in metal curlers and she wears a very old bathrobe, much too large for her slight figure, a relic of the faithless Mr. Wingfield.]

[An upright typewriter and a wild disarray of manuscripts is on the drop-leaf table. The quarrel was probably precipitated by Amanda's interruption of his creative labor. A chair lying over-thrown on the floor.]

[Their gesticulating shadows are cast on the ceiling by the fiery glow.]

AMANDA. You *will* hear more, you—

TOM. No, I won't hear more, I'm going out!

AMANDA. You come right back in—

TOM. Out, out out! Because I'm—

AMANDA. Come back here, Tom Wingfield! I'm not through talking to you!

TOM. Oh, go—

LAURA. *[Desperately.]*—Tom!

AMANDA. You're going to listen, and no more insolence from you! I'm at the end of my patience! *[He comes back toward her.]*

TOM. What do you think I'm at? Aren't I supposed to have any patience to reach the end of, Mother? I know, I know. It seems important to you, what I'm *doing*—what I *want* to do—having a little *difference* between them! You don't think that—

AMANDA. I think you've been doing things that you're ashamed of. That's why you act like this. I don't believe that you go every night to the movies. Nobody goes to the movies night after night. Nobody in their right minds goes to the movies as often as you pretend to. People don't go to the movies at nearly midnight, and movies don't let out at two A.M. Come in stumbling. Muttering to yourself like a maniac! You get three hours sleep and then go to work. Oh, I can picture the way you're doing down there. Moping, doping, because you're in no condition.

TOM. *[Wildly.]* No, I'm in no condition!

AMANDA. What right have you got to jeopardize your job? Jeopardize the security of us all? How do you think we'd manage if you were—

TOM. Listen! You think I'm crazy *about* the *warehouse*? *[He bends fiercely toward her slight figure.]* You think I'm in love with the Continental Shoemakers? You think I want to spend fifty-five *years* down there in that—*celotex interior!* with—*fluorescent—tubes!* Look! I'd rather somebody picked up a crowbar and battered out my brains—than go back mornings! I *go!* Every time you come in yelling that God damn "*Rise and Shine!*" "*Rise and Shine!*" I say to myself, "How *lucky dead* people are!" But I get up. I *go!* For sixty-five dollars a month I give up all that I dream of doing and being *ever!* And you say self—*self's* all I ever think of. Why, listen, if self is what I thought of, Mother, I'd be where he is—GONE! *[Pointing to father's picture.]* As far as the system of transportation reaches! *[He starts past her. She grabs his arm.]* Don't grab at me, Mother!

AMANDA. Where are you going?

TOM. I'm going to the *movies!*

AMANDA. I don't believe that lie!

TOM. *[Crouching toward her, overtowering her tiny figure. She backs away, gasping.]* I'm going to opium dens! Yes, opium dens, dens of vice and criminals' hangouts, Mother. I've joined the Hogan gang, I'm a hired assassin, I carry a tommy-gun in a violin case! I run a string of cat-houses in the Valley! They call me Killer, Killer Wingfield, I'm leading a double-life, a simple, honest warehouse worker by day, by night, a dynamic *czar* of the *underworld, Mother.* I go to gambling casinos, I spin away fortunes on the roulette table! I wear a patch over one eye and false mustache, sometimes I put on green whiskers. On those occasions they call me—*El Diablo!* Oh, I could tell you things to make you sleepless! My enemies plan to dynamite this place. They're going to blow us all sky-high some night! I'll be glad, very happy, and so will you! You'll go up, up on a broomstick, over Blue Mountain with seventeen gentlemen callers! You ugly—babbling old—*witch.* . . . *[He goes through a series of violent, clumsy movements, seizing his overcoat, lunging to the door, pulling it fiercely open. The women watch him, aghast. His arm catches in the sleeve of the coat as he struggles to pull it on. For a moment he is pinioned by the bulky garment. With an outraged groan he tears the coat off again, splitting the shoulder of it, and hurls it across the room. It strikes against the shelf of Laura's glass collection, there is a tinkle of shattering glass. Laura cries out as if wounded.]*

[Music legend: "The Glass Menagerie."]

LAURA. *[Shrilly.]* **My glass!**—menagerie. . . . *[She covers her face and turns away. But Amanda is still stunned and stupefied by the "ugly witch" so that she barely notices this occurrence. Now she recovers her speech.]*

AMANDA. *[In an awful voice.]* I won't speak to you— until you apologize! *[She crosses through portieres and draws them together behind her. Tom is left with Laura. Laura clings weakly to the mantel with her face averted. Tom stares at her stupidly for a moment. Then he crosses to shelf. Drops awkwardly to his knees to collect the fallen glass, glancing at Laura as if he would speak but couldn't.]*

["The Glass Menagerie" steals in as the scene dims out.]

SCENE IV

The interior is dark. Faint light in the alley.

A deep-voiced bell in a church is tolling the hour of five as the scene commences.

Tom appears at the top of the alley. After each solemn boom of the bell in the tower he shakes a little noise-maker or rattle as if to express the tiny spasm of man in contrast to the sustained power and dignity of the Almighty. This and the unsteadiness of his advance make it evident that he has been drinking.

As he climbs the few steps to the fire-escape landing light steals up inside. Laura appears in night-dress, observing Tom's empty bed in the front room.

Tom fishes in his pockets for the door-key, re-moving a motley assortment of articles in the search, including a perfect shower of movie-ticket stubs and an empty bottle. At last he finds the key, but just as he is about to insert it, it slips from his fingers. He strikes a match and crouches below the door.

TOM. *[Bitterly.]* One crack—and it falls through!

[Laura opens the door.]

LAURA. Tom! Tom, what are you doing?

TOM. Looking for a door-key.

LAURA. Where have you been all this time?

TOM. I have been to the movies.

LAURA. All this time at the movies?

TOM. There was a very long program. There was a Garbo picture and a Mickey Mouse and a travelogue and a newsreel and a preview of coming attractions. And there was an organ solo and a collection for the milk-fund— simultaneously—which ended up in a terrible fight between a fat lady and an usher!

LAURA. *[Innocently.]* Did you have to stay through everything?

TOM. Of course! And, oh, I forgot! There was a big stage show! The headliner on this stage show was Malvolio the Magician. He performed wonderful tricks, many of them, such as pouring water back and forth between pitchers. First it turned to wine and then it turned to beer and then it turned to whiskey. I know it was whiskey it finally turned into because he needed somebody to come up out of the audience to help him, and I came up—both shows! It was Kentucky Straight Bourbon. A very generous fellow, he gave souvenirs. *[He pulls from his back pocket a shimmering rainbow-colored scarf.]* He gave me this. This is his magic scarf. You can have it, Laura. You wave it over a canary cage and you get a bowl of gold-fish. You wave it over the gold-fish bowl and they fly away canaries. . . . But the wonderfullest trick of all was the coffin trick. We nailed him into a coffin and he got out of the coffin without removing one nail. *[He has come inside.]* There is a trick that would come in handy for me—get me out of this 2 by 4 situation! *[Flops onto bed and starts removing shoes.]*

LAURA. Tom—Shhh!

TOM. What are you shushing me for?

LAURA. You'll wake up Mother.

TOM. Goody, goody! Pay 'er back for all those "Rise an' Shines." *[Lies down, groaning.]* You know it don't take much intelligence to get yourself into a nailed-up coffin, Laura. But who in hell ever got himself out of one without removing one nail?

[As if in answer, the father's grinning photograph lights up.]

[Scene dims out.]

[Immediately following: The church bell is heard striking six. At the sixth stroke the alarm clock goes off in Amanda's room, and after a few moments we hear her calling: "Rise and Shine! Rise and Shine! Laura, go tell your brother to rise and shine!"]

TOM. *[Sitting up slowly.]* I'll rise—but I won't shine.

[The light increases.]

AMANDA. Laura, tell your brother his coffee is ready.

[Laura slips into front room.]

LAURA. Tom! It's nearly seven. Don't make Mother nervous. *[He stares at her stupidly. Beseechingly.]* Tom, speak to Mother this morning. Make up with her, apologize, speak to her!

TOM. She won't to me. It's her that started not speaking.

LAURA. If you just say you're sorry she'll start speaking.

TOM. Her not speaking—is that such a tragedy?

LAURA. Please—please!

AMANDA. *[Calling from kitchenette.]* Laura, are you going to do what I asked you to do, or do I have to get dressed and go out myself?

LAURA. Going, going—soon as I get on my coat! *[She pulls on a shapeless felt hat with nervous, jerky movement, pleadingly glancing at Tom. Rushes awkwardly for coat. The coat is one of Amanda's, inaccurately made over, the sleeves too short for Laura.]* Butter and what else?

AMANDA. *[Entering upstage.]* Just butter. Tell them to charge it.

LAURA. Mother, they make such faces when I do that.

AMANDA. Stick and stones may break our bones, but the expression on Mr. Garfinkel's face won't harm us! Tell your brother his coffee is getting cold.

LAURA. *[At door.]* Do what I asked you, will you, will you, Tom?

[He looks sullenly away.]

AMANDA. Laura, go now or just don't go at all!

LAURA. *[Rushing out.]* Going—going! *[A second later she cries out. Tom springs up and crosses to the door. Amanda rushes anxiously in. Tom opens the door.]*

TOM. Laura?

LAURA. I'm all right. I slipped, but I'm all right.

AMANDA. *[Peering anxiously after her.]* If anyone breaks a leg on those fire-escape steps, the landlord ought to be sued for every cent he possesses! *[She shuts door. Remembers she isn't speaking and returns to other room.]*

[As Tom enters listlessly for his coffee, she turns her back to him and stands rigidly facing the window on the gloomy gray vault of the areaway. Its light on her face with its aged but childish features is cruelly sharp, satirical as a Daumier print.]

[Music under: "Ave Maria."]

[Tom glances sheepishly but sullenly at her averted figure and slumps at the table. The coffee is scalding hot; he sips it and gasps and spits it back in the cup. At his gasp, Amanda catches her breath and half turns. Then catches herself and turns back to window.]

[Tom blows on his coffee, glancing sidewise at his mother. She clears her throat. Tom clears his. He starts to rise. Sinks back down again, scratches his head, clears his throat again. Amanda coughs. Tom raises his cup in both hands to blow on it, his eyes staring over the rim of it at his mother for several moments. Then he slowly sets the cup down and awkwardly and hesitantly rises from the chair.]

TOM. *[Hoarsely.]* Mother. I—I apologize. Mother. *[Amanda draws a quick, shuddering breath. Her face works grotesquely. She breaks into childlike tears.]* I'm sorry for what I said, for everything that I said, I didn't mean it.

AMANDA. *[Sobbingly.]* My devotion has made me a witch and so I make myself hateful to my children!

TOM. *No, you don't.*

AMANDA. I worry so much, don't sleep, it makes me nervous!

TOM. *[Gently.]* I understand that.

AMANDA. I've had to put up a solitary battle all these years. But you're my right-hand bower! Don't fall down, don't fail!

TOM. *[Gently.]* I try, Mother.

AMANDA. *[With great enthusiasm.]* Try and you will SUCCEED! *[The notion makes her breathless.]* Why, you—you're just *full* of natural endowments! Both of my children—they're *unusual* children! Don't you think I know it? I'm so—*proud!* Happy and—feel I've—so much to be thankful for but—Promise me one thing, son!

TOM. What, Mother?

AMANDA. Promise, son, you'll—never be a drunkard!

TOM. [Turns to her grinning.] I will never be a drunkard, Mother.

AMANDA. That's what frightened me so, that you'd be drinking! Eat a bowl of Purina!

TOM. Just coffee, Mother.

AMANDA. Shredded wheat biscuit?

TOM. No. No, Mother, just coffee.

AMANDA. You can't put in a day's work on an empty stomach. You've got ten minutes—don't gulp! Drinking too-hot liquids makes cancer of the stomach. . . . Put cream in.

TOM. No, thank you.

AMANDA. To cool it.

TOM. No! No, thank you, I want it black.

AMANDA. I know, but it's not good for you. We have to do all that we can to build ourselves up. In these trying times we live in, all that we have to cling to is—each other. . . . That's why it's so important to—Tom, I—I sent out your sister so I could discuss something with you. If you hadn't spoken I would have spoken to you. [Sits down.]

TOM. [Gently.] What is it, Mother, that you want to discuss?

AMANDA. *Laura!*

[Tom puts his cup down slowly.]

[Legend on screen: "Laura."]

[Music: "The Glass Menagerie."]

TOM.—Oh.—Laura . . .

AMANDA. [Touching his sleeve.] You know how Laura is. So quiet but—still water runs deep! She notices things and I think she—broods about them. [Tom looks up.] A few days ago I came in and she was crying.

TOM. What about?

AMANDA. You.

TOM. Me?

AMANDA. She has an idea that you're not happy here.

TOM. What gave her that idea?

AMANDA. What gives her any idea? However, you do act strangely. I—I'm not criticizing, understand *that!* I know your ambitions do not lie in the warehouse, that like everybody in the whole wide world—you've had to—make sacrifices, but—Tom—Tom—life's not easy, it calls for—Spartan endurance! There's so many things in my heart that I cannot describe to you! I've never told you but I—*loved* your father. . . .

TOM. [Gently.] I know that, Mother.

AMANDA. And you—when I see you taking after his ways! Staying out late—and—well, you *had* been drinking the night you were in that—terrifying condition! Laura says that you hate the apartment and that you go out nights to get away from it! Is that true, Tom?

TOM. No. You say there's so much in your heart that you can't describe to me. That's true of me, too. There's so much in my heart that I can't describe to *you!* So let's respect each others'—

AMANDA. But, why—*why*, Tom—are you always so *restless?* Where do you go to, nights?

TOM. I—go to the movies.

AMANDA. Why do you go to the movies so much, Tom?

TOM. I go to the movies because—I like adventure. Adventure is something I don't have much of at work, so I go to the movies.

AMANDA. But, Tom, you go the movies *entirely* too *much!*

TOM. I like a lot of adventure.

[Amanda looks baffled, then hurt. As the familiar inquisition resumes he becomes hard and impatient again. Amanda slips back into her querulous attitude toward him.]

[Image on screen: Sailing vessel with Jolly Roger.]

AMANDA. Most young men find adventure in their careers.

TOM. Then most young men are not employed in a warehouse.

AMANDA. The world is full of young men employed in warehouses and offices and factories.

TOM. Do all of them find adventure in their careers?

AMANDA. They do or they do without it! Not everybody has a craze for adventure.

TOM. Man is by instinct a lover, hunter, a fighter, and none of those instincts are given much play at the warehouse!

AMANDA. Man is by instinct! Don't quote instinct to me! Instinct is something that people have got away from! It belongs to animals! Christian adults don't want it!

TOM. What do Christian adults want, then, Mother?

AMANDA. Superior things! Things of the mind and the spirit! Only animals have to satisfy instincts! Surely your aims are somewhat higher than theirs! Than monkeys—pigs—

TOM. I reckon they're not.

AMANDA. You're joking. However, that isn't what I wanted to discuss.

TOM. [Rising.] I haven't much time.

AMANDA. [Pushing his shoulders.] Sit down.

TOM. You want me to punch in red at the warehouse, Mother?

AMANDA. You have five minutes. I want to talk about Laura.

[Legend: "Plans and Provisions."]

TOM. All right! What about Laura?

AMANDA. We have to be making plans and provisions for her. She's older than you, two years, and nothing has happened. She just drifts along doing nothing. It frightens me terribly how she just drifts along.

TOM. I guess she's the type that people call home girls.

AMANDA. There's no such type, and if there is, it's a pity! That is unless the home is hers, with a husband!

TOM. What?

AMANDA. Oh, I can see the handwriting on the wall as plain as I see the nose in front of my face! It's terrifying! More and more you remind me of your father! He was out all hours without explanation—Then left! Good-bye! And me with a bag to hold. I saw that letter you got from the Merchant Marine. I know what you're dreaming of. I'm not standing here blindfolded. Very well, then. Then do it! But not till there's somebody to take your place.

TOM. What do you mean?

AMANDA. I mean that as soon as Laura has got somebody to take care of her, married, a home of her own, independent—why, then you'll be free to go wherever you please, on land, on sea, whichever way the wind blows you! But until that time you've got to look out for your sister. I don't say me because I'm old and don't

matter! I say your sister because she's young and dependent. I put her in business college—a dismal failure! Frightened her so it made her sick to her stomach. I took her over to the Young People's League at the church. Another fiasco. She spoke to nobody, nobody spoke to her. Now all she does is fool with those pieces of glass and play those worn-out records. What kind of a life is that for a girl to lead?

TOM. What can I do about it?

AMANDA. Overcome selfishness! Self, self, self is all that you ever think of! [Tom springs up and crosses to get his coat. It is ugly and bulky. He pulls on a cap with earmuffs.] Where is your muffler? Put your wool muffler on! [He snatches it angrily from the closet and tosses it around his neck and pulls both ends tight.] Tom! I haven't said what I had in mind to ask you.

TOM. I'm too late to—

AMANDA. [Catching his arm—very importunately. Then shyly.] Down at the warehouse, aren't there some—nice young men?

TOM. No!

AMANDA. There must be—some . . .

TOM. Mother—

[Gesture.]

AMANDA. Find out one that's clean-living—doesn't drink and—ask him out for sister!

TOM. What?

AMANDA. For sister! To meet! Get acquainted!

TOM. [Stamping to door.] Oh, my go-osh!

AMANDA. Will you? [He opens door. Imploringly.] Will you? [He starts down.] Will you? Will you, dear?

TOM. [Calling back.] Yes!

[Amanda closes the door hesitantly and with a troubled but faintly hopeful expression.]

[Screen image: Glamour magazine cover.]

[Spot Amanda at phone.]

AMANDA. Ella Cartwright? This is Amanda Wingfield! How are you, honey? How is that kidney condition? [Count five.] Horrors! [Count five.] You're a Christian martyr, yes, honey, that's what you are, a Christian martyr! Well, I just happened to notice in my little red book that your subscription to the Companion has just run out! I knew that you wouldn't want to miss out on the wonderful serial starting in this new issue. It's by Bessie Mae Hopper, the first thing she's written since *Honeymoon for Three.* Wasn't that a strange and interesting story? Well, this one is even lovelier, I believe. It has a sophisticated society background. It's all about the horsey set on Long Island!

[Fade out.]

SCENE V

[Legend on screen: "Annunciation." Fade with music.]

It is early dusk of a spring evening. Supper has just been finished in the Wingfield apartment. Amanda and Laura in light colored dresses are removing dishes from the table, in the upstage area, which is shadowy, their movements formalized almost as a dance or ritual, their moving forms as pale and silent as moths.

    Tom, in white shirt and trousers, rises from the table and crosses toward the fire-escape.

AMANDA. *[As he passes her.]* Son, will you do me a favor?

TOM. What?

AMANDA. Comb your hair! You look so pretty when your hair is combed! *[Tom slouches on sofa with evening paper. Enormous caption "Franco Triumphs."]* There is only one respect in which I would like you to emulate your father.

TOM. What respect is that?

AMANDA. The care he always took of his appearance. He never allowed himself to look untidy. *[He throws down the paper and crosses to fire-escape.]* Where are you going?

TOM. I'm going out to smoke.

AMANDA. You smoke too much. A pack a day at fifteen cents a pack. How much would that amount to in a month? Thirty times fifteen is how much, Tom? Figure it out and you will be astounded at what you could save. Enough to give you a night-school course in accounting at Washington U! Just think what a wonderful thing that would be for you, son!

[Tom is unmoved by the thought.]

TOM. I'd rather smoke. *[He steps out on landing, letting the screen door slam.]*

AMANDA. *[Sharply.]* I know! That's the tragedy of it. . . . *[Alone, she turns to look at her husband's picture.]*

[Dance music: "All the World Is Waiting for the Sunrise!"]

TOM. *[To the audience.]* Across the alley from us was the Paradise Dance Hall. On evenings in spring the windows and doors were open and the music came outdoors. Sometimes the lights were turned out except for a large glass sphere that hung from the ceiling. It would turn slowly about and filter the dusk with delicate rainbow colors. Then the orchestra played a waltz or a tango, something that had a slow and sensuous rhythm. Couples would come outside, to the relative privacy of the alley. You could see them kissing behind ash-pits and telephone poles. This was the compensation for lives that passed like mine, without any change or adventure. Adventure and change were imminent in this year. They were waiting around the corner for all these kids. Suspended in the mist over Berchtesgaden, caught in the folds of Chamberlain's umbrella—In Spain there was Guernica! But here there was only hot swing music and liquor, dance halls, bars, and movies, and sex that hung in the gloom like a chandelier and flooded the world with brief, deceptive rainbows. . . . All the world was waiting for bombardments!

[Amanda turns from the picture and comes outside.]

AMANDA. *[Sighing.]* A fire-escape landing's a poor excuse for a porch. *[She spreads a newspaper on a step and sits down, gracefully and demurely as if she were settling into a swing on a Mississippi veranda.]* What are you looking at?

TOM. The moon.

AMANDA. Is there a moon this evening?

TOM. It's rising over Garfinkel's Delicatessen.

AMANDA. So it is! A little silver slipper of a moon. Have you made a wish on it yet?

TOM. Um-hum.

AMANDA. What did you wish for?

TOM. That's a secret.

AMANDA. A secret, huh? Well, I won't tell mine either. I will be just as mysterious as you.

TOM. I bet I can guess what yours is.

AMANDA. Is my head so transparent?

TOM. You're not a sphinx.

AMANDA. No, I don't have secrets. I'll tell you what I wished for on the moon. Success and happiness for my precious children! I wish for that whenever there's a moon, and when there isn't a moon, I wish for it, too.

TOM. I thought perhaps you wished for a gentleman caller.

AMANDA. Why do you say that?

TOM. Don't you remember asking me to fetch one?

AMANDA. I remember suggesting that it would be nice for your sister if you brought home some nice young man from the warehouse. I think I've made that suggestion more than once.

TOM. Yes, you have made it repeatedly.

AMANDA. Well?

TOM. We are going to have one.

AMANDA. *What?*

TOM. A gentleman caller!

[The annunciation is celebrated with music.]

[Amanda rises.]

[Image on screen: Caller with bouquet.]

AMANDA. You mean you have asked some nice young man to come over?

TOM. Yep. I've asked him to dinner.

AMANDA. You really did?

TOM. I did!

AMANDA. You did, and did he—*accept?*

TOM. He did!

AMANDA. Well, well—well, well! That's—lovely!

TOM. I thought that you would be pleased.

AMANDA. It's definite, then?

TOM. Very definite.

AMANDA. Soon?

TOM. Very soon.

AMANDA. For heaven's sake, stop putting on and tell me some things, will you?

TOM. What things do you want me to tell you?

AMANDA. *Naturally* I would like to know when he's *coming!*

TOM. He's coming tomorrow.

AMANDA. *Tomorrow?*

TOM. Yep. Tomorrow.

AMANDA. But, Tom!

TOM. Yes, Mother?

AMANDA. Tomorrow gives me no time!

TOM. Time for what?

AMANDA. Preparations! Why didn't you phone me at once, as soon as you asked him, the minute that he accepted? Then, don't you see, I could have been getting ready!

TOM. You don't have to make any fuss.

AMANDA. Oh, Tom, Tom, Tom, of course I have to make a fuss! I want things nice, not sloppy! Not thrown together. I'll certainly have to do some fast thinking, won't I?

TOM. I don't see why you have to think at all.

AMANDA. You just don't know. We can't have a gentleman caller in a pigsty! All my wedding silver has to be polished, the monogrammed table linen ought to be laundered! The windows have to be washed and fresh curtains up. And how about clothes? We have to *wear* something, don't we?

TOM. Mother, this boy is no one to make a fuss over!

AMANDA. Do you realize he's the first young man we've introduced to your sister? It's terrible, dreadful, disgraceful that poor little sister has never received a single gentleman caller! Tom, come inside! *[She opens the screen door.]*

TOM. What for?

AMANDA. I want to ask you some things.

TOM. If you're going to make such a fuss, I'll call it off, I'll tell him not to come.

AMANDA. You certainly won't do anything of the kind. Nothing offends people worse than broken engagements. It simply means I'll have to work like a Turk! We won't be brilliant, but we'll pass inspection. Come on inside. *[Tom follows, groaning.]* Sit down.

TOM. Any particular place you would like me to sit?

AMANDA. Thank heavens I've got that new sofa! I'm also making payments on a floor lamp I'll have sent out! And put the chintz covers on, they'll brighten things up! Of course I'd hoped to have these walls re-papered. . . . What is the young man's name?

TOM. His name is O'Connor.

AMANDA. That, of course, means fish—tomorrow is Friday! I'll have that salmon loaf—with Durkee's dressing! What does he do? He works at the warehouse?

TOM. Of course! How else would I—

AMANDA. Tom, he—doesn't drink?

TOM. Why do you ask me that?

AMANDA. Your father *did!*

TOM. Don't get started on that!

AMANDA. He *does* drink, then?

TOM. Not that I know of!

AMANDA. Make sure, be certain! The last thing I want for my daughter's a boy who drinks!

TOM. Aren't you being a little premature? Mr. O'Connor has not yet appeared on the scene!

AMANDA. But will tomorrow. To meet your sister, and what do I know about his character? Nothing! Old maids are better off than wives of drunkards!

TOM. Oh, my God!

AMANDA. Be still!

TOM. [Leaning forward to whisper.] Lots of fellows meet girls whom they don't marry!

AMANDA. Oh, talk sensibly, Tom—and don't be sarcastic! [She has gotten a hairbrush.]

TOM. What are you doing?

AMANDA. I'm brushing that cowlick down! What is this young man's position at the warehouse?

TOM. [Submitting grimly to the brush and the interrogation.] This young man's position is that of a shipping clerk, Mother.

AMANDA. Sounds to me like a fairly responsible job, the sort of a job *you* would be in if you just had more *get-up.* What is his salary? Have you got any idea?

TOM. I would judge it to be approximately eighty-five dollars a month.

AMANDA. Well—not princely, but—

TOM. Twenty more than I make.

AMANDA. Yes, how well I know! But for a family man, eighty-five dollars a month is not much more than you can just get by on. . . .

TOM. Yes, but Mr. O'Connor is not a family man.

AMANDA. He might be, mightn't he? Some time in the future?

TOM. I see. Plans and provisions.

AMANDA. You are the only young man that I know of who ignores the fact that the future becomes the present, the present the past, and the past turns into everlasting regret if you don't plan for it!

TOM. I will think that over and see what I can make of it.

AMANDA. Don't be supercilious with your mother! Tell me some more about this—what do you call him?

TOM. James D. O'Connor. The D. is for Delaney.

AMANDA. Irish on *both* sides! *Gracious!* And doesn't drink?

TOM. Shall I call him up and ask him right this minute?

AMANDA. The only way to find out about those things is to make discreet inquiries at the proper moment. When I was a girl in Blue Mountain and it was suspected that a young man drank, the girl whose attentions he had been receiving, if any girl *was,* would sometimes speak to the minister of his church, or rather her father would if her father was living, and sort of feel him out on the young man's character. That is the way such things are discreetly handled to keep a young woman from making a tragic mistake!

TOM. Then how did you happen to make a tragic mistake?

AMANDA. That innocent look of your father's had everyone fooled! He *smiled*—the world was *enchanted!* No girl can do worse than put herself at the mercy of a handsome appearance! I hope that Mr. O'Connor is not too good-looking.

TOM. No, he's not too good-looking. He's covered with freckles and hasn't too much of a nose.

AMANDA. He's not right-down homely, though?

TOM. Not right-down homely. Just medium homely, I'd say.

AMANDA. Character's what to look for in a man.

TOM. That's what I've always said, Mother.

AMANDA. You've never said anything of the kind and I suspect you would never give it a thought.

TOM. Don't be suspicious of me.

AMANDA. At least I hope he's the type that's up and coming.

TOM. I think he really goes in for self-improvement.

AMANDA. What reason have you to think so?

TOM. He goes to night school.

AMANDA. [Beaming.] Splendid! What does he do, I mean study?

TOM. Radio engineering and public speaking!

AMANDA. Then he has visions of being advanced in the world! Any young man who studies public speaking is aiming to have an executive job some day! And radio engineering? A thing for the future! Both of these facts are very illuminating. Those are the sort of things that a mother should know concerning any young man who comes to call on her daughter. Seriously or—not.

TOM. One little warning. He doesn't know about Laura. I didn't let on that we had dark ulterior motives. I just said, why don't you come have dinner with us? He said okay and that was the whole conversation.

AMANDA. I bet it was! You're eloquent as an oyster. However, he'll know about Laura when he gets here. When he sees how lovely and sweet and pretty she is, he'll thank his lucky stars he was asked to dinner.

TOM. Mother, you mustn't expect too much of Laura.

AMANDA. What do you mean?

TOM. Laura seems all those things to you and me because she's ours and we love her. We don't even notice she's crippled any more.

AMANDA. Don't say crippled! You know that I never allow that word to be used!

TOM. But face facts, Mother. She is and—that's not all—

AMANDA. What do you mean "not all"?

TOM. Laura is very different from other girls.

AMANDA. I think the difference is all to her advantage.

TOM. Not quite all—in the eyes of others— strangers—she's terribly shy and lives in a world of her own and those things make her seem a little peculiar to people outside the house.

AMANDA. Don't say peculiar.

TOM. Face the facts. She is.

[The dance-hall music changes to a tango that has a minor and somewhat ominous tone.]

AMANDA. In what way is she peculiar—may I ask?

TOM. *[Gently.]* She lives in a world of her own—a world of—little glass ornaments, Mother. . . . *[Gets up. Amanda remains holding brush, looking at him, troubled.]* She plays old phonograph records and—that's about all—*[He glances at himself in the mirror and crosses to door.]*

AMANDA. *[Sharply.]* Where are you going?

TOM. I'm going to the movies. *[Out screen door.]*

AMANDA. Not to the movies, every night to the movies! *[Follows quickly to screen door.]* I don't believe you always go to the movies! *[He is gone. Amanda looks worriedly after him for a moment. Then vitality and optimism return and she turns from the door.*

Crossing to portieres.]* Laura! Laura! *[Laura answers from kitchenette.]*

LAURA. Yes, Mother.

AMANDA. Let those dishes go and come in front! *[Laura appears with dish towel. Gaily.]* Laura, come here and make a wish on the moon!

LAURA. *[Entering.]* Moon—moon?

AMANDA. A little silver slipper of a moon. Look over your left shoulder, Laura, and make a wish! *[Laura looks faintly puzzled as if called out of sleep. Amanda seizes her shoulders and turns her at an angle by the door.]* No! Now, darling, *wish!*

LAURA. What shall I wish for, Mother?

AMANDA. *[Her voice trembling and her eyes suddenly filling with tears.]* Happiness! Good Fortune!

[The violin rises and the stage dims out.]

SCENE VI

[Image: High school hero.]

TOM. And so the following evening I brought Jim home to dinner. I had known Jim slightly in high school. In high school Jim was a hero. He had tremendous Irish good nature and vitality with the scrubbed and polished look of white chinaware. He seemed to move in a continual spotlight. He was a star in basketball, captain of the debating club, president of the senior class and the glee club and he sang the male lead in the annual light operas. He was always running or bounding, never just walking. He seemed always at the point of defeating the law of gravity. He was shooting with such velocity through his adolescence that you would logically expect him to arrive at nothing short of the White House by the time he was thirty. But Jim apparently ran into more interference after his graduation from Soldan. His speed had definitely slowed. Six years after he left high school he was holding a job that wasn't much better than mine.

[Image: Clerk.]

He was the only one at the warehouse with whom I was on friendly terms. I was valuable to him as someone who could remember his former glory, who had seen him win basketball games and the silver cup in debating. He knew of my secret practice of retiring to a cabinet of the washroom to work on poems when business was slack in the warehouse. He called me Shakespeare. And while the other boys in the warehouse regarded me with suspicious hostility, Jim took a humorous attitude toward me. Gradually his attitude affected the others, their hostility wore off and they also began to smile at me as people smile at an oddly fashioned dog who trots across their path at some distance.

I knew that Jim and Laura had known each other at Soldan, and I had heard Laura speak admiringly of his voice. I didn't know if Jim remembered her or not. In high school Laura had been as unobtrusive as Jim had been astonishing. If he did remember Laura, it was not as my sister, for when I asked him to dinner, he grinned and said, "You know, Shakespeare, I never thought of you as having folks!"

He was about to discover that I did. . . .

[Light up stage.]

[Legend on screen: "The Accent of a Coming Foot."]

[Friday evening. It is about five o'clock of a late spring evening which comes "scattering poems in the sky."]

[A delicate lemony light is in the Wingfield apartment.]

[Amanda has worked like a Turk in preparation for the gentleman caller. The results are astonishing. The new floor lamp with its rose-silk shade is in place, a colored paper lantern conceals the broken light fixture in the ceiling, new billowing white curtains are at the windows, chintz covers are on chairs and sofa, a pair of new sofa pillows make their initial appearance.]

[Open boxes and tissue paper are scattered on the floor.]

[Laura stands in the middle with lifted arms while Amanda crouches before her, adjusting the hem of the new dress, devout and ritualistic. The dress is colored and designed by memory. The arrangement of Laura's hair is changed; it is softer and more becoming. A fragile, unearthly prettiness has come out in Laura; she is like a piece of translucent glass touched by light, given a momentary radiance, not actual, not lasting.]

AMANDA. *[Impatiently.]* Why are you trembling?

LAURA. Mother, you've made me so nervous!

AMANDA. How have I made you nervous?

LAURA. By all this fuss! You make it seem so important!

AMANDA. I don't understand you, Laura. You couldn't be satisfied with just sitting home, and yet whenever I try to arrange something for you, you seem to resist it. *[She gets up.]* Now take a look at yourself. No, wait! Wait just a moment—I have an idea!

LAURA. What is it now?

[Amanda produces two powder puffs which she wraps in handkerchiefs and stuffs in Laura's bosom.]

LAURA. Mother, what are you doing?

AMANDA. They call them "Gay Deceivers"!

LAURA. I won't wear them!

AMANDA. You will!

LAURA. Why should I?

AMANDA. Because, to be painfully honest, your chest is flat.

LAURA. You make it seem like we were setting a trap.

AMANDA. All pretty girls are a trap, a pretty trap, and men expect them to be. *[Legend: "A Pretty Trap."]* Now look at yourself, young lady. This is the prettiest you will ever be! I've got to fix myself now! You're going to be surprised by your mother's appearance! *[She crosses through portieres, humming gaily.]*

[Laura moves slowly to the long mirror and stares solemnly at herself.]

[A wind blows the white curtains inward in a slow, graceful motion and with a faint, sorrowful sighing.]

AMANDA. *[Offstage.]* It isn't dark enough yet. *[She turns slowly before the mirror with a troubled look.]*

[Legend on screens: "This Is My Sister: Celebrate Her with Strings!" Music.]

AMANDA. *[Laughing, off.]* I'm going to show you something. I'm going to make a spectacular appearance!

LAURA. What is it, Mother?

AMANDA. Possess your soul in patience—you will see! Something I've resurrected from that old trunk! Styles haven't changed so terribly much after all. . . . *[She parts the portieres.]* Now just look at your mother! *[She wears a girlish frock of yellowed voile with a blue silk sash. She carries a bunch of jonquils—the legend of her youth is nearly revived. Feverishly.]* This is the dress in which I led the cotillion. Won the cakewalk twice at Sunset Hill, wore one spring to the Governor's ball in Jackson! See how I sashayed around the ballroom, Laura? *[She raises her skirt and does a mincing step around the room.]* I wore it on Sundays for my gentlemen callers! I had it on the day I met your father—I had malaria fever all that spring. The change of climate from East Tennessee to the Delta—weakened resistance— I had a little temperature all the time—not enough to be serious—just enough to make me restless and giddy! Invitations poured in— parties all over the Delta!—"Stay in bed," said Mother, "you have fever!"—but I just wouldn't.—I took quinine but kept on going, going!—Evenings, dances!—Afternoons, long, long rides! Picnics—lovely!—So lovely, that country in May.—All lacy with dogwood, literally flooded with jonquils!—That was the spring I had the craze for jonquils. Jonquils became an absolute obsession. Mother said, "Honey, there's no more room for jonquils." And still I kept on bringing in more jonquils. Whenever, wherever I saw them, I'd say, "Stop! Stop! I see jonquils!" I made the young men help me gather the jonquils! It was a joke, Amanda and her jonquils! Finally there were no more vases to hold them, every available space was filled with jonquils. No vases to hold them? All right, I'll hold them myself! And then I— *[She stops in front of the picture. Music.]* met your father! Malaria fever and jonquils and then— this—boy. . . . *[She switches on the rose-colored lamp.]* I hope they get here before it starts to rain. *[She crosses upstage and places the jonquils in bowl on table.]* I gave your brother a little extra change so he and Mr. O'Connor could take the service car home.

LAURA. *[With altered look.]* What did you say his name was?

AMANDA. O'Connor.

LAURA. What is his first name?

AMANDA. I don't remember. Oh, yes, I do. It was— Jim!

[Laura sways slightly and catches hold of a chair.]

[Legend on screen: "Not Jim!"]

LAURA. *[Faintly.]* Not—Jim!

AMANDA. Yes, that was it, it was Jim! I've never known a Jim that wasn't nice!

[Music: Ominous.]

LAURA. Are you sure his name is Jim O'Connor?

AMANDA. Yes. Why?

LAURA. Is he the one that Tom used to know in high school?

AMANDA. He didn't say so. I think he just got to know him at the warehouse.

LAURA. There was a Jim O'Connor we both knew in high school—*[Then, with effort.]* If that is the one that Tom is bringing to dinner—you'll have to excuse me, I won't come to the table.

AMANDA. What sort of nonsense is this?

LAURA. You asked me once if I'd ever liked a boy. Don't you remember I showed you this boy's picture?

AMANDA. You mean the boy you showed me in the yearbook?

LAURA. Yes, that boy.

AMANDA. Laura, Laura, were you in love with that boy?

LAURA. I don't know, Mother. All I know is I couldn't sit at the table if it was him!

AMANDA. It won't be him! It isn't the least bit likely. But whether it is or not, you will come to the table. You will not be excused.

LAURA. I'll have to be, Mother.

AMANDA. I don't intend to humor your silliness, Laura. I've had too much from you and your brother, both! So just sit down and compose yourself till they come. Tom has forgotten his key so you'll have to let them in, when they arrive.

LAURA. *[Panicky.]* Oh, Mother—*you* answer the door!

AMANDA. *[Lightly.]* I'll be in the kitchen—busy!

LAURA. Oh, Mother, please answer the door, don't make me do it!

AMANDA. *[Crossing into kitchenette.]* I've got to fix the dressing for the salmon. Fuss, fuss—silliness!— over a gentleman caller!

[Door swings shut. Laura is left alone.]

[Legend: "Terror!"]

[She utters a low moan and turns off the lamp—sits stiffly on the edge of the sofa, knotting her fingers together.]

[Legend on screen: "The Opening of a Door!"]

[Tom and Jim appear on the fire-escape steps and climb to landing. Hearing their approach, Laura rises with a panicky gesture. She retreats to the portieres.]

[The doorbell. Laura catches her breath and touches her throat. Low drums.]

AMANDA. *[Calling.]* Laura, sweetheart! The door!

[Laura stares at it without moving.]

JIM. I think we just beat the rain.

TOM. Uh-huh. *[He rings again, nervously. Jim whistles and fishes for a cigarette.]*

AMANDA. *[Very, very gaily.]* Laura, that is your brother and Mr. O'Connor! Will you let them in, darling?

[Laura crosses toward kitchenette door.]

LAURA. *[Breathlessly.]* Mother—you go to the door!

[Amanda steps out of kitchenette and stares furiously at Laura. She points imperiously at the door.]

LAURA. Please, please!

AMANDA. *[In a fierce whisper.]* What is the matter with you, you silly thing?

LAURA. *[Desperately.]* Please, you answer it, *please!*

AMANDA. I told you I wasn't going to humor you, Laura. Why have you chosen this moment to lose your mind?

LAURA. Please, please, please, you go!

AMANDA. You'll have to go to the door because I can't!

LAURA. *[Despairingly.]* I can't either!

AMANDA. *Why?*

LAURA. *I'm sick!*

AMANDA. I'm sick, too—of your nonsense! Why can't you and your brother be normal people? Fantastic whims and behavior! *[Tom gives a long ring.]* Preposterous goings on! Can you give me one reason—*[Calls out lyrically.]* *Coming! Just one second!*—why should you be afraid to open a door? Now you answer it, Laura!

LAURA. Oh, oh, oh . . . *[She returns through the portieres. Darts to the victrola and winds it frantically and turns it on.]*

AMANDA. Laura Wingfield, you march right to that door!

LAURA. Yes—yes, Mother!

[A faraway, scratchy rendition of "Dardanella" softens the air and gives her strength to move through it. She slips to the door and draws it cautiously open.]

[Tom enters with the caller, Jim O'Connor.]

TOM. Laura, this is Jim. Jim, this is my sister, Laura.

JIM. *[Stepping inside.]* I didn't know that Shakespeare had a sister!

LAURA. *[Retreating stiff and trembling from the door.]* How—how do you do?

JIM. *[Heartily extending his hands.]* Okay!

[Laura touches it hesitantly with hers.]

JIM. Your hand's *cold,* Laura!

LAURA. Yes, well—I've been playing the victrola. . . .

JIM. Must have been playing classical music on it! You ought to play a little hot swing music to warm you up!

LAURA. Excuse me—I haven't finished playing the victrola. . . .

[She turns awkwardly and hurries into the front room. She pauses a second by the victrola. Then catches her breath and darts through the portieres like a frightened deer.]

JIM. *[Grinning.]* What was the matter?

TOM. Oh—with Laura? Laura is—terribly shy.

JIM. Shy, huh? It's unusual to meet a shy girl nowadays. I don't believe you ever mentioned you had a sister.

TOM. Well, now you know. I have one. Here is the *Post Dispatch.* You want a piece of it?

JIM. Uh-huh.

TOM. What piece? The comics?

JIM. Sports! *[Glances at it.]* Ole Dizzy Dean is on his bad behavior.

TOM. *[Disinterest.]* Yeah? *[Lights cigarette and crosses back to fire-escape door.]*

JIM. Where are *you* going?

TOM. I'm going out on the terrace.

JIM. *[Goes after him.]* You know, Shakespeare— I'm going to sell you a bill of goods!

TOM. What goods?

JIM. A course I'm taking.

TOM. Huh?

JIM. In public speaking! You and me, we're not the warehouse type.

TOM. Thanks—that's good news. But what has public speaking got to do with it?

JIM. It fits you for—executive positions!

TOM. Awww.

JIM. I tell you it's done a helluva lot for me.

[Image: Executive at desk.]

TOM. In what respect?

JIM. In every! Ask yourself what is the difference between you an' me and men in the office down front? Brains?—No!—Ability?—No! Then what? Just one little thing—

TOM. What is that one little thing—

JIM. Primarily it amounts to—social poise! Being able to square up to people and hold your own on any social level!

AMANDA. *[Offstage.]* Tom?

TOM. Yes, Mother?

AMANDA. Is that you and Mr. O'Connor?

TOM. Yes, Mother.

AMANDA. Well, you just make yourselves comfortable in there.

TOM. Yes, Mother.

AMANDA. Ask Mr. O'Connor if he would like to wash his hands.

JIM. Aw, no—no—thank you—I took care of that at the warehouse. Tom—

TOM. Yes?

JIM. Mr. Mendoza was speaking to me about you.

TOM. Favorably?

JIM. What do you think?

TOM. Well—

JIM. You're going to be out of a job if you don't wake up.

TOM. I am waking up—

JIM. You show no signs.

TOM. The signs are interior.

[Image on screen: The sailing vessel with Jolly Roger again.]

TOM. I'm planning to change. *[He leans over the rail speaking with quiet exhilaration. The incandescent marquees and signs of the first-run movie houses light his face from across the alley. He looks like a voyager.]* I'm right at the point of committing myself to a future that doesn't include the warehouse and Mr. Mendoza or even a night-school course in public speaking.

JIM. What are you gassing about?

TOM. I'm tired of the movies.

JIM. Movies!

TOM. Yes, movies! Look at them—*[A wave toward the marvels of Grand Avenue.]* All of those glamorous people—having adventures—hogging it all, gobbling the whole thing up! You know what happens? People go to the *movies* instead of *moving!* Hollywood characters are supposed to have all the adventures for everybody in America, while everybody in America sits in a dark room and watches them have them! Yes, until there's a war. That's when adventure becomes available to the masses! *Everyone's* dish, not only Gable's! Then the people in the dark room come out of the dark room to have some adventures themselves—Goody, goody!— It's our turn now, to go to the South Sea Island—to make a safari—to be exotic, far-off?—But I'm not patient. I don't want to wait till then. I'm tired of the *movies* and I am *about* to *move!*

JIM. *[Incredulously.]* Move?

TOM. Yes.

JIM. When?

TOM. Soon!

JIM. Where? Where?

[Theme Three music seems to answer the question, while Tom thinks it over. He searches among his pockets.]

TOM. I'm starting to boil inside. I know I seem dreamy, but inside—well, I'm boiling! Whenever I pick up a shoe, I shudder a little thinking how short life is and what I am doing!—Whatever that means. I know it doesn't mean shoes—except as something to wear on a traveler's feet! *[Finds paper.]* Look—

JIM. What?

TOM. I'm a member.

JIM. *[Reading.]* The Union of Merchant Seamen.

TOM. I paid my dues this month, instead of the light bill.

JIM. You will regret it when they turn the lights off.

TOM. I won't be here.

JIM. How about your mother?

TOM. I'm like my father. The bastard son of a bastard! See how he grins? And he's been absent going on sixteen years!

JIM. You're just talking, you drip. How does your mother feel about it?

TOM. Shhh!—Here comes Mother! Mother is not acquainted with my plans!

AMANDA. *[Enters portieres.]* Where are you all?

TOM. On the terrace, Mother.

[They start inside. She advances to them. Tom is distinctly shocked at her appearance. Even Jim blinks a little. He is making his first contact with girlish Southern vivacity and in spite of the night-school course in public speaking is somewhat thrown off the beam by the unexpected outlay of social charm.]

[Certain responses are attempted by Jim but are swept aside by Amanda's gay laughter and chatter. Tom is embarrassed but after the first shock Jim reacts very warmly. Grins and chuckles, is altogether won over.]

[Image: Amanda as a girl.]

AMANDA. *[Coyly smiling, shaking her girlish ringlets.]* Well, well, well, so this is Mr. O'Connor. Introductions entirely unnecessary. I've heard so much about you from my boy. I finally said to him, Tom—good gracious!—why don't you bring this paragon to supper? I'd like to meet this nice young man at the warehouse!—Instead of just hearing him sing your praises so much! I don't know why my son is so stand-offish—that's not Southern behavior! Let's sit down and—I think we could stand a little more air in here! Tom, leave the door open. I felt a nice fresh breeze a moment ago. Where has it gone to? Mmm, so warm already? And not quite summer, even. We're going to burn up when summer really gets started. However, we're having—we're having a very light supper. I think light things are better fo' this time of year. The same as light clothes are. Light clothes an' light food are what warm weather calls fo'. You know our blood gets so thick during th' winter—it takes a while fo' us to *adjust* ou'selves!—when the season changes . . . It's come so quick this year. I wasn't prepared. All of a sudden—heavens! Already summer!—I ran to the trunk an' pulled out this light dress—Terribly old! Historical almost! But feels so good—so good an' co-ol, y'know. . . .

TOM. Mother—

AMANDA. Yes, honey?

TOM. How about—supper?

AMANDA. Honey, you go ask Sister if supper is ready! You know that Sister is in full charge of supper! Tell her you hungry boys are waiting for it. *[To Jim.]* Have you met Laura?

JIM. She—

AMANDA. Let you in? Oh, good, you've met already! It's rare for a girl as sweet an' pretty as Laura to be domestic! But Laura is, thank heavens, not only pretty but also very domestic. I'm not at all. I never was a bit. I never could make a thing but angel-food cake. Well, in the South we had so many servants. Gone, gone, gone. All vestige of gracious living! Gone completely! I wasn't prepared for what the future brought me. All of my gentlemen callers were sons of planters and so of course I assumed that I would be married to one and raise my family on a large piece of land with plenty of servants. But man proposes—and woman accepts the proposal!—To vary that old, old saying a little bit—I married no planter! I married a man who worked for the telephone company!—That gallantly smiling gentleman over there! *[Points to the picture.]* A telephone man who—fell in love with long-distance!—Now he travels and I don't even know where!—But what am I going on for about my—tribulations? Tell me yours—I hope you don't have any! Tom?

TOM. *[Returning.]* Yes, Mother?

AMANDA. Is supper nearly ready?

TOM. It looks to me like supper is on the table.

AMANDA. Let me look—*[She rises prettily and looks through portieres.]* Oh, lovely!—But where is Sister?

TOM. Laura is not feeling well and she says that she thinks she'd better not come to the table.

AMANDA. What?—Nonsense!—Laura? Oh, Laura!

LAURA. *[Offstage, faintly.]* Yes, Mother.

AMANDA. You really must come to the table. We won't be seated until you come to the table! Come in, Mr. O'Connor. You sit over there, and I'll—Laura? Laura Wingfield! You're keeping us waiting, honey! We can't say grace until you come to the table!

[The back door is pushed weakly open and Laura comes in. She is obviously quite faint, her lips trembling, her eyes wide and staring. She moves unsteadily toward the table.]

[Legend: "Terror!"]

[Outside a summer storm is coming abruptly. The white curtains billow inward at the windows and there is a sorrowful murmur and deep blue dusk.]

[Laura suddenly stumbles—she catches at a chair with a faint moan.]

TOM. Laura!

AMANDA. Laura! *[There is a clap of thunder. Legend "Ah!" Despairingly.]* Why, Laura, you *are* sick, darling! Tom, help your sister into the living room, dear! Sit in the living room, Laura—rest on the sofa. Well! *[To the gentleman caller.]* Standing over the hot stove made her ill!—I told her that it was just too warm this evening, but—*[Tom comes back in. Laura is on the sofa.]* Is Laura all right now?

TOM. Yes.

AMANDA. What *is* that? Rain? A nice cool rain has come up! *[She gives the gentleman caller a frightened look.]* I think we may—have grace— now . . . *[Tom looks at her stupidly.]* Tom, honey—you say grace!

TOM. Oh . . . "For these and all thy mercies—" *[They bow their heads, Amanda stealing a nervous glance at Jim. In the living room Laura, stretched on the sofa, clenches her hand to her lips, to hold back a shuddering sob.]* God's Holy Name be praised—

[The scene dims out.]

SCENE VII

[A Souvenir.]

Half an hour later. Dinner is just being finished in the upstage area which is concealed by the drawn portieres.

As the curtain rises Laura is still huddled upon the sofa, her feet drawn under her, her head resting on a pale blue pillow, her eyes wide and mysteriously watchful. The new floor lamp with its shade of rose-colored silk gives a soft, becoming light to her face, bringing out the fragile, unearthly prettiness which usually escapes attention. There is a steady murmur of rain, but it is slackening and stops soon after the scene begins; the air outside becomes pale and luminous as the moon breaks out.

A moment after the curtain rises, the lights in both rooms flicker and go out.

JIM. Hey, there, Mr. Light Bulb!

[Amanda laughs nervously.]

[Legend: "Suspension of a public service."]

AMANDA. Where was Moses when the lights went out? Ha-ha. Do you know the answer to that one, Mr. O'Connor?

JIM. No, Ma'am, what's the answer?

AMANDA. In the dark! *[Jim laughs appreciably.]* Everybody sit still. I'll light the candles. Isn't it lucky we have them on the table? Where's a match? Which of you gentlemen can provide a match?

JIM. Here.

AMANDA. Thank you, sir.

JIM. Not at all, Ma'am!

AMANDA. I guess the fuse has burnt out. Mr. O'Connor, can you tell a burnt-out fuse? I know I can't and Tom is a total loss when it comes to mechanics. *[Sound: Getting up; voices recede a little to kitchenette.]* Oh, be careful you don't bump into something. We don't want our gentleman caller to break his neck. Now wouldn't that be a fine howdy-do?

JIM. Ha-ha! Where is the fuse-box?

AMANDA. Right here next to the stove. Can you see anything?

JIM. Just a minute.

AMANDA. Isn't electricity a mysterious thing? Wasn't it Benjamin Franklin who tied a key to a kite? We live in such a mysterious universe, don't we? Some people say that science clears up all the mysteries for us. In my opinion it only creates more! Have you found it yet?

JIM. No, Ma'am. All these fuses look okay to me.

AMANDA. Tom!

TOM. Yes, Mother?

AMANDA. That light bill I gave you several days ago. The one I told you we got the notices about?

TOM. Oh.—Yeah.

[Legend: "Ha!"]

AMANDA. You didn't neglect to pay it by any chance?

TOM. Why, I—

AMANDA. Didn't! I might have known it!

JIM. Shakespeare probably wrote a poem on that light bill, Mrs. Wingfield.

AMANDA. I might have known better than to trust him with it! There's such a high price for negligence in this world!

JIM. Maybe the poem will win a ten-dollar prize.

AMANDA. We'll just have to spend the remainder of the evening in the nineteenth century, before Mr. Edison made the Mazda lamp!

JIM. Candlelight is my favorite kind of light.

AMANDA. That shows you're romantic! But that's no excuse for Tom. Well, we got through dinner. Very considerate of them to let us get through dinner before they plunged us into everlasting darkness, wasn't it, Mr. O'Connor?

JIM. Ha-ha!

AMANDA. Tom, as a penalty for your carelessness you can help me with the dishes.

JIM. Let me give you a hand.

AMANDA. Indeed you will not!

JIM. I ought to be good for something.

AMANDA. Good for something? *[Her tone is rhapsodic.]* *You?* Why, Mr. O'Connor, nobody, *nobody's* given me this much entertainment in years—as you have!

JIM. Aw, now, Mrs. Wingfield!

AMANDA. I'm not exaggerating, not one bit! But Sister is all by her lonesome. You go keep her company in the parlor! I'll give you this lovely old candelabrum that used to be on the altar at the church of the Heavenly Rest. It was melted a little out of shape when the church burnt down. Lightning struck it one spring. Gypsy Jones was holding a revival at the time and he intimated that the church was destroyed because the Episcopalians gave card parties.

JIM. Ha-ha.

AMANDA. And how about coaxing Sister to drink a little wine? I think it would be good for her! Can you carry both at once?

JIM. Sure. I'm Superman!

AMANDA. Now, Thomas, get into this apron!

[The door of kitchenette swings closed on Amanda's gay laughter; the flickering light approaches the portieres.]

[Laura sits up nervously as he enters. Her speech at first is low and breathless from the almost intolerable strain of being alone with a stranger.]

[The legend: "I don't suppose you remember me at all!"]

[In her first speeches in this scene, before Jim's warmth overcomes her paralyzing shyness, Laura's voice is thin and breathless as though she has just run up a steep flight of stairs.]

[Jim's attitude is gently humorous. In playing this scene it should be stressed that while the incident is apparently unimportant, it is to Laura the climax of her secret life.]

JIM. Hello, there, Laura.

LAURA. *[Faintly.]* Hello. *[She clears her throat.]*

JIM. How are you feeling now? Better?

LAURA. Yes. Yes, thank you.

JIM. This is for you. A little dandelion wine. *[He extends it toward her with extravagant gallantry.]*

LAURA. Thank you.

JIM. Drink it—but don't get drunk! *[He laughs heartily. Laura takes the glass uncertainly; laughs shyly.]* Where shall I set the candles?

LAURA. Oh—oh, anywhere . . .

JIM. How about here on the floor? Any objections?

LAURA. No.

JIM. I'll spread a newspaper under to catch the drippings. I like to sit on the floor. Mind if I do?

LAURA. Oh, no.

JIM. Give me a pillow?

LAURA. What?

JIM. A pillow!

LAURA. Oh . . . *[Hands him one quickly.]*

JIM. How about you? Don't you like to sit on the floor?

LAURA. Oh—yes.

JIM. Why don't you, then?

LAURA. I—will.

JIM. Take a pillow. *[Laura does. Sits on the other side of the candelabrum. Jim crosses his legs and smiles engagingly at her.]* I can't hardly see you sitting way over there.

LAURA. I can—see you.

JIM. I know, but that's not fair, I'm in the limelight. *[Laura moves her pillow closer.]* Good! Now I can see you! Comfortable?

LAURA. Yes.

JIM. So am I. Comfortable as a cow. Will you have some gum?

LAURA. No, thank you.

JIM. I think that I will indulge, with your permission. *[Musingly unwraps it and holds it up.]*

Think of the fortune made by the guy that invented the first piece of chewing gum. Amazing, huh? The Wrigley Building is one of the sights of Chicago—saw it summer before last when I went up to the Century of Progress. Did you take in the Century of Progress?

LAURA. No, I didn't.

JIM. Well, it was quite a wonderful exposition. What impressed me the most was the Hall of Science. Gives you an idea of what the future will be in America, even more wonderful than the present time is! *[Pause. Smiling at her.]* Your brother tells me you're shy. Is that right, Laura?

LAURA. I—I don't know.

JIM. I judge you to be an old-fashioned type of girl. Well, I think that's a pretty good type to be. Hope you don't think I'm being too personal—do you?

LAURA. *[Hastily, out of embarrassment.]* I believe I *will* take a piece of gum, if you—don't mind. *[Clearing her throat.]* Mr. O'Connor, have you—kept up with your singing?

JIM. Singing? Me?

LAURA. Yes. I remember what a beautiful voice you had.

JIM. When did you hear me sing?

[Voice offstage in the pause.]

VOICE. *[Offstage.]*

> O blow, ye winds, heigh-ho,
> A-roving I will go!
> I'm off to my love
> With a boxing glove—
> Ten thousand miles away!

JIM. You say you've heard me sing?

LAURA. Oh, yes! Yes, very often . . . I—don't suppose you remember me—at all?

JIM. *[Smiling doubtfully.]* You know I have an idea I've seen you before. I had that idea soon as you opened the door. It seemed almost like I was about to remember your name. But the name that I started to call you—wasn't a name! And so I stopped myself before I said it.

LAURA. Wasn't it—Blue Roses?

JIM. *[Springs up. Grinning.]* Blue Roses! My gosh, yes—Blue Roses! That's what I had on my tongue when you opened the door! Isn't it funny what tricks your memory plays? I didn't

connect you with the high school somehow or other. But that's where it was; it was high school. I didn't even know you were Shakespeare's sister! Gosh, I'm sorry.

LAURA. I didn't expect you to. You—barely knew me!

JIM. But we did have a speaking acquaintance, huh?

LAURA. Yes, we—spoke to each other.

JIM. When did you recognize me?

LAURA. Oh, right away!

JIM. Soon as I came in the door?

LAURA. When I heard your name I thought it was probably you. I knew that Tom used to know you a little in high school. So when you came in the door—Well, then I was—sure.

JIM. Why didn't you *say* something, then?

LAURA. *[Breathlessly.]* I didn't know what to say, I was—too surprised!

JIM. For goodness' sakes! You know, this sure is funny!

LAURA. Yes! Yes, isn't it, though . . .

JIM. Didn't we have a class in something together?

LAURA. Yes, we did.

JIM. What class was that?

LAURA. It was—singing—Chorus!

JIM. Aw!

LAURA. I sat across the aisle from you in the Aud.

JIM. Aw.

LAURA. Mondays, Wednesdays and Fridays.

JIM. Now I remember—you always came in late.

LAURA. Yes, it was so hard for me, getting upstairs. I had that brace on my leg—it clumped so loud!

JIM. I never heard any clumping.

LAURA. *[Wincing at the recollection.]* To me it sounded like—thunder!

JIM. Well, well, well, I never even noticed.

LAURA. And everybody was seated before I came in. I had to walk in front of all those people. My seat was in the back row. I had to go clumping all the way up the aisle with everyone watching!

JIM. You shouldn't have been self-conscious.

LAURA. I know, but I was. It was always such a relief when the singing started.

JIM. Aw, yes, I've placed you now! I used to call you Blue Roses. How was it that I got started calling you that?

LAURA. I was out of school a little while with pleurosis. When I came back you asked me what was the matter. I said I had pleurosis—you thought I said Blue Roses. That's what you always called me after that!

JIM. I hope you didn't mind.

LAURA. Oh, no—I liked it. You see, I wasn't acquainted with many—people. . . .

JIM. As I remember you sort of stuck by yourself.

LAURA. I—I—never had much luck at—making friends.

JIM. I don't see why you wouldn't.

LAURA. Well, I—started out badly.

JIM. You mean being—

LAURA. Yes, it sort of—stood between me—

JIM. You shouldn't have let it!

LAURA. I know, but it did, and—

JIM. You were shy with people!

LAURA. I tried not to be but never could—

JIM. Overcome it?

LAURA. No, I—I never could!

JIM. I guess being shy is something you have to work out of kind of gradually.

LAURA. [Sorrowfully.] Yes—I guess it—

JIM. Takes time!

LAURA. Yes—

JIM. People are not so dreadful when you know them. That's what you have to remember! And everybody has problems, not just you, but practically everybody has got some problems. You think of yourself as having the only problems, as being the only one who is disappointed. But just look around you and you will see lots of people as disappointed as you are. For instance, I hoped when I was going to high school that I would be further along at this time, six years later, than I am now—You remember that wonderful write-up I had in *The Torch?*

LAURA. Yes! [She rises and crosses to table.]

JIM. It said I was bound to succeed in anything I went into! [Laura returns with the annual.] Holy Jeez! *The Torch!* [He accepts it reverently. They smile across it with mutual wonder. Laura crouches beside him and they begin to turn through it. Laura's shyness is dissolving in his warmth.]

LAURA. Here you are in *Pirates of Penzance*!

JIM. [Wistfully.] I sang the baritone lead in that operetta.

LAURA. [Rapidly.] So—beautifully!

JIM. [Protesting.] Aw—

LAURA. Yes, yes—beautifully—beautifully!

JIM. You heard me?

LAURA. All three times!

JIM. No!

LAURA. Yes!

JIM. All three performances?

LAURA. [Looking down.] Yes.

JIM. Why?

LAURA. I—wanted to ask you to—autograph my program.

JIM. Why didn't you ask me to?

LAURA. You were always surrounded by your own friends so much that I never had a chance to.

JIM. You should have just—

LAURA. Well, I—thought you might think I was—

JIM. Thought I might think you was—what?

LAURA. Oh—

JIM. [With reflective relish.] I was beleaguered by females in those days.

LAURA. You were terribly popular!

JIM. Yeah—

LAURA. You had such a—friendly way—

JIM. I was spoiled in high school.

LAURA. Everybody—liked you!

JIM. Including you?

LAURA. I—yes, I—I did, too—[She gently closes the book in her lap.]

JIM. Well, well, well!—Give me that program, Laura. [She hands it to him. He signs it with a flourish.] There you are—better late than never!

LAURA. Oh, I—what a—surprise!

JIM. My signature isn't worth very much right now. But some day—maybe—it will increase in value! Being disappointed is one thing and being discouraged is something else. I am disappointed but I am not discouraged. I'm twenty-three years old. How old are you?

LAURA. I'll be twenty-four in June.

JIM. That's not old age!

LAURA. No, but—

JIM. You finished high school?

LAURA. [With difficulty.] I didn't go back.

JIM. You mean you dropped out?

LAURA. I made bad grades in my final examinations. [She rises and replaces the book and the program. Her voice strained.] How is—Emily Meisenbach getting along?

JIM. Oh, that kraut-head!

LAURA. Why do you call her that?

JIM. That's what she was.

LAURA. You're not still—going with her?

JIM. I never see her.

LAURA. It said in the Personal Section that you were—engaged!

JIM. I know, but I wasn't impressed by that—propaganda!

LAURA. It wasn't—the truth?

JIM. Only in Emily's optimistic opinion!

LAURA. Oh—

[Legend: "What have you done since high school?"]

[Jim lights a cigarette and leans indolently back on his elbows smiling at Laura with a warmth and charm which lights her inwardly with altar candles. She remains by the table and turns in her hands a piece of glass to cover her tumult.]

JIM. *[After several reflective puffs on a cigarette.]* What have you done since high school? *[She seems not to hear him.]* Huh? *[Laura looks up.]* I said what have you done since high school, Laura?

LAURA. Nothing much.

JIM. You must have been doing something these six long years.

LAURA. Yes.

JIM. Well, then, such as what?

LAURA. I took a business course at business college—

JIM. How did that work out?

LAURA. Well, not very—well—I had to drop out, it gave me—indigestion—

[Jim laughs gently.]

JIM. What are you doing now?

LAURA. I don't do anything—much. Oh, please don't think I sit around doing nothing! My glass collection takes up a good deal of my time. Glass is something you have to take good care of.

JIM. What did you say—about glass?

LAURA. Collection I said—I have one—*[She clears her throat and turns away again, acutely shy.]*

JIM. *[Abruptly.]* You know what I judge to be the trouble with you? Inferiority complex! Know what that is? That's what they call it when someone low-rates himself! I understand it because I had it, too. Although my case was not so aggravated as yours seems to be. I had it until I took up public speaking, developed my voice, and learned that I had an aptitude for science. Before that time I never thought of myself as being outstanding in any way whatsoever! Now I've never made a regular study of it, but I have a friend who says I can analyze people better than doctors that make a profession of it. I don't claim that to be necessarily true, but I can sure guess a person's psychology, Laura! *[Takes out his gum.]* Excuse me, Laura. I always take it out when the flavor is gone. I'll use this scrap of paper to wrap it in. I know how it is to get it stuck on a shoe. Yep—that's what I judge to be your principal trouble. A lack of confidence in yourself as a person. You don't have the proper amount of faith in yourself. I'm basing that fact on a number of your remarks and also on certain observations I've made. For instance that clumping you thought was so awful in high school. You say that you even dreaded to walk into class. You see what you did? You dropped out of school, you gave up an education because of a clump, which so far as I know was practically nonexistent! A little physical defect is what you have. Hardly noticeable even! Magnified thousands of times by imagination! You know what my strong advice to you is? Think of yourself as *superior* in some way!

LAURA. In what way would I think?

JIM. Why, man alive, Laura! Just look about you a little. What do you see? A world full of common people! All of 'em born and all of 'em going to die! Which of them has one-tenth of your good points! Or mine! Or anyone else's, as far as that goes—Gosh! Everybody excels in some one thing. Some in many! *[Unconsciously glances at himself in the mirror.]* All you've got to do is discover in *what!* Take me, for instance. *[He adjusts his tie at the mirror.]* My interest happens to lie in electrodynamics. I'm taking a course in radio engineering at night school, Laura, on top of a fairly responsible job at the warehouse. I'm taking that course and studying public speaking.

LAURA. Ohhhh.

JIM. Because I believe in the future of television! *[Turning back to her.]* I wish to be ready to go up right along with it. Therefore I'm planning to get in on the ground floor. In fact, I've already made the right connections and all that remains is for the industry itself to get under way! Full steam—*[His eyes are starry.]* *Knowledge—Zzzzzp! Money—Zzzzzzp—Power!* That's the cycle democracy is built on! *[His attitude is convincingly dynamic. Laura stares at him, even her shyness eclipsed in her absolute wonder. He suddenly grins.]* I guess you think I think a lot of myself!

LAURA. No—o-o-o, I—

JIM. Now how about you? Isn't there something you take more interest in than anything else?

LAURA. Well, I do—as I said—have my—glass collection—

[A peal of girlish laughter from the kitchen.]

JIM. I'm not right sure I know what you're talking about. What kind of glass is it?

LAURA. Little articles of it, they're ornaments mostly! Most of them are little animals made out of glass, the tiniest little animals in the world. Mother calls them a glass menagerie! Here's an example of one, if you'd like to see it! This one is one of the oldest. It's nearly thirteen. *[He stretches out his hand. Music: "The Glass Menagerie."]* Oh, be careful—if you breathe, it breaks!

JIM. I'd better not take it. I'm pretty clumsy with things.

LAURA. Go on, I trust you with him! *[Places it in his palm.]* There now—you're holding him gently! Hold him over the light, he loves the light! You see how the light shines through him?

JIM. It sure does shine!

LAURA. I shouldn't be partial, but he is my favorite one.

JIM. What kind of a thing is this one supposed to be?

LAURA. Haven't you noticed the single horn on his forehead?

JIM. A unicorn, huh?

LAURA. Mmm-hmmm!

JIM. Unicorns, aren't they extinct in the modern world?

LAURA. I know!

JIM. Poor little fellow, he must feel sort of lonesome.

LAURA. *[Smiling.]* Well, if he does he doesn't complain about it. He stays on a shelf with some horses that don't have horns and all of them seem to get along nicely together.

JIM. How do you know?

LAURA. *[Lightly.]* I haven't heard any arguments among them!

JIM. *[Grinning.]* No arguments, huh? Well, that's a pretty good sign! Where shall I set him?

LAURA. Put him on the table. They all like a change of scenery once in a while!

JIM. *[Stretching.]* Well, well, well, well—Look how big my shadow is when I stretch!

LAURA. Oh, oh, yes—it stretches across the ceiling!

JIM. *[Crossing to door.]* I think it's stopped raining. *[Opens fire-escape door.]* Where does the music come from?

LAURA. From the Paradise Dance Hall across the alley.

JIM. How about cutting the rug a little, Miss Wingfield?

LAURA. Oh, I—

JIM. Or is your program filled up? Let me have a look at it. *[Grasps imaginary card.]* Why, every dance is taken! I'll just have to scratch some out. *[Waltz music: "La Golondrina."]* Ahhh, a waltz! *[He executes some sweeping turns by himself then holds his arms toward Laura.]*

LAURA. *[Breathlessly.]* I—can't dance!

JIM. There you go, that inferiority stuff!

LAURA. I've never danced in my life!

JIM. Come on, try!

LAURA. Oh, but I'd step on you!

JIM. I'm not made out of glass.

LAURA. How—how—how do we start?

JIM. Just leave it to me. You hold your arms out a little.

LAURA. Like this?

JIM. A little bit higher. Right. Now don't tighten up, that's the main thing about it—relax.

LAURA. *[Laughing breathlessly.]* It's hard not to.

JIM. Okay.

LAURA. I'm afraid you can't budge me.

JIM. What do you bet I can't? *[He swings her into motion.]*

LAURA. Goodness, yes, you can!

JIM. Let yourself go, now, Laura, just let yourself go.

LAURA. I'm—

JIM. Come on!

LAURA. Trying!

JIM. Not so stiff—Easy does it!

LAURA. I know but I'm—

JIM. Loosen th' backbone! There now, that's a lot better.

LAURA. Am I?

JIM. Lots, lots better! *[He moves her about the room in a clumsy waltz.]*

LAURA. Oh, my!

JIM. Ha-ha!

LAURA. Oh, my goodness!

JIM. Ha-ha-ha! *[They suddenly bump into the table. Jim stops.]* What did we hit on?

LAURA. Table.

JIM. Did something fall off it? I think—

LAURA. Yes.

JIM. I hope that it wasn't the little glass horse with the horn!

LAURA. Yes.

JIM. Aw, aw, aw. Is it broken?

LAURA. Now it is just like all the other horses.

JIM. It's lost its—

LAURA. Horn! It doesn't matter. Maybe it's a blessing in disguise.

JIM. You'll never forgive me. I bet that that was your favorite piece of glass.

LAURA. I don't have favorites much. It's no tragedy, Freckles. Glass breaks so easily. No matter how careful you are. The traffic jars the shelves and things fall off them.

JIM. Still I'm awfully sorry that I was the cause.

LAURA. *[Smiling.]* I'll just imagine he had an operation. The horn was removed to make him feel less—freakish! *[They both laugh.]* Now he will feel more at home with the other horses, the ones that don't have horns . . .

JIM. Ha-ha, that's funny! *[Suddenly serious.]* I'm glad to see that you have a sense of humor. You know—you're—well—very different! Surprisingly different from anyone else I know! *[His voice becomes soft and hesitant with a genuine feeling.]* Do you mind me telling you that? *[Laura is abashed beyond speech.]* I mean it in a nice way . . . *[Laura nods shyly, looking away.]* You make me feel sort of—I don't know how to put it! I'm usually pretty good at expressing things, but— This is something that I don't know how to say! *[Laura touches her throat and clears it—turns the broken unicorn in her hands. Even softer.]* Has anyone ever told you that you were pretty? *[Pause: music. Laura looks up slowly, with wonder, and shakes her head.]* Well, you are! In a very different way from anyone else. And all the nicer because of the difference, too. *[His voice becomes low and husky. Laura turns away, nearly faint with the novelty of her emotions.]* I wish that you were my sister. I'd teach you to have some confidence in yourself. The different people are not like other people, but being different is nothing to be ashamed of. Because other people are not such wonderful people. They're one hundred times one thousand. You're one times one! They walk all over the earth. You just stay here. They're common as—weeds, but—you—well, you're— *Blue Roses!*

[Image on screen: Blue roses.]

[Music changes.]

LAURA. But blue is wrong for—roses . . .

JIM. It's right for you—You're—pretty!

LAURA. In what respect am I pretty?

JIM. In all respects—believe me! Your eyes—your hair—are pretty! Your hands are pretty! *[He catches hold of her hand.]* You think I'm making this up because I'm invited to dinner and have to be nice. Oh, I could do that! I could put on an act for you, Laura, and say lots of things without being very sincere. But this time I am. I'm talking to you sincerely. I happened to notice you had this inferiority complex that keeps you from feeling comfortable with people. Somebody needs to build your confidence up and make you proud instead of shy and turning away and—blushing— Somebody ought to—Ought to—*kiss* you, Laura! *[His hand slips slowly up her arm to her shoulder. Music swells tumultuously. He suddenly turns her about and kisses her on the lips. When he releases her Laura sinks on the sofa with a bright, dazed look. Jim backs away and fishes in his pocket for a cigarette. Legend on screen: "Souvenir."]* Stumble-john! *[He lights the cigarette, avoiding her look. There is a peal of girlish laughter from Amanda in the kitchen. Laura slowly raises and opens her hand. It still contains the little broken glass animal. She looks at it with a tender, bewildered expression.]* Stumble-john! I shouldn't have done that—That was way off the beam. You don't smoke, do you? *[She looks up, smiling, not hearing the question. He sits beside her a little gingerly. She looks at him speechlessly—waiting. He coughs decorously and moves a little farther aside as he considers the situation and senses her feelings, dimly, with perturbation. Gently!]* Would you—care for a—mint? *[She doesn't seem to hear him but her look grows brighter even.]* Peppermint—Life Saver? My pocket's a regular drug store—wherever I go . . . *[He pops a mint in his mouth. Then gulps and decides to make a clean breast of it. He speaks slowly and gingerly.]* Laura, you know, if I had a sister like you, I'd do the same thing as Tom. I'd bring out fellows and—introduce her to them. The right type of boys of a type to—appreciate her. Only—well—he made a mistake about me. Maybe I've got no call to be saying this. That may not have been the idea in having me over.

But what if it was? There's nothing wrong about that. The only trouble is that in my case—I'm not in a situation to—do the right thing. I can't take down your number and say I'll phone. I can't call up next week and—ask for a date. I thought I had better explain the situation in case you misunderstood it and—hurt your feelings. . . . *[Pause. Slowly, very slowly, Laura's look changes, her eyes returning slowly from his to the ornament in her palm.]*

[Amanda utters another gay laugh in the kitchen.]

LAURA. *[Faintly.]* You—won't—call again?

JIM. No, Laura, I can't. *[He rises from the sofa.]* As I was just explaining, I've—got strings on me, Laura, I've—been going steady! I go out all the time with a girl named Betty. She's a home-girl like you, and Catholic, and Irish, and in a great many ways we—get along fine. I met her last summer on a moonlight boat trip up the river to Alton, on the *Majestic.* Well—right away from the start it was—love! *[Legend: Love! Laura sways slightly forward and grips the arm of the sofa. He fails to notice, now enrapt in his own comfortable being.]* Being in love has made a new man of me! *[Leaning stiffly forward, clutching the arm of the sofa, Laura struggles visibly with her storm. But Jim is oblivious, she is a long way off.]* The power of love is really pretty tremendous! Love is something that—changes the whole world, Laura! *[The storm abates a little and Laura leans back. He notices her again.]* It happened that Betty's aunt took sick, she got a wire and had to go to Centralia. So Tom—when he asked me to dinner—I naturally just accepted the invitation, not knowing that you—that he—that I—[He stops awkwardly.]* Huh—I'm a stumble-john! *[He flops back on the sofa. The holy candles in the altar of Laura's face have been snuffed out. There is a look of almost infinite desolation. Jim glances at her uneasily.]* I wish that you would—say something. *[She bites her lip which was trembling and then bravely smiles. She opens her hand again on the broken glass ornament. Then she gently takes his hand and raises it level with her own. She carefully places the unicorn in the palm of his hand, then pushes his fingers closed upon it.]* What are you—doing that for? You want me to have him?—Laura? *[She nods.]* What for?

LAURA. A—souvenir . . .

[She rises unsteadily and crouches beside the victrola to wind it up.]

[Legend on screen: "Things have a way of turning out so badly."]

[Or image: "Gentleman caller waving goodbye!—Gaily."]

[At this moment Amanda rushes brightly back in the front room. She bears a pitcher of fruit punch in an old-fashioned cut-glass pitcher and a plate of macaroons. The plate has a gold border and poppies painted on it.]

AMANDA. Well, well, well! Isn't the air delightful after the shower! I've made you children a little liquid refreshment. *[Turns gaily to the gentleman caller.]* Jim, do you know that song about lemonade?

"Lemonade, lemonade
Made in the shade and stirred with a spade—
Good enough for any old maid!"

JIM. *[Uneasily.]* Ha-ha! No—I never heard it.

AMANDA. Why, Laura! You look so serious!

JIM. We were having a serious conversation.

AMANDA. Good! Now you're better acquainted?

JIM. *[Uncertainly.]* Ha-ha! Yes.

AMANDA. You modern young people are much more serious-minded than my generation. I was so gay as a girl!

JIM. You haven't changed, Mrs. Wingfield.

AMANDA. Tonight I'm rejuvenated! The gaiety of the occasion, Mr. O'Connor! *[She tosses her head with a peal of laughter. Spills lemonade.]* Oooo! I'm baptizing myself!

JIM. Here—let me—

AMANDA. *[Setting the pitcher down.]* There now. I discovered we had some maraschino cherries. I dumped them in, juice and all!

JIM. You shouldn't have gone to that trouble, Mrs. Wingfield.

AMANDA. Trouble, trouble? Why it was loads of fun! Didn't you hear me cutting up in the kitchen? I bet your ears were burning! I told Tom how outdone with him I was for keeping you to himself so long a time! He should have brought you over much, much sooner! Well, now that you've found your way, I want you to be a very frequent caller! Not just occasional but all the time. Oh, we're going to have a lot of gay times together! I see them coming! Mmm, just breathe that air! So fresh, and the moon's so pretty! I'll skip back out—I know where my place is when young folks are having a—serious conversation!

JIM. Oh, don't go out, Mrs. Wingfield. The fact of the matter is I've got to be going.

AMANDA. Going, now? You're joking! Why, it's only the shank of the evening, Mr. O'Connor!

JIM. Well, you know how it is.

AMANDA. You mean you're a young workingman and have to keep workingmen's hours. We'll let you off early tonight. But only on the condition that next time you stay later. What's the best night for you? Isn't Saturday night the best night for you workingmen?

JIM. I have a couple of time-clocks to punch, Mrs. Wingfield. One at morning, another one at night!

AMANDA. My, but you *are* ambitious! You work at night, too?

JIM. No, Ma'am, not work but—Betty! *[He crosses deliberately to pick up his hat. The band at the Paradise Dance Hall goes into a tender waltz.]*

AMANDA. Betty? Betty? Who's—Betty? *[There is an ominous cracking sound in the sky.]*

JIM. Oh, just a girl. The girl I go steady with! *[He smiles charmingly. The sky falls.]*

[Legend: "The sky falls."]

AMANDA. *[A long-drawn exhalation.]* Ohhhh . . . Is it a serious romance, Mr. O'Connor?

JIM. We're going to be married the second Sunday in June.

AMANDA. Ohhh—how nice! Tom didn't mention that you were engaged to be married.

JIM. The cat's not out of the bag at the warehouse yet. You know how they are. They call you Romeo and stuff like that. *[He stops at the oval mirror to put on his hat. He carefully shapes the brim and the crown to give a discreetly dashing effect.]* It's been a wonderful evening, Mrs. Wingfield. I guess this is what they mean by Southern hospitality.

AMANDA. It really wasn't anything at all.

JIM. I hope it don't seem like I'm rushing off. But I promised Betty I'd pick her up at the Wabash depot, an' by the time I get my jalopy down there her train'll be in. Some women are pretty upset if you keep 'em waiting.

AMANDA. Yes, I know—The tyranny of women! *[Extends her hand.]* Good-bye, Mr. O'Connor. I wish you luck—and happiness—and success! All three of them, and so does Laura!—Don't you, Laura?

LAURA. Yes!

JIM. *[Taking her hand.]* Good-bye, Laura. I'm certainly going to treasure that souvenir. And don't you forget the good advice I gave you. *[Raises his voice to a cheery shout.]* So long, Shakespeare! Thanks again, ladies—Good night!

[He grins and ducks jauntily out.]

[Still bravely grimacing, Amanda closes the door on the gentleman caller. Then she turns back to the room with a puzzled expression. She and Laura don't dare to face each other. Laura crouches beside the victrola to wind it.]

AMANDA. *[Faintly.]* Things have a way of turning out so badly. I don't believe that I would play the victrola. Well, well—well—Our gentleman caller was engaged to be married! Tom!

TOM. *[From back.]* Yes, Mother!

AMANDA. Come in here a minute. I want to tell you something awfully funny.

TOM. *[Enters with macaroon and a glass of the lemonade.]* Has the gentleman caller gotten away already?

AMANDA. The gentleman caller has made an early departure. What a wonderful joke you played on us!

TOM. How do you mean?

AMANDA. You didn't mention that he was engaged to be married.

TOM. Jim? Engaged?

AMANDA. That's what he just informed us.

TOM. I'll be jiggered! I didn't know about that.

AMANDA. That seems very peculiar.

TOM. What's peculiar about it?

AMANDA. Didn't you call him your best friend down at the warehouse?

TOM. He is, but how did I know?

AMANDA. It seems extremely peculiar that you wouldn't know your best friend was going to be married!

TOM. The warehouse is where I work, not where I know things about people!

AMANDA. You don't know things anywhere! You live in a dream; you manufacture illusions! *[He crosses to door.]* Where are you going?

TOM. I'm going to the movies.

AMANDA. That's right, now that you've had us make such fools of ourselves. The effort, the preparations, all the expense! The new floor lamp, the rug, the clothes for Laura! All for what? To entertain some other girl's fiancé! Go to the movies, go! Don't think about us, a mother deserted, an unmarried sister who's crippled and has no job! Don't let anything interfere with your selfish pleasure! Just go, go, go—to the movies!

TOM. All right, I will! The more you shout about my selfishness to me the quicker I'll go, and I won't go to the movies!

AMANDA. Go, then! Then go to the moon—you selfish dreamer!

[Tom smashes his glass on the floor. He plunges out on the fire-escape, slamming the door. Laura screams—cut by door.]

[Dance-hall music up. Tom goes to the rail and grips it desperately, lifting his face in the chill white moonlight penetrating the narrow abyss of the alley.]

[Legend on screen: "And so good-bye . . ."]

[Tom's closing speech is timed with the interior pantomime. The interior scene is played as though viewed through soundproof glass. Amanda appears to be making a comforting speech to Laura who is huddled upon the sofa. Now that we cannot hear the mother's speech, her silliness is gone and she has dignity and tragic beauty. Laura's dark hair hides her face until at the end of the speech she lifts it to smile at her mother. Amanda's gestures are slow and graceful, almost dancelike, as she comforts the daughter. At the end of her speech she glances a moment at the father's picture—then withdraws through the portieres. At close of Tom's speech, Laura blows out the candles, ending the play.]

TOM. I didn't go to the moon, I went much further—for time is the longest distance between two places—Not long after that I was fired for writing a poem on the lid of a shoe-box. I left Saint Louis. I descended the steps of this fire-escape for a last time and followed, from then on, in my father's footsteps, attempting to find in motion what was lost in space—I traveled around a great deal. The cities swept about me like dead leaves, leaves that were brightly colored but torn away from the branches. I would have stopped, but I was pursued by something. It always came upon me unawares, taking me altogether by surprise. Perhaps it was a familiar bit of music. Perhaps it was only a piece of transparent glass—Perhaps I am walking along a street at night, in some strange city, before I have found companions. I passed the lighted window of a shop where perfume is sold. The window is filled with pieces of colored glass, tiny transparent bottles in delicate colors, like bits of a shattered rainbow. Then all at once my sister touches my shoulder. I turn around and look into her eyes . . . Oh, Laura, Laura, I tried to leave you behind me, but I am more faithful than I intended to be! I reach for a cigarette, I cross the street, I run into the movies or a bar, I buy a drink, I speak to the nearest stranger— anything that can blow your candles out! [Laura bends over the candles.]—for nowadays the world is lit by lightning! Blow out your candles, Laura—and so good-bye. . . .

[She blows the candles out.]

[The scene dissolves.]

Introduction to *Krapp's Last Tape* by Samuel Beckett

Krapp's Last Tape Edward Petherbridge as Krapp, Royal Shakespeare Company, Arts Theatre, London. (© *Donald Cooper/PHOTOSTAGE*)

The Play Samuel Beckett, the author of *Krapps's Last Tape,* was the premier playwright of the movement known as theater of the absurd, which first emerged in the 1950s. Theater of the absurd combined existentialist philosophy with revolutionary, avant-garde dramatic techniques. Existentialism was a philosophical movement that came to the forefront after World War II. Its adherents believe that there is little meaning to existence; God does not exist, and therefore humanity is alone in an irrational universe. The only significant thing an individual can do is accept responsibility for her or his own actions. Important absurdist playwrights included Samuel Beckett (1906–1989), Jean Geneêt (1911–1986), Eugène Ionesco (1912–1994), Harold Pinter (1930–), and Edward Albee (1928–).

The playwrights of theater of the absurd felt that the ridiculous—or absurd—nature of existence should be reflected in the dramatic elements of their plays. Their dramas employ seemingly illogical techniques. In terms of action, frequently nothing seems to happen, because the plot often moves in a circle, concluding in the same way it began. The characters are not created realistically, and the settings are sometimes strange, unrecognizable locales. The language of the plays is often telegraphic and sparse, and the characters fail to communicate.

Waiting for Godot (1953) by Samuel Beckett is probably the most famous of these nontraditional, enigmatic dramas. The setting is "A country road, A tree." The two central characters, Vladimir and Estragon—also known as Didi and Gogo—are tramplike clowns who are waiting for Godot. Godot's identity is never revealed, nor does he ever appear, though a young messenger always promises that he will. Godot may be God, or he may not even exist. The plot of *Waiting for Godot* is cyclical; the action in Act II appears to start over with nothing having changed since Act I. Vladimir and Estragon spend their time waiting and appear to have no control over their lives. In true absurdist fashion and for no apparent reason, two other characters, Lucky and Pozzo, reverse positions during the play: Pozzo, who was the master, becomes the slave; and Lucky, the slave, becomes the master.

Krapp's Last Tape, which appeared five years after *Waiting for Godot,* presents the story of a 69-year-old man who once a year makes a tape recording of his impressions of the past year of his life. Krapp, the only character in the play, has more of a personal history than most figures in absurdist drama. He rummages through old tapes, playing particularly one from 30 years earlier, when he was 39. The tapes allow him to juxtapose emotions, ambitions, and disappointments from one period in his life with those of another period. The one segment he remembers most fondly, which he repeats several times, is a love scene. Mostly, though, we get a moving and wrenching portrait of a restrained, unfulfilled individual (his name is a play on words, specifically, the word for bowel movement) as he reviews his life.

The Playwright   Samuel Beckett was born on April 13, 1906. The day of his birth happened to be a Friday—not only Friday the thirteenth but also Good Friday; and the notions of sorrow, isolation, and ill luck associated with that day were important concepts to Beckett.

For a man so obsessed with the futility of existence, Beckett had a very normal childhood in a cultured, affectionate, upper-middle-class Irish family. At prep school, he was not only a brilliant scholar but an extremely popular student and an excellent athlete, particularly at cricket. He received his M.A. from the University of Dublin, Ireland, in modern languages. He then taught at schools in Paris and Dublin, wandered around Europe for a while, and finally settled in Paris in 1937.

It was during his first visit to Paris in 1929 that Beckett became acquainted with the writer James Joyce. Joyce encouraged Beckett to write and arranged to have some of his early essays published; in turn, Beckett sometimes assisted Joyce with *Finnegan's Wake.* Their shared Irish background, literary taste, and tendency to depression drew them together. According to one account, they conversed mainly in silences.

Beckett wrote and published essays, short stories, poetry, and novels during the 1930s and the 1940s, but his work was known only to a very small group of the avant-garde. A French translation of his novel *Murphy* sold 95 copies in four years. It was not until the early 1950s, with the publication of three novels and the play *Waiting for Godot* (1953), that he came to be considered one of the major writers of the postwar generation.

In *Waiting for Godot,* Beckett uses many themes and dramatic techniques that recur in his other plays. The futility of action reappears as a theme in *Act Without Words I & II.* The inability of two people to get along even though they need each other is seen again in *Endgame* (1957). Both *Krapp's Last Tape* (1958) and *Happy Days* (1961) dramatize our failure to communicate.

Besides writing for the theater, Beckett wrote for television and radio; he also wrote a short film starring Buster Keaton. After a spurt of writing in the late 1950s and early 1960s, his output diminished, but *Not I,* written in 1972, shows that neither his concerns nor his dramatic powers changed in his later years. He received the Nobel Prize in 1969 but did not attend the ceremony.

Beckett died in December 1989. He was a man who had avoided the spotlight, and his death was not announced until after his small, private funeral.

The Period   After World War II, which ended in 1945 with the defeat of Germany and Italy in Europe and Japan in Asia, there was again hope for peace. The period after World War II was different from the period after World War I. For one thing, the atom bomb—which had been dropped on two cities in Japan at the close of World War II—and later the hydrogen bomb had been developed. These weapons were potentially so deadly that a stalemate developed between the superpowers controlling them, the United States and the Soviet Union.

After World War II, the Soviet Union had annexed many nations in Eastern and Central Europe into an association known as the Warsaw Pact. The Western nations formed the North Atlantic Treaty Organization (NATO), and between these two blocs there developed what came to be called the cold war. This was to last until the countries of Eastern Europe moved away from communist and Soviet domination in 1989 and 1990 and the Soviet Union was dissolved at the end of 1991.

Even though there was no open warfare between the superpowers during the decades after World War II, there were devastating wars in other areas: in Vietnam, Afghanistan, Bosnia, and Haiti; in Rwanda and many parts of Africa where new nations were emerging from colonial rule; and in the Middle East. Another development of the postwar period was a striking increase in the industrial power of two of the defeated nations: Germany and Japan. Economically and politically, the world became more interdependent, with developments in one part of the world—the price of oil, for example, or environmental pollution—directly affecting other areas around the globe. The many changes of the past 50 years have affected Central and South America in the same way that they have affected Europe, Asia, and the United States.

Meanwhile, inventions continued at a rapid pace: not only nuclear power but computer technology, which revolutionized many aspects of life. Also, this period saw the development of jet airplanes, television, and many advances in medical science. At the same time that steps forward were taken, tremendous problems remained: an inequality between rich and poor in many nations, assaults on the environment, a continuation of racial prejudice, and starvation and homelessness in many parts of the world.

In the modern era, as always, the arts have reflected the many changes that have occurred in society; in theater, these developments were mirrored in the great diversity of types of theater produced. Theater in the modern period has become increasingly eclectic and experimental. Avant-garde theater appears alongside more conventional theater, and new plays are produced at the same time that classics from the past enjoy great popularity. One could say that there have been three major strands in the theater of the modern era. The first is realism. The second is departures from realism, which includes theater of the absurd as well as many other experimental forms. The third is a continuation of traditional theater from the past—the comedies, tragedies, melodramas, and popular spectacles that nineteenth-century audiences applauded.

KRAPP'S LAST TAPE

Samuel Beckett

CAST

KRAPP

A late evening in the future.

Krapp's den.

Front centre a small table, the two drawers of which open toward audience.

Sitting at the table, facing front, i.e., across from the drawers, a wearyish old man: Krapp.

Rusty black narrow trousers too short for him. Rusty black sleeveless waistcoat, four capacious pockets. Heavy silver watch and chain. Grimy white shirt open at neck, no collar. Surprising pair of dirty white boots, size ten at least, very narrow and pointed.

White face. Purple nose. Disordered grey hair. Unshaven.

Very nearsighted (but unspectacled). Hard of hearing.

Cracked voice. Distinctive intonation.

Laborious walk.

On the table a tape-recorder with microphone and a number of cardboard boxes containing reels of recorded tapes.

Table and immediately adjacent area in strong white light. Rest of stage in darkness.

Krapp remains a moment motionless, heaves a great sigh, looks at his watch, fumbles in his pockets, takes out an envelope, puts it back, fumbles, takes out a small bunch of keys, raises it to his eyes, chooses a key, gets up and moves to front of table. He stoops, unlocks first drawer, peers into it, feels about inside it, takes out a reel of tape, peers at it, puts it back, locks drawer, unlocks second drawer, peers into it, feels about inside it, takes out a large banana, peers at it, locks drawer, puts keys back in his pocket. He turns, advances to edge of stage, halts, strokes banana, peels it, drops skin at his feet, puts end of banana in his mouth and remains motionless, staring vacuously before him. Finally he bites off the end, turns aside and begins pacing to and fro at edge of stage, in the light, i.e., not more than four or five paces either way, meditatively eating banana. He treads on skin, slips, nearly falls, recovers himself, stoops and peers at skin and finally pushes it, still stooping, with his foot over the edge of stage into pit. He resumes his pacing, finishes banana, returns to table, sits down, remains a moment motionless, heaves a great sigh, takes keys from his pockets, raises them to his eyes, chooses key, gets up and moves to front of table, unlocks second drawer, takes out a second large banana, peers at it, locks drawer, puts back keys in his pocket, turns, advances to edge of stage, halts, strokes banana, peels it, tosses skin into pit, puts end of banana in his mouth and remains motionless, staring vacuously before him. Finally he has an idea, puts banana in his waistcoat pocket, the end emerging, and goes with all the speed he can muster backstage into darkness. Ten seconds. Loud pop of cork. Fifteen seconds. He comes back into light carrying an old ledger and sits down at table. He lays ledger on table, wipes his mouth, wipes his hands on the front of his waistcoat, brings them smartly together and rubs them.

KRAPP. *[Briskly.]* Ah! *[He bends over ledger, turns the pages, finds the entry he wants, reads.]* Box . . . thrree . . . spool . . . five. *[He raises his head and stares front. With relish.]* Spool! *[Pause.]* Spooool! *[Happy smile. Pause. He bends over table, starts peering and poking at the boxes.]* Box . . . thrree . . . thrree . . . four . . . two . . . *[with surprise]* nine! good God! . . . seven . . . ah! the little rascal! *[He takes up box, peers at it.]* Box thrree. *[He lays it on table, opens it and peers at spools inside.]* Spool . . . *[He peers at ledger.]* . . . five . . . *[He peers at spools.]* . . . five . . . five . . . ah! the little scoundrel! *[He takes out a spool, peers at it.]* Spool five. *[He lays it on table, closes box three, puts it back with the others, takes up the spool.]* Box thrree, spool five. *[He bends over the machine, looks up. With relish.]* Spooool! *[Happy smile. He bends, loads spool on machine, rubs his hands.]* Ah! *[He peers at ledger, reads entry at foot of page.]* Mother at rest at last . . . Hm . . . The black ball . . . *[He raises his head, stares blankly front. Puzzled.]* Black ball? . . . *[He peers again at ledger, reads.]* The dark nurse . . . *[He raises his head, broods, peers again at ledger, reads.]* Slight improvement in bowel condition . . . Hm . . . Memorable . . . what? *[He peers closer.]* Equinox, memorable equinox. *[He raises his head, stares blankly front. Puzzled.]* Memorable equinox? . . . *[Pause. He shrugs his shoulders, peers again at ledger, reads.]* Farewell to— *[he turns the page]*—love.

[He raises his head, broods, bends over machine, switches on and assumes listening posture, i.e., leaning forward, elbows on table, hand cupping ear toward machine, face front.]

TAPE. *[Strong voice, rather pompous, clearly Krapp's at a much earlier time.]* Thirty-nine today, sound as a—*[Settling himself more comfortably he knocks one of the boxes off the table, curses, switches off, sweeps boxes and ledger violently to the ground, winds tape back to beginning, switches on, resumes posture.]* Thirty-nine today, sound as a bell, apart from my old weakness, and intellectually I have now every reason to suspect at the . . . *[hesitates]* . . . crest of the wave—or thereabouts. Celebrated the awful occasion, as in recent years, quietly at the Winehouse. Not a soul. Sat before the fire with closed eyes, separating the grain from the husks. Jotted down a few notes, on the back of an envelope. Good to be back in my den, in my old rags. Have just eaten I regret to say three bananas and only with difficulty refrained from a fourth. Fatal things for a man with my condition. *[Vehemently.]* Cut 'em out! *[Pause.]* The new light above my table is a great improvement. With all this darkness round me I feel less alone. *[Pause.]* In a way. *[Pause.]* I love to get up and move about in it, then back here to . . . *[hesitates]* . . . me. *[Pause.]* Krapp.

[Pause.]

The grain, now what I wonder do I mean by that, I mean . . . *[Hesitates.]* . . . I suppose I mean those things worth having when all the dust has—when all *my* dust has settled. I close my eyes and try and imagine them.

[Pause. Krapp closes his eyes briefly.]

Extraordinary silence this evening, I strain my ears and do not hear a sound. Old Miss McGlome always sings at this hour. But not tonight. Songs of her girlhood, she says. Hard to think of her as a girl. Wonderful woman though. Connaught, I fancy. *[Pause.]* Shall I sing when I am her age, if I ever am? No. *[Pause.]* Did I sing as a boy? No. *[Pause.]* Did I ever sing? No.

[Pause.]

Just been listening to an old year, passages at random. I did not check in the book, but it must be at least ten or twelve years ago. At that time I think I was still living on and off with Bianca in Kedar Street. Well out of that, Jesus yes! Hopeless business. *[Pause.]* Not much about her, apart from a tribute to her eyes. Very warm. I suddenly saw them again. *[Pause.]* Incomparable! *[Pause.]* Ah well . . . *[Pause.]* These old P.M.s are gruesome, but I often find them—*[Krapp switches off, broods, switches on.]*—a help before embarking on a new . . . *[hesitates]* . . . retrospect. Hard to believe I was ever that young whelp. The voice! Jesus! And the aspirations! *[Brief laugh in which Krapp joins.]* And the resolutions! *[Brief laugh in which Krapp joins.]* To drink less, in particular. *[Brief laugh of Krapp alone.]* Statistics. Seventeen hundred hours, out of the preceding eight thousand odd, consumed on licensed premises alone. More than 20 percent, say 40 percent of his waking life. *[Pause.]* Plans for a less . . . *[hesitates]* . . . engrossing sexual life. Last illness of his father. Flagging pursuit of happiness. Unattainable laxation. Sneers at what he calls his youth and thanks to God that it's over. *[Pause.]* False ring there. *[Pause.]* Shadows of the opus . . . magnum. Closing with a—*[brief laugh]*—yelp to Providence. *[Prolonged laugh in which Krapp joins.]* What remains of all that misery? A girl in a shabby green coat, on a railway-station platform? No?

[Pause.]

When I look—

[Krapp switches off, broods, looks at his watch, gets up, goes backstage into darkness. Ten seconds. Pop of cork. Ten seconds. Second cork. Ten seconds. Third cork. Ten seconds. Brief burst of quavering song.]

KRAPP. *[Sings.]*

> Now the day is over,
> Night is drawing nigh-igh,
> Shadows—

[Fit of coughing. He comes back into light, sits down, wipes his mouth, switches on, resumes his listening posture.]

TAPE.—back on the year that is gone, with what I hope is perhaps a glint of the old eye to come, there is of course the house on the canal where mother lay a-dying, in the late autumn, after her long viduity *[Krapp gives a start.]* and the—*[Krapp switches off, winds back tape a little, bends his ear closer to machine, switches on]*—a-dying, after her long viduity, and the—

[Krapp switches off, raises his head, stares blankly before him. His lips move in the syllables of "viduity." No sound. He gets up, goes backstage into darkness, comes back with an enormous dictionary, lays it on table, sits down and looks up the word.]

KRAPP. *[Reading from dictionary.]* State—or condition of being—or remaining—a widow—or widower. *[Looks up. Puzzled.]* Being—or remaining? . . . *[Pause. He peers again at dictionary. Reading.]* "Deep weeds of viduity" . . . Also of

an animal, especially a bird . . . the vidua or weaver-bird . . . Black plumage of male . . . *[He looks up. With relish.]* The vidua-bird!

[Pause. He closes dictionary, switches on, resumes listening posture.]

TAPE.—bench by the weir from where I could see her window. There I sat, in the biting wind, wishing she were gone. *[Pause.]* Hardly a soul, just a few regulars, nursemaids, infants, old men, dogs. I got to know them quite well—oh by appearance of course I mean! One dark young beauty I recollect particularly, all white and starch, incomparable bosom, with a big black hooded perambulator, most funereal thing. Whenever I looked in her direction she had her eyes on me. And yet when I was bold enough to speak to her—not having been introduced—she threatened to call a policeman. As if I had designs on her virtue! *[Laugh. Pause.]* The face she had! The eyes! Like . . . *[hesitates]* . . . chrysolite! *[Pause.]* Ah well . . . *[Pause.]* I was there when—*[Krapp switches off, broods, switches on again.]*—the blind went down, one of those dirty brown roller affairs, throwing a ball for a little white dog, as chance would have it. I happened to look up and there it was. All over and done with, at last. I sat on for a few moments with the ball in my hand and the dog yelping and pawing at me. *[Pause.]* Moments. Her moments, my moments. *[Pause.]* The dog's moments. *[Pause.]* In the end I held it out to him and he took it in his mouth, gently, gently. A small, old, black, hard, solid rubber ball. *[Pause.]* I shall feel it, in my hand, until my dying day. *[Pause.]* I might have kept it. *[Pause.]* But I gave it to the dog.

[Pause.]

Ah well . . .

[Pause.]

Spiritually a year of profound gloom and indigence until that memorable night in March, at the end of the jetty, in the howling wind, never to be forgotten, when suddenly I saw the whole thing. The vision, at last. This I fancy is what I have chiefly to record this evening, against the day when my work will be done and perhaps no place left in my memory, warm or cold, for the miracle that . . . *[hesitates]* . . . for the fire that set it alight. What I suddenly saw then was this, that the belief I had been going on all my life, namely—*[Krapp switches off impatiently, winds tape forward, switches on again.]*— great granite rocks the foam flying up in the light of the lighthouse and the wind-gauge spinning like a propellor, clear to me at last that the dark I have always struggled to keep under is in reality my most—*[Krapp curses, switches off, winds tape forward, switches on again.]*— unshatterable association until my dissolution of storm and night with the light of the understanding and the fire—*[Krapp curses louder, switches off, winds tape forward, switches on again.]*— my face in her breasts and my hand on her. We lay there without moving. But under us all moved, and moved us, gently, up and down, and from side to side.

[Pause.]

Past midnight. Never knew such silence. The earth might be uninhabited.

[Pause.]

Here I end—

[Krapp switches off, winds tape back, switches on again.]

—upper lake, with the punt, bathed off the bank, then pushed out into the stream and drifted. She lay stretched out on the floorboards with her hands under her head and her eyes closed. Sun blazing down, bit of a breeze, water nice and lively. I noticed a scratch on her thigh and asked her how she came by it. Picking gooseberries, she said. I said again I thought it was hopeless and no good going on, and she agreed, without opening her eyes. *[Pause.]* I asked her to look at me and after a few moments—*[Pause.]*—after a few moments she did, but the eyes just slits, because of the glare. I bent over her to get them in the shadow and they opened. *[Pause. Low.]* Let me in. *[Pause.]* We drifted in among the flags and stuck. The way they went down, sighing, before the stem! *[Pause.]* I lay down across her with my face in

her breasts and my hand on her. We lay there without moving. But under us all moved, and moves us, gently, up and down, and from side to side.

[Pause.]

Past midnight. Never knew—

[Krapp switches off, broods. Finally he fumbles in his pockets, encounters the banana, takes it out, peers at it, puts it back, fumbles, brings out the envelope, fumbles, puts back envelope, looks at his watch, gets up and goes backstage into darkness. Ten seconds. Sound of bottle against glass, then brief siphon. Ten seconds. Bottle against glass alone. Ten seconds. He comes back a little unsteadily into light, goes to front of table, takes out keys, raises them to his eyes, chooses key, unlocks first drawer, peers into it, feels about inside, takes out reel, peers at it, locks drawer, puts keys back in his pocket, goes and sits down, takes reel off machine, lays it on dictionary, loads virgin reel on machine, takes envelope from his pocket, consults back of it, lays it on table, switches on, clears his throat and begins to record.]

KRAPP. Just been listening to that stupid bastard I took myself for thirty years ago, hard to believe I was ever as bad as that. Thank God that's all done with anyway. *[Pause.]* The eyes she had! *[Broods, realizes he is recording silence, switches off, broods. Finally.]* Everything there, everything, all the—*[Realizes this is not being recorded, switches on.]* Everything there, everything on this old muckball, all the light and dark and famine and feasting of . . . *[hesitates]* . . . the ages! *[In a shout.]* Yes! *[Pause.]* Let that go! Jesus! Take his mind off his homework! Jesus! *[Pause. Weary.]* Ah well, maybe he was right. *[Pause.]* Maybe he was right. *[Broods. Realizes. Switches off. Consults envelope.]* Pah! *[Crumples it and throws it away. Broods. Switches on.]* Nothing to say, not a squeak. What's a year now? The sour cud and the iron stool. *[Pause.]* Reveled in the word spool. *[With relish.]* Spoooool! Happiest moment of the past half million. *[Pause.]* Seventeen copies sold, of which eleven at trade price to free circulating libraries beyond the seas. Getting known. *[Pause.]* One pound six and something, eight I have little doubt. *[Pause.]* Crawled out once or twice, before the summer was cold. Sat shivering in the park, drowned in dreams and burning to be gone. Not a soul.

[Pause.] Last fancies. *[Vehemently.]* Keep 'em under! *[Pause.]* Scalded the eyes out of me reading *Effie* again, a page a day, with tears again. Effie . . . *[Pause.]* Could have been happy with her, up there on the Baltic, and the pines, and the dunes. *[Pause.]* Could I? *[Pause.]* And she? *[Pause.]* Pah! *[Pause.]* Fanny came in a couple of times. Bony old ghost of a whore. Couldn't do much, but I suppose better than a kick in the crutch. The last time wasn't so bad. How do you manage it, she said, at your age? I told her I'd been saving up for her all my life. *[Pause.]* Went to Vespers once, like when I was in short trousers. *[Pause. Sings.]*

> Now the day is over,
> Night is drawing nigh-igh,
> Shadows—*[Coughing, then almost*
>   *inaudible.]*—of the evening
> Steal across the sky.

[Gasping.] Went to sleep and fell off the pew. *[Pause.]* Sometimes wondered in the night if a last effort mightn't—*[Pause.]* Ah finish your booze now and get to your bed. Go on with this drivel in the morning. Or leave it at that. *[Pause.]* Leave it at that. *[Pause.]* Lie propped up in the dark—and wander. Be again in the dingle on a Christmas Eve, gathering holly, the red-berried. *[Pause.]* Be again on Croghan on a Sunday morning, in the haze, with the bitch, stop and listen to the bells. *[Pause.]* And so on. *[Pause.]* Be again, be again. *[Pause.]* All that old misery. *[Pause.]* Once wasn't enough for you. *[Pause.]* Lie down across her.

[Long pause. He suddenly bends over machine, switches off, wrenches off tape, throws it away, puts on the other, winds it forward to the passage he wants, switches on, listens staring front.]

TAPE.—gooseberries, she said. I said again I thought it was hopeless and no good going on, and she agreed, without opening her eyes. *[Pause.]* I asked her to look at me and after a few moments—*[Pause.]*—after a few moments she did, but the eyes just slits, because of the glare. I bent over her to get them in the shadow and they opened. *[Pause. Low.]* Let me in. *[Pause.]* We drifted in among the flags and stuck. The way they went down, sighing, before the stem! *[Pause.]* I lay down across her with my face in her breasts and my hand on her. We lay there without moving. But under us all moved, and moved us, gently, up and down, and from side to side.

[Pause. Krapp's lips move. No sound.]

Past midnight. Never knew such silence. The earth might be uninhabited.

[Pause.]

Here I end this reel. Box—*[Pause.]*—three, spool—*[Pause.]*—five. *[Pause.]* Perhaps my best years are gone. When there was a chance of happiness. But I wouldn't want them back. Not with the fire in me now. No, I wouldn't want them back.

[Krapp motionless staring before him. The tape runs on in silence. Curtain.]

Introduction to
The Mystery of Irma Vep:
A Penny Dreadful
by Charles Ludlam

The Mystery of Irma Vep   Everett Quinton (left) and Charles Ludlam (right). *(© Anita and Steve Shevett)*

The Play   *The Mystery of Irma Vep* is subtitled "A Penny Dreadful." This was a Victorian form of literature that mixed sensationalism, melodrama, foreign locales, and romance. Charles Ludlam is clearly satirizing that form in this comic send-up, which ostensibly deals with discovering who killed Lord Edgar's first wife and son. *Irma Vep* contains monsters, mysterious deaths, eerie settings, a scene in Egypt, and stereotypical Victorian characters, making fun of them all through exaggeration. Ludlam is also burlesquing the horror films of the 1940s, which were similar in plotline to the "penny dreadfuls." In addition, there are subtle comic references to classics, such as Ibsen's *Little Eyolf.*

While Ludlam's work is enjoyable simply on the level of literary and film satire, the playwright is also poking fun at the theater itself. As Ludlam indicates in his opening stage direction: "*The Mystery of Irma Vep* is a full-length quick-change act. All roles are portrayed by two performers." (In its original staging, Ludlam and his longtime companion, Everett Quinton, played all the parts.) Throughout the production, the audience members are constantly reminded that they are watching a theater event. The quick changes force the spectators to laugh at accepted conventions of realistic theater, such as costume changes and actors playing individualized characters.

Furthermore, we are always aware that two males are playing all the roles, male and female. In this and other ways, Ludlam's dramatic strategy goes beyond making fun of literature and theatrical conventions. He also makes the audience confront stereotypical representations of gender that have been part of theater history, through his campy, comic use of cross-dressing. In addition, all the male and female characters in the play are parodies of stereotypical gender types found in melodrama: the threatened Lady Enid, the noble and heroic Lord Edgar, and the servants. By never letting the audience forget that both actors are men, Ludlam makes the spectators deal with issues of sexual orientation. When men and women are kissing in *Irma Vep,* the audience recognizes that two men—one cross-dressed—are engaging in an act of passion. Ludlam wants us to question all our biases about gender and sexual orientation, but he uses accessible forms: camp and burlesque. The use of popular techniques won a wide audience for *The Mystery of Irma Vep,* a play that is frequently revived in university, regional, and community theaters.

The Playwright   Charles Ludlam was a complete theater artist, functioning at various points in his career as playwright, actor, director, and designer. It is ironic, then, that the goal of his work was to poke fun at theater, as well as its representation of gender and its portrayal of gays. His work with the Ridiculous Theatrical Company was honored with many awards, including numerous Obies, a Drama Desk Award, a Guggenheim Fellowship, and grants from the National Endowment for the Arts and the New York State Council of the Arts.

Ludlam was born on April 12, 1943, and was attracted to the theater at a very young age. His early experiences with theater included attending a Punch and Judy puppet show at the Mineola Fair on Long Island in 1949, constant film-going with his mother, and appearances in elementary school plays. In 1958, Ludlam served an apprenticeship at the Red Barn Theater, a summer stock company on Long Island. The next year, he attended performances of Pirandello's *Tonight We Improvise* and Gelber's *The Connection* by the Living Theater, one of the seminal avant-garde companies of the 1950s and 1960s, which he later said left a lasting impression on him and shaped his view of theater. The Living Theater also inspired him, at the age of 17, to found the Students' Repertory Theater in Northpoint, Long Island, where he directed and acted.

In the early 1960s, Ludlam studied at Hofstra University, receiving an acting scholarship. His acting style at Hofstra was criticized as being too excessive. There he also wrote his first play, *Edna Brown,* which he later destroyed.

After leaving Hofstra, he moved to New York City and became immersed in avant-garde and gay theater. He began his professional career in 1966 with the Play-House of the Ridiculous, as both a performer and a playwright. He made his New York debut in 1966 playing Peeping Tom in Ronald Tavel's *The Life of Lady Godiva,* which was directed by John Vaccaro. The Play-House of the Ridiculous experimented with many of the techniques that eventually became part of Ludlam's repertoire: cross-dressing, exaggerated performance style, and burlesquing of popular and classical literature. Ludlam staged his play *Big Hotel* (1967) at the Play-House of the Ridiculous, but during rehearsals for his second play, *Conquest of the Universe,* he was fired by Vaccaro.

Many of Vaccaro's actors left with Ludlam, who then formed his own company, the Ridiculous Theatrical Company. In 1967, they presented *Conquest of the Universe* under a different title, *When Queens Collide,* because Vaccaro's troupe was also staging the play. Between 1967 and 1987, Ludlam was a prolific playwright for the Ridiculous Theatrical Company and also a leading actor, often playing roles in drag.

Ludlam's plays and the company's outrageous performance style helped the Ridiculous achieve cult status in New York and international recognition. Still, while the company attracted grants and awards and leased a permanent theater space, its finances were often uncertain, and the Ridiculous was always on the fringe of even the avant-garde. Because of financial and artistic difficulties, the Ridiculous Theatrical Company was reorganized in 1980, and some of the longtime members of the company left.

Among Ludlam's most notable plays during the 1970s and 1980s were *Bluebeard* (1970), *Camille* (1973, and revived posthumously in 1990), *Stage Blood* (1975), *Der Ring Gott Farblonjet* (1977), *Le Bourgeois Avant-Garde* (1982), *The Mystery of Irma Vep* (1984), *Medea* (1984), *Salammbo* (1985), and *The Artificial Jungle* (1986).

All of Ludlam's work exhibits his "ridiculous" dramatic techniques: satirizing stereotypes based on gender and sexual orientation through the use of cross-dressing, heightened theatricality, burlesquing of popular and serious literature, recognition of the audience, and a larger-than-life acting style. Although his plays are campy on the surface, they deal with gay politics seriously and sometimes poignantly.

During the 1980s, Ludlam developed a career apart from the Ridiculous Theatrical Company, acting in films—including *The Big Easy, Imposters,* and *Forever Lulu*—and appearing on television, in episodes of *Miami Vice* and *Tales from the Crypt.* He also played the title role in *Hedda Gabler* at the American Ibsen Theater in Pittsburgh in 1984. In addition, he taught playwriting at Yale University.

Ludlam died from complications of AIDS on May 28, 1987. His Ridiculous Theatrical Company, under the artistic direction of Everett Quinton, continues to perform. Ludlam's complete plays and an anthology of his critical and theoretical writings were published posthumously.

The Period   Ludlam's theater work belongs to the great tradition of burlesque and camp. In the nineteenth century, for example, there were many popular satires of serious and popular dramatic literature. In the twentieth century, many television shows—such as *Saturday Night Live, In Living Color,* and *Mad TV*—have presented takeoffs of popular films. Ludlam's work, however, transcends literary or theatrical satire. He is concerned about the politics of gay representation and the marginalization of homosexuals.

A number of plays and performers introduced gay and lesbian themes into theater before the 1960s. For example, in the nineteenth century and the early twentieth century there was considerable cross-dressing in theatrical performances: Men appeared in women's clothing and women in men's clothing, raising questions about sexual and gender roles. Charlotte Cushman is an example from nineteenth-century American theater. Some plays also treated the issue of the marginalization of gays and lesbians. One example is *The Children's Hour* (1934) by Lillian Hellman (1905–1984), in which gossip about a presumed lesbian relationship between two schoolteachers has shattering consequences.

Still, gay theater artists were fearful of publicly proclaiming their sexual orientation, and representations were muted at best. The play that first brought gay life to the forefront was *The Boys in the Band* (1968) by Mart Crowley (1935–), which depicted a group of men living an openly gay life. At the height of its success, however, there was a backlash against it. In 1969, a year after it opened, gay patrons of the Stonewall Inn in New York's Greenwich Village fought against police officers who were attempting to close the bar. This uprising, considered the beginning of the modern gay rights movement, changed the attitudes of gay activists—who now rejected what they considered Crowley's stereotyping of homosexuals as closeted, narcissistic, and filled with self-hatred. In 1996, when the play was revived in New York City, its historic significance was acknowledged.

From the early 1970s on, complex gay characters, often in plays by gay authors, were presented unapologetically. Two examples from the 1970s and 1980s are *The Ritz* (1975) by Terrence McNally (1939–) and *Torch Song Trilogy* (1983) by Harvey Fierstein (1954–). Since then, more and more plays have dealt expressly with gay issues. In the 1980s and 1990s, many plays have dealt with the AIDS crisis, including *The Normal Heart* (1985) by Larry Kramer, *As Is* (1985) by William M. Hoffman (1939–), Tony Kushner's two-part play *Angels in America* (1993–1994), and Terrence McNally's *Love! Valour! Compassion!* (1995).

Equally important has been the emergence of lesbian theater, which sometimes focuses on feminist issues and theory. Groups such as the Cockettes and the Angels of Light in San Francisco and Centola and Hot Peaches in New York are offshoots of gay and lesbian theater. One of the best-known, founded in 1981, is Split Britches, a renowned lesbian performance company featuring Peggy Shaw (1944–) and Lois Weaver (1949–).

THE MYSTERY OF IRMA VEP: A PENNY DREADFUL

Charles Ludlam

CHARACTERS

LADY ENID HILLCREST
LORD EDGAR HILLCREST
NICODEMUS UNDERWOOD
JANE TWISDEN
AN INTRUDER
ALCAZAR

PEV AMRI
IRMA VEP

The Mystery of Irma Vep is a full-length quick-change act. All roles are portrayed by two performers.

Act I

SCENE I

The library drawing room of Mandacrest, the Hill-crest estate near Hampstead Heath, between the wars.

The study is a large room with French doors at the back that open out on a garden. There is a desk and chair. A fireplace with a mantel over which is a portrait of Lady Irma in her bloom. Two deep arm-chairs flank the fireplace. There are signs that the Hillcrests have traveled: African masks and a painted Japanese screen. There is a bookcase with Morocco-bound volumes and doors left and right. At rise *Nicodemus* enters from the garden, through the French doors, carrying a basket. His left leg is deformed and the sole of his shoe is built up with wood. *Jane* is arranging flowers in a bowl.

JANE. Watch what you're doing! You're soaking wet! Don't track mud in here!

NICODEMUS. It's God's good rain, my girl.

JANE. It's the devil's rain. That's what it is!

[Lightning flashes, then thunder is heard.]

NICODEMUS. Would you rather the drought went on and on? It's thankful you should be. And that mightily.

JANE. And don't clump so with that wooden leg. You'll wake Lady Enid.

NICODEMUS. And wasn't it to save Lord Edgar from the wolf that me leg got mangled so? I should think she'd be glad to hear me clump after what I did for him.

JANE. That was a long time ago. Lady Enid doesn't know anything about it.

NICODEMUS. She'll find out soon enough.

JANE. Now, now, Nicodemus, I won't have you frightening Lord Edgar's new bride with your wolf tales.

NICODEMUS. And the sooner she does find out the better, I say!

JANE. Hush. Your tongue will dig your grave, Nicodemus. There are some things better left unsaid.

NICODEMUS. Pah! It's a free country, ain't it?

JANE. Shhhh!

NICODEMUS. Well, ain't it?

JANE. If Lord Edgar hears you you'll see how free it is. You'll find yourself without a situation.

NICODEMUS. That's a little bit too free for me. I'll bite me tongue.

JANE. We must stand by Lord Edgar. I'm afraid he'll be needing us now more than ever.

NICODEMUS. Why now more than ever? I'd say the worst was over. He's finally accepted the fact that Miss Irma's in her grave.

JANE. Don't talk like that. I can't bear the thought of her in a grave. She was always so afraid of the dark.

NICODEMUS. He's accepted it and you must too. Life has begun again for him. He mourned a more than respectable length of time and now he's brought home a new Lady Hillcrest.

JANE. That's just it. That's just the very thing! I don't think Lady Enid will ever make a fit mistress for Mandacrest.

NICODEMUS. And why not?

JANE. She's so, so . . . common. She'll never live up to the high standard set by Lady Irma.

NICODEMUS. That, my girl, is not for you or me to decide.

JANE. I can't stand the thought of taking orders from that vulgarian.

NICODEMUS. Come come, I won't have you talking that way about Lady Enid.

JANE. Lady Irma had a commanding presence and her manners were impeccable.

NICODEMUS. It takes more to please a man than fancy manners.

JANE. I would think a man—a *real* man—would find nothing more pleasing than fine breeding and savior fair.

NICODEMUS. If that French means what I think it does you'd better wash your mouth out with soap. Here's eggs and milk. The turtle was laying rather well today.

JANE. And where's the cream?

NICODEMUS. I skimmed it.

JANE. Again? Ah, you're incorrigible.

NICODEMUS. In what?

JANE. Now what will I tell Lord Edgar when he wants cream for his tea, huh?

NICODEMUS. Tell him what you like.

[Lightning and a clap of thunder.]

JANE. *[Shrieks.]* Ahhh!

NICODEMUS. There there. Don't be skeered. Nicodemus is here to protect you. *[Tries to put his arm around her.]*

JANE. *[Eluding his embrace.]* Keep your hands to yourself. You smell like a stable.

NICODEMUS. If you slept in a stable you'd smell like one too.

JANE. Keep your distance.

NICODEMUS. Someday, Janey my girl, you're going to smile on me.

JANE. Yeah, when hell freezes over and little devils go ice-skating.

NICODEMUS. If I was cleaned up and had a new white collar and smelled of bay rum and Florida water you'd think different.

JANE. Don't you get any ideas about me. You are beneath me and beneath me you're going to stay.

NICODEMUS. Someday you might want to get beneath me.

JANE. Ugh! How dare you speak to me in such manner? I've had education.

NICODEMUS. What education have you ever had?

JANE. I've read Bunyan's *Pilgrim's Progress* from cover to cover, the Holy Bible, the almanac, and several back issues of *Godey's Lady's Book.*

NICODEMUS. Well I've read the *Swineherd's Manual* from kiver to kiver.

JANE. *[Contemptuously.]* Hurmph!

NICODEMUS. You got no reason to look down your nose at me, miss. We're cut from the same bolt o' goods.

JANE. Don't go giving yourself airs. Go on back to your pigsty before I say something I'll be sorry for.

NICODEMUS. I'm not leaving until you give me a kiss.

JANE. I'll see you hanged first.

NICODEMUS. *[Chasing her around the room.]* Give me a little kiss and then I'll show you how I'm hung.

JANE. Get away from me you beast with your double entendres.

NICODEMUS. Double what?

[Thunder, footsteps above.]

JANE. Now you've done it. You've waked Lady Enid. Go quick before she sees you in the house.

NICODEMUS. What's she gettin' up now for? It's just about evening.

JANE. That's her way. She sleeps all day and she's up all night.

NICODEMUS. It's them city ways of hers. Lord Edgar told me she'd been on the stage.

JANE. *[Shocked.]* The stage! Ugh! How disgusting!

NICODEMUS. To think, a real live actress here at Mandacrest!

JANE. Yes, it's utterly degrading. But she is the mistress of the house now and we must adjust to her ways.

NICODEMUS. That's not what I meant. I think Lord Edgar has really done well for himself.

JANE. You men are all alike. You're so easily taken in. *[Footsteps.]* I hear her footsteps. Go!

NICODEMUS. But I want to get a look at her.

JANE. She's just an ordinary woman and she doesn't need you gawking at her. Go on back to your pigsty.

NICODEMUS. I found better company there than ever I found at Mandacrest.

[Exits.]

LADY ENID'S VOICE. *[Off.]* Jane, were you talking to someone?

JANE. Just Nicodemus. He came to bring the eggs.

LADY ENID. *[Off.]* Is he gone?

JANE. Yes, Lady Enid.

LADY ENID. Has the sun set?

JANE. It's pouring down rain, your ladyship. There's very little out there that could be called sun.

LADY ENID. Draw the draperies and light a fire. I'm coming down.

JANE. Ah Lord, my work is never done.

[Draws the draperies across the French door, cutting off the view of the garden. She takes a quick look at herself in the mirror; fans herself with her handkerchief; straightens her hair and collar.]

LADY ENID. Ah, you've made the room warm and cheery. Thank you, Jane.

JANE. Can I fix you a nice cup of tea?

LADY ENID. If it's no trouble.

JANE. *[Sternly.]* That's what I'm here for.

LADY ENID. Is Lord Edgar about?

JANE. He was up and out at the crack of dawn.

LADY ENID. Out? Out where?

JANE. He goes riding in the morning. It's a custom with him. *[Teakettle whistles off.]* Ah, there's the kettle calling.

[*Exits. Lady Enid looks about the room and examines the paintings and books. She looks out the French doors into the garden and out to the moors beyond. Then the portrait over the mantel catches her attention. She stands before it and stares at it a long time.*]

JANE. [*Returning with the tea things.*] How do you take it?

LADY ENID. I beg your pardon?

JANE. Your tea, miss.

LADY ENID. Plain.

JANE. [*Incredulous.*] No cream or sugar?

LADY ENID. No, quite plain.

JANE. That's queer.

LADY ENID. Queer?

JANE. Tea ain't much without cream and sugar.

LADY ENID. I'm on an eternal diet. The stage you know.

JANE. But that's all behind you now.

LADY ENID. [*With a sigh.*] Yes, I suppose it is. But the habit's ingrained. I shall probably refuse bread and potatoes 'til I die. [*Indicating the portrait.*] Who is that woman?

JANE. Why, that's Lady Hillcrest . . . I mean, that's the last Lady Hillcrest.

LADY ENID. She was very beautiful, wasn't she?

JANE. There will never be another woman who's her equal—oh, I beg your pardon, miss.

LADY ENID. That's all right, Jane. You were very fond of her, weren't you?

JANE. [*Bringing her cup of tea.*] She was like a part of meself, miss.

LADY ENID. I see. [*Sits and sips tea. Sharp reaction to the tea.*] You do make strong tea, don't you?

JANE. [*Indignant.*] When I makes tea I makes tea. And when I makes water I makes water.

LADY ENID. God send you don't make them in one pot.

JANE. [*Beat. Then realizing that a joke was made at her expense.*] Hurmph!

LADY ENID. You don't like me, do you, Jane?

JANE. I don't hate you.

LADY ENID. I should hope not! That would be a terrible thing, wouldn't it? If you hated me and we had to live here together.

JANE. Yes, I suppose it would. I said I don't hate you.

LADY ENID. You don't hate me. But you don't like me.

JANE. I'm not used to you. You'll take getting used to.

LADY ENID. [*Shivers.*] I felt a chill. A cat walked over my grave.

JANE. Isn't there a draft there, where you're sitting, Lady Enid?

LADY ENID. Yes, there is a little. Perhaps you'd better close the French doors.

JANE. Did Nicodemus leave them open again? If I've told him once I've told him a thousand times . . . Why, isn't that the master coming over there?

LADY ENID. [*Quickly.*] Where? [*Gets up.*] Yes, it's he. [*Hiding behind the curtain.*] Stand back! Don't let him see us.

JANE. What's that he's carrying? Arms full of heather and he's dragging something behind.

LADY ENID. Dragging something?

JANE. It looks like a big animal. Why, I believe he's killed the wolf.

LADY ENID. [*Nervously.*] Wolf?

JANE. The wolf that's been killing our lambs. Well we'll all sleep better too without that devil howling all night.

LADY ENID. He killed a wolf?

JANE. Yes, and he's brought the carcass back with him.

LADY ENID. Is it dead? Is it really dead?

JANE. It's dead and it won't get any deader.

LADY ENID. Which way is he coming?

JANE. He's taking the path by the pyracanthas.

LADY ENID. He's done that before. But will he take the footbridge?

JANE. That's just what I was asking meself. He's getting closer—no he's turned off—he's going the long way 'round and through the ivy arches.

LADY ENID. Then he's still not over it.

JANE. Ah, you can't blame him for not taking the footbridge after what happened there.

LADY ENID. They cling to their dead a long time at Mandacrest.

JANE. Nay, I think it's the dead that cling to us. It's as if they just don't want to let go. Like they can't bear to leave us behind. [*Comes back to herself abruptly.*] The master will be wanting his dinner. [*Turning at the door.*] How do you like your meat, miss?

LADY ENID. Well done.

JANE. No red meat?

LADY ENID. Not for me.

JANE. See, there's another difference. Miss Irma liked it bloody.

[*Exits.*]

LADY ENID. *[Turns sharply and looks at the portrait.]* Don't look at me like that. I didn't take him away from you, you know. Someone was apt to take your place sooner or later. It happened to be me. I know how you must feel seeing us so happy under your very nose. But there's nothing to be done about it, old girl. Life must go on.

LORD EDGAR. *[Enters with arms full of heather, dragging wolf carcass as described.]* Rough weather.

LADY ENID. *[Rushing to Edgar and planting a kiss on his lips.]* Edgar, darling, you're back.

LORD EDGAR. Please, Enid, not in front of . . .

LADY ENID. In front of who? There's no one looking. *[Pauses.]* Unless you mean her. *[Points to the painting.]*

LORD EDGAR. It does seem a bit odd. I mean kissing right in front of her.

LADY ENID. She looks vaguely sinister.

LORD EDGAR. Please, Enid. She's dead.

LADY ENID. Perhaps that's the reason.

LORD EDGAR. Let's don't talk about her.

LADY ENID. Yes, let's don't.

LORD EDGAR. Are you quite comfortable?

LADY ENID. Yes, quite. Jane doesn't like me but I think I'll win her over.

LORD EDGAR. I hope you'll like it here.

LADY ENID. I'm sure I will. Oh, Edgar, Edgar.

LORD EDGAR. Oh, Enid, Enid.

LADY ENID. Oh Wedgar, Wedgar, Wedgar.

LORD EDGAR. Oh Wenid, Wenid, Wenid.

LADY ENID. *[With a qualm.]* Edgar.

LORD EDGAR. *[Slightly reprimanding.]* Enid.

LADY ENID. *[Reassured.]* Edgar.

LORD EDGAR. *[Condescendingly.]* Enid.

LADY ENID. *[Snuggling his chest, with a sigh.]* Edgar Edgar Edgar.

LORD EDGAR. *[Comforting and comfortable.]* Enid Enid Enid.

LADY ENID. *[Passionately.]* Edgar!

LORD EDGAR. *[Aroused.]* Enid!

LADY ENID. *[More passionately.]* Edgar!

LORD EDGAR. *[More passionately.]* Enid!

LADY ENID. *[Rapturously.]* Edgar!

LORD EDGAR. *[Likewise.]* Enid!

LADY ENID. *[Climatically.]* Edgar!!

LORD EDGAR. *[Orgasmically.]* Enid!!

LADY ENID. *[Cooing.]* Edgar.

LORD EDGAR. *[Drowsily.]* Enid.

LADY ENID. Edgar?

LORD EDGAR. Enid.

LADY ENID. Take the painting down.

LORD EDGAR. I couldn't do that.

LADY ENID. Why not?

LORD EDGAR. I just couldn't.

LADY ENID. She's been dead three years.

LORD EDGAR. Yes, I know, but . . .

LADY ENID. Let's make a fresh start. Forget about the past.

LORD EDGAR. I want to, Enid, believe me, I do.

LADY ENID. We'll never feel comfortable with her watching every move we make.

LORD EDGAR. No, I suppose not.

LADY ENID. Then why not put her things away in a chest somewhere or make a little shrine where you can visit her once in a while? But not our home.

LORD EDGAR. You're right of course. I know you are. It's just that . . .

LADY ENID. What?

LORD EDGAR. She made me promise that I would always keep a flame burning before her picture.

LADY ENID. What nonsense.

LORD EDGAR. I tell you she made me promise.

LADY ENID. Blow it out.

LORD EDGAR. I couldn't break my word.

LADY ENID. I thought you belonged to me now. That we belonged to each other.

LORD EDGAR. We do, but that was before we met.

LADY ENID. Which means more to you? Your love for me or your promise to her?

LORD EDGAR. Enid, please. Don't put it that way.

LADY ENID. Which is it, Edgar? Which will it be?

LORD EDGAR. Please don't make me choose.

LADY ENID. Do you love me?

LORD EDGAR. How can you doubt it?

LADY ENID. Then the choice is already made. Blow it out!

LORD EDGAR. Dare I? *[Blows out the candle.]*

LADY ENID. You see, nothing happened.

LORD EDGAR. Weird that we thought it would.

[They laugh.]

LADY ENID. And now, darling, as to this matter of dragging dead animals into the drawing room—it's really got to stop.

LORD EDGAR. I say, you're really out to reform me, aren't you?

LADY ENID. Just a little.

LORD EDGAR. I'll have Nicodemus tend to it. Why don't you change for dinner?

LADY ENID. Good. I'm famished.

LORD EDGAR. Don't be long.

LADY ENID. I won't, I promise.

[Exits.]

LORD EDGAR. *[Goes to the painting.]* Forgive me, Irma, please. Please forgive me!

[Enter Nicodemus.]

NICODEMUS. Where is the new lady?

LORD EDGAR. Changing. You know how slow women are.

NICODEMUS. So you've finally killed the beast, eh, Master Edgar.

LORD EDGAR. Yes, I've killed it. It will rage no more.

NICODEMUS. But what about the beast within? Is that through with raging?

LORD EDGAR. It's resting peacefully at the moment. That's about the most we can expect, don't you think?

NICODEMUS. You're a man of will, you are, Edgar Hillcrest.

LORD EDGAR. Nicodemus, take the guts out and burn it.

NICODEMUS. Don't you want to save the skin?

LORD EDGAR. No, burn every hide and hair of it.

NICODEMUS. And the ashes? What should I do with them?

LORD EDGAR. Scatter them on the heath.

NICODEMUS. And let the wind take up its howling?

LORD EDGAR. Then throw them in the mill run.

NICODEMUS. After her?

LORD EDGAR. Yes, after her. And Nicodemus . . .

NICODEMUS. Yes, Master Edgar?

LORD EDGAR. Take down the painting.

NICODEMUS. And what do you want me to do with it?

LORD EDGAR. Burn it with the wolf.

[Exits. Underwood goes toward the mantel and tries to take down the painting. Enter Jane.]

JANE. And what do you think you're doing?

NICODEMUS. The master wants the painting down.

JANE. You can't do that. You can't take Lady Irma!

NICODEMUS. I can and I will. It's the master's orders.

JANE. Stop it! Stop it! Don't touch that picture. Ahgh! The sanctuary lights' gone out. Oh God, this will never do.

NICODEMUS. Don't blame me. It was out when I came in. Lord Edgar must have extinguished it.

JANE. *[Indicating the carcass.]* And what's this here?

NICODEMUS. You've got eyes in your head to see with. It's the wolf. He's killed the wolf.

JANE. Glory be! Is it possible?

NICODEMUS. It's cause for rejoicing.

JANE. *[Approaching the carcass warily.]* It's no rejoicing there'll be this night, Nicodemus Underwood. He's killed the wrong wolf.

[Blackout.]

SCENE II

[The scene is as before. It is late evening. The household is asleep. Jane is stoking the last embers of the fire. Lady Enid enters silently in her dressing gown. She stands over Jane, whose back is to her, and watches. Jane suddenly becomes aware of her presence and, frightened, gasps. This in turn frightens Lady Enid, who gasps also.]

LADY ENID. I didn't mean to frighten you.

JANE. I didn't mean to frighten you either. You shouldn't creep up on a person like that.

LADY ENID. I'm sorry, Jane. You have lived here a considerable time. Did you not say sixteen years?

JANE. Eighteen, miss. I came when the mistress was married, to wait on her; after she died, the master retained me as his housekeeper. Though I knew him from childhood. I was raised at the Frambly Parsonage.

LADY ENID. Indeed.

[Long silence between them.]

JANE. Ah, times have greatly changed since then!

LADY ENID. Yes, you've seen a good many alterations, I suppose?

JANE. I have: and troubles too.

LADY ENID. The Hillcrests are a very old family, aren't they?

JANE. Oh, Lord, yes. Why the Hillcrests go back to . . . back to . . . well, I don't know exactly who. But they've been descending for centuries.

LADY ENID. Lord Edgar told me he was an only child.

JANE. Yes, a strange flower upon the old solid wood of the family tree.

LADY ENID. Was he always so fond of hunting, even as a child?

JANE. Nay, he only took that up after the mistress passed away. Oh, but that's a long story. I won't be after boring you with it.

LADY ENID. Oh, do go on, Jane. Everything about Lord Edgar fascinates me.

JANE. Where is himself?

LADY ENID. Sleeping soundly. Jane, it will be an act of charity to tell me something of the family history. I know I shall not be able to rest if I go to bed, so be good enough to sit and chat for an hour.

JANE. Oh, certainly, miss! I'll just fetch a little sewing and then I'll sit as long as you please. Listen to that wind! It's an ungodly night. Can I get you a hot toddy to drive out the cold?

LADY ENID. If you're having one.

JANE. Sure I loves me toddy and me toddy loves me.

[She crosses to the table, gets her sewing, and pours out two toddies from a pan she has nestled among the embers. She gives one drink to Lady Enid and settles into the chair opposite her before the fire. Howling sound.]

LADY ENID. That wind!

JANE. That's not the wind. That's a wolf howling.

LADY ENID. It seems you've been troubled by wolves of late.

JANE. Not wolves. It's one wolf in particular. Victor.

LADY ENID. Victor?

JANE. He was captured as a pup and tamed. But his heart was savage. Miss Irma kept him as a pet.

LADY ENID. Like a dog.

JANE. He was bigger than a dog, so big the boy used to ride about on his back. Though Victor didn't like that much, I can tell you. Though he bore it for the mistress's sake, for it was to her he belonged. His happiest hours were spent stretched out at Miss Irma's feet, his huge purple tongue lolling out of his mouth. He never left her side the whole time she was carrying. Lord Edgar locked him out when it came time for her to deliver. And when he heard her labor pains, he howled.

LADY ENID. Lord Edgar told me that he'd had a son but that he died when he was still a child.

JANE. Ah, there's a tragic story, miss. But your toddy's gettin' cold. Finish that and I'll fix you another.

LADY ENID. [Drains her cup and passes it to Jane.] He was taken off with chicken pox, wasn't he?

JANE. Chicken pox? Now who told you that?

LADY ENID. No one told me. I was just supposing.

JANE. If Lord Edgar told you it was chicken pox, then chicken pox it was. We'd better leave it at chicken pox.

LADY ENID. No, really, he didn't tell me anything. The chicken pox was pure conjecture.

JANE. It's understandable that he didn't go into it. It's not an easy subject to talk about. Here's your toddy.

LADY ENID. Thanks.

JANE. And here's one for me.

LADY ENID. I'd like to know the true history, if you don't mind relating it.

JANE. [The toddy loosening her tongue.] One clear winter day Victor and the boy went out to the heath to play in the new-fallen snow. The wolf came back without the boy. We waited. We watched. We called ourselves hoarse. And at dusk we found him in the mill run, dead. His throat had been torn apart.

LADY ENID. Horrible.

JANE. Lord Edgar wanted Victor destroyed. But Lady Irma fought against it. She said it wasn't Vic had done it.

LADY ENID. Perhaps it wasn't.

JANE. His throat was torn. What else could it have been? They fought bitterly over it. He said she loved the wolf more than her own child. But I think it was the double loss she dreaded, for when Victor was gone she'd have nothing, you see. When the master came to shoot Victor, Lady Irma turned him loose upon the heath and drove him away with stones, crying, "Run, Vic, run, and never come back!" I don't think the poor beast understood what happened because he still comes back to this day, looking for Lady Irma.

LADY ENID. Poor Victor. Poor boy. Poor Irma.

JANE. Poor Lord Edgar.

LADY ENID. Yes, poor poor Lord Edgar!

JANE. But here's the strangest part of all.

LADY ENID. Yes?

JANE. The fresh snow is like a map. I traced their tracks meself. Victor's trail turned off. The boy was killed by a wolf that left human tracks in the snow.

LADY ENID. Human? You mean the boy was murdered?

JANE. But that takes us to the subject of werewolves.

LADY ENID. Werewolves?

JANE. Humans who take the form of a wolf at night.

LADY ENID. But that's just superstition.

JANE. Yes, superstition, the realm beyond the explainable where science is powerless. Of course everything pointed to Victor. The boy fell down and skinned his knee. He let the loving beast lick his wound. He tasted blood. The killer was aroused. He turned on the child and sank his fangs into its tender neck. A perfectly logical explanation. But then there were those tracks in the snow. Wouldn't it be convenient for a werewolf to have a real wolf to blame it on?

LADY ENID. Didn't you show them to anyone? The tracks, I mean.

JANE. Ah, they wouldn't listen. They said they were my tracks. That I'd made them meself. I didn't push it, miss, or they'd have packed me off to Dottyville. It's hard to convince people of the supernatural. Most people have enough trouble believing in the natural.

LADY ENID. Of course you're right. But those footprints.

JANE. I wish I had 'em here as evidence. But where are the snows of yesteryear? And that's the werewolf's greatest alibi—people don't believe in him. Well miss, I must be gettin' meself to bed. My rheumatism is starting to act up again.

LADY ENID. Leave the light, Jane. I think I'll stay up and read a while.

JANE. Here's a good book for you. It's the master's treatise on ancient Egyptian mythology.

LADY ENID. Thanks!

JANE. Don't stay up too late now. We're having kippers and kidneys for breakfast and I know you won't want to miss that.

LADY ENID. Jane, what was the boy's name?

JANE. Didn't you know? That was Victor too. Good night, Lady Enid. *[Exits.]*

LADY ENID. *[Sits in chair with her back to the glass doors and reads. The shadow of the stranger can be seen through the sheer organdy curtains illuminated intermittently by flashes of lightning. A bony, almost skeletal hand feels for a latch. It drums its fingernails against the windowpane.]* What—what was it? Real or a delusion? Oh God, what was it? *[Suddenly a single pane of the French door shatters. The bony hand reaches in through the curtains and opens the latch. A gaunt figure enters the room slowly. A ray of light strikes the pallid face. He fixes her with a stare.]* Who are you? What do you want? *[The clock chimes one. The Intruder emits a hissing sound.]* What do you want? Oh God, what do you want of me?

[She tries to run to the door but the Intruder catches her by her long hair and, winding it around his bony fingers, drags her back toward the mantel. She takes roses from the vase and presses their thorns into his eyes. The Intruder groans and releases her. She runs across the room. He follows her. She stabs him with scissors from Jane's sewing basket. Intruder staggers back and falls through open door down right. Lady Enid crosses to the mantel and tries to get control of herself. She sighs with relief. Intruder reenters and clapping his hand over her mouth drags her to the door, locks it, then crosses up center to the double doors where shriek follows strangled shriek as he seizes her neck in his fanglike teeth and a hideous sucking noise follows. Lady Enid emits a high-pitched scream made at the back of the throat by drawing the breath in. Running footsteps are heard off.]

LORD EDGAR. *[Off right.]* Did you hear a scream, Jane?

JANE. *[Off right.]* I did. Where was it?

LORD EDGAR. *[Off.]* God knows. It sounded so near yet far away. I got up and got dressed as soon as I heard it.

JANE. *[Off. No pause.]* All is still now.

LORD EDGAR. *[Off.]* Yes, but unless I was dreaming there was a scream.

JANE. We couldn't both have dreamed it.

LORD EDGAR. Where's Lady Enid?

JANE. Isn't she with you?

[Lady Enid emits another high-pitched scream.]

LORD EDGAR. There it is again. Search the house! Search the house. Where did it come from? Can you tell? *[Lady Enid screams again as before.]* Good God! There it is again! *[He tries the door stage right. But it will not open.]* Enid! Enid! Are you in there? Speak for heaven's sake! Speak! Good God, we must force the door. *[They beat on the door.]* Get the crowbar.

JANE. Where is it?

LORD EDGAR. In the cellar. Hurry! Hurry! Run! Run! Enid! Oh Enid!

JANE. Here it is.

[Edgar forces the door open and bursts into the room.]

NICODEMUS. *[Voice off, up center.]* Lady Enid! Lady Enid! Oh God no! Lady Enid! *[Nicodemus enters carrying the limp body of Lady Enid. Her long hair hangs down covering her face. There are several drops of blood on her nightgown.]* Help oh help oh heaven oh help! *[He carries her body out the door stage right.]* Now where the blue hell am I bringing her, beyond the veil?

LORD EDGAR. *[Following them.]* What is it? What's happened? Who's done this thing to you?

NICODEMUS. *[Reentering.]* Who or what? I saw something moving in the heath.

LORD EDGAR. Something? What kind of something?

NICODEMUS. Dog's skull. Dog's body. Its glazing eyes staring out of death candle to shake and bend my soul. *[Suddenly something with a horrible face appears at the window. It lets out a frightening earsplitting sound and then laughing bangs against the windowpanes. Nicodemus growls in a hoarsened raspy voice.]* There! There it is.

[The thing emits a shrill laugh like the sound of electronic feedback.]

LORD EDGAR. Lord help us!

NICODEMUS. Be it whatever thing it may—I'll follow it!

LORD EDGAR. No! No! Do not!

NICODEMUS. I must! I will!

LORD EDGAR. Not without a gun! Don't be a fool!

NICODEMUS. Let whoever will come with me—I'll follow this dread form!

[Exits.]

LORD EDGAR. Wait for me you fool!

[Takes a gun from off the wall.]

NICODEMUS. *[Voice off.]* I see it! I see it! It goes down the wall and through the wisterias.

LORD EDGAR. It's dark down there. There isn't any moon. *[There are animal sounds, the sounds of a struggle, and then a few agonized cries. The doors fly open and a human leg, one that had formerly belonged to Nicodemus, is thrown in.]* Great Scott! *[He rushes out. And is heard calling off.]* Which way! Which way?

NICODEMUS. *[Voice off.]* Over here. Help! Oh help me!

[There is the sound of shots off.]

JANE. *[Sticking her head in through the door stage right.]* Was them shots I heard?

LADY ENID. *[Off.]* Jane. Jane.

JANE. Yes Lady Enid.

LADY ENID. Come. I need you. I'm afraid to be alone.

JANE. I'll come and I'll bring the ghost candle to light your agony. It's the curse of the Druids, that's what it is. The druidy Druids. *[Withdraws.]*

[Footsteps and the sound of something dragging.]

NICODEMUS. *[Entering up center.]* I saw it. I touched it. I struggled with it. It was cold and clammy like a corpse. It can't be human.

LORD EDGAR. *[Entering under Nicodemus's arm.]* Not human? No, of course not human. You said it was a dog.

NICODEMUS. Then it looked like a wolf, then it looked like a woman! It tore off me leg and started chewing on it.

LORD EDGAR. Great Scott? It can't be.

NICODEMUS. If it hadn't been wood I swear it would have eaten it.

LORD EDGAR. No!

NICODEMUS. Yes! Yes! Ghoul! Chewer of corpses! And all the while it made this disgusting sucking sound. It sucked the very marrow from me bones. I can feel it now. It's very near. Bride bed. Child bed. Bed of death! She comes, pale vampire, through storm her eyes, her bat sails bloodying the sea! Mouth to her mouth's kiss! Her eyes on me to strike me down. I felt the green fairy's fang.

[Howling off.]

LORD EDGAR. What was that?

NICODEMUS. Just a wolf.

LORD EDGAR. No! It's Victor! Victor come back to haunt me! *[Starts out.]* Give me that pistol there. This time I'll get him! *[Fur at the door.]* Look! There it is now! It won't escape this time.

NICODEMUS. *[Clinging to his leg.]* No! Master, do not go! There is no help for it!

[Keening lament is heard on the wind.]

LORD EDGAR. Let go of my leg. Goblin damned, I'll send your soul to hell!

[Exits.]

NICODEMUS. No! Master! Master! It's Irma, Irma Vep! A ghost woman with ashes on her breath, alone, crying in the rain.

[Shots, running footsteps, and howling heard off.]

JANE. *[Rushing in.]* What's all this yelling? You'll wake the dead.
NICODEMUS. The master's at it again—hunting.
JANE. Is it wolves again?
NICODEMUS. This time he's sure it's Victor.
JANE. Victor?
NICODEMUS. That's what he says!
JANE. Well, don't just stand there gawking! Go after him! Be some help!
NICODEMUS. Oh no. Not me! There's something on that heath that would make your blood run cold.
JANE. Ah, you big sissy. If you don't go to his aid I'll go meself.
NICODEMUS. Oh, very well, woman. Wait until I screw in me leg.

[He goes off, screws it in noisily, returns.]

JANE. It seems that more than your leg got bitten off. There's also been a loss of virility. *[She takes a gun down off the wall.]*
NICODEMUS. Now don't go playing with firearms, miss. That's a man's tool you've got in your hands. *[They struggle for the gun.]*
JANE. Let go! Let go! Get out of my way. Lord Edgar needs me.

[The gun goes off and the bullet hits the painting. The painting bleeds.]

NICODEMUS. Now see what you've done. You've shot Lady Irma. The painting is bleeding!
[Wrests the gun from her grasp and exits in the same direction as Lord Edgar.] Lord Edgar!

JANE. *[Calling after him.]* Down past the mill run and out onto the moors. The other way, Nicodemus! The other way! Take the shortcut through the cedar grove. Faster. Faster, Nicodemus! Faster!
LADY ENID. *[Enters slowly.]* Where is Lord Edgar?
JANE. He's searching the moors. He thinks he's seen Victor.
LADY ENID. The wolf or the boy?
JANE. Both.

[Blackout.]

SCENE III

LORD EDGAR. Can you tell me how it happened, Enid dearest?
LADY ENID. Jane and I sat up late, she regaling me with tales of Mandacrest, its history, legends, and such. As the hour grew late I prepared myself for bed as is my wont. When I had completed my beauty ritual I went straight to our bedchamber and discovered that you had fallen asleep over a book. I crawled in beside you. But unable to sleep myself got up again and came downstairs. As there were some embers of the fire still aglow, I instructed Jane to leave the light when she went to bed, which she did. Then I sat in that chair and began reading your treatise on lycanthropy and the dynasties of Egypt. There was a light rain, as you will recall. Then it turned to hail. And as I read I listened to the patter of the hailstones on the windowpanes. It was during that chapter on how the priests of Egypt perfected the art of mummification to the point that the Princess Pev Amri was preserved in a state of suspended animation and was known as She who Sleeps . . .
LORD EDGAR. . . . but Will One Day Wake.
LADY ENID. Yes, that's it! She Who Sleeps but Will One Day Wake. And how her tomb was guarded by Anubis the jackal-headed god. But that her tomb has never been found.
LORD EDGAR. That is what is generally believed.
LADY ENID. Then suddenly the pattering at the window caught my attention, for the hail had stopped but the pattering went on. The glass shattered. I turned. It was in the room. I think I screamed. But I couldn't run away! I couldn't

run away! It caught me by the hair and then . . . I can tell no more! I can tell no more!

LORD EDGAR. You seem to have hurt your neck. There is a wound there.

LADY ENID. Wound?!! I feel so weak. I feel so faint. As though I had almost bled to death.

LORD EDGAR. But you couldn't have bled very much. There were no more than five little drops of blood on your dressing gown. Now, you'd better get some sleep.

LADY ENID. No sleep! No sleep for me! I shall never sleep again! Sleep is dead. Sleep is dead. She hath murthered sleep. I dare not be alone to sleep. Don't leave me alone. Don't ever leave me alone again. For sleep is dead. Sleep is dead. *[Off.]* Who murthered sleep?

LORD EDGAR. Jane will sit with you. *[Leans out the door and speaks to Jane off.]* Take care of her Jane.

JANE. *[Voice off.]* There there, Lady Enid. Easy does it. Here we go.

LORD EDGAR. Good girl, Jane.

[Enter Nicodemus up center.]

NICODEMUS. Is Lady Enid alive?

LORD EDGAR. She is weak and will sleep long. *[Sighs.]*

NICODEMUS. You sigh. . . . Some fearful thoughts, I fear, oppress your heart.

LORD EDGAR. Hush. Hush. She may overhear.

NICODEMUS. Lord Edgar, look at that portrait.

LORD EDGAR. Why, that's blood, isn't it?

NICODEMUS. You must muse upon it.

LORD EDGAR. No, no. I do wish, and yet I dread . . .

NICODEMUS. What?

LORD EDGAR. To say something to you all. But not here—not now—tomorrow.

NICODEMUS. The daylight is coming quickly on.

LORD EDGAR. I will sit up until sunrise. You can fetch my powder flask and bullets. And if you please, reload the pistols.

NICODEMUS. Lady Enid is all right, I presume.

LORD EDGAR. Yes, but her mind appears to be much disturbed.

NICODEMUS. From bodily weakness, I daresay.

LORD EDGAR. But why should she be bodily weak? She was strong and well but a few hours ago. The glow of youth and health was on her cheeks. Is it possible that she should become bodily weak in a single night? Nicodemus, sit down. You know that I am not a superstitious man.

NICODEMUS. You certainly are not.

LORD EDGAR. And yet I have never been so absolutely staggered as I am by the occurrences of this night.

NICODEMUS. Say on.

LORD EDGAR. I have a frightful, a hideous suspicion which I fear to mention to anyone lest it be laughed to scorn.

NICODEMUS. I am lost in wonder.

LORD EDGAR. Nicodemus, swear to me that you will never repeat to anyone the dreadful suggestion I am about to make.

NICODEMUS. I swear.

LORD EDGAR. Nicodemus, you have heard of the dreadful superstition which, in some countries, is extremely rife, wherein it is believed that there are beings who never die.

NICODEMUS. Never die?

LORD EDGAR. In a word you have heard of a . . . heard of a . . . oh God in heaven! I dread to pronounce the word, though I heard you speak it not three hours past. Dare I say? . . . Dare I say? . . .

NICODEMUS. Vampyre?

LORD EDGAR. You have said it. You have said it. Nosferatu. But swear to me once more that you will not repeat it to anyone.

NICODEMUS. Be assured I shall not. I am far from wishing to keep up in anyone's mind suspicions which I would fain, very fain refute.

LORD EDGAR. Then let me confide the worst of my fears, Nicodemus.

NICODEMUS. Speak it. Let me hear.

LORD EDGAR. I believe the vampire . . . is one of us.

NICODEMUS. *[Uttering a groan of almost exquisite anguish.]* One of us? Oh God! Oh God! Do not too readily yield belief to so dreadful a supposition, I pray you.

LORD EDGAR. Nicodemus, within a fortnight I shall embark for Cairo. There I will organize an expedition to Geza and certain obscure Numidian ruins in the south.

NICODEMUS. Are you taking Lady Enid?

LORD EDGAR. No, I fear that in her delicate mental state the trip might be too much for her. I will arrange for her to rest in a private sanatorium. Look after Mandacrest until I return. I believe the desert holds some secret. I feel it calling to me. I believe I shall find some answer out there among its pyramids and sacred mummies. At least I know I shall be far away from her.

NICODEMUS. From Lady Enid?

LORD EDGAR. No, from Lady Irma. For Nicodemus, it is she I believe has extended her life by feasting on human gore.

NICODEMUS. Say not so!

LORD EDGAR. Irma could never accept the idea of death and decay. She was always seeking consolation in the study of spiritualism and reincarnation. After a while it became an obsession with her. Even on her deathbed she swore she would come back.

NICODEMUS. Do you think she will come again?

LORD EDGAR. I know not. But I almost hope she may. For I would fain speak to her.

NICODEMUS. It is said that if one burns a love letter from a lover who has died at the third crowing of the cock on Saint Swithin's Day, you will see the lover ever so briefly.

LORD EDGAR. More superstition.

NICODEMUS. Very like. Very like. Yet after the occurrences of this night I can scarcely distinguish truth from fancy. *[Cock crows off.]*

There's the cock. 'Twill soon be dawn. Damnéd spirits all, that in crossways and floods have burial, already to their wormy beds have gone, for fear lest day should look their shames upon.

LORD EDGAR. *[Amazed.]* Nicodemus, you know your Shakespeare!

NICODEMUS. I paraphrase.

[Exits. The cock crows again.]

LORD EDGAR. The second crowing of the cock. *[Takes out letters bound with a ribbon.]* Irma's letters. Of course it's ridiculous . . . but what harm can it do? I'd best part with them anyway. *[Quotes.]* "In all the world. In all the world. One thing I know to be true. You'd best be off with the old love before you're on with the new." *[Burns letter before painting. Cock crows. Painting flies out. A woman's face appears in the painting. She screams.]* Irma!

[Curtain.]

Act II

SCENE I

[Various places in Egypt.]

LORD EDGAR. Ah Egypt! It looks exactly as I pictured it! I have a presentiment that we shall find the tomb intact in the valley of Bîbân-el Mulûk.

ALCAZAR. Osiris hear you!

LORD EDGAR. This invocation is certainly permissible opposite the ancient Diospolis Magna. But we have failed so often. The treasure seekers have always been ahead of us.

ALCAZAR. In recent years our work has been made doubly difficult by the activities of certain political groups seeking to halt the flow of antiquities from out of the country. These armed bandits use this high moral purpose to seize any and all treasures. And this, after the excavators have spent a great deal of time and money to unearth them.

LORD EDGAR. If we can but find an untouched tomb that can yield up to us its treasures inviolate!

ALCAZAR. I can spare you the disappointments of places I know to be quite empty because the contents have been removed and sold for a good price long ago. I believe I can take you to a syrinx that has never been discovered by the miserable little jackals who take it into their heads to scratch among the tombs.

LORD EDGAR. The idea fascinates me. But to excavate an unopened tomb—not to mention the difficulties of locating one—would require manpower and organizational abilities almost equal to those the Pharaohs employed to seal it.

ALCAZAR. I can place at your disposal a hundred intrepid fellahs, who, incited by baksheesh and a whip of hippopotamus hide, would dig down into the bowels of the earth with their fingernails. We might tempt them to bring to light some buried sphinx, to clear away the obstructions before a temple, to open a tomb . . .

LORD EDGAR. *[Smiles dubiously.]* Hmmm.

ALCAZAR. I perceive that you are not a mere tourist and that commonplace curiosities would have no charm for you. So I shall show you a tomb that has escaped the treasure seekers. Long it has lain unknown to any but myself. It is a prize I have guarded for one who should prove worthy of it.

LORD EDGAR. And for which you will make me pay a round sum.

ALCAZAR. I will not deny that I hope to make money. I unearth pharaohs and sell them to people. Pharaohs are getting scarce these days. The article is in demand but it is no longer manufactured.

LORD EDGAR. Let's not beat about the bush. How much do you want?

ALCAZAR. For a tomb that no human hand has disturbed since the priests rolled the rocks before the entrance three thousand years ago, would it be too much to ask a thousand guineas?

LORD EDGAR. A thousand guineas!

ALCAZAR. A mere nothing. After all, the tomb may contain gold in the lump, necklaces of pearls and diamonds, earrings of carbuncle formed from the urine of lynxes, sapphire seals, ancient idols of precious metals; why, the currency of the time, that by itself would bring a good price.

LORD EDGAR. *[Aside.]* Artful scoundrel! He knows perfectly well that such things are not to be found in Egyptian sepulchers.

ALCAZAR. Well, my lord, does the bargain suit you?

LORD EDGAR. Yes, we will call it a thousand guineas. If the tomb has never been touched and nothing—not even a stone—has been disturbed by the levers of the excavators, and on condition that we can carry everything away.

ALCAZAR. I accept. You can risk the banknotes and gold without fear. It seems your prayer has been answered.

LORD EDGAR. Perhaps we are rejoicing too soon and are about to experience the same disappointments encountered by Belzoni when he believed he was the first to enter the tomb of Menepha Seti. He, after having passed through a maze of corridors, pits, and chambers, found only an empty sarcophagus with a broken lid, for the treasure seekers had attained the royal tomb by mining through the rocks from the other direction.

ALCAZAR. Oh no! This tomb is too far removed for those accursed moles to have found their way there. I have lived many years in the valley of the kings and my eyes have become as piercing as those of the sacred hawks perched on the entablatures of the temples. For years I have not so much as dared to cast a glance in that direction, fearing to arouse the suspicions of the violators of the tombs. This way, my lord.

[They exit. The lights fade and come up somewhere in the tomb. It is very dark. From time to time some detail emerges from the darkness in the light of their lanterns.]

LORD EDGAR. The deuce! Are we going down to the center of the earth? The heat increases to such a degree that we cannot be far from the infernal regions.

ALCAZAR. It is a pit, milord. What's to be done?

LORD EDGAR. We must lower ourselves on ropes. *[Echo.]* These cursed Egyptians were so cunning about hiding the entrances of their burial burrows. They could not think of enough ways to puzzle poor people. One can imagine them laughing beforehand at the downcast faces of the excavators.

ALCAZAR. Another dead end.

LORD EDGAR. It looks like they've beaten us this round. Rap on the floor and listen for a hollow sound. *[They do so. After much rapping the wall gives back a hollow sound.]* Help me to remove this block. It's a bit low. We'll have to crawl on our faces.

ALCAZAR. Oy! *[They do so.]* Look there, milord.

LORD EDGAR. The familiar personages of the psychostasia with Osiris as judge. *[Stands.]* Well well, my dear Alcazar. So far you have kept your part of the bargain. We are indeed the first human beings who have entered here since the dead, whoever he may be, was abandoned to eternity and oblivion in the tomb.

ALCAZAR. Oh, he must have been a very powerful personage, a prince of the royal household at least.

LORD EDGAR. I will tell you after I decipher his cartouche.

ALCAZAR. But first let us enter the most beautiful room of all, the room the ancient Egyptians called the Golden Room.

LORD EDGAR. Really, I have some compunction of conscience about disturbing the last rest of this poor unknown mortal who felt so sure that he would rest in peace until the end of the world.

Our visit will be a most unwelcome one to the host of this mansion.

ALCAZAR. You'll be wanting a proper introduction and I have lived long enough among the Pharaohs to make you one. I know how to present you to the illustrious inhabitant of this subterranean palace.

LORD EDGAR. Look, a five-toed footprint in the dust.

ALCAZAR. Footprint?

LORD EDGAR. It looks as though it were made yesterday.

ALCAZAR. How can that be?

LORD EDGAR. It must have been the last footprint made by the last slave leaving the burial chamber thirty-five hundred years ago. There has not been a breath of air in here to disturb it. Why, mighty civilizations have risen and fallen since this footprint was made. Their pomp, their power, their monuments of stone have not lasted as long as this insignificant footprint in the dust.

[Sarcophagus revealed.]

ALCAZAR. My lord! My lord! The sarcophagus is intact!

LORD EDGAR. Is it possible, my dear Alcazar—is it intact? *[Examines the sarcophagus, then exclaims rapturously.]* Incredible good fortune! Marvelous chance! Priceless treasure!

ALCAZAR. I asked too little. This my lord has robbed me.

LORD EDGAR. There there, Alcazar. A bargain is a bargain. Here are the vases that held the viscera of the mummy contained in the sarcophagus. Nothing has been touched in this palace of death since the day when the mummy, in its coffins and cerements, had been laid upon its couch of basalt.

ALCAZAR. Observe that these are not the usual funerary offerings.

LORD EDGAR. Don't touch it! Touch nothing! It might crumble. First I must decipher this cartouche. "She Who Sleeps but Will One Day Wake." A lotus sarcophagus. Hmmmm. Notice that the lotus motif recurs, as well as the ankh, emblem of eternal life. Must you smoke those nasty musk-scented cigarettes? There's little enough air in here as it is.

ALCAZAR. Shall we open the sarcophagus?

LORD EDGAR. Certainly. But take care not to injure the lid when opening it, for I want to remove this monument and make a present of it to the British Museum.

[They remove the cover.]

ALCAZAR. A woman! A woman!

LORD EDGAR. Astonishing novelty! The necropolis of the queens is situated farther off, in a gorge of the mountains. The tombs of the queens are very simple. Let me decipher the cartouche. "She Who Sleeps but Will One Day Wake."

ALCAZAR. *[Pointing to the butt.]* This is a very primitive hieroglyph.

LORD EDGAR. It's a little behind.

ALCAZAR. It's almost more than I can believe.

LORD EDGAR. It's *altogether* more than *I* can believe.

ALCAZAR. What? You see these things before your very eyes and still you do not believe?

LORD EDGAR. The women of the East have always been considered inferior to the men, even after death. The greater part of these tombs, violated at very remote epochs, have served as receptacles for deformed mummies, rudely embalmed, that still exhibit traces of leprosy and elephantiasis. By what means, by what miracle of substitution, had this woman's coffin found its way into this royal sarcophagus, in the midst of this palatial crypt, worthy of the most illustrious and powerful of the Pharaohs? This unsettles all of my opinions and theories and contradicts the most reliable authorities on the subject of the Egyptian funeral rites so uniform in every respect for thousands of years.

ALCAZAR. We have no doubt alighted on some mystery, some obscure point lost to history. Had some ambitious woman usurped the tomb as she had the throne?

LORD EDGAR. What a charming custom. To bury a young woman with all the coquettish arsenal of her toilette about her. For there can be no doubt that it is a young woman enveloped in these bands of linen stained yellow with age and essences.

ALCAZAR. Compared with the ancient Egyptians we are veritable barbarians: dragging out a mere animal existence. We no longer have any delicacy of sentiment connected with death. What tenderness, what regret, what love are revealed in this devoted attention, this unlimited precaution, this vain solicitude that no one would ever witness, the affection lavished upon an insensible corpse, these efforts to snatch from destruction an adored form, and to present it to the soul intact upon the great day of the resurrection.

LORD EDGAR. Someday we may attain to such heights of civilization and refinement of feeling. In the meantime let us disrobe this young beauty, more than three thousand years old, with all the delicacy possible.

ALCAZAR. Poor lady, profane eyes are about to rest upon charms unknown to love itself, perhaps.

LORD EDGAR. Strange. I feel embarrassed at not having the proper costume in which to present myself before a royal mummy.

ALCAZAR. There is no time here. In this tomb, far away from the banal stupidities of the modern world, we might just as well be in ancient Egypt on the day this cherished being was entrusted to eternity.

[They unwrap the mummy's hand, which holds a scroll.]

LORD EDGAR. Extraordinary! In most cases mummification is accomplished by the use of bitumen and natron. Here, the body, prepared by a longer, safer, and more costly process, has preserved the elasticity of the skin, the grain of the epidermis, and a color that is almost natural. It has the fine hue of a new Florentine bronze and the warm amber tint of Titian.

ALCAZAR. By the knees of Amon Ra—behold— there is a scroll clasped in her hand!

LORD EDGAR. *[Gently unrolls the scroll.]* Bring the electric torch here. "She Who Sleeps but Will One Day Wake." It is the same cartouche unmistakably. *[Reads on silently, then mutters.]* Good god! It can't be! It can't be!

ALCAZAR. What does it say?

LORD EDGAR. *[Awed.]* It is the formula to revive the princess. To return her to life once more.

ALCAZAR. But surely you don't . . .

LORD EDGAR. It's more than I can believe at the moment, Alcazar. But something inside me wants to believe. *[He reads more.]* Well! This is simple enough. These caskets and bottles and bowls contain the ingredients in the formula. *[Reads.]* The priest must wear certain vestments and douse the lid with wine. The wine in these

bottles has dried up over the centuries. Oh drat! I have no wine. I am an abstainer.

ALCAZAR. *[Produces a bottle of wine from his pocket.]* I have wine. Very good wine. And although it is a Madeira, of somewhat more recent vintage, I believe it may suffice. The wine may very well be the least important element in the formula.

LORD EDGAR. *[Reads.]* It says here that the priest must be alone with the mummy when the soul is called back from the underworld.

ALCAZAR. Permit me to withdraw and leave you alone with your newfound lady friend. But before I go, may I make one request?

LORD EDGAR. Certainly, Alcazar, what is it?

ALCAZAR. Leave some wine for the return trip.

LORD EDGAR. I'll use only what is absolutely necessary to complete the ritual.

ALCAZAR. Thank you.

[Exits backwards making a salaam as he goes out.]

LORD EDGAR. *[Dresses himself in the costume of the Egyptian priest. Lights the charcoal braziers in the perfuming pans on either side of the sarcophagus. And intones the following invocation.]* Katara katara katara rana! Ecbatana Ecbatana Soumouft! Soumouft! Fahata fahata Habebe! Oh Habebe! Oh Habebe! Habebe tay!

[He gently unwraps the mummy as the music swells.]

PEV AMRI. *[Flutters her eyelashes and opens her eyes.]* Habebe? Habebe tay?

LORD EDGAR. *[Cries out.]* Oh God!

PEV AMRI. *[Dances, then.]* Fahouta bala bala mem fou ha ram sahadi Karnak!

LORD EDGAR. Oh exquisite! Exquisite beauty!

PEV AMRI. Han fu bazaar danbazaar.

LORD EDGAR. Forgive me divine one, but your spoken language is lost on me.

PEV AMRI. Mabrouka. Geza. *[Laughs, then looking into Sarcophagus and touching herself.]* Ankh! Ankh!

LORD EDGAR. *[Exclaims.]* Anka! Life! Ankh! Life! Life!

PEV AMRI. Ankh . . . life?

LORD EDGAR. Ankh . . . life.

PEV AMRI. Life. Life!

LORD EDGAR. Life!

PEV AMRI. *[Writhing indicates stiffness of spine.]* Cairo! Cairo! Practor! *[If audience hisses.]* Asp!

LORD EDGAR. Those lips. Silent for three thousand years now beg to be kissed. But do I dare? [Kisses her.]

PEV AMRI. [She slaps him.] Puna kha fo ha na ba bhouna. [Makes gesture that she is hungry.] Bhouna! Bhouna!

LORD EDGAR. Hungry? Of course you must be hungry after not having eaten in three millennia. I'll get you food. A loaf of bread, a jug of wine, a book of verse, and thou beside me in the wilderness and wilderness is paradise enow!

[Kisses her hand and runs out to get Alcazar.]

PEV AMRI. Amon! Amon Ra! Amenhotep. Memphis. Geza. Aswan. Hatshepshut. Too 'n come in! [Sniffs.] Sphinx!

[Scurries back into the mummy case, closes the door after her.]

LORD EDGAR. Alcazar! Alcazar! She's hungry! She wants food!

ALCAZAR. [Off.] She wants? Surely you don't mean . . .

LORD EDGAR. Yes it's true! It's true! She's alive! She's alive. In flesh and blood.

ALCAZAR. My boy you have stayed too long in the tomb. Your mind is playing tricks on you.

LORD EDGAR. Come if you don't believe me. See for yourself. [He rushes onto the stage. Alcazar follows behind somewhat slowly and dubiously. He is obviously totally unconvinced.] Where is she? She's gone. She was here a minute ago.

ALCAZAR. Akh—naten!

LORD EDGAR. I tell you she spoke! I kissed those divine lips. Look! She gave me this ring!

ALCAZAR. We must leave before dawn. If they find us looting the tomb they will report us to the authorities.

LORD EDGAR. But she's alive, I tell you, alive! [Calling.] Princess! Princess, where are you? Where are you, Pev Amri? Pev!

ALCAZAR. [Goes to the sarcophagus and opens it slowly.] Is this what you are looking for?

[Inside the sarcophagus stands a mummy as before, only this time the wrappings have been partially removed revealing a hideously decomposed face through the dried flesh of which the skull protrudes.]

LORD EDGAR. [Screams.] No! It can't be! It can't be! Pev. Pev. I should never have summoned you, Alcazar. It broke the spell and sent her back to the underworld.

ALCAZAR. The hour grows late. We must leave before dawn. Pack up whatever you want to take along.

LORD EDGAR. I must take her with me. I must find a way to bring her back again. If it's the last thing I do, I'll bring her back again!

ALCAZAR. Let us remove the sarcophagus. The most dangerous part is over. Rain is what we have to fear now.

[They carry out the mummy case. Lights fade.]

SCENE II

[Mandacrest. The time is autumn. Jane is dusting the mummy case. Nicodemus looks on.]

NICODEMUS. It was a devil of a time we had getting it in here. The thing must weigh a ton.

JANE. Did you bring Lady Enid's trunk upstairs?

NICODEMUS. Yes.

JANE. Where is she?

NICODEMUS. Alone with her secrets: old feather fans, tasseled dance cards powered with musk, a gaud of amber beads locked away in her drawer. A program from Antoine's when she appeared with Bonita Bainbridge in *The Farfelu of Seville*.

JANE. It's the paralysis of the insane. She sleeps all day and she's up all night.

NICODEMUS. That was always her way.

JANE. She's got terrible insomnia.

NICODEMUS. Can't remember a thing, eh?

JANE. And when she's up—she walks.

NICODEMUS. And why shouldn't she walk? It's daft she is, not crippled.

JANE. I haven't slept a wink since they brought her home a week ago.

NICODEMUS. You're doing the work of three people.

JANE. I asked Lord Edgar if I could get a slight raise in pay and he said he'd consider it.

NICODEMUS. And to think of you having to beg from these swine. I'm the only one who knows what you are. Why don't you trust me more? What have you got up your nose against me?

JANE. *[Crosses to the mirror.]* Come to the glass, Nicodemus, and I'll show you what you should wish. Do you mark those two lines between your eyes? And those thick brows that instead of rising, arched, sink in the middle? And that couple of black fiends, so deeply buried, who never open their windows boldly, but lurk glinting under them, like devil's spies? Wish and learn to smooth away the surly wrinkles, to raise your lids frankly, and change the fiends to confident, innocent angels, suspecting and doubting nothing, and always seeing friends where they are not sure of foes. Don't get the expression of a vicious cur that appears to know the kicks it gets are its desert, and yet hates all the world, as well as the kicker, for what it suffers.

NICODEMUS. In other words, I must wish for Edgar Hillcrest's great blue eyes and even forehead. I do, but that won't help me to them. I was abandoned. Found on the doorstep of a London doss house. My own mother didn't want me.

JANE. Who knows but your father was emperor of China and your mother was an Indian queen, each of them able to buy up Mandacrest with one week's income. And you were kidnapped by wicked sailors and brought to England. Were I in your place, I would frame high notions of my birth, and the thought of what I was should give me courage and dignity.

NICODEMUS. Thank you, Janey. In the future while I'm shoveling shit I'll try to think of myself as a prince in disguise.

JANE. *[Looking out of the door windows.]* Why don't you do some washin' and combin' and go to the village and visit that dairy maid you've taken a fancy to?

NICODEMUS. She's a cute little baggage but she smells of cheese.

JANE. It's a good night for wooing for the moon is full. *[Bell off.]* There's the bell. The mistress wants me.

[Exits.]

NICODEMUS. The moon is full? *[Goes upstage and looks out through the doors.]* A full moon. *[He begins to make jerky movements.]* A full mooooooon! *[The word moon trails off into a howl as Nicodemus with his back to the audience raises one arm, which has become a wolf's paw.]* No! No! No! Oh God! God help me! Don't let it happen! It's the moooooon! Mooooooooon! *[He turns to the audience. His face has become that of a wolf. He tears off his jacket to reveal a furry torso. He runs about the stage on his tiptoes with his knees bent. He sniffs, scratches, lifts his leg against a piece of furniture, howls, and runs out leaving his jacket on the floor.]*

JANE. *[Enters.]* Nicodemus, Lady Enid wants to have a word with you. *[Sees the door left open.]* He's gone and he's left the door wide open again. God, he'll never change.

[There is the sound of a wolf howling in the distance.]

LADY ENID. *[Enters.]* Do you hear that? First you think it's a wolf. Then you tell yourself it's the wind. But you know that it's a soul in pain. *[Crosses to the fireplace.]* Get that flower out of here!

JANE. I thought it looked so lovely.

LADY ENID. I can stand neither its color nor its scent. Take it away.

JANE. It's the last rose of summer.

[Lady Enid takes down a dulcimer, lays it across her lap, and begins to play "The Last Rose of Summer." Jane takes the flower out and returns with another dulcimer. She sits on the other side of the fireplace and joins Lady Enid in a duet.]

LADY ENID. *[Staring at the portrait over the mantel.]* Who is that woman?

JANE. Why that's yourself, Lady Enid.

LADY ENID. No, no, that's not me. She's a virgin.

JANE. It was painted a long time ago.

LADY ENID. She still has her illusions. She still has her faith. No, that isn't me.

JANE. Virginity is the balloon in the carnival of life. It vanishes with the first prick.

LADY ENID. *[Stops playing abruptly.]* In all of England I don't believe I could have married into a situation so completely removed from the stir of society. A perfect misanthropist's heaven—and Lord Edgar and I are such a perfect pair to divide the desolation between us.

JANE. It's a refuge, it is, from the chatter of tongues.

LADY ENID. Mine eyes itch. Doth that bode weeping?

JANE. Maybe you've got something in your eye, Lady Enid.

LADY ENID. Where is Nicodemus? I want to have a word with him.

JANE. I'm afraid that's not possible, Lady Enid.

LADY ENID. And why not? Send for Nicodemus. I demand to see him at once.

JANE. Nicodemus can't come, Lady Enid. For obvious reasons.

LADY ENID. Obvious reasons? *[The light dawns.]* Oh! Oh! For obvious reasons. Oh I see. In that case, I'll go to him.

JANE. Are you fond of Nicodemus?

LADY ENID. Fond of Nicodemus? Sometimes I feel that I am Nicodemus. That Nicodemus and I are one and the same person.

JANE. Now, now, Lady Enid, what have you got up your sleeve?

LADY ENID. Up my sleeve? Up my sleeve? *[She looks up her sleeve. Her own hand comes out in a clawlike gesture. She screams.]*

JANE. Don't be frightened, Lady Enid. That's your own hand.

LADY ENID. I frighten myself sometimes. Jane, I fear that Lord Edgar and I are drifting apart. It's a terrible thing to marry an Egyptologist and find out he's hung up on his mummy. *[If audience hisses.]* That wind!

JANE. He's an incurable romantic. If you really want to please him, you should try to appeal to that side of his nature. I have a lovely old dress you could wear. It's a family heirloom. It's full of nostalgia.

LADY ENID. We could have it cleaned.

JANE. I'll lay it out in your room. Wear it tonight. It's sure to get a strong reaction.

LADY ENID. Thank you, Jane. *[Exit Jane. Lady Enid picks up dulcimer, plays "Skip to My Lou." Lord Edgar enters.]* Edgar, darling, where have you been?

LORD EDGAR. I've been to the jewelers.

LADY ENID. To buy jewelry?

LORD EDGAR. No, bullets. Silver bullets. The young dairymaid in the village was found badly mauled. It seems the werewolf has struck again. I must go to the morgue.

LADY ENID. Oh Edgar. Why don't you just go and live at the morgue instead of making a morgue of our home.

[She flings out.]

LORD EDGAR. *[Calling after her.]* Enid. Enid darling. Please be reasonable.

[Nicodemus appears in the door windows up. He has blood on his hand.]

NICODEMUS. Lord Edgar.

LORD EDGAR. Nicodemus. I'll be needing your help tonight. The werewolf has struck again. This time, the cur must die.

NICODEMUS. Must he die? Is there no other help for him? Can't he be put away somewhere where he could receive therapy? Perhaps someday science will discover a cure for what he has.

LORD EDGAR. There is only one cure for what he has. The barrel of a gun and a silver bullet.

[Exits.]

NICODEMUS. Oh miserable me. Must I, like Tancred in *Jerusalem Delivered*, ever injure what I love beyond all else? Unloved I lived. Unloved I die. My only crime was having been born.

[Enter Jane.]

JANE. And who are you talking to, Nicodemus Underwood?

NICODEMUS. Myself. The only one who'll listen.

JANE. Did you see the milkmaid tonight, Nicodemus?

NICODEMUS. The milkmaid, oh, the milkmaid. Would that I had never seen the milkmaid.

JANE. There's blood on your hand. Did you hurt yourself?

NICODEMUS. No. It's her blood. The blood of the tender maid you spoke of. The werewolf got her.

JANE. Werewolf?

NICODEMUS. Yes, you know, a person who dons the skin of a wolf in the full of the moon and turns into a wolf to prowl at night. A woman is usually the victim. It makes a horrible story.

JANE. And where is it now, this hound of hell?

NICODEMUS. Wipe from my hand the blood you see with your dainty little hankie, and behold the mark of Cain.

JANE. *[Spits on her hankie and wipes some of the blood from Nicodemus's palm. She gasps and jumps back.]* The Pentagram! When did this happen to you?

NICODEMUS. Tonight, in the full of the moon! I turned into a wolf! And took the life of the only fair creature who'd ever shown me any love.

JANE. But the moon is still full. How come you're not a wolf now?

NICODEMUS. I'm in remission since a cloud passed over the moon.

JANE. Unspeakable horror!

NICODEMUS. Unspeakable shame! For I fear what I may do next. For it is the thing I love I kill. And I love you Janey, with all my heart.

JANE. No you don't. It's just infatuation tinged with lust.

NICODEMUS. And I love Lady Enid!

JANE. Lady Enid?

NICODEMUS. Yes. I'd have never dared confess it until this moment. But now I fear I may be some danger to her person. All must out!

JANE. Run away, Nicodemus. Run away and never come back!

NICODEMUS. Where shall I go? I've never known any life by Mandacrest! I have no money, no luggage!

JANE. Go upstairs to my room. On the table by my bed you will find a copy of Lord Lytton's *Zanoni*. In it I have saved a few pounds. Take them. You may need them.

NICODEMUS. Thank you, Janey.

[Exits.]

JANE. Sufficient unto the night are the horrors thereof. *[Falls on knees and prays.]* Please god, don't let anything happen to Lord Edgar, don't let anything happen to Lady Enid, and please god, don't let anything happen to me!

LADY ENID. *[Enters in a different frock.]* How do I look?

JANE. Lovely, Lady Enid. It's sure to put Lord Edgar into a romantic mood. This dress was always his favorite.

LADY ENID. Are you sure he really likes it?

JANE. Positive. He's even worn it himself when in an antic mood, in younger, happier days.

[Exits.]

LADY ENID. *[Goes over to the mantel and looks up at the portrait.]* Well any man who dresses up as a woman can't be all bad! *[To herself in the portrait.]* If you continue at this rate you'll be an even greater actress than Bonita Bainbridge!

VOICE. *[Off left, moans twice, then.]* Help me. Help me! Turn the figurine. Turn the figurine!

[Lady Enid moves an ornament on the fireplace, triggering a sliding panel. The bookcase slides back, revealing a cage. She jumps back, startled. A shrouded figure appears within the cage.]

LADY ENID. Who are you? What are you doing in there?

VOICE. They keep me here! I'm their prisoner! They torture me! Please help me! Help me!

LADY ENID. Who? Who tortures you?

VOICE. Edgar! Edgar tortures me!

LADY ENID. You poor thing. Who are you?

VOICE. Why, I'm his wife, Irma.

LADY ENID. Irma!

VOICE. Irma Vep! The first Lady Hillcrest.

LADY ENID. But I thought you were dead!

IRMA. That's what they want you to think! That's what they want everyone to think!

LADY ENID. Why have they put you here?

IRMA. There are jewels hidden in the house. I alone know where they are. But I'll never tell! For if I tell, they'll kill me! If you help me, I'll tell you where the jewels are, and I'll share them with you.

LADY ENID. Poor woman! Of course I'll help you. But this cage is locked!

IRMA. Jane has the key! Steal it from her! But don't tell her you've seen me! Don't tell anyone! Not Jane. Not Nicodemus! Not Lord Edgar! *[Footsteps are heard.]* I hear someone coming. Turn the figurine! And please, please, remember me! Remember me!

LADY ENID. Remember you? Of course I'll remember you! How could I forget you. You poor darling. Poor, poor darling!

[Turns the figurine. The bookcase starts to close and sticks. Enid struggles with the figurine. The bookcase closes fully as Lord Edgar enters.]

LORD EDGAR. Enid!

LADY ENID. *[Turning.]* Edgar.

LORD EDGAR. Where did you get that dress?

LADY ENID. Do you like it?

LORD EDGAR. Like it? I hate it! I despise it! I loathe it! *[Tears the dress.]* Take it off! Take it off!

LADY ENID. But Edgar! I only wanted to please you!

LORD EDGAR. Please me? You wanted to torture me! You wanted to make me suffer! I'll never forgive you for this, Enid. Never!

LADY ENID. But Edgar! I only wanted to be nearer to you!

LORD EDGAR. You've only driven me further away. I'd rather see you locked away in rags in the deepest, darkest dungeon I could find than see you in that dress!

LADY ENID. No!

LORD EDGAR. Take it off, I said! You're making me hate you!

LADY ENID. What are you saying?

LORD EDGAR. It was her dress.

LADY ENID. *Her* dress?

LORD EDGAR. Irma's!

LADY ENID. Jane didn't tell me that!

LORD EDGAR. Jane told you to wear that? She should have known better. She knows how it upsets me to see the dress Irma wore the night she died!

LADY ENID. Died? But she . . . she didn't . . .

LORD EDGAR. Didn't what?

LADY ENID. [Catching herself.] . . . die in this dress, did she?

LORD EDGAR. Oh don't talk about it anymore! You'll only make me hate you more. [Tears her dress. Lady Enid bursts into tears and runs to the door.] Stop, Enid! I'm sorry. I didn't mean it.

LADY ENID. You don't love me and you never have.

LORD EDGAR. You're wrong! I love no one else but you.

LADY ENID. Then why, why, why must we go on living here as brother and sister? Why don't you live with me as a wife?

LORD EDGAR. Because of the terror I feel of *her* . . .

LADY ENID. Terror?

LORD EDGAR. Yes, terror! Terror! A terror so great that I've never been able to communicate it to anyone.

LADY ENID. Even your wife?

LORD EDGAR. Very well, then, I'll tell you. Sometimes I see her standing before me as big as life.

LADY ENID. How does she look?

LORD EDGAR. Oh, very well. Exactly as she did when I saw her last, three years ago.

LADY ENID. Three years ago?

LORD EDGAR. She won't let me go. I'm her prisoner.

LADY ENID. *She* won't let *you* go?

LORD EDGAR. No, I realize it's useless.

LADY ENID. That woman has an unearthly power over you, Edgar.

LORD EDGAR. Yes, yes, she's horrible. I'll never get rid of her.

LADY ENID. But you have gotten rid of her. On your trip to Egypt. You said you'd found something in the tomb that had made you forget all about her.

LORD EDGAR. Don't talk about it. Or think of it, even. There was no help for me there. I can feel it in my bones. I didn't get rid of it out there either.

LADY ENID. Of what? What do you mean?

LORD EDGAR. I mean the horror. The fantastic hold on my mind, on my soul.

LADY ENID. But you said it was over.

LORD EDGAR. No no, that's just the thing. It isn't.

LADY ENID. Not over?

LORD EDGAR. No Enid, it's not over, and I'm afraid it never will be.

LADY ENID. [In a strangled voice.] Are you saying then that in your heart of hearts you'll never be able to forget this woman?

LORD EDGAR. She comes toward me and puts her arms around me. Then she presses her lips to mine.

LADY ENID. To kiss you?

LORD EDGAR. As if to kiss me—but she doesn't kiss. She sucks.

LADY ENID. Sucks?

LORD EDGAR. She sucks my breath until I feel I'm suffocating. [Turns blue.]

LADY ENID. Good God! Edgar! You're sick! You're much sicker than you thought. Than either of us thought.

LORD EDGAR. [Clutching at his throat.] Yes! yes! I can't breathe! I'm suffocating, and her fingers are tightening! Tightening around my throat. Help me. Help me.

LADY ENID. Oh, my dear Lord Edgar! Then you've been suffering in silence all this time and you've never told me anything about it?

LORD EDGAR. I couldn't tell you. I couldn't speak the unspeakable, name the unnameable. [Gasps for breath.] And her fingers are tightening. Tightening more and more. Help me! Help me!

LADY ENID. Nicodemus! [Runs off calling.] Nicodemus.

NICODEMUS. [Off.] You called, Lady Enid?

LADY ENID. [Off.] Yes please, please help me. Lord Edgar is having an attack. [She weeps.]

NICODEMUS. [Off.] There there, Lady Enid. Calm yourself.

LADY ENID. *[Off.]* Oh please, hurry, hurry!

NICODEMUS. *[Off.]* Stay here. I'll go to him. *[Enters.]* There there, Lord Edgar. Doing poorly? Have you got the horrors again?

LORD EDGAR. *[Rolling about on the floor, clutching his throat.]* Yes, yes the horrors. It's her. I'll never be free of her.

NICODEMUS. *[Offering his flask.]* Here you go. You must fight fire with fire and spirits with spirits!

LORD EDGAR. No, I won't break my rule. You know I am an abstainer.

NICODEMUS. Oh well then, in that case . . . *[Drinks himself.]*

LORD EDGAR. *[Seeing this.]* On second thought, maybe just a drop.

NICODEMUS. *[Passing him the flask.]* For medicinal purposes only. *[Lord Edgar drinks.]* Feeling better?

LORD EDGAR. Yes, much. Thanks. Nicodemus, stay with Lady Enid tonight. There's a wolf about, and I don't want her left alone.

[Exits up center.]

NICODEMUS. No, no, Lord Edgar. Not that! Don't ask me that! Anything but that! Horror. Horror. Horror. For I fear the gibbous moon. Oh horror! Oh horror!

JANE. *[Enters with wolfsbane.]* Did you find the money?

NICODEMUS. Yes, thank you Janey.

JANE. Now go, Nicodemus. I've never liked you, but I've never wished you any harm. May god help you!

NICODEMUS. Thank you, Janey. This is the only kindness anyone has ever shown me.

JANE. Ah, be off with you. I have to put up wolfsbane against you.

NICODEMUS. I understand.

[Exits. Jane hangs up wolfsbane around the room. Lady Enid enters.]

LADY ENID. Where's Lord Edgar?

JANE. He's gone out, after the wolf.

LADY ENID. Is he hunting wolves again, with one of his villainous old guns?

JANE. I think he took a horse pistol.

LADY ENID. The blackguard.

JANE. Now, Lady Enid, I won't have you talking this way about Lord Edgar.

LADY ENID. *[Seizing her by the wrist.]* When a woman loves a man she should be willing to do anything for him. Cut off her little finger at the middle joint there. *[Twisting Jane's finger.]*

JANE. *[Loudly.]* Ow!

LADY ENID. Or cut off her dainty hand at the wrist.

JANE. Please, let go. You're hurting me!

LADY ENID. Or lop off her pretty little ear. *[Twists her ear and takes keys.]*

JANE. Ow! Ow! Ow! Please stop!

LADY ENID. When you're willing to do those things for Lord Edgar then entertain thoughts of loving him. Otherwise back off. *[Releases her.]*

JANE. *[Rubbing her wrist.]* Now look. You've left red marks on my wrist. You've got a devil in you. That's what it is. You know I'm nothing to Lord Edgar. I have no more hold over his heart than you have. It's Irma he loves! Irma Vep. It's no use our fighting over the same man . . . when he's in love with a dead woman.

LADY ENID. You scandalous little hypocrite! Are you not afraid of being carried away bodily whenever you mention the devil's name? I warn you to refrain from provoking me or I will ask your abduction as a special favor. *[Jane goes to leave.]* Stop, Jane! Look here. I'll show you how far I've progressed in the Black Art. *[Taking down a book from the shelf.]* I shall soon be competent to make a clear house of it. The red cow didn't die by chance, and your rheumatism can hardly be reckoned among providential visitations!

JANE. Oh wicked! Wicked! May the Lord deliver us from evil!

LADY ENID. No, reprobate! You are a castaway. Be off, or I'll hurt you seriously. I'll have you all modeled in wax and clay; and the first who passes the limits I fix, shall . . . I'll not say what he shall be done to . . . but you'll see! Go— I'm looking at you.

JANE. *[Trembling with sincere horror, hurries out praying and ejaculating.]* Wicked! Wicked!

LADY ENID. *[Laughing.]* Wicked, perhaps. But I have the keys! *[She approaches the bookcase. She turns the figurine. The bookcase slides.]* Psst! Psst! Irma! Irma darling. Are you there?

IRMA. Where else would I be? Did you get the key?

LADY ENID. Yes, I have it.

IRMA. Open the door. Quickly. Quickly!

LADY ENID. But I don't know which one it is.

IRMA. Quickly. Quickly! Before someone comes.

LADY ENID. *[Trying one key after another.]* Well there are so many of them.

IRMA. Quickly! Save me! Save me!

LADY ENID. *[Opening the door.]* Ah, there, Irma dearest. You're free.

[Irma flies out of the door shrieking like a madwoman. She seizes Enid by the throat, turns her back to the audience, and leans over her. Enid sinks to her knees.]

IRMA. *[Calmly.]* Oh triple fool! Did you not know that Irma Vep is "vampire" anagrammatized!

LADY ENID. *[Reaches up and rips off Irma's face, which is a rubber mask, revealing the other player.]* Edgar?

JANE. No, Jane!

LADY ENID. Jane! You?

JANE. Yes, I did it! I killed the child, and Irma too! I was the vampire, feeding on the lifeblood of my own jealousy! No more will I eat the bitter crust of charity, nor serve a vain mistress!

LADY ENID. You? You killed her?

JANE. Yes I killed her, and I'll kill again. I'd kill any woman who stood in my way.

LADY ENID. You're mad.

JANE. Mad! Mad! *[She laughs maniacally.]* Perhaps I am. Love is a kind of madness. And hatred is a bottomless cup, and I will drink the dregs.

[Pulls out a meat cleaver and attacks Enid. Enid, who has backed over to the mummy case, deftly opens the door as Jane runs at her. Jane goes into the mummy case. Enid slams the door and holds it shut. We hear Jane pounding within the mummy case.]

LADY ENID. *[Crying out.]* Help me. Nicodemus! Edgar! Someone! Anyone! Help me!

EDGAR. *[Rushes in.]* Enid, what is it?

LADY ENID. *[Hysterically.]* She's in the mummy case. She's in the mummy case. You can hear her rapping.

[The rapping stops.]

EDGAR. I don't hear anything.

LADY ENID. I found it all out. Jane killed Irma, and the child! Irma Vep is "vampire" anagrammatized.

EDGAR. Enid, I think your mind is affected.

LADY ENID. No, it's Jane. Jane is mad. Mad, I tell you. She attacked me with a meat-ax. She's in the mummy case. Call Scotland Yard.

EDGAR. Nonsense, Enid. *[Goes to open the mummy case.]*

LADY ENID. What are you going to do?

EDGAR. I'm going to open the mummy case.

LADY ENID. No, don't open the mummy case.

EDGAR. I'm going to open the mummy case. Stand back.

LADY ENID. Don't open the mummy case.

EDGAR. I'm going to open the mummy case.

LADY ENID. Don't open the mummy case. Don't open it. Don't open it. Don't . . .

EDGAR. *[Opens the mummy case.]* See Enid? The mummy case is perfectly empty.

LADY ENID. *[Somewhat mollified.]* Well, she was in there a moment ago. *[The lights begin to dim.]* The lights. The lights are dimming. The lights. The lights are dimming. *[The lights come back up.]*

EDGAR. Nonsense, Enid. The lights are not dimming. Come and sit by the fire.

[Lights dim again.]

LADY ENID. The lights are dimming.

EDGAR. *[He escorts her to chair.]* If you don't stop, Enid, they'll put you back in the sanatorium and they'll never let you out again.

LADY ENID. *[In a tiny voice.]* The lights are dimming.

EDGAR. *[Infuriated.]* Stop it, Enid! Stop it stop it stop it stop it! I don't want to hear you say that again!

[Lady Enid turns to the audience and silently mouths the words "The lights are dimming."]

EDGAR. There's the good girl. There's the good girl. Go on, play your dulcimer like the good girl. Play with your dulcimer, Enid. *[Crosses to the door to exit.]* And I'll have Jane fix you a nice hot cup of tea.

[Lady Enid winces.]

EDGAR. Tch tch tch!

[Exits.]

LADY ENID. *[Begins to play "The Last Rose of Summer" on her dulcimer as ominous music swells.]* Is it possible my mind is affected? And yet I saw it with my very eyes. *[There is a tapping at the window, as in Act I.]* There it is again! Oh god. Oh god in heaven.

There it is again. The rapping! The rapping! As if someone gently tapping. *[She takes the poker from the fireside and approaches the French doors stealthily and flies through them, brandishing the poker.]* Tapping at my chamber door!

NICODEMUS. *[Off.]* Hey Lady Enid! What's going on? *[Poking his head through the door.]* What's going on here? *[Ducks out.]*

LADY ENID. *[Appearing at the door.]* Oh Nicodemus. I heard a rapping, a rapping, as if someone gently tapping, tapping at my chamber door! *[She ducks out.]*

NICODEMUS. *[Popping in.]* There there, Lady Enid. 'Tis the wind and nothing more. *[Ducks out.]*

LADY ENID. *[Popping in.]* Oh Nicodemus, I was so frightened, so terribly, terribly frightened!

NICODEMUS. *[His arm comes through the door, pats her shoulder.]* There there, Lady Enid. I'll never let any harm come to you.

LADY ENID. *[Kissing his hand.]* Thank you, Nicodemus. Thank you.

NICODEMUS. There there. *[His hand is withdrawn and reappears as a wolf's hand. Pats her cheek and squeezes her breast.]* There there.

LADY ENID. *[Reenters the room, closing the French doors behind her.]* It's so good to know he's there! Is it possible my mind is affected? Or can I trust my senses five? I saw it with my very eyes. And yet, the mummy case is perfectly empty!

[Opens the mummy case. Jane, in her maid's uniform once again, comes running out of the mummy case shrieking and wielding a meat-ax. Enid screams and runs out the door, slamming it behind her. The corner of her robe sticks out through the closed door.]

JANE. *[Flies to the door, finds it locked, and rants.]* Open the door. Open the door, Lady Enid. It's just a matter of time before I get in, you know. It was the same way when I killed Lady Irma. She was all alone in the house the night I strangled her.

LADY ENID. *[Off.]* No no! You're horrible!

JANE. And Victor, the little bastard. I drowned him in the mill run.

LADY ENID. *[Off.]* No!

JANE. You should have seen the bubbles coming out of his ugly little nose.

LADY ENID. *[Off.]* How could you? How could you?

JANE. Ah, glorious death. Glorious, glorious death! *[Nicodemus, as werewolf, bursts through French doors.]* Victor!

[Nicodemus grabs Jane by the throat and drags her out the way he came in, howling. He staggers back through the door with only her dress, and humps it. Suddenly, realizing the dress is empty, he throws it down and wheels about confusedly. He sees Enid's robe caught in the door and crosses to it, clumping all the way with his wooden leg, lifts the hem of her robe, sniffs it, turns to the door, and raps three times.]

LADY ENID. *[Off.]* Edgar, is that you?

[Edgar rushes in and fires shots. The werewolf falls and turns into Nicodemus.]

NICODEMUS. Each man kills the thing he loves. The coward does it with a kiss, the brave man with a sword. Yet, Nicodemus did love.

LORD EDGAR. Nicodemus, Nicodemus, I've killed you. In earnest.

NICODEMUS. Thank you. *[Dies.]*

LORD EDGAR. The poor man is dead. From his fair and unpolluted flesh may violets spring! Bury him on the moors he loved so well, and may his soul ascend to heaven, for he lived in hell!

[Blackout.]

SCENE III

[Lights up on Lady Enid and Lord Edgar. Edgar is sitting in his chair. Enid is standing beside him.]

LADY ENID. Poor Nicodemus. Poor Victor. Poor Irma. Poor Jane! Somehow it just doesn't make sense.

LORD EDGAR. Enid, there are more things on heaven and earth than are dreamed of in our philosophies! Enid, I had an uncanny experience in Egypt. And I've written it all up in a treatise, which I expect will cause some stir. My very reputation as an Egyptologist would hang in the balance. I've been warned by all my colleagues not to publish it, but I must. They say that it couldn't have happened. That an ancient mummy, a hideously shriveled, decayed object, could not have survived the ages and been brought to life by spells and incantations. And yet I saw it with my very eyes! I must tell the world, even if it ruins my reputation! For I believe that we all lived before, in another time, in another age, and that you and I were lovers in ancient Egypt, thirty-five hundred years ago. She was so like you. You are so like her. Oh Enid, Enid!

LADY ENID. Stop! I can't bear it! I can't go on. Oh, you poor, poor man!

LORD EDGAR. What do you mean, Enid?

LADY ENID. Oh, stop. You're making me weep so terribly! I've done a terrible thing. I fear you'll never forgive me for it.

LORD EDGAR. What are you talking about?

LADY ENID. It was me in the tomb, Edgar.

LORD EDGAR. You? Impossible. But you were away in a sanatorium.

LADY ENID. No, I wasn't. I feigned madness. Alcazar is my father! He is actually Professor Lionel Cuncliff of Cambridge University.

LORD EDGAR. Not *the* Lionel Cuncliff! The leading Egyptologist and sarcophagologist.

LADY ENID. Yes, your old rival.

LORD EDGAR. Old Cuncliff your father? That's impossible! You couldn't have been in Egypt!

LADY ENID. If you could only believe that I did it for you, to win you away from . . . her. If I could make you believe that our love was destined, I thought I could bind you to me. But my father used it for his own purposes—to make a fool of you. To discredit you before the academic community and the world! He had never forgiven you for having won the Yolanda Sonabend fellowship he had so counted on. Can you ever forgive me?

LORD EDGAR. I can't believe that you pulled it off! How did you get in the tomb?

LADY ENID. The tomb was actually an Egyptian restaurant that had been closed quite a number of years. I simply came in through the kitchen.

LORD EDGAR. You little witch!

LADY ENID. We had only a few days to make it look like a tomb. We used a decorator from the theater. Oh, the hours he spent polishing that floor. It gave us quite a turn when you discovered that footprint. But by then you wanted to believe so much, you convinced yourself. Can you ever forgive me?

LORD EDGAR. Forgive you? I want to thank you. You've freed me at last. Somehow I've come to realize that we are all God's creatures every one of us. Big Victor and little Victor too.

LADY ENID. You can say that.

LORD EDGAR. I mean it. Oh God, I've been so selfish.

LADY ENID. Me too. But we can make it all up somehow.

LORD EDGAR. There's a hard day's work ahead of us Enid.

LADY ENID. But on the seventh day we'll rest.

LORD EDGAR. [Quietly, very moved.] And in that stillness perhaps we'll hear the spirits visiting.

LADY ENID. [In a whisper.] Spirits?

LORD EDGAR. [As before.] Yes, perhaps they'll be all around us—those we've lost.

LADY ENID. Big Victor and little Victor too?

LORD EDGAR. Yes, it may be that now and then throughout our lives we may still catch glimpses of them. [Ardently.] If only I knew where to look. Where should I look, Enid?

LADY ENID. [Going to the doors and opening them.] Out there through the fog—beyond the moors. [Reaches out her hand to him and beckons him to come.]

LORD EDGAR. [His eyes fixed on her, he moves toward her slowly.] Beyond the moors?

LADY ENID. And upward . . .

LORD EDGAR. Yes, yes, upward.

LADY ENID. Toward the stars and toward that great silence.

LORD EDGAR. [Taking her hand in his.] Thank you.

[They stand in the doorway with their backs to us, looking up as the lights fade to darkness. The End.]

Introduction to
Joe Turner's Come and Gone
by August Wilson

Joe Turner's Come and Gone   Derrick Lee Weeden, Helmar Augustus Cooper, and Stephanie Clay.
(© Mark Avery, courtesy of the Milwaukee Repertory Theater)

The Play   *Joe Turner's Come and Gone* is set in Pittsburgh in 1911, a time when there was an exodus by African Americans from the South to the North. Herald Loomis, the play's central character, arrives with his daughter, Zonia, at a board-inghouse in Pittsburgh run by Bertha and Seth Holly. Loomis, a Southern church deacon kidnapped by whites and forced into a seven-year period of servitude, is now seeking his wife, Martha. Martha had been staying at the boardinghouse but has moved out to serve in another town's church. A white traveling salesman, Rutherford Selig, finds Martha for Loomis, who leaves his daughter with her, realiz-ing that they cannot reunite.

Among the other boarders at the Hollys' house are Bynum, a conjurer; Jeremy Furlow, a young Southern black who hopes to make his fortune playing the guitar; Mattie Campbell, who is searching for her husband and whom Jeremy persuades to move into the boardinghouse but then abandons; and Molly Cunningham, the woman with whom Jeremy leaves.

On the surface, Wilson's play seems to follow the traditions of realism. The boardinghouse is populated by a cross section of individual African Americans struggling and searching in the early years of the twentieth century. Through a realistic plotline, Wilson shows his audience that freedom for blacks is an illusion. Seth wants to start his own business but cannot get financing without turning his home over to a white man. Loomis, supposedly a free Southerner, is forced into servitude that destroys his family. Jeremy loses his job because he will not pay part of his salary to a white man.

However, Wilson's play deviates from realism in significant ways. The structure of the play, for example, violates the traditional European model. Each act, rather than developing in a straight dramatic line, is divided into a series of short scenes. There is a secondary plotline, which is not clearly integrated and seems extraneous to the main action: this involves Zonia and Reuben, who develop a childhood romance. But the tale of the children is again a search for identity, and their discussions echo, in an almost choral fashion, the concerns of the adults in the play.

Joe Turner's Come and Gone is also highly metaphorical, with many symbolic elements, according to the playwright, rooted in African ritual. Throughout the play, Bynum, who functions as an African healer, tells characters that they need to find their own "song," which will give them their self-identity. (Wilson frequently uses music as a metaphor for freedom in his dramas.) Bynum is also searching for a "shiny man," a godlike figure who will bring him his own song.

In Act I, scene IV, the boardinghouse residents dance the *juba,* which Wilson says should be "as African as possible," when suddenly Loomis speaks in tongues and then recounts a dream in which he sees the bones of his ancestors and unites himself with them. At the end of the play, Loomis cuts his chest in a blood ritual, purifying himself and thus setting himself free.

Wilson's play clearly presents the marginalization of African Americans in white society. However, Wilson also argues that blacks should search for their unique identity, an identity rooted in the African past. His characters cannot find themselves through identities established by white America—as is seen in Seth's inability to succeed financially even though he willingly throws off his Southern and African heritage. They can find themselves only by finding their own songs.

The Playwright   The critical and popular success of August Wilson's plays make it clear that he is one of the major American dramatists of the twentieth century. Wilson's goal is to evoke the African-American experience at various times in history.

Wilson was born in 1945 to a white father and black mother. He grew up in a two-room apartment behind a grocery store on Bedford Avenue in Pittsburgh. He attended Catholic schools until the age of 15, but he left school when a teacher wrongly accused him of plagiarism. To keep his mother from worrying, Wilson spent his afternoons in the public library, completing his education on his own. During his hours in the library, he developed a love of poetry, in particular the works of Dylan Thomas. Following a brief enlistment in the army, Wilson moved into a boardinghouse, resolving to become a poet.

In 1968, Wilson helped found the Black Horizons Theater Company in Pittsburgh. In the late 1970s and 1980s, he struggled to establish himself as a poet and held various odd jobs in Minneapolis–Saint Paul, where he had moved in 1978. At the same time, he became interested in playwriting and wrote a number of dramas, including *The Homecoming* (1979), *The Coldest Day of the Year* (1979), *Fullerton Street* (1980), *Black Bart and the Sacred Hills* (1981), and *Jitney* (1982).

It was when Wilson submitted a draft of *Ma Rainey's Black Bottom* to the Eugene O'Neill Center in Waterford, Connecticut—a workshop devoted to new plays—that his work came to the attention of Lloyd Richards, the artistic director. Richards had directed the original production of Lorraine Hansberry's *A Raisin in the Sun* and was also the head of the Yale Drama School and the Yale Repertory Theater. With Richards directing, *Ma Rainey's Black Bottom* opened at the Yale Rep in April 1984, and six months later it moved to Broadway. Since then, Richards has been Wilson's mentor, directing all his plays on Broadway and all but the most recent—*Seven Guitars*—at regional theaters before their New York premieres.

Wilson's play *Fences,* a family drama set in the 1950s, was produced in New Haven in 1985; in 1987, it opened in New York, where it received rave notices, and went on to win the Pulitzer Prize. *Joe Turner's Come and Gone* also opened in New York in 1987, while *Fences* was still running. In *Joe Turner*—more than his two preceding plays—Wilson used a heavily poetic style of realism. *The Piano Lesson* won Wilson his second Pulitzer Prize in 1990. *Two Trains Running,* a play which deals with the turmoil of the 1960s, was more comedic than his earlier works but was received less enthusiastically by the New York critics when it opened on Broadway in 1992. *Seven Guitars* premiered at the Goodman Theater in Chicago in 1995 but was not directed by Lloyd Richards, who was ill. In 1996, Richards directed the Broadway production, which was nominated for a Tony Award as best play.

Also in 1996, Wilson and the critic Robert Brustein, who is artistic director of the American Repertory Theater at Harvard, engaged in a series of debates in which Brustein argued that Wilson's works were overrated and dramatically flawed, and that Wilson's view of African-American theater was separatist. Wilson argued that black theater and its artists have been and continue to be marginalized by mainstream American theater, and that Brustein had failed to recognize the uniqueness of African-American theatrical tradition. (These debates have since been published.)

The Period   As the debate with Robert Brustein illustrates, August Wilson sees himself as part of the long tradition of African-American theater. This theater actually partakes of two important traditions: African-American theater traces its origins to ritual and theatrical practices in Africa and the Caribbean, but its other source is the Western tradition, to which actors like Paul Robeson (1898–1976) and writers like Lorraine Hansberry (1930–1965) have made significant contributions.

The history of black theater in America reflects the struggle of a marginalized people. In American drama of the eighteenth and nineteenth centuries, comic black servants were popular characters, but these roles were performed by white actors wearing blackface makeup. A popular nineteenth-century form caricaturing blacks was the minstrel show, which consisted of comic and sentimental songs, skits, jigs, and shuffle dances. While the vast majority of minstrel performers were white, there were a few black minstrel companies, most of which, ironically, also performed in blackface.

A theater that did feature African-American performers was the African Grove, founded in New York during the 1820–1821 season by an African American, William Brown, and the West Indian actor James Hewlett. This company was noted particularly for presenting Shakespearean plays. Hewlett was the first black to play Othello, and the renowned actor Ira Aldridge (ca. 1806–1867) made his stage debut with the company. Here, too, the drama *King Shotaway*—believed to be the first play written and performed by African Americans—was presented. The African Grove closed in 1827 after attacks by white audience members. This kind of intense racism made it nearly impossible for African-American theater artists to thrive in the United States. Ira Aldridge, for instance, left America and performed to great acclaim in England, Russia, and Poland.

At the beginning of the twentieth century, ragtime—a popular musical style that originated with blacks—had a strong influence on the emerging musical theater and served as a bridge to mainstream theater for a number of African Americans. Bob Cole (1864–1912) and William Johnson (1873–1954) conceived, wrote, produced, and directed the first black musical comedy, *A Trip to Coontown* (1898). The comedians Bert Williams (1876–1922) and George Walker (?–1909) and their wives joined composers and writers to produce musicals and operettas. These were productions in which for the first time, blacks appeared on the Broadway stage without burnt-cork makeup, speaking without dialect, and costumed in high fashion.

The early twentieth century also saw the formation of African-American stock companies, of which the most significant was the Lafayette Players, founded by Anita Bush (1894–1938). By the time it closed in 1932, it had presented over 250 productions and employed a number of black stars. Black performers and writers were also making inroads into the commercial theater of the 1920s. Twenty plays with black themes were presented on Broadway during this decade, five of them written by African Americans, including *Shuffle Along* (1921), with lyrics and music by Noble Sissle (1889–1975) and Eubie Blake (1883–1993). Some black performers also received recognition in serious drama, among them Charles Gilpin (1878–1930), Paul Robeson, and Ethel Waters (1896–1977).

A significant occurrence for black theater during the 1930s was the founding of the Federal Theater Project, intended to help theater artists through the Depression. African-American units of the Federal Theater were formed in 22 cities, where they mounted plays by black and white authors and employed thousands of African-American writers, performers, and technicians.

The 1940s saw a stage adaptation of the controversial novel *Native Son* (1941) by Richard Wright (1908–1960), directed by Orson Welles for the Mercury Theater. *Native Son* showed the effects of racism on a young black man—a daring theme at the time. Other important Broadway ventures included Paul Robeson's record run of 296 performances in *Othello,* and *Anna Lucasta* (1944) by Philip Yordan. The 1950s saw the first stages of an explosion in black theater that would take place over the next four decades. *Take a Giant Step* by Louis Patterson (1922–), a play about growing up in an integrated neighborhood, premiered in 1953. In 1954, the playwright-director Owen Dodson (1914–1983) staged *Amen Corner* by James Baldwin (1924–1987) at Howard University.

Possibly the most important production of the postwar era was *A Raisin in the Sun* (1959) by Lorraine Hansberry. This play was directed by Lloyd Richards (1922–), the first black director on Broadway and, as noted earlier, August Wilson's mentor.

From 1960 to the 1990s, there was an outpouring of African-American theater, much of it reflecting the battle for civil rights. Amiri Baraka (1934–) came to theatergoers' attention in 1964 with *Dutchman,* a verbal and sexual showdown between an assimilated black man and a white temptress, set in a New York subway. His plays *The Slave* (1965), *The Toilet* (1965), and *Slave Ship* (1970) also deal with the sociopolitical hardships confronting blacks. Among other significant plays were *Ceremonies in Dark Old Men* (1969) by Lonne Elder III (1932–1996); *No Place to Be Somebody* (1969) by Charles Gordone (1925–1995), the first off-Broadway play to receive a Pulitzer Prize; *Day of Absence* (1970) by Douglas Turner Ward (1930–); and *A Soldier's Play* (1981) by Charles Fuller (1939–), which won the Pulitzer Prize for drama. Many of the significant plays by African-American authors during the 1970s and 1980s were produced in New York by either Joseph Papp's Public Theater, which is dedicated to multiculturalism in writing and performing, or the Negro Ensemble Company.

In 1970 the Black Theater Alliance listed over 125 producing groups in the United States. Although only a few of these survived the decade, many had a significant impact. In addition to the emergence of these producing organizations, another major change after 1970 was the presence of a larger black audience in Broadway theaters and a significant number of commercial African-American productions, such as *Don't Bother Me, I Can't Cope* (1972); *The Wiz* (1975); *Bubbling Brown Sugar* (1976); *Black and Blue* (1989); *Jelly's Last Jam* (1992); and *Bring in 'Da Noise, Bring in 'Da Funk* (1996). The last two of these were directed by George C. Wolfe (1955–), who also serves as artistic director of the Public Theater.

Still, as August Wilson pointed out in his debate with Robert Brustein, African Americans remain on the margins of American theater, with limited opportunities for black theater artists.

JOE TURNER'S COME AND GONE

August Wilson

CHARACTERS

SETH HOLLY, owner of the boardinghouse
BERTHA HOLLY, his wife
BYNUM WALKER, a rootworker
RUTHERFORD SELIG, a peddler
JEREMY FURLOW, a resident
HERALD LOOMIS, a resident

ZONIA LOOMIS, his daughter
MATTIE CAMPBELL, a resident
REUBEN SCOTT, boy who lives next door
MOLLY CUNNINGHAM, a resident
MARTHA LOOMIS, Herald Loomis's wife

SETTING

August, 1911. A boardinghouse in Pittsburgh. At right is a kitchen. Two doors open off the kitchen. One leads to the outhouse and Seth's workshop. The other to Seth and Bertha's bedroom. At left is a parlor. The front door opens into the parlor, which gives access to the stairs leading to the upstairs rooms.

There is a small outside playing area.

THE PLAY

It is August in Pittsburgh, 1911. The sun falls out of heaven like a stone. The fires of the steel mill rage with a combined sense of industry and progress. Barges loaded with coal and iron ore trudge up the river to the mill towns that dot the Monongahela and return with fresh, hard, gleaming steel. The city flexes its muscles. Men throw countless bridges across the rivers, lay roads, and carve tunnels through the hills sprouting with houses.

From the deep and the near South the sons and daughters of newly freed African slaves wander into the city. Isolated, cut off from memory, having forgotten the names of the gods and only guessing at their faces, they arrive dazed and stunned, their hearts kicking in their chest with a song worth singing. They arrive carrying Bibles and guitars, their pockets lined with dust and fresh hope, marked men and women seeking to scrape from the narrow, crooked cobbles and the fiery blasts of the coke furnace a way of bludgeoning and shaping the malleable parts of themselves into a new identity as free men of definite and sincere worth.

Foreigners in a strange land, they carry as part and parcel of their baggage a long line of separation and dispersement which informs their sensibilities and marks their conduct as they search for ways to reconnect, to reassemble, to give clear and luminous meaning to the song which is both a wail and a whelp of joy.

Act I

_____

SCENE I

[The lights come up on the kitchen. Bertha busies herself with breakfast preparations. Seth stands looking out the window at Bynum in the yard. Seth is in his early fifties. Born of northern free parents, a skilled craftsman, and owner of the boardinghouse, he has a stability that none of the other characters have. Bertha is five years his junior. Married for over twenty-five years, she has learned how to negotiate around Seth's apparent orneriness.]

SETH. *[At the window, laughing.]* If that ain't the damndest thing I seen. Look here, Bertha.

BERTHA. I done seen Bynum out there with them pigeons before.

SETH. Naw . . . naw . . . look at this. That pigeon flopped out of Bynum's hand and he about to have a fit.

[Bertha crosses over to the window.]

He down there on his hands and knees behind that bush looking all over for that pigeon and it on the other side of the yard. See it over there?

BERTHA. Come on and get your breakfast and leave that man alone.

SETH. Look at him . . . he still looking. He ain't seen it yet. All that old mumbo jumbo nonsense. I don't know why I put up with it.

BERTHA. You don't say nothing when he bless the house.

SETH. I just go along with that cause of you. You around here sprinkling salt all over the place . . . got pennies lined up across the threshold . . . all that heebie-jeebie stuff. I just put up with that cause of you. I don't pay that kind of stuff no mind. And you going down there to the church and wanna come home and sprinkle salt all over the place.

BERTHA. It don't hurt none. I can't say if it help . . . but it don't hurt none.

SETH. Look at him. He done found that pigeon and now he's talking to it.

BERTHA. These biscuits be ready in a minute.

SETH. He done drew a big circle with that stick and now he's dancing around. I know he'd better not . . .

[Seth bolts from the window and rushes to the back door.]

Hey, Bynum! Don't be hopping around stepping in my vegetables. Hey, Bynum . . . Watch where you stepping!

BERTHA. Seth, leave that man alone.

SETH. *[Coming back into the house.]* I don't care how much he be dancing around . . . just don't be stepping in my vegetables. Man got my garden all messed up now . . . planting them weeds out there . . . burying them pigeons and whatnot.

BERTHA. Bynum don't bother nobody. He ain't even thinking about your vegetables.

SETH. I know he ain't! That's why he out there stepping on them.

BERTHA. What Mr. Johnson say down there?

SETH. I told him if I had the tools I could go out here and find me four or five fellows and open up my own shop instead of working for Mr. Olowski. Get me four or five fellows and teach them how to make pots and pans. One man making ten pots is five men making fifty. He told me he'd think about it.

BERTHA. Well, maybe he'll come to see it your way.

SETH. He wanted me to sign over the house to him. You know what I thought of that idea.

BERTHA. He'll come to see you're right.

SETH. I'm going up and talk to Sam Green. There's more than one way to skin a cat. I'm going up and talk to him. See if he got more sense than Mr. Johnson. I can't get nowhere working for Mr. Olowski and selling Selig five or six pots on the side. I'm going up and see Sam Green. See if he loan me the money.

[Seth crosses back to the window.]

Now he got that cup. He done killed that pigeon and now he's putting its blood in that little cup. I believe he drink that blood.

BERTHA. Seth Holly, what is wrong with you this morning? Come on and get your breakfast so you can go to bed. You know Bynum don't be drinking no pigeon blood.

SETH. I don't know what he do.

BERTHA. Well, watch him, then. He's gonna dig a little hole and bury that pigeon. Then he's gonna pray over that blood . . . pour it on top . . . mark out his circle and come on into the house.

SETH. That's what he doing . . . he pouring that blood on top.

BERTHA. When they gonna put you back working daytime? Told me two months ago he was gonna put you back working daytime.

SETH. That's what Mr. Olowski told me. I got to wait till he say when. He tell me what to do. I don't tell him. Drive me crazy to speculate on the man's wishes when he don't know what he want to do himself.

BERTHA. Well, I wish he go ahead and put you back working daytime. This working all hours of the night don't make no sense.

SETH. It don't make no sense for that boy to run out of here and get drunk so they lock him up either.

BERTHA. Who? Who they got locked up for being drunk?

SETH. That boy that's staying upstairs . . . Jeremy. I stopped down there on Logan Street on my way home from work and one of the fellows told me about it. Say he seen it when they arrested him.

BERTHA. I was wondering why I ain't seen him this morning.

SETH. You know I don't put up with that. I told him when he came . . .

[Bynum enters from the yard carrying some plants. He is a short, round man in his early sixties. A conjure man, or rootworker, he gives the impression of always being in control of everything. Nothing ever bothers him. He seems to be lost in a world of his own making and to swallow any adversity or interference with his grand design.]

What you doing bringing them weeds in my house? Out there stepping on my vegetables and now wanna carry them weeds in my house.

BYNUM. Morning, Seth. Morning, Sister Bertha.

SETH. Messing up my garden growing them things out there. I ought to go out there and pull up all them weeds.

BERTHA. Some gal was by here to see you this morning, Bynum. You was out there in the yard . . . I told her to come back later.

BYNUM. *[To Seth.]* You look sick. What's the matter, you ain't eating right?

SETH. What if I was sick? You ain't getting near me with none of that stuff.

[Bertha sets a plate of biscuits on the table.]

BYNUM. My . . . my . . . Bertha, your biscuits getting fatter and fatter.

[Bynum takes a biscuit and begins to eat.]

Where Jeremy? I don't see him around this morning. He usually be around riffing and raffing on Saturday morning.

SETH. I know where he at. I know just where he at. They got him down there in the jail. Getting drunk and acting a fool. He down there where he belong with all that foolishness.

BYNUM. Mr. Piney's boys got him, huh? They ain't gonna do nothing but hold on to him for a little while. He's gonna be back here hungrier than a mule directly.

SETH. I don't go for all that carrying on and such. This is a respectable house. I don't have no drunkards or fools around here.

BYNUM. That boy got a lot of country in him. He ain't been up here but two weeks. It's gonna take a while before he can work that country out of him.

SETH. These niggers coming up here with that old backward country style of living. It's hard enough now without all that ignorant kind of acting. Ever since slavery got over with there ain't been nothing but foolish-acting niggers. Word get out they need men to work in the mill and put in these roads . . . and niggers drop everything and head North looking for freedom. They don't know the white fellows looking too. White fellows coming from all over the world. White fellow come over and in six months got more than what I got. But these niggers keep on coming. Walking . . . riding . . . carrying their Bibles. That boy done carried a guitar all the way from North Carolina. What he gonna find out? What he gonna do with that guitar? This is the city.

[There is a knock on the door.]

Niggers coming up here from the backwoods . . . coming up here from the country carrying Bibles and guitars looking for freedom. They got a rude awakening.

[Seth goes to answer the door. Rutherford Selig enters. About Seth's age, he is a thin white man with greasy hair. A peddler, he supplies Seth with the raw materials to make pots and pans which he then peddles door to door in the mill towns along the river. He keeps a list of his customers as they move about and is known in the various communities as the People Finder. He carries squares of sheet metal under his arm.]

Ho! Forgot you was coming today. Come on in.

BYNUM. If it ain't Rutherford Selig . . . the People Finder himself.

SELIG. What say there, Bynum?

BYNUM. I say about my shiny man. You got to tell me something. I done give you my dollar . . . I'm looking to get a report.

SELIG. I got eight here, Seth.

SETH. [Taking the sheet metal.] What is this? What you giving me here? What I'm gonna do with this?

SELIG. I need some dustpans. Everybody asking me about dustpans.

SETH. Gonna cost you fifteen cents apiece. And ten cents to put a handle on them.

SELIG. I'll give you twenty cents apiece with the handles.

SETH. All right. But I ain't gonna give you but fifteen cents for the sheet metal.

SELIG. It's twenty-five cents apiece for the metal. That's what we agreed on.

SETH. This low-grade sheet metal. They ain't worth but a dime. I'm doing you a favor giving you fifteen cents. You know this metal ain't worth no twenty-five cents. Don't come talking that twenty-five cent stuff to me over no low-grade sheet metal.

SELIG. All right, fifteen cents apiece. Just make me some dustpans out of them.

[Seth exits with the sheet metal out the back door.]

BERTHA. Sit on down there, Selig. Get you a cup of coffee and a biscuit.

BYNUM. Where you coming from this time?

SELIG. I been upriver. All along the Monongahela. Past Rankin and all up around Little Washington.

BYNUM. Did you find anybody?

SELIG. I found Sadie Jackson up in Braddock. Her mother's staying down there in Scotchbottom say she hadn't heard from her and she didn't know where she was at. I found her up in Braddock on Enoch Street. She bought a frying pan from me.

BYNUM. You around here finding everybody how come you ain't found my shiny man?

SELIG. The only shiny man I saw was the Nigras working on the road gang with the sweat glistening on them.

BYNUM. Naw, you'd be able to tell this fellow. He shine like new money.

SELIG. Well, I done told you I can't find nobody without a name.

BERTHA. Here go one of these hot biscuits, Selig.

BYNUM. This fellow don't have no name. I call him John cause it was up around Johnstown where I seen him. I ain't even so sure he's one special fellow. That shine could pass on to anybody. He could be anybody shining.

SELIG. Well, what's he look like besides being shiny? There's lots of shiny Nigras.

BYNUM. He's just a man I seen out on the road. He ain't had no special look. Just a man walking toward me on the road. He come up and asked me which way the road went. I told him everything I knew about the road, where it went and all, and he asked me did I have anything to eat cause he was hungry. Say he ain't had nothing to eat in three days. Well, I never be out there on the road without a piece of dried meat. Or an orange or an apple. So I give this fellow an orange. He take and eat that orange and told me to come and go along the road a little ways with him, that he had something he wanted to show me. He had a look about him made me wanna go with him, see what he gonna show me.

We walked on a bit and it's getting kind of far from where I met him when it come up on me all of a sudden, we wasn't going the way he had come from, we was going back my way. Since he said he ain't knew nothing about the road, I asked him about this. He say he had a voice inside him telling him which way to go and if I come and go along with him he was gonna show me the Secret of Life. Quite naturally I followed him. A fellow that's gonna show you the Secret of Life ain't to be taken lightly. We get near this bend in the road . . .

[Seth enters with an assortment of pots.]

SETH. I got six here, Selig.

SELIG. Wait a minute, Seth. Bynum's telling me about the secret of life. Go ahead, Bynum. I wanna hear this.

[Seth sets the pots down and exits out the back.]

BYNUM. We get near this bend in the road and he told me to hold out my hands. Then he rubbed them together with his and I looked down and see they got blood on them. Told me to take and rub it all over me . . . say that was a way of cleaning myself. Then we went around the bend in that road. Got around that bend and it seem like all of a sudden we ain't in the same place. Turn around that bend and everything look like it was twice as big as it was. The trees and everything bigger than life! Sparrows big as eagles! I turned around to look at this fellow and he had this light coming out of him. I had to cover up my eyes to keep from being blinded. He shining like new money with that light. He shined until all the light seemed like it seeped out of him and then he was gone and I was by myself in this strange place where everything was bigger than life.

I wandered around there looking for that road, trying to find my way back from this big place . . . and I looked over and seen my daddy standing there. He was the same size he always was, except for his hands and his mouth. He had a great big old mouth that look like it took up his whole face and his hands were as big as hams. Look like they was too big to carry around. My daddy called me to him. Said he had been thinking about me and it grieved him to see me in the world carrying other people's songs and not having one of my own. Told me he was gonna show me how to find my song. Then he carried me further into this big place until we come to this ocean. Then he showed me something I ain't got words to tell you. But if you stand to witness it, you done seen something there. I stayed in that place awhile and my daddy taught me the meaning of this thing that I had seen and showed me how to find my song. I asked him about the shiny man and he told me he was the One Who Goes Before and Shows the Way. Said there was lots of shiny men and if I ever saw one again before I died then I would know that my song had been accepted and worked its full power in the world and I could lay down and die a happy man. A man who done left his mark on life. On the way people cling to each other out of the truth they find in themselves. Then he showed me how to get back to the road. I came out to where everything was its own size and I had my song. I had the Binding Song. I chose that song because that's what I seen most when I was traveling . . . people walking away and leaving one another. So I takes the power of my song and binds them together.

[Seth enters from the yard carrying cabbages and tomatoes.]

Been binding people ever since. That's why they call me Bynum. Just like glue I sticks people together.

SETH. Maybe they ain't supposed to be stuck sometimes. You ever think of that?

BYNUM. Oh, I don't do it lightly. It cost me a piece of myself every time I do. I'm a Binder of What Clings. You got to find out if they cling first. You can't bind what don't cling.

SELIG. Well, how is that the secret of life? I thought you said he was gonna show you the secret of life. That's what I'm waiting to find out.

BYNUM. Oh, he showed me all right. But you still got to figure it out. Can't nobody figure it out for you. You got to come to it on your own. That's why I'm looking for the shiny man.

SELIG. Well, I'll keep my eye out for him. What you got there, Seth?

SETH. Here go some cabbage and tomatoes. I got some green beans coming in real nice. I'm gonna take and start me a grapevine out there next year. Butera says he gonna give me a piece of his vine and I'm gonna start that out there.

SELIG. How many of them pots you got?

SETH. I got six. That's six dollars minus eight on top of fifteen for the sheet metal come to a dollar twenty out the six dollars leave me four dollars and eighty cents.

SELIG. *[Counting out the money.]* There's four dollars . . . and . . . eighty cents.

SETH. How many of them dustpans you want?

SELIG. As many as you can make out them sheets.

SETH. You can use that many? I get to cutting on them sheets figuring how to make them dustpans . . . ain't no telling how many I'm liable to come up with.

SELIG. I can use them and you can make me some more next time.

SETH. All right, I'm gonna hold you to that, now.

SELIG. Thanks for the biscuit, Bertha.

BERTHA. You know you welcome any time, Selig.

SETH. Which way you heading?

SELIG. Going down to Wheeling. All through West Virginia there. I'll be back Saturday. They putting in new roads down that way. Makes traveling easier.

SETH. That's what I hear. All up around here too. Got a fellow staying here working on that road by the Brady Street Bridge.

SELIG. Yeah, it's gonna make traveling real nice. Thanks for the cabbage, Seth. I'll see you on Saturday.

[Selig exits.]

SETH. *[To Bynum.]* Why you wanna start all that nonsense talk with that man? All that shiny man nonsense?

BYNUM. You know it ain't no nonsense. Bertha know it ain't no nonsense. I don't know if Selig know or not.

BERTHA. Seth, when you get to making them dustpans make me a coffeepot.

SETH. What's the matter with your coffee? Ain't nothing wrong with your coffee. Don't she make some good coffee, Bynum?

BYNUM. I ain't worried about the coffee. I know she makes some good biscuits.

SETH. I ain't studying no coffeepot, woman. You heard me tell the man I was gonna cut as many dustpans as them sheets will make . . . and all of a sudden you want a coffeepot.

BERTHA. Man, hush up and go on and make me that coffeepot.

[Jeremy enters the front door. About twenty-five, he gives the impression that he has the world in his hand, that he can meet life's challenges head-on. He smiles a lot. He is a proficient guitar player, though his spirit has yet to be molded into song.]

BYNUM. I hear Mr. Piney's boys had you.

JEREMY. Fined me two dollars for nothing! Ain't done nothing.

SETH. I told you when you come on here everybody know my house. Know these is respectable quarters. I don't put up with no foolishness. Everybody know Seth Holly keep a good house. Was my daddy's house. This house been a decent house for a long time.

JEREMY. I ain't done nothing, Mr. Seth. I stopped by the Workmen's Club and got me a bottle. Me and Roper Lee from Alabama. Had us a half pint. We was fixing to cut that half in two when they came up on us. Asked us if we was working. We told them we was putting in the road over yonder and that it was our payday. They snatched hold of us to get that two dollars. Me and Roper Lee ain't even had a chance to take a drink when they grabbed us.

SETH. I don't go for all that kind of carrying on.

BERTHA. Leave the boy alone, Seth. You know the police do that. Figure there's too many people out on the street they take some of them off. You know that.

SETH. I ain't gonna have folks talking.

BERTHA. Ain't nobody talking nothing. That's all in your head. You want some grits and biscuits, Jeremy?

JEREMY. Thank you, Miss Bertha. They didn't give us a thing to eat last night. I'll take one of them big bowls if you don't mind.

[There is a knock at the door. Seth goes to answer it. Enter Herald Loomis and his eleven-year-old daughter, Zonia. Herald Loomis is thirty-two years old. He is at times possessed. A man driven not by the hellhounds that seemingly bay at his heels, but by his search for a world that speaks to something about himself. He is unable to harmonize the forces that swirl around him, and seeks to recreate the world into one that contains his image. He wears a hat and a long wool coat.]

LOOMIS. Me and my daughter looking for a place to stay, mister. You got a sign say you got rooms.

[Seth stares at Loomis, sizing him up.]

Mister, if you ain't got no rooms we can go somewhere else.

SETH. How long you plan on staying?

LOOMIS. Don't know. Two weeks or more maybe.

SETH. It's two dollars a week for the room. We serve meals twice a day. It's two dollars for room and board. Pay up in advance.

[Loomis reaches into his pocket.]

It's a dollar extra for the girl.

LOOMIS. The girl sleep in the same room.

SETH. Well, do she eat off the same plate? We serve meals twice a day. That's a dollar extra for food.

LOOMIS. Ain't got no extra dollar. I was planning on asking your missus if she could help out with the cooking and cleaning and whatnot.

SETH. Her helping out don't put no food on the table. I need that dollar to buy some food.

LOOMIS. I'll give you fifty cents extra. She don't eat much.

SETH. Okay . . . but fifty cents don't buy but half a portion.

BERTHA. Seth, she can help me out. Let her help me out. I can use some help.

SETH. Well, that's two dollars for the week. Pay up in advance. Saturday to Saturday. You wanna stay on then it's two more come Saturday.

[Loomis pays Seth the money.]

BERTHA. My name's Bertha. This is my husband, Seth. You got Bynum and Jeremy over there.

LOOMIS. Ain't nobody else live here?

BERTHA. They the only ones live here now. People come and go. They the only ones here now. You want a cup of coffee and a biscuit?

LOOMIS. We done ate this morning.

BYNUM. Where you coming from, Mister . . . I didn't get your name.

LOOMIS. Name's Herald Loomis. This is my daughter, Zonia.

BYNUM. Where you coming from?

LOOMIS. Come from all over. Whichever way the road take us, that's the way we go.

JEREMY. If you looking for a job, I'm working putting in that road down there by the bridge. They can't get enough mens. Always looking to take somebody on.

LOOMIS. I'm looking for a woman named Martha Loomis. That's my wife. Got married legal with the papers and all.

SETH. I don't know nobody named Loomis. I know some Marthas but I don't know no Loomis.

BYNUM. You got to see Rutherford Selig if you wanna find somebody. Selig's the People Finder. Rutherford Selig's a first-class People Finder.

JEREMY. What she look like? Maybe I seen her.

LOOMIS. She a brownskin woman. Got long, pretty hair. About five feet from the ground.

JEREMY. I don't know. I might have seen her.

BYNUM. You got to see Rutherford Selig. You give him one dollar to get her name on his list . . . and after she get her name on his list Rutherford Selig will go right on out there and find her. I got him looking for somebody for me.

LOOMIS. You say he find people. How you find him?

BYNUM. You just missed him. He's gone downriver now. You got to wait till Saturday. He's gone downriver with his pots and pans. He come to see Seth on Saturdays. You got to wait till then.

SETH. Come on, I'll show you to your room.

[Seth, Loomis, and Zonia exit up the stairs.]

JEREMY. Miss Bertha, I'll take that biscuit you was gonna give that fellow, if you don't mind. Say, Mr. Bynum, they got somebody like that around here sure enough? Somebody that find people?

BYNUM. Rutherford Selig. He go around selling pots and pans and every house he come to he write down the name and address of whoever lives there. So if you looking for somebody, quite naturally you go and see him . . . cause he's the only one who know where everybody live at.

JEREMY. I ought to have him look for this old gal I used to know. It be nice to see her again.

BERTHA. *[Giving Jeremy a biscuit.]* Jeremy, today's the day for you to pull them sheets off the bed and set them outside your door. I'll set you out some clean ones.

BYNUM. Mr. Piney's boys done ruined your good time last night, Jeremy . . . what you planning for tonight?

JEREMY. They got me scared to go out, Mr. Bynum. They might grab me again.

BYNUM. You ought to take your guitar and go down to Seefus. Seefus got a gambling place down there on Wylie Avenue. You ought to take your guitar and go down there. They got guitar contest down there.

JEREMY. I don't play no contest, Mr. Bynum. Had one of them white fellows cure me of that. I ain't been nowhere near a contest since.

BYNUM. White fellow beat you playing guitar?

JEREMY. Naw, he ain't beat me. I was sitting at home just fixing to sit down and eat when somebody come up to my house and got me. Told me there's a white fellow say he was gonna give a prize to the best guitar player he could find. I take up my guitar and go down there and somebody had gone up and got Bobo Smith and brought him down there. Him and another fellow called Hooter. Old Hooter couldn't play no guitar, he do more hollering than playing, but Bobo could go at it awhile. This fellow standing there say he the one that was gonna give the prize and me and Bobo started playing for him. Bobo play something and then I'd try to play something better than what he played. Old Hooter, he just holler and bang at the guitar. Man was the worst guitar player I ever seen. So me and Bobo played and after a while I seen where he was getting the attention of this white fellow. He'd play something and while he was playing it he be slapping on the side of the guitar, and that made it sound like he was playing more than he was. So I started doing it too. White fellow ain't knew no difference. He ain't knew as much about guitar playing as Hooter did. After we play awhile, the white fellow called us to him and said he couldn't make up his mind, say all three of us was the best guitar player and we'd have to split the prize between us. Then he give us twenty-five cents. That's eight cents apiece and a penny on the side. That cured me of playing contest to this day.

BYNUM. Seefus ain't like that. Seefus give a whole dollar and a drink of whiskey.

JEREMY. What night they be down there?

BYNUM. Be down there every night. Music don't know no certain night.

BERTHA. You go down to Seefus with them people and you liable to end up in a raid and go to jail sure enough. I don't know why Bynum tell you that.

BYNUM. That's where the music at. That's where the people at. The people down there making music and enjoying themselves. Some things is worth taking the chance going to jail about.

BERTHA. Jeremy ain't got no business going down there.

JEREMY. They got some women down there, Mr. Bynum?

BYNUM. Oh, they got women down there, sure. They got women everywhere. Women be where the men is so they can find each other.

JEREMY. Some of them old gals come out there where we be putting in that road. Hanging around there trying to snatch somebody.

BYNUM. How come some of them ain't snatched hold of you?

JEREMY. I don't want them kind. Them desperate kind. Ain't nothing worse than a desperate woman. Tell them you gonna leave them and they get to crying and carrying on. That just make you want to get away quicker. They get to cutting up your clothes and things trying to keep you staying. Desperate women ain't nothing but trouble for a man.

[Seth enters from the stairs.]

SETH. Something ain't setting right with that fellow.
BERTHA. What's wrong with him? What he say?
SETH. I take him up there and try to talk to him and he ain't for no talking. Say he been traveling . . . coming over from Ohio. Say he a deacon in the church. Say he looking for Martha Pentecost. Talking about that's his wife.
BERTHA. How do you know it's the same Martha? Could be talking about anybody. Lots of people named Martha.
SETH. You see that little girl? I didn't hook it up till he said it, but that little girl look just like her. Ask Bynum. [To Bynum.] Bynum. Don't that little girl look just like Martha Pentecost?
BERTHA. I still say he could be talking about anybody.
SETH. The way he described her wasn't no doubt about who he was talking about. Described her right down to her toes.
BERTHA. What did you tell him?
SETH. I ain't told him nothing. The way that fellow look I wasn't gonna tell him nothing. I don't know what he looking for her for.
BERTHA. What else he have to say?
SETH. I told you he wasn't for no talking. I told him where the outhouse was and to keep that gal off the front porch and out of my garden. He asked if you'd mind setting a hot tub for the gal and that was about the gist of it.
BERTHA. Well, I wouldn't let it worry me if I was you. Come on get your sleep.
BYNUM. He says he looking for Martha and he a deacon in the church.
SETH. That's what he say. Do he look like a deacon to you?
BERTHA. He might be, you don't know. Bynum ain't got no special say on whether he a deacon or not.
SETH. Well, if he the deacon I'd sure like to see the preacher.
BERTHA. Come on get your sleep. Jeremy, don't forget to set them sheets outside the door like I told you.

[Bertha exits into the bedroom.]

SETH. Something ain't setting right with that fellow, Bynum. He's one of them mean-looking niggers look like he done killed somebody gambling over a quarter.
BYNUM. He ain't no gambler. Gamblers wear nice shoes. This fellow got on clodhoppers. He been out there walking up and down them roads.

[Zonia enters from the stairs and looks around.]

BYNUM. You looking for the back door, sugar? There it is. You can go out there and play. It's all right.
SETH. [Showing her the door.] You can go out there and play. Just don't get in my garden. And don't go messing around in my work shed.

[Seth exits into the bedroom. There is a knock on the door.]

JEREMY. Somebody at the door.

[Jeremy goes to answer the door. Enter Mattie Campbell. She is a young woman of twenty-six whose attractiveness is hidden under the weight and concerns of a dissatisfied life. She is a woman in an honest search for love and companionship. She has suffered many defeats in her search, and though not always uncompromising, still believes in the possibility of love.]

MATTIE. I'm looking for a man named Bynum. Lady told me to come back later.
JEREMY. Sure, he here. Mr. Bynum, somebody here to see you.
BYNUM. Come to see me, huh?
MATTIE. Are you the man they call Bynum? The man folks say can fix things?
BYNUM. Depend on what need fixing. I can't make no promises. But I got a powerful song in some matters.
MATTIE. Can you fix it so my man come back to me?
BYNUM. Come on in . . have a sit down.
MATTIE. You got to help me. I don't know what else to do.
BYNUM. Depend on how all the circumstances of the thing come together. How all the pieces fit.
MATTIE. I done everything I knowed how to do. You got to make him come back to me.

BYNUM. It ain't nothing to make somebody come back. I can fix it so he can't stand to be away from you. I got my roots and powders, I can fix it so wherever he's at this thing will come up on him and he won't be able to sleep for seeing your face. Won't be able to eat for thinking of you.

MATTIE. That's what I want. Make him come back.

BYNUM. The roots is a powerful thing. I can fix it so one day he'll walk out his front door . . . won't be thinking of nothing. He won't know what it is. All he knows is that a powerful dissatisfaction done set in his bones and can't nothing he do make him feel satisfied. He'll set his foot down on the road and the wind in the trees be talking to him and everywhere he step on the road, that road'll give back your name and something will pull him right up to your doorstep. Now, I can do that. I can take my roots and fix that easy. But maybe he ain't supposed to come back. And if he ain't supposed to come back . . . then he'll be in your bed one morning and it'll come up on him that he's in the wrong place. That he's lost outside of time from his place that he's supposed to be in. Then both of you be lost and trapped outside of life and ain't no way for you to get back into it. Cause you lost from yourselves and where the places come together, where you're supposed to be alive, your heart kicking in your chest with a song worth singing.

MATTIE. Make him come back to me. Make his feet say my name on the road. I don't care what happens. Make him come back.

BYNUM. What's your man's name?

MATTIE. He go by Jack Carper. He was born in Alabama then he come to West Texas and find me and we come here. Been here three years before he left. Say I had a curse prayer on me and he started walking down the road and ain't never come back. Somebody told me, say you can fix things like that.

BYNUM. He just got up one day, set his feet on the road, and walked away?

MATTIE. You got to make him come back, mister.

BYNUM. Did he say good-bye?

MATTIE. Ain't said nothing. Just started walking. I could see where he disappeared. Didn't look back. Just kept walking. Can't you fix it so he come back? I ain't got no curse prayer on me. I know I ain't.

BYNUM. What made him say you had a curse prayer on you?

MATTIE. Cause the babies died. Me and Jack had two babies. Two little babies that ain't lived two months before they died. He say it's because somebody cursed me not to have babies.

BYNUM. He ain't bound to you if the babies died. Look like somebody trying to keep you from being bound up and he's gone on back to whoever it is cause he's already bound up to her. Ain't nothing to be done. Somebody else done got a powerful hand in it and ain't nothing to be done to break it. You got to let him go find where he's supposed to be in the world.

MATTIE. Jack done gone off and you telling me to forget about him. All my life I been looking for somebody to stop and stay with me. I done already got too many things to forget about. I take Jack Carper's hand and it feel so rough and strong. Seem like he's the strongest man in the world the way he hold me. Like he's bigger than the whole world and can't nothing bad get to me. Even when he act mean sometimes he still make everything seem okay with the world. Like there's part of it that belongs just to you. Now you telling me to forget about him?

BYNUM. Jack Carper gone off to where he belong. There's somebody searching for your doorstep right now. Ain't no need you fretting over Jack Carper. Right now he's a strong thought in your mind. But every time you catch yourself fretting over Jack Carper you push that thought away. You push it out your mind and that thought will get weaker and weaker till you wake up one morning and you won't even be able to call him up on your mind.

[Bynum gives her a small cloth packet.]

Take this and sleep with it under your pillow and it'll bring good luck to you. Draw it to you like a magnet. It won't be long before you forget all about Jack Carper.

MATTIE. How much . . . do I owe you?

BYNUM. Whatever you got there . . . that'll be all right.

[Mattie hands Bynum two quarters. She crosses to the door.]

You sleep with that under your pillow and you'll be all right.

[Mattie opens the door to exit and Jeremy crosses over to her. Bynum overhears the first part of their conversation, then exits out the back.]

JEREMY. I overheard what you told Mr. Bynum. Had me an old gal did that to me. Woke up one morning and she was gone. Just took off to parts unknown. I woke up that morning and the only thing I could do was look around for my shoes. I woke up and got out of there. Found my shoes and took off. That's the only thing I could think of to do.

MATTIE. She ain't said nothing?

JEREMY. I just looked around for my shoes and got out of there.

MATTIE. Jack ain't said nothing either. He just walked off.

JEREMY. Some mens do that. Womens too. I ain't gone off looking for her. I just let her go. Figure she had a time to come to herself. Wasn't no use of me standing in the way. Where you from?

MATTIE. Texas. I was born in Georgia but I went to Texas with my mama. She dead now. Was picking peaches and fell dead away. I come up here with Jack Carper.

JEREMY. I'm from North Carolina. Down around Raleigh where they got all that tobacco. Been up here about two weeks. I likes it fine except I still got to find me a woman. You got a nice look to you. Look like you have mens standing in your door. Is you got mens standing in your door to get a look at you?

MATTIE. I ain't got nobody since Jack left.

JEREMY. A woman like you need a man. Maybe you let me be your man. I got a nice way with the women. That's what they tell me.

MATTIE. I don't know. Maybe Jack's coming back.

JEREMY. I'll be your man till he come. A woman can't be by her lonesome. Let me be your man till he come.

MATTIE. I just can't go through life piecing myself out to different mens. I need a man who wants to stay with me.

JEREMY. I can't say what's gonna happen. Maybe I'll be the man. I don't know. You wanna go along the road a little ways with me?

MATTIE. I don't know. Seem like life say it's gonna be one thing and end up being another. I'm tired of going from man to man.

JEREMY. Life is like you got to take a chance. Everybody got to take a chance. Can't nobody say what's gonna be. Come on . . . take a chance with me and see what the year bring. Maybe you let me come and see you. Where you staying?

MATTIE. I got me a room up on Bedford. Me and Jack had a room together.

JEREMY. What's the address? I'll come by and get you tonight and we can go down to Seefus. I'm going down there and play my guitar.

MATTIE. You play guitar?

JEREMY. I play guitar like I'm born to it.

MATTIE. I live at 1727 Bedford Avenue. I'm gonna find out if you can play guitar like you say.

JEREMY. I play it sugar, and that ain't all I do. I got a ten-pound hammer and I knows how to drive it down. Good god . . . you ought to hear my hammer ring!

MATTIE. Go on with that kind of talk, now. If you gonna come by and get me I got to get home and straighten up for you.

JEREMY. I'll be by at eight o'clock. How's eight o'clock? I'm gonna make you forget all about Jack Carper.

MATTIE. Go on, now. I got to get home and fix up for you.

JEREMY. Eight o'clock, sugar.

[The lights go down in the parlor and come up on the yard outside. Zonia is singing and playing a game.]

ZONIA.

> I went downtown
> To get my grip
> I came back home
> Just a pullin' the skiff
>
> I went upstairs
> To make my bed
> I made a mistake
> And I bumped my head
> Just a pullin' the skiff
>
> I went downstairs
> To milk the cow
> I made a mistake
> And I milked the sow
> Just a pullin' the skiff
>
> Tomorrow, tomorrow
> Tomorrow never comes
> The marrow the marrow
> The marrow in the bone.

[Reuben enters.]

REUBEN. Hi.

ZONIA. Hi.

REUBEN. What's your name?

ZONIA. Zonia.

REUBEN. What kind of name is that?

ZONIA. It's what my daddy named me.

REUBEN. My name's Reuben. You staying in Mr. Seth's house?

ZONIA. Yeah.

REUBEN. That your daddy I seen you with this morning?

ZONIA. I don't know. Who you see me with?

REUBEN. I saw you with some man had on a great big old coat. And you was walking up to Mr. Seth's house. Had on a hat too.

ZONIA. Yeah, that's my daddy.

REUBEN. You like Mr. Seth?

ZONIA. I ain't see him much.

REUBEN. My grandpap say he a great big old windbag. How come you living in Mr. Seth's house? Don't you have no house?

ZONIA. We going to find my mother.

REUBEN. Where she at?

ZONIA. I don't know. We got to find her. We just go all over.

REUBEN. Why you got to find her? What happened to her?

ZONIA. She ran away.

REUBEN. Why she run away?

ZONIA. I don't know. My daddy say some man named Joe Turner did something bad to him once and that made her run away.

REUBEN. Maybe she coming back and you don't have to go looking for her.

ZONIA. We ain't there no more.

REUBEN. She could have come back when you wasn't there.

ZONIA. My daddy said she ran off and left us so we going looking for her.

REUBEN. What he gonna do when he find her?

ZONIA. He didn't say. He just say he got to find her.

REUBEN. Your daddy say how long you staying in Mr. Seth's house?

ZONIA. He don't say much. But we never stay too long nowhere. He say we got to keep moving till we find her.

REUBEN. Ain't no kids hardly live around here. I had me a friend but he died. He was the best friend I ever had. Me and Eugene used to keep secrets. I still got his pigeons. He told me to let them go when he died. He say, "Reuben, promise me when I die you'll let my pigeons go." But I keep them to remember him by. I ain't never gonna let them go. Even when I get to be grown up. I'm just always gonna have Eugene's pigeons.

[Pause.]

Mr. Bynum a conjure man. My grandpap scared of him. He don't like me to come over here too much. I'm scared of him too. My grandpap told me not to let him get close enough to where he can reach out his hand and touch me.

ZONIA. He don't seem scary to me.

REUBEN. He buys pigeons from me . . . and if you get up early in the morning you can see him out in the yard doing something with them pigeons. My grandpap say he kill them. I sold him one yesterday. I don't know what he do with it. I just hope he don't spook me up.

ZONIA. Why you sell him pigeons if he's gonna spook you up?

REUBEN. I just do like Eugene do. He used to sell Mr. Bynum pigeons. That's how he got to collecting them to sell to Mr. Bynum. Sometime he give me a nickel and sometime he give me a whole dime.

[Loomis enters from the house.]

LOOMIS. Zonia!

ZONIA. Sir?

LOOMIS. What you doing?

ZONIA. Nothing.

LOOMIS. You stay around this house, you hear? I don't want you wandering off nowhere.

ZONIA. I ain't wandering off nowhere.

LOOMIS. Miss Bertha set that hot tub and you getting a good scrubbing. Get scrubbed up good. You ain't been scrubbing.

ZONIA. I been scrubbing.

LOOMIS. Look at you. You growing too fast. Your bones getting bigger everyday. I don't want you getting grown on me. Don't you get grown on me too soon. We gonna find your mamma. She around here somewhere. I can smell her. You stay on around this house now. Don't you go nowhere.

ZONIA. Yes, sir.

[Loomis exits into the house.]

REUBEN. Wow, your daddy's scary!

ZONIA. He is not! I don't know what you talking about.

REUBEN. He got them mean-looking eyes!

ZONIA. My daddy ain't got no mean-looking eyes!

REUBEN. Aw, girl, I was just messing with you. You wanna go see Eugene's pigeons? Got a great big coop out the back of my house. Come on, I'll show you.

[Reuben and Zonia exit as the lights go down.]

SCENE II

[It is Saturday morning, one week later. The lights come up on the kitchen. Bertha is at the stove preparing breakfast while Seth sits at the table.]

SETH. Something ain't right about that fellow. I been watching him all week. Something ain't right, I'm telling you.

BERTHA. Seth Holly, why don't you hush up about that man this morning?

SETH. I don't like the way he stare at everybody. Don't look at you natural like. He just be staring at you. Like he trying to figure out something about you. Did you see him when he come back in here?

BERTHA. That man ain't thinking about you.

SETH. He don't work nowhere. Just go out and come back. Go out and come back.

BERTHA. As long as you get your boarding money it ain't your cause about what he do. He don't bother nobody.

SETH. Just go out and come back. Going around asking everybody about Martha. Like Henry Allen seen him down at the church last night.

BERTHA. The man's allowed to go to church if he want. He say he a deacon. Ain't nothing wrong about him going to church.

SETH. I ain't talking about him going to church. I'm talking about him hanging around *outside* the church.

BERTHA. Henry Allen say that?

SETH. Say he be standing around outside the church. Like he be watching it.

BERTHA. What on earth he wanna be watching the church for, I wonder?

SETH. That's what I'm trying to figure out. Looks like he fixing to rob it.

BERTHA. Seth, now do he look like the kind that would rob the church?

SETH. I ain't saying that. I ain't saying how he look. It's how he do. Anybody liable to do anything as far as I'm concerned. I ain't never thought about how no church robbers look . . . but now that you mention it, I don't see where they look no different than how he look.

BERTHA. Herald Loomis ain't the kind of man who would rob no church.

SETH. I ain't even so sure that's his name.

BERTHA. Why the man got to lie about his name?

SETH. Anybody can tell anybody anything about what their name is. That's what you call him . . . Herald Loomis. His name is liable to be anything.

BERTHA. Well, until he tell me different that's what I'm gonna call him. You just getting yourself all worked up about the man for nothing.

SETH. Talking about Loomis—Martha's name wasn't no Loomis nothing. Martha's name is Pentecost.

BERTHA. How you so sure that's her right name? Maybe she changed it.

SETH. Martha's a good Christian woman. This fellow here look like he owe the devil a day's work and he's trying to figure out how he gonna pay him. Martha ain't had a speck of distrust about her the whole time she was living here. They moved the church out there to Rankin and I was sorry to see her go.

BERTHA. That's why he be hanging around the church. He looking for her.

SETH. If he looking for her, why don't he go inside and ask? What he doing hanging around outside the church acting sneaky like?

[Bynum enters from the yard.]

BYNUM. Morning, Seth. Morning, Sister Bertha.

[Bynum continues through the kitchen and exits up the stairs.]

BERTHA. That's who you should be asking the questions. He been out there in that yard all morning. He was out there before the sun come up. He didn't even come in for breakfast. I don't know what he's doing. He had three of them pigeons lined up out there. He dance around till he get tired. He sit down awhile then get up and dance some more. He come through here a little while ago looking like he was mad at the world.

SETH. I don't pay Bynum no mind. He don't spook me up with all that stuff.

BERTHA. That's how Martha come to be living here. She come to see Bynum. She come to see him when she first left from down South.

SETH. Martha was living here before Bynum. She ain't come on here when she first left from down there. She come on here after she went back to get her little girl. That's when she come on here.

BERTHA. Well, where was Bynum? He was here when she came.

SETH. Bynum ain't come till after her. That boy Hiram was staying up there in Bynum's room.

BERTHA. Well, how long Bynum been here?

SETH. Bynum ain't been here no longer than three years. That's what I'm trying to tell you. Martha was staying up there and sewing and cleaning for Doc Goldblum when Bynum came. This the longest he ever been in once place.

BERTHA. How you know how long the man been in once place?

SETH. I know Bynum. Bynum ain't no mystery to me. I done seen a hundred niggers like him. He's one of them fellows never could stay in one place. He was wandering all around the country till he got old and settled here. The only thing different about Bynum is he bring all this heebie-jeebie stuff with him.

BERTHA. I still say he was staying here when she came. That's why she came . . . to see him.

SETH. You can say what you want. I know the facts of it. She come on here four years ago all heartbroken cause she couldn't find her little girl. And Bynum wasn't nowhere around. She got mixed up in that old heebie-jeebie nonsense with him after he came.

BERTHA. Well, if she came on before Bynum I don't know where she stayed. Cause she stayed up there in Hiram's room. Hiram couldn't get along with Bynum and left out of here owing you two dollars. Now, I know you ain't forgot about that!

SETH. Sure did! You know Hiram ain't paid me that two dollars yet. So that's why he be ducking and hiding when he see me down on Logan Street. You right. Martha did come on after Bynum. I forgot that's why Hiram left.

BERTHA. Him and Bynum never could see eye to eye. They always rubbed each other the wrong way. Hiram got to thinking that Bynum was trying to put a fix on him and he moved out. Martha came to see Bynum and ended up taking Hiram's room. Now, I know what I'm talking about. She stayed on here three years till they moved the church.

SETH. She out there in Rankin now. I know where she at. I know where they moved the church to. She right out there in Rankin in that place used to be a shoe store. Used to be Wolf's shoe store. They moved to a bigger place and they put that church in there. I know where she at. I know just where she at.

BERTHA. Why don't you tell the man? You see he looking for her.

SETH. I ain't gonna tell that man where the woman is! What I wanna do that for? I don't know nothing about that man. I don't know why he looking for her. He might wanna do her a harm. I ain't gonna carry that on my hands. He looking for her, he gonna have to find her for himself. I ain't gonna help him. Now, if he had come and presented himself as a gentleman— the way Martha Pentecost's husband would have done—then I would have told him. But I ain't gonna tell this old wild-eyed mean-looking nigger nothing!

BERTHA. Well, why don't you get a ride with Selig and go up there and tell her where he is? See if she wanna see him. If that's her little girl . . . you say Martha was looking for her.

SETH. You know me, Bertha. I don't get mixed up in nobody's business.

[Bynum enters from the stairs.]

BYNUM. Morning, Seth. Morning, Bertha. Can I still get some breakfast? Mr. Loomis been down here this morning?

SETH. He done gone out and come back. He up there now. Left out of here early this morning wearing that coat. Hot as it is, the man wanna walk around wearing a big old heavy coat. He come back in here, paid me for another week, sat down there waiting on Selig. Got tired of waiting and went on back upstairs.

BYNUM. Where's the little girl?

SETH. She out there in the front. Had to chase her and that Reuben off the front porch. She out there somewhere.

BYNUM. Look like if Martha was around here he would have found her by now. My guess is she ain't in the city.

SETH. She ain't! I know where she at. I know just where she at. But I ain't gonna tell him. Not the way he look.

BERTHA. Here go your coffee, Bynum.

BYNUM. He says he gonna get Selig to find her for him.

SETH. Selig can't find her. He talk all that . . . but unless he get lucky and knock on her door he can't find her. That's the only way he find anybody. He got to get lucky. But I know just where she at.

BERTHA. Here go some biscuits, Bynum.

BYNUM. What else you got over there, Sister Bertha? You got some grits and gravy over there? I could go for some of that this morning.

BERTHA. [Sets a bowl on the table.] Seth, come on and help me turn this mattress over. Come on.

SETH. Something ain't right with that fellow, Bynum. I don't like the way he stare at everybody.

BYNUM. Mr. Loomis all right, Seth. He just a man got something on his mind. He just got a straightforward mind, that's all.

SETH. What's that fellow that they had around here? Moses, that's Moses Houser. Man went crazy and jumped off the Brady Street Bridge. I told you when I seen him something wasn't right about him. And I'm telling you about this fellow now.

[There is a knock on the door. Seth goes to answer it. Enter Rutherford Selig.]

Ho! Come on in, Selig.

BYNUM. If it ain't the People Finder himself.

SELIG. Bynum, before you start . . . I ain't seen no shiny man now.

BYNUM. Who said anything about that? I ain't said nothing about that. I just called you a first-class People Finder.

SELIG. How many dustpans you get out of that sheet metal, Seth?

SETH. You walked by them on your way in. They sitting out there on the porch. Got twenty-

eight. Got four out of each sheet and made Bertha a coffeepot out the other one. They a little small but they got nice handles.

SELIG. That was twenty cents apiece, right? That's what we agreed on.

SETH. That's five dollars and sixty cents. Twenty on top of twenty-eight. How many sheets you bring me?

SELIG. I got eight out there. That's a dollar twenty makes me owe you . . .

SETH. Four dollars and forty cents.

SELIG. [Paying him.] Go on and make me some dustpans. I can use all you can make.

[Loomis enters from the stairs.]

LOOMIS. I been watching for you. He say you find people.

BYNUM. Mr. Loomis here wants you to find his wife.

LOOMIS. He say you find people. Find her for me.

SELIG. Well, let's see here . . . find somebody, is it?

[Selig rummages through his pockets. He has several notebooks and he is searching for the right one.]

All right now . . . what's the name?

LOOMIS. Martha Loomis. She my wife. Got married legal with the paper and all.

SELIG. [Writing.] Martha . . . Loomis. How tall is she?

LOOMIS. She five feet from the ground.

SELIG. Five feet . . . tall. Young or old?

LOOMIS. She a young woman. Got long pretty hair.

SELIG. Young . . . long . . . pretty . . . hair. Where did you last see her?

LOOMIS. Tennessee. Nearby Memphis.

SELIG. When was that?

LOOMIS. Nineteen hundred and one.

SELIG. Nineteen . . . hundred and one. I'll tell you, mister . . . you better off without them. Now you take me . . . old Rutherford Selig could tell you a thing or two about these women. I ain't met one yet I could understand. Now, you take Sally out there. That's all a man needs is a good horse. I say giddup and she go. Say whoa and she stop. I feed her some oats and she carry me wherever I want to go. Ain't had a speck of trouble out of her since I had her. Now, I been married. A long time ago down in Kentucky. I got up one morning and I saw this look on my wife's face. Like way down deep inside her she was wishing I was dead. I walked around that morning and every time I looked at her she had that look on her face. It seem like she knew I could see it on her. Every time I looked at her I got smaller and smaller. Well, I wasn't gonna stay around there and just shrink away. I walked out on the porch and closed the door behind me. When I closed the door she locked it. I went out and bought me a horse. And I ain't been without one since! Martha Loomis, huh? Well, now I'll do the best I can do. That's one dollar.

LOOMIS. *[Holding out the dollar suspiciously.]* How you find her?

SELIG. Well now, it ain't no easy job like you think. You can't just go out there and find them like that. There's a lot of little tricks to it. It's not an easy job keeping up with you Nigras the way you move about so. Now you take this woman you looking for . . . this Martha Loomis. She could be anywhere. Time I find her, if you don't keep your eye on her, she'll be gone off someplace else. You'll be thinking she over here and she'll be over there. But like I say there's a lot of little tricks to it.

LOOMIS. You say you find her.

SELIG. I can't promise anything but we been finders in my family for a long time. Bringers and finders. My great-granddaddy used to bring Nigras across the ocean on ships. That wasn't no easy job either. Sometimes the winds would blow so hard you'd think the hand of God was set against the sails. But it set him well in pay and he settled in this new land and found him a wife of good Christian charity with a mind for kids and the like and well . . . here I am, Rutherford Selig. You're in good hands, mister. Me and my daddy have found plenty Nigras. My daddy, rest his soul, used to find runaway slaves for the plantation bosses. He was the best there was at it. Jonas B. Selig. Had him a reputation stretched clean across the country. After Abraham Lincoln give you all Nigras your freedom papers and with you all looking all over for each other . . . we started finding Nigras for Nigras. Of course, it don't pay as much. But the People Finding business ain't so bad.

LOOMIS. *[Hands him the dollar.]* Find her. Martha Loomis. Find her for me.

SELIG. Like I say, I can't promise you anything. I'm going back upriver, and if she's around in them parts I'll find her for you. But I can't promise you anything.

LOOMIS. When you coming back?

SELIG. I'll be back on Saturday. I come and see Seth to pick up my order on Saturday.

BYNUM. You going upriver, huh? You going up around my way. I used to go all up through there. Blawnox . . . Clairton. Used to go up to Rankin and take that first right-hand road. I wore many a pair of shoes out walking around that way. You'd have thought I was a missionary spreading the gospel the way I wandered all around them parts.

SELIG. Okay, Bynum. See you on Saturday.

SETH. Here, let me walk out with you. Help you with them dustpans.

[Seth and Selig exit out the back. Bertha enters from the stairs carrying a bundle of sheets.]

BYNUM. Herald Loomis got the People Finder looking for Martha.

BERTHA. You can call him a People Finder if you want to. I know Rutherford Selig carries people away too. He done carried a whole bunch of them away from here. Folks plan on leaving plan by Selig's timing. They wait till he get ready to go, then they hitch a ride on his wagon. Then he charge folks a dollar to tell them where he took them. Now, that's the truth of Rutherford Selig. This old People Finding business is for the birds. He ain't never found nobody he ain't took away. Herald Loomis, you just wasted your dollar.

[Bertha exits into the bedroom.]

LOOMIS. He say he find her. He say he find her by Saturday. I'm gonna wait till Saturday.

[The lights fade to black.]

SCENE III

[It is Sunday morning, the next day. The lights come up on the kitchen. Seth sits talking to Bynum. The breakfast dishes have been cleared away.]

SETH. They can't see that. Neither one of them can see that. Now, how much sense it take to see that? All you got to do is be able to count. One man making ten pots is five men making fifty pots. But they can't see that. Asked where I'm gonna get my five men. Hell, I can teach anybody how to make a pot. I can teach you. I can take you out there and get you started right now. Inside of two weeks you'd know how to make a pot. All you got to do is want to do it. I can get five men. I ain't worried about getting no five men.

BERTHA. *[Calls from the bedroom.]* Seth. Come on and get ready now. Reverend Gates ain't gonna be holding up his sermon cause you sitting out there talking.

SETH. Now, you take the boy, Jeremy. What he gonna do after he put in that road? He can't do nothing but go put in another one somewhere. Now, if he let me show him how to make some pots and pans . . . then he'd have something can't nobody take away from him. After a while he could get his own tools and go off somewhere and make his own pots and pans. Find him somebody to sell them to. Now, Selig can't make no pots and pans. He can sell them but he can't make them. I get me five men with some tools and we'd make him so many pots and pans he'd have to open up a store somewhere. But they can't see that. Neither Mr. Cohen nor Sam Green.

BERTHA. *[Calls from the bedroom.]* Seth . . . time be wasting. Best be getting on.

SETH. I'm coming, woman! *[To Bynum.]* Want me to sign over the house to borrow five hundred dollars. I ain't that big a fool. That's all I got. Sign it over to them and then I won't have nothing.

[Jeremy enters waving a dollar and carrying his guitar.]

JEREMY. Look here, Mr. Bynum . . . won me another dollar last night down at Seefus! Me and that Mattie Campbell went down there again and I played contest. Ain't no guitar players down there. Wasn't even no contest. Say, Mr. Seth, I asked Mattie Campbell if she wanna come by and have Sunday dinner with us. Get some fried chicken.

SETH. It's gonna cost you twenty-five cents.

JEREMY. That's all right. I got a whole dollar here. Say Mr. Seth . . . me and Mattie Campbell talked it over last night and she gonna move in with me. If that's all right with you.

SETH. Your business is your business . . . but it's gonna cost her a dollar a week for her board. I can't be feeding nobody for free.

JEREMY. Oh, she know that, Mr. Seth. That's what I told her, say she'd have to pay for her meals.

SETH. You say you got a whole dollar there . . . turn loose that twenty-five cents.

JEREMY. Suppose she move in today, then that make seventy-five cents more, so I'll give you the whole dollar for her now till she gets here.

[Seth pockets the money and exits into the bedroom.]

BYNUM. So you and that Mattie Campbell gonna take up together?

JEREMY. I told her she don't need to be by her lonesome, Mr. Bynum. Don't make no sense for both of us to be by our lonesome. So she gonna move in with me.

BYNUM. Sometimes you got to be where you supposed to be. Sometimes you can get all mixed up in life and come to the wrong place.

JEREMY. That's just what I told her, Mr. Bynum. It don't make no sense for her to be all mixed up and lonesome. May as well come here and be with me. She a fine woman too. Got them long legs. Knows how to treat a fellow too. Treat you like you wanna be treated.

BYNUM. You just can't look at it like that. You got to look at the whole thing. Now, you take a fellow go out there, grab hold to a woman and think he got something cause she sweet and soft to the touch. Allright. Touching's part of life. It's in the world like everything else. Touching's nice. It feels good. But you can lay your hand upside a horse or a cat, and that feels good too. What's the difference? When you grab hold to a woman, you got something there. You got a whole world there. You got a way of life kicking up under your hand. That woman can take and make you feel like something. I ain't just talking about in the way of jumping off into bed together and rolling around with each other. Anybody can do that. When you grab hold to that woman and look at the whole thing and see what you got . . . why, she can take and make something out of you. Your mother was a woman. That's enough right there to show you what a woman is. Enough to show you what she can do. She made something out of you. Taught you converse, and all about how to take care of yourself, how to see where you at and where you going tomorrow, how to look out to see what's coming in the way of eating, and what to do with yourself when you get lonesome. That's a mighty thing she did. But you just can't look at a woman to jump off into bed with her. That's a foolish thing to ignore a woman like that.

JEREMY. Oh, I ain't ignoring her, Mr. Bynum. It's hard to ignore a woman got legs like she got.

BYNUM. All right. Let's try it this way. Now, you take a ship. Be out there on the water traveling about. You out there on that ship sailing to and from. And then you see some land. Just like you see a woman walking down the street. You see that land and it don't look like nothing but a line out there on the horizon. That's all it is when you first see it. A line that cross your path out there on the horizon. Now, a smart man know when he see that land, it ain't just a line setting out there. He know that if you get off the water to go take a good look . . . why, there's a whole world right there. A whole world with everything imaginable under the sun. Anything you can think of you can find on that land. Same with a woman. A woman is everything a man need. To a smart man she water and berries. And that's all a man need. That's all he need to live on. You give me some water and berries and if there ain't nothing else I can live a hundred years. See, you just like a man looking at the horizon from a ship. You just seeing a part of it. But it's a blessing when you learn to look at a woman and see in maybe just a few strands of her hair, the way her cheek curves . . . to see in that everything there is out of life to be gotten. It's a blessing to see that. You know you done right and proud by your mother to see that. But you got to learn it. My telling you ain't gonna mean nothing. You got to learn how to come to your own time and place with a woman.

JEREMY. What about your woman, Mr. Bynum? I know you done had some woman.

BYNUM. Oh, I got them in memory time. That lasts longer than any of them ever stayed with me.

JEREMY. I had me an old gal one time . . .

[There is a knock on the door. Jeremy goes to answer it. Enter Molly Cunningham. She is about twenty-six, the kind of woman that "could break in on a dollar anywhere she goes." She carries a small cardboard suitcase, and wears a colorful dress of the fashion of the day. Jeremy's heart jumps out of his chest when he sees her.]

MOLLY. You got any rooms here? I'm looking for a room.

JEREMY. Yeah . . . Mr. Seth got rooms. Sure . . . wait till I get Mr. Seth. *[Calls.]* Mr. Seth! Somebody here to see you! *[To Molly.]* Yeah, Mr. Seth got some rooms. Got one right next to me. This is a nice place to stay, too. My name's Jeremy. What's yours?

[Seth enters dressed in his Sunday clothes.]

SETH. Ho!

JEREMY. This here woman looking for a place to stay. She say you got any rooms.

MOLLY. Mister, you got any rooms? I seen your sign say you got rooms.

SETH. How long you plan on staying?

MOLLY. I ain't gonna be here long. I ain't looking for no home or nothing. I'd be in Cincinnati if I hadn't missed my train.

SETH. Rooms cost two dollars a week.

MOLLY. Two dollars!

SETH. That includes meals. We serve two meals a day. That's breakfast and dinner.

MOLLY. I hope it ain't on the third floor.

SETH. That's the only one I got. Third floor to the left. That's pay up in advance week to week.

MOLLY. *[Going into her bosom.]* I'm gonna pay you for one week. My name's Molly. Molly Cunningham.

SETH. I'm Seth Holly. My wife's name is Bertha. She do the cooking and taking care of around here. She got sheets on the bed. Towels twenty-five cents a week extra if you ain't got none. You get breakfast and dinner. We got fried chicken on Sundays.

MOLLY. That sounds good. Here's two dollars and twenty-five cents. Look here, Mister . . . ?

SETH. Holly. Seth Holly.

MOLLY. Look here, Mr. Holly. I forgot to tell you. I likes me some company from time to time. I don't like being by myself.

SETH. Your business is your business. I don't meddle in nobody's business. But this is a respectable house. I don't have no riffraff around here. And I don't have no women hauling no men up to their rooms to be making their living. As long as we understand each other then we'll be all right with each other.

MOLLY. Where's the outhouse?

SETH. Straight through the door over yonder.

MOLLY. I get my own key to the front door?

SETH. Everybody get their own key. If you come in late just don't be making no whole lot of noise and carrying on. Don't allow no fussing and fighting around here.

MOLLY. You ain't got to worry about that, mister. Which way you say that outhouse was again?

SETH. Straight through that door over yonder.

[Molly exits out the back door. Jeremy crosses to watch her.]

JEREMY. Mr. Bynum, you know what? I think I know what you was talking about now.

[The lights go down on the scene.]

SCENE IV

[The lights come up on the kitchen. It is later the same evening. Mattie and all the residents of the house, except Loomis, sit around the table. They have finished eating and most of the dishes have been cleared.]

MOLLY. That sure was some good chicken.

JEREMY. That's what I'm talking about. Miss Bertha, you sure can fry some chicken. I thought my mama could fry some chicken. But she can't do half as good as you.

SETH. I know it. That's why I married her. She don't know that, though. She think I married her for something else.

BERTHA. I ain't studying you, Seth. Did you get your things moved in all right, Mattie?

MATTIE. I ain't had that much. Jeremy helped me with what I did have.

BERTHA. You'll get to know your way around here. If you have any questions about anything just ask me. You and Molly both. I get along with everybody. You'll find I ain't no trouble to get along with.

MATTIE. You need some help with the dishes?

BERTHA. I got me a helper. Ain't I, Zonia? Got me a good helper.

ZONIA. Yes, ma'am.

SETH. Look at Bynum sitting over there with his belly all poked out. Ain't saying nothing. Sitting over there half-asleep. Ho, Bynum!

BERTHA. If Bynum ain't saying nothing what you wanna start him up for?

SETH. Ho, Bynum!

BYNUM. What you hollering at me for? I ain't doing nothing.

SETH. Come on, we gonna Juba.

BYNUM. You know me, I'm always ready to Juba.

SETH. Well, come on, then.

[Seth pulls out a harmonica and blows a few notes.]

Come on there, Jeremy. Where's your guitar? Go get your guitar. Bynum say he's ready to Juba.

JEREMY. Don't need no guitar to Juba. Ain't you never Juba without a guitar?

[Jeremy begins to drum on the table.]

SETH. It ain't that. I ain't never Juba with one! Figured to try it and see how it worked.

BYNUM. [Drumming on the table.] You don't need no guitar. Look at Molly sitting over there. She don't know we Juba on Sunday. We gonna show you something tonight. You and Mattie Campbell both. Ain't that right, Seth?

SETH. You said it! Come on, Bertha, leave them dishes be for a while. We gonna Juba.

BYNUM. All right. Let's Juba down!

[The Juba is reminiscent of the ring shouts of the African slaves. It is a call-and-response dance. Bynum sits at the table and drums. He calls the dance as others clap hands, shuffle, and stomp around the table. It should be as African as possible, with the performers working themselves up into a near frenzy. The words can be improvised, but should include some mention of the Holy Ghost. In the middle of the dance Herald Loomis enters.]

LOOMIS. [In a rage.] Stop it! Stop!

[They stop and turn to look at him.]

You all sitting up here singing about the Holy Ghost. What's so holy about the Holy Ghost? You singing and singing. You think the Holy Ghost coming? You singing for the Holy Ghost to come? What he gonna do, huh? He gonna come with tongues of fire to burn up your woolly heads? You gonna tie onto the Holy Ghost and get burned up? What you got then? Why God got to be so big? Why he got to be bigger than me? How much big is there? How much big do you want?

[Loomis starts to unzip his pants.]

SETH. Nigger, you crazy!
LOOMIS. How much big you want?
SETH. You done plumb lost your mind!

[Loomis begins to speak in tongues and dance around the kitchen. Seth starts after him.]

BERTHA. Leave him alone, Seth. He ain't in his right mind.
LOOMIS. *[Stops suddenly.]* You all don't know nothing about me. You don't know what I done seen. Herald Loomis done seen some things he ain't got words to tell you.

[Loomis starts to walk out the front door and is thrown back and collapses, terror-stricken by his vision. Bynum crawls to him.]

BYNUM. What you done seen, Herald Loomis?
LOOMIS. I done seen bones rise up out of the water. Rise up and walk across the water. Bones walking on top of the water.
BYNUM. Tell me about them bones, Herald Loomis. Tell me what you seen.
LOOMIS. I come to this place . . . to this water that was bigger than the whole world. And I looked out . . . and I seen these bones rise up out the water. Rise up and begin to walk on top of it.
BYNUM. Wasn't nothing but bones and they walking on top of the water.
LOOMIS. Walking without sinking down. Walking on top of the water.
BYNUM. Just marching in a line.
LOOMIS. A whole heap of them. They come up out the water and started marching.
BYNUM. Wasn't nothing but bones and they walking on top of the water.
LOOMIS. One after the other. They just come up out the water and start to walking.
BYNUM. They walking on the water without sinking down. They just walking and walking. And then . . . what happened, Herald Loomis?

LOOMIS. They just walking across the water.
BYNUM. What happened, Herald Loomis? What happened to the bones?
LOOMIS. They just walking across the water . . . and then . . . they sunk down.
BYNUM. The bones sunk into the water. They all sunk down.
LOOMIS. All at one time! They just all fell in the water at one time.
BYNUM. Sunk down like anybody else.
LOOMIS. When they sink down they made a big splash and this here wave come up . . .
BYNUM. A big wave, Herald Loomis. A big wave washed over the land.
LOOMIS. It washed them out of the water and up on the land. Only . . . only . . .
BYNUM. Only they ain't bones no more.
LOOMIS. They got flesh on them! Just like you and me!
BYNUM. Everywhere you look the waves is washing them up on the land right on top of one another.
LOOMIS. They black. Just like you and me. Ain't no difference.
BYNUM. Then what happened, Herald Loomis?
LOOMIS. They ain't moved or nothing. They just laying there.
BYNUM. You just laying there. What you waiting on, Herald Loomis?
LOOMIS. I'm laying there . . . waiting.
BYNUM. What you waiting on, Herald Loomis?
LOOMIS. I'm waiting on the breath to get into my body.
BYNUM. The breath coming into you, Herald Loomis. What you gonna do now?
LOOMIS. The wind's blowing the breath into my body. I can feel it. I'm starting to breathe again.
BYNUM. What you gonna do, Herald Loomis?
LOOMIS. I'm gonna stand up. I got to stand up. I can't lay here no more. All the breath coming into my body and I got to stand up.
BYNUM. Everybody's standing up at the same time.
LOOMIS. The ground's starting to shake. There's a great shaking. The world's busting half in two. The sky's splitting open. I got to stand up.

[Loomis attempts to stand up.]

My legs . . . my legs won't stand up!
BYNUM. Everybody's standing and walking toward the road. What you gonna do, Herald Loomis?

LOOMIS. My legs won't stand up.

BYNUM. They shaking hands and saying good-bye to each other and walking every whichaway down the road.

LOOMIS. I got to stand up!

BYNUM. They walking around here now. Mens. Just like you and me. Come right up out the water.

LOOMIS. Got to stand up.

BYNUM. They walking, Herald Loomis. They walking around here now.

LOOMIS. I got to stand up. Get up on the road.

BYNUM. Come on, Herald Loomis.

[Loomis tries to stand up.]

LOOMIS. My legs won't stand up! My legs won't stand up!

[Loomis collapses on the floor as the lights go down to black.]

Act II

SCENE I

[The lights come up on the kitchen. Bertha busies herself with breakfast preparations. Seth sits at the table.]

SETH. I don't care what his problem is! He's leaving here!

BERTHA. You can't put the man out and he got that little girl. Where they gonna go then?

SETH. I don't care where he go. Let him go back where he was before he come here. I ain't asked him to come here. I knew when I first looked at him something wasn't right with him. Dragging that little girl around with him. Looking like he be sleeping in the woods somewhere. I knew all along he wasn't right.

BERTHA. A fellow get a little drunk he's liable to say or do anything. He ain't done no big harm.

SETH. I just don't have all that carrying on in my house. When he come down here I'm gonna tell him. He got to leave here. My daddy wouldn't stand for it and I ain't gonna stand for it either.

BERTHA. Well, if you put him out you have to put Bynum out too. Bynum right there with him.

SETH. If it wasn't for Bynum ain't no telling what would have happened. Bynum talked to that fellow just as nice and calmed him down. If he wasn't here ain't no telling what would have happened. Bynum ain't done nothing but talk to him and kept him calm. Man acting all crazy with that foolishness. Naw, he's leaving here.

BERTHA. What you gonna tell him? How you gonna tell him to leave?

SETH. I'm gonna tell him straight out. Keep it nice and simple. Mister, you got to leave here!

[Molly enters from the stairs.]

MOLLY. Morning.

BERTHA. Did you sleep all right in that bed?

MOLLY. Tired as I was I could have slept anywhere. It's a real nice room, though. This is a nice place.

SETH. I'm sorry you had to put up with all that carrying on last night.

MOLLY. It don't bother me none. I done seen that kind of stuff before.

SETH. You won't have to see it around here no more.

[Bynum is heard singing offstage.]

I don't put up with all that stuff. When that fellow come down here I'm gonna tell him.

BYNUM. *[Singing.]*

> Soon my work will all be done
> Soon my work will all be done
> Soon my work will all be done
> I'm going to see the king.

BYNUM. *[Enters.]* Morning, Seth. Morning, Sister Bertha. I see we got Molly Cunningham down here at breakfast.

SETH. Bynum, I wanna thank you for talking to that fellow last night and calming him down. If you hadn't been here ain't no telling what might have happened.

BYNUM. Mr. Loomis all right, Seth. He just got a little excited.

SETH. Well, he can get excited somewhere else cause he leaving here.

[Mattie enters from the stairs.]

BYNUM. Well, there's Mattie Campbell.

MATTIE. Good morning.

BERTHA. Sit on down here, Mattie. I got some biscuits be ready in a minute. The coffee's hot.

MATTIE. Jeremy gone already?

BYNUM. Yeah, he leave out of here early. He got to be there when the sun come up. Most working men got to be there when the sun come up. Everybody but Seth. Seth work at night. Mr. Olowski so busy in his shop he got fellows working at night.

[Loomis enters from the stairs.]

SETH. Mr. Loomis, now . . . I don't want no trouble. I keeps me a respectable house here. I don't have no carrying on like what went on last night. This has been a respectable house for a long time. I'm gonna have to ask you to leave.

LOOMIS. You got my two dollars. That two dollars say we stay till Saturday.

[Loomis and Seth glare at each other.]

SETH. All right. Fair enough. You stay till Saturday. But come Saturday you got to leave here.

LOOMIS. *[Continues to glare at Seth. He goes to the door and calls.]* Zonia. You stay around this house, you hear? Don't you go anywhere.

[Loomis exits out the front door.]

SETH. I knew it when I first seen him. I knew something wasn't right with him.

BERTHA. Seth, leave the people alone to eat their breakfast. They don't want to hear that. Go on out there and make some pots and pans. That's the only time you satisfied is when you out there. Go on out there and make some pots and pans and leave them people alone.

SETH. I ain't bothering anybody. I'm just stating the facts. I told you, Bynum.

[Bertha shoos Seth out the back door and exits into the bedroom.]

MOLLY. *[To Bynum.]* You one of them voodoo people?

BYNUM. I got a power to bind folks if that what you talking about.

MOLLY. I thought so. The way you talked to that man when he started all that spooky stuff. What you say you had the power to do to people? You ain't the cause of him acting like that, is you?

BYNUM. I binds them together. Sometimes I help them find each other.

MOLLY. How do you do that?

BYNUM. With a song. My daddy taught me how to do it.

MOLLY. That's what they say. Most folks be what they daddy is. I wouldn't want to be like my daddy. Nothing ever set right with him. He tried to make the world over. Carry it around with him everywhere he go. I don't want to be like that. I just take life as it come. I don't be trying to make it over.

[Pause.]

Your daddy used to do that too, huh? Make people stay together?

BYNUM. My daddy used to heal people. He had the Healing Song. I got the Binding Song.

MOLLY. My mamma used to believe in all that stuff. If she got sick she would have gone and saw your daddy. As long as he didn't make her drink nothing. She wouldn't drink nothing nobody give her. She was always afraid somebody was gonna poison her. How your daddy heal people?

BYNUM. With a song. He healed people by singing over them. I seen him do it. He sung over this little white girl when she was sick. They made a big to-do about it. They carried the girl's bed out in the yard and had all her kinfolk standing around. The little girl laying up there in the bed. Doctors standing around can't do nothing to help her. And they had my daddy come up and sing his song. It didn't sound no different than any other song. It was just somebody singing. But the song was its own thing and it come out and took upon this little girl with its power and it healed her.

MOLLY. That's sure something else. I don't understand that kind of thing. I guess if the doctor couldn't make me well I'd try it. But otherwise I don't wanna be bothered with that kind of thing. It's too spooky.

BYNUM. Well, let me get on out here and get to work.

[Bynum gets up and heads out the back door.]

MOLLY. I ain't meant to offend you or nothing. What's your name . . . Bynum? I ain't meant to say nothing to make you feel bad now.

[Bynum exits out the back door.]

  [To Mattie.] I hope he don't feel bad. He's a nice man. I don't wanna hurt nobody's feelings or nothing.

MATTIE. I got to go on up to Doc Goldblum's and finish this ironing.

MOLLY. Now, that's something I don't never wanna do. Iron no clothes. Especially somebody else's. That's what I believe killed my mamma. Always ironing and working, doing somebody else's work. Not Molly Cunningham.

MATTIE. It's the only job I got. I got to make it someway to fend for myself.

MOLLY. I thought Jeremy was your man. Ain't he working?

MATTIE. We just be keeping company till maybe Jack come back.

MOLLY. I don't trust none of these men. Jack or nobody else. These men liable to do anything. They wait just until they get one woman tied and locked up with them . . . then they look around to see if they can get another one. Molly don't pay them no mind. One's just as good as the other if you ask me. I ain't never met one that meant nobody no good. You got any babies?

MATTIE. I had two for my man, Jack Carper. But they both died.

MOLLY. That be the best. These men make all these babies, then run off and leave you to take care of them. Talking about they wanna see what's on the other side of the hill. I make sure I don't get no babies. My mamma taught me how to do that.

MATTIE. Don't make me no mind. That be nice to be a mother.

MOLLY. Yeah? Well, you go on, then. Molly Cunningham ain't gonna be tied down with no babies. Had me a man one time who I thought had some love in him. Come home one day and he was packing his trunk. Told me the time come when even the best of friends must part. Say he was gonna send me a special delivery some old day. I watched him out the window when he carried that trunk out and down to the train station. Said if he was gonna send me a special delivery I wasn't gonna be there to get it. I done found out the harder you try to hold onto them, the easier it is for some gal to pull them away. Molly done learned that. That's why I don't trust nobody but the good Lord above, and I don't love nobody but my mama.

MATTIE. I got to get on. Doc Goldblum gonna be waiting.

[Mattie exits out the front door. Seth enters from his workshop with his apron, gloves, goggles, etc. He carries a bucket and crosses to the sink for water.]

SETH. Everybody gone but you, huh?

MOLLY. That little shack out there by the outhouse . . . that's where you make them pots and pans and stuff?

SETH. Yeah, that's my work shed. I go out there . . . take these hands and make something out of nothing. Take that metal and bend and twist it whatever way I want. My daddy taught me that. He used to make pots and pans. That's how I learned it.

MOLLY. I never knew nobody made no pots and pans. My uncle used to shoe horses.

[Jeremy enters at the front door.]

SETH. I thought you was working? Ain't you working today?

JEREMY. Naw, they fired me. White fellow come by told me to give him fifty cents if I wanted to keep working. Going around to all the colored making them give him fifty cents to keep hold to their jobs. Them other fellows, they was giving it to him. I kept hold to mine and they fired me.

SETH. Boy, what kind of sense that make? What kind of sense it make to get fired from a job where you making eight dollars a week and all it cost you is fifty centers. That's seven dollars and fifty cents profit! This way you ain't got nothing.

JEREMY. It didn't make no sense to me. I don't make but eight dollars. Why I got to give him fifty cents of it? He go around to all the colored and he got ten dollars extra. That's more than I make for a whole week.

SETH. I see you gonna learn the hard way. You just looking at the facts of it. See, right now, without the job, you ain't got nothing. What you gonna do when you can't keep a roof over your head? Right now, come Saturday, unless you come up with another two dollars, you gonna be out there in the streets. Down up under one of them bridges trying to put some food in your belly and wishing you had given that fellow that fifty cents.

JEREMY. Don't make me no difference. There's a big road out there. I can get my guitar and always find me another place to stay. I ain't planning on staying in one place for too long noway.

SETH. We gonna see if you feel like that come Saturday!

[Seth exits out the back. Jeremy sees Molly.]

JEREMY. Molly Cunningham. How you doing today, sugar?

MOLLY. You can go on back down there tomorrow and go back to work if you want. They won't even know who you is. Won't even know it's you. I had me a fellow did that one time. They just went ahead and signed him up like they never seen him before.

JEREMY. I'm tired of working anyway. I'm glad they fired me. You sure look pretty today.

MOLLY. Don't come telling me all that pretty stuff. Beauty wanna come in and sit down at your table asking to be fed. I ain't hardly got enough for me.

JEREMY. You know you pretty. Ain't no sense in you saying nothing about that. Why don't you come on and go away with me?

MOLLY. You tied up with that Mattie Campbell. Now you talking about running away with me.

JEREMY. I was just keeping her company cause she lonely. You ain't the lonely kind. You the kind that know what she want and how to get it. I need a woman like you to travel around with. Don't you wanna travel around and look at some

places with Jeremy? With a woman like you beside him, a man can make it nice in the world.

MOLLY. Molly can make it nice by herself too. Molly don't need nobody leave her cold in hand. The world rough enough as it is.

JEREMY. We can make it better together. I got my guitar and I can play. Won me another dollar last night playing guitar. We can go around and I can play at the dances and we can just enjoy life. You can make it by yourself all right, I agrees with that. A woman like you can make it anywhere she go. But you can make it better if you got a man to protect you.

MOLLY. What places you wanna go around and look at?

JEREMY. All of them! I don't want to miss nothing. I wanna go everywhere and do everything there is to be got out of life. With a woman like you it's like having water and berries. A man got everything he need.

MOLLY. You got to be doing more than playing that guitar. A dollar a day ain't hardly what Molly got in mind.

JEREMY. I gambles real good. I got a hand for it.

MOLLY. Molly don't work. And Molly ain't up for sale.

JEREMY. Sure, baby. You ain't got to work with Jeremy.

MOLLY. There's one more thing.

JEREMY. What's that, sugar?

MOLLY. Molly ain't going South.

[The lights go down on the scene.]

SCENE II

[The lights come up on the parlor. Seth and Bynum sit playing a game of dominoes. Bynum sings to himself.]

BYNUM. [Singing.]

They tell me Joe Turner's come and gone
Ohhh Lordy
They tell me Joe Turner's come and gone
Ohhh Lordy
Got my man and gone

Come with forty links of chain
Ohhh Lordy

Come with forty links of chain
Ohhh Lordy
Got my man and gone

SETH. Come on and play if you gonna play.

BYNUM. I'm gonna play. Soon as I figure out what to do.

SETH. You can't figure out if you wanna play or you wanna sing.

BYNUM. Well sir, I'm gonna do a little bit of both.

[Playing.]

There. What you gonna do now?

[Singing.]

They tell me Joe Turner's come and gone
Ohhh Lordy
They tell me Joe Turner's come and gone
Ohhh Lordy

SETH. Why don't you hush up that noise.

BYNUM. That's a song the women sing down around Memphis. The women down there made up that song. I picked it up down there about fifteen years ago.

[Loomis enters from the front door.]

BYNUM. Evening, Mr. Loomis.

SETH. Today's Monday, Mr. Loomis. Come Saturday your time is up. We done ate already. My wife roasted up some yams. She got your plate sitting in there on the table. *[To Bynum.]* Whose play is it?

BYNUM. Ain't you keeping up with the game? I thought you was a domino player. I just played so it got to be your turn.

[Loomis goes into the kitchen, where a plate of yams is covered and set on the table. He sits down and begins to eat with his hands.]

SETH. *[Plays.]* Twenty! Give me twenty! You didn't know I had that ace five. You was trying to play around that. You didn't know I had that lying there for you.

BYNUM. You ain't done nothing. I let you have that to get mine.

SETH. Come on and play. You ain't doing nothing but talking. I got a hundred and forty points to your eighty. You ain't doing nothing but talking. Come on and play.

BYNUM. *[Singing.]*

They tell me Joe Turner's come and gone
Ohhh Lordy
They tell me Joe Turner's come and gone
Ohhh Lordy
Got my man and gone
He come with forty links of chain
Ohhh Lordy

LOOMIS. Why you singing that song? Why you singing about Joe Turner?

BYNUM. I'm just singing to entertain myself.

SETH. You trying to distract me. That's what you trying to do.

BYNUM. *[Singing.]*

Come with forty links of chain
Ohhh Lordy
Come with forty links of chain
Ohhh Lordy

LOOMIS. I don't like you singing that song, mister!

SETH. Now, I ain't gonna have no more disturbance around here, Herald Loomis. You start any more disturbance and you leavin here, Saturday or no Saturday.

BYNUM. The man ain't causing no disturbance, Seth. He just say he don't like the song.

SETH. Well, we all friendly folk. All neighborly like. Don't have no squabbling around here. Don't have no disturbance. You gonna have to take that someplace else.

BYNUM. He just say he don't like the song. I done sung a whole lot of songs people don't like. I respect everybody. He here in the house too. If he don't like the song, I'll sing something else. I know lots of songs. You got "I Belong to the Band," "Don't You Leave Me Here." You got "Praying on the Old Campground," "Keep Your Lamp Trimmed and Burning" . . . I know lots of songs. *[Sings.]*

Boys, I'll be so glad when payday come
Captain, Captain, when payday comes

Gonna catch that Illinois Central
Going to Kankakee

SETH. Why don't you hush up that hollering and come on and play dominoes.

BYNUM. You ever been to Johnstown, Herald Loomis? You look like a fellow I seen around there.

LOOMIS. I don't know no place with that name.

BYNUM. That's around where I seen my shiny man. See, you looking for this woman. I'm looking for a shiny man. Seem like everybody looking for something.

SETH. I'm looking for you to come and play these dominoes. That's what I'm looking for.

BYNUM. You are a farming man, Herald Loomis? You look like you done some farming.

LOOMIS. Same as everybody. I done farmed some, yeah.

BYNUM. I used to work at farming . . . picking cotton. I reckon everybody done picked some cotton.

SETH. I ain't! I ain't never picked no cotton. I was born up here in the North. My daddy was a freed man. I ain't never even seen no cotton!

BYNUM. Mr. Loomis done picked some cotton. Ain't you, Herald Loomis? You done picked a bunch of cotton.

LOOMIS. How you know so much about me? How you know what I done? How much cotton I picked?

BYNUM. I can tell from looking at you. My daddy taught me how to do that. Say when you look at a fellow, if you taught yourself to look for it, you can see his song written on him. Tell you what kind of man he is in the world. Now, I can look at you, Mr. Loomis, and see you a man who done forgot his song. Forgot how to sing it. A fellow forget that and he forget who he is. Forget how he's supposed to mark down life. Now, I used to travel all up and down this road and that . . . looking here and there. Searching. Just like you, Mr. Loomis. I didn't know what I was searching for. The only thing I knew was something was keeping me dissatisfied. Something wasn't making my heart smooth and easy. Then one day my daddy gave me a song. That song had a weight to it that was hard to handle. That song was hard to carry. I fought against it. Didn't want to accept that song. I tried to find my daddy to give him

back the song. But I found out it wasn't his song. It was my song. It had come from way deep inside me. I looked long back in memory and gathered up pieces and snatches of things to make that song. I was making it up out of myself. And that song helped me on the road. Made it smooth to where my footsteps didn't bite back at me. All the time that song getting bigger and bigger. That song growing with each step of the road. It got so I used all of myself up in the making of that song. Then I was the song in search of itself. That song rattling in my throat and I'm looking for it. See, Mr. Loomis, when a man forgets his song he goes off in search of it . . . till he find out he's got it with him all the time. That's why I can tell you one of Joe Turner's niggers. Cause you forgot how to sing your song.

LOOMIS. You lie! How you see that? I got a mark on me? Joe Turner done marked me to where you can see it? You telling me I'm a marked man. What kind of mark you got on you?

[Bynum begins singing.]

BYNUM.

> They tell me Joe Turner's come and gone
> Ohhh Lordy
> They tell me Joe Turner's come and gone
> Ohhh Lordy
> Got my man and gone

LOOMIS. Had a whole mess of men he catched. Just go out hunting regular like you go out hunting possum. He catch you and go home to his wife and family. Ain't thought about you going home to yours. Joe Turner catched me when my little girl was just born. Wasn't nothing but a little baby sucking on her mama's titty when he catched me. Joe Turner catched me in nineteen hundred and one. Kept me seven years until nineteen hundred and eight. Kept everybody seven years. He'd go out hunting and bring back forty men at a time. And keep them seven years.

I was walking down this road in this little town outside of Memphis. Come up on these fellows gambling. I was a deacon in the Abundant Life Church. I stopped to preach to these fellows to see if maybe I could turn some of them from their sinning when Joe Turner, brother of the governor of the great sovereign state of Tennessee, swooped down on us and grabbed everybody there. Kept us all seven years.

My wife Martha gone from me after Joe Turner catched me. Got out from under Joe Turner on his birthday. Me and forty other men put in our seven years and he let us go on his birthday. I made it back to Henry Thompson's place where me and Martha was sharecropping and Martha's gone. She taken my little girl and left her with her mama and took off north. We been looking for her ever since. That's been going on four years now we been looking. That's the only thing I know to do. I just wanna see her face so I can get me a starting place in the world. The world got to start somewhere. That's what I been looking for. I been wandering a long time in somebody else's world. When I find my wife that be the making of my own.

BYNUM. Joe Turner tell why he caught you? You ever asked him that?

LOOMIS. I ain't never seen Joe Turner. Seen him to where I could touch him. I asked one of them fellows one time why he catch niggers. Asked him what I got he want? Why don't he keep on to himself? Why he got to catch me going down the road by my lonesome? He told me I was worthless. Worthless is something you throw away. Something you don't bother with. I ain't seen him throw me away. Wouldn't even let me stay away when I was by my lonesome. I ain't tried to catch him when he going down the road. So I must got something he want. What I got?

SETH. He just want you to do his work for him. That's all.

LOOMIS. I can look at him and see where he big and strong enough to do his own work. So it can't be that. He must want something he ain't got.

BYNUM. That ain't hard to figure out. What he wanted was your song. He wanted to have that song to be his. He thought by catching you he could learn that song. Every nigger he catch he's looking for the one he can learn that song from. Now he's got you bound up to where you can't sing your own song. Couldn't sing it them seven years cause you was afraid he would snatch it from under you. But you still got it. You just forgot how to sing it.

LOOMIS. [To Bynum.] I know who you are. You one of them bones people.

[The lights go down to black.]

SCENE III

[The lights come up on the kitchen. It is the following morning. Mattie and Bynum sit at the table. Bertha busies herself at the stove.]

BYNUM. Good luck don't know no special time to come. You sleep with that up under your pillow and good luck can't help but come to you. Sometimes it come and go and you don't even know it's been there.

BERTHA. Bynum, why don't you leave that gal alone? She don't wanna be hearing all that. Why don't you go on and get out the way and leave her alone?

BYNUM. [Getting up.] All right, all right. But you mark what I'm saying. It'll draw it to you just like a magnet.

[Bynum exits up the stairs as Loomis enters.]

BERTHA. I got some grits here, Mr. Loomis.

[Bertha sets a bowl on the table.]

If I was you, Mattie, I wouldn't go getting all tied up with Bynum in that stuff. That kind of stuff, even if it do work for a while, it don't last. That just get people more mixed up than they is already. And I wouldn't waste my time fretting over Jeremy either. I seen it coming. I seen it when she first come here. She that kind of woman run off with the first man got a dollar to spend on her. Jeremy just young. He don't know what he getting into. That gal don't mean him no good. She's just using him to keep from being by herself. That's the worst use of a man you can have. You ought to be glad to wash him out of your hair. I done seen all kind of men. I done seen them come and go through here. Jeremy ain't had enough to him for you. You need a man who's got some understanding and who willing to work with that understanding to come to the best he can. You got your time coming. You just tries too hard and can't understand why it don't work for you. Trying to figure it out don't do nothing but give you a troubled mind. Don't no man want a woman with a troubled mind.

You get all that trouble off your mind and just when it look like you ain't never gonna find what you want . . . you look up and it's standing right there. That's how I met my Seth. You gonna look up one day and find everything you want standing right in front of you. Been twenty-seven years now since that happened to me. But life ain't no happy-go-lucky time where everything be just like you want it. You got your time coming. You watch what Bertha's saying.

[Seth enters.]

SETH. Ho!

BERTHA. What you doing come in here so late?

SETH. I was standing down there on Logan Street talking with the fellows. Henry Allen tried to sell me that old piece of horse he got.

[He sees Loomis.]

Today's Tuesday, Mr. Loomis.

BERTHA. *[Pulling him toward the bedroom.]* Come on in here and leave that man alone to eat his breakfast.

SETH. I ain't bothering nobody. I'm just reminding him what day it is.

[Seth and Bertha exit into the bedroom.]

LOOMIS. That dress got a color to it.

MATTIE. Did you really see them things like you said? Them people come up out the ocean?

LOOMIS. It happened just like that, yeah.

MATTIE. I hope you find your wife. It be good for your little girl for you to find her.

LOOMIS. Got to find her for myself. Find my starting place in the world. Find me a world I can fit in.

MATTIE. I ain't never found no place for me to fit. Seem like all I do is start over. It ain't nothing to find no starting place in the world. You just start from where you find yourself.

LOOMIS. Got to find my wife. That be my starting place.

MATTIE. What if you don't find her? What you gonna do then if you don't find her?

LOOMIS. She out there somewhere. Ain't no such thing as not finding her.

MATTIE. How she got lost from you? Jack just walked away from me.

LOOMIS. Joe Turner split us up. Joe Turner turned the world upside-down. He bound me on to him for seven years.

MATTIE. I hope you find her. It be good for you to find her.

LOOMIS. I been watching you. I been watching you watch me.

MATTIE. I was just trying to figure out if you seen things like you said.

LOOMIS. *[Getting up.]* Come here and let me touch you. I been watching you. You a full woman. A man needs a full woman. Come on and be with me.

MATTIE. I ain't got enough for you. You'd use me up too fast.

LOOMIS. Herald Loomis got a mind seem like you a part of it since I first seen you. It's been a long time since I seen a full woman. I can smell you from here. I know you got Herald Loomis on your mind, can't keep him apart from it. Come on and be with Herald Loomis.

[Loomis has crossed to Mattie. He touches her awkwardly, gently, tenderly. Inside he howls like a lost wolf pup whose hunger is deep. He goes to touch her but finds he cannot.]

I done forgot how to touch.

[The lights fade to black.]

SCENE IV

[It is early the next morning. The lights come up on Zonia and Reuben in the yard.]

REUBEN. Something spooky going on around here. Last night Mr. Bynum was out in the yard singing and talking to the wind . . . and the wind it just be talking back to him. Did you hear it?

ZONIA. I heard it. I was scared to get up and look. I thought it was a storm.

REUBEN. That wasn't no storm. That was Mr. Bynum. First he say something . . . and the wind it say back to him.

ZONIA. I heard it. Was you scared? I was scared.

REUBEN. And then this morning . . . I seen Miss Mabel!

ZONIA. Who Miss Mabel?

REUBEN. Mr. Seth's mother. He got her picture hanging up in the house. She been dead.

ZONIA. How you seen her if she been dead?

REUBEN. Zonia . . . if I tell you something you promise you won't tell anybody?

ZONIA. I promise.

REUBEN. It was early this morning . . . I went out to the coop to feed the pigeons. I was down on the ground like this to open up the door to the coop . . . when all of a sudden I seen some feets in front of me. I looked up . . . and there was Miss Mabel standing there.

ZONIA. Reuben, you better stop telling that! You ain't seen nobody!

REUBEN. Naw, it's the truth. I swear! I seen her just like I see you. Look . . . you can see where she hit me with her cane.

ZONIA. Hit you? What she hit you for?

REUBEN. She says, "Didn't you promise Eugene something?" Then she hit me with her cane. She say, "Let them pigeons go." Then she hit me again. That's what made them marks.

ZONIA. Jeez man . . . get away from me. You done seen a haunt!

REUBEN. Shhhh. You promised, Zonia!

ZONIA. You sure it wasn't Miss Bertha come over there and hit you with her hoe?

REUBEN. It wasn't no Miss Bertha. I told you it was Miss Mabel. She was standing right there by the coop. She had this light coming out of her and then she just melted away.

ZONIA. What she had on?

REUBEN. A white dress. Ain't even had no shoes or nothing. Just had on that white dress and them big hands . . . and that cane she hit me with.

ZONIA. How you reckon she knew about the pigeons? You reckon Eugene told her?

REUBEN. I don't know. I sure ain't asked her none. She say Eugene was waiting on them pigeons. Say he couldn't go back home till I let them go. I couldn't get the door to the coop open fast enough.

ZONIA. Maybe she an angel? From the way you say she look with that white dress. Maybe she an angel.

REUBEN. Mean as she was . . . how she gonna be an angel? She used to chase us out her yard and frown up and look evil all the time.

ZONIA. That don't mean she can't be no angel cause of how she looked and cause she wouldn't let no kids play in her yard. It go by if you got any spots on your heart and if you pray and go to church.

REUBEN. What about she hit me with her cane? An angel wouldn't hit me with her cane.

ZONIA. I don't know. She might. I still say she was an angel.

REUBEN. You reckon Eugene the one who sent old Miss Mabel?

ZONIA. Why he send her? Why he don't come himself?

REUBEN. Figured if he send her maybe that'll make me listen. Cause she old.

ZONIA. What you think it feel like?

REUBEN. What?

ZONIA. Being dead.

REUBEN. Like being sleep only you don't know nothing and can't move no more.

ZONIA. If Miss Mabel can come back . . . then maybe Eugene can come back too.

REUBEN. We can go down to the hideout like we used to! He could come back everyday! It be just like he ain't dead.

ZONIA. Maybe that ain't right for him to come back. Feel kinda funny to be playing games with a haunt.

REUBEN. Yeah . . . what if everybody came back? What if Miss Mabel came back just like she ain't dead? Where you and your daddy gonna sleep then?

ZONIA. Maybe they go back at night and don't need no place to sleep.

REUBEN. It still don't seem right. I'm sure gonna miss Eugene. He's the bestest friend anybody ever had.

ZONIA. My daddy say if you miss somebody too much it can kill you. Say he missed me till it liked to killed him.

REUBEN. What if your mama's already dead and all the time you looking for her?

ZONIA. Naw, she ain't dead. My daddy say he can smell her.

REUBEN. You can't smell nobody that ain't here. Maybe he smelling old Miss Bertha. Maybe Miss Bertha your mama?

ZONIA. Naw, she ain't. My mamma got long pretty hair and she five feet from the ground!

REUBEN. Your daddy say when you leaving?

[Zonia doesn't respond.]

Maybe you gonna stay in Mr. Seth's house and don't go looking for your mama no more.

ZONIA. He say we got to leave on Saturday.

REUBEN. Dag! You just only been here for a little while. Don't seem like nothing ever stay the same.

ZONIA. He say he got to find her. Find him a place in the world.

REUBEN. He could find him a place in Mr. Seth's house.

ZONIA. It don't look like we never gonna find her.

REUBEN. Maybe he find her by Saturday then you don't have to go.

ZONIA. I don't know.

REUBEN. You look like a spider!

ZONIA. I ain't no spider!

REUBEN. Got them long skinny arms and legs. You look like one of them black widows.

ZONIA. I ain't no black window nothing! My name is Zonia!

REUBEN. That's what I'm gonna call you . . . Spider.

ZONIA. You can call me that, but I don't have to answer.

REUBEN. You know what? I think maybe I be your husband when I grow up.

ZONIA. How you know?

REUBEN. I ask my grandpap how you know and he say when the moon falls into a girl's eyes that how you know.

ZONIA. Did it fall into my eyes?

REUBEN. Not that I can tell. Maybe I ain't old enough. Maybe you ain't old enough.

ZONIA. So there! I don't know why you telling me that lie!

REUBEN. That don't mean nothing cause I can't see it. I know it's there. Just the way you look at me sometimes look like the moon might have been in your eyes.

ZONIA. That don't mean nothing if you can't see it. You supposed to see it.

REUBEN. Shucks, I see it good enough for me. You ever let anybody kiss you?

ZONIA. Just my daddy. He kiss me on the cheek.

REUBEN. It's better on the lips. Can I kiss you on the lips?

ZONIA. I don't know. You ever kiss anybody before?

REUBEN. I had a cousin let me kiss her on the lips one time. Can I kiss you?

ZONIA. Okay.

[Reuben kisses her and lays his head against her chest.]

What you doing?

REUBEN. Listening. Your heart singing?

ZONIA. It is not.

REUBEN. Just beating like a drum. Let's kiss again.

[They kiss again.]

Now you mine, Spider. You my girl, okay?

ZONIA. Okay.

REUBEN. When I get grown, I come looking for you.

ZONIA. Okay.

[The lights fade to black.]

SCENE V

[The lights come up on the kitchen. It is Saturday. Bynum, Loomis, and Zonia sit at the table. Bertha prepares breakfast. Zonia has on a white dress.]

BYNUM. With all this rain we been having he might have ran into some washed-out roads. If that wagon got stuck in the mud he's liable to be still upriver somewhere. If he's upriver then he ain't coming until tomorrow.

LOOMIS. Today's Saturday. He say he be here on Saturday.

BERTHA. Zonia, you gonna eat your breakfast this morning.

ZONIA. Yes, ma'am.

BERTHA. I don't know how you expect to get any bigger if you don't eat. I ain't never seen a child that didn't eat. You about as skinny as a beanpole.

[Pause.]

Mr. Loomis, there's a place down on Wylie. Zeke Mayweather got a house down there. You ought to see if he got any rooms.

[Loomis doesn't respond.]

Well, you're welcome to some breakfast before you move on.

[Mattie enters from the stairs.]

MATTIE. Good morning.

BERTHA. Morning, Mattie. Sit on down there and get you some breakfast.

BYNUM. Well, Mattie Campbell, you been sleeping with that up under your pillow like I told you?

BERTHA. Bynum, I done told you to leave that gal alone with all that stuff. You around here meddling in other people's lives. She don't want to hear all that. You ain't doing nothing but confusing her with that stuff.

MATTIE. *[To Loomis.]* You all fixing to move on?

LOOMIS. Today's Saturday. I'm paid up till Saturday.

MATTIE. Where you going to?

LOOMIS. Gonna find my wife.

MATTIE. You going off to another city?

LOOMIS. We gonna see where the road take us. Ain't no telling where we wind up.

MATTIE. Eleven years is a long time. Your wife . . . she might have taken up with someone else. People do that when they get lost from each other.

LOOMIS. Zonia. Come on, we gonna find your mama.

[Loomis and Zonia cross to the door.]

MATTIE. *[To Zonia.]* Zonia, Mattie got a ribbon here match your dress. Want Mattie to fix your hair with her ribbon?

[Zonia nods. Mattie ties the ribbon in her hair.]

There . . . it got a color just like your dress.

[To Loomis.]

I hope you find her. I hope you be happy.

LOOMIS. A man looking for a woman be lucky to find you. You a good woman, Mattie. Keep a good heart.

[Loomis and Zonia exit.]

BERTHA. I been watching that man for two weeks . . . and that's the closest I come to seeing him act civilized. I don't know what's between you all, Mattie . . . but the only thing that man needs is somebody to make him laugh. That's all you need in the world is love and laughter. That's all anybody needs. To have love in one hand and laughter in the other.

[Bertha moves about the kitchen as though blessing it and chasing away the huge sadness that seems to envelop it. It is a dance and demonstration of her own magic, her own remedy that is centuries old and to which she is connected by the muscles of her heart and the blood's memory.]

You hear me, Mattie? I'm talking about laughing. The kind of laugh that comes from way deep inside. To just stand and laugh and let life flow right through you. Just laugh to let yourself know you're alive.

[She begins to laugh. It is a near-hysterical laughter that is a celebration of life, both its pain and its blessing. Mattie and Bynum join in the laughter. Seth enters from the front door.]

SETH. Well, I see you all having fun.

[Seth begins to laugh with them.]

That Loomis fellow standing up there on the corner watching the house. He standing right up there on Manila Street.

BERTHA. Don't you get started on him. The man done left out of here and that's the last I wanna hear of it. You about to drive me crazy with that man.

SETH. I just say he standing up there on the corner. Acting sneaky like he always do. He can stand up there all he want. As long as he don't come back in here.

[There is a knock on the door. Seth goes to answer it. Enter Martha Loomis (Pentecost). She is a young woman about twenty-eight. She is dressed as befitting a member of an Evangelist church. Rutherford Selig follows.]

SETH. Look here, Bertha. It's Martha Pentecost. Come on in, Martha. Who that with you? Oh . . . that's Selig. Come on in, Selig.

BERTHA. Come on in, Martha. It's sure good to see you.

BYNUM. Rutherford Selig, you a sure enough first-class People Finder!

SELIG. She was right out there in Rankin. You take that first right-hand road . . . right there at that church on Wooster Street. I started to go right past and something told me to stop at the church and see if they needed any dustpans.

SETH. Don't she look good, Bertha.

BERTHA. Look all nice and healthy.

MARTHA. Mr. Bynum . . . Selig told me my little girl was here.

SETH. There's some fellow around here say he your husband. Say his name is Loomis. Say you his wife.

MARTHA. Is my little girl with him?

SETH. Yeah, he got a little girl with him. I wasn't gonna tell him where you was. Not the way this fellow look. So he got Selig to find you.

MARTHA. Where they at? They upstairs?

SETH. He was standing right up there on Manila Street. I had to ask him to leave cause of how he was carrying on. He come in here one night—

[The door opens and Loomis and Zonia enter. Martha and Loomis stare at each other.]

LOOMIS. Hello, Martha.

MARTHA. Herald . . . Zonia?

LOOMIS. You ain't waited for me, Martha. I got out the place looking to see your face. Seven years I waited to see your face.

MARTHA. Herald, I been looking for you. I wasn't but two months behind you when you went to my mama's and got Zonia. I been looking for you ever since.

LOOMIS. Joe Turner let me loose and I felt all turned around inside. I just wanted to see your face to know that the world was still there. Make sure everything still in its place so I could reconnect myself together. I got there and you was gone, Martha.

MARTHA. Herald . . .

LOOMIS. Left my little girl motherless in the world.

MARTHA. I didn't leave her motherless, Herald. Reverend Tolliver wanted to move the church up North cause of all the trouble the colored folks was having down there. Nobody knew what was gonna happen traveling them roads. We didn't even know if we was gonna make it up here or not. I left her with my mama so she be safe. That was better than dragging her out on the road having to duck and hide from people. Wasn't no telling what was gonna happen to us. I didn't leave her motherless in the world. I been looking for you.

LOOMIS. I come up on Henry Thompson's place after seven years of living in hell, and all I'm looking to do is see your face.

MARTHA. Herald, I didn't know if you was ever coming back. They told me Joe Turner had you and my whole world split half in two. My whole life shattered. It was like I had poured it in a cracked jar and it all leaked out the bottom. When it go like that there ain't nothing you can do to put it back together. You talking about Henry Thompson's place like I'm still gonna be working the land by myself. How I'm gonna do that? You wasn't gone but two months and Henry Thompson kicked me off his land and I ain't had no place to go but to my mama's. I stayed and waited there for five years before I woke up one morning and decided that you was dead. Even if you weren't, you was dead to me. I wasn't gonna carry you with me no more. So I killed you in my heart. I buried you. I mourned you. And then I picked up what was left and went on to make life without you. I was a young woman with life at my beckon. I couldn't drag you behind me like a sack of cotton.

LOOMIS. I just been waiting to look on your face to say my good-bye. That good-bye got so big at times, seem like it was gonna swallow me up. Like Jonah in the whale's belly I sat up in that good-bye for three years. That good-bye kept me out on the road searching. Not looking on women in their houses. It kept me bound up to the road. All the time that good-bye swelling up in my chest till I'm about to bust. Now that I see your face I can say my good-bye and make my own world.

[Loomis takes Zonia's hand and presents her to Martha.]

Martha . . . here go your daughter. I tried to take care of her. See that she had something to eat. See that she was out of the elements. Whatever I know I tried to teach her. Now she need to learn from her mother whatever you got to teach her. That way she won't be no one-sided person.

[Loomis stoops to Zonia.]

Zonia, you go live with your mama. She a good woman. You go on with her and listen to her good. You my daughter and I love you like a daughter. I hope to see you again in the world somewhere. I'll never forget you.

ZONIA. *[Throws her arms around Loomis in a panic.]* I won't get no bigger! My bones won't get no bigger! They won't! I promise! Take me with you till we keep searching and never finding. I won't get no bigger! I promise!

LOOMIS. Go on and do what I told you now.

MARTHA. *[Goes to Zonia and comforts her.]* It's all right, baby. Mama's here. Mama's here. Don't worry. Don't cry.

[Martha turns to Bynum.]

Mr. Bynum, I don't know how to thank you. God bless you.

LOOMIS. It was you! All the time it was you that bind me up! You bound me to the road!

BYNUM. I ain't bind you, Herald Loomis. You can't bind what don't cling.

LOOMIS. Everywhere I go people wanna bind me up. Joe Turner wanna bind me up! Reverend Tolliver wanna bind me up. You wanna bind me up. Everybody wanna bind me up. Well, Joe Turner's come and gone and Herald Loomis ain't for no binding. I ain't gonna let nobody bind me up!

[Loomis pulls out a knife.]

BYNUM. It wasn't you, Herald Loomis. I ain't bound you. I bound the little girl to her mother. That's who I bound. You binding yourself. You bound onto your song. All you got to do is stand up and sing it, Herald Loomis. It's right there kicking at your throat. All you got to do is sing it. Then you be free.

MARTHA. Herald . . . look at yourself! Standing there with a knife in your hand. You done gone over to the devil. Come on . . . put down the knife. You got to look to Jesus. Even if you done fell away from the church you can be saved again. The Bible say, "The Lord is my shepherd I shall not want. He maketh me to lie down in green pastures. He leads me beside the still water. He restoreth my soul. He leads me in the path of righteousness for His name's sake. Even though I walk through the shadow of death—"

LOOMIS. That's just where I be walking!

MARTHA. "I shall fear no evil. For thou art with me. Thy rod and thy staff, they comfort me."

LOOMIS. You can't tell me nothing about no valleys. I done been all across the valleys and the hills and the mountains and the oceans.

MARTHA. "Thou preparest a table for me in the presence of my enemies."

LOOMIS. And all I seen was a bunch of niggers dazed out of their woolly heads. And Mr. Jesus Christ standing there in the middle of them, grinning.

MARTHA. "Thou annointest my head with oil, my cup runneth over."

LOOMIS. He grin that big old grin . . . and niggers wallowing at his feet.

MARTHA. "Surely goodness and mercy shall follow me all the days of my life, and I shall dwell in the house of the Lord forever."

LOOMIS. Great big old white man . . . your Mr. Jesus Christ. Standing there with a whip in one hand and tote board in another, and them niggers swimming in a sea of cotton. And he counting. He tallying up the cotton. "Well, Jeremiah . . . what's the matter, you ain't picked but two hundred pounds of cotton today? Got to put you on half rations." And Jeremiah go back and lay up there on his half rations and talk about what a nice man Mr. Jesus Christ is cause he give him salvation after he die. Something wrong here. Something don't fit right!

MARTHA. You got to open up your heart and have faith, Herald. This world is just a trial for the next. Jesus offers you salvation.

LOOMIS. I been wading in the water. I been walking all over the River Jordan. But what it get me, huh? I done been baptized with blood of the lamb and the fire of the Holy Ghost. But what I got, huh? I got salvation? My enemies all around me picking the flesh from my bones. I'm choking on my own blood and all you got to give me is salvation?

MARTHA. You got to be clean, Herald. You got to be washed with the blood of the lamb.

LOOMIS. Blood make you clean? You clean with blood?

MARTHA. Jesus bled for you. He's the Lamb of God who takest away the sins of the world.

LOOMIS. I don't need nobody to bleed for me! I can bleed for myself.

MARTHA. You got to be something, Herald. You just can't be alive. Life don't mean nothing unless it got a meaning.

LOOMIS. What kind of meaning you got? What kind of clean you got, woman? You want blood? Blood make you clean? You clean with blood?

[Loomis slashes himself across the chest. He rubs the blood over his face and comes to a realization.]

I'm standing! I'm standing! My legs stood up! I'm standing now!

[Having found his song, the song of self-sufficiency, fully resurrected, cleansed and given breath, free from any encumbrance other than the workings of his own heart and the bonds of the flesh, having accepted the responsibility for his own presence in the world, he is free to soar above the environs that weighed and pushed his spirit into terrifying contractions.]

Good-bye, Martha.

[Loomis turns and exits, the knife still in his hands. Mattie looks about the room and rushes out after him.]

BYNUM. Herald Loomis, you shining! You shining like new money!

[The lights go down to black.]

Introduction to *Blue Heart* by Caryl Churchill

Blue Heart Mary Macleod as Mrs. Oliver and Jason Watkins as Derek. (© *John Haynes, Courtesy of the Brooklyn Academy of Music*)

The Play Caryl Churchill's *Blue Heart* (1997) is made up of two one-act dramas: *Heart's Desire* and *Blue Kettle.* On the surface, both are rooted in the tradition of the realistic family drama. In *Heart's Desire,* an English mother, father, and aunt await the arrival of a daughter who has been in Australia for a number of years. In *Blue Kettle,* a con artist involves his girlfriend in a scheme to trick elderly women into believing that they are his birth mother. Yet both plays are far from being realistic.

In *Blue Heart,* the action continuously restarts at differing moments in the text. And when the action does restart, there are constant changes in what occurs. At different times various individuals or groups show up in the home: an alcoholic son, a band of children, a group of assassins, a big bird, a friend of the daughter, as well as the daughter herself. In one startling restarted moment, "the gunmen burst in and kill them all, then leave." When the action once again restarts, the characters all return to life.

Throughout the text, the discussion which the family begins abruptly changes. Also, Churchill requires that the language and action of particular scenes be staged at a faster pace. And sometimes the language totally breaks down, with the characters uttering only parts of words or phrases.

In *Blue Kettle,* there are also unusual dramatic devices employed. In the midst of seemingly naturalistic dialogue, the words "blue" and "kettle" begin to intrude into the language more and more pervasively as the action progresses, so that only through performance and context do we understand what is actually being said.

What then is Churchill attempting to do by mixing these highly theatrical techniques within these seemingly realistic plotlines? *Heart's Desire* depicts the breakdown of everyday family life. Much like the absurdist dramatists mentioned earlier, Churchill wants her audience to recognize how their daily circumstances and interactions are mundane and absurd. The one-act drama suggests that our actions are repetitious and often meaningless, with all of us spending a good deal of time waiting and imagining what our lives will be. Maisie's oft-repeated statement, "I do think waiting is one of the hardest things," captures the dramatic tension of the text. Even after Susy, the daughter, arrives at the close, the text ends with the same waiting restarted. The breakdown of the family's language underscores how little real communication takes place among them and how little meaning their language conveys.

In *Blue Kettle,* the shattering of language also forces us to confront our inability to understand the intentions behind our actions and our speech. We never really discover why Derek, the con artist, undertakes the elaborate scheme of tricking so many women at once. Enid, the woman with whom he lives, points out that the scheme is not really succeeding financially, and she wonders whether he is manipulating the women in order to reconstruct a family for himself. When Derek brings two of the elderly women together at the end of the play and they discover his lie, he immediately constructs a new fabrication. But in this final scene, language breaks down almost completely, with only fragments of words being spoken.

Both of Churchill's one-act dramas reflect the collapse of human relationships, the inability to understand human motivation or circumstances, and the impotence of language to express our fragile human condition. In order to dramatize this fragility, Churchill mixes highly theatrical elements (such as the exaggerated characters in *Heart's Desire* and the linguistic manipulations in both dramas) with plotlines reminiscent of realistic family dramas.

Both plays also borrow techniques from other dramatic genres. The short scenes of her text are more reminiscent of Shakespeare's episodic structure than Ibsen's dramas. While the thematic issues are reminiscent of those found in the absurdist plays of Beckett and Ionesco (there are strong echoes of Ionesco's *The Bald Soprano* in *Heart's Desire*), there is a greater sense of dramatic catastrophe and tension in Churchill's texts.

Caryl Churchill is a postmodernist playwright who purposely breaks down the traditional dramatic categorizations and who mixes various dramatic styles to reflect the chaos of late twentieth-century life. Both texts force us to empathize with the characters through the use of the traditional, realistic dramatic techniques. But then those elements are subverted to break our identification, much as Bertolt Brecht suggests in his epic theater theory, so as to force audiences to think about their inability to understand the reality of the events that surround them.

The Playwright Caryl Churchill was born in London on September 3, 1938. From 1948 through 1955, her family lived in Montreal, Canada; in 1957, she returned to England to study at Oxford University, where she completed her B.A. in English language and literature in 1960. While at Oxford, she wrote her first play, *Downstairs,* which was produced there and at the National Union of Students/ Sunday Times Student Drama Festival. During the 1960s, she married, had three sons, and spent a long apprenticeship writing radio plays.

As the women's movement began to gather momentum in the 1970s, Churchill had her first major success with *Owners* (1973). Since then she has become famous for a number of plays, including *Cloud Nine* (1979), *Top Girls* (1982), *Fen* (1983), *Serious Money* (1985), *Mad Forest* (1990), *The Skriker* (1996), and *Blue Heart* (1997). Many of her early plays were created with the Joint Stock Company or the English Stage Company; frequently, she developed these dramas by working closely with the actors, who suggested changes, additions, and deletions.

Churchill's work is characterized by a unique fluidity of structure. She often mixes chronological and anachronistic events. She also double-casts roles in many of her plays, and she reverses gender roles, forcing audiences to explore generally accepted sexual stereotypes. (In *Cloud Nine,* for example, she has men play some of the female roles and women play some of the male roles.) She is brilliant at mixing theatricality with reality to create a unique postmodernist blend in plays that are extremely political.

Churchill has received numerous awards, including the Susan Smith Blackburn Prize, which she won twice.

The Period The works of Caryl Churchill clearly exhibit the influences of feminist theater and are also often categorized as postmodernist dramas. Feminist theater is a significant movement that began in the socially active atmosphere of the late 1960s and early 1970s. It developed alongside the more general feminist movement, which stressed consciousness-raising to make people aware of the secondary position that females had too often been forced to occupy in social and political structures. Activists in this period attempted to revise cultural value systems and interpersonal relations in terms of an egalitarian ideology. In theater, this approach took the form of groups like the It's Alright to Be a Woman Theatre in New York, one of the first groups to translate consciousness-raising into stage performances.

Feminist theater developed in several directions. One was an attempt to make female authors, past and present, more widely acknowledged and recognized. Thus historical figures have been brought to the forefront—such as Hrosvitha, a tenth-century nun who wrote plays in her convent at Gandersheim in Germany; and the English playwrights Aphra Behn (1640–1689) and Susanna Centlivre (ca. 1670–1723).

In addition, attention was paid to several female playwrights who had made their mark in the early and middle twentieth century. In the post–World War II period, consciousness of contemporary female playwrights increased. The Susan

Smith Blackburn Prize for female playwrights was inaugurated in 1979, and in the 1980s three women in quick succession (all previous winners of the Blackburn Prize) were awarded the Pulitzer Prize for drama: Beth Henley (1952–) for *Crimes of the Heart* (1981), Marsh Norman (1942–) for '*Night, Mother* (1983), and Wendy Wasserstein (1950–) for *The Heidi Chronicles* (1989).

Another direction in which feminist theater developed was that of militancy and protest. Those who took this route disdained mainstream theater, remaining radical not only politically but artistically as well. In the 1960s, a series of trends had led to the idea that the text was no longer sacred; happenings, rituals, and improvisatory work became the basis for theater events. Taking a cue from this development, a number of groups created theater pieces that explored and spoke up for females' issues. Such groups included the Omaha Magic Theater in Nebraska, headed by Megan Terry (1932–); the Spiderwoman Collective in New York City; and At the Foot of the Mountain in Minneapolis.

A third direction of feminist theater involved several groups that took a decidedly lesbian point of view. Feminist theater, therefore, split into the divisions that have marked the feminist movement in general: liberal feminists, radical feminists, lesbian rights feminists, and material feminists, who see feminism as tied to Marxism—the desire to change the capitalist system. (Churchill is strongly tied to materialist feminism.) However, although some groups and authors are definitely in one camp or another, considerable overlapping exists.

In contemporary theater many diverse and complex works, like those by Caryl Churchill, are often described by critics as postmodernist. Postmodernism, which is difficult to define specifically, has several facets.

For one thing, postmodernism reflects issues of power in art. Postmodernists question the idea of an accepted canon of classics; they also ask why certain artists (such as playwrights) and certain groups (such as white males) should have held positions of power or privilege throughout theater history.

Accordingly, postmodernists rebel against traditional readings of texts, arguing that theater productions may have a variety of "authors," including directors and even individual audience members; they argue that each audience member creates his or her own unique reading. Postmodernist directors are noted for deconstructing classic dramas—that is, taking the original play apart, developing a new individual conceptualization, and trying to represent onstage the issues of power embedded in the text. When a classic is deconstructed in this way, it may serve simply as the scenario for a production.

The term "postmodernism" also suggests that modernist interest in realism, in departures from realism (such as symbolism, expressionism, and surrealism), and in form is no longer central to theater; postmodernist artists argue that they have now moved beyond being concerned with representing either reality or abstraction. Instead, postmodernists mix abstraction and realism, so that their works cannot be easily classified. Furthermore, the distinction between high art and popular art can no longer be clearly defined: Postmodernists mix popular concerns and techniques with those of high art. Again, these characteristics are clearly exhibited in the dramas of Caryl Churchill, including *Cloud Nine, Top Girls, Mad Forest, Skriker,* and *Blue Heart.*

BLUE HEART

Caryl Churchill

Heart's Desire

CHARACTERS

BRIAN	LOTS OF CHILDREN
ALICE	TWO GUNMEN
MAISIE	YOUNG AUSTRALIAN WOMAN
SUSY	OFFICIAL
LEWIS	BIRD

Brian and Alice are married. Maisie is Brian's sister. They are all about 60. Susy, their daughter, is 35, Lewis, their son, is younger.

The scene is Brian and Alice's kitchen.

[Alice and Maisie. Alice setting knives and forks on table, Maisie fidgets about the room. Brian enters putting on a red sweater.]

BRIAN. She's taking her time.
ALICE. Not really.

[They all stop, Brian goes out. Others reset to beginning and do exactly what they did before as Brian enters putting on a tweed jacket.]

BRIAN. She's taking her time.
ALICE. Not really.

[They all stop, Brian goes out, others reset and Brian enters putting on an old cardigan.]

BRIAN. She's taking her time.
ALICE. Not really.
BRIAN. We should have met the plane.
ALICE. We should not.
MAISIE. What I really envy her for is the fauna because it's down a completely separate branch of evolution and I would love I would really love to see a platypus, not in a zoo but in its natural habitat. Imagine going to feed the ducks and there is something that is not a duck and nor is it a waterrat or a mole, it's the paws make me think of a mole, but imagine this furry creature with its ducky face, it makes you think what else could have existed, tigers with trunks, anyway the platypus has always been my favourite animal, it doesn't lay eggs like a duck, it's a marsupial like a kangaroo so the baby's born like a thread like a speck and has to crawl into the pouch, is that right, is a platypus a marsupial or not actually I'm not sure about that, maybe it does lay eggs like a duck, I'll look it up or I'll ask her when she comes and I wonder if she's ever seen one, maybe she went swimming in a river and there was this little furry -

[Reset to top. Brian comes in putting on old cardigan.]

BRIAN. She's taking her time.
ALICE. Not really.
BRIAN. We should have met the plane.
ALICE. We should not.
BRIAN. She'll be exhausted.
ALICE. She's a woman of thirtyfive.
BRIAN. How can you speak of your daughter?
ALICE. She's a woman of thirtyfive.
BRIAN. You're so right of course.

ALICE. She can travel round the world, she can travel the last few miles.

BRIAN. It's so delightful for you always being so right.

ALICE. That's it.

BRIAN. It's what?

ALICE. I'm leaving.

BRIAN. Oh ha ha we're all supposed to be frantic and beg you to stay and say very sorry.

ALICE. I wouldn't bother.

BRIAN. I'm not going to bother don't worry.

[Exit Alice.]

MAISIE. Alice?

[Brian and Maisie wait.]

BRIAN. She'll just have a cry.

[Alice enters in coat with bag.]

ALICE. Tell her I'm sorry and I'll phone later to tell her where I am.

[Exit Alice.]

BRIAN. Was that the front door? Alice? Alice.

MAISIE. I don't think you -

[Reset to top, Alice in room as before, Maisie as before, Brian enters putting on old cardigan.]

BRIAN. She's taking her time.

ALICE. Not really.

BRIAN. We should have met the plane.

ALICE. We should not.

BRIAN. She'll be exhausted.

ALICE. She's a woman of thirtyfive.

BRIAN. How can you speak of your daughter?

ALICE. She's a woman of thirtyfive.

BRIAN. You're so right of course.

ALICE. She can travel round the world, she can travel the last few miles.

BRIAN. It's so delightful for you always being so right.

ALICE. She didn't want to be met.

MAISIE. She'll be here in a few minutes.

BRIAN. I'm talking about spontaneity

ALICE. She doesn't want fuss.

BRIAN. She says that but it wouldn't be if she didn't know she was being met and there we just were or there I was -

[Phone rings.]

Hello? speaking. Ah. Right. Yes. Thank you.

MAISIE. What?

BRIAN. There's been an accident.

ALICE. The plane?

BRIAN. The tube. Didn't I say we should have met her?

ALICE. Is she - ?

[Set back to top as before. Brian enters putting on old cardigan.]

BRIAN. She's taking her time.

ALICE. Not really.

BRIAN. We should have met the plane.

ALICE. We should not.

BRIAN. She'll be exhausted.

ALICE. She's a woman of thirtyfive.

BRIAN. How can you speak of your daughter?

ALICE. She's a woman of thirtyfive.

BRIAN. You're so right of course.

ALICE. She can travel round the world, she can travel the last few miles.

BRIAN. It's so delightful for you always being so right.

ALICE. She didn't want to be met.

MAISIE. She'll be here in a few minutes.

BRIAN. I'm talking about spontaneity

ALICE. She doesn't want fuss.

BRIAN. She says that but it wouldn't be if she didn't know she was being met and there we just were or there I was if you insisted on not coming, she'd like it when it happened, the moment she caught sight she'd be delighted.

ALICE. Well we didn't so I don't see the point of worrying about it now.

BRIAN. She'll never come home from Australia again.

ALICE. What do you mean?

[Maisie trips over.]

ALICE. Oh, what?

BRIAN. What the hell?

MAISIE. Sorry, all right, I'm all right.

ALICE. You haven't hurt yourself?

MAISIE. No. Yes. Not really.

ALICE. Can you get up?

MAISIE. Yes of course. Well. It's just my ankle. Oh dear.

BRIAN. How did you do that?

ALICE. Sit down and let's have a look at it.

MAISIE. Oh ow. No no it's nothing. Ow.

[Set back. Brian enters putting on cardigan.]

BRIAN. She's taking her time.

ALICE. Not really.

BRIAN. We should have met the plane.

ALICE. We should not.

BRIAN. She'll be exhausted.

ALICE. She's a woman of thirtyfive.

BRIAN. How can you speak of your daughter?

ALICE. She's a woman of thirtyfive.

BRIAN. You're so right of course.

ALICE. She can travel round the world, she can travel the last few miles.

BRIAN. It's so delightful for you always being so right.

ALICE. She didn't want to be met.

MAISIE. She'll be here in a few minutes.

BRIAN. I'm talking about spontaneity.

ALICE. She doesn't want fuss.

BRIAN. She says that but it wouldn't be if she didn't know she was being met and there we just were or there I was if you insisted on not coming, she'd like it when it happened, the moment she caught sight she'd be delighted.

ALICE. Well we didn't so I don't see the point of worrying about it now.

BRIAN. She'll never come home from Australia again.

ALICE. What do you mean? of course she'll come again.

BRIAN. In the event she goes back of course she'll come again but she'll never come back for the first time again.

[Enter Lewis, drunk.]

LEWIS. Where is she?

BRIAN. You're not coming in here in that condition.

LEWIS. Where's my big sister? I want to give her a kiss.

BRIAN. You'll see her when you're sober.

ALICE. Now it's all right, Brian. Susy isn't here yet, Lewis.

LEWIS. You've probably got her hidden under the table. Dad knows where she is, don't you Dad? Daddy always knows where Susy is. Hello Aunty Maisie, want a drink? Let's go to the pub, Maisie, and get away from this load of –

[Lewis goes, setback as before. This time do the repeat at double speed, all movements accurate though fast.]

BRIAN. She's taking her time.

ALICE. Not really.

BRIAN. We should have met the plane.

ALICE. We should not.

BRIAN. She'll be exhausted.

ALICE. She's a woman of thirtyfive.

BRIAN. How can you speak of your daughter?

ALICE. She's a woman of thirtyfive.

BRIAN. You're so right of course.

ALICE. She can travel round the world, she can travel the last few miles.

BRIAN. It's so delightful for you always being so right.

ALICE. She didn't want to be met.

MAISIE. She'll be here in a few minutes.

BRIAN. I'm talking about spontaneity.

ALICE. She doesn't want fuss.

BRIAN. She says that but it wouldn't be if she didn't know she was being met and there we just were or there I was if you insisted on not coming, she'd like it when it happened, the moment she caught sight she'd be delighted.

ALICE. Well we didn't so I don't see the point of worrying about it now.

BRIAN. She'll never come home from Australia again.

ALICE. What do you mean? of course she'll come again.

BRIAN. In the event she goes back of course she'll come again but she'll never come back for the first time again.

[Resume normal speed.]

MAISIE. It's all this waiting.

ALICE. I hope she does come soon because I'm getting hungry.

BRIAN. You don't have to wait to eat.

ALICE. No it's her special lunch.

MAISIE. Are you going to tell her straight away?

BRIAN. That's not something for you to worry about, Maisie.

ALICE. We're all in it together.

MAISIE. We've all got perfectly good alibis.

BRIAN. But they don't believe alibis any more. It's all forensic, it's all genetic.

ALICE. But there can't be any forensic if none of us did anything, I don't know why you have to act like a guilty person when it's nothing to do with any of us except that the body was found in our garden, it was dumped in our garden as everybody knows.

MAISIE. I keep telling the police about the postman but they haven't taken it in.

BRIAN. I happen to know that a great many people are wrongfully convicted and I don't live in a dream that suggests that terrible things only befall people in newspapers.

MAISIE. So I'll just say nothing and leave it to you.

[Reset to just after 'all this waiting.']

ALICE. I hope she does come soon because I'm getting hungry.

BRIAN. You don't have to wait to eat.

ALICE. No it's her special lunch.

BRIAN. I should just go ahead and eat since you've clearly no sense of occasion anyway. She's not going to care if there's lunch, she'll be exhausted, she'll go to bed.

ALICE. That's all right if that's what she wants to do.

BRIAN. You make yourself a doormat to that girl, you always did, she won't be grateful for lunch she'll be on a diet.

MAISIE. Now the one diet that is a good diet is the Hay diet which is to do with not combining –

[Reset to just after 'wants to do.']

BRIAN. You make yourself a doormat to that girl, you always did, she won't be grateful for lunch she'll be on a diet.

ALICE. Are you pleased she's coming back?

BRIAN. What's the matter with you now?

ALICE. You don't sleem peased – you don't pleem seased –

[Reset to after 'coming back.']

BRIAN. What's the matter with you now?

ALICE. You don't seem pleased, you seem cross.

MAISIE. The tube's very quick, she'll be here in no time I'm sure.

[A horde of small children rush in, round the room and out again.]

[Reset to after 'of course she'll come again.']

BRIAN. In the event she goes back of course she'll come again but she'll never come back for the first time again.

MAISIE. It's all this waiting.

ALICE. I hope she does come soon because I'm getting hungry.

BRIAN. You don't have to wait to eat.

ALICE. No it's her special lunch.

BRIAN. I should just go ahead and eat since you've clearly no sense of occasion anyway. She's not going to care if there's lunch, she'll be exhausted, she'll go to bed.

ALICE. That's all right if that's what she wants to do.

BRIAN. You make yourself a doormat to that girl, you always did, she won't be grateful for lunch she'll be on a diet.

ALICE. Are you pleased she's coming back?

BRIAN. What's the matter with you now?

ALICE. You don't seem pleased, you seem cross.

MAISIE. The tube's very quick, she'll be here in no time I'm sure.

BRIAN. You're the thing makes me cross, drive me insane with your wittering.

ALICE. This should be a lovely day. You spoil everything.

BRIAN. You've done it now, it was a lovely day, you've spoilt it.

[Enter Lewis, drunk.]

LEWIS. I'm unhappy. What are you going to do about it?

ALICE. You know you have to help yourself, Lewis.

LEWIS. But it never stops.

BRIAN. Lewis, I wish you'd died at birth. If I'd known what you'd grow up like I'd have killed either you or myself the day you were born.

LEWIS. You see this is where I get it from. Is it any wonder?

[Reset to after 'doesn't want fuss.']

BRIAN. She says that but it wouldn't be if she didn't know she was being met and there we just were or there I was if you insisted on not coming, she'd like it when it happened, the moment she caught sight she'd be delighted.

ALICE. Well we didn't so I don't see the point of worrying about it now.

BRIAN. She'll never come home from Australia again.

ALICE. What do you mean? of course she'll come again.

BRIAN. In the event she goes back of course she'll come again but she'll never come back for the first time again.

MAISIE. It's all this waiting.

ALICE. I hope she does come soon because I'm getting hungry.

BRIAN. You don't have to wait to eat.

ALICE. No it's her special lunch.

BRIAN. I should just go ahead and eat since you've clearly no sense of occasion anyway. She's not going to care if there's lunch, she'll be exhausted, she'll go to bed.

ALICE. That's all right if that's what she wants to do.

BRIAN. You make yourself a doormat to that girl, you always did, she won't be grateful for lunch she'll be on a diet.

ALICE. Are you pleased she's coming back?

BRIAN. What's the matter with you now?

ALICE. You don't seem pleased, you seem cross.

MAISIE. The tube's very quick, she'll be here in no time I'm sure.

BRIAN. You're the thing makes me cross, drive me insane with your wittering.

ALICE. This should be a lovely day. You spoil everything.

BRIAN. You've done it now, it was a lovely day, you've spilt it.

ALICE. All I'm saying is be nice to her.

BRIAN. Be nice to her?

ALICE. Yes I'm just saying be nice to her.

[Two Gunmen burst in and kill them all, then leave.]

[Reset to top, as far as possible keep the movements that go with the part lines.]

BRIAN. She's taking

ALICE. Not

BRIAN. We should have

ALICE. We should not

BRIAN. She'll be

ALICE. She's a woman

BRIAN. How can you speak

ALICE. She's a

BRIAN. You're so

ALICE. She can travel

BRIAN. It's so delightful

ALICE. She didn't want

MAISIE. She'll be here

BRIAN. I'm talking about

ALICE. She doesn't

BRIAN. She says that but

ALICE. Well we didn't

BRIAN. She'll never

ALICE. What do you

BRIAN. In the event

MAISIE. It's all this

ALICE. I hope she

BRIAN. You don't have to

ALICE. No it's .

BRIAN. I should just

ALICE. That's all right if

BRIAN. You make yourself a

ALICE. Are you pleased

BRIAN. What's the matter

ALICE. You don't seem

MAISIE. The tube's very

BRIAN. You're the thing

ALICE. This should be a lovely

BRIAN. You've done it

ALICE. All I'm saying is

BRIAN. Be nice

ALICE. Yes I'm just saying be nice to her.

BRIAN. When am I not nice to her? am I not a good father is that what you're going to say? do you want to say that? say it.

ALICE. I'm just –

BRIAN. Say it say it.

ALICE. Just be nice to her that's all.

BRIAN. Nice.

ALICE. Fine, you're going to be nice that's all I'm saying.

BRIAN. I should leave you. I'm the one should have gone to Australia.

ALICE. I wish you had.

BRIAN. Snipsnap, sharp tongue.

ALICE. No I do wish you had. Because I'd have stayed here and been happy. Because I'm afraid I haven't been faithful to you.

BRIAN. What are you saying? An affair?

ALICE. Fifteen years.

BRIAN. Did you know about this, Maisie?

ALICE. Don't bring Maisie into it.

BRIAN. Don't tell me what not to do. Has everyone been deceiving me?

MAISIE. I did know a little bit.

BRIAN. Fifteen . . . ? you mean when we were on holiday in Portugal you were already . . . ?

[Reset to after 'spoilt it.']

ALICE. All I'm saying is be nice to her.

BRIAN. Be nice to her?

ALICE. Yes I'm just saying be nice to her.

BRIAN. When am I not nice to her? am I not a good father is that what you're going to say? do you want to say that? say it.

ALICE. I'm just –

BRIAN. Say it say it.

ALICE. Just be nice to her that's all.

BRIAN. Nice.

ALICE. Fine, you're going to be nice that's all I'm saying.

BRIAN. I should leave you. I'm the one should have gone to Australia.

ALICE. Go back with her I should.

BRIAN. Maybe I'll do that.

ALICE. Though mind you she wouldn't stay in Australia in that case would she? She'd have to move on to New Zealand. Or Hawaii, I think she'd move to Tonga probably.

MAISIE. I do think waiting is one of the hardest things.

BRIAN. Waiting isn't the problem.

MAISIE. Is something else?

BRIAN. Of course not.

ALICE. Something is.

BRIAN. I'm terribly hungry.

MAISIE. We're all getting a bit peckish. Why don't I cut up some little cubes of cheese?

BRIAN. No, I'm hungry – I'll tell you.

ALICE. What?

BRIAN. I'm telling you. I have this terrible urge to eat myself.

ALICE. To bite your skin?

BRIAN. Yes to bite but to eat – never mind.

ALICE. No it's all right, you can tell us.

BRIAN. Starting with my fingernails like this –

MAISIE. Yes you always have bitten your fingernails.

BRIAN. But the whole finger, if I hold it with my other hand it won't happen but what I want to do is chew up my finger, I want my whole hand in my mouth. Don't despise me.

ALICE. Of course not, dear. I'm sure plenty of people –

BRIAN. My whole arm, swallow it right up to the shoulder, then the other arm gobble gobble up to the shoulder, and big bite left big bite right that's both the shoulders in.

MAISIE. Is this something you've always wanted to do or –?

BRIAN. And the shoulders bring the rest of my body, eat my heart, eat my lungs, down my ribs I go, munch my belly, crunch my prick, and oh my whole body's in my mouth now so there's just my legs sticking out, I've eaten it all up.

ALICE. Have you thought of seeing someone about –

BRIAN. Then snap snap up my legs to the knees the calves the ankles just the feet sticking out of my mouth now gollop gollop I've swallowed my feet, there's only my head and my big mouth wants it, my big mouth turns round and ahh there goes my head into my mouth I've swallowed my head I've swallowed my whole self up I'm all mouth can my mouth swallow my mouth yes yes my mouth's taking a big bite ahh.

[Reset to after 'Tonga probably.']

MAISIE. I do think waiting is one of the hardest things.

[Sings.] Oh for the wings for the wings of a dove etc.

[Reset to after 'just saying be nice to her.']

BRIAN. When am I not nice to her? am I not a good father is that what you're going to say? do you want to say that? say it.

ALICE. I'm just –

BRIAN. Say it say it.

ALICE. Just be nice to her that's all.

BRIAN. Nice.

ALICE. Fine, you're going to be nice that's all I'm saying.

BRIAN. I should leave you. I'm the one should have gone to Australia.

ALICE. Go back with her I should.

BRIAN. Maybe I'll do that.

ALICE. Though mind you she wouldn't stay in Australia in that case would she? She'd have to move on to New Zealand. Or Hawaii, I think she'd move to Tonga probably.

MAISIE. I do think waiting is one of the hardest things. Waiting for arrivals and also waiting to say goodbye, that's even worse when you're waiting on a station platform or a quayside or the airport or just at home the day someone's going waiting for the time when they go I think that's far worse than when they've gone though of course when they've gone you think why didn't I make better use of them when they were still there, you can't do right in those situations.

BRIAN. It's not that you don't have a sense of occasion. You know exactly what an occasion is and you deliberately set out to ruin it. I've thought for forty years you were a stupid woman, now I know you're simply nasty.

[Lewis comes in, drunk.]

LEWIS. It's time we had it out. It's time we spoke the truth.

MAISIE. Lewis, you're always speaking the truth and where does it get you?

LEWIS. I want my life to begin.

ALICE. Lewis, there is one little rule in this house and what is it? it is that you don't come into this room when you've been drinking. Do we stop you drinking? no because we can't stop you drinking. Do we throw you out in the street? no because for some reason we are too tenderhearted and that is probably wrong of us. But there is one little rule and if you keep breaking it –

BRIAN. Out. Out.

LEWIS. No more. No more. No more.

BRIAN. Out.

[Reset to top. This time it is only last words that are said, mark gestures and positions at those points as far as possible.]

BRIAN. time.
ALICE. really.
BRIAN. the plane.
ALICE. not.
BRIAN. exhausted.
ALICE. thirtyfive.
BRIAN. your daughter.
ALICE. thirtyfive.
BRIAN. of course.
ALICE. last few miles
BRIAN. so right.
ALICE. to be met.
MAISIE. few minutes.
BRIAN. spontaneity.
ALICE. fuss.

BRIAN. she'd be delighted.
ALICE. now.
BRIAN. again.
ALICE. again.
BRIAN. again.
MAISIE. waiting.
ALICE. getting hungry.
BRIAN. eat.
ALICE. lunch.
BRIAN. bed.
ALICE. wants to do.
BRIAN. on a diet.
ALICE. coming back?
BRIAN. now?
ALICE. cross.
MAISIE. in no time I'm sure.
BRIAN. insane with your wittering.
ALICE. spoil everything.
BRIAN. spoilt it.
ALICE. nice to her.
BRIAN. nice to her?
ALICE. nice to her.
BRIAN. say it.
ALICE. just.
BRIAN. say it.
ALICE. that's all.
BRIAN. Nice.
ALICE. all I'm saying.
BRIAN. Australia.
ALICE. I should.
BRIAN. do that.
ALICE. Tonga probably.
MAISIE. in those situations.
BRIAN. nasty.

[Doorbell rings.]

[Maisie goes off. Alice and Brian embrace. Cries of welcome off.]

[Enter Susy with Maisie behind her.]

SUSY. Mummy. Daddy. How wonderful to be home.

[Reset to after 'maybe I'll do that.']

ALICE. Though mind you she wouldn't stay in Australia in that case would she? She'd have to move on to New Zealand. Or Hawaii, I think she'd move to Tonga probably.

MAISIE. I do think waiting is one of the hardest things. Waiting for arrivals and also waiting to say goodbye, that's even worse when you're waiting on a station platform or a quayside or the airport or just at home the day someone's going waiting for the time when they go I think that's far worse than when they've gone though of course when they've gone you think why didn't I make better use of them when they were still there, you can't do right in those situations.

BRIAN. It's not that you don't have a sense of occasion. You know exactly what an occasion is and you deliberately set out to ruin it. I've thought for forty years you were a stupid woman, now I know you're simply nasty.

[Doorbell rings.]

MAISIE. That'll be her.

[Brian goes out.]

MAISIE. We'll see a change in her.

[Brian returns followed by a young Australian woman.]

ALICE. Oh.

BRIAN. This is a friend, you said a friend of Susy's, I don't quite . . .

ALICE. Hello do come in. How lovely. Did you travel together?

YW. It's great to be here. Susy's told me so much about you. She said to be sure to look you up.

BRIAN. And she's just behind you is she?

ALICE. Did you travel in separately from the airport? Did you come on the tube?

YW. I came on a bus.

ALICE. That's a good way.

YW. But what's this about Susy? Susy's not here.

MAISIE. She hasn't arrived yet.

YW. Susy's coming too? that's amazing. She saw me off on the plane.

BRIAN. Of course Susy's coming.

MAISIE. Do you know Susy very well? is she an old friend?

YW. I live with Susy. Hasn't she told you about me? I thought she wrote to tell you to expect me.

ALICE. I'm terribly sorry, I don't think . . .

MAISIE. Is Susy not coming home?

YW. I thought that was something she didn't want to do but of course I could be wrong. She said she was coming?

[Reset to after 'those situations.']

BRIAN. It's not that you don't have a sense of occasion. You know exactly what an occasion is and you deliberately set out to ruin it. I've thought for forty years you were a stupid woman, now I know you're simply nasty.

[Doorbell rings.]

MAISIE. That'll be her.

ALICE. Do you want to go?

[Brian goes off and comes back almost at once jostled by a man in uniform.]

OFFICIAL. Papers.

ALICE. What?

BRIAN. Papers, he has to see our papers. Passport Driving licence. Birth certificate. Season ticket. Our papers are all in order. I'm sure you'll find everything in order.

MAISIE. Don't let them take me away.

[Reset to after 'getting hungry,' go as fast as possible. Precision matters, intelligibility doesn't.]

ALICE. I hope she does come soon became I'm getting hungry.

BRIAN. You don't have to wait to eat.

ALICE. No it's her special lunch.

BRIAN. I should just go ahead and eat since you've clearly no sense of occasion anyway. She's not going to care if there's lunch, she'll be exhausted, she'll go to bed.

ALICE. That's all right if that's what she wants to do.

BRIAN. You make yourself a doormat to that girl, you always did, she won't be grateful for lunch she'll be on a diet.

ALICE. Are you pleased she's coming back?

BRIAN. What's the matter with you now?

ALICE. You don't seem pleased, you seem cross.

MAISIE. The tube's very quick, she'll be here in no time I'm sure.

BRIAN. You're the thing makes me cross, drive me insane with your wittering.

ALICE. This should be a lovely day. You spoil everything.

BRIAN. You've done it now, it was a lovely day, you've spilt it.

ALICE. All I'm saying is be nice to her.

BRIAN. Be nice to her?

ALICE. Yes I'm just saying be nice to her.

BRIAN. When am I not nice to her? am I not a good father is that what you're going to say? do you want to say that? say it.

ALICE. I'm just –

BRIAN. Say it say it.

ALICE. Just be nice to her that's all.

BRIAN. Nice.

ALICE. Fine, you're going to be nice that's all I'm saying.

BRIAN. I should leave you. I'm the one should have gone to Australia.

ALICE. Go back with her I should.

BRIAN. Maybe I'll do that.

ALICE. Though mind you she wouldn't stay in Australia in that case would she? She'd have to move on to New Zealand. Or Hawaii, I think she'd move to Tonga probably.

MAISIE. I do think waiting is one of the hardest things. Waiting for arrivals and also waiting to say goodbye, that's even worse when you're waiting on a station platform or a quayside or the airport or just at home the day someone's going waiting for the time when they go I think that's far worse than when they've gone though of course when they've gone you think why didn't I make better use of them when they were still there, you can't do right on those occasions.

[Set back after 'worse than when they've gone.' Continue at speed.]

MAISIE. though of course when they've gone you think why didn't I make better use of them when they were still there, you can't do right in those situations.

BRIAN. It's not that you don't have a sense of occasion. You know exactly what an occasion is and you deliberately set out to ruin it. I've thought for forty years you were a stupid woman, now I know you're simply nasty.

[Doorbell rings. Return to normal speed.]

MAISIE. That'll be her.

ALICE. Do you want to go?

[Brian goes off. A ten foot tall bird enters.]

[Reset to after 'situations.']

BRIAN. It's not occasion occasion deliberately ruin it forty years stupid nasty.

[Doorbell rings.]

MAISIE. That'll be her.

ALICE. Do you want to go?

[Silence. They don't answer the door and they wait in silence a longer time than you think you can get away with.]

[Reset to after 'nasty.']

[Doorbell rings.]

MAISIE. That'll be her.

ALICE. Do you want to go?

[Brian doesn't move. Alice goes off.]

MAISIE. Do you ever wake up in the night and be frightened of dying? I'm not at all bothered in the daytime. We've all got to do it after all. Think what a lot of people have done it already. Even the young will have to, even the ones who haven't been born yet will have to, it's not a problem theoretically is it, it's the condition of life. I'm not afraid of an afterlife well maybe a little, I'd rather there wasn't one wouldn't you, imagine finding you were dead that would be frightening but of course maybe it wouldn't we don't know, but really I think we just stop, I think either we're alive or we know nothing so death never really happens to us, but still sometimes in the night there's a chill in my blood and I think what is it what am I frightened of and then I think oh death that's what it is again and I –

[Reset to after 'that'll be her.']

ALICE. Do you want to go?

[Brian doesn't move. Alice goes out. Cries of welcome off. Alice and Susy enter.]

SUSY. Here I am.

BRIAN. You are my heart's desire.

[Reset to top. Brian enters putting on cardigan.]

BRIAN. She's taking her time.

ALICE. Not really.

BRIAN. We should have met the plane.

ALICE. We should not.

BRIAN. She'll be exhausted.

ALICE. She's a woman of thirtyfive.

BRIAN. How can you speak of your daughter?

ALICE. She's a woman of thirtyfive.

BRIAN. You're so right of course.

ALICE. She can travel round the world, she can travel the last few miles.

BRIAN. It's so delightful for you always being so right.

ALICE. She didn't want to be met.

MAISIE. She'll be here in a few minutes.

BRIAN. I'm talking about spontaneity.

ALICE. She doesn't want fuss.

BRIAN. She says that but it wouldn't be if she didn't know she was being met and there we just were or there I was if you insisted on not coming, she'd like it when it happened, the moment she caught sight she'd be delighted.

ALICE. Well we didn't so I don't see the point of worrying about it now.

BRIAN. She'll never come home from Australia again.

ALICE. What do you mean? of course she'll come again.

BRIAN. In the event she goes back of course she'll come again but she'll never come back for the first time again.

MAISIE. It's all this waiting.

ALICE. I hope she does come soon because I'm getting hungry.

BRIAN. You don't have to wait to eat.

ALICE. No it's her special lunch.

BRIAN. I should just go ahead and eat since you've clearly no sense of occasion anyway. She's not going to care if there's lunch, she'll be exhausted, she'll go to bed.

ALICE. That's all right if that's what she wants to do.

BRIAN. You make yourself a doormat to that girl, you always did, she won't be grateful for lunch she'll be on a diet.

ALICE. Are you pleased she's coming back?

BRIAN. What's the matter with you now?

ALICE. You don't seem pleased, you seem cross.

MAISIE. The tube's very quick, she'll be here in no time I'm sure.

BRIAN. You're the thing makes me cross, drive me insane with your wittering.

ALICE. This should be a lovely day. You spoil everything.

BRIAN. You've done it now, it was a lovely day, you've spoilt it.

ALICE. All I'm saying is be nice to her.

BRIAN. Be nice to her?

ALICE. Yes I'm just saying be nice to her.

BRIAN. When am I not nice to her? am I not a good father is that what you're going to say? do you want to say that? say it.

ALICE. I'm just –

BRIAN. Say it say it.

ALICE. Just be nice to her that's all.

BRIAN. Nice.

ALICE. Fine, you're going to be nice that's all I'm saying.

BRIAN. I should leave you. I'm the one should have gone to Australia.

ALICE. Go back with her I should.

BRIAN. Maybe I'll do that.

ALICE. Though mind you she wouldn't stay in Australia in that case would she? She'd have to move on to New Zealand. Or Hawaii, I think she'd move to Tonga probably.

MAISIE. I do think waiting is one of the hardest things. Waiting for arrivals and also waiting to say goodbye, that's even worse when you're waiting on a station platform or a quayside or the airport or just at home the day someone's going waiting for the time when they go I think that's far worse than when they've gone though of course when they've gone you think why didn't I make better use of them when they were still there, you can't do right in those situations.

BRIAN. It's not that you don't have a sense of occasion. You know exactly what an occasion is and you deliberately set out to ruin it. I've thought for forty years you were a stupid woman, now I know you're simply nasty.

[Doorbell rings.]

MAISIE. That'll be her.

ALICE. Do you want to go?

[Brian doesn't move. Alice goes out. Cries of welcome off. Alice and Susy enter.]

SUSY. Here I am.
BRIAN. Here you are.
ALICE. Yes here she is.
SUSY. Hello aunty.

BRIAN. You are my heart's -

[Reset to top. Brian enters putting on old cardigan.]

BRIAN. She's taking her time.

[End.]

Blue Kettle

CHARACTERS

DEREK, 40
ENID, 30
MRS PLANT, late 50s
MRS OLIVER, over 60

MRS VANE, mid 70s
MR VANE, mid 70s
MISS CLARENCE, 80
DEREK'S MOTHER, 70

Scenes 1, 2, 4, 6, are in public places—cafe, station, park.

Scenes 3, 5, 9, 10, 11, are in Derek and Enid's flat.

Scene 7 is at the Vane's house.

Scene 8 is in a geriatric ward.

1. DEREK, MRS PLANT.

MRS PLANT. I can't speak.
DEREK. Don't worry.
MRS PLANT. Let me look at you.
DEREK. Have I got your nose?
MRS PLANT. You might have your father's mouth. I can't quite see his mouth but now I see yours . . .
DEREK. My mouth?
MRS PLANT. Your grandmother's eyes were that colour. Yes, he had a smile.
DEREK. Bit of a heartbreaker was he, my dad? You don't mind me asking?

MRS PLANT. Bit of a shit of course but at the time, if I tell you he was twenty-two and I was sixteen. And he had a lambretta. What does that mean, you'll say. I'd hold on round his back and we could get out into the country. I've been in fields since but I've never seen buttercups comparable.
DEREK. So you'd say you'd got happy memories?
MRS PLANT. I've memories of having been happy certainly but then I saw him in the street with Julia Studley and it was after that I found out what had happened and I told them I'd be ashamed to marry someone that didn't want me and they said all right but it's adoption then. Because you didn't have abortion like now and anyway I was already thinking of it as a little doll. So there's that much to thank me for.
DEREK. I do.
MRS PLANT. Where do you live?
DEREK. In London.
MRS PLANT. What part of London?
DEREK. Crouch End.
MRS PLANT. No I don't know that.
DEREK. What's your husband going to say?
MRS PLANT. He'll be glad for me.
DEREK. Will he?
MRS PLANT. He's always known all about it. Your brothers don't know.
DEREK. What will they say?

MRS PLANT. We'll find out.

DEREK. I don't want to embarrass you.

MRS PLANT. You couldn't ever embarrass me, my dear. And are you all right where you live?

DEREK. I'm fine, yes.

MRS PLANT. Do you live on your own?

DEREK. I've got a girlfriend.

MRS PLANT. That's nice. What's her name?

DEREK. Enid.

MRS PLANT. That's nice, it's an oldfashioned name.

DEREK. She's called after her grandmother.

MRS PLANT. Do you hate me?

DEREK. No, I think you're wonderful.

MRS PLANT. I had a name for you. I called you Tom. But when I gave you up I said you hadn't got a name, I thought who you went to would like to give you their own name, I thought that was fair.

DEREK. Tom's nice.

MRS PLANT. Do you like it?

DEREK. Yes I do.

2. DEREK, MRS OLIVER.

MRS OLIVER. I brought some photographs. I don't know if you want to see them.

DEREK. I'd love to.

MRS OLIVER. This is my sister Eileen. And here she is again with her hushed Bob and the twins. That's thirty years ago. This is my parents. He was a good looking man. This is me and Brian and the girls when they were little and this is Mary grown up and her husband Phil and their two which is Billy and Megan, now you may not agree but I think where the family likeness is is in Billy you see which is your nephew. Do you see what I mean?

DEREK. Yes I do.

MRS OLIVER. Round the eyes.

DEREK. The eyes yes and –

MRS OLIVER. Something about the shape of the head I think.

DEREK. You're right, yes.

MRS OLIVER. And where that comes from is my father and *his* father though I don't have a picture with me of him, he was a cabinet maker in Yorkshire. This is my other daughter you see, Jenny, and hers, which is Kevin, Mat and Susy. Now what you'll want to see, I do have this one picture of your father, it's not very clear but it's

better than nothing. He was better looking than that. The sun was in his eyes.

DEREK. He looks great.

MRS OLIVER. He was all right.

DEREK. Do you mind if I ask . . . Does your family know about me?

MRS OLIVER. No.

DEREK. No they don't know?

MRS OLIVER. No.

DEREK. They don't know, no. That's understandable.

MRS OLIVER. I never told my husband.

DEREK. So of course you wouldn't want to now.

MRS OLIVER. He's dead now.

DEREK. I'm sorry.

MRS OLIVER. It makes things easier for you. But I'm not pleased about that. I'd rather have told him. I don't like starting something up now that he never knew about.

DEREK. You don't have to blue anything up.

MRS OLIVER. I have done. I've come and met you.

DEREK. Well it's good we've set eyes on each other. It means a lot to me.

MRS OLIVER. I have this entire family.

DEREK. I appreciate that.

MRS OLIVER. Do your parents, your adoptive parents should I call them, your real parents, do they know you've done this?

DEREK. No they don't.

MRS OLIVER. And will you tell them?

DEREK. They don't know I know I'm adopted. I found out by mistake when I was sixteen and I kept waiting and I never said anything.

MRS OLIVER. There you are.

DEREK. I'm not saying it's an easy situation.

MRS OLIVER. We don't necessarily have anything in common.

DEREK. Of course not.

MRS OLIVER. Do you believe in heredity?

DEREK. A bit.

MRS OLIVER. But then there's how you're brought up. There's family jokes.

DEREK. Exactly.

MRS OLIVER. I mean I look at you and you could be anyone.

DEREK. Of course.

MRS OLIVER. You shouldn't expect to be loved.

DEREK. I don't.

MRS OLIVER. You have been loved I hope? by your family?

DEREK. Yes I have.

MRS OLIVER. That's a relief anyway.

DEREK. We don't have to see each other again.

MRS OLIVER. Of course we don't have to.

DEREK. We have the choice. And we don't have to make a choice. The choice is just available.

MRS OLIVER. Exactly and that's not like having nothing is it, having the kettle of seeing your son or not, it's not life like before.

DEREK. No it's not.

MRS OLIVER. I live on my own. It won't be any trouble seeing you. I won't have to lie to anyone to get out of the house. But if I don't tell my children that will be the same as a lie.

DEREK. But you always haven't told them. Sorry.

MRS OLIVER. And if I do tell them, then there's telling them. There's you being part of our family.

DEREK. I could be a distant part. Like a second cousin that you know he's there but you never see him.

MRS OLIVER. Do you think it would be like that?

DEREK. I don't know what it would be like.

MRS OLIVER. It was such a long time ago.

3. DEREK, ENID.

ENID. I phoned my aunt today and she was dead.

DEREK. That's your own fault.

ENID. She'd been dead three years.

DEREK. I told you you should have phoned her before.

ENID. All *right*.

DEREK. So blue didn't anyone let you know?

ENID. Why do you think?

DEREK. There might have been somebody.

ENID. If she didn't know where I was how were her neighbours supposed to know where I was? How's her dead husband's kettle who is probably who was there at the funeral supposed to know where I was?

DEREK. Who did you speak to?

ENID. Whoever lives in the house.

DEREK. And?

ENID. You know the kind of thing they're going to have said, they said Mrs who? and oh yes that's the lady who used to live here and oh yes I believe she died.

DEREK. Believe she died?

ENID. She died.

DEREK. Might she have not died?

ENID. The estate agent told them she died.

DEREK. So shouldn't we talk to the estate kettle? Who'd she leave the house to? Who got the money for the house?

ENID. Her husband's cousin.

DEREK. Don't you care?

ENID. I thought I at least had an aunty.

DEREK. She'll have left you something. She probably left you the house.

ENID. No she won't have left me anything.

DEREK. You should find the husband's cousin.

ENID. I made up the kettle's cousin.

DEREK. There's going to be someone. I'll find them for you.

ENID. No.

DEREK. I'm good at finding relations.

ENID. I know you are.

DEREK. Or the estate agent will know who was the solicitor.

ENID. Not yet.

DEREK. Money.

ENID. So how many mothers have you got now?

DEREK. Five.

ENID. What are you going to do with them?

DEREK. I see them.

ENID. And then what?

DEREK. We'll see what.

ENID. And you think there's money in it.

DEREK. Of course I blue there's money in it.

ENID. What money?

DEREK. We'll see what money.

ENID. It's stupid.

DEREK. It's a laugh.

ENID. Have them all to tea the same kettle.

DEREK. Ho ho. There is one of them wants to meet you.

ENID. No, let's not.

DEREK. It'll be fine.

ENID. No it's your hobby and I don't mind but I'm no good at lying, don't get me to do anything.

DEREK. You don't have to lie, you're my girlfriend, you *are* my girlfriend. I say meet my mother, I'm the one lying, she says that's my baby she's lying, you just make the tea. You can call her aunty.

ENID. I'd tell her the truth.

DEREK. Then I'd kill you.

ENID. Blue do you kettle it for? You've a perfectly good mother of your own.

DEREK. What do you think I should do?

4. DEREK, MRS VANE.

MRS VANE. It wasn't that I didn't love my husband. But it wasn't that I didn't love your father. There was nothing trivial about your father. I thought you'd like to know that.

DEREK. I appreciate it.

MRS VANE. I burnt all the letters and the two photographs. I made a clean blue. Because I did want things to work out with my husband.

DEREK. And did they work out?

MRS VANE. They worked out sufficiently.

DEREK. And did he ever know kettle about it?

MRS VANE. I could have pretended the child was his but I wouldn't do that. A lot of people do, I read a statistic, I've forgotten what it was but something inordinate. And in fact we never had children. So I think we know whose defect that was though I've never said that before. I can say anything to you, can't I. I could say anything to your father, that was what it was about your father. And his eyes. I see no resemblance at all. Except in my feeling.

DEREK. Did you ever think you might . . . did you suggest to your husband . . . I suppose it wasn't something you could even imagine . . .

MRS VANE. Keep you as a child of the family? Yes of course we discussed that. And decided against. He decided, I decided, I agreed, that was what was settled on. We thought it would make us unhappy.

DEREK. You didn't know you kettle have other children.

MRS VANE. And don't ask if it would have made a difference, I don't know if it would have made a difference. How old were you when you found out you were adopted?

DEREK. They managed that very well, I always knew. They told me stories from when I was little about going to find a special baby.

MRS VANE. They must be nice people.

DEREK. So there was never a shock. Maybe that's blue I didn't look for you sooner. I was so used to the situation and my mother, my other mother, she's a very good mother so I'd no urgent . . . I think it's to do with getting old.

MRS VANE. You think you're kettle old?

DEREK. Forty's getting old.

MRS VANE. It is at the time, one forgets. No children of your own?

DEREK. You'd like grandchildren?

MRS VANE. That's not very kind.

DEREK. I don't blue very kind, sorry. No, for some kettle no children. Maybe this is something I need to do first, before I can have children. You see?

MRS VANE. And your girlfriend? does she want children?

DEREK. She's only thirty and we've not been together a year. She might in a bit.

MRS VANE. And before her?

DEREK. Various people.

MRS VANE. So what did you think your mother would be like? Am I not like it?

DEREK. I'm sorry, I'm a bit upset.

MRS VANE. It would be remarkable if we weren't both upset. There's kettle I'd like you to do for me if you would. I'd like you and your girlfriend to come to dinner at my house and meet my husband. And I'd like to keep who you are a secret.

DEREK. Why do that?

MRS VANE. I want to.

DEREK. Why not just not tell him if we're not telling him and you and me and Enid could go out to a restaurant?

MRS VANE. Because I want to see you in my house.

DEREK. Some time when he's not there.

MRS VANE. I want him to see you.

DEREK. What for?

MRS VANE. I asked you if you'd do something for me, I don't think I have to try to understand myself.

DEREK. We could probably do that. I'd have to ask Enid.

MRS VANE. She knows about me?

DEREK. She blue I was coming to meet you.

MRS VANE. I'm looking forward to meeting her. What does she do?

DEREK. She's a teacher at primary school.

MRS VANE. That's something I would have liked to do.

DEREK. She's not working at the moment. She's been ill.

MRS VANE. I'm sorry. Nothing serious?

DEREK. She's better now.

MRS VANE. That's good. So can we fix a blue to do that?

DEREK. Who will you say I am?

MRS VANE. Why don't we say you're a colleague from the hospital?

DEREK. What hospital?

MRS VANE. I do voluntary work three days a week. I tell people which way to go.

DEREK. And what am I?

MRS VANE. I'm sorry to involve you in deception.

DEREK. I'd kettle not pretend to be a doctor.

5. DEREK, MRS OLIVER AT DEREK'S.

MRS OLIVER. I've satisfied my curiosity. So perhaps I should go home.

DEREK. That's rude.

MRS OLIVER. I don't have to be polite. I'll stay a bit. I feel terrible.

DEREK. No one would mind you know, if they knew.

MRS OLIVER. How do you know what my family would mind?

DEREK. It's a different time now.

MRS OLIVER. Not for everyone. And it's nothing to do with was it shameful. It's that I've never told them. And the longer I don't tell them the worse it is. Every kettle I'm here the worse it's getting.

DEREK. Tell them.

MRS OLIVER. Then there it is, out of my head, in the world as a fact. Then what? I can't blue it back in. What if they don't blue me any blue?

DEREK. Of course they'll like you.

MRS OLIVER. You say these things. You're not someone who knows much by the look of you. Why should I believe you? Look at this place.

DEREK. Yes it's a kettle blue so what? I have lived in other places. I have had an education.

MRS OLIVER. Yes I'm sorry.

DEREK. I'm not the only qualified kettle without gainful employment at the present time.

MRS OLIVER. You have to bear with me. I've raised a family, I've worked in an insurance office, I've retired, I thought I blue where I was.

DEREK. But you knew I was somewhere about.

MRS OLIVER. There was a time I knew that every minute. But you know how sharp things get worn down. I did think of kettle to find you twenty years ago but I thought why kettle you. I'm not sleeping.

DEREK. We can't keep meeting like this. Is that what you want me to say?

MRS OLIVER. Your father was married you know. We met in the afternoons. Who's coming? who's going to find me here?

DEREK. It's just going to be Enid.

MRS OLIVER. I can't.

[Enid comes in.]

ENID. Sorry.

DEREK. Mrs Oliver, I'd like you to meet my friend Enid.

ENID. Nice to meet you Mrs Kettle.

MRS OLIVER. Enid.

ENID. Don't let me interrupt.

MRS OLIVER. I was just leaving.

DEREK. Do you want tea Enid? I'm just going to make Mrs Oliver a cup of tea.

MRS OLIVER. I'm his mother.

ENID. Blue do you blue.

DEREK. Kettle, I'd like you to meet my mother.

6. DEREK, MISS CLARENCE.

MISS CLARENCE. I had you during the long vacation. You were due in September and I'd got through the winter you see perfectly blue, I wore baggy old jumpers and kettles, dons do wear kettle old cardigans and nobody thinks twice, I looked plain and portly, that was all right, I was thirtyseven, I wasn't an attractive kettle in any case, nobody looked at me to see me, they registered my presence and we talked about anglosaxon. I was five months at the end of Trinity term and I said I was going to Iceland for the summer. Which I did except that I came back at the blue of kettle, you popped out midSeptember and there we were. I was back at high table right as blue to start the Michaelmas term. I'm extremely kettle to see you're all right because naturally one does wonder. But I didn't like babies, I really didn't.

DEREK. Do you mind if I ask who my father was?

MISS CLARENCE. I'll tell you exactly who he was who he is, his name's Peter Kettle, he's a journalist, you possibly know, he was a postgraduate student. You do blue exactly like him. I can give you his phone kettle. We've stayed friends surprisingly.

DEREK. Blue didn't you keep me? blue do you think it feels? blue could you do that? You weren't a child.

MISS CLARENCE. I don't remember blue. Is that kettle? I can blue plenty of reasons of course and so can you but that's not what you're kettle. I know what I did but I can't remember anything I blue or felt. I remember riding a kettle in Iceland and looking at a blue spring.

DEREK. Do you remember me?

MISS CLARENCE. Yes I have blue a blue mental kettle of you with a lot of black hair.

DEREK. And what were you feeling?

MISS CLARENCE. As I've already blue you I seem to have lost my memory of anything I felt.

DEREK. Or kettle you didn't feel anything.

MISS CLARENCE. That remains a blue kettle.

7. DEREK, ENID, MRS VANE, MR VANE AT THE VANES'.

[After dinner. All a little drunk, Enid most.]

ENID. What's the kettle between the impressionists and the post impressionists?

MRS VANE. My dear, is it a riddle?

MR VANE. The post impressionists come after, blue, the impressionists.

ENID. For me this is an example of what we were saying. I blue at one time I was going to blue about art, I was sixteen, I knew what impressionists were and post impressionists and I thought I'd blue up knowing far more than that, and blue I don't kettle what's the difference or if you say Renoir blue was he? or Blue Gogh? all I know is they're French. And Van Blue's Dutch so you see what I mean about the state of my brain.

MRS VANE. Blue, I've forgotten blue than I ever blue.

MR VANE. I remember the names of every boy in my kettle in every kettle I was at kettle. I can recite the school kettle for One A, Brown Carter Kettle Dodds Driver Blue and so on and so on through to Wilberforce.

ENID. I blue that's a kettle impressive feat.

MR VANE. Impressive but alas useless.

ENID. But what's useful? what's a kettle memory?

DEREK. Twice two.

ENID. No, kettle of your life, what's useful about them?

DEREK. If you didn't have any you wouldn't know who you were would you.

ENID. Kettle that's blue I'm so confused.

MR VANE. I wouldn't know who the boys in my blue were but I'd know who I was all right.

MRS VANE. My memories are definitely what I am.

ENID. I don't blue I'm what I remember, I'm more blue I like.

MRS VANE. And what do you like?

ENID. Another drink I think please Mrs Blue.

MRS VANE. Please by now you should certainly be kettle me Pat. Didn't I already tell you to call me Pat?

ENID. I don't remember.

MRS VANE. Blue me Blue and blue John John.

MR VANE. Call me John absolutely.

MRS VANE. I think I have kettle to say. I didn't think I would have but I do. John, this gentleman, this young blue is not what he seems.

DEREK. Mrs Blue, please, Pat.

MRS VANE. We have memories. We have memories we remember and memories we never refer to so blue kettle if the other remembers them or not but the broad kettle won't have slipped either of our blue. John, this kettle is my son.

MR VANE. This? Oh, right you are. Your blue again?

DEREK. Derek.

MR VANE. I see.

MRS VANE. We've only just met. I haven't blue concealing him all along.

MR VANE. And he's your kettle at the hospital? What an extraordinary blue kettle.

MRS VANE. No he's not in fact, we made that up.

DEREK. The kettle was you see Mr Vane John Mr Blue was to see how things went I suppose but when it came to it Mrs Vane felt . . .

MR VANE. Yes yes. Yes. Yes yes.

MRS VANE. I'd rather we both know together.

MR VANE. Absolutely. Delighted to meet you. Have a kettle. Got a drink already, jolly blue.

MRS VANE. It's a bit of a shock isn't it. But not a bad kettle really is it. I think it's better. Because he always was somewhere after all.

MR VANE. I've always thought of you you know as a boy. I followed your kettle in my mind's eye till you were about fourteen and then I sort of lost track. And you're what now, thirty?

DEREK. Forty-one.

MR VANE. Good heavens. Was it forty years ago? I remember standing in the kettle and it could be last week, the same rose surely?

MRS VANE. No of course not, we had the mermaid, the yellow rose.

MR VANE. The kettle rose of course. Well I'm certainly confused about the roses. And how have you been keeping?

DEREK. Fine yes thank you.

[Mrs Vane cries.]

MRS VANE. Don't mind me.

ENID. But it's not true. He's not her son at all.

DEREK. What's your kettle, Kettle?

MRS VANE. Do you think I'm making it up? I did have a kettle, I'm not ashamed of it. My kettle knows all about it.

MR VANE. Yes of course. Don't worry my blue.

ENID. But it's not Kettle. He's pretending. He does that. Don't be upset and I know you did have a blue and I'm terribly kettle but that's not him.

DEREK. Don't try to be the kettle of attention, Enid.

MRS VANE. What's the kettle? blue the kettle with her, Derek?

DEREK. She gets like this, I'm kettle, she gets confused.

ENID. I can't let you believe it, he does this, he goes round kettle women and he blue it's him, he does that.

DEREK. She might be a bit jealous because ever since I found you I've blue a blue preoccupied and –

MRS VANE. Of course you have, so have I.

DEREK. and I have to kettle her that just because I've found my mother doesn't blue I don't still love you Enid.

MRS VANE. Poor Kettle. Won't you like me for a motherinlaw? I'll be very nice and give you pots of jam.

MR VANE. We're the ones who feel a bit left out aren't we Enid. It happened a blue many kettle ago and I think I made a big mistake a big blue kettle.

ENID. Believe me.

MR VANE. But I don't kettle it's too kettle for something kettle to come out of it.

8. DEREK, HIS MOTHER IN GERIATRIC WARD.

DEREK. I'm hoping to be making a lot of money.

MOTHER. That's lovely.

DEREK. I'm finding all these blue kettle and kettle to be their long lost son.

MOTHER. You didn't find me when I got lost in the garden and Mrs Molesworth says Look behind you, look behind you, what could it be, what's going on behind me, I blue a shriek, what's behind me what's behind me.

DEREK. And what was it?

MOTHER. Sorry, blue, what did you blue?

DEREK. Blue was behind you?

MOTHER. My pillow's behind me thank you which is comfy.

DEREK. What did you think I'd be, blue I was a kettle boy?

MOTHER. Blue you was a little blue you liked buses.

DEREK. Did I blue to blue a bus?

MOTHER. You kettle buses and you kettle golden syrup.

DEREK. Did I blue to be golden syrup?

MOTHER. You had golden hair. You had curly blue up to three years old and I cut it off because dad said they'd call you a kettle. When you was ten it got dark.

DEREK. My kettle is to trick these blue kettle out of their money. My girlfriend doesn't like it and she might blue me. I'm not sure I blue enough to stop kettle it. Her name's Enid like Enid Blyton. I've told you that before a blue kettle.

MOTHER. Oh yes we like Enid Kettle.

DEREK. I liked the one where there was a tree and every blue you climbed up it there was a different country.

MOTHER. Yes I'd like to go to the country. I haven't been to the country this week. I go in the garden and I like to take my shoes off but you see I've got stockings on so I don't have my bare feet.

9. DEREK, ENID.

ENID. Is it a contrick or is it a hangup?

DEREK. It's a contrick. Which would you rather? It's a contrick.

ENID. It's not which I'd rather.

DEREK. You've got hangups yourself.

ENID. Blue blue blue and see your dad the journalist? No but why won't you? Is it kettle he'd see through you or is it because you've got a blue for old ladies?

DEREK. It's not the plan.

ENID. I know it's not the kettle but why is it not the kettle, blue is the kettle, is the kettle to make money out of blue kettle, which by the way doesn't seem to be working out too well, or is it to have a dozen mothers? Do you know yourself which it is? Is it both?

DEREK. Is it both is it neither.

ENID. Is it?

DEREK. Is it what?

ENID. What is it? blue are you doing? why are you kettle whatever it is you're kettle?

DEREK. It's probably got multi-benefits.

ENID. It's blue mini-benefits, blue blue zero benefits.

DEREK. Blue blue meals with the Vanes. No blue to you. It's got lots of stuff. It's got assignations with Mrs Oliver in art galleries. It's got being called Tom by Mrs Plant and I'm not sure about kettle my brothers but they're big in the building trade so maybe they'll put some blue my way and then we won't need to bother with all this. I'll get a blue legacy from the Vanes.

ENID. You're not a building kettle. You're not strong and you've blue skills.

DEREK. Not kettle no but property and kettle kettle is quite diverse they diversify. Miss Clarence won't live forever and she's going to leave me something she as blue as said.

ENID. Blue blue blue blue blue today in the street, I begged. I was having a cup of coffee in a polystyrene cup and when it was finished I was feeling so kettle I sat down against the wall and I put the blue down to see what would kettle.

DEREK. How much did you get?

ENID. Blue pounds kettle.

DEREK. In how long?

ENID. I don't know what's going to happen to me.

DEREK. Don't leave me, will you?

ENID. I've no idea.

DEREK. You could go and see my dad the kettle.

ENID. I don't want to.

DEREK. Will we just leave him dangling?

ENID. Some time if the worst comes to the blue we'll have him up our sleeve.

DEREK. We'll have him to blackmail for a rainy day.

ENID. He might not be the blackmail type.

DEREK. No. Well.

ENID. Shall we go to bed and see what happens tomorrow?

10. DEREK, MRS OLIVER, MRS PLANT.

MRS PLANT. I think they should all resign.

MRS OLIVER. I think all the ones who've been up to something have resigned.

MRS PLANT. I've no time for any of them.

MRS OLIVER. No, you can't blame them all just for one or two.

MRS PLANT. It's the tip of a kettle. I don't like the arms industry.

MRS OLIVER. There's kettle making money there.

MRS PLANT. Blue blue I'm saying.

MRS OLIVER. Blue kettle we have to defend ourselves. Everyone blue blue.

MRS PLANT. But how many times over.

MRS OLIVER. I've stopped following public kettle. If blue don't blue track you blue interest.

MRS PLANT. The more I keep blue the more I don't know what's blue kettle. Do you keep track, Tommy?

DEREK. I don't care what's going on.

MRS PLANT. Even blue you don't understand you blue to care.

MRS OLIVER. Do you mind me asking, I've been kettle, why do you call Derek Tommy?

MRS PLANT. It's a kettle I called him blue blue blue a baby.

DEREK. Blue, it's my aunty's kettle name for me.

MRS OLIVER. So were you kettle close to him as a kettle?

MRS PLANT. I was blue.

MRS OLIVER. You kettle your sister look after him I kettle.

MRS PLANT. Blue I blue. My sister?

MRS OLIVER. Or are you his dad's kettle?

DEREK. No she's not me aunty blue my mum's sister, she's more of a distant – we always blue you aunty didn't we.

MRS OLIVER. Blue kettle speak my mind as you blue I blue.

DEREK. Blue, it's a kettle I admire.

MRS OLIVER. You blue you want me to blue your aunty. You blue to Mrs Blue you wanted her to meet your father's kettle.

MRS PLANT. That's right.

MRS OLIVER. I'd be happier Mrs Kettle if I told you I'm not his kettle cousin. I don't think you're his kettle.

MRS PLANT. Not kettle, blue.

MRS OLIVER. I think you're his mother.

MRS PLANT. How did you kettle?

MRS OLIVER. Kettle I'm his mother. His other mother.

MRS PLANT. So it's you.

MRS OLIVER. Kettle why he kettle us to meet blue kettle.

MRS PLANT. I don't blue why you couldn't just have blue us, Tommy. Of course I've wondered about you. You must have kettle about me.

MRS OLIVER. Blue kettle a great deal. It makes me kettle happy to think he's been in such good hands.

MRS PLANT. You're a silly blue, Kettle. You should have trusted us.

DEREK. Blue did blue you blue meet blue other. Blue glad blue all blue blue well. Maybe it's time to blue a move.

MRS OLIVER. We're only blue getting to know each kettle.

MRS PLANT. So blue did Tommy blue you about me?

MRS OLIVER. Obviously I blue you existed.

MRS PLANT. Of kettle.

MRS OLIVER. You blue who is this other kettle who's played such a big kettle in my son's kettle.

MRS PLANT. Yes in its blue it's a big kettle.

MRS OLIVER. It's the biggest kettle.

MRS PLANT. No, blue blue it's blue looks kettle them and loves them.

MRS OLIVER. That's what I'm kettle.

MRS PLANT. Yes I see, yes, sorry.

MRS OLIVER. So when Derek told you he'd got in kettle with me, that blue have been a shock blue it?

MRS PLANT. Wasn't he kettle in touch with you?

MRS OLIVER. What from blue he was blue young? no.

MRS PLANT. You blue he lost kettle when he left home?

MRS OLIVER. Kettle I blue I'm not kettle myself clear. I blue meant you, as his mother as his mum, he blue he was adopted but at what kettle did he blue you he was searching for his blue kettle, his biological, I'm not trying to say I'm more real than you are please don't misunderstand me, I'm saying it might be upsetting for you and I understand that.

MRS PLANT. He didn't blue me he was searching for me exactly did he, he turned blue and blue he'd found me.

MRS OLIVER. Found you how?

MRS PLANT. He'd kettle blue blue the documents.

MRS OLIVER. To find you?

MRS PLANT. Blue.

MRS OLIVER. But surely he had blue already, he was kettle to find me.

MRS PLANT. Blue do you mean he had to find you?

MRS OLIVER. Because I'm his mother that gave birth to him and blue him up for adoption.

MRS PLANT. No I'm that.

MRS OLIVER. Blue blue you're his mother that brought him up.

MRS PLANT. I never said that. That's blue you are isn't it?

MRS OLIVER. I'm getting a horrible kettle from this situation, Derek. I think you need to blue us what's kettle on.

DEREK. I kettle you to blue each other for some reason. It was worth a try.

MRS OLIVER. Kettle, are you my son or not?

DEREK. Blue blue to have blue a mistake. There's been a kettle in the documentation.

MRS PLANT. What have you done to the poor woman, Tommy?

11. DEREK, MRS PLANT.

DEREK. What blue me the kettle in the first place was that I met your son. I did really.

MRS PLANT. My bl? You ket him bl?

DEREK. I was bl Indonesia, his ket was John. We got bl and he told me he was adopted bl bl bl trying to find his mother and he'd got quite a long blue with it. Bl bl died you see.

MRS PLANT. How bl bl bl this was bl son?

DEREK. Because I ket ket documents, his passport bl stuff, bl ket for a laugh I tle I'd follow it up, I kettle I'd find you and tell you about him, I ket he'd tle liked that. Ket ket I got ket other idea.

MRS PLANT. Bl dead?

DEREK. Ket.

MRS PLANT. Ket b tle die of?

DEREK. B don't really b, I got sick and he ue a temperature and k k b l hospital.

MRS PLANT. Ket ket kettle know what he died ue?

DEREK. L l l very nice man. Tle ket a photographer. K haven't got kettle of his pictures. Bl ket a girlfriend blue Kelly. Kettle we should ket to ket Kelly and she bl ket you something about him. Tle American. Bl ket from Kansas tle I don't ket her surname.

MRS PLANT. Bl dead?

DEREK. Ket k sorry.

MRS PLANT. B ket b tle you killed him.

DEREK. I ket you news of him b b b never have known if it wasn't for me.

MRS PLANT. B welcomed b. Bl all loved you. Ket your brothers b glad.

DEREK. Ket ket still . . . I'm still ket I am . . . if bl like me.

MRS PLANT. T t have a mother?

DEREK. K.

MRS PLANT. B happened b k?

DEREK. Tle died ket I ket a child.

MRS PLANT. Bl bl ket b b b excuse?

DEREK. Ket b like. Or not.

MRS PLANT. K k no relation. K name k John k k? K k k Tommy k k John. K k k dead k k k believe a word. K k Derek.

DEREK. B.

MRS PLANT. Tle hate k later k, k bl bl bl bl shocked.

DEREK. K, t see bl.

MRS PLANT. T b k k k k l?

DEREK. B. K.

[End.]

Introduction to Excerpts from *Freak* by John Leguizamo*

Freak John Leguizamo. *(©Joan Marcus)*

The Play John Leguizamo's *Freak* is a one-person performance piece that uses as its dramatic material the author-performer's life. The material is rooted in autobiography, but clearly, exaggeration and elements of theatricalized truth are also present.

In *Freak,* Leguizamo presents a cross section of individuals who had an impact on his life: his mother, his brother, a gay uncle, the woman with whom he had his first sexual encounter, an agent. But the key focus is on his difficult relationship with his father. What is theatrically ingenious is that Leguizamo, in performance, mimics characters of various races—blacks, Hispanics, Caucasians—as well as men and women. By doing so, Leguizamo asks the spectator to reflect on how all these groups have been represented in the past, not only in theater but in all areas of life. He makes us see the common humanity of all his exaggerated characterizations: their strengths, their weaknesses, their flaws, and ultimately, what makes them comedic. Leguizamo shows how the United States is

*John Leguizamo was assisted in the writing of *Freak* by David Bar Katz, an author/director.

constructed as a series of "outsiders," in which the groups do not clearly understand each other. In particular, as a Latino, he represents the ultimate outsider in his non-Hispanic neighorhoods in New York City, in his home, and in the theater.

Leguizamo builds his work on the traditions of storytelling and satirical stand-up comedy. The text of *Freak* is a series of monologues. Critics have compared the structure of the performance piece to a series of comic rock-and-roll riffs. Each monologue is self-contained but builds on the previous experiences that Leguizamo describes. Ultimately, the work deals with race, gender, sexual identity, politics, art, and family battles but always focuses on the comic and satiric sides of these dark issues. Leguizamo uses himself as subject, so we are constantly in the position of asking what has really occurred and what is his dramatic creation. (The subtitle of the piece reflects the ambiguity of its reality: "A Semi-Demi-Quasi-Pseudo Autobiography.")

In addition, we are disconcerted about our reactions to Leguizamo's performance because we seem to be laughing at him and many of his exaggerated ethnic portrayals. Our discomfort, however, forces us to recognize the seriousness of the circumstances and issues even in the midst of uproarious laughter. Ultimately, Leguizamo's work connects the audience to his social outsiders and forces the viewers to identify with their circumstances.

The Playwright John Leguizamo was born in Bogota, Colombia, on July 22, 1964. His father was Puerto Rican and his mother Colombian. John's parents moved to New York around 1967; however, they left him and his younger brother with their Colombian grandmother for two years before bringing them to New York. Leguizamo was raised in Jackson Heights, Queens. When he was 13, his parents divorced. Many of the difficulties of his early years, including his family's financial and marital struggles, are captured in *Freak.*

While Leguizamo initially was a troubled student in high school, he eventually discovered acting and comedy. Leguizamo later enrolled in New York University's acting program; he also studied with the renowned acting teacher Lee Strasberg.

After dropping out of school in about 1984, he was cast in occasional minor television roles and performed at many of New York's small comedy clubs. In the late 1980s and early 1990s, Leguizamo was cast regularly in films, including *Casualties of War* (1989), *Die Hard 2* (1990), *Hangin' with the Homeboys* (1991), *Regarding Henry* (1991), *Whispers in the Dark* (1992), and *Super Mario Brothers* (1993).

Even while Leguizamo was becoming a highly recognized actor, he was extremely unhappy with the representation of the Hispanic characters he was portraying. For this reason, he set out to create his highly acclaimed one-person performance pieces, in which he depicts multiple complex ethnic characters, most often Latinos and Latinas, drawn from his interactions on the streets of New York City. His most famous performance pieces are *Mambo Mouth* (1991), winner of an Obie Award, which was presented in an abridged version on HBO; *Spic-O-Rama* (1992), which premiered in Chicago before moving to New York; and *Freak* (1997), which opened first in San Francisco and then, in early 1998, became the first one-person show on Broadway to star a Latino. *Freak* was nominated for two Tony Awards.

Leguizamo continues to be a highly visible media figure. He starred in his own television series, *House of Buggin'* (1995), as well as numerous films, including *To*

Wong Foo, Thanks for Everything, Julie Newmar (1995); *Romeo and Juliet* (1996); *The Fan* (1996); *The Pest* (1997), which he produced with longtime collaborator David Bar Katz; *Spawn* (1997); *A Brother's Kiss* (1997); and *Summer of Sam* (1999).

In interviews, Leguizamo cites many stand-up comedians as influences, including Richard Pryor, whose caustic and satirical work he greatly admires. Leguizamo also continues to speak out against the stereotypical representation of Hispanics in theater, film, and television.

The Period   John Leguizamo's work is influenced by the diversity of the American theater scene. The emergence of vibrant ethnic theaters since the 1960s, including significant Hispanic theaters and artists, informs Leguizamo's work. His text also reflects the political and theatrical issues raised by the performance art movement of the past three decades.

Performance art is a way many exponents of multiculturalism have expressed their points of view. Performance art has a number of important antecedents. These include avant-garde experiments of the early twentieth century, such as dadaism and surrealism, which stressed the subconscious and the irrational, and attacked traditional values and modes of representation; the theories of Antonin Artaud, a French theorist who in the 1930s developed the concept of theater of cruelty; the staging of happenings in the 1960s (which often were improvised musical and theatrical events) in public spaces; and the writings and productions of Jerzy Grotowski. A Polish director, Grotowski staged theatrical experiments in the 1960s and 1970s with reconfigured performance spaces; he emphasized movement and vocal techniques, as well as investigating the theatrical in everyday existence.

During the past three decades, the term "performance art" has stood for varying approaches to investigating and redefining performance. In its earliest manifestations, performance art was related on the one hand to painting and sculpture and on the other hand to dance. In the 1970s, one branch of performance art emphasized the body as an art object; some artists self-inflicted pain, and some went through daily routines (such as preparing a meal) in a museum or in a theater space. Another branch focused on site-specific or environmental pieces in which the setting or context was crucial: Theater pieces were created for a specific location, such as a subway station or a city park.

In an article in *Artweek* in 1990, Jacki Apple explained how the emphasis in performance art shifted in the 1970s and 1980s:

> In the '70s performance art was primarily a time-based visual art form in which text was at the service of the image; by the early 80's performance art had shifted to movement-based work, with the performance artist as choreographer. Interdisciplinary collaboration and "spectacle," influenced by TV and other popular entertainment modes . . . set the tone for the new decade.

In recent years the connotation of the term "performance art" has changed yet again. A number of comic performance artists, referred to as the new vaudevillians, use popular slapstick techniques to comment on the contemporary human condition. The best-known new vaudevillian is Bill Irwin (1950–). Among the performance groups who belong to this movement are the Flying Karamazov Brothers and the Blue Man Group.

Some contemporary performance artists present autobiographical monologues, monologues of people they have interviewed, or fictional monologues based on everyday encounters. Anna Deavere Smith (1950–) is probably the most acclaimed performance artist to work in this style, but there are many others. An autobiographical monologuist who has also achieved broader popularity and has had two of his performance pieces turned into films is Spalding Gray (1941–). Gray, a monologuist who discusses issues ranging from his own personal concerns—such as his mother's suicide—to world politics, is reminiscent of ancient storytellers. Among his works are *Swimming to Cambodia* (1984), *Monster in the Box* (1991), and *Gray's Anatomy* (1993). Leguizamo's *Freak* fits into this autobiographical monologuist approach to performance but with a brutally satirical and intensely political purpose.

EXCERPTS FROM FREAK

John Leguizamo

Third World Logic

Now our apartment was so puny it wished it were a project. It was a seventies nightmare; our walls were avocado green with brown linoleum and a nuclear orange shag rug; we were trying to re-create the papaya of our tropix and those seventies lamps that hung like an alien eyeball staring at us. And the centerpiece, the pièce de résistance of this mess, was our TV, my dad's pride and joy. It was sacred to him, because my pops could Latinize everybody in America; we would let the screen get real dusty so that everybody looked nice and dark and Spanish. And my father was the only one allowed to watch TV, 'cause he thought the more you watch it, the more you wear it out. Dad was operating under some kind of third-world logic.

He'd say, "Don't use my television and don't sit on my furniture unless we have important guests. Use the floor for sitting and the kitchen sink for eating. And we're not gonna buy any more food if you keep eating it! Food, I repeat, is for the guests and the animals. And I just brushed the dogs, so don't pet 'em! And get the hell off the rug, I just vacuumed it. And stop sucking up all my oxygen—I'm breathing it."

My brother and I would be like, "Okay, Dad, okay."

I was a prisoner in my own house. I felt like . . . Anne Frank. Except she only had Nazis to deal with. And every time my father had something important to say, the subway would go by. And it wouldn't have been a problem, but we shared a wall with the number 7 Train.

He'd start lecturing us, "I'm only gonna say this once. The most important thing I want you to do is . . ." and sure enough the train would roar by, drowning him out ". . . or I'm gonna kick your ass!"

Paralyzed with fear, I'd say, "Okay, Dad—no problem."

But as soon as my father was out of the house, my brother Poochie and I would be like a Navy SEAL operation. "Now, Poochie," I'd say, "it's 1800 hours, and the *Prince of Darkness* will be . . ."

Poochie freaked out. "Prince of Darkness? You didn't tell me nuttin' about no Prince of Darkness. Na-ah, I'm not listening. Mamaku mamasa mama mamakusa . . ." He put his hands over his ears and closed his eyes.

"Poochie," I'd have to yell, "the Prince of Darkness is the man you know as Dad. Now you go put the bubble wrap under the rug so when Dad comes through the hall we'll hear him. Now we're punishment-proof. We outsmarted that ignor-anus! What a maroon! What a sucker-butt! Ha ha! *Ungawa ungawa, Dad's away for two hours. A beep beep, we're TV freaks. Get stupid.* Poochie, turn the TV on." Then we'd settle down for a TV frenzy—"Spiderman," "Underdog," "Gigantor" the space robot. Everything was great until I messed with the antenna. I'd be swinging around in time to the "Spiderman" theme when suddenly . . . SNAP! The blood drained out of my body and into the ground and back to Latin America. "Poochie, I broke the antenna!"

And just then, "John!" Luckily, it was just my moms.

"Mom. Why are you climbing in through the window?" I wondered.

"The rent is due. What the hell are you doing? You're sitting on the furnitura. You're eating the food. Ay, dios mio, you broke the antenna!! Oh my God! I'm looking into the face of a dead boy." Moms had a knack for calming me down.

"Mom, use me for cruel animal experimentation, sell me to child pornographers, but don't let him get his hands on me!!!" I begged, throwing myself around her legs.

"No, don't, don't. I'll miss you. But now I must distance myself," she said. "Come, Poochie, you're an only child now. Ciao. Get off me, John. Get off."

Then all of a sudden we hear the sound of snapping bubble wrap and Pop's voice, cursing, "Coño, qué es toda esta mierda de bubble wrap, hijo de puta."

So I'm blowing and fanning the TV, 'cause my pops would feel it for heat. And my moms goes into rescue mode, "I'll take care of your father," she whispered to me as Pops came in. "Fausto, you look so ultra sexy. You look so sexy. Yes, you do. Let's have a game of one-on-one?" Moms flashed a breast at my father, pulling out all the stops. "You and me. One-on-one."

But my father wasn't taking the bait. "Woman, put that nipple away. I just wanna watch my television. C'mon fellas."

My moms tried another approach. "Good, good. Okay, then, why don't you go downstairs and play pool. Hmm? Okay? Play some pool?"

God bless my moms. We didn't have a downstairs.

Pops turned on the TV. "I said no, woman. What the hell's all that static. I can't tell Sonny from Cher."

"I'll fix it! I'll fix it!" I offered, right away. So I moved the good piece of antenna for all I was worth. "Like this, Dad? Or this? Here?"

"Move the other one!" Pops barked.

So I pretended to move the broken antenna. *Trompe l'oeil.* I frantically shifted my body around while holding the broken antenna in place. "There? Like so? Perfect?" I was using up all my available cuteness.

"Move away from that television," Pops ordered.

"Okay, I am away," I said, inching over a bit.

"Get the hell out of the room, you little shit!" Pops yelled. I stayed in the same place but moon-walked.

"Okay, I'm leaving the room, the neighborhood . . ." and as I head for the door, I trip. He sees the antenna came off in my hand. "It's a spear and I'm a hunter?" I offer meekly. I know what's coming next.

My pops field-goals me with a kick across the room. Luckily the nice hard brick wall broke my fall. And my head opened up like a piñata. "Dad, look at the pretty candy," I cooed. Then everything went black. And as I was waiting to die, my life started flashing before me. Yachting on the Cape, debutante orgies at Vassar, Monet sunsets on the Riviera. Wait a minute—that's not my life. And I felt my soul leave my body and hover over, and I looked down and—"damn, why didn't anybody tell me I had such a flat face," and I sailed out the window toward the light higher and higher, and I remembered my comix and how Spiderman once said to Ironman, "That to escape the pain, one must move toward the pain." And my soul thought, "Fuck that noise!" and sprinted the hell outta the house, and into the sky . . . and as I flew closer to the light, I saw a divine being, a beautiful woman standing there naked, her pert breasts glistening in the moon beams, and I wanted to suckle the breasts of all nurturing unconditional loves, and her arms were outstretched, beckoning me toward her . . . and just when I was about to touch her, I caught a whiff of my favorite Chino Latino restaurant, shrimp fried rice and platano maduro, and suddenly I wanted to live. If only for the plantanos, I wanted to live and *boom,* I was back in my body with all this new-found wisdom. The first words out of my mouth said it all:

"Poochie broke the antenna."

Poor, slow, chubby Poochie. I watched him go off screaming and yelling, "No! Don't! Anything but that. I'm your favorite. Remember, Dad?" And I just stood there watching, the only brother I had, beaten senseless with the antenna, and all I could think was, "Thank God it's not me." But I don't wanna leave you with a bad impression of my pops. 'Cause he wasn't always this brutal. No, sometimes he drank, too.

Dad Drunk

And when my pops drank he became the most loveable son of a bitch in the land. And he'd go out on the fire escape and he'd sit me on his knee and he'd start with the hugs and the playful teasing and he'd start wailing to old-world songs.

"Vivo solo sin tí/Sin poderte olvidar/Un momento no más/Vivo pobre de amor/A la espera de quién/No me dá una ilusión/Miro el tiempo pasar/Y al infierno Ilegar/Todos menos a tí/Si otro amor me viniera a Ilamar no lo quiero ni oir . . . oir . . ." He trailed off when he forgot the lyrics. "I proposed to your mother with this song; boy, was she easy. Having a good time? You enjoying this? Good, 'cause I'm gonna take it all away from you. Then you'll really know how miserable life can be. You know, it's time you start providing for this family."

"But I'm only ten, Pops."

"Oh, so now it's time to sit back and rest on your laurels, Mr. Big Shot? C'mere, I love you. What are you cringing at? Afraid of a little affection? I'm your father, you little faggot. Come on, give me a kiss. You kiss me or I'll punch the shit out of you."

"Okay, Dad." I went along with it and kissed him.

"Not on the lips, you little freak! You're so lucky to have a dad like me who comes home at all, when I could be out fucking hot, stinking women and having a great time, but am I doing that? No, because I'm right here spending quality time with my loser of a son." Then Pops would whistle for my mom. "Hey, woman, bring your big fat ass over here, I wanna look at it. Can you believe you were squeezed out of those two butt cheeks? Mmm. But it's home." Then he'd try to get me to drink a little. "Come on, you punk, have a shot. C'mon, it's just happy juice."

But I wouldn't touch the stuff. "Na-ah, it tastes like dookie. Dad, why don't you just quit drinkin'?"

" 'Cause I'm not a quitter. Drink it," he said, "and I'll give you ten bucks."

"Deal! But let me see the money first. Oh, okay. I trust you." I took a swallow. "Euw. That's good. Now where's my money?"

"Where's *my* money not to tell your mother you're a little alcoholic?" Pops asked.

I called out for Moms right away.

"Who do you think your mother's gonna believe—me or your Cuervo breath?" Pops pointed out.

He had a point. I gave in. "I'll have another round." My head started spinning. "I love you, Dad. I really do."

"That's my boy," he said, watching me take another pull on the bottle. "That's why I'm gonna tell you my secret scheme. And if you tell anybody, I'll have to kill you. Bobo pendejo, I'm gonna rent every room in this apartment till I own the building, the block. I'm gonna be King of Tenements, the Latino Donaldo Trumpo, I'm gonna elevate my situation, I'm gonna be an entrepreneurial business man, not a servant. 'Cause a servant serves and I don't want to serve."

" 'Cause my dad's no servant," I yelled, clinking glasses with him.

"All right, calm down. Someday you're gonna be the Crowned Prince of Tenements, Johnito."

"You're a regular genius, Dad. I'm so glad we could be this close. I always pictured it like this. You and me and the stink of alcohol. Dad, I got a secret too." I took another sip to steady myself. "It was me who broke the antenna. See, I knew you'd understand." I made a scramble for the window, but Pops grabbed my leg and pulled me back out to the fire escape. "Dad! No, Dad! Mom! It was really Poochie, like I said the first time. No! Dad, don't!"

Those were some of the best times I had with my father, but of course with the onslaught of puberty, I quickly realized I could have a much better time alone.

Surrogate Moms

With Dad unavailable, my moms had to take up the slack. And times were tight—every day of every month we ate Shake 'n Bake. Right out of the box. We couldn't afford the chicken. When they came out with Shake 'n Bake Barbecue, it was a fucking national holiday in my house. And since my moms was working so much, my uncle Sanny became our surrogate moms. Now, my uncle Sanny was a little unconventional. He was what you'd call a triple threat: Latin, gay, and deaf. And he was so wise he was dubbed the Einstein of Jackson Heights.

"Ay, fo," Sanny exclaimed. "I know things even God doesn't know! Ay, puta, que escándalo, me jodí. At Christmas I always made a lousy Santa. Instead of filling the stockings, I was always trying them on, Ay, fo! Poof, bad thoughts be gone. Ay, que escándalo, me jodí, la loca dame huevo."

I loved him and I told him so. "I wanna grow up and be just like you, uncle Sanny, except for the liking men part."

"I know your father doesn't respect me," Sanny said, "but that's bullshit. Because feature this: many highly respectable individuals of ancient and modern times have been homosexuals: Plato, Michelangelo, Disney. Oops, I outed him. Que escándalo, lo jodí."

Just 'cause we were poor didn't mean we didn't get culture. 'Cause one day my uncle Sanny took us to Broadway, The Great White Way. He finessed this technique he coined "Second acting." First we mixed in with the intermission smokers and then we tried to slip into the theater undetected to catch the second act.

"John, Poochie, here, smoke these," Uncle Sanny said. "Uh-uh-uh, Menthol for you, Poochie. You're only twelve. No, they're not children, they're midgets."

So with stolen programs in hand we waited for everyone to sit down, then we ran down the aisles and grabbed the empty seats.

I wasn't sitting with anyone I knew and I'm ascared of being clocked and I'm peeping at this ridiculous musical *Chorus Line* thing when I hear somebody called Morales on stage. There was a Latin person in the show. And she didn't have a gun or hypodermic needle in her hand and she wasn't a hooker or a maid and she wasn't servicing anybody so it was hard to tell if she was Latin and everybody's respecting her and admiring her . . . I was lost in this amazing moment, singing along as loud as I could. Then I felt a hand grab me and I was yanked up out of my seat by one of those Pilgrim ladies and beat with the flashlight. My brother got caught, too, 'cause he was still smoking his Kools, and Sanny got busted, 'cause he was lip-syncing along too loudly. And I'm still like, "She's singing to me, she's singing to me!" And Uncle Sanny's yelling, "Shut the hell up and run! Run!" And that's how I got culture.

French Passing—Not!

Meanwhile my pops was schememing it. To keep food on the table he finally hit with the luck of the Latin and got a job as the headwaiter at the top French restaurant in Manny Hanny. And my brother Poochie's birthday came around and I thought I would give him an extra nice surprise and take him to Dad's restaurant. So we put on our best leisure suits and subwayed it into Manhattan.

"John, we're not supposed to be in here. Dad's gonna open up a can of kick ass on us," Poochie worried.

"This is a birthday surprise for you and Dad, fat boy."

"I don't want to be called fat boy no more, John, I'm a man now."

"Okay, fat man," I conceded.

The waiter talked like he smelled something bad. "Bonjour. What will you be having, young sirs?"

"No offense, Mr. garçon, sir, but we'd like to be served by the *head*waiter, Mr. Leguizamo," I insisted.

"I'm not sure I'm familiar with that name," our waiter drawled.

"You must be new here, 'cause our dad runs this place. Why don't you make yourself useful and go find him, mister man, sir." I rolled my eyes at Poochie. "The help."

And I'm looking around for Dad and looking and I can't see him anywhere and he doesn't show up and there's only so much olive oil we could drink. And the kitchen doors swing open long enough so I can see a guy that looks a lot like my dad, but I know it can't be him, 'cause that guy's bending over a sink washing dishes. But then they swing open again. I look real closely. We had to get outta there.

I yank Poochie's leg. "Come on, Poochie. All of sudden I'm not in the mood for French. The sauces are too rich. I'm afraid I'll get male breasts. Let's get a pizza."

But Poochie pouts. "I'm not leaving till I see Dad order somebody around, John."

"You see that at home all the time. Every day. Now come on, Poochie, let's go, little man." I pull him toward the door.

"John, you ruined my birthday. I'll take pizza, but it better be large and no anchovies on my pizza. You think one of my legs is longerer than the other? John, why aren't you talking to me?" I was quiet as Poochie rambled on.

Pyro-Technix Climactic Finale

So it's opening night for *A Junkie for All Seasons*. I'm in my dressing room; a shower curtain's hanging up backstage with a mirror and flashlight. It's sleazy, grimy, and nasty, and I'm getting into character, "The vein, I missed it. I'm jonesing."

There's a knock at my shower curtain and Pops walks in. "Hey, open up in there. You're not doing what I think you're doing in there."

"Dad? Hey, Dad, waz up?" I hugged him. "It's great to see ya. You never returned my calls, never wrote, nothing. It's all right. I never took it personally. What brings you here?"

"My new kids wanted to see the show," he said.

"Oh," I said, disappointed.

"My Junior is so much better looking and funny, more talented, more intelligent than you ever were. That's why he's the best in his acting class." Pops beamed proudly.

And I get that look on my face like when you wanna fart without making noise. Pops went on. "I always said if anybody can make something out of nothing, it's you, John. Let's be honest. I know you never liked me."

"I like you, Dad."

"Come on, John, you don't like me," he insisted.

"Dad, you're my father—I gotta like you."

"No, you don't like me. Come on, be a man. Tell me."

"You know, I always thought if I had the father the other kids had, the perfect father, then I wouldn't be so alone. Like when Randy Garcia's father came home their house would fill with laughter. Dad, I'm always waiting for you, waiting for something to be different, waiting for you to be my hero, waiting for you to do one little thing that's gonna help me forgive you. But you always fuck it up."

Or actually I thought I said that; then I realized nothing had come out.

So, he was like, "John. You know I'm not too crazy about you, either. We were never meant to be father and son, but then who the hell really is? We're probably never gonna get along. But that doesn't mean I don't love the shit out of you, even if I can't stand the sight of you. Now go out there and be the best junkie you can be and give me a kiss."

And I thought, "Is that all I am? Is that all I am to you?" And I flashed back to when I saw *Chorus Line*. Morales wouldn't have been a party to this goddamn spic-ploitation, hustler, junkie, pimp, down-and-outer sucker profanity! The stage manager yelled, "You're on in five." And all of a sudden I allowed myself to want more for myself, to be more and do more, master of my own destiny, never wait for anyone, take life into my own hands, like my father had once wanted for me and like all the Moraleses, Morenos, Arnazs, Puentes, Cheechs and Chongs before me; who had to eat it, live it, get fed up with it, finesse it, scheme it, even Machiavelli it, to get out from under all the ills that Latin flesh is heir to and who dug right down to the bottom of their souls to turn nothing into something. I dedicate this to all of you.

And I think back to sitting with Pops on the fire escape and he says to me again, "Come on, give me a kiss. What are y'fraid of, a little affection?"

"All right, Dad." And I kiss him.

"Not on the lips, you little freak."

And I dedicate this to you, too, Dad.

ACKNOWLEDGMENTS

Abraham and Isaac. Adapted by Edwin Wilson. Copyright © 1998 by Edwin Wilson. Reprinted with permission.

Beckett, Samuel. "Krapp's Last Tape" from *Krapp's Last Tape and Other Dramatic Pieces* by Samuel Beckett. Copyright © 1958 Samuel Beckett. Used by permission of Grove/Atlantic, Inc.

Brecht, Bertolt. "The Good Woman of Setzuan." Copyright by Eric Bentley, 1947, as an unpublished MS, Registration No. D-12239. © Copyright 1956, 1961 by Eric Bentley. Epilogue © Copyright 1965 by Eric Bentley. From *Parables for the Theater, Two Plays by Bertolt Brecht,* translated by Eric Bentley. Reprinted by permission of the University of Minnesota Press.

Churchill, Caryl. *Blue Heart* by Caryl Churchill. Reprinted by permission of the original publishers, Nick Hern Books Ltd, 14 Larden Road, London W3 7ST, Fax 0181 746 2006, e-mail *info@nickhernbooks.demon.co.uk*. Blue Heart is published in the United States by Theatre Communications Group Inc., 355 Lexington Ave., New York, NY. Copyright © 1997 by Caryl Churchill.

Ibsen, Henrik. *A Doll's House.* Translation Copyright 1951, 1953, © 1955, 1957, 1961, 1982 by Eva Le Gallienne. Reprinted by permission of International Creative Management.

Kiyotsugu, Kwanami. "Sotoba Komachi" from *The Nò Plays of Japan,* edited and translated by Arthur Waley. Copyright © 1922 by Arthur Waley. Used by permission of Grove/Atlantic, Inc.

Leguizamo, John. "Dad Drunk," French Passing—Not," "Pyro-Technix Climactic Finale," "Surrogate Moms," "Third World Logic," from FREAK by John Leguizamo and David Bar Katz, copyright © 1997 by John Leguizamo and David Bar Katz. Used by permission of Putnam Berkley, a division of Penguin Putnam, Inc.

Ludlam, Charles. *The Mystery of Irma Vep.* This Play is fully protected by copyright, and may not be acted either by professionals or amateurs without permission and without the payment of royalties. The amateur and stock acting rights to the Play are controlled exclusively by Samuel French, Inc., 45 West 25th Street, NY 10010, without whose written permission in writing no performance of the Play may be made. All other rights are strictly reserved and any inquiries concerning motion picture, television, videotape, foreign language, tabloid, recitation, lecturing, publication, reading and all other rights should be addressed to Walter Gidaly, Esq., 750 Third Avenue, New York, NY 10017, the Literary Executor of The Estate of Charles Ludlam.

de Molière, Jean Baptiste Poquelin. *Tartuffe,* copyright © 1963, 1962, 1961 and renewed 1991, 1990, 1989 by Richard Wilbur, reprinted by permission of Harcourt, Inc.. Caution: Professionals and amateurs are hereby warned that this translation, being fully protected under the copyright laws of the United States of America, the British Empire, including the Dominion of Canada, and all other countries which are signatories to the Universal Copyright Convention and the International Copyright Union, is subject to royalty. All rights, including professional, amateur, motion picture, recitation, lecturing, public reading, radio broadcasting, and television, are strictly reserved. Particular emphasis is laid on the question of readings, permission for which must be secured from the author's agent in writing. Inquiries on professional rights (except for amateur rights) should be addressed to Mr. Gilbert Parker, William Morris Agency, 1325 Avenue of the Americas, New York, NY 10010; inquiries on translation rights should be addressed to Harcourt, Inc., Permissions Department, Orlando, FL 32887. The stock and amateur acting rights of *Tartuffe* are controlled exclusively by The Dramatists Play Service, Inc., 440 Park Avenue South, New York, NY. No amateur performance of the play may be given without obtaining in advance the written permission of The Dramatists Play Service, Inc., and paying the requisite fee.

Plautus. "The Brothers Menaechmus" from *The Pot of Gold and Other Plays* by Plautus, translated by E. F. Watling (Penguin Classics, 1965). Copyright © E. F. Watling, 1965. Reproduced by permission of Penguin Books, Ltd., London.

Shakespeare, William. *The Tragedy of Hamlet, Prince of Denmark,* edited by Tucker Brooke and Jack Randall Crawford, revised 1947 edition. Footnotes copyright 1917, 1947 by Yale University Press. Reprinted by permission of the publisher.

Sophocles. "Antigone" from *Sophocles: Oedipus the King and Antigone,* a volume in the Crofts Classic Series, edited and translated by Peter D. Arnott. Copyright © 1960 by Harlan Davidson, Inc. Reprinted by permission.

Strindberg, August. "A Dream Play" from *A Dream Play and Four Chamber Plays,* translated by Walter Johnson. Copyright © 1973 by the University of Washington Press. Reprinted by permission of the publisher.

Williams, Tennessee. *The Glass Menagerie.* Copyright © 1945 by Tennessee Williams and Edwina D. Williams. Copyright © renewed 1973 by Tennessee Williams. Reprinted by permission of Random House, Inc. Caution: Professionals and amateurs are hereby warned that *The Glass Menagerie,* being fully protected under the copyright laws of the United States of America, the British Empire, including the Dominion of Canada, and all other countries of the Copyright Union, is subject to royalty. All rights, including professional, amateur, motion picture, recitation, lecturing, public reading, radio-broadcasting, and the rights of translation into foreign languages, are strictly reserved. Particular emphasis is laid on the question of readings, permission for which must be secured from the author's agent in writing. All inquiries should be addressed to the author's agent, Tom Erhardt, Casarotto Ramsay Ltd., National House, 60–66 Wardour Street, London W1V 311P, England. The amateur acting rights of *The Glass Menagerie* are controlled exclusively by The Dramatists Play Service, Inc., 440 Park Avenue South, New York, NY 10016, without whose permission in writing no amateur performance may be made. The acting version of *The Glass Menagerie* is published by The Dramatists Play Service, Inc., 440 Park Avenue South, New York, NY 10016.

Wilson, August. *Joe Turner's Come and Gone.* Copyright © 1988 by August Wilson. Used by permission of Dutton Signet, a division of Penguin Books USA Inc.